P9-BYO-736

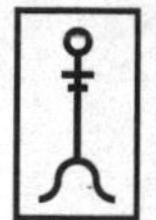

Also by Bill James

The New Bill James Historical Baseball Abstract
The Bill James Guide to Baseball Managers
Whatever Happened to the Hall of Fame?
This Time Let's Not Eat the Bones

Also by Rob Neyer

Rob Neyer's Big Book of Baseball Lineups
Feeding the Green Monster
Baseball Dynasties (with Eddie Epstein)

THE NEYER/JAMES GUIDE TO PITCHERS

An Historical Compendium of Pitching, Pitchers, and Pitches

BILL JAMES
and ROB NEYER

A FIRESIDE BOOK
PUBLISHED BY SIMON & SCHUSTER
NEW YORK LONDON TORONTO SYDNEY

I want to thank Dick Beverage, Dave Smith, Dick Thompson, and all the other SABR members who delve into baseball's history for nothing more than the sheer joy of the thing. This book is for you guys.

—Rob

For Reuben James, my unique and wonderful son.

—Bill

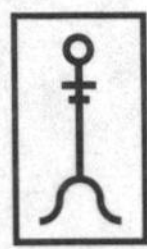
FIRESIDE
Rockefeller Center
1230 Avenue of the Americas
New York, NY 10020

FIRESIDE and colophon are registered trademarks
of Simon & Schuster, Inc.

For information about special discounts for bulk purchases,
please contact Simon & Schuster Special Sales:
1-800-456-6798 or business@simonandschuster.com

Designed by Ruth Lee-Mui

Manufactured in the United States of America

10 9 8 7 6 5 4 3 2 1

Library of Congress Cataloging-in-Publication Data

James, Bill and Neyer, Rob
The Neyer/James guide to pitchers : an historical compendium of pitching, pitchers, and pitches / Bill James and Rob Neyer.
p. cm.
1. Pitchers (Baseball)—United States—Biography. 2. Pitching (Baseball)—United States—History. I. Title.
GV865.A1J36 2004
796.357'22—dc22 13518856

ISBN 0-7432-6158-5

CONTENTS

CEREMONIAL FIRST PITCH

Hello, I'm Rob Neyer.

And I'm Bill James.

This book began the way that wars, scandals, and co-authored books usually begin: over lunch. This was more than ten years ago; the two of us worked together from 1989 through 1992. It was lunch one day in 1991 . . . Neyer was probably eating a cheese sandwich, James was probably munching on a large slab of some dead animal . . . and the two of us were talking about some pitcher from the 1950s. Memory suggests that it was Harvey Haddix. Between the two of us, we probably knew a couple of hundred facts about Harvey Haddix. We knew that he was small, that he threw left-handed, that he was very quick and an outstanding fielder. We knew that he won twenty games for the Cardinals in 1953, and also hit .289 that year. We knew of course about the twelve perfect innings in a 1959 game that he eventually lost, we knew that he helped the Pirates win the World Championship in 1960, and we knew that later on he was an effective reliever for the Orioles.

However, one of us happened to ask, "What did he throw?"

Was he a curveball specialist? Was he sneaky fast? Did he live on the sinker, or did he have a trick pitch? We didn't have a clue. We knew nicknames and anecdotes and stats by the gross, but about this very basic element of his career—what he did on the mound—we drew a blank.

We thought about that for a minute, and then the conversation moved on. Ten minutes later, twenty minutes later, we were talking about another old pitcher . . . Paul Derringer or Larry French or somebody. Same thing. We knew many facts about the pitcher, but in this fundamental area, central to his career, we were about as useful as a gorilla with a sewing machine. A few minutes later, a third pitcher, and by this time we were primed to focus on the blank, like your tongue feeling out a missing tooth.

Both of us are compulsive collectors and readers of old baseball books. Both of us spend too many hundreds of dollars every year on our baseball libraries. Yet not only did we not *know* what many pitchers threw, we discovered that we had no reliable way to find out. There was no reference book, anywhere, that passed along this information. The encyclopedias were entirely silent on the subject. The *Baseball Registers,* a basic source for so many types of information, were no help at all. The old baseball guides were of little use. There were books about pitchers and pitching, of course, but these were hit and miss; finding specific information about a specific pitcher was always a long shot.

And so, realizing there was a hole in the baseball reference library, we simply set out to accumulate information about the subject. Rob went through *Total Baseball* and made a list of every pitcher in history who had pitched at least one thousand innings in the major leagues—through 1990, there were 905 of them—and we went to work, finding whatever information we could find about each pitcher.

In many ways this project was simply blessed. The systematic pursuit of this simple question—*What did he throw?*—was like opening a door into a vast, green area of the game that neither of us was ever really aware of before. One thing led to another, led to another, led to another. We wound up *understanding* things that we had never understood before; perhaps, in a few cases, understanding things that no one had understood before, because no one had pursued this question before. We started with a little cigar box in which to store information, more empty than full, and pushed out one side of it, and pushed out another, and rebuilt another, until we wound up with a very large pile of very interesting information.

The first thing we realized—we figured this out at lunch—was that if we were to accumulate this information, it would be of little use unless we documented it. How do we *know* Vean Gregg threw a drop ball? How do we *know*

Herb Pennock threw an overhand curve, a sidearm curve, a change, a fastball and an occasional screwball?

"Because we said so" not only isn't a good answer for you; it isn't an answer that is helpful to us, either. Very often there are conflicts between sources. One source says that Nelson Potter's best pitch was a screwball; another describes him as a knuckleball pitcher. How do you know what to believe? A documentary trail is essential to sorting out those conflicts, so from the first minute that we began working on this, we have maintained a complete record of the sources that we used.

And what a record it has become. In the process of compiling these files, we have used (and documented) thousands upon thousands of sources; we have no idea how many thousands. But this is getting a little ahead of the story. What did we mean by saying that this project was, in some ways, simply blessed?

At that time, James was the employer, Neyer the employee. James is not organized enough to keep track of his own wallet, let alone keep track of what somebody else is doing all day, and so being James' employee involves long hours of sitting around waiting for an assignment. This project gave Neyer something he could *do*, consuming an essentially limitless number of hours; not only something he could do, but something which was fun, interesting, and actually productive.

We had several hundred old issues of *The Sporting News* in the office. They're a lot of fun to read, but we might go a year without looking at them. This project created a *reason* to look through them, page by page, article by article. *I'm not wasting time reading through a stack of* Sport *magazines from the 1950s* (we could tell ourselves), *I'm looking for information about pitches.*

Over time, the quest to find which pitches everybody threw began to shape our libraries. In making a book-buying decision, we would tend to purchase books based, at least in part, on how promising they seemed as possible sources of pitch information. But this, again, is getting a little ahead of the story.

Within two or three months, we had located some information about probably 350 pitchers. Within a year, we were over 500—more than half the pitchers on our original list. Of course, looking backward, that information was sketchy, and a lot of it wasn't accurate—really, now it seems like nothing—but we didn't know that at the time. That was probably as much information as we *expected* to get.

We soon realized, however, that there were pitchers who pitched in the major leagues for fifteen years, seventeen years, even longer, who didn't pitch 1,000 major-league innings. Paul Assenmacher didn't pitch 1,000 major-league innings, Randy Myers didn't. Jeff Montgomery, Larry Andersen, Tom Henke . . . none of these guys pitched 1,000 innings in the majors. We changed the standard from "1,000 innings" to "1,000 innings or 400 games."

For probably the first year of the project, we didn't make or save notes about pitchers who didn't qualify for the list. But often, when searching for information about Bud Daley, we would stumble across information about Jim Archer, or Dan Pfister. What do you do with that information?

For the first year or so, we would just ignore it. Eventually it occurred to us that information about pitchers who *didn't* qualify for the list was often just as interesting as information about pitchers who did. There was a Yankees pitcher in the 1920s named Walter Beall who pitched only 124 innings in the major leagues, but who nonetheless had a very famous curveball. Why throw that information away? What good does that do anybody?

So then we started saving information about pitchers who didn't "qualify" for the list, just when we happened to see it. Many times, when looking for information about pitchers' pitches, we would find notes about *how fast* pitchers threw. We started collecting those. More significantly, we would very often find, in the course of our research, notes about *how* the pitcher threw—whether he threw sidearm or overhand, whether he had a compact delivery or an awkward delivery, whether there was anything unusual about his actions on the mound.

Anything that helped the reader to visualize the pitcher on the mound, helped the reader to understand specifically how this pitcher differed from the next pitcher, we began to collect. Descriptions, notes, quotes . . . we put them all into the files. Later we realized there are some pitchers who become historically significant even though they don't pile up innings *or* games (Herb Score, Bo Belinsky, David Clyde, scores of others), and that we really should reach out and find information about those guys, as well. We added Negro League pitchers. Just for the hell of it, we added a few pitchers who live only in our imaginations (if you look carefully, you'll find them).

And of course, with the passage of time, the "qualifying" list swelled in number; this was, after all, back when Dubya's daddy was still running the country and Bill Clinton could date in cheerful anonymity. The information in the files swelled and swelled and swelled, not because we were trying to build it up into a book, but simply because, once you begin collecting very specific information about pitchers, it is hard to know where to stop.

Neyer left James' employment in 1993, but the two of us continued to work together on this project, just in a casual way. James kept the list, and would occasionally add to it. Neyer, if he found any information, would e-mail James, and James would add that to the files.

John Sickels worked for James for a few years, and he also pitched a few items into the files, although his interest was never drawn to the project the way ours was (John built his own areas of expertise). Neyer, however, remained interested, and continued to work on it for nine years after leaving Lawrence, Kansas, where the project began. Sometimes he might go for months without sending any information—but sometimes he might send twenty-five or thirty items in a month. It never went away. The tooth was still missing.

Finally, in the summer of 2002, James happened to find a note about the pitches thrown by Cy Falkenberg, a pitcher of no special note who threw his last major-league pitch in 1917. Entering a now-familiar ritual, James pulled up the file (Pitch1.doc) and began to make the entry—and discovered that we already had information about Cy Falkenberg. Multiple pieces of information about Cy Falkenberg.

Days later, he found a note about Cecil Upshaw, went to enter this new information (Pitch2.doc)—and discovered that we already had multiple sources of information about Cecil Upshaw (1966–1975, 34 wins and 36 losses).

At this point, we realized that the time had come to publish the information in the files. This book is the consequence of that realization.

Since then, we have dealt with the problem of trying to "finish" (as a piece of furniture is "finished") a project which could never be "finished" in the sense of being complete. Although we somehow had come up with a wealth of redundant information about Cy Falkenberg and Cecil Upshaw, we were still missing information about a couple of hundred "qualifying" pitchers, and for many others our information was thin. We began an aggressive outreach program to fill in the gaps.

Matthew Namee, who has worked with Bill for the last two years, was as interested in the project as we were, and he accepted the challenge of pulling the files together into something like a book form. This isn't an acknowledgments section, but Matthew was almost a third co-author, in a way; he spent hundreds of hours revising and polishing the files, filling in gaps for the many pitchers whose careers have been played since the files were originally established (who are easy to research, because of the scouting report–type books which now are published every year, but who still need to be included). James made pilgrimages to *The Sporting News* archives in St. Louis, to pore through their clipping files. Neyer spent a few days in the Paul Ziffren Sports Resource Center at the Amateur Athletic Foundation in Los Angeles, and many days looking at microfilm in various other places. We hired Bill Deane and Eric Enders, in Cooperstown, to go to the Hall of Fame's library and do research for us there.

To make the research files into a book, we have also added some miscellaneous articles about pitchers and pitching, some of them almost random, and some of them calculated to fill gaps. We wrote little biographies about a certain class of pitchers—pitchers who

a) pitched at least thirty years ago,

b) are not in the Hall of Fame,

c) have never been the subject of a book-length biography, but

d) had careers of Hall of Fame caliber.

Lon Warneke and Bucky Walters and Billy Pierce were every bit as good and every bit as interesting as Dazzy Vance and Rube Waddell and Don Drysdale; they just didn't happen to make the Hall of Fame cut, and so less attention is paid to them. It seemed to us to be consistent with what we are doing here to fill that gap, to even the playing field a little bit between Tommy Bridges and Dizzy Dean. Other stuff is more random—lists of the pitchers with the best curveballs, the best fastballs of the 1890s and so on, because it is fun to compile those lists and fun to read them, and an article about pitchers who have unique records (only major-league pitcher ever to go 24-5, etc.) because . . . well, one of us got interested in the subject, and it's a book about pitching, so it qualifies.

We haven't filled every gap; we haven't thickened every thin spot. We have come astonishingly close. If you had told us twelve years ago that we would wind up with actual, documented information about the pitches thrown by roughly ninety-eight percent of the pitchers with substantial major-league careers, plus hundreds who had not-very-substantial careers, I don't think we would have believed you. But that's what we've got, and we hope you like it.

ACKNOWLEDGMENTS

Bill James says . . .

The term "acknowledgments" is a combination of the ancient Eritrean word "know", meaning "I know", and the revered comic strip expression "ACK!!!", as in "ACK! I KNOW I forgot somebody." Who it is I forgot, I don't know, but psychologically, I am out on a LEDGE, having gone MENTAL with remorse.

Well, let's remember who we can. First of all, I should thank Matthew Namee, who worked nearly as hard on this book as Rob and I did, at least over the last year of the project, when the hardest work was done. Mike Webber works with us; he also was most helpful with this project, most helpful. I should thank my agents, Chuck Verrill and Liz Darhansoff, and our editor on this book, Brant (let's get ready to) Rumble. (Is that too obvious? Sorry—but see, this way, his name will stick in your head a little better. Also, I'll pay you a dollar if you can come up with a good Bermanism for "Darhansoff.")

I should thank Rob, who did more work on this book than I did. I am grateful to Bill Deane, who did research for us at the Hall of Fame library, and also to Steve Gietschier, who opened the files of *The Sporting News* morgue to me for four days in 1999, when I was operating under one of my periodic delusions that I was near the end of the project.

John Sickels did a little work on this. Tim Wiles from the Hall of Fame sent to me research files on the pitchers who were subjects of biographies, and on several others; thank you, Casey.

My wife, Susan McCarthy, made it through another entire book crunch without hiring a hit man to get rid of me; thank you, darlin'. My kids—Rachel, Isaac and Reuben—were equally tolerant.

A very, very large number of people flipped info to me at one point or another, and I have little chance of remembering them all here, but I salve my conscience by pretending that I acknowledged them all as source notes. I didn't, of course, and I send my apologies to those of you that I missed.

Rob Neyer says . . .

I'm grateful to Adam Ulrey and Mark Armour for opening up their homes and their wonderful magazine collections to me. Jason Brannon, Mike Curto, Richard Lally, Steve Schulman, Peter Bjarkman, and Steve Steinberg all helped us find specific information about specific pitchers. Eric Enders, of Triple E Productions, did a lot of great detective work in Cooperstown.

Mary Brace, Bill Burdick, Tom Gilbert, Mark Rucker, and especially Clay Luraschi of the Topps Company were immensely helpful when I was tracking down photos. I'm also grateful to the Los Angeles Dodgers, Arizona Diamondbacks, Florida Marlins, Baltimore Orioles, and San Francisco Giants for supplying photos.

Eileen Canepari, who presides over the SABR Lending Library, was incredibly helpful when I was trying to cram a bunch of stuff into the book at the last minute.

Late in the process, I realized that there were probably a great number of interesting pitchers who 1) didn't meet any of the various criteria, statistical and otherwise, I'd come up with, and 2) had otherwise escaped my attention. So I asked some friends for help, and Eddie Epstein, Chris Marcil, Geoff Reiss, Burdett Loomis, Bobby Plapinger, John Sickels, Alan Schwarz, and Mat Olkin all responded with lists of pitchers who needed to be in the book, but in many cases weren't. Now, most of them are. A bit of extra credit goes to Mat for the sheer volume of his list, and to Chris for his brilliant idea of allowing fictional pitchers into the book.

Jay Mandel of the William Morris Agency continues to serve as my liaison with the business world (and if anybody ever needed a liaison it's me). Thanks, buddy. Bill already thanked Brant Rumble (but if anybody ever deserved to be thanked twice it's Brant).

I'm eternally grateful to Kristien, my wife, and Micah, my son, for giving me two great reasons to get up every morning.

And finally, I have to thank Bill. When he hired me fifteen years ago, it was a dream come true. This book is another.

PART I
PITCHES

WHAT DO YOU CALL THAT THING?

It has been our policy, since we began this effort, simply to call every pitch by whatever name its author called it.

Many times this is not as straightforward as it seems. Many times—most times, we suppose—the information about a pitch does not come from the pitcher himself, but from somebody who played with him or somebody who wrote about him. What the other person calls the pitch is not necessarily what the pitcher would have called it.

Also, many times the best descriptions of a pitcher's work are not contemporary descriptions, but descriptions written down fifteen or twenty years later. The language of the game changes substantially in every generation; a rising fastball becomes a four-seam fastball which becomes a four-seamer, a forkball becomes a split-fingered fastball which becomes a splitter, a drop curve becomes an overhand curve which becomes a 12-to-6 curve, an incurve becomes a fadeaway, a fadeaway becomes a screwball, and now almost nobody throws a screwball but people throw a circle change-up that does the same thing, sort of.

A pitcher will say, forty years after the fact, that he threw a knuckle curve, although we know for certain that

a) the term "knuckle curve" hadn't been invented at that time, and

b) even now, there is no consistent definition of what a knuckle curve is or what it does.

In fact, in many cases there is not a consistent definition of what some pitch is. One guy will call a pitch a slider; another guy will call the *same pitch* a curve. Don Newcombe, according to some sources, had an outstanding slider—but Newcombe never threw a slider. He threw a pitch that looked like a slider, but he and those close to him called it a curve.

Sometimes old timers would call the David Wells pitch, the pitch we now call a 12-to-6 curveball, a "drop"—but other people might use the term "drop" to mean the forkball, or some version of sinker.

It is our policy to call each pitch whatever the pitcher called it, but this is of no use to you if you don't know what the damn thing *was.* We had not anticipated when we began this effort how difficult it would become to trace the changes in the language, and to tie those changes in the language to the pitches that are being thrown. Both things change, over time—the language changes, and the pitches in common use change. Documenting those changes, and tying one to another, is perhaps the fundamental challenge of this book.

This will require several articles to explain, but let us begin in this way.

At the start of major league baseball in 1871, pitchers were not supposed to be the focus of the game. A pitcher's job was to deliver the ball, to start the action—but not to get the batter out.

By 1870, half a dozen pitchers were experimenting with curve balls. You know this story, but bear with us; we have a point. Some physicists, nineteenth-century Robert Adair know-it-alls, claimed that it was impossible to make a ball curve, and for many years this argument raged, even well after various pitchers had actually demonstrated that yes, it damn well could be done (see biographic article about Tommy Bond).

Now, visualize Candy Cummings throwing a curve ball. Little bitty guy, 120 pounds, square hat and a uniform with a collar like the one your father wears to church; picture it in your mind . . . Got it?

At least eighty-eight percent of you just made a very basic mistake. Candy Cummings threw underhand. Submarine style. That first generation of curveball pitchers, who battled science to demonstrate that a baseball could be curved—they all threw underhand, because the rules said they had to.

And they didn't throw very hard. The rules in the 1870s required that a pitch be thrown with a stiff wrist and a stiff elbow. This constraint was there, essentially, to prohibit the pitcher from throwing hard (remember, they weren't supposed to be getting the hitters out, not all by themselves).

Well . . . they weren't supposed to throw hard, but they did. The rule against using your wrist, the rule requiring a stiff arm, was all but impossible to enforce, and so pitchers, from the very beginning of professional baseball, *did* throw hard—not anything like as hard as major-league pitchers throw now, but they threw as hard as they could under the constraints placed upon them, and it looked pretty hard to the hitters.

And probably—this is just an opinion—but probably they made that ball curve like you wouldn't believe. Why? The baseballs.

If a baseball isn't perfectly centered, it will break unpredictably. A lopsided baseball will break in ways that you can't imagine, if you're accustomed to twenty-first-century baseballs. The manufacturing standards of baseballs in the 1870s weren't anything like what they are now. The baseballs were probably very often a little bit lopsided when they were brand new—and they didn't throw them out and get new ones eight or ten times an inning. They used baseballs until they couldn't use them any more.

So that's baseball in the 1870s—underhanded pitching, supposed to be a stiff arm and stiff wrist, balls probably not thrown more than seventy-five miles an hour, but curves like Pamela Anderson. There were basically three pitches in the 1870s: the curve, the fastball, and the change, all thrown underhanded.

This is not an article about the rules, but we're just saying . . . you have to implant the rules within your mind before you can understand anything about the game. By the early 1880s, the "stiff arm, stiff wrist" regulation was completely gone, and pitchers were whittling away at the regulation about throwing underhanded. They were pushing the limits, swinging the arm out away from the body a little bit as they delivered the pitch, then throwing sidearm, and then, by the mid-1880s, throwing overhand (see article about Tony Mullane).

As overhand pitching developed, pitch selections developed. The drop curve and the down shoot became common in the second half of the 1880s. Some pitchers in the 1880s, most notably Old Hoss Radbourn, began to throw a wide variety of pitches. And they certainly threw harder than pitchers had thrown in the 1870s—this, after all, was the driving force behind the switch from underhand to overhand pitching. They switched to overhand because they could throw harder that way.

Within a very few years, between 1882 and 1887, underhand pitching became virtually extinct. Between 1889 and 1892 the first *real* hard throwers entered baseball. The 1890 Spalding Guide, edited by Henry Chadwick, reported that "The most effective work in the box since overhand throwing succeeded the straight-arm delivery of the ball to the bat, was that accomplished in 1889. There was far more of strategic skill exhibited to the position, for one thing, and the tendency to depend upon mere speed for success was not resorted to except among the less intelligent class of pitchers."

Baseball men today, early in the twenty-first century, often complain about the way the radar guns have redefined pitching; it's as if everything revolves around speed, and the strategy of getting the batter out with movement, deception, and location is not respected as it should be. There were no radar guns in 1890, but what Chadwick was saying then was exactly the same thing—and, of course, it was true then and it is true now.

By 1892 Chadwick was still sounding the same theme, but coming at it from a different angle.

> *The season of 1891 was marked by some exhibitions of swift pitching unequaled in the annals of the game,* and yet it was not effective in placing the team, which had the cyclone pitchers, in the lead. If the speed is too great for catchers to handle even with the protection the defensive paraphernalia at command which the breast pads, the masks, and the padded gloves of the period yields, why then it is worse than useless. It was skilled strategic pitching which helped to win the pennant in 1891 and not "cyclone" pitching.

> Speed is all very well as an aid to success, but without . . . thorough command of the ball to give it full effect, it is more costly than otherwise.

(Italics ours; not in original.) The team to which Chadwick referred here, which "had the cyclone pitchers" but did not place "in the lead" was, of course, the New York Giants, with Amos Rusie. Rusie, who threw harder than anyone before him, led the National League that year in strikeouts, with 337, but also in walks, with 262, and the Giants finished third.

Rusie did not succeed in driving the Giants to the pennant—but Rusie and a few other hard-throwing pitchers who came up about the same time (Cy Young, Jouett Meekin) forced the National League to move the pitcher's mound back, and they forced the League to switch from a pitcher's "box" to a pitcher's "slab" (or "rubber," as it is called now). Remember—this is the other mistake we inevitably make in visualizing the early game—from 1881 to 1892 the pitchers were throwing from fifty feet away.

And they took a running start.

Well, in 1892 the National League batting average was .245, and frankly it's kind of amazing that it was that high. You get a guy with a major-league fastball taking a jump start and throwing at you from fifty feet—that's hard to hit. Within a few years, had they not done something about it, the league batting average would probably have been .210.

In 1893, however, they moved the pitching mound back to sixty feet, six inches, and they locked the pitcher to a little slab, rather than allowing him a "box" in which to shuffle his feet as he went into his delivery.

This opened the door to a ten-year period of massive experimentation in pitching. Apart from speed, there is a big, big difference between pitching from fifty feet and pitching from sixty. It is very difficult to make a baseball do anything from fifty feet. You take a knuckleball pitcher pitching from fifty feet, the batting average against him would be about .748, because the ball doesn't really break until the last few feet. Of course, you can make the ball break earlier if you do things a little differently, but still, it's a lot easier to get the ball to do something over the course of sixty feet than fifty feet.

The hitters ruled baseball for three or four years in the mid-1890s, but then the pitchers began to catch up. Inshoots, outshoots, drop curves, hard curves, slow curves, raise balls, spit balls, slow balls, overhand curves, sidearm curves . . . these guys threw everything.

Modern pitching really began in the years following the 1893 rules changes. Yes, it is true that Mickey Welch and a couple of other guys had thrown a primitive in-shoot in the mid-1880s, which may have been a screwball/fadeaway, or may actually have been closer to Greg Maddux' cut fastball. It was something that drifted in on a right-handed hitter (from a right-handed pitcher).

But really, it was the pitchers of the 1890s—Rusie, Cy Young, Kid Nichols, Clark Griffith, Kid Gleason, Bill Hutchison, Brickyard Kennedy, Pink Hawley—who invented the modern pitching repertoire. By 1903, not literally but generally speaking, the pitchers were throwing everything we throw now. The forerunner of every modern pitch was in use somewhere by 1910.

Many years ago, in the early 1980s, one of us (Bill) wrote, "Babe Ruth was a hurricane who swept up the precious strategies of the previous generation and scattered them like ashes. You cannot oppose a home run offense with a one-run offense; you'll get beat." What he was saying is, Babe Ruth simplified the game, from an offensive standpoint. The baseball of the years 1910–1919 was very, very rich in strategy—lots of bunts, huge numbers of stolen-base attempts, constant efforts to hit and run. A full-fledged war was fought: hitters and runners vs. pitchers and catchers. Babe Ruth stopped all of that, because he proved that you could do more damage with long-range artillery than you could by fighting the war one base at a time.

What we had never understood, until we began this effort, was that the exact opposite happened, at the same time, with pitching. Offenses were complex and rich in strategy before 1920; simple and direct after that. But pitching was simple and direct in the years just before 1920, and became much more rich and complicated just after that.

Why? The spitball. Not just the spitball, but the emery ball, the tar ball, the licorice ball, the grease ball, the mud ball, the shine ball, the scuff ball, the paraffin ball . . . anything you can think of (and a lot you can't), they tried it.

The scuff ball was perfected in the minor leagues in 1908, and brought to the majors in 1910. It was originally held secret by its inventor, Russ Ford, but the secret was picked up by George Kahler in 1911 or 1912, and became common knowledge within a year after that.

The spitball, developed in approximately 1902, had already begun to put an end to the rich experimentation in pitching which characterized the years after 1893. The emery ball brought strategy in pitching to a screeching halt.

You have to understand, these guys were not subtle about defacing the baseballs. They rubbed dirt on the ball, rubbed tar on it, spit tobacco juice on it. They spiked it, rubbed as much sweat into it as they could get in there, did everything they could do to make the baseball dark, heavy and lifeless. If they could find a pool of water, they'd drop it in the water. This was all either legal or ignored by the officials.

Well, think about it. If you can openly do that stuff to the baseball, are you going to mess around with a dinky little curve and a screwball used as a change? Of course not. The silliest question that people ask about this era is how many pitchers threw the spitball. *Everybody* threw the spitball. Walter Johnson threw the spitball. You couldn't help it. That was what the ball was.

And—this is an overstatement, but it contains more truth than falsehood—everything else was dying out. Why mess around with a nickel curve, when you can just rub shoe polish on the ball and fill it up with sweat, and it takes Ty Cobb to get the thing out of the infield?

We came to this realization while following up on two things that puzzled us about the information we had: One realization was that there were a number of pitchers from the late 1910–1919 era who were hard to document . . . hard to find specific references for. Why? Because, when everybody is throwing the scuff ball, the press will stop reporting that such-and-such a pitcher is throwing the scuff ball. It's assumed; it's unstated, and therefore difficult to document.

The other thing we noticed was that, just after 1920, there was another explosion of experiments in pitching.

The things that are written about pitching just after 1920 are night and day different from the things written about pitching just before 1920. As to the "explosion of experiments" in pitching . . . look at the comments, in the pages that follow, on Vic Aldrige, on Virgil Barnes, on Jesse Haines, on Rosy Ryan. Aldridge is talking about using the curve more in Wrigley Field, but switching to the fastball more in other parks. Barnes is talking about the difference between a roundhouse curve and a sharp-breaking curve. The Rosy Ryan comment reveals that, by 1923, John McGraw had his men charting pitches—the first known reference to this practice.

In 1920 or '21, Joe Bush came up with a forkball. In 1921 or '22, Jesse Haines began using the knuckleball. The knuckleball had been invented earlier, in 1906 or thereabouts, but was used as more than a waste pitch by only a few pitchers before 1920. Just after 1920 you have star pitchers in both leagues (Haines and Eddie Rommel) throwing clearly and unmistakably *different* pitches, but both calling it a knuckle ball.

Lefty Grove came to the majors in 1925, using what is really the first "modern" delivery. Dead Ball Era pitchers did a lot of stuff with their arms; Grove brought to the majors a power delivery, getting a lot of drive out of his legs. It was copied by everybody, and eventually became the standard delivery of the 1950s and '60s. Shortly after that, the slider begins to emerge as a distinct pitch, rather than being simply the "curve" that is used by some pitchers—the so-called nickel curve.

The *language* changes. The pitch which was known as the fadeaway becomes the screwball, sometime between 1921 and 1928. The old terms "inshoot" and "outshoot" and "drop curve" disappear, and are replaced by new terms like "sinker" and "sailer." From 1870 until the early 1920s, the word "curve" was a generic term which meant "any breaking pitch." Articles would include mention of a pitcher's "fastball and curves," which could mean just about anything. Beginning in the 1920s, pitches begin to develop—knuckleballs and forkballs and, later, sliders—which are clearly "breaking pitches" in the sense that they are not simple fastballs or changes, but which are not called "curves." The term "breaking ball" replaces that meaning of the term "curve."

Urban Shocker, one of the great pitchers of the era, maintains meticulous notes about every hitter in the league. Catchers—who, as late as 1925, would often stand to receive the pitch when there was nobody on base—go into a full squat on every pitch. The origin of the slider, although it can legitimately be dated earlier or later, really traces to that era, to the mid-1920s, when George Uhle and then Red Ruffing began throwing the pitch that became known as the slider.

At first, we were puzzled by this. Why is all of this stuff happening at the same time? Why are there so *many* interesting things happening in pitching, all at once?

And then it hit us. Oh, of course; it's the flip side of

the Babe Ruth phenomenon. When they took the spitball away from pitchers in 1920, the pitchers went to school. The league ERA was going through the roof, and the pitchers were scrambling to catch up.

The great pitchers of the Dead Ball Era—and don't get us wrong, they *were* great pitchers—were basically one-pitch pitchers. Walter Johnson didn't worry much about refining his curve ball until he was in his mid-thirties. Pete Alexander was called "Old Low and Away" because he would throw that same pitch, that little sinker or curve or slider or whatever it was, probably eighty-eight miles an hour and tailing away from a right-handed hitter—he would throw that until the sun went down and the umpires had to stop the game. Eddie Cicotte . . . well, he was anything but a one-pitch pitcher, but he's the exception. There is one of those in every generation. Most great pitchers had either a great fastball or a great spitball, and that was all they needed.

Johnson and Alexander could pitch that way because

a) they had fantastic arms, and, in the case of Alexander, fantastic control, and

b) the game was working for them.

They could make mistakes and get away with most of them, because the ball didn't jump. The pitchers who came along after 1920 couldn't afford to think that way. They needed every edge they could find.

The most enduring pitches to emerge from this "era of experimentation," 1920–1927, were the slider and the forkball. The origins of the slider, as we said before, are difficult to trace. The earliest pitcher who clearly and absolutely threw the slider, in our opinion (actually, in Bill's opinion; Rob thinks Bill is a lunatic), was Chief Bender. Bender did not have a name for the pitch, which in that era was not really unusual (because any breaking pitch could just be called "a curve"; a pitcher might throw three or four curves—a drop, an outcurve, etc.). The pitch now called the slider was one of Bender's curves.

Bender, however, was probably *not* the first pitcher to throw the slider; he was merely the earliest pitcher to whom the modern slider can clearly be traced. Clark Griffith (1891–1914) relied heavily on a hard, late-breaking curve ball very much like a slider. Cy Young, who threw a wide-breaking curve the first half of his career, rejuvenated his career in 1901 when he switched to a harder, slider-like curve with a smaller break.

Arthur Daley once suggested that the "secret" of Pete Alexander's greatness may have been that he was throwing a slider as his bread-and-butter pitch, and a really good slider at that, at a time when nobody had seen the slider and didn't know what to do with it. That's one theory, but another theory is that maybe a lot of pitchers from that generation were throwing the pitch now known as the slider, but, like Bender, just never articulated it as a separate pitch.

But Bender, while he clearly threw the pitch, threw it once in a while. George Uhle, late in his career, threw it a lot (and is sometimes credited with inventing the pitch). Red Ruffing threw the slider (and is also sometimes credited with inventing it).

Lefty Grove, in the late 1950s when the slider was the hot pitch, said the pitch he had called the "sailer" was actually the same pitch as the slider. (A lot of people in the '20s and '30s threw a sailer, but probably most of them were using that name for what we would now call a cut fastball—a fastball that "sails.")

Anyway, isolated pitchers in the 1920s were probably throwing the slider, but it never quite emerged, somehow, as a big-name pitch.

The eventual breakthrough of the slider, in the late 1930s, can be traced to three things: the pitch getting its own name, Red Ruffing's successful career, and Bucky Walters' MVP season in 1939. Walters, a converted infielder, was taught to throw the slider—with no name attached to it, just a generic curve—in 1935, by Chief Bender. Perfecting the pitch, Walters rode it to a 27-11 mark in 1939—oddly enough, the same record George Uhle posted in 1926.

In 1938, only a very few pitchers were throwing the slider, and the average baseball fan probably would never have heard the term "slider." By 1948, everybody and his friggin' brother was throwing the pitch, and the name had become a permanent part of the game. It was the pitch of the 1950s, and it was very controversial. Old-timers, for reasons you probably have to be well over seventy years old to understand, hated the pitch, and blamed everything that was wrong with the game of baseball on the slider. Well, the slider and the Red Communists. When Bob Feller suggested that George Blaeholder be put in the Hall of Fame for inventing the slider, Frankie Frisch said, "Blaeholder goes in the Hall of Fame for inventing the pitch that enabled Roger Maris to hit 61 home runs?" (Frankie wasn't quite seventy at the time, but he was prematurely grouchy.)

In the 1940s, teams began hiring pitching coaches. We think the first true pitching coach might have been Earle Brucker with the A's, in the early '40s. The Indians hired Mel Harder in 1948. Casey Stengel had Jim Turner and relied heavily on him, and Leo Durocher had Frank Shellenback; by the mid-1950s everybody had to have a pitching coach (another thing which irritated the grouchy old-timers, by the way, unless they were lucky enough to get one of the jobs).

One practical effect of every team having a pitching coach was to add weight to conventional thinking. Since 1920, many major-league pitchers had thrown a knuckleball as a part of a standard repertoire. Fastball, curveball, maybe the slider, and a change-up which might be a knuckleball or a palmball or something else. But there has always been a strong irrational prejudice against the knuckleball; if there wasn't, there would be a hundred knuckleball pitchers in the major leagues today.

One manifestation of this gut-level dislike of the knuckler was the argument that a pitcher shouldn't throw the knuckleball as a part of a mixed repertoire; instead, the pitch should be left to specialists. This argument had been around at least since the 1930s (see entry on Joe Bowman), but it gained momentum when pitching coaches were hired. It was a way that guys like Frank Shellenback could explain why it was okay for Hoyt Wilhelm to throw the knuckleball (about which Shellenback probably didn't know the first thing), but not okay for a young pitcher like you.

When I became a baseball fan in 1960 (this is James; Neyer wasn't even born in 1960), a fan would hear this argument several times every summer, served like communion. As I look back on it, this seems exceedingly strange. For forty years, there had been pitchers who mixed a knuckleball in with other pitches, quite successfully, and in 1960 there were still many such pitchers. Early Wynn won the Cy Young Award in 1959, mixing the knuckleball in with fastballs and curves and sliders, and Bob Purkey went 23-5 in 1962, doing the same thing. Vern Law, Cy Young Award winner in 1960, would bust out an occasional knuckler, and Frank Lary threw some knuckleballs when he went 23-9 in 1961. Many other pitchers of that era did the same thing—yet pitching coaches were actively and successfully pushing the idea that you couldn't do this. You'd hurt your arm, they would say, and you wouldn't be consistent enough with the knuckleball to make it effective. Jim Bouton was told to stop throwing that damn knuckleball, so that's what he did until he blew out his arm and didn't have a choice.

So the knuckleball, as a part of a mixed repertoire, essentially disappeared after 1960. Another consequence of the hiring of pitching coaches was the beginning of the movement toward streamlined, "efficient" pitching deliveries. If you watch films of games from the 1950s, the deliveries of pitchers seem extraordinary—arms and legs flying like torpedoes. Even Bob Gibson's delivery, from the late 1960s, looks quite extraordinary today. Any modern pitching coach, given a young Bob Gibson, would immediately set out to expunge all that unnecessary flailing about.

From 1950 to the present, pitching mechanics have gotten more and more streamlined, and more and more compact. This continues to this day; even the deliveries of the early 1980s, compared to those of the early twenty-first century, look a little bit quaint and melodramatic. Speaking as a guy who doesn't know shit about it but has strong opinions anyway (this is Bill again), I don't believe there is any valid reason for this change; I don't believe there is any actual reason to streamline the deliveries. Give me Bob Gibson any day; I don't care about the noise in the delivery. But the real Bob Gibson struggled for years before emerging as a star—and in modern baseball, the coaches would beat that excessive motion out of him and bury him in the bullpen.

All of that traces back to about 1950—the hiring of pitching coaches, the elimination of the knuckler as a part of a mixed repertoire, and the simplification of pitching mechanics. There is a fourth thing that traces to 1950: the two fastballs.

In modern baseball, the four-seam and the two-seam fastball are completely distinct pitches, and it is relatively easy to distinguish one from the other. Trying to walk backward on this . . . when did this occur? When did pitchers start throwing multiple and distinct varieties of the fastball?

The first pitcher who is known to have thrown both a rising and a sinking fastball is Curt Simmons, 1950. (Satchel Paige threw two distinct fastballs, but neither of them was a sinker.) Simmons, who had a great fastball, emerged as a star in 1950, and gave interviews talking about throwing both a rising and a sinking fastball.

Here the two of us, the two authors of this book, diverge. Bill is of the opinion that Simmons most likely was among the very first pitchers to do this. There probably was an antecedent to it, in the way that Chief Bender is an antecedent to Bucky Walters, but, in Bill's opinion, it probably was not at all common before 1950.

Neyer disagrees. Rob is more of the opinion that Simmons is merely the earliest pitcher we can *document* throwing the two distinct fastballs, and that there is little reason to believe that the practice was not common before then.

This is James again. My argument is that the practice could not have been common much before 1950, because there is simply no awareness of the two fastballs as distinct pitches. In the Lon Warneke biographic article, I quote Tom Meany as talking about how much Warneke looked like Dazzy Vance, on the mound. But Warneke obviously threw a two-seam fastball; Vance obviously threw a four-seamer. Meany didn't see that, because this distinction wasn't meaningful to him. It wasn't meaningful to anybody in that generation.

This is Neyer. My argument is that many, many pitchers before Curt Simmons were said to have "a weirdly sinking fast ball" or something similar, and one can find photos of pitchers gripping their fastball along the seams, even though most of the instructional books of the time told young pitchers to hold the ball *across* the seams, to get that "rise" (which does not, of course, literally exist). I think that pitchers tried different things, and some of them discovered that if they used the two-seam grip, they could make the ball do funny things. Sinking things. And it's likely that they used that funny fastball in conjunction with the regular one. In fact, there are multiple references to pitchers who threw both a fastball *and* a "sinker," which I think was, in some cases, a two-seam fastball.

In any case, there is little hard evidence of other pitchers throwing the two fastballs until the mid-1960s, when the practice suddenly exploded in popularity. The next successful pitcher who can be documented as throwing the two fastballs, after Curt Simmons, is Wally Bunker, the teenager who went 19-5 in 1964. Bunker was a teammate of Robin Roberts that summer; Roberts, of course, had for many years been a teammate of Curt Simmons.

Bob Shaw, in a 1972 book about pitching, specifically warned young pitchers *against* trying to throw the two fastballs. It would be interesting to know what the hell he was thinking. Shaw may have tried to throw the two fastballs, and found that it wasn't helpful to him, or he may have been parroting something *he* had been told by a pitching coach when he was young.

In any case, by the time Shaw published his warning, the battle was lost. Bob Gibson—also a teammate of Curt Simmons for several years—threw both a rising and a sinking fastball (although we don't know the exact date when he began to throw both; Gibson expanded his repertoire throughout his major-league career). There were a large number of star pitchers born in the years 1940 through '44 who reached the majors between 1964 and 1967: Don Sutton, Tom Seaver, Ferguson Jenkins, Jim Palmer, Steve Carlton. Most or all of these pitchers threw both the sinking and the rising fastball. By the time Shaw was telling young pitchers not to do this, most of the great young pitchers were doing it.

For some reason, sometime in the late 1980s the language changed; the "rising" fastball became a "four-seam" fastball, the "sinking" fastball became a "two-seam" fastball. We believe that the catalyst for this change was Syd Thrift. Thrift, who wrote a 1990 book (*The Game According to Syd*), was a popular figure in the mid- to late 1980s, and he talked about the two-seam and four-seam fastball. One of his theories was that he could help a pitcher throw harder by teaching him to switch from a two-seam to a four-seam fastball; the four-seamer, which rises, tends to come in two to four miles an hour faster. Almost every pitcher who throws the two fastballs throws the four-seamer a few miles an hour faster.

Let's see, what else is changing . . . Around 1980 the forkball was more or less replaced by the split-fingered fastball. A short description of what happened to the forkball, 1940–1975, is that it became an old man's pitch, and it became impossible to teach young pitchers to throw it.

In the early 1940s, the forkball was moderately popular, competing with the knuckleball to become the "freak delivery" of choice. In the late 1940s the slider became even hotter, but the forkball remained a popular pitch to teach a young pitcher.

The forkball, as thrown by Joe Bush or Ernie Bonham or Joe Page, was a hard thrown ball—like a splitter. Dizzy Trout threw a forkball; he probably threw it 90 miles an hour. [This paragraph and the next are solely Bill's opinion; Rob's not at all convinced.] But what happened was, as the generation of pitchers who learned the forkball from 1945 to 1955 aged, it became an old man's pitch. By the late 1960s, virtually the only people left who threw the forkball were old guys like Elroy Face and Diego Segui. They threw the forkball about 78 miles an hour, because that was as hard as they could throw.

The forkball, then, wasn't "cool"; you couldn't teach a young pitcher to throw a forkball, because he thought you were dissin' him, trying to get him to throw that slop. The appeal of the split-fingered fastball was that it was a *fastball*, man; it had cachet.

The splitter is not *exactly* the same pitch as the forkball; a lot of people think that it's just the same pitch with a different name, but there actually is a subtle difference. But the splitter, and Bruce Sutter, brought the forkball back to life. Bruce Sutter was taught to throw the forkball in the minor leagues in 1973, by Freddie Martin; he called it a forkball at the time. Sutter became a superstar in 1977, and the split-fingered fastball took hold at about the same time. Sutter switched to calling his a splitter, and the pitch came back to life.

Actually, *both* pitches came back to life; after Sutter there were a lot of pitchers, and several star pitchers, who threw the forkball as a key pitch. Bob Welch and Dave Stewart threw the forkball, and the forkball is alive and well today. And everybody and his friggin' uncle threw the splitter. The splitter was often called the "pitch of the '80s."

Tony Kubek would say that the *real* pitch of the eighties was the circle change. That was true, too; for three years there you couldn't get through the turnstile without being hit by a circle change.

The next big thing in pitching—and, for now, the last big thing—is the cut fastball. Up-to-the-minute history tends not to age well, so we'll pass over the cutter fairly lightly.

In writing about the knuckleball, I noted that, in the 1920s, there were two quite distinct pitches being thrown, both *called* the knuckleball. One was the pitch we now call the knuckleball; the other was a pitch thrown much harder and with a different break, but also called a knuckleball (see entries on Eddie Rommel, Ben Cantwell, Jesse Haines and Freddie Fitzsimmons).

To a modern reader, this seems very odd, that you would have distinct pitches sharing the same name. But if you think about it, we're doing the same thing now with the cut fastball. There are all kinds of different things right now being called a cut fastball. There is a cutter that breaks in; there is a cutter that breaks out. Pitchers talk about "cutting" the fastball in or "cutting" it out. The cut fastball is a pitch that is thrown like a fastball, but held a little bit off-center so that it spins out of the hand with a different rotation. Greg Maddux throws what is called a cut fastball, but which is a pitch that drifts to the plate like a falling leaf; it seems bizarre, to me, to call that damn thing any kind of a fastball.

The key figure in the popularity of the cut fastball is Mariano Rivera, the magnificent Yankee relief ace who bears an uncanny resemblance to the young Henry Fonda. Mariano throws a hard fastball that explodes in on a left-handed hitter. And, as is always the case, this has antecedents going back many years.

Another thing that is happening right now is that more pitchers are throwing underhand/low sidearm than at any time since 1887. From 1890 to 1990 there were never more than a couple of pitchers at a time who threw underhanded or used a low-sidearm delivery (see entry on Joe McGinnity; see also list of underhand/low sidearm pitchers since 1901, page 436). Now we have . . . who knows how many? There must be a couple dozen of them in the major leagues, and some teams have two or three of them.

Bill James is on record as predicting, many years ago, that underhanded pitching would eventually return, and become a standard, if not *the* standard, way of pitching. It may be that it's starting to happen. It may also be that this little boomlet will soon bust. Unless there is a dramatic success story—Byun-Hyung Kim or Chad Bradford wins the Cy Young Award—the revival is not likely to catch fire. The down side of underhanded pitching is that it limits the pitcher's repertoire. Well, maybe not, but the repertoire of pitches which have been successfully thrown by underhanded pitchers, to this point in time, is fairly limited. This is where we are in 2004, anyway; we'll just have to see what happens next.

This is not everything there is to say about the history of pitch selections; this is just a very general overview. We'll follow with a few other articles to flesh it out.

ALL THE PITCHES WE COULD FIND

(okay, most of them)

ROB NEYER

This is not designed as an instructional book; there are plenty of good ones out there already. But we hope that when you run across a pitch in the middle of this book that you don't recognize, you can find a decent description of its origins and physical characteristics here. You'll find all the *big* pitches mentioned below, but they also get their own essays in the pages that follow.

BLOOPER *a.k.a. Floater* According to *The Pitcher* (John Thorn and John Holway, 1987), this high, arching pitch was "brought into popularity by Indianapolis' Bill Phillips (formerly of Cincinnati)."

Phillips pitched for the Reds from 1899 through 1903, then spent 1904 with Indianapolis (as both pitcher and manager), so we can guess that Phillips showed off his floater that season. To say he brought anything into popularity is a stretch, though, because it would be another forty years until another pitcher would be well-known for throwing a floater/blooper.

What's unique about the Blooper is that it's been thrown so rarely that oftentimes the pitch is nicknamed after (or by) its practitioner. The most famous floater/blooper was named "Eephus" by Rip Sewell. Steve Hamilton, a side-arming relief pitcher of the late '60s and early '70s, threw a blooper called the "Folly Floater." And in the 1980s, Dave LaRoche's ultra-slow ball was called the "LaLob."

In recent years, only Orlando "El Duque" Hernandez has shown off a version of the blooper. He used the pitch, thrown at approximately fifty miles per hour and rarely for a strike, a few times per game in 2002, and on August 26 he made the highlight reels when Alex Rodriguez took one blooper for a ball, then hit the next one over the fence for his forty-sixth home run of the season.

BREAKING BALL Term used to describe a curveball, a slider, or as a catch-all for any pitch that either can't be identified or falls somewhere in between the curve and slider.

CHANGE-UP *a.k.a. Change of Pace, Slow Ball, Change* Any pitch that's designed to fool the batter because of its lack of speed. There are "specialty" change-ups—circle change, palmball, slip pitch, and others—but "change" often simply means "taking something off" the fastball or curveball.

Also see Circle Change, Forkball, Foshball, Palmball, and Slip Pitch.

CIRCLE CHANGE If the split-finger fastball was the pitch of the '80s, then the Circle Change-up was the Pitch of the '90s (or one of them; the Cut Fastball probably belongs in there somewhere, too).

The first printed reference I've found to "circle change" is in *The Scouting Report: 1990*. What's more, the first edition of Paul Dickson's *The Dickson Baseball Dictionary,* published in 1989, does not include "circle change" (or "circle change-up") among the 5,000-some baseball terms listed. So there's good reason to think the *term* didn't gain any sort of currency until the early 1990s.

But when was the pitch itself invented?

Jim Slaton recently said, "We didn't have the circle change back then"—Slaton pitched in the majors from

1971 through 1986—"so for a change-up I just took something off my two-seam fastball."

On the other hand . . . Wayne Twitchell told me he threw the circle change late in his career (which ended in 1979). Tim McCarver has described Johnny Podres' change-up as a circle change.[1] And I believe that Warren Spahn was throwing the circle-change—or something very much like it—in the 1950s.

Warren Spahn? Yes, Warren Spahn.

While everybody *knew* that Spahn threw a great screwball in the latter part of his career, for years Spahn denied throwing a screwball at all. It seems likely, to me at least, that he was actually throwing the pitch that is now known as the circle change (or something like it). In *The New Yorker,* Roger Angell wrote about watching and listening as Spahn tutored an apathetic Mickey Mahler in 1987 . . .

> "Look, it's easy," Spahnie said. "You just do this." His left thumb and forefinger were making a circle, with the three other fingers pointing up, exactly as if he were flashing the "O.K." sign to someone nearby. The ball was tucked comfortably up against the circle, without being held by it, and the other fingers stayed up and apart, keeping only a loose grip on the pill. Thrown that way, he said, the ball departed naturally off the inside, or little-finger side, of the middle finger, and would then sink and break to the left as it crossed the plate. "There's nothing to it," he said optimistically. "Just let her go, and remember to keep your hand up so it stays inside your elbow. Throw it like that, and you turn it over naturally—a nice, easy movement, and the arm follows through on the same track."[2]

Sounds a lot like the circle change to me, though Angell, probably taking a cue from Spahn, calls the pitch a "sinker-screwball." That's apparently what Spahn called the pitch when he actually used it, but the description of both the technique *and* the movement of the pitch . . . well, that's the circle change-up. That's the pitch that Pedro Martinez throws (though it's unlikely that anybody, even Warren Spahn, has ever thrown it as *well* as Pedro throws it).

1. Tim McCarver with Danny Peary, *Tim McCarver's Baseball for Brain Surgeons and Other Fans* (1998).
2. Roger Angell, *Season Ticket* (1988).

The key to the success of the circle change, in the marketplace of pitches, is what Spahn said: "There's nothing to it."

CROSSFIRE Not a pitch, but a style of pitching that once enjoyed a certain degree of popularity. Basically, the idea is that a right-handed pitcher (for example) works from the extreme right edge of the pitching rubber, and instead of stepping toward the plate, he steps toward the third-base dugout and throws with sidearm delivery, thus launching the ball from a position designed to make the batter very uncomfortable.

CUT FASTBALL *a.k.a. Cutter* A cut fastball is a pitch thrown at full speed, but released slightly off-center, so that it has a sharp horizontal break near the plate.

It's hard to say exactly when people first started using the *term,* "cut fastball." However, it probably happened in the early 1980s. In Tom Seaver's 1984 book about pitching, he (or his ghost) wrote, "You hear a lot of TV talk these days about the 'cut fastball.' This is just another kind of moving fastball that tails away from a right-hand hitter and into a leftie [*sic*]. It looks like a slider but lacks the sharp downward movement of a good slider. It is effective because of its different kind of movement in the hitting zone."[3]

But while the term's been around for something like twenty years, the pitch itself has been around for a long, long time. In 1953, Ethan Allen wrote in his instructional book, "Johnny Allen, also an overhand pitcher, threw a fastball that was unique because it slid or broke like a curve. It was somewhat like a fast ball (wrist rigid instead of relaxed), but he threw over the side of the index finger to a greater extent. This off-center pressure caused the break."

Nearly fifty years later in *The Act of Pitching,* Dr. John Bagonzi wrote, "With a cutter pressure comes from the middle finger and the ball is gripped more to the outside."

There are some who will tell you that a cut fastball and a slider are the same pitch, and it's probably true that one term has often been used when the other should have been. But there's no doubt that they're distinct pitches (or, rather, that they *can* be). Quoting Tom Candiotti in a recent column for ESPN.com, answering

3. Tom Seaver with Lee Lowenfish, *The Art of Pitching* (1984), page 112.

the question, "What's the difference between a cutter and a slider?"

> A cutter (or cut fastball) and a slider have several distinct features. A slider is 6 to 8 mph slower than a fastball, and it breaks horizontally (or laterally) *and* vertically—not with the same pronounced break of a curveball, but with a similar rotation.
>
> A cutter is thrown with a fastball grip as well as a fastball rotation, and it's only 2 or 3 mph slower than a fastball. But it breaks a few inches—more horizontally than vertically—because the pitcher places slight pressure on his second (non-index) finger upon release.
>
> The grip on a slider is similar to a curveball grip—it's released with a break of the wrist—but it's designed to look like a fastball as it approaches the plate. The pitcher wants to make the batter think the slider is a fastball so he commits to his swing as the pitch breaks.
>
> A right-handed pitcher who throws a cutter, such as . . . Mariano Rivera usually will attempt to run the cutter away from a right-handed hitter, working the outside part of the plate. But against a left-handed batter, he'll throw the cutter inside and hand-high, which often enough will break the bat. That's a tough pitch for a lefty to handle and hit fair.
>
> The cutter has been around baseball for as long as I can remember (my career began in the early 1980s). Rivera has arguably the best cut fastball in baseball history. Two left-handers with excellent cutters are his teammate, Andy Pettitte, and New York Mets starter Al Leiter.

Candiotti makes the difference between the slider and the cutter sound pretty clear-cut, but it's not always so easy.

In *The Man in the Dugout*, Paul Richards says of Roy Parmelee, "He had a sailing slider-fastball kind of pitch which was effective." Was that a slider, a fastball, or maybe a cutter? We'll never know.

According to a *Daily News* article in 2002, "Hall of Famer Juan Marichal used to throw [the cut fastball], though he called it a slider . . ."[4]

There are numerous contemporary references to a pitcher relying on a cutter one season, and a slider the next . . . but most of the time, the pitcher didn't change; the reporter did.

Generally, though, even if you don't know how the pitcher is gripping the ball and snapping his wrist (or not), you can tell the difference between a cutter and a slider by checking the speed of the pitch and its movement.

4. T.J. Quinn in the New York *Daily News* (June 9, 2002).

DROP BALL *see Overhand Curve*

DROP CURVE *see Overhand Curve* It's simplistic to suggest World War II as the strict dividing line between terminology, but it's probably true that the term "drop curve" was frequently used before World War II, and not so frequently afterward. "Overhand curve" was already taking over before the war, but it became the standard term in the 1940s.

(Similarly, in the same period "slow ball" was largely replaced in the vernacular by "change of pace" and other, more specific terms.)

The term "Drop Ball" was probably also used by some reporters to refer to a forkball or to any other pitch that broke straight down as it neared the plate.

DRY SPITTER Sounds like an oxymoron, right? The term was occasionally used, from roughly 1908 through the 1930s, to describe various pitches that behaved like the spitball: not much spin, sharp downward break.

In May of 1908, one newspaper—*The Sporting News*, probably—ran etchings of two "Young Pitchers of Promise": Ed Summers and Eddie Cicotte.

Cicotte's key pitch is identified as the "knuckle ball," which "starts toward the batsman at a high rate of speed, but slows up and breaks quickly just before reaching the plate." It's difficult to see detail, but it appears that Cicotte is gripping the ball with the first knuckles on his first three fingers, the thumb and pinky serving as support.

Meanwhile, the dry spitter, "introduced by Summers, Detroit's 1908 pitching find, is also projected above the shoulder and acts as erratically as the saliva-covered sphere, but, as it is dry, it is handled by the catcher and other fielders without the danger of a wild throw."

Nearly twenty years later, John J. Ward wrote of Fred

Fitzsimmons, "In fact, some batters refer to Fitzsimmons' knuckle ball as a 'dry spitter.' "

This shouldn't be a surprise, because the pitch as described by Ward sounds *exactly* like the pitch attributed to Ed Summers.

> Fitzsimmons' knuckle ball . . . is something else again. He holds it by doubling up the first two fingers of his pitching hand, gripping the ball rather lightly against these doubled fingers between his thumb and the third and fourth finger of the pitching hand. He throws the ball with a good deal of speed. As it leaves his hand, it slips gently out from under the knuckles of his two bent fingers and it breaks down very much like a spit ball.[5]

(It's important to note that Ward, elsewhere in the article, makes a very clear distinction between Fitzsimmons' knuckler/dry spitter and the other sort of knuckleball: the "floater" that travels slower and in less predictable fashion than Fitzsimmons' pet pitch.)

Anyway, that was in 1927. In 1936 Big Jim Weaver said of his forkball, "It acts very much like the old, much abused spitball. In fact, batters sometimes call it a dry spitter. Like the spitball, it comes up to the batter, then ducks . . ."[6]

In the early '40s, the Chicago *Daily News'* John P. Carmichael also referred to a forkball as a "dry spitter," but the term seems to have disappeared shortly thereafter.

EEPHUS *see Blooper* Made famous by Ewell Blackwell in the late 1940s. *Most* famously, Ewell threw an Eephus to Ted Williams in the 1946 All-Star Game, and Williams hit it over the fence.

In the last five years, people have been using the term "blooper" or "eephus" to refer to what we might call a ridiculously slow curveball. But the original blooper, as thrown by Sewell or Bobo Newsom or a surprising number of other aging pitchers of the 1940s and 1950s, was a pitch thrown 20 to 30 feet into the air, which crossed the plate on a downward trajectory. The "blooper" of Orlando Hernandez isn't anything like that; it's just a real big schoolyard curve ball that El Duque is able to get by with because nobody is expecting to see a pitch like that in a major league game.

5. John J. Ward, *Baseball Magazine* (February 1927).
6. F.C. Lane, *Baseball Magazine* (June 1936).

EMERY BALL A specific sort of scuff ball, invented by Russ Ford in 1908 and brought by him to the majors in 1910. Essentially, Ford secreted a piece of sandpaper inside his glove, and roughed up one side of the ball with it. This was technically illegal, even then, but the authorities weren't real big into enforcement, and Ford pitched some wonderful ball before hurting his arm. Ford's secret got out within a couple of years and other pitchers threw the emery ball, though not with the same success.

FADEAWAY *see Screwball* The pitch that Christy Mathewson made famous, and an antecedent of the screwball. It's not clear exactly how Mathewson threw his fadeaway, but we do know that, as thrown by the right-handed Mathewson, it was an off-speed pitch—or "slow ball," in the parlance of the time—that broke down and away from a left-handed hitter.

For more on the fadeaway and the screwball, see article on page 52.

FINGERNAIL BALL *a.k.a. Fingertip Ball; see Knuckleball* Early in the history of the knuckleball, pitchers experimented with a number of different grips. Some pitchers gripped the pitch with their knuckles, some with their fingertips, and some with a combination thereof. Oddly, though the fingertip grip wound up being the grip of choice, it was the term "knuckleball" that stuck. However, for another fifty years or so, pitchers and writers would feel compelled to apologize for "knuckleball." In the 1948 *Baseball Register,* Gene Bearden says, "My knuckler probably should be called a fingertip ball. I file my nails down and grasp the ball with my thumb and little finger, resting the tips of my three other fingers on the ball."

Eddie Summers must have been proud.

For more on the fingernail ball, see article about knuckleball on page 40.

FASTBALL The king of all pitches, the only one that's been around since the very beginning. Until (roughly) the 1920s, you would see only one term: "fast ball." Gradually, though, players and writers started talking about different kinds of fastballs: sinking fastballs (commonly, the "sinker"), rising fastballs, tailing fastballs, sailing fastballs, even sliding fastballs. Most of those terms remained in standard use until the 1990s, when for some reason they were replaced by terms that described how the ball looked to the hitter ("two-seam" and "four-seam") or how the pitch was thrown ("cut fastball" and "split-fingered fastball"), rather than how it seemed to behave.

For more about the fastball, see article on page 23.

FORKBALL Precursor to the Split-Finger Fastball, the Forkball was popularized shortly after World War I by Bullet Joe Bush, then with the Red Sox. Basically a sort of change-up, Bush's forkball was gripped with the index and middle finger spread as far apart as possible, and when thrown correctly would travel plateward with little spin, almost like a knuckleball, and appear to dip suddenly upon its arrival at the plate.

Over the years, it's likely that the pitch was generally thrown with the fingers held closer together, and more spin.

What distinguishes the forkball from the splitter? As thrown by Bush and Roy Face (its most famous practitioners), the forkball is held deeper in the hand and thrown with less velocity than the split-finger fastball (think of the hard curve vs. the slow curve).

For more about the forkball, see article on page 45.

FOSHBALL *a.k.a. Fosh Change* According to an article about Tom Gordon in April of 1996, the foshball is "a cross between a split-finger pitch and a straight change-up."[7]

According to another article, "It's held like a fastball, except the fingers are spread slightly apart. It works like an off-speed split-fingered fastball, or a changeup that breaks."[8]

It's not clear who invented the "fosh," but the first pitcher known for throwing it was Mike Boddicker, who won sixteen games as a rookie with the Orioles in 1983. There are numerous references to pitchers throwing the fosh in the years since, but these days you can watch a game on TV every night and hear nary a mention of the pitch, probably because it's easier to just call every change-up a "change-up."

There are no fewer than three stories about how the fosh got its name. One holds that Earl Weaver thought it looked like a cross between a fastball and a dead fish. Another has David Nied, one of the later practitioners, saying that fosh "sounded like the perfect word for the movement of the pitch."[9] And finally, Al Nipper suggested that fosh is an acronym for the feeling the batters had when the pitch sailed past them for a strike: "F" for "full," "O" for "of," and "SH" for . . .[10]

HARD CURVE Like a slow curve, but faster.

Just kidding. The term "hard curve" has been used over the years to describe many pitches, and in the 1950s and 1960s was often used interchangeably with "slider."

INCURVE *a.k.a. Inshoot* "Inshoot" was a term popular in the 1890s. "Incurve" was more popular after the turn of the century, and was used until about 1930.

One might assume that the incurve is simply the reverse of the outcurve, which would be the reverse of the curveball . . . which is to say, a screwball.

But it's not. The opposite of the curveball was first named "fadeaway"—once somebody bothered to name it—and later "screwball."

So what was the incurve? According to John McGraw, it was something like nothing. Or rather, it was just another name for a fastball.

> All balls that are twisted out of their natural course are called curves. The outcurve, the drop, down shoot, and so on, are simply a curve ball to the professional player. To us there is no such thing as an incurve. That is what we call a fast ball. Of course, I am assuming that the pitcher is right-handed. A so-called incurve is nothing more than a ball thrown in a natural way with great force. A ball thus thrown will naturally curve inward, to a certain extent. If it takes a sharp jump, due to the speed, we call that the "break on his fast one." In other words, the inshoot is the natural course of a ball. A curve is unnatural, due to a reverse twist being put on it.[11]

7. Sean McAdam (New England Sports Service), "A fresh start for Gordon" (April 3, 1996).
8. Jimmy Golen (Associated Press), "Sox pitchers hit with 'fosh fever' " (March 10, 1996).
9. Paul Dickson, *The New Dickson Baseball Dictionary* (1999), page 204.
10. Golen, ibid.
11. John J. McGraw, *My Thirty Years in Baseball.*

This makes sense, if you think about it. If a fastball thrown overhand can be perceived as "rising" (even though it doesn't, really), then it follows that a fastball thrown three-quarters or sidearm by a right-handed pitcher might be seen as "curving" toward (into) a right-handed batter.

There are, to be sure, some sources suggesting that "incurve" was the first term used to describe the pitch that eventually became known as the screwball, but these sources aren't particularly convincing.

INSHOOT *see Incurve* In many sources, "inshoot" and "incurve" are used interchangeably, but in others they're apparently considered different pitches, with the "incurve" actually being some sort of curveball (perhaps an early screwball) and the "inshoot" being simply a fastball with movement in the opposite direction of a regular curveball. It would be nice if "curves" and "shoots"—two popular terms in the nineteenth century—were clearly differentiated, but they're not. That said, we suspect that the term "shoot" generally referred to some variety of fastball.

KNUCKLEBALL *a.k.a. Fingernail Ball, Fingertip Ball, Floater, Butterfly Ball, Flutterball, Dry Spitter* The knuckleball is a pitch thrown with very little rotation, usually thrown less than 80 MPH, so that the buildup of air pressure causes the ball to dive sharply a few feet in front of the plate.

The best evidence suggests that the knuckleball—the pitch that is thrown with very little spin, off either the knuckles or, more commonly, the fingertips—was invented by Eddie Cicotte and modified by Eddie "Kickapoo" Summers, in 1906 when both were pitching for Indianapolis.

For more about the knuckleball, see article on page 40.

KNUCKLE CURVE *see Spike Curve* Three pitchers have been well-known for throwing a "knuckle curve," and the most interesting thing about that is that all three pitchers threw different pitches.

The first pitcher was Dave Stenhouse, who started the second All-Star Game for the American League in 1962 (they played two that year). A couple of years ago, Stenhouse described his knuckle curve to me . . .

> . . . I put my knuckles on the ball and threw it like you'd throw a fastball. And so when I threw the knuckleball, it had a semi-knuckleball, semi-fastball spin on it. And the pitch came in and broke straight down. I said to myself, "Geez, that's a pretty good pitch." So starting in high school, I developed this knuckle-curve. I threw my fastball 88 or 89, and I'd guess the knuckle-curve came in around 82–83, almost the same speed as my slider. Everybody thought I was throwing a spitball when I came up to the majors.

(By the way, as Stenhouse describes the speed and the trajectory of his knuckle-curve, it sounds very much like the "knuckleball" thrown by Freddie Fitzsimmons and Jesse Haines.)

The second was Burt Hooton, who made a big splash in the early 1970s with the Cubs. Not as big a splash as Mark Prior would make thirty years later, but close. According to Brent Strom, who saw Hooton pitch many times, Hooton's knuckle curve was thrown with the pitcher placing his "fingernails on the ball much like a knuckleball pitcher, but instead of maintaining position of the fingernails as the ball is thrown, will actually 'push' hard, with the fingers elongating, creating overspin, something the knuckleball pitcher does not want to do."

And the third is Mike Mussina, whose "knuckle curve" isn't any such thing. The pitch Mussina throws is the same curveball that was thrown by Don Sutton, Darryl Kile, and many others. Essentially, Mussina's knuckle curve is thrown like a regular curveball, but with the index finger dug into the ball to provide leverage. The term "spike curve" was invented to describe this pitch, but for some reason it's never really entered the vernacular, except among some pitching coaches.

OUTCURVE Basically, a fancy name for a curveball that's not thrown overhand. That is, if a right-handed pitcher throws a curveball with a three-quarters delivery to a right-handed batter, the ball will curve away—out—from the batter.

This term has been traced back to 1865, and was still in use through the 1920s.

OVERHAND CURVE *a.k.a. Overhand Drop, Drop Ball, Downer, 12-to-6 Curve* Not to make a value judgment or anything, but the overhand curveball is the best curveball.

Why? Sidearm curves and three-quarter curves are fine pitches . . . if the batter bats the same way the pitcher pitches. That is, a sidearm curve thrown by a right-handed pitcher can be devastating to a right-handed hitter. A good sidearm curve thrown by a right-handed pitcher makes a right-handed hitter flinch (or worse), and if you flinch you're lost. However, that same pitch thrown to a left-handed hitter is often easy pickings. This, of course, is 1) why hitters are platooned, and 2) why Jesse Orosco has been in the majors since a peanut farmer was President.

The overhand curve doesn't break horizontally, however. It breaks straight down, which means it's equally effective, or very nearly so, against both left- and right-handed hitters.

Generally, it takes great arm strength to throw a great overhand curveball and it's not an easy pitch to control . . . so not many pitchers have great ones, or even good ones.

Just in the last few years, "12-to-6 Curve" has, for some reason, generally replaced "Overhand Curve" in the popular vernacular.

For more about the curveball, see article on page 33.

PALM BALL *a.k.a. Wiggle Ball* In *Blackball Stars*, John Holway quotes Chet Brewer on Joe "Bullet" Rogan, who first pitched professionally in 1917:

> Rogan could throw a curve ball faster than most pitchers could throw a fast ball. And he was the inventor of the palm ball. He had such a terrific fast ball, then he'd palm the ball and just walk it up there. Hitters were well off stride. I saw him one winter just make Al Simmons crawl trying to hit that ball.

There's no way to know if Rogan really did invent the palm ball, because for many years all forms of the change-up were generally described by the same term: "slow ball."

Seems unlikely, though. We've got a photo of a young Walter Johnson demonstrating the "Slow Ball as it Leaves the Hand," and the grip looks exactly like that used for what later became known as the palm ball. It's likely that the palm ball, though not known by that term, was one of many options, and perhaps the most popular option, for pitchers casting about for a slow ball (or in our vernacular, a change-up).

By the 1940s, "slow ball" was out and terms like "change of pace" and "palm ball" were in. The June 1948 issue of *Baseball Magazine* includes a photo of a smiling Ewell Blackwell demonstrating "how he holds his new pitch, the 'Palm Ball,' which he has added to his repertoire this year." The photo shows the baseball held in the palm by the thumb and pinky finger, with the other three fingers just along for the ride.

In 1950, Phillies reliever Jim Konstanty won the National League's MVP Award. And though he didn't actually rely on his palm ball—his best pitch was his slider—the palm ball probably was his second-best pitch, and it's the palm ball for which Konstanty is remembered.

Similarly, 1970s reliever Dave Giusti became well known for his palm ball, even though (as he told Roger Angell), "The fastball is my best pitch . . ."

Today, Eddie Guardado is the only well-known pitcher who features the palm ball, as most major leaguers prefer the circle change or the split-finger fastball, both of which are apparently easier to control and/or more baffling to the hitters.

Finally, it should be said that some versions of the palm ball are indistinguishable from the Slip Pitch (see below), which was taught by Paul Richards.

In an early-1970s photo of Giusti demonstrating his palm ball (as the caption says), "The ball is stuffed into the palm of the hand. The rest of the fingers lie gently and slightly curved around the ball. The pitcher releases the ball with a fast ball motion by letting the ball float out of the hand, controlled by the pressure of the inside joint of the thumb."[12]

In Stan Musial's autobiography, he says about Bob Friend, "And he came up with a 'slip' pitch, a kind of palm-ball change-up." In some books, photos purporting to show the slip pitch show something that looks like the palm ball, and vice versa.

Like the knuckleball, there are different ways to throw the palm ball. Essentially, it's thrown without much help from the fingertips, and with as little spin as possible. It was a popular pitch for a long time, but has generally been superseded by the circle change-up and the splitter.

12. Walter Alston and Don Weiskopf, *The Complete Baseball Handbook: Strategies and Techniques for Winning* (1972), page 112.

PUFF BALL Invented, and perhaps thrown exclusively by, Gaylord Perry. As Tim Tucker described the pitch in *The Sporting News*, "As the 'puff ball' is thrown, a cloud of resin dust emerges, distracting the hitter, if not rendering him helpless."

There's only one documented occasion on which Perry threw the puff ball: April 22, 1981, against the Reds. However, Perry said he developed the pitch in 1980, when he was pitching for Texas (later in '80, he also pitched for the Yankees), and so he may have thrown some that season, too.

Perry explained himself by saying, "I figure if the resin bag is out there, you're supposed to use it, right?"

Major League Baseball disagreed. As *The Sporting News* tersely reported in the May 30 issue, "Gaylord Perry's puffball was outlawed."

RAISE BALL Joe McGinnity was careful to distinguish between his Raise Ball and the Jump Ball. The latter was—at least according to McGinnity—simply a fastball with (apparently) a late "hop," as thrown by Kid Nichols and Nig Cuppy. McGinnity's raise ball, on the other hand, was a sort of fastball thrown underhand, "from any angle in the vicinity of the knee."[13]

RISING FASTBALL No, a fastball can't actually "rise," unless it's thrown underhand. But if you throw a fastball overhand with enough force, it will *appear* to rise because it's not dropping as much as the batter's brain thinks it should.

So please don't bother sending us letters. While we attribute the Rising Fastball to a number of pitchers in this book, we do know what we're talking about.

For more about various fastballs, see article on page 23.

ROUNDHOUSE CURVE A big, looping curveball. Thrown by a right-handed pitcher to a right-handed hitter, a roundhouse curve would start high and inside and finish low and outside. Distinguished from the Overhand Curve, which drops straight down.

SAILER *see Cut Fastball* The term "sailer" has been used, over the years, to describe more than one pitch, but there's evidence suggesting that "sailer" was often used to describe the pitch that's now known as the Cut Fastball.

> **ITEM 1:** In 1927, Ted Lyon's sailer was described in *Baseball Magazine* as a "peculiar fast ball that . . . will swerve from a straight line as much as a foot or more, breaking somewhat like a curve. Lyons throws this ball with great speed and with an overhand motion."

> **ITEM 2:** In 2002, Charlie Metro told me that Stubby Overmire, who Metro both caught and batted against in the mid-'40s, "had a little bit of a cut fastball. He had stubby fingers, he wasn't a tall guy; he'd cut the fastball a little. They call that a cut fastball now, but it's what we used to call a sailer."

Lyons was a right-hander, which means his curveball broke from right to left, which means his sailer broke from right to left. And an overhand fastball, thrown by a right-handed pitcher, that moves right to left with great speed makes one think of Mariano Rivera, who of course throws the best cutter around.

Metro's not a young man, but he's got an excellent memory—or if he doesn't, he's very good at faking it—and he was a professional player, manager, coach, or scout from 1937 through 1984, so he probably knows a cut fastball when he sees one.

Granted, the term "sailer" was also used to describe the pitch that became known as the slider, but 1) I believe it was more often used to describe the cut fastball, and 2) anyway, I think what people called a "slider" in the 1930s and '40s was often, and perhaps usually, more like the cut fastball than anything else. (Yes, it can all become quite confusing.)

SCREWBALL *a.k.a. Fadeaway* The origins of the screwball are even murkier than those of most pitches, as nobody yet has stepped forward to take credit for inventing the pitch. Christy Mathewson, of course, was the first major leaguer identified as throwing the fadeaway—which, by most accounts, became the screwball—and we have good reason to believe that Mathewson learned the pitch from minor-league teammate Dave Williams in 1898.

But that's about all we know. We're not sure the screwball was exactly the same pitch as the fadeaway. We're not sure who threw the first screwball, or who named it.

13. James B. Foster, *How to Pitch* (1908).

For more information about the screwball, see article on page 52.

SHINE BALL Eddie Cicotte wasn't the only pitcher who threw the Shine Ball, but he's certainly the most famous. Cicotte, while still active, adamantly denied any funny business with the baseball, claiming instead that the knuckleball was the secret to his success. As he told *Baseball Magazine* in 1918,

> Last season I was credited with the discovery of a new invention along this line known as the shine ball. This mysterious ball aroused a good deal of interest in various quarters. Ban Johnson must have a whole trunk full of balls that were thrown out of various games and forwarded to him for inspection. I understand that a number of these balls were analyzed by a chemist to determine if any foreign substances were rubbed on the surface. This analysis, so I am informed, showed that the ball had been treated with tobacco juice. But a good many pitchers use the spitball occasionally, and most of them chew tobacco. None of the many investigations ever involved me in criminal practices with the ball and my own contention that the Shine ball was a myth was never successfully refuted.[14]

But as *Baseball Magazine* had reported in 1917, "Clark Griffith calls this delivery illegal and nearly every opposing American League club has protested that Cicotte does something to the ball to give it that peculiar, unhittable 'sail' effect."[15]

Eventually, the secret got out. In 1948, Frank Shellenback—a spitball pitcher for decades who also happened to have been Cicotte's teammate with the White Sox in 1918 and 1919—said,

> Cicotte, a natural fast ball pitcher, doubled his effectiveness with the shine ball he developed.
>
> Eddie darkened the ball on one side by rubbing it in the dirt. Then, he slickened the ball by rubbing it vigorously on his pants.
>
> The process camouflaged the ball perfectly. The ball, thrown with blazing speed, rotating quickly, and showing the white side only at split-second intervals, baffled batters completely.

Four years later, Cicotte himself finally admitted it. When asked by H.G. Salsinger about his "mystery pitch," the one that nobody seemed quite sure about, Cicotte replied, "It was a shine ball, one over which I had perfect, or near perfect, control. I could break it either to the right or left and I was generally able to keep the ball low, around the knees. It was the manner in which I delivered it that made the pitch successful."[16]

Russ Ford, and Clark Griffith before him, had discovered that if you scuffed a baseball, it would break in the direction of the scuff when you threw it. Cicotte took that one step further. Not only did he darken or scuff one side of the ball, he made the other side white and slick, perhaps with the aid of paraffin on his uniform pants. And not only did this make the ball do strange things, it was confusing as hell for the batsmen.

Spitballs, of course, were generally outlawed in 1920. Physically defacing the ball had always been illegal, technically, but nobody seemed able to catch Cicotte in the act (and there's not a lot of evidence suggesting they tried). In 1921, Cicotte was banned for conspiring to throw the '19 World Series, so we don't know if he could have kept getting away with cheating. But the leagues generally cracked down on such tactics—Dave Danforth was, from 1921 forward, harassed constantly by the officials—and Cicotte probably would have been in trouble.

SHORT CURVE *a.k.a. Fast Curve a.k.a. Slurve?* This one doesn't actually appear anywhere else in this book, but that's almost certainly because of a deficiency in our research rather than the absence of the "short curve" in the real world.

Johnny Sain was Jim Kaat's pitching coach in 1965 and '66, and as Kaat relates in his autobiography, "From Sain, I also learned what he called a short curve, which is somewhere between a slider and a curve. He called it a controlled breaking ball. If I had a hitter 3-0 and I was concerned about him having the hit sign, I had confidence that I could throw that pitch for a strike just about any time I wanted to."[17]

Before Sain worked with Kaat in Minnesota, he

14. Eddie Cicotte, *Baseball Magazine* (July 1918).
15. *Baseball Magazine* (November 1917, page 166).
16. H.G. Salsinger, *Baseball Digest* (June 1952).
17. Jim Kaat with Phil Pepe, *Still Pitching* (2003), page 118.

worked with Jim Bouton in New York. And according to a 1967 article in *Baseball Digest*, Bouton threw "a combination between a curve and a slider. It's a harder curve than most curves."[18]

Sain himself, a few years after he worked with Bouton and Kaat, referred to his trademark pitch not as the "short curve" or the "controlled breaking ball," but as the "fast curve" and even as the "Slider (fast curve)."

If all of this makes you think of the "slurve," you're not alone. And according to *The New Dickson Baseball Dictionary*, in 1973 a newspaper headline read, "Kaat 'Slurves' Yanks."

All this is confusing, but really points out something that keeps coming up when you research questions like this: we know that Randy Johnson throws a slider and that Barry Zito throws a curve, but everywhere in between there's room for interpretation.

SINKER *a.k.a. Sinking Fastball* The terms "sinker" and "sinking fastball" were, for many years, used interchangeably. But are they the same pitches?

Not necessarily. "Sinking fastball" is, today, synonymous with "two-seam fastball" (see below). Basically, grip the ball along—as opposed to across—two seams, and throw like hell. A baseball thrown like this will naturally sink, because (as I understand it) the seams aren't doing much to counteract gravity.

But there's more to the sinker than just throwing the hell out of it.

In 1980, long-ago Yankees shortstop Mark Koenig said of Wilcy Moore, "He had one of the first good sinker balls. He'd go in with three men on and they'd never score."[19]

Moore certainly was not the first pitcher to throw a sinker, but he probably was the first pitcher to become famous for throwing one.

In Walter Alston's instructional book, he (or, more likely, one of his anonymous helpers), described the sinking fastball like this:

> **Sinking Fast Ball** (with the seams). The "sinking" fast ball is released with an over-the-top, then outside-in, flip of the wrist. For a right-handed pitcher, this ball drives down and in on a right-handed hitter, and down and away from a left-handed swinger. In releasing the ball, the pitcher has to turn the ball over at the last moment, placing more pressure on the index finger.
>
> This fast ball is gripped with the middle finger and forefinger curled snugly, not tightly, along the two parallel short seams. The thumb underneath pinches across the short seams on the lower half of the baseball.
>
> Known as a sinker, it is a little more difficult to throw than the rising fast ball because of the over-the-top wrist flip. When a ground ball is needed, this pitch can be very effective.[20]

Here, we've got the two basic elements, at least one of which always shows up when baseball people talk about the sinker: gripping the ball along the seams (rather than across them), and "turning the ball over."

SINKING FASTBALL *a.k.a. Two-Seam Fastball*
see Sinker

SLIDER *a.k.a. Slide Ball, Slide Piece* A slider is a pitch thrown almost as hard as a fastball, much harder than a curve, and which breaks later and sharper than a curveball. If you attend a game and see a pitcher throwing one pitch ninety-two miles per hour, one pitch eighty-seven miles per hour, and one pitch seventy-eight miles per hour, the slider is the pitch thrown eighty-seven.

The slider is said to have been invented by George Blaeholder, or maybe George Uhle. Or Cy Young, or Pete Alexander, or Johnny Allen, or perhaps Red Ruffing.

Because the slider is, or was initially, simply a variation of the fastball, there's really no inventor, though Uhle took credit for inventing the name, presumably sometime in the 1930s. The term, and perhaps the pitch, didn't become truly popular until just after World War II; before long, more pitchers threw one than didn't.

Essentially, the slider is thrown with a fastball motion, but with the ball held off-center. Some pitchers snap their wrist slightly as they're releasing the ball, and some let their natural finger pressure do the slider-making work.

For more about the slider, see article on page 37.

18. Charles Dexter, *Baseball Digest* (March 1967).
19. Dave Newhouse, *The Sporting News* (July 5, 1980), page 11.
20. Alston and Weiskopf, ibid.

SLIP PITCH Forever identified with Paul Richards, who must have taught his favorite pitch for more than thirty years, as a minor-league manager, major-league manager, and team executive.

I've seen a few photos of supposed grips used for the slip pitch, and I've been drawn to the conclusions that "slip pitch" 1) means different things to different people, and 2) was little more than a slightly different version of the palm ball.

SLOW BALL *see Change-up and Palm Ball* "Slow ball" was, until the second half of the twentieth century, widely used as a catch-all term for anything that wasn't a fastball or curveball. Fadeaways, knuckleballs, forkballs . . . all of them were simply described as "slow ball," at least occasionally. However, "slow ball" was *most* commonly used to describe the pitch that eventually became known as the "palm ball." Photos of pitchers demonstrating the slow ball almost always showed the thumb and little finger exerting most of the pressure, with the ball held near the base of the three middle fingers. And that's what later became generally known as the palm ball.

SLOW CURVE Sort of a catch-all category that might include both the Roundhouse Curve and the Overhand Curve, but generally the Overhand variety will be specified as either that or the Drop Curve (or, today, the 12-to-6).

SLURVE *see Short Curve* Today, Kerry Wood throws an outstanding breaking ball that he calls a slider but breaks downward, like a curve. Is that a slurve? All we really know is that some pitchers throw a pitch that doesn't break as much as they think a curve should, but more than they think a slider should, and that some of *those* pitchers call that pitch a slurve. There's no textbook definition, though, or at least not one that I could find.

SNEAK-BALL In the September 1937 issue of *Baseball Magazine*, Dan Daniel wrote, "The sneak-ball is a fast delivery which is effective because the ball is on top of the hitter before he knows it. That type of pitching owes its baffling qualities not so much to speed as to motion and a certain something which is given to the pitch by the wrist."

In that same article, Daniel says the "best sneak-ball pitchers are Oral Hildebrand, Browns, and Roy Henshaw, Dodgers," and in another article Lou Fette is said by Braves coach Hank Gowdy to throw the "sneak ball."

We're still not sure what it means. Sneaky fastball, probably.

see Sneaky Fastball

SNEAKY FASTBALL There's no technical definition of a sneaky fastball, but essentially it's a fastball that looks, to the batter, faster than it really is. Typically, this deception can be caused by two things: 1) a pitching motion that obscures the baseball until the last possible instant, and/or 2) a pitching motion that looks slow and easy, but propels the ball with at least a fair degree of speed. The sneakiest fastball I ever saw was the one thrown by Sid Fernandez.

SPIKE CURVE A better name, if rarely used, for the so-called "knuckle curve" thrown by Mike Mussina, and before him Don Sutton and others.

see Knuckle Curve

SPINNER According to Dickson, "spinner" is just another term for "breaking ball," but occasionally an old-time pitcher will refer to his curveball *and* his spinner, and to this point we're not exactly sure what to make of this.

SPITBALL *a.k.a. Spitter* An early twentieth century pitcher named Elmer Stricklett has widely been credited with inventing the spitball, but he denied it. According to Stricklett, he learned it from George Hildebrand, who had learned it from Frank Corridon (and there's decent evidence that Corridon wasn't the first to throw it).[21]

For more information about the spitball, see article on page 56.

SPLIT-FINGERED FASTBALL *a.k.a. Splitter* Invented by Fred Martin, perfected by Bruce Sutter in the late 1970s, and popularized by Roger Craig in the early '80s, the splitter looks to the hitter like a fastball until it takes an abrupt dip. What's the difference between a forkball and a splitter? Not always a lot. But according to Sutter, "The way Martin taught it and I threw it, the pitch wasn't the same as a forkball. You threw it a lot harder. And the ball has spin on it . . . It's like a changeup except harder."[22]

21. Dickson (1999), page 469.
22. Rob Cairns, *Pen Men* (1992), page 330.

For more on the split-fingered fastball, see article on page 45.

TWO-SEAM FASTBALL *a.k.a. Sinking Fastball* There don't seem to be any rules governing the words used for various pitches. "Two-seam fastball" is now more commonly used than "sinking fastball," though it's the latter term that's more visually vivid. Meanwhile, the visually vivid "12-to-6 curve" has largely replaced "overhand curve."

Actually, if there is a governing principle, it's the trend toward newness. We'll never see a return to "drop curve," but it's likely that in fifty years "12-to-6 curve" will have been replaced.

WIGGLE BALL *see Palm Ball* We've found exactly one reference to the Wiggle Ball: in the caption for a series of six photographs showing the grips that Hugh McQuillan used for his pitches. It's clear, from the photo, that the wiggle ball—held in the palm by the thumb and pinky, with the three middle fingers raised off the ball—is what had generally been known as the "regular" slow ball, and would later become known as the palm ball.

THE MIGHTY FASTBALL

BILL JAMES

Throwing a fastball is different from throwing a curve, throwing a slider, or throwing a knuckleball in that it is not so much a skill as it is a talent. Thus, a history of the fastball is not so much a history of the skill as simply a record of the talent. This may overstate the fact; there *are* different ways to throw a fastball, and there is much skill involved in the use of the animal.

From the beginning of baseball, long before baseball separated itself from the cluster of other games with which it shares an ancestry, throwing hard has been a part of the game. George Zettlein, a pitcher whose glory years were the years of the National Association (1871–1875), was alleged by old-timers to have thrown as hard as Walter Johnson. I don't *believe* them, but then, I wasn't there with a radar gun, so what do I know?

The rules of baseball, in its infancy, discriminated against throwing the ball hard. This understates the fact; the rules deliberately tried to keep the pitchers from throwing the ball too hard. The basis of the game was the interaction between fielders and hitters; the pitcher was not supposed to upset the apple cart by striking people out or walking them.

Thus, it is hard to really believe that any pitcher from the 1870s, throwing underhanded and supposedly with a stiff wrist and a stiff elbow, could have gotten speed on the pitch comparable to Walter Johnson. The Zettlein comment is a characteristic comment, in two ways:

1) Everybody in history—or at least everybody before Bob Feller—who had a decent fastball was, at some point, described as being faster than Walter Johnson, and

2) The old-timers get faster and faster as they get older and older.

I don't mean (2) above in a snide sense, that old players are inclined to romanticize their youth. That's true also, of course, but what I meant was this: that players are most impressed with the *first* really good fastball that they see. Honus Wagner, who batted against Cy Young in the 1890s and faced Walter Johnson in several exhibition matches, said that Young threw harder than Johnson. Charlie Gehringer, who batted against the young Lefty Grove and, many years later, the young Bob Feller, said that Grove threw much harder than Feller. That's the typical response; it doesn't provide much *real* evidence that Grove was faster than Feller. When Charlie Gehringer first saw Bob Feller, he had been in the major leagues for ten years. He had seen a lot of fastballs. When he first saw Grove, he was more like "Wow, never saw anything like that before."

In the first half of the 1880s, baseball switched gradually from underhand to overhand pitching. This increased the speed with which the ball was thrown, and thus brought into the game the first generation of true fastball pitchers. But when that switch was made (1882–1887) there was a generation of young boys who began working with an overhand delivery when they were twelve, thirteen, fourteen years old. As you would expect to be the case, when those boys matured, they were faster than the pitchers before, who had mastered the overhand delivery in mid-career.

The fastest of that generation is easy to identify: it was Amos Rusie. Rusie, Cy Young, and Jouett Meekin, who all threw harder than anyone had ever seen before, forced the National League in 1893 to move the pitching mound back from fifty feet (where it had been since 1881) to sixty feet and six inches.

So far, I have been equating "thrown real hard" with "good fastball." It is, of course, not simply being thrown hard that makes a fastball a good pitch. There is also the issue of movement. Jeremy Hill, a minor leaguer currently the property of the New York Mets, has been known to hit triple digits on the radar gun, and throws 98–99 consistently. But his pitch is fairly straight and his motion is not deceptive, so people still hit it.

From the time baseball switched to overhand pitching, some pitchers have known how to make a baseball "hop" or "jump," and some people have known how to make a baseball sink. (Yes, yes, Egbert; we all know that a baseball does not literally jump in mid-air, it merely appears to do so to the batter. Very good; now sit down and shut up.) Ted Breitenstein, a .500 pitcher for the Cardinals and Reds through the 1890s, threw a rising fastball. Nig Cuppy, a minor star with the Cleveland Spiders, threw what he called a "jump ball"—a rising fastball.

In the Dead Ball Era (1903–1919), a "hopping" fast ball was prized, because it led to strikeouts, pop ups, and fly balls, which generally were not dangerous in that era. In the lively ball era (beginning in 1920), the "sinking" fast ball was more prized, because it kept the ball in the infield, and kept down the number of home runs.

However, while some pitchers could make a ball hop and some people could make a ball "sink," there is no evidence of any major-league pitcher, before 1950, doing both, or switching between one and the other (Satchel Paige threw two distinct fastballs in the 1930s, when he pitched in the Negro Leagues. But neither of them was a sinking fastball). Pitchers universally seemed to regard the movement of their fastball not as a function of strategy, but as a gift from the heavens. "My fastball had a natural sink to it," they would say, or "My fastball had a pretty good hop to it," or "I had pretty good speed, but my fastball was straight, so I had to keep it away from the middle of the plate." Although certainly some very few pitchers would learn how to make "their" fastball hop or how to make "their" fastball sink, there is little evidence, before 1950, of an understanding that the movement on a pitcher's fastball was not simply an endowment of nature, but was a consequence of grip, release, and spin.

Nick Cuppy expressed this idea succinctly in 1908, in a book called *How to Pitch* (John Foster). "That there is such a thing as a jump ball I believe is universally conceded," said Cuppy, "but like other pitchers I am in the dark as to its cause. I am positive that it exists, for I have been able to get it myself." Forty years later, there is little evidence of much better understanding. Dan Daniel reported of Wilcy Moore that Moore "owed his relief success to his strange sinker, which he never could explain. It was a natural delivery and he really did not know how to throw it." About Curt Davis in 1939, John J. Ward

Bill's got a four-part definition of "best"; here's my one-part definition: "Was this pitch so good that he could, and often did, get hitters out using this and very little else?" No, I don't think that Walter Johnson threw as hard in 1910 as, say, Mark Prior did in 2003. But in Johnson's time, the hitters were more impressed by Johnson's fastball than the hitters today are impressed by Prior's.

BEST FASTBALLS, STARTERS

1. Walter Johnson
2. Amos Rusie
3. Lefty Grove
4. Roger Clemens
5. Rube Waddell
6. Dick Redding
7. Satchel Paige
8. Robin Roberts
9. Bob Feller
10. Dazzy Vance

Where is Nolan Ryan? Nolan Ryan didn't always know where his fastball was going, so he just missed my cut. Randy Johnson just missed because the fastball hasn't always been his best pitch (often it's that slider). Same thing with Sandy Koufax (who had an awesome curveball). Other starters who just missed for various reasons are Bartolo Colon, Jim Maloney, Sudden Sam McDowell, Jouett Meekin, Joe Rogan, Curt Schilling, Herb Score, Virgil Trucks, Bob Turley, Joe Wood, and Cy Young. And please, don't write; I know there are a few dozen others who deserve to be mentioned here.

—ROB NEYER

BEST FASTBALLS, RELIEVERS

1. Goose Gossage
2. Mariano Rivera
3. Dick Radatz
4. Billy Wagner
5. Rob Dibble
6. Firpo Marberry
7. Tom Henke
8. Joe Page
9. Lee Smith
10. John Wetteland

This is the only place where I'll make the distinction between starters and relievers, but in the other articles about the pitches I'll offer more top-ten lists.

—ROB NEYER

wrote, "His fast ball is a natural sinker." Sam Nahem, an early-1940s pitcher, said, "I often wish that God had given me movement on my fastball, but he didn't." Floyd Bevens, quoted in 1947: "I have a sinker, but it is a natural delivery." Mel Harder said, years after his career, "My fastball was a natural sinker." Bob Lemon, same exact words. Phil Marchildon, a 1940s pitcher, said in his book that "it was estimated that my fastball traveled about ninety five miles per hour. The movement on it was so distinctive that it became known around the American League by the name 'Johnny Jump-Up.' "

The apparently universal assumption was that each pitcher was endowed by nature with a unique movement on his fastball, and that was simply what he had. Curt Simmons (see Curt Simmons entry) changed that, and probably Curt Simmons didn't figure it all out by himself; probably he was taught something by an older pitcher, and built on it.

In any case, Simmons threw both a sinking and a rising fastball, and by the mid-1960s, many pitchers had begun to do this. Teenagers Wally Bunker (1964) and Larry Dierker (1965) threw the two fastballs, even as very young pitchers. Fergie Jenkins emerged as a star in 1967, throwing a rising fastball to right-handers, a sinking fastball to lefties, and Tom Seaver won the Rookie of the Year Award, also mixing up his fastballs. Don Sutton threw the two fastballs, as did Bill Stoneman. Bob Veale (mid-1960s) said his two best pitches were his fastball and his low fastball. The practice just exploded in the mid- to late-'60s; all of a sudden everybody was doing it (although the press *never* picked up on this; there was never a spate of stories discussing the new trend).

By the mid-1970s, even more variety in fastballs was beginning to appear. Goose Gossage, though he never used the term "cut fastball," could make his fastball "ride" or "tail." Other pitchers of that era also could, but they lacked any very specific vocabulary to talk about it, and thus our understanding of how these pitchers used their fastballs is far from perfect.

The term "split-fingered fastball," which emerged about 1980, is somewhat misleading, since no one *really* thinks of a splitter as a variation of a fastball. The term "cut fastball," which emerged in the mid-1980s and is now used to describe almost everything, is an example of the language trying not very successfully to catch up to the complexity of real life.

Fastballs do different things . . . they sink, tail, hop, sail, ride, etc. We have, at this point, three terms in common usage to describe these pitches: four-seam fastball (or rising fastball), two-seam fastball (or sinking fastball), and cut fastball (which is used for any pitch which is released without a snap of the wrist, but which breaks either left or right as it nears the batter).

For many years, some pitchers would be described as

George Brace Collection

Phil Marchildon

throwing a "light" ball (an easy pitch for the catcher to catch) or throwing a "heavy" ball. You don't hear that much anymore.

It seems clear, to me, that the specific part of the language has not really caught up with the diversity of fastballs which are thrown by major-league pitchers, and that more terms will develop over the next twenty years to fill in the gaps. We have lots of adjectives for fastballs, but very few nouns. Over time, the term "cut fastball" is likely to develop a more clear and limited definition, just as the term "slider" did, and just as the term "curve" did. The term "cut fastball" at this point has a very general and imprecise description. As time passes, the language will continue to evolve.

THE BEST FASTBALLS OF EACH HALF-DECADE

BILL JAMES

In the article about fastballs, I wrote that a history of the fastball is not so much a history of the skill as simply a record of the talent. I said this to set up the following set of lists, which are intended to be simply a careful and fairly extensive record of the talent.

Who had the best fastball of the years 1955–1959? There are four necessary characteristics of a great fastball:

1. It is thrown very hard,
2. It moves enough, or is thrown with enough deception, that it is difficult to hit,
3. The pitcher has some control over it, and
4. The pitcher is able to throw it consistently over time.

The first and fourth characteristics are the most important ones. Control . . . sure, that's tremendously important, but "having good control" is not what we mean by "having a great fastball." It is common to hear said, "He's got a great heater, but he doesn't have control of it." This phrase, if you think about it, clearly implies that control is *not* what we mean when we say a pitcher has a great fastball. It's a separate characteristic, necessary to make the fastball *useful*.

If a guy can throw a fastball 100 miles an hour, but he can only throw it a few times a game, you don't think of that as being in the same class with the Nolan Ryan/Roger Clemens fastball, because those guys could throw the fastball 100 times a game. This feeds also into what I might describe as the David Clyde problem. When David Clyde passed the thirty-year anniversary of his pathetic few major-league successes, many stories were written about him, and in those stories old players were quoted as raving about David Clyde's fastball . . . greatest fastball I ever saw, buddy.

I drew up a list of the best fastballs of the early 1970s, and David Clyde doesn't make the list. People will read the list, and some of you will look at the early 1970s, and you'll look for David Clyde, and he's not there, and so you'll think that I'm just not *aware* of the things that batters said who had to face him, or that I'm aware of them but I don't believe them.

But that's not true; I am aware of them, and I do believe them. It's just that . . . well, does that make him Nolan Ryan? Does that make him Vida Blue? There are too many other guys with better evidence.

In any five-year period, there are forty guys who are claimed by *somebody* to be as fast as Walter Johnson, or as fast as Bob Feller, or as fast as Nolan Ryan, as fast as whoever the standard is at the moment. People made the same exact sort of comments about Pete Broberg that they did about David Clyde. We have the same kind of quotes about Gary Gentry, claiming he was faster than Seaver. The fastest known radar reading from that era, other than Nolan Ryan, was for John D'Acquisto. You've got Goose Gossage in that pot—a *young* Goose Gossage. You have to sort out those claims somehow. Steve Busby threw a no-hitter as a rookie, threw another the next year, won TSN's Rookie Pitcher of the Year award, and won 40 games over the next two years, although he was injured and ineffective for the last two months of that second year. He was throwing a sinking fastball. Don't you reckon the batters who faced him, when he was throwing a no-hitter (or one of his several *near* no-hitters) were fairly impressed with his fastball? Steve Carlton went 27-10 with a terrible team one year

George Brace Collection

Bob Brown

in there, throwing high fastballs (the slider didn't become his best pitch until two years later). We have quotes about Steve Carlton when he first came up, comparing him to Sandy Koufax—but, since he is Carlton, those kind of quotes don't even make the file for him, because there is so much other stuff. Which is better evidence about the quality of his fastball: 27 wins and 300 strikeouts, or some guy thirty years later talking about what an awesome fastball David Clyde threw that one afternoon?

Bob Brown, a pitcher with the Braves in the 1930s, went 14-7 in 1932, but won only sixteen games in his career. Beans Reardon, a longtime umpire, insisted that Brown was the fastest pitcher he ever saw—faster than Grove, faster than Feller. Well, okay . . . but does a fastball that wins sixteen games rate higher than a fastball that wins 300? Not usually.

Of course, the business of rating the best fastballs of each era is somewhat haphazard. I didn't bat against any of these guys, and I haven't read every word written about them. Take the lists for what they're worth. The best fastballs of each half-decade, beginning in 1880:

Best Fastballs of 1880–1884

1. Pud Galvin
2. Jim McCormick
3. Jim Whitney
4. Lee Richmond
5. Tony Mullane
6. Jumbo McGinnis
7. Larry Corcoran
8. Old Hoss Radbourn
9. Tim Keefe
10. Jersey Bakely

Best Fastballs of 1885–1889

1. Pud Galvin
2. Silver King
3. Bob Caruthers
4. Matt Kilroy
5. Jesse Duryea
6. Darby O'Brien
7. Dave Foutz
8. Charlie Ferguson
9. Mark Baldwin
10. Dan Casey

Best Fastballs of 1890–1894

1. Amos Rusie
2. Cy Young
3. Jouett Meekin
4. Kid Nichols
5. Bill Hutchison
6. Ted Breitenstein
7. Nig Cuppy
8. Jack Stivetts
9. Sadie McMahon
10. George Hemming

Best Fastballs of 1895–1899

1. Cy Young
2. Amos Rusie
3. Jouett Meekin
4. Jack Powell
5. Kid Nichols
6. Cy Seymour
7. Ted Breitenstein
8. Jack Taylor
9. Ad Gumbert
10. Nig Cuppy

Best Fastballs of 1900–1904

1. Jack Powell
2. Rube Waddell

3. Addie Joss
4. Rube Foster
5. Christy Mathewson
6. Cy Young
7. Wild Bill Donovan
8. Deacon Phillippe
9. Kid Nichols
10. Luther Taylor

Best Fastballs of 1905–1909

1. Walter Johnson
2. Smokey Joe Williams
3. Rube Waddell
4. Ed Reulbach
5. Red Ames
6. Addie Joss
7. Rube Foster
8. Jack Powell
9. Howie Camnitz
10. Harry Buckner

Best Fastballs of 1910–1914

1. Walter Johnson
2. Dick Redding
3. Joe Wood
4. Smokey Joe Williams
5. George Baumgardner
6. Rube Benton
7. Harry Buckner
8. Bullet Joe Bush
9. Rube Marquard
10. Bob Harmon

Best Fastballs of 1915–1919

1. Walter Johnson
2. Dick Redding
3. Smokey Joe Williams
4. Joe Bush
5. Hippo Vaughn
6. Bert Gallia
7. Dave Davenport
8. Carl Mays
9. Pol Perritt
10. Babe Ruth

Best Fastballs of 1920–1924

1. Dazzy Vance
2. Walter Johnson
3. Dick Redding
4. Carl Mays
5. Bullet Rogan
6. Rip Collins
7. Slim Harriss
8. Waite Hoyt
9. Smokey Joe Williams
10. George Uhle

Best Fastballs of 1925–1929

1. Lefty Grove
2. Dazzy Vance
3. George Earnshaw
4. Satchel Paige
5. Pat Malone
6. Bullet Rogan
7. Tommy Thomas
8. Rube Walberg
9. Johnny Miljus
10. Firpo Marberry

Best Fastballs of 1930–1934

1. Lefty Grove
2. Van Mungo
3. Satchel Paige
4. Dizzy Dean
5. George Earnshaw
6. Lefty Gomez
7. Lon Warneke
8. Pat Malone
9. Schoolboy Rowe
10. Johnny Allen

Best Fastballs of 1935–1939

1. Bob Feller
2. Atley Donald
3. Johnny Allen
4. Van Lingle Mungo
5. Leon Day
6. Johnny Vander Meer
7. Bobo Newsom
8. Lefty Grove
9. Dizzy Dean
10. Bill Dietrich

Best Fastballs of 1940–1944

1. Bob Feller
2. Hal Newhouser

3. Virgil Trucks
4. Dizzy Trout
5. Atley Donald
6. Bill Zuber
7. Johnny Vander Meer
8. Kirby Higbe
9. Phil Marchildon
10. Claude Passeau

Best Fastballs of 1945–1949

1. Bob Feller
2. Rex Barney
3. Hal Newhouser
4. Ewell Blackwell
5. Virgil Trucks
6. Allie Reynolds
7. Don Newcombe
8. Warren Spahn
9. Dizzy Trout
10. Allie Reynolds

Best Fastballs of 1950–1954

1. Robin Roberts
2. Curt Simmons
3. Mike Garcia
4. Mickey McDermott
5. Don Newcombe
6. Billy Pierce
7. Johnny Antonelli
8. Warren Spahn
9. Carl Erskine
10. Ron Necciai or Karl Spooner

Best Fastballs of 1955–1959

1. Herb Score
2. Ryne Duren
3. Bob Turley
4. Don Drysdale
5. Sandy Koufax
6. Steve Dalkowski
7. Turk Farrell
8. Jim Bunning
9. Billy Pierce
10. Robin Robcrts

Best Fastballs of 1960–1964

1. Don Drysdale
2. Sandy Koufax

George Brace Collection

Curt Simmons

3. Dick Radatz
4. Bob Gibson
5. Steve Barber
6. Jim Maloney
7. Bob Veale
8. Jim Bunning
9. Turk Farrell
10. Al Downing

Best Fastballs of 1965–1969

1. Sam McDowell
2. Bob Gibson
3. Don Wilson
4. Tom Seaver
5. Sandy Koufax
6. Jim Maloney
7. Luis Tiant
8. Steve Carlton
9. Bob Veale
10. Larry Dierker

Best Fastballs of 1970–1974

1. Nolan Ryan
2. Vida Blue
3. Goose Gossage
4. Steve Carlton
5. Tom Seaver

6. Don Wilson
7. Steve Busby
8. Sam McDowell
9. Bert Blyleven
10. Gary Gentry

Best Fastballs of 1975–1979

1. Nolan Ryan
2. Goose Gossage
3. Frank Tanana
4. Ron Guidry
5. J. R. Richard
6. Dennis Eckersley
7. Jim Kern
8. Bob Welch
9. Tom Seaver
10. Vida Blue

Best Fastballs of 1980–1984

1. Nolan Ryan
2. Goose Gossage
3. Juan Berenguer
4. Mike Scott
5. Joaquin Andujar
6. Floyd Bannister
7. Jack Morris
8. Mario Soto
9. Len Barker
10. Rick Sutcliffe

Best Fastballs of 1985–1989

1. Roger Clemens
2. Dwight Gooden
3. Nolan Ryan
4. Bobby Witt
5. Bret Saberhagen
6. Lee Smith
7. Mark Langston
8. Tom Henke
9. David Cone
10. Chuck Finley

Best Fastballs of 1990–1994

1. Rob Dibble
2. Randy Johnson

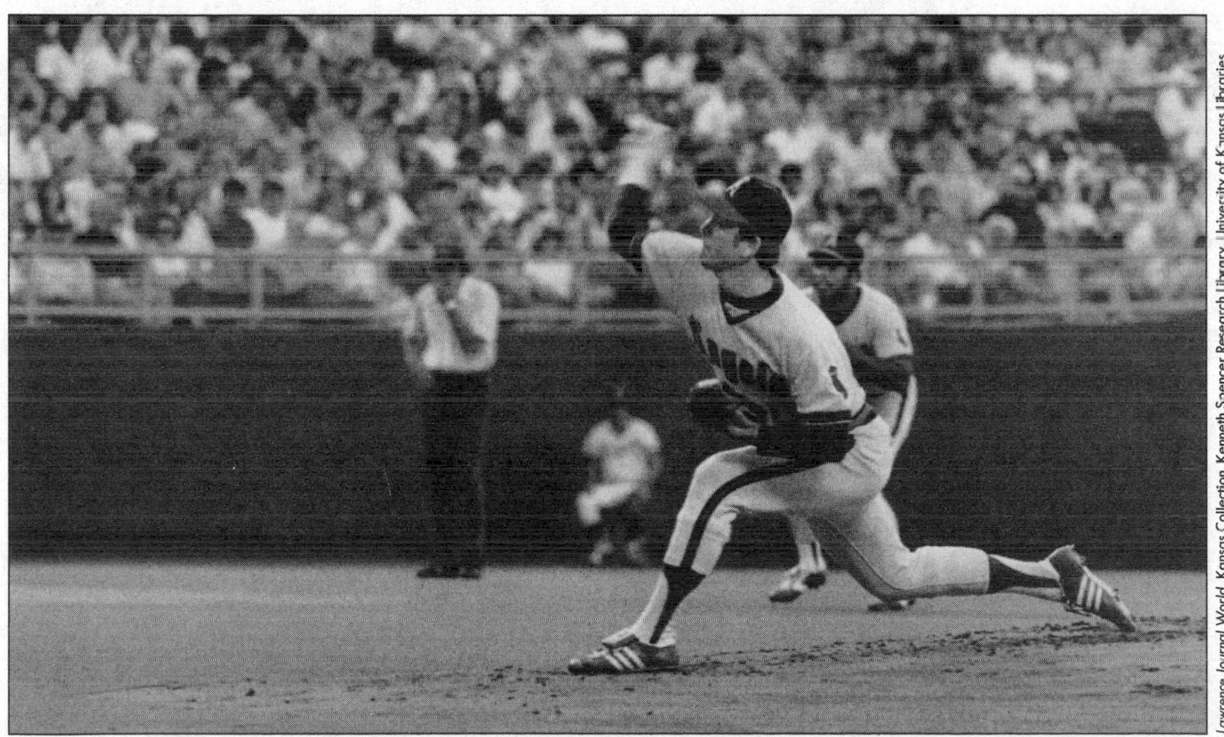

Lawrence Journal World, Kansas Collection, Kenneth Spencer Research Library, University of Kansas Libraries

Nolan Ryan

3. Roger Clemens
4. Bobby Witt
5. Juan Guzman
6. Pedro Martinez
7. Kevin Brown
8. John Wetteland
9. Mark Langston
10. David Cone

Best Fastballs of 1995–1999

1. Randy Johnson
2. Billy Wagner
3. Pedro Martinez
4. Curt Schilling
5. Kerry Wood
6. Roger Clemens
7. Armando Benitez
8. Bartolo Colon
9. Jose Mesa
10. John Rocker

Best Fastballs of 2000–present

1. Billy Wagner
2. Armando Benitez
3. Bartolo Colon
4. Kerry Wood
5. Randy Johnson
6. Mark Prior
7. Curt Schilling
8. Jason Schmidt
9. Jose Contreras
10. Johan Santana

THE CURIOUS CURVE

ROB NEYER

Candy Cummings has a plaque in the Hall of Fame because he supposedly invented the curveball, so we'll let him tell his own story, which was published in the September 1908 issue of *Baseball Magazine* . . .

HOW I PITCHED THE FIRST CURVE

By William Arthur Cummings

I have often been asked how I first got the idea of making a ball curve. I will now explain. It is such a simple matter, though, that there is not much explanation.

In the summer of 1863 a number of boys and myself were amusing ourselves by throwing clam shells (the hard shell variety) and watching them sail along through the air, turning now to the right, and now to the left. We became interested in the mechanics of it and experimented for an hour or more.

All of a sudden it came to me that it would be a good joke on the boys if I could make a baseball curve the same way. We had been playing "three-old-cat" and town-ball, and I had been doing the pitching. The joke seemed so good that I made a firm decision that I would try to play it.

I set to work on my theory and practiced every spare moment that I had out of school. I had no one to help me and had to fight it out alone. Time after time I would throw the ball, doubling up into all manner of positions, for I thought that my pose had something to do with it; and then I tried holding the ball in different shapes. Sometimes I thought I had it, and then maybe again in twenty-five tries I could not get the slightest curve. My visionary successes were just enough to tantalize me. Month after month I kept pegging away at my theory.

In 1864 I went to Fulton, New York, to a boarding school, and remained there a year and a half. All that time I kept experimenting with my curved ball. My boy friends began to laugh at me, and to throw jokes at my theory of making a ball go sideways. I fear that some of them thought it was so preposterous that it was no joke, and that I should be carefully watched over.

I don't know what made me stick at it. The great wonder to me now is that I did not give up in disgust, for I had not a single word of encouragement in all that time, while my attempts were a standing joke among my friends.

After graduating I went back to my home in Brooklyn, New York, and joined the "Star Juniors," an amateur team. We were very successful. I was solicited to join as a junior member of the Excelsior club, and I accepted the proposition.

In 1867 I, with the Excelsior club, went to Boston, where we played the Lowells, the Tri-Mountains, and Harvard clubs. During these games I kept trying to make the ball curve. It was during the Harvard game that I became fully convinced that I had succeeded in doing what all these years I had been striving to do. The batters were missing a lot of balls; I began to watch the flight of the ball through the air, and I distinctly saw it curve.

A surge of joy flooded over me that I shall never forget. I felt like shouting out that I had made a ball curve; I wanted to tell everybody; it was too good to keep to myself.

BEST CURVEBALLS OF ALL TIME

1. Sandy Koufax
2. Mordecai Brown
3. Bert Blyleven
4. Toothpick Sam Jones
5. Tommy Bridges
6. Hilton Smith
7. Camilo Pascual
8. Herb Pennock
9. Sal Maglie
10. David Wells

Others: Tom Gordon, Ted Trent, Gregg Olson, Barry Zito, Mike Witt, Dwight Gooden (early career), Darryl Kile, Dave McNally, Johnny Morrison, Guy Morton, Rosy Ryan, Johnny Schmitz, Earl Whitehill, Vic Aldridge, Clem Labine, Johnny Sain

Cummings concluded his account with this: "I get a great deal of pleasure now in my old age out of going to games and watching the curves, thinking that it was through my blind efforts that all this was made possible."

Of course, others have been credited with inventing the curveball, most notably Bobby Matthews (who's also been described as the inventor of both the fadeaway/screwball and the spitball; a clever lad, he must have been), but also Phonie Martin, Fred Goldsmith, Terry Larkin, and at least a few more.

When Cummings started throwing his curve, the pitchers were required by the rules to throw underhand, so their curving options were fairly limited. But as they found ways to get around the rules, and as the rules were liberalized, the pitchers came up with all sorts of different curves, one for every arm angle. Most notably,

- the sidearm curve, which typically moves laterally, more or less,
- the "outcurve," later known as the "roundhouse," which moves laterally *and* down, and
- the "drop curve," later known as the "overhand curve," today sometimes known as the "12-to-6 curve," which is thrown overhand (naturally) and drops straight down (or very nearly so).

Despite all the stories being told by puzzled batters, for many decades there were people who simply didn't believe that a man could make a baseball curve. Various pitchers were forever conducting demonstrations involving two poles set fifty feet apart to prove that baseballs really could be curved but, this being in the days before moving pictures and videotape, the great majority of the skeptics weren't able to actually witness these demonstrations.

Nevertheless, by the 1950s most caring Americans did believe that a man could throw a curveball. Of course, by then not as *many* men were throwing curveballs, because they'd discovered the slider. There's still plenty of life in the ol' curveball yet, though, and if you want to see a great drop ball, watch Barry Zito or Josh Beckett pitch sometime.

Transcendental Graphics/ruckerarchive.com

Trade Card, 1885

THE CHANGING CHANGE-UP

ROB NEYER

> The original slow ball was merely a ball thrown slowly, the pitcher depending entirely upon a false motion to deceive the batter into believing he was pitching a fast ball. Keefe, O'Day, and most of the oldtime pitchers used that kind of a slow ball.
>
> —John J. Evers and Hugh S. Fullerton, *Touching Second* (1910)

After years of "study," I've come to believe there are two running themes throughout baseball's history: the owners' efforts to cheat the players, and the pitchers' efforts to come up with the perfect change-up.

I'm serious about this. Talk to a pitcher from any era, and he's likely to say something like, "Well, I had a good fastball and a pretty good curve [or slider], but I never really did develop a good change-up. I wish I'd have worked on it more."

While it's not technically true that every pitcher needs a third pitch—you don't need one if you've already got one great pitch or two very good ones—many pitchers have fallen short of stardom because they couldn't develop that third pitch, and often as not that third pitch was a reliable change-up.

Last season, twenty-six-year-old Kip Wells said on television that he was still searching for a change-up that works for him.

In Tom Seaver's 1973 book about pitching, he said, "The change is a very hard pitch to learn . . . I've had a lot of difficulty learning it, but there are days when things are going so right that the change is right along with the other pitches."[23] (Mind you, by 1973 Seaver already had three twenty-win seasons under his belt; he did eventually discover a sort of circle change-up that worked for him.)[24]

Not that it's always so difficult. Shortly after Larry Dierker signed with the Houston Colt .45s out of high school, Paul Richards tried to teach Dierker the slip pitch. Dierker couldn't get the hang of it . . . so instead, within a matter of weeks he came up with an effective variation on the forkball, all by himself.

All this points to a running theme: the Quest for the Perfect Change-up. It's a quest that's been taken collectively by all of baseball, and individually by thousands and thousands of pitchers, and when you do what Bill and I have done in this book, you can't help but notice it.

In the nineteenth century, a number of pitchers were well-known for their "slow ball," which was for many years the generic term often used to describe any pitch that wasn't a fastball or curve. As Evers and Fullerton suggest in the quote that leads off this essay, the original slow ball was a "motion pitch"; instead of altering the grip on the ball, the pitcher might slow down his motion

BEST CHANGE-UPS OF ALL TIME

1. Stu Miller
2. Jean Dubuc
3. Ed Lopat
4. Jamie Moyer
5. Pedro Martinez
6. Trevor Hoffman
7. Doug Jones
8. Ellis Kinder
9. Bill Sherdel
10. Andy Messersmith

Others: John Franco, Johnny Podres, Kirk Rueter, Mark Eichhorn, Nap Rucker (late career), John Tudor (late career), Mike Boddicker, Mario Soto

23. Tom Seaver with Steve Jacobson, *Pitching with Tom Seaver* (1973), page 99.
24. Tom Seaver with Lee Lowenfish, *The Art of Pitching* (1984), pages 136–137.

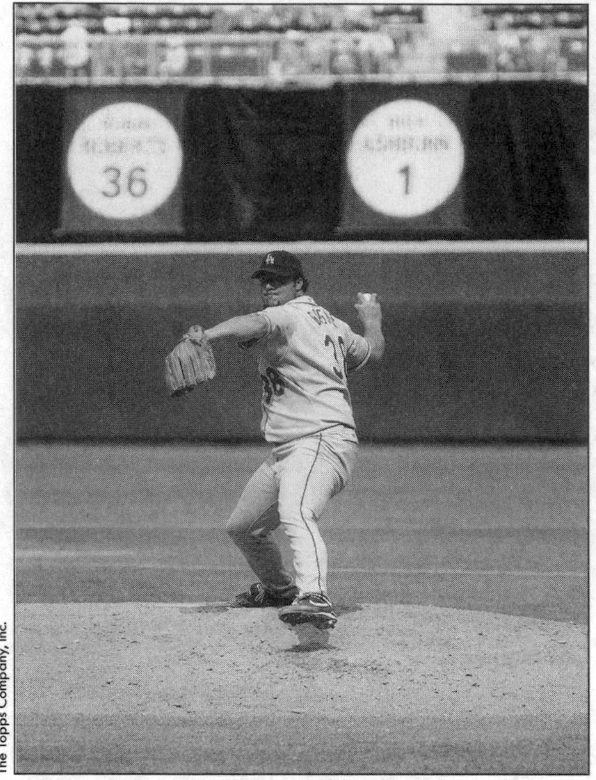

The Topps Company, Inc.

Eric Gagne throwing his change-up

at the last possible moment, or drag his rear foot. Later, this became known as the "let-up pitch" and, more recently, the "straight change."

By early in the twentieth century, however, a lot of pitchers were throwing a different kind of slow ball. They achieved deception not by altering their motion, but by altering their grip. Early on, the most popular version of the slow ball was thrown by holding the ball back in the palm of the hand, with only the thumb and pinky finger applying real pressure to the ball. When thrown correctly, the result was a pitch with little speed or spin, which sometimes would wobble like a knuckleball. Many years later, probably in the 1940s, this version of the slow ball became commonly known as the "palm ball," and shortly thereafter a manager named Paul Richards invented (or was said to have invented) a variation he called the "slip pitch."

In the meantime, other pitches were described as "slow balls," among them Christy Mathewson's fadeaway and Eddie Cicotte's knuckleball. In 1920, Joe Bush popularized the forkball, which was essentially another slow ball (in my opinion; Bill disagrees).

After 1920, it was a long time before anybody came up with a radically different slow ball. But there's some evidence that in the 1950s, the pitch that we now call the "circle change" gained some currency among major leaguers. Johnny Podres has been said to have thrown the pitch, and I believe that Warren Spahn might have, too. In the 1980s, some bright boy came up with the "fosh change," a variation on the forkball which might actually be nothing more than the *original* version of the forkball, before the label was corrupted by the split-fingered fastball.

Today, all those pitches are thrown by major leaguers, though the palm ball is rarely seen and the knuckleball isn't used as a change-up by anybody (it's not a change-up when the batter knows it's coming, as they do when Tim Wakefield and Steve Sparks are pitching). In the marketplace of ideas, the big winners today are the circle change, the forkball/splitter, and the straight change.

THE UNDEFINABLE SLIDER

ROB NEYER

> Perhaps the newest of the breaking pitches is one called the slider, which almost every pitcher uses these days.
>
> The late George Blaeholder is generally credited with the development of the pitch in the early thirties, but I cannot testify to the truth of this.
>
> —BOB FELLER IN *Pitching to Win* (1948)

I cannot testify to the truth of that, either.

There is no *Eureka!* moment for the slider, in large part because nobody really knows when, or even approximately when, the first slider was thrown. In the literature, the slider is generally attributed to one of two Georges (if not both): the aforementioned Blaeholder, and Uhle.

In 1936, John J. Ward wrote a *Baseball Magazine* article about Blaeholder titled, "He Hurls the 'Slide Ball.' " Reading the article, we realize there's something of a problem with thinking about Blaeholder's pet pitch as a "modern" slider: Ward calls it a fastball.

> . . . There was something about his loose jointed delivery and his sideways, sloping fast ball that Yankees sluggers didn't like.
>
> Blaeholder's strong point is his fast ball. He generally throws this with a side-arm motion which gives the ball a curious sweep to one side as it crosses the plate. Disconcerted batters have christened it the "slide ball." Evidently this deceptive sweep is due to some peculiarity in holding and throwing the ball. But Blaeholder takes no special credit.
>
> "It's just my natural style," he says . . .

This sounds like the pitch that today we would call a cut fastball, and what players in Blaeholder's time often called a "sailer" (though maybe they had a good reason for not calling Blaeholder's pitch a sailer).

Speaking of the sailer, here's what George Uhle said about *his* slider:

> . . . It just came to me all of a sudden, letting the ball go along my index finger and using my ring finger and pinky to give it just a little bit of a twist. It was a sailing fastball, and that's how come I named it the slider. The real slider is a sailing fastball. Now they call everything a slider, including a nickel curve.

Now, contrast the descriptions of Blaeholder's and Uhle's slider with that of Bob Feller's:

> The delivery is almost identical with that of a fast ball until the point of release. I think the release can be best described by comparing it with the passing of a football. The index finger controls the release, even as it does a football, and the hand is about in the same position.
>
> Unlike the curve, the snap of the wrist is late and the arm turns in only half as much as it does for the curve. To carry the metaphor further, the release of the slider is similar to the motion which would be used in pointing the index finger at home plate.[25]

This is only twelve years after the *Baseball Magazine* article about Blaeholder, but Feller is talking about a completely different pitch. He's throwing the pitch with a fastball motion, but with a twist of the wrist roughly half what it would be for a curveball.

While it's true that, today, the slider is generally described as Feller describes it, snapping the wrist was not then, *and is not now*, necessary when throwing a slider.

25. Bob Feller, *Pitching to Win* (1952 edition), page 88.

Here's what longtime pitching coach Bob Cluck recently wrote about the slider:

> The slider is also [like the cut fastball] gripped off-center and simply thrown like a fastball. Because you have more surface of the ball in contact with the middle finger than you have with the cutter, the ball will break down and across 10 to 12 inches. If the break on the ball is big one time and short the next, the pitcher is twisting or turning around the ball and the pitch will never be consistent. Remember, *if you twist the ball, it is not only tough on your elbow but the break will never be the same from pitch to pitch.* [italics mine]

While writing this article, I got into a heated argument with Bill. *If the pitcher wasn't breaking his wrist,* I e-mailed Bill, *then it wasn't really a slider.*

I won't print Bill's rebuttals here, because it got a little ugly; for a few minutes, it looked like we might both take our names off this book. Suffice to say, he thought I was daft.

Still, I wouldn't come around . . . until, a few days later, I happened to run across Cluck's editorial, which demonstrates beyond a shadow of a doubt that indeed you don't have to snap your wrist to throw a slider. It's still true, I think, that we'll never *know* if Blaeholder and Uhle threw what we would consider sliders, or cut fastballs (or something in between; there's plenty of room there). But they called them sliders, and that's probably the best we'll ever do.

BEST SLIDERS OF ALL TIME

1. Steve Carlton
2. Randy Johnson
3. Bob Gibson
4. Larry Andersen
5. Sparky Lyle
6. Ron Guidry
7. Dave Stieb
8. Bob Lemon
9. Dick Donovan
10. J.R. Richard

Others: Johnny Allen, Bob Feller, Mike Jackson, Larry Jansen, Vern Law, Jeff Nelson, Red Ruffing, Jim Bunning

Gerorge Brace Collection

George Blaeholder

So who threw the first great slider? Red Ruffing and Johnny Allen are real possibilities, and Bob Feller also is a candidate. With most of the great pitchers drafted during World War II (Feller actually enlisted), there weren't a lot of great *pitches* thrown from 1943 through 1945. But Feller came back after the war, and wrote in his book, "It was the slider which was of the greatest help to me in 1946 when I established a strikeout record of 348 for a season. I used it in many spots where I had used a curve before."

Feller pitched for the Indians, of course, and he soon was joined by another great slider. In the late 1940s, Indians outfielder Bob Lemon became Indians *pitcher* Bob Lemon, and he learned the slider from pitching coach Mel Harder. Lemon's in the Hall of Fame, and he probably wouldn't be there without his slider.

Dick Donovan's not in the Hall of Fame, but he did come up with a Hall of Fame slider in the 1950s, and in 1961 his 2.40 ERA was the lowest in the majors. Meanwhile, Jim Bunning was throwing a great slider of which Ted Williams later said, "unlike most sliders, Bunning's tended to rise, he kind of slung it sidearm . . ." And Bunning, like Lemon, eventually wound up in the Hall of Fame.

Courtesy of Arizona Diamondbacks

Randy Johnson

Bob Gibson probably threw the best slider of the 1960s, but the decade didn't see a lot of *great* sliders. Most of the best pitchers of the '60s threw overpowering fastballs and tough curveballs (overhand or sidearm), in part because the conditions of the time rewarded pitchers with that style.

In the 1970s, though, things changed. One of the most vivid memories of my youth involves listening to Royals games on the radio, and hearing Denny Matthews or Fred White refer to an opposition starter as a "sinker/slider guy." Those were the two pitches of the '70s: good sinker, hard slider.

The slider's a great pitch, but not everybody's a fan. Back in the 1950s, it was disdained by a lot of the old-timers, the basic sentiment, I think, being that the slider was for pansies. As noted tough guy Sal Maglie said, "All pitchers today are lazy. They all look for the easy way out, and the slider gives them that pitch."[26]

26. Paul Votano, *Late and Close: A History of Relief Pitching* (2002), page 41.

There were also those who thought throwing the slider would likely lead to an injury. In *The Dodger Way to Play Baseball*, a 256-page book written by Al Campanis and published in 1954, the word "slider" does not appear once. Nearly twenty years later, Dodgers manager Walter Alston put together a huge instructional book, *The Complete Baseball Handbook*, and while Alston admitted the slider "can be a highly effective pitch and has attained considerable prominence among present-day major league pitchers," he also said, "The general feeling among pitching authorities is that the young pitcher should stay away from the slider until he is physically equipped and has sufficient talent to throw it properly."

To this day, there are coaches and entire organizations that will teach the slider only as a last resort, because they're afraid of what might happen. But does throwing the slider really increase the risk of an injury? We don't know. But if you'd like to find out for yourself, this book's not a bad starting point.

THE DANCING KNUCKLEBALL

ROB NEYER

The origins of the knuckleball are a bit murky, as four different pitchers have been said to have invented a non-spinning pitch thrown off the knuckles or the fingertips at roughly the same time.

- In 1907, Nap Rucker arrived in the major leagues with the Dodgers, and quickly established himself as one of the better pitchers in the National League. At that time he threw very hard, but before long he also came up with an effective knuckleball.
- In 1908, the New York *Press* described Phillies right-hander Lew "Hicks" Moren, pitching in his second season, as the knuckleball's "inventor."
- Also in 1908, Eddie Cicotte reached the majors for good—he'd pitched briefly for the Tigers in 1905—and quickly got hung with the nickname, "Knuckles."
- *Also* in 1908, Ed Summers became known for a pitch called a "dry spitter," but a photo shows a pitch gripped with the first knuckles on the index and middle finger; that is, a knuckleball in the most literal sense.

Moren's story has apparently been lost to history (at least for now), but Cicotte's has not. In 1952 he told H.G. Salsinger, "They say I invented the knuckle ball but Eddie (Kickapoo) Summers deserves a full share of the credit. We worked on it together and developed it at Indianapolis in 1906, where Detroit had us farmed out."

Makes sense, because we know that Cicotte and Summers were two of the first to throw the pitch, and they apparently *were* together in Indianapolis, in 1906.

But what should we make of the fact that in *1905*, Cicotte and Rucker pitched together with the Augusta club in the South Atlantic League? It's certainly possible that Rucker and/or Cicotte came up with the pitch in 1905, and then Summers helped Cicotte refine it in 1906.

And what of Hicks Moren? Your guess is as good as ours.

The key to the safe is probably an article in the July 1908 issue of *Baseball Magazine.* The article is titled "The Finger-Nail Ball," and it's all about Ed Summers.

> I thought I had this knuckle-ball they talk so much about. I at least got my idea from that. I watched Eddie Cicotte, who first used it, and followed him. He rested the ball on his knuckles, but I couldn't see the value of that, because I couldn't control it, and one can put but little speed on it. The knuckle ball is practically a deviation of the slow ball, or floater. I found by holding the ball with my finger tips and steadying it with my thumb alone I could get a peculiar break to it and send it to the batters with considerable speed and good control. I worked on it for two years, and used it quite a lot last summer. This spring I succeeded in getting it down right. It is not like a "spitter"; it isn't a knuckle-ball; it isn't a slow ball. It's—I don't know what; it's just this.[27]

Here's what I *think* happened. I think that Cicotte probably came up with the knuckleball (perhaps with the help of Rucker, in 1905), and Summers figured out a different (if not better) way of getting something like

27. James C. Mills, *Baseball Magazine* (July 1908), "The Finger-Nail Ball."

the same results. Why did Cicotte, years later, give Summers half the credit? Well, his memory might have failed him, but perhaps he shared the credit because Cicotte himself didn't wait long before adopting Summers' fingertip grip.

But wherever and whenever the knuckleball was invented, it seems pretty likely that Cicotte was somehow involved. And as it happened, he was the first pitcher to enjoy great success with the pitch. In 1909, Cicotte's second full season with the Red Sox, he went 14-5 with a 1.94 ERA. In 1913—by which point Cicotte might have been throwing his infamous "shine ball," too—he went 18-11 with a 1.58 ERA.

But while Cicotte might have been the only successful "knuckleball pitcher" in that era, he was far from the only pitcher who threw the knuckleball. After reading a great number of articles about pitchers that were published in *Baseball Magazine* in the Dead Ball Era, I've concluded that a great *number* of pitchers threw the knuckleball during that time. We'll never have an accurate count, though, because often the knuckler was simply lumped under the heading of "slow ball."

In a booklet called "Pitching Course" and published in 1914, Nap Rucker says, "The Knuckler and an *ordinary* slow ball are my change of pace deliveries."

The italics there are mine, and I use them to suggest that the knuckleball fell under the heading of "slow ball," along with the fadeaway, the palm ball (the "ordinary" slow ball, commonly used but not yet specifically named), and other deliveries designed to screw up the batter's timing.

Cicotte's last season was 1920, and 1920 was Eddie Rommel's first season. When Rommel came up with the Athletics, his knuckleball was probably his second—or third—best pitch, but by 1922 he relied on his knuckler and led the majors with twenty-seven wins.

Also in 1920, Jesse Haines reached the majors for good, and wound up getting into the Hall of Fame while

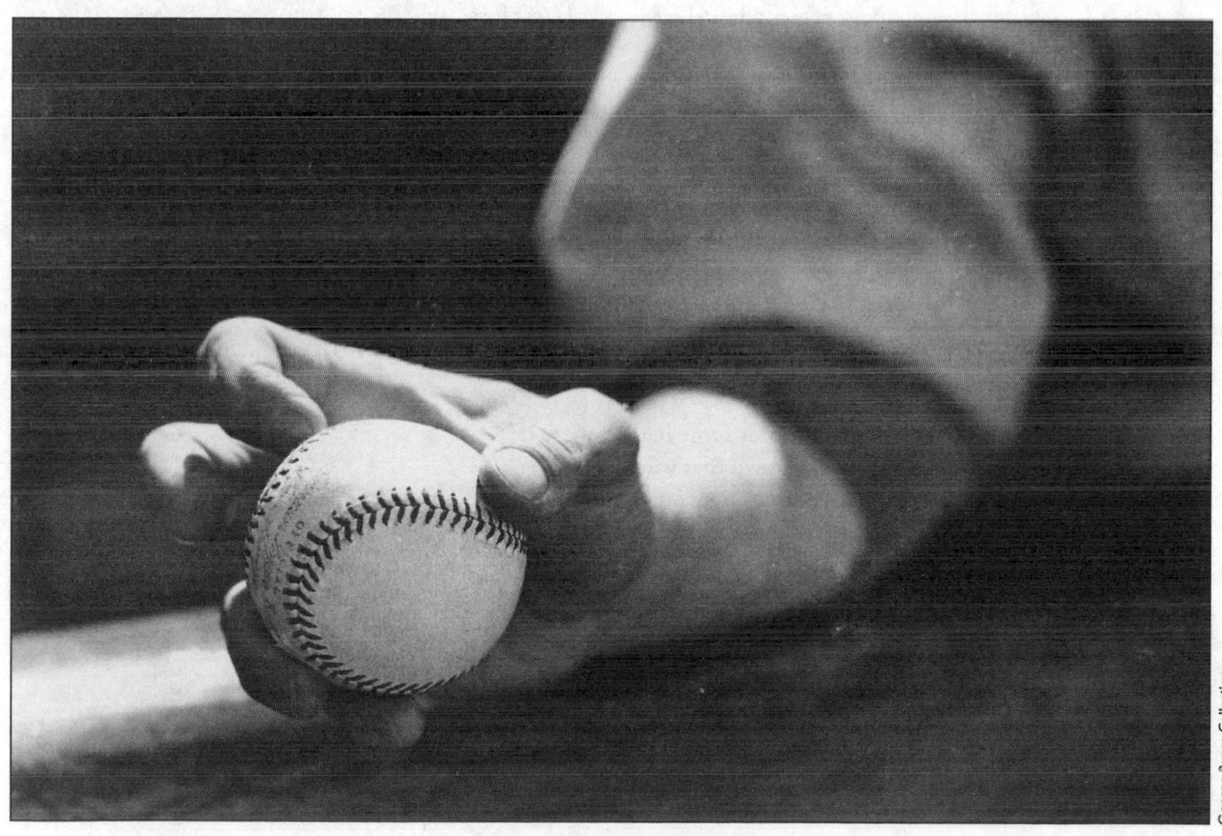

George Brace Collection

George Caster's knuckleball grip

BEST KNUCKLEBALLS

1. Hoyt Wilhelm
2. Phil Niekro
3. Wilbur Wood
4. Eddie Rommel
5. Charlie Hough
6. Tom Candiotti
7. Dutch Leonard
8. Tim Wakefield
9. Joe Niekro
10. Eddie (Fisher or Cicotte)

Others: Ken Johnson, Bob Purkey, Nap Rucker, Ed Summers, Jim Tobin; perhaps it wasn't fair to leave Fred Fitzsimmons and Jesse Haines off this list, but their "knuckleballs" weren't the same sort of pitch as thrown by the fellows on the list.

depending largely on a pitch that everybody called a knuckleball. In 1925 Fred Fitzsimmons arrived, featuring a fast knuckleball similar to Haines', and while Fitzsimmons didn't wind up in the Hall of Fame, he was a better pitcher than Haines.

Whereas Rommel's knuckleball danced, Fitzsimmons' and Haines' knucklers came in harder and moved in the same direction—straight down—just about every time. Does that mean they weren't "true" knuckleballs as we think of them now? Depends on how you look at it. Fitzsimmons and Haines did use their knuckles to grip their best pitches, and they probably did *not* twist their wrists when they released the ball. It's hard to say what we would call their pitches today, because for some reason it's been a long time since anyone's thrown that way.

In the early 1930s, the knuckleball became something of a fad. As William E. Brandt wrote in the March 1932 issue of *Baseball Magazine*,

> . . . Statistics are not available, so it's fairly safe to say, without fear of contradiction, that more knuckle-balls were knuckled in the major leagues in 1931 than in any season since Abner Cooperstown Doubleday decided that ninety feet is the right handicap to give a grounder.
>
> . . . it is a good ball only for those that can control it and that are absolutely positive it will "knuck" every time they turn it loose. The other boys use it best as a "surprise" pitch and at their own risk.
>
> Socks Seibold uses it a lot. Vance throws about four a game, and is very choosy just when to throw them, although he is credited with chucking a very mean one. Red Lucas once in a while. Gaston, Coffman, Stiles, and a dozen other American Leaguers are likely to flop one at you when you've got two strikes and not much else . . .

Adding Eddie Rommel to "Gaston, Coffman, Stiles, and a dozen other American Leaguers" gives us sixteen pitchers who threw the knuckleball at least occasionally, among only eight teams. That's a fad.

On the other hand, if we define "fad" as something that is taken up for just a brief period of time, then the knuckleball should *not* be considered a fad, because the pitch remained at least moderately popular for decades. Sure, every few years there were *stories* suggesting that the knuckleball was enjoying new life. But that was just players forgetting recent history and writers trying to be original. From the early 1930s through the 1950s, a con-

George Brace Collection

Fred Fitzsimmons

siderable number of pitchers featured the knuckleball as a complementary pitch.

Still, with the retirement of Rommel in 1932, there were only two "knuckleball pitchers" in the major leagues; that is, two pitchers (Haines and Fitzsimmons) who relied on the pitch and were well-known for it. And that's where it stayed for about five seasons . . . until the late 1930s, when for some reason there was a mini-explosion of knuckleball pitchers.

From the late '30s through the end of World War II, something like a dozen pitchers reached the majors with the knuckleball as their best pitch. This movement of sorts is best epitomized by the Washington Senators in 1944 and '45: in those two seasons, four knuckleballers—Dutch Leonard, Mickey Haefner, Roger Wolff, and Johnny Niggeling—accounted for seventy-two percent of their team's starts. But these specialists were actually the exception; I suspect that something like half the pitchers in the majors occasionally threw a knuckleball. In 1945, Ed Rumill wrote of Senators catcher Rick Ferrell, "He has been a stylist behind the plate for a long time, some years before the knuckler became the most popular specialty pitch."[28]

Things did slow down some after the war. Knuckleballers Gene Bearden (1948) and Hoyt Wilhelm (1952) were both runners-up in their leagues' Rookie of the Year balloting, but the 1950s were a relatively fallow period for the pitch. While a number of pitchers continued to employ it as a complementary pitch, there really weren't any knuckleballing stars in the decade.

This was due, in part, to the odd notion that knuckleball pitchers belonged in the bullpen. It might have started with Wilhelm, who'd been a successful starter in the minors but was turned into a reliever by Leo Durocher when he came up with the Giants in 1952. From then through the late 1960s, when Phil Niekro established himself, it wasn't easy to find a "knuckleball pitcher" in a major-league rotation (the notable exception being Ken Johnson, who spent most of 1962 through '67 starting for the Colt .45s/Astros and Braves).

There were, on the other hand, a great number of knuckleballing relievers. In addition to Wilhelm—who eventually became the first reliever elected to the Hall of Fame—there were something like a dozen knuckleballing relievers in the 1950s and '60s, and many more who used the pitch at least occasionally.

28. Ed Rumill in *Baseball Magazine* (February 1945), page 294.

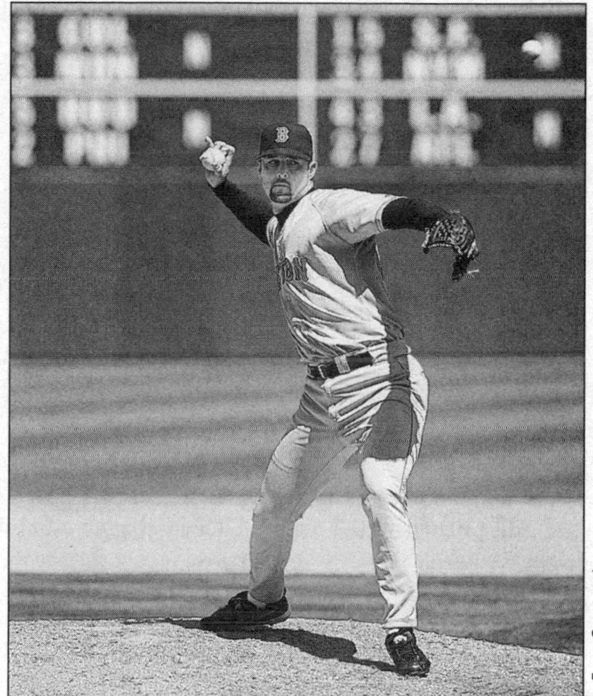
The Topps Company, Inc.

Tim Wakefield

September of 1981 was a signal point in the history (if not the evolution) of the knuckleball pitcher. On September 3, Charlie Hough made his 415th career relief appearance. On September 8, he started against the A's and pitched well (but lost). Hough started four more games in September, won all of them . . . and his long career as a reliever was over. He would pitch in the majors for thirteen more seasons, and pitch only three more games as a reliever.

Wilhelm had pitched his last game in 1972, Eddie Fisher in 1973, which left Hough as the last of the knuckleball relievers. He vacated his title in 1981, and the position went unfilled for nearly twenty years. In 1999, Tim Wakefield spent much of the season in the Red Sox bullpen, and then in 2003 Steve Sparks worked purely as a reliever for the Tigers and the Athletics. For nearly thirty years, though, the general prejudice against knuckleballers extended to an *extreme* prejudice against knuckleball relievers.

Theoretically, a knuckleballer is ill-suited for relief work because relievers often enter a game with runners on base, when an errant floater can be particularly costly. But wasn't this equally true in the 1960s, when Hoyt Wilhelm, Eddie Fisher, and Wilbur Wood thrived in relief?

Or maybe we've got it backwards. Maybe it was the managers of the 1950s and '60s who were biased . . . against knuckleballing *starters*. Maybe everybody finally realized that Phil Niekro and Wilbur Wood and Charlie Hough and the rest were simply too good to be tucked away in the bullpen and used for one hundred innings rather than two hundred (or in the case of Wood and Niekro, well upwards of three hundred).

Actually, the more interesting question is, "Why did pitchers stop using the knuckleball as a complementary pitch?"

I think there are a couple of reasons.

One, pitchers didn't need the knuckleball as much. In the 1960s just about everything was going their way, so there wasn't the same pressure to find an edge over the hitter. And by the 1970s, when the pendulum swung the other way, the circle change-up (or something like it), the forkball, the slip pitch, and others gave pitchers options when looking for a dependable off-speed pitch.

Two, it became popular to suggest that you couldn't throw a knuckleball *effectively* unless you threw it almost *exclusively*. Hoyt Wilhelm, by far the most famous knuckleball pitcher in the 1960s, said this all the time. But is it true? Well, it depends on what you mean by "effectively." It may well be true that a "knuckleball pitcher" has to throw finely tuned knuckleballs to win, and to throw finely tuned knuckleballs he has to throw a *lot* of them. But I think it's silly to suggest that a pitcher today couldn't occasionally throw a knuckleball as his third- or fourth-best pitch, and get some hitters out with it.

Nobody will try it, though. John Smoltz is the only pitcher in recent years who has. He threw a few knuckleballs in 1999 and talked about making the pitch an important part of his repertoire. But then Smoltz got hurt, came back as a reliever and didn't think he needed the knuckleball any more (he was right).

Does the knuckleball have a future? These days, when a knuckleball pitcher throws a "fast" ball and the batter knows it's coming, a home run becomes a distinct possibility. When a knuckleballer throws a knuckleball that doesn't "knuck," a home run becomes a distinct possibility. Times are tough all over.

In May of 1991, *The Sporting News* ran an article titled "Endangered Species: the Amazing Unpredictable Knuckleball is on the Verge of Extinction."

Alarmist? Perhaps. But at the time, there were only two knuckleball pitchers in the major leagues, and one of them (Charlie Hough) was forty-three years old. The other (Tom Candiotti) was thirty-three—young, of course, for a knuckleballer—and it looked like Candiotti would soon be alone, as there weren't any promising knuckleball pitchers in the minor leagues.

But slightly more than a year later, Tim Wakefield made his major-league debut. Three years later, Steve Sparks and Dennis Springer arrived, and in 2001 a "fast" knuckleballer named Jared Fernandez made it.

What happens if Fernandez doesn't stick, and Wakefield goes where all knuckleballers eventually go? There will be another. There always is. At this writing, our hopes lie with a Red Sox farmhand named Charlie Zink. Signed in 2002 on the recommendation of Luis Tiant, Zink is very young for a knuckleball pitcher but has already made great progress in harnessing the pitch. Don't be surprised if he winds up pitching for twenty years in the major leagues.

THE FORKBALL FAST AND SLOW

ROB NEYER

This essay was rewritten at the last moment, when we discovered that we didn't know what we thought we knew.

We thought that a pitcher named Joe Bush invented the forkball.

When Bush came up with the Philadelphia Athletics in 1913, he impressed everybody with his fastball. Ten years later, though, Bush was famous for throwing the "fork ball." Early in 1923, F.C. Lane wrote in *Baseball Magazine*,

> . . . There was a day when Bush could get by on sheer speed. Those were the years when he picked up the nickname of "Bullet Joe." Nowadays, however, Bush couples speed with his fork ball and a few, a very few, judiciously placed curves. These are his repertoire and the prize of the lot is the fork ball. This peculiar delivery is hardly a secret, though, of course, Bush as the originator cannot be expected to explain the intricacies of his pet delivery while it is still the basis of his pitching success.

Joe Bush. Forkball. Originator.

Seems clear enough. But when did Bush originate the forkball?

The answer is "1920." One source says Bush discovered the pitch in 1921, but the more credible stories suggest that he came up with the pitch in 1920 but didn't realize what he had until 1921. In 1929, Bush told *The Saturday Evening Post*,

> Probably one of the most bewildering balls ever pitched was my own invention—the fork ball, which I discovered in 1920 when I was essaying my comeback with the Boston Red Sox after I had hurt my arm several years before and was forced to stop throwing curve balls. I haven't thrown fifteen since. My arm had lost the power and snap it had when I first started to pitch, and I knew I had to evolve a new delivery of my own if I were to stay in the Big Show.
>
> It was while experimenting on different deliveries that I placed the ball between my index and middle fingers, resting the bottom of the sphere on my thumb, and threw it. I discovered that the ball took a funny hop. I tried it again, moving my thumb to the inside of the ball. It took another peculiar hop as it passed over the plate. I repeated the same thing a number of times, moving my thumb in different positions under the ball and noticed that it broke over the pan in all sorts of strange ways. It struck me as somewhat like the spitter, breaking sharply over the plate. I kept working on this delivery day after day until my fingers and thumb would get so sore from stretching around the ball that they would ache for hours, even though my hand is large. A pitcher with a small hand would have great difficulty controlling this pitch.
>
> After developing and perfecting this delivery I gave it the name of fork ball. When I first used it in the league I was almost unhittable. This one pitch had everything to do with my comeback.
>
> I used my thumb as a propeller to guide the ball the way I wanted it to break over the plate. I threw it both overhand and side-arm. When I threw the ball overhand it took a sharp break much like the spit ball. By turning my thumb underneath to the inside I

> could make the ball break away from the hitter, and by turning my thumb to the outside I could make it break in to the batter.
>
> Of course, when I first used it the opposing hitters had no idea I had such a breaking ball and they were so nonplused they had little success hitting against me. The first time Ty Cobb, the greatest batter of all time, hit at it he complained to Umpire Bill Evans that I was using a spit ball, which had been banned.
>
> Evans examined the ball, found no wet spot on it, handed it back to the catcher and told Cobb to go on batting. I heaved another forkie. Ty swung hard and missed it a mile. He insisted I was doing something illegal to the ball and demanded that Evans investigate.
>
> The umpire walked out to the pitcher's mound and asked me what I was doing to give the ball such a freak hop. In as much as I was doing nothing illegal, I was not obliged to disclose my secret and I informed him of the fact in so many words.
>
> Later, of course, the secret got out and everybody in the league knew about my pet pitch, but that made it none the less hard to hit. In the several years following I used it continually to good advantage.[29]

That's a long quote, but it's not often that we're witness to the supposed invention and unveiling of a famous pitch, in detail.

There's only one problem with this story, which is that while Bush might have *thought* he invented the forkball, he certainly did not invent "forkball" the *term*, and there's pretty good evidence that he didn't invent the pitch, either.

There's a story about the forkball's beginnings in a 1987 book called *The Pitcher*, by John Thorn and John Holway . . .

> The paternity of the pitch actually goes back . . . to Chattanooga in about 1905, when outfielder Mike Lynch, who had had a cup of coffee with the White Sox a few years before, experimented with the pitch and found he could get "astonishing" breaks. But the style tired his fingers, and he could not control it.
>
> Three years later, playing with the Tacoma Tigers, he taught it to pitcher Bert Hall, who experimented with it in secret for about three weeks, learning to control it. Finally, on September 8, 1908, he sprang it on the unsuspecting Seattle club and shut them down on four hits. BERT HALL HAS NEW FANGLED BALL WORSE THAN SPITTER, the local paper headlined. That day the pitch—and the name *forkball*—were both born.

29. Joe Bush, "On the Mound," *The Saturday Evening Post* (June 8, 1929).

BEST FORKBALLS & SPLITTERS OF ALL TIME

1. Bruce Sutter (split)
2. Mike Scott (split)
3. Roy Face (fork)
4. Joe Bush (fork)
5. Jack McDowell (split/fork)
6. Tiny Bonham (fork)
7. Jack Morris (split)
8. Mort Cooper (fork)
9. Kazuhiro Sasaki (split)
10. Big Jim Weaver (fork)

I was, until just before the deadline for submitting *our* book, highly skeptical about this story. For one thing, that season, 1908, was also the first season that the knuckleball became well-known in the major leagues, and we know of instances when "fork" was used to mean something else. For another, it seems strange that *nobody* would have mentioned Hall in the early 1920s, when Joe Bush unveiled his forkball. Granted, Hall wasn't famous by any means, but he did pitch briefly in the majors (in 1911).

And finally, while *The Pitcher* is generally well-researched, there's a big hole in their material on the forkball. According to Thorn and Holway, after Hall's (supposed) use of the forkball, "It was thirty years before another hurler used the pitch in the majors."

Of course, this ignores not only Bush, but also quality pitchers like Milt Gaston, Larry French, and Big Jim Weaver, along with a few other 1930s forkballers who didn't enjoy much success but did pitch in the majors. What's more, nobody named Lynch ever played for the White Sox . . . though a Mike Lynch did play for the Cubs in 1902, so that checks out. Sort of.

In the end—which is to say, when I realized that this book wouldn't be complete unless I did—I felt com-

National Baseball Hall of Fame, Cooperstown, NY

Bert Hall

pelled to check out old Bert Hall . . . and what I found was pretty compelling.

Thorn and Holway got the year right but the date wrong; it was not September 8, but rather September 18. As the *Seattle Times* reported the next day,

> The Seattle sluggers could not have hit young Burt Hall yesterday with a canoe paddle. The young fellow simply put the ball between his first two fingers, drew back his arm and let fly. The result was a lot of wiggles on the ball that had the local help completely mystified, and when they hit the ball at all they were so surprised that they sometimes forgot to run.
>
> Hall's assortment yesterday beats all the spit-ball and knuckle ball combinations to death, for he used it overhand, side arm and any old way and kept the ball breaking over the plate. The Seattle team has a habit of making all pitchers look good but young Hall really was good yesterday.

Gosh, that sure sounds like an original forkball to me, right down to the wiggles (many years later, Joe Bush would say, "It dances, too, like a knuckle ball . . ."), and what's really interesting is that the distinction is specifically made between Hall's pitch and the knuckleball.

That item in the *Times* did not specifically name Hall's baffling pitch, but for the rest of the season the *Tacoma Daily Tribune* repeatedly referred to Hall's "fork ball." The *Tribune* also confirmed that the September 18 game in Seattle was the first in which Hall had thrown the pitch.

Hall pitched for Tacoma until late in the 1911 season, when he jumped from the low-grade Northwestern League all the way to the National League, debuting with the Phillies on August 21. On October 9 he made his first start, against the Braves in Philadelphia, and gave up eight runs in a couple of innings. It was the Phillies' last game of the season, and Hall's only game in the majors. He pitched for Tacoma again in 1912, after which I lose track of his career as a professional baseball pitcher.

Hall died in 1948. Babe Ruth and Hack Wilson also passed away that year, and were eulogized in the *Official Baseball Guide.* Also mentioned in the *Guide* were Miss Dorothy Hummel ("secretary to American League President Will Harridge and an employee of the league office for 34 years"), Maurice I. Block ("vice-president of the Southeastern League and former Selma president"), and twenty-one others, most of whom you've never heard of. No mention, however, of Bert Hall, who just might have been the first real forkballer.

If Bert Hall had any impact at all, if anybody saw Hall's forkball or heard about Hall's forkball and adopted the pitch as his own, we've not found any clue.

With Bush's success, on the other hand, the forkball became moderately famous moderately quickly, but for some reason the forkball did not spread quickly (moderately or otherwise). There were few pitchers who did more than fool around with it, and for a while the only pitchers who relied on it were pitchers who'd learned it from Joe Bush himself. Bennie Karr, a journeyman, learned the forkball from Bush, probably in 1921, when both were Red Sox. Milt Gaston, the first well-known forkball artist after Bush, probably learned the pitch from Bush in 1924 when both were Yankees.

Bush last pitched in the majors in 1928, Gaston in 1934, and for the rest of the 1930s there really wasn't anybody who was particularly noted for throwing the forkball. Larry French and Dizzy Trout threw good ones, and Big Jim Weaver relied on it. But it might be argued that since Bush there have been two, and *only* two, famous forkballers: Ernie "Tiny" Bonham and Elroy Face.

It's not that nobody threw a forkball. A lot of pitchers threw it. But it was just one of many off-speed pitches—what used to be called "slow balls"—fighting for a place in the arsenal. With the abolition of the spitball in 1920, almost every pitcher began casting about for a third pitch, something to complement his fastball and curveball. The forkball wasn't as easy to pick up as the knuckleball or the screwball or the other change-ups, but there's little doubt that a significant number of hurlers did fool around with it.

The forkball was Tiny Bonham's best pitch, though, and he became a star. In 1940, he went 9-3 with a 1.90 ERA, and the Yankees probably would have won the pennant if they'd brought him to the majors in April rather than August. Bonham was used sparingly in 1941, but he clinched the World Series that fall with a four-hitter to beat the Dodgers, and then in 1942 he went 21-5 and led the majors in winning percentage.

In August of 1949, Bonham had just turned thirty-six but was still pitching effectively (by then, for the Pirates). On the 27th he beat the Phillies, 8-2. On September 8, Bonham underwent an appendectomy and other abdominal surgery. On the 15th, he died (and became a footnote to history when his wife became the first to receive death benefits from the new pension fund).[30]

The next real forkball pitcher really *was* tiny—"Tiny" Bonham had tipped the scales at well over 200 pounds—as Roy Face stood five-eight and weighed somewhere in the neighborhood of 150 pounds. As a twenty-five-year-old Pirates rookie in 1953, Face went 6-8 with a (gulp) 6.58 ERA. So in 1954, Pirates general manager Branch Rickey sent Face to New Orleans and told him to work on an off-speed pitch. That spring, Joe Page had been in the Pirates' camp. Page threw a forkball, and that gave Face an idea.

"Page didn't show me how to throw it," Face later told interviewer Jim O'Brien. "I learned that myself. I just thought if the forkball made Page so successful, I would give it a try."[31]

30. The Sporting News, *Official Guide and Record Book 1950*, page 84.
31. Jim O'Brien, *Maz and the '60 Bucs* (1993).

Face worked on the forkball, and in the middle of the season he started throwing it in games. He finished the season with a 4.45 ERA, but pitched well enough to break camp with the Pirates in 1955, and for the next fifteen seasons he ranked as one of the game's best relievers.

What's odd is that nobody followed in Face's footsteps. It's not *literally* true that nobody else threw the forkball in the 1960s—most notably, Lindy McDaniel used the pitch to great effect—but it's true enough that only a small number of people on this planet could easily prove me wrong.

Bill James thinks the forkball lost favor with major leaguers because young pitchers thought the pitch a bit . . . well, a bit unmanly. Maybe he's right about that. I think there's another, simpler explanation, which is that the forkball simply lost out in the marketplace. From the day Joe Bush came up with the forkball, there never were more than a few major-league pitchers who used it more than occasionally, probably because 1) it wasn't easy to control (see Milt Gaston entry on page 216), and 2) it was said to cause injuries (also, Bush later said that throwing the forkball eventually resulted in a looser grip on the ball, which made the pitch less effective). Flipping through the instructional books published in the 1940s, the forkball is barely even mentioned, and it's essentially never suggested as a quality pitch. And if the forkball's limitations (or perceived limitations) weren't already damaging enough, in the 1950s

- Paul Richards was teaching his slip pitch to everybody in sight,
- a *lot* of guys were throwing spitballs, and
- at some point, probably in this same period, somebody came up with the circle change-up or something very much like it.

I think the forkball was on life support in the 1950s and '60s because the pitchers believed they had better options, which they probably did. But rather than dying, the forkball made a comeback in the 1970s . . . in the guise of the split-fingered fastball.

Where did the splitter come from? In *Think Better Baseball*, longtime pitcher and coach Bob Cluck wrote,

> My partner Roger Craig and I developed the "split" with the help of others at the San Diego School of

> Baseball during a winter of the late 1970s . . . The original name was actually the "split-fingered change." Roger Craig took it to Detroit and changed the name to "split-fingered fastball" so pitchers would think "fastball" as they threw it. He taught it to the major league pitchers, and it took off from there.

There is a big problem with this story, though, which is that Bruce Sutter, the most famous split-fingered fastball pitcher ever, specifically said that he learned his splitter in 1973 from Cubs minor-league pitching instructor Fred Martin.[32]

A couple of things about Sutter . . . when he first reached the majors and began pitching well, his key pitch was labeled a forkball. And years *after* he reached the majors, he was said to have been taught his best pitch by Cubs pitching coach Mike Roarke.

However, 1) multiple contemporary accounts have him learning the pitch from Fred Martin, and 2) by 1979, there was definitely a distinction being made between Sutter's pitch and the old-style forkball. As Ron Fimrite wrote in *Sports Illustrated*, "This [Sutter's] grip is not to be confused with the one used in throwing the forkball. The fingers also are spread in delivering that pitch, but the ball is wedged back in the palm of the hand, and the thumb plays no real role in the delivery."[33]

Speaking of Sutter, he's adamant in his assertion that Roger Craig doesn't deserve all the credit he's received for inventing the splitter.

> I keep hearing Roger Craig's name associated with the pitch. He has become the guru of the pitch, but I'll tell you what pisses me off about that. I taught Roger Craig the split-finger. That still doesn't set right with me. I understand that he's teaching it and he's doing a good job with it. Some of the guys he's taught have been very successful. I don't think that just because Fred Martin and I started throwing it that we should have a patent on it or that anybody that wants to learn has got to come to me. Roger is a very qualified coach but here's how Roger Craig learned the split-finger fastball. He was the pitching coach of the San Diego Padres. In fact, this happened one of those times when the Cubs had Fred [Martin] . . . up in the major leagues working with me. We were in San Diego playing and Roger called us over by the batting cage and wanted to know all about the split-finger fastball, how to hold the ball and that crap. So now, when the split-finger is mentioned, all you ever hear is Roger Craig. This was during batting practice. He just wanted to know how to hold the ball and we told him. When people start talking about the split-finger, Fred Martin should get the credit. Roger is doing a good job and he deserves everything he can get as a major league coach and manager, that's his job. But as far as being the guru of the split-finger, that doesn't sit right with me.[34]

San Francisco Giants

Roger Craig

So there you have it, folks. Fred Martin invented the split-fingered fastball, Bruce Sutter perfected it, and Roger Craig stole all the credit.

No, it's probably not that simple. Craig may have al-

32. Ron Fimrite, *Sports Illustrated* (September 19, 1979), "This Pitch in Time Saves Nine."
33. Fimrite, ibid.
34. Bruce Sutter in *Pen Men* (Rob Cairns, 1993), page 329–330.

ready known plenty about the pitch, and was just quizzing Martin and Sutter in case they knew something he didn't. And either way, Craig deserves an immense amount of credit for popularizing the splitter. When he was the Tigers' pitching coach in the early '80s, Craig had almost everybody on the staff throwing it, then he taught it to Mike Scott in the middle '80s, and then in the late '80s, as manager of the Giants, he taught the splitter to most of his pitchers *there.*

Here's how Peter Gammons told the story, in 1983, of Craig and the splitter:

> The infatuation with this pitch started in 1978 and '79, when Craig was managing the Padres and had a school for Little League pitchers in San Diego. "I talked to a lot of orthopedic surgeons," said Craig, "and they agreed that no one should ever teach a Little League pitcher to throw a breaking ball until he's 14, 15 or 16. But when they have only one type of pitch, a fastball, they want something else, and if you don't teach them something that won't hurt their arms and still allow them to develop their mechanics, they'll learn something on their own and only hurt themselves.
>
> "I came up with two ideas. One was to hold the baseball like a football; it didn't work too well. But the other was to spread the fingers out in some form of forkball and throw a regular fastball. I was absolutely amazed at what 14- and 15-year-olds could make the ball do, and I thought to myself, 'hey, if they can do it, what about major leaguers?"[35]

Well, again, here we've got Craig working on the splitter in the late 1970s, and we know that Sutter was throwing it five years earlier. You be the judge.

POSTSCRIPT: After reading what I wrote about the forkball, Bill James kindly attempted to save me from myself. You see, Bill doesn't agree with me about the forkball being a "slow ball," and he was afraid that, if left to my own devices, I would come across as something of a fool on this subject. Bill argues that while the forkball, as thrown by Joe Bush and others, probably was not thrown quite as hard as the modern split-fingered fastball, it also was not really an "off-speed pitch" as I've characterized it.

Faced with Bill's dubiousness, I went searching for anything that might speak to the question. Here's what I found . . .

- In their 1941 book, *Play Ball! Advice for Young Ballplayers*, scouts Al Chapman and Hank Severeid co-wrote about slow balls, "Many so-called pitches are merely indicative of the way in which this slow ball is held, such as the finger-nail ball, the fork ball, and the knuckle ball." This passage, coming in the middle of a broad discussion of "the slow ball," clearly indicates that the forkball was considered a form of change-up.
- In a 1943 *Baseball Magazine* article titled "Change-of-Pace," the forkball is grouped with the knuckleball, both of which were said by author Ed Rumill to have started "the pitching parade of the junkers . . ."
- In a 1949 *Baseball Magazine* article about A's pitching coach Earle Brucker, Brucker says of Phil Marchildon, "He hated the knuckle ball when he tried it, his hand wasn't big enough for the palm ball. So the last trial was a fork ball. And Phil adopted that pitch for his 'sneaker.' "
- In 1953, Joe Bush said of the forkball, "It dances, too, like a knuckle ball, but it's thrown much harder than a knuckler."
- In his 1964 autobiography, Stan Musial said of Ken Raffensberger's forkball, "The fork ball looked as big as a grapefruit, but fell off the table, low."
- In 2002, Ted Gray told me that his forkball—he pitched in the late '40s and early '50s—was the same pitch that's known today as the split-fingered fastball.

Of these six references, four suggest that the forkball was, indeed, an off-speed pitch. One exception is Bush's quote, which I consider questionable because it requires us to guess 1) what Bush means by "much harder," and 2) whose knuckler he's talking about. The other is Gray's claim, which I consider questionable because old pitchers *generally* resist the notion that today's pitchers do anything that they didn't do just as well (or just as fast).

The way I interpret the evidence, the score is Rob 4, Bill 2 (though Bill might take issue with my scorekeeping).

35. Peter Gammons, *The Sporting News* (March 21, 1983), "Craig Calls Forkball Key Pitch."

It's hard to pin down just how hard the forkball was thrown before 1940, because very few major-league pitchers *threw* the forkball before 1940. However, I'm confident that *by* the 1940s, the forkball was placed squarely among the various pitches generically known as "slow balls" (though it may well have been thrown somewhat harder than the other slow balls).

I'm also confident, if not to the same degree, that the forkball/splitter has evolved from the beginning, with the two gripping fingers moving closer and closer together. Bert Hall's forkball was described as a pitch that wiggled; Joe Bush said his danced like a knuckleball. A pitch simply can't wiggle or dance unless it's spinning very, very slowly. And you can't make a pitch spin very, very slowly with a forkball grip unless your fingers are spread very, very wide.

But that probably wasn't how the forkball was thrown in the 1930s. I've got a little book called *How to Pitch*, published in 1928, that features photos of various pitchers gripping a variety of pitches, six pitches per pitcher. Granted, it's not likely that each pitcher actually threw all six pitches he's shown gripping, but it's worth noting that the two pitchers shown gripping a forkball, Walter Johnson (!) and Freddy Fitzsimmons, are using grips that look very much like those used by pitchers today, to throw the splitter.

Granted, neither Johnson nor Fitzsimmons were known to actually throw a forkball in games, so we have to take those photos for what they're worth. But in 1942, Herbert Simons wrote in *Baseball Magazine*, "Although, unlike the knuckler, the course of the fork ball usually is predetermined, it is just as hard to control." That just doesn't sound, to me at least, like the same pitch that Joe Bush (and Bert Hall, probably) had thrown twenty and thirty years earlier.

BONUS POSTSCRIPT: Literally moments before I positively, absolutely had to stop making significant changes to this book, I found yet *another* pitcher who might have been the first to throw the forkball. His name was apparently Michael Propreski but he preferred James Swift, and in 1908 he pitched for the Wilkes-Barre club in the New York State League. Propreski/Swift relied on his spitball, but that wasn't all he had. According to *The Sporting News* (October 15, 1908),

> A previous reference to the proposed legislation against the "spit ball" not affecting Swift is the fact that he has a substitute for this species of delivery that acts identically the same. Swift has it under absolute control, having used it in the past two or three years. There is a word used in the Polish language, meaning good, which is "dobre"; and Swift terms this ball his "dobre ball." He has exceptionally long fingers and is able to place the ball between the index and second finger of his left hand. The two first joints of the fingers clasp one side of the ball, while the thumb remains underneath it, so that the ball is clasped almost as tightly as though in a vise. This "dobre ball" acts exactly the same as the "spit ball." It breaks in different directions and is in every sense as difficult to hit as the "spit ball," while the catcher necessarily must exercise the same caution in catching it. Whenever Swift uses this ball it renders him remarkably effective, and no matter what difficulty he finds himself in, this species of delivery proves of great value. No man can use this "dobre ball" unless he is favored with a hand such as Swift carries, and even then it is doubtful if he could use it, because it required years of practice while his hand was developing for Swift to acquire this feat and particular delivery.

Maybe I've become fork-happy, but the "dobre ball" certainly sounds like a forkball to me. Or rather, it sounds like the dancing version of the forkball thrown by Bert Hall and Joe Bush. All I know about James Swift is 1) what you've already read, and 2) that he never did pitch in the major leagues. But it's certainly possible that *he* invented the forkball, and he deserves at least a footnote when the story is told.

THE SCREWBALL: FADING AWAY

ROB NEYER

Nobody knows who threw the first screwball. The earliest pitcher who has been *credited* with throwing the screwball is Mickey Welch, a big star in the 1880s. A startlingly handsome fellow who probably stood about five-eight in his baseball shoes, Welch wound up winning 307 games.

In a recent *Sporting News* book titled *Heroes of the Hall*, Ron Smith wrote, "When asked the secret of his success, Welch smiled and attributed it to drinking beer. More likely it had to do with the fastball, curve and changeup he mastered while carving up hitters—and an unusual screwball he might have been the first to throw."

There are a couple of problems with this. The first, minor problem is, what in hell is an "unusual screwball"? And the second, major problem is that we've not seen a primary source supporting the notion that Welch threw the pitch that would later become known first as the fadeaway and later the screwball.

In *Baseball's First Stars* (SABR, 1996), Irv Bergman quotes Welch on his repertoire: "I had a pretty good fast ball, but I depended chiefly on change of pace and an assortment of curve balls."

It's certainly possible that a screwball-like pitch was just part of that assortment, and it's also possible that, years later, Welch said, "I threw the fadeaway back in my day, but we didn't have a name for it." We haven't seen a quote like that, though.

Another supposed early screwball artist was Charlie Sweeney. In *A Century of Baseball* (1938), A.H. Tarvin wrote,

> So far as it is known, Charlie Sweeney is the father of the "fadeaway." At any rate, it was that style of delivery that he used when he immortalized himself, when pitching for Providence, in 1884, by fanning 19 batters in that nine-frame contest. However, that very feat nearly ended Charlie's career as a boxman, because it affected his arm. He never tried it again.

By the time Sweeney pitched that game against Providence, Welch had already won a hundred National League games (Sweeney was pitching in his second season). Old Hoss Radbourn, Tim Keefe, John Clarkson . . . all of these pitchers were big stars, and all have been rumored to have thrown a precursor to the screwball.

All we really know is that *somebody* was throwing the screwball in the nineteenth century, because that's when Christy Mathewson learned the pitch. It was 1898, and he was tutored by a minor-league teammate named Dave Williams. Nobody's ever seriously suggested that Williams invented the pitch—which became famous as the "fadeaway" when Mathewson became a household name—and nobody's figured out who tutored Williams.

But just about anybody could have invented it. Once everybody realized that you could make a baseball curve *that* way by twisting your wrist *this* way, it wouldn't have taken a genius to realize that reversing the process should be possible, the result being what we might call—and what might actually have been called—a "reverse curve."

Or "incurve," a term commonly used as the nineteenth century became the twentieth. According to *The New Dickson Baseball Dictionary*, the incurve was the "pitch now known as a screwball."

Maybe. But in the early '20s, John McGraw (or his

BEST SCREWBALLS OF ALL TIME

1. Carl Hubbell
2. Fernando Valenzuela
3. Christy Mathewson
4. Mike Cuellar
5. Mike Marshall
6. Tug McGraw
7. Luis Tiant, Sr.
8. Harry Brecheen
9. Jim Bagby, Sr.
10. Ruben Gomez

Others: Luis Arroyo, Jack Baldschun, Huck Betts, Cy Blanton, Jim Brewer, Willie Hernandez, Carmen Hill, Jim Mecir, Fred Norman, Nels Potter, Sloppy Thurston

ghostwriter) denied this, saying the incurve was merely a riding fastball.

In a 1908 instructional book called *How to Pitch*, Bill Dineen says of the incurve/inshoot (he used the terms interchangeably), "Speed is necessary for an inshoot . . . Do not become discouraged if you fail to see the ball positively change its course as it does in an outcurve . . . Practice will succeed in giving a sharp break to the ball, which may not amount to more than an inch or two . . ."

Anyway, I'm getting off the track. "Incurve" might have been used, as a number of terms have, to describe more than one pitch.

What's more, I'm not completely convinced that the fadeaway and the screwball were the same pitch. Reading the description of the fadeaway, I can't help but wonder if the fadeaway wasn't more like the pitch we now call the circle change-up.

Here's Sloppy Thurston, one of the top fadeaway specialists after Christy Mathewson, in 1924: "My favorite ball is a kind of fade-away that breaks away from a left-handed batter. It's a slow ball and I use a lot of them. Perhaps out of a hundred pitched balls, I'll use as many as twenty-five slow balls."

Notice that Thurston doesn't remotely suggest that he's throwing what would essentially be the reverse of a curveball. He says he's throwing a slow ball—that is, some sort of change-up—that happens to break away from the left-handed hitter (Thurston threw right-handed).

Thurston enjoyed some fine seasons, as did Ned Garvin and Jim Bagby, Sr. And yet, in another, later edition of *How to Pitch*, J.E. Wray wrote, "The fadeaway is a one-man ball. There is no record of another pitcher having made a notable success by using this form of delivery."

Maybe Wray just didn't know what the hell he was talking about. Or maybe those other pitchers weren't thought to be throwing the same pitch that Mathewson threw. In the same book, Virgil Barnes' right hand is pictured demonstrating the grips for six pitches . . . including, according to the captions, the "Screw ball" *and* the "Fadeaway ball."

That presents a problem. That edition of *How to Pitch* was published in 1928, which was Carl Hubbell's first season in the major leagues. According to *The New Dickson Baseball Dictionary*,

> **ETYMOLOGY.** George Vecsey interviewed Hubbell (*New York Times*, July 9, 1984). After establishing the fact that Hubbell first threw the pitch in the minor leagues, Vecsey concluded: "If the pitch was thrown before Hubbell, it certainly had no mystique until a catcher in Oklahoma City—Hubbell says his name was Earl Walgamot—warmed him up before a game and said, "That's the screwiest thing I ever saw."

If all this is true, we have to believe the term "screwball" was invented in 1925—when Hubbell pitched for Oklahoma City—and then picked up by Barnes within a couple of years, because presumably *How to Pitch* was put together *before* the 1928 season, when Hubbell debuted with the Giants a month *after* Barnes had been traded from the Giants to the Braves.

Now, if you look up Hubbell and Virgil Barnes, you'll see that both pitched for the New York Giants in 1928. They don't overlap—Barnes got traded to the Braves in June, Hubbell debuted in July—but you might guess that they were teammates in spring training.

They weren't. Hubbell was the property of the Detroit Tigers that spring, and didn't become a Giant until just before he reached the majors.

Back in the 1930s, with the events still fresh in his mind, Hubbell wasn't nearly so specific. In 1934 he told Frank Graham about coming up with his screw ball.

> I wasn't even thinking about a screw ball. In fact, I wouldn't have known a screw ball if I had seen one. It

> was in 1925, when I was with Oklahoma City. I had a fast ball and a curve ball but everybody else had that much. I noticed that there were a couple of other pitchers in the league who had a sinker and that they could do a little better than anybody else. So I set out to develop a sinker and finally I got it. Then everybody began to call it a screw ball. And so, I guess, that's what it is.[36]

A sinker?

The more research into these things you do, the more you realize that you don't know anything. All we can do is the best that we can. But the evidence strongly suggests that the term "screwball" was *not* invented to describe Hubbell's pitch. In the February 1928 issue of *Baseball Magazine,* F.C. Lane off-handedly mentioned that Willis Hudlin did not throw a screw ball. Would Lane use a term that had been invented to describe a pitch thrown by someone (Hubbell) who hadn't even pitched in the major leagues yet?

So we don't know who threw the first fadeaway, and we don't know who came up with "screwball," or when.

One thing we do know is that for a long, long time, there's been a prejudice against the fadeaway/screwball, because of what it supposedly does to a pitcher's arm.

Way back in 1912, Christy Mathewson (or his ghost writer) wrote,

> Many persons have asked me why I do not use my "fade-away" oftener when it is so effective, and the only answer is that every time I throw the "fade-away" it takes so much out of my arm. It is a very hard ball to deliver. Pitching it ten or twelve times in a game kills my arm, so I save it for the pinches.[37]

If you don't believe that throwing a screwball puts a strain on your arm, I want you to conduct a little experiment (don't worry, it'll take just a few seconds and doesn't involve a Bunsen burner).

First, raise your right arm, with your elbow pointing toward third base (work with me here) and your hand pointing straight up.

Now, quickly bring your hand forward and downward, and just as your arm is nearly straight, twist your wrist violently clockwise, so that your palm winds up facing skyward and your thumb is pointing toward third base.

Not bad, huh? That was a curveball.

Now, start over and do the same thing . . . except instead of twisting your wrist clockwise, twist it counterclockwise.

Hurts a little, doesn't it? That's a screwball. Carl Hubbell threw so many screwballs that he was left permanently disfigured. As Jim Murray wrote of Hubbell, many years after he'd retired, "The only eccentric thing about him is his left arm. He looks as if he put it on in the dark."

In his 1942 book, *How to Pitch,* ex-major leaguer Lew Fonseca wrote, "The screwball is another trick ball that can ruin a beginner's arm."

In the 1947 edition of his book, *Baseball: Individual Team Play and Strategy,* ex-major leaguer Jack Coombs wrote, "The screw ball, which has in the last decade made a number of professional pitchers famous in the baseball world, should never be taught to a young man before he has mastered the fundamentals of pitching. It is doubtful whether it should *ever* be taught to a young man, as it calls for muscle movements in the wrist, forearm, and elbow that are *contrary to the laws of nature.*"

Italics are mine. Coombs is essentially saying that while throwing the screwball can lead to great things, it's probably not worth the risk.

And he might be right. Generally, the top screwballing starters haven't enjoyed particularly long careers.

- Christy Mathewson's last big season came when he was thirty-two.
- Carl Hubbell's last big season came when he was thirty-four.
- Harry Brecheen's last big season came when he was thirty-three.
- Mike Cuellar's last good season came when he was thirty-eight.
- Fernando Valenzuela's last good season came when he was . . . well, who knows how old he was? Late twenties, probably.

Okay, so Cuellar doesn't really make my point. He enjoyed his best year at twenty-nine, and was still better

36. Frank Graham, *Baseball Magazine* (October 1934), "The Wizard of the Screw Ball."
37. Christy Mathewson, *Pitching in a Pinch* (1912), page 11.

than the league when he was thirty-seven. But the others didn't last as long as we expect great pitchers to last.

To this day, young pitchers are discouraged from throwing the screwball. Here's what Pat Jordan wrote about the pitch in *Sports Illustrated Pitching: The Keys to Excellence* (1988): "A screwball—the pitch—got its name because it must be thrown in a way that is the opposite of every pitch; because the ball spins in a way that is the reverse of a curveball; and, finally, because only a demented person would specialize in such a perverse pitch that is so hard to master and so damaging to a pitcher's arm."

Only a demented person.

A few years ago, I asked Stan Williams and Larry Dierker why the screwball seemed to have fallen into disfavor (Williams was Seattle's pitching coach, Larry Dierker was Houston's manager, and both pitched in the 1960s).

Williams: "I think the advent of the forkball and the split-fingered pitch has probably supplanted the need for the screwball."

Dierker: "The screwball is a tough pitch to throw. The splitter is a lot easier to throw and it gives you something against a guy who hits the other way."

And we haven't even mentioned the circle change-up, which does almost precisely what the screwball—or at least a slow screwball—does. The screwball is hard to learn, it's rough on the ol' soupbone, and there are other pitches that serve the same purpose.

New pitches come, and old pitches go. The screwball's not dead yet, but when you see one, treasure the moment. Because it might be your last.

THE UNSANITARY SPITBALL

ROB NEYER

> Elmer Stricklett has been called the inventor of the "spit ball." By that I take it that he went further trying to control a ball with a wet surface than any of his predecessors. After he had a little success others followed in his footsteps.
>
> —JACK CHESBRO, 1908

Chesbro was the most famous spitball pitcher for a few years—until Ed Walsh became a big star—and when it comes to the origin of his best pitch, he nailed it. Stricklett has widely been credited with inventing the spitball; in 1913, P.A. Meaney wrote in *Baseball Magazine*, "About 90% of the players and sporting writers throughout the United States are under the impression that Elmer Stricklett was the man who invented and first used the 'spit ball.' "

But as Meaney went on to argue, Stricklett wasn't any such thing. According to Meaney, the spitball was 1) discovered by a minor-league pitcher named Frank Corridon in 1902, 2) demonstrated by Corridon to one of his teammates, an outfielder named George Hildebrand, who 3) moved to another minor-league team, and showed the spitball to Elmer Stricklett.

Stricklett wasn't a great pitcher, but he figured out how to throw a pretty good spitball. In 1903 he was witnessed by Chesbro,[38] in 1904 by Big Ed Walsh, and both of them developed outstanding spitballs. Chesbro burned out quickly, but Walsh was a great pitcher for seven years (1906–1912), and did more than anybody to popularize the spitball.

But was Meaney right? Did Corridon invent the spitball?

No, probably not. In 1931, *Baseball Magazine* ran a profile of a nineteenth-century pitcher named Bobby Matthews, and the article included:

> I was a pitcher and captain of the old Eckfords in 1868, when we took a trip to Baltimore to play the Lord Baltimores, then a famous club. Bobby Matthews was pitching for the Baltimores at that time and well do I remember the sensation he occasioned. We managed to beat the Baltimores the first game, but they put it all over us the second game and all because of Matthews' pitching, which was a revelation to us. Matthews rubbed the ball with his hands and kept one side of it perfectly white, then he would moisten it with his fingers and let it go. The ball not only would take a decided outcurve at times but at other times would drop and curve as the exact counterpart, in fact, of Christy Mathewson's fadeaway. You may not believe it but I know I am right for I saw it.[39]

There are other accounts, in the literature, of this nineteenth-century pitcher or that one fooling around with a spitball. There's nothing suggesting that any particular pitcher relied on the spitball, and for some reason it apparently didn't sweep across the game. Corridon might never have heard of the spitball, when he came up with it. But he wasn't the first, and Stricklett *certainly* wasn't the first.

Anyway, with Walsh carving up American League hitters every season, the spitball got real popular. He was the best spitballer, but there were plenty of good ones: Bugs Raymond, Marty O'Toole, Jeff Tesreau . . .

And if a pitcher couldn't get the hang of the spitter, he had plenty of options. Russ Ford and Cy Falkenberg threw the emery ball, Eddie Cicotte and Dave Danforth threw the shine ball, other pitchers threw these and var-

38. P.A. Meaney, *Baseball Magazine* (May 1913), page 59.

39. H.H. Westlake, *Baseball Magazine* (April 1931), page 513.

ious other "freak deliveries" with varying degrees of success. If a pitcher did *not* do something to the baseball, at least occasionally, it was cause for mention.

As a result, in the teens you could hardly open an issue of *Baseball Magazine* without coming across an article like "Why the Spit Ball Should Be Abolished," or "Who Needs the Spit Ball?" or "Why Freak Deliveries Must Go."

The men who wrote these articles had a variety of arguments, but essentially it boiled down to one thing: the pitchers were making a mockery of the game. It was one thing to apply a bit of saliva to the baseball, but the pitchers didn't know when to stop. They slathered every manner of slippery substance on the ball, and also competed with each other trying to come up with new ways of scuffing and discoloring it. Frankly, it became a joke.

So finally, prior to the 1920 season a rule was introduced:

> At no time during the progress of the game shall the pitcher be allowed to: (1) Apply a foreign substance of any kind to the ball; (2) Expectorate either on the ball or his glove; (3) Rub the ball on his glove, person, or clothing; (4) Deface the ball in any manner; (5) or to deliver what is called the "shine" ball, "spit" ball, "mud" ball, or "emery" ball. For violation of any part of this rule the umpire shall at once order the pitcher from the game, and in addition he shall be automatically suspended for a period of 10 days, on notice from the president of the league.

National Baseball Hall of Fame, Cooperstown, NY

Ed Walsh

At the same time, those designated by their teams as "bona fide spitball pitchers" were allowed to continue throwing the spitball through the duration of their careers. Why every team didn't list all or most of their pitchers as spitballers, I don't know, but the final list consisted of only seventeen pitchers.

Here's the list, chronologically according to the last season each pitched in the majors: Ray Fisher (1920), Doc Ayers (1921), Earl Caldwell (1921), Phil Douglas (1922), Dana Fillingim (1925), Marvin Goodwin (1925), Hub Leonard (1925), Allan Russell (1925), Allen Sothoron (1926), Dick Rudolph (1927), Stan Coveleski (1928), Urban Shocker (1928), Bill Doak (1929), Clarence Mitchell (1932), Red Faber (1933), Jack Quinn (1933), and Burleigh Grimes (1934).

Coveleski, Faber, and Grimes all wound up in the Hall of Fame, Quinn pitched in the majors until he was fifty, and one might reasonably argue that these guys benefited from something like an unfair advantage.

Oddly, it's very difficult to find references to pitchers throwing the spitball between 1920 and 1940, aside from those who were still permitted to throw it. I don't have the slightest idea why this would be the case, but it is.

And then, beginning in the early 1940s, suddenly a great number of pitchers are accused of throwing spitballs (and some of them would eventually admit it). Perhaps most famously, Hugh Casey's pitch that escaped catcher Mickey Owen in the 1941 World Series is widely supposed to have been a spitball. Tommy Bridges threw spitballs, Joe Page threw spitballs, and Claude Passeau was thought to throw spitballs (he always denied it). In 1956, Milton Gross wrote an article for *Sport* titled "Are They Still Throwing the Spitter?" Gross polled players on all sixteen major-league teams, and came up with seventeen pitchers suspected of cheating.

BEST SPITBALLS OF ALL TIME

1. Ed Walsh
2. Stan Coveleski
3. Gaylord Perry
4. Red Faber
5. Jack Quinn
6. Burleigh Grimes
7. Jack Chesbro
8. Phil Douglas
9. Jeff Tesreau
10. Frank Shellenback

Others: Walter Ball (negro leaguer), Lou Burdette, Bill Byrd (negro leaguer), Ray Caldwell, Larry Cheney, Phil Cockrell (negro leaguer), Bill Doak, Dutch (Hub) Leonard, Marty O'Toole, Bugs Raymond, Allan "Rubberarm" Russell

One of them was Lou Burdette, the most famous spitball pitcher of the 1950s. Everybody thought Burdette threw a spitball, and after retiring he admitted it. Don Drysdale was also thought to throw the spitball, at least occasionally, and when he got around to writing his autobiography, he wasn't shy about admitting that he'd thrown a lot of them, especially late in his career.

Of course, you know about Gaylord Perry.

Aside from Perry, though, the suspected spitballers have been few and far between since the 1960s. Yes, Doug Corbett's sinker was suspected of being a wet one, and Mike Scott's splitter was suspected of being a scuffball. A few others. But when was the last time you were watching a game on TV and heard somebody suggest the pitcher was throwing a spitball?

So what's happened to the spitball and the various other illegal deliveries?

A couple of things, I think.

For one thing, the widespread use of the split-fingered fastball and the circle change-up has largely obviated the need for a pitch like the spitball. And for another, every baseball game is now recorded from multiple angles, which would make it pretty tough for a suspected spitballer to get away with anything for long.

PART II

PITCHERS

TOMMY BOND

ROB NEYER

There's a wonderful "creation myth"—at least I think it's a myth—about Thomas Henry Bond. The way the story goes, when he was a boy Tommy moved to Brooklyn, home of the famous Atlantics, one of the top semi-pro clubs of the early 1870s. One afternoon, sportswriter Henry Chadwick—later to gain entry to the Hall of Fame as the "Father of Baseball"—happened across Bond pitching on a sandlot, and recommended the youngster to Bob Ferguson, captain of the Atlantics.

Ferguson told Chadwick to have the boy report to Coney Island the following Sunday, to see how he might fare against strong competition. Bond got hit hard, but (so the story goes) Ferguson later visited Bond with some advice.

> Ferguson told boy to pitch up against door and showed him how to make lines on wood. Bond padded door and started throwing at it, but landlord strenuously protested. Landlord threatened to get his son, who was sheriff of county, after lad. Ferguson saw sheriff, however, and patched things up, so Tom could practice his pitching.

It's not at all clear when this supposedly happened, but one source says Bond was sixteen, and we do know that when he was eighteen, Ferguson finally invited him to pitch for the Atlantics. (And you know, maybe it's all true. As a professional concern, baseball in the early 1870s was still an infant, and it probably wasn't all that uncommon for a player to be discovered by a random passer-by.)

In 1874, the Atlantics played fifty-six league games—National Association games, that is—and eighteen-year-old Tommy Bond started fifty-five of them. He went just 22–32, but the Atlantics had a poor hitting attack, and his ERA was slightly better than the league average.

In *America's National Game* (1911), Al Spalding wrote, "In 1874 Tom Bond inaugurated the present style of pitching or, rather, underhand throwing, with its in-curves and out-shoots. This style of delivery was then in violation of the straight-arm pitching rules, but umpires were disposed to let it go, and thus gradually, in spite of legislation, the old style gave way to the new."

It's hard to know exactly what to make of that, and accounts of Bond's pitching style vary widely. It does seem that Bond was doing *something* different, though; another source says Bond was "the pioneer in the art of underhand hurling. In the days when he broke into the league pitchers used to serve 'em up in stiff-arm fashion, standing with their feet together. Bond's delivery, although classed as underhanded, more resembled a side-arm motion than it did the submarine style of Carl Mays."

Whatever Bond was doing, it apparently allowed him to generate greater speed than people were used to seeing, as he was often referred to as a "cannon ball" thrower, though he weighed only 160 pounds.

On October 19 of his rookie season, Bond employed his new style with great effect, nearly fashioning the first no-hitter in the recorded history of professional baseball. Before some 500 fans at Brooklyn's Union Grounds, Bond faced off against the New York Mutuals, and held them hitless through eight innings. According to David Nemec in *The Great Encyclopedia of 19th-Century Major League Baseball*, "The eighteen-year-old rookie began the ninth frame by easily retiring Dick Higham and Doug Al-

Transcendental Graphics/ruckerarchive.com

lison. With only one more out between him and immortality, Bond faced Joe Start. The lefty-hitting Mutuals' first sacker took Bond the opposite way, slapping a pitch to left field that fell in for a double."

Bond then gave up another hit, but got the next man on a deep fly to clinch the shutout, his only whitewash of the season.

In case you're wondering how a pitcher could pitch fifty-five complete games—yes, he completed every game he started—and post a 2.02 ERA, yet record only one shutout, the answer is "unearned runs." Players in 1874 didn't wear gloves; for that and other reasons, the unearned runs far outnumbered the earned runs. So while Bond gave up only two *earned* runs per nine innings, he allowed nearly eight *runs* per nine innings. Which made the shutouts hard to come by.

In 1875, Ferguson moved to Hartford, and he took Bond with him. However, Bond did not maintain his position as Ferguson's favorite pitcher, because the Hartford club also had Candy Cummings.

Cummings, of course, is credited with inventing the curveball; that's how he got into the Hall of Fame. Now, it's open to debate whether or not Cummings really did invent the curve, but for our purposes what's relevant is that in 1875, Bond and Cummings were teammates with Hartford. In those days, most teams employed only one pitcher, so for the first two months of the season Cummings pitched while Bond played right field . . . and learned.

By July, though, Bond had mastered the curveball and supplanted Cummings (still one of the league's best pitchers) as Hartford's top hurler. And in 1876, with Hartford playing in the new National League—previously, the Atlantics and Hartford competed in the loosely-organized National Association—Cummings sat on the bench and watched Bond start 45 of the team's first 47 league games.

On August 19, though, Bond got hammered by the Boston club, 13-4. On the 20th, Cummings started for Hartford and beat the Bostons, 10-4.

Bond would not pitch another game for Hartford.

A note in the next day's Hartford *Daily Courant* said, "Cummings appeared between the pitcher's paints for the first time in a championship game since the Hartford-Cincinnati games, the change being necessitated by the lameness of Bond's arm, he having strained some of the tendons of his fore-arm in his recent games . . ."

But there was more to the story. On August 24, the following item appeared in *The Boston Globe:*

> HARTFORD, Conn., August 23—The Times of this evening has the following: We have refrained for several days from noticing in any way the many street rumors afloat in regard to a misunderstanding between Captain Ferguson and Mr. Bond, the pitcher of the Hartford nine. Mr. Bond, as we are credibly informed, boldly charged Captain Ferguson with selling the game in Boston on Saturday last, the Athletic game in Philadelphia on Saturday August 12th, and two or three of the Mutual games, and on these grounds asked for his release from the club. The release was refused him. These are grave charges, and Captain Ferguson, who has always stood well with the patrons and admirers of the game in Hartford, owes it to himself and the club with which he is connected to relieve himself of these accusations. Cap-

tain Ferguson should demand an investigation at once.

That evening, Ferguson himself published a "card" in which he "pronounce[d] false in every particular the charges made against his character by Mr. Bond, who accused him of selling out games."

And finally, on August 28 the *Daily Courant* published a short note: "Bond now writes a letter, taking back his charges against Captain Ferguson, of selling games, and declaring that he made the charges when he was mad; in short, that he pitched a wide ball."

On September 11 the *Globe* reported, "Mr. Thomas H. Bond, formerly of the Hartfords, has signed an agreement to pitch for the Bostons next season. It is alleged that the reason of his withdrawal from the Hartfords is because of trouble with Captain Ferguson. He is young, not yet twenty-one, of gentlemanly deportment and correct habits. He plays for his side more than for individual record, is a fair third baseman and outfielder and will add to the batting strength of the club which he is to join."

What happened between August 28 and September 11? I wasn't able to find out, but it's obvious that Bond was released from his Hartford contract, one way or another. And it's worth repeating that just a few weeks after accusing his employer of throwing ball games, Bond was described as being "of gentlemanly deportment and correct habits."

Whatever happened between Bond and Ferguson, it was the young pitcher who would have the last laugh.

In 1877, Boston won forty-two games, and Bond won forty of them. In 1878, Boston won forty-one games, and Bond again won forty of them. In both seasons, the Bostons finished with the best record in the National League. Meanwhile, Hartford finished third in 1877 and dropped out of the league; in '78, Ferguson joined the Chicago club, which finished fourth.

As late as 1878—and for quite a long time after that, actually—there were still many, many people who didn't believe that a pitcher could make a baseball curve, that it was nothing more than an optical illusion, or the whimsy of the prevailing wind. Harry Wright was then managing Boston, and he set out to prove the skeptics wrong. As Harold Kaese wrote in *The Boston Braves*,

> The experiment was made in Cincinnati in 1878. The two fences were placed twenty yards apart, with the post midway in the gap—all three being on the same line. Bond then stood to the left of one fence and made the ball curve around the post so that it passed the left of the second fence.
>
> Cincinnati doubters watched Bond curve the ball around the post several times, then shook their heads, and said, "Nope. It's a good trick, but you can't get away with it. The wind is blowing the ball off its course."
>
> But Wright wasn't considered the shrewdest baseball man of his time for nothing. He immediately called on a left-handed pitcher, one Lefty Mitchell, to make the ball curve against the wind. When Mitchell did this, all but a few of the most stubborn skeptics were converted to the theory that it was possible to make a ball curve. Baseball had passed another milestone.

In 1879, with the National League schedule expanded, Bond set career highs with sixty-four starts and forty-three victories. He didn't lead the league in wins, as he had the two previous seasons, but he did lead with eleven shutouts and a 1.96 ERA.

In 1880, all of Bond's hard work over the previous six seasons finally had its way with his right arm. (In retrospect, the only surprise is that he lasted as long as he did; none of Bond's contemporaries were able to pitch as well as he did for as long.) His 2.67 ERA doesn't look bad, but the league ERA was just 2.38 and Bond's mark was the worst of his career.

Bond started three games for Boston in 1881, and got hammered. He pitched twice for the Worcester club in 1882 (and managed briefly; sources differ regarding the exact length of his tenure), but spent most of '82 and '83 coaching the Harvard baseball team and umpiring in the National League (and also the New England League, according to one account). In 1884, Bond came back to pitch for Boston's entry in the new Union Association. He won 13 games and earned $1,800 (or at least had a contract for that sum, his highest salary ever), but the U.A. didn't last the season. Bond joined Indianapolis in the American Association, lost all five of his starts, and thereafter his retirement stuck.

Bond umpired a few National League games in 1885, reportedly went into the "leather business," and then in 1891 he took a position with the Assessor's Department in Boston, holding that position for 35 years before retiring in 1926.

In his last years, Bond became something of a celebrity at both Boston ballparks. He never drank or smoked, and by the late 1930s was billed as the sole survivor from the National League's first season. Bond held that title—real or imagined—until January of 1941, when he died just a few months shy of his eighty-fifth birthday.

At his death (and before), Bond was always said to have been born in New York. But in 1965, one of his sons informed Lee Allen that Bond was actually born in Granard, County Longford, Ireland.

TONY MULLANE

BILL JAMES

Remembering a character as rich as Tony Mullane for something so simple as pitching with both hands is like remembering Bill Clinton as the President who once installed AstroTurf in the back of a pickup truck, but such is history. We don't have the time or the energy to keep track of all the things that happened before we were born.

The Mullane family came to America from their native Ireland in 1864. Tony was five years old. Immigrating to a country engulfed in Civil War might seem odd, but in Mullane's case it was prophetic: conflict was true north to Tony's compass. The Mullane family settled in Erie, Pennsylvania. As a youth, Mullane excelled at roller skating, boxing, and baseball. In 1876, there being no professional roller skating at the time, Mullane signed to play baseball for a team in Geneva, Ohio, for one dollar a day plus room and board.

Baseball was just getting organized. In 1876 the National League emerged from the wreckage of the National Association, and limped through the 1879 season in danger of bleeding to death from its internal injuries. In 1879 Mullane signed a contract for a tryout with Buffalo of the National League, but departed Buffalo without appearing in any league games. In 1880 he was pitching for Akron, an independent team, and the National League, led by Cap Anson's Colts, began to catch on as a commercial product. In an exhibition game between Akron and Chicago (Anson's men), Mullane limited the Colts to two hits.

In 1881 Mullane pitched a 19-inning complete game, the game ending in a 2-2 tie. Late in the season he was purchased by Detroit, made his first appearance against the Colts, and, at least according to an 1885 newspaper article, limited Chicago to "one unearned run and several scattering safe hits" in his first outing. His fortunes faded soon; by season's end he had given up 42 runs in 44 innings and lost 4 of 5 decisions, and was let go.

But after the season the American Association formed as a competitor to the National League, which was by now making money. The American Association was formed out of independent teams like the Akron team Mullane had pitched for, and Mullane was well known in that group. Mullane signed with Louisville for 1882—the same team that he had pitched the 19-inning game *against* in 1881. He led the American Association in games pitched with 54 and finished 30-24, marking him as one of the new league's premier pitchers. On September 11, 1882, Mullane pitched a no-hitter against the Cincinnati team, and then, pitching again the next day (which was common at that time) pitched more no-hit ball through the first six innings—15 consecutive no-hit innings against one opponent over a stretch of two days.

In 1883 Mullane pitched for St. Louis, and was once more one of the best pitchers in the American Association, finishing 35-15 (or with some similar won-lost record if you prefer some other source). This was Mullane's only year with St. Louis; in 1884 he was pitching for Toledo, same league. Toledo in that summer engaged in an historic but ill-fated effort to integrate baseball. They hired a black catcher, Moses Fleetwood Walker. Mullane was his pitcher. Although the Toledo ball club should be remembered for its courage, the effort backfired, and triggered instead the quasi-official establishment of segregation in baseball. Walker "was the best catcher I ever worked with," Mullane told the New

York *Age* in 1919, "but I disliked a Negro and whenever I had to pitch to him I used to pitch anything I wanted without looking at his signals. One day he signaled me for a curve and I shot a fast ball at him. He caught it and walked down to me. He said, 'I'll catch you without signals, but I won't catch you if you are going to cross me when I give you signals.' And all the rest of that season he caught me and caught anything I pitched without knowing what was coming."

After the 1884 season there arose another controversy, this one with Mullane at the epicenter. Here is an entry from the 1885 Spalding Guide:

> The "Mullane Case" which occupied considerable attention at the American Association convention in December, 1884, merits passing notice in the GUIDE from the fact of the lesson it teaches of the folly of a dishonorable course of conduct by a professional player. A. J. Mullane, a noted pitcher of the American Association clubs made himself notorious early in the season of 1884 by "jumping" his contract with the St. Louis Union Club and leaving its service to play in the Louisville team in 1884. In the fall of the year he left the Louisville Club under a promise to sign with the American Club of St. Louis, and then broke his written pledge to that club to sign with the Cincinnati Club under the influence of a higher salary, together with an advance of $2,000 down. This case came up before the convention through charges made by the St. Louis Club, and after a full hearing the convention adopted the following resolution.
>
> Whereas, A. J. Mullane having been found guilty of conduct calculated to bring discredit on the professional fraternity, and of setting an example of sharp practice almost equivalent to actual dishonesty, therefore it is
>
> Resolved, That the Board of Directors feel that such conduct cannot be passed by without punishment, and they therefore decree the suspension of said A. J. Mullane for and during the season of 1885; and they also require that he shall refund to the Cincinnati Club, before Jan. 1, 1885, $1,000 of the money advanced to him by that club; and, furthermore, that said Mullane shall not be eligible to play baseball in any professional club during the season of 1885; the violation of this decree to be punished by final expulsion.

"An example of sharp practice almost equivalent to actual dishonesty" . . . you've got to love the way these guys write. Here's a more sympathetic (and more dramatic) account of Mullane's 1884 negotiations, from an un-identified newspaper clipping at the Hall of Fame files, dated February 5, 1898:

> ## TONY WAS TEMPTED
>
> ### How the Cincinnati Club Secured Mullane's Signature to a Contract
>
> It isn't every man that is hunted like a thief until caught only to be offered a soft job with the salary of a prince attached . . . A singular instance of this sort was that by which Anthony Mullane, the famous pitcher, became a member of the Cincinnati club. Mullane, in the year 1884, was the star pitcher of the Toledo club, which was then a member of the American Association. At that time the rules of base ball were not as rigid as they are now and as there was broadness in the competition for the services of players that is unknown at the present day. It happened, too, at this particular time that the Toledo club was on the ragged edge and was about to break up at the end of the season. Of course, all the other clubs wanted Mullane's services in the worst way and were ready to pay him a fancy salary would he only consent to be theirs. And Mullane, having his eye on the main chance, was not to be done out of a few dollars more or less when nothing but a little diplomacy to call it nothing more, stood between him and net profit.
>
> As the season drew near the close the Louisville Club saw Mullane and made him a very generous offer. This he promised to accept. Then when he went to St. Louis, the manager there offered him better terms, and Tony also accepted these. Louisville's offer was $3,000 for the year and that of St. Louis was $3,500. This was pretty good pay. Each club felt certain of the man but in order not to be behind with the business managers of both teams turned up in Toledo on the day when Mullane's contract with Toledo would expire. Time and again did the two

hunters cross each other's path in their wild search through the town for Antonio, but nary an Antonio could they find. They had begun early in the afternoon and had scoured the city until midnight and were as yet unsuccessful.

At 12 o'clock that night Mullane's contract with Toledo would expire and it was clear that the man could first lay hands upon him would have the advantage. (But) where was Mullane? Had the rival managers known where he was and what he was doing while they were pursuing their fruitless hunt for him they would have suffered more than they suffered when they found out at last.

At the time that St. Louis and Louisville were turning the thriving little city of Toledo inside out to find the ball player that gentleman himself was riding through the contiguous country in a carriage with a President Stern and Manager Caylor of Cincinnati. These two wily workers had arrived in town before their opponents, and had carried Mullane away bodily and had held him by sheer force from negotiating with or even seeing any rival managers. Just on the stroke of midnight the carriage was drawn up before a hotel in town and the three men repaired to a room. Here Mr. Stern took a huge wallet from his pocket and counted out $2,000 in ten and twenty dollar bills on the table. Mr. Caylor at the same time threw a contract all ready to be signed on the table near the cash. A pen was placed in the hand of the bewildered ball player, and he was told that if he would only sign his name to the paper the $2,000 in cash would be given him then and there and that a like sum would be paid him in addition for his services during the year.

The sight of that money stifled in Mullane's breast all thought of other offers. Here was the cash itself—a million times better than any promise. His human nature was not proof against the temptation. He yielded, signed the bond and took the money. A few minutes afterward the agents from St. Louis and Louisville found him, but it was then too late. He was already the property of Cincinnati. The two clubs who were defeated by the clever tactics of the Cincinnatis made a vigorous protest against the matter at the next general meeting of the American Association, and their pull was strong enough to have Mullane declared incompetent for one year, which

Transcendental Graphics/ruckerarchive.com

he spent—at a liberal salary—doing nothing on the bench of the Cincinnati Club.

Figuring out exactly what happened here is almost impossible, but I think I have most of it. By late 1884 the American Association and the National League had made an arrangement not to raid one another's talent, but by that time a *new* upstart league, the Union Association, was trying to sign players, mostly paying them with promises. Mullane signed to play with the St. Louis Union team in 1884, but jumped back to the American Association, and pitched that year for the Toledo Blue Stockings—and quite well, too, going 36-26 for what was otherwise a pretty awful team. (The Spalding Guide, which says incorrectly that Mullane pitched for Louisville in 1884, was apparently simply confused for half a sentence by Mullane's endless wanderings.)

By late 1884 the Toledo team was breaking up, and three American Association teams—St. Louis, Louisville and Cincinnati—all wanted Mullane, the best player on his team. Tony agreed to terms, at various times, with all three teams. The Association, determined to enforce some order in contract negotiations, then suspended him for the 1885 season—and carried through on the suspension; Mullane spent that summer, according to various sources, pitching in St. Joseph, Missouri, sitting on the Cincinnati bench, sitting in the Cincinnati stands smoking cigarettes, or pitching for Cincinnati but only in non-league contests.

The game was changing at extraordinary speed, and Mullane was caught in the vortex. All of the following were happening in 1880–1884:

1) The "league" or "official" schedule was getting longer each year,

2) Exhibition games against non-league competitors were rapidly becoming less important,

3) New teams and new leagues were quickly forming and, almost as quickly, going out of business,

4) Baseball player salaries were exploding,

5) Teams were trying desperately to establish respect among one another for contract rights to players they had signed, and even for a reserve clause carrying over those rights beyond the consent of the player,

6) Teams were switching from one pitcher who pitched every day to two- or three-man pitching rotations.

7) Baseball was switching gradually from underhanded pitching to overhand pitching, which was theoretically illegal, but was becoming the dominant practice by 1882.

8) Baseball was feeling out its place in society, trying to figure out how it should relate to African Americans and at the same time trying to figure out how it should relate to society in a thousand different ways—whether baseball should be played on Sunday, whether beer should be sold at the games, whether athletes should be treated as gentlemen or ruffians or heroes.

With the possible exception of Cap Anson, no player was more smack in the middle of all this than Mullane. He was the American Association's second-best pitcher—behind Will White—and its leading contract-jumper. The Cincinnati team, which had White, wanted Mullane as well, and would not balk at chicanery to acquire him.

The baseball rules of the 1870s required . . . well, here, let me quote the rules from 1878:

> Rule III—Pitching
>
> Sec. 2 . . . The ball must be delivered to the bat with the arm swing nearly perpendicular at the side of the body, and the hand in swinging forward must pass below the waist.
>
> Sec. 3 Should the pitcher deliver the ball by an overhand throw, a "foul balk" shall be declared. Any outward swing of the arm, or any other swing save that of the perpendicular movement refered to in Section 2 of this rule, shall be considered an overhand throw.
>
> Sec. 4. When a "foul balk" is called, the umpire shall warn the pitcher of the penalty incurred by such unfair delivery, and should such delivery be continued until *three foul balks* have been called in one inning, the umpire shall declare the game forfeited. (Italics in original)

In other words, the ball could not be thrown overhand, and it could not be thrown sidearm. It had to be pure underhand.

A cadre of well-trained umpires could no doubt have enforced this rule. But baseball games in the 1870s and '80s were officiated by one umpire with no training of any kind, working alone, and contending with players who cut across the infield, took non-standard defensive positions, fought, were sometimes abusive, were sometimes drunk, and were often very seriously engaged in efforts to subvert the rulebook. Also, nature abhors a forfeit. The umpire's specified way of enforcing this rule was to declare a forfeit, but how often are you really going to do that? The umpires, overwhelmed with a thousand responsibilities, found this rule to be unenforceable.

Mullane was one of many pitchers of the 1880–1884 era who tested and eventually eroded the rule. When the umpires enforced a straight underhand throw, he moved his arm to the side. When other pitchers moved their arm to the side, he swung his arm out a little further. By 1883 the rules were amended to allow a pitcher to throw from shoulder height. In 1884 the American Association abolished the rule entirely, permitting an overhand delivery, although the National League continued to try to enforce the shoulder-high limit.

By 1884, with the schedules lengthening, teams were using two or three starting pitchers. That was Mullane's summer with the Toledo Blue Stockings. The Blue Stockings, 10-32 when Mullane didn't pitch, were 36-26 when he did. The demand for pitching was increasing, and Mullane was by now clearly established as one of the league's very best. This set up the wild scramble for his services when the Akron team folded in late 1884.

So Mullane signed with Cincinnati in 1885, but was banned from pitching in league contests for a year. By the mid-1880s the leagues were making peace, and were getting out of the business of stealing one another's players. Mullane would remain in Cincinnati for eight adventurous years, until the middle of the 1893 season. Here are a couple of his exploits, recounted from various newspapers . . . sometimes these stories make perfect sense, and sometimes you apparently had to be there, but I quote them because I like the picture of the time that they create:

> Tony Mullane and Jimmie Peoples, of the Cincinnati team, skated a three-mile race at the Queen City Rink, Cincinnati, April 4 (1885) for the championship of the three cities. The track was twelve laps to the mile. Mullane won the race easily with a lap and a half to spare. He made the distance in the remarkable time of 12 m. and 10s. The race was witnessed by about 1,500 people. Old sports who saw Mullane's work say they think he can beat anybody in Cincinnati.
>
> —Unidentified clipping

A COUPLE ON MULLANE

Little Adventures in the Career of Antonio, of Cincinnati

> Tony Mullane seems to have enjoyed the visits of the Cincinnatis to New York if the *Cincinnati Times-Star* reporter who travels with the team is to be believed. Mulford tells a couple of good ones on Mullane. Here is one:
>
> Whenever a coterie of ball players get ticketed for Coney Island the West Brighton fakirs are in for a siege. It isn't often they get the best of the diamond kings. One of the wrinkles down there is to cover a great spot on the table with five copper plates, and if you make it you get one dollar and if you don't the fakir gets your ten cents. "The Only Antoine" went against the game, and he commenced covering the spots so neatly that the fellow in charge got an attack of the heart disease. No less than three dollars did Antoine win in as many throws, and he was as fresh as a daisy to keep it up. The fakir grew pale as he saw the tricks turned, and he commenced shoving the table back just as Mullane pitched the plate. The trick was discovered by "Long John" Reilly, whose kick was met with a growl.
>
> "What yer puttin' yer lip in it fer?"
>
> "This is my brother," retorted "Long John." "I don't want to see him robbed!"
>
> The fakir quit and put up the bars. He had had all the exhibition of the skills of the Reds' pitcher that he wanted.

And Another

> The only Antoine enjoyed himself immensely over at the Eden Musee the other morning. He took the daughter of the household there with him and little Ina went to sleep in the chamber of horrors. Sinking back in a chair in one of the darkest corners, Tony sat perfectly still and kept his eye fasted upon the face of the sleeping heir of the Mullanes. A dozen visitors gathered and thumbed their catalogues to see just what horror was depicted there. When the dozen had increased to fully a score Antoine snickered and the hood-winked souls joined in the laugh and then stood aside to see the next delegation fooled. For an hour Tony and the baby were one of "the attractions" not on the bill and in speaking of it afterward, Tom Loftus declared "And Tony had on his St. Patrick's coat at that time. All that he needed was a label on him reading, "I was a real lord in Ireland!"

Mullane was a thin-faced man, extremely handsome, with large dark eyes shaded by large dark eyebrows and the rich waxed moustache which was the fashion of the 1880s. He would sometimes pull up the sleeves of his uniform and flex his muscles, showing off his exceptional arms. He dressed sharply, and showered attention on the lady fans. He was called "The Apollo of the Box" and "the Adonis of pitchers." It has been written so often as to be common knowledge that the custom of "Ladies Day" at the ballpark, which lasted into the 1970s, was invented in Cincinnati in the 1880s, as a way of taking advantage of Mullane's immense popularity with female fans. According to a July 1916 article in

Cincinnati Enquirer, "Baseball history tells the story of how the gay and festive 'Count' used to have a class of beautiful young girls or ladies to whom he taught the intricacies of baseball. There may be a tinge of laundry blueing in this . . ." I do not know what is meant by "a tinge of laundry blueing," but modern readers are encouraged to keep their filthy comments to themselves. The *Washington Post* in 1899 reported that "Tony's blue-black locks are still innocent of frost, and the spring and vigor of youth still burns in his piercing eye."

But beyond the roguish charm, the quixotic sense of humor and the almost too-pretty face, Mullane was a complex and difficult man. It was his nature to think himself better than those around him. On May 21, 1887, the *Sporting Life* reported

> Pitcher Tony Mullane, who has already figured in a number of disagreeable scrapes, is once more the central figure in a base ball sensation, and has gotten into a scrape out of which he will not be able to crawl without humiliation, as he has been fined by his club and suspended and will be still further punished at the end of the season unless he makes his peace with the management of the club.
>
> "On Wednesday Mullane and Baldwin were assigned as the battery against the Brooklyn Club, and their names appeared on the official scorecard. Just before Umpire Knight called play Tony Mullane arose from the bench in a surly manner and said to Manager Schmelz—"You might as well put in somebody else; I don't intend to pitch."
>
> "Why not," inquired Manager Schmelz, "is your arm sore?"
>
> "No, but I don't intend to pitch in extra games unless I get extra pay for it."
>
> "This isn't an extra game, my friend," said Mr. Schmelz. "You pitched your last game last Sunday, and you certainly ought to be willing to go in and take a turn three days after."
>
> "I don't care. I don't intend to do any more work than the rest of the pitchers," retorted Mullane.

"Anybody acquainted with Mullane's past record will not be surprised at his action," opined *The Sporting Life*. "He has always had the reputation of being the most avaricious and ungrateful player in the profession . . . in 1885 he sat on the seats of the Cincinnati Park the whole season smoking cigarettes, and drew $3,200 out of the club treasury for so doing."

He was out a month, at one point referring to the team President as "a little bow-legged son of a bitch." A month later the *Sporting Life* reported that "It was a wise piece of work on the part of President Stern, showing the clear-headed way in which he does business. He had courage enough to set aside his pride and his prejudice for the good of his club. The advice I gave him here in New York was cordially received. Manager Schmelz, acting on the advice of President Stern, visited Rutland, Vermont, Wednesday, and after a long conference with Tony, came to New York bringing him along. Gus tells me that it would have been hard work to get Tony to return had it not been for Mrs. Mullane, who persuaded her husband to do the right thing and accept the overtures. With Mullane and Smith in the points the Cincinnati team will yet give the winner a good race. Mark the prediction."

OK, we marked it. It was wrong.

> Before his suspension in May, Mullane had lost but two games. Since his reinstatement he has lost nearly five times that many. There is a chapter of that trouble that has never been published. Tony's "strike" was not a surprise. He had volunteered to do more of the club's pitching than he had been doing, and asked as a recompense a slice of the salary of one of "the moss agate pitchers then on the bench"—to quote his own words.
>
> —Unidentified clipping

Nor was this to be his last brush with infamy, in and out of contract negotiation. In July 1892, the *Sporting Life* reported once more that "Pitcher Tony Mullane is not the manager of the Cincinnati team nor in the confidence of the management, yet he presumes to publicly criticize the team of which he is a member. He was asked by the Cincinnati *Commercial Gazette* His opinion of the Cincinnati team, and this is his answer:

" 'Well, it might be a little stronger. Comiskey ought to secure another first class pitcher even if he is forced to sacrifice the best man in his club. One of us may break down, and then the club would be in a bad fix.'

" 'What about Morgan Murphy?' asked the reporter.

" 'I would rather have seen Boyle with the club,' Mullane replied. "He is a better batter and could have been used as a general utility player.' "

Later that summer (June 30, 1892) Mullane pitched a 20-inning complete game, a National League record at the time which, as long games did to many pitchers in that era, pretty much finished his career. After the season, his arm gone, he was offered a substantial pay cut. He refused, jumped the club again, and spent the 1892 season pitching for an independent team in Butte, Montana. He rejoined the Reds in 1893, was traded to Baltimore, didn't pitch any better for Baltimore than he had for Cincinnati, was traded to Cleveland, and was out of the majors by 1895.

At some point in the early 1880s, Mullane began to occasionally pitch left-handed. According to an article in *The Sporting News* at the time of his death, Mullane's "ambidexterity on the diamond was the result of a sore right arm that threatened to end his career after he joined Detroit. The injury resulted from his efforts in a field meet, in which he was credited with throwing a ball 416 feet 7¾ inches. Experimenting with his left, Mullane became proficient as a southpaw, but resumed throwing regularly with his right arm when it became sound again."

In an 1899 interview with the *Washington Post* (published on October 20), Mullane said, "I was an ambidextrous pitcher, but as a rule I never called on my left hand unless we were playing an exhibition game or in practice for the amusement of a few friends." Over time, reports of Mullane's ambidexterity grew like wedding invitation lists. By 1916, Sam Crane insisted that "Mullane was able to pitch both right-handed and left-handed and was just as effective from both sides. He used his left-handed delivery quite frequently, too, when left-handed batters faced him, but he had much more speed pitching from the starboard."

Since the development of the Society for American Baseball Research, efforts have been made to pin down exactly where and when Mullane pitched left-handed. The consensus is that he certainly did do this, but that he apparently did not do so routinely. But it may also be that some or even many news accounts simply failed to make note of Mullane's pitching left-handed, since it was a generally known fact that he would sometimes do this. Perhaps the most clear result of Mullane's ambidexterity is that, since he wore no glove and could throw quickly to the base with either hand, he had a devastating selection of pickoff moves.

After leaving the majors Mullane spent three full years pitching for St. Paul in the Western League, pitched a few games for Toronto in the Eastern League, and retired in 1899, aged 40. In 1902, umpiring in the Pacific Northwest League, he attempted a comeback, and pitched in 20 games in that league before retiring once more.

He was hired by the city of Chicago as a police officer, became a detective, and worked for the department until his retirement in 1926. He remained in Chicago until his death in 1944. He was married and divorced several times. David Porter wrote in the *Biographical Dictionary of American Sports* that "Mullane's showmanship, independence, and all-around athletic ability made him the embodiment of the nineteenth century baseball hero" and the entry on him in *Nineteenth Century Baseball Stars* (SABR) says that "Mullane was as talented as he was showy." Perhaps. He was a great pitcher, and he was a spoiled, self-indulgent *prima donna,* a bit of a bully, a racist, and a pioneer who explored the depths of tactlessness and selfishness in contract negotiations.

WILBUR COOPER

ROB NEYER

As trivia questions go, this one shouldn't be too tough. . . .

Who owns the record for pitching victories by a Pittsburgh Pirate?

The answer is Wilbur Cooper, who won 202 games in his thirteen seasons with the Pirates. But how many of you knew that before this very moment?

Arley Wilbur Cooper got his professional start in 1911, with the Marion Diggers in the Ohio State League. The Marion club's majority owner was a newspaper owner and ex-lieutenant governor named Warren Harding. At the time, Harding held no public office, having been defeated in his bid to become governor of Ohio a year earlier. (In 1914, Harding returned to politics with an easy victory in his campaign for the Senate. And according to Fred Lieb, "After Harding became President [in 1920], he knew Cooper's Pirate record to the minute.")

Cooper went 16-11 for the Diggers, and in 1912 he jumped all the way to Columbus in the fast American Association. He did well there, and on August 24 both Cooper and teammate George Sisler (still a pitcher then) were acquired by the Pittsburgh Pirates.

Cooper pitched well for the Pirates that September, but saw limited action in 1913. Like most major leaguers, Cooper received an offer to jump to the Federal League for the 1914 season. The Feds offered him a two-year contract for $5,500 per season—considering that his top salary with the Pirates would eventually be $12,500, that was real good money—but Cooper talked to Pirates manager Fred Clarke and decided to stay put. "I never regretted it," Cooper said in 1947. "Fred Clarke was like a father to me and when he advised me not to jump I accepted that as sound advice."

When tales of Cooper were told many years later, three games in particular were remembered . . .

On September 6, 1912, Cooper got his first major-league start, against the Cardinals in St. Louis. He tossed a nine-hit shutout, his first of two whitewashes on the season. Cooper would always recall one specific thing about that game. A bouncer went over his head, and he turned to see Honus Wagner scoop it up and throw out the runner. "On the way to the bench I said, 'Mr. Wagner, if they field like that behind me I will stay up here a long time,' and Honus said, 'You make 'em hit it, Lefty, and we'll do the rest.' I guess it was the first time Wagner had spoken to me and I never forgot it." Cooper finished his rookie campaign with a 3-0 record and a 1.66 ERA.

On August 1, 1918 in Boston, the Pirates and Braves played twenty scoreless innings before the Bucs pushed across two runs in the top of the twenty-first frame. Art Nehf pitched all twenty-one innings for the Braves, but two Pirates shared the mound duties. Erskine Mayer pitched the first fifteen and one-third, departing in the sixteenth with runners on first and second. Cooper shut the door, then went the rest of the way to earn the victory.

On August 8, 1919 in Pittsburgh, Cooper gave up a triple to Dodgers leadoff man Ivy Olson . . . and didn't surrender another hit the rest of the game. Olson died on third base, and Cooper wound up with a 3-0 shutout. (He'd previously pitched a one-hitter, in 1918, but lost that game 1-0.)

Cooper was tall enough for his day—he stood just a hair short of six feet—but very thin, right around 165 pounds. Cooper would say, many years later, "The good Lord blessed me with an easy motion, a sneaky fast ball, a sharp curve, a change of pace and wonderful control for a lefthander." He also said, "I never used a spitter or a

Transcendental Graphics/ruckerarchive.com

scuff ball, but I did have one little trick." Cooper chewed gum and tobacco at the same time, and spit the juice into his glove. After an inning or two—remember, in those days one baseball might last three innings or more—the ball would darken, and become a bit more difficult for the hitters to see (of course, the opposing hurler would gain the same advantage).

Pie Traynor took over at third base for the Pirates in 1922. "We had a trick play that became famous," Traynor recalled in 1969. "Cooper would take the signal from the catcher just in back of the rubber. The minute he would open his glove, I was to run toward the base and he would throw with a sidearm motion and we'd pick off the runner by six feet."

Cooper was well-known for both his fielding and his hitting, and he worked hard at both. "He always kept himself in great shape," Traynor said. "He ran the outfield every day, and during the pre-game practices, he would go to the outfield and make some great catches. He had great range."

Cooper was also famous for working fast. "He was a little fella with a great delivery," Traynor remembered. "He threw a sinker, and when he got the ball back, he threw it right away."

In 1953, Pittsburgh sportswriter Harry Keck asked both Cooper and Honus Wagner to name their all-time National League teams. For his left-handed pitcher, Cooper split his vote between Art Nehf and Eppa Rixey. At that, Wagner interrupted, "No, take out those last two. Cooper belongs in there as the left-hander. Look at his record: Eight straight seasons with an average of better than 20 victories for a club that didn't win a pennant, and 212 victories in 12 years.

"I'm glad I didn't have to hit against him. He had a ball that broke opposite to the way you expected. Instead of breaking away from a right-handed batter, it broke in on him. He got it on the handle."

Old Honus's math was off, but not by much. In Cooper's twelve best years, he won 206 games (not 212). But from 1917 through 1924 ("eight straight seasons"), Cooper did average almost exactly twenty wins per season. And Cooper's 1924 season was right in line: 20-14 with a 3.28 ERA and four shutouts. He was only thirty-two years old, and he'd already won 202 games in the major leagues.

But the Pirates, in the middle of the pennant race until the last week, finished three games behind the pennant-winning Giants after getting swept by New York in a late September series. It wasn't the first time the Giants had knocked out the Pirates, and owner Barney Dreyfuss wasn't happy. And so shortly after the World Series, Dreyfuss worked out a blockbuster trade with the Cubs. Coming to Pittsburgh: infielder George Grantham, pitcher Vic Aldridge, and minor-league first baseman Al Niehaus. Going to Chicago: first baseman Charlie Grimm, shortstop Rabbit Maranville . . . and pitcher Wilbur Cooper.

"I got rid of my banjo players," Dreyfuss harrumphed. And as Fred Lieb wrote in The Pittsburgh Pirates, "The remark fitted Charley Grimm, who still likes to strum on his banjo, and the impish Rabbit, but not the serious-minded Wilbur Cooper, who had never been one of the club's playboys. 'Where do I fit into that picture?' Wilbur asked."

It should be said that apparently Cooper wasn't always the easiest man in the world to get along with. In 1919, an anonymous writer noted,

> Wilbur Cooper . . . is a slim youth with a good curve, a fast ball that fairly sears the atmosphere between the box and the plate, and a world of confidence in

> himself . . . Cooper, it is said, often seriously refers to himself as a "star," but as long as he makes good in the role to which he has nominated himself, with the approval of Smoky City fans, there will be none to argue the point with him.

Forty-one years later, newspaper columnist Chester Smith wrote that Cooper's "only fault, if it could be called that, was his impatience with any show of mediocrity or failure around him. He made it very plain by his actions that he regarded errors and mental lapses inexcusable."

And still later, a Cooper biographer wrote that he ". . . came equipped with a temper that was as sensitive as the trigger on a squirrel gun. A bobble or a case of plain stupidity on the field drove him wild, but he was fair about it—to him a misplay of his own was just as inexcusable as a misdemeanor by a teammate."

Anyway, the trade "worked," as the 1925 Pirates won the National League pennant and the World Series. It's hard to say how much the trade actually *helped* the Pirates, though. Aldridge won fifteen games for the Bucs, and Cooper won twelve games for the Cubs. Grantham played well at first base for the Pirates, and Grimm played well at first base for the Cubs. Niehaus played fifteen games for Pittsburgh before being sold to Cincinnati; Maranville missed half the season with an injury, and was pretty awful for the Cubs when he did play.

Many years later, Pittsburgh baseball writer Chilly Doyle wrote, "I do not want to see again in baseball a spectacle like that of the lonely, homesick Cooper trying to pitch a game against his longtime teammates at Wrigley Field in Chicago. If the saddened hurler had turned in his uniform right there the whole effect could not have been harder on him than it was when he was relieved. Wilbur carried that grief for less than two seasons before he retired."

Actually, Cooper did not "retire" (but we'll get to that in a minute). On balance, the big trade may have gained the Pirates a couple of wins . . . and they finished eight-and-a-half games ahead of the second-place Giants. You can't argue with success, though, and Aldridge did win Games 1 and 5 in the World Series.

All of it was rough on Cooper. After a dozen seasons with the Pirates, he's exiled and they finally win. And the 1925 Chicago Cubs? They finished last, for the first time in their long history. Nearly fifty years later, Cooper told an interviewer that his biggest disappointment was that he never got to pitch in a World Series.

In 1926, things went from bad to worse. Cooper got off to a slow start with the Cubs—4.42 ERA in eight starts—and they cut him loose. He signed with Ty Cobb's Tigers, went 0-4 with an 11.20 ERA in fourteen innings, and got cut again.

Rather than retire, Cooper just kept playing baseball, as was customary in those days. He finished up that season with Toledo, then spent a couple of years in the Pacific Coast League. Cooper enjoyed a decent 1929 season with Shreveport in the Texas League, then got off to a horrible start in 1930 but hung around with San Antonio as an outfielder. He developed bursitis in his left shoulder after running into a fence, and quit before the season ended.

Still, he pitched in semi-pro leagues for a few more years. He also worked for a spell as a guard at Western Penitentiary in Pittsburgh. In 1935, Cooper took a job managing in the Class D Pennsylvania State Association, and in three years he managed three different teams to fifth-, first-, and second-place finishes.

Cooper later worked in the real-estate business in Pittsburgh. In 1963, by then retired, he and his wife Edith moved to southern California, where two of their daughters lived. On August 6, 1973, six men, including Roberto Clemente, were inducted into the Hall of Fame. Wilbur Cooper died the next day. He was eighty-one years old, and his death meant, for the most part, the end of a vigorous campaign in Pittsburgh to get him into Cooperstown, too. In 1969, Cooper was named in a Pittsburgh poll as the Pirates' greatest pitcher ever. If that poll were taken today, it's unlikely that Cooper would come out on top again. He remains the greatest starting pitcher in Pirates history, but even in Pittsburgh he's been nearly forgotten.

EDDIE ROMMEL

ROB NEYER

If a great pitcher throws a great fastball or curve, nobody bothers asking him how he learned to throw it. But if a great pitcher throws a great knuckleball, then how he learned to throw it is always a part of his story. So that's where we'll start. . . .

The tale was told differently over the years, but the most credible account comes straight from Edwin Americus Rommel, who generally credited his discovery of the knuckleball to a fellow Baltimorean named Cutter Druery. In a 1932 interview, Rommel remembered,

> . . . That's a funny thing. He wasn't even a pitcher. I was a kid on the lots trying to learn to throw a spitball. I nearly wore out my arm and my mouth. But I couldn't make the ball behave.
>
> So Cutter Druery—he played first base around with the rest of us semi-pros—he said, "Why didn't I try the knuckleball?" He showed me how to hold it and, believe it or don't, the first one I threw actually broke.
>
> Not a big break, of course, but more than I'd ever seen on any alleged spitter of my manufacture. So I decided I must be a natural knuckle man. And here I am.

It's not clear, among all the various tellings of the story, exactly *when* Druery taught Rommel the knuckleball. We do suspect that Rommel broke into semiprofessional baseball in 1916 with the Seaford, Delaware, team in the Peach League, and we know that in 1918, skipping the lower rungs of Organized Baseball, Rommel joined the Newark Bears of the top-flight International League.

At the conclusion of Rommel's 1918 season with Newark—he went 12-15 but posted a 2.22 ERA—John McGraw purchased his contract in an optional deal. Rommel went to spring training with the Giants in 1919, and the evidence suggests that he nearly made the club. He survived a round of cuts on April 10—the Giants were scheduled to open their season on the 23rd—and pitched four strong innings on the 13th. At some point between the 13th and the 23rd, however, McGraw returned Rommel to Newark. A few years later, Rommel said, "I do not blame McGraw or anyone else for this. I do not recall that McGraw looked me over very much himself. He was too busy. His associates no doubt gave him their best judgment."

Rommel's ERA went up in 1919, but so did his innings and his wins. On May 12 he pitched a no-hitter against Toronto, winning 1-0. In his next start, he lost 1-0 while allowing just one hit that didn't figure in the scoring. Newark was managed that season by Connie Mack's son, Earle, and near the end of the season Connie himself traveled to Newark to watch Rommel pitch. As Rommel would later remember,

> We were playing a double-header with Toronto that afternoon, and I was overjoyed when told that Mack was in the stands. Here, I thought, is a chance to break into the majors. I had shut out Toronto in the opening game of the season and I expected no trouble that day. Well, I was knocked out of the box in the second inning of the first game. I was sent back to start the second game and was knocked loose again in the third inning! Despite my poor showing, Connie bought me. He told me later that I was breaking my

Associated Press

curve on the inside instead of on the outside. Boy, was I lucky!

When Rommel joined the Athletics in 1920 at their spring-training site in Lake Charles, Louisiana, he was twenty-two. He stuck with the A's and pitched well during the regular season, perhaps due to Mack's babying. Rommel started only a dozen games (tossing two shutouts) and relieved in twenty-one more, finishing the season with a 7-7 record and a 2.85 ERA over 174 innings.

Having proved his mettle in 1920, in 1921 Rommel pitched 285 innings and won sixteen games. That was the good news. The bad news was that he also lost twenty-three games. In Rommel's defense, it should be noted that he went 16–23 for a team that lost 100 games on the nose, and none of his teammates managed more than eleven wins.

Mack apparently wasn't impressed, or at least he wasn't as impressed as Rommel thought he should be. Based on correspondence between Mack and Commissioner Landis, it seems that Rommel considered Mack's 1922 contract offer something of an insult. Quoting from Mack's letter to Landis on the matter, dated March 7:

> When I sent this player his contract some time ago he took the letter I inclosed [*sic*] with it to the office of a Baltimore newspaper the very first thing and had the letter published in full. In all my experience in base ball it is the very first time I ever heard of a player taking his manager's letter to a newspaper office for publication . . .
>
> Rommel commented at the time that the salary offered him was a minor league salary . . .
>
> If Rommel had not gone with his grievance to the newspapers but had followed my instructions that if not satisfied with the salary offered him to take the matter up with you I would then have been more than willing to have done something better for him after receiving your letter.

Mack went on to say that, much as he might *like* to increase Rommel's salary, he couldn't very well do it *now*, because that would only encourage other players to take their grievances to the newspapers. However, "If the player comes to our club and shows an inclination to do the right thing and has a good year in 1922 our club will surely satisfy him in the way of a contract for 1923."

Rommel had a good year in 1922.

The Athletics had finished last in 1921; in fact, they'd finished last in 1920, they'd finished last in 1919, they'd finished last in 1918 . . . the A's had finished last in every season since 1914, when they were swept by the Braves in the World Series. The Athletics, from 1915 through 1921, put together one of the worst seven-year stretches in major-league history.

But the Athletics wouldn't finish last in 1922, thanks in large part to Rommel, who led the American League with fifty-one appearances (including thirty-one starts) and twenty-seven victories. During or shortly after the season, St. Louis Browns first baseman George Sisler—who batted .420 in '22—provided a detailed analysis of Rommel's knuckleball:

> The bat has to meet the ball squarely for a clean wallop. I have found myself not only topping Rommel's knuckler but getting under it. Which results in grounders to the infield or soft flies. The ball does not

> seem to do its stuff until it is about six feet from the plate.
>
> If it made a one-way hop the batter would be able to set himself and familiarize himself with the break. But that's just where Rommel's success comes in. It goes down one time and the next will take an upward break.
>
> I believe I hit more infield flies against Rommel than any other pitcher in the league. With the golfer who hooks and slices it is: "What am I doing?" I know blame well what I'm doing against Rommel. I'm getting under it too much. I'm prepared to meet that sharp drop the next time and Rommel is giving me that break which shoots from the belt to the shoulders.

That same season, Rommel said of his knuckler, "It's sure some ball, and for a finisher there's nothing like it. I use it for third strikes, or when I've got something on the batter. Outside of that I use a fast ball and a curve. If I'm going with those I can change to that floater and it naturally becomes harder to hit through unexpectedness."

In 1923, Rommel told *Baseball Magazine*'s F.C. Lane, "Roughly speaking, I throw a knuckleball one out of three tries on the slab. The remaining two tries will be about evenly divided between curves and fast balls. You know it doesn't do to throw all one thing, no matter how good that one thing may be. You have to mix them up to keep batters guessing."

We might guess that as Rommel's right arm got older and his knuckleball got more refined, he'd have thrown more of them. We might be wrong about that, though. If Rommel did eventually become something like a strict knuckleball pitcher—the way we think of Tim Wakefield today—he took plenty of time doing it.

On Opening Day in 1926, the Athletics met the Senators in Washington. Edwin Rommel against Walter Johnson. Nobody scored until the bottom of the fifteenth, when the Nats finally pushed across a run to beat the A's and Rommel, who went the distance (as did Johnson). And how many of his famous knuckle balls did Rommel throw in fifteen innings?

Zero. At least if you believe F.C. Lane in the September, 1926 *Baseball Magazine.*

> We will venture to say that Rommel has never pitched a headier, more brilliant game than that great battle he lost to Walter Johnson on Opening Day. And how many knuckle balls do you suppose he pitched in those fifteen innings? We have it not only upon his own word, which is good enough for us, but also upon the evidence of his catcher, that he threw not a single knuckle ball during that long struggle. Speed and a limited curve, with excellent control, were his entire stock in trade on that memorable day.
>
> And we might refer to a great game that Rommel pitched last year against the White Sox in which he used just one knuckle ball and not a single curve. So-called experts who refer to Rommel as a specialist, are talking decidedly wide of the mark. He is a great pitcher first, and a specialist afterwards.

Something else that was usually forgotten as the years went by: Rommel did *not* arrive in the majors with a refined knuckleball. As Connie Mack told Lane in '23,

> His knuckle ball is a very effective delivery. He didn't use it much when he first came to the club, but last year he perfected it so much that it was valuable to him. I know of no pitcher in the league who throws such a ball. Not a few have tried to master it, but they didn't succeed. The ball has been compared to Eddie Cicotte's shiner, but it is altogether different. Cicotte used to doctor the ball. Rommel has a perfectly legal delivery . . .

Rommel followed up 1922 with another fine season, winning eighteen games (and again leading the league in losses, with nineteen) in 1923 as the Athletics moved up one more notch in the standings, to sixth. As the seasons progressed and the Athletics kept moving up, the one constant was Eddie Rommel; from 1922 through 1925 he won eighty-four games, including a league-best twenty-one victories in '25.

Primarily a starter, Rommel worked plenty in relief, too. Over the aforementioned four-season stretch, he started 126 games and relieved in seventy-six more. Rommel topped the AL with fifty-one appearances in 1922, and then again with fifty-six in '23.

Writing in 1938 for *The Sporting News,* Charley Scully theorized, "Just how many games Rommel's relief pitching pulled out of the fire to swell the mound average of his teammates is not known, but if statisticians should some day delve into the archives to compute the number, rest assured the resultant total will be imposing, to say the least."

Roughly thirty years later, the statisticians did delve,

and the resultant total is indeed imposing, at least by the standards of Rommel's time. In both 1928 and '29, he won eight games in relief to lead the American League, and he also saved four games in each season.

By then, he wasn't starting often. In 1926, Rommel pitched in thirty-seven games, starting twenty-six of them; both were his lowest figures since his rookie season. In 1927, he saw even less action, with thirty games, seventeen starts, and a career-low 147 innings, and his workload dwindled even as the Athletics improved.

Yet there's little evidence that Rommel was becoming less effective. In 1928, he went 13-5 with a 3.06 ERA, the lowest since he was a rookie, and in 1929 he went 12-2 with a 2.85 ERA. Early that season, somebody (Lane again?) wrote in *Baseball Magazine*, "Rommel was not used as a finishing pitcher last season because he was unable to go the distance. He was used as a finishing pitcher because such a pitcher was a vital necessity in the Athletic hurling corps, and Rommel was, by all odds, best fitted to play the role."

Indeed, from 1927 through 1931, Rommel, working mostly out of the bullpen, won fifty-two games while losing only nineteen. In the latter three of those five seasons, of course, the Athletics won American League pennants, with Lefty Grove, George Earnshaw, and Rube Walberg doing most of the heavy lifting in the pitching department. In the three World Series—the A's won in 1929 and '31—Rommel pitched only two innings (but did win Game 4 in 1929 when the A's scored ten runs in the bottom of the seventh).

In 1932, Sunday baseball was still illegal in Philadelphia. So as they often did, on July 10 the Athletics traveled—to Cleveland, in this case—to play a single game in the middle of a home stand. When the A's made these one-day trips, Connie Mack, to save train fare, would bring along only as many players as he thought he'd need. So for this game, Mack had available exactly two pitchers: Lew Krausse and Eddie Rommel.

Rommel pitched batting practice, then sat on the bench and watched Krausse start the game.

He wouldn't sit for long.

Krausse got lit up in the bottom of the first, so Mack sent Rommel out for the bottom of the second. Four hours and *seventeen innings* later, Rommel staggered off the mound, having allowed twenty-nine hits, fourteen runs . . . and gaining credit for the Athletics' 18–17 win.

That bizarre victory, coming in his thirteenth season in the American League, easily ranked as Rommel's most famous. It was the 171st win of his career . . . and the last. As Rommel would later recall, "I was thirty-four at the time, and I had worked the two previous days. It never occurred to me that I'd have to go more than a couple of innings, if any. It was the end of me as a pitcher, too."

The Athletics had hosted the White Sox for three double-headers on the three days before their trip to Cleveland, and Rommel had worked two innings on Friday and three more on Saturday. A lot of people think that knuckleball pitchers are impervious to fatigue, but if that were true, Phil Niekro would have started eighty games every season. Knuckleballers get tired, too, and that seventeen-inning stint really was the end of Eddie Rommel as an effective pitcher.

He remained with the A's for the rest of the season, but finished with just that single victory, two losses, and a 5.51 ERA in seventeen games. On October 21, Mack released Rommel, the Athletics' last link—aside from Mack himself—to their "American League cellar days."

In *The Sporting News* that October, Bill Dooly wrote, "It is almost certain that a National League club will take on the veteran hurler, for Rommel would be a sure bet to help a team in the elder circuit. His knuckle ball would be almost entirely new around the league and, aside from that advantage, Eddie also knows all the answers in pitching to hitting weaknesses."

What's more, Dooly noted, Rommel's arm was as sound as ever. "Indeed, in all his years in baseball, the knuckle-ball artist never suffered with a lame wing. This is probably due to a graceful, natural delivery; an easy motion that never severely strained his arm."

No National League team showed any interest. Or perhaps one did, but Rommel didn't reciprocate. Still only thirty-five—young for a knuckleballer, even if nobody back then knew it—Rommel remained with the Athletics as a coach in 1933 and '34. (He supposedly developed an outstanding curveball while pitching batting practice, leading to speculation that he might be reactivated. Nothing came of that, though.)

On September 28, 1934, the United Press reported that coach Rommel had been released to make room for Connie Mack Jr., who was then a *sophomore* at Duke University (however, the references don't list Junior as a coach for the Athletics in 1935, or any other year).

In 1935, Rommel managed the Piedmont League's

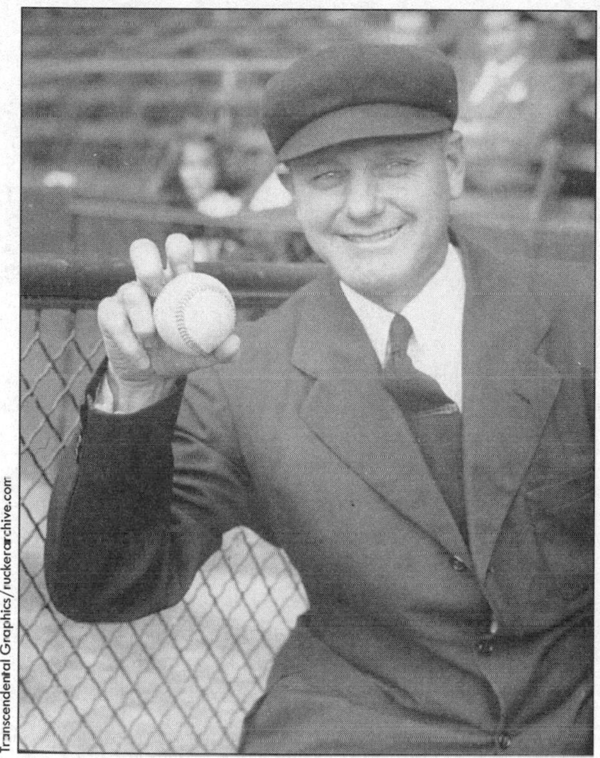
Transcendental Graphics/ruckerarchive.com

Richmond Colts—one of Mack's two farm teams—to a third-place finish in the regular season, and a first-place finish in the league's championship series. Those successes notwithstanding, Rommel didn't much care for managing, but he did want to stay in baseball. Which was a problem, because in those days there were few coaching jobs available in the major leagues, and virtually none in the minors. Most of the major-league clubs employed the manager and one coach. A famous figure from the club's past might, if he were lucky, secure a position as press-box attendant or something, but the great majority of ex-players were forced to find a new line of work.

Ah, but what about umpiring? On June 10, 1936, Fred Marberry pitched his last game in the major leagues. Almost immediately, he was given—and "given" is the correct verb here—a job as a major-league umpire, a job for which he proved ill-suited. As Joe Williams wrote a few years later, "Typical of most veterans, Marberry didn't have the slightest conception of the job. He was passably competent in making routine decisions, but he could never get over the fact he was a ballplayer. Before the game he would go into the dressing room and play cards with the home players. On trips he would ride with the teams. He never developed the independent, isolated attitude of an umpire and as a consequence he was a complete failure."

A noble experiment, perhaps, but one that would not be repeated. That same year, ex-American League pitching stars Eddie Rommel and George Pipgras applied for positions as arbiters. League president Will Harridge told them he'd give them a chance, but they'd have to spend three years in the minor leagues, working for minor-league salaries.

Both agreed, and both became American League umpires in 1938 after serving abbreviated apprenticeships. (Harridge actually hoped that one day *all* of his umpires would be ex-American League players, but of course that didn't happen.)

In 1939, just his second season, Rommel worked at second base in the All-Star Game. He was behind the plate for the All-Star Game in 1943, and would eventually work in six All-Star Games (but only two World Series, along with the American League's pennant playoff game in 1948).

In 1946, Rommel worked his third All-Star Game, and Commissioner Happy Chandler promised the All-Star umpires he would honor them with watches. On December 3, with no watch yet in evidence, Rommel fired off the following missive to Chandler . . .

December 3, 1946

One Day Nearer Xmas.

Mr. A.B. Chandler
Carew Bldg.
Cincinnati, Ohio

Dear Commissioner:

The War has been won,
The All-Star game has been played,
The Football season is done,
And Xmas is not long delayed

BUT

Winter is here,
And I may survive,
Yet my watch has not arrived.

Respectfully yours,
Ed. Rommel

(Two weeks later, Chandler responded with a short note, not nearly so entertaining, in which he explained that when he first promised the watches, he didn't know that the league presidents had already made arrangements to present the umpires with gifts for their All-Star service.)

On April 15, 1954, the city of Baltimore returned to the major leagues for the first time since 1902. And at Rommel's request, the lifelong Baltimorean was behind the plate to call the Orioles' 3-1 win against the White Sox; four years later, he served as plate umpire in the 1958 All-Star Game, Baltimore's first.

On the second day of the 1956 season, Rommel reportedly became the first umpire in major-league history to call a game while wearing eyeglasses. He wore spectacles for the rest of his career—he was forced to retire after the 1959 season, at sixty-two—but only during night games in which he did *not* work behind the plate.

As an umpire, Rommel had little patience with delays, whether due to argumentative managers or dawdling pitchers.

"To say an umpire never makes a bad call is an outright lie," he said. "What I used to do is say, 'Okay, I missed it. Now what do we do?' That always stopped 'em because there wasn't any answer."

About the pitchers, Rommel said in 1964, "[Pedro] Ramos and [Orlando] Peña just don't want to pitch. They do anything they can to keep from throwing the ball in a close game. Somebody might hit it. . . . [Chuck] Estrada is not only slow-moving but he seems to feel he's not earning his money if he doesn't run the count to three and two." (That's just a snippet from Rommel's cranky article, "Baseball is a Big Bore," published in *True* magazine.)

Rommel also had little tolerance for pitchers throwing at hitters. "That doesn't belong in baseball," he said. "It's dishonest and I don't think the fans come to the park for baseball wars."

He claimed to have thrown at only one batter in his long career. "Cy Perkins was catching for the A's," Rommel recalled, "and he wanted me to throw at Ray Schalk. I did and the results were disastrous. I hit Schalk in the back and he later scored, costing me the game."

After leaving baseball in 1959, Rommel hired on as a senior clerk with Maryland Governor Millard Tawes, working at that job for seven years. He began suffering kidney problems in 1966, and died in 1970.

MEL HARDER

ROB NEYER

On May 16, 1928, Mel Harder—a rookie right-hander, all of eighteen years old, and pitching in his third game for the Cleveland Indians—fell behind in the count against Ty Cobb. He threw his next pitch down the middle, and the ball wound up flying over the right-field wall. It was Cobb's first home run of the season, and the last of his career.

Harder spent all of '28 with the Tribe and racked up a 6.61 ERA in forty-nine innings. He spent most of the next season in New Orleans, and reestablished himself as a prospect—not that he'd ever actually unestablished himself—by going 7-2 with a 2.50 ERA in sixteen games. That got him back to Cleveland in 1930, and that's where he stayed for a long, long time.

Early on, Harder picked up a nickname. As Cleveland *Plain Dealer* sportswriter Gordon Cobbledick wrote in 1931, "His only nickname is Chief. Bib Falk invented it and Harder says he doesn't know why, but it probably was suggested by his rather high cheek bones and straight black hair. There's no Indian blood in his veins, but Chief seemed apt enough and has stuck."

In 1932, Harder may not have been the ace of the staff—not yet, anyway—but on July 31 he received an honor normally accorded an ace. The Indians were scheduled to play their first game at massive Cleveland Stadium that afternoon, and Wes Ferrell was supposed to start. But Ferrell had a sore shoulder. So two days before the big game, manager Roger Peckinpaugh told Harder that instead the assignment was his.

Cleveland Stadium could hardly have been more different than League Park, where the Tribe had been playing their home games. League Park held fewer than 25,000 fans; the new Stadium could accommodate more than three times that, and in that first game the Indians set a new record for professional baseball, with 80,184 fans.

Harder was still only twenty-two years old, but he was more excited than nervous.

"Cleveland Stadium was a pitcher's park, 460 to center field, 320 down the line left and right, and Lefty Grove and I had a real pitchers' duel going," Harder would recall, sixty-four years later. "I was getting good calls from my catcher, Luke Sewell, mixing up my fastball-sinker, curve and change-of-pace, handling their hitters pretty well. And we weren't able to do much with Lefty's stuff. We both had shutouts going through seven innings."

With two outs in the eighth, Philadelphia's Mickey Cochrane grounded a single up the middle to drive in Max Bishop from second base with the game's first run. And that was how it ended: 1-0, with Grove tossing a four-hit shutout. Though Harder got hung with the loss, he always regarded that day as the greatest of his career.

Harder lost thirteen games that season, but he also won fifteen (after winning eleven and thirteen the two previous seasons). Harder would eventually register exactly fifteen victories in four different seasons, and the shorthand description of him was "Come hell or high water, he'll win fifteen for you every year."

Harder didn't mess around with any trick pitches. He didn't need to, because in his prime he threw two *outstanding* pitches: a sinking fastball with great natural movement and a curveball widely considered among the best in the American League. After reaching the majors, Harder did his best to mimic the pitching motion of White Sox ace Ted Lyons. As Harder told Fred Lieb in

1939, "He was already well established as a star when I came into the league. I observed the freedom and ease of his delivery, and I did my best to copy it." And many years later, Harder told Ed Rumill, "Both Ted and I specialized in the curve ball, so I picked him out as my model. I studied him and tried to copy every move. He could 'spot it' and he threw it at changing speeds. When we were playing the White Sox, I wouldn't take my eyes off him."

Harder's prime lasted three and a half seasons: from 1933 through the first three months of the 1936 season. Over that span, there wasn't a better pitcher in the American League, as he won seventy-one games and lost only forty-six. After running his record to 14-6 on July 21, 1936, Harder could boast 101 career victories . . . and he was still three months shy of his twenty-seventh birthday.

But that was as good as it got. Here's how Harder would later recall the second half of the '36 season:

> I didn't have any physical problems until 1936. I was having a real good year, because I had 13 victories and only 3 defeats going into the All-Star game break. After I pitched in the All-Star game in Boston we went to Philadelphia and I pitched after my normal three days' rest.
>
> In the fourth inning I felt this twinge and when I went into the dugout I told our trainer, Lefty Weisman, that something happened to my shoulder. He massaged it and put some hot stuff on it and I went out and pitched the rest of the game. I won that game 6-4.
>
> My shoulder got worse that night and the next day I could hardly lift it. They gave me ten days' rest and my next start I lasted only three innings. So I rested again for two weeks and the same thing happened. It was the same all through the second half of the season. The rest of the year I only won two more games and lost twelve. I had a lousy second half.

Harder was nearly ninety years old when he gave that interview, so he can certainly be excused for missing a few of the details.

He was actually 11-6 at the All-Star break, and his first start after the break was not in Philadelphia; it was in New York, where he beat the Yankees handily. It was his *second* start that came in Philadelphia (and he did indeed beat the A's, 6-4). But he did *not* get ten days of rest after that game. Five days later, Harder beat the Red Sox in Cleveland, 6-5.

After which, everything fell apart, as the Indians lost Harder's next four starts: 0-13, 7-11, 4-9, and 7-9. After that fourth straight loss, Harder got a twelve-day break before coming back to beat the Browns, 4-2.

Problem solved? Hardly. That win over the Browns would be Harder's last in 1936, as he lost five of his last six starts and got hammered in the other.

What was the state of sports medicine in 1936?

> In the fall the club sent me up to Mayo Clinic, but in those years they didn't know how to treat rotator cuff or other shoulder injuries. Well, they couldn't find anything wrong with me. I had to tell *them* what was wrong. So, of all things, at the end of my three-day exam they finally told me that I should have my four wisdom teeth taken out. That's all they knew!

When Harder got to spring training in '37, he had no idea what would happen. Eventually, he got up the nerve to cut loose . . . and his arm didn't hurt. He could still pitch. Maybe not as hard as before (a couple of years later, *The Sporting News* would refer to Harder as a "curve specialist"). But he could still pitch.

His moment had passed, though. Two days after Harder's last win in '36, seventeen-year-old Bob Feller started (and won) his first game for the Indians, and Harder would never again be the club's ace. Granted, he did pitch well in the first half in '37, well enough to earn a start in the All-Star Game. It was his fourth straight All-Star berth—and his last, as it turned out—and Harder pitched three shutout innings, winding up his All-Star career with a record that's not been matched: in thirteen innings, he didn't allow a single run.

For all his All-Star success, Harder never pitched in the World Series. His best chance—his only chance, really—came in 1940, but instead of lasting postseason glory, the Indians gained for themselves a measure of perpetual ignominy.

Ossie Vitt managed the Tribe that season, and he wasn't what you'd call a player's manager. Vitt got the job in 1938, and basically did everything he could think of to alienate his players. So for two years, simmering.

And then in June of 1940, the kettle boiled over. On June 7 in New York, Feller lost to the Yankees, and during the game Vitt supposedly said, "There's my star out

Transcendental Graphics/ruckerarchive.com

there, the great Feller. How can I win a pennant with him?"

Mel Harder and Hal Trosky had seen and heard enough. They organized a meeting, mostly of the club's veterans, and a plan was hatched. When the Indians got back to Cleveland, Harder called owner Alva Bradley and asked for an appointment. Bradley told Harder to come on over, and within an hour Harder and roughly a dozen other players appeared.

Harder, who had been with the club far longer than anybody else, was the spokesman. "We think we've got a good chance to win," he told Bradley. "But we'll never win it with Vitt as manager. If we can get rid of him, we can win. We all feel sure of that."

Bradley might have wanted to fire Vitt, but he couldn't do it because a number of the writers already had the story. If Bradley fired Vitt, everybody would know the inmates were running the asylum.

So Vitt stayed. And it became a huge story anyway, not just in Cleveland but around the country. The Indians became infamous as the "Cleveland Cry Babies," and things got particularly nasty in Detroit, where the fans threw "everything from baby bottle nipples to jars of baby food at the Indians."

It's often said that the Indians fell apart after the failed rebellion, but that's not at all what happened. When Chief Harder and his little band of Indians trooped into Alva Bradley's office, the Tribe was two games out of first place with a 28-21 (.571) record. They went 61-44 (.581) the rest of the way—some said that Vitt did change his ways, at least somewhat, and some also said that the players invented their own system of signals, thus bypassing Vitt in certain situations—and they were in the pennant race until the very end.

In late September, with the Indians and Tigers tied for first place, the two clubs met in Detroit for a three-game series. Harder started the opener, and pitched brilliantly for seven innings, permitting three singles and one run. He got into a spot of trouble in the eighth, though: with one out, he walked Barney McCosky and gave up a single to Charlie Gehringer. Vitt headed for the mound and, after a conference that reportedly lasted five minutes, he sent Harder to the dugout and summoned Feller from the bullpen. Feller had pitched a complete game two days earlier, didn't have anything, and the Tigers wound up winning, 6-5, to take a one-game lead over the Indians.

Four days later, Harder lost a critical game to the Browns, dropping the Tribe to one-and-a-half lengths behind the Tigers (who were idle). That was on the 24th. The Indians won on the 25th but so did the Tigers . . . twice. That gave Detroit a two-game lead, with the clubs slated for a season-ending series in Cleveland, starting on the 27th. The Indians would have to win all three or be eliminated, and the drama ended quickly when a thirty-year-old rookie named Floyd Giebell, making his second major-league start, beat Feller in the opener, clinching the pennant for the Tigers.

Vitt finally got fired after the season, but in 1941 the Indians went down in the standings, not up. Harder spent seven more seasons in Cleveland, and the *closest* the Indians got to first place was eleven games, in 1945. Harder wasn't a lot of help. When he was healthy enough to pitch (which wasn't all that often), he was roughly a league-average pitcher . . . and that's a league significantly weakened by the war.

Harder pitched his last game in 1947, and it was a

good one; on September 7 he started against the Yankees and beat them, 3-2. With that victory, he extended his franchise record for victories to 223. Harder is still number two on the all-time list, behind only Feller, and to this day only Walter Johnson (21) and Ted Lyons (ditto) have pitched more seasons for one club than Mel Harder (20) did.

For 1948, Indians owner Bill Veeck hired Harder as a coach at large; shortly after the season opened, Harder became the Indians' first-base coach (giving him a great view as the Indians finally did win the pennant). The next season he took over as pitching coach, and held that job for fifteen years. In the mid-1950s, the Indians put together one of the great rotations in baseball history, featuring Early Wynn, Bob Lemon, and Mike Garcia (along with first Bob Feller, and then Herb Score), and Harder received a great deal of credit for the staff's success. Score later said, "If Mel Harder couldn't teach you a curveball, then no one could."

Fired by the Indians after the '63 season, Harder then spent a year with the Mets, three years with the Reds, and one year with the expansion Royals. That season in Kansas City was Harder's forty-second in a major-league uniform, and his last.

Harder retired to Sun City, Arizona, with his wife Hazel; they'd been married since 1932, and raised two daughters. In 1983, Mel and Hazel moved back to the Cleveland area. In 1990, the Indians retired Harder's number: 19. And on October 3, 1993, the man who had thrown the first official pitch at Cleveland Stadium, sixty-one years earlier, threw the ceremonial last pitch at Cleveland Stadium.

There was, over the years, some talk of getting Harder in the Hall of Fame. Veterans Committeeman Ted Williams was, publicly at least, a big supporter even though he didn't actually see Harder pitch until Harder was well past his prime. But Williams died on July 5, 2002. And Harder—who in 1976 said about the Hall of Fame, "If I live long enough maybe I'll get in."—passed away on October 20. He had just turned ninety-three, and we've not yet found anyone with less than a kind word about those ninety-three years.

LON WARNEKE

BILL JAMES

Cy Slapnicka was among the most famous scouts in baseball history. He looked under rocks and over prospects for the Cleveland Indians for many years, eventually becoming the general manager of the Indians, and remaining active for many years after that.

In 1929 the Indians loaned $5,000 to the Shreveport team in the Texas League, a condition of the loan being that the Indians had their pick of anybody on the Shreveport roster. There wasn't anybody on the Shreveport team the Indians liked, but Shreveport had an arrangement with Alexandria, in the Cotton States League, allowing Shreveport to purchase players from Alexandria. Alexandria had two star players: Lon Warneke, and Odell "Bad News" Hale. The Indians bought Hale (by way of Shreveport) for $1,500 and dispatched Slapnicka to look at Warneke.

On the day that Slapnicka went to look at Warneke, however, there were torrential rains, and a dam near the ballpark broke, flooding the field. Slapnicka got to the park and there was nothing going on except fans huddling under the overhang and two players, in uniform, sitting out near second base on barrel staves, pretending to row with their bats.

"Who is the nut putting on the show?" Slapnicka asked.

"That's Lon Warneke," somebody told him. "Our best pitcher."

Slapnicka waded back to the train station and left town without bothering to watch the nut case pitch. Patsy Flaherty saw him pitch shortly after that, and persuaded the Cubs to purchase him.

Lon Warneke hailed from Mt. Ida, Arkansas, a thriving metropolis of 512 people, give or take a few. The two best pitchers ever born in the state of Arkansas, Lon Warneke and Dizzy Dean, were almost the same age, were both originally signed by the Cardinals, both made their major league debuts in 1930, and both emerged as stars in 1932. Both were hard-throwing right-handed hillbillies, and both pitched for the Cardinals and Cubs.

There, however, the two depart. Dean was a gregarious, egocentric man with an obsessive need to be the center of attention. Warneke, although he had a robust sense of humor and also enjoyed being center stage, was a quiet, modest man whose humor was often so low-key that it was impossible to tell for sure whether he was pulling your leg. Warneke graduated from high school, and worked a couple of summers on farm crews traveling through the wheat belt up into North Dakota; Dean never really attended school after the third grade, and joined the army when he was sixteen.

In the winter of 1927–1928, the eighteen-year-old Warneke hopped a freight train and rode from Mt. Ida to Houston, where he stayed with one of his older sisters. He got a job as a bicycle messenger, delivering telegrams for Western Union. His sister was married to a man named Buck Weaver, not the old player, but a fanatic baseball fan of the same name. Weaver thought Warneke had ability as a pitcher, and encouraged him to try out with the Cardinals, who had a top minor-league affiliate in Houston. Warneke bicycled to the ballpark, and asked to see the boss. "What do you want?" asked the boss, who turned out to be Pancho Snyder. Warneke informed Snyder that he was a pitcher. Snyder, impressed by the young man's aggressive attitude, promised to let him know when and where the Cardinals were conducting tryouts.

When the tryouts were announced, they were 27 miles from the house where Warneke was staying. He got on his bicycle, rode the 27 miles, and impressed the Cardinal scouts as much with his fastball as he had with his attitude. The Cardinals signed him and sent him to the Laurel, Mississippi, team in the Cotton States League.

Warneke, who was thin at his thickest, was sick most of that summer, lost thirty pounds, pitched dreadfully, and was released in mid-summer. The Alexandria manager in the same league, however, was desperate for pitching, and thought Warneke was worth another look. Warneke worked hard and guzzled milk and bacon all winter to get his strength back, and in 1929 had a breakout season in the minors.

The other stories told about Warneke's minor-league career involve snakes. One time the team bus broke down on the border of a swamp. The players were standing on the edge of the blacktop, trying to keep their shoes dry, when one of them spotted a huge blacksnake slithering through the wet grass. Warneke charged into the muck, grabbed the snake by its tail and came out, cracking the snake like a bullwhip.

George Brace Collection

A few days later, having discovered that some of his teammates were squeamish about snakes, Warneke smuggled a snake onto the bench in a sack, and turned it loose during the game. The players bolted out of the dugout, clearing the bench except for Warneke and the snake. Warneke was ejected, and told to take his snake with him.

As much as his pitching, it may have been incidents like this that led to his release. Warneke was an easygoing, laconic man, and he didn't seem to the Cardinals—as he didn't seem to Cy Slapnicka—to be serious about his work. He never seemed to be running quite as hard as he could have run, and he took defeat perhaps a little too much in stride.

But he won 16 games in 1929. The Cubs bought him in late '29; he got one major-league inning in 1930, put in another year in the minors, and spent 1931 back in the majors, working mostly in long relief. The story told about his 1931 season involves not snakes, but suits. Coming to Chicago, Warneke was reportedly astonished to discover that city people owned more than one suit. After visiting a haberdasher, Warneke returned with thirteen suits. Actually, the number of suits depends on the retelling; we have sources giving the total as high as eighteen. He bought a bunch of suits.

I think the suit episode is instructive about Warneke's character. There is a parallel story about Dizzy Dean, which involves Jimmie Wilson. The first time Dean visited New York, Jimmie Wilson loaned him a white silk shirt, explaining as tactfully as possible that he did not think it would reflect well on the St. Louis Cardinals to allow their star rookie to walk around New York City in a plaid cotton shirt with several buttons missing. Dean accepted the shirt gratefully, but the next day Wilson was astonished to discover that his closet had been cleaned out; Dean had taken all of his shirts. Wilson confronted Dean with fire in his eyes, but Dizzy smiled disarmingly and explained that he jus' *knew* the St. Louis Cardinals would not want to let a great young pitcher like him run around New York City with only one silk shirt.

What is never said, in the profligate published versions of the suit story, is what prompted Warneke to go on his suit-buying spree. What had to have happened is that somebody said something to him about his clothes—and that punched his "I'll show *you* button." Warneke probably didn't respond very much, and never passed along to reporters what the slight was, but there was more to Lon Warneke than met the eye. He had a very strong desire to *be* somebody. He didn't lash out, and he didn't *talk* about what he wanted to be or what he wanted to do. He diverted attention with backwoods humor—but he would tramp trains and cadge a bicycle and ride the bicycle thirty miles to a tryout. He didn't hang his head, after he was released by the Cardinals; he got another job, and he made the adjustments he needed to make to be successful. If somebody made a slighting remark about his clothes, he would go get a better wardrobe than anybody else had.

In 1931, mostly because of his control, he was not effective. In modern terminology, he had a lot of noise in his delivery. He had the habit of looking at his feet while pitching, not *taking* his eye off the plate so much as *keeping* his eye off the plate. When this was pointed out to him, he corrected it. He would sit on the bench during games with a baseball in his hand, spinning it off his fingers again and again and again, trying to make the act of spinning a curveball second nature. In a way, Warneke *wanted* people to underrate him; he wanted people to sell him short, because he knew what he was made of.

Rogers Hornsby made him a starting pitcher in 1932, and Warneke emerged suddenly as the best pitcher in the National League, going 22-6 with a 2.37 ERA. The Cubs, 84-70 in 1931, won the National League pennant. The 1932 season made Warneke a star—one reporter rated him the second-best player in the majors that season, behind Jimmie Foxx—and the newspapers of late 1932 were filled with Lon Warneke stories, which form the basis of this biography. Warneke had used his major-league money to buy cattle, 200 head of cattle at $2 a head. His father, Lon Warneke Sr., missed the 1932 World Series; because he was stuck tending the cattle, which Warneke had been unable to sell. "What are you going to do with all those cattle?" a reporter asked Lonnie.

"We'll just keep 'em as pets," Warneke replied with a straight face.

Although the spotlight passed from Warneke to Carl Hubbell and Dizzy Dean, Warneke remained a sensational pitcher for three years following his 1932 breakout, winning twenty games every season from 1932 through 1935 except 1933, when he pitched 287 innings with a 2.00 ERA, but finished only 18-13 due to abysmal offensive support. In 1934 Warneke pitched two consecutive one-hitters to start the season.

A few descriptions of him may serve to sharpen our image. Westbrook Pegler described him as "a tall, gaunt youth whose starved appearance belies the generous feeding policy of his employers."

Dan Daniel, *New York World-Telegram*, September 23, 1932: "The other Cubs call Warneke Dick. A man named Dick, in Mount Ida, lost his nose in an accident and the local impression is that Len has Dick's as well as his own schnozzle."

Unidentified clipping, Hall of Fame files: "Warneke is extremely modest and quiet off the field but is right at home in a game. He possesses an unlimited amount of nerve and never loses his head."

Tom Meany, *New York World-Telegram*, reporting on Warneke in advance of the 1935 World Series: "I hadn't seen Mr. Warneke since that (1932) series. To me at that time he was the perfect hill-billy. The mercurial tempo of big-time doings meant nothing to him, there was no accelerated heartbeat, no change from the lazy, slumbering, contented life in Mount Ida . . . It is a pleasure to report that Mr. Warneke is still the perfect hill-billy and when I write this I write it in complete applause. Geographically and mentally he is still in Mount Ida . . . You have to take a close-up of Mr. Warneke, with his thin, tobacco-stained lips and Billy DeBeck stage setting to appreciate the enduring love of the hill-billies for the hills. And to make it positive all you have to do is listen to Mr. Warneke before he goes to the hill to pitch the first game of the world series.

" 'Maybe I'll beat 'em and maybe I won't. I ain't worrying. Should you?' "

James A. Burchard, *New York World-Telegram*, reporting on Ladies Day at the Polo Grounds, 1937: "The most obliging of the ball players was Lon Warneke. Chewing a cud that would have choked a horse, he signed his name about two hundred times.

" 'What the hell,' said the gallant Warneke. 'It's Ladies Day, ain't it?' " (Warneke later would be featured in advertisements for Beechnut chewing tobacco. "When there's 2 On and Ott Coming up—*Beechnut* helps me out of the pinch.")

Tom Meany, *New York World-Telegram*, March 19, 1938: "Lon Warneke has been yanked from the pitcher's box occasionally, but he has never had a tooth yanked. In fact, Warneke has never visited a dentist." (In 1932

Warneke had been ordered by the Cubs to see a doctor about some late-season back trouble. He flatly refused to go. "No doctor or dentist has ever laid a hand on me since the day I was born," he explained. "And it's a poor idea to have them tinkering with me at this late date." He relented several years later, when he needed to have his tonsils removed, and eventually became a regular consumer of professional medical care. Well, semi-regular.)

F. C. Lane in *Baseball Magazine* (November, 1932) wrote that Rogers Hornsby "contended that Warneke was the speediest pitcher in the league," although Lane expressed the opinion that Dazzy Vance, then 41 years old, still threw harder.

Lane also said "Warneke is a side-arm pitcher with a tendency to keep his fast ball low," and numerous other sources also say very specifically that Warneke threw a *low* fastball as his stock in trade. However, as to the "side arm" comment, Tom Meany in the *New York World-Telegraph* (August 5, 1932) wrote, "The kid resembles Vance a great deal. He has the same square-rigged shoulders, the same direct, almost violent overhand motion and a lot of the stuff that Daz had a few seasons ago. Warneke is fast and he has a good hook to use in complement with his fast ball. Most of the other Cub flingers effect a side-arm style, largely due to the construction of Wrigley Field. The centre field bleachers there are in the range of vision of the batter . . . This gives the pitcher a white background and a very poor one for the batter if the pitcher happens to be a side-armer. Warneke has so much stuff, however, that he comes down straight overhand, without the benefit of camouflage to dazzle the hitters."

Both Lane and Meany are respected writers who usually know what they are talking about. In this case, however, the Meany quote is more credible, because it is much more specific. An irony of the Meany quote, which could never have been anticipated by the author, was that Warneke would wind up with an extraordinarily similar *record* to Dazzy Vance. Vance in his career made 347 starts, with a career record of 197-140, 30 shutouts, 11 saves and a 3.24 ERA. Warneke made 343 starts, with a career record of 192-121, 31 shutouts, 13 saves and a 3.18 ERA.

Warneke was called "The Arkansas Hummingbird" as an allusion to his love of singing. The nickname, unlike many of the nicknames which now decorate the encyclopedias, was very commonly used throughout his career. An Associated Press story (September 28, 1932) reported that "The sputtering of village square arc lights on concert night in Mount Ida, Ark., means more to Lonnie Warneke than the big league calcium glare. . . . The National League pitching sensation expects to 'beat it' back to his job directing the Mount Ida town band as soon as he has got his World Series chores done. Far more willing to talk about his prowess with a baton than of his cannonading of baseballs past enemy batters, Lonnie admits his greatest love is hunting. He is as proud of his four fine bird dogs as of any big league pitching feats."

The story about directing the town band may have been a goof on the reporters. Warneke also claimed to be able to play a musical saw, a guitar, a concertina and a harmonica, but, when confronted with the actual instruments, was unable (or unwilling) to demonstrate a working knowledge of any of them. "He's the best rifle shot in the majors, though," asserted *The Sporting News*. "They haven't exploded that one on him and never will. And he's still an Ozark exponent of the homely axiom. Independent as hell and don't cater to no city slickers."

Before the 1932 World Series it was suggested to Warneke that the Cubs were outclassed by the Yankees, who had won 107 games with Ruth and Gehrig having their last great year together, and Ruffing and Gomez their first. "Why?" asked Warneke. "They put their pants on one leg at a time like anybody else, don't they?" Although the Yankees seemed hardly human and certainly not vulnerable in the 1932 World Series, this remark entered the lexicon of all sports; it is still used by coaches today to try to draw a feared opponent back to the level of mere mortals. It would be interesting to know whether it *truly* originated with Warneke, or whether Warneke was borrowing a phrase from his native culture, but unfortunately nobody knows.

The Cubs, after strong races in '33 and '34, made it back to the World Series in 1935. They had two twenty-game winners, Warneke (20-13) and Big Bill Lee (20-6), backed by Larry French (17-10) and Charlie Root (15-8); all four pitchers had earned-run averages within a few points of 3.00. Warneke, who had won his last seven starts, started the first game, matched against Schoolboy Rowe of the Tigers, another Arkansas fire-baller, who had won 24 games in '34 and 19 more in '35. Warneke pitched a four-hit shutout, beating the Tigers 3-0.

The 1935 World Series was played on six consecutive days, with no day of rest. Root started the second game and was hammered; Bill Lee started the third game, and carried a 3-1 lead into the eighth. The Tigers got a walk, a double and a single, tying the game with one out. Warneke, with one day of rest after the shutout in Game One, came in to pitch. He quickly gave up two more singles, pushing across a run that was charged to Lee (Tigers now lead, 4-3), and putting runners on first and third. The runner on first, Billy Rogell, broke for second, drew a throw, got into a rundown, and the runner from third scored during the rundown (a play that was very common during the 1930s, incidentally). Warneke got the third out, and Larry French replaced him in the ninth inning.

The Cubs then tied the game, but lost it in the eleventh inning. The reports of this game were dominated by an injury to Hank Greenberg, who suffered a broken arm early in the game, and an on-field altercation in which Charlie Grimm (Cub manager) was thrown out after arguing a call at second base, and such strong language was used that Grimm, Billy Jurges, Woody English, Billy Herman and the umpire, George Moriarty, were all fined by Commissioner Landis.

Escaping notice was Grimm's decision to use both Warneke and French in relief. The use of two of his starters in relief, in a series with no off days, forced the Cubs to use their fifth starter to start the fourth game. Warneke had started the first game and relieved in the third; he was out. Root had been pasted in the second game and had only one day of rest; he was out. Lee had started the third game; he was out. And French had pitched two innings of relief in Game Three; with no day of rest, he was out.

The fifth starter, Tex Carleton, pitched well enough in Game Four, but lost. Warneke went back to the mound for Game Five, and pitched six shutout innings—and then something ruptured in his shoulder.

Given the state of 1935 sports medicine, we have no idea what went wrong, but it was apparent that Warneke, who had pitched fifteen shutout innings in two starts, would be unable to pitch again. The Cubs held on to win that game, 3-1, but then lost for the fourth time in Game Six.

Whatever was wrong with Warneke's arm, it was assumed that a winter's rest would clear it up. It didn't. Warneke, although he remained a rotation anchor for seven more years and was always able to win more than he lost, was never again the brilliant pitcher he had been from 1932 to 1935.

Charlie Grimm avoided any serious second-guessing. He wasn't fired, and the press apparently accepted his use of two starting pitchers in relief in one game. This was 1935; teams didn't really have bullpens in 1935, and Grimm didn't have any relievers that he trusted. But . . . just stating the facts, Grimm pushed Warneke very hard; Warneke suffered a serious injury. He had four good starters—but he used three of them in an ill-fated effort to salvage one game, which forced him to put his fifth starter on the mound in Game Four, down two games to one. I wasn't there, but it doesn't look very bright to me.

Warneke remained an effective pitcher into the early 1940s, occasionally interrupted by injuries, but never by ineffectiveness; he never had a losing season until 1943 (4-5), and won 16 to 18 games four more times, giving him a total of eight seasons of sixteen or more wins.

After a subpar 1936 season (16-13), Warneke was traded to the Cardinals. He was right at home in St. Louis: closer to his home, and surrounded by a team full of players with similar backgrounds—Dizzy Dean, Pepper Martin, and the rest of the Gashouse Gang. Some of the guys formed a band, the Mudcat band, which performed around St. Louis and also appeared at least once on national radio, on *Ripley's Believe It or Not* radio show in May, 1937. According to Frankie Frisch in *The Fordham Flash*, "The band made a hit wherever we went. In fact it became such a popular feature that on one trip to Rochester for an exhibition game, the billboards, which were supposed to advertise the ball game between the Cardinals and the Redwings, chose to publicize instead the fact that, 'The Mississippi Mudcat Band Is in Town.' I think it was about that time that Sam Breadon and Branch Rickey decided that it might be better if the talented athletes confined their activities to the business of playing baseball." (Think of the movie, *O Brother, Where Art Thou?* Same time frame, same place, same type of music. Also the greatest movie in years.)

In late May, 1938, Cookie Lavagetto drilled a ball off Warneke's ankle, putting him out of commission for several weeks—an odd echo of the injury suffered by Dizzy Dean in the 1937 All-Star game.

Warneke pitched a no-hitter in 1941, against the defending World Champion Cincinnati Reds.

In March 1944, Warneke told reporters in Hot Springs, Arkansas, that he had agreed to report for his pre-induction physical for the United States Army.

> Warneke, 35, father of two children, played in major league baseball for almost 14 years. He is the owner of a service station and has an interest in a wholesale feed store (in Hot Springs).
>
> "Whatever Uncle Sam wants me to do, I am going to try to do with the best of my ability," he said.
>
> —*The Sporting News*, March 1944

Warneke got out of the Army in '45 and pitched a few more games. He was effective enough, but there was a funny thing about Warneke: he *wanted* to be an umpire. In 1942—while still a rotation anchor—Warneke told a reporter that he hoped to be a major-league umpire in two or three years. In typical Warneke fashion, he followed through. In November 1945, the *New York World-Telegram* reported that "Lon Warneke has left the Cubs to become an umpire in the Pacific Coast League . . . he needs only eight games to achieve the 200 victory mark, but may forego the chance." Though still a reasonably effective major-league pitcher, he retired to go to the minor leagues and become an umpire.

He umpired in the PCL for three years, returning to the majors in 1949. Leo Durocher, Warneke's teammate in 1937, said that Warneke was the worst umpire he ever saw. He may not have been a bad umpire, but it must certainly be said that he was inexpert at dodging controversy. In May 1951, Warneke had a loud confrontation with Durocher, then managing the Giants. The problem started when Warneke threw Eddie Stanky, Durocher's second baseman and pet player, out of a game after a relatively modest outburst. Later in the same game (or perhaps the next day) the Cardinal second baseman, Red Schoendienst, got the short end of a close call, and stormed all over Warneke, making—at least it appeared to the New York reporters—a much bigger stink than Stanky had stunk, but without being ejected. When Schoendienst was allowed to continue in the game, Durocher went ballistic.

"Well, maybe he had a kick coming," Warneke said, in explaining why he had decided not to eject Schoendienst. "It was a pretty tough decision and I wish I had another look at it. Besides, Schoendienst did not use abusive language. But Durocher's language was pretty rough." Both Warneke and Durocher denied reports that they had met under the stands to sort it out with their fists later on, and Warneke continued to deny these reports many years later.

"Durocher didn't swing at me, like some people said," Warneke told a reporter in the mid-1960s. "I'm sorry he didn't. He'd have gotten a receipt for it." This incident, like many things that happened in New York City baseball in the 1950s, became famous out of all proportion to its merit, the fountain of literally hundreds of newspaper stories. It was the most famous of the many controversies that dogged Warneke's umpiring career. In June of 1953, he warned a Cincinnati pitcher named Howie Judson about throwing at batters, after Judson had flattened Junior Gilliam and made another hitter or two nervous. This was 30 years before there were any clearly established policies about warning both benches, and the warning made more news when Warneke, apparently figuring it was nobody's business what he had talked to the pitcher about, denied that he had warned him about throwing at the Dodger hitters, and insisted he had just been cautioning him about how close he was to balking when he threw to the bases.

This has little to do with Lon Warneke, but is noteworthy for other reasons. In May 1955, Red Schoendienst came to bat with the bases loaded, and lined a clean single, or what looked like a clean single, into right field. Right fielder Monte Irvin, however, picked up the ball and gunned it home in time to retire the runner from third base, Solly Hemus—a force out, 9-2. Warneke, umpiring the game, said that in twenty-seven years in baseball he had never seen anything like it. I would think not.

Warneke umpired through the 1958 season, retired from baseball and returned home to Hot Springs, Arkansas. In 1960 he stood for election to be a local magistrate—an elected judge. Among his supporters was Col. Reed Landis, the son of Kennesaw Mountain Landis. "We're going to put the ole boy to work," explained Landis. "He's loafed long enough." Adlai Stevenson, when he ran for president, said he had walked so far in campaigning he had worn a hole in his shoe. "I must have walked twice as far as he did," Lon deadpanned. "I finished the campaign with holes in both shoes." In November 1960—the same day Kennedy was elected President—Warneke was elected as the County Judge of

Garland County (Hot Springs), Arkansas. He was elected by a margin of 192 votes—his lucky number, apparently.

Warneke served as county judge until the early 1970s, when he was forced into retirement by his health. He died of a heart attack in 1976.

Lon Warneke had a kid brother, Lester Warneke, who pitched several years in the minors. Lester had the same body as Lonnie, the same fastball, the same laconic manner. When the scouts saw him, they were excited, because they knew what a pitcher could do with that body and that fastball. But Lester never pitched in the majors.

It wasn't the fastball that made Lester's big brother who he was. It was the spunk, the determination. Warneke's secret was his "I'll show you" button. I don't really *know* why Lester Warneke didn't pitch in the majors, but I'm guessing that he was like most people. When there was an obstacle in front of him, he waited for it to go away. He didn't have that *thing* that Lonnie had, that drove him to push over whatever obstacle arose in his path. The scouts thought Lester looked just like Lonnie, but they missed the point of Lon Warneke. Baseball didn't come looking for Lonnie; Lonnie went looking to bust into baseball. That was what made him what he was.

TOMMY BRIDGES

ROB NEYER

Tommy Bridges' father and grandfather were both doctors, but he always wanted to be . . . a writer. Well, not always. Bridges, who grew up in a small town forty-five miles from Memphis, pursued a Bachelor's degree at the University of Tennessee for two years, then enrolled in the business school. In those days, major leaguers who attended a few years of college were, almost invariably, eventually said to be "graduates" of that college, and this was true of Bridges, as well. He did spend four years in Knoxville and he did star for the Vols on the diamond, but before earning a degree he left to play professional ball.

In 1929, Tigers scout Billy Doyle signed Bridges to his first pro contract. Pitching that summer for Wheeling in the Middle Atlantic League, he went 10-3 with a 3.11 ERA.

The Middle Atlantic League was Class C. In 1930, Bridges moved up to Evansville in the Class A Illinois-Indiana-Iowa League. When the Three-I league finished its schedule he ranked twenty-eighth in the league with 140 innings . . . and first with 189 strikeouts. He was twenty-three years old, and he was playing a different game than everybody else. Those strikeouts were plenty enough for the Tigers, who brought Bridges to the majors well before Evansville completed its season.

His first outing with the Tigers came on August 13 in the Bronx, and it was a humdinger. According to columnist Sam Murphy ("The Old Scout"), manager Bucky Harris asked Bridges, "Tom, you think you'd be ready to face those fellows the next inning?"

Bridges nodded.

"You know who you're going to face, don't you?" asked Harris. "Well, Babe Ruth, Gehrig and Lazzeri are going to come up. It is a hard test."

"I'll be ready," Bridges said.

Supposedly. It all sounds like something invented by a half-looped baseball writer on deadline. But the record shows that in the sixth inning, with the Tigers trailing the Yankees 10-6, Bridges did face those three future Hall of Famers in his first major-league game. He got Ruth on a pop-up, gave up a single to Lazzeri, struck out Gehrig, and retired Harry Rice (who does *not* have a plaque in Cooperstown) to escape the inning with no damage done.

Twelve days later, Bridges made his first major-league start, against the Browns in Detroit, and he beat them, 7-5. Not that it was easy. Bridges walked a dozen St. Louis hitters, including the first four in the ninth inning before he finally got lifted in favor of reliever Waite Hoyt, who got a double play to preserve the rookie's victory.

He never walked twelve hitters in one game again, but Bridges did struggle with his control. In 1931 he walked 108 hitters in 173 innings, and in 1932 he walked 119 hitters in 201 innings. So in 1933, Tigers manager Bucky Harris told Bridges to avoid using his curve—even then, "rated about the best in the big leagues"—until he was ahead of the hitter. As Ralph Cannon later wrote, "It is easier, of course, to control a fast ball, and so by relying more on it—and he has a very good fast ball, too, as well as a good change of pace—Bridges gradually acquired the control that was all he needed to make him a great pitcher."

History is rarely as tidy as we'd like. While it's true

He isn't big and husky, as you see him in the box. He's inches less than six feet tall when standing in his sox. He seems, in fact, a little frail, this Tiger pitching vet, who doesn't scale a hundred sixty pounds when soaking wet. But, still, for all his lack of size, the lad is hard and tough, with guile and power in his arm, and lots of pitching stuff. With loads of moxie in the clutch, and, when the chips are down, he throws the batters gobs of grief, and surely goes to town. Some other guys are faster when they let their hard one sail. But, kid, he's got the sweetest curve along the Big Time trail. And when he's got it hooking right, and when he's feeling grim, the bombers at the dusty plate all look alike to him. He's steady in the pinches when the sluggers start to clout. He knows the different batters, and he knows his way about. And when he's in a spot that gives a lot of lugs the shakes, he's cagy and he's nervy, and he's got just what it takes. Oh, the big and husky hurlers are impressive blokes to view whenever they get out there fogging hooks and fast ones through. But when you *gotta* have that game, with big dough on the line, it's little Tommy Bridges that I'll take out there for mine.

—W.R. HOEFER IN *BASEBALL MAGAZINE* (SEPTEMBER, 1939)

that Bridges' control did improve in '33, it's also true that he continued to walk his share of batters. And there's also good reason to think the advice from Bucky Harris might have come before 1933. Because on August 2, 1932, Bridges pitched the greatest game of his major-league career.

Going against the Senators in Detroit, Bridges sailed through the first eight innings. On the advice of Harris, Bridges relied mainly on his fastball and set down the first twenty-four Washington hitters in order. Meanwhile, the Tigers were building a huge lead, and when the ninth inning rolled around the score was 13-0.

Bridges retired the first two Senators in the ninth. Due next was Bob Burke, a pitcher. Would manager Walter Johnson send up a pinch-hitter for Burke? He would: Dave Harris, a good fastball hitter. Would Bridges continue to rely on his fastball? He would, and Harris lined Bridges' first pitch, a fastball, over shortstop Billy Rogell's head for a clean single. Bridges got the next guy, but the perfect game was gone.

There were people who thought it something less than sporting, for Johnson to send up a pinch-hitter with the Senators so far behind. That's silly, of course, and Bridges knew it. "I didn't want the perfect game to be given me on a platter," he said. "I wanted it with the opposition doing its best to keep me from winning."

If Bridges didn't spend a lot of time worrying about the perfect game that wasn't, he did always worry about throwing strikes. According to a 1941 article in *Baseball Magazine*, "Being a college man, Bridges is only moderately superstitious. He carries only one luck piece and that is a constructive item. It contains the story of a ball game he lost to Oglethorpe College while he was pitching for the University of Tennessee. Tommy lost that game on a wild pitch. During the years he was struggling to perfect his control with the Tigers he would occasionally take that yellowed clipping out and look at it. He never again wants to lose a game on a wild pitch."

Bridges pitched two famous games in his career.

The first was the nearly perfect game against the Senators in 1932. (Twice in 1933, Bridges again flirted with no-hitters. On April 23 against the Browns, he pitched no-hit ball for seven innings before giving up a single to Sammy West with one out in the eighth. And on July 20 in Washington, he pitched six hitless innings before giving up a home run to Joe Kuhel in the seventh. In all three of Bridges' brushes with greatness, he finished with a one-hitter. When Frank Graham asked Bridges if he thought he'd ever throw a no-hitter, he replied, "No. The odds are too heavy against a pitcher, and I've come so close three times it doesn't look as though I'll ever make it.")

The second was Game 6 of the 1935 World Series. The score was tied at three runs apiece heading into the ninth. Stan Hack led off for the Cubs, and drove Bridges' second pitch to the flagpole in deep center field for a triple. Man on third base, nobody out. As Joe Williams wrote in the *New York World-Telegram*, "The odds were 5 to 1 that at least one run would score. Under the circumstances, what with more than $2,000 riding on every thrown ball, that being the difference between the individual winners' and losers' share, the odds were probably 25 to 1. A passed ball, a wild pitch, an ordinary fly, an infield error—any of these could produce a run."

Billy Jurges came up next. Bridges threw three curveballs. Jurges swung three times and missed three times. One down.

Cubs pitcher Larry French came up next. Bridges threw two curveballs. French swung two times and missed two times. Bridges threw another curveball, and French tapped the ball back to the mound. Two down, and Hack was still on third.

Augie Galan came up next. A ball, a strike, a ball, "and then Galan lifted an easy fly to old Goose Goslin out in left, and to all intents and purposes the series was over."

Well, not really. The Tigers still had to score. And they did, thanks to Goslin's RBI single with two outs in the bottom of the ninth. Bridges didn't see it, though. In the locker room after the game, Tigers player-manager Mickey Cochrane, who'd scored the winning run, asked Bridges, "Boy, did you see that hit Goslin got?"

Replied Bridges, "No, I didn't. I was hunched down in the dressing room tunnel having a smoke. I heard the roar of the crowd when you got a hit and I decided to stay put for the rest of the inning just for luck."

A few minutes later, Cochrane said of Bridges, "Just look at him. That's what I said, just look at him and feel proud you were ever on the same team with him. I can say it only one way, he's 150 pounds of sheer guts!" (This perfectly sums up what Bridges' teammates thought about him. *Decades* later, Doc Cramer would say, "Tommy Bridges was 150 pounds of guts.")

The Tigers were World Series winners for the first time in franchise history, and the party in the city's streets and taverns lasted until dawn the next day. As Fred Lieb wrote, "Detroit had a terrible hang-over, but, gosh, it was worth it."

Remember, this came just a year after the Tigers had *lost* the World Series, to the Cardinals. And Bridges had pitched well in that one, too. He got knocked out in the fifth inning of the third game, but came back just two days later and pitched a complete game to beat St. Louis, 3-1. The '34 Series ended badly, with the 11-0 loss in Game 7, but of course it also made the World Championship in '35 all that much sweeter.

What was the key to Bridges' performance in Game 6 of the '35 Series? According to a press release sent out by the Cincinnati Reds (and why the Reds were sending out a press release about Tommy Bridges, I don't have the foggiest idea), "He had been pitching fast balls all through the game and then, after Hack tripled, he changed to curve ball pitching and no pitcher ever broke sharper curves to three successive batters than Bridges

Transcendental Graphics/ruckerarchive.com

did. For the space of the few minutes that it took him to retire three men he was unhittable by any three batters you can name."

This merely solidified the reputation of Bridges' phenomenal curveball, which was universally rated the best in the league, and perhaps the best anybody had seen since Three Finger Brown was pitching for the Cubs.

In 1933, Ralph Cannon wrote, "Hitters say that Bridges has one of the best curves in baseball, a fast, sharp-breaking ball that drops down and out."

Also in 1933, Jimmy Dykes said, "He has a hook that is a hook, and when he's on his game and can lay it where he wants to, you might as well bring a match up to the plate as a bat. Give Bridges control and he'll curve you right back to the bench."

In 1934, Dan Daniel wrote, "Bridges boasts the best right-hand curve in the American League."

As great as that curveball was, Bridges was far from a

one-pitch pitcher. Contemporary stories about Bridges rarely failed to mention his outstanding fastball—in fact, sometimes there's no mention of his curveball at all—and Mickey Cochrane always said that Bridges actually won more games with his fastball than his curve. Bridges himself said, "A curve isn't worth a hoot unless they respect your fastball."

Then again, Bridges' curve was so good that it usually didn't matter much if the hitters knew it was coming. As Birdie Tebbetts, who caught Bridges for eight seasons, remembered many years later, "Bridges won for 12 years with a curve every hitter knew was coming. He tipped off every curve, but if he got rid of the tip-off, he wouldn't have been able to throw the curve."

And like a lot of pitchers in those days, Bridges had at least one trick up his sleeve, which was especially useful after he'd lost the good zip on his fastball. Charlie Metro was a teammate of Bridges' with the Tigers in 1943. Nearly six decades later, Metro recalled,

> Tommy Bridges was in Detroit toward the end of his career. He had an absolutely great curve ball. Every once in a while, I would catch batting practice. Tommy would say, "Hey, Rook, get that glove." I'd get the glove, and we'd start warming up. Without telling me, he'd break off a curve that would drop down and hit me on the toes. Finally he would let me know. Then he'd say, "Now watch this. You haven't seen this." And he'd throw me the dangedest spitter you ever saw! That thing would hit me all over. I had a heck of a time catching it. I said, "When do you throw this?" He said, "You watch. You just keep watching me. You'll recognize it." Boy, if he'd get two strikes on a guy and maybe he had just one guy out or maybe this was the deciding hitter in the ball game, here would come that spitter. I never saw how he did it, and I watched him real close.

How Bridges threw his spitball may have been a mystery, but *that* he threw it wasn't much of a secret around the league. Paul Richards told a story about catching Bridges one day against the Senators. Richards put down his signal for the curve. Bridges shook him off. Richards put down his signal for the fastball. Bridges shook him off. Richards put down his signal for the change-up. Bridges shook him off.

"Well," Richards thought, "the only thing left is the spitter."

Richards was right, and Bridges struck out Stan Spence with three straight wet ones. Spence flung his bat to the ground, protesting to umpire Bill Summers. Senators manager Ossie Bluege came out and joined the fray. After a bit of that, Bluege, Spence, Richards, and Summers all trooped out to the supposed scene of the crime.

"Tommy," Summers said, "these gentlemen say you've been throwing spitters."

"Why, Mr. Summers," Bridges said, "don't you know the spitter has been outlawed for years? How would I ever learn to throw one?"

Thus assured, the delegation headed back toward the plate. Before they got far, though, Bridges put his glove next to his mouth and addressed Summers in a stage whisper.

"Hey, Bill. Wasn't that last one a sweetheart, though?"

(Speaking of Summers, in 1945 he was asked which pitcher was the toughest for him. His response? Bridges. "Tommy had an overhand curve that dropped off the table. It could be caught in the dirt and yet be a strike. Working with Bridges outside Detroit often meant taking an awful lot from the fans.")

Baseball players in the 1930s weren't nearly as big as they are today, of course, but even then, few could write about Bridges without mentioning his slight build. In just the first few years of his career, Bridges was described at various weights ranging from 144 to 165 pounds. Whatever the correct figure, there's no question that he was very small for a major-league pitcher, even in those days.

And it might have been Bridges' size that resulted in a significant change to his job description in 1938. From 1934 through '36, Bridges averaged thirty-six starts, twenty-two wins, and about 280 innings per season. But in 1937 he started only thirty-one games and pitched 245 innings, and in no season thereafter did Bridges start more than twenty-eight games or pitch 200 innings.

It wasn't that he couldn't still pitch. Bridges had an off year in '38 (13-9, 4.59 ERA), but in each of the next five seasons his ERA was significantly better than league average.

He just didn't pitch as often, due to both injuries and (apparently) his managers figuring he couldn't handle the strain of pitching every four or five days. In 1941 *and* 1942 *and* 1943, Bridges started twenty-two games. This was not completely a coincidence. There were, in those days, twenty-two weeks in the baseball season, and over those three seasons Bridges was generally a once-a-week pitcher. In 1941, he started on each of the season's last five Sundays. In 1942, seven of his twenty-two starts came on Sunday. And in 1943, twelve of his twenty-two starts came on Sunday, including each of the season's last nine Sundays (and eleven of the last twelve).

He'd become a Sunday pitcher, just like Ted Lyons. Could he still pitch? In '43, Bridges posted a 2.37 ERA, the lowest of his career. Granted, most of the boys were in the service . . . and that's where Bridges went in 1943, too. He was old but still sound of body. So that November, just a few weeks shy of his thirty-seventh birthday, Bridges was inducted into the army and he reported for duty at Fort Sheridan, Illinois. "I'm ready to go wherever the Army thinks I can be most useful," he said.

Which turned out to be Camp Crowder, Missouri, where Bridges played a lot of baseball. He was discharged in late August of 1945, and just a few days later he started for the Tigers against the White Sox. He got the victory but didn't pitch all that well, and saw action in only three more games—all in relief—the rest of the way as the Tigers out-dueled the Senators for the American League pennant. He pitched a couple of innings in the World Series, out of the bullpen, and gave up three runs in a game the Tigers wound up losing, 8-7.

In 1946 Bridges returned to the Tigers as a coach. Or at least that was the plan. A couple of months before the season started, Bridges asked to be dropped as a coach and added as a player. Manager Steve O'Neill said, "I'll use him as a spot pitcher. Tommy needs only seven more victories to break into the 200 victory class. He thinks he can make it, and so do I."

Bridges agreed, saying, "I'm a cinch to do it."

He didn't. Bridges won just once, in the second game of a doubleheader on May 5th, and he lost once (at Fenway Park on May 2nd, when Ted Williams homered in the bottom of the tenth). On September 16th, having worked in only nine games all season, and not at all since a relief outing nearly two months earlier, Bridges got his release.

And then, like a lot of star pitchers in those days, Bridges went to the minors. He had to earn a living and pitching was his livelihood, so he pitched.

In 1947 Bridges hooked up with the Pacific Coast League's Portland Beavers, and in his first start he pitched a two-hitter. Afterward, manager Jim Turner said, "My intention is to use Bridges as our 'Sunday pitcher,' much as the Chicago White Sox used Ted Lyons so effectively for many years.' "

Bridges was effective, too. And on April 20, he finally got his no-hitter.

It was Bridges' first start in Portland, the San Francisco Seals were in town, and Bridges beat the Seals, 2-0. Bones Sanders, who walked in the eighth, was the sole baserunner. With two outs in the top of the ninth, Bridges again faced a pinch-hitter, just like he had in 1933 . . . but this time the pinch-hitter, Sal Taormina, didn't get a hit, as Bridges recorded the game-ending out on Taormina's grounder to the first baseman.

Afterward, Turner said,

> In 24 years in professional baseball, and starting on my 25th, Tommy Bridges' no-run, no-hitter Sunday was the best pitched game I have ever seen. Not one of the best—the best of all, by far . . . I saw Vander Meer of Cincinnati shut out our Boston club in '38, the first of his two consecutive no-run no-hitters and 21 no-hit innings . . . and it didn't compare with Tommy's game . . . I said when we signed Tommy Bridges I felt sure he was still a major league pitcher, and repeated it emphatically after his first game in Los Angeles. Now let me add that Tommy could still take his pitching turn with any club in either major league and win his 15 games a season.

Perhaps, but Bridges didn't get that chance.

Injuries limited him to thirteen games in '47, but he went 7-3 with a 1.64 ERA. Healthy in 1948, Bridges went 15-11—including nine straight wins, the last a twelve-inning, 1-0 victory against the Seals on August 31—with a 2.86 ERA that was good for fourth in the league.

Last summer I talked to Charlie Silvera, Portland's catcher in 1947 and '48, and Silvera told me that Bridges could have returned to the major leagues in 1948 . . . with the New York Yankees.

> Back in 1948, Portland had a partial agreement with the Yankees. The Yankees were in a pennant race, in '48, and in Portland we had a chance to get into the

playoffs. Tommy missed his assignment, and I went to Turner and I said, "Jim, what's wrong with Tommy?"

"Well," he says, "I'll tell you what happened. The Yankees want to bring him back for the stretch drive, for the last month or so. Tommy's been thinking about it, and I'm going to hold him out one more day and he's going to give me his decision." And Tommy decided not to go.

But Tommy still had great stuff. Still had the great curveball. He was a little erratic at that time, though, and his fastball was erratic. I don't think he could see. Of all the pitchers I caught, Tommy Bridges crossed me up more than anybody else. I'd go out there sometimes and I'd look at him, and I'd doubt where he could see. I think that's one of the reasons that he didn't want to go back.

So Bridges stayed in Portland, and in 1949 he pitched again for the Beavers. He was forty-two years old, and went 11-11 with a still-decent 3.82 ERA. Late that season, a number of PCL players, including Bridges, were asked about their "toughest things in baseball." To which Bridges replied, "trying to throw the same stuff as I did ten years ago."

He pitched again in 1950, but washed out with both Seattle and San Francisco after brief trials. And shortly afterward, we lose track of Tommy Bridges . . . for a while, anyway.

For the entire 1930s, Billy Rogell played shortstop behind Bridges. In 1942, shortly after his career ended, Rogell won a seat on the Detroit city council, and he stayed for thirty-eight years.

When I'd drive down to council meetings, I'd go down First Street. That was a one-way street. There was a sporting goods shop. One day, as I was crossing Michigan Avenue, I noticed this guy lying by this store. I drove about two stores down and I thought, "Goddamn, that looked like Bridges." So I backed the car up and got out and sure enough, it's Tommy Bridges. Jesus Christ, he looked terrible.

So I took him over to City Hall, the old one, and got him cleaned up. Got him some coffee to drink, took him out to breakfast, talked to him. I said, "Tom, where the hell do you live? I didn't know you were in Detroit." He says, "I live in Toledo." See, he'd gotten divorced from his wife and married this waitress he'd met in Seattle or some damned place. The husband was after him to kill him and all that crap. He came to Detroit looking for a job.

Rogell got Bridges a job selling beer for a local brewery. In retrospect, that might not seem like the perfect place for a man down on his luck. A few days later, somebody from the brewery called Rogell, wanting to know, "Where the hell's Tommy?"

As Rogell remembered, "Well, how the hell do I know where Bridges is? He never showed up. He went way down. It was terrible to see that. But nice guys go, too, you know."

From Rogell's account, it's hard to tell when this actually happened. Sometime in the 1950s, probably. Bridges did coach for the Reds in 1951, but if he had a significant impact on any of Cincinnati's young pitchers, it's escaped our attention. Afterward, he falls off the baseball map, though according to his Associated Press obituary, Bridges did work for a while as a tire salesman in Detroit. In 1968, Bridges died in Nashville. He was sixty-one, and the cause of death was listed as "carcinoma of liver."

BUCKY WALTERS

BILL JAMES

The Philadelphia Phillies could be counted on to lose just about 100 games every year, and Jimmie Wilson was doing his damnedest to change that. The Phillies' young third baseman, Bucky Walters, was a standout defensive player who hit .260 that year, a little pop, but he was basically the kind of third baseman you get if you're going to lose 100 games a year. Wilson thought that Walters' career was going nowhere as a third baseman, but that he had a real future if he would convert to the pitching mound.

Bucky told him no, he was going to stay at third base.

William Henry Walter Jr. was born near Philadelphia in 1909. His father, of the same name, was a telephone company employee, also called "Bucky." Little Bucky dropped out of school in 1925, intent on becoming an electrician. In 1929 a scout named Howard Lohr spotted him playing sandlot baseball—he was the shortstop—and recommended him to Montgomery of the Southeastern League. He signed with Montgomery and was farmed out by them to the Piedmont League.

In 1929 Walters (sportswriters for some reason had appended an *s*) played all over the field, more at third base than anywhere else, and had a 5-6 record as a pitcher—four of the wins, at least according to reports by journalists who I will guarantee you never double-checked, coming against the league champion, Greensboro.

From 1930 to 1933 Walters worked his way through the minor leagues, and also played center for the Philadelphia Elks, a professional basketball team. (Bucky was a hair over six foot tall. Pro basketball was a little different then.) He had a cup of coffee with the Boston Braves in 1931, got married that winter, returned to the minors, played for Montreal in 1932, had a little longer cup of coffee in 1932, and then ate the Pacific Coast League for breakfast in 1933, batting .376 with 92 RBI in 91 games for Mission. The numbers are a little phony; Mission was a great place to hit. The Mission team that year scored 1,027 runs, leading the Pacific Coast League, but finished 79-108.

Tom Yawkey had just purchased the Red Sox, and Eddie Collins was trolling the PCL with a loaded checkbook. Collins purchased Bucky for the Red Sox (who have a very bad history with players with "Buck" in their name). Walters broke his finger shortly after the purchase, but played respectably for the Red Sox, hitting .256 with four homers and 26 RBI in 52 games.

He started slowly in 1934, however, and was sold to the Phillies for $15,000. He had a hot streak after joining the Phillies, played well for a while, then had a serious attack of poison ivy that kept him on the sidelines for several weeks. When he got back in the lineup he didn't hit, and lost his job at third base. Seeing Walters sitting on the bench, Jimmie Wilson wondered if he could get something out of Walters as a pitcher, since Walters had a wonderful arm and had pitched a little in the minors.

The story of Bucky's conversion to the mound was often and dramatically retold in the early 1940s, after Bucky had won an MVP award and been the best pitcher in the league two or three times. The details vary a little, of course, but the hero of the narrative, whether told by Walters or by Wilson, is always Jimmie Wilson; it was Wilson who thought that Walters, a humdrum infielder, could be a great pitcher. Walters threw a natural sinker. Wilson, a catcher, knew that that was rare, and that it was very hard to *teach* a pitcher to throw a sinker. Walters was given by nature not only a great arm, but a great weapon. Wilson just couldn't stand to see him wasting it as a third baseman.

Walters, however, was *not* convinced that he could be a star pitcher. A cautious man by nature and a so-so pitcher in the minors, he thought he would be better off as an infielder. Finally . . . distilling what seems like a credible account from a number of reporters' more colorful variations . . . in the spring of 1935, the Reds were training in Orlando, Florida, which was their spring training home for eons. At the instigation of Jimmie Wilson, two of his coaches, Dick Spalding and Hans Lobert, dragged Walters to a road house on the edge of town, and began plying him with the best wine available. Then they began telling him what a sucker he was for plodding along as a second-rate infielder, when he had the makings of a first-rate pitcher who could be making five or six times as much money. Walters listened politely, and, after a while, Wilson "happened" to join the group. Spalding and Lobert "explained" the discussion, and Wilson chimed in, "What's the use of talking to him? If he's satisfied to be a bush leaguer, that's his privilege, isn't it?"

Walters finally snapped, told Wilson that he was no bush leaguer, and that he would pitch tomorrow to prove it. And he did pitch, and he did pitch well. The conversion was under way. Walters was 9-9 with a 4.17 ERA in 1935—pretty good for a raw pitcher on a 64-win team with a 4.76 team ERA. In '36 he led the National League in losses (he was 11-21), but then, the team lost 100 games, and Walters, as their best pitcher, had to take his share of the abuse, plus his arm hurt the second half of the season. In 1937 he was 14-15 with a team that lost another 92 games.

In June 1938, Walters was traded/sold to the Cincinnati Reds. A word of background: the Reds by the early 1930s had become the worst team in the National League, even worse than the Phillies. They had finished dead last in 1931, 1932, 1933, and 1934. They had scrambled out of the basement in '35 and '36, but fallen back into it in '37.

After the '37 season Bill McKechnie was hired to manage the Reds, with attendant promises from ownership to provide the resources to improve the team. McKechnie began buying players—not high-priced stars, but useful players whose abilities had not been fully utilized by other teams. His judgment was extraordinary. He collected men of good values, good work habits, all-around athletic ability and a willingness to work, but men who, for one reason or another, simply had not been highly successful in the major leagues. By doing this he built not only a championship team, but probably the *nicest*, most *likable* championship team of all time.

Negotiating with the Phillies for a pitcher, McKechnie agreed to a price reported as $47,500 or $55,000, plus two players, for his choice of any pitcher on the Philadelphia staff. The feeling among reporters was that he would and probably should take either Hugh Mulcahy or Claude Passeau. The man he wanted was Walters—the team's best pitcher the previous year, but struggling along with a 4-8 record, 5.23 ERA.

Walters, however, was what McKechnie wanted: a good man, no ego, good work habits, and a terrific athlete. In moving from Philadelphia to Cincinnati, Walters moved from the worst pitcher's park in the National League to the second-best. He moved, simultaneously, from a team with a terrible defense to a team with perhaps the best defensive infield in major league history up to that point—four Gold Glove-quality infielders behind him. Half of his ERA disappeared in an instant. He emerged almost immediately as the premier pitcher in the National League.

In 1939 Walters not only went 27-11 with a 2.29 ERA, but also hit .325 and drove in 16 runs, leading the Reds to their first National League pennant in 20 years. He was elected the National League's Most Valuable Player, with one of the highest vote totals ever (with that particular voting system, which was in place from 1938 through 1960). That winter he attended, by actual count, 65 banquets and awards ceremonies. He lived during the off-season in Germantown, Pennsylvania, very near to a well-equipped YMCA. He made it to the Y three times a week without fail, and survived the banquet circuit without falling out of his usual superb physical condition. Let me quote his description of his training routine, given to Ed Burns in Philadelphia that winter:

> I have no difficulty in picking up some fellow who wants to play a little easy handball, or squash. I avoid those guys who play as though they were defending a world championship. I'm out for a lot of leg work, a fair sweat, but no fatigue. The minute I feel the least

> tired, I quit exercising, take a short cabinet bath, then go on the rubbing table. My masseur doesn't know, so far as his operations indicate, whether I pitch with my right or left arm. He knows I walk and run on two legs . . .
>
> During the season my weight ranges from 175 to 185, mostly according to the weather. Today I weigh 188. I'll weigh about that when I go to Tampa very soon and will knock off those three pounds in golf . . . I haven't discovered any symptoms of "old age" and until I do, I'm not going to worry about diet. I eat anything I like, and that includes potatoes and the milder desserts, like sherbet and ice cream. I eat a good breakfast, frequently skip lunch and bear down at dinner.
>
> I never take any training advice from Old John Barley corn, but I smoke too much, I think, especially in the off-season, when I get a little fidgety.

His seriousness about conditioning enabled him to follow his MVP season with another almost as good, going 22-10 with a league-leading 2.48 ERA. He was third in the voting for the National League's MVP award. The Reds made it back to the World Series in 1940, and this time they won it, Walters pitching a three-hitter in Game Two (a 5-3 victory) and a five-hit shutout in Game Six (4-0); he also doubled and scored in the first game, and hit a two-run homer in the second. Reporting the game for the *New York World-Telegram*, Joe Williams wrote that "Walter slapped the American Leaguers right in the puss with a bucket of whitewash . . . By way of adding parsley to the mackerel Walters gave the Joe Louis to one of (Fred) Hutchinson's fast balls in the eighth and hit it out of the park for a home run." You know, if I ever start my own newspaper, I'm going to bring back that kind of reporting.

In an irony that only Bucky could have enjoyed, Walters—the natural hero of the 1940 World Series—was bumped from that spot by Jimmie Wilson, the man who had converted him to a pitcher many years earlier. Wilson, a coach with the Reds, had been virtually retired for three years when a series of accidents and tragedies left the Reds without competent catching. Wilson stepped into the breech, hit .353 in the World Series—and stole Bucky's thunder.

This, however, is getting just a tiny bit ahead of the story. In June 1940, Walters struck Billy Jurges in the head with a pitch, putting him in the hospital for several days. Walters, well known as a sensitive man, was shaken by the accident. Almost a decade later, hired to manage a major league baseball club, Walters located Jurges and sent him a telegram offering him a job as a coach. Jurges, already well employed, declined the offer.

In August 1940, the Reds' backup catcher, Willard Hershberger, committed suicide in a Boston hotel room. Walters, whose normal roommate was Billy Werber, had reserved a single room for the trip to Boston, expecting his wife to join him. His wife stayed home due to a minor illness of their son, however, and so Walters was alone in the hotel. Werber recalled in his autobiography many years later that Walters, shaken up by the suicide, had asked Werber to join him in his room; he just couldn't stand the emptiness. Werber said no; he had already moved in all of his stuff, he couldn't easily switch rooms. But while Werber went to dinner, Bucky got into his room and moved all of his stuff down to Bucky's room. He just could not stand to be alone.

That's a bit of an odd story, and here's an even odder one. In November 1939, Otto Knabe, second baseman for the Phillies from 1907 to 1913, was put on trial in Philadelphia on a charge of operating a gambling house. His co-defendant, a former light heavyweight boxing champion named Battling Barney Levinsky, pleaded guilty and was placed on probation. Knabe pleaded innocent, and called Bucky Walters and Gerald Nugent, president of the Phillies, who both testified that Knabe was a man of good character and not no stinkin' gambler. Knabe was acquitted. This is all I know about that story.

Here's another anecdote, actually a quote from Harold Kaese, *Famous American Athletes of Today, Eighth Series*, who interviewed the Reds' clubhouse attendant for insights into the superstar:

> Bucky's a nice quiet fellow, not fat-headed, and not a pop-off; but he's got some humor. You know, he must spend a couple of dollars a season buying Vaseline to put on the handle of my broom. Every time I pick it up to sweep something, it's squirting out of my hands. Then I know Bucky has been up to his tricks again.

In addition to his natural sinker, his batting skill and his near-legendary ability to field his position, Walters relied heavily on the pitch now known as the slider. He was taught to throw the pitch in 1935 by Chief Bender, then a coach/hanger-on with the Philadelphia A's. This fact is well documented, but never clearly explained is how Bender came to be working with Walters. I would assume the nexus between the two is Philadelphia. In any case, Walters never *called* the pitch a slider. Since Bender never gave him a name for the pitch, he just called it his curve ball—the term "curve ball" still being used, in the 1930s, to mean any breaking pitch. But by the time Walters retired the slider had become a fairly common pitch, and it is very clear that Walters' curve was, in fact, a slider, and a good one. McKechnie never liked the slider, and discouraged its use, but Walters threw it anyway.

After 1940 the Reds began to slide out of contention. Bill McKechnie believed in pitching and defense all the way, with no compromises. As an organizing principle in constructing a team, this was great. As a fixed object in maintaining the team, it was disastrous. The Reds won the World Championship in 1940 with a team that scored only 29 runs more than the league average. In 1941 they were 42 runs below average; in '42 they were 71 runs below average. In 1944 they were 89 runs below average. In 1945 they were 153 below average—yet McKechnie continued to preach pitching and defense, pitching and defense. Pitching and defense are going to turn this thing around for us. Walters continued to post outstanding ERAs, but his won-lost records in '41 and '42 were 19-15, 15-14. In '43 he injured his leg jumping hurdles in spring training; troubled by that and an irregular appendix, he pitched just as much but not quite as well, finishing 15-15. After the 1943 season Walters was scheduled to go on a tour of the Pacific with Stan Musial, Frankie Frisch and others, but had to back out at the last minute due to an emergency appendectomy. In a perhaps-related note—who knows?—he snapped back in '44 with a 23-8 record, 2.40 ERA, making him once more the best pitcher in the league. His .280 batting average helped alleviate the Reds' chronic shortage of run support.

On November 27, 1944, Walters left for Europe with a group of baseball stars; Walters, Mel Ott, Frankie Frisch, and a few others would tell baseball stories, sign autographs, back-slap and answer questions for groups of soldiers. The tour lasted through December and most of January—among the fiercest and deadliest months of the war in Europe, incidentally—and Bucky returned to the United States with pain in his elbow, diagnosed as arthritis. He continued to pitch well in '45 and '46, but not nearly as much as he had before, and in '47 he was no longer effective.

In August 1948—still an active player in theory, although nearly a permanent fixture on the disabled list—Walters was named to manage his team, which was then staggering toward a seventh-place finish. This was not a happy experience. The Reds, about ten players short of a contender, staggered miserably to another seventh-place finish in '49. In August of that year, Dan Daniel opined, "It is expected that the next resignation among the pilots of the majors will come from the ailing Bucky Walters of Cincinnati. Walters, who could take the jolts as they came when he was pitching, is not built for the rigors of managerial life and has been warned by doctors to get out as fast as he can." Disdaining the hints and the medical guidance, Bucky was fired in the last week of the season. Joe Williams, bumping into Walters at a mid-winter function, reported that "I was shocked at the change in the former pitching great. Where once he was cheerful and articulate now he seemed hurt, and depressed. To questions he was tight lipped."

For several years after that his health was less than perfect. At one point, coaching in the minors, he passed out on the bench in the middle of a game, and had to be rushed to the hospital by ambulance. The trouble was traced to an ulcer. He remained in the game, however; he coached for the Boston Braves from 1950 to mid-season, 1952, went to the minors to manage the Braves' top farm club for half a season, took the team to the pennant, then returned to the majors as the pitching coach. Bill Rigney was hired to manage the New York Giants in 1956, and decided he wanted Bucky Walters to be his pitching coach. (Where Rigney and Walters had hooked up, and why Rigney liked Walters so much in this role, I do not know.) Anyway, Horace Stoneham, owner of the Giants, contacted Walters and offered him the job. This turned out to be a mistake. Walters was still under contract to the Milwaukee Braves, who took umbrage at the offer. Apologies, mumbles . . . apologies accepted, permission granted; Walters got the job, and the tampering flap stamped him as a valuable man, one of the most visible pitching coaches of the 1950s.

The smile was back on his face. Walters coached with the Giants for two years, 1956 and '57. Johnny Antonelli credited him with getting his career restarted after a lackluster season in '55 and a poor start in '56. He didn't seem to do much for the rest of the staff, as the Giants fell hopelessly out of contention and, at the end of the '57 season, broke and ran for California. Walters was offered $25,000, in those days a premium salary for a coach, to move west with the team, but he turned it down because he didn't want to be so far away from his family. A few days later he did an about-face, called Stoneham and tried to accept the offer, but was informed that the position had already been filled. He landed on his feet; just a few days later, he was hired to be the farm director for the Phillies, his hometown team. He held that job for just a couple of years, drifted out of baseball, and landed a public relationship job with a Philadelphia custom machine company, a job he held until his retirement in the mid-1970s. He died peacefully in 1991, one day after his 82nd birthday.

BILLY PIERCE

ROB NEYER

To suggest that Billy Pierce got his professional career off to a good start would be something of an understatement. He was born in Detroit, the son of a druggist. In the spring of 1944, a few months before he graduated from high school, Pierce signed with the Tigers. He went to spring training in 1945 and started the season on the major-league roster (in 1945, there were a great number of very young and very old players on major-league rosters). As Pierce later recalled,

> For the first six weeks of the season I sat on the Tigers' bench and didn't pitch. Then I was sent to Buffalo. I returned to the Tigers before September 1, so I was on Detroit for three-fifths of the year and we won the World Championship. I pitched only 10 innings all year and didn't pitch in the World Series—but I was eligible to pitch and received a ring at the age of 18! I didn't know it would be my only world title.

(Oops, didn't mean to give away too much there. But trust me, there's still plenty of drama left in our story.)

In 1946, with the veterans back from the war, Pierce went back to the minors, but pitched only ten games for Buffalo before hurting his back in June. "I was in the Ford hospital for a while," he remembered. "During the winter they would bake me in an oven three days a week. They decided the pain came from my being a boy doing a man's work. So I rested."

In 1947 Pierce returned to Buffalo, where Paul Richards had taken over as catcher-manager. It wasn't the first time they'd met. As Richards later told Donald Honig,

> Billy Pierce is quite a pitcher. You know, I first ran into him when I was playing with Detroit in 1945 and he was working out with them. In fact, he got into a few games that year. He was just a kid. His father owned a drugstore about a block from where I was living. I'd go in now and then to buy something, and there was this kid clerking behind the counter. I never paid any attention to him. Then out at the ball park we had this little left-hander who I'd warm up occasionally. One day he walked up to me on the field and said, "You know, you won't even speak to me when you come into our drugstore."
>
> "What are you talking about?" I asked.
>
> "That's my father's drugstore," he said. "You were in there last night."
>
> I took a good hard look at him and, sure enough, he was the clerk.

Pierce pitched well in '47 and would later say of Richards, "He said Detroit wanted me to pitch only on occasion because of my back. He'd catch when I pitched and tried to slow me down by holding on to the ball." Pierce started only twenty-three games (and relieved in five more), but his 14-8 record and 3.87 ERA were enough to get him back into the majors in '48, all of which he spent with the big club (though he rarely pitched; twenty-two games and fifty-five innings). He struggled with the Tigers, but still figured as a big part of the team's future. Until . . .

> In November, I went over to my fiancee's house. We turned on the radio and I learned from a disk jockey that I had been traded to the White Sox. I was traded for Aaron Robinson and 10 grand because the Tigers wanted a left-handed-hitting catcher who could take advantage of the short porch in right field. The Tigers wanted to give the Sox Ted Gray instead of me, but Chicago wouldn't go for it . . . It was a bad shock to be traded from Detroit.

For the first few years he was in the majors, Pierce—all five feet, ten inches, and 160-some pounds of him—just reared back and let 'er loose. And Pierce could certainly throw hard. As Joe DiMaggio supposedly said after batting against him, "That little so-and-so is a marvel. So little—and all that speed. And I mean speed! He got me out of there on a fastball in the ninth that I'd have needed a telescope to see."

But early on, the speed wasn't enough. Well, it was enough to make Pierce a *good* pitcher; in 1949 and '50 with Chicago, he posted better-than-league-average ERA's. But he also walked more hitters than he struck out.

And then in 1951, Paul Richards came into Billy Pierce's life yet again, this time as the White Sox's new manager.

Richards got a lot of the credit for Hal Newhouser becoming one of the league's best pitchers in the 1940s, and likewise he would get a lot of the credit for Billy Pierce becoming one of the league's best pitchers in the 1950s. According to Richards, "I worked a little with him on his windup to help his delivery and convinced him that he had to throw a slider and an occasional change of pace, and that was all he needed."

In Richards' first season in Chicago, Pierce went 15-14 with a 3.03 ERA after entering with career marks of 22-31 and 4.18. The most striking improvement was in his control of the strike zone. In 391 innings over the previous two seasons, Pierce had walked 249 hitters while striking out only 213. Under Richards, Pierce's strikeout rate actually fell slightly (and temporarily, as it turned out), but his walk rate fell *significantly,* from one walk every two innings to one walk every three.

Forty years later, Pierce said of his transformation, "I learned to control my fastball better and, at Richards' request, learned a third pitch to go with my fastball and curve—a slider. Developing the slider helped me tremendously because it gave me a third out pitch. I threw it almost as hard as my fastball, but I could throw it for strikes better than the fast ball or good curve . . . Richards made me work on it, and it took me about two years before it was consistent."

Pierce didn't really begin to refine his slider until near the end of the '51 season. The change really showed up in 1952 (15-12, 2.57), and then he got off to a fast start in 1953. "Pierce primarily is a fast ball pitcher," Richards said that spring. "He can blast the ball past anybody pretty regularly. But he has improved the past two seasons because he has learned to mix speed with curves and an occasional slider."

He started the '53 All-Star Game (and would start in '55 and '56, too), and in three innings the only blemish was Stan Musial's single to center field. Pierce finished the season with eighteen wins, and for the first time he led the American League in something (strikeouts, with 186). That wasn't the only time, though. He would also lead the league in ERA (1.97 in 1955; he was the only major leaguer between 1946 and '63 to post a sub-2.00 ERA), wins (20 in 1957), and complete games (three straight seasons, beginning in 1956).

Pierce's tenure with the White Sox might be classed as just short of brilliant. He threw four one-hitters, and on June 27, 1958, he just missed becoming the first left-hander in major-league history to twirl a perfect game. Facing the Senators before 11,300 fans at Comiskey Park, Pierce retired the first twenty-six batters he faced, and owned a 3-0 lead with two outs in the top of the ninth. But Washington manager Cookie Lavagetto—who, as a pinch-hitter, famously broke up a World Series no-hitter in 1947—sent up a pinch-hitter, Ed Fitz Gerald, and Fitz Gerald doubled. Afterward, Pierce said, "The pitch . . . was a good one that had a sharp break but he still was able to get around on it."

In 1982 Pierce told Bill Madden, "The book on Fitz Gerald was that he was a fastball hitter on the first ball and liked it inside where he could pull it. So we threw him a curve away and he hit it into right for a solid hit . . . I didn't feel that badly about it, really. It didn't mean that much at the moment. But now . . . well, now I wish I had got it. It would have been nice." (Pierce did strike out Albie Pearson to seal his third straight shutout.)

That 1958 season was Pierce's last great one. In '59, his ERA jumped nearly a full run (from 2.68 to 3.62), he went 14-15, and he wasn't given a starting assignment in

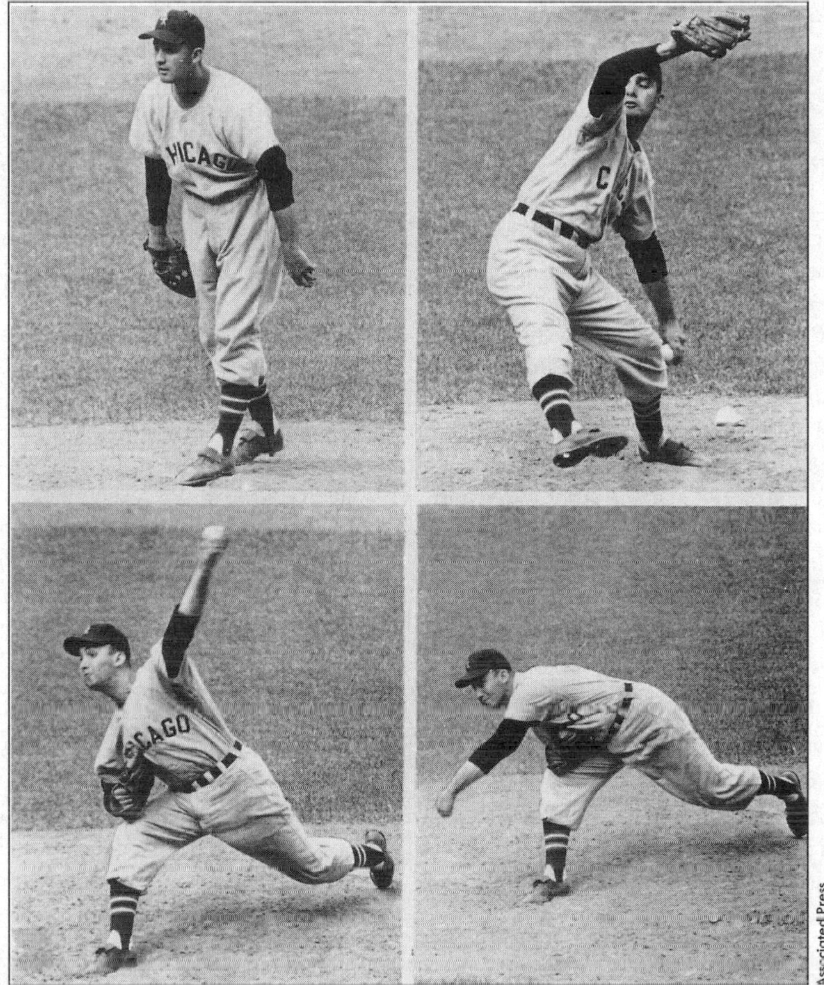

Associated Press

the White Sox's first World Series in forty years (they lost to the Dodgers).

Why didn't Pierce start in the Series? Early Wynn started three times, which made sense because Wynn won twenty-two games that season. Bob Shaw started twice, which made sense because he went 18-6 with a 2.69 ERA (and he pitched well in the Series). The other start went to Dick Donovan, who'd gone 9–10 with a 3.66 ERA (nearly identical to Pierce's). So if there's a question here, it's "Why did Donovan start instead of Pierce?"

If anybody knows, apparently they're not talking. More than thirty years later, White Sox outfielder Al Smith told Danny Peary, "I was surprised that Al Lopez didn't start Billy Pierce. We all knew why Lopez didn't pitch him, but we never told anyone and I won't say now. I will say that I thought he should have pitched. He'd been pitching all year, hadn't he?"

Actually, no. Pierce missed three weeks in August and September because of what was called a "chronic hip condition." He did return to the rotation on September 7 and pitched decently down the stretch, and it's also true that Donovan hadn't won a game since the 2nd of September.

Smith's support isn't surprising, because Pierce was as well-liked as anybody on the team. He didn't drink, but once said, "If another player wanted to drink, fine. I could go along and have a coke. I never had problems with other ballplayers, where if I didn't drink I wasn't part of the group. They understood that I'd rather be at the movies."

Pierce and Nellie Fox (his longtime roommate) were considered the leaders on the club, and Pierce was for years the club's union player representative. Later, Pierce pitched for San Francisco (oops, giving away too much again . . .), and Giants pitching coach Larry Jansen would say, "Never a bad word about anybody—the nicest man you'd ever want to meet."

Reading through newspaper clippings about Pierce's career, one finds only one instance in which he comes across as something less than a hail fellow well met. On November 30, 1961, the White Sox traded Billy Pierce and Don Larsen to the Giants for pitchers Eddie Fisher, Dom Zanni, and outfielder Bob Farley. Pierce's reaction: "I am not surprised. But it's a rotten trick and I will make Al Lopez sorry he did it." (Granted, Pierce quite possibly still held a grudge over not starting in the '59 World Series.)

The word around the American League was that Pierce was damaged goods, that his hip problem and a sore shoulder weren't going to get better. And a few months later, Pierce pitched like a man with a hip problem and a sore shoulder, posting a 16.45 ERA during spring training with the Giants.

Nevertheless, he broke camp with a slot in the rotation, and in his first start, on April 13 in San Francisco, he beat the Reds 7-2, giving up just two hits and three walks in seven and one-third innings.

Pierce also won his second decision, and his third, and he just kept on winning, running his record to 8-0 in his eighth start on June 1 before finally losing a close one to the Cubs on June 7. Pierce's luck got worse in his next start. Pitching against the Reds in Cincinnati, he got spiked in the first inning and wound up taking a dozen stitches. He next pitched on July 15, got hammered in three-plus innings, and then not again until August 2 when he re-assumed his spot in the rotation.

On September 26, the last (scheduled) Wednesday of the regular season, Pierce beat the Cardinals to keep the Giants just two games behind the first-place Dodgers. On Thursday, both contenders lost. Friday, the Dodgers lost to the Cardinals and the Giants and Astros were rained out at Candlestick. Saturday, the Dodgers lost again and the Giants split a doubleheader with Houston.

That left the Giants one game behind the Dodgers, with one game to play. The story of that Sunday afternoon has been told well in other places, so suffice to say the Dodgers lost 1-0, the Giants won 2-1 . . . and so just like in 1951, the Dodgers and Giants would play a best-of-three series to decide the National League pennant.

The Giants had a weird staff that season. Among the four pitchers who started more than fifteen games, nobody had an ERA higher than 3.53 (Billy O'Dell) . . . or lower than 3.36 (Juan Marichal). In the middle were Pierce and Jack Sanford. The playoff series would begin on October 1, a Monday. Sanford and Marichal had started in the doubleheader on Saturday, O'Dell on Sunday.

Which left Billy Pierce. To face Sandy Koufax.

It wasn't any contest, as Pierce pitched a three-hitter to shut out the Dodgers (and run his Candlestick winning streak to twelve games: twelve wins, zero losses on the season).

Pierce was, by most accounts, relying mostly on slow stuff by the time he joined the Giants, but he could still throw the ball hard when he wanted to. Watching that first playoff game from the press box, longtime National League umpire Babe Pinelli exclaimed, "Look at him fire that fast one! He's been in so many clutch games that they're nothing to him!" And according to Pierce, the fastball *still* was his best pitch.

The playoff series shifted south for the second game. Heading to the bottom of the sixth the Giants held a 5-0 lead; to that point, they'd skunked L.A. in the two games, 13-0. But the Dodgers scored seven runs in the sixth, then one more in the bottom of the ninth to break a 7-7 tie and force a third game.

What ensued was a near-replay of what had happened eleven years earlier between the same two teams (but a continent away). Just as they had in 1951, the Dodgers owned a lead after eight innings. And just as they had in 1951, the Giants jumped ahead in the ninth. This time the Giants were the road team, though, so the Dodgers would have one last chance. Juan Marichal had pitched the first seven innings for the Giants, and was replaced by Don Larsen in the eighth. Larsen got bumped in the ninth by pinch-hitter Matty Alou (who started the Giants' four-run rally with a base hit).

Pierce had pitched a complete game just two days earlier, but now manager Alvin Dark called on his thirty-five-year-old lefty again.

He retired the Dodgers in order, and the Giants were National League champs.

Lee Walls made the final out, lifting an easy fly ball to center field. Just before making the catch, Willie Mays reminded himself to save the ball for Pierce. But the moment got the better of him and he "changed his mind and heaved it into the center-field bleachers in a cathartic act of pure, unadulterated ecstasy."

Pierce pitched well against the Yankees in the World Series. He tossed six shutout innings before faltering in the seventh inning of Game 3 (which he lost at the Stadium), then beat the Yankees, 5-2, with a three-hitter in Game 6 (at Candlestick).

The Giants lost Game 7, of course, but Pierce was one of the big stories. Including their playoff series against the Dodgers, Pierce pitched in four postseason games, won two of them and saved another, posted a 1.44 ERA, and allowed only eleven hits and three walks in twenty-five innings.

In the Giants' 1963 home opener, Pierce ran his Candlestick winning streak to fourteen straight (including the World Series), tossing a six-hit shutout against Houston's Colt .45s. (According to Charles Einstein, Pierce got some help at home. In *Willie's Time,* Einstein wrote that Giants groundskeeper Matty Schwab had a habit of "wetting down the grass on the left side of the infield hours before game time on days when Pierce was scheduled to pitch. This had the effect of slowing down ground balls that righthanded batsmen would get off lefthanded pitching, reducing the number of hits that would go through to the outfield.")

The streak finally ended four days later, though, with a 4-0 loss to the Cubs. And it was, for the most part, all downhill from there; Pierce finished the season with three wins, eleven losses, and a 4.27 ERA, the highest since he was a rookie with the Tigers back in '48.

That December, the Giants asked for waivers on Pierce. He wanted to keep pitching and he thought he would, saying, "I'm sure there is at least one big league club that wants me." There was; Pierce went to camp with the Giants in the spring of '64 and signed a contract on Opening Day. But Bobby Bolin was ready for a spot in the rotation and the Giants had traded for Bob Hendley, who had good stuff and was a dozen years younger than Pierce. So the veteran coming off a lousy season got sent to the bullpen, from where he pitched effectively, if rarely in critical spots: four saves, two wins, zero losses.

On September 10, he started for the first time in more than a year, and beat the Dodgers with seven and two-thirds strong innings. Afterward, somebody asked him if he knew how many strikeouts he had. "Right to the dot," he replied. "I had 1,994 going into the game. I added three more and that leaves me three short of the 2,000 mark." Pierce wouldn't get another start, and for some reason he pitched just once more. On October 3, the next-to-last day of the season, Pierce picked up two more strikeouts in three innings, which left him just one short of 2,000 career K's.

And that's where his quest ended. Though Pierce had gone 3-0 with a 2.20 ERA in '64, he announced his retirement on the last day of the season.

After leaving the game, Pierce made his permanent home in the Chicago area. He co-owned an Oldsmobile and Cadillac dealership for two years, worked briefly as a stockbroker, and occasionally served as a scout without portfolio for the White Sox (he's been credited with discovering Ron Kittle). In the early 1970s Pierce hooked up with the Continental Envelope Company, and worked for them in sales and public relations for twenty-three years before retiring in 1997.

That same year, the Nellie Fox Society—of which Pierce was a member in good standing—saw its *raison d'être* inducted into the Hall of Fame . . . and promptly renamed itself the Billy Pierce Society.

BOB FRIEND

BILL JAMES

A gentleman in every sense, respected universally by fellow players (who put his business sense to work long ago by making him a league player representative), Friend is articulate, cooperative and knowledgeable. His blue eyes twinkle with a humor that's softer than Whitey Ford's, but rich enough. And if there is such a thing as big league atmosphere, Friend exudes it.

—Leonard Koppett

In February 1969, Bob Friend was assigned to round up guests for the annual Dapper Dan banquet in Pittsburgh. Among those he brought in were two football stars of different eras, and differing fame: Byron "Whizzer" White, a former Pittsburgh Steeler who achieved even greater fame as a member of the United States Supreme Court, and O. J. Simpson, then in college. Must have been a hell of a conversation up on the dais, don't you reckon? It seems like a premise for a movie . . . "My Dinner with Whizzer and O.J.," or one of those movies that re-creates imagined conversations between Freud and Hitler, bumping into one another on the streets of Vienna, or bedroom banter between Thomas Jefferson and Sally Hemmings.

"O.J., what do you want to do with your life after you leave football?"

"I'm not sure yet, Mr. Justice; I thought maybe I'd make some silly movies and then maybe kill a couple of people."

"Did you ever think of entering the legal profession?"

"Which side?"

Bob Friend was born in Lafayette, Indiana, on November 24, 1930. His father, a graduate of Purdue University, was an orchestra leader; according to a 1956 article in the *Saturday Evening Post* he was "the kind who conducts Sunday concerts in the park." Bob (Bobby, he was then) started piano lessons at the age of five, and was very good; for several years he spoke more often of a future as a concert pianist than as an athlete. He was an all-state halfback in high school, however, and an all-state pitcher in baseball, striking out 21 of 22 batters he faced in one game. He gave up the piano at sixteen, supposedly after an embarrassing incident in which he snapped a piano string during a recital. His father died about the same time, and his interest in the piano rested alongside his father.

Three brothers, three sisters, and numerous other relatives were alumni of or students at Purdue University, as well as his father, and Friend dreamed of playing football for Purdue, but also of pitching in the major leagues. An injury to his right shoulder, suffered while playing high school football, forced him to choose between the two; Friend knew that if he played football at Purdue, he would probably re-injure the shoulder, which would end his pitching career. Baseball was the big sport at that time, and baseball had the money, so Friend signed a contract with the Pirates for a handsome bonus (variously reported as $15,000, $17,500, and $25,000), and reported to Waco of the Big State League for the 1950 season. Although he enrolled at Purdue in the fall of 1949, he was ineligible for college athletics.

He went 12-9 for Waco, pitched a no-hitter in his last start there (having been told before the game that he had been promoted), and moved up to Indianapolis. Branch Rickey became the Pirates' General Manager in November 1950, and began acquainting himself with the Pirates talent or lack thereof. The Pirates had precious little to work with, and Rickey took an immediate liking to Friend. In a spring training game in 1951 Friend pitched six shutout innings, defeating Bob Feller. The manager had told him he needed a third pitch, but Rickey emphatically disagreed. "You've got everything you need," Rickey told him after that game. "Fast ball, curve, and change on both. Boy, you can be great." Rickey decided, probably over the objections of his manager, that the best place for Friend to learn to pitch in the majors was in the majors, and so Friend, after one season in the minor leagues, began the 1951 season on the Pirate roster.

As a rookie he was nicknamed by teammates "Nervous Nervous Friend," a moniker adapted from a Damon Runyon character named Nicely Nicely Johnson. He was nervous but not all that bad, considering; his 4.27 ERA in 1951 was second on the Pittsburgh staff. He was 6-10 that year, 7-17 in '52, 8-11 in '53, 7-12 in '54. After four years in the major leagues he was 28-50, which actually was better than the won-lost record of his teams over those four years (209-407, a .339 percentage.)

Still, Friend had shown little evidence of improvement, and Branch Rickey's enthusiasm was waning. After the 1954 season Rickey called Friend into his office, invited him to lunch, and told him that he was going to spend the 1955 season with Hollywood of the Pacific Coast League. "Young man," said Rickey. "You're going backward, not forward." Friend said, let's skip lunch; I can't eat.

"Later, he told me that he had been testing my confidence," said Friend, "that if I had shown any hesitation in my reaction, he would have sent me down." Another version is that Rickey *did* ask waivers to send Friend to Hollywood, but that Friend didn't clear the waivers. Anyway, he opened the 1955 season on the major league roster, but buried in the Pirate bullpen. Teams at that time, and particularly *bad* teams, didn't *have* bullpens, in the modern sense of the word. They had starting pitchers, and they had extras. Friend was not high on the list of extras.

He pitched well in mop-up roles, however, and earned a start on May 31. Branch Rickey listened to the game on the radio. When he heard that Friend was starting, he called the manager (Fred Haney) on the phone, and bawled him out for giving Friend the start (at least according to Haney). Branch was giving Friend a major league wake-up call. Leading the Dodgers 1-0 in the fourth inning, Friend gave up three consecutive home runs, then took a line drive off his shin. He survived that onslaught, and won the game 6-3, thus moving into the rotation. That game was the turning point of his career. Although the rest of the Pirates were as bad as they had ever been (their won-lost percentage without Friend was .351), Friend finished the season 14-9 with an ERA of 2.83, which led the National League. He was the first pitcher in major league history to lead the league in ERA while pitching for a last-place team.

Friend continued to pitch well in 1956, starting the season 11-3, starting several games on two days rest, and finishing 17-17. He started 42 times that season, a modern record for a Pittsburgh pitcher (then and now), and started the All-Star Game for the National League. In June 1956, Joe King reported that "Bob Friend of the Pirates is generally regarded as the best pitcher in the National League." In 1957, although he finished just 14-18 (the Pirates were still bad), he had a sharp 3.38 ERA (seventh in the league), and led the league in starts and innings for the second straight season.

After Friend became a success, Branch Rickey and Fred Haney engaged in a public tug-of-war to take credit for his emergence. Haney, let go by the Pirates after losing 299 games in three years (1953–55), insisted that it was *he* who had always believed in Friend, and that he had kept Friend from being sent to the minors several times. Rickey declared that this was nonsense, that he

George Brace Collection

had just been trying to shake Friend up, talking about sending him to the minors.

Friend's life outside of baseball was also coming together. Attending Purdue in the off-seasons for eight years, he earned a Bachelor's degree in economics in January, 1957. In 1953, as a 22-year-old kid, he had become the Pirates' Player Representative. Now, as a mature player and a college graduate, he became the National League Player Representative—effectively the National League's union leader.

In September 1957, he married Patricia Koval, who had been a nurse in the office of the Pirates' team doctor. It was a permanent marriage, complete with family. In the off season he began work with a large Pittsburgh bank, moving from that to a job as the district manager for Federated Investors, Inc. ("a world-wide investment firm specializing in mutual funds"). In 1958 he had his best major league season—or not, depending on how you look at it. Friend in 1958 won 22 games, lost 14, and finished third in the voting for the Cy Young Award, which was then a two-league award; Friend finished third behind one National League pitcher and one American League pitcher. It was the only time in his fine career that he was mentioned in the Cy Young voting.

However, if you look at Friend's ERA, his hits allowed, his runs allowed, the 1958 season was far from his best. The Sabermetric Encyclopedia has a stat called "Runs Saved Against Average," which compares the pitcher to a league-average pitcher, park-adjusted. Friend shows as positive—that is, better than average—every year from 1955 through 1965—except 1958, when he shows as -1.

In any case, a pitcher in that era was evaluated almost entirely by his won-lost record, and Friend was thus regarded as having had an outstanding season—as did his team. The Pirates, adding Roberto Clemente in 1955 and Bill Mazeroski in '56, finally became a competitive ballclub in '58, vaulting to 84 wins and a second-place finish.

In that era, when $20,000 was a good salary for a baseball player, a player could make $100, $200, once in awhile $500 by attending an off-season baseball dinner and telling a couple of jokes. The better year a player had, the more invitations he had to do off-season dinners. With 22 wins, Friend was the Pirates' big star in 1958, and he spent the off-season doing dinners (as well as working in the bank). He showed up at spring training 18 pounds overweight. He was nearing 30 now; his metabolism was changing. He thought he could sweat the weight off in a few weeks and never notice it. He was wrong. He went 8–19, leading the National League in losses.

"The harder I worked, the tougher it became," Friend said later. "Then I developed an infection and this, plus the added weight, left me weak. I couldn't do as much running as I wanted and didn't get in enough pitching. When the season opened, I thought I was in shape. I'd pitch good ball for five or six innings, then run out of gas. My legs felt weak—more like rubber—and everything was an effort. I certainly paid the price."

The Pirates—70-57 when Friend wasn't on the mound—finished nine games behind the Dodgers in a race that was ripe for the plucking. Friend took considerable criticism for dragging the Pirates out of the pennant race, but Pirate manager Danny Murtaugh was firmly against getting rid of him. "What would you do if a Cadillac broke down?" he asked. "You wouldn't junk it. You'd get the trouble fixed. So why should I give up on Bob?"

How bad the year really was is debatable. The Sabermetric Encyclopedia, which shows Friend one run worse than an average pitcher in 1958, shows him as one run better than average in '59. One suspects that further research would show that the reason Friend went 22-14 in '58 and 8–19 in '59 was that the Pirates didn't score any runs for him in '59, and Roy Face picked up what victories were there to be had. Still, he did show up overweight, he did lose 19 games. In later years Friend would re-tell the story of the spring he showed up out of shape to any reporter who needed a story. This story thus appears in print dozens of times in slightly varying versions. In re-tellings it is always the 1959 season when he got out of shape, although in reality, if you read the contemporaneous records, Friend had a weight problem the first half of his career, was described as "chunky" as early as 1952, and showed up at spring training overweight several times as late as 1961.

After the 1959 season Friend and his wife Pat embarked on a six-week tour of Europe, visiting twelve countries including Russia. A young Russian woman, hired to show them around Moscow, asked Bob what he did for a living. Bob told her he played baseball. That's nice, she said, "but what do you *really* do for a living?" Friend told her that he also sold stocks and bonds.

"Ah," the girl said understandingly. "Wall Street. It is the American tragedy."

In 1960, of course, the Pirates won the World Championship. Friend won 18 games that year, was the starting and winning pitcher in the first of two All-Star Games, and threw four shutouts, but was battered twice in the World Series. He struck out 183 batters that year, a Pittsburgh record at the time (and still, remarkably enough, one of the top ten figures of all time for a Pirate. One 19th century Pittsburgh pitcher had struck out more, Mark Baldwin in 1891, but 19th century records were almost totally discounted at that time). Friend was named the National League Comeback Player of the Year.

The rest of his career was more or less a glide path. Having struggled to the top of the mountain, Friend skied toward the bottom, winning 18 more games in 1962 and 17 in 1963, but also losing 19 in 1961—which led the league for the second time in three years—and 18 more in 1964. Friend pitched 200 innings every year from 1955 through 1965—an average of 255 per season—and posted better-than-league ERAs every year except 1958, when he won 22 games. In 1963, although he finished just 17-16, he was third in the National League in ERA, at 2.34, as baseball broke into a pitcher's era.

He became something of a fitness fanatic, working hard to keep the weight off. Stories written about him in his early thirties regularly observed that he was in the best shape of his career, while Friend himself talked often about pitching into his forties, as Warren Spahn had done. "I don't baby my arm," Friend said. "Robin Roberts once told me to keep on throwing and I'd never have trouble with my arm. He was so right. If there's a slight stiffness, I throw it out." Nonetheless, he was traded to the Yankees after losing records in '64 and '65 (13–18, 8–12 . . . he had still pitched a lot of innings with better-than-league ERAs), then to the Mets, by whom he was released at the age of 35.

Friend's career record is pretty awful, 197 wins against 230 losses. There is an argument here that I don't want to get into: was Friend actually a good pitcher? I'm not here to argue the issue, but let me make a series of true statements that would be a part of the argument:

1) Friend's career record is poor.
2) He did pitch for several terrible teams, and only one really good team (the '60 Pirates).
3) Friend's career won-lost record is no worse than that of his teams, but it is also no better. If Friend had had the same winning percentage as the rest of his team every year, his career record would be the same as it is—197–230.
4) Nonetheless, Friend was regarded, while active, as an outstanding and valuable pitcher.
5) His ERAs were very good. In terms of earned runs, he was 84 runs better than an average pitcher, park adjusted.
6) Although regarded as a superb athlete, Friend was a horrible hitter. Some of the discrepancy between his expected and actual won-lost records can be attributed to his own inability to hit.
7) Ground ball pitchers, like Friend, give up more *unearned* runs than normal. Friend in his career gave up 15 unearned runs for each 100 earned runs; the league average was 13 per 100. The difference is 20 runs over the course of his career.

Friend had anticipated a long career. Released by the Mets with 197 wins, he wanted to get to 200. He went to the winter meetings in '66 looking for a job, but when you have been released by a team that has just lost 112 games, people tend to take that as a sign that you no longer have your best stuff.

One other odd note about his career. Friend never pitched a no-hitter in the major leagues, but pitched two one-hitters—one in 1955, one in 1965, both against the Cubs, and both in Wrigley Field. "What are you guys so excited about?" Friend asked reporters after the second game. "I pitch a one-hitter here every ten years." The men who got the hits were Frankie Baumholtz and Don Landrum, who was commonly known as the Frankie Baumholtz of the 1960s, or anyway should have been. Both hits were infield singles, one fielded by the second baseman, one by the shortstop.

In 1966 Friend became involved in a kind of feud with Harry Walker, then managing the Pirates, who he thought was a bush-league individual (a fairly common opinion of Harry, by the way). Harry had a habit of throwing up his hands in annoyance when his players didn't play well, so Friend, playing for the Mets against the Pirates, would sit on the other bench and fling up his hands in mock exasperation after almost every pitch. Remembering that the Pirates had used a squeeze bunt against him in an earlier game when they were already five runs ahead—a tactic he had described as "unprocessed organic plant food"—he signaled frantically for a bunt every time the Pirates got a runner to third base. This led to other gestures back and forth between the two dugouts, and eventually, Friend charged across the field and into the Pirate dugout, then occupied by approximately twenty of his old teammates and a scrawny little manager that many of the ex-teammates wouldn't have minded taking a whack at themselves if the opportunity had arisen. The incident ended with no real damage.

In baseball in Friend's era there were four pitchers who had what might be called obvious political futures: Friend (born 1930), Vinegar Bend Mizell (also born 1930), Larry Jackson (born 1931) and Jim Bunning (born 1931). All four were handsome, self-confident, articulate men who were just pretty much certain that they knew what ought to be done almost all of the time. If you were going to bet on one of those guys to become President one day, Friend would have been the guy you would have bet on. Friend was the National League Player Representative in the early 1960s, when the Player's Association was searching for a leader—a search that eventually landed Marvin Miller, which changed baseball forever.

In the early 1960s it was reported that Friend had been his team's player representative longer than any other player in history—a distinction he might still hold, for all I know. In early 1960 the Pirates had a game rained out in Philadelphia—actually, rained out twice, on April 24 and again on June 4. The Phillies and Pirates rescheduled the game as a part of a Sunday double-header on July 10. The Pirate players, already facing a double-header on July 8 and a night game on July 9, objected to playing another double-header on July 10, which incidentally was getaway day for the All-Star break. The Pirate players, with Friend as their spokesman and leader, argued that the scheduling violated an agreement not to play an double-header after a night game, and threatened to walk out on the game. This strike threat was an historic act, an almost unprecedented action at that time. The National League backed off, and moved the rescheduled game to another date.

In February 1964, Friend testified before Congress in one of their periodic anti-trust grumblings. After leaving baseball he began the political career to which he had long been pointing. He had the perfect name for a politician; in fact, if I ever run for office, I'm going to change my name to Bob Friend. He ran for Comptroller of Allegheny County (Pittsburgh), as a Republican in a Democratic County, and he won handily (November 1967),

FRIEND '58, FRIEND '59

In the Bob Friend comment I speculated that the difference between Bob Friend in '58 and Bob Friend in '59 was probably mostly that the Pirates didn't score any runs for him in '59. Mike Webber, reading the article, realized that this was easy to check with the data available from Project Retrosheet, and so we did.

It turns out that the differences between Friend in '58 and Friend in '59 may be summarized in three areas:

1. **Offensive support.** In Friend's 38 starts in 1958 the Pirates scored 173 runs, or 4.55 per game. In 1959 they scored 136 runs, or 3.89 per game.

2. **Bullpen support.** In 1958 Friend's relievers surrendered only 13 runs in (approximately) 68 innings, or 1.72 per nine innings (based on the assumption that the games averaged nine innings.) In 1959 the bullpen gave up 40 runs in about 80 innings, or 4.50 per nine innings.

3. **Defensive support.** In 1958 Friend gave up only eight unearned runs, or 0.26 per nine innings. In 1959 he gave up 24 unearned runs, or 0.92 per nine innings. (The Pirates did have a poor defensive season in '59.)

The Pirates in '58 outscored their opponents 173–133 when Friend was the starting pitcher, creating an expected won-lost record of 23-15, an actual record of 24-14. In '59 they were outscored 136–169 in Friend's starts, creating an expected record of 14–21, and an actual record the same. The actual decline is eight and a half games, but it looks like ten and a half in Friend's record because almost half of the wins in '59 (six of fourteen) went to the bullpen. Three of those went to Elroy Face, who was having the 18-1 season, and three to other relievers.

getting more votes than any other Republican on the ballot. He was popular in the position, and was re-elected four years later, despite—or perhaps even because of, who knows—an endless diet of politics-as-baseball metaphors:

(On trailing by 10,000 votes early on election eve): "The game isn't over yet. Only one-third of the returns are in. This is just the third inning."

(On winning the election): "I'm 1-and-0, but if I have to go to the post 197 times in this business, I won't live very long. It's a hell of a big county, and when you're campaigning there's no three-day rotation."

(On his election co-workers): "I've never seen such teamwork."

(On the election business): "You don't have as much control over the results of an election as you do a ball game. You go all out and meet the public, and they decide the outcome of the contest."

(On what he had learned about politics): "You have to battle in baseball, and you have to battle in politics, too."

In February 1970, *The Sporting News* reported that Friend was giving serious consideration to a run for the Pennsylvania governor's office. That failing, he might run for Lieutenant Governor. For some reason he decided not to pursue a political career beyond the Comptroller's office. He didn't run for re-election in '75, giving "personal bankruptcy" as the reason. Bankruptcy? Friend, who came from a family of some means, was widely believed to be wealthy in the late 1960s. He was a co-founder and co-owner of the Allegheny Planned Income Corporation, reported to be a thriving business at the end of Friend's career. In the winter of 1963–64 it was reported that he had traveled to Asia to establish an import-export business. How he wound up bankrupt after two terms as the county Comptroller is surely not a pretty story, but whatever it was, he succeeded in keeping the details out of the newspapers.

"I got out of it after my two terms," Friend said years later. "I guess I just got tired of it. I don't think politics was for me." He was not destined to become President, or even a Senator, like Jim Bunning, or even a representative, like Vinegar Bend or Larry Jackson, whose baseball career parallels Friend's almost perfectly. He returned to work in the financial industry, accepting a Vice Presidency with Babb, Inc., an insurance broker. He worked in the insurance business, to the best of my knowledge, until his retirement in the mid-1990s.

PITCHER CENSUS

DON AASE 6'3" 190-pound righty
66-60, 3.80, 82 Saves 1977 1990

Pitch Selection: 1. Fastball 2. Slider
3. Slow Curve (developed in 1986)
Sources: *The Scouting Report* (1987 and 1990)

GLENN ABBOTT 6'6" 200-pound righty
62-83, 4.39, 0 Saves 1973 1984

Pitch Selection: 1. Slider 2. Sinking Fastball
Source: *The Sporting News* (5/3/1980, Hy Zimmerman)

JIM ABBOTT 6'3" 200-pound lefty
87-108, 4.25, 0 Saves 1989 1999

Pitch Selection: 1. Fastball 2. Curve 3. Forkball
4. Change
Sources: *The Scouting Report: 1992; 1994 Baseball Almanac*

Description: "His fastball has a lot of life, his slider breaks real late, and his change-up is coming along. One thing that hurts him is his pitches are real easy to follow. Without that hand, he can't use his glove to create deception."
Source: *Bill Mazeroski's Baseball* (1993 edition)

PAUL ABBOTT 6'2" 203-pound righty
40-26, 4.68, 0 Saves 1990 2003

Pitch Selection: 1. Fastball (low-90s)
2. Hard Sinker/Split-Fingered Fastball
3. Curve (occasional)
Source: *The Scouting Notebook: 2000*

Pitch Selection: 1. Straight Change
2. Fastball (low-90s) 3. Hard Slider
Sources: *The Scouting Notebook* (2001 and 2002 editions)

AL ABER 6'2" 195-pound lefty
24-25, 4.18, 14 Saves 1950 1957

Quote: "I could catch [Billy] Hoeft with a fielder's glove. Although he's fast, he throws a 'light' ball that makes it easy on the catcher. Al Aber, another leftie on our staff, is tough to catch because he throws a 'heavy' ball."
Source: Tigers catcher Frank House in *Sport* (June 1956, Tommy Devine)

TED ABERNATHY 6'4" 215-pound righty
63-69, 3.46, 148 Saves 1955 1972

Pitch Selection: 1. Sinking Fastball 2. Curve
3. Rising Fastball 4. Knuckleball
Note: After a 1957 arm injury, Abernathy adopted an underhand delivery; thereafter, he threw from so low that his knuckles sometimes scraped the ground.
Sources: *The Relief Pitcher* (John Thorn, 1979); *Major League Baseball: 1971* (Brenda Zanger and Dick Kaplan)

Pitch Selection, mid-1960s: 1. Sinking Fastball (75%)
2. Knuckleball
Source: Abernathy quoted in *Baseball Digest* (January 1966, Jim Ferguson)

Description: "With the unique underhand motion, Abernathy's curveball rises and his fastball sinks . . . He's almost impossible to hit when you get only one shot at him. You see the overhanded stuff all the time,

then this guy comes in there throwing the ball from out of the ground."
Source: *1971 Kansas City Royals Yearbook*

JUAN ACEVEDO 6'2" 245-pound righty
28-40, 4.33, 53 Saves 1995 2003

Pitch Selection: 1. Four-Seam Fastball (mid-90s)
2. Cut Fastball
Source: *The Scouting Notebook: 1999*

JIM ACKER 6'2" 210-pound righty
33-49, 3.97, 30 Saves 1983 1992

Pitch Selection: 1. Sinking Fastball 2. Slider
3. Change
Sources: *The Scouting Report* (1990 and 1992)

ACE ADAMS 5'10" 182-pound righty
41-33, 3.47, 49 Saves 1941 1946

Pitches: 1. Fastball 2. Slider 3. Curve 4. Slow Curve
5. Change
Adams: "The fastball and change, I threw them all, used everything. Fastball, curve, slow curve, that's the way I pitched. And then when I got to the big leagues I started practicing up on a slider, and there weren't many sliders in those days. Jelly Collier, a pitcher with Nashville, taught me the pitch."
Source: Interview in *Pen Men* (Bob Cairns, 1992)

BABE ADAMS 5'11" 185-pound righty
194-140, 2.76, 15 Saves 1906 1926

Pitch Selection: 1. Fastball 2. Hard Curve
Sources: *Baseball Digest* (May 1950, page 30); *The National Game* (Alfred H. Spink, 1911); *Baseball in the Big Leagues* (Johnny Evers and Hugh Fullerton, 1910)

Adams: "Pitching is an art only perfected by constant practice. It can not be learned in a day. There must be perfect harmony between the pitcher and catcher. I use about ten different forms of the curve ball, and when speed is a factor it gives me a wide scope in putting in a mixture of balls that only the best have a right to negotiate."
Source: *Baseball Magazine* (February 1910, Orel R. Geyer)

TERRY ADAMS 6'3" 205-pound righty
45-56, 3.97, 39 Saves 1995 2003

Pitches: 1. Two-Seam Fastball (mid-90s)
2. Hard Slider (86) 3. Curve (occasional)
Sources: *The Scouting Notebook* (1996, 1997, and 2000 editions); curve mentioned only in the 1997 book.

DEWEY ADKINS 6'2" 195-pound righty
2-4, 5.64, 0 Saves 1942 1949

Pitch Selection: 1. Curve 2. Fastball
Description: "Adkins has the curve ball, one of those kind that dips and twists like a feather in a wind tunnel. His fast ball is capable and his control has been good."
Source: *Pacific Coast Baseball News* (8/25/1948)

JUAN AGOSTO 6'2" 190-pound lefty
40-33, 4.01, 29 Saves 1981 1993

Pitch Selection: 1. Sinker 2. Curve 3. Screwball
Sources: *The Scouting Report* (1990 and 1992 editions)

RICK AGUILERA 6'4" 195-pound righty
86-81, 3.57, 318 Saves 1985 2000

Pitches: 1. Rising Fastball 2. Split-Fingered Fastball
3. Slider 4. Curve
Sources: *The Scouting Report* (1990 and 1992 editions)

Description: "He might not knock your eyes out, but has three above-average pitches (fastball, slider, forkball) and can use any of them to finish off a batter."
Source: *Bill Mazeroski's Baseball* (1993 edition)

HANK AGUIRRE 6'4" 205-pound lefty
75-72, 3.24, 33 Saves 1955 1970

Pitch Selection: 1. Fastball 2. Screwball
Source: *The Sporting News* (3/5/1966, Warren Spoelstra)

JACK AKER 6'2" 190-pound righty
47-45, 3.28, 123 Saves 1964 1974

Pitch Selection: 1. Sinker 2. Curve
3. Slider (added in 1966)
Source: *The Kansas City Athletics* (John E. Peterson, 2003)

Key Pitch: Sinker
Sources: *The Relief Pitcher* (John Thorn, 1979); *Baseball Digest* (March 1964, Page 99)

Description: ". . . now throws sidearm and owns a good slider, sinker, and curve."
Source: *Major League Baseball—1969* (Jack Zanger)

SCOTT ALDRED 6'4" 220-pound lefty
20-39, 6.02, 1 Save 1990 2000

Key Pitch: Fastball (low-90s)
Sources: *The Scouting Report* (1992 and 1993 editions)

Pitch Selection: 1. Fastball (90) 2. Curve
Source: *The Scouting Notebook: 1997*

VIC ALDRIDGE 5'9" 175-pound righty
97-80, 3.76, 6 Saves 1917 1928

Pitch Selection, 1922–24: 1. Curve 2. Fastball 3. Screwball
Pitch Selection, 1925–29: 1. Fastball 2. Curve 3. Screwball (used mainly as Change)
Sources: *Baseball Magazine* (December 1925 and July 1927); *Terre Haute Tribune* (4/18/1973, Obituary)

Quote from obituary: "He was known for a fast, sharp breaking curve, which prompted Rogers Hornsby to note in an interview that Aldridge has one of the three best curve balls he ever faced." *Baseball Magazine* said in 1927 that "he has one of the best curves on the diamond," and also specifies that it was a hard, sharp-breaking curve, rather than a slow roundhouse curve.

Aldridge in 1925 *Baseball Magazine*: "In the Cubs' relatively small field with encroaching bleacher seats, the pitcher had to guard particularly against a fluky home run. A curve is less likely to be changed into a homer than a fast ball. When I came to Pittsburgh, however, with a larger field in which to navigate, I found it advisable to depend more upon my fast ball."

DOYLE ALEXANDER 6'3" 190-pound righty
194-174, 3.76, 3 Saves 1971 1989

Pitches, early career: 1. Sinking Fastball 2. Change 3. Curve 4. Slider
Pitches, late career: 1. Sinker 2. Slider 3. Change 4. Fastball (82–86) 5. Curve 6. Knuckleball (occasional until 1989, when he threw a lot of them)
Note: Alexander generally threw overhand, but often dropped to three-quarters and occasionally sidearm.

Quote: "Alexander usually starts batters off with a slider, which he keeps low. He will come back with breaking balls, spot the fastball on the corner, then tinker with a change, whether ahead or behind in the count. He does not give in to batters by walking them, and will make them hit a low breaking ball if he can."
Source: *The Scouting Report: 1984*
Other Sources: *The Sporting News* (7/19/1980, Ken Picking); *The Scouting Report* (1982, 1985, and 1990 editions)

PETE ALEXANDER 6'1" 185-pound righty
373-208, 2.56, 32 Saves 1911 1930

Pitch Selection: 1. Sinking Fastball 2. Hard Curve 3. Change 4. Fadeaway
Source: Bill Killefer in *Kings of the Diamond* (Lee Allen and Tom Meany, 1965)

Pitch Selection: 1. Curve 2. Fastball 3. Change
Source: Alexander in *Baseball Magazine* (May 1913, C.P. Stack)

Alexander in *Baseball Magazine*: "I consider my curve ball my main strong point. I have pretty good speed and a good change of pace, which is important; but the main thing with me is curves . . . In fact, when I am in a tight place and the batter has me in a hole, I generally feed him a good curve, for I am surer of being able to get it over the plate about where I want it than I am of a fast one . . .

"In addition to curves and speed I have tried to develop a special knack of delivery which is very helpful. I believe that the side arm motion is much more baffling to the batter than the overhand delivery. For that reason I have developed the side arm delivery and have cultivated it so that I have it down pretty well. It has been very effective."

Notes: John Ogden, longtime scout for the Giants, said that Alexander had the best change-up he ever saw (source: Lee Allen's "Cooperstown Corner" column in *The Sporting News*, 11/16/1963).

The 1924 *Reach Guide* included Alexander on a list of curve-ball pitchers (Page 47). Arthur Daley, in the *New York Times* (July, 1953), speculated that Alexander's effectiveness may have been due to the fact that he was throwing what was, in effect, a slider as his curve ball, at a time when everybody else was throwing bigger and slower curves.

In *Baseball Digest* (September 1947, Harry Sheer), Charlie Grimm said, "The best motionless motion was Grover Cleveland Alexander's. He'd just put his hands over his head, drop 'em to his waistline, then wham!"

Rogers Hornsby: "Alexander has as much speed as anybody in the National League and he is the best pitcher I ever saw . . ."
Source: *Baseball Magazine* (April 1919, Hornsby)

Quote: "There are not many side-arm pitchers. In fact, I do not consider even [Walter] Johnson a true side-arm pitcher. He uses a half side-arm motion, but his arms are so long he is in a class by himself. Alexander, however, is a true side-arm pitcher."
Source: Hippo Vaughn in *Baseball Magazine* (August 1919, F.C. Lane)

Quote: ". . . He threw right-handed with an easy, relaxed and seemingly effortless side-arm motion, but with almost perfect control."

" 'My fast ball broke in and down to a right-handed batter,' [Alexander] explained to me one day. 'As I brought my arm around, I rolled my hand over slightly forward, releasing the ball off the inside of my second finger tip. This gave the ball a slight downward spin, but at an angle that made it act like a screwball, or a fadeaway, as they called it in Christy Mathewson's day. I kept it low and made sure it was also doing something around the edge of the plate.'

"Alexander had a curve and a good one, but he depended most on the sinking fast ball. His hand was small, but the fingers were long. His wrist was rubbery, and loose from many years of twisting to throw the side-arm curve . . ."
Source: Arthur Daley (in *The New York Times*?)

Quote: "When Aleck sticks two strikes over on a batter, that batter is almost a goner. There is no wasting that next one as so many pitchers do. For that next one would just be inches off the corner of the plate. He might even decide, in such a case, to throw that next one right to the batter's known strength but just off enough to make it a bad ball to hit."
Source: Bill Doak in *Baseball Magazine* (October 1938, John Drebinger)

Description: "Alex threw hard in those days [1915], but he continued to win for years even when he no longer had a hummer. He not only could pinpoint the fast ball and curve, low and away, but he also had the knack of taking something off his fast one by degrees and he came up with a screwball about which little has been written. He also threw deceptively.

"The delivery was labeled as side-armed, but it really wasn't, as hitters who faced him remember, because he short-armed the ball, bringing it up across his chest and throwing his out of his uniform front. The ball was especially difficult to pick up when it came out of his white home uniform."
Source: Bob Broeg in *Super Stars of Baseball* (Bob Broeg, 1971)

Jesse Haines: "I called him Old Low-and-Away, because that's the way he pitched everybody, down at the knees and nicking the outside corner, with his good fast ball or his short, sharp curve."
Source: *Super Stars of Baseball*

ANTONIO ALFONSECA 6'5" 250-pound righty
23-30, 4.11, 121 Saves 1997 2003

Pitches: 1. Sinker (94–95)
2. Four-Seam Fastball (high-90s)
3. Slider (occasional) 4. Change (occasional)
Sources: *The Scouting Notebook* (1999, 2001–2003 editions)

JOHNNY ALLEN 6'0" 180-pound righty
142-75, 3.75, 18 Saves 1932 1944

Pitch Selection: 1. Fastball 2. Slider
3. Overhand Curve 4. Change
Sources: *Baseball Play and Strategy* (Ethan Allen, 1959); *Strikeout Story* (Bob Feller, 1947); *Fiery Fast-Baller* (Wint Capel, 2001)

Note: Ethan Allen (1959; other versions printed earlier) says that Allen was "an overhand pitcher."

However, Lew Fonseca in "How to Pitch Baseball" (1942) listed Allen among three "present-day pitchers who successfully employ the sidearm type of delivery." In *The Greatest Team of All Time* (Nicholas Acocella and Donald Dewey, 1994), former teammate Bill Dickey says of Allen, "He had good control and could come completely sidearm or straight overhand."

Description: "Johnny Allen, also an overhand pitcher, threw a fast ball that was unique because it slid or broke like a curve. It was somewhat like a fast ball (wrist rigid instead of relaxed), but he threw over the side of the index finger to a greater extent. For this reason, he gripped the ball mainly with the middle finger. This off-center pressure caused the break."
Source: *Baseball: Major League Technique and Tactics* (Ethan Allen, 1953)

Johnny Allen: "The best delivery a pitcher can have is an overhand curve ball. I know, there have been games when I've only thrown four curves all afternoon. It just depends . . ."
Note: According to his son, Allen claimed to have been the creator of the slider. Maybe so, but others thought they were—before Allen. Allen named his slider "My Out-pitch." He threw it when he needed strike three, or to make the batter hit a ball easy to catch.
Source: *Fiery Fast-Baller*

Quote: "His sidearm fastball, especially when it comes out of a white-shirted bleacher background, sneaks up on the hitter with malign effect."
Source: Dan Daniel in *The Hurlers* (Kevin Kerrane, 1989)

Description: "Allen pitches both side-arm and overhand and in the parlance of the game has plenty of stuff."
Source: *Baseball Magazine* (February 1932, Clifford Bloodgood)

NEIL ALLEN 6'3" 185-pound righty
58-70, 3.88, 75 Saves 1979 1989

Pitch Selection: 1. Rising Fastball 2. Hard Curve
Note: Allen's fastball and curve were both outstanding pitches, and at times he could effectively change speeds on both. But he never did develop a reliable change-up.
Sources: *The Sporting News* (5/13/1978, page 38); *The Scouting Report* (1983 and 1985 editions)

NICK ALTROCK 5'10" 197-pound lefty
84-75, 2.67, 7 Saves 1898 1924

Pitch Selection: 1. Curve 2. Changes 3. Fastball
Source: *The Sporting News* (2/22/1934)
Note: Altrock was famous for having the best pickoff move of his generation.

WILSON ALVAREZ 6'1" 175-pound lefty
94-82, 3.93, 3 Saves 1989 2003

Pitches, early career: 1. Fastball (low-90s) 2. Curve 3. Change 4. Slider
Sources: *The Scouting Notebook: 1996; 1995 Baseball Almanac*

Pitch Selection, late career: 1. Fastball (upper-80s) 2. Change 3. 12-to-6 Curve
Description: "Though the former fireballer's four-seamed fastball now tops out in the upper 80s, Alvarez is not afraid to come inside with it. The key for Alvarez is to have good command of two other pitches, both of which have good downward movement. He gets righthanders out with a turnover change and hammers lefties with an excellent 12-to-six curveball."
Source: *The Scouting Notebook 2004*

RED AMES 5'10" 185-pound righty
183-167, 2.63, 36 Saves 1903 1919

Pitch Selection: 1. Fastball 2. Slow Curve
Sources: *New York Tribune* (5/23/1913); *The National Game* (Alfred H. Spink, 1911)

Quote from Spink: "He is a giant, with a world of speed."

Key Pitch: Curve
Description: "Personally, we have never seen the twirler with a curve like Leon Ames.' Reulbach, when right, is a more or less close rival, but Ames is unbeatable."
Source: *Baseball Magazine* (November 1913, F.C. Lane)

LARRY ANDERSEN 6'3" 200-pound righty
40-39, 3.15, 49 Saves 1975 1994

Pitch Selection: 1. Slider 2. Slider 3. Slider 4. Sinker
Source: *The Scouting Report: 1990*; see below for other sources.

Quote: "Former big leaguers James Rodney Richard and Larry Andersen had the best sliders of any pitchers that I ever coached."
Source: *Think Better Baseball* (Bob Cluck, 2002)

Quote: "I had a good slider but Larry Andersen had the best slider I have ever seen . . . I would estimate that 90 percent of the pitches he threw were sliders—he could throw it up, down, in, out. He almost had to throw it

when he was behind in the count because he had better control with his slider than he did with his fastball. When I asked Larry how he threw his slider he said that he gripped it tightly with his middle finger and crimped his hand toward his head and threw it as hard as he could. Since then, I have asked a lot of pitchers who have good sliders how they threw them. All but one, Mike Jackson, said they gripped it more tightly with their middle finger . . ."
Source: Larry Dierker, *This Ain't Brain Surgery: How to Win the Pennant Without Losing Your Mind* (Dierker, 2003)

ALLAN ANDERSON 6'0" 201-pound lefty
49-54, 4.11, 0 Saves 1986 1991

Pitch Selection: 1. Change 2. Mediocre Fastball

Commentary: Anderson lived by changing speeds off his 86 MPH fastball.
Source: *The Scouting Report: 1990*

BOB ANDERSON 6'4" 210-pound righty
36-46, 4.26, 13 Saves 1957 1963

Pitch Selection: 1. Curve 2. Forkball
Source: *Don Schiffer's Major League Baseball Handbook—1964*

BRIAN ANDERSON 6'1" 195-pound lefty
75-69, 4.58, 1 Save 1993 2003

Pitch Selection: 1. Fastball (87–91) 2. Change 3. Slider 4. Curve
Sources: *The Scouting Report* (1995 and 1996 editions); *The Scouting Notebook* (1998 and 1999 editions)

Pitch Selection: 1. Fastball 2. Change 3. Cut Fastball/Slider
Sources: *The Scouting Notebook* (2002 and 2003 editions)

MATT ANDERSON 6'4" 200-pound righty
15-7, 4.89, 26 Saves 1998 2003

Pitch Selection: 1. Fastball (95–101)
2. Knuckle Curve (high-80s)
3. Split-Fingered Fastball (occasional; added about 2001)
Sources: *The Scouting Notebook* (1999, 2002, and 2003 editions)

IVY ANDREWS 6'1" 200-pound righty
50-59, 4.14, 8 Saves 1931 1938

Pitches: 1. Fastball 2. Curve 3. Change
Description: "He is a strictly overhand pitcher whose fine winning record has been compiled by judicious use of a blazing fast ball, a good curve and a fair change of pace. They have proved to be all the assortment he needs.

"Andrews says, 'My method of pitching is hardly a secret, it can be read in many guide books. I try to keep my fast ball inside and my curve ball away from the hitter. On the wild swingers I find it advisable to mix up my delivery with a change of pace.' "
Source: *Baseball Magazine* (June 1933, Clifford Bloodgood)

Note: At some point after 1933, Andrews added both a knuckleball and screwball to his repertoire. In the September 1937 issue of *Baseball Magazine*, Dan Daniel wrote, "In addition to Fred Fitzsimmons, traded by the Giants to Brooklyn, our knuckle-ball dynasty in the majors includes George Caster, of the Athletics; Ted Lyons, White Sox; Jack Knott, Browns; and Paul Andrews, Indians. Andrews also pitches the screw-ball, which was taught to him by Hubbell."

Also, in 1939, Yankees catcher Bill Dickey said, "Now the worst pitch to receive is the knuckle-ball. And with Andrews gone, we haven't a knuckler on the club."

JOAQUIN ANDUJAR 6'0" 170-pound righty
127-118, 3.58, 9 Saves 1976 1988

Pitch Selection: 1. Fastball 2. Slider
Note: Andujar would pitch from over the top, three-quarters, and sidearm.
Source: *The Scouting Report: 1987*

RICK ANKIEL 6'1" 210-pound lefty
12-10, 3.84, 1 Save 1999 2001

Pitches: 1. Fastball (mid-90s) 2. Curve 3. Slider 4. Change (occasional)
Source: *The Scouting Notebook: 2001*

Note: Ankiel walked eleven batters in four postseason innings in 2000, and at this writing still hasn't got his career back on track.

JOHNNY ANTONELLI 6'1" 185-pound lefty
126-110, 3.34, 21 Saves 1948 1961

Pitch Selection: 1. Fastball 2. Curve
3. Change

Note: Basically a fastball pitcher, but sometimes threw more changes in a game than fastballs.

Sources: *The Incredible Giants* (Tom Meany, 1955), *We Played the Game* (Danny Peary, 1994)

Stan Musial: "Antonelli was a good pitcher with great control for several years. In his 20-game peak he came up with a terrific change of pace that made him outstanding. But a little later he lost that change, the pitch that went away from a righthanded hitter, and he never got it back. Losing that pitch cost him something in the way of effectiveness."

Source: *Stan Musial: The Man's Own Story* (Musial, as told to Bob Broeg, 1964)

Quote: "Antonelli credits Bucky Walters, Giants pitching coach, and Roy Campanella, Brooklyn catcher, no less, for a large measure of his success this season.

" 'Before the All-Star game Bucky told me I ought to concentrate more on throwing three-quarters,' Johnny recalls. 'During the game Campy told me my over-the-top pitch gets to the batter faster and doesn't have the tail on the end of it. I still use the three-quarters occasionally for variety, though.' "

Source: Unidentified clipping dated September, 1956 (Hall of Fame files, article by Lou Miller)

Notes: In *Tim McCarver's Baseball for Brain Surgeons and Other Fans* (McCarver with Danny Peary, 1998), McCarver includes Antonelli in a list of "screwball specialists."

Antonelli was listed by *The Sporting News* (8/29/1956) as having one of the best fastballs in the league.

KEVIN APPIER 6'2" 180-pound righty
169-136, 3.72, 0 Saves 1989 2003

Pitch Selection: 1. Fastball
2. Forkball or Split-Fingered Fastball 3. Slider
4. Curve

Sources: *The Scouting Report: 1996; 1995 Baseball Almanac*

PETE APPLETON 5'11" 180-pound righty
57-66, 4.31, 26 Saves 1927 1945

Key Pitch: Overhand Curve

Sources: Shirley Povich in the *Washington Post; Baseball Digest* (May 1946)

See also Guy Morton.

LUIS AQUINO 6'1" 190-pound righty
31-32, 3.68, 5 Saves 1986 1995

Pitches: 1. Fastball 2. Slider 3. Curve 4. Change

Sources: *The Scouting Report* (1990, 1992, and 1993 editions)

JIM ARCHER 6'0" 190-pound lefty
9-16, 3.94, 5 Saves 1961 1962

Pitch Selection: 1. Curve 2. Change 3. Fastball

Source: *Baseball Digest* (September 1962)

JACK ARMSTRONG 6'5" 220-pound righty
40-65, 4.58, 0 Saves 1988 1994

Pitch Selection: 1. Fastball (low-90s) 2. Curve
3. Slider 4. Change

Sources: *The Scouting Report* (1990, 1993, and 1994 editions)

ROLANDO ARROJO 6'4" 240-pound righty
40-42, 4.55, 6 Saves 1998 2002

Pitch Selection: 1. Fastball 2. Slider
3. Split-Fingered Change 4. Curve

Note: Uses many different arm angles.

Source: *The Scouting Notebook: 1999*

LUIS ARROYO 5'8" 178-pound lefty
40-32, 3.93, 44 Saves 1955 1963

Pitch Selection: 1–2. Screwballs 3. Fastball

Arroyo: "Naturally the hitter is expecting the screwball. They know that's my bread-and-butter pitch. He knows what's coming and I have to stop him, even so. But I have two speeds on the screwball—and once in a while I can throw a fastball past a hitter."

Source: Arroyo quoted in *Late and Close: A History of Relief Pitching* (Paul Votano, 2002)

Notes: Arroyo had a good fastball until 1951, when he hurt his arm while pitching for the Cardinals' Rochester

farm team. Arroyo learned his screwball from Al Hollingsworth, his manager in Puerto Rico in the winter of 1956.
Source: Arroyo quoted in *Baseball Monthly* (June 1962, Francis Stann)

MIGUEL ASENCIO 6'2" 190-pound righty
6-8, 5.14, 0 Saves 2002 2003

Pitches, 2002: 1. Sinking Fastball 2. Change 3. Slider (occasional)
Source: *Kansas City Star* (6/4/2002, Dick Kaegel)

ANDY ASHBY 6'5" 180-pound righty
98-110, 4.13, 1 Save 1991 2003

Pitches: 1. Sinking Fastball 2. Cut Fastball 3. Sharp-breaking Curve 4. Change 5. Slider
Sources: *The Scouting Report: 1996; The Scouting Notebook 1999*
Note: Ashby in 1998, under pitching coach Dave Stewart, added a split-fingered fastball to his sinking and cut fastballs.

PAUL ASSENMACHER 6'3" 195-pound lefty
61-44, 3.53, 56 Saves 1986 1999

Pitch Selection: 1. Overhand Curve 2. Just-fair Fastball 3. Slider (occasional)
Sources: *The Scouting Report: 1990; 1995 Baseball Almanac*

PEDRO ASTACIO 6'2" 174-pound righty
118-109, 4.58, 0 Saves 1992 2003

Pitch Selection: 1. Sinking Fastball 2. Slider 3. Big, Slow Curve 4. Change
Sources: *1994 Baseball Almanac; The Scouting Notebook 1999*

KEITH ATHERTON 6'4" 200-pound righty
41-26, 3.99, 47 Saves 1983 1989

Pitch Selection: 1. Fastball (low-90s) 2. Slider 3. Change
Source: *The Scouting Report: 1985*

TOMMY ATKINS 5'10" 165-pound lefty
3-2, 2.86, 2 Saves 1909 1910

Key Pitches: 1. "Fingernail Fling" 2. Fastball 3. Curve
Source: 1911 *Reach Guide* (page 225)
Quote: "Tommy has a fingernail fling which is a grand ball." With the terminology not yet standardized, this fingernail fling was quite likely what we now call a knuckleball.

ELDEN AUKER 6'2" 194-pound righty
130-101, 4.42, 2 Saves 1933 1942

Pitch Selection: 1. Sinker 2. Curve
Note: Auker pitched submarine style. He separated his shoulder while playing football for Kansas State, and pitched sidearm during his college career. While pitching for Decatur in the Three-I League, his manager, Bob Coleman, convinced Auker to drop down even further, to submarine.
Sources: Auker in *Sleeper Cars and Flannel Uniforms* (Auker with Tom Keegan, 2001); Auker in *The Crooked Pitch* (Martin Quigley, 1984); *How to Pitch Baseball* (Lew Fonseca, 1942)

Quote: "The easiest pitcher I ever caught was Elden Auker. His underhand deliveries came over the plate nice and soft."
Source: Birdie Tebbetts in *Baseball Digest* (October 1949)

STEVE AVERY 6'4" 180-pound lefty
96-83, 4.19, 0 Saves 1990 2003

Pitch Selection, 1990: Fastball, period
Pitch Selection, as young pitcher, 1991–1993: 1. Fastball 2. Curve 3. Change
Pitch Selection, later in career: 1. Sinker 2. Change 3. Curve 4. "Fast" ball
Sources: *The Scouting Report: 1992; The Scouting Notebook 1999*

BOBBY AYALA 6'2" 190-pound righty
37-44, 4.78, 59 Saves 1992 1999

Pitch Selection: 1. Fastball (low-90s) 2. Slider 3. Forkball
Sources: *1995 Baseball Almanac, The Scouting Report: 1998*

Note: Early in his career, Ayala had a 95 MPH fastball, but it was pretty straight.

DOC AYERS 6'1" 185-pound righty
64-79, 2.84, 15 Saves 1913 1921

Key Pitch: Spitball
Note: Ayers was one of the grandfather-clause spitballers.
Source: 1923 *Reach Guide* (Page 38)

JOHNNY BABICH 6'1" 185-pound righty
30-45, 4.93, 1 Save 1934 1941

Key Pitch: Slider
Sources: Al Lopez in the *Baseball Digest* (Dec.–Jan. 1961, Page 45); "Greg's Gossip" column in the Portland *Oregonian* (7/28/1947, L.H. Gregory)

Quote from "Greg's Gossip": "Back in 1933, when no one had ever heard of 'sliders' as such, a young fellow named Johnny Babich, pitching for the San Francisco Missions (the present Hollywood) had a sensational 20 game first year winning record on what now probably would be classed as a 'slider,' but then, in lieu of any other name for it, was called 'Babich's sailer.' Thrown fast, it acted much as present-day 'sliders' do, but with this important addition: it not only took an ungodly swerve sharply to the side, but at the same time shot downward, a combination present 'slider' pitchers have not yet achieved. Still more freakily, Babich himself didn't know what he did to make it act that way. He just pitched naturally, and the ball 'sailed,' but after the Philadelphia Athletics had paid big money for him on the strength of this pitch, he entirely lost it and never did get it back. To this day he can't tell you how he threw it. Whether he unconsciously 'overweighted' one side of the ball he doesn't know. With Seattle many years later he didn't even possess an ordinary 'slider.' "

LES BACKMAN 6'0" 195-pound righty
9-18, 3.61, 2 Saves 1909 1910

Key Pitch: Fastball
Quote: "He is a great big strapping fellow, possessed of a great deal of speed."
Source: *The National Game* (Alfred H. Spink, 1911)

JIM BAGBY SR. 6'0" 170-pound righty
127-87, 3.11, 29 Saves 1912 1923

Key Pitch: Screwball or Fadeaway
Sources: *The Pitch That Killed* (Mike Sowell, 1989); Frank Gibbons in the *Cleveland Plain Dealer* (12/14/1940); unidentified article in TSN morgue, dated April 1941

Notes: The 1941 article gives the most specific and credible account of Bagby's key pitch.

According to that article, Bagby, a minor league outfielder, was recuperating from a broken arm, playing catch with teammate Buck Weaver. Just messing around on the sidelines, Bagby said "Watch me throw Mathewson's fadeaway." To the astonishment of both Bagby and Weaver, the ball broke about a foot—and Bagby never returned to the outfield.

In 1963, Lee Allen identified Bagby as a "change-of-pace boy" (*The Sporting News,* 3/9/1963). This is incorrect, although Bagby may have become an off-speed pitcher after hurting his arm in 1921. Numerous accounts of the career of Bagby Jr. (below) talk about Bagby Sr. teaching his son to throw his famous fadeaway.

JIM BAGBY JR. 6'2" 170-pound righty
97-96, 3.96, 9 Saves 1938 1947

Pitch Selection: 1. Fastball 2. Screwball 3. Knuckleball 4. Forkball (early 1940s, occasional and perhaps replacing Knuckleball)
Sources: *New York World-Telegram* (4/21/1938); unidentified article in TSN morgue, dated April 1941; article by Dennis Lusting, unidentified newspaper (July 1970); *Baseball Magazine* (September 1942, Herbert Simons)
Description of Bagby's fastball: "And it's a fast ball with a difference. When it takes off it doesn't rise. It shoots to the right and to the left."
Source: Attributed to "Flame Hose catchers" in *Baseball Magazine* (November 1938, Harold C. Burr)

STAN BAHNSEN 6'2" 185-pound righty
146-149, 3.60, 20 Saves 1966 1982

Pitch Selection: 1. Rising Fastball 2. Curve 3. Slider 4. Change
Note: Bahnsen switched from an overhand delivery to three-quarters in 1971. According to Dick Kaplan, "Carl

Yastrzemski says the Iowa-born hurler is the hardest thrower in the league."
Sources: *The Sporting News* (6/26/1971, Jim Ogle); *Major League Baseball: 1971* (Brenda Zanger and Dick Kaplan)

Note: In *Talkin' Baseball* (Phil Pepe, 1988), Jeff Torborg says that in 1973, when Bahnsen made forty-two starts, he "started [the season] throwing overhand, and by the time the season was over, he was throwing sidearm."

SCOTT BAILES 6'2" 171-pound lefty
39-44, 4.95, 13 Saves 1986 1998

Pitch Selection: 1. Fastball (87–88) 2. Slider
3. Change (used when pitching as a starter)
Source: *The Scouting Report: 1987*

BILL BAILEY 5'11" 165-pound lefty
37-76, 3.56, 0 Saves 1907 1922

Notes: In *The National Game* (1911) Alfred H. Spink says that "Bailey . . . has everything a pitcher should have but weight." *The New York Press* (2/20/1910) describes him as a "side-wheeler."

DOUG BAIR 6'0" 170-pound righty
55-43, 3.63, 81 Saves 1976 1990

Pitch Selection, mid-career: 1. Fastball (88-90)
2. Slider 3. Curve 4. Change
Pitch Selection, late career: 1. Fastball 2. Sharp Curve
Note: Bair threw overhand.
Sources: *The Scouting Report* (1982, 1984, and 1990 editions)

JERSEY BAKELY 6'2" 220-pound righty
76-125, 3.66, 0 Saves 1883 1891

Key Pitch: Fastball
Quote: "Bakely is a perfect wonder having great speed with good command of the ball."
Source: 1884 newspaper quote from *The 1884 Kansas City Unions: A History of Kansas City's First Major League Baseball Team* (H.L. Dellinger, 1977)

JACK BALDSCHUN 6'1" 175-pound righty
48-41, 3.69, 60 Saves 1961 1970

Pitches: 1. Screwball 2. Fastball 3. Slider 4. Curve
Sources: *View From the Dugout* (Ed Richter, 1963); *Baseball Digest* (June 1963)

JAMES BALDWIN 6'3" 210-pound righty
79-70, 5.02, 1 Save 1995 2003

Pitch Selection: 1. Curve 2. Fastball (high 80s)
3. Change
Sources: *The Scouting Notebook* (1997 and 2001 editions)

Pitch Selection: 1. Curve 2. Fastball (high-80s)
3. Cut Fastball
Sources: *The Scouting Notebook* (2002 and 2003 editions)

Quote: "Seattle's James Baldwin doesn't have the stuff of an ace, but he gets the most out of what he has. His fastball doesn't have a lot of life, his curve is average at best, and his backdoor slider hangs more than you would like."
Source: "Scouts Views" section of *The Sporting News* (7/15/2003)

LADY BALDWIN 5'11" 160-pound lefty
72-41, 2.85, 1 Save 1884 1890

Pitch Selection: 1. Fastball 2. Curve
Source: *Nineteenth Century Stars* (SABR, 1989, see Deacon McGuire article by Joe Overfield)

Pitch Selection: 1. Straight Ball 2. Down Shoot
3. Underhand Curve
Description: "When the batsman takes his position Baldwin faces right short and glances over his shoulder at the player he proposes to bowl out. Seizing the ball firmly in his 'south paw'—for the 'Lady' is left-handed—he brings it up to his breast and moves his left foot quickly towards first base. Swinging suddenly around he steps out briskly with his right foot and hurls the sphere towards the plate with a quick, powerful movement. His delivery is marked by both over and under hand throwing. With the overhand style he pitches a straight ball and a 'down shoot,' while the several curves of which he is master, are executed with the underhand delivery. With men on the bases, Baldwin grows uneasy in his movements in the points and frequently shifts his position. He rarely becomes 'rattled,' however. As a strategist, he has few superiors."

Source: Article titled "How Men Pitch Base-Ball: The Famous Pitchers of the National League of 1886." No author or publisher is given, though the information in the article is said to have come from photographic studies done by the *New York World* newspaper.

Quote: "His drop and inshoot balls are the most effective with right-handed batters."
Source: *Reach's American Association Base Ball Guide* (1888)

Description: "Baldwin's weird snake ball—a ball that broke either in or out; his overhand ball that made a curve drop in toward the right-handed batter and his straight jump ball were working well against the opposition in 1886 and 1887. Baldwin says the fact that he threw them all with the same overhand delivery fooled the batters and he says most of the pitchers today 'give themselves away' by their delivery."
Source: *Baseball Magazine* (February 1929, Louis F. Chamberlain)

MARK BALDWIN 6'0" 190-pound righty
154-164, 3.36, 7 Saves 1887 1893

Key Pitch: Fastball
Quote: "Although never known for a good curve or changeup, he had plenty of speed and the gumption to challenge the best hitters."
Source: *Baseball's First Stars* (published by SABR in 1996, article by Robert L. Tiemann)

WALTER BALL righty
NEGRO LEAGUES 1903 1923

Key Pitch: Spitball
Source: *The Biographical Encyclopedia of the Negro Baseball Leagues* (James A. Riley, 1994)

JEFF BALLARD 6'0" 209-pound lefty
41-53, 4.71, 2 Saves 1987 1994

Pitch Selection: 1. Change
2. Sinker away from the hitter
Source: *From 33rd Street to Camden Yards* (John Eisenberg, 2001), comments by Cal Ripken Jr., Billy Ripken, and Ballard

JAY BALLER 6'6" 215-pound righty
4-9, 5.24, 6 Saves 1982 1992

Pitch Selection: 1. Slider 2. Fastball (90)
Source: *A Baseball Winter* (edited by Terry Pluto and Jeffrey Neuman, 1986)

EDDIE BANE 5'9" 160-pound lefty
7-13, 4.69, 2 Saves 1973 1976

Twins manager Frank Quilici: "He didn't throw hard enough to break a pane of glass . . . He was very cute out there and didn't give in to hitters. You just had the idea that, long-term, his stuff wasn't going to be good enough."
Description: "Bane did throw from an assortment of angles, including a back-to-the-hitter, Luis Tiant-style delivery from which a hitter might expect the little lefty's best fastball and wind up getting a big, slow curve."
Source: *Minneapolis Star-Tribune* (7/5/2003, Patrick Reusse)

Note: Bane went straight from pitching for Arizona State to pitching for the Twins, and made his MLB debut on July 4, 1973.

DAN BANKHEAD 6'1" 184-pound righty
9-5, 6.53, 4 Saves 1947 1951

Key Pitch: Fastball
Description: "With a good fastball, an array of breaking pitches, and a herky-jerky delivery . . ."
Source: *Crossing the Line: Black Major Leaguers 1947–1959* (Larry Moffi and Jonathan Kronstadt, 1994)

Comment: "Satchel Paige opines that Dan Bankhead, youngest member of the Bankhead Baseball Brothers, throws a faster ball than Cleveland's speedy Bobby Feller."
Source: *The Baltimore Afro-American* (8/24/1948, Lula Garrett)

Description: "What I remember most about him was how he used to stamp his foot down so hard, whoom, stamp the hell out of the rubber when he pitched."
Source: Al Gionfriddo in *Bums: An Oral History of the Brooklyn Dodgers* (Peter Golenbock, 1984)

Note: Bankhead was the first acknowledged black pitcher in the major leagues.

SCOTT BANKHEAD 5'10" 185-pound righty
57-48, 4.18, 1 Save 1986 1995

Pitches: 1. Sinking Fastball (83–89) 2. Slider 3. Change 4. Curve
Sources: *The Scouting Report* (1987, 1990, and 1993 editions)

WILLIE BANKS 6'1" 200-pound righty
33-39, 4.75, 2 Saves 1991 2002

Pitch Selection: 1. Sinking Fastball (88–92) 2. Change 3. Curve (occasional)
Sources: *The Scouting Report: 1993; The Scouting Notebook: 1995*

Pitch Selection: 1. Fastball 2. Curve
Comment: "Inspired by a late-night viewing of a Satchel Paige documentary, Banks has gone to a bent-over, arm-pumping windup."
Source: *The Scouting Notebook: 1999*

FLOYD BANNISTER 6'1" 190-pound lefty
134-143, 4.06, 0 Saves 1977 1992

Pitch Selection: 1. Fastball 2. Change 3. Curve
Source: *The Scouting Report: 1990*

STEVE BARBER 6'0" 195-pound lefty
121-106, 3.36, 13 Saves 1960 1974

Pitch Selection: 1. Sinking Fastball 2. Slider 3. Curve (rarely)
Sources: *Baseball Stars of 1964* (article by George Vecsey); *From 33rd Street to Camden Yards: An Oral History of the Baltimore Orioles* (John Eisenberg, 2001)
Note: After the 1960 season, *Time* brought six pitchers to Miami, Florida, with a high-speed camera, and attempted to determine who was the hardest-throwing pitcher in baseball. The six pitchers were Barber, Drysdale, Koufax, Ryne Duren, Herb Score and Bob Turley. Barber won the contest, throwing a pitch clocked at 95.55 miles per hour.
Note: In *From 33rd Street to Camden Yards,* Barber says, "My first trip into Boston in '60, Clint [Courtney] was catching and it was the ninth . . . I'd thrown fastballs and sliders the whole game, but as bad as my curve was, I thought I could throw one in the dirt and get a swing." However, Don Schiffer in the *1963 Major League Handbook* said that Barber "Has tremendous breaks on his curve balls." This contrast implies that either

a) Barber developed a curve between 1960 and 1962, or

b) Schiffer didn't know what he was talking about.

Brooks Robinson: "Barber could throw up to 95 mph but I thought of him as a sinkerball pitcher."
Source: *We Played the Game* (Danny Peary, 1994)

Jim Palmer: "A few sidearmers, such as Dean Chance and Steve Barber, can throw across the body successfully—mainly because the optical effect contributes to fear on the part of right-handed batters."
Source: *Pitching* (Palmer, edited by Joel H. Cohen, 1975)

CURT BARCLAY 6'3" 210-pound righty
10-9, 3.48, 0 Saves 1957 1959

Description: "Barclay, although 25, is a polished pitcher with professional manners and know-how. He has noteworthy control of curve balls of various speeds, and is a master at brushing back the too-eager batsman."
Source: *The Sporting News* (4/17/1957, Joe King)

CLYDE BARFOOT 6'0" 172-pound righty
8-10, 4.10, 5 Saves 1922 1926

Story: "It probably will be a big alibi winter for supporters of the Washington club, but one of the best alibi stories ever told is related by Joe Engel, president of the Chattanooga Southern Association club, and scout for the Washington Senators, who wouldn't mind if lightning struck and made him president of the Chicago Cubs. The story has to do with Clyde Barfoot, one of Engel's pitchers at Chattanooga and who was once with the St. Louis Cardinals and the Detroit Tigers.

"With the opposing pitcher at bat and two strikes on him, Barfoot tossed up a knuckle ball, which the batter hit for a double.

" 'What kind of baseball is that,' asked Engel. 'You had two strikes on the guy. He couldn't hit a fast ball and still you throw him 'dink' stuff.'

"Clyde studied for a moment and then replied: 'Well, it was in the repertory, that's all.' "
Source: *The Sporting News* (10/19/1933, Edgar G. Brands' "Between Innings")

Note: Barfoot won 314 games in the minor leagues.

CY BARGER 6'0" 160-pound righty
47-62, 3.56, 9 Saves 1906 1915

Pitch Selection: 1. Sharp Curve 2. Fadeaway
Source: *Dodger Classics* (Robert L. Tiemann, 1983)

LEN BARKER 6'5" 225-pound righty
74-76, 4.34, 5 Saves 1976 1987

Pitch Selection: 1. Fastball 2. Curve 3. Change
Sources: *The Sporting News* (9/8/1979, Bob Sudyk); *The Sporting News* (4/16/1984)

Comment: "Fastball has been clocked at 96 mph."
Source: *The Complete Handbook of Baseball: 1982 Season* (edited by Zander Hollander)

Note: In Barker's perfect game on May 15, 1981, he threw 75 percent curveballs, with his fastball averaging 91 miles per hour.
Source: *The Sporting News* (5/30/1981, Bob Sudyk)

JESSE BARNES 6'0" 170-pound righty
152-150, 3.22, 13 Saves 1915 1927

Key Pitches: 1. Fastball 2. Change 3. Curve
Notes and Sources: The best source is an article by John J. Ward in *Baseball Magazine* (September 1925). Quote from that source: "When I was with the Giants I had to pitch more curves for those were the orders from the bench. Now I pitch a fair number of curves, but my favorite ball is still the fast ball. Surely out of a hundred balls that I throw over the plate, two-thirds will be fast balls." Norman Macht's entry on Barnes in *The Ballplayers* (1990) identifies Barnes as "a hard thrower." The 1923 *Reach Guide*, reporting on Barnes' performance in the 1922 World Series, says that "Jesse Barnes slow-balled the heavy hitters to death." *Baseball Magazine* (September 1926) quotes Virgil Barnes as saying, "Jesse always threw a curve off the tips of his fingers and I do the same."

VIRGIL BARNES 6'0" 165-pound righty
61-59, 3.66, 11 Saves 1919 1928

Pitch Selection: 1. Fastball 2. Curve
Barnes: "It's possible to get the ball to break several feet by pitching a roundhouse curve, but that wouldn't deceive any smart batter. It's the sudden, sharp dart to one side and down that fools the batter. Some pitchers' curves break straight down. Mine breaks down and on a long slant."
Source: *Baseball Magazine* (September 1926)

Note: The book *How to Pitch* (J.E. Wray, 1928) has pictures of Barnes gripping a Fast Ball, a Drop Ball, a Screw Ball, a Slow Ball, a Curve Ball, and a Fadeaway Ball, and also says that Barnes "has a long swing, the whip of which helps him to get the ball to the plate in a manner to fool the batter." The inclusion of both the Fadeaway and the screwball on the list is puzzling, since we usually think that a "fadeaway" is simply a screw ball thrown by a right-handed pitcher . . . perhaps Wray had something else in mind. In any case, Wray posed pitchers as they *would* throw a given pitch, even if the pitcher never threw that pitch in a game . . . thus, we cannot conclude that Barnes actually threw any of these pitches.

REX BARNEY 6'3" 185-pound righty
35-31, 4.34, 1 Save 1943 1950

Pitch Selection: 1. Fastball 2. Curve 3. Change
Description: "Barney had blazing speed, a tricky curve, and a tantalizing change-up . . ."
Source: *Bums* (Peter Golenbock, 1984)

Note: Babe Pinelli, home plate umpire at Rex Barney's no-hitter in September, 1948, said Barney "throws the fastest ball I've ever seen, and that includes Bob Feller."
Source: *The Giants and the Dodgers* (Lee Allen, 1964)

Quote: "I mean, nobody threw harder than Rex Barney, but he couldn't win. He couldn't get anything over but his fastball, and when he got his fastball over it was right down the middle and people hit it."
Source: Del Crandall in *This Side of Cooperstown* (Larry Moffi, 1996)

Quote: "There's an awful lot of guys that will tell you Rex Barney was the fastest pitcher they ever saw. Speed to burn."
Source: Bobby Bragan in *The Man in the Dugout* (Donald Honig, 1977)

Quote: "Rex Barney would be the league's best pitcher if the plate were high and outside."
Source: Bob Cooke in *Voices of Baseball* (ed. Bob Chieger, 1983)

Commentary: By all accounts, after Barney's control problems cost him his job in the majors, he could still throw hard and he could still throw strikes . . . when warming up. However, the minute he went into a game, he couldn't throw strikes at all. Barney might be the first known sufferer of what later was called Steve Blass Disease.

JIM BARR 6'3" 205-pound righty
101-112, 3.56, 12 Saves 1971 1983

Pitch Selection: 1. Fastball 2. Hard Slider 3. Curve
Source: *The Sporting News* (7/6/1974, Pat Frizzell)

KEWPIE DICK BARRETT 5'9" 175-pound righty
35-58, 4.30, 2 Saves 1933 1945

Pitches: 1. Curves 2. Fastball 3. Change 4. Slider (occasional)
Barrett: "First, I make my leg, back and shoulder do most of the work. Second, I stick pretty much to the old routine—the same form and rhythm, the same pitches. Two curves, a fast one and a change. I stay away from screwballs, knuckleballs and the rest and only rarely throw a slider. So my muscles and bones and nerves just keep on doing what they're used to. Third, I like it out there."
Source: *Pacific Coast League Baseball News* (4/25/1948; at the time, Barrett was forty-one years old and had recently recorded his 200th Pacific Coast League victory and his 316th as a professional pitcher.)

RED BARRETT 5'11" 183-pound righty
69-69, 3.53, 7 Saves 1937 1949

Pitch Selection: 1. Change 2. Curve 3. Fastball
Source: *1947 Scout Report* (Wid Matthews); *Great American Sports Humor* (Mac Davis, 1949) says that Barrett "won his share of games with a mystifying nothing-ball," and other sources support the notion that Barrett didn't throw hard, at all.

Note: In 1955, Barrett admitted that he'd frequently thrown a spitball.
Source: *The Sporting News* (7/13/1955, Brad Wilson)

Pitch Selection: 1. Fastball 2. Curve
Source: Lee Allen in *The Sporting News* (1/25/1969, Allen's "Cooperstown Corner" column)

Note: In the late 1940s, Barrett was moderately famous for having thrown only 58 pitches in a 1944 nine-inning shutout.

FRANK BATES ?-pound righty
3-19, 6.33, 0 Saves 1898 1899

Pitch Selection: 1. Curve 2. Fastball
Quote: "He has only average speed, very poor command of the ball, and relies almost entirely on the outcurve."
Source: *New York Times* (8/13/1899)

MIGUEL BATISTA 6'1" 197-pound righty
42-50, 4.39, 1 Save 1992 2003

Pitch Selection: 1. Fastball 2. Slider 3. Change
Sources: *1993 Montreal Expos Media Guide; The Scouting Notebook: 1999*

Pitches: 1. Cut Fastball 2. Slider 3. Split-Fingered Fastball 4. Curve (occasional) 5. Fastball (94)
Source: *The Scouting Notebook: 2002*

Pitches: 1. Sinking Fastball (low-90s) 2. Slider 3. Change 4. Split-Fingered Fastball (occasional)
Description: "Batista's repertoire consists of three quality pitches, but everything works off his low-90s fastball (he also throws a breaking ball and a changeup). He has dabbled with a split-fingered fastball, which he throws occasionally. He becomes more vulnerable when he tries to overthrow and leaves the ball up in the zone. But when he keeps his focus and keeps the ball down by the knees, he gets ground balls with a good sinking fastball. When Batista needs a strikeout, he has a nasty slider, and he has good control with it—he can throw it for strikes."
Source: Tom Candiotti, writing for ESPN.com's Insider (7/1/2003)

RUSS BAUERS 6'3" 195-pound righty
31-30, 3.53, 5 Saves 1936 1950

Pitch Selection: 1. Fastball 2. Curve
Description: "Bauers' fast ball fairly sings as it whizzes plateward and his curve has as sharp a break as a dip of a scenic railway."
Source: *Baseball Magazine* (March 1938, Arthur O. W. Anderson)

FRANK BAUMANN 6'0" 205-pound lefty
45-38, 4.11, 13 Saves 1955 1965

Key Pitch: Sinking Fast Ball
Source: *Major League Baseball 1965* (Jack Zanger)

Note: According to the 1963 *Major League Handbook* (Don Schiffer), Baumann had developed a new curve and improved his slider late in 1962. What role they played post-1962, we do not know.

Quote: "He was impressive with a fastball in the mid-ninety's and a fair curve ball."
Source: Russ Kemmerer in *Ted Williams: 'Hey Kid, Just Get It Over the Plate!'* (Kemmerer with W.C. Madden, 2002)

GEORGE BAUMGARDNER 5'11" 178-pound righty
36-47, 3.22, 4 Saves 1912 1916

Key Pitch: Fastball
Note: Baumgardner was described in a 1912 newspaper article as "faster than Walter Johnson."
Source: Lee Allen in *The Sporting News* (6/1/1968, Allen's "Cooperstown Corner" column)

JOSE BAUTISTA 6'2" 205-pound righty
32-42, 4.62, 3 Saves 1988 1997

Pitch Selection: 1. Forkball 2. Fastball 3. Curve 4. Slider
Note: Throws forkball at two speeds.
Source: *The Scouting Notebook: 1995*

Pitch Selection: 1. Fastball (high-80s) 2. Slider 3. Change 4. Forkball
Note: According to the 1996 *Scouting Notebook,* in 1995 Bautista gave up a number of home runs on hanging forkballs.
Source: *The Scouting Notebook* (1996 and 1997 editions)

WALTER BEALL 5'10" 178-pound righty
5-5, 4.43, 1 Save 1924 1929

Key Pitch: Curve
Babe Ruth: "The best curve ball I ever saw . . . Beall could make a baseball sit up and sing bass, no kidding. His curve broke down, and I'll swear he could break it three or four inches. But he never knew whether it was going over the plate or down the left field foul line . . ."
Source: *Babe Ruth's Own Book of Baseball* (Ruth, 1928)

Commentary: Ruth didn't actually write his "Own Book of Baseball," but his ghost writer (Ford Frick, probably) was echoing a widely-held sentiment around baseball, that Beall had the most amazing curveball in the game but couldn't consistently throw it for strikes. That may be true, but it's also true that he pitched only 124 innings in the majors, and did well in the high minors.

See also Guy Morton entry.

GENE BEARDEN 6'3" 198-pound lefty
45-38, 3.96, 1 Save 1947 1953

Pitches: 1. Knuckleball (80%) 2. Fastball 3. Curve 4. Slider 5. Screwball (occasional)
Sources: *Baseball Magazine* (September 1948, Ed Rumill); *Baseball Register* (1949 edition); *Baseball Digest* (October 1950, Gordon Cobbledick)

Notes: Bearden learned his slider from Mel Harder in 1947. Citation for 80-percent knuckleballs comes from *Player-Manager* (Lou Boudreau with Ed Fitzgerald, 1952 edition).

Bearden in the *Baseball Register:* "My knuckler probably should be called a fingertip ball. I file my nails down and grasp the ball with my thumb and little finger, resting the tips of my three other fingers on the ball. I soon developed calluses where my nails were. The ball dips, wiggles or waves depending upon how I throw it and the direction of the wind."

LARRY BEARNARTH 6'2" 203-pound righty
13-21, 4.13, 8 Saves 1963 1971

Pitch Selection: 1. Slider 2. Fastball
Sources: *Don Schiffer's Major League Baseball Handbook—1964; Baseball Digest* (March 1963)

Casey Stengel: "He is an inexperienced pitcher, but he gets out of that hole. Big uniforms and big names don't frighten him. He throws those double-play sinkers to them all."
Source: *The Gospel According to Casey* (Ira Berkow and Jim Kaplan, 1992)

JIM BEATTIE 6'5" 210-pound righty
52-87, 4.17, 1 Save 1978 1986

Pitch Selection: 1. Hard Slider 2. Fastball 3. Change
Description: "He has an excellent slider, as quick as any in the American League . . . He is the type who can be flirting with a no-hitter when he has his excellent stuff."
Source: Denny Matthews in *The Scouting Report: 1985*

Note: Beattie began suffering from shoulder tendinitis in 1980, and first underwent surgery at the end of 1984. Before the surgery, he'd thrown a low-90s fastball, but afterward he was usually clocked in the high 80s.
Sources: *The Scouting Report: 1986; The Sporting News* (6/30/1986, Jim Street)

JOHNNY BEAZLEY 6'1" 190-pound righty
31-12, 3.01, 3 Saves 1941 1949

Pitches: 1. Fastball 2. Curve 3. Changes
Beazley: "What more does a guy have to have? I slow up on both the fast ball and the curve. But none of those screw ball pitches for me. I don't want no part of 'em."
Source: *Baseball Magazine* (December 1942, Herbert Goren)

Stan Musial: ". . . Johnny had everything to be a great pitcher. He had confidence, courage, control, a good fast ball and a good curve. If he hadn't hurt his arm, he would have had many, many big years."
Source: *Stan Musial: The Man's Own Story* (Musial, as told to Bob Broeg, 1964)

BOOM-BOOM BECK 6'2" 200-pound righty
38-69, 4.30, 6 Saves 1924 1945

Pitch Selection, 1924–1928: 1. Fastball
Pitch Selection, 1933 on: 1. "Sneaky" Fastball 2. Curve 3. Change
Sources: Thomas Holmes in the *Brooklyn Eagle* (3/16/1933); *Pueblo Chieftain* (3/23/1933)

Note: Beck threw with a loose, sweeping sidearm delivery that somewhat resembled Walter Johnson's.

Quote: "Beck is a side-armer with varied material."
Source: *Who's Who in Major League Baseball* (Harold "Speed" Johnson, 1933)

ROD BECK 6'1" 215-pound righty
38-43, 3.21, 286 Saves 1991 2003

Pitch Selection: 1. Sinker 2. Slider 3. Split-Fingered Fastball or Forkball
Sources: *1994 Baseball Almanac; The Scouting Notebook 1999*

JOSH BECKETT 6'5" 216-pound righty
17-17, 3.32, 0 Saves 2001 2003

Pitches: 1. Four-Seam Fastball (96–98) 2. 12-to-6 Curve 3. Two-Seam Fastball (low-90s) 4. Change
Source: *The Scouting Notebook 2003*

JOE BECKWITH 6'3" 200-pound righty
18-19, 3.54, 7 Saves 1979 1986

Pitch Selection: 1. Fastball (high-80s) 2. Curve 3. Slider 4. Change
Sources: *The Scouting Report* (1984 and 1985)

STEVE BEDROSIAN 6'3" 200-pound righty
76-79, 3.38, 184 Saves 1981 1995

Pitch Selection: 1. Fastball 2. Slider
Source: *The Scouting Report: 1990*

JOE BEGGS 6'1" 182-pound righty
48-35, 2.96, 29 Saves 1938 1948

Key Pitch: Sinker
Source: Junior Thompson in *Dugout to Foxhole* (Rick Van Blair, 1994)

TIM BELCHER 6'3" 210-pound righty
146-140, 4.16, 5 Saves 1987 2000

Pitch Selection, early in career: 1. Fastball (95) 2. Slider
Pitches, later in career: 1. Fair Fastball 2. Slider 3. Split-Fingered Fastball 4. Curve
Sources: *The Scouting Report: 1990; The Scouting Notebook: 1997*

STAN BELINDA 6'3" 185-pound righty
41-37, 4.15, 79 Saves 1989 2000

Pitch Selection: 1. Sidearm Fastball 2. Split-Fingered Fastball
Sources: *1994 Baseball Almanac; The Scouting Notebook: 1996*

BO BELINSKY 6'2" 191-pound lefty
28-51, 4.10, 2 Saves 1962 1970

Pitch Selection: 1. Fastball 2. Screwball 3. Curve

Note: In 1966, Belinsky frequently threw a spitball that he'd learned from Hal Newhouser in 1959.
Source: *Bo: Pitching and Wooing* (Maury Allen, 1973)

Pitch Selection: 1. Live, Riding Fastball 2. Hard Curve 3. Screwball
Source: Associated Press obituary (11/24/2001) quoting Belinsky's catcher, Buck Rodgers

GARY BELL 6'1" 196-pound righty
121-117, 3.68, 51 Saves 1958 1969

Pitch Selection: 1. Fastball 2. Curve 3. Slider
Sources: *The Impossible Dream Remembered* (Coleman and Valenti, 1987; In *Major League Baseball—1969*, Jack Zanger wrote, "During Gary's heyday with Cleveland . . . his fastball racked up a lot of strikeouts. But he depended on his slider more last year and fanned only 105."

WILLIAM BELL 5'11" 185-pound righty
Negro Leagues 1923 1937

Pitch Selection: 1. Fastball 2. Curve 3. Change 4. Slider
Source: *The Biographical Encyclopedia of the Negro Baseball Leagues* (James A. Riley, 1994)

CHIEF BENDER 6'2" 185-pound righty
212-127, 2.46, 33 Saves 1903 1925

Pitch Selection: 1. Fast Curves 2. Fastball 3. Submarine Fadeaway 4. Slow Ball (occasional)
Bender: "I use fast curves, pitched overhand and side arm, fast balls, high and inside, and an underhand fadeaway pitch with the hand almost down to the level of the knees. These are my most successful deliveries, though a twisting slow one mixed up with them helps at times."
Source: *Baseball Magazine* (August 1911, "Big Chief Bender")

Pitch Selection: 1. Change 2. Curve 3. Fastball
Sources: Bob Shawkey in *The Man in the Dugout* (Donald Honig, 1977); *Memories of Twenty Years in Baseball* (Ty Cobb)

Shawkey: "The Chief had a great curveball, but I'd say his greatest success came on the change-up he threw off his fastball. They'd swing at his motion, and that ball would come floating up there. It was beautiful to watch."
Comment: Bender may have thrown a knuckleball. In *The Bobby Shantz Story* (1953), Shantz (as told to Ralph Bernstein) credits Bender with teaching him to throw the pitch. And when Bender refers above to his "twisting slow one," he might be talking about a knuckleball, which at that time often was lumped under the general heading of "slow ball."

ANDY BENES 6'6" 235-pound righty
155-139, 3.97, 1 Save 1989 2002

Pitch Selection, early career: 1. Fastball 2. Slider 3. Change
Pitches, later career: 1. Rising Fastball 2. Sinking Fastball 3. Hard Slider 4. Slurve 5. Change 6. Split-Fingered Fastball (added mid-season 2002)
Sources: *The Scouting Report: 1992; The Scouting Notebook: 1997*; ESPN's "Baseball Tonight" (9/1/2002)

Note: According to the "Baseball Tonight" feature, a few days after Benes came off the disabled list in July 2002, the Cardinals acquired Chuck Finley, who taught Benes how to throw a splitter. Benes threw his first splitter in a game on July 30, 2002, and it quickly became one of his better pitches.

RAY BENGE 5'9" 160-pound righty
101-130, 4.52, 19 Saves 1925 1938

Pitch Selection: 1. Three-Quarter Sidearm Curve 2. Fastball 3. Change 4. Knuckleball 5. Screwball
Sources: Cullen Cain, National League Service Bureau (2/15/1931); *Baseball Magazine* (February 1934); unidentified clippings of April 5, 1934, and March 7, 1935, in the *TSN* Morgue, possibly from the *Brooklyn Eagle*

1931 Description: "He has a lot of 'smoke' to use with his curves."

Benge in *Baseball Magazine*: "Even a curve pitcher serves up more fast balls than any other variety. But he usually plans to tempt the batter to hit his curve."

Note: The knuckleball and screwball were used only occasionally until Benge got older.

ARMANDO BENITEZ 6'4" 220-pound righty
30-31, 3.03, 197 Saves 1994 2003

Pitch Selection: 1. Overpowering Fastball
2. Split-Fingered Fastball 3. Slider
Source: *The Scouting Notebook 1999*

DENNIS BENNETT 6'3" 192-pound lefty
43-47, 3.69, 6 Saves 1962 1968

Pitch Selection: 1. Curve 2. (Sneaky) Fastball
Sources: *1963 Major League Handbook* (Don Schiffer); *Sport* (July 1964, Stan Hochman)

JACK BENTLEY 5'11" 200-pound lefty
46-33, 4.01, 9 Saves 1913 1927

Description of Bentley's delivery: "Bentley whirled around, somewhat like Fitzsimmons, but he swung his arms and shoulders through a series of pretzel convolutions that eventually tired him out. 'When it got to be the seventh inning,' said Bentley, 'I feel the effects. And yet, I can't seem to pitch without that wind-up.' "
Source: *Baseball Magazine* (June 1935, F.C. Lane)

AL BENTON 6'4" 215-pound righty
98-88, 3.66, 66 Saves 1934 1952

Pitch Selection, 1934–1935: 1. Fastball
Pitch Selection, 1938–1940: 1. Fastball 2. Slider
Pitch Selection, 1941–1945: 1. Slider 2. Curve
3. Fastball
Pitches, 1948–1950: 1. Sinker 2. Curve 3. Slider
4. Fastball
Pitches, 1952: 1. Sinker 2. Curve 3. Fastball
Commentary: Pitching for the A's in the mid-'30s, Benton tried hard to learn a curve, but simply could not. He learned the slider in the minors in 1937, and that brought him back to the majors. H. G. Salsinger wrote in 1945 that Benton's slider was "probably the best pitch of its kind seen in the big leagues this year." However, in 1949 Benton gave a very specific ranking of his pitches to Bill Conlin, and listed the sinker as his best pitch. He stopped throwing the slider in 1951 because he thought it was taking away from his curve.

Even as a 40-year-old pitcher, Benton could still throw hard when the occasion required. And his durability allowed him to give up home runs to both Babe Ruth and Mickey Mantle.

Sources: Henry P. Edwards, American League Service Bureau (January 18, 1942); Salsinger in *The Sporting News* (3/26/1942 and May, 1945); Bill Conlin in the *Sacramento Union* (1/11/1949); Franklin Lewis in the *Cleveland Plain-Dealer* (3/8/1950); Frank Finch in *The Sporting News* (5/28/1952)

LARRY BENTON 5'11" 165-pound righty
127-128, 4.03, 22 Saves 1923 1935

Key Pitch: Fastball
Quote: "Benton is essentially a speed ball pitcher. He has a fine hop on the fast ball."
Source: John J. Ward in *Baseball Magazine* (February 1927)

Quote: "He has not been a strikeout hurler, averaging only three per game, but he has control and a curve that baffles the foe."
Source: *Who's Who in Major League Baseball* (Harold "Speed" Johnson, 1933)

RUBE BENTON 6'1" 190-pound lefty
154-145, 3.09, 21 Saves 1910 1925

Pitch Selection: 1. Fastball 2. Curve 3. Change
Source: unsigned article circulated by the North American Newspaper Alliance, July 16, 1932

JOE BENZ 6'1" 196-pound righty
76-75, 2.44, 3 Saves 1911 1919

Pitch Selection: 1. Spitball 2. Knuckleball
Source: *The Ballplayers* (1990, article by Richard C. Lindberg); *The 1917 White Sox* (Warren N. Wilbert and William C. Hageman, 2003)

JASON BERE 6'3" 185-pound righty
71-65, 5.14, 0 Saves 1993 2003

Pitches: 1. Fastball (90s) 2. Fosh Change
3. Slider 4. Curve
Source: *The Scouting Notebook: 1996*

Pitch Selection: 1. Fastball (high 80s) 2. Change
3. Curve 4. Cut Fastball
Source: *The Scouting Notebook: 1999*

JUAN BERENGUER 5'11" 186-pound righty
67-62, 3.90, 32 Saves 1978 1992

Pitch Selection, 1983–84: 1. Fastball (low-90s) 2. Hard Slider 3. Hard Curve
Pitch Selection, 1985–92: 1. Fastball (88–92) 2. Split-Fingered Fastball 3. Slider
Note: Berenguer developed a split-fingered fastball under the tutelage of Tigers pitching coach Roger Craig.
Sources: *The Scouting Report: 1985; Inside Pitch* (Roger Craig, 1985); *The Scouting Report:* (1990 and 1992 editions)

BRUCE BERENYI 6'3" 205-pound righty
44-55, 4.03, 0 Saves 1980 1986

Pitch Selection: 1. Fastball (mid-90s) 2. Slider 3. Curve
Source: *The Scouting Report: 1983*

Pitch Selection: 1. Fastball (90s) 2. Slider 3. Curve 4. Straight Change
Note: It appears that Berenyi added the straight change in 1983.
Source: *The Scouting Report: 1984*

SEAN BERGMAN 6'4" 225-pound righty
39-47, 5.28, 0 Saves 1993 2000

Pitches: 1. Sinking Fastball (88–94) 2. Hard Slider 3. Change
Sources: *The Scouting Notebook* (1996 and 1999 editions)

BILL BERNHARD 6'1" 205-pound righty
116-82, 3.04, 3 Saves 1899 1907

Key Pitch: Slow Ball
Source: *The Detroit News* (4/12/1929, H.G. Salsinger column)

JOE BERRY 5'10" 145-pound righty
21-22, 2.45, 18 Saves 1942 1946

Pitches: 1. Curves 2. Slider 3. Fastball 4. Screwball (used as Change)
Description: "Berry is this effective not because he has a great deal of natural stuff, which he hasn't, but because every pitch he throws is different. He has a curve with three different speeds. He'll waste one fast ball, then throw another with a little taken off the top, easing it up there where the batter can hit it, but not well.

"He has a slider with varying speeds. He changes up with an evil little screwball. In dugout parlance, every pitch 'does something.' "
Source: *Baseball Digest* (March 1945, Red Smith)

Pitch Selection: 1. Curve 2. Knuckle Ball
Source: *Veeck's Medicine Mine for 1947* (1947 Cleveland Indians Media Guide)

FRANK BERTAINA 5'11" 177-pound lefty
19-29, 3.84, 0 Saves 1964 1970

Pitch Selection: 1. Fastball 2. Slider 3. Curve 4. Change
Source: *Major League Baseball—1969* (Jack Zanger)

DON BESSENT 6'0" 175-pound righty
14-7, 3.33, 12 Saves 1955 1958

Note: Listed by *The Sporting News* (8/29/1956) as having one of the best fastballs in the league.

HUCK BETTS 5'11" 170-pound righty
61-68, 3.93, 16 Saves 1920 1935

Pitch Selection: 1. Screwball 2. Curve 3. Fastball 4. Slow Curve
Sources: *Diamond Greats* (Rich Westcott, 1984), F. C. Lane in *Baseball Magazine* (August 1935 article about Carl Hubbell); in *Masters of the Diamond* (Rich Westcott, 1994), Ethan Allen describes Betts as a "slowball" pitcher.

Pitches: 1. Fastball 2. Change 3. Curve 4. Screwball
Quote: "What is Betts' pitching repertoire? He can burn over a fairly fast ball, he has a good change of pace, a fine curve and a deceptive screw ball.

" 'My fast ball is possibly my best delivery, but I won't say I depend upon it most in a jam.' "
Source: *Baseball Magazine* (January 1933, Clifford Bloodgood)

FLOYD BEVENS 6'3" 210-pound righty
40-36, 3.08, 0 Saves 1944 1947

Pitches: 1. Fastball 2. Curve 3. Change 4. Sinker
Bevens: "I do not use anything odd or unorthodox. I have a sinker, but it is a natural delivery. Fast ball, curve,

change, and change in speeds. That is my repertoire. You know how that sinker acts. It could make you a bit wild. One day it will behave, another it will act up. However, I am getting control of it."
Source: *Baseball Magazine* (June 1947, Daniel M. Daniel; in same article, Bevens goes out of his way to stress that he doesn't fool around with the knuckleball, that he's working on a screwball but hasn't thrown one in a game yet, and that Spud Chandler tried to teach him the slider but it didn't take.)

JIM BIBBY 6'5" 235-pound righty
111-101, 3.76, 8 Saves 1972 1984

Pitches: 1. Fastball 2. Curve 3. Slider
Sources: *The Sporting News* (8/7/1971, George McClelland; 7/30/1977, Russ Schneider; and 8/25/1979, Charley Feeney)

VERN BICKFORD 6'0" 180-pound righty
66-57, 3.71, 2 Saves 1948 1954

Pitch Selection: 1. Slider 2. Curve 3. Fastball 4. Change
Sources: *Baseball Magazine* (February 1949); Bickford quoted in *The No-Hit Hall of Fame* (Rich Coberly, 1985)

ROCKY BIDDLE 6'3" 230-pound righty
16-22, 5.09, 35 Saves 2000 2003

Pitches: 1. Fastball (low-90s) 2. Slurve (mid-80s) 3. Curve (high-70s)
Source: Expos-Dodgers broadcast on Fox Sports Net, 8/20/2003

MIKE BIELECKI 6'3" 195-pound righty
70-73, 4.18, 5 Saves 1984 1997

Pitch Selection: 1. Fastball 2. Forkball 3. Curve 4. Change
Sources: *The Scouting Report: 1990; The Scouting Notebook: 1997*
Quote: Bielecki "shows no preference and will use any of [his four pitches] during any count."

JACK BILLINGHAM 6'4" 195-pound righty
145-113, 3.83, 15 Saves 1968 1980

Pitch Selection: 1. Fastball 2. Curve
Source: *The Sporting News* (9/4/1976, Earl Lawson)
Note: According to *Major League Baseball: 1971* (Brenda Zanger and Dick Kaplan), Billingham threw "with a sidearm motion that's hard on righthanded hitters."

Note: Listed as a suspected spitball pitcher.
Source: *The Cincinnati Game* (Lonnie Wheeler and John Baskin, 1988)

DOUG BIRD 6'4" 180-pound righty
73-60, 3.99, 60 Saves 1973 1983

Pitch Selection: 1. Fastball 2. Slider 3. Palm Ball
Sources: *The Sporting News* (6/26/1976, Sid Bordman); unidentified clipping of article by Ray Didinger (TSN Morgue)

RALPH BIRKOFER 5'11" 213-pound lefty
31-28, 4.19, 2 Saves 1933 1937

Pitch Selection: 1. Sinking Fastball 2. Curve
Description: "Birkofer not only has bulk, but power and strength to go with it. When he cuts loose he can throw one of the fastest balls in the business, and from his left hand which is an added advantage. Moreover Ralph's hard one sinks as it reaches the plate and when he has it in control is almost unhittable even if the batsman knows it is coming. But speed, while it is his chief dependence in a jam, does not exhaust his stock in trade. Birkofer's curve is better than fair."
Source: *Baseball Magazine* (March 1935, Clifford Bloodgood)

BUD BLACK 6'2" 180-pound lefty
121-116, 3.84, 11 Saves 1981 1995

Pitches, 1982–88: 1. Fastball (84–88) 2. Slider 3. Curve 4. Change
Pitches, 1989–90: 1. Fastball 2. Slider 3. Curve 4. Cut Fastball 5. Change
Pitches, 1991: 1. Fastball 2. Slider 3. Change 4. Curve 5. Forkball
Sources: *The Scouting Report* (1982, 1985, 1987, 1990, and 1992 editions)

JOE BLACK 6'2" 220-pound righty
30-12, 3.91, 25 Saves 1952 1957

Pitch Selection: 1. Fastball 2. Curve
Note: Black's curve was often mistaken for a slider.

Source: Mike Gaven in the *New York Journal-American* (October 1952)

Quote: "He possessed only a fast ball and a small, sharp curve. Dressen liked pitchers with varied weapons and he was reluctant to believe that Black could win with just two pitches."
Source: Roger Kahn in *The Boys of Summer* (1971)

Note: Listed as a suspected spitball pitcher
Source: *The Cincinnati Game* (Lonnie Wheeler and John Baskin, 1988)

EWELL BLACKWELL 6'6" 195-pound righty
82-78, 3.30, 10 Saves 1942 1955

Pitches: 1. Sinking Fastball 2. Curve 3. Change 4. Slider 5. Palm Ball (added in 1948)
Notes and sources: *1947 Scout Report* (Wid Matthews); *Stan Musial* (Musial with Bob Broeg, 1964); column by Lou Smith in unidentified newspaper, 6/1/1960, TSN Morgue; *Baseball Magazine* (June 1948; includes photo of Blackwell holding his palm ball). Blackwell threw with a sidearm motion that terrified right-handed hitters.

Description: "Moreover, he possesses one of the most unusual—and physically trying—windups in baseball . . . He kicks his long left leg until the batter fears for his personal safety, whirls with the ball hidden from view, and then whips the ball sidearm."
Source: *Sport* (September 1952, Lou Smith)

Description: "Blackwell perhaps isn't as fast as Feller was in his prime. Maybe not even as fast as Newhouser at his best. But he IS fast, he has an exceptional sidearm sinker and, most of all, he has a contortionist motion that baffles the best batters."
Lou Boudreau: "His speed is terrific, he is around the plate all the time, his curve is deadly and his sidearm sinker spectacular."
Pee Wee Reese: "They ought to have a rule making that sidearm pitch of his illegal. He's got a little of everything, too. That sinker can shoot down and in, or down and away."
Source: *Baseball Digest* (September 1947, Harold Sheldon)

Description: "One of the last remaining hurlers who still can overpower the opposition. He throws a crossfire pitch and a sinking sidearm fastball that often is almost impossible to hit squarely. The hitters are confident on one score—Blackwell never changes up."
Source: *Baseball Digest* (January 1951, Milton Richman)

GEORGE BLAEHOLDER 5'11" 175-pound righty
104-125, 4.54, 12 Saves 1925 1936

Pitches: 1. Fastball/Slider 2. Curve 3. Change (ineffective)
Quote: "Blaeholder's strong point is his fastball. He generally throws this with a side arm motion which gives the ball a curious sweep to one side as it crosses the plate. Disconcerted batters have christened it the 'slide ball.' Evidently this deceptive sweep is due to some peculiarity in holding and throwing the ball. But Blaeholder takes no special credit.

" 'It's just my natural style,' he says. 'I've developed control, but that's all.' Blaeholder also has a fair curve, though not much change of pace. He has never bothered with the screw ball or other patented deliveries. A regulation pitcher with a slightly freaky fast ball describes him."
Source: *Baseball Magazine* (August 1936, John J. Ward, "He Hurls the 'Slide Ball' ")

Key Pitch: Slider
Sources: *Who's Who in the American League (1935)* (Page 71); also, the 1936 edition of *Who's Who* says, "One of his most effective deliveries is popularly known as a 'slider' and it has annoyed Jimmie Foxx to no end."

Note: Blaeholder has been often credited with inventing the slider. Specific citations for this include *Baseball Digest* (Dec.–Jan. 1961) and *The Sporting News* (9/24/1952)

Quote: "Jimmy Foxx, of the Athletics, a hitter of parts as everyone knows, admits that of all pitchers he is called upon to face, Blaeholder is the toughest to solve."
Source: *Who's Who in Major League Baseball* (Harold "Speed" Johnson, 1933)

WILLIE BLAIR 6'1" 185-pound righty
60-86, 5.04, 4 Saves 1990 2001

Pitch Selection: 1. Fastball 2. Slider 3. Curve
Source: *The Scouting Notebook 1998*

SHERIFF BLAKE 6'0" 180-pound righty
87-102, 4.13, 8 Saves 1920 1937

Pitches, through 1928: 1. Curve 2. Fastball
3. Slow Ball 4. Knuckleball (occasional)
Pitches, post-1928: 1. Fastball 2. Curve 3. Change?
Sources: *Baseball Magazine* (January 1928, "Comprising an Interview with John Fred (Sheriff) Blake"); *Baseball Players and Their Times: Oral Histories of the Game, 1920–1940* (Eugene Murdock, 1991)

Quote from 1928 *Baseball Magazine* article: "I've experimented with the knuckle ball, but I very seldom use it and I haven't what I'd call a good slow ball, either. Yes, I guess I'm a curve ball pitcher, all right."

Note: Blake's fingers were jammed and bent by a line drive in the closing weeks of the 1928 season. The injury left him unable to grip the curve properly, which sent his career into a tailspin, as that was his best pitch. He adjusted his delivery to try to compensate—even, at times, throwing the ball underhanded.

TED BLANKENSHIP 6'1" 170-pound righty
77-79, 4.29, 4 Saves 1922 1930

Key Pitch: Fastball
Quote: "[He] had a lot of stuff for a pitcher. He could, as the boys say, make the ball whistle."
Source: F.C. Lane in *Baseball Magazine* (March 1927)

CY BLANTON 5'11" 180-pound righty
68-71, 3.55, 5 Saves 1934 1942

Pitches: 1. Screwball 2. Fastball 3. "Downer"
4. Curve 5. Change (added 1935)
Sources: Damon Kerby, *St. Louis Post-Dispatch*, May 9, 1935; Sam Murphy in unidentified newspaper, 1935; unidentified 1938 article (TSN Morgue); Harry Keck, *Pittsburgh Sun-Telegraph* (3/20/1960); *The Crooked Pitch* (Martin Quigley, 1984), *Baseball Magazine* (January 1935, Kirk L. Stiles; and August 1935, F.C. Lane); Stiles says Blanton "specializes in a blinding fastball that hitters often fail to see."

Commentary: Blanton's fastball was excellent, although he favored the screwball as his best pitch. The "Downer" was a pitch that broke straight down, like a forkball, spitball, splitter or drop curve. This pitch often hit the dirt in front of home plate. It is unclear to us whether Blanton threw another curve as well or whether the "downer" is the "big curve" cited by several writers.

As a semi-pro pitcher in 1929, Blanton pitched a no-hitter in which he struck out 23 men. He ruined his arm pitching a complete game no-hitter early in spring training, 1938.

WADE BLASINGAME 6'1" 185-pound lefty
46-51, 4.52, 5 Saves 1963 1972

Pitch Selection: 1. Sneaky Fastball
2. Wide, sweeping curve 3. Mediocre Change
Sources: *Baseball Digest* (March 1963, Page 16), *Major League Baseball 1965* (Jack Zanger)

STEVE BLASS 6'0" 165-pound righty
103-76, 3.63, 2 Saves 1964 1974

Pitch Selection: 1. Slider 2. Fastball
3. Big, Slow Curve 4. Sinking Fastball 5. Curve
Sources: *Five Seasons* (Roger Angell, 1977); *Major League Baseball—1969* (Jack Zanger)

Angell: "I can still recall how Blass looked that afternoon [in 1972]—his characteristic, feet-together stance at the outermost, first-base edge of the pitching rubber, and then the pitch, delivered with a swastikalike scattering of arms and legs and a final lurch to the left . . ."

Comment: In 1973, Blass developed an inexplicable inability to throw strikes, from which he never recovered.

JOE BLONG ?-pound righty
10-9, 2.68, 0 Saves 1876 1877

Key Pitch: Fastball
Quote: "A fine, speedy pitcher was Joe."
Source: *The National Game* (Alfred H. Spink, 1911)

VIDA BLUE 6'0" 189-pound lefty
209-161, 3.26, 2 Saves 1969 1986

Pitch Selection: 1. Fastball 2. Curve 3. Change
4. Blue developed a slider in 1978.
Sources: *Vida* (Bill Libby and Vida Blue, 1972); *The Sporting News* (5/19/1979, Nick Peters)

Description: "Vida Blue, I discovered, is a pitcher in a hurry. Each inning, he ran to the pitcher's mound to

begin his work and ran back to the dugout when it was done. In the field, he worked with immense dispatch, barely pausing to get his catcher's sign before firing; this habit, which he shares with Bob Gibson and a few others, adds a pleasing momentum to the game. His motion looked to be without effort or mannerism: a quick, lithe body-twist toward first base, a high lift and crook of the right leg, a swift forward stride—almost a leap—and the ball, delivered about three-quarters over the top, abruptly arrived, a flick of white at the plate."
Source: Roger Angell in *The New Yorker* (reprinted in *The Summer Game,* 1972)

BERT BLYLEVEN 6'3" 200-pound righty
287-250, 3.31, 0 Saves 1970 1992

Pitch Selection: 1. Hard Curve 2. Fastball 3. Change 4. Developed a Slow Curve in 1983
Source: *The Sporting News* (April 1984)

Pitch Selection: 1. Roundhouse Curve 2. Overhand Drop Curve 3. Fastball
Source: Blyleven in *Baseball Digest* (September 1989, Tom Capezzuto.)

Minnesota Twins

Bert Blyleven

DOUG BOCHTLER 6'3" 200-pound righty
9-18, 4.57, 6 Saves 1995 2000

Pitch Selection: 1. Fastball (mid-90s) 2. Slider 3. Change
Note: Threw with a herky-jerky delivery
Sources: *The Scouting Notebook* (1996 and 1997 editions)

MIKE BODDICKER 5'11" 172-pound righty
134-116, 3.80, 3 Saves 1980 1993

Pitch Selection: 1. Slow Curve 2. Change 3. Fastball
Note: Boddicker sometimes threw what he called a "foshball," a combination of a forkball and a change. He was an artist at changing speeds and tantalizing hitters with curves so slow it was impossible to wait on them, and he would sometimes throw a 70 MPH fastball right down the middle of the plate and get by with it.
Sources: *The Scouting Report: 1987* and *1989*

JOE BOEHLING 5'11" 168-pound lefty
55-50, 2.94, 5 Saves 1912 1920

Description: "Joseph packs a world of stuff in that south side fin, has a slashing curve that sweeps in with a sharp break and mixes 'em up well. His control is perhaps his weak point."
Source: *Baseball Magazine* (September 1917, John J. Ward)

BRIAN BOEHRINGER 6'2" 192-pound righty
25-31, 4.35, 3 Saves 1995 2003

Pitch Selection: 1. Fastball (low-90s) 2. Slider (85) 3. Change (occasional)
Source: *The Scouting Notebook* (1999 and 2002 editions)

JOE BOEVER 6'1" 200-pound righty
34-45, 3.93, 49 Saves 1985 1996

Pitch Selection: 1. Palm Ball 2. Fastball 3. Slider
Source: *1994 Baseball Almanac*
Note: Boever could make the palm ball break either right or left as it sunk. It was essentially a trick pitch.

TOMMY BOGGS 6'2" 195-pound righty
20-44, 4.22, 0 Saves 1976 1985

Pitches: 1. Fastball (92) 2. Curve 3. Slider (added in 1980)
Source: *The Sporting News* (4/18/1981, Tim Tucker)

BRIAN BOHANON 6'2" 215-pound lefty
54-60, 5.19, 2 Saves 1990 2001

Pitch Selection: 1. Change 2. Fastball 3. Cut Fastball 4. Slow Curve (occasional)
Sources: *The Scouting Notebook* (1996 and 2000 editions)

BERNIE BOLAND 5'8" 168-pound righty
68-53, 3.25, 12 Saves 1915 1921

Key Pitch: Sharp Curve
Source: *The Ballplayers* (1990, article by Norman Macht)

BOBBY BOLIN 6'4" 185-pound righty
88-75, 3.40, 50 Saves 1961 1973

Key Pitch: Sidearm Fastball
Source: *1963 Major League Handbook* (Don Schiffer); Schiffer says, "some say [Bolin] is as overpowering as Don Drysdale."
Comment: "His problem has been to develop an effective curve to complement his overpowering speeder."
Source: *Don Schiffer's Major League Baseball Handbook—1964*

TOM BOLTON 6'2" 185-pound lefty
31-34, 4.56, 1 Save 1987 1994

Pitch Selection: 1. Fastball 2. Change 3. Curve
Source: *The Scouting Report: 1992*

TOMMY BOND 5'7" 160-pound righty
193-115, 2.25, 0 Saves 1876 1884

Pitch Selection: 1. Curve 2. Fastball
Sources: *The National Game* (Alfred H. Spink, pages 122–124); *Nineteenth Century Stars* (SABR, 1989, article by Bob Richardson)

RICKY BONES 5'10" 175-pound righty
63-82, 4.85, 1 Save 1991 2001

Pitch Selection: 1. Rising Fastball 2. Forkball 3. Curve
Source: *1995 Baseball Almanac*

JULIO BONETTI 6'0" 180-pound righty
6-14, 6.03, 1 Save 1937 1940

Key Pitch: Sinker
Description: "Ordinary fast ball, but good 'sinker.' Makes most batters top ball and hit on the ground."
Source: *The Sporting News* (9/21/1939)

BILL BONHAM 6'3" 190-pound righty
75-83, 4.01, 11 Saves 1971 1980

Pitch Selection: 1. Sinking Fastball 2. Change 3. Curve
Source: *The Sporting News* (5/6/1978, Earl Lawson)

TINY BONHAM 6'2" 215-pound righty
103-72, 3.06, 9 Saves 1940 1949

Pitch Selection: 1. Forkball 2. Fastball
Sources: *Baseball Magazine* (September 1942, Herbert Simons); *The Pitcher* (John Thorn and John Holway, 1987); *The Sporting News* (10/2/1941, Page 1; and 9/24/1952, Page 4)

Joe McCarthy: "Tiny reminds me a good deal of Grover Alexander. His control is so good that the hitters never get a good shot at the ball. He just keeps nicking those corners and mixing 'em up on the batters. Another thing. He pitches fast, like Old Alex. I remember when the concessions people would squawk because Alex raced through a game so quick, firing the ball back to the catcher almost as soon as he got it. I don't know what the concessionaires think of Ernie, but I know what the rest of us think of him. He has come along fine, is a game guy and a swell kid."
Source: *The Sporting News* (6/18/1942, Page 10)

Quote: "Bonham's fast ball rises a little. His fork ball sinks. You can see what this can do to a batter."
Source: Yankees coach Johnny Schulte in *Baseball Magazine*

JOE BONIKOWSKI 6'0" 175-pound righty
5-7, 3.88, 2 Saves 1962 1962

Pitch Selection: 1. Fastball
Source: *1963 Major League Handbook* (Don Schiffer, who describes it as "crackling" fastball)

DAN BOONE 5'8" lefty
2-1, 3.36, 4 Saves 1981 1990

Description: "Besides a below average fastball, Boone throws a curve, slider, knuckler and screwball. The latter is one of his most effective pitches."

Source: *The Sporting News* (6/13/1981, Phil Collier)

Key Pitch, 1990: Knuckleball (80–85%)
Source: *Baltimore Evening Sun* (9/17/1990, Ken Rosenthal)

Notes: Boone stopped playing professional baseball in 1984, and was rediscovered while pitching in the Senior League in 1989.

When Boone returned to the majors in 1990, he was said in one source to weigh 139 pounds, which would have made him the lightest major-league pitcher since Jose Acosta in the early 1920s.

PEDRO BORBON 6'2" 185-pound righty
69-39, 3.52, 80 Saves 1969 1980

Pitch Selection: 1. Fastball
Quote from Sparky Anderson: "His ball is really alive now . . . really moves."
Source: *The Sporting News* (4/27/1974, article by Earl Lawson)

Note: Reviewing several TSN articles and books about the Big Red Machine, there are numerous references to Borbon's "live" fastball, but no mention of him throwing any other pitch (which doesn't mean he didn't have others).

PEDRO BORBON JR. 6'1" 230-pound righty
16-16, 4.68, 6 Saves 1992 2003

Pitch Selection: 1. Fastball (mid-90s) 2. Hard Slider 3. Change
Source: *The Scouting Notebook: 1996*

Pitch Selection: 1. Curve 2. Fastball (below average) 3. Change
Note: Threw from a three-quarters delivery.
Source: *The Scouting Report: 1996*

Pitch Selection: 1. Fastball (mid-80s) 2. Big, Flat Curve
Source: *The Scouting Notebook: 2000*

FRANK BORK 6'2" 175-pound righty
2-2, 4.07, 2 Saves 1964

Pitch Selection: 1. Fastball 2. Knuckle Curve
Source: *The Sporting News* (1/11/1964, Les Biederman)

JOE BOROWSKI 6'2" 225-pound righty
11-14, 3.41, 35 Saves 1995 2003

Pitches: 1. Fastball (low-90s) 2. Slider 3. Change
Source: *The Scouting Notebook 2003*

HANK BOROWY 6'0" 175-pound righty
108-82, 3.50, 7 Saves 1942 1951

Pitch Selection: 1. Fastball 2. Curve 3. Change
Commentary: Borowy's fastball had excellent movement. The Smith article (below) says that he "has a free, rhythmic delivery with great wrist action which gives him a live ball." Struggling in 1946–48, Borowy switched to a sidearm delivery. He returned to an overhand motion in 1949.

Borowy was plagued throughout his career by blisters on his pitching hand, and also by digestive problems. Reviewing his clipping file at *The Sporting News,* there are stories every year about how some doctor, fan, or wise old teammate has finally helped him to lick the problem with the blisters, but none of the cures ever lasted.

Borowy was accused by Luke Sewell in 1944 of throwing a spitball.
Sources: Michael F. Gaven in *The Sporting News* (July 20, 1939); Jack Smith *Sunday News,* April 6, 1941); Fred Lieb in *TSN* (January 28, 1943); Stan Baumgartner in *TSN* (1949); John Lardner in *The Saturday Evening Post* (June 17, 1950)

Description: "Hank Borowy was the kind of pitcher who sent batters back to the bench muttering, 'He's got nothing. He won't be around the next time I hit.' He pitched a one-hitter against us and that's when I learned to be leery whenever I heard batters talk that way."
Source: *Rex Barney's Thank Youuuu for 50 Years in Baseball from Brooklyn to Baltimore* (Barney with Norman L. Macht, 1993)

CHRIS BOSIO 6'3" 220-pound righty
94-93, 3.96, 9 Saves 1986 1996

Pitches: 1. Fastball 2. Sinking Fastball 3. Change 4. Slider 5. Split-Fingered Fastball
Sources: *The Scouting Report* (1990 and 1993 editions)

Description: "Bosio throws strikes . . . He has only marginally good stuff, but succeeds by throwing a variety of

breaking pitches at constantly changing speeds, keeping the ball down, working fast, working inside and making hitters beat him."
Source: *Bill Mazeroski's Baseball* (1993 edition)

SHAWN BOSKIE 6'3" 210-pound righty
49-63, 5.14, 1 Save 1990 1998

Pitch Selection: 1. Curve 2. Fastball (mid-80s) 3. Split-Fingered Fastball (added 1991)
Sources: *The Scouting Report* (1992 and 1993 editions)

Note: *The Scouting Report: 1992* mentions that Boskie threw four pitches, but does not name all of them.

Pitch Selection: 1. Fastball (mid-80s) 2. Curve 3. Split-Fingered Fastball 4. Change 5. Cut Fastball
Note: Boskie's cut fastball is also called a sinker.
Sources: *The Scouting Report* (1992–1994 editions); *The Scouting Notebook: 1995*

DICK BOSMAN 6'2" 195-pound righty
82-85, 3.67, 2 Saves 1966 1976

Pitch Selection: 1. Sinking Fastball 2. Curve 3. Slider 4. Change
Source: *The Sporting News* (8/3/1974, Russ Schneider)

DAVE BOSWELL 6'3" 185-pound righty
68-56, 3.52, 0 Saves 1964 1971

Pitch Selection: 1. Overhand Fastball 2. Curve 3. Change
Source: *Sport* (May 1967, Maury Allen)

Pitch Selection: 1. Slow Curve 2. Fastball
Source: *Winning!* (Earl Weaver, edited by John Sammis, 1972)

RICKY BOTTALICO 6'1" 200-pound righty
28-38, 4.03, 114 Saves 1994 2003

Pitch Selection: 1. Fastball 2. Hard Curve
Sources: *The Scouting Notebook* (1997 and 1998 editions)

KENT BOTTENFIELD 6'3" 240-pound righty
46-49, 4.54, 10 Saves 1992 2001

Pitch Selection: 1. Fastball 2. Curve 3. Slider 4. Change
Source: *1993 Montreal Expos Media Guide*

Pitch Selection: 1. Sinking Fastball 2. Slider 3. Change
Source: *The Scouting Notebook 2000*

JIM BOUTON 6'0" 170-pound righty
62-63, 3.57, 6 Saves 1962 1978

Pitches, through 1968: 1. Fastball 2. Overhand Curve 3. Change (added in 1964)
Key Pitch, after 1968: Knuckleball
Notes: Bouton's Grade A Fastball disappeared in late 1964, and he added the change-up. After 1964 he relied more on his curveball, and beginning in 1969 he threw the knuckleball almost exclusively.
Sources: *Ball Four* (Jim Bouton, 1970); *Diamond Greats* (Rich Westcott, 1983); *The Sporting News* (7/2/1966, Til Ferdenzi), *Major League Baseball 1965* (Jack Zanger)

Mickey Mantle: "He throws that big curve like Pascual, and his fastball is better than Pascual's."
Comment: ". . . Bouton, who used to experiment with trick pitches, including a knuckler, credits ex-Yankee pitching coach Johnny Sain with giving him some invaluable advice. 'Sain told me my four or five pitches were all right, but that none of them were outstanding,' Jim says. 'He urged me to concentrate on my fastball and curve—which I did. They're still the pitches I get big hitters out with.' "
Source: *1964 Official Baseball Almanac* (Don Wise)

Description: "For eight innings [of Game 3 of the 1964 World Series], Curt Simmons and Jim Bouton pitched marvelously—Simmons, the veteran, with a selection of soft, in-and-out sliders, curves, and other junk, and Bouton with a rearing fast ball delivered with such energy that his cap flew off on every second or third pitch."
Source: Roger Angell in *The New Yorker* (October 1964, and reprinted in *The Summer Game*)

Bouton: "I throw a combination between a curve and a slider. It's a harder curve than most curves. I can make it break large or small, depending on the situation. You might say I have the standard stuff, fast ball, change and breaking ball. Sometimes I can make the curve break flatter, sometimes straight down."
Source: *Baseball Digest* (March 1967, Charles Dexter)

JOE BOWMAN 6'2" 190-pound righty
77-96, 4.40, 11 Saves 1932 1945

Pitch Selection, after World War II: 1. Knuckleball 2. Fastball 3. Sinker

Bowman in 1945: "I'm just using something I always had—a knuckleball. Something that a lot of managers and catchers talked me out of pitching when I was young, because they said I would hurt my arm. I might have been a great pitcher, one of those fellows who win 17 or 18 games a year over a long period of time, if I had started using my knuckler as regularly as I do now. I knew how to throw it when I first started pitching in Portland, and I was successful there. Then, when I got to the big leagues, a couple of managers, who didn't know any more about pitching than I know about raising bees, and a couple of catchers who used their heads only as hat-racks, said, 'Don't throw that knuckler—it will hurt your arm.' "

Source: *The Sporting News* (Dan Daniel, 8/16/1945)

OIL CAN BOYD 6'1" 155-pound righty
78-77, 4.04, 0 Saves 1982 1991

Pitch Selection: 1. Fastball 2. Curve 3. Slider 4. Change

Note: Boyd would throw each of his pitches from different angles.

Sources: *The Scouting Report: 1987; 1990 Montreal Expos Media Guide*

HENRY BOYLE 6'1" 205-pound righty
89-111, 3.06, 1 Save 1884 1889

Pitch Selection: 1. Fastball 2. "Up In-Shoot"

Quote: "Possessing a fine physique, his attitudes in the points are very striking. Standing with right foot a few inches in advance, he raises both hands to his breast, holding the ball in the fingers of the right hand. Swinging the left foot around to the middle of the box, he elevates the left elbow and pivoting on the left leg, sends the sphere in with both over and under-hand throws. Boyle depends chiefly upon the effectiveness of the 'up in-shoot' and the terrific speed with which he drives in the straight pitch."

Source: Article titled "How Men Pitch Base-Ball: The Famous Pitchers of the National League of 1886." No author or publisher is given, though the information in the article is said to have come from photographic studies done by the *New York World* newspaper.

GENE BRABENDER 6'5" 225-pound righty
35-43, 4.25, 6 Saves 1966 1970

Pitches: 1. Slider 2. Sinking Fastball 3. Tailing Fastball 4. Change (occasional)

Source: *The Sporting News* (10/4/1969, Hy Zimmerman; and 7/4/1970, Larry Whiteside)

TOM BRADLEY 6'2" 180-pound righty
55-61, 3.72, 2 Saves 1969 1975

Pitch Selection: 1. Fastball 2. Curve 3. Slider 4. Change

Sources: *The Sporting News* (6/26/1971, Edgar Munzel; and 4/13/1974, Pat Frizzell)

Bradley in 1971: "The controlled breaking pitch that [Johnny Sain] teaches already has saved me in a couple of games . . . and it's certainly easier on my arm, and easier to control, than the full curve or regular slider."

Source: *Baseball Digest* (August 1971, Dave Nightingale)

RALPH BRANCA 6'3" 220-pound righty
88-68, 3.79, 19 Saves 1944 1956

Pitch Selection: 1. Fastball 2. Curve

Source: Branca quoted in *Bums* (Peter Golenbock, 1984)

Note: The pitch that Bobby Thomson hit was a fastball, slightly inside and slightly high. The many published reports that it was a high curve are incorrect.

Sources: Branca quoted *Splendor on the Diamond* (Rich Westcott, 2000); interview with Branca conducted by Joshua Prager

ED BRANDT 6'1" 190-pound lefty
121-146, 3.86, 17 Saves 1928 1938

Pitch Selection: 1. Fastball 2. Curve 3. Change of Pace

Source: *Baseball Magazine* (September 1931, John J. Ward)

Description: "He is a powerful left-hander with blinding speed and a curve that is far better than the average."

Source: *Who's Who in Major League Baseball* (Harold "Speed" Johnson, 1933)

Key Pitch: Forkball
Source: *The Ballplayers* (1990, article by Morris Eckhouse)

JEFF BRANTLEY 5'11" 180-pound righty
43-46, 3.39, 172 Saves 1988 2001

Pitch Selection: 1. Split-Fingered Fastball or Forkball 2. Sinker 3. Slider 4. Curve
Sources: *The Scouting Report: 1992; 1995 Baseball Almanac.*

Quote: "He's a tough little guy, a bulldog. And he's developed the split-finger to the point where he can throw it anytime. Plus, his curve has improved and he's developed a 94 mile-an-hour fastball."
Source: Giants pitching coach Norm Sherry in *Giants Magazine* (Vol. 5, No. 5, 1990, article by Nick Peters)

Note: According to the same source, Brantley learned the splitter *not* from Roger Craig (as most would guess), but from Giants minor-league instructor Marty DeMerritt, and he perfected the pitch while playing winter ball in Puerto Rico following the 1988 season.

GARLAND BRAXTON 5'11" 152-pound lefty
50-53, 4.13, 32 Saves 1921 1933

Key Pitch: Screwball
Description: "Braxton has no great speed, but he has a baffling screwball which he uses effectively."
Source: Muddy Ruel in *Baseball Magazine* (August 1930, F.C. Lane)
Other Source: *The Relief Pitcher* (John Thorn, 1979)

AL BRAZLE 6'2" 185-pound lefty
97-64, 3.31, 60 Saves 1943 1954

Pitch Selection: 1. Sinking Fastball 2. Curve
Note: Brazle threw sidearm.
Sources: *1947 Scout Report* (Wid Matthews); *How to Play Winning Baseball* (Arthur Mann, 1953)

Stan Musial: "Old Alfie was a terrific relief pitcher because he was a lefthander with good control and a great natural sinker that dipped better the more he worked and the more tired he became. He didn't have much of a curve, but somehow his knee action when he sidearmed lefthander hitters seemed to drive some pretty good ones crazy . . . Brazle was a loosey-goosey guy with a durable arm, but he couldn't field."
Source: *Stan Musial: The Man's Own Story* (Musial, as told to Bob Broeg, 1964)
Quote: "If I needed a left-hander to pitch to one batter: Alpha Brazle."
Source: *Rex Barney's Thank Youuuu for 50 Years in Baseball from Brooklyn to Baltimore* (Barney with Norman L. Macht, 1993)

HARRY BRECHEEN 5'10" 160-pound lefty
133-92, 2.92, 18 Saves 1940 1953

Pitch Selection: 1. Screwball 2. Fastball 3. Curve
Sources: *Redbirds Revisited* (David Craft & Tom Owens, 1990); *1947 Scout Report* (Wid Matthews)

Description: "Control and cunning have been Brecheen's bywords ever since he first learned in the distant past that he couldn't power the ball past the big guys with the big bats."
Source: *Baseball Magazine* (Nov.–Dec. 1952); article notes that Brecheen is relying more on his curve than he had in the past.

Note: In *Baseball Digest* (January 1951), Milt Richman says Brecheen "owns a hard-to-hit screwball and depends largely on slow breaking stuff."

TED BREITENSTEIN 5'9" 167-pound lefty
162-166, 4.04, 2 Saves 1891 1901

Pitch Selection: 1. Rising Fastball 2. Drop curve 3. Inshoot 4. Change
Source: *Nineteenth Century Stars* (SABR, 1989, article by Robert L. Tiemann)

KEN BRETT 6'0" 190-pound lefty
83-85, 3.93, 11 Saves 1967 1981

Key Pitch: Fastball
Source: *The George Brett Story* (John Garrity, 1981)

MARV BREUER 6'2" 185-pound righty
25-26, 4.03, 3 Saves 1939 1943

Key Pitch: Curve
Quote: "Breuer, possessing a remarkable curveball, was called in from Kansas City."

Source: *The Sporting News* (10/2/1941, Page 1)

Note: According to *The Sporting News* (8/28/1941, Page 10), during the 1941 season, "Breuer discovered he could control a knuckle ball . . ."

BILLY BREWER 6'1" 200-pound lefty
11-11, 4.79, 5 Saves 1993 1999

Pitch Selection: 1. Fastball 2. Hard Slider
Source: *The Scouting Notebook: 1995*

CHET BREWER 6'4" 187-pound righty
NEGRO LEAGUES 1925 1948

Pitch Selection: 1. Drop Ball 2. Fastball 3. Screwball 4. Cut Ball (occasional)
Brewer: "I threw an overhand curve ball, what we called a drop ball. It started about letter-high, then dropped down by the knees. Of course I could throw a screw ball and had a good, live, running fast ball. We'd play on those rough diamonds, when the ball hit the ground, it got roughed up. I could screw it real good then.

"A cut ball? I got credit for that. If I picked up a rough one, I didn't throw it out of the game. I didn't exactly put the cuts on it myself, but I could pitch it . . . but with that curve ball I had, I could win without scratching the ball. When I learned the screw ball, they said, 'Heck, he's scratching the ball,' so I knew that I was getting on them. I'd face the outfield and rub the ball up, turn around, throw a screw ball: 'Oh, he cut it!' But it was more a psychological thing."
Source: Interview with Brewer in *Black Diamonds* (John Holway, 1989)

JIM BREWER 6'1" 186-pound lefty
69-65, 3.07, 132 Saves 1960 1976

Pitch Selection: 1. Screwball 2. Fastball 3. Sidearm Curve
Sources: *The Sporting News* (9/2/1972, Bob Hunter); *Major League Baseball: 1971* (Brenda Zanger and Dick Kaplan)

Quote: "Jim Brewer . . . a left-handed relief specialist, throws from the right side of the rubber because his best pitch is a screwball."
Source: *Pitching* (Bob Shaw, 1972)

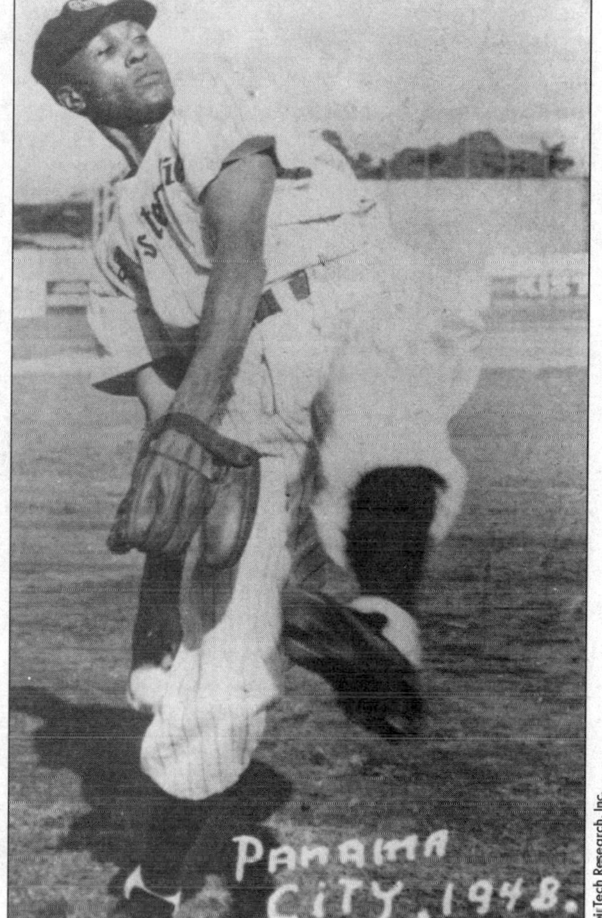

Noir Tech Research, Inc.

Chet Brewer

Note: According to Paul Votano in *Late and Close: A History of Relief Pitching* (2002), Brewer learned his screwball from Warren Spahn in 1964.

TOM BREWER 6'1" 175-pound righty
91-82, 4.00, 3 Saves 1954 1961

Pitch Selection: 1. Hard Curve 2. Fastball
Sources: *Baseball Digest* (April 1957, Hy Hurwitz); *The Sporting News* (8/29/1956)

Note: In *The Crooked Pitch*, Martin Quigley wrote that Brewer "depended mainly upon" his Screwball, though it's possible Quigley had Tom Brewer confused with Jim Brewer.

MARSHALL BRIDGES 6'1" 165-pound lefty
23-15, 3.75, 25 Saves 1959 1965

Pitch Selection: 1. Fastball 2. Low Curve
Source: *1963 Major League Handbook* (Don Schiffer)

TOMMY BRIDGES 5'10" 155-pound righty
194-138, 3.57, 10 Saves 1930 1946

Pitches: 1. Curve 2. Fastball 3. Change
4. Spitball (later career, occasional)
Note: Bridges was universally regarded as having the best curve of his generation.
Sources: *Baseball's Famous Pitchers* (Ira L. Smith, 1954); *The Detroit Tigers* (Fred Lieb, 1946); *The Crooked Pitch* (Martin Quigley, 1984) *Who's Who In the American League, 1935* (Harold Johnson), *Baseball Between the Wars* (Eugene Murdock, 1992), *The Sporting News* (5/1/1957)

Description: "Hitters say that Bridges has one of the best curves in baseball, a fast, sharp-breaking ball that breaks down and out. He has an unusual way of gripping the ball in his long, powerful fingers, using mostly the second finger instead of the first two fingers to grip the ball, and gripping it somewhat below the equator."
Source: Ralph Sampson in *The Sporting News* (4/26/1933)

NELSON BRILES 5'11" 195-pound righty
129-112, 3.43, 22 Saves 1965 1978

Pitch Selection: 1. Sinking Fastball 2. Overhand Curve
3. Change (ineffective)
Sources: *The Sporting News* (10/24/1964, Neal Russo); *Baseball Digest* (June 1968, Bob Broeg); Briles in *That Was Part of Baseball Then* (Victor Debs, Jr., 2002); *Major League Baseball—1969* (Jack Zanger)

Description: "Briles, who occasionally falls on the mound because of the effort he puts into his delivery, has caused alarm among Royals fans, but his knee has held up."
Source: *The Sporting News* (5/31/1975, Joe McGuff)

LOU BRISSIE 6'4" 210-pound lefty
44-48, 4.07, 29 Saves 1947 1953

Pitch Selection: 1. Fastball 2. Curve 3. Change
Sources: *Splendor on the Diamond* (Rich Westcott, 2000); *The Boston Herald* (4/19/1951)
Pitch Selection: 1. Knuckle Ball
Source: *Baseball Magazine* (February 1949, Clifford Bloodgood)

JOHNNY BROACA 5'11" 190-pound righty
44-29, 4.08, 3 Saves 1934 1939

Pitch Selection: 1. Fastball 2. Curve
Quote: "Johnny has a good fast ball . . . he mixes it with an effective curve, but paces himself nicely so that he always has the fireball in reserve."
Source: *New York World-Telegram* (8/20/1934)

Quote: "The writer saw John throw a few curves the like of which he did not possess last season . . . Broaca had been doing some experimenting out of hours with a better type of curve ball."
Source: *New York World-Telegram* (3/28/1936)

Note: A *World-Telegram* article from March 8, 1935 says that Broaca learned "how to hold the ball for a curve and a fast ball" from a magazine article.
Comment: "He is blessed with an abundance of 'swift.' "
Source: *Who's Who in the American League, 1935* (Harold "Speed" Johnson)

PETE BROBERG 6'3" 205-pound righty
41-71, 4.56, 1 Save 1971 1978

Key Pitch: Fastball
Comment: "People all around the league said that Broberg threw as hard as any pitcher in the game. Ted Williams said that Broberg would never see a day in the minor leagues."
Source: *Kiss It Goodbye* (Shelby Whitfield, 1973)

DOUG BROCAIL 6'5" 235-pound righty
28-36, 3.87, 5 Saves 1992 2000

Pitch Selection, up to 1997: 1. Fastball 2. Slider
Pitches, since 1997: 1. Fastball 2. Knuckle Curve
3. Slider 4. Change
Sources: *The Scouting Notebook* (1998 and 2000 editions)

DICK BRODOWSKI 6'1" 182-pound righty
9-11, 4.76, 5 Saves 1952 1959

Note: Listed by *The Sporting News* as having one of the best fastballs in the league, August 29, 1956.

ERNIE BROGLIO 6'2" 200-pound righty
77-74, 3.74, 2 Saves 1959 1966

Pitches: 1. Fastball 2. Curve 3. Slider 4. Change
Broglio: "When I first started, I was two pitches: fastball, curveball. That's it. And then after you get rocked around a little, you have to start adding pitches to your repertoire . . . When the Giants bought me, I started working on a slider and a change-up. And that's what I ended up with: fastball, curveball, slider, and change-up. Straight change. And of course I'd change up on my other pitches, too."
Source: Interview with Broglio (8/2/2003, Rob Neyer)
Other Source: *Sport* (May 1961, Al Hirshberg)

Note: Nearly forty years before talking to Neyer, Broglio said, "I used to lean heavily on my fast ball, and on my curve, which was pretty sharp breaking. Then my fast ball slowed down a little and I had to start mixing in a slider and a change-up. I think I'm a much better pitcher today than I ever was previously."
Source: *1964 Official Baseball Almanac* (Don Wise; following the publication of this quote, Broglio won exactly ten games in the major leagues.)

Pitches: 1. Curve 2. Change 3. Fastball
Source: *1963 Major League Handbook* (Don Schiffer)

Note: Schiffer says that Broglio's "curve is the most feared in the circuit." Similarly, the January 1963 *Baseball Digest* says that in 1959, Broglio "had a remarkable curve ball. It came right down—but he went with the slider for some reason. Now even though he had great success with it the next year (1960) it hurt his curve ball."

JIM BROSNAN 6'4" 197-pound righty
55-47, 3.54, 67 Saves 1954 1963

Pitch Selection: 1. Slider 2. Fastball 3. Curve 4. Change
Note: Brosnan was accused of throwing a spitball in the early 1960s.
Sources: *The Long Season* (Brosnan, 1960); *Sports Illustrated* (6/3/1963)

Note: According to Brosnan in *Splendor on the Diamond* (Rich Westcott, 2000), he learned to throw his slider (which was outstanding) from Max Lanier.

BOB BROWN 6'0" 190-pound righty
16-21, 4.48, 1 Save 1930 1936

Key Pitch: Fearsome Fastball
Quote: "Bob Brown, who pitched for the Braves in the thirties, was the fastest pitcher I ever saw. I saw Lefty Grove and Bob Feller in their prime, but they couldn't match Brown for speed. Too bad he couldn't get his fastball over the plate."
Source: Umpire Beans Reardon in *The Men in Blue* (Larry Gerlach, 1980)

CHARLIE BROWN 4'2" 87-pound righty

Theoretical Pitch Selection: 1. Fastball 2. Curve 3. Drop 4. Knuckleball
Actual Pitch Selection: 1. Straight Ball 2. Straight Ball 3. Straight Ball 4. Straight Ball
Note: Brown gave up an unusual number of line drives up the middle.
Source: *Sandlot Peanuts* (Charles M. Schulz, 1977)

CLINT BROWN 6'1" 190-pound righty
89-93, 4.26, 64 Saves 1928 1942

Pitch Selection: 1. Submarine Screwball 2. Curve 3. Sinker
Sources: *The Relief Pitcher* (John Thorn, page 76), 1935 and 1936 *Who's Who in the American League*

Notes: The 1935 *Who's Who in the American League* describes Brown as "a right-handed submarine screwball pitcher," while the '36 edition says "his most effective delivery on the firing line is a submarine screwball." Thorn says that Brown threw underhand, sidearm, and three-quarters.

In a 1933 issue of *Baseball Magazine,* Brown said that when he warmed up, he threw "three fast ones, three curves and three screw balls at top speed . . ."

HAL (SKINNY) BROWN 6'2" 180-pound righty
85-92, 3.81, 11 Saves 1951 1964

Key Pitches: Knuckleball and Slip Pitch
Sources: *The Ballplayers* (1990, article by Jane Charnin-Aker); undated clipping from the *Baltimore News-Post* of article by John F. Steadman (apparently 1957)

JUMBO BROWN 6'4" 295-pound righty
33-31, 4.07, 29 Saves 1925 1941

Key Pitch: Fastball
Sources: *Baseball Between the Wars* (Eugene C. Murdock, 1992), *Baseball Magazine* (August 1943, Harold C. Burr).

Note: Brown had very short, stubby fingers, which made it difficult for him to grip a baseball, almost impossible for him to throw a curve. According to Burr, "Brownie would moodily compare his fingers with those of any chance acquaintance in wistful envy."

Enos Slaughter: "And Jumbo Brown . . . now there was a big, *big* man . . . 300 pounds. He just threw fastballs, but he'd kinda short-arm his delivery, so when he released the ball it would come outta that big ol' body of his and I would lose the flight of the ball."
Source: *Redbirds Revisited* (David Craft and Tom Owens, 1990)

KEVIN BROWN 6'4" 195-pound righty
197-131, 3.16, 0 Saves 1986 2003

Pitches: 1. Two-Seam (Sinking) Fastball
2. Four-Seam (Rising) Fastball 3. Hard Slider
4. Curve 5. Change 6. Split-Fingered Fastball
Sources: *The 1994 Baseball Almanac, The Scouting Report: 1995*, and *The Scouting Notebook 2000*

Tim McCarver: "Kevin Brown throws a hard, top-heavy sinker, but don't be as interested in the velocity of his pitches as in their movement. His sinker explodes in on the hands, the same as a tailer. He has the best natural sinker in the game today. The bottom falls out, and it resembles a splitter. It's very tough to hit the bottom part of the ball against him and get any lift on it. Ground balls don't go out of the ballpark. Brown, a righty, is especially tough on right-handed batters. Also, he has benefited from being in the National League because umpires are more likely to call the low strike."
Source: *Tim McCarver's Baseball for Brain Surgeons and Other Fans* (McCarver with Danny Peary, 1998)

Quote: "At 6'4" and 200 pounds, he has the wingspan and wiry strength of a basketball player. 'He can scratch his knees without bending over,' [Tom] House says. Though Brown's windup is unorthodox—he has an exaggerated hip turn, leading with his butt, and can throw any pitch from any arm angle—he maintains flawless balance, and his amazing extension maximizes the whip effect of his long arm."
Quote: "He is unique; a power sinkerball pitcher."
Source: *Sports Illustrated* (3/29/1999, Tom Verducci)

Paul LoDuca: "He can be hard to catch. I told him sometimes I just go out there trying to knock it down. His fastball moves so much, and he can throw it 95, 96 miles an hour, just right by you. When he needs to reach back, he can. The previous two years, he couldn't.

"His split-finger is 90, 91 miles an hour with unbelievable movement. He's got a great slider, too. He's got so many weapons."
Source: *Baseball Digest* (November 2003, David Leon Moore)

Description: "He's throwing his four-seam fastball in the mid-90s and his sinker in the low 90s. He also changes speeds so well on his sinker that it looks like a change-up at times. He has an extremely deceptive motion; the ball is on the hitter very quickly. A tip for lefthanded batters: Your first pitch is going to be a high fastball running away. For righthanders: When he is ahead in the count, he likes to drop down to a sidearm delivery and throw a two-seam fastball or hard slider."
Source: Scout Lewis Shaw in *The Sporting News* (4/21/2003)

LLOYD BROWN 5'9" 170-pound lefty
91-105, 4.20, 21 Saves 1925 1940

Pitch Selection: 1. Fastball 2. Change 3. Curve
Note: Brown had a good curve, but had what was called "Curve Ball Elbow," meaning that he had recurring elbow trouble which got worse when he tried to throw a curve.
Source: *Baseball Magazine* (May 1933, Clifford Bloodgood)

Quote: "Each spring finds him afflicted with a sore arm. He has sought to offset this annoyance by perfecting a 'screw ball.' "
Source: *Who's Who in Major League Baseball* (Harold "Speed" Johnson, 1933)

MACE BROWN 6'1" 190-pound righty
76-57, 3.46, 48 Saves 1935 1946

Pitch Selection, 1930s: 1. Overhand Curve
2. Overhand Drop Ball 3. Fastball

Pitch Selection, 1940s: 1. Slider 2. Curve 3. Fastball 4. Drop Ball
Note: Brown developed a slider in 1941. It became his best pitch, although he had a good fastball and an outstanding curve.
Sources: Undated article from *The Paris* (Texas) *News* (TSN Morgue); *The Relief Pitcher* (John Thorn, 1979)

Description: "He pitches hard once he is in the box and employs a fast ball and curve to advantage."
Source: *Baseball Magazine* (October 1938, Clifford Bloodgood)

Quote: "I hit against Mace Brown of the Pirates. He had a real good curveball. It was so good that I used to stand up in the front part of the batters box on him so I could hit his curve before it broke."
Source: Goody Rosen in *Dugout to Foxhole* (Rick Van Blair, 1994)

Note: Gabby Hartnett's famous "Homer in the Gloamin' " was hit off a Mace Brown curveball.
Source: Brown in *Dugout to Foxhole*

MORDECAI BROWN 5'10" 175-pound righty
239-129, 2.06, 49 Saves 1903 1916

Pitches: 1. Overhand Curve 2. Fastball 3. Slow Ball 4. Sidearm Curve 5. Underhand Fastball
Brown: "I think my best ball is the curve the fellows call the 'hook.' I pitch it over-handed with a half-round arm motion, starting slowly and finishing with a fast snap with the hand and wrist bent. My next best ball is a speedy one. I always make the ball twist, no matter what I pitch. My first ball I let off the third finger on the side, but near the tip, with the stub of the little finger pressed hard under the ball. I have a twisting slow ball, and a sidearm curve, also a fast underhand ball."
Source: Brown in *Baseball Magazine* (July 1911, "Mordecai Brown and His Favorite Curves")

Pitch Selection: 1. Big Curve 2. Fastball 3. Slow Ball
Source: *Pitching in a Pinch* (Christy Mathewson, 1912)

Quote: "All curves are developments of the 'barrel hoop,' the same principle entering into each, whether it is Mordecai Brown's marvelous 'hook' curve, George Mullin's meteoric shoot, or the wonderful curves of Camnitz, Overall, Wiltse, Krause, [Babe] Adams, [George] Ferguson and others.

"Brown's 'hook' curve is the highest present development of the fast overhand curve pitch which breaks sharply down and outward . . . Brown pitches the 'hook' overhand, releasing the ball at various points after his hand swings past his body. By the point at which he releases the ball he regulates the point at which it breaks in the air. He can make the ball either describe a wide fast arc, or by jerking his hand at the proper instant, make the ball go in almost a straight line, perhaps fifty feet, and then dart suddenly down and outward."
Source: *Touching Second* (John J. Evers and Hugh S. Fullerton, 1910)

Quote: "Expert after expert developed the slowball, until its perfection was reached in the hands of Brown, Frank Sparks, of Philadelphia, and 'Doc' White of the Chicago Americans."
Source: *Touching Second* (Evers and Fullerton, 1910)

RAY BROWN 6'1" 195-pound righty
NEGRO LEAGUES 1930 1948

Pitch Selection: 1. Curve 2. Fastball 3. Sinker 4. Slider

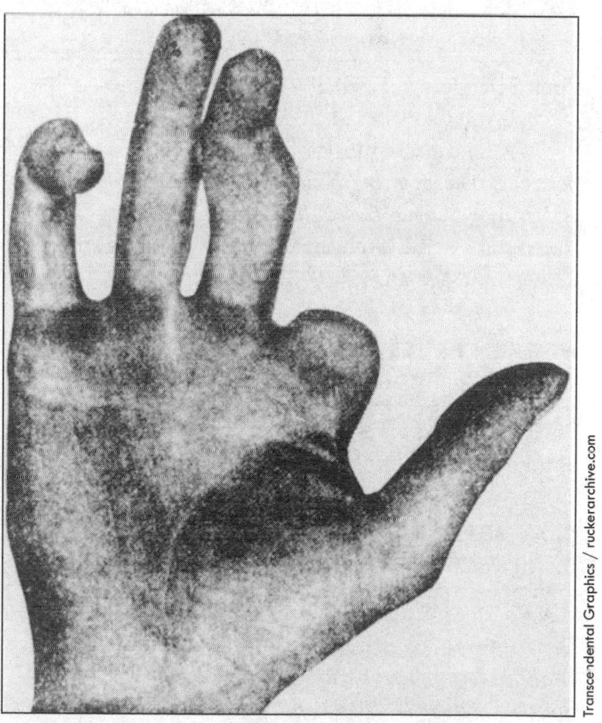
Transcendental Graphics / ruckerarchive.com

The secret of Miner Brown's success?

Sources: *The Biographical Encyclopedia of the Negro Baseball Leagues* (James A. Riley, 1994); *Catching Dreams* (Frazier "Slow" Robinson with Paul Bauer, 1999)

Key Pitch: Knuckleball
Source: Napoleon Gulley interview in *The Negro Leagues Revisited* (Brent Kelley, 2000); *My Life in the Negro Leagues* (Wilmer Fields, 1992)

TOM BROWNING 6'1" 190-pound lefty
123-90, 3.94, 0 Saves 1984 1995

Pitches: 1. Screwball 2. Fastball 3. Curve 4. Slider 5. Change
Sources: *The Scouting Report* (1987 and 1990)

BOB BRUCE 6'3" 200-pound righty
49-71, 3.85, 1 Save 1959 1967

Pitch Selection: 1. Curve 2. Change 3. Fastball
Sources: *Inside the Astrodome* (1965); Jack Zanger's *Major League Baseball 1965* says Bruce "throws curves of varying speeds, as well as a slider."

GEORGE BRUNET 6'1" 195-pound lefty
69-93, 3.62, 4 Saves 1956 1971

Pitch Selection: 1. Fastball
2. Brunet developed change-up in 1966
3. Added a slider in 1968.
Sources: *The Sporting News* (7/30/66, Ross Newhan), and *Major League Baseball—1969* (Jack Zanger); *TSN* also reported, 3/21/64, that Brunet was "experimenting with a knuckle ball."

WARREN BRUSSTAR 6'3" 200-pound righty
28-16, 3.51, 14 Saves 1977 1985

Pitch Selection: 1. Fastball 2. Curve 3. Slider
Source: *The Scouting Report: 1984*

CLAY BRYANT 6'2" 195-pound righty
32-20, 3.73, 7 Saves 1935 1940

Key Pitch: Fastball
Description: "He has plenty of 'swift,' some say he is about as fast as anyone in the league."
Source: *Baseball Magazine* (January 1939, Clifford Bloodgood)

RON BRYANT 6'0" 190-pound lefty
57-56, 4.02, 1 Save 1967 1975

Pitches: 1. Fastball 2. Curve 3. Slider 4. Change
Source: Bryant in *The Sporting News* (4/5/1975, Pat Frizzell)

Description: "Bryant is not overpowering. He is sneaky fast and his ball tails away from righthanded batters."
Source: *The Sporting News* (5/31/1975, Neal Russo)

GARLAND BUCKEYE 6'0" 260-pound lefty
30-39, 3.91, 1 Save 1918 1928

Pitches: 1. Fastball 2. Curve
3. Knuckleball (occasional)
Description: "Buckeye is a left hander in delivery only. He's a first rate normal citizen in all other respects. The speed ball is his specialty, though he has a good curve and occasionally uses a knuckle ball."
Source: *Baseball Magazine* (January 1926, F.C. Lane)

Buckeye: "I weighed over 250 all the time I was in the big leagues, and in 1928, when Billy Evans was general manager of the Indians and Roger Peckinpaugh manager, Evans had me come to Cleveland to sign my 1928 contract. I got on a scale in the Cleveland ball club office and weighed 269. I played pro football for years at the time I played baseball, and one winter I had to play handball continually to keep under 275."
Source: *The Sporting News* (3/16/1968, Lee Allen's "Cooperstown Corner" column)

HARRY BUCKNER
NEGRO LEAGUES 1896 1918

Key Pitch: Fastball
Quote: "He . . . was called the 'speed marvel' of the Brooklyn Royal Giants in 1910."
Source: *The Biographical Encyclopedia of the Negro Baseball Leagues* (James A. Riley, 1994)

MARK BUEHRLE 6'2" 200-pound lefty
53-35, 3.71, 0 Saves 2000 2003

Pitch Selection: 1. Fastball (low-90s) 2. Slider
3. Curve 4. Change
Source: *The Scouting Notebook: 2001*

Pitch Selection: 1. Fastball (low-90s) 2. Curve
3. Change 4. Cut Fastball (added 2001)

Sources: *The Scouting Notebook* (2002 and 2003)

Pitches: 1. Fastball (86–90) 2. Sinker 3. Slider
Note: Buehrle has a good pickoff move to first base.
Source: Interview with White Sox pitching coach Don Cooper, aired during NESN broadcast of White Sox–Red Sox game (9/3/2003)

CHARLIE BUFFINTON 6'1" 180-pound righty
233-151, 2.96, 3 Saves 1882 1892

Pitch Selection: 1. Fastball 2. Down Shoot
Quote: "Unlike the majority of pitchers, when about to deliver the ball, Buffinton squarely faces the batsman. Holding the ball in both hands at arm's length before his face, he nervously twists the sphere about for a moment or two. Then tossing his hands above his head he lifts his left foot from the ground and hops forward on the right. Swinging his right arm down to his side he sends the ball in with but little effort, but with considerable force. Buffinton as well as Stemmyer practices an effective 'down shoot' that proves very deceptive to the average batsman."
Source: Article titled "How Men Pitch Base-Ball: The Famous Pitchers of the National League of 1886." No author or publisher is given, though the information in the article is said to have come from photographic studies done by the *New York World* newspaper.

Key Pitch: Overhand Curve
Source: *Nineteenth Century Stars* (SABR, 1989, article by Joe Overfield)

Comment: "It was in 1883, or about that time, that Buffington of the Boston club, became prominent as a drop ball pitcher, and he could make the ball talk."
Source: *Baseball Magazine* (May 1911, "The Discoveries of the Curve and Drop")

Key Pitch: Drop Ball/Spitball
Source: *The Sporting News* (4/11/1918)
Quote from that source: "Buffington, of Boston [was known for] his drop ball, which in later years they called a spitball."

Commentary: This is the only time we've ever seen someone equate the Drop Ball with the Spitball, and so must be considered with a healthy dose of skepticism.

BOB BUHL 6'2" 180-pound righty
166-132, 3.55, 6 Saves 1953 1967

Pitch Selection: 1. Slider 2. Fastball
Note: Buhl threw with a herky-jerky motion.
Sources: *Milwaukee's Miracle Braves* (Tom Meany, 1954); *View from the Dugout* (Ed Richter, 1964)

Pitch Selection, 1957: 1. Fastball 2. Curve 2. Slider 4. Change 5. Knuckleball (occasional)
Source: Braves catcher Del Rice quoted in *Sport* (October 1957, Bob Wolf); Rice is described as Buhl's "personal catcher."

Key Pitch: Fastball
Source: *1963 Major League Handbook* (Don Schiffer)

Note: Listed by *The Sporting News* (8/29/1956) as having one of the best fastballs in the league.

JIM BULLINGER 6'2" 180-pound righty
34-41, 5.06, 11 Saves 1992 1998

Pitch Selection: 1. Overhand Curve 2. Fastball (87–89) 3. Change
Source: *The Scouting Report: 1993*

Pitch Selection: 1. Curve
2. Cut Fastball (added about 1995)
3. Sinking Fastball
Source: *The Scouting Report: 1996*

Note: This is the only source we've found that mentions Bullinger's cut fastball. The next two editions of *The Scouting Report* make no mention of it.

WALLY BUNKER 6'2" 197-pound righty
60-52, 3.51, 5 Saves 1963 1971

Pitches: 1. Rising Fastball 2. Sinking Fastball 3. Curve 4. Change
Sources: *The Sporting News* (5/23/1964, Doug Brown); *Sport* (June 1965, Fred Katz)

Mickey Mantle: "Wally Bunker of Baltimore has one of those sinkers you can break your back on."
Source: *The Education of a Baseball Player* (Mantle with Bob Smith, 1967)

Harry Brecheen: "He has a good fast ball that he can make sink or rise. That's very unusual for one so young.

And he's got a good curve and a change-up. But most of all he's got control . . ."
Source: *1965 Official Baseball Almanac* (Bill Wise)

JIM BUNNING 6'3" 190-pound righty
224-184, 3.27, 16 Saves 1955 1971

Pitches: 1. Slider 2. Fastball 3. Curve 4. Change
Note: Bunning threw with a "sweeping sidearm delivery." He was accused of throwing a spitball, although his natural stuff was so outstanding he certainly didn't need to.
Sources: *Baseball's Star Pitchers* (Bill Libby); Sandy Grady in the *Philadelphia Bulletin* (June 1964); *1963 Major League Handbook* (Don Schiffer); *Sports Illustrated* (6/3/1963)

Description: "For his part, [Ted] Williams always remembered that Bunning slider, which seemed to rise instead of drop as it approached the plate. At least that's the way it looked—a result of Jim's sidearm delivery that ended with him hurtling off the mound to the first base side, often with his gloved left hand actually touching the ground."
Source: *Jim Bunning: Baseball and Beyond* (Frank Dolson, 1998)

Note: In his first no-hitter (7/20/1958), Bunning threw 51 fastballs, 49 sliders, 25 curves and 7 change-ups.
Source: *The Story of Jim Bunning* (Bunning, as told to Ralph Bernstein, 1965)

DAVE BURBA 6'4" 220-pound righty
111-86, 4.50, 1 Save 1990 2003

Pitch Selection, through 1997: 1. Fastball 2. Slider 3. Change
Pitches, 1998–1999: 1. Fastball 2. Splitter 3. Slider 4. Curve 5. Change
Sources: *The 1995 Baseball Almanac; The Scouting Notebook* (1998 and 2000 editions)

BILL BURBACH 6'4" 215-pound righty
6-11, 4.47, 0 Saves 1969 1971

Key Pitch: Fastball
Note: Burbach was the Yankees' first pick in the first amateur draft (1965).
Source: *Dog Days: The New York Yankees' Fall from Grace and Return to Glory, 1964–1976* (Philip Bashe, 1994)

LOU BURDETTE 6'2" 180-pound righty
203-144, 3.66, 31 Saves 1950 1967

Pitch Selection: 1. Sinker (Sinking Fastball) 2. Slider 3. Change 4. Sidearm Curve 5. Spitball
Sources: The best source is an interview with Burdette in *Bombers*, a book by Richard Lally about the New York Yankees. Other sources include *Lew Burdette of the Braves* (Gene Schoor) and *Sports Illustrated* (9/28/1959)

Notes: According to Whitey Ford in *Slick* (1987), "Burdette had the reputation of throwing the best spitter in baseball."

The rule that a pitcher is allowed to moisten his fingers while pitching as long as he doesn't do it on the mound originated in a 1957 ruling by Warren Giles, who was trying to clarify the enforcement policies after a series of confrontations about charges that Burdette was throwing a spitter. Giles said that Burdette—and thus, by inference, all other pitchers—was permitted to moisten his fingertips while pitching, but must step off the mound to do so.

Quote: "Occasionally there would be a pitcher you could only call one pitch on, but that's all you would need, that one pitch. Like Burdette. I could only call his spitter. When our careers were over he wanted to know, 'How'd you hit me like you did?"

"I said, 'Well, it was the spitter, if you remember.'

"He said, 'How'd you think I did it?'

"I said, 'You only wet one finger.'

"Well, that really amazed him. He said, 'Where do you think I got it?'

"I said, 'You spit in your hand. When you got your hand to your cap you spit right then.'

"That amazed him again. I said, 'There's another way you can tell. If you reached at the resin bag with two fingers up it was loaded. If the two fingers were down it wasn't.' "
Source: Dave Philley in *This Side of Cooperstown* (Larry Moffi, 1996)

Comment: "Lew Burdette of the Braves, who likes to forego the fast ball in favor of a screwball."
Source: *Sport* (July 1956, Milton Richman); this is the

only reference we've seen to Burdette throwing a screwball, which doesn't mean he didn't throw one.

TOM BURGMEIER 5'11" 185-pound lefty
79-55, 3.23, 102 Saves 1968 1984

Pitch Selection: 1. Sinker 2. Slider 3. Fastball
Sources: Hy Zimmerman in *The Sporting News* (May, 1965); Sid Bordman in the *Kansas City Star* (3/7/1969); Peter Gammons in TSN (6/6/1981)
Commentary: Burgmeier's fastball was just fair. He could throw a curve, and used it a lot as a minor-league starting pitcher, but threw it from a different delivery than his fastball, which telegraphed it to the hitter. When he came to the majors he was a reliever, and largely junked the curve in favor of the slider, which was taught to him by Tom Morgan and Bob Lemon in 1964–65.

Bob Lemon stated numerous times that Burgmeier was "the best fielding pitcher since Bobby Shantz." As an older pitcher Burgmeier was suspected of throwing a spitball.

BOBBY BURKE 6'0" 150-pound lefty
38-46, 4.29, 5 Saves 1927 1937

Pitch Selection: 1. Fastball 2. Curve
Quote: "In this no-hit game I threw only about five curve balls. All the rest were fast balls."
Source: Burke in *Who's Who in Major League Baseball* (Harold "Speed" Johnson, 1933)

TIM BURKE 6'3" 205-pound righty
49-33, 2.72, 102 Saves 1985 1992

Pitch Selection: 1. Sinking Fastball 2. Slider
Source: *Scouting Report 1990*

JOHN BURKETT 6'2" 175-pound righty
166-136, 4.31, 1 Save 1987 2003

Pitch Selection: 1. Fastball 2. Slider 3. Curve 4. Split-Fingered Fastball
Sources: *1994 Baseball Almanac; The Scouting Notebook 1998*

Leo Mazzone: "Burky was a guy who came here with a full assortment of pitches. When he was getting banged around a little bit, he started trying to trick everybody. . . . So the emphasis with Burky was on the fastball. It was: Work down, and away—work off that and practice that. That made his curve and his change more effective. But the key was to practice banging the fastball down and away."
Source: article by Jayson Stark on ESPN.com (2/25/2003); Mazzone was Burkett's pitching coach with the Braves in 2000 and 2001.

Note: According to Burkett, he was taught the change-up by his pitching coach in A-ball in 1984. He demonstrated the pitch, which he called "basically a palmball." Burkett also explained that, to change speeds, he shortens his stride. According to broadcaster Jeff Brantley, that method of changing speeds is both rare and difficult.
Source: ESPN broadcast of Red Sox–Royals game (5/7/2003)

Note: Burkett stopped throwing his splitter in the late 1990s. According to Ian Browne of MLB.com (August 11, 2003), Burkett's mid-season resurgence came after he rediscovered his splitter in early July 2003. The story I heard is that he re-discovered the splitter when he was role-playing himself in a video game. In the video game he threw a splitter, and he thought, "Oh, yeah, that was a good pitch. Why did I stop throwing that?"
Source: Bill James, reporting Red Sox front office gossip.

KEN BURKHART 6'1" 190-pound righty
27-20, 3.85, 7 Saves 1945 1949

Description: "Not blessed with blinding speed, he depends on control and use of oddly-breaking knuckleball."
Source: *The Sporting News* (10/23/1946, Page 6)

Stan Musial: "He had a frozen shoulder, a strange shot-put delivery, and only limited skill."
Source: *Stan Musial: The Man's Own Story* (Musial, as told to Bob Broeg, 1964)

WALLY BURNETTE 6'0" 178-pound righty
14-21, 3.56, 1 Save 1956 1958

Key Pitch: Knuckleball
Sources: *The Artful Dodger* (Tommy Lasorda and David Fisher, 1985); *The Kansas City Athletics* (John E. Peterson, 2003)

BRITT BURNS 6'5" 215-pound lefty
70-60, 3.66, 3 Saves 1978 1985

Pitch Selection, 1980–82: 1. Fastball (90) 2. Slider 3. Curve 4. Change
Pitch Selection, 1983–85: 1. Slider 2. Fastball (mid-80s) 3. Curve 4. Change
Note: Burns suffered a shoulder injury in 1982 that cost him the good velocity on his fastball. And then after 1985, just as he was getting back to where he'd once been, a congenital hip problem virtually ended his career.
Sources: *The Scouting Report* (1983, 1984, and 1986 editions)

TODD BURNS 6'2" 195-pound righty
21-23, 3.47, 13 Saves 1988 1993

Pitch Selection: 1. Fastball 2. Curve 3. Forkball 4. Change
Source: *The Scouting Report: 1990*

Pitch Selection: 1. Fastball (high-80s) 2. Change 3. Slider 4. Curve
Source: *The Scouting Report: 1993*

RAY BURRIS 6'5" 200-pound righty
108-134, 4.17, 4 Saves 1973 1987

Pitch Selection: 1. Fastball 2. Slider 3. Curve 4. Change
Source: *The Sporting News* (4/26/1975, page 17, article by Jerome Holtzman)

STEVE BUSBY 6'2" 205-pound righty
70-54, 3.72, 0 Saves 1972 1980

Pitch Selection: 1. Sinking Fastball 2. Slider 3. Curve
Sources: *The No-Hit Hall of Fame* (Rich Coberly, 1985); *The Sporting News* (8/3/1974, Sid Bordman)

GUY BUSH 6'0" 175-pound righty
176-136, 3.86, 34 Saves 1923 1945

Pitches: 1. Fastball 2. Slow Ball 3. Curve (occasional)
Description: "Bush says that Dazzy Vance is the only pitcher in the league who can get by on sheer speed. And yet, last season he pitched two full games against the Giants, 18 consecutive innings, with just one curve ball. And that curve ball was pitched in the ninth inning of the second game. However effective sheer speed can be when it is speedy enough was disclosed in those two contests, for the Giants made just two hits in each game and swallowed a painful dose of whitewash in both.

"Naturally Bush does not always pitch fast balls. He is learning to diversify his defence. He has developed a fair curve ball and a good slow ball. This he uses as an effective change of pace."
Source: *Baseball Magazine* (August 1927, F.C. Lane)

Pitch Selection: 1. Fastball 2. Screwball
Source: Interview with Riggs Stephenson in *Baseball History, An Annual of Original Research* (1989 edition); the Slow Ball mentioned above in *Baseball Magazine* may well have been a screwball, or something that behaved like a screwball. Then again, in a 1937 issue of *Baseball Magazine,* Dan Daniel suggests that Bush developed his screwball in 1932.

Description: "Bush is long and lanky. He has nothing of the brute strength of Malone or the chunky sturdiness of Charley Root. He looks rather frail. In truth, he would be a better pitcher if he weighed more . . .

"On the hurling mound Bush has developed a curious 'hop-toad' lunge that is unique. When he really bears down on a ball, he actually springs forward and finishes up in a squat position like a catcher reaching for a low pitch. This freakish hop forward would be impossible to many pitchers. Bush can do it by virtue of his lithe and wiry build, his long thin legs."
Source: *Baseball Magazine* (November 1930, F.C. Lane)

JOE BUSH 5'9" 173-pound righty
195-183, 3.51, 20 Saves 1912 1928

Pitch Selection, 1912–1919: 1. Fastball 2. Change 3. Curve
Sources: *Babe Ruth's Own Book of Baseball* (Ruth, 1928); *The Crooked Pitch* (Martin Quigley, 1984), Waite Hoyt in *Baseball Between the Wars* (Eugene Murdock, 1992), *The Sporting News* (9/24/1952)

Pitches, 1920s: 1. Forkball 2. Fastball 3. Curve (occasional)
Quote: "There was a day when Bush could get by on sheer speed. Those were the years when he picked up the nickname of 'Bullet Joe.' Nowadays, however, Bush couples speed with his fork ball and a few, a very few, judiciously placed curves. These are his repertoire and the

prize of the lot is the fork ball. This peculiar delivery is hardly a secret, though, of course, Bush as the originator cannot be expected to explain the intricacies of his pet delivery while it is still the basis of his pitching success. Suffice it to say that the ball is held firmly between the first and second fingers as illustrated in the accompanying photograph. Thrown with a good degree of speed it breaks rather sharply, neither the batter nor Bush knows in advance exactly where. But it breaks and when it is working nicely for its inventor, it is a very tidy delivery indeed and one well calculated to deceive the opposing slugger.

"Bush estimates that perhaps thirty balls out of a hundred that he throws are of the fork variety. The great majority of pitches are simply fast balls. Like all other pitchers he finds it advisable to mix up his delivery for the batter is fooled quite as much by variety as by anything else."

Source: *Baseball Magazine* (February 1923, F.C. Lane)

Commentary: Bush was widely said to have invented the forkball and he never disputed the notion, but we've got solid evidence that two minor leaguers threw the pitch more than a decade before Bush first threw his.

JOHN BUTCHER 6'4" 185-pound righty
36-49, 4.42, 6 Saves 1980 1986

Pitch Selection: 1. Slider 2. Sinker 3. Fastball
Sources: *The Scouting Report* (1984 and 1985)
Note: Butcher's sinker suspected of occasionally being a spitball. According to *The Scouting Report: 1987*, he abandoned the pitch in 1986.

MAX BUTCHER 6'2" 220-pound righty
95-106, 3.73, 9 Saves 1936 1945

Pitch Selection, 1936–1937: 1. Fastball 2. Curve 3. Sinker
Pitch Selection, 1938–1939: 1. Fastball 2. Sinker 3. Slider 4. Curve
Pitch Selection, 1940s: 1. Slider 2. Fastball 3. Sinker 4. Curve
Sources: Dick Farrington writing in *The Sporting News* in 1938 (TSN Morgue, publication date unknown); Herb Simons in *Baseball Magazine* (July 1945)

Quotes from Simons article: " 'When I first came up to the big league, I had a big curve, but I started messing around with other pitches and I lost it.' With the help of [Burleigh] Grimes, he started working on his slider. 'I was one of the first to use it—now everybody's using it.' . . . Now Butcher estimates that three out of every five pitches he throws are sliders."

BILL BUTLER 6'2" 210-pound lefty
23-35, 4.21, 1 Save 1969 1977

Pitch Selection: 1. Curve 2. Change 3. Fastball
Quote: "His fast ball isn't fast enough to overpower hitters and he gets hurt a lot by it. Has a lot of motion. Curve, change, and poise are better than average and if he comes up with another pitch, has chance."
Source: *Baseball Digest* (March 1967, "Official Scouting Reports on 1967 Major League Rookies")

JOHN BUZHARDT 6'2" 195-pound righty
71-96, 3.66, 7 Saves 1958 1968

Pitch Selection: 1. Fastball 2. Change 3. Slider
Note: Buzhardt's strengths were that he had excellent control, and virtually never got the ball above the belt. His fastball was just fair.
Source: The Philadelphia *Bulletin* (3/5/1960, Sandy Grady)

BILL BYRD 6'1" 210-pound righty
NEGRO LEAGUES 1932 1950

Pitch Selection: 1. Spitball 2. Fast Knuckleball 3. Slow Knuckleball 4. Roundhouse Curve 5. Fastball 6. Sinker
Sources: *Catching Dreams* (Frazier "Slow" Robinson with Paul Bauer, 1999); *Buck Leonard: The Black Lou Gehrig* (Buck Leonard with James A. Riley, 1995); *The Biographical Encyclopedia of the Negro Leagues* (James A. Riley, 1994); Gene Benson quoted in *Black Diamonds* (John Holway, 1989)

Quote from Slow Robinson in *Catching Dreams:* "Bill Byrd was an old-timer who had been pitching since the early thirties. He was past his prime and got by on a variety of knucklers, spitters, and big looping curves . . . Now Billy Byrd was a good pitcher, although he did throw a spitball—used that slippery elm—and a lot of times he might shake his glove for another signal. If he had thrown you two of those spitballs and they moved, he might throw you a fastball down the middle."

Quote from *The Biographical Encyclopedia of the Negro Leagues:* "He learned the spitball from Roosevelt Davis while playing with the Columbus Blue Birds in 1933, and would often fake throwing the pitch for psychological reasons."

PAUL BYRD 6'1" 185-pound righty
52-46, 4.39, 0 Saves 1995 2002

Pitches: 1. Fastball 2. Cut Fastball 3. Slider 4. Curve 5. Change 6. Screwball
Source: *Kansas City Star* (5/17/2002, Bob Dutton)
Note: Byrd was perhaps the only pitcher of his generation to pitch with a full wind-up.

TOMMY BYRNE 6'1" 182-pound lefty
85-69, 4.11, 12 Saves 1943 1957

Pitch Selection: 1. Fastball 2. Curve 3. Change 4. Sent to the minors in 1954, Byrne developed a slow curve and a slider.
Sources: *Dynasty* (Peter Golenbock, 1975); *The DiMaggio Albums* (Richard Whittingham, page 616); *The Sporting News* (March 1956, Harold Kaese; and 4/11/1956, Dan Daniel); *Sport* (September 1952, Tommy Byrne)

Note: Byrne, a talkative eccentric, made a trip to Japan in the winter of 1955–56, and came back throwing a pitch he called the "Kimono Ball," which was apparently a kind of a blooper pitch or slow change thrown from behind his back. Byrne threw the pitch in spring training, 1956, and talked about throwing it in the regular season, but to the best of my knowledge never did.

MARTY BYSTROM 6'5" 200-pound righty
29-26, 4.26, 0 Saves 1980 1985

Pitches: 1. Fastball 2. Slider 3. Change 4. Curve
Source: Phillies pitching coach Claude Osteen in *The Sporting News* (9/26/1983, Hal Bodley)

GREG CADARET 6'3" 200-pound lefty
38-32, 3.99, 14 Saves 1987 1998

Pitch Selection: 1. Fastball 2. Curve 3. Forkball 4. Change
Sources: *The Scouting Report* (1990 and 1992 editions)
Note: Cadaret threw 70 percent fastballs. Everything else was spotted.

LEON CADORE 6'1" 190-pound righty
68-72, 3.14, 3 Saves 1915 1924

Key Pitch: Curve
Source: *The Ol' Ball Game* (article by Norman Macht)

Description: "Leon Cadore, a foxy fellow on Brooklyn . . . used to wear a piece of sandpaper on the side of his pants. Or so his opponents claimed."
Source: *Baseball Magazine* (June 1936, Hugh Bradley, "Freak Pitching Deliveries—Past and Present")

BOB CAIN 6'0" 165-pound lefty
37-44, 4.50, 8 Saves 1949 1954

Pitch Selection: 1. Fastball 2. Curve 3. Change
Sources: *Baseball Magazine* (January 1951, page 283), and *We Played the Game* (Danny Peary, 1994)
Cain in *We Played the Game:* "I was a little wild, but I threw hard and had a pretty good curveball. I threw overhand or three-quarters. Only on occasion would I throw sidearm to a left-handed batter. For some reason—maybe I didn't concentrate enough or got lazy—I had less luck with left-handed batters than right-handers . . ."
Description from *Baseball Magazine:* "Bob goes according to the pitch that is working best for him. One day it may be the curve and the next outing his fast ball . . . He doesn't have any trick deliveries in his repertoire."

MIKE CALDWELL 6'0" 185-pound lefty
137-130, 3.81, 18 Saves 1971 1984

Pitch Selection: 1. Sinker 2. Fastball
Note: Caldwell's sinker was widely suspected of being a spitball.
Sources: *Nine Innings* (Dan Okrent, 1985); *The Sporting News* (6/6/1981, Peter Gammons)

Pitch Selection: 1. Sinker 2. Slider 3. Curve 4. Fastball 5. Change
Note: Caldwell threw from a three-quarter delivery, sometimes dropping to sidearm, especially against left-handed hitters.
Sources: *The Scouting Report* (1983–1985 editions)

RAY CALDWELL 6'2" 190-pound righty
133-120, 3.22, 9 Saves 1910 1921

Key Pitch: Spitball

Note: Caldwell was one of the "grandfathered" pitchers allowed to continue to throw the spitball after it was otherwise banned in 1921.
Source: 1923 *Reach Guide* (Page 38)

Key Pitch: Knuckleball
Source: *The Pitch That Killed* (Mike Sowell, 1989)

Description: "Ask any American League batter the half dozen toughest pitching propositions he faces in a season, and nine out of ten of them will include Caldwell's name in the list. Not only is he rated a pitcher with great natural gifts in speed and control, but he is universally considered one of those wise players who uses his head."
Source: *Baseball Magazine* (February 1919, "Leading Stars of the Winter Trades")

DICK CALMUS 6'4" 187-pound righty
3-1, 3.19, 0 Saves 1963 1967

Pitch Selection: 1. Fastball 2. Curve
Source: *Don Schiffer's Major League Baseball Handbook—1964*

ERNIE CAMACHO 6'1" 180-pound righty
10-20, 4.21, 45 Saves 1980 1990

Pitch Selection: 1. Fastball (92–95) 2. Slider 3. Forkball (occasional)
Quote from Pat Corrales: "Ernie needs to do one thing—let me do his thinking for him. Here is a guy who throws harder than Al Holland and all he wants to do is throw forkballs. Thinking is the reason he has been with six different organizations."
Source: *A Baseball Winter* (edited by Terry Pluto and Jeff Neuman, 1986)

HOWIE CAMNITZ 5'9" 169-pound righty
133-107, 2.75, 15 Saves 1904 1915

Pitch Selection: 1. Fastball 2. Curves
Description: "He is a right-handed pitcher with great speed, sharp curves, and excellent control."
Source: *Baseball Magazine* (December 1909, Page 69)

Key Pitch: Curve
Source: *Touching Second* (John J. Evers and Hugh S. Fullerton, 1910)

RICK CAMP 6'1" 185-pound righty
56-49, 3.37, 57 Saves 1976 1985

Pitch Selection: 1. Heavy Sinker (mid-80s) 2. Slider 3. Mediocre Curve 4. Change (occasional)
Sources: *The Scouting Report* (1983 and 1984 editions)

BILL CAMPBELL 6'3" 185-pound righty
83-68, 3.54, 126 Saves 1973 1987

Pitch Selection: 1. Screwball 2. Sinker
Source: *The Relief Pitcher* (John Thorn, 1979)

JOHN CANDELERIA 6'7" 205-pound lefty
177-122, 3.33, 29 Saves 1975 1993

Pitch Selection: 1. Fastball 2. Hard Curve 3. Slider 4. Change
Source: *The Scouting Report: 1987*

TOM CANDIOTTI 6'3" 205-pound righty
151-164, 3.73, 0 Saves 1983 1999

Pitch Selection, 1983–84: 1. Slow Curve 2. Slow Slider 3. Fastball
Pitch Selection, rest of career: 1. Knuckleball 2. Slow Curve 3. Fastball
Sources: *The Scouting Report* (1983 and 1990 editions)
Note: Candiotti went to the minors in 1985 to work on the knuckleball, and returned to the majors in 1986 as Phil Niekro's teammate (and pupil) with the Indians.

BEN CANTWELL 6'1" 168-pound righty
76-108, 3.91, 21 Saves 1927 1937

Pitches: 1. Curve 2. Slow Ball 3. Knuckle Ball 4. Slower Change 5. Sinking Fastball
Sources: *The Sporting News* (3/9/1933); Harold K. George in the *Lowell Courier Citizen* (9/14/1933); *The Boston Braves* (Fred Lieb, 1948)

Pitch Selection: 1. Curve 2. Sinking Fastball 3. Knuckleball (as Change)
Source: *Baseball Magazine* (January 1934, Clifford Bloodgood)

Commentary: Lieb describes Cantwell as "sidewheeling." When Cantwell was in the high minor leagues, a scout said that he "has no fastball." He was a change-of-speeds pitcher, a slowball pitcher. This came to be the defining description of him, repeated almost by rote when his name was mentioned, the pitcher without a fastball. He finally turned the corner in 1932 and had a great season in 1933 when he realized that although his fastball wasn't outstanding, he nonetheless could throw it and *had* to throw it in order to be successful.

Cantwell was a handsome, polite, articulate man, highly intelligent, and a graduate of the University of Tennessee. His knuckleball was a "floater," like a modern knuckleball, rather than the hard knuckleball thrown by Freddie Fitzsimmons and other pitchers in the thirties.

BUZZ CAPRA 5'10" 168-pound righty
31-37, 3.88, 5 Saves 1971 1977

Description: "Capra, 26, is a fidgety craftsman who mixes off-speed breaking pitches with a sneaky fastball. A righthander, he dips so low off the mound that he seems to deliver the ball from the vicinity of his kneecaps."
Source: *Sports Illustrated* (7/8/1974, Ray Kennedy)

PAT CARAWAY 6'4" 175-pound lefty
22-40, 5.35, 3 Saves 1930 1932

Pitches: 1. Change of Pace 2. Fastball 3. Curve 4. Knuckleball (refined in 1931)
Description: "This affable young Texan has a repertoire that would rouse envy in a grizzled veteran of the mound. His lanky build and sweeping left-hand shoots are puzzle enough to the harassed batsman who faces him. Caraway has a deceptive underhand delivery, a good fast ball, a good curve, and excellent change of pace. These things are the arrow in the quiver of a pitcher's talents. But Caraway has added another quirk to his assortment of pitching tricks, namely, the knuckle ball."
Source: *Baseball Magazine* (September 1931, John J. Ward)

DON CARDWELL 6'4" 210-pound righty
102-138, 3.92, 7 Saves 1957 1970

Pitches: 1. Fastball 2. Curve 3. Slider 4. Sinker 5. Change 6. Spitball (occasional)
Cardwell: "It took me ten years to throw a curve that satisfied me. What I threw then was more like a slider. I've never gone in for fancy stuff. Fast ball, curve, slider, sinker and change-up and all controlled satisfies me. I go three-quarters with the curve. I don't use the overhand curve because if you do you've got to come overhand with your fast one or the hitters will know it's coming . . .

"Once in a while I load one up. I've got a pretty good teacher in the spitball in one of our Met pitchers and if I can get away with it I'm going to use it."
Source: *Baseball Digest* (July 1967, Charles Dexter)
Pitch Selection: 1. Sinking Fastball 2. Change 3. Sidearm Curve
Sources: *The No-Hit Hall of Fame* (Rich Coberly, 1985); *The New Era Cubs: 1941–1985* (Eddie Gold and Art Ahrens, 1985)

Note: Cardwell, after having difficulty hiding his pitches, developed a unique delivery in which he pumped his arms over his head with the ball in his glove, his right hand empty. He would grab the ball at the top of the windup, and get his grip for the pitch he wanted while following through on the delivery.

TEX CARLETON 6'1" 180-pound righty
100-76, 3.91, 9 Saves 1932 1940

Pitch Selection: 1. Sinking Fastball 2. Curve 3. Slow Curve
Source: *The Gashouse Gang* (Robert E. Hood, 1976)

Description: "He is generally regarded as a side-arm pitcher, but not infrequently he shoots an overhand or underhand ball plateward. He marches toward his greatest heights when keeping the ball low."
Source: *Baseball Magazine* (February 1934, Clifford Bloodgood)

HAL CARLSON 6'0" 180-pound righty
114-120, 3.97, 19 Saves 1917 1930

Key Pitch, before 1920: Spitball
Pitch Selection, 1920 on: 1. Fastball 2. Curve 3. Change 4. Screwball
Sources: *Chicago Tribune* (8/24/1929); *The Phillies Encyclopedia* (Frank Bilovsky and Rich Westcott, 1984); *Rockford Journal* (4/2/1986); unidentified clippings from the Hall of Fame Library

Quote from *Chicago Tribune:* "Officials neglected to register him as one entitled to salivate the orb . . . (He proceeded to) concentrate on curves and speed and a slow ball with his fast ball delivery."

Quote from *Rockford Journal:* "As an administrative oversight, the Pittsburgh Pirates failed to register such a designation for Carlson, and use of the spitball was forever lost to him. To offset that handicap, he polished a standard technique: fast ball, curve and change of pace."

Quote: "Last of the spitball pitchers . . . when the spitter was outlawed, Carlson drifted back to the minors."
Quote: "He perfected his screw ball and came back to the big leagues with the Phillies."
Source: unidentified clippings from the Hall of Fame Library

Note: A poem composed after Carlson's death in 1930 said that Carlson had "a motion swift and hard . . . blazing speed . . . [and] spectral curves."
Source: unidentified clipping from the Hall of Fame Library

STEVE CARLTON 6'4" 210-pound lefty
329-244, 3.22, 2 Saves 1965 1988

Pitches, 1965–1968: 1. Rising Fastball 2. Curve
Pitches, 1969: 1. Rising Fastball 2. Slider 3. Curve
Pitches, 1970: 1. Rising Fastball 2. Curve
3. Slider (occasional)
Pitches, 1971: 1. Rising Fastball 2. Curve
3. Change (developed in 1971)
Pitches, 1972–1974: 1. Rising Fastball 2. Curve
3. Slider
Pitches, after 1974: 1. Slider 2. High Fastball (88–90)
3. Sweeping Curve
Sources: *The Sporting News* (5/8/1971, Neal Russo; 6/24/1972, Allen Lewis; 3/2/1974, Neal Russo; and 6/6/1983, Jayson Stark); *Sports Illustrated* (8/21/1972, William Leggett); *The Heart of the Order* (Tom Boswell, page 266)

Commentary: Carlton first learned to throw the slider on a postseason trip to Japan in 1968, and it became one of his best pitches shortly into the 1969 season. But he had trouble throwing his slider effectively in 1970, and essentially junked it early in 1971. He rediscovered the slider in the spring of '72, however, and—though he basically lost it again in '73—eventually the slider became his best pitch. In 1972, when Carlton went 27-10 for a Phillies team that finished 59–97, there were some who thought that *each* of Carlton's three pitches was as good as the *best* pitch of almost any other pitcher in the majors. It's also worth noting that in the early '70s, many considered Carlton's curveball the best in the majors.

Description: "Carlton had classic form on the mound. He began his motion with his head down, which helped him keep his weight forward. As he brought his right leg up his head would rise, too, and he lifted his right knee almost to shoulder height as he rocked into his windup. Pivoting on his left leg, he brought his left arm forward and whipped the ball with an easy pinwheel motion, the throwing arm ending up below his right hip before whiplashing back into proper defensive position.

"Lefty's grip was a bit unorthodox but effective. He held the baseball out toward his fingertips, keeping his index and middle fingers near each other at the very top of the ball. He generally threw his curve almost straight overhand, his slider about three-quarter arm. Because he threw the fastball equally well from either motion, batters couldn't figure out what pitch was coming simply by following his delivery."
Source: *Baseball's Greatest Players: The Saga Continues* (David Shiner, 2001)

Willie Stargell in 1972: "Hitting against Steve Carlton is like eating soup with a fork."
Source: *The Sporting News* (3/2/1974, Ray Kelly)

Bob Brenly in 1983: "You see more guys swing through [Carlton's slider] than any other pitch. With that slider, you see guys take some of the funniest hacks you ever want to see. You tell yourself you don't want to swing at a bad one, but then that thing comes up there and it just freezes you."
Source: *The Sporting News* (6/6/1983, Jayson Stark)

Keith Hernandez: "When I played with the Cardinals, Steve Carlton threw me (and most batters) 95 percent sliders. It was a great pitch, as good as J.R. Richards's, but he had even better control of it than Richard. Carlton threw the slider like an automaton: outside corner black, at the knees, every time . . ."
Source: *Pure Baseball: Pitch by Pitch for the Advanced Fan* (Keith Hernandez and Mike Bryan, 1994)

DON CARMAN 6'3" 195-pound lefty
53-54, 4.11, 11 Saves 1983 1992

Pitch Selection: 1. Fastball (90)
2. Change (occasional)

Source: *The Scouting Report: 1987*
Pitch Selection: 1. Fastball 2. Curve 3. Change
Source: *The Scouting Report: 1990*

CHRIS CARPENTER 6'6" 230-pound righty
49-50, 4.83, 0 Saves 1997 2002

Pitches: 1. Four-Seam Fastball (91-95)
2. Two-Seam Fastball 3. Curve 4. Circle Change
5. Slider
Note: The only mention we've found of Carpenter's slider is in the 2002 edition of *The Scouting Notebook.*
Sources: *The Scouting Notebook* (1998–2002 editions)

Pitches: 1. Four-Seam Fastball (92–93)
2. Sweeping Curve 3. Cut Fastball 4. Change
Source: *The Scouting Notebook: 2003*

CRIS CARPENTER 6'1" 198-pound righty
27-22, 3.91, 7 Saves 1988 1996

Pitch Selection: 1. Fastball (high-80s) 2. Slider
3. Forkball
Sources: *The Scouting Report: 1990; The Scouting Notebook: 1995*

Pitches: 1. Slider 2. Sinking Fastball 3. Curve
4. Forkball 5. Change
Source: *The Scouting Report: 1995*

HECTOR CARRASCO 6'2" 175-pound righty
30-42, 4.22, 16 Saves 1994 2003

Pitch Selection: 1. Heavy Fastball 2. Hard Slider
3. Split-Fingered Fastball
Source: *The Scouting Notebook 1999*

ALEX CARRASQUEL 6'1" 182-pound righty
50-39, 3.73, 16 Saves 1939 1949

Key Pitches: 1. Sharp-breaking Curve 2. Fastball
3. Change of Pace
Source: *The Washington Post* (Shirley Povich, report dated 2/22/1939); *Baseball Magazine* (June 1943, Clifford Bloodgood)

Description: "Alejandro is by far the most picturesque ball player in the major leagues. He is tall, thin and fiery, and has black and glossy hair. Close up, he has a ferocious and formidable appearance. There is an intriguing air of mystery about him in that nobody seems to know where he came from or how he got where he was going."
Source: Marvin McCarthy's column in unidentified newspaper (6/2/1939)

Comment: "Carrasquel not only knew how to pitch, but it was quickly evident that he knew how to field his position, too. There were debates on the Washington bench about who was the best fielding pitcher in the league—Sid Hudson or Carrasquel."
Source: Shirley Povich in *The Washington Post* (7/8/1949, "This Morning" column)

Commentary: The following paragraphs of the Bloodgood article are reprinted because they reflect the prevalence of sidearm pitching at that time. Basically, almost every pitcher at that time would, at least sometimes, drop down sidearm . . .

> His first experience with the New York Yankees is worth a paragraph in this sketch. Alex was called in to relieve with the bases filled, two out, and catcher Joe Glenn, noted for his love of flashy sports jackets and his distaste for side arm deliveries, at bat.
>
> When Carrasquel came in from the bullpen Ossie Bluege, who was coach then, tried to tell the Venezuelan to pitch side-arm to Glenn, but he couldn't make himself understood. Manager Bucky Harris then had to send his Spanish speaking utility man Roberto Estalella out to the mound to give Alex the instructions. The pair jabbered a few minutes, the pitcher nodded, and proceeded to strike out the Yankee on three side-arm pitches.

BILL CARRICK 6'1" 192-pound righty
63-88, 4.14, 0 Saves 1898 1902

Key Pitch: Curve
Source: *Misfits!* (J. Thomas Hetrick, 1991)

CLAY CARROLL 6'1" 178-pound righty
96-73, 2.94, 143 Saves 1964 1978

Pitch Selection: 1. Fastball 2. Curve 3. Slider
4. Slip pitch
Sources: *The Relief Pitcher* (John Thorn, 1979); *The Sporting News* (8/1/1970, Earl Lawson)

OWNIE CARROLL 5'10" 165-pound righty
64-90, 4.43, 5 Saves 1925 1934

Pitch Selection: 1. Curve 2. Fastball 3. Change
Sources: *New York World* (6/24/1925 and 1/25/1930); *New York World-Telegram* (3/23/1934); unidentified clipping in the Hall of Fame Library (12/30/1928)

Babe Ruth: "He seems to have lots of speed and a clever drop ball."
Ty Cobb: ". . . [He has] as pretty a hook as you ever saw."
Source: *New York World* (6/24/1925)

Comment: "An overhand pitcher, he always has had a good curve ball and his fast ball has improved as he has matured."
Source: *New York World* (1/25/1930)

Carroll: "I would say my change of pace is my favorite delivery . . . I used to alternate between my curve and my fast ball. There's no real break to it, either out or in, but it may sink a little."
Source: *New York World-Telegram* (3/23/1934)
Comment: "He has developed one of the best slow curves in the business . . . tossing up the floater when the [opposition is] expecting fast ones."
Source: unidentified clipping in the Hall of Fame Library (12/30/1928)

KID CARSEY 5'7" 168-pound righty
116-138, 4.95, 5 Saves 1891 1901

Pitch Selection: 1. Slow Curve 2. Slow Change 3. Slower Change
Sources: *Misfits!* (J. Thomas Hetrick, 1991); *Baseball's First Stars* (SABR, 1996, article by Joan M. Thomas)

Comment: "Another delivery that has gone, but mainly through the change of rules, was the cross-fire, Kid Carsey's best stock in trade. When a man's foot is glued to a small slab, he can't do much cross-firing.

"But when the pitchers had a box to rove in, several of them could get a delightful angle to their deliveries, by changing from one corner to the other. It can easily be seen that a pitcher, by thus changing, could get a wide slant for either right or left hand hitters, and Carsey, years after he had no speed remaining, won in the big league on that style of foxy pitching."
Source: *Baseball Magazine* (January 1917; no author listed)

BOB CARUTHERS 5'7" 138-pound righty
217-98, 2.83, 4 Saves 1884 1892

Key Pitch: Fastball
Quote: "Caruthers had wonderful speed and perfect control."
Source: *The National Game* (Alfred H. Spink, 1911)

Description: "Caruthers first advances his right leg, fumbles the ball on his hip a second and then with a sour look throws to the batter. He pitches without effort and seemingly does not care whether the batter hits the ball or not. His delivery looks like it would be easy to bat, but the reverse is the case."
Source: Brooklyn *Daily Eagle* (11/25/1888), reprinted in *A Tale of Four Cities* (Jean-Pierre Caillault, 2003)

DAN CASEY 6'0" 180-pound lefty
96-90, 3.18, 0 Saves 1884 1890

Pitch Selection: 1. Fastball 2. Curve
Quote: "I had the same kind of stuff on the ball that the present-day pitchers do, plenty of steam and some curves."
Source: Interview with Casey in the *New York Times* (4/30/1935)

HUGH CASEY 6'1" 207-pound righty
75-42, 3.45, 55 Saves 1935 1949

Pitch Selection: 1. Slider 2. Fastball 3. Curve
Sources: *Bums* (Peter Golenbock, 1984), *The DiMaggio Albums* (Richard Whittingham, Page 384, game account by John Drebinger)

Key Pitch: Sinker
Source: Spider Jorgensen in *We Played the Game* (Danny Peary, 1989)

CARL CASHION 6'2" 200-pound righty
12-13, 3.70, 1 Save 1911 1914

Key Pitch: Fastball
Comment: "Another boxman who had Rusie's speed, but in this instance never gained control, was Carl Cashion, a giant tried out by Griffith a few years ago. Cash

had so much stuff that it was hard to follow the pill as it flashed across the plate. The pity is that he was unable to tame it; otherwise Washington, no doubt, would have a pennant or so to its credit, a consummation devoutly to be wished."
Source: *Baseball Magazine* (May 1919, Edmund K. Goldsborough, "Famous Speed Kings of the Past")

LARRY CASIAN 6'0" 175-pound lefty
11-13, 4.56, 2 Saves 1990 1998

Pitch Selection: 1. Fastball 2. Curve 3. Slider 4. Change
Source: *The Scouting Notebook: 1995*

GEORGE CASTER 6'1" 180-pound righty
76-100, 4.54, 39 Saves 1934 1946

Pitch Selection, early career: 1. Fastball 2. Curve 3. Knuckleball
Pitch Selection, later: 1. Knuckleballs 2. Fastball 3. Curve (occasional)
Sources: *Baseball Magazine* (January 1938, Robert C. Milne); *Baseball Magazine* article about A's pitching coach Earle Brucker (April 1949, Frank Yeutter); *Baseball Magazine* article about knuckleball pitchers (April 1947, Yeutter); *Baseball Magazine* article about Athletics catcher Hal Wagner (September 1942, Yeutter); Red Hayworth in *The Pastime in Turbulence: Interviews with Baseball Players of the 1940s* (Brent Kelley, 2001); Dario Lodigiani in *Dugout to Foxhole* (Rick Van Blair, 1994)

Quote: "Caster threw his knuckler at two speeds. He'd throw his fast knuckler first, then follow with a good fast ball, then toss up the dancer. I've seen a lot of good hitters take all three pitches for strikes. And when they did swing at the fast one they'd better hit it for they wouldn't see it again."
Source: Ex-Athletics catcher Earle Brucker in 1947 *Baseball Magazine*

Key pitch, 1936: Hard Sinker
Source: *Who's Who in the Major Leagues* (1937 ed.)

Description: "George has a peculiar delivery, practically lacking any windup."
Source: *Who's Who in the American League, 1935* (Harold Johnson)

BOBBY CASTILLO 5'10" 170-pound righty
38-40, 3.94, 18 Saves 1977 1985

Pitch Selection: 1. Screwball 2. Fastball (86) 3. Curve 4. Slider
Sources: *The Scouting Report* (1983 and 1984 editions); *The Sporting News* (2/2/1980, Gordon Verrell)

Note: Castillo taught his screwball to Fernando Valenzuela during the winter of 1979/1980.
Source: *The Sporting News* (10/18/1980, Gordon Verrell)

FRANK CASTILLO 6'1" 190-pound righty
82-103, 4.55, 2 Saves 1991 2002

Pitch Selection: 1. Fastball (mid-80s) 2. Change 3. Slider 4. Curve
Sources: *The Scouting Report: 1993* and *The Scouting Notebook 1998*

TONY CASTILLO 5'10" 177-pound lefty
28-23, 3.93, 22 Saves 1988 1998

Pitch Selection: 1. Fastball 2. Curve 3. Change
Source: *The Scouting Report: 1996*

BILL CAUDILL 6'1" 190-pound righty
35-52, 3.68, 106 Saves 1979 1987

Pitches: 1. Fastball (low-90s) 2. Cut Fastball 3. Slider 4. Change (occasional)
Note: Caudill threw a high percentage of fastballs, and never really did develop anything like a reliable off-speed pitch.
Sources: *The Scouting Report* (1983–1985 editions, and 1987)

JOHN CERUTTI 6'2" 195-pound lefty
49-43, 3.94, 4 Saves 1985 1991

Pitches, 1985–1988: 1. Curve 2. Four-Seam Fastball 3. Forkball 4. Sinker 5. Change 6. Slider (occasional)
Pitches, 1989–1991: 1. Sinker 2. Curve 3. Four-Seam Fastball 4. Change 5. Forkball 6. Slider (occasional)
Sources: *The Scouting Notebook* (1987 and 1990 editions); e-mail correspondence between Cerutti and Rob Neyer (5/29/2002)

Quote from e-mail: "When I first came to the big leagues, my best pitch was probably my curveball, even though I only threw it 25–35 percent of the time. As I learned to throw a better sinker, that became my best pitch. I wish I had developed (and thrown) more change-ups. But that's another story. I used the forkball early in my career, but got away from it later in my career. By the way, I did throw a slider occasionally. I would throw the slider to very good left-handed hitters, like Don Mattingly, but not often."

ELTON (ICEBOX) CHAMBERLAIN

5'9" 168-pound righty
156-120, 3.57, 2 Saves 1886 1896

Note: Pitched with both hands on May 9, 1888, and October 1, 1891.
Quote: ". . . [He] is able to pitch both left handed and right handed."
Source: *New York Clipper* (8/22/1891)

CLIFF CHAMBERS 6'3" 208-pound lefty

48-53, 4.29, 1 Save 1948 1953

Pitch Selection: 1. Fastball 2. Change
Quote: "Seldom changes up and tries to go it on fast balls alone. Pirates board of strategy attempted to interest him in a curve but he preferred to stick with swift."
Source: *Baseball Digest* (January 1951, Milt Richman)

Note: Oddly enough, less than a year earlier in *Baseball Magazine* (August 1950), Chambers told Hub Miller, "Now I have confidence in my curve and can use it as effectively as my fast ball."

DEAN CHANCE 6'3" 200-pound righty

128-115, 2.92, 23 Saves 1961 1971

Pitch Selection: 1. Sinking Fastball 2. Sweeping Curve
3. Slider
Sources: *Sport* (August 1963, Page 86); *Baseball Stars of 1965* (article by Ray Robinson)

Pitch Selection: 1. Fastball 2. Slider
3. Changeup Screwball
Source: *Don Schiffer's Major League Baseball Handbook—1964*

Jim Palmer: "A few sidearmers, such as Dean Chance and Steve Barber, can throw across the body successfully—mainly because the optical effect contributes to fear on the part of right-handed batters."
Source: *Pitching* (Jim Palmer, edited by Joel H. Cohen, 1975)

SPUD CHANDLER 6'0" 181-pound righty

109-43, 2.84, 6 Saves 1937 1947

Pitches: 1. Fastball (90) 2. Curve 3. Sinker
4. Slider (added in 1941) 5. Forkball
6. Screwball (as Change)
7. Knuckleball (occasional)
Sources: *Famous American Athletes of Today: Ninth Series* (Gordon Campbell); *Diamond Greats* (Rich Westcott, 1988); *Baseball Magazine* (July 1943, Clifford Bloodgood; and September 1944, Ed Rumill)
Source for Slider: *The Sporting News* (8/28/1941, Page 10)

Description from Bloodgood article: "Spurgeon is all business when he is on the pitching parapet, so serious one could get the erroneous impression that he lacks a sense of humor. He's restless out there, forever picking up the resin bag, scraping the sod with his cleats, punching his glove, blowing into his bare hand." Same article says that Chandler learned his slider from Red Ruffing in 1942.

Comment: "There are only two overhand sinker-ball pitchers—Hal Schumacher, of the Giants, and Spurgeon Chandler, of the Yankees. This variety of the pitch entails tremendous strain on the arm. The overhand sinker has no complete follow through."
Source: *Baseball Magazine* (September 1937, Daniel M. Daniel)

Chandler on pitching in 1946: "It was the end of the line for me, and over the years I had come up with the five [pitches]. Fast ball, curve, slider, screw ball, and (I hope some of the San Francisco Giants see this) a fork ball."
Source: *Yogi: It Ain't Over . . .* (Yogi Berra with Tom Horton, 1986)

NORM CHARLTON 6'3" 195-pound lefty

51-54, 3.71, 97 Saves 1988 2001

Pitch Selection: 1. Fastball 2. Splitter 3. Slider
Sources: *The Scouting Report* (1990 and 1996 editions); *Bill Mazeroski's Baseball* (1993)

KEN CHASE 6'2" 210-pound lefty
53-84, 4.27, 1 Save 1936 1943

Note: Chase prior to 1940 was a side-arm pitcher who relied heavily on his fastball. In 1940 he switched to an overhand delivery and developed "an overhand curve that comes up to the plate waist high and looks very inviting to the hitter, but it breaks suddenly to the batter's knees."
Source: *Baseball Magazine* (August 1940, Robert C. Milne)

Description: "A prominent heavy ball thrower in [the American League] is Ken Chase of the Senators. He serves up a ball that made Rick Ferrell, who was his battery mate, think he had caught a bowling ball when it landed in his mitt."
Source: *Baseball Magazine* (July 1941, Edward T. Murphy)

LARRY CHENEY 6'1" 185-pound righty
116-100, 2.70, 19 Saves 1911 1919

Pitch Selection: 1. Spitball 2. Fastball
Sources: *The Brooklyn Dodgers* (Frank Graham, 1947); *Dodger Classics* (Robert L. Tiemann, 1983)

Description: "Larry Cheney, the spitball pitcher who once worked for Brooklyn . . . had no wind-up at all, principally because he had one bad knee and couldn't throw his legs around carelessly."
Source: *Baseball Magazine* (June 1936, Hugh Bradley, "Freak Pitching Deliveries—Past and Present")

TOM CHENEY 5'11" 170-pound righty
19-29, 3.77, 2 Saves 1957 1966

Pitch Selection: 1. Cut Fastball 2. Curve
Cheney: "Out of 10 pitches, I threw 7 or 8 fastballs. My strikeout pitch was a high fastball . . . All my career, I much preferred pitching to a left-hander than a right-hander, and I know that's just backward thinking because I was a righty. But my fastball ran. They called it a cut fastball. I could jam a left-hander but had trouble pitching a right-handed hitter inside."
Source: *We Played the Game* (Danny Peary, 1994)

Pitches: 1. Fastball 2. Curve 3. Slider 4. Change 5. Knuckleball
Source: *The Sporting News* (4/11/1964, Page 23)

JACK CHESBRO 5'9" 180-pound righty
198-132, 2.68, 5 Saves 1899 1909

Key Pitch, 1899–1903: Fastball
Key Pitch, 1904–1909: Spitball
Comment: "Gripping it like a curve and throwing it from three-quarters motion, he claimed he could control both the direction and degree of the drop from 2 to 18 inches. By midseason [1904] he was able to signal to his catcher just how far the ball was going to drop and later admitted, 'Over the last 30 games of the season I pitched spitballs entirely. In those 30 games I didn't pitch a half-dozen balls that weren't spitballs.' "
Source: *Yankees Century* (Glenn Stout and Richard A. Johnson, 2002)

Notes: Clark Griffith insisted in *The Sporting News* (4/6/1955) that while Hildebrand and Stricklett had fiddled with the spitball on the sidelines, Chesbro was the first to throw it in a game.

Yankees Century quotes Chesbro as saying he discovered the spitball in the spring of 1903 when "he saw it demonstrated by Elmer Stricklett." Stricklett supposedly said to himself, "Mr. Chesbro, that is something you must learn," but whether this happened during a game or not, we don't know.

BOB CHESNES 6'0" 180-pound righty
24-22, 4.66, 1 Save 1948 1950

Pitch Selection: 1. Fastball 2. Curve
Quote: "Bob Chesnes . . . had a fastball about as fast as anyone could throw. We didn't have measurements in those days, but I imagine he was in the mid 90s. He had a good curveball and all the physical equipment to be a superstar, but I understand he got a sore arm and eventually gave up baseball."
Source: Jack Brewer in *The San Francisco Seals, 1946–1957* (Brent Kelley, 2002)

Description: "His arm 'swings through the air with the greatest of ease' aptly describes the pitching motion of Seal ace, Bob Chesnes, hailed as one of the greatest prospects ever developed on the Pacific Coast . . . Chesnes simply looks lazy on the mound, but his blazing fast ball and hurling artistry has piled up the victories to such an extent that virtually every major league club has its scout, with pen in hand, ready to do 'business.' "
Source: *Pacific Coast League Baseball News* (7/15/1947)

Jack Chesbro

Commentary: It's perhaps worth mentioning that Chesnes' strikeout rates in both the Pacific Coast League and the National League were not particularly high, though in 1946, pitching in the Class C Pioneer League, he did strike out 278 hitters in 225 innings.

BOB CHIPMAN 6'2" 190-pound lefty
51-46, 3.72, 14 Saves 1941 1952

Warren Spahn: "He didn't have any speed, otherwise he could have been a helluva pitcher. But he knew change of speeds. He could make a baseball almost walk up to that plate."
Source: *Warren Spahn: Immortal Southpaw* (Al Silverman, 1961)

LARRY CHRISTENSON 6'4" 215-pound righty
83-71, 3.79, 4 Saves 1973 1983

Pitch Selection: 1. Fastball 2. Curve 3. Slider
Source: *The Sporting News* (8/9/1975, Ray Kelly)

JASON CHRISTIANSEN 6'5" 241-pound lefty
17-22, 4.17, 13 Saves 1995 2003

Pitch Selection: 1. Fastball 2. Curve
Source: *The Scouting Notebook: 1996*

Pitch Selection: 1. Fastball (mid-90s) 2. Slider
3. Curve (occasional) 4. Change (occasional)
Sources: *The Scouting Notebook* (1999 and 2000 editions)

Pitch Selection: 1. Fastball (high-80s)
2. Slider (82–84)
Note: Velocity dropped after shoulder surgery in October 2000.
Source: *The Scouting Notebook: 2002*

RUSS CHRISTOPHER 6'3" 170-pound righty
54-64, 3.37, 35 Saves 1942 1948

Key Pitch: Sinking Fastball
Note: Christopher was converted to submarine style by Athletics pitching coach Earle Brucker in 1942 or '43.
Source: *To Absent Friends* (Red Smith, Page 88)

Quote: "It is his underhand delivery that makes Russ Christopher of the Athletics so effective."
Source: Minneapolis manager Frank Shellenback in *Baseball Digest* (April 1948, George A. Barton)

BUBBA CHURCH 6'0" 180-pound righty
36-37, 4.10, 4 Saves 1950 1955

Pitch Selection: 1. Fastball 2. Curve
3. Change off the Fastball 4. Change off the Curve
Source: *The Whiz Kids and the 1950 Pennant Race* (Robin Roberts and C. Paul Rogers III, Page 210)

Andy Seminick: "His good control lets him keep most of his stuff low. He keeps his fast ball below the batter's waist and inside, where it can do the least damage. He does the same thing with his curve. He doesn't seem to be putting much on the ball, yet every pitch does something. His ball is alive. And he rarely wastes a pitch. He gets it over and makes them hit. He surprised me with

his control. Few kids his age are as sharp hitting the corners of the plate."
Source: *Baseball Magazine* (April 1951, Ed Rumill)

EDDIE CICOTTE 5'9" 175-pound righty
209-149, 2.38, 24 Saves 1905 1920

Pitch Selection: 1. Shine Ball 2. Fastball 3. Curve 4. Knuckleball
Note: After Cicotte was traded to the White Sox, he learned the shine ball from Red Faber.
Sources: *The National Game* (Alfred H. Spink, 1911); Cicotte in *Baseball Digest* (June 1952); *The Crooked Pitch* (Martin Quigley, 1984); *Eight Men Out* (Eliot Asinof); *The Great Baseball Mystery* (Victor Luhrs, 1966); *The Boston Red Sox* (Fred Lieb, 1947); unidentified clipping dated June 21, 1955

Cicotte: "The knuckle ball has been of great value to me. I confess that I depend upon it a good deal in my work. I think it is no exaggeration to say that out of 100 average balls that I throw, 75 are knuckle balls."
Source: *Baseball Magazine* (May 1917, John J. Ward)

Comment: "Cicotte, a natural fast ball pitcher, doubled his effectiveness with the shine ball he developed.

"Eddie darkened the ball on one side by rubbing it in the dirt. Then, he slickened the ball by rubbing it vigorously on his pants.

"The process camouflaged the ball perfectly. The ball, thrown with blazing speed, rotating quickly, and showing the white side only at split-second intervals, baffled batters completely."
Source: Frank Shellenback in *Baseball Digest* (April 1948, George A. Barton); Shellenback, Cicotte's teammate in 1918 and '19, presumably knew what he was talking about.

Comment: "Perhaps no pitcher in the world has such a varied assortment of wares in his repertory as Cicotte. He throws with effect practically every kind of ball known to pitching science.

" 'All the pitching deliveries concocted by the imagination were tabooed in certain quarters after Cicotte made a success of fooling the batters last year,' said Manager Rowland. 'They talked about the mud ball, the talcum ball and about every other kind of delivery.'

"The baffled baseball men who tried to diagnose Cicotte's delivery last year forgot the gum ball. Some day some one will think of that, and it will stick.

"The real inside dope is that Cicotte is the best little mixer on the slab in the world. In pitching for a batter's weakness and cutting corners when he wants to he has no superior in the game. His success is founded on these little things. He was the same crafty Eddie on the hill before he even thought of rubbing the ball on his uni."
Source: *The Sporting News* (5/2/1918)

Note: In this issue of TSN, Cicotte claimed that "the so-called shine ball is a pure freak of the imagination." He rubbed the ball on his sleeve simply to play with the batter's mind, he said, but was really just throwing a knuckleball.

Key Pitch: Sailor
Quote: "For instance, nobody knows to this day—not even his own manager and the coaches—what it was that Eddie Cicotte did to a ball to make it sail in that peculiar manner so completely puzzling to batters.

"Eddie Cicotte's great success was due almost entirely to his 'sailor.' This ball would start out like an ordinary pitch and then would sail much in the same manner of a flat stone thrown by a small boy . . . When he was thrown out of organized baseball his secret went with him."
Source: *Memoirs of Twenty Years in Baseball* (Ty Cobb, Pages 65, 68)

GALEN CISCO 6'0" 200-pound righty
25-56, 4.57, 2 Saves 1961 1969

Pitch Selection: 1. Sinker 2. Fastball
Source: *Don Schiffer's Major League Baseball Handbook—1964*

JIM CLANCY 6'4" 220-pound righty
140-167, 4.23, 10 Saves 1977 1991

Pitch Selection: 1. Fastball 2. Slider 3. Forkball 4. Straight Change (developed in 1982)
Note: Clancy threw with a three-quarters delivery.
Source: *The Scouting Report: 1983*

Pitch Selection: 1. Slider 2. Fastball 3. Slow curve
Source: *The Scouting Report: 1990*

Comment: "When Cox took over as manager a year ago, the staff was struggling through growing pains . . . 'We're a power staff,' says Cox, and they went back to

the power. Widmar took away Clancy's forkball, got him to keep his fastball down and the 6-4 righthander became one of the league's premier pitchers."
Source: *The Sporting News* (6/13/1983, Peter Gammons)

BRYAN CLARK 6'2" 185-pound lefty
20-23, 4.15, 4 Saves 1981 1990

Pitch Selection: 1. Hard Slider 2. Fastball (high-80s) 3. Slow Curve
Sources: *The Scouting Report* (1983 and 1984 editions)

MARK CLARK 6'5" 225-pound righty
74-71, 4.61, 0 Saves 1991 2000

Pitch Selection: 1. Slider 2. Sinking Fastball 3. Forkball or Split-Fingered Fastball 4. Change
Sources: *1995 Baseball Almanac, The Scouting Notebook 1999*

Tim McCarver: "The only sinkerballer who consistently throws four-seamers is Mark Clark, a strange pitcher. He has to keep the ball down because he doesn't have overpowering stuff, but he's still not a ground-ball pitcher because his four-seam sinker is light and easy to lift. I'm surprised at how effective he is because if his erratic splitter isn't working, he doesn't really have an out pitch."
Source: *Tim McCarver's Baseball for Brain Surgeons and Other Fans* (McCarver with Danny Peary, 1998)

RICKEY CLARK 6'2" 170-pound righty
19-32, 3.38, 2 Saves 1967 1972

Pitch Selection: 1. Sinker 2. Curve
Source: Angels coach Mike Roarke in *Baseball Digest* (August 1968, Ed Rumill)

WATTY CLARK 6'0" 175-pound lefty
111-97, 3.66, 16 Saves 1924 1937

Pitch Selection: 1. Curve 2. Fastball
Clark: "I'll pitch a curve roughly half the time. I like to pitch curves. Even when my arm is sore I'd rather pitch a curve than a fast ball. That's probably because my arm gets sore at the shoulder. Curve balls give your arm a twist at the elbow that never seems to bother me."
Source: *Baseball Magazine* (August 1930, F.C. Lane)

Pitch Selection: 1. Fastball 2. Slow Curve
Source: *The Sporting News* (7/16/1931; 7/7/1932; and 3/25/1972)

Quote: "It was a boyfriend of one of his sisters who induced him to try out for the [Mississippi College] team. 'Jim Edwards was a sophomore pitcher and he had me throw to him a couple of times,' Clark recalled. 'He was impressed by my speed and natural curve.' "
Source: Clark's obituary in *TSN* (3/25/1972)

JOHN CLARKSON 5'10" 155-pound righty
329-177, 2.81, 4 Saves 1882 1894

Pitch Selection: 1. Drop Curve 2. Rising Fastball 3. Change
Source: *A Ball Player's Life* (Cap Anson, 1900)

Key Pitch: Fastball
Source: Billy Sunday in *The Fireside Book of Baseball* (Page 334)

Key Pitch: Curve
Source: *The Boston Braves* (Harold Kaese, 1948)

Description: "Clarkson, of Boston, faces second base first, then quickly whirls around and throws the ball over the plate, startling the batter. He is a swift thrower."
Source: Brooklyn *Daily Eagle* (11/25/1888), reprinted in *A Tale of Four Cities* (Jean-Pierre Caillault, 2003)

Comment: "John Clarkson was one of the best exponents of the opposite idea: that the enemy should be made to hit the ball, and that nine men were paid to go get it when it was hit. Clarkson held that constant change of pace and angle, with annoying curves and tempting twists, would deceive the foe into hitting them but feebly, and well within the reach of fielding clutches."
Source: *Baseball Magazine* (November 1910, George Morton)

Commentary: According to the 1923 *Reach Guide*, Clarkson had "Curves, speed, control and wisdom that stamped him as a pitching marvel." According to Lee Allen in *The Sporting News* (4/6/1963), Clarkson threw a "singing fastball" early in his career, but relied later in his career on "a remarkable drop, the pitch now referred to as the sinker." Perhaps the most reliable description is Alfred H. Spink's, in *The National Game* (1910): "Clarkson was a man of medium size, but with only moderate speed. His great success was due to magnificent judgment, level head and wonderful control." Ted Sullivan, quoted by Spink in his description of Old Hoss Radbourn, credits Clarkson with one of the best change-ups ever thrown.

Description: "In taking position in the points John faces short field, with one foot firmly planted in either corner of the lower end of the square."
Source: Article titled "How Men Pitch Base-Ball: The Famous Pitchers of the National League of 1886." No author or publisher is given, though the information in the article is said to have come from photographic studies done by the *New York World* newspaper.

Comment: "John Clarkson's trick of wearing a huge and glittering belt-buckle, from which the sun flashed into the batters' eyes, would be, of course, illegal now. It was illegal then, and the umpires called him down, but before they could get to John he usually had several batsmen stowed away in the put-out column, and every out counts in the winning or losing of a ball-game."
Source: *Baseball Magazine* (April 1910, William Arnold, "Baseball Tricks of Long Ago")

Description: "John Clarkson was an extremely handsome man, not very tall or heavy, but he seemed to have at all times a reserve of strength that never failed him. In his early days his speed was his big asset and when his famous fast ball fell by the wayside he developed a curve ball with a peculiar drop to it and cultivated a change of pace. In his later years his wonderful control and precise knowledge of the batters who faced him still enabled him to continue pitching winning ball long after his famous curve and fast ball were but memories."
Source: *Baseball Magazine* (January 1931, H.H. Westlake)

MARK CLEAR 6'4" 200-pound righty
71-49, 3.85, 83 Saves 1979 1990

Pitch Selection: 1. Curve 2. Fastball
3. Clear developed a slider in 1986.
Source: *The Sporting News* (9/1/1986, Tom Flaherty)

JOE CLEARY 5'9" 150-pound righty
0-0, 189.00, 0 Saves 1945 1945

Pitch Selection: 1. Curve 2. Fastball 3. Change
Source: *The Pastime in Turbulence: Interviews with Baseball Players of the 1940s* (Brent Kelley, 2001)

ROGER CLEMENS 6'4" 205-pound righty
310-160, 3.19, 0 Saves 1984 2003

Pitch Selection: 1. Rising Fastball 2. Forkball
3. Curve 4. Slider
Source: *Tom Seaver's 1989 Scouting Notebook*

Pitch Selection: 1. Four-Seam Fastball (mid-90s)
2. Forkball 3. Two-Seam Fastball 4. Slider
5. Change
Source: *The Scouting Notebook: 2002*

Pitches, 2001–2003: 1. Fastballs (64%)
2. Splitter (23%) 3. Slider (12%)
4. Curve (occasional) 5. Change (occasional)
Source: *USA Today Sports Weekly* (6/3/2003, data from Inside Edge)

Note: According to Inside Edge, Clemens threw two fastballs: four-seamer at 91–96 m.p.h. and two-seamer at 87–91. His splitter went from 85 to 91, and his slider from 83 to 88 with sinking action.

MATT CLEMENT 6'3" 210-pound righty
60-62, 4.46, 0 Saves 1998 2003

Pitch Selection: 1. Sinking Fastball (low-90s)
2. Hard Slider 3. Four-Seam Fastball 4. Change
Source: *The Scouting Notebook* (2000–2003 editions)

PAT CLEMENTS 6'0" 175-pound lefty
17-11, 3.77, 12 Saves 1985 1992

Key Pitch: Curve
Source: *The Scouting Report: 1990*

REGGIE CLEVELAND 6'1" 195-pound righty
105-106, 4.01, 25 Saves 1969 1981

Pitch Selection: 1. Fastball 2. Slider
Note: Cleveland's fastball was thrown high and moved in on a right-handed hitter.
Sources: *The Sporting News* (7/27/1974, Peter Gammons; and 9/27/1975, Gammons)

TRUMAN CLEVENGER 6'1" 180-pound righty
36-37, 4.18, 30 Saves 1954 1962

Note: In 1956, Clevenger was listed by *The Sporting News* (August 29 issue) as having one of the best fastballs in the league.

TONY CLONINGER 6'0" 210-pound righty
113-97, 4.07, 6 Saves 1961 1972

Pitch Selection: 1. Fastball 2. Change 3. Curve
Source: Baltimore Orioles scouting report prior to 1970 World Series, reported in *Putting It All Together* (Brooks Robinson with Fred Bauer, 1971)

Quote from same source: "Has average stuff. Will not throw curve when behind. Depends on fast ball and change. He is a nibbler." This, of course, describes him in 1970; he was not a nibbler in 1965 or 1966 (see below).

Description: "That's his pitch, the hard one. His fastball is in the same class with Bob Gibson's, Bob Veale's, Jim Maloney's, Don Drysdale's, and those fellows. He's not a finesse man yet. When he gets to be, he'll be one of the great ones."
Source: Bobby Bragan in *Sport* (February 1966, Furman Bisher)

BRAD CLONTZ 6'1" 203-pound righty
22-8, 4.34, 8 Saves 1995 2000

Pitch Selection: 1. Fastball (high-80s) 2. Slider 3. Sinker
Note: Threw with a submarine delivery.
Source: *The Scouting Notebook: 1996*

DAVID CLYDE 6'1" 180-pound lefty
18-33, 4.63, 0 Saves 1973 1979

Pitches, when he debuted: 1. Fastball (low-90s) 2. Curve
Pitches, later in his career: 1. Fastball (low-90s) 2. Curve 3. Change 4. Slider (occasional)
Quote: "When I first signed, I was strictly fastball and curveball. I developed an okay change-up and also worked with the slider at times, when my curve ball wasn't working."
Source: Clyde in ESPN.com chat on May 30, 2003
Other Source: *The Sporting News* (5/16/1981, Ed Hinton)

Quote: "I faced Vida Blue, [and] he had a fastball that would come over the top and *whooom* . . . just like that. Well, David was the same way. It had that little giddy-up at the end. And he had some movement on it, too, that was just unbelievable. Man, that guy was a great, great pitcher . . ."
Source: Dave Nelson in *The Dallas Observer* (5/16/2003, John Gonzalez)

ANDY COAKLEY 6'0" 165-pound righty
58-59, 2.35, 3 Saves 1902 1911

Key Pitch: Slow Ball
Source: *The Unforgettable Season* (G.H. Fleming)

Description: "Dr. Coakley was only a shade less effective than the great Mathewson. The eminent dentist had his famous slow ball frequently on exhibition, and it was a puzzler for fair."
Source: Jack Ryder in the *Cincinnati Enquirer* (quoted in *The Unforgettable Season*)

Description: "There is nothing about the gentle art of pitching unknown to Dr. Coakley. Physically frail, he faces the hardest hitters with calm courage, outwits and outguesses them and holds them in check."
Source: *The Sporting News* (9/17/1908)

JIM COATES 6'4" 192-pound righty
43-22, 4.01, 18 Saves 1956 1967

Pitch Selection: 1. Fastball 2. Curve 3. Change
Note: Coates injured his arm in 1958 trying to learn a slider, and absolutely never threw a slider after that.
Source: *Baseball Digest* (September 1960)

Vic Power: "Jim Coates was a bad guy. He used to throw at me all the time."
Minnie Minoso: "I don't want to name the pitchers who threw at me on purpose . . . but if you guessed Jim Coates, I wouldn't say you were wrong."
Johnny Klippstein: "Coates was one of the few pitchers who would deliberately throw at a batter's head. I couldn't condone that. Pitchers tried to get him but never got him good. I wouldn't have felt sorry for him."
Source: *We Played the Game* (Danny Peary, 1994)

PHIL COCKRELL 5'8" 160-pound righty
NEGRO LEAGUES 1917 1934

Pitch Selection: 1. Spitball 2. Fastball
Quote: "Phil Cockrell was a great pitcher, but you hated to play behind him because he threw that spit ball and you'd get ahold of the goddamn spit sometimes. You just couldn't throw true."

Source: Paul "Jake" Stephens interview in *Black Diamonds* (John B. Holway, 1989)
Other Sources: *Blackball Stars* (John Holway, 1988); *The Biographical Encyclopedia of the Negro Baseball Leagues* (James A. Riley, 1994)

CHRIS CODIROLI 6'1" 160-pound righty
38-47, 4.87, 3 Saves 1982 1990

Pitch Selection: 1. Fastball (high-80s) 2. Slider
Note: Throws with a sidearm delivery. After the 1983 season, he went to winter ball to develop a curve and a change.
Source: *The Scouting Report: 1984*

Pitch Selection: 1. Fastball (high-80s)
2. Slider 3. Change (occasional)
4. Curve (abandoned after 1984 season)
Source: *The Scouting Report: 1985*

Pitch Selection: 1. Fastball (high-80s) 2. Sinker
3. Slider 4. Change (occasional)
Source: *The Scouting Report: 1987*

DICK COFFMAN 6'2" 195-pound righty
72-95, 4.65, 38 Saves 1927 1945

Key Pitch: Low Curve
Description: "Dick is a tall, slim chap of 31 who does all his talking with a low curve ball."
Source: *The Sporting News* (5/26/1938, Harry Forbes)

Description: "He has plenty of swift and a good curve."
Source: *Who's Who in Major League Baseball* (Harold "Speed" Johnson, 1933)

ROCKY COLAVITO 6'3" 190-pound righty
1-0, 0.00, 0 Saves 1958 1968

Pitches: 1. Overhand Fastball 2. Change (occasional)
3. Slider (occasional)
Source: *Dog Days: The New York Yankees' Fall from Grace and Return to Glory, 1964–1976* (Philip Bashe, 1994)

Note: Colavito, a near–Hall of Fame quality right fielder, pitched in two games, ten years apart. He totaled five and two-thirds innings, and allowed no runs on one hit and five walks.

JIM COLBORN 6'0" 185-pound righty
83-88, 3.80, 7 Saves 1969 1978

Pitch Selection: 1. Fastball 2. Slider
Source: *The Sporting News* (9/23/72, Larry Whiteside)

KING COLE 6'1" 170-pound righty
56-27, 2 Saves, 3.12 1909 1915

Pitch Selection: 1. Fastball 2. Curve 3. Change
Source: Cole's obituary in Bay City, Michigan newspaper (1/16/1916); *Dodger Classics* (Robert L. Tiemann, 1983)

JOE COLEMAN SR. 6'2" 200-pound righty
52-76, 4.38, 6 Saves 1942 1955

Pitch Selection: 1. Fastball 2. Slider
Note: Coleman, a journeyman pitcher since 1942, had an excellent season in 1954 after he learned to throw the slider while pitching in Cuba the previous winter.
Source: James Ellis in the *Baltimore Sun* (April, 1954)

JOE COLEMAN JR. 6'3" 175-pound righty
142-135, 3.70, 7 Saves 1965 1979

Pitch Selection: 1. Fastball 2. Forkball
3. Sidearm Sinker 4. Sidearm Curve
Sources: *The Sporting News* (7/1/72, Watson Spoelstra); and *Major League Baseball: 1971* (Brenda Zanger and Dick Kaplan).

Note: In *Major League Baseball—1969*, Jack Zanger says that Coleman throws "a fastball, sinkerball, a lot of breaking pitches, and last year started to develop a forkball." By 1972 the forkball had apparently replaced the sinker and off-speed stuff.

PHIL COLLINS 5'11" 175-pound righty
80-85, 4.66, 24 Saves 1923 1935

Pitch Selection: 1. Curve 2. Screwball 3. Fastball
Sources: unidentified article by Cullen Cain (December 1930); *The Sporting News* (8/14/1948)

Quote from Cain article: "He has a cool head and a brave heart and a most baffling screw ball."

Quote from *TSN* article: "[on 8/19/1930] Phil said he shook off the fast ball signal several times, but his catcher insisted on that type of pitch. [After the batter hit a home run], he pitched only curves for the remaining eight innings."

Note: The *TSN* article cited above also says that "[t]he nickname Fidgety was tacked on Collins before he came up to the Phils because of his mannerisms around the mound. He had a habit of hitching his pants, stamping around the rubber, jerking at his cap, swinging his arms aimlessly and going through other motions that probably contributed to his success. Undoubtedly, they threw the batter off balance, especially since Phil followed with a herky-jerky windup and delivery."

RAY COLLINS 6'1" 185-pound lefty
84-62, 2.51, 4 Saves 1909 1915

Pitch Selection: 1. Change 2. Fastball
Source: *Babe Ruth's Own Book of Baseball* (Ruth, 1928), which includes an excellent description of Collins' pitching style.

Description: "Some pitchers have a peculiar hook delivery, a species of curve which owes its chief baffling influence to the fact that it comes from an unexpected angle while the eye is deceived by a complicated wind-up motion. Wiltse of the Giants is generally known as Hooks on account of his delivery; Ray Collins of the Red Sox, the man who broke Johnson's great winning streak, has a similar hook delivery. Needless to say, the pitchers who are proficient at this art are left-handers."
Source: *Baseball Magazine* (November 1913, F.C. Lane)

RIP COLLINS 6'1" 205-pound righty
108-82, 3.99, 5 Saves 1920 1931

Pitch Selection: 1. Fastball 2. Curve 3. Change
Quote: "He had blinding speed, more sheer stuff, perhaps, than any pitcher has shown since Walter Johnson . . . [Collins said,] 'When I came to the Yankees, all I had was speed . . . I developed a better curve and a pretty good slow ball.' "
Source: *Baseball Magazine* (August 1926)

BARTOLO COLON 6'0" 185-pound righty
100-62, 3.86, 0 Saves 1997 2003

Pitch Selection: 1. Two-Seam Fastball (low-90s)
2. Four-Seam Fastball (94–98)
3. Hard Curve (85–88) 4. Change (low-80s)
Sources: *The Scouting Notebook* (1999–2003 editions)

Nomar Garciaparra: "I know that physics says there's no way a ball can rise, but with this pitch [Colon's four-seamer] you have the perception that it does."
Colon: "For righthanded hitters I throw it [the four-seamer] to the outside, either high or low. For left-handed hitters I throw it inside mostly or outside every so often. I can throw it at that high speed, or I can take something off and paint it."
Source: *Sports Illustrated* (3/31/03, Page 64)

LARRY COLTON 6'3" 200-pound righty
0-0, 4.50, 0 Saves 1968 1968

Pitches: 1. Fastball 2. Curve 3. Slider
Source: *Baseball Digest* (March 1966, "Scouting Reports on 1966 Major League Rookies")

Note: Colton's very brief time in the majors was ended by an injury; he later became a writer and authored *Goat Brothers* (1993) and *Counting Coup* (2002).

DAVID CONE 6'1" 180-pound righty
194-126, 3.46, 1 Save 1986 2003

Pitches as young pitcher: 1. Fastball (95) 2. Slider
3. Sharp Curve 4. Change
Pitches as mature pitcher: 1. Fastball (92)
2. Splitter 3. Slider 4. Overhand Curve
5. Sidearm (Laredo) Curve 6. Change
Sources: *The Scouting Report: 1990; The Scouting Notebook 1999*

Umpire Durwood Merrill: "The Yankees' David Cone, who could have played linebacker, is what I call a junk-yard dog because he'll knock you out of the box without blinking. He's got a better-than-average fastball and a real hard slider. Those two pitches help set up one of the best change-ups in either league."
Source: *You're Out and You're Ugly, Too* (Merrill with Jim Dent, 1998)

Tom Candiotti: "David Cone had one of the best repertoires I've ever seen a pitcher possess. He had phenomenal natural stuff. He never looked like a classic power pitcher—he wasn't a big guy—but he had a mid-90s fastball with about eight different arm angles. He threw a Frisbee slider that started out *behind* right-handed hitters, yet he could paint the outside corner with it. He

was also able to throw a curveball and a devastating splitter, so he was as tough on left-handed hitters as on right-handers."
Source: Candiotti in an ESPN.com article, 5/30/2003

DICK CONGER 6'0" 185-pound righty
3-7, 5.14, 0 Saves 1940 1943

Key Pitch: Fastball
Source: *Pacific Coast Baseball News* (4/10/1950)

GENE CONLEY 6'8" 225-pound righty
91-96, 3.82, 9 Saves 1952 1963

Pitch Selection: 1. Sidearm Fastball 2. Change
3. Sidearm Curve 4. Overhand Curve
5. Overhand Fastball
Source: *Saturday Evening Post* (Al Hirshberg, 5/28/55)

Description: "Pitch? He could deal it any way you liked. From his towering but athletic height of 6-8, Conley could come straight overhand and deliver a fast ball that jumped with life. Or he could crack a curve that dropped off an invisible table. He could deliver both pitches off a three-quarter overhand delivery as well, and he could 'take a little off' for a change-of-pace that made even the wiliest hitters lunge and flail."
Source: *Sport* (March 1957, Emmett Watson)

Note: Listed by *The Sporting News* (8/29/1956) as having one of the best fastballs in the league.

SARGE CONNALLY 5'11" 170-pound righty
49-60, 4.30, 31 Saves 1921 1934

Key Pitch: Fastball
Source: Arthur Daley in the *New York Times,* 1955 (quoting Arthur Mann)

JIM CONSTABLE 6'1" 185-pound lefty
3-4, 4.87, 2 Saves 1956 1963

Description: "His repertoire includes a little of everything."
Source: *1963 Major League Handbook* (Don Schiffer)

SANDY CONSUEGRA 5'11" 165-pound righty
51-32, 3.37, 26 Saves 1950 1957

Key Pitch: Slider
Quote: "Little Sandy Consuegra was a pretty good pitcher who fooled batters with an array of pitches, including an effective slider, and motions."
Source: Les Moss in *We Played the Game* (Danny Peary, 1994)

JOSE CONTRERAS 6'4" 224-pound righty
7-2, 3.30, 0 Saves 2003 2003

Pitches: 1. Fastball (mid-90s) 2. Forkball (82–83)
3. Slider 4. Change
Sources: New York *Daily News* (8/24/2003, Sam Borden; and 9/20/2003, Anthony McCarron); Sean McAdam's ESPN.com column (3/4/2003); Fox broadcast of 2003 ALCS Game 3

PETE CONWAY 5'10" 162-pound righty
61-61, 3.59, 0 Saves 1885 1889

Key Pitch: Down Shoot
Quote: "Peter Conway, the down-shoot pitcher of the team . . ."
Source: *Reach's American Association Base Ball Guide* (1888)

Description: "When about to pitch the ball, Conway faces third base with his right foot slightly advanced.

Jose Contreras

Drawing his arm back, he steps quickly forward, executing the delivery while in the act of moving through the box. The movement is finished with the arm very high. With men on the bases, Conway follows the example of the veteran pitchers by facing the bag held by the runner . . . His favorite pitch is a kind of overhand throw that is hard for batsmen to keep from knocking flies. This gives plenty of work to the outfielders."
Source: Article titled "How Men Pitch Base-Ball: The Famous Pitchers of the National League of 1886." No author or publisher is given, though the information in the article is said to have come from photographic studies done by the *New York World* newspaper.

DENNIS COOK 6'3" 185-pound lefty
64-46, 3.91, 9 Saves 1988 2002

Pitch Selection: 1. Fastball (high-80s) 2. Split-Fingered Sinker 3. Slider
Sources: *The Scouting Report: 1990* and *The Scouting Notebook 1999*

Note: Cook's sinker was also sometimes called a forkball.

STEVE COOKE 6'6" 245-pound lefty
26-36, 4.31, 1 Save 1992 1998

Pitch Selection: 1. Sinking Fastball (mid-80s) 2. Curve 3. Slider 4. Change
Source: *The Scouting Notebook: 1998*

JACK COOMBS 6'0" 185-pound righty
158-110, 2.78, 9 Saves 1906 1920

Pitch Selection: 1. Drop Curve 2. Fastball
Sources: *The National Game* (Alfred H. Spink, page 126); *Baseball's Famous Pitchers* (Ira L. Smith, 1954); *Washington Star* (5/15/1957)

Malachi Kittredge in *The National Game:* "Coombs . . . has mastered the greatest of all pitching assets, the drop ball that does not break from the right-handed batters. I don't mean one of those outdrops, but a ball that comes up to the plate squarely in the center and falls from one to two feet without changing its lateral direction."

Description: "Take Coombs, for instance. The Athletic twirler has great speed but he has pitched so many curves that his arm is actually shortened by the stiffening of the cords at the elbow, caused by curve pitching."
Source: *Baseball Magazine* (November 1913, F.C. Lane)

JOHNNY COONEY 5'10" 165-pound lefty
34-44, 3.72, 6 Saves 1921 1930

Key Pitch: Fastball
Description: "As a pitcher Cooney depended most of all upon speed. He had a good fast ball, but he used his creative fancy by developing a new type of delivery which he called 'the hesitation.' He found this delivery particularly effective when throwing a curve to a left handed batter. The theory of the thing was simple. He would start his wind up, then, in the act of hurling the ball, pause a fraction of a second before letting go of the sphere. This, when properly done, would throw the batter off balance. However, batters study pitchers and when one of their hereditary enemies upon the slab invents a freak variation like Cooney's specialty, they learn to watch for it. In baseball the expected play is already half defeated."
Source: *Baseball Magazine* (April 1927, John J. Ward)

Key Pitch: Forkball
Casey Stengel: "He's got one of the best fork balls I ever saw. Over a four or five inning stretch, I think John would be unbeatable."
Source: *Baseball Magazine* (May 1940, Herbert Goren); by this point, Cooney was a 39-year-old outfielder and hadn't pitched in a major-league game in almost ten years.

ANDY COOPER 6'2" 220-pound lefty
NEGRO LEAGUES 1920 1941

Pitch Selection: 1. Curve 2. Change 3. Slider 4. Screwball
Source: *The Biographical Encyclopedia of the Negro Baseball Leagues* (James A. Riley, 1994)

MORT COOPER 6'2" 210-pound righty
128-75, 2.97, 14 Saves 1938 1949

Pitch Selection, 1938–1941: 1. Fastball 2. Screwball 3. Curve
Pitch Selection, 1941–1949: 1. Fastball 2. Forkball
Note: Cooper was taught the screwball by Mike Ryba when he was with Houston in 1938.

Sources: *Baseball Magazine* (March 1940, Clifford Bloodgood; September 1942, Herbert Simons); *Baseball's Famous Pitchers* (Ira L. Smith, 1954); *Stan Musial: The Man's Own Story* (Musial with Bob Broeg, 1964); *Famous American Athletes of Today* (Ninth Series, 1945)

Description: "Cooper's 1939 record was fashioned mainly by the use of a fast ball mixed with a deceptive screw ball which he employed as a change of pace. He really needed the two in the National League . . . Mort has had trouble with his control, but this past season was able to locate the plate with a fair degree of certainty."
Source: Bloodgood in *Baseball Magazine*

Comment: "Cooper first started flashing the fork ball to National League hitters last year, when he substituted it for a screwball he used in the past. This year it has stood him in even better stead."
Source: Simons in 1942 *Baseball Magazine*

Stan Musial: "This great pitcher used to chew aspirins on the mound to dull the pain caused by bone chips in his elbow. Mort had a very good fast ball and good fork ball. He didn't walk anybody. It was a pleasure to play behind him because he knew where he was going to pitch the hitters and you could play them accordingly, confident of Cooper's control."
Source: *Stan Musial: The Man's Own Story*

Description: "Mort Cooper was a big heavyset guy who knew how to pitch, a Rick Reuschel type."
Source: *Rex Barney's Thank Youuuu for 50 Years in Baseball from Brooklyn to Baltimore* (Barney with Norman L. Macht, 1993)

WILBUR COOPER 5'11" 175-pound lefty
216-178, 2.89, 14 Saves 1912 1926

Pitch Selection: 1. "Sneaky" Fastball 2. Curve
3. Change
Sources: Henry Boyle in the *Pittsburgh Post-Gazette* (2/25/1939); Al Abrams in the *Pittsburgh Post-Gazette* (1/27/1959); John Carroll, UPI, (9/30/1959)

Note: Cooper said in 1959 that he never threw a spitter or a scuff ball, but that he would chew tobacco and spit into his glove, gradually darkening the baseball.

Cooper: "The good Lord blessed me with an easy motion, a sneaky fast ball, a sharp curve, a change of pace and wonderful control."
Source: Abrams in the *Post-Gazette* (1/27/1959)

Description: "He owned the easiest and most graceful throwing motion of his time . . . he tossed a ball up to the plate with less effort than any hurler in the league."
Source: Boyle in the *Post-Gazette* (2/25/1939)

DOUG CORBETT 6'1" 185-pound righty
24-30, 3.32, 66 Saves 1980 1987

Pitch Selection: 1. Sinker (low-80s)
2. Slider (occasional)
3. Change (occasional, to left-handed batters)
Notes: Some suspected that Corbett's sinker, on which he relied to a great degree, was actually a spitball. He threw from three-quarters, almost sidearm.
Sources: *The Sporting News* (5/9/1981, Pat Reusse; 6/6/1981, Peter Gammons); *The Scouting Report* (1983, 1984, and 1987 editions)

LARRY CORCORAN 5'10" 120-pound righty
177-89, 2.36, 2 Saves 1880 1887

Pitch Selection: 1. Fastball 2. Curve
Sources: *The National Game* (Alfred H. Spink, Page 116); *Nineteenth Century Stars* (SABR, 1989, article by John O'Malley)

Note: On at least one occasion in 1884, Corcoran pitched with both hands.

FRANCISCO CORDOVA 6'1" 190-pound righty
42-47, 3.96, 12 Saves 1996 2002

Pitch Selection: 1. Sinking Fastball 2. Curve 3. Slider
4. Change
Note: Cordova varies his arm angle and his delivery to keep hitters off-stride.
Source: *The Scouting Notebook 1999*

Description: "Cordova is a side-arming right-hander with good sinking action on his fastball and great control of a knee-buckling curve."
Source: Larry Dierker in *This Ain't Brain Surgery: How to Win the Pennant Without Losing Your Mind* (Dierker, 2003)

RHEAL CORMIER 5'10" 185-pound lefty
61-54, 4.04, 2 Saves 1991 2003

Pitch Selection: 1. Sinker 2. Fastball 3. Soft Slider
4. Forkball (as Change)

Sources: *The Scouting Report* (1992, 1996, and 1997 editions); *The 1994 Baseball Almanac*

Pitch Selection: 1. Sinker 2. Slider
3. Split-Fingered Fastball (against lefties)
Source: *The Scouting Notebook* (2000–2002 editions)

EDWIN CORREA 6'2" 192-pound righty
16-19, 5.16, 0 Saves 1985 1987

Pitch Selection: 1. Change 2. Fastball 3. Curve
Description: "He is a power pitcher with an above-average fastball, but he uses it to set up his out pitch, a terrific change-up.

"He hides the ball well during his windup and then delivers his pitches straight overhand from a herky-jerky motion."
Source: *The Scouting Report: 1997*

FRANK CORRIDON 6'0" 170-pound righty
70-68, 2.80, 7 Saves 1904 1910

Key Pitch: Spitball
Source: Lee Allen in *The Sporting News* (3/7/64, Allen's "Cooperstown Corner" column)
Note: Corridon is regarded by some as the inventor of the spitball.

JIM CORSI 6'1" 230-pound righty
22-24, 3.25, 7 Saves 1988 1999

Pitch Selection: 1. Fastball 2. Slider 3. Sinker
Source: *The Scouting Report: 1992*

AL CORWIN 6'1" 170-pound righty
18-10, 3.98, 5 Saves 1951 1955

Key Pitch: Sinking Fastball
Note: Listed as a sidearm pitcher.
Source: *How to Play Winning Baseball* (Arthur Mann, 1953)

FRITZ COUMBE 6'0" 152-pound lefty
38-38, 2.79, 13 Saves 1914 1921

Key Pitch: Big, Slow Curve
Source: *The Cleveland Indians* (Franklin Lewis, 1949)

HARRY COVELESKI 6'0" 180-pound lefty
81-55, 2.39, 9 Saves 1907 1918

Pitch Selection: 1. Fastball 2. Curve
Quote: "[He] has plenty of speed, all that any pitcher wants, and he has a great curved ball. His fast ball has a jump on it."
Source: Cubs' pitcher Rube Kroh in *The Sporting News* (12/3/1908, Hugh Fullerton)

STAN COVELESKI 5'11" 166-pound righty
215-142, 2.89, 21 Saves 1912 1928

Pitch Selection: 1. Spitball 2. Curve 3. Fastball
4. Slow Ball
Note: Coveleski was one of the "grandfathered" pitchers allowed to continue to throw the spitball after it was otherwise banned in 1921.
Sources: *The Glory of Their Times* (Lawrence Ritter, 1966); 1923 *Reach Guide* (Page 38); 1924 *Reach Guide* (Page 48)

Quote from 1924 *Reach:* "Coveleski is dependent entirely on [the spitball] for his success."

Coveleski: "I got so I had as good control over the spitball as I did over my other pitches. I could make it break any of three ways: down, out, or down and out. And I always knew which way it would break. Depended on my wrist action. For the spitball, what you do is wet these first two fingers. I used alum, had it in my mouth. Sometimes it would pucker your mouth some, get gummy. I'd go to my mouth on *every* pitch. Not every pitch would be a spitball. Sometimes I'd go two or three innings without throwing one. But I'd always have them looking for it."
Source: *The Glory of Their Times*

DANNY COX 6'4" 235-pound righty
74-75, 3.64, 8 Saves 1983 1995

Pitch Selection: 1. Change 2. Slider 3. Fastball
Source: *Tom Seaver's 1989 Scouting Notebook*

TIM CRABTREE 6'4" 220-pound righty
21-22, 4.20, 9 Saves 1995 2001

Pitch Selection: 1. Hard Slider 2. Sinking Fastball
Source: *The Scouting Notebook: 1996*

Pitch Selection: 1. Sinking Fastball (92) 2. Hard Slider
3. Circle Change (added 1996)
Source: *The Scouting Notebook: 1997*

Pitch Selection: 1. Fastball (98) 2. Hard Slider
Quote: "His fastball sinks when he takes something off it . . ."
Source: *The Scouting Notebook: 2000*

ROGER CRAIG 6'4" 185-pound righty
74-98, 3.83, 19 Saves 1955 1966

Key Pitch: Slider
Sources: Craig in *Baseball Digest* (December 1962, Robert Riger; also, January 1963)

DOC CRANDALL 5'10" 180-pound righty
102-62, 2.92, 25 Saves 1908 1918

Pitch Selection: 1. Sweeping Curve 2. Fastball
Source: *Pitching in a Pinch* (Christy Mathewson, 1912)

Key Pitch: Change
Story: "Doc Crandall . . . used to give his catcher on the Giants, the late Roger Bresnahan, most of the credit for the peculiar change of pace ball that was Do's specialty in clutches . . . As Doc once told us, he was fooling around in a warmup with Bresnahan at the Polo Grounds when a ball he threw did funny things. Instantly Bresnahan started to run toward him, shouting: 'How did you throw that? Think quick! Try to remember what you did!'

" 'I had thrown it off my thumb, just experimenting,' Doc explained. 'If Bresnahan had not been so insistent I wouldn't have paid much attention to the pitch, nor remembered what I had done. He made me repeat it, and work on the delivery until I could throw it any time; and many a hole that change of pace pulled me out of. Unlike most changes I could throw it on any pitch, to any hitter, and to almost any spot, for it came up perfectly concealed out of my natural pitching move.' "
Source: "Greg's Gossip" column in the Portland *Oregonian* (5/16/1947, L.H. Gregory)

ED CRANE 5'10" 204-pound righty
72-97, 3.99, 2 Saves 1884 1893

Key Pitch: Fastball
Source: *A Tale of Four Cities* (Jean-Pierre Caillault, 2003)

Quote: "He soon developed into a speedy pitcher."
Source: *The Sporting Life* (9/26/1896)

Note: Crane set records of over 400 feet in long-distance throwing contests.
Sources: *The Sporting Life* (1/29/1890); *Baseball Magazine* (1908)

STEVE CRAWFORD 6'5" 225-pound righty
30-23, 4.17, 19 Saves 1980 1991

Pitch Selection: 1. Fastball (mid-80s) 2. Curve 3. Slider 4. Change
Source: *The Scouting Report: 1985*

Pitch Selection: 1. Cross-Seam (Four-Seam) Fastball (90+) 2. Hard Sinker (90+) 3. Slow Curve
Source: *The Scouting Report: 1987*

Pitch Selection: 1. Fastball 2. Straight Change
Source: *The Scouting Report: 1990*

JACK CREEL 6'0" 165-pound righty
5-4, 4.14, 2 Saves 1945 1945

Key Pitch: Curve
Source: *Pacific Coast Baseball News* (4/25/1950)

TIM CREWS 6'0" 195-pound righty
11-13, 3.44, 15 Saves 1987 1992

Pitch Selection: 1. Fastball 2. Curve 3. Change
Source: *The Scouting Report: 1990*

Pitch Selection: 1. Slider 2. Fastball 3. Forkball
Source: *The Scouting Report: 1992*

CHUCK CRIM 6'0" 175-pound righty
47-43, 3.83, 45 Saves 1987 1994

Pitch Selection: 1. Sinker 2. Slider 3. Fastball
Source: *The Scouting Report: 1990*

RAY CRONE 6'2" 165-pound righty
30-30, 3.87, 4 Saves 1954 1958

Note: Listed by *The Sporting News* (8/29/1956) as having one of the best fastballs in the league.

GENERAL CROWDER 5'10" 170-pound righty
167-115, 4.12, 22 Saves 1926 1936

Pitches: 1. Fastball 2. Change 3. Curve 4. Screwball
Description: "Crowder is the craftiest of the Detroit pitchers, by a big margin . . . Crowder has a fast ball that

slides. He has a fine change of pace, a fair curve, a screwball—and a noodle."
Source: Dan Daniel in a 1934 "Daniel's Dope" column, published just before the World Series

Description: "[Cowder threw] a fast ball that didn't look fast. What it had after Crowder came out of his lazy delivery was considerable 'sneak.' And what Crowder had otherwise was considerable shrewdness and a motion to first base that discouraged base stealers."
Source: *The Washington Senators* (Shirley Povich, 1954)

Note: A 1935 *Baseball Magazine* article about Crowder was subtitled, "No Dazzling Fast Ball, No Miraculous Curve Had Been the Secret of Crowder's Pitching Success. But Read His Comments on Control and You Understand."

Quote: "[Crowder threw] a lot of junk and screwballs and sinkers and sliders."
Source: Ray Hayworth in *In the Shadow of the Babe* (Brent Kelley, 1995); Hayworth caught Crowder toward the end of his career.

MIKE CUELLAR 6'0" 165-pound lefty
185-130, 3.14, 11 Saves 1959 1977

Pitches: 1. Screwball 2. Fastball 3. Slider 4. Slow Curve 5. Change
Notes: In the *Philadelphia Bulletin* (4/6/1980), Herm Starrette said Cuellar and Tug McGraw threw the best screwballs he ever saw.

Kaplan and Zanger in *Major League Baseball: 1971* (Dick Kaplan and Brenda Zanger) said that Cuellar threw his screwball at three separate speeds and that he had "a first-rate fastball."
Other Sources: *Unsung Heroes of the Major Leagues* (Art Berke); *Winning!* (Earl Weaver, 1972)

Description: "At its best, Cuellar's attack on the plate reminds one of a master butcher preparing a standing roast of beef—a sliver excised here, a morsel trimmed off the bottom, two or three superfluous swishes of the knife through the air, and then a final slice of white off the ribs: *Voila!*"
Source: Roger Angell in *The New Yorker* (1974, reprinted in *Five Seasons,* 1977)

NICK CULLOP 5'11" 172-pound lefty
57-53, 2.73, 4 Saves 1913 1921

Pitch Selection: 1. Curve 2. Fastball

Quote: "Cullop, the ex-Fed southpaw, had his first real chance to show what he is worth in Thursday's battle. Cullop had almost perfect control of a wide curve ball and corking speeder."
Source: *The Sporting News* (5/18/1916, Page 1)

RAY CULP 6'0" 200-pound righty
122-101, 3.58, 1 Save 1963 1973

Pitch Selection: 1. Fastball 2. Slider
Note: Upon arrival in Boston in 1968, Culp added a curve and palm ball to his repertoire.
Sources: *View from the Dugout* (Ed Richter, 1964); *The Sporting News* (6/28/69, Larry Claflin), *Major League Baseball—1969* (Jack Zanger)

GEORGE CULVER 6'2" 185-pound righty
48-49, 3.62, 23 Saves 1966 1974

Key Pitch: Fastball
Source: *Baseball Digest* (March 1967, "Official Scouting Reports on 1967 Major League Rookies")

JOHN CUMBERLAND 6'0" 185-pound lefty
15-16, 3.82, 2 Saves 1968 1974

Pitch Selection: 1. Fastball 2. Curve 3. Screwball
Source: *The Sporting News* (5/8/1971, Pat Frizzell)

CANDY CUMMINGS 5'9" 120-pound righty
21-22, 2.78, 0 Saves 1876 1877

Key Pitch: Curve
Note: Cummings claimed to be the inventor of the curveball, and was inducted into the Hall of Fame because of this.
Sources: *Baseball's First Stars* (SABR, 1996, Joseph M. Overfield); *When Johnny Came Sliding Home* (William J. Ryczek, 1998)

Baseball's First Stars: "In the version of the discovery most often heard, Cummings developed the curved pitch after watching the erratic flights of clam shells picked up on a beach near his Brooklyn home and flung into the wind. Martin Quigley, in his book *The Crooked Pitch* (1984), quotes Cummings, somewhat fancifully, it seems: 'I thought what a wonderful thing it would be if I could make a baseball curve like that.' As the story goes, he started to experiment with the curve in games played among boys in the neighborhood, learning along the way that finger pressure and wind direction had a great deal to do with the result."

When Johnny Came Sliding Home: "By the mid-1860's, Arthur Cummings of the Excelsiors (later of the Stars) had developed the first curve ball. Cummings was small but had 'long, sinewy' wrists and made the ball curve by squeezing it tightly between the ends of his fingers and twisting his wrist when he released the ball. On wet days, the ball developed further deceptive qualities. Because of the sphere's loose stitching, Cummings' tight grip disfigured it and caused it to lopsidedly approach the plate. Although he first discovered the curve while pitching for the Star Juniors of Brooklyn in 1864, Cummings never used the pitch in a game while performing for that club or the Excelsiors. His first competitive curve was delivered in 1867 after he had joined the Stars."

BERT CUNNINGHAM 5'5" 187-pound righty
142-170, 4.22, 2 Saves 1887 1901

Pitch Selection, 1887–1891: 1. Fastball 2. Nothing
Pitch Selection, 1895–1901: 1. Slow Curve
Source: *Baseball's First Stars* (SABR, 1996, William E. McMahon)

Comment: "Shadowing the ball, which was an art in the former days, is almost lost. A few pitchers try it, but without the skill of Bert Cunningham, Mattie Kilroy, Willie McGill and many others of the old school. Shadowing consists of the pitcher sidestepping and placing his body on the line of the batter's vision, so that the ball has no background except the pitcher's body and the batter cannot see it plainly until the ball is almost upon him."
Source: *Touching Second* (John J. Evers and Hugh S. Fullerton, 1910)

NIG CUPPY 5'7" 160-pound righty
161-97, 3.48, 7 Saves 1892 1901

Key Pitch: Jump Ball (Rising Fastball)
Charley Nichols: "That there is such a thing as a jump ball I believe is universally conceded, but like other pitchers I am in the dark as to its cause. I am positive that it exists, for I have been able to get it myself, and I have batted against other pitchers whom, I am sure, possessed it. George Cuppy, the famous Cleveland pitcher, for example, was one man whose whole success was due to a jump ball . . . I know this much about it. Speed is the first requirement to obtain it. None but overhand pitchers seem able to get it."
Source: *How to Pitch* (John B. Foster, 1908 edition)

Commentary: In *Baseball's First Stars* (SABR, 1996) there is an extremely interesting article by Rich Eldred, one of the best articles in that fine book. However, Eldred says that Cuppy "was known as 'the famous slow pitcher,' " which according to Eldred referred not only to his repertoire of off-speed stuff but also to the time he took between pitches. However, it seems to us that the Nichols quote is specific and credible, that Nichols was in a position to know what he was talking about, and that therefore it is most likely that Cuppy did in fact rely heavily on the rising fastball, and that the term "the famous slow pitcher" was intended to refer *only* to Cuppy's dawdling around on the mound, and not to his repertoire.

JOHN CURTIS 6'1" 175-pound lefty
89-97, 3.96, 11 Saves 1970 1984

Pitch Selection: 1. Curve 2. Fastball 3. Change 4. Slider (occasional)
Sources: *The Scouting Report: 1983*; *The Wrong Stuff* (Bill Lee with Dick Lally, 1984)

ED CUSHMAN 6'0" 177-pound lefty
62-80, 3.86, 1 Save 1883 1890

Pitch Selection: 1. Fastball 2. Curve
Quote: "He has a very peculiar delivery, which, combined with pace and curve, makes his pitching prove puzzling to the best of batsmen."
Source: Article in what appears to be the *New York Clipper*, circa 1886

OMAR DAAL 6'3" 160-pound lefty
68-78, 4.55, 1 Save 1993 2003

Pitch Selection: 1. Fastball 2. Curve 3. Change
Source: *1996 Montreal Expos Media Guide*

Pitch Selection: 1. Slider/Curve Cross 2. Change 3. Fastball
Source: *The Scouting Notebook 2000*

JOHN D'ACQUISTO 6'2" 205-pound righty
34-51, 4.56, 15 Saves 1973 1982

Pitch Selection: 1. Overpowering Fastball 2. Curve 3. Slider
Sources: *The Sporting News* (10/13/1973, Pat Frizzell; 6/1/1974, Frizzell; 9/28/1974, Frizzell)

Giants manager Charlie Fox: "This kid is a foot and a half faster than McDowell. Can you imagine that? Nobody throws as hard as Sudden Sam. But this guy does. I can't believe it. I wish he were closer to Candlestick Park. I'd like him right now on arm alone. But he needs experience."
Source: *The Sporting News* (4/1/1972, Wells Twombly column)

Note: According to *The Sporting News* (6/19/1976, Phil Collier), D'Acquisto's fastball was once clocked at 98 miles per hour.

ED DAILY 5'11" 174-pound righty
66-70, 3.39, 1 Save 1885 1891

Description: "Daily's delivery is simple, direct and speedy. Facing third base, he strides out into the middle of the box with the left foot. Following quickly with the right, he throws the ball while poised on the toes of the left, and then, after standing an instant with eyes on the batsman, returns to the lower end of the box."
Source: Article titled "How Men Pitch Base-Ball: The Famous Pitchers of the National League of 1886." No author or publisher is given, though the information in the article is said to have come from photographic studies done by the *New York World* newspaper.

ONE ARM DAILY 6'2" 180-pound righty
73-87, 2.92, 1 Save 1882 1887

Pitch Selection: 1. Drop Curve
Sources: *Baseball Research Journal 1979* (article by Al Kermisch)

BUD DALEY 6'1" 185-pound lefty
60-64, 4.03, 10 Saves 1955 1964

Pitches: 1. Roundhouse Curve 2. Knuckleball 3. Slip Pitch 4. Slider 5. Fastball
Source: *Sports Illustrated* (7/11/60, Roy Terrell)

JEFF D'AMICO 6'7" 255-pound righty
44-50, 4.49, 0 Saves 1996 2003

Pitch Selection: 1. Fastball (90) 2. Curve 3. Change 4. Forkball
Source: *The Scouting Notebook: 1997*
Pitch Selection: 1. Four-Seam Fastball (90s) 2. Two-Seam Fastball 3. Slider 4. Change
Note: D'Amico's 1998 entry in *The Scouting Notebook* refers to his "new" four-seam fastball.
Source: *The Scouting Notebook: 1998*
Pitch Selection: 1. Slow Curve 2. Fastball (high-80s) 3. Change
Note: D'Amico missed all of 1998 and most of 1999 due to multiple shoulder surgeries.
Sources: *The Scouting Notebook* (2001–2003 editions)

STEVE DALKOWSKI
MINOR LEAGUES 1957 1965

Pitches: 1. Terrifying Fastball 2. "Vicious Slider"
Source: *It's What You Learn After You Know It All That Counts* (Earl Weaver with Berry Stainback, 1982)

Baltimore Orioles

Steve Dalkowski

Story: "In the days before radar guns, the Baltimore organization sent him out to the Aberdeen Proving Grounds the night after throwing a complete game. They set up a tubelike device on a tripod above home plate that could measure the speed of an object in flight. The problem was, of course, Dalko couldn't hit the damn thing. He threw for forty minutes before sneaking a fastball down the tube: 98.6 miles an hour—without a mound. A fresh, sober Bob Feller threw 5 miles an hour slower through the same machine. Some say Dalko would've stopped a radar gun at 120 mph."
Source: Ron Shelton in *Cult Baseball Players* (ed. Danny Peary, 1990)

DAVE DANFORTH 6'0" 167-pound lefty
71-66, 3.89, 23 Saves 1911 1925

Key Pitch: Shine Ball
Sources: *The Relief Pitcher* (John Thorn, 1979); *The Sporting News* (9/24/1952, Page 3)

Note: TSN reference says that Danforth invented the trick of cutting the ball with his fingernail to make it dive. According to *Baseball Between the Wars* (Eugene Murdock, 1992), Danforth was suspended by American League for throwing the emery ball after it was banned.

Quote: "Dave Danforth, another member of the White Sox pitching staff with Cicotte and myself, went Eddie one better by treating the ball with talcum powder.

"Dave, after discoloring half of the ball by rubbing it in dirt, slickened the other half by polishing it with talcum powder which was concealed in his right pants leg."
Source: Frank Shellenback in *Baseball Digest* (April 1948, George A. Barton)

Quote: "Danforth had a tricky move to first base that many thought was a balk. (*Post-Dispatch*'s J. Roy) Stockton commented: 'It's impossible to tell whether Danforth is about to throw to first or the plate. He starts with the same windup, kicks with his right foot in either case and as he throws he steps either toward first or toward the plate."
Source: *The 1922 St. Louis Browns* (Roger A. Godin, 1991)

Comment: "Danforth, if you believe the boys in the dugouts, did everything to the ball. The possessor of exceptionally large and strong hands, he is supposed to have loosened the cover of the ball, raised the seams, and sometimes nicked it with a specially sharpened thumb nail so as to make it sail."
Source: *Baseball Magazine* (June 1936, Hugh Bradley, "Freak Pitching Deliveries—Past and Present")

Note: Danforth was suspended twice for 10 days for throwing "loaded" baseballs. On July 27, 1922, he was kicked out by Brick Owens in St. Louis in a game against the Yankees (Godin, pages 115–118). The second time was August 1, 1923, in Philadelphia against the Athletics, when George Moriarity ejected him for discoloring the ball (page 201).

Quote: "In the case of Dave Danforth it was found that he used paraffin on the seam of the ball, making it appear smooth and legal. He and others discovered that by delicately slitting the little raised places between the stitches in the seam a raised edge could be had whenever desired. These slits were made with a safety razor blade. Then the seam was pressed back into place, covered with paraffin and rubbed in. There was absolutely nothing to show the ball had been tampered with."
Source: *Memoirs of Twenty Years in Baseball* (Ty Cobb, Page 69)

VIC DARENSBOURG 5'8" 170-pound lefty
7-15, 5.10, 2 Saves 1998 2003

Pitches: 1. Fastball (91–94) 2. Slider 3. Change
Sources: *The Scouting Notebook* (1999 and 2002 editions)

RON DARLING 6'3" 195-pound righty
136-116, 3.87, 0 Saves 1983 1995

Pitch Selection: 1. Fastball 2. Curve 3. Change 4. Slider 5. Forkball
Source: *Tom Seaver's 1989 Scouting Notebook*

Description: "Darling isn't as forceful a pitcher as Roger Clemens, although he can get the ball up to the plate in a hurry. But his forkball is his 'out' pitch. He tries to get ahead of the hitter with his fastball or curve, then he'll come in with his forkball. So you'd better jump on his first few pitches."
Source: Red Sox scout Sam Mele quoted in *The Boston Herald* (10/27/1986)

Note: According to Peter Gammons in *Sports Illustrated* (4/6/1987), Darling added a split-fingered fastball in

1987. Gammons says that Darling threw an 88-MPH fastball, which would be equivalent to 90–92 on today's radar guns, which read faster than the guns in use at that time.

DANNY DARWIN 6'3" 185-pound righty
171-182, 3.84, 32 Saves 1978 1998

Pitch Selection, as Reliever: 1. Fastball 2. Slider
Pitch Selection, as Starter: 1. Fastball 2. Slider 3. Curve 4. Change 5. Split-Fingered Fastball
Sources: *Tom Seaver's 1989 Scouting Notebook; The Scouting Report: 1990; USA Today* (8/14/90, Rod Beaton)

HOOKS DAUSS 5'10" 168-pound righty
222-182, 3.30, 40 Saves 1912 1926

Pitch Selection: 1. Curve 2. Fastball 3. Sinker 4. Screwball or Fadeaway (added 1923 at insistence of Ty Cobb)
Sources: 1924 *Reach Guide* (Page 48); *Baseball Magazine* (April 1925, F.C. Lane); *The Indianapolis Times* (10/26/1958, Tev Laudeman); *Baseball Nicknames* (James Skipper)

Note: Dauss was always called "George" by press and public while he was active. His nickname, used by other players, was not "Hooks" but "Hookie." How he became "Hooks" in the encyclopedias, we don't know.

DAVE DAVENPORT 6'6" 220-pound righty
73-83, 2.93, 12 Saves 1914 1919

Pitch Selection: 1. Fastball 2. Curve
Description: "Only Walter Johnson has more speed . . . and when the hop on his fast one is zipping just right, Davenport is almost unhittable . . . He packs a pretty stylish curve with his tremendous speed."
Source: *Baseball Magazine* (February 1917, W.R. Hoefer)

Description: "Long Dave Davenport, a real pitching thunderbolt with any sort of backing, worked in a flock of games, apparently without injuring his sinewy, giraffe-like figure to any marked degree. Davenport seemed, barring some hard luck in the early part of the season, about as classy a speed merchant as any manager could wish to gaze upon."
Source: *Baseball Magazine* (January 1917, William A. Phelon)

CURT DAVIS 6'2" 185-pound righty
158-131, 3.42, 33 Saves 1934 1946

Pitch Selection: 1. Sinking Fastball 2. Curve 3. Change
Sources: *Baseball Magazine* (February 1935, John J. Ward); *Who's Who in the Major Leagues* (1939 edition); *Rowdy Richard* (Dick Bartell and Norman L. Macht, 1987)

Commentary: The Ward article gives such an excellent description of Davis on the mound that we feel compelled to quote from it. "He has an easy motion," Ward says, "an air of serious-minded confidence. His control is excellent and so is his mental poise. In build he is decidedly loose jointed and rangy. His pitching repertoire includes about everything a master hurler could wish—speed, curves and change of pace. His prime asset is his peculiar fast ball.

"The fast ball is a natural sinker. At times it will drop four or five inches. Most pitchers, needless to say, throw a fast ball that jumps and is quite likely to jump upwards. Fast balls that sink are a decided rarity and for that reason difficult to hit. Grover Alexander had such a fast ball and it was one of the key notes of his extraordinary career. Jimmy Wilson, master of the Phillies, who caught Alexander for several years, says Curt Davis reminds him of Big Alec. 'His control and general delivery are quite similar,' says Wilson.

"Davis makes no secret of his fast ball. 'It is not patented, and other pitchers are welcome to copy it, if they can. I throw it,' he says, 'with a snap of my wrist and the ball spins off the end of my middle finger, slightly inside, though not so much as a screw ball. This delivery was not difficult for me to master for it seemed to be my natural way of throwing a fast ball. It has never been hard on my arm or given me any difficulty whatever. I can control it better than any other type of delivery."

Bartell, with Macht, also likens Davis to Pete Alexander. Davis pitched for Salt Lake City in 1928, going 16-8 there, but with a high ERA. "The air is so light at Salt Lake," Davis said in the Ward article, "that it offers lessened resistance to the ball. Hence, it travels faster and farther than it will do nearer sea level. That naturally favors the batter. The batter is favored in another way because the pitcher finds it difficult to throw curve balls. The ball won't break properly."

DIXIE DAVIS 5'11" 155-pound righty
75-71, 3.97, 2 Saves 1912 1926

Quote: "Considered great control artist, clever pitcher."
Source: unidentified clipping from the Hall of Fame Library in Cooperstown

Quote: "He was wiry, had a lot of stuff and endurance, and was one of the gamest pitchers ever to step on the mound."
Source: *The Sporting News* (2/10/1944)

GEORGE DAVIS 5'10" 175-pound righty
7-10, 4.48, 0 Saves 1912 1915

Key Pitch: Spitball
Source: 1915 *Reach Guide* (Page 85)

JIM DAVIS 6'0" 180-pound lefty
24-26, 4.01, 10 Saves 1954 1957

Key Pitch: Knuckleball
Sources: *The Sporting News* (4/17/1957, Bob Broeg); *The Quality of Courage* (Mickey Mantle, 1964)

Description: "His specialties are a screw ball and knuckler."
Source: *Chicago Daily Tribune* (4/16/1954)

MARK DAVIS 6'3" 180-pound lefty
51-84, 4.17, 96 Saves 1980 1997

Pitch Selection: 1. Hard Curve 2. Fastball
Note: Davis' hard curve described as "half-curve, half-slider."
Source: *The Scouting Report: 1987*

RON DAVIS 6'4" 205-pound righty
47-53, 4.05, 130 Saves 1978 1988

Pitches: 1. Fastball (90+) 2. Slider
3. Curve (occasional) 4. Change (occasional)
Sources: *The Scouting Report* (1983 and 1987 editions)

STORM DAVIS 6'4" 207-pound righty
113-96, 4.02, 11 Saves 1982 1994

Pitch Selection: 1. Fastball 2. Overhand curve
3. Forkball (1988 on)
Source: *The Scouting Report: 1990*

BILL DAWLEY 6'5" 235-pound righty
27-30, 3.42, 25 Saves 1983 1989

Pitch Selection: 1. Sinking Fastball (90–92)
2. Hard Slider 3. Curve (occasional)
4. Change (occasional)
Source: *The Scouting Report: 1984*

LEON DAY 5'9" 170-pound righty
NEGRO LEAGUES 1934 1950

Pitch Selection: 1. Fastball 2. Curve 3. Change
Leon Day: "When I threw overhand, it would hurt my shoulder. But from here (his ear), I'd feel nothing. I threw my fastball straight up. I couldn't throw overhand, so I jerked it at them. It fooled a lot of hitters."
Roy Campanella: "Day was a short-arm. He used very little motion, but was very quick, had good control, plus a breaking pitch and a change of speed."
George Giles: "He looked like he was too small to be a batboy. Little bitty guy, but oh, could he throw hard."
Source: *Blackball Stars* (John Holway, 1988)

Quote: "As you can imagine, with no windup it was hard to steal on Leon. Plus he was quick and had a good pick-off move."
Source: Slow Robinson in *Catching Dreams* (Frazier "Slow" Robinson with Paul Bauer, 1999)

KEN DAYLEY 6'0" 171-pound lefty
33-45, 3.64, 39 Saves 1982 1993

Pitch Selection: 1. Fastball (low-90s) 2. Curve
3. Slider 4. Change (occasional)
Sources: *The Scouting Report* (1983 and 1984 editions)

CHUBBY DEAN 5'11" 181-pound lefty
30-46, 5.08, 9 Saves 1937 1943

Quote: "Chubby was one of the game's great eccentrics, and one of the few men I've ever known who could make [Connie] Mack visibly angry. A southpaw who seemed to have all the talent in the world, he never managed to win more than eight games in any of his seven big-league seasons."
Source: Phil Marchildon in *Ace: Phil Marchildon* (Marchildon with Brian Kendall, 1993)

YES, YOU'VE GUESSED IT!
IT'S THAT EMINENT
RIGHTHANDER, "DIZZY" DEAN
WINDING UP FOR
ONE OF THOSE
ZIPPING SPEEDBALLS
WHERE THE FAMED
"DIZZY" GETS HIS SPEED,
NOTE THE LONG STRIDE
STRIKE THREE! YER OUT
Seewald

Baseball Magazine, 1936

DIZZY DEAN 6'2" 182-pound righty
150-83, 3.02, 30 Saves 1930 1947

Pitch Selection: 1. Fastball 2. Curve 3. Change
Note: Dean would throw sidearm, overhand, and three-quarters.
Source: Leo Durocher in *Dizzy Dean: His Story in Baseball* (Lee Allen, 1967)

Description: " 'Dizzy's' fast ball is a thing to marvel at. It's really faster than it looks. 'Dizzy' has an easy side-arm motion, and his immense length of limb enables him to shoot the ball over the plate with little apparent effort. It gives the batter scant time to make up his mind. It is his favorite weapon in clinching a strikeout."
Source: *Baseball Magazine* (October 1933, F.C. Lane); same source says that Dean "has a fair curve, which is improving, and he is developing a good change of pace. More modern quirks of pitching, such as the screw ball and the knuckle ball are not for him."

Babe Herman: "Something most people don't know about Dizzy Dean is that he had the best motion on a change of pace that I ever saw . . . With a three and two count he would throw you that motion and come in with that change of pace."
Source: *Legends of Baseball* (Walter M. Langford, 1987)

Umpire Lee Ballanfant: "Dizzy Dean was the best pitcher I ever saw. He was fast, had a good curve and great control. And he had more confidence than any pitcher I ever knew. He'd yell to a batter, 'Can you hit a curve?' Damn if he wouldn't throw a curve right by him."
Source: *The Men in Blue* (Larry Gerlach, 1980)

PAUL DEAN 6'0" 175-pound righty
50-34, 3.75, 8 Saves 1934 1943

Pitch Selection: 1. Fastball 2. Nickel Curve
Sources: *Baseball Complete* (Russ Hodges, 1952); Terry Moore in *Legends of Baseball* (Walter M. Langford, 1987); *Cobb Would Have Caught It* (Richard Bak, 1991); *Baseball Magazine* (October 1934, F.C. Lane)

Terry Moore: "Paul never had the good curveball and also he didn't have a change-up . . . He had what we call a nickel curve."

See also Dizzy Trout.

WAYLAND DEAN 6'1" 178-pound righty
24-36, 4.87, 1 Save 1924 1927

Pitch Selection: 1. Sweeping Curve 2. Fastball
Description: "He has EVERYTHING that a good pitcher needs, including a dandy fast ball, a peach of a curve, oodles of gameness, and most of all, control . . . His chief asset is a wide sweeping curve ball, which he serves with a side-arm delivery with speed. Unlike most pitchers who specialize with the curve ball, Dean has excellent control . . . Time after time Dean will curve over the third strike with the count standing at 3 and 2 on the hitter . . ."
Source: *Baseball Magazine* (March 1924, Duke Ridgley)

DAVE DEBUSSCHERE 6'6" 225-pound righty
3-4, 2.90, 0 Saves 1962 1963

Key Pitch: Fastball

Source: *Don Schiffer's Major League Baseball Handbook—1964*

Description: "In those days a lot of pitchers held the ball in their hand [as they started their windup], and they'd show you more ball on the breaking ball than they would on the fast ball when they were coming up to their glove. I remember Dave DeBuscherre—he pitched for the White Sox—he had good stuff, but you could read every pitch that he threw. Probably to this day he wonders why he wasn't more successful."
Source: Frank Malzone in *Jim Bunning: Baseball and Beyond* (Frank Dolson, 1998)

JEFF DEDMON 6'2" 200-pound righty
20-16, 3.84, 12 Saves 1983 1988

Pitch Selection: 1. Sinking Fastball 2. Slider
Source: *The Scouting Report: 1985*

Pitch Selection: 1. Knuckle Curve 2. Fastball
Source: *The Scouting Report: 1987*

MIKE DeJEAN 6'4" 217-pound righty
24-24, 4.26, 52 Saves 1997 2003

Pitch Selection: 1. Split-Fingered Fastball 2. Two-Seam Fastball (low-90s) 3. Slider
Sources: *The Scouting Notebook* (1999, 2002, and 2003 editions)

JOSE DeLEON 6'3" 210-pound righty
86-119, 3.76, 6 Saves 1983 1995

Pitches: 1. Forkball 2. Fastball 3. Slider 4. Change 5. Curve
Sources: *Tom Seaver's 1989 Scouting Notebook; The Scouting Report* (1990 and 1992 editions)

Commentary: In *Baseball Digest* (September 1989), Bill Chastain reported that while DeLeon was with the White Sox (1986–1987), he added a sinker. "Before then I didn't have much movement on my fastball. The sinker added velocity to my fastball as well as movement," DeLeon said. His former catcher in Pittsburgh, Tony Pena, said, "At Pittsburgh, Jose just used his fastball and forkball." We have not found a mention of DeLeon's sinker in any other source, but it is likely that the "fastball" to which other sources refer is actually both the two-seam and four-seam fastballs.

LUIS DeLEON 6'1" 160-pound righty
17-19, 3.12, 32 Saves 1981 1989

Pitch Selection: 1. Fastball (88) 2. Hard Sinker 3. Slider
Source: *The Scouting Report: 1983*

IKE DeLOCK 5'11" 175-pound righty
84-75, 4.03, 31 Saves 1952 1963

Pitch Selection: 1. Sinker 2. Curve
Source: Yogi Berra by way of Dale Berra by way of Rob Neyer on August 15, 2002

RICH DeLUCIA 6'0" 190-pound righty
38-51, 4.62, 7 Saves 1990 1999

Pitch Selection: 1. Slider 2. Curve 3. Change 4. Fastball
Source: *The Scouting Report: 1993*

AL DEMAREE 6'0" 170-pound righty
80-72, 2.77, 9 Saves 1912 1919

Pitch Selection: 1. Curve 2. Fastball 3. Change
Sources: *New York Globe* (9/18/1912); numerous unidentified clippings from the Hall of Fame Library in Cooperstown; *New York Herald* (3/7/1919)

Description: "He has a good curve ball (and) knows how to pitch . . . While Demaree uses his curve to advantage, his most effective ball, according to Southern League critics, is a fast one that has lots of 'stuff' on it without appearing to have anything."
Source: *New York Globe* (9/18/1912)

Description: "He is a curve ball pitcher, who resorts to speed and an iron wrist for effectiveness to baffle the opposition rather than the application of digestive juice to the leather."
Source: unidentified clipping from the Hall of Fame Library (September 1912)

Description: "Simple and open motions . . . He has a very deceptive change of pace and a fast ball with a jump to it. His curves break close up to the batter."
Source: article by J.W. McConaughy (October 1913, unidentified source)

Description: "Has considerable smoke when he wants to cut loose. He also has a good assortment of benders

and the weight to put a mighty mean shoulder behind them."
Source: article by Jack Veiock (October 1917, unidentified source)

Note: Demaree threw sidearm.
Source: *Baseball's Greatest Teams* (Tom Meany, 1949)

RYAN DEMPSTER 6'3" 215-pound righty
50-55, 5.01, 0 Saves 1998 2003

Pitch Selection: 1. Fastball (92–94) 2. Slider 3. Change
Source: *The Scouting Notebook: 2000*

JOHN DENNY 6'3" 185-pound righty
123-108, 3.59, 0 Saves 1974 1986

Pitch Selection, early career: 1. Fastball 2. Hard Curve 3. Change
Pitch Selection, late career: 1. Curve 2. Fastball (85) 3. Slider 4. Change
Sources: *The Sporting News* (9/13/1975, Neal Russo); *The Scouting Report: 1983*

PAUL DERRINGER 6'3" 205-pound righty
223-212, 3.46, 29 Saves 1931 1945

Pitch Selection: 1. Overhand Curve 2. Fastball 3. Knuckleball (added in 1940 or shortly before)
Note: Derringer threw overhand.
Sources: *Major League Baseball* (Ethan Allen, Page 26); *Stan Musial* (Musial with Bob Broeg, 1984); *The St. Louis Cardinals* (Fred Lieb, 1945); Damon Phillips in *The Pastime in Turbulence: Interviews with Baseball Players of the 1940s* (Brent Kelley, 2001); *The Detroit News* (October 1940); *The Sporting News* (8/15/1940, Page 4)

Comment: "He depends upon no freak stuff to fool the batters. He has no fancy screw ball or knuckler to achieve renown. He succeeds with a good old-fashioned curve, mixed with a fast ball and a change of pace. His curve ball is no dinky that comes up begging to be murdered, nor is it a telegraphed roundhouse. It is a hook that breaks sharply downward and it has the batters hitting into the ground.

"One big factor in his development has been his ability to hide his pitch. When Derringer's right arm is arched back for the throw, his left leg is raised high, so high that it entirely conceals his right hand. The batter can't spot the ball until it is on its way plateward."
Source: *Baseball Magazine* (November 1931, Clifford Bloodgood)

Damon Phillips: "Derringer used to throw a real heavy-type ball. All the players used to talk about it . . . if you didn't get it on the center of the bat it just vibrated right up your arms."

Quote: "Paul Derringer had a great curve. He rolled that curveball right off the table and had a good fastball, too. If I had to pick the toughest pitcher I ever hit against, it would be Paul Derringer. I'll tell you, he was tough on me!"
Source: Pinky May in *Dugout to Foxhole* (Rick Van Blair, 1994)

Derringer: "Don't believe what you may hear about me throwing lots of knuckle balls. I've never thrown more than half a dozen in any one game."
Source: *The Sporting News* (6/19/1941, Page 5)

Description: "Derringer of the Cincinnati Reds has perhaps the most energetic wind-up on the major mound. All pitchers raise one foot as they stride forward to get their body weight and momentum behind the pitch. But Derringer elevates that foot sometimes higher than his head. It travels in a great sweeping arc of spikes and leather across the batter's range of vision and isn't designed to help the latter a bit in following the course of the ball. It acts as a purely mental distraction."
Source: *Baseball Magazine* (January 1937, F.C. Lane)

Note: According to columnist Dan Daniel, Derringer admitted to writer Joe Williams that he'd thrown a spitball to retire Earl Averill for the last out of the 1940 World Series.
Source: "Daniel's Dope" column in the *New York World-Telegram* (6/6/1941)

JIM DeSHAIES 6'4" 222-pound lefty
84-95, 4.14, 0 Saves 1984 1995

Pitches: 1. High Fastball 2. Change 3. Slider 4. Curve
Sources: *Tom Seaver's 1989 Scouting Notebook: The Scouting Report* (1990 and 1992 editions)

CHARLES DEVENS 6'1" 180-pound righty
5-3, 3.73, 0 Saves 1932 1934

Pitch Selection: 1. Fastball 2. Curve 3. Change
Devens: "I was mostly a fastball pitcher, and it was that pitch that caught the Yankees' interest. If they'd had radar guns in the thirties, I know my fastball was in the nineties. Despite some control problems, I also had a decent curve and change of pace."
Source: *Yankees Century* (Glenn Stout and Richard A. Johnson, 2002)

JIM DEVLIN 5'11" 175-pound righty
65-60, 1.89, 0 Saves 1876 1877

Note from *The Sporting Life* (10/15/1883): "While [at Louisville], he invented the 'down shoot' delivery and there were but few men who could hit him, so effectual was his peculiar pitching."

MARK DEWEY 6'0" 216-pound righty
12-7, 3.65, 8 Saves 1990 1996

Pitch Selection: 1. Sinking Fastball (90) 2. Slider 3. Change
Source: *The Scouting Notebook: 1995*

Pitch Selection: 1. Three-quarter/Sidearm Curve 2. Sinker (88) 3. Slider 4. Change
Source: *The Scouting Notebook: 1996*

ROB DIBBLE 6'4" 230-pound righty
27-25, 2.98, 89 Saves 1988 1995

Pitch Selection: 1. Fastball 2. Slider
Source: *USA Today* (5/25/1989, Rod Beaton)

Description: "He's the hardest thrower in the league, bar none. Some people say his fastball doesn't have much movement. Hell, how much movement do you need when you throw 100?"
Source: *Bill Mazeroski's Baseball* (1993 edition)

MURRY DICKSON 5'10" 157-pound righty
172-181, 3.66, 23 Saves 1939 1959

Pitches: 1. Fastball 2. Curve 3. Sinker 4. Slider 5. Knuckleball 6. Screwball 7. Forkball
Note: Dickson continually varied his position on the rubber and his windup. Also, he threw overhand, sidearm and underhand. *Baseball Digest* (January 1963, Page 48) cites Dickson as being one of the first pitchers to rely heavily on the slider.
Sources: *Stan Musial* (Musial with Bob Broeg, 1964); Dickson's obituary in *The Sporting News* (10/2/1989); *The Crooked Pitch* (Martin Quigley, 1984), and *Baseball Digest* (January 1963)

Stan Musial: "Murry was a great competitor, but he never worried about anything. They called him the Tom Edison of the mound because he liked to experiment with pitches. He had the widest assortment I ever saw—fast ball, curve, slider, knuckler, sinker, screwball—and a remarkable arm that stood it all. Dickson wouldn't have given his mother anything good to hit."

Gil Hodges: "He has everything to make him a great pitcher. His control is magnificent and his curves—well, you can just call them baffling. There's no other word for them. The most devastating is his slider. Contrary to the general belief, this isn't a slow ball. It comes at you like a bullet, breaks about six inches from the plate, and when you swing, all you hit is the air."
Source: *Sport* (May 1952, Ed Burkholder)

Notes: In *Baseball Is a Funny Game* (1960), Joe Garagiola tells a story about Dickson throwing eight straight curve balls on a 3-2 count to Carl Furillo, at different speeds and from different arm angles.

In *A Glimpse of Fame* (Dennis Snell, 1993), Ron Necciai said of Dickson (his teammate, briefly), "He could throw you six different curveballs from six different places at six different speeds, and have them all wind up in the same spot."

Branch Rickey: "Dickson is a scatterbrain, which may explain a scatter-arm. A pitching staff of ten Dicksons would finish about mid-way in the race. A good club could spot him and find him helpful. His record for the past three years shows that it takes him half the season to get ready to pitch the second half. He has an assortment of a great number of pitches—adjustments of rotation to velocity—varying both the direction and rapidity of rotation to velocity—so much so that he is continuously flabbergasted in making a decision of what pitch to make. He reminds me of the fellow in the army who complained of every job given to him and was unsatisfactory in all of them and finally he was given the job of sorting potatoes. At the end of two days, the sergeant

asked him how he liked his new work, and he said, 'Terrible, I don't like it at all—it almost worries me to death.' 'What worries you,' said the sergeant, and the reply was, 'The damn decisions.' I will say Dickson reminds me of that chap. He ought to be a really great pitcher. He fields his position splendidly and he can hit."
Source: Letter from Rickey to Pirates owner John W. Galbreath (3/7/1951), reprinted in *Branch Rickey in Pittsburgh* (Andrew O'Toole, 2000)

LARRY DIERKER 6'4" 215-pound righty
139-123, 3.31, 1 Save 1964 1977

Pitches: 1. Fastball (two-seam and four-seam) 2. Slider 3. Change 4. Curve
Note: Shortly after Dierker signed out of high school with Houston, general manager Paul Richards tried to teach him to throw the slip pitch. But he couldn't get the hang of it, and instead came up with a forkball that was good enough that he'd get strikeouts with it. Dierker threw the forkball until the early 1970s, when he hurt one of his pitching fingers playing basketball and couldn't throw the pitch effectively afterward. From that point, to change up on right-handed hitters he took something off his curveball, and to change up on left-handed hitters he took something off his fastball.
Dierker: "Almost from the beginning, I was a two-seam/four-seam/slider pitcher. Early in a game, I'd get a feel for which fastball was working, and then I'd mostly stick with that one. It was rare, but there were occasions when both of them were good, and on those days I didn't really have to use a breaking ball or a change-up."
Source: Interview with Dierker (7/1/2003, Rob Neyer)
Other Sources: *This Ain't Brain Surgery: How to Win the Pennant Without Losing Your Mind* (Larry Dierker, 2003); *The Sporting News* (5/29/1976, Harry Shattuck)

BILL DIETRICH 6'0" 185-pound righty
108-128, 4.48, 11 Saves 1933 1948

Key Pitch: Fastball
Source: *Baseball Magazine* (May 1944, Herbert Simons)

Notes: Simons wrote, "Old-timers were comparing him—and favorably—with Walter Johnson . . . 'He actually threw so hard that when his game was over, he was physically exhausted,' coach Muddy Ruel told us once."

Dietrich's lack of success, despite his tremendous fastball, was attributed both to a lack of control and to his inability to control his temper.

Dietrich on his 1936 no-hitter: "My best pitch, I consider, is a fast ball, but I depended almost entirely on slow stuff for the first five innings. They may have thrown the hitters off. They may have been expecting speed."
Source: *Baseball Magazine* (December 1937, Clifford Bloodgood)

Dietrich: "I tried the knuckle ball once. I worked on it a long while and finally, a couple of years ago, I threw two of them at Cleveland. One was a homer and the other a triple—and the triple was hit farther than the homer!"
Source: *Baseball Magazine* (September 1942, Herbert Simons)

MARTIN DiHIGO 6'3" 190-pound righty
Negro Leagues 1923 1945

Pitch Selection: 1. Fastball 2. Curve
Source: *Blackball Stars* (John B. Holway, 1988)
Quote from Cuban fan Pedro Cardona, same source: "I don't think he had much of a curve. But he had a lot of speed and a lot of control."

BILL DILLMAN 6'2" 180-pound righty
7-12, 4.54, 3 Saves 1967 1970

Description: "Has better than average curve. Everything else good, except change, which is just fair."
Source: *Baseball Digest* (March 1967, "Official Scouting Reports on 1967 Major League Rookies")

BILL DINNEEN 6'1" 190-pound righty
170-176, 3.01, 7 Saves 1898 1909

Pitch Selection: 1. Fastball 2. Sharp Curve
Source: *The Story of the World Series* (Fred Lieb, 1965)
Note: Dinneen wrote the chapter, "How to Pitch an Inshoot" in the 1908 book, *How to Pitch*.

Description: "I would have the boys taught that a good step helps very much in pitching, and that it is essential to cultivate a powerful body swing, especially to follow the ball well with the arm and the body after it is delivered. Dinneen, the great pitcher of the St. Louis Browns, has an especially stylish delivery in this respect, and should be a model for youth to imitate."
Source: *Baseball Magazine* (June 1909, J.B. Sheridan)

FRANK DiPINO 5'10" 175-pound lefty
35-38, 3.83, 56 Saves 1981 1993

Pitch Selection: 1. Fastball 2. Slider 3. Change
Source: *The Scouting Report 1990*

JERRY DiPOTO 6'2" 208-pound righty
27-24, 4.05, 49 Saves 1993 2000

Pitch Selection: 1. Hard Slider 2. Two-Seam Fastball 3. Four-Seam Fastball
Source: *The Scouting Notebook 2000*

ART DITMAR 6'2" 185-pound righty
72-77, 3.98, 14 Saves 1954 1962

Pitches: 1. Fastball 2. Slider 3. Curve
Ditmar: "I used an inside fastball and a slider . . . Overall, though, I had trouble with lefties. My curve just wasn't good enough."
Source: *The Berkshire Eagle* (4/6/2003, Brian Sullivan)

Pitch Selection: 1. Sinker 2. Slider 3. Curve (especially in 1961)
Source: Ditmar in *Sweet Seasons* (Dom Forker, 1989)

Note: Listed by *The Sporting News* (8/29/1956) as having one of the best fastballs in the league.

BILL DOAK 6'0" 165-pound righty
169-157, 2.98, 16 Saves 1912 1929

Pitches: 1. Spitball 2. Fastball 3. Curve (occasional)
Doak: "It makes me smile when I remember what they used to say about the spitter in the old days and the havoc it would wreck with a pitcher's elbow and shoulder. Really it's the easiest ball in the world to pitch, far easier than the curve, less trying to the arm than the fast ball, which is supposed to be the most natural of all deliveries. For the spitter is thrown with the same arm motion as the fast ball, only you don't have to put so much stuff on it to fool the batter. If I were obliged to depend on sheer speed, I'd have to burn up a lot more energy. I pitch some curves, but not many. The spitter and curve seldom mix in a pitcher's repertoire. The fast ball and the spitter are natural allies."
Source: *Baseball Magazine* (March 1928, John J. Ward)
Other Sources: *Bob Broeg's Redbirds* (Bob Broeg, 1988), 1924 *Reach Guide* (Page 47), 1923 *Reach Guide* (Page 38)

CHUCK DOBSON 6'4" 200-pound righty
74-69, 3.78, 0 Saves 1966 1975

Pitches: 1. Low Fastball 2. Slider 3. Curve 4. Change
Reggie Jackson in 1969: "Chuck is going to be the next (Bob) Gibson."
Dick Williams in 1971: "He's got an arm as good as Vida Blue's . . . I don't mean necessarily that he has the same speed, but he is more equipped to get the same results."
Sources: Ron Bergman in *The Sporting News* (5/24/1969, 8/14/1971, and 2/16/1974)

JOE DOBSON 6'2" 197-pound righty
137-103, 3.62, 18 Saves 1939 1954

Pitch Selection: 1. Curve 2. Fastball 3. Change
Sources: Ed Rumill in *The Sporting News* (6/16/1948); Rumill in unidentified newspaper (May 1952, TSN Morgue); *Fenway Voices* (Jack Lautier); *Baseball Digest* (July 1950, Clif Keane)

Quote from Rumill: "Having had a closeup of the Dobson curve, the writer wonders how hitters ever get a piece of it." (According to Rumill, Dobson disliked trick pitches, and never would have anything to do with them.)

Description: "Dobson throws more curves in three innings . . . than most pitchers throw in two games."
Source: Milt Richman in *Baseball Digest* (January 1951)

Quote: "A few years ago one of our popular magazines ran a pseudo-scientific article designed to prove that there is no such thing as a curve ball. There are upwards of two hundred right-handed batters who have faced Sain and Feller and Dobson and Blackwell, to mention but four hurlers among dozens, who would be pretty hard to convince!"
Source: *The Way to Better Baseball* (Tommy Henrich and A.L. Plaut, 1951)

PAT DOBSON 6'3" 190-pound righty
122-129, 3.54, 19 Saves 1967 1977

Pitch Selection: 1. Overhand curve 2. Fastball 3. Slider
Source: *The Sporting News* (6/21/69, Watson Spoelstra)

ED DOHENY 5'10" 165-pound lefty
77-83, 3.75, 2 Saves 1895 1903

Key Pitch: Curve
Quote: "Only six home runs were made off the perverse curves of Doheny in the nine years he faced big league batsmen."
Source: *The Great Teams of Baseball* (MacLean Kennedy, 1929)

Note: Doheny in fact allowed 13 home runs in the major leagues, which is a very low total.

JOHN DOHERTY 6'4" 215-pound righty
32-31, 4.87, 9 Saves 1992 1996

Pitch Selection: 1. Sinking Fastball 2. Curve 3. Change 4. Slider
Source: *The Scouting Notebook: 1995*

RED DONAHUE 6'0" 187-pound righty
165-172, 3.61, 3 Saves 1893 1906

Key Pitch: Curve
Quote: "Curved and worked with a high degree of success."
Source: unidentified clipping from the Hall of Fame Library (August 1913)

Quote: "Long after his once good right arm was practically useless he earned his salary working for big league by using his brains."
Source: unidentified clipping from the Hall of Fame Library (July 1913)

Quote: "He was known as the brainiest boxman in the history of latter-day baseball."
Source: *The National Game* (Alfred H. Spink, 1911)

ATLEY DONALD 6'1" 186-pound righty
65-33, 3.52, 1 Save 1938 1945

Pitch Selection: 1. Fastball 2. Curve 3. Slider (added in 1941)
Note: Donald was clocked throwing a fastball at 94.7 MPH at Municipal Stadium in Cleveland in 1939. This was the record speed for a fastball at that time, and remained so until Bob Feller faced a radar gun on August 20, 1946.
Sources: *Bill Stern's Favorite Baseball Stories* (Pocket Books, 1949); Letter in files of *The Sporting News* morgue; *The Sporting News* (9/7/1974) incorrectly reports that Donald's record-making throw was made in 1958.
Source for Slider: *The Sporting News* (8/28/1941, Pagc 10)

Description: ". . . a tremendous conniver, a guy without the best stuff, but who had control of his curveball, and that was rare in the '30s."
Source: *A Legend in the Making: The New York Yankees in 1939* (Richard J. Tofel, 2002)

JOHN DONALDSON 6'0" 185-pound lefty
Negro Leagues 1913 1934

Pitch Selection: 1. Hard Curve 2. Fastball 3. Change
Sources: *Only the Ball Was White* (Robert W. Peterson, 1970); *The Biographical Encyclopedia of the Negro Baseball Leagues* (James A. Riley, 1994)

John McGraw: "If Donaldson were a white man, or if the unwritten law of baseball didn't bar negroes from the major leagues, I would give $50,000 for him—and think I was getting a bargain."
Source: *Sporting Life* (7/3/1915; reprinted in Janet Bruce's *The Kansas City Monarchs,* 1985)

Quote from *Only the Ball Was White:* "John Donaldson was noted for his grace on the mound and a sharp-breaking curve ball that was faster than most pitchers' fastballs . . . His money pitch was a hard, sharp-breaking curve . . . His beautiful drop and wide assortment of curves, combined with a good fastball and change-up, made him one of the best left-handers in the history of black baseball."

BLIX DONNELLY 5'10" 178-pound righty
27-36, 3.49, 12 Saves 1944 1951

Key Pitch: Curve
Comment: "Perhaps the most beautiful curve in the major leagues today is the one pitched by Blix Donnelly of the Phillies. However, possession of that terrific asset has not done quite as much for Blix as had been expected."
Source: *The Sporting News* (10/30/1946, Page 20)

PETE DONOHUE 6'2" 185-pound righty
134-118, 3.87, 12 Saves 1921 1932

Pitch Selection: 1. Curve 2. Change
Source: *The Cincinnati Reds* (Lee Allen, 1948)

DICK DONOVAN 6'3" 190-pound righty
122-99, 3.67, 5 Saves 1950 1965

Pitches: 1. Slider 2. Sinking Fastball 3. Curve 4. Change
Sources: *Baseball Stars of 1963* (article by Lee Greene); *Sport* (November 1962, Sandy Grady); *Sports Illustrated* (10/12/1959); *Baseball Digest* (September 1955, Page 45); *Baseball Digest* (March 1964, page 32) says Donovan "has the best slider in the majors." In *We Played the Game* (Danny Peary, 1994), Les Moss said that Donovan "could throw a slider for a strike any time he wanted."

Note: According to Al Hirshberg in *Sport* (February 1957), Donovan was taught to throw the slider by Whitlow Wyatt in Atlanta in 1954. Hirshberg also says Donovan threw the best slider of his generation.

Quote: "You've got to see Donovan's curve. Can't tell about the curve on TV. Got to catch it, try to catch it, to see what the thing does. It breaks so you can almost hear it."
Source: Billy Pierce in *Out of My League* (George Plimpton, 1961; considering what people said about Donovan's slider, it's quite possible that Pierce was actually referring to Donovan's slider, rather than his curve.)

WILD BILL DONOVAN 5'11" 190-pound righty
186-139, 2.69, 8 Saves 1898 1918

Key Pitch: Fastball
Source: *The National Game* (Alfred H. Spink, 1911)
Quote: "When in good shape Donovan has fine speed, a wonderful break on his fast ball and is one of the best fielding pitchers in the country."

Road West Publishing—*Baseball Magazine* Collection

1925 Cincinnati Reds Pitching Staff: Neal Brady, Harry Biemiller, Tom Sheehan, Eppa Rixey, Pete Donohue, Rube Benton, Carl Mays, Dolph Luque and Jackie May.

Luque, Rixey and Donohue finished 1-2-3 in the NL ERA standings and the Reds' staff had a team ERA nearly half a run better than the second best team. They finished 80-73 in third place, because their offense finished last in the league in runs scored.

JOHN DOPSON 6'4" 230-pound righty
30-47, 4.27, 1 Save 1985 1994

Pitch Selection: 1. Sinker 2. Slider
3. Forkball (occasional)
Source: *The Scouting Report: 1993*

HARRY DORISH 5'11" 204-pound righty
45-43, 3.83, 44 Saves 1947 1956

Pitch Selection: 1. "Cosmic" Pitch 2. Sinker
Quote: "A sinker ball which induces batsmen to hit the ball on the ground, mastery of the 'cosmic' pitch, a baffling delivery taught by Manager Paul Richards, and the ability to get the ball in the strike zone has made the 206-pounder one of the finest relief pitchers in modern baseball."
Source: *Chicago White Sox Yearbook, 1954* (Arch Ward)

Pitch Selection: 1. Slip Pitch 2. Fastball 3. Curve
4. Slider (experimental)
Source: *The Sporting News* (6/15/1955, Jesse A. Linthicum)

Note: In the *Baseball Digest* in 1952, Richards explains that Dorish's best pitch was a slip pitch on which Dorish was able to get a screwball type action. Undated clipping from *Baltimore News-Post* of article by John F. Steadman leaves little doubt that the "Cosmic" Pitch (also known as "The Thing") was the pitch that later became known as the Slip Pitch.

RICH DOTSON 6'1" 190-pound righty
111-113, 4.23, 0 Saves 1979 1990

Pitch Selection, before 7/85 arm surgery: 1. Fastball
2. Curve 3. Slider
Source: *The Scouting Report: 1987*

Pitch Selection, after 7/85 arm surgery: 1. Change
2. Fastball 3. Curve
Source: *The Kansas City Star* (4/12/90, Dick Kaegel)

Comment: "Had problems with his control, but made the big breakthrough in 1980 when he mastered the changeup."
Source: *The Complete Handbook of Baseball: 1982 Season* (edited by Zander Hollander)

PHIL DOUGLAS 6'3" 190-pound righty
94-93, 2.80, 8 Saves 1912 1922

Pitch Selection: 1. Spitball 2. Curve 3. Fastball
4. Change
Note: Douglas was on the list of pitchers "grandfathered in," allowed to continue throwing the spitball after it was banned in 1921.
Sources: *One Last Round for the Shuffler* (Tom Clark, 1979); *The New York Giants* (Frank Graham, 1947), 1923 *Reach Guide* (Page 38)

AL DOWNING 5'11" 175-pound lefty
123-107, 3.22, 3 Saves 1961 1977

Pitches: 1. High Fastball 2. Slider 3. Change
4. Curve
Sources: *Catching* (Elston Howard, 1967); Downing in *Sweet Seasons* (Dom Forker, 1989)

Quote: "Learned how to pitch the hard way, bouncing from team to team after his fast ball evaporated . . . 'I realize now I'll never throw that hard again,' Downing said last season. 'I'm fortunate I learned how to make it as a pitcher.' "
Source: *The Complete Handbook of Baseball* (1972 edition, edited by Zander Hollander)

Note: Hank Aaron's 715th home run came on a low-and away fastball.
Source: Downing in *Talkin' Baseball: An Oral History of Baseball in the 1970s* (Phil Pepe, 1998)

KELLY DOWNS 6'4" 195-pound righty
57-53, 3.86, 1 Save 1986 1993

Pitch Selection: 1. Split-Fingered Fastball 2. Fastball
3. Curve
Sources: *The Scouting Report* (1987 and 1993 editions)

JOE DOYLE 5'8" 150-pound righty
22-21, 2.85, 1 Save 1906 1910

Description: "He wants eight to ten days between the games in which he works. He is a slow chap, anyhow. He claims that his arm needs rest. He is one of the greatest pitchers there is. You never see him throw a ball hard. He just tosses them."
Source: *Baseball Magazine* (February 1910, John D. Chesbro)

DOUG DRABEK 6'1" 185-pound righty
155-134, 3.73, 0 Saves 1986 1998

Pitch Selection: 1. Fastball (88–92) 2. Slider 3. Curve 4. Change
Source: *The Scouting Report: 1987*

Pitch Selection: 1. Overhand Curve 2. Slider 3. Fastball 4. Change
Source: *The Scouting Report: 1990*

Pitch Selection: 1. Slider 2. Sinking Fastball 3. Cut Fastball 4. Curve 5. Change
Source: *USA Today* (9/14/1990, Rod Beaton)

Pitch Selection: 1. Slider 2. Curve 3. Fastball 4. Change
Sources: *The Scouting Report* (1992 and 1993 editions)

MOE DRABOWSKY 6'3" 190-pound righty
88-105, 3.71, 55 Saves 1956 1972

Pitch Selection: 1. Fastball 2. Slider 3. Curve
Sources: *Sport* (January 1967, Doug Brown); Drabowsky in *Pen Men* (Bob Cairns, 1992); *Baseball Digest* (August 1958, Charles Dexter)

DICK DRAGO 6'1" 190-pound righty
108-117, 3.62, 58 Saves 1969 1981

Pitches: 1. Sinking Fastball 2. Rising Fastball 3. Slider 4. Change
Source: *The Sporting News* (6/14/1969, Joe McGuff)

Pitch Selection: 1. Slider 2. Change
Source: *The Sporting News* (5/12/1979, Larry Whiteside)

DAVE DRAVECKY 6'1" 195-pound lefty
64-57, 3.13, 10 Saves 1982 1989

Pitch Selection: 1. Fastball 2. Slider
Note: Dravecky threw sidearm.
Source: *The Scouting Report: 1987*

DARREN DREIFORT 6'2" 211-pound righty
47-56, 4.36, 10 Saves 1994 2003

Pitch Selection: 1. Tailing Fastball (mid-90s) 2. Slider (high-80s) 3. Change
Note: The 1998 edition of *The Scouting Notebook* says that Dreifort was developing a splitter to use as his change. This is the only mention we've found of Dreifort throwing that pitch.
Source: *The Scouting Report: 1995; The Scouting Notebook* (1995, 1997–2002 editions)

TRAVIS DRISKILL 6'0" 215-pound righty
11-13, 5.23, 1 Save 2002 2003

Pitch Selection: 1. Two-Seam Fastball (low-90s) 2. Split-Fingered Fastball (82–84) 3. Slider (occasional)
Source: Personal observation (5/25/2002, Rob Neyer)

DICK DROTT 6'0" 185-pound righty
27-46, 4.78, 0 Saves 1957 1963

Pitch Selection: 1. Fastball 2. Curve
Sources: *Baseball Digest* (August 1958, Charles Dexter); *Take Me Out to the Cubs Game* (John C. Skipper, 2000)

LOUIS DRUCKE 6'1" 188-pound righty
18-15, 2.90, 1 Save 1909 1912

Key Pitch: Drop Curve
Description: "Drucke is 21 years old and a strapping, long-armed fellow. He has been well advised by Mathewson, and to some extent has copied the delivery of the 'Big Six.' Like Mathewson, he indulges in no preliminary swing, but simply raises both hands above his head and lets go. He has a very effective drop curve, something like Matty's 'fadeaway.' "
Source: *The National Game* (Alfred H. Spink, 1911)

DON DRYSDALE 6'5" 190-pound righty
209-166, 2.95, 6 Saves 1956 1969

Pitches: 1. Fastball 2. Curve 3. Change 4. Slider 5. Spitball
Source: *Sport* (September 1962, Steve Gelman); *Once a Bum, Always a Dodger* (Don Drysdale with Bob Verdi, 1990)

Drysdale on his Spitball: "Through the years, I called on my spitter at times to get out of jams. I wasn't the only one, believe me. Gaylord Perry wrote a book on it. Bob Shaw and my fellow Dodger, Phil Regan, had fingers pointed at them, too. You'll have to ask them. But my good buddy, Gene Mauch, singled me out. He said I threw the best spitter in the National League because I threw it the hardest. Thanks, Gene.

"I was accused of applying all sorts of foreign substances to the ball, from KY jelly to Vaseline. Bill Rigney, the manager of the Giants for a while, swore I had some gook on the inside of my belt. All I was doing, though, was drying off my thumb after going to my mouth to get some saliva. I wet the index and middle fingers and then spread the moisture around with my thumb. Some guys could throw the spitter with their thumb wet, but I couldn't."

Drysdale: "I had control from the beginning, although it was nowhere near as sharp as it is now. I came up with only a fastball and a curve.

"Then Joe Becker (now Cub coach) began teaching the change-up. I kept experimenting and now it's a sort of mongrel pitch.

"I learned the 'dead leg' technique from Gordie Holt, a scout, and a loose wrist action from Johnny Podres. That's similar to the slip pitch that Paul Richards invented. Then Sal Maglie joined our club and taught me how to throw the slider."
Source: *Baseball Digest* (August 1968, George Vass)

Walter Alston: "Don's fast ball always did have a tendency to sink and bear in on a right-handed batter. This was (and is) his best pitch, the kind of delivery that often breaks the bat in the hitter's hands."
Source: *Alston and the Dodgers* (Alston and Si Burick, 1966)

Jim Bunning: "If I had as good a greaseball as Drysdale at that time [1968], I'd have had fifty-eight straight scoreless innings, too. He had one of the best I've ever seen. Whoo-o-o.

"I started a game against Drysdale in that streak for Pittsburgh when he was shutting everybody out. You couldn't hit him. He had everything going, including control. He had great stuff, and he added this slippery pitch. The bottom fell out, and it was about 93–94 miles an hour. It was unhittable."
Source: *Jim Bunning: Baseball and Beyond* (Frank Dolson, 1998)

Umpire Tom Gorman: "Toward the end Drysdale loaded up a few. I'd say he had a very good spitter, just like Gaylord Perry's. But Drysdale didn't seem to use it as much as Perry, just when he needed a strikeout, or when he was in a jam in the late innings."
Three and Two! (Tom Gorman as told to Jerome Holtzman, 1979)

Description: "If your elbow is even with your shoulder and your wrist above your elbow, call it three-quarters . . . Don Drysdale look(s) like (a) sidearmer because (he is) so tall and reach(es) out so far, but at the point of release (he) still (has) the wrist above the elbow . . . Don Drysdale looked like a sidearm pitcher because he was so tall, but he took his stride straight ahead and reached out wide."
Source: *Pitching with Tom Seaver* (Seaver and Steve Jacobson, 1973)

Gene Mauch: "I'd say the inshoot as we knew it as kids was just like Don Drysdale's fast ball—tails into a right-hand batter. Not many guys have one."
Source: unidentified clipping, by Sandy Grady, 1964

Notes: Drysdale's fastball broke in on a right-handed hitter. Drysdale was timed at 95.31 miles per hour by *Time* Magazine in 1960 (see Steve Barber). A good guess is that he might register at 96 or 98 on modern radar guns. According to Jack Zanger in *Major League Baseball 1965*, Drysdale also threw a pitch that he described as a "knuckle fork ball." This may have been a code name for his spitball.

JEAN DUBUC 5'10" 185-pound righty
85-76, 3.04, 13 Saves 1908 1919

Key Pitch: Slow Ball
Quote: "There is not a doubt in the world that Dubuc to-day possesses the greatest control of a slow ball and has a more effective type of delivery in this particular field than any other pitcher in the game."
Source: *Baseball Magazine* (January 1913, F.C. Lane; article titled "The Slow Ball Wizard")

Dubuc: "In slow ball pitching I make all the motions of a fast ball, but at the last minute I hold back. It is like reversing an engine at full speed; it wrenches the arm from wrist to shoulder. But it is a good delivery."
Source: *Baseball Magazine* (November 1913, F.C. Lane)

Marty O'Toole on Dubuc's Slow Ball: "Dubuc, who is one of the best slow ball pitchers, uses the same delivery as he does in pitching a fast ball, only he lets the ball slide

out from under his two first fingers with hardly a contact. It is something like a slow spitball, only he doesn't wet the ball."
Source: *Baseball Magazine* (October 1914, F.C. Lane)

JIM DUCKWORTH 6'4" 194-pound righty
7-25, 5.25, 4 Saves 1963 1966

Key Pitch: Fastball
Source: *Don Schiffer's Major League Baseball Handbook—1964*

GEORGE DUMONT 5'11" 163-pound righty
10-23, 2.85, 3 Saves 1915 1919

Key Pitch: Fastball
Note: Dumont was said to throw almost as hard as Walter Johnson.
Source: *The 1917 White Sox* (Warren N. Wilbert and William C. Hageman, 2003)

JACK DUNN 5'9" 180-pound righty
63-58, 4.11, 4 Saves 1897 1904

Key Pitch: Curve
Source: *Misfits* (J. Thomas Hetrick, 1991)

STEVE DUNNING 6'2" 205-pound righty
23-41, 4.57, 1 Save 1970 1977

Pitch Selection: 1. Fastball 2. Slider
Source: *Sport* (October 1970, Pat Jordan)

RYNE DUREN 6'2" 190-pound righty
27-44, 3.83, 57 Saves 1954 1965

Pitches: 1. Fastball 2. Slider 3. Sinker 4. Knuckleball
Note: Duren was probably the fastest pitcher in baseball from 1958 through 1960. He was accused of throwing a spitball in 1963, in a comeback season.
Sources: *Baseball Digest* (August 1958, Charles Dexter); *The Sporting News* (7/27/1963, Page 7); *The Relief Pitcher* (John Thorn, 1979)

Minor-league scouting report: "Big guy. Throws like hell. Hitter can't see it. But he can't see you either. He's practically blind. Can't hit, field or run. Curve not much. Neither is sinker. Just throws fast one. Unpredictable where it'll go."
Source: *Late and Close: A History of Relief Pitching* (Paul Votano, 2002)

JESSE DURYEA 5'10" 175-pound righty
60-62, 3.45, 3 Saves 1889 1893

Key Pitch: Fastball
Sources: *The Sporting Life* (2/12/1890 and 3/26/1892)
Quote: "Ted [Sullivan, St. Paul owner] was favorably 'impressed' with Jim's terrific speed . . . It was Ted who dubbed Duryea the 'Cyclone,' and he still relates how Jim pitched a ball through a six-inch plank."
Source: *The Sporting Life* (2/12/1890)

FRANK DWYER 5'8" 145-pound righty
177-141, 3.84, 6 Saves 1888 1899

Pitch Selection: 1. Curves 2. Fastball
Description: "Dwyer did not have an overpowering fastball . . . But he could 'distribute an assortment of variegated curves, elipses, hyperbolae and parabolae with . . . judgement,' according to a St. Louis writer. He also had a nervous tic that caused him to wink his eye at the batter."
Source: *Baseball's First Stars* (SABR, 1996; article by Robert Tiemann)

JIMMY DYGERT 5'10" 115-pound righty
56-49, 2.65, 2 Saves 1905 1910

Key Pitch: Spitball
Source: 1911 *Reach Guide* (Page 224)

GEORGE EARNSHAW 6'4" 210-pound righty
127-93, 4.38, 12 Saves 1928 1936

Pitches, early career: 1. Fastball 2. Change 3. Curve (occasional)
Quotes: "Earnshaw is strictly a speed ball pitcher, and in his case speed is spelled with capital letters. There are no fancy frills, just a bullet-like delivery, with a perplexing change of pace.

" 'I have pitched more than one game,' says Earnshaw, 'in which I didn't use a single curve. All that I showed was my fast ball and a ball that wasn't so fast.'

" 'Once in a while,' says [A's catcher Mickey] Cochrane, 'Earnshaw uses a kind of half screw ball that is quite slow. He really has a beautiful change of pace. That makes his fast ball all the more unhittable.' "

Source: *Baseball Magazine* (November 1929, F.C. Lane)

Pitch Selection, middle career: 1. Fastball
2. Overhand Curve (25%)

Earnshaw: "I am tall and pitch with an overhand motion most of the time. My fast ball, which is my best ball, naturally sweeps low. Does the batter facing me prefer a low ball? Perhaps he does. I don't care. It's my best ball and that's what he'll get, if I can give it to him.

"I pitch an overhand curve that breaks sharply down. To be effective, that curve must also be low. The low ball hitter gets it just the same . . ."

"If there is anything original in my pitching style, it is my curve ball. There I think I am a little different. Perhaps twenty-five percent of the balls I pitch are curves. My curve is fast because I throw it in a way to get the maximum result with a minimum of effort. All the pitchers I have known snap their wrist in throwing a curve. This results in a kink in their elbow. In pitching a curve they let the ball slip out from the under side of the first two fingers of their pitching hand. In pitching a fast ball, they let it roll off the tips of these first two fingers.

"I throw a curve exactly the same way I throw a fast ball, only I hold my hand bottom side up. The back of my hand is roughly parallel to the ground when I release a curve ball. It doesn't slip out from under the side of my fingers, either. It rolls off the tips of my fingers. Mickey Cochrane has summed it up in one sentence when he says my curve ball is exactly like my fast ball, upside down.

"My style of pitching curves puts the minimum strain on the elbow and gives the greatest possible play to the wrist. It also produces a lot of speed. I've had batters swing at my curve ball when it hit the dirt in front of the plate. They misjudged it that badly."

Source: *Baseball Magazine* (September 1932, "Comprising an Interview with George Earnshaw")

Earnshaw: "I admire curve pitching and slower stuff myself, because I am strictly a speed pitcher. Generally you admire what you haven't got."

Source: *Baseball Magazine* (January 1934, F.C. Lane)

Note: *Baseball Players and Their Times* (Eugene Murdock, 1991) quotes an unidentified *Baseball Magazine* writer as saying that Ted Lyons "does not possess Earnshaw's blinding speed."

Quote: "Earnshaw's blinding speed, particularly in World's Series games, is still a live topic."

Source: *Baseball Magazine* (February 1930)

Quote: "Grove's best pitch is his speed ball. Earnshaw's is his curve."

Source: Athletics catcher Cy Perkins in *Baseball Magazine* (October 1930, F.C. Lane) . . . and Perkins was in a pretty good position to know (even though by that time he rarely played).

Quote: "The best fast curve ball I ever saw belonged to George Earnshaw. The curve of most pitchers cannot compare in speed with a fast ball, but Earnshaw's could."

Source: Longtime Giants scout John Ogden in *The Sporting News* (11/16/1963, Lee Allen's "Cooperstown Corner" column)

Quote: "George Earnshaw . . . had a great curve ball. The nearest thing to him in recent years was Koufax."

Source: Jocko Conlan in *Jocko* (Conlan and Robert Creamer, 1967)

Commentary: Editorializing just a bit, it's clear that various people were awed by Earnshaw for various reasons. He clearly had one of the better fastballs of his time, a curve among the most impressive in the game, and a change-up that apparently behaved something like Pedro Martinez's. Earnshaw was an outstanding pitcher for three years.

JAMIE EASTERLY 5'9" 180-pound lefty
23-33, 4.62, 14 Saves 1974 1987

Pitch Selection: 1. Fastball (87) 2. Hard Slider
3. Curve (occasional) 4. Change (occasional)

Source: *The Scouting Report: 1984*

RAWLY EASTWICK 6'3" 180-pound righty
28-27, 3.31, 68 Saves 1974 1981

Pitch Selection, 1974–78: 1. Sinking Fastball 2. Slider
3. Change

Sources: *Men of the Machine* (Ritter Collett, 1977); *The Sporting News* (10/28/1978, Ray Kelley; 3/31/1979, Hal Bodley)

Pitch Selection, 1980–81: 1. Split-Fingered Fastball
2. Fastball 3. Change

Sources: *The Sporting News* (4/18/1981, Joe Goddard);

Herm Starrette in *Philadelphia Bulletin* (4/6/1980); unidentified clipping of article by Ray Didinger (TSN Morgue)

Comment: "Phillie reliever Rawley Eastwick has experimented with the split-fingered fastball this season—and used it to beat Sutter last week—but he is still wary of using it in critical situations . . ."
Source: *Sports Illustrated* (9/17/1979, Ron Fimrite)

DENNIS ECKERSLEY 6'2" 190-pound righty
197-171, 3.50, 390 Saves 1975 1998

Pitch Selection, as Starter: 1. Fastball 2. Curve 3. Slider
Pitch Selection, as Reliever: 1. Fastball 2. Slider
Note: Eckersley threw between three-quarters and sidearm.
Sources: *The Scouting Report* (1987 and 1990 editions); *Tom Seaver's 1989 Scouting Notebook*

Description: "With a whip-like delivery, he lives on the black, willing to pitch inside but going away when he needs an out. Eckersley uses his fastball on right-handed hitters and goes after lefties with his slider. His reputation and quick work give him marginal calls, making batters swing at pitches just off the plate."
Source: *Bill Mazeroski's Baseball* (1993 edition)

HOWARD EHMKE 6'3" 190-pound righty
166-166, 3.75, 14 Saves 1915 1930

Pitch Selection: 1. Fastball 2. Change of Pace 3. Curve
Sources: *Baseball Magazine* (May 1924, F.C. Lane); *Baseball's Famous Pitchers* (Ira L. Smith, 1954); *The No-Hit Hall of Fame* (Rich Coberly, 1985); 1924 *Reach Guide*

Note: Ehmke threw sidearm. In the 1924 *Reach Guide,* Joe Tinker implicitly cites Ehmke as having one of the best curves in baseball. At the time pitchers were complaining that the "fresh" baseballs kept constantly in play were impossible to grip properly, and thus impossible to throw good curves with. Tinker pooh-poohed this theory, saying that "Howard Ehmke and Sam Jones certainly made it break beautifully. They made it talk." (p. 193) However, the best source, the article by F.C. Lane in *Baseball Magazine,* explicitly states that "Ehmke pitches some curves, though not many."

Quote from Lane article: "Probably he has the slimmest pitching arm of anyone in the Major Leagues. One day while he was conversing with the late President Harding, the President took hold of his pitching arm and said: "I don't see where all the power comes from." Nevertheless, there is in that long, bony right arm of his a snap like a steel spring."

Comment: "Some pitchers resort to eccentric movements in an attempt to disconcert the batsman. This brings to mind Alex Ferguson, who pitched for Washington a few years ago. In every wind-up, he used a little twist of the wrist motion, similar to that employed by the sleight of hand artist. Ehmke of the Athletics, is the originator of the 'hesitation' delivery that he effects by coming to a slight pause after he takes the forward step in his effort to the plate . . ."
Source: *Baseball Magazine* (July 1927, umpire George Moriarty)

Quote: "He never once shot a fast ball at the Cubs. In fact, there is no fast one anymore. The fastest he has is merely a change of pace ball for the faster pitchers. He used a slow, hesitating curve. He used a sharp-breaking, shoulder high 'duster.' He curved a cross-fire, inside. He threw a floating outside curve. But NOT ONCE did the Cubs get a good ball to hit."
Babe Ruth: "I've always thought Ehmke was one of the smartest pitchers in baseball and wished many times he was with the Yankees. But who ever had an idea he could throw curves like that. He was a right handed Pennock today. And that's the greatest compliment I can pay him."
Source: *Baseball Magazine* (December 1929, Franklin W. Yeutter) reporting on Ehmke's victory over the Cubs in Game 1 of the '29 World Series, by which point Ehmke's once-vaunted fastball was long gone.

Description: "Ehmke's arm is about as large as a bill clerk's wrist. He is so long and bony that one is led to strain his ears to hear him rattle when he walks. But Ehmke, in spite of his emaciated appearance, is a sterling hurler, with much more than average speed, in his prime . . ."
Source: *Baseball Magazine* (July 1930, F.C. Lane)

Description: "Howard Ehmke was another pitcher with a lot of stuff who employed pitching psychology whenever it would serve his purpose. Ehmke had an angular wind-up that suggested a professional contortionist. His

thin arms and legs sprawled all over the landscape, or so it seemed to the harassed batter. Ehmke had a trick of delivering the ball so that it came at the batter against this background of undulating arms and legs. When he was in form and had his control, he was a difficult proposition, indeed. But one of his chief assets was his aptitude in diverting the batter's mind from the task in hand—namely, keeping his eyes on the ball."
Source: *Baseball Magazine* (January 1937, F.C. Lane)

JUAN EICHELBERGER 6'2" 195-pound righty
26-36, 4.10, 0 Saves 1978 1988

Pitches: 1. Fastball 2. Curve 3. Slider 4. Change 5. Sinker (occasional)
Source: *The Scouting Report: 1983*

MARK EICHHORN 6'4" 200-pound righty
48-43, 3.00, 32 Saves 1982 1996

Pitch Selection: 1. Slow, Slow Change 2. Fastball 3. Slider
Sources: *The Scouting Report* (1987 and 1992 editions)

Note: Eichhorn threw from a low sidearm/submarine angle as a result of a shoulder injury in 1983.

Quote: "Normally hitters argue about how hard a pitcher throws but in Eichhorn's case, the opposite is true. Even the most veteran hitters say they have never seen a major league pitcher throw a pitch as *slow* as Eichhorn does."
Source: *The Scouting Report: 1987*

HARRY EISENSTAT 5'11" 185-pound lefty
25-27, 3.84, 14 Saves 1935 1942

Key Pitch: Curve Ball

Description: "Harry Eisenstat, a stocky left-hander with a tantalizing curve ball . . . He had enough heart to make up for the lack of a fast ball."
Source: *The Cleveland Indians* (Franklin Lewis, 1949)

SCOTT ELARTON 6'8" 240-pound righty
36-27, 5.03, 3 Saves 1998 2003

Pitch Selection: 1. Sinking Fastball (92–93) 2. Curve 3. Straight Change
Note: Experimented with a slider in 2000.
Sources: *The Scouting Notebook* (1999 and 2001 editions)

CAL ELDRED 6'4" 215-pound righty
81-72, 4.52, 8 Saves 1991 2003

Pitch Selection: 1. Fastball 2. Overhand Curve 3. Change
Sources: *The Scouting Report: 1993* and *The Scouting Notebook 1998*

RUBE ELDRIDGE
MINOR LEAGUES 1904 1934

Pitch Selection: 1. Knuckle Ball 2. Change 3. Fastball
Source: *Fiery Fastball: The Life and Times of Johnny Allen, World Series Pitcher* (Wint Capel, 2001)

Note: Eldridge never pitched in the major leagues, but won 285 games in the minors. His description of his fastball: "I never had no frightening fastball. But sometimes when I was stinking sweaty, I could throw real hard in a pinch."

HOD ELLER 5'11" 185-pound righty
60-40, 2.62, 5 Saves 1917 1921

Key Pitch: Shine Ball
Note: Eller's career basically ended with the outlawing of his best pitch.
Sources: *The Cincinnati Reds* (Lee Allen, 1948); 1924 *Reach Guide* also specifies that Eller threw the Shine Ball (page 47), as does John Lardner in *The Saturday Evening Post* (6/17/1950). In *Baseball's Greatest Teams* (1949), Tom Meany says Eller "specialized in trick deliveries."

JUMBO ELLIOTT 6'3" 235-pound lefty
63-74, 4.24, 12 Saves 1923 1934

Pitch Selection: 1. Fastball 2. Change 3. Curve (occasional)
Sources: *Brooklyn Daily Eagle* (7/31/1925); *Baseball Magazine* (June 1928); unidentified clipping from the Hall of Fame Library

Quote: "He has terrific speed when he chooses to use it and a curve ball that breaks quickly."
Source: *Brooklyn Daily Eagle* (7/31/1925)

Quote: "He has a beautiful fast ball . . . Elliott's favorite ball is a fast ball. This is a deceptive delivery and won the instant respect of the best hitters in the National circuit . . . Somehow he can sneak over that fast ball of his from around his huge bulk so that it seems to be halfway to home plate before the batter ever gets a glimpse of it. Elliott makes the delivery still more effective by change of pace. 'I pitch the same way,' he says, 'but sometimes I'll hold back a little on the ball and it won't come so fast.' Elliott also throws curve balls, but he doesn't like them particularly [because they are] hard on the arm."
Source: *Baseball Magazine* (June 1928)

Quote: "With the power he can easily put behind a ball, and his loose-jointed supple delivery, his left-handed slants and hooks are very hard to fathom."
Source: unidentified clipping from the Hall of Fame Library

DOCK ELLIS 6'3" 205-pound righty
138-119, 3.46, 1 Save 1968 1979

Pitches: 1. Sinking Fastball 2. Slider 3. Curve 4. Change 5. Palmball
Sources: *Dock Ellis in the Country of Baseball* (Donald Hall with Ellis, 1976); *The Sporting News* (8/21/1971, Page 3)

SAMMY ELLIS 6'1" 175-pound righty
63-58, 4.15, 18 Saves 1962 1969

Pitches: 1. Curve 2. Fastball 3. Slider
Source: *Baseball Digest* (March 1963, Page 9)
Note: *Major League Baseball 1965* (Jack Zanger) says that Ellis has "a flaming fastball and a snapping curve."

DICK ELLSWORTH 6'3" 180-pound lefty
115-137, 3.72, 5 Saves 1958 1971

Pitches: 1. Sinker 2. Slider (developed in 1963) 3. Curve 4. Fastball 5. Change
Sources: *Sport* (December 1963, George Vecsey); *Baseball Stars of 1964* (article by Robert G. Deindorfer); *Take Me Out to the Cubs Game* (John C. Skipper, 2000)

Note: *View From the Dugout* (Ed Richter, 1963) describes Ellsworth as a "fastballer" and says that "his fastball was blazing" in one particular game.

DON ELSTON 6'0" 165-pound righty
49-54, 3.69, 63 Saves 1953 1964

Pitches: 1. Fastball 2. Curve 3. Knuckleball 4. Screwball 5. Blooper (*very* occasional)
Note: Elston threw a Blooper Pitch about a half-dozen times a year.
Sources: *Baseball Digest* (August 1959, Si Burick); *The Sporting News* (5/24/1961, Jerome Holtzman)

Note: Elston was the first pitcher for whom "Saves" were figured. Jerome Holtzman, who was covering the Cubs in Elston's heyday, developed "saves" as a way of tracking Elston's contribution to the team.

ALAN EMBREE 6'3" 185-pound lefty
26-26, 4.43, 7 Saves 1992 2003

Pitch Selection: 1. Fastball (low-90s) 2. Slider
Source: *The Scouting Notebook: 1996*

RED EMBREE 6'0" 165-pound righty
31-48, 3.72, 1 Save 1941 1949

Key Pitch: Curve
Source: *Baseball Magazine* (July 1946, Ed McAuley)

EDDIE ERAUTT 5'11" 185-pound righty
15-23, 4.86, 2 Saves 1947 1953

Key Pitch: Fastball
Source: *Pacific Coast League Baseball News* (6/15/1947)

PAUL ERICKSON 6'2" 200-pound righty
37-48, 3.86, 6 Saves 1941 1948

Pitch Selection: 1. Fastball 2. Slow Curve
Source: *The Cubs Win the Pennant!* (John C. Skipper, 2004)

SCOTT ERICKSON 6'4" 220-pound righty
140-128, 4.51, 0 Saves 1990 2002

Pitch Selection, 1990–1992:
1. Hard, Hard Sinking Fastball 2. Change 3. Overhand Curve
Pitch Selection, as mature pitcher:
1. Hard, Sinking Two-Seam Fastball 2. Slider 3. Three-Quarters Curve 4. Change
Sources: *The Scouting Report: 1992* and *The Scouting Notebook 1999*

Commentary: As a young pitcher Erickson would vault off the mound so that his right knee actually dragged the ground just in front of the mound. Later he didn't do that, but he has other unique features. He'll switch his pitching patterns in mid-season. He'll beat people for a couple of months with that phenomenal sinking fastball, then he'll hit a rough patch and switch to throwing something else, using the fastball to set up a change as a strikeout pitch, for example, or using the change to set up the slider. He's one of a kind. Kevin Brown is the only guy in the majors who is even remotely like him.

CARL ERSKINE 5'10" 165-pound righty
122-78, 4.00, 13 Saves **1948 1959**

Pitch Selection: 1. Fastball 2. "Rainbow" Curve
3. Change
Sources: *Bums* (Peter Golenbock, 1984); *Baseball Stars of 1954*

Pitch Selection: 1. Fastball 2. Slider 3. Curve
4. Change
Source: Erskine quoted in *The No-Hit Hall of Fame* (Rich Coberly, 1985)

Whitey Herzog: "Carl Erskine . . . was known throughout baseball for a breaking ball that swooped down on you like a falcon on a chipmunk."
Source: *You're Missin' a Great Game* (Herzog and Jonathan Pitts, 1999)

Enos Slaughter: "I'm sure I got my hits off him, but Carl Erskine was one guy who caused me problems. He caused me as much trouble as anybody in the National League. He had a good, live fastball, a good change and two different kinds of curves. He was tough."
Source: *Redbirds Revisited* (David Craft and Tom Owens, 1990)

Enos Slaughter: "Most curveballers from the right side have trouble with lefties, but not him. He came right over the top, and that ball didn't take prisoners when he got it where he wanted it."
Source: *The Greatest Team of All Time* (Nicholas Acocella and Donald Dewey, 1994)

Note: Listed by *The Sporting News* (8/29/1956) as having one of the best fastballs in the league.

KELVIM ESCOBAR 6'1" 210-pound righty
58-55, 4.58, 58 Saves **1997 2003**

Pitches: 1. Four-Seam Fastball (mid-90s)
2. Split-Fingered Fastball (high-80s)
3. Two-Seam Fastball (low-90s) 4. Curve
5. Change 6. Cut Fastball (88–90; added 2002)
Sources: *The Scouting Notebook* (1998–2003 editions)

SHAWN ESTES 6'2" 185-pound lefty
77-73, 4.53, 0 Saves **1995 2003**

Pitches, 1995–2000: 1. Hard Curve
2. Four-Seam Fastball (91–95)
3. Two-Seam Fastball (88–90) 4. Change
Pitches, 2001–2002: 1. 12-to-6 Curve
2. Fastball (mid-80s) 3. Sinking Change
4. Cut Fastball
Sources: *The Scouting Notebook* (1997–2003 editions)

CHUCK ESTRADA 6'1" 185-pound righty
50-44, 4.07, 2 Saves **1960 1967**

Key Pitch: High Fastball
Source: *From 33rd Street to Camden Yards* (John Eisenberg, 2001)

BILL EVANS 6'2" 180-pound righty
0-1, 4.98, 0 Saves **1949 1951**

Key Pitch: Sinker
Source: *Pacific Coast Baseball News* (7/25/1950)

BOB EWING 6'1" 170-pound righty
124-118, 2.49, 4 Saves **1902 1912**

Key Pitch: Spitball
Source: *Deadball Stars of the National League* (SABR, 2004)

Quote: "Ewing pitches with tremendous speed."
Source: *The National Game* (Alfred H. Spink, 1911)

RED FABER 6'2" 180-pound righty
254-213, 3.15, 29 Saves **1914 1933**

Pitch Selection: 1. Spitball 2. Sinking Fastball
3. Curve
Note: Faber was one of the "grandfathered" pitchers who were allowed to continue to throw the spitball after it was otherwise banned in 1921.

Sources: *Baseball's Famous Pitchers* (Ira Smith, 1954); *My Baseball Diary* (James T. Farrell, 1957); Ted Lyons in *Baseball Players and Their Times* (Eugene Murdock, 1991); 1923 *Reach Guide* (Page 38); 1924 *Reach Guide* (Page 48)

Quote from 1924 *Reach:* "Coveleskie is dependent entirely on (the spitball) for his success, while the same is largely true of Faber."

Ray Hayworth: ". . . Red Faber could break his spitter down or away making it harder to hit . . . I heard Ty Cobb say one day when Faber was pitching against us in Detroit, 'that man is the toughest man I have ever hit against; the most difficult to hit"—because the ball just moves so fast your eye cannot adjust quickly enough to it."
Source: *Baseball Players and Their Times* (Eugene Murdock, 1991)

Faber: "A spitter has to be thrown moderately fast and the ball slips away from under the front two fingers of the pitching hand and sails up to the batter rotating very slowly. Then it breaks down and to one side . . . I never wet the ball but merely the ends of the first two fingers on my right hand. The whole theory of the spit ball is to let the ball slide away from a smooth surface. Wetting the fingers gives this smooth surface . . . A spit ball pitcher always chews something. It's an odd thing, but I have had to experiment with things to chew. Some spit ball pitchers use slippery elm. Slippery elm doesn't work with me. It's too slippery and I can't control the ball. I have tried chewing gum. But that wasn't quite slippery enough. So I have had to fall back on the good old custom, now much abused, of chewing tobacco. Tobacco juice fills the bill. And I don't chew it because I like it either. In fact, I never chew except when I am pitching. But it seems to be an indispensable part of my business like a mason's trowel or a carpenter's hammer.

"Of course I depend a great deal on the spit ball. But I do not use spitters exclusively. I throw a lot of fast balls and some curves. There are batters in this league who seem to like spitters. They have solved the problem of hitting under where the ball looks to be and meeting it as it breaks. There are batters that I wouldn't give a spitter to in a pinch, I would feed them a curve . . ."
Source: *Baseball Magazine* (September 1922, "comprising an interview with Red Faber")

ELROY FACE 5'8" 155-pound righty
104-95, 3.48, 193 Saves 1953 1969

Pitch Selection, 1953: 1. Fastball 2. Curve
Pitch Selection, 1955–1956: 1. Forkball 2. Fastball 3. Curve
Pitch Selection, 1957 on: 1. Forkball 2. Fastball 3. Slider 4. Curve
Note: Face developed his forkball in 1954, when Branch Rickey sent him to New Orleans to work on an off-speed pitch.
Source: *Maz and the '60 Bucs* (Jim O'Brien, 1993)
Other Sources: See below.

Face: "I think I was the only one at that time throwing [the forkball]. They accused me of throwing a spitball, because it would sink. If it was working I might use it sixty or seventy percent of the time. If it wasn't, I may have used it twenty percent."
Source: *Twin Killing: The Bill Mazeroski Story* (John T. Bird, 1995)

Face: ". . . Because I had good control, I threw all pitches on all counts. I'd throw harder stuff to a breaking-ball hitter and more breaking stuff to a fastball hitter. I didn't have a real pattern. If a guy had me timed on the fastball, I might throw my slider at the same speed and the little bit of movement took the ball to the end of the bat instead of the sweet part. If my forkball was working I might throw it 70 percent of the time. Even if my forkball didn't work, I'd throw it around 30 percent of the time to keep batters honest. There was no such thing as a good forkball hitter. Some batters would swing a foot over it. I was hurt by hanging curves and sliders but not with the forkball, if it broke properly."
Source: *We Played the Game* (Danny Peary, 1994)

Pitch Selection: 1. Slider 2. Curve 3. Sneaky Fastball
Source: *Sport* (September 1957, Page 72); considering the other sources, this must be considered with great skepticism.

PETE FALCONE 6'2" 185-pound lefty
70-90, 4.07, 7 Saves 1975 1984

Pitch Selection: 1. Knuckle Curve 2. Palm ball
Source: *The Sporting News* (5/3/1975, Pat Frizzell)

CY FALKENBERG 6'5" 180-pound righty
130-123, 2.68, 8 Saves 1903 1917

Key Pitch, 1903–1911: Fadeaway
Key Pitch, 1913–1917: Emery Ball?
Sources: *Touching Second* (John J. Evers and Hugh S. Fullerton, 1910); *The Sporting News* (10/1/1914); interview with Russ Ford in *The Sporting News* (April, 1935)

Note: Falkenberg denied in the 1914 TSN interview that he threw the emery ball. However, Russ Ford in 1935 claimed that Falkenberg did indeed throw the emery ball, and that it was taught to him by one of Ford's old Yankee teammates (unnamed).

Pitches: 1. Fall-Away 2. Fastball 3. Curve
Falkenberg: "I never think of my curve ball. I don't think I have much of a curve—just a wrinkle at best. I have tried the spit ball, but never with any brilliant success. I never use it in a game.

"My best ball is a fall-away. It is a slow ball, not so very slow, but it has a good break. I use a great many of these fall-away balls in the course of a game, but at that I don't depend upon them so much. Perhaps fifty per cent of the balls I pitch are of this variety but its main use is that it furnishes me with good change of pace."
Source: Falkenberg in *Baseball Magazine* (August 1913, F.C. Lane); it's quite possible that "fall-away" was Falkenberg's code name for his emery ball.

Description: "No one could call Falkenberg 'ideal' as to formation. He is built on bean-pole lines, stands several inches over 6 feet and carries just enough flesh to knit his bones together."
Source: *The Sporting News* (11/16/1911)

Description: "They tell me that this elongated veteran twirler could make a ball almost stop at will in midair about where he wished to, like a Hindoo magician."
Source: *Baseball Magazine* (August 1919, Charles Webb Murphy, "Why Freak Deliveries Must Go")

Quote: "I always thought that a lot of old Cy Falkenburg's [*sic*] latter day effectiveness was due to the fact that he kept the ball just above or below the knee, rather than to the emery or shine ball with which he was credited."
Source: John B. Sheridan in unknown newspaper, dated March 28, 1929

ED FARMER 6'5" 200-pound righty
30-43, 4.30, 75 Saves 1971 1983

Pitch Selection: 1. Curve 2. Fastball (90)
3. Slider (occasional)
Tim McCarver: "Farmer's stuff has never been questioned; it's his consistency in throwing strikes."
Source: *The Scouting Notebook: 1983*
Comment: "Farmer's forte is changing speeds on his curve ball. 'He's the first relief pitcher I've ever seen with a curve like that,' said pitching coach Ron Schueler. 'Against Boston, he threw one to Jim Rice on a 1-2 count that Rice must have swung at three times.' "
Source: *The Sporting News* (6/14/1980, Joe Goddard)

STEVE FARR 5'10" 198-pound righty
48-45, 3.25, 132 Saves 1984 1994

Pitch Selection: 1. Fastball 2. Slider 3. Curve
Sources: *The Scouting Report* (1990 and 1992 editions)

JOHN FARRELL 6'4" 210-pound righty
36-46, 4.56, 0 Saves 1987 1996

Pitch Selection: 1. Fastball 2. Slider 3. Change
Source: *The Scouting Report: 1990*

TURK FARRELL 6'4" 215-pound righty
106-111, 3.45, 83 Saves 1956 1969

Pitch Selection: 1. Fastball 2. Slider 3. Slip Pitch
4. Spitball (occasional)
Sources: *Inside the Astrodome* (1965, Page 116), *Major League Baseball 1965* (Jack Zanger)

Note: Farrell had one of the best fastballs of his generation. On July 5, 1959, he appeared on the CBS pre-game show, which had arranged for him to be tested by a primitive radar devise. He threw three pitches, timed at 91.2, 94.0, and 93.5 miles per hour. Given a modern radar gun, he might get very different results.
Source: *The Sporting News* (7/15/1959)

Quote: " 'When sweat rolls off my arm, I apply it to the ball when I'm in a tight spot and want a strikeout,' Farrell said.

"Farrell told [Houston sportswriter Zarko] Franks he throws the spitball three or four times in a game. He said he learned how to do it from watching Lew Burdette of

the Milwaukee Braves, frequently accused of being a spitballer."
Source: *Los Angeles Times* (3/22/1962, UPI)

JEFF FASSERO 6'1" 180-pound lefty
113-108, 4.00, 25 Saves 1991 2003

Pitch Selection: 1. Sinking Fastball 2. Forkball 3. Slider 4. Change or Slower Fastball
Sources: *The Scouting Notebook* (1997 and 1999 editions)

BILL FAUL 5'10" 184-pound righty
12-16, 4.71, 2 Saves 1962 1970

Key Pitch: Fastball
Description: "A side-arm motion, good fast ball, overwhelming desire and confidence that tells him 'I'm the best' could earn him a permanent berth."
Source: *Don Schiffer's Major League Baseball Handbook—1964*

BOB FELLER 6'0" 185-pound righty
266-162, 3.25, 21 Saves 1936 1956

Pitch Selection, 1936–1942: 1. Fastball 2. Curve
Pitch Selection, mid-'40s (at least): 1. Fastball 2. Curve 3. Slider
Pitch Selection, late career: 1. Fastball 2. Slider 3. Curve 4. Change
Sources: Too numerous to catalog, but including *Pitching to Win* (Feller, 1948); *Baseball's Famous Pitchers* (Ira Smith, 1954); and *Stan Musial: The Man's Own Story* (Musial with Bob Broeg, 1964)

Feller on his motion: "In the early stages of my career, I used an extraordinarily high left leg kick, but I gave it up. It tended to destroy balance and it added little speed, if any."
Source: *The Hurlers* (Kevin Kerrane, 1989)

Note: *The Sporting News* of September 7, 1974, reported that Feller threw a fastball clocked at 98.6 miles per hour in 1946, which was the record speed until broken by Nolan Ryan.

Phil Rizzuto: "Every time I thought I had Feller's fastball timed he would blink at me and one of those big overhand curves of his would come out of the white shirts in center field and I'd be out again."
Source: *The Greatest Team of All Time* (Nicholas Acocella and Donald Dewey, 1994)

Note: In a 1953 interview which is included on a videotape of highlights from the 1948 World Series, Feller, interviewed by Marty Glickman, lists his pitches at that time as 1. Fastball 2. Slider 3. Curve 4. Change, and says that he has been working on a sinker and a knuckleball.

ALEX FERGUSON 6'0" 180-pound righty
61-85, 4.93, 10 Saves 1918 1929

Pitch Selection: 1. Curve 2. Fastball
Description: "Ferguson has a nice curve ball and a fair amount of speed."
Source: newspaper article by William S. Hennigan, datelined Feb. 26, 1921

Key Pitch: Screwball
Quote: "He's a screw ball pitcher, but he hasn't developed a curve. Give him a curve, and he'll be a world beater."
Source: Miller Huggins in 1921 Fred Lieb column from Hall of Fame files

Key Pitch: Forkball
Source: *Who's Who in Baseball History* (Lloyd Johnson and Brenda Ward, 1994)

Commentary: We've obviously got contradictory information about Ferguson, but the first source listed doesn't seem particularly dependable, and our best guess is that in 1921, when Ferguson got his first real taste of major-league action, the screwball was his best pitch (assuming that Miller Huggins, Ferguson's manager, was accurately quoted by Lieb). In 1922 he was traded to the Red Sox, where he may well have learned the forkball from teammate Benn Karr, who had probably learned it the year before from Joe Bush (who went to the Yankees in the trade that sent Ferguson to the Red Sox). And yes, this is more speculating than we generally prefer to engage in.

Description: "Some pitchers resort to eccentric movements in an attempt to disconcert the batsman. This brings to mind Alex Ferguson, who pitched for Washington a few years ago. In every wind-up, he used a little twist of the wrist motion, similar to that employed by the sleight of hand artist."

Source: *Baseball Magazine* (July 1927, umpire George Moriarty's column)

CHARLIE FERGUSON 6'0" 165-pound righty
99-64, 2.67, 4 Saves 1884 1887

Key Pitch: Fastball
Quote: "Ferguson was perhaps the greatest pitcher that ever lived. He combined all the points to make him great. He had a magnificent arm, a clear eye, pluck and control. He could throw a ball with terrific speed, and he had absolute control of the sphere at all times."
Source: *The National Game* (Al Spink, 1911)

Quote: "When first facing a batsman Ferguson stands awkwardly, and the half dozen balls delivered at the beginning of the game give a very imperfect idea of his work when finally warmed up. Casting aside all superfluous gestures, he walks rapidly through the box and throws the ball with arm bent at the elbow and held at right angles to the body. His arm does not go as far forward in the delivery as is usual among pitchers as speedy as Ferguson, the sphere being sent in with a short, overhand jerk."
Source: Article titled "How Men Pitch Base-Ball: The Famous Pitchers of the National League of 1886." No author or publisher is given, though the information in the article is said to have come from photographic studies done by the *New York World* newspaper.

GEORGE FERGUSON 5'10" 165-pound righty
29-47, 3.34, 8 Saves 1906 1911

Key Pitch: Curve
Source: *Touching Second* (John J. Evers and Hugh S. Fullerton, 1910)

ALEX FERNANDEZ 6'1" 205-pound righty
107-87, 3.74, 0 Saves 1990 2000

Pitch Selection: 1. Fastball 2. Curve 3. Slider 4. Change
Sources: *The 1994 Baseball Almanac; The Scouting Notebook 1998*

JARED FERNANDEZ 6'1" 225-pound righty
4-7, 4.26, 0 Saves 2001 2003

Pitches: 1. Knuckleball 2. Fastball 3. Slider
Fernandez: "I throw my knuckleball differently than they do. They dig their fingernails right in and do a push; I put my knuckles right on it and I throw it."
Source: *Cincinnati Enquirer* (7/15/2002, John Erardi)
Other Source: Fox Sports Cincinnati broadcast of Reds game, 7/19/2002

Commentary: Fernandez, unlike other contemporary knuckleball pitchers, actually grips the ball with his knuckles rather than his fingernails. Fernandez throws both a slow and hard knuckleball. He is probably the first pitcher to regularly throw a hard knuckleball—that is, in the low seventies—since Joe Niekro, and there's no telling who the last pitcher was to actually throw a knuckleball with his knuckles.

SID FERNANDEZ 6'1" 220-pound lefty
114-96, 3.36, 1 Save 1983 1997

Pitch Selection: 1. Rising Fastball 2. Slow Curve 3. Hard Curve 4. Change
Sources: *Tom Seaver's 1990 Scouting Notebook; The Scouting Report: 1990*

DON FERRARESE 5'9" 170-pound lefty
19-36, 4.00, 5 Saves 1955 1962

Pitches: 1. Overhand Curve 2. Fastball 3. Change (occasional)
Ferrarese: "I had an outstanding curveball, an overhand curve that broke straight down . . . Mine was a hard curve. My weakness was two things, as a major leaguer. First, [in]consistency. And secondly, I did not have a change-up that was worth a—Charlie Dressen tried to teach me a change like Johnny Podres threw. I had coaches everywhere, and managers, trying to teach me a damn change-up. And then when I did finally throw one, I was so excited I wasn't consistent. So therefore I was a power pitcher, even though I was a little guy. Every pitch I threw, I threw hard."
Source: Interview with Ferrarese (8/2/2003, Rob Neyer)

Quote: "[Paul] Richards has come up with a fast-ball phenom in Southpaw Don Ferrarese . . . Ferrarese throws a jet ball with sharp-breaking radar-controlled curve."
Source: *The Sporting News* (8/29/1956, Joe King)
Note: Ferrarese's name is pronounced "fer-EES-ee."

WES FERRELL 6'2" 195-pound righty
193-128, 4.04, 13 Saves 1927 1941

Pitches: 1. Fastball 2. Curve 3. Change 4. Change Curve 5. Slider
Source: Ferrell in *Baseball When the Grass Was Real* (Donald Honig, 1975)

Description: "His best ball, of course, is his fast ball. But he also has a most serviceable curve, such a curve as many pitchers fail to acquire in years of patient practice. And young and inexperienced as he is, he has developed a baffling change of pace."
Source: *Baseball Magazine* (March 1930, F.C. Lane)

Ferrell: "Anything I pitch to a batter is the best ball for that particular time. It makes no difference what your specialty may be—fast ball, curve or change of pace, you can't depend upon that specialty alone. I like a fast ball? Every pitcher does. But I depend just as much upon my curve and change of pace. Besides, my fast ball hasn't been so fast these last two years. By bearing down hard, I could show a batter, once in a while, that I still had my fast ball, but I couldn't keep the pace."
Source: *Baseball Magazine* (June 1933, F.C. Lane)

Note: According to *Total Baseball*, Ferrell lost his good fastball in 1933 and was forced to make the adjustment to junkballer. However, in the 1933 *Baseball Magazine* article, Ferrell claimed that his arm "started to go bad two years ago."

Ferrell in 1937: "I use a lot of slow curves and mix them up."
Source: *Baseball Magazine* (June 1937, John J. Ward)

TOM FERRICK 6'2" 220-pound righty
40-40, 3.47, 56 Saves 1941 1952

Pitch Selection: 1. Sinker 2. Slider 3. Forkball 4. Fastball (occasional)
Sources: *Baseball Digest* (January 1951, Milt Richman; and Dec.–Jan. 1961, Page 45)

BOO FERRISS 6'2" 208-pound righty
65-30, 3.64, 8 Saves 1945 1950

Pitch Selection: 1. Sinking Fastball 2. Slider
Source: Bobby Doerr in *Fenway* (Peter Golenbock, 1992)

Description: "I studied Dave Ferris [*sic*] carefully and came away from watching him and discussing pitching with him with certain new ideas. The main thing I learned about Ferris is contained in a remark made by an American League hitter. This hitter said: 'I know why I can't hit Ferris. He hides that ball behind his back and he uses his glove to shield the ball from the hitter. The glove screens the ball, and the hitter doesn't get a look at the ball at all until it is almost on top of him.' "
Source: Bert Dunne in *Play Ball!* (Doubleday and Co., 1947)

LOU FETTE 6'1" 200-pound righty
41-40, 3.15, 1 Save 1937 1945

Key Pitches: Curves
Description: "Fette has a curve for every hitter, it seems. He has a roundhouse and a dipsy-do, he has a sharp breaker and a lazy looper which loafs around that plate and gets the hitter to break his back in futile gesture, or go off fishing in foolish adventure.

"Fette hasn't enough speed to 'knock your hat off.' That is the expression among the players . . .

"Fette has about the finest curve ball I have seen since the Yankees flashed the wild Walter Beall on an astonished world. Beall had the wonder curve, but could not restrain it. Fette can make his geni obey. Control is one of his glorious superlatives."
Source: *Baseball Magazine* (September 1937, Daniel M. Daniel)

Description: "He is a deceiving pitcher. If you ask me for his particular strong point, I would say it was the 'sneak ball.' He stands out there on the mound, easy, loose-jointed, cool, pitching with apparently little effort. It is that 'apparently little effort' which deceives the opposing batter. He isn't looking for anything very difficult and all at once the ball comes sneaking over the plate for a strike."
Source: Braves coach Hank Gowdy in *Baseball Magazine* (September 1937, John J. Ward)

Comment: "Neither [Jim] Turner nor Fette was a strikeout pitcher. Both relied on good control. They kept the ball low, so that enemy batters hit the ball on the ground, which was kept damp and slow by the canny McKechnie."
Source: *The Boston Braves* (Harold Kaese, 1948)

Note: In 1937, Fette and Braves teammate Jim Turner were a big story, as both won twenty games as rookies in their thirties.

MIKE FETTERS 6'4" 200-pound righty
31-40, 3.73, 99 Saves 1989 2003

Pitch Selection, early 1990s: 1. Curve 2. Fastball 3. Slider
Pitch Selection, later in 1990s: 1. Split-Finger Fastball 2. Fastball
Sources: *The Scouting Report: 1993* and *The Scouting Notebook 1998*

MARK FIDRYCH 6'3" 175-pound righty
29-19, 3.10, 0 Saves 1976 1980

Pitches: 1. Fastball 2. Slider 3. Change
Source: Fidrych in *No Big Deal* (Fidrych and Tom Clark, 1977)

Roger Angell: "On the mound, Fidrych represented the classic profile and demeanor of a very young hurler—long legs and a skinny, pleasing gawkiness (he is six-three); a pre-delivery flurry of overexcited twitches, glances, and arm-loosening wiggles; and a burning anxiety to get rid of the ball, to see what would happen next, to get *on* with this, man! The results were something altogether different. His pitching was cool and intelligent, built around some middling-good fastballs and down-slanting sliders, all delivered with excellent control just above or below the hemline of the strike zone . . ."
Source: *Five Seasons* (Angell, 1977)

Ralph Houk: "He had unbelievable control with a fastball that moved. Breaking stuff wasn't really that great, but the ball always moved."
Rusty Staub: "Just hard slider, sinking fastball, hard slider, sinking fastball, and he just had location. On the mound, whatever the antics were, his concentration about where he wanted the ball to go was as good as anybody I ever saw."
Source: *Talkin' Baseball: An Oral History of Baseball in the 1970s* (Phil Pepe, 1998)

ED FIGUEROA 6'1" 190-pound righty
80-67, 3.51, 1 Save 1974 1981

Pitch Selection, 1974: 1. Fastball 2. Curve 3. Change
Pitch Selection, 1975–78: 1. Fastball 2. Slider 3. Sinker 4. Curve 5. Change
Pitch Selection, 1979–81: 1. Slider 2. Curve 3. Sinker 4. Change
Sources: *The Sporting News* (1/24/1976, Phil Pepe; and an article from 1981)

DANA FILLINGIM 5'10" 175-pound righty
47-73, 3.56, 5 Saves 1915 1925

Key Pitch: Spitball
Note: Fillingim was on the list of "grandfathered" pitchers allowed to continue to throw the spitball after it was otherwise banned in 1921.
Sources: 1923 *Reach Guide* (Page 38); 1924 *Reach Guide* (Page 47)

SIDD FINCH 6'3" 182-pound righty
2-0, 0.00, 0 Saves 1985 1985

Only Pitch: Fastball (168)
Mets catcher Ronn Reynolds: "A real good fastball will make a sound like ripping silk. But not Finch's. It just arrives. Or to put it another way, suddenly it's *there. Pft-boom!*"
Source: *The Curious Case of Sidd Finch* (George Plimpton, 1987)
Note: Finch faced fifty-three batters in his brief career, and struck out all fifty-three of them.

ROLLIE FINGERS 6'4" 190-pound righty
114-118, 2.90, 341 Saves 1968 1985

Pitch Selection: 1. Fastball 2. Slider 3. Forkball (developed in 1979)
Sources: *The Relief Pitcher* (John Thorn, 1979); *The Sporting News* (5/10/1980, Phil Collier); Tony Kubek in NBC broadcast of Brewers-Tigers game (10/3/1981)

CHUCK FINLEY 6'6" 220-pound lefty
200-173, 3.85, 0 Saves 1986 2002

Pitches: 1. Fastball 2. Change 3. Curve
4. Forkball (added in 1990)
5. Split-Fingered Fastball (added about 1992)
6. Slurve (added in mid-1990s)
Sources: *The Scouting Report: 1990; 1994 Baseball Almanac; The Scouting Notebook: 1998*

Note: According to the *Seattle Times* (10/15/2001), Finley in 2001 threw 50 percent fastballs, 28 percent changeups, 14 percent sliders and 8 percent curves. According to the same source, Finley threw three fastballs: a four-seamer thrown 85–87 m.p.h., a two-seamer with a slight sink at 83–85, and a cutter thrown 82–84. His curve was slow with an 11-to-5 break. His slider was a slurve thrown 72–78, and his changeup had "good sink/run."

STEVE FIREOVID 6'2" 195-pound righty
3-1, 3.39, 0 Saves 1981 1992

Pitches: 1. Fastball 2. Slider
3. Change-up (occasional)
Source: *The 26th Man: One Minor Leaguer's Pursuit of a Dream* (Fireovid and Mark Winegardner, 1991)

BILL FISCHER 6'0" 190-pound righty
45-58, 4.34, 13 Saves 1956 1964

Pitches, 1956–1961: 1. Sinker 2. Slider
Pitches, 1962: 1. Slow Curve (against left-handed hitters) 2. Sinker 3. Slider
Source: *Baseball Digest* (Oct.–Nov. 1962, Joe McGuff)

HANK FISCHER 6'0" 190-pound righty
30-39, 4.23, 7 Saves 1962 1967

Key Pitch: "Hopping Fast Ball"
Source: 1961 Milwaukee Braves Guide for Press/Radio/TV

BRIAN FISHER 6'4" 210-pound righty
36-34, 4.39, 23 Saves 1985 1992

Pitch Selection: 1. Fastball (90s) 2. Slider 3. Change
Note: This source clearly states that Fisher did not have a curve in 1986.
Source: *The Scouting Report: 1987*

Pitch Selection: 1. Fastball (high-80s) 2. Curve
3. Slider 4. Change
Source: *The Scouting Report: 1990*

EDDIE FISHER 6'2" 200-pound righty
85-70, 3.41, 81 Saves 1959 1973

Pitches: 1. Knuckleball 2. Curve 3. Slider
4. Fastball
Sources: *The Sporting News* (5/23/1964, Jerome Holtzman); *The Relief Pitcher* (John Thorn, 1979); *Sports Illustrated* (8/3/1959)

JACK FISHER 6'2" 215-pound righty
86-139, 4.06, 9 Saves 1959 1969

Pitch Selection: 1. Fastball 2. Curve 3. Slider
4. Change
Source: *Major League Baseball—1966* (Jack Zanger)

RAY FISHER 5'11" 180-pound righty
100-94, 2.82, 7 Saves 1910 1920

Key Pitch: Spitball
Note: Fisher was one of the "grandfathered" pitchers allowed to continue to throw the spitball after it was otherwise banned in 1921.
Sources: *The Crooked Pitch* (Martin Quigley, 1984); 1923 *Reach Guide* (Page 38)

AL FITZMORRIS 6'2" 190-pound righty
77-59, 3.65, 7 Saves 1969 1978

Pitch Selection: 1. Sinker 2. Slider
Sources: *The Sporting News* (6/29/1974, Sid Bordman; and 9/14/1974, Joe McGuff)

FREDDIE FITZSIMMONS 5'11" 185-pound righty
217-146, 3.51, 13 Saves 1925 1943

Pitch Selection: 1. Knuckleball 2. Fastball 3. Curve
Sources: *Baseball's Famous Pitchers* (Ira L. Smith, 1954), Jesse Haines in *Baseball Magazine* (February 1931)
Note: According to Haines, Fitzsimmons threw a *hard* knuckleball that broke straight down like a spitball, as Haines's did, rather than a "floater" like Eddie Rommel threw.

Description: "That Fitzsimmons was a fifth infielder on defense belied the pitcher's physical characteristics, which were more closely related to those of a hod-carrier or, athletically speaking, more like the circumferential dimensions of a shortwinded entry in a Fat Men's Bowling League.

Fitz was 'out to lunch' when necks were handed out. His head plumps squarely between wide shoulders of a bulging torso that dwarfs short legs. Pigeon-toed feet held up 210 pounds . . . as you could see any time Fat Freddie waddled out, his face aglow like a neon sign, to give an umpire a piece of his mind. Fitz's right arm, just in case you never noticed, is so crooked from a twenty-year supply of knucklers employed in baffling batters that it appears constantly akimbo, and the palm always faces in the direction from which Freddie has just trundled, giving him the appearance of a track relay man waiting for the baton to be passed to him.

Besides a girth absolutely not conducive to defensive agility, Fat Freddie included among his pitching assets a peculiar pivot. Just before delivering the ball, he swung completely around to face second base, thereby committing what for another pitcher would have been the cardinal sin of taking his eye off the target. . . . Nevertheless, Fitzsimmons was a great fielding pitcher."
Source: Bob Broeg and Bob Burrill, *Don't Bring THAT Up* (1946, A. S. Barnes and Company, page 23)

Description: "Freddy Fitzsimmons threw hard but he also had a knuckle-curveball."
Source: Harry Danning in *Dugout to Foxhole* (Rick Van Blair, 1994)

Fitzsimmons in 1953: "Nowadays these fellows call theirs the wobbly type. It doesn't turn like a curve. It floats. Some of them call it a floater. They never know which way it will break. Sometimes it breaks down and sometimes it breaks up. That's why they are so hard to catch.

"When I threw a knuckler—the right way—I pushed my two fingers forward and usually knew where the ball was going."
Source: *The Sporting News* (6/10/1953, Frank Eck)

Commentary: From Fitzsimmons' description, and Harry Danning calling Fitzsimmons' best pitch a "knuckle-curveball," we might reasonably assume that Fitzsimmons' knuckleball was actually the pitch later thrown by Burt Hooton and called the "knuckle curve."

Gabby Hartnett: "When Fitz was good he used to give you two knucklers and then come through with a high fast ball. The next time you would look for the fast one and he'd throw another knuckler. He was a whizz at giving you the pitch you weren't looking for at that particular time. When you were expecting a low breaking knuckle ball that high fast one would come and you wouldn't be ready to hit it. And when you did happen to get a knuckler when you were expecting it you would have to be lucky not to pound the ball into the dirt for an infield out."
Source: *Baseball Magazine* (November 1940, Edward T. Murphy)

Description: "Fitzsimmons has short fingers and, like all pitchers with short fingers, cramps them a great deal to bear down in an effort to get a spin to the ball. Fitzsimmons' speed is in reality the best qualification that a pitcher of his type has for major league success. With it he manages to get a certain amount of hop on the ball which makes itself manifest just as the ball reaches the batsman."
Source: *How to Pitch* (J.E. Wray, 1928)

Description: "Fitz has a peculiar delivery. He turns away from the batter before throwing. He has a fast ball of rare speed, but throws with an easy motion and the pellet is upon the batsman before he is aware of its approach. The late Addie Joss pitched that way with great effect."
Source: *Who's Who in Major League Baseball* (Harold "Speed" Johnson, 1933)

Description: "McGraw had seen Fitzsimmons at Indianapolis the previous spring. One of the Giants, in watching Fitzsimmons's strange delivery, remarked that the young pitcher 'looked like a guy swinging Indian clubs.' "
Source: *The Giants of the Polo Grounds* (Noel Hynd, 1988)

Fitzsimmons on his delivery: "There is real merit to the delivery. The batter, you know, has one thing in mind, to keep his eye on the ball. Even when the pitcher is indulging in his customary wind-up, swinging his arms around his head and all the rest of it, the batter watches that ball. But if you turn your back on him as I do, he loses sight of it. When he gets his next glimpse, the ball is already traveling towards him. From his viewpoint, it is disconcerting. That, of course, is what the pitcher wants. Never play into the batter's hands, and if you can bother him, do so.

"With my delivery, I have been reasonably successful. Take it away from me and I wouldn't gamble on my success. That's how important I rate it. And I don't think I'm overenthusiastic."
Source: *Baseball Magazine* (June 1935, F.C. Lane, "Freddy Fitzsimmons and his Freak Wind-Up")

Description: "Freddy Fitzsimmons . . . has a knuckle ball that sinks and he is listed as a heavy ball thrower. The batters pound his pitches into the dirt and when he is working infielders must be on the alert."
Source: *Baseball Magazine* (July 1941, Edward T. Murphy)

Description: "Incidentally, they say the Fitzsimmons butterfly was the fastest of its type ever thrown in the majors. It looked from the sidelines like a medium fast ball."
Source: Ed Rumill writing about the knuckleball in *Baseball Magazine* (September 1944)

Note: When active, Fitzsimmons was universally considered the best fielding pitcher in the majors.

PATSY FLAHERTY 5'8" 165-pound lefty
67-84, 3.10, 2 Saves 1899 1911

Key Pitch: Spitball
Source: *Honus Wagner: The Life of Baseball's "Flying Dutchman"* (Arthur D. Hittner, Page 131)

Description: "Pat Flaherty's return-ball was enough to set people raving. He would deliver the ball slowly and lazily; the catcher would fairly drive it back at him, and he would push it back with lightning quickness, getting the batsman totally unprepared."
Source: *Baseball Magazine* (November 1910, George Morton)

MIKE FLANAGAN 6'0" 185-pound lefty
167-143, 3.90, 4 Saves 1975 1992

Pitch Selection: 1. Slow Curve 2. Heavy Sinker 3. Fastball 4. Flanagan was taught a change by Scott McGregor in 1979.
Sources: *The Sporting News* (8/9/1980, Ken Nigro); *The Scouting Report: 1987;* Rick Dempsey in *From 33rd Street to Camden Yards* (John Eisenberg, 2001)

Rick Dempsey: "On the days he didn't have good stuff, he just kept coming at you. He would change his rhythm, change his speed, drop down, throw a sidearm curveball—use every weapon in his arsenal to get you out. And then on the days when he had good stuff, you had no chance against him."

DAVE FLEMING 6'3" 205-pound lefty
38-32, 4.67, 0 Saves 1991 1995

Pitches: 1. Fastball 2. Curve 3. Slider 4. Change
Lance Parrish: "You stand on the sideline, and it's pretty obvious he doesn't have a great fastball, or a great curve, or a great slider, but he knows what he's doing. He knows when to throw strikes, and he knows when to go outside the strike zone. He knows when to throw a hard curve, and when to throw a soft curve."
Source: *The Scouting Report: 1993*

JESSE FLORES 5'10" 175-pound righty
44-59, 3.18, 6 Saves 1942 1950

Pitch Selection, 1947: 1. Screwball 2. Fastball 3. Curve
Quote: "There's nothing to getting Jesse ready. He tosses that screwball just about as well the first day of the season as he does the last. He's fast enough when he has to be, has as good a curve ball as a pitcher needs and can 'thread a needle' with his screwball."
Source: Athletics pitching coach Earle Brucker in *Baseball Magazine* (September 1947, Frank Yeutter)

Pitch Selection, 1949: 1. Curve 2. Slider 3. Fastball
Quote: ". . . his curve ball, slider and fast one are working at their peak."
Source: *Pacific Coast Baseball News* (8/10/1949)

Key Pitch: Sinker
Quote: ". . . the chunky Mexican sinker specialist . . ."
Source: *Pacific Coast Baseball News* (8/25/1949)

Description: "Flores is not only the top winner in the majors, but the slowest worker. He is in a baseball sense the direct descendant of Slow Joe Doyle, who pitched for the Yankees from 1906 through 1910. In a day of low scores Slow Joe specialized in performances verging on the 2.45 limit. Doyle was just naturally slow. But Flores works that way to drive the batters daffy. He is far and away the most infuriating hurler in the big time."
Source: Dan Daniel in the New York *World-Telegram* (6/2/1943, "Daniel's Dope" column); Flores recorded his seventh win of the season in late May, but managed only five the rest of the way (the A's finished 49–105 that year).

BRYCE FLORIE 5'11" 195-pound righty
20-24, 4.47, 2 Saves 1994 2001

Pitch Selection: 1. Sinking Fastball (92–93) 2. Slider 3. Change

Description from the 1996 *Scouting Notebook:* "Florie's fastball normally tails down and away from left-handed hitters, but sometimes it simply drops and sometimes it comes in straight."

Source: *The Scouting Notebook* (1996 and 1999 editions)

RUSS FORD 5'11" 175-pound righty
99-71, 2.59, 9 Saves 1909 1915

Pitch Selection: 1. Scuff Ball 2. Spitball 3. Fastball 4. Knuckle Ball

Sources: *The National Game* (Alfred H. Spink, 1911); *Pitching in a Pinch* (Christy Mathewson, 1912)

Note: Ford is widely credited with inventing the scuff ball.

Key Pitch: Emery Ball

Quote: "Ford, a most intelligent fellow, had an odd delivery that was almost unhittable. He had an overhand swing that was noticeably good and his form was not up to that of the really great pitchers. Still he would send a ball up at the batter that would suddenly dart away. . . .

"Russel Ford was pitching in Atlanta one day when a wild pitch went over Catcher Sweeney's head and struck a concrete post. This roughed up one side of the ball. On the next pitch Sweeney noticed that the ball took a peculiar shoot and almost got away from him.

" 'What are you throwing?,' he asked Ford. 'It jumped half a foot.'

"Ford himself didn't know exactly but he began to study this odd phenomenon.

"After many experiments he reached the conclusion that the roughed up side of the ball caught the wind and the friction gave the ball a lopsided motion, causing it to veer off from a straight course at odd angles. . . .

"It was two years before we learned his trick.

"Russel Ford always wore a ring while pitching and he and Sweeney conceived the idea of having this ring made of emery. As a darkly mounted ring it did not attract unusual attention and nobody suspected its real purpose.

"For two years this mystery remained. Then (George) Kahler of Cleveland, having learned the trick some way in the minors, came up with it. Next (Cy) Falkenberg got it."

. . . "I forgot to say in discussing Russel Ford that he kept his secret a long time by pretending he was pitching a spitter. He would deliberately show his finger to the batter and then wet it with saliva."

Source: *Memoirs of Twenty Years in Baseball* (Ty Cobb, Pages 65–67, 70)

WHITEY FORD 5'10" 178-pound lefty
236-106, 2.75, 10 Saves 1950 1967

Pitch Selection: 1. Fastball 2. Curve 3. Change 4. Sinker 5. Slider (refined in 1961)
6. Ford developed a number of illegal pitches in the early sixties.

Sources: *Baseball Stars of 1964* (article by Paul Jablow); *Slick* (Whitey Ford with Phil Pepe, Page 192); *New York Times* (September 1968, Joe Durso)

Pitch Selection, mid-'50s: 1. Slider 2. Change 3. Fastball

Ford: "You'll see me throwing fast balls out there, but not half as many as you think. The fast ball isn't generally a pitch you can get the hitters out with. In that respect, I've had much better success with my slider and change. They're the pitches I go to when it comes right down to brass tacks."

Source: *Sport* (July 1956, Milton Richman)

Johnny Sain: "His pitches were more alive than Lopat's: there was an active spin on the ball. His breaking ball was very sharp. He had three speeds on his curveball. (What would really make him a great pitcher—in 1961 . . . was when he started sinking the ball and throwing more of a controlled breaking ball.)"

Source: *We Played the Game* (Danny Peary, 1994)

Elston Howard: "Ford's got a real good slider, one of the best, and it doesn't hurt his curve any. But his fast ball is real live. It goes up or sinks down and the slider going the other way lets him mix 'em up."

Source: *Baseball Digest* (January 1963)

Description: "Ford stands on the mound like a Fifth Avenue bank president. Tight-lipped, absolutely still between pitches, all business and concentration, he personifies the big-city, emotionless perfection of his team."

Source: Roger Angell in *The New Yorker* (October 1962, and reprinted in *The Summer Game*)

Listed by *The Sporting News* (8/29/1956) as having one of the best fastballs in the league.

Description: "[Whitey Ford] throws three-quarter-arm . . ."
Source: *Pitching* (Bob Shaw, 1972)
Also see Bob Friend

FRANK FOREMAN 6'0" 160-pound lefty
95-91, 3.94, 5 Saves 1884 1902

Pitch Selection: 1. Fastball 2. Curve of some sort 3. Drop Curve
Quote: "He has fairly good speed, but his curves and drops are not worth speaking about."
Source: clipping from the Hall of Fame Library (9/13/1890); the source is referred to as "F.I." and was describing Foreman's struggle to pitch with a broken finger.

MIKE FORNIELES 5'11" 155-pound righty
63-64, 3.96, 55 Saves 1952 1963

Pitches: 1–3. Fastball, Curve and Knuckleball 4–5. Slider and Screwball
Red Sox catcher Russ Nixon: "He's got five different pitches, and regardless of which one he throws, it's usually thrown for a strike . . . the pitch is working best for him on a particular day is the one he keeps throwing. Sometimes it's the fast ball; sometimes it's the curve or the knuckler."
Source: *The Sporting News* (10/14/1960, Hy Hurwitz)

BOB FORSCH 6'4" 200-pound righty
168-136, 3.76, 3 Saves 1974 1989

Pitch Selection: 1. Fastball 2. Curve 3. Change
Source: *The Sporting News* (8/23/1975, Neal Russo)

KEN FORSCH 6'4" 195-pound righty
114-113, 3.37, 51 Saves 1970 1986

Pitch Selection: 1. Slider 2. Forkball
Source: *The No-Hit Hall of Fame* (Rich Coberly, 1985)

TERRY FORSTER 6'3" 200-pound lefty
54-65, 3.23, 127 Saves 1971 1986

Pitch Selection: 1. Fastball 2. Slider 3. Change
Source: *The Scouting Report: 1987*

TONY FOSSAS 6'0" 195-pound lefty
17-24, 3.90, 7 Saves 1988 1999

Pitch Selection: 1. Slider 2. Tailing Fastball
Sources: *The Scouting Report: 1992* and *The Scouting Notebook 1998*

ALAN FOSTER 6'0" 180-pound righty
48-63, 3.74, 0 Saves 1967 1976

Pitch Selection: 1. Fastball 2. Curve
Ted Simmons: "Foster had a very live fastball and an excellent curveball."
Source: Phone interview with Simmons (10/8/2002, Rob Neyer)

Note: Foster pitched consecutive no-hitters against Seattle in 1967.

BILL FOSTER 6'1" 195-pound lefty
NEGRO LEAGUES 1923 1938

Pitches: 1. Fastball 2. Overhand Curve 3. Slider 4. Sidearm Curve 5. Change
Foster: "I had a pretty good fast ball, and I had a good overhand curve ball, which was known as the 'drop' ball. And then I had what they call sliders now. I had what is called a sidearm curve ball—palm down. I had a slider, an 'out-shoot' and a curve ball all on the same pitch."
Source: *Voices from the Great Black Baseball Leagues* (John Holway, 1975)

Quote: "Willie Foster's greatness was that he had this terrific speed and a great, fast-breaking curve ball and a drop ball, and he was really a master of the change-of-pace. He could throw you a real fast one and then use the same motion and bring it up a little slower, and then a little slower yet. And then he'd use the same motion again, and Z-zzzz!"
Source: Dave Malarcher in *Only the Ball Was White* (Robert W. Peterson, 1970)

Additional Source: *The Biographical Encyclopedia of the Negro Baseball Leagues* (James A. Riley, 1994)

KEVIN FOSTER 6'1" 175-pound righty
32-30, 4.86, 0 Saves 1993 2001

Pitches: 1. Four-Seam Fastball 2. Straight Change 3. Curve 4. Two-Seam Fastball (added 1997)
Source: *The Scouting Notebook* (1995 and 1998 editions)

RUBE FOSTER 6'2" 200-pound righty
NEGRO LEAGUES 1902 1926

Pitch Selection: 1. Fastball 2. Curves 3. Submarine Screwball
Sources: *The Best Pitcher in Baseball* (Robert Charles Cottrell, 2001); *The Biographical Encyclopedia of the Negro Baseball Leagues* (James A. Riley, 1994); Larry Lester in *The Negro Leagues Book* (ed. Dick Clark and Larry Lester, 1994)

Note: A number of sources—including two of John Holway's books and the Ken Burns documentary—report that Christy Mathewson learned his fadeaway pitch from Foster. However, clearly that's not what happened. Foster apparently picked up the pitch in 1902, while Mathewson learned it from minor-league pitcher Dave Williams in 1898.
Sources: Larry Lester in *The Negro Leagues Book;* Dick Thompson in *The Baseball Research Journal 25* (SABR, 1996)

Foster: "Some pitchers when they have three balls and two strikes on a batter, often bring the ball straight over the plate and as the batter is always looking for it that way he will possibly 'break up' the game for you. I use a curve ball mostly when in the hole. In the first place, the batter is not looking for it, and secondly, they will hit at a curve quicker as it may come over the plate, and if not, they are liable to be fooled . . ."
Source: *Sol White's Official Base Ball Guide* (1908)

Description: "Foster, the Great, was in prime form. A girl in the grandstand proclaimed him 'Procrastination' Foster. He had such an aggravating way of taking his time. He is a man of huge frame. His arms are like those of a windmill. He would swing them like the pendulum of a clock, looking the while, about the diamond. Suddenly he would twist up like a Missouri grasshopper about to make a spring and the ball would shoot from the pitcher's box . . ."
Source: *Philadelphia Item* (3/5/1915)

STEVE FOUCAULT 6'0" 205-pound righty
35-36, 3.21, 52 Saves 1973 1978

Pitch Selection: 1. Sidearm Curve 2. Fastball
Source: *The Sporting News* (6/8/1974, Merle Heryford)

KEITH FOULKE 6'0" 210-pound righty
28-25, 3.16, 143 Saves 1997 2003

Pitches, 1997–1998: 1. Sinker 2. Slider 3. Fastball
Pitches, 1999–2003: 1. Straight Change (75) 2. Fastball (85–91)
Note: The 2001 edition of *The Scouting Notebook* says that Foulke throws breaking pitches to right-handed batters, but recent sources agree that he throws his fastball and outstanding change-up—basically a palmball—almost exclusively.
Sources: *The Scouting Notebook* (1998–2003 editions); observation of ESPN broadcast of Athletics–Red Sox game, 10/1/2003.

DAVE FOUTZ 6'2" 161-pound righty
146-66, 2.84, 5 Saves 1884 1894

Pitch Selection: 1. Fastball 2. Curve
Note: Foutz threw sidearm.
Sources: *The National Game* (Alfred H. Spink, 1911); *Nineteenth Century Stars* (SABR, 1989, article by Robert L. Tiemann)

Quote from Spink: "Foutz was perhaps the tallest and slimmest pitcher in the history of the game. He was from all outward appearances a consumptive. But despite his appearance he was the possessor of considerable strength and [was] one of the speediest of pitchers . . . As a thoroughly gentlemanly player Foutz had few equals on the diamond. In his whole career no one ever saw him lose his temper or heard him speak a harsh word to his most formidable opponent."

ART FOWLER 5'11" 180-pound righty
54-51, 4.03, 32 Saves 1954 1964

Pitch Selection: 1. Fastball 2. Slider 3. Breaking Pitch
Quote: "All he'd do was throw a little fastball and hold it a little off-center and it would sail. He had such great control that he could throw it through knotholes."
Source: Billy Moran in *We Played the Game* (Danny Peary, 1994)

Comment: "He throws a knuckleball and a neat slider."
Source: *The Sporting News* (3/21/1951, Page 18)

Note: Listed as a suspected spitball pitcher
Source: *The Cincinnati Game* (Lonnie Wheeler and John Baskin, 1988)

DICK FOWLER 6'4" 215-pound righty
66-79, 4.11, 4 Saves 1941 1952

Pitch Selection: 1. Fastball 2. Change 3. Curve 4. Fork-slider

Sources: Buddy Rosar in *The No-Hit Hall of Fame* (Rich Coberly, 1985); *Baseball Digest* (November 1948, Ed Rumill)

HOWIE FOX 6'3" 210-pound righty
43-72, 4.33, 6 Saves 1944 1954

Pitches: 1. Fastball 2. Sinker 3. Curve 4. Change

Note: Until the middle of the 1950 season, Fox alternated between pitching overhand and sidearm. He dropped the sidearm delivery in mid-1950, and also improved his change of pace at that time.

Source: *Baseball Magazine* (July 1951, Jack Smart)

JIMMIE FOXX 6'0" 195-pound righty
1-0, 1.50, 0 Saves 1939 1945

Pitches: 1. Fastball 2. Change 3. Screwball 4. Knuckleball (occasional)

Source: *Jimmie Foxx: The Life and Times of a Baseball Hall of Famer, 1907–1967* (W. Harrison Daniel, 1996)

PAUL FOYTACK 5'11" 175-pound righty
86-87, 4.14, 7 Saves 1953 1964

Pitches: 1. Fastball 2. Curve 3. Slider 4. Change 5. Knuckleball (added in 1962)

Source: *Baseball Digest* (October 1956, Hal Middlesworth); Bill Fischer quoted in *Baseball Digest* (Oct.–Nov. 1962, Joe McGuff)

JOHN FRANCO 5'10" 170-pound lefty
88-79, 2.74, 424 Saves 1984 2003

Pitch Selection: 1. Sinking Fastball 2. Slider 3. Screwball

Source: *The Scouting Report 1990*

Pitch Selection: 1. Change/Screwball 2. Fastball 3. Slider

Source: *The Scouting Report 1992*

FRED FRANKHOUSE 5'11" 175-pound righty
106-97, 3.92, 12 Saves 1927 1939

Pitch Selection: 1. Curve 2. Fastball 3. Slow Screwball (used as Change) 4. Spitball?

Sources: *Who's Who in the Major Leagues* (1935 edition); *Baseball Magazine* (February 1935, Clifford Bloodgood)

Frankhouse: "Manager McKechnie has helped me a lot since I came to Boston. He has given me regular assignments when I have been in good health and he changed my style of pitching from sidearm to overhand. The result has been better control and more stuff on the ball. My curve ball especially is more effective . . .

"My curve is fashioned by the snap of my wrist and the position of my fingers on the ball. My middle fingers are bent under, pressing the cover."

Source: *Baseball Magazine* (March 1932, Clifford Bloodgood)

Comment: "Freddy Frankhouse, of the Brooklyn Dodgers, is another pitcher who throws curves, and then more curves."

Source: *Baseball Magazine* (September 1937, Daniel M. Daniel)

Description: "Fred Frankhouse, a present-day Dodger, helps hide the ball by swinging his gloved hand before him as he comes around with a sidearm pitch."

Source: *Baseball Magazine* (June 1936, Hugh Bradley, "Freak Pitching Deliveries—Past and Present")

Notes: Frankhouse had one of the best curves in baseball. *Who's Who* describes him as "one of the outstanding curveball flingers of the National League," and Bloodgood wrote, "his curve is still definitely wicked to even curve ball hitters." He spotted the fastball (at that time) and used the screwball mostly against left-handed hitters. In *The Sporting News* (7/20/1955), longtime umpire Bill Stewart said that Frankhouse was the only pitcher he ever warned about throwing a spitball. Just a week earlier, TSN reported that Babe Pinelli had also warned Frankhouse.

JOHN FRASCATORE 6'1" 223-pound righty
20-17, 4.00, 1 Save 1994 2001

Pitch Selection: 1. Fastball (low-90s) 2. Curve 3. Hard Slider

Source: *The Scouting Notebook 2000*

WILLIE FRASER 6'1" 206-pound righty
38-40, 4.47, 7 Saves 1986 1995

Pitch Selection: 1. Fastball (mid-80s) 2. Slider 3. Forkball (as Change)

Source: *The Scouting Report* (1987, 1990, and 1992 editions)

VIC FRASIER 6'0" 182-pound righty
23-38, 5.77, 4 Saves 1931 1939

Key Pitch: Fastball
Quote: "His most effective pitching weapon, according to batters who have faced him, is a blinding fast ball delivered with a deceptive motion."
Source: *Who's Who in Major League Baseball* (compiled by Harold "Speed" Johnson, 1933)

Description: "His forte is speed and he had plenty of it."
Source: *Baseball Magazine* (January 1932, Robert Milne)

GEORGE FRAZIER 6'5" 205-pound righty
35-43, 4.20, 29 Saves 1978 1987

Pitch Selection: 1. Fastball 2. Big, Sweeping Curve 3. Sharp-breaking Slider
Source: *The Scouting Report: 1983*

Note: Frazier would use three arm angles, mixing up overhand, three-quarters, and sidearm deliveries to keep the hitters off-stride.

HERSHELL FREEMAN 6'3" 220-pound righty
30-16, 3.74, 37 Saves 1952 1958

Pitches: 1. Sinking Fastball 2. Curve 3. Forkball (added in 1956)
Freeman: "I was primarily a fastball pitcher with a three-quarters delivery. I threw in the 90s and my fastball sank, breaking down and in to a right-handed hitter. It was a heavy pitch . . . I also threw a curveball. In 1956 I started messing around with a forkball . . . I found it easy to pick up, but my out pitch was still my fastball."
Source: *We Played the Game* (Danny Peary, 1994)

MARVIN FREEMAN 6'7" 222-pound righty
35-28, 4.64, 5 Saves 1986 1996

Pitch Selection: 1. Fastball 2. Slider 3. Split-Fingered Fastball (used as Change)
Sources: *The Scouting Report* (1992, 1993, and 1996 editions); *The Scouting Notebook: 1995*

Pitch Selection: 1. Fastball (88–92) 2. Curve 3. Change
Source: *The Scouting Notebook: 1996*

TONY FREITAS 5'8" 161-pound lefty
25-33, 4.48, 4 Saves 1932 1936

Pitches: 1. Curve 2. Change 3. Fastball 4. Screwball (developed in 1936)
Freitas: "I never did have what you could call a fastball. For me, it was control, a change-up, the curveball."
Source: *Baseball's Forgotten Heroes* (Tony Salin, 1999)

Note: Freitas won 342 games in the minor leagues.

LARRY FRENCH 6'1" 195-pound lefty
197-171, 3.44, 17 Saves 1929 1942

Pitches, 1929–1941: 1. Forkball 2. Screwball 3. Slow Curve 4. Fastball
Pitches, 1942: 1. Knuckleball 2. Curve 3. Fastball 4. Screwball
Sources: *Who's Who in the Major Leagues* (1937 ed.); *Baseball for Everyone* (Joe DiMaggio); Phil Cavaretta in *Wrigleyville* (Peter Golenbock, 1996); *Baseball Magazine* (August 1935, F.C. Lane article about Carl Hubbell; and October 1942, Roscoe McGowen)

Note: According to *The Sporting News* (5/14/1942), French first threw his knuckleball in a game on May 5, 1942 (he threw sixteen knucklers that day). Also according to *The Sporting News* (7/3/1940), French learned his knuckleball from Fred Fitzsimmons and his screwball from Hub Pruett.

Pitches: 1. Fastball 2. Screwballs (15%) 3. Curve
French: "My screw ball isn't so good as Carl Hubbell's. He throws his with more of an overhand motion. Mine is more side arm. A screw ball is a troublesome ball for a right-hander to hit, for, thrown by a left-handed pitcher, it breaks away from him. Its break is not so sharp as that of a curve, but it seems even more deceptive. As the batters say, it fades away.

"There are other tricks that a pitcher can play on a screw ball. I throw it with two different speeds. That adds an element of timing which also bothers a batter. Out of a hundred pitched balls perhaps fifteen that I throw will be screw balls."
Source: *Baseball Magazine* (January 1934, F.C. Lane); no mention of forkball in this profile of French

Comment: In the spring of '42, French learned the knuckleball from Fred Fitzsimmons, took to the pitch immediately, and might have pitched for years afterward

. . . but he went into the Navy after that season, and remained in the service for many years after the war.

All sources, except F.C. Lane in the 1934 article, agree that French did not throw hard.

BENNY FREY 5'10" 165-pound righty
57-82, 4.50, 8 Saves 1929 1936

Key Pitch: Fastball
Source: Frey's obituary in *The Sporting News* (11/4/1937)

Note: Frey added a knuckleball to his repertoire in 1933.
Source: *The Sporting News* (1/4/1934, Page 2)

Note: Frey threw sidearm.
Source: *The Ballplayers* (1990, article by Jack Kavanaugh)

STEVE FREY 5'9" 170-pound lefty
18-15, 3.76, 28 Saves 1989 1996

Pitch Selection: 1. Fastball 2. Slider 3. Curve
Source: *1990 Montreal Expos Media Guide*

Pitch Selection: 1. Curve 2. Fastball 3. Slider 4. Change (occasional)
Source: *The Scouting Report* (1992 and 1993 editions)

BOB FRIEND 6'0" 190-pound righty
197-230, 3.58, 11 Saves 1951 1966

Pitch Selection: 1. Sinking Fastball 2. Hard Curve 3. Slow Curve 4. Change or Slip Pitch
Note: Later in career, third pitch is Slider.
Sources: Having written a 4,000-word article on Friend, we have dozens of sources about his stuff. Among these are *Baseball Digest* (June 1956, quote from George Susce); a 1956 article in *The Saturday Evening Post* (Myron Cope); *Sport* (September 1957), *Baseball Stars of 1959* (article by Dick Schaap); a newspaper article by Dan Daniel dated 2/16/1962 (newspaper unidentified); the *Philadelphia Daily News* (6/26/1963, Stan Hochman); *The Sporting News* (8/7/1965, Les Biederman); an article by Steve Jacobson (unknown newspaper, 6/25/1964); and the book *Maz and the '60 Bucs* (Jim O'Brien, 1993).

Commentary: At the start of his career, Friend threw only two pitches: a sinking fastball, and a hard curve. Most people thought he would need to go back to the minors to add a pitch; however, Branch Rickey realized that, since both pitches were outstanding *and* Friend could change speeds on both of them, he had all that he needed to be a successful pitcher—and that was all that he threw for several years, whether you want to call that two pitches or four. The fastball was a hard, sinking fastball—presumably a two-seam fastball in the modern vernacular—which was sometimes described as a sinker. His ground ball rates were probably very, very high, and Jim Brosnan said that he broke more bats than any pitcher in the league. He threw the sinking fastball approximately 50 percent of the time.

What confuses the record with regard to Friend is the slider. Throughout the second half of Friend's career—from 1958 on—there are constant stories that "Friend has added a slider this year." Part of this confusion may stem from the fact that Friend's hard curve was so hard and flat that it broke almost like a slider, and some people would describe it as a slider, although Friend called it a curve.

However, even allowing for that, it is very clear that Friend told different reporters over a period of several years that he had just added a slider—and credited different people with teaching him to throw it. As late as 1965 he credited Clyde King with having taught him to throw a slider that spring—although he had made similar comments about other pitching coaches in 1958, '60, '62, and '63, and had been described as having a top-flight slider as early as 1956, granted that that was probably his curve.

One explanation for this is that Friend experimented with various ways of throwing the slider unsuccessfully for years before finally adding one late in his career. Another explanation is that Friend, an engaging fellow who went out of his way to be helpful to reporters, was simply trying to give the writers something to write about, or give the hitters something to think about, real or imagined.

In 1953 Fred Haney, taking over the Pirates, thought that Friend's delivery needed to be completely re-worked, and Haney re-constructed Friend's entire delivery. Whether this facilitated Friend's development or delayed it is a debatable point. "It is interesting to note that Friend's form, even after having been refined, violates a cardinal rule of pitching," wrote Myron Cope in 1956. "He takes his eye off the target. As he winds up and brings his hind end around, he looks briefly toward left field . . . This unorthodox behavior worries the devil out of the batter, who can't help feeling that Bobby may bounce one off his head if he doesn't look where he's throwing. Some of the Brooklyn Dodgers have frankly admitted that's one reason why he's so effective against their team."

Also see entry on Jim Maloney

DANNY FRISELLA 6'0" 185-pound righty
34-40, 3.32, 57 Saves 1967 1976

Pitches through 1969: 1. Overhand Curve 2. Slider 3. Fastball
Source: *The Sporting News* (5/4/1968, Jack Lang)

Key Pitch after 1969: Forkball (taught to him by Diego Segui in the winter of 1969/1970)
Sources: *Baseball Digest* (August 1971, George Vass); *The Sporting News* (7/1/1972, Jack Lang); *The Complete Handbook of Baseball* (1972 edition, edited by Zander Hollander)

TODD FROHWIRTH 6'4" 205-pound righty
20-19, 3.60, 11 Saves 1987 1996

Pitch Selection: 1. Sinking Fastball 2. Change 3. Slurve
Note: Threw with a submarine delivery.
Source: *The Scouting Report: 1993*

Comment: "Once a non-prospect, Frohwirth rescued his career by dropping his arm angle from sidearm to submarine. He decided to give it a try after watching Kent Tekulve on television. Frohwirth's fastball and slurve are hard to track because of the deception he creates with his body motion."
Source: *Bill Mazeroski's Baseball* (1993 edition)

ART FROMME 6'0" 178-pound righty
80-90, 2.90, 4 Saves 1906 1915

Key Pitch: Fastball
Quote: "Have my speed and my arm is strong."
Source: Telegram from Fromme to Cincinnati manager Clark Griffith (9/14/1910)

WOODIE FRYMAN 6'3" 197-pound lefty
141-155, 3.77, 58 Saves 1966 1983

Pitch Selection: 1. Fastball 2. Change 3. Slider
Source: *The Sporting News* (6/3/1972, Allen Lewis)

Fryman: "I was pretty well a strikeout pitcher in my earlier days in the game. I'd say for the first six or seven years I pitched in the major leagues, I was a strikeout pitcher . . . But then after I got older and hurt my arm a few times I become more of a ground-ball pitcher . . . What helped me, more than anything else, to alter my style was when they put me in the bullpen. I didn't think that was something that I could do, because I didn't think my arm would let me throw every day, enough where I could pitch in the bullpen. But it did . . . And then I could throw hard for one inning . . . I pitched inside all my career, and I liked to throw the ball on the knuckles . . ."
Source: Fryman interviewed by Dan DiNardo (8/10/1991, SABR Oral History Committee)

ERIC GAGNE 6'2" 195-pound righty
17-18, 3.50, 107 Saves 1999 2003

Pitches as starter (1999–2001): 1. Curve 2. Fastball (low-90s) 3. Cut Fastball
Pitches as Reliever (2002–2003): 1. Fastball (mid-90s) 2. Change (87) 3. Slow Curve 4. Slider (occasional)
Source: *The Scouting Notebook 2002;* SportingNews.com (7/3/2003, Ken Rosenthal); Baseball Canada News (6/17/2002, Stephen Cannella); *Sports Illustrated* (6/2/2003, Daniel G. Habib); *The Orange County Register* (9/3/2003, Mark Whicker)

Description: "Most closers depend on one pitch that becomes synonymous with their success: Trevor Hoffman's changeup, Mariano Rivera's cut fastball. Gagne thrives on the dizzying oscillation between his changeup and his fastball. They have the same release point and the same arm speed. The fastball is straight gas . . . but the changeup is a devious thing, a bowling ball rolled off a picnic table. It travels some 10 mph slower than his fastball, anywhere from 83–88 mph, and like a splitter it breaks late and sharp."
Source: Habib in *Sports Illustrated*

Habib on Gagne's change-up: "He split his middle and ring fingers wide and curled them perpendicular to the seams, creating a four-seam changeup, which he threw in the same stress-free motion as his fastball. 'I just get on top of the ball and throw it as hard as I can,' Gagne says. 'I don't have to think about movement; the grip takes care of it.' "

Quote: "Hitters might see a splitter or slider that hard, but they never see a straight change that hard."
Source: Dodgers catcher Paul LoDuca in Cannella article

Preston Wilson: "The curveball is just like a Bugs Bunny curveball. It's ridiculous. When he throws it, you see hitters lock up, they're so geared up."
Source: CNNSI.com's "Inside Baseball" column (8/6/2003, John Donovan)

Note: Some sources list Gagne's slider as his best breaking pitch, but in 2003 LoDuca said Gagne "throws a slider that's terrible and he always wants to throw it. I give him crap because I don't want him to throw it because it's the worst pitch he has."
Source: Torrance (Cal.) *Daily Breeze* (9/8/2003, Bill Cizek)

Quote: "I'll tell you what: he has four quality major-league pitches. That is what makes him unique, and outstanding."
Source: Ross Porter during broadcast of Dodgers-Astros game, 9/2/2003

RICH GALE 6'7" 225-pound righty
55-56, 4.54, 2 Saves 1978 1984

Pitch Selection: 1. Fastball (90) 2. Slider
3. Curve (occasional)
Source: *The Scouting Report: 1983*

DENNY GALEHOUSE 6'1" 195-pound righty
109-118, 3.97, 13 Saves 1934 1949

Key Pitch: Fastball
Source: *Who's Who in the American League* (1935 edition)

BERT GALLIA 6'0" 165-pound righty
66-68, 3.14, 10 Saves 1912 1920

Comment: "Manager Griffith and Nick Altrock . . . consider Gallia as having more stuff than any pitcher on the local staff, not even barring Walter Johnson."
Source: unidentified clipping from the Hall of Fame Library

PUD GALVIN 5'8" 190-pound righty
360-305, 2.87, 1 Save 1879 1892

Pitch Selection: 1. Fastball

Comment: "Galvin . . . paid no attention to developing a curve ball but combined dazzling speed with uncanny control and continued to rely solely upon his speed and control to the last game he pitched in the big league."
Source: *Baseball Magazine* (February 1931, H.H. Westlake)

Description: "There was not much curve to the ball that Jim Galvin pitched, but there was as much speed to it as though it had been hurled from a Gatling gun."
Source: *The National Game* (Alfred H. Spink, 1911)

GIL GAMESH 6'2" 205-pound lefty
42-1, 0.42, 0 Saves 1933 1933

Key Pitch: Fastball (120+)
Description: "Rubbing the ball around in those enormous paws that hung down practically to his knees, he would glare defiantly at the man striding up to the plate (some of them stars when he was still in the cradle) and announce out loud his own personal opinion of the fellow's abilities. 'You couldn't lick a stamp. You couldn't beat a drum. Get your belly button in there, bud, you're what I call duck soup.' Then, sneering away, he would lean way back, kick that right leg up sky-high like a chorus girl, and that long left arm would start coming around by way of Biloxi—and next thing you knew it was strike one."
Source: *The Great American Novel* (Philip Roth, 1973)

GENE GARBER 5'10" 175-pound righty
96-113, 3.34, 218 Saves 1969 1988

Pitch Selection: 1. Change 2. Slider
3. Sinking Fastball 4. Curve
Note: Garber threw sidearm.
Source: *The Scouting Report: 1987*

RICH GARCES 6'0" 250-pound righty
23-10, 3.74, 7 Saves 1990 2002

Pitches: 1. Fastball (low-90s) 2. Hard Curve
3. Split-Fingered Fastball (added about 1999)
Source: *The Scouting Notebook* (1997, 2000–2002 editions)

FREDDY GARCIA 6'4" 240-pound righty
72-43, 3.97, 0 Saves 1999 2003

Pitch Selection: 1. Fastballs 2. Curve 3. Change
4. Slider (occasional)

Source: *Seattle Times* (10/18/2001)
Note: According to the Times article, Garcia in 2001 threw 63 percent fastballs, 17 percent curves, 17 percent change-ups, and 3 percent sliders. According to the same article, Garcia threw two fastballs: a straight four-seamer thrown 92–96 m.p.h., and a tailing two-seamer thrown 86–92. His change was thrown 78–85, and would sink and run away from a right-handed hitter. His curve had a small break and was thrown 70–79, while his slider (thrown only occasionally) was thrown 80–83.

MIKE GARCIA 6'1" 195-pound righty
142-97, 3.27, 23 Saves 1948 1961

Pitch Selection: 1. Sinking Fastball 2. Curve 3. Slider
Sources: *Cleveland Plain Dealer* (3/5/1949, Franklin Lewis); *The Sporting News* (4/5/1950, Frank Finch); *Baseball Digest* (April 1951, Harry Jones); *The Sporting News* (8/22/1951, Ed McAuley); Cleveland Indians Press Guide, 1953; *Distant Drums: The 1949 Cleveland Indians Revisited* (Bruce Dudley); *Baseball Magazine* (January 1950, Hub Miller)

Notes: Garcia's fastball was outstanding. Ed McAuley, interviewed by another writer in 1950, said, "No, he's not as fast as the Feller I once knew, but he's plenty swift." In 1951, Bob Lemon said, "Mike throws the league's best fast ball." The 1953 Cleveland Press Guide said that he was "reputed to be one of the hardest throw ing pitchers in the game." Mel Harder taught Garcia to throw a curve during spring training, 1949, but Garcia didn't really gain control of it until 1951.

The *Baseball Magazine* article, written when Garcia was a rookie, describes the slider as Garcia's "pet" pitch.

In 1977, Harder told Cleveland *Plain Dealer* columnist Russell Schneider that Garcia had "a real good spit ball."

Garcia on his slider: "Sometimes it slides into the hitter, and sometimes it slides out. Other times, it just goes straight, but it always seems to catch a piece of the plate."
Source: *Baseball Digest* (October 1949, Milton Richman, who describes the slider as "the pride of Mike's pitching repertoire.")

Quote: "The Big Bear, on the other hand, utilizing a rather lazy, deceptively leisurely motion, would be content to cut down American League batters four days out of the week, and twice on Sundays."
Source: *Sports Stars* (August 1952)

MARK GARDNER 6'1" 190-pound righty
99-93, 4.56, 1 Save 1989 2001

Pitch Selection: 1. Fastball 2. Curve 3. Change
Source: *1990 Montreal Expos Media Guide*

Pitch Selection: 1. Big Curve 2. Slurve
3. Fastball (mid-80s)
Sources: *The Scouting Report: 1993* and *The Scouting Notebook 1999*

WAYNE GARLAND 6'0" 195-pound righty
55-66, 3.89, 6 Saves 1973 1981

Pitches: 1. Curve 2. Slider 3. Screwball 4. Fastball
5. Knuckleball
Source: *The Sporting News* (7/5/1980, Bob Sudyk)

Commentary: One gets the impression that Garland didn't always have all these pitches.

Key Pitch: Fastball
Maury Wills: "Poise is the one word that comes to mind when I think of Wayne Garland. Although Wayne has an assortment of pitches, his hard fastball is what impresses me the most. He's a pitcher who doesn't nibble around. He charges the batter."
Source: *How to Steal a Pennant* (Wills with John Freeman, 1976)

SCOTT GARRELTS 6'4" 210-pound righty
69-53, 3.29, 48 Saves 1982 1991

Pitch Selection: 1. Fastball 2. Slider
3. Split-Fingered Fastball
Source: *The Scouting Report: 1990*

NED GARVER 5'10" 180-pound righty
129-157, 3.73, 12 Saves 1948 1961

Pitch Selection: 1. Slider 2. Fastball 3. Change
4. Curve
Sources: Arthur Richman, unidentified clipping in *TSN* Morgue, June, 1951; Robert L. Burnes, unidentified newspaper, July, 1957

Garver: "I was a sinker-slider pitcher. I had a pretty good sinker, and I had a pretty good slider. Ted Williams will

tell you that my slider was a pitch that he had trouble picking up the spin on."
Source: *Splendor on the Diamond* (Rich Westcott, 2000)

Note: Garver was cited as the best of the modern sidearmers in *How to Play Winning Baseball* (Arthur Mann, 1953).

VIRGIL (NED) GARVIN 6'3" 160-pound righty
57-98, 2.72, 4 Saves 1896 1904

Key Pitch: Screwball/Fadeaway
Source: *The Year They Called Off The World Series* (Benton Stark, 1991); *Touching Second* (Johnny Evers and Hugh Fullerton, 1910)

Note: Evers said that Garvin had "extraordinarily long fingers" and that he "pitched the same ball in even more wonderful style . . . before Mathewson, but he did not understand its use or worth."

MILT GASTON 6'1" 185-pound righty
97-164, 4.55, 8 Saves 1924 1934

Pitch Selection: 1. Fastball 2. Forkball
Sources: *Sports Collectors Digest* (3/24/1995, Jim Sargent); Henry P. Edwards, American League Service Bureau (12/21/1930)

Gaston in *Sports Collectors Digest:* "My best pitch was the fastball. I always threw a number of pitches, but my main pitch was the fastball.

"I was one of the first pitchers to throw the forkball . . . I had good success with it for a while, but I couldn't control it. So later on, I didn't use it too much because I couldn't always get it over."

Quote from Edwards article: "In New York, Gaston . . . learned how to toss the fork ball. That particular deceiver is a great ball to throw in the pinches—when it is accompanied by control but Gaston, himself, admits it is difficult to control. The official averages also show that Gaston had eleven wild pitches during the season of 1930 and probably most of them were in trying to throw that same fork ball.

"It is also rumored that the real reason St. Louis traded Milt to Washington is that Phil Ball, president of the Browns, became somewhat annoyed because he had to dodge so many fork balls that Milt threw into the grand stand.

"Along that line, William McKinley Hargrave, who caught Gaston at St. Louis, says that no catcher can successfully handle Gaston's forker, saying the receiver merely has to guess where it is going. Hargrave, as an illustration, tells of a game in which New York filled the bases with none out. Gaston threw a fork ball. The batter swung and missed. Hargrave grabbed and missed. One run across. Gaston threw another fork ball. Batter swung and missed again. Hargrave grabbed and missed again. Two runs across. Whereupon Hargrave went into executive secret session with Gaston and intimated that while it was all right to fool the batter, it was carrying it just a trifle too far when he fooled the catcher also and that if St. Louis were going to get the Yankees out that afternoon, it might be just as well if he ceased toying with the fork ball. Gaston did and the next three batters were easy."

HANK GASTRIGHT 6'2" 190-pound righty
72-65, 4.20, 3 Saves 1889 1896

Quote: "Henry Gastright had all the St. Louis Browns guessing the location of his curves, inshoots, and drops."
Note: Gastright pitched a one-hitter for Columbus on May 8, 1890. The one hit was a double by the Browns' pitcher, and was said to be on a slow drop.
Source: *Ohio State Journal* (May 9, 1890) (thanks to John Lewis)

JOE GENEWICH 6'0" 174-pound righty
73-92, 4.29, 12 Saves 1922 1930

Key Pitch: Slow Curve
Note: Genewich threw his slow curve "by dragging his back foot slowly across the pitching rubber instead of swinging it around quickly."
Source: *Major League Baseball* (Ethan Allen, Page 34)

GARY GENTRY 6'0" 170-pound righty
46-49, 3.56, 2 Saves 1969 1975

Pitch Selection: 1. Fastball 2. Curve 3. Change
Source: *Major League Baseball—1970* (Jack Zanger)

Description: "His stuff was every bit as good as Seaver's. Aw, shit yeah, man. He had just as live an arm. When I wasn't playing I used to warm him up in the bullpen just to keep my reflexes sharp . . .

"I remember warming this guy up a few times, and

let me tell you something, his ball was all over the place. It just jumped and ran . . . He was a cowboy, a skinny kid with a tremendous arm. He was great."
Source: Ron Swoboda in *Amazin': The Miraculous History of New York's Most Beloved Baseball Team* (Peter Golenbock, 2002)

JOHN GELNAR

Pitch Selection: 1. Fastball 2. Curve
Quote: "Good fast ball. Better than average curve."
Source: *Baseball Digest* (March 1966, "Scouting Reports on 1966 Major League Rookies")

CHARLIE GETZIEN 5'10" 172-pound righty
145-140, 3.46, 1 Save 1884 1892

Pitch Selection: 1. Curve 2. Fastball 3. Drop Curve
Description: "When about to deliver the ball, 'Getz' faces third base with one foot in either corner of the lower end of the box. Bending the left knee slightly, he draws his right arm well back. Then, straightening up quickly, he slides the left foot forward with a characteristic little skip, and, bringing his arm around with a swift overhand swing, drives the ball in at a lively pace. Getzein [*sic*] has a weakness for a peculiar drop curve, which he considers very effective. He is also partial to a speedy straight pitch, with which he frequently follows the slower ball."
Source: Article titled "How Men Pitch Base-Ball: The Famous Pitchers of the National League of 1886." No author or publisher is given, though the information in the article is said to have come from photographic studies done by the *New York World* newspaper.
Other Source: *Nineteenth Century Stars* (SABR, 1989, article by Robert L. Tiemann)

RUBE GEYER 5'10" 170-pound righty
17-26, 3.67, 1 Save 1910 1913

Key Pitch: Drop Ball
Quote: "He possesses a peculiar drop ball and is a splendid fielding pitcher."
Source: *The National Game* (Alfred H. Spink, 1911)

JOE GIBBON 6'4" 200-pound lefty
61-65, 3.52, 32 Saves 1960 1972

Pitch Selection: 1. Fastball 2. Sinker 3. Slider
Sources: *Pittsburgh Post-Gazette* (February, 1959, Chester L. Smith); *San Francisco Examiner* (3/8/1966, Jack McDonald)

Quote: "Ever hear of a major league pitcher without a curve ball? Gibbon is one. 'I come out of a three-quarters overhand delivery or sidearm and the curve is a flat pitch for me. I make my slider do its work.' "

BOB GIBSON 6'1" 189-pound righty
251-174, 2.91, 6 Saves 1959 1975

Pitch Selection: 1. Rising Fastball 2. Slider 3. Sinking Fastball 4. Curve 5. Change
Gibson: "It was said that I threw, basically, five pitches—fastball, slider, curve, change-up, and knockdown. I don't believe that assessment did me justice, though. I actually used about nine pitches—two different fastballs, two sliders, a curve, a change-up, knockdown, brushback, and hit-batsman."
Source: *Stranger to the Game: The Autobiography of Bob Gibson* (Gibson and Lonnie Wheeler, 1994)
Other Source: *Late Innings* (Roger Angell, Page 262)

Roger Angell: "Gibson, hardly taking a deep breath between pitches, was simply overpowering, throwing fast balls past the hitters with his sweeping right-handed delivery, which he finished with a sudden lunge toward first base."
Source: Angell in *The New Yorker* (October, 1968, reprinted in *The Summer Game*)

Umpire Tom Gorman: ". . . Gibson knew how to pace himself. He was one of the very few pitchers whose fastball was as good in the eighth and ninth innings as it was in the first and second."
Source: *Three and Two!* (Gorman as told to Jerome Holtzman, 1979)
Comment: "The so-called wise observers used to knock Gibson because he couldn't hold runners on first base, but what was the point? He couldn't hold runners on, so just let the guy pitch without distraction."
Source: *Oh, Baby, I Love It!* (Tim McCarver with Ray Robinson, 1987)

Description: "If your elbow is even with your shoulder and your wrist above your elbow, call it three-quarters. Bob Gibson is a three-quarters pitcher."
Source: *Pitching with Tom Seaver* (Seaver and Steve Jacobson, 1973)

PAUL GIBSON 6'1" 195-pound lefty
22-24, 4.07, 11 Saves 1988 1996

Pitch Selection: 1. Sinker 2. Slider
Sources: *The Scouting Report* (1992 and 1993 editions)

SAM GIBSON 6'2" 198-pound righty
32-38, 4.28, 5 Saves 1926 1932

Key Pitch: Knuckleball
Source: Ray Hayworth in *Baseball Between the Wars* (Eugene Murdock, 1992)

FLOYD GIEBELL 6'2" 172-pound righty
3-1, 4.03, 0 Saves 1939 1941

Pitch Selection: 1. Sinker 2. Slider
Giebell: "I could throw ninety-one, ninety-two. I wasn't a softball pitcher."
Source: *A Glimpse of Fame* (Dennis Snelling, 1992)
Note: In 1940, Giebell beat Bob Feller to clinch the American League pennant for Detroit.

PAUL GIEL 5'11" 185-pound righty
11-9, 5.40, 0 Saves 1954 1961

Description: "Although his fast ball is alive—the high one takes off, the low one dips—the somewhat chunky 178-pounder doesn't consider himself another supple-armed Bob Feller. Good control, therefore, is highly important when Paul is out there on the mound."
Source: *Baseball Digest* (February 1958, Dick Gordon)

DAVE GIUSTI 5'11" 190-pound righty
100-93, 3.60, 145 Saves 1962 1977

Pitch Selection: 1. Fastball 2. Slider 3. Palm Ball 4. Curve
Sources: *The Relief Pitcher* (John Thorn, 1979); *The New York Times* (5/16/1965, Page 3S)

Note: Giusti was best-known for his palm ball, but in 1975 he told Roger Angell, "The fastball is my best pitch . . ."

FRED GLADDING 6'1" 220-pound righty
48-34, 3.13, 109 Saves 1961 1973

Key Pitch: Sinking Fastball
Source: *The Sporting News* (9/6/1969, John Wilson)

FRED GLADE 5'10" 175-pound righty
52-68, 2.62, 2 Saves 1902 1908

Key Pitch: Fastball
Sources: unidentified clipping from the Hall of Fame Library (11/4/1907); manuscript "The Much Maligned Mr. Glade" (Tracy Thibeau, 1988)

Quote: "If he had a slow ball he would be the game's greatest pitcher. When requested to cultivate a change of pace, Fred would explain that it hurt and weakened his arm to deliver a slow ball."
Source: unidentified clipping from the Hall of Fame Library (11/4/1907)

TOM GLAVINE 6'0" 175-pound lefty
251-157, 3.43, 0 Saves 1987 2003

Pitch Selection: 1. Fastball 2. Circle Change 3. Curve 4. Slider 5. Added a Cut Fastball in 2000
Sources: *The Scouting Report: 1993; 1995 Baseball Almanac; The Scouting Report: 1996* and *The Scouting Notebook 2000*

Commentary: Glavine actually has two pitches that he uses as a slider, one to lefties and one to right-handers, and in a career as long as he has had, obviously he has changed and re-emphasized his stuff somewhat. The Change is probably his best pitch, but he isn't the kind of pitcher for whom we would list a changeup as his number one pitch, because he has a good fastball. Normally if you say that a guy's number one pitch is a change, you're saying that he's a junkballer, which Glavine is not.

Note: Glavine added a cut fastball in 2000. He kept most of his pitches away from lefties, but the cutter broke in on them.
Source: article by Tom Verducci on CNNSI.com, 5/10/2000

Glavine: "If I throw 100 pitches in a game, I'll probably throw as many as 70 fastballs. . . . Too many guys pitch backward. They throw their breaking ball so much that it's almost like their fastball is their off-speed pitch. What you have to realize is that a breaking ball is tough to throw for strikes. That means you have more pitchers pitching behind in the count, and that's when you get hit."
Source: *As Koufax Said . . . : The 400 Best Things Ever*

Said About How to Play Baseball (compiled by Randy Voorhees and Mark Gola, 2003)

KID GLEASON 5'7" 158-pound righty
138-133, 3.79, 7 Saves 1888 1895

Pitch Selection: 1. Curve 2. Fastball 3. Change
Sources: *Biographical Dictionary of Baseball; Philadelphia Enquirer* (4/4/1915); clipping labeled *Evening Telegram*, from the Hall of Fame Library

Quote from *Biographical Dictionary of Baseball:* "Attracted attention as a curveball pitcher in Camden while a teenager."

Quote from *Philadelphia Enquirer* article: "[In an 1887 game, the Johnstown team] got after his curves from the jump, at the end of the third inning had the Kid and his pet curves massacred to the tune of 13-4."

Quote from *Evening Telegram:* "With the assistance of a good drop ball, at that time a popular manner in which to baffle the batters, he could stand such venerable old chaps as 'Pop' Anson and 'Dan' Brouthers on their heads . . . With the speed of which he was possessed he had a nice slow one that sailed on and on with the lulling smoothness of a Great South Bay catboat 'boosted' from behind by a favoring wind. It looked easy to hit, but such great men as Ewing, Gore, 'Jeems' O'Rourke, and others of the old school have popped their bats against it only to be fooled."

JERRY DON GLEATON 6'3" 205-pound lefty
15-23, 4.25, 26 Saves 1979 1992

Pitch Selection: 1. Fastball 2. Curve
Source: *The Scouting Report: 1992*

FRED GOLDSMITH 6'1" 195-pound righty
112-68, 2.73, 1 Save 1879 1884

Key Pitch: Curve
Sources: *Bury My Heart at Wrigley Field* (Larry D. Names, page 210); *Baseball: 1845–1881* (Preston D. Orem, 1961)

DAVE GOLTZ 6'4" 200-pound righty
113-109, 3.69, 8 Saves 1972 1983

Pitch Selection: 1. Sinking Fastball 2. Knuckle Curve
Source: *The Sporting News* (6/28/1980, Gordon Verrell)

WAYNE GOMES 6'2" 225-pound righty
30-23, 4.60, 29 Saves 1997 2002

Pitch Selection: 1. Fastball (low-90s) 2. Sharp Curve
Source: *The Scouting Notebook: 1998*

LEFTY GOMEZ 6'2" 173-pound lefty
189-102, 3.34, 9 Saves 1930 1943

Pitch Selection: 1. Fastball 2. Gomez refined a Slow Curve midway through his career
Sources: *Inside Baseball* (Arthur Daley, Page 127); *The New York Yankees* (Frank Graham, 1952 edition); Gomez's obituary in *The Sporting News* (2/27/1989)

Quote: "Lefty Grove is the greatest pitcher, left or right-hander, that I have ever seen. In my humble opinion he throws the fastest ball in existence, but Gomez is not far behind him in speed. Just a shade."
Source: Catcher Cy Perkins in *Baseball Magazine* (April 1932, Clifford Bloodgood)

RUBEN GOMEZ 6'0" 170-pound righty
76-86, 4.09, 5 Saves 1953 1967

Pitch Selection: 1. Fastball 2. Screwball 3. Curve
Source: *Sport* (September 1957, Page 72)

Description: "He has a fastball that bursts in on you, a good curveball, and the best screwball of any right-handed pitcher I ever saw."
Source: Giants scout Tom Sheehan in *Crossing the Line: Black Major Leaguers 1947–1959* (Larry Moffi and Jonathan Kronstadt, 1994)

Pitch Selection: 1. Screwball 2. Fastball 3. Slider
Description: "He has great pitching equipment, with special stress on his screwball, and, thanks to understanding handling by Wes Westrum, he knows how to mix it up effectively. He has a good fast ball, which he uses as Sal Maglie does his, and he has added the third pitch so necessary to hurlers these days, a slider."
Source: *The Incredible Giants* (Tom Meany, 1955)

DWIGHT GOODEN 6'2" 190-pound righty
194-112, 3.51, 3 Saves 1984 2000

Pitch Selection, 1980s: 1. Fastball 2. Sweeping Curve 3. Change
Pitch Selection, 1990s: 1. Curve 2. Four-Seam Fastball 3. Slider 4. Change

Sources: *Tom Seaver's 1989 Scouting Notebook; The Scouting Report: 1990; The Scouting Report: 1987*

Commentary: In Gooden's first two seasons, when he was the dominant pitcher in the league, his fastball had great movement. Beginning in 1986 his fastball began to flatten out, and he was never quite able to get back where he had been.

Pitches: 1. Fastball 2. Hard Curve 3. Slow Curve 4. Change
Source: Gooden in *The Hurlers* (Kevin Kerrane, 1989)

MARV GOODWIN 5'11" 168-pound righty
21-25, 3.30, 2 Saves 1916 1925

Key Pitch: Spitball

Note: Goodwin was one of the "grandfathered" pitchers allowed to continue to throw the spitball after it was otherwise banned in 1921.
Source: 1923 *Reach Guide* (Page 38)

TOM GORDON 5'9" 160-pound righty
113-107, 4.07, 110 Saves 1988 2003

Pitch Selection: 1. Big, Hard Curve 2. Slow, Soft Curve 3. Fastball
Source: *The Scouting Notebook 1999*

Note: Gordon threw perhaps the best curve of his generation. He was taught to throw the curve as a boy by his father, Tom Gordon Sr., and the pitch was refined by his high school coach, Ronnie Jackson.
Source: *The Kansas City Star* (8/27/1989, Bill Richardson)

TOM GORMAN 6'1" 190-pound righty
36-36, 3.77, 42 Saves 1952 1959

Pitch Selection: 1. Sinker 2. Curve 3. Slider 4. Knuckle Ball
Note: Gorman threw sidearm.
Source: *Baseball Digest* (September 1955, Page 62); *The Sporting News* (7/13/1955, Ernest Mehl)

JOHNNY GORSICA 6'2" 180-pound righty
31-39, 4.18, 17 Saves 1940 1947

Pitch Selection: 1. Sinker 2. Curve 3. Fastball
Source: *Baseball Magazine* (September 1940, Charles P. Ward)

Pitch Selection: 1. Fastball 2–3. Overhand Sinker and Curve
Source: *Baseball Magazine* (May 1941, Henry P. Edwards)

GOOSE GOSSAGE 6'3" 180-pound righty
124-107, 3.01, 310 Saves 1972 1994

Pitches: 1. Rising Fastball 2. Sinking Fastball 3. Slider (refined in 1975) 4. Change (occasional)
Note: Gossage, like so many others, learned his slider from Johnny Sain.
Source: *The Goose Is Loose* (Gossage with Russ Pate, 2000)

Pitch Selection, early 1980s: 1. Fastball (mid-90s) 2. Slider
Pitch Selection, late 1980s: 1. Fastball (low-90s) 2. Slider
Pitch Selection, early 1990s: 1. Fastball (high-80s) 2. Slider
Commentary: In his prime, Gossage threw from a three-quarters delivery with apparent great effort, as hard as any reliever in the majors. He almost never threw his breaking pitch—which he sometimes described as a slurve—to left-handed hitters.
Sources: *The Scouting Report* (1983, 1985, 1987, 1989, and 1995 editions)

Comment: ". . . hitters quake at facing his fastball, which is clocked regularly at 96 mph."
Source: *The Complete Handbook of Baseball: 1982 Season* (edited by Zander Hollander)

JIM GOTT 6'4" 215-pound righty
56-74, 3.87, 91 Saves 1982 1995

Pitch Selection: 1. Fastball 2. Slider 3. Curve
Sources: *The Scouting Report* (1990 and 1992 editions)

Quote: " 'He probably has the best raw stuff on the staff,' says [Blue Jays manager Bobby] Cox. 'After Rich Gossage and maybe Juan Berenguer, he probably throws as hard as any righthander in the league, and when he gets his slider over, he's virtually unhittable.' "
Source: *The Sporting News* (6/13/1983, Peter Gammons)

HENRY GRAMPP 6'1" 185-pound righty
0-1, 16.20, 0 Saves 1927 1929

Story: "Henry Grampp appeared in only three games during the 1920s, but as a batting-practice pitcher in the '30s he was the Cubs' secret weapon. [Photographer George] Brace says Grampp could imitate the style of any opposing pitcher, both righty and lefty, and he went so far as to use putty and paint his face so he looked *and* pitched like the upcoming opponent."
Source: *The Game That Was* (Richard Cahan and Mark Jacob, 1996)

WAYNE GRANGER 6'2" 165-pound righty
35-35, 3.14, 108 Saves 1968 1976

Key Pitch: 1. Sinker 2. Slow Sidearm Curve
3. Quick slider-like curve, thrown three-quarters
Sources: *The Sporting News* (8/1/1970, Earl Lawson); Baltimore Orioles scouting report prior to 1970 World Series, reported in *Putting It All Together* (Brooks Robinson with Fred Bauer, 1971)
Note: Granger threw "almost cross-fire from sidearm delivery."

MARK GRANT 6'2" 195-pound righty
22-32, 4.31, 8 Saves 1984 1993

Pitch Selection: 1. Fastball 2. Slider
3. Change (developed in 1989)
Source: *The Scouting Notebook: 1990*

MUDCAT GRANT 6'1" 186-pound righty
145-119, 3.63, 53 Saves 1958 1971

Pitch Selection, early career: 1. Fastball 2. Slider
3. Curve 4. Change
Quote from Bob Swift, Washington's pitching coach: ". . . his curve isn't much and that Mudcat has trouble throwing his change-up."
Source: *Baseball Digest* (September 1960)

Pitch Selection, late career: 1. Curve 2. Fastball
Source: *Catfish: My Life in Baseball* (Jim "Catfish" Hunter with Armen Keteyian, 1988)

DANNY GRAVES 6'0" 185-pound righty
39-36, 3.89, 131 Saves 1996 2003

Pitch Selection: 1. Fastball (high-80s) 2. Sinker
3. Change
Source: *The Scouting Notebook: 1999*

Pitch Selection: 1. Two-Seam Fastball (92–96)
2. Straight Change 3. Wide-Breaking Slider
4. Slow Curve
Source: *The Scouting Notebook* (2000–2003 editions)

SAM GRAY 5'10" 175-pound righty
111-115, 4.18, 22 Saves 1924 1933

Pitch Selection, early career: 1. Fastball
2. Curve (occasional)
Pitches, later career: 1. Curves 2. Fastball
3. Knuckleball
Sources: *Baseball Magazine* (May 1926, F.C. Lane; September 1929, Lane); *Who's Who in Major League Baseball* (compiled by Harold "Speed" Johnson, 1933); *The Sporting News* (9/24/1952, Page 3)

Description: "The secret of Gray's success is still something of a debatable problem. Ira Thomas says that he can do things to a fast ball that nobody else can do. His fast ball seems to sail and breaks in an opposite direction from most fast balls . . .

"Gray does not depend exclusively on his baffling speedball. He also has a good curve, though he uses it but sparingly. 'Perhaps I'll pitch half a dozen curves a game,' he says. 'Against certain fellows, at some particular stage in the game, I don't like to pitch too many curves. They're hard on your arm. I've never had a sore arm, yet, and I don't want one.'

"Pitchers naturally swap ideas. In teaching others how to throw his peculiar fast ball, Gray has also been open to suggestions. 'I can throw Rommel's knuckle ball,' he says, 'but I can't control it. It would take me maybe a couple of years to control it. In the meantime I wouldn't amount to much. I'll stick to my own style.' "
Source: *Baseball Magazine* (May 1926, F.C. Lane)

Gray in 1929 *Baseball Magazine:* "I pitch a curve with three speeds: fast, medium, and slow . . . I particularly like a slow curve. It's the best thing on earth, in my opinion, to feed a slugger."

Gray in *Who's Who:* "Connie Mack had the most to do with my success. He told me what two balls had to be pitched in the major leagues and I went out and pitched them—a good curve and a fast ball. I have never forgot how."

Note: TSN article says that Gray relied heavily on his knuckleball when the wind was in his face, but didn't throw it much when the wind was behind him.

TED GRAY 5'11" 175-pound lefty
59-74, 4.37, 4 Saves 1946 1955

Pitch Selection: 1. Fastball 2. Curve 3. Forkball
Interview:
Gray: I was a fastball pitcher.
Neyer: Did you have any secondary pitches?
Gray: Well, I threw a curve, and a split-finger fastball.
Neyer: Did you call it a forkball back then?
Gray: Sure, we called it a forkball. It's the same pitch.
Neyer: Were you basically fastball-curve-forkball your entire career?
Gray: Yes.
Source: Phone interview with Gray (6/5/2002, Rob Neyer)

Note: According to an article by Joe Overfield in "*Bisonogram*," the newsletter of the Buffalo Bisons (April/1989), Gray threw 20 forkballs in his first major-league start in August 1948. Overfield contrasted Gray with Billy Pierce, his teammate in Buffalo and later in the major leagues, by saying that "though built alike and looking alike, (Pierce and Gray) had different pitching styles. Pierce came over the top, threw hard and worked fast . . . Gray threw more from the side, had greater movement on his pitches and a greater variety."

Ted Williams: "He's tough. He's real quick (fast) and he has the moxie to throw the ball in here. He throws it and dares you to hit it. I like that in a pitcher. He's one of the toughest for me to hit."
Source: *Baseball Magazine* (October 1950, Ed Rumill)

TOMMY GREENE 6'5" 222-pound righty
38-25, 4.14, 0 Saves 1989 1997

Pitch Selection: 1. Two-Seam Fastball (low-90s) 2. Hard Curve 3. Change
Source: *The Scouting Report: 1992; The Scouting Notebook: 1995*

KENT GREENFIELD 6'1" 180-pound righty
41-48, 4.54, 1 Save 1924 1929

Pitches: 1. Fastball 2. Curve
Quote: "Greenfield not only has an unusual amount of stuff, but he gets a peculiar hop on his fast ball. This, he believes, is primarily because he is an over-hand pitcher. There are not many such: Vance, Morrison, two or three others. Most pitchers mix up a side-arm and over-hand delivery. The true over-hander is rare in the major leagues."
Source: *Baseball Magazine* (January 1926, John J. Ward)

VEAN GREGG 6'1" 185-pound lefty
92-63, 2.70, 12 Saves 1911 1925

Pitches: 1. Curves 2. Fastball 3. Change
Gregg: "I have always had a good deal of speed, and suppose that a speed ball is about as effective as any delivery. Still I have depended very largely on curves . . . I think I can control my curves even better than I can fast straight ones.

" . . . I never use the spit-ball myself and have no intention of trying at present."
Source: *Baseball Magazine* (December 1912, E.D. Soden)

Description: "One of the all-time great pitchers from the standpoint of natural stuff was the famous southpaw Vean Gregg. They tell me that the last year he was in the Coast League, before he came to the majors, he had as much on the ball as anybody who ever lived. He hurt his arm before the next season but still went on to have a long and phenomenal major-league career. He was near the end of it in 1925 when both of us were with the champion Washington club but he still had plenty. One day I asked Vean how he went to work pitching for the corners. 'Hank,' he replied, 'I aim for the middle and I get plenty of corners!' "
Source: Hank Severeid in *Play Ball! Advice for Young Ballplayers* (Al Chapman and Severeid, 1941)

Key Pitch: Drop Ball
Source: 1915 *Reach Guide*, page 327, poem by Grantland Rice
First stanza of poem:

I do not pose as one who knows
The Final word in perfect pitching;
As one would say the "fadeaway"
Which Matty shoots is most bewitching;
Or Vean Gregg's drop, or Joe Wood's hop,
Or Walsh's magic necromancy;
Though class is there, I'd hate to swear
Which one of these styles struck my fancy.

TOM GRIFFIN 6'3" 210-pound righty
77-94, 4.07, 5 Saves 1969 1982

Pitch Selection: 1. Hard Slider 2. Fastball
Source: *The Sporting News* (6/14/1969, John Wilson)

CLARK GRIFFITH 5'6" 156-pound righty
236-143, 3.31, 7 Saves 1891 1914

Pitch Selection: 1. Sharp Curve 2. Scuff Ball 3. Spitball
Source: *They Played the Game* (Harry Grayson, Page 57)

Key Pitch: Slow Ball
Source: *Touching Second* (Johnny Evers and Hugh Fullerton, 1910)

Note: In a *Baseball Magazine* article (July 1917, "Why The Spit Ball Should Be Abolished"), Griffith acknowledged that he'd often doctored the baseball by banging it against his spikes, but said he never threw an actual spitball.

BOB GRIM 6'1" 175-pound righty
61-41, 3.61, 37 Saves 1954 1962

Pitch Selection: 1. Sneaky Fastball 2. Curve 3. Change 4. Slider
Source: *The Saturday Evening Post* (4/23/1955, Arthur Mann)
Quote from Yankees pitching coach Jim Turner, same source: "No one factor made him a standout. He isn't that kind of pitcher. He did enough things well to make us like him . . . He has a sneaky fast ball and he throws it low. He has a good curve, and he's not afraid to throw the change-up on any delivery. What did I teach him? I don't know. Maybe nothing. You'll have to ask the boy."

Yogi Berra: "Bob had a good sneaky fastball. That was his best pitch, followed by a curve, a little slider and change-up."
Source: Yogi Berra by way of Dale Berra by way of Rob Neyer (e-mail interview, 8/15/2002)

BURLEIGH GRIMES 5'10" 175-pound righty
270-212, 3.53, 18 Saves 1916 1934

Pitch Selection: 1. Spitball 2. Fastball 3. Curve
Source: *Baseball's Famous Pitchers* (Ira L. Smith, 1954); 1923 *Reach Guide* (Page 38), 1924 *Reach Guide* (Page 48)

Transcendental Graphics / ruckerarchive.com

Clark Griffith

Pitches: 1. Fastball 2. Spitball 3. Curve 4. Slider 5. Change 6. Screwball

Grimes: "I used to chew slippery elm—the bark, right off the tree. Come spring the bark would get nice and loose and you could slice it free without any trouble. What I checked was the fiber from inside, and that's what I put on the ball. That's what they called the foreign substance. The ball would break like hell, away from right-handed hitters and in on lefties.

"It wasn't necessarily my number one pitch—the fastball generally was. The spitter was always a threat . . . People meet me today and they say, 'Oh, Burleigh Grimes? You were the spitball pitcher.' Well, hell, I threw a fastball, curve, slider, change, screwball. One

time I pitched 18 innings against the Cubs, beating Hippo Vaughn 3-2, and I threw only three slow spitballs in the ball game. The rest were all fastballs."
Source: *The Man in the Dugout* (Donald Honig, 1977)

Grimes: "Mike Kelly, then manager of the St. Paul club of the American Association, was a friend of my father. In 1909, I visited St. Paul and Mike took me to see a game in which Hank Gehring, the old spit-baller, was pitching. I was so impressed with his delivery that when I returned home, I immediately started practicing on a spitball delivery."
Source: Article by J.G. Taylor Spink in Burleigh Grimes file at the Hall of Fame, quoted in SABR-L posting of August 13–14, 2002 (#2002-273), posted by Steve Steinberg.

Grimes: "I believe I could get by without the spit-ball, provided I took time to develop a good curve. Spit balls and curves don't mix. It's either one thing or the other. In throwing the spit-ball a pitcher throws overhand and brings his arm straight down. You don't use that delivery in throwing curves. Still, I have developed a kind of an imitation curve that I throw with a sort of overhand, side arm motion.

"This curve is just to give the batter something to think about. To pep him up a little and add something to the spice of his existence. This curve I speak of doesn't break very much, perhaps twice the thickness of a bat. But it has been one of my most effective deliveries this summer. I mix it up with my other things, of course, but the spitter is my main defence, that and my fastball."
Source: *Baseball Magazine* (May 1924, "Comprising an interview with Burleigh Grimes")

JASON GRIMSLEY 6'3" 205-pound righty
35-47, 4.81, 4 Saves 1989 2003

Pitch Selection: 1. Sinking Fastball 2. Curve
Source: *The Scouting Report: 1992*

Pitch Selection: 1. Fastball (86–88) 2. Slider
3. Split-Fingered Fastball
Source: *The Scouting Notebook: 1995*

Pitch Selection: 1. Fastball (mid-90s) 2. Sinker
3. Split-Fingered Fastball (occasional)
Source: *The Scouting Notebook* (2001–2003 editions)

Pitches, 2002–2003: 1. Sinker (low-90s)
2. Four-Seam Fastball (mid-90s)
3. Slider (occasional)
Source: Rob Neyer's observation of far too many Royals games

ROSS GRIMSLEY 6'3" 195-pound lefty
124-99, 3.81, 3 Saves 1971 1982

Pitch Selection: 1. Change 2. Curve 3. Slow Curve
4. Slider 5. Screwball 6. Fastball
Note: Grimsley was a master at varying the speeds on all his pitches.
Sources: *The Sporting News* (4/29/1978, Ian McDonald); Spring 1979 *Baseball Factbook* (article by K. D. Thornton titled "Ross Grimsley: Baseball's Change-Up King")

DAN GRINER 6'1" 200-pound righty
28-55, 3.49, 6 Saves 1912 1918

Description: ". . . Marquard has a good, fast waist-high ball for the right-hand sluggers. Griner, the new St. Louis pitcher, has the same slant for right-handers and can also throw it to a left-handed hitter—a trick nobody else seems to possess, and one which makes this Griner a far better pitcher than many critics have imagined."
Source: *Baseball Magazine* (August 1913, "The Vagaries of Pitching")

LEE GRISSOM 6'3" 200-pound lefty
29-48, 3.89, 7 Saves 1934 1941

Key Pitch: Fastball
Source: *Baseball Magazine* (September 1937, Clifford Bloodgood)

MARV GRISSOM 6'3" 190-pound righty
47-45, 3.41, 58 Saves 1946 1959

Key Pitch: Fastball
Source: *The Long Season* (Jim Brosnan, 1960)
Key Pitch as young man/starter: Fastball
Key Pitches as old man/reliever: 1. Screwball
2. Fastball
Source: *A Day in the Bleachers* (Arnold Hano, 1952)

STEVE GROMEK 6'2" 180-pound righty
123-108, 3.41, 23 Saves 1941 1957

Pitch Selection, 1945: 1. Fastball 2. Hard Curve
3. Change

Note: Gromek threw no speciality pitches at that time.
Source: *Baseball Magazine* (October 1945, Ed McAuley)
Note: McAuley says that George Susce, a Cleveland coach, had "taught Gromek to throw his curve . . . as a fast ball with a hook to it," and adds, "Under the tutelage of the Cleveland coaches, he has become almost exclusively a sidearm pitcher."

Description: "Steve Gromek of Cleveland throws the ball harder than any other American League pitcher now that Hughson is gone. I can see both of their fast balls rise. It comes up that far—about six inches—as it nears the batter."
Source: anonymous American League umpire quoted by Shirley Povich in *The Sporting News* (8/17/1944, Page 10)

Pitch Selection: 1. Fastball 2. Change
Source: *Baseball Digest* (March 1949, Frank Gibbons); according to Gibbons, Gromek tried to learn the curveball and the knuckleball, failed at both, and wound up going with just his "jumping fast ball and his letup pitch."

Pitch Selection: 1. Fastball 2. Change
3. Knuckle Curve
Source: *The Ballplayers* (1990, article by Morris Eckhouse)

BOB GROOM 6'2" 175-pound righty
119-150, 3.10, 13 Saves 1909 1918

Key Pitch: Curve
Quote: "Groom undoubtedly has a fine selection of curves and promises one day to be one of the greatest pitchers in the baseball world."
Source: *The National Game* (Alfred H. Spink, 1911)

BUDDY GROOM 6'2" 200-pound lefty
26-30, 4.62, 26 Saves 1992 2003

Pitch Selection: 1. Fastball (high-80s) 2. Slider
3. Curve 4. Change
Source: *The Scouting Notebook: 1997*

KEVIN GROSS 6'5" 203-pound righty
142-158, 4.11, 5 Saves 1983 1997

Pitch Selection: 1. Hard Curve 2. Fastball 3. Change
4. Slider
Sources: *The Scouting Report: 1987; Tom Seaver's 1989 Scouting Notebook*

LEFTY GROVE 6'3" 190-pound lefty
300-141, 3.06, 55 Saves 1925 1941

Pitch Selection: 1. Fastball 2. Curve
3. Forkball (late career)
Note: An excellent discussion of Grove's pitch selection can be found in Moe Berg's article "Pitchers and Catchers" in the *Atlantic Monthly*, September 1941. The gist of it is that Grove threw mostly fastballs early in his career, gradually began mixing in more curves, and added a forkball in 1935, after his arm injury (though a *Baseball Magazine* article says Grove threw the forkball only in his last two seasons).
Sources: *Atlantic Monthly* (September 1941, Moe Berg); *The Fireballers* (Jack Newcombe, 1964); Wes Ferrell in *Baseball When the Grass Was Real* (Donald Honig, 1975)

Walter Johnson: "And there are different kinds of fast balls. Take Lefty Grove, for instance. He probably uses more stuff right now than any pitcher. But he's not what I would call a vicious pitcher, a fellow you have to watch. His fast ball comes at you as straight as a string."

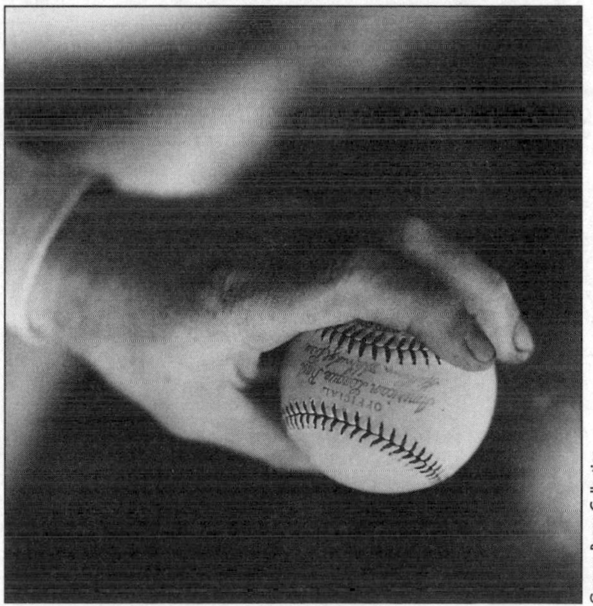
George Brace Collection

Lefty Grove's fastball grip

Source: *Baseball Magazine* (July 1930, "Comprising an Interview with Walter Johnson")

Description: "He has the hands of an artist, long, thin fingers. His wrists are slender. But there's a world of deception in those thin arms, long fingers and slender wrists. He is, in fact, tremendously powerful. Without an ounce of bulky weight on his person, there is a whip-cord, leathery strength to his long, lean muscles and close-knit joints."
Mickey Cochrane: "I'll admit when Grove broke into the circuit he had little else except his fast ball. But he has learned a lot. He has a pretty fair change of pace and a very serviceable curve."
Source: *Baseball Magazine* (May 1934, F.C. Lane); same source, both Lane and Cochrane confirm that while Grove's fastball is certainly excellent, it's straight, with no "hop."

Comment: "Lefty Grove is the greatest pitcher, left or right-hander, that I have ever seen. In my humble opinion he throws the fastest ball in existence . . ."
Source: Catcher Cy Perkins in *Baseball Magazine* (April 1932, Clifford Bloodgood)

Note: As a young pitcher Grove threw a pitch he called a "sailor," which he later stated was the same pitch that came to be called the slider.
Source: *Sport* (February 1957, Al Hirshberg)

Commentary: In *Two Spectacular Seasons* (William B. Mead, 1990), Doc Cramer says that Grove "didn't have the curve," and Charlie Gehringer in the same book says that Grove "hardly ever threw a curve." Cramer and Gehringer, however, were speaking many years after the fact, when their memories had long since simplified the past. The other sources are more credible.

ORVAL GROVE 6'3" 196-pound righty
63-73, 3.78, 4 Saves 1940 1949

Pitch Selection: 1. Sinker 2. Curve 3. Fastball
Quote: "It was in camp that year (1940) that Ted Lyons . . . predicted greatness for the big boy. 'They'll never drive that sinker very far,' he said."

Note: Grove matured as a pitcher after Muddy Ruel showed him that he was gripping the ball too loosely, resulting in a loss of control.
Source: *Baseball Magazine* (September 1943, Herbert Simons)

HENRY GRUBER 5'9" 155-pound righty
60-78, 3.67, 2 Saves 1887 1891

Note from *New Haven Journal-Courier* (9/27/1932): "He worked for the New Haven team [after his major league career] for quite a few seasons, and then faded from the picture, the old 'stuff' gone from the arm which had thrown many a strike past the best hitters in the big leagues."

CECILIO GUANTE 6'3" 205-pound righty
29-34, 3.48, 35 Saves 1982 1990

Pitch Selection: 1. Fastball 2. Forkball 3. Curve
Note: Guante was knock-kneed. Source says he threw two types of curveballs. He also threw from multiple angles.
Source: *The Scouting Report: 1984*

Pitch Selection: 1. Fastball (90s) 2. Slider
Source: *The Scouting Report: 1987*

EDDIE GUARDADO 5'10" 200-pound lefty
36-47 4.50, 116 Saves 1993 2003

Pitch Selection: 1. Fastball (90–92) 2. Hard Curve 3. Palm Ball
Sources: *The Scouting Notebook* (1997, 1999, and 2002 editions); broadcast of Twins-Angels game (5/30/2002)

MARK GUBICZA 6'6" 215-pound righty
132-136, 3.96, 2 Saves 1984 1997

Pitch Selection: 1. Fastball 2. Slider 3. Curve
Sources: *Tom Seaver's 1989 Scouting Notebook; The Scouting Report: 1990*

LEE GUETTERMAN 6'8" 225-pound lefty
38-36, 4.33, 25 Saves 1984 1996

Pitch Selection: 1. Fastball (88–90) 2. Slider 3. Sinker 4. Curve 5. Straight Change
Source: *The Scouting Report: 1990*

Pitch Selection: 1. Sinker 2. Curve 3. Slider 4. Change
Note: Guetterman threw mostly sinkers.
Source: *The Scouting Report: 1992*

RON GUIDRY 5'11" 161-pound lefty
170-91, 3.29, 4 Saves 1975 1988

Pitch Selection: 1. Fastball 2. Slider
Source: *The Scouting Report: 1987*

Quote: "The consensus around baseball is that the best sliderball pitcher now at work is Ron Guidry of the Yankees, who, not incidentally, also has one of the best fastballs."
Source: Frederick C. Klein, July 1979, unidentified clipping in *The Sporting News* morgue.

Quote: "Owns the best slider in the AL."
Source: *The Complete Handbook of Baseball: 1982 Season* (edited by Zander Hollander)

DON GULLETT 6'0" 190-pound lefty
109-50, 3.11, 11 Saves 1970 1978

Pitch Selection: 1. Fastball 2. Hard Slider
3. Forkball (later career) 4. Curve
Sources: Gullett in *The Pastime in the Seventies* (Bill Ballew, 2002); *The Sporting News* (4/17/1976, Earl Lawson; 9/6/1975, Lawson); *Baseball Digest* (January 1971, Wells Twombly); *Men of the Machine* (Ritter Collett, 1977)

Gullett: "I think early in my career I went basically with the fastball and a hard slider. Then I started using the curveball during my second season in the major leagues. The last few years of my career I got to the point where I could throw the forkball and it was a very effective pitch for me. It made pitching easier for me—not that pitching is ever easy—but it made my fastball a lot quicker and it made me a more complete pitcher by having four pitches I could throw for strikes and get batters out."
Source: *The Pastime in the Seventies* (Ballew)

Gullett on his Forkball: "I use it as my change of pace. I was getting a reputation around the league as only being a fastball pitcher. I still rely on my fastball, but the forkball has made me a much better fastball pitcher because hitters can't always expect it now."
Source: *Baseball Digest* (October 1974, Rick Van Sant)

Description: "Has excellent fastball, fair curve. Can really bring smoke for 3 innings."
Source: Baltimore Orioles scouting report prior to 1970 World Series, from *Putting It All Together* (Brooks Robinson with Fred Bauer, 1971)

Quote: "Throwing across the body can cause career-ending injuries if it is not corrected. In recent times, Don Gullett . . . had a brilliant career curtailed because he could not correct this flaw and caused major damage to his left arm and shoulder."
Source: *The Art of Pitching* (Tom Seaver with Lee Lowenfish, 1984)

BILL GULLICKSON 6'3" 200-pound righty
162-136, 3.93, 0 Saves 1979 1994

Pitch Selection: 1. Fastball 2. Sinker 3. Curve
Source: *The Scouting Report: 1987*

Description: "His fastball hits 84 mph on a good day—nothing more than a batting-practice pitch unless he cuts it or sinks it. Keeping hitters off balance is the key for Gullickson, who throws two kinds of curves and a slider, and hides the ball extremely well."
Source: *Bill Mazeroski's Baseball* (1993 edition)

AD GUMBERT 5'10" 200-pound righty
128-99, 4.27, 1 Save 1888 1896

Key Pitch: Fastball
Quote: "He is a powerful young fellow, though, and pitches a wonderfully speedy and accurate ball. His delivery appears to be devoid of curves, but is singularly difficult to hit. Many times this season he has had two or three balls on a man and then would pitch ball after ball over the plate, compelling the batsman to strike out or hit out."
Source: *The Sporting Life* (11/15/1890)

HARRY GUMBERT 6'2" 185-pound righty
143-113, 3.68, 48 Saves 1935 1950

Pitches: 1. Curve 2. Fastball 3. Change
Notes: Gumbert's breakthrough in 1938 was credited to a better fastball and increased reliance on his fastball, although his curve was always his best pitch.

His improved fastball in 1938–39 was attributed to working harder in the off season, and to catcher Harry Danning, who convinced him that he was throwing too many curves.
Sources: *The Sporting News* (5/18/1939, Tom Meany);

Dugout to Foxhole (Rick Van Blair, 1994); in latter source, Gumbert refers to his "nothing-ball changeup."

RANDY GUMPERT 6'3" 185-pound righty
51-59, 4.17, 7 Saves 1936 1952

Pitch Selection: 1. Fastball 2. Screwball
Notes: An 18-year-old sensation for a few weeks in 1936, Gumpert disappeared for ten years after that when, according to Gumpert, the Philadelphia coaches tried to change his natural three-quarters delivery to an overhand motion. Despite going 11-3 with a 2.31 ERA for the Yankees in 1946, he failed to gain the confidence of Yankee manager Bucky Harris, who traded him to Chicago, where he had a second comeback. He attributed that second comeback (1949) purely to throwing his screwball to left-handed hitters, which he had never done before.
Sources: Articles by Al Cartwright and "The Old Scout" (Sam Murphy) in *The Sporting News* morgue.

ERIC GUNDERSON 6'0" 190-pound lefty
8-11, 4.95, 2 Saves 1990 2000

Pitch Selection: 1. Fastball 2. Sinker
Source: *The Scouting Notebook: 1998*

LARRY GURA 6'0" 170-pound lefty
126-97, 3.76, 14 Saves 1970 1985

Pitches: 1. Curve 2. Slider 3. Fastball 4. Change
Source: *The Sporting News* (9/30/1978, Sid Bordman)

MARK GUTHRIE 6'4" 215-pound lefty
51-54, 4.05, 14 Saves 1989 2003

Pitches: 1. Forkball/Splitter 2. Fastball 3. Curve 4. Change
Sources: *The Scouting Report: 1992; The Scouting Notebook: 1997*

JOSE GUZMAN 6'2" 160-pound righty
80-74, 4.05, 0 Saves 1985 1994

Pitch Selection: 1. Hard Sinking Fastball 2. Change 3. Slider
Source: *The Scouting Report: 1992*

JUAN GUZMAN 6'0" 190-pound righty
91-79, 4.08, 0 Saves 1991 2000

Pitch Selection: 1. Sinking Fastball 2. Rising Fastball 3. Slider 4. Curve added after arm injury in mid-1990s
Sources: *1994 Baseball Almanac; The Scouting Notebook 1999*

Description: "Incredible stuff, and he's just wild enough for hitters to have that in the back of their minds. His fastball has a late jump, he intimidates with his slider, and he has a great change-up. The only drawback is his delivery. It's just a matter of time before he breaks down."
Source: *Bill Mazeroski's Baseball* (1993 edition)

MOOSE HAAS 6'0" 180-pound righty
100-83, 4.01, 2 Saves 1976 1987

Pitches: 1. Fastball 2. Slider 3. Change (developed in 1983)
Source: *The Sporting News* (8/29/1983, Tom Flaherty; 6/14/1980, Flaherty)

JOHN HABYAN 6'2" 195-pound righty
26-24, 3.85, 12 Saves 1985 1996

Pitch Selection: 1. Slider 2. Sinking Fastball
Source: *The Scouting Report: 1992*

WARREN HACKER 6'1" 185-pound righty
62-89, 4.21, 17 Saves 1948 1961

Pitch Selection: 1. Fastball 2. Knuckleball 3. Sinker
Source: Hacker in *Take Me Out to the Cubs Game* (John C. Skipper, 2000)

Pitch Selection: 1. Knuckleball 2. Fastball 3. Curve
Source: *The Sporting News* (5/28/1952)

Pitches: 1. Fastball 2. Slow Curve 3. Change 4. Knuckleball
Note: Hacker threw sidearm.
Source: Hacker in the *Kansas City Times* (3/11/1957, AP story)

Note: Listed by *The Sporting News* (8/29/1956) as having one of the best fastballs in the league.

HARVEY HADDIX 5'9" 170-pound lefty
136-113, 3.63, 21 Saves 1952 1965

Pitch Selection: 1. Fastball 2. Slider 3. Curve 4. Change
Source: *Baseball Monthly* (June 1962, by Harvey Haddix)
Other Sources: *Best Sports Stories 1960* (article by Lester J. Biederman); *The Crooked Pitch* (Martin Quigley, 1984)

Haddix on his twelve-inning perfect game: "I was to work a two-pitch game—fastball and slider. You could count the number of changeups and curves I threw on the fingers of one hand."

Stan Musial: "Haddix, a good fielder and hitter, was a good pitcher who would have been great, in my opinion, if he hadn't lost something off his curve ball. He never was quite the same after Joe Adcock hit a line drive off his knee one day in 1954 when he was just about the most effective pitcher around."
Source: *Stan Musial: The Man's Own Story* (Musial, as told to Bob Broeg, 1964)

GEORGE HADDOCK 5'11" 155-pound righty
94-88, 4.07, 2 Saves 1888 1894

Comment: "He had excellent command of the sphere, and was as elusive in his twists and drops as could be wished for . . ."
Source: *The Washington Post* (9/5/1894, Page 6)

BUMP HADLEY 5'11" 190-pound righty
161-165, 4.24, 25 Saves 1926 1941

Pitch Selection: 1. Fastball 2. Curve 3. Half-Speed Fastball (as Change)
Description: "Hadley's stock in trade is his fast ball, which is plenty fast. He pitches a few curves, but he has never developed a particularly serviceable bender. His change of pace is mainly a shift from a fast ball to a ball that isn't quite so fast."
Source: *Baseball Magazine* (June 1933, John J. Ward)

Pitch Selection: 1. Slow Curve 2. Fastball
Sources: *Who's Who in the Major Leagues* (1937 edition: ". . . always been regarded as a curve-ball specialist."); *Who's Who in the Major Leagues* (1939 edition); Bobby Doerr in *Fenway* (Peter Golenbock, 1992)

MICKEY HAEFNER 5'8" 160-pound lefty
78-91, 3.50, 13 Saves 1943 1950

Pitch Selection: 1. Knuckleball 2. Curve 3. Screwball 4. Spitball
Source: Haefner in *The Sporting News* (12/23/1943, Shirley Povich)

Pitch Selection: 1. Knuckleball 2. Curve 3. Fastball
Sources: *The Crooked Pitch* (Martin Quigley, 1984); Ernie Stewart in *The Men in Blue* (Larry Gerlach, 1980); *The Washington Post* (3/3/1948, Shirley Povich column)

NOODLES HAHN 5'9" 160-pound lefty
130-93, 2.55, 0 Saves 1899 1906

Key Pitch: Jump ball
Source: *Cincinnati Commercial Tribune* (7/13/1900)

JESSE HAINES 6'0" 190-pound righty
210-158, 3.64, 10 Saves 1918 1937

Pitch Selection, 1920: 1. Fastball 2. Curve
Pitch Selection, 1921–23: 1. Fastball 2. Knuckleball 3. Curve
Pitch Selection, 1924–25: 1. Fastball 2. Change 3. Curve
Pitch Selection, 1926–31: 1. Knuckleball 2. Fastball 3. Change 4. Curve
Pitch Selection, 1932–37: 1. Knuckleball 2. Change 3. Fastball 4. Curve
Notes: When I (Bill) was nearly finished with this book, I realized that I had divergent and incompatible information about Haines, one source describing him as a fastball pitcher, another as a curve ball pitcher, two others describing him as a knuckleball pitcher. I thus added him to the list of pitchers to be researched at *The Sporting News* morgue.

When Haines came to the major leagues in 1920, he had an excellent fastball with a natural hop to it. He lost 20 games as a rookie, however, and realized that he needed a second pitch. He tried to develop a curve, but according to Haines (Cullen Cain article) "it was not much of a curve." In other discussions, he speaks more kindly of his curve, and several sources describe him as having a good curve. He began to experiment with a knuckle ball, which he used as his number two pitch 1921–1922 and mastered in 1923, winning 20 games. In 1924 the knuckleball deserted him, leading to two poor seasons, but he rediscovered the knuckler in early season, 1926, and it became his "out" pitch at that time, although he still had a better-than-fair fastball.

Haines called his key pitch a knuckleball, and he is referred to hundreds of times in contemporary articles as a knuckleball pitcher. Nonetheless, the pitch probably was *not* a knuckleball in the modern meaning of the term. He threw the pitch hard, as hard as he threw his fastball. It broke sharply downward as it neared the plate, like a spitball, a forkball or a split-fingered fastball. The best description of his two key pitches and how he threw them is in the Haley article, referenced below:

> Haines . . . points out that his fast ball "jumps" as it nears the plate. In other words, it "defies gravity" and rises a few inches above its regular course. This is caused by the manner in which Jess grips the ball and by the terrific speed with which he throws it, plus air resistance. Jess grips the ball so that it revolves in an upward motion, from back to front, as Haines sees it. Then, as it nears the plate, the spin meeting air friction carries the ball upward.
>
> Haines holds the ball for fastball pitchering between his thumb and the first and second fingers of his right hand. When he wants to use his knuckleball he closes his first two fingers, pressing the ball tightly with his thumb against the first joints of the fingers. He delivers this pitch in such a way that the ball, approaching the plate, revolves sharply downward and away from a right-hand batter and toward a left-hand batter."

The grip, the spin, and the fact that the ball was thrown hard, I feel, identify the pitch not as a modern knuckleball, but as a distinct pitch, probably no longer thrown, but probably closer to a knuckle curve or a cut fastball. As Haley stated, "his 'knuckler' is simply a variation of his fast ball." The sharp downward break of a hard-thrown ball made the ball break down like a spitball, which was commonly observed, but, oddly enough, reviewing more than 40 articles about Haines, I found *no* allegations that he threw a spitball.

A quote from *Baseball Magazine*, February 1927: "The number of knucklers I use in a game depends largely on how good my fast ball and curve happen to be. Some days when they're good, I'll not use more than a dozen knucklers in a game. There are other games when I'll pitch as many as fifty . . . The knuckler, no doubt, has made me a successful pitcher."

A statement in *Babe Ruth's Own Book of Baseball* (page 85) that "Jess Haines of the Cardinals is another chap who depends upon his curve ball to get him out of trouble" is clearly wrong, unless one considers his knuckleball to be a form of a curve.

Sources: Unidentified clipping of Haines' no-hitter (July 17, 1924); John J. Ward in *Baseball Magazine,* 1927; C. William Duncan in *Baseball Magazine* (August 1927); Cullen Cain, *National League Service Bureau* (January 15, 1928); interview with Haines in *Baseball Magazine* (February 1931); Martin J. Haley in the *St. Louis Globe-Democrat,* March 20, 1932; undated story in *The Sporting News* (1934); *Baseball's 50 Greatest Games* (Bert Sugar, page 34); Ed Rumill in *The Christian Science Monitor* (October 1972); *The Sporting News* (8/19/1978, page 53, Obit)

Haines: "My favorite ball is the knuckler. I hold the ball tight against the knuckles of my pitching hand and throw it with every ounce of speed I can put behind it. When it's breaking right, it swoops down a good deal like a curve, only faster and with a sharper break than a curve. I don't believe any batter in uniform likes to face a good knuckle ball when it's sweeping in with a lot of zip and breaking right."

Source: *Baseball Magazine* (May 1928, "Comprising an Interview with Jesse Haines")

Haines: "I have a pretty good curve and a fast ball, but the knuckle ball is always something that I carry in reserve. The number of knucklers I use in a game depends largely on how good my fast ball and curve happen to be. Some days when they're good, I'll not use more than a dozen knucklers in a game. There are other games when I'll pitch as many as fifty."

Source: *Baseball Magazine* (March 1931, Jesse Haines)

JOHN HALAMA 6'5" 215-pound lefty
45-37, 4.49, 0 Saves 1998 2003

Pitch Selection: 1. Sinking Fastball (mid-80s) 2. Change 3. Slow Curve 4. Four-Seam Fastball

Sources: *The Scouting Notebook* (2000–2001 editions)

ED HALICKI 6'7" 220-pound righty
55-66, 3.62, 1 Save 1974 1980

Pitch Selection: 1. Fastball 2. Slider 3. Change

Sources: *The Sporting News* (8/7/1976, Art Spander); *The No-Hit Hall of Fame* (Rich Coberly, 1985)

BERT HALL 5'10" 178-pound righty
0-1, 4.00, 0 Saves 1911 1911

Key Pitch: Forkball?
Source: *The Seattle Times* (9/19/1908); various editions of *The Tacoma Daily Tribune*

Note: Hall pitched only a few games in the major leagues, but previously was well known for throwing his "fork ball" with Tacoma in the Northwestern League, and we believe he's the first to throw a pitch with that name in the professional game.

DICK HALL 6'6" 200-pound righty
93-75, 3.32, 68 Saves 1955 1971

Pitch Selection: 1. Fastball 2. Curve 3. Slider
Sources: *The Kansas City Star* (5/11/1960, Page 9C); *The Ballplayers* (1990, article by Morris Eckhouse)

Roger Angell: "Dick Hall is a Baltimore institution, like crab cakes. He is six feet six and one-half inches tall and forty years old, and he pitches with an awkward, sidewise motion that suggests a man feeling under his bed for a lost collar stud. He throws a sneaky fast ball and never, or *almost* never, walks batters . . ."
Source: *The New Yorker* (October 1970, reprinted in *The Summer Game*)

Dick Hall: "There is a statistic that I am quite proud of. In my last seven years in the majors (1965–71), I only allowed twenty-three bases on balls that were not intentional walks. I also had only one wild pitch in my career, that came when I was experimenting with a knuckle ball. At Pittsburgh, Branch Rickey wanted everyone to experiment with a knuckleball."
Source: *Yesterday's Heroes* (Marty Appel, 1988)

SEA LION HALL 6'1" 187-pound righty
54-47, 3.08, 16 Saves 1906 1918

Key Pitch: Fastball
Source: *St. Paul Dispatch* (12/7/1943, Gordon Gilmore)

TOM HALL 6'0" 150-pound lefty
52-33, 3.27, 32 Saves 1968 1977

Pitch Selection: 1. Fastball 2. Curve 3. Slider 4. Change (developed in 1972)
Source: Missing (sorry).

Quote: "Hall is a guy who can enter a game in a tough situation and strike out the side."
Source: Royals scout Tom Ferrick in *The Sporting News* (12/8/1971, Earl Lawson)

BILL HALLAHAN 5'10" 170-pound lefty
102-94, 4.03, 8 Saves 1925 1938

Pitch Selection: 1. Fastball 2. Overhand Curve 3. Slow Ball (added in 1930)
Sources: *Baseball Magazine* (December 1930, Clifford Bloodgood); *The Gashouse Gang* (Robert E. Hood, 1976)

Comment: "When Hallahan has control, he is a mighty hard man to beat. He puts more stuff on the ball, I believe, than Grove, of the Athletics, and he has almost as much speed. If he could clip the corners like a Grover Alexander, he would seldom lose a ball game."
Source: Charlie Grimm in 1930 *Baseball Magazine*

Description: "Bill Hallahan certainly has great speed, but he has something besides speed, a lot of stuff on the ball. The old ball certainly hops and shoots when Bill is having a good day."
Source: *Baseball Magazine* (July 1932, "Comprising an Interview with Ray Kremer")

Note: Hallahan struggled with his control and was known as "Wild Bill," but when Hallahan missed it was very rarely at the expense of the hitter. In 1930 and '31, Hallahan walked 238 hitters (leading the National League both seasons) . . . and hit only *one*. This was typical, as he finished his career with 779 walks allowed, and eight hit batters. We weren't there, but it's probably safe to assume that Hallahan almost never worked the inside of the plate.

EARL HAMILTON 5'8" 160-pound lefty
116-147, 3.16, 13 Saves 1911 1924

Pitch Selection: 1. Change 2. Fastball 3. Curve
Quote: "Chances are that Ham will quit the game he ornamented with a slow ball . . . So passeth a nice chap with a fine slow ball, some speed, a good curve."
Source: *New York Sun* (5/16/1915)

Description: "Hamilton is one of the under-sizlings of the American League. Furthermore he, like Rube Mar-

quard, has a 'wry' neck, that may have come from looking over his shoulders at runners on first base."
Source: *The Sporting News* (11/16/1911)

JACK HAMILTON 6'0" 200-pound righty
32-40, 4.53, 20 Saves 1962 1969

Note: Hamilton was frequently accused of throwing a spitball.
Source: *The Sporting News* (12/23/1967)

JOEY HAMILTON 6'4" 220-pound righty
74-73, 4.44, 1 Save 1994 2003

Pitch Selection: 1. Sinking Fastball 2. Slider 3. Curve 4. Change (added in 1998)
Sources: *The Scouting Notebook* (1997 and 1999 editions)

STEVE HAMILTON 6'6" 190-pound lefty
40-31, 3.05, 42 Saves 1961 1972

Note: In the late sixties, Hamilton developed a blooper pitch he called the "Folly Floater."
Source: *The Sporting News* (9/6/1969, Page 6)

Hamilton on the Folly Floater: "I combined Satch's hesitation pitch with Rip's high blooper, and it has been so effective that I've made it an important part of my pitching repertoire . . .

"It never was a joke to me. A pitcher just can't get by with a fast ball and a curve or slider. He's got to find another avenue to throw off the batters. But I couldn't throw a screwball and I never had a real good slow curve. I tried a palm ball and slip pitches and couldn't master them either."
Source: *Baseball Digest* (August 1971, George Vass)

Notes: According to Ferguson Jenkins in *Inside Pitching* (with Dave Fisher, 1972), Hamilton "was one of the great sidearm specialists of all time. He's about 6'7", and he'd lean way over to the right to throw his pitch."

According to Tom Seaver in *Pitching with Tom Seaver* (with Steve Jacobson, 1973), "The greatest advantage a pitcher has against a hitter hitting from the same side is demonstrated by a sidearmer. Take a tall fellow like Steve Hamilton—six feet, seven inches and appropriately long arms—reaching all the way out to pitch: A left-handed hitter must think the first baseman is throwing the ball. He was a devastating relief pitcher to left-handed hitters."

Indeed. From 1967 through 1969, covering 198 at-bats, Hamilton held left-handed hitters to a .167 batting average.

LUKE HAMLIN 6'2" 168-pound righty
73-76, 3.77, 9 Saves 1933 1944

Pitch Selection: 1. Sailer (Fastball) 2. Slider 3. Curve
Source: Harold Parrott in *The Sporting News* (10/26/1939)

Notes: Parrott says (1939) that Hamlin seldom threw a curve. He may have thrown a change, although this is not specifically mentioned by Parrott.

In *The Pastime in Turbulence: Interviews with Baseball Players of the 1940s* (Brent Kelley, 2001), Red Hayworth says that he hit his one major-league home run against Hamlin, and that Hamlin "was a curveball pitcher." The fact that Hayworth's home run was hit off Hamlin checks out . . . Hamlin probably was throwing the curve ball a lot more by then, as his fastball was no longer very good.

ATLEE HAMMAKER 6'3" 200-pound lefty
59-67, 3.66, 5 Saves 1981 1995

Pitch Selection: 1. Slider 2. Fastball
Note: Hammaker suffered a rotator cuff injury in 1984, which drastically reduced the effectiveness of his fastball.
Source: *The Scouting Report: 1990*

CHRIS HAMMOND 6'1" 190-pound lefty
56-59, 4.16, 2 Saves 1990 2003

Pitch Selection: 1. Change 2. Fastball 3. Curve 4. Slider
Source: *The Scouting Report: 1992*

Pitch Selection: 1. Change 2. Slider 3. Fastball (mid-80s)
Source: *The Scouting Notebook: 1996*

Description: ". . . For him, the changeup is a devastating weapon, evaluated at a score of 80—the highest possible—by the Yankee scouts.

" 'It has different action on it,' [Mark] Newman said. He has great arm speed and command of it. The funny term people use for it is 'Bugs bunny change,' because it's like it stops in midair. It's so good he throws it to left-handers and right-handers.'

"... He delivers his changeup awkwardly, stomping hard on the mound with his right foot and then releasing it. The harder he stomps, the more he is concentrating."

" 'It looks funny,' Newman said, 'but more importantly, hitters think it looks funny.' "

Source: *New York Times* (2/16/2003, article by Tyler Kepner)

Leo Mazzone: "He came to us with a great changeup. In fact, he had more confidence in the changeup than he had in the fastball. So again, the emphasis was put on the fastball. We told him if the (quality of his) fastball ever equaled the changeup, it would just make the changeup that much better because it would be easier to throw it. It wouldn't have to be great anymore. It could just be good. Changing speeds doesn't just mean pulling the throttle. It means pushing it, too."

Source: article by Jayson Stark on ESPN.com (2/25/2003); Mazzone was Hammond's pitching coach with the Braves in 2002.

GRANNY HAMNER 5'10" 163-pound righty
0-2, 5.40, 0 Saves 1956 1962

Key Pitch: Knuckleball

Source: *Kansas City Times* (7/26/1962)

Note: Hamner, an infielder with the Phillies in the 1950s, pitched a few games in 1956 (and one in '57), then returned to the minors as a manager *and* refined his knuckleball, which earned him a brief return to the majors in 1962 with the Kansas City A's. It's not clear whether or not he relied on the knuckler in 1956 and '57, but it seems likely.

RALPH HAMNER 6'3" 165-pound righty
8-20, 4.58, 1 Save 1946 1949

Description: "He pitched for the Cubs and the White Sox a little bit, tall thin guy. He'd throw more ground balls than anyone I'd ever seen."

Source: Cal McLish in *The Side of Cooperstown* (Larry Moffi, 1996)

MIKE HAMPTON 5'10" 180-pound lefty
120-89, 3.96, 1 Save 1993 2003

Pitch Selection: 1. Two-Seam Fastball 2. Four-Seam Fastball 3. Cut Fastball 4. Change 5. Cut Fastball/Slider 6. Sweeping Curve

Sources: *The Scouting Notebook 2000;* Hampton quoted in the *Rocky Mountain News* (3/19/2002, Tracy Ringolsby)

Commentary: Hampton told Ringolsby that in his good years, he threw the two-seam fastball (which came in at about 88 MPH but with a sinking action) 85 percent of the time (presumably meaning 85 percent of his fastballs, and not 85 percent of his pitches). In Coors Field, he had gotten away from that, and was throwing the four-seam fastball, which came in about 92, more often.

Hampton got his career back on track in 2003 after joining the Braves. According to *Sports Illustrated* (8/18/2003), "Hampton credits his turnaround to better mechanics. He took some velocity off his sinker and focused on throwing it with more movement. After Hampton's 7-1 win over the Brewers last Thursday . . . pitching coach Leo Mazzone said Hampton had thrown 'the best sinker I've ever seen.' "

BILL HANDS 6'2" 185-pound righty
111-110, 3.35, 14 Saves 1965 1975

Pitch Selection: 1. Sinking Fastball 2. Slider 3. Curve

Sources: *The Sporting News* (7/19/1969, Jerome Holtzman); *The Cubs of '69* (Rick Talley, 1969); *Sport* (August 1970, Pat Jordan)

Description: "To understand just how conscious an effort Bill Hands' pitching is, you have to watch him warm up before a game. At first glance he seems smooth and natural, and only later do you notice that his motion is just a little too stiff and formal. When he kicks his left leg high and is about to pounce on the batter, he pauses a second and his eyes suddenly dart from the plate to his leg, as if he is examining his movements in mid-form. It is then that you realize that his motion is not some spontaneous inspiration, like that of Bob Gibson's, but rather, a more conscious, deliberate and disciplined creation."

Source: Jordan in *Sport*

Quote: "His fastball is only average, but he throws a wicked slider."

Source: *Major League Baseball: 1971* (Brenda Zanger and Dick Kaplan)

CHRIS HANEY 6'3" 210-pound lefty
38-52, 5.07, 1 Save 1991 2002

Pitch Selection: 1. Fastball (high-80s)
2. Cut Fastball (high-80s) 3. Curve
4. Slider 5. Change
Sources: *The Scouting Notebook* (1996 and 1997 editions)

GERRY HANNAHS 6'3" 210-pound lefty
3-7, 5.07, 1 Save 1976 1979

Key Pitch: Knuckle Curve
Source: *The Sporting News* (3/1/1980, Gordon Verrell)

JIM HANNAN 6'3" 205-pound righty
41-48, 3.88, 7 Saves 1962 1971

Description: "An old-fashioned blow-em-down guy . . . who tosses the curve as his clutch pitch."
Source: *1963 Major League Handbook* (Don Schiffer)

ERIK HANSON 6'6" 210-pound righty
89-84, 4.15, 0 Saves 1988 1998

Pitch Selection, early career: 1. Fastball 2. Curve
3. Change
Pitch Selection, mid-1990s: 1. Big Curve 2. Change
3. Fastball 4. Cut Fastball
Sources: *The Scouting Report: 1992; The Scouting Notebook: 1996*

MEL HARDER 6'1" 195-pound righty
223-186, 3.80, 23 Saves 1928 1947

Pitches, 1928–1936: 1. Sinking Fastball 2. Curve
3. Change
Pitches, 1937–1947: 1. Curve 2. Sinking Fastball
3. Slider 4. Change
Note: Harder threw overhand.
Sources: Harder in *Baseball Digest* (July 1952); *Major League Baseball* (Ethan Allen, Page 28); Harder in *Voices from the Pastime* (Nick Wilson, 2000)

Harder: "My fastball was a natural sinker. I had that from the time I started to play . . . I didn't have much of a curveball until I got to professional ball. I also had to learn a change-up when I made it to the pros. I got a lot of batters out with that fastball sinker. But over the years, I had to mix it up more. I eventually came up with a real good curveball."
Source: Mel Harder in on-line chat with ESPN SportsZone (7/22/1998)

Commentary: Harder came to the majors with a great sinker and not much else, but learned to throw an excellent curveball within a few years. He suffered a severe arm injury in 1936 and afterward wasn't the same pitcher, though he was able to pitch effectively by relying on his curveball more.

STEVE HARGAN 6'3" 170-pound righty
87-107, 3.92, 4 Saves 1965 1977

Pitch Selection: 1. Fastball 2. Slider 3. Change
Sources: *The Sporting News* (7/2/1966, Russell Schneider)

Quote: "[Hargan in 1970] wasn't throwing as hard as he used to, but . . . his slider, which was his best pitch before the arm acted up, was sharp again."
Source: *Major League Baseball: 1971* (Brenda Zanger and Dick Kaplan)

MIKE HARKEY 6'5" 220-pound righty
36-36, 4.49, 0 Saves 1988 1997

Pitch Selection: 1. Fastball (90) 2. Curve 3. Slider
Source: *The Scouting Report: 1993*

Pitch Selection: 1. Fastball (mid-80s) 2. Change
3. Forkball 4. Curve
Source: *The Scouting Notebook: 1996*

JOHN HARKINS 6'1" 205-pound righty
51-83, 4.09, 0 Saves 1884 1888

Key Pitch: Fastball
Quote: "When he threw the ball it came at you like a cannon ball."
Source: former amateur teammate William Major, quoted in an unidentified New Brunswick, New Jersey, newspaper, circa 1929.

BOB HARMON 6'0" 187-pound righty
107-133, 3.33, 12 Saves 1909 1918

Key Pitch: Fastball
Quote: "Bresnahan considers him one of the best and speediest young pitchers in America. Harmon is a fine

fielding pitcher, being intelligent and having all the ear marks of a comer."
Source: *The National Game* (Alfred H. Spink, 1911)

PETE HARNISCH 6'1" 195-pound righty
111-103, 3.89, 0 Saves 1988 2001

Pitches: 1. High Hard One 2. Slider 3. Change
4. Overhand Curve (added in mid-1990s)
Sources: *The Scouting Report: 1992; The Scouting Notebook 2000*

HARRY HARPER 6'2" 165-pound lefty
57-76, 2.87, 5 Saves 1913 1923

Pitch Selection: 1. Fastball 2. Curve 3. Change
Sources: unidentified clippings from the Hall of Fame Library (July 1913, August 1914, 12/4/1915)
Quote from July 1913 clipping: "He is loose as ashes, has amazing control for a southpaw, fair speed and a most deceptive delivery, shooting the ball out of his pocket at the batsman."
Quote from August 1914 clipping: "With fully as good a curve ball as [Joe] Boehling's, Harper has far greater speed and his control now is better."
Quote from 12/4/1915 clipping: "Harper seems to have mastered control at last, and also has a very deceptive slow ball, and, as change of pace was one of the few essentials lacking in his repertoire, he is now doped by the wise men as one of the best southpaws for next year."

JACK HARPER 6'0" 178-pound righty
80-63, 3.55, 1 Save 1899 1906

Harper: "I was horsing around with another player and hurt my shoulder . . . When the game began, I found if I threw more sidearm than usual, it didn't hurt . . . Then, about the fifth inning, I worked the kink out of my shoulder and went back to my natural pitching style, more of an overhand."
Source: Harper in a 1946 interview, discussing a game played in 1899, from *The Sporting News* (8/30/1961)

GREG A. HARRIS 6'0" 165-pound righty
74-90, 3.69, 54 Saves 1981 1995

Pitch Selection: 1. Slow Curve 2. Fastball 3. Slider
Sources: *The Scouting Report* (1987 and 1990 editions)

Note: Harris pitched with both hands on September 28, 1995.

GREG W. HARRIS 6'2" 191-pound righty
45-64, 3.98, 16 Saves 1988 1995

Pitch Selection: 1. Fastball 2. Curve 3. Change
4. Slider (occasional)
Note: Harris worked with pitching coach Mike Roarke to develop a change in 1991.
Sources: *The Scouting Report* (1990, 1992, and 1993 editions)

JOE HARRIS 6'1" 198-pound righty
3-30, 3.35, 2 Saves 1905 1907

Note: Joe Harris had a major league record of 3 wins, 30 losses—I believe the worst record in major-league history, 25 or more decisions. He disappeared from the majors in 1907. Nonetheless, the entry on him in Alfred H. Spink's *The National Game* (1911) is long and glowing, credits Harris with "great speed" and attributes his poor record to bad luck.

LUM HARRIS 6'1" 180-pound righty
35-63, 4.16, 3 Saves 1941 1947

Pitches: 1. Knuckleball 2. Fastball 3. Curve
4. Knuckle Curve (occasional in 1942)
Harris: "I don't throw as many knucklers as [Roger] Wolff does but when I do it's only a wild guess on my part where it is going. I experimented with the knuckle ball and had pretty good luck with it both in the minors and the majors and this year I've tried to throw a 'knuckle curve.' Instead of merely throwing the ball I twist my wrist once in a while. When the twist takes you get a pitch that's liable to do anything. But I've been spared by Hal. He's a wonder."
Source: *Baseball Magazine* article (September 1942, Frank Yeutter) about A's catcher Hal Wagner

MICKEY HARRIS 6'0" 195-pound lefty
59-71, 4.18, 21 Saves 1940 1952

Pitch Selection: 1. Fastball 2. Curve 3. Change
(added while in U.S. Army during World War II)
Source: *Baseball Magazine* (August 1946, Hub Miller)

SLIM HARRISS 6'6" 180-pound righty
95-135, 4.25, 16 Saves 1920 1928

Pitch Selection: 1. Tailing Fastball 2. Curve

Quote: "What makes Slim a pitcher is the wickedest side-arm fast ball ever turned loose upon an unsuspecting batsman. Slim's fast ball breaks as wide as a lot of big leaguers' curves, and the real mystery about his pitching is how anybody ever hits it at all, with the curve breaking a foot and a half one way, and the fast ball swerving fully that far in the opposite direction . . . [Giants' scout Dick Kinsella] told him he would never make the grade to the big league unless he changed his side-arm delivery to a straight over-arm, thus taking full advantage of his prodigious altitude. So Slim tried it that way, with little effectiveness."
Source: unidentified clipping from the Hall of Fame Library

Description: "He throws with an underhand delivery suggestive of Carl Mays. His great height, immense reach and wiry frame give him an ideal build for speed pitching, and he is impressively fast."
Source: *Baseball Magazine* (September 1926, "Comprising an Interview with Bryan Harriss")

Description: "His fast ball was often compared to that of Walter Johnson but the Texan lacked control."
Source: Harriss' obituary in *The Sporting News* (10/12/1963)

EARL HARRIST 6'0" 178-pound righty
12-28, 4.34, 10 Saves 1945 1953

Key Pitch: Knuckleball
Source: *The Sporting News* (7/2/1952, Page 7)

JACK HARSHMAN 6'2" 178-pound lefty
69-65, 3.50, 7 Saves 1952 1960

Pitches: 1. Curve 2. Fastball
3. "The Thing" (Slip Pitch) 4. Slider 5. Change
Sources: unidentified clipping in *The Sporting News* morgue; article in TSN Morgue by John F. Steadman from the *Baltimore News-Post*, date unknown but apparently 1957.

Quote: " 'One [scout] said he had a fine curve but no speed,' said Frank Lane, general manager of the White Sox. 'Another one said he threw a good slider, but his curve wasn't good enough. Another one said that his change-up was great, but he didn't have the speed to make it work. Well, I decided that a guy with all those pitches ought to be able to pitch.' "

Note: In *Baseball Digest* (August 1958), Charles Dexter identified Harshman as a "fireballer" and implied that he had among the best fastballs in the majors.

BILL HART 5'10" 163-pound righty
69-118, 4.65, 1 Save 1886 1901

Key Pitch: Fastball
Source: *The National Game* (Alfred H. Spink, 1911)
Quote: "William Hart, an old major league pitcher, was in his day one of the speediest pitchers in the business."
Note: Hart, 45 years old at that time, was still pitching in the minor leagues, and insisted to Spink that he could still throw as hard as ever once he got loose.

MIKE HARTLEY 6'1" 195-pound righty
19-13, 3.70, 4 Saves 1989 1995

Pitch Selection: 1. Split-Fingered Fastball 2. Curve
Source: *The Scouting Report: 1992*

CLINT HARTUNG 6'5" 210-pound righty
29-29, 5.02, 1 Save 1947 1950

Pitch Selection: 1. Fastball
Description: "Hartung did not have a curve ball to speak of. His fast ball did not seem to break with any life. Walker Cooper was asked about it. 'That's right. His pitch just comes in there straight. It doesn't jump.'

" 'But it is awful fast,' he continued with a grin, as he held up a left hand swollen like a balloon. 'It's awful fast,' he repeated. 'Isn't that enough?' "
Source: *Sport* (August 1947, Joe King)

BRYAN HARVEY 6'2" 212-pound righty
17-25, 2.49, 177 Saves 1987 1995

Pitch Selection: 1. Fastball (92) 2. Forkball
Quote: ". . . was playing with his father on a nationally-known slo-pitch softball team, Howard's Furniture, when he was discovered by Angels scout Alex Cosmidis in 1985."
Source: *The Scouting Report: 1990*
Other Source: *USA Today* (6/10/1991, Mel Antonen)

SHIGETOSHI HASEGAWA 5'11" 180-pound righty
40-34, 3.47, 33 Saves 1997 2003

Pitches: 1. Fastball (high-80s) 2. Change 3. Curve
Source: *The Scouting Notebook: 1998*

The Topps Company, Inc.

Shigetoshi Hasegawa

Pitches: 1. Sinking Fastball 2. Running Fastball 3. Forkball (used as Change) 4. Slider
Source: *The Scouting Notebook: 2001*

Description: "Hasegawa may not have the intimidating fastball of Eric Gagne or John Smoltz, but he gets it done by inducing ground balls with his forkball and slider."
Source: *ESPN The Magazine* (9/15/2003, Jim Caple)

ANDY HASSLER 6'5" 220-pound lefty
44-71, 3.83, 29 Saves 1971 1985

Pitch Selection: 1. Live Fastball 2. Hard Slider
Sources: *The Scouting Report* (1983 and 1984 editions)
Note: Hassler experimented with a submarine delivery toward the end of his career.

JOE HATTEN 6'0" 176-pound lefty
65-49, 3.87, 4 Saves 1946 1952

Pitches: 1. Overhand Curve 2. Fastball 3. Change
Source: *Baseball Magazine* (July 1949, Roscoe McGowen)

BRAD HAVENS 6'1" 180-pound lefty
24-37, 4.81, 3 Saves 1981 1989

Pitch Selection: 1. Fastball (high-80s) 2. Curve 3. Straight Change
Source: *The Scouting Report: 1983*

ANDY HAWKINS 6'4" 200-pound righty
84-91, 4.22, 0 Saves 1982 1991

Pitches: 1. Fastball 2. Cut Fastball 3. Slider 4. Change
Sources: *Tom Seaver's 1989 Scouting Notebook; The Scouting Report: 1990*

LATROY HAWKINS 6'5" 214-pound righty
44-57, 5.05, 44 Saves 1995 2003

Pitches: 1. Fastball (mid-90s) 2. Slider 3. Curve 4. Change 5. Split-Fingered Fastball 6. Cut Fastball (added 2001)
Note: Neither the 2002 nor the 2003 editions of *The Scouting Notebook* mention a cut fastball for Hawkins.
Sources: *The Scouting Notebook* (1998–2003 editions)

WYNN HAWKINS 6'3" 195-pound righty
12-13, 4.17, 1 Save 1960 1962

Pitch Selection: 1. "Low curve"
Source: *1963 Major League Handbook* (Don Schiffer)

PINK HAWLEY 5'10" 185-pound righty
165-175, 3.96, 6 Saves 1892 1901

Key Pitch: Fastball
Source: *Nineteenth Century Stars* (SABR, 1989, article by Joe Overfield)

JIMMY HAYNES 6'4" 175-pound righty
63-86, 5.32, 1 Save 1995 2003

Pitches, early career: 1. Fastball (low-90s) 2. Curve 3. Slider 4. Change (occasional)
Pitches, 2001–2002: 1. Four-Seam Fastball (low-90s) 2. Two-Seam Fastball (low-90s) 3. Overhand Curve 4. Split-Fingered Fastball 5. Straight Change
Commentary: It appears that Haynes has had trouble with a change-up throughout his career. Early on, he never threw it very often, and by 2001 he seemed to

have junked it, instead using a splitter as his change. In 2002, he continued to throw the splitter, but also added a straight change.
Sources: *The Scouting Notebook* (1997, 1999, 2002, and 2003 editions)

Quote from *The Scouting Notebook: 2003:* "Like so many other pitchers, it has taken Haynes several seasons to begin harnessing his considerable ability. He is in the low 90s with both his four-seam and two-seam fastballs, which he now throws the majority of the time. He mixes in a big-breaking curve and a split, and he also has started throwing a straight change."

JOE HAYNES 6'2" 190-pound righty
76-82, 4.01, 21 Saves 1939 1952

Pitches: 1. Fastball 2. Change 3. Curve
Description: "He was more of a fireballer type. In today's terms, his fastball probably would have been around 90. He had a small curve, but he had a good change-up, and he threw it often. He'd throw you one, and then he'd come right back with another."
Source: Phone interview with Charlie Metro (6/13/2002, Rob Neyer)

ED HEAD 6'1" 175-pound righty
27-23, 3.48, 11 Saves 1940 1946

Pitch Selection: 1. Fastball 2. Curve
Source: *Baseball Magazine* (August 1942, Roscoe McGowen)

EGYPTIAN HEALY 6'2" 158-pound righty
78-136, 3.84, 0 Saves 1885 1892

Key Pitch: Fastball
Quote: "He gave ample proof that he brought his speed along with him."
Source: unidentified clipping from the Hall of Fame Library (4/14/1890)

JIM HEARN 6'3" 205-pound righty
109-89, 3.81, 8 Saves 1947 1959

Pitch Selection: 1. Sinker 2. Slider
Source: *The Miracle at Coogan's Bluff* (Thomas Kiernan, 1975)

Key Pitch: Fastball
Source: *Baseball Complete* (Russ Hodges, 1952)

Hearn: "When I came over from St. Louis I was basically a straight overhand pitcher. I threw hard and had an overhand curve, but I wasn't having a lot of success. Then I hooked up with [Giants coaches] Frank [Shellenback] and Freddie [Fitzsimmons]. After they watched me for awhile they told me to drop down a little with my delivery. So instead of throwing directly overhand, I threw from the three-quarter position. The ball came off my fingers at a different angle and my fastball started to drop. It became like a sinker with the new angle and I started to win."
Bobby Thomson: "For opponents, Jim Hearn was a pain-in-the-ass pitcher. He was always a fussbudget on the mound. He had to rub the ball up just right before he made the pitch."
Source: *The Giants Win the Pennant! The Giants Win the Pennant!* (Bobby Thomson with Lee Heiman and Bill Gutman, 1991)

Note: Listed by *The Sporting News* (8/29/1956) as having one of the best fastballs in the league.

NEAL HEATON 6'1" 197-pound lefty
80-96, 4.37, 10 Saves 1982 1993

Pitch Selection: 1. Fastball 2. Slider 3. Curve 4. Change
Source: *The Scouting Report: 1990*

Pitch Selection, 1990–1991: 1. Fastball 2. "Screw-Knuckle-Change" 3. Slider
Source: *The Scouting Report 1992*
Note: Heaton pitched well enough in the first half of the 1990 season to earn a spot on the National League All-Star team, and his success was generally credited to his invention of a new pitch, the so-called "screw-knuckle-change." Years later, though, Ray Miller—Heaton's pitching coach in 1990—said that Heaton was simply throwing a Circle Change-up, and came up with the funny name because Miller hated the circle change and didn't want one of his pitchers known for throwing it.

GUY HECKER 6'0" 190-pound righty
173-148, 2.92, 1 Save 1882 1890

Key Pitch: Hard Overhand Drop Curve

Source: *Nineteenth Century Stars* (SABR, 1989, article by Bob Bailey)

Note: According to Bailey, Hecker

a) Used a "running start" type of delivery until that was banned in 1887,

b) Was a power pitcher early in his career, switched to a finesse pitcher after arm injuries beginning in 1886,

c) Had to cut down on his use of the drop curve after the arm injuries.

BOB HEFFNER 6'4" 200-pound righty
11-21, 4.50, 6 Saves 1963 1968

Pitch Selection: 1. Slider 2. Fastball
Source: *Don Schiffer's Major League Baseball Handbook—1964*

FRED HEIMACH 6'0" 175-pound lefty
62-69, 4.46, 7 Saves 1920 1933

Pitch Selection: 1. Fastball 2. Curve (see sources)
Sources: *New York Telegram* (7/19/1930, 4/3/1931); *New York World* (7/20/1930). The *Telegram* on 7/19/1930 says of Heimach, "While he has no baffling curve ball, he has enough steam and know-how to fit." The very next day, the *World* said that Heimach "is still a young man with a real curve and a fast ball."

Quote: " 'Go back to the minors and get a curve and some control,' were the parting words of Lee Fohl, then the Red Sox manager."
Source: *Boston Sunday Advertiser* (9/9/1928); this would've occurred in 1926, which was Heimach's only season with Boston and Fohl's last year as manager of the Red Sox.

KEN HEINTZELMAN 5'11" 185-pound lefty
77-98, 3.93, 10 Saves 1937 1952

Pitch Selection, early career: 1. Fastball 2. Curve
Sources: *Who's Who in the Major Leagues* (1937 ed.); *The Sporting News* (9/3/1937)

Quote: "Heintzelman is only a boy, but he can powerhouse his fast ball [and] throw a fine hook."

Pitch Selection, later: 1. Change 2. Fastball
Source: *1947 Scout Report* (Wid Matthews)

RICK HELLING 6'3" 215-pound righty
90-78, 4.77, 0 Saves 1994 2003

Pitch Selection: 1. Fastball 2. Slider
Source: *The Scouting Report: 1995*

Pitch Selection: 1. Sinking Fastball 2. Cut Fastball 3. Circle Change
Source: *The Scouting Notebook* (1997 and 1998 editions)

Pitch Selection: 1. Curve 2. Fastball (high-80s) 3. Change
Source: *The Scouting Notebook: 1999*

Pitches: 1. High Fastball 2. Curve 3. Change 4. Slider
Sources: *The Scouting Notebook* (2002 and 2003 editions)

GEORGE HEMMING 5'11" 170-pound righty
94-84, 4.52, 5 Saves 1890 1897

Pitch Selection: 1. Fastball 2. Curve
Quote: "He has great speed, good command of the ball and enough curves to fool the best of them."
Source: teammate Larry Twitchell, quoted in an unidentified clipping from the Hall of Fame Library, 1890

BOB HENDLEY 6'2" 190-pound lefty
48-52, 3.97, 12 Saves 1961 1967

Pitch Selection: 1. Curve 2. Fastball
Source: *Jocko* (Jocko Conlan and Robert Creamer, 1967)

CLAUDE HENDRIX 6'0" 195-pound righty
144-117, 2.65, 17 Saves 1911 1920

Key Pitch: Spitball
Source: *The Pittsburgh Pirates* (Fred Lieb, 1948)

Quote: "Hendrix of the Pirates is supposed to be a spitball pitcher, but at that [Pirates owner] Barney Dreyfus smiled discreetly and relieved himself of the following cryptic statement: 'I don't know, but I doubt if he pitches over half a dozen spit-balls in an entire game.' In other words, Hendrix bluffs. The batters expect a spitball and don't get it. It acts just as well that way."
Source: *Baseball Magazine* (November 1913, F.C. Lane)

TOM HENKE 6'5" 215-pound righty
41-42, 2.67, 311 Saves 1982 1995

Pitches: 1. Fastball 2. Forkball 3. Slider
Sources: *The Scouting Report* (1987 and 1990 editions)

MIKE HENNEMAN 6'4" 205-pound righty
57-42, 3.21, 193 Saves 1987 1996

Pitch Selection: 1. Sinking Fastball 2. Forkball 3. Slider
Sources: *The Scouting Report* (1990 and 1992 editions)

BILL HENRY 6'2" 180-pound lefty
46-50, 3.26, 90 Saves 1952 1969

Pitches: 1. Fastball 2. Change 3. Screwball 4. Slider (occasional)
Source: *Baseball Digest* (May 1960, Si Burdick); Burdick's article, titled "Reliever Without a Curve," is very specific about Henry's stuff.

Duke Snider: "He was a lefty who threw nothing but fastballs. I could usually hit the fastball, but the harder he threw, the more I popped up."
Source: *The Greatest Team of All Time* (Nicholas Acocella and Donald Dewey, 1994)

Eddie Mathews: "And Cincinnati had an old reliever named Bill Henry. He was tough. I used to say, I kept him in the league for an extra four or five years. He had a very unorthodox delivery with a high kick. He threw his pitches at two or three different angles, and he had good control."
Source: *Splendor on the Diamond* (Rich Westcott, 2000)

BUTCH HENRY 6'1" 205-pound lefty
33-33, 3.83, 7 Saves 1992 1999

Pitches: 1. Change 2. Sinking Fastball (mid-80s) 3. Curve 4. Slider
Source: *The Scouting Report* (1993, 1995, and 1996 editions); *The Scouting Notebook* (1995, 1996, and 1998 editions)

Pitch Selection: 1. Fastball 2. Curve 3. Change
Source: *1994 Montreal Expos Media Guide*

DOUG HENRY 6'4" 185-pound righty
34-42, 4.19, 82 Saves 1991 2001

Pitch Selection: 1. High Fastball 2. Slider 3. Split-Fingered Fastball (occasional)
Source: *The Scouting Notebook 1999; Bill Mazeroski's Baseball* (1993 edition)

DWAYNE HENRY 6'3" 230-pound righty
14-15, 4.65, 14 Saves 1984 1995

Pitches: 1. Fastball (low-90s) 2. Slider (high-80s) 3. Change (occasional)
Sources: *The Scouting Report* (1992 and 1993 editions)

PAT HENTGEN 6'2" 210-pound righty
129-103, 4.21, 1 Save 1991 2003

Pitches: 1. Cut Fastball 2. Four-Seam Fastball 3. Big Curve 4. Change
Sources: *The Scouting Notebook* (1998 and 1999 editions)

RON HERBEL 6'1" 195-pound righty
42-37, 3.83, 16 Saves 1963 1971

Pitch Selection: 1. Straight Fastball 2. Sidearm Curve
Source: *Baseball Digest* (March 1963, Page 109)

RAY HERBERT 5'11" 185-pound righty
104-107, 4.01, 15 Saves 1950 1966

Pitch Selection: 1. Fastball 2. Curve 3. Change (refined in 1960)
Note: Herbert's breakthrough in 1959, after years of struggling, was generally credited to him finally gaining control of his curve; prior to that, the fastball was his only quality pitch.
Sources: Edgar Munzel in *The Sporting News* (9/1/1962 and 5/25/1963); *The Kansas City Athletics* (John E. Peterson, 2003); Yogi Berra in *Don Schiffer's Major League Baseball Handbook—1964*

FELIX HEREDIA 6'0" 180-pound lefty
27-18, 4.27, 6 Saves 1996 2003

Pitch Selection: 1. Fastball (high-80s) 2. Slider
Source: *The Scouting Notebook: 1997*

GIL HEREDIA 6'1" 221-pound righty
57-51, 4.46, 4 Saves 1991 2001

Pitches: 1. Two-Seam Fastball 2. Four-Seam Fastball 3. Cut Fastball 4. Split-Fingered Fastball 5. Slider
Source: *The Scouting Notebook 2000*

DUSTIN HERMANSON 6'3" 195-pound righty
65-65, 4.28, 5 Saves 1995 2003

Pitch Selection: 1. Fastball (mid-90s) 2. Hard Slider 3. Change
Source: *The Scouting Notebook 1999*

LIVAN HERNANDEZ 6'2" 220-pound righty
84-79, 4.22, 0 Saves 1996 2003

Pitch Selection, early career: 1. Fastball (mid-90s) 2. Slider 3. Change
Sources: *The Scouting Notebook* (1998 and 2000 editions)

Pitches, later career: 1. Fastballs (87-92) 2. Curve 3. Slider 4. Change
Note: Midway through the 2003 season, Hernandez began throwing all of his pitches from the same arm slot, and his strikeout rate jumped dramatically.
Source: Interview with Expos pitching coach Randy St. Claire (9/4/2003, Rob Neyer)

ORLANDO HERNANDEZ 6'2" 220-pound righty
53-38, 4.04, 1 Save 1998 2002

Pitches: 1. Fastball (88–92) 2. Curve 3. Slider 4. Change
Source: *The Scouting Notebook: 1999*
Note: Following is the report submitted by Yankees scouts Gordon Blakeley and Lin Garrett, prior to the Yankees' signing of Hernandez . . .

> Very easy, loose and free arm, TQ [three-quarters] to LTQ [low three-quarters] angle, sudden violent leg lift (Len Barker) then goes easy with the arm—ball gets in on you (Rivera), FB [fastball] 88–92 with sink or bore/sink or riding life or occ. Straight. LTQ angle CB [curveball]—has occ. Hump but plus rotation—will vary angle, depth and velocity, threw all strikes, located away but will come inside with a high rider, mixes pitches well, very confident, poised, athletic and strong, likes being out there, likes the attention, enjoys the game . . .

Source: *The Duke of Havana* (Steve Fainaru and Ray Sanchez, 1991); Hernandez didn't have a change-up when he signed, but developed a pretty good one shortly thereafter.

ROBERTO HERNANDEZ 6'4" 220-pound righty
53-54, 3.30, 320 Saves 1991 2003

Pitch Selection: 1. Overhand, Sinking Fastball 2. Slider 3. Split-Fingered Fastball
Sources: *The Scouting Report: 1995; The Scouting Notebook: 1997*

WILLIE HERNANDEZ 6'3" 180-pound lefty
70-63, 3.38, 147 Saves 1977 1989

Pitch Selection: 1. Screwball 2. Fastball
Source: *The Scouting Report: 1987*

XAVIER HERNANDEZ 6'2" 185-pound righty
40-35, 3.90, 35 Saves 1989 1998

Pitch Selection: 1. Forkball or Split-Fingered Fastball 2. Fastball 3. Slider
Sources: *The Scouting Report: 1993; The Scouting Notebook: 1997*

OREL HERSHISER 6'3" 190-pound righty
204-150, 3.48, 5 Saves 1983 2000

Pitches: 1. Sinker 2. Cut Fastball 3. Curves 4. Straight Change
Hershiser: "I have a sinking fastball to either side of the plate, a cutter (which changes the direction of my fastball so it breaks instead of sinking) to either side of the plate, a curveball I throw at three speeds and three angles, a straight change—using the same arm speed and position as a fastball but with a grip and a release that slows it dramatically, and changeups to different locations that I throw off my sinker and which look like batting practice fastballs. Different locations, different speeds, and slightly different arm angles on all those pitches give me a wide palette of choices."
Source: *Out of the Blue* (Hershiser with Jerry B. Jenkins, 1989)

Note: According to *The Scouting Notebook: 1991*, "The chapters [in Hershiser's book] on pitching and preparation are considered a textbook by other pitchers."

Note: Hershiser added a Slider in the early 1990s.
Source: *The Scouting Notebook: 1998*

JOE HESKETH 6'2" 173-pound lefty
60-47, 3.78, 21 Saves 1984 1994

Pitch Selection: 1. Slider 2. Fastball
Source: *The Scouting Report: 1987*

Pitch Selection: 1. Sinker 2. Straight Change
Source: *Bill Mazeroski's Baseball* (1993 edition)

ED HEUSSER 6'0" 187-pound righty
56-67, 3.69, 18 Saves 1935 1948

Pitch Selection: 1. Sinker 2. Curve
Sources: *The Sporting News* (8/29/1935); unidentified clippings from the Hall of Fame Library (9/5/1935; 1940)

Quote: "[Heusser] had shown Frisch a sinker which actually sank in batting practice."
Source: *The Sporting News* (8/29/1935)

Description: "Strong arm, a natural sinker and no imagination."
Source: unidentified clipping from the Hall of Fame Library (9/5/1935)

Description: "[Heusser] is a matured curver . . . His best pitch is his 'sinker,' but he has a wide variety of trajectories."
Source: unidentified clipping from the Hall of Fame Library (1940)

JOE HEVING 6'1" 185-pound righty
76-48, 3.90, 63 Saves 1930 1945

Key Pitch: Sidearm Sinker
Source: *The Relief Pitcher* (John Thorn, 1979); Billy Rogell in *Masters of the Diamond* (Rich Wescott, 1994); *Baseball Digest* (May 1943)

Heving: "You know the kind of pitcher I am. I throw a side arm fast ball that sinks. Well, I've noticed that on the days when I seem to be a little faster than usual my sinker doesn't break and I get my ears pinned back. So I'm satisfied to go along with just medium speed, and if I lose some more of that as I get older maybe it'll make my sinker still better."
Source: *Baseball Digest* (May 1943, Gordon Cobbledick)

Note: Heving started throwing his sinker as a minor leaguer in 1926, after he'd spent three years as an outfielder.
Source: Heving quoted in *The Sporting News* (5/25/1944, Ed McAuley)

GREG HIBBARD 6'0" 185-pound lefty
57-50, 4.05, 1 Save 1989 1994

Pitches: 1. Change 2. Sinking Fastball 3. Curve 4. Slider
Source: *The Scouting Report: 1992*

BRYAN HICKERSON 6'2" 190-pound lefty
21-21, 4.72, 2 Saves 1991 1995

Pitch Selection: 1. Split-Fingered Fastball 2. Riding Fastball 3. Slider
Source: *The Scouting Report: 1993*

Pitch Selection: 1. Split-Fingered Fastball 2. Cross-Seam Fastball (high-80s) 3. Big Curve
Source: *The Scouting Notebook: 1995*

KEVIN HICKEY 6'1" 170-pound lefty
9-14, 3.91, 17 Saves 1981 1991

Pitch Selection: 1. Fastball (88–90) 2. Slider 3. Curve (occasional) 4. Straight Change (occasional)
Note: Hickey was discovered by the White Sox while playing 16-inch softball in Chicago. He patterned his baseball delivery after Tug McGraw. According to *The Scouting Report: 1990,* Hickey began the 1989 season with only a fastball, later adding a slider.
Sources: *The Scouting Report* (1983 and 1990 editions)

KIRBY HIGBE 5'11" 190-pound righty
118-101, 3.69, 24 Saves 1937 1950

Pitches: 1. Fastball 2. Curve 3. Change 4. Knuckleball (developed late in career)
Sources: *The High Hard One* (Higbe with Martin Quigley, 1967); *Stan Musial* (Musial with Bob Broeg, 1964); *We Played the Game* (Danny Peary, 1994)

Quote: "Kirby Higbe, who was a fast-ball pitcher when he was with Philadelphia, Chicago and Brooklyn, experimented with the knuckle-ball while with Pittsburgh, and for two years threw almost nothing else for New York!"
Source: *The Way to Better Baseball* (Tommy Henrich with A.L. Plaut, 1951)

TEDDY HIGUERA 5'10" 178-pound lefty
94-64, 3.61, 0 Saves 1985 1994

Pitch Selection: 1. Fastball 2. Slider 3. Change
Sources: *The Scouting Report: 1987; Tom Seaver's 1989 Scouting Notebook*

ORAL HILDEBRAND 6'3" 175-pound righty
83-78, 4.35, 13 Saves 1931 1940

Pitch Selection: 1. Fastball
2. Slow Curve (used as Change) 3. Curve
Quote: "Oral employs scarcely no windup yet specializes in a high-calibered fast ball that whistles past enemy batsmen. In addition he packs a baffling curve, but his chief stock in trade is a change of pace, a curve which he slows down with no perceptible change in his motion."
Sources: *Who's Who in Major League Baseball* (compiled by Harold "Speed" Johnson, 1933); Oral Hildebrand oral history, Hall of Fame files

Quote: "I took an option to purchase Hildebrand for twenty-five thousand dollars after seeing him work in only one game. He was devoting his energies then to speed, and I was impressed with it. Today he has, I believe, the finest change of pace in the American League. He rears up and discharges that ball with the same action as if he were pouring every ounce of his power into the pitch. He conducts this deception so expertly that the timing of the best batters suffers severely. Yet this great change of pace has only been perfected within the past year."
Source: Indians general manager Billy Evans in *Baseball Magazine* (August 1933, Clifford Bloodgood)

Hildebrand: "I could throw harder than hell."
Source: Hildebrand oral history, Hall of Fame files

Photo caption: "Oral Hildebrand at the finish and follow-through of a three-quarter sidearm pitch, of which he is a leading exponent."
Source: *How to Pitch Baseball* (Lew Fonseca, 1942)

CARMEN HILL 6'1" 180-pound righty
49-33, 3.39, 8 Saves 1915 1930

Pitches: 1. Screwball 2. Fastball 3. Change
4. Slow Curve
Sources: *Baseball Between the Wars* (Eugene Murdock, 1992); *Baseball Magazine* (November 1927, F.C. Lane)
Lane: "He has good speed, a good curve and a particularly effective screwball."

Note: Hill was one of the first major leaguers to wear eyeglasses on the field.

KEN HILL 6'4" 200-pound righty
117-109, 4.06, 0 Saves 1988 2001

Pitch Selection: 1. Fastball 2. Forkball 3. Change
Source: *1993 Montreal Expos Media Guide*

Pitch Selection: 1. Forkball 2. Fastball 3. Slider
Sources: *The Scouting Report: 1993; The Scouting Notebook: 1995*

SHAWN HILLEGAS 6'3" 205-pound righty
24-38, 4.61, 10 Saves 1987 1993

Pitch Selection: 1. Fastball (high-80s) 2. Curve
3. Change
Source: *The Scouting Report: 1990*

Pitch Selection: 1. Fastball 2. Split-Fingered Fastball
Source: *The Scouting Report: 1992*

FRANK HILLER 6'0" 200-pound righty
30-32, 4.42, 4 Saves 1946 1953

Key Pitch: Fastball
Source: *The Sporting News* (10/22/1952)

JOHN HILLER 6'1" 185-pound lefty
87-76, 2.83, 125 Saves 1965 1980

Pitch Selection: 1. Fastball 2. Curve 3. Change
Source: *The Sporting News* (6/1/1974, Jim Hawkins)

Quote: "Curve, fast ball, change and control are this big strong southpaw's features. Has a weight problem but this can be cured. Looks promising."
Source: *Baseball Digest* (March 1967, "Official Scouting Reports on 1967 Major League Rookies")

STERLING HITCHCOCK 6'1" 195-pound lefty
74-73, 4.77, 3 Saves 1992 2003

Pitches: 1. Fastball 2. Split-Fingered Fastball 3. Sinker 4. Slider
Source: *The Scouting Notebook 1998*

GLEN HOBBIE 6'2" 195-pound righty
62-81, 4.20, 6 Saves 1957 1964

Pitch Selection: 1. Curve 2. Fastball
Source: *The New Era Cubs 1941–1985* (Eddie Gold and Art Aherns, 1985)

BILLY HOEFT 6'3" 180-pound lefty
97-101, 3.94, 33 Saves 1952 1966

Pitch Selection: 1. Fastball 2. Curve 3. Slider 4. Slip Pitch (developed in 1961)
Sources: *Sport* (April 1962, "Good Pitcher, Good Quipper"); *The Sporting News* (3/21/1964, Bob Wolf)

Notes: Listed by *The Sporting News* as having one of the best fastballs in the league, August 29, 1956.

In the *Sport* article, the slip pitch is called a "change-up." In at least one other place, it's called a slider. And in some places it's a totally unique pitch. Our best guess is that it was a slow slider used as a change, in the modern vernacular. Also, Hoeft learned the slip pitch from Paul Richards, as did many others.

JOE HOERNER 6'1" 200-pound lefty
39-34, 2.99, 99 Saves 1963 1977

Pitch Selection: 1. Sidearm Sinking Fastball 2. Slider 3. Change
Notes: Hoerner switched to a sidearm delivery after suffering a heart attack on the mound in a minor-league game in 1958. He threw the sinking fastball probably 80 percent of the time. Allen Lewis said that he was "pretty much of a one-pitch pitcher," and also said that he was "difficult to follow because of his slingshot motion."

Craft and Owens quoted Hoerner as saying, "I was a fastball, slider pitcher. Mostly fastball. I might pitch an inning or more and never throw anything but a fastball."
Sources: Hoerner in *Redbirds Revisited* (David Craft and Tom Owens, 1990); Ray Kelly in *The Evening Bulletin* (Philadelphia, 3/4/1970); Allen Lewis in *The Sporting News* (5/1/1971); Jim Murray in *The Sporting News* (6/26/1971)

Hoerner: "Grady Hatton was the one that came to me, he said, 'Joe, you don't have enough pitches to be a starting pitcher. You throw hard enough, you've got good movement on your ball, you've got good control, you get left-handers out real well. I think you've got an opportunity to be a relief pitcher, and a good relief pitcher, in the major leagues. You're going to be strictly . . . in the eighth and ninth innings, that's all I'm going to use you. I think that'll get you to the big leagues.' And of course, after eight or nine years you're willing to do anything to get to the big leagues . . . And it worked."

Hoerner: "I mainly kept everything away from the right-handed batter all the time. And with my ball running away and sinking, I really didn't give up a lot of home runs in my career."
Source: Hoerner in an interview by Dan DiNardo (8/10/1991, SABR Oral History Committee)

Note: Jack Zanger in *Major League Baseball—1969* identifies (or mis-identifies) Hoerner's key pitch as a slider.

Tom Seaver: "Drag Arm. This is a flaw that really isn't a flaw. With a drag-arm motion, the release is a fraction behind the impact of the foot. The front of the body is a little more opened at the time of release. Drag-arm pitchers don't throw the ball so much as they sling it. Joe Hoerner pitches that way. So did Ron Perranoski . . ."
Source: *Pitching with Tom Seaver* (Tom Seaver with Steve Jacobsen, 1973)

BILL HOFFER 5'9" 155-pound righty
93-46, 3.75, 4 Saves 1895 1901

Pitch Selection: 1. Fastball 2. Curve
Sources: *Nineteenth Century Stars* (SABR, 1989, article by Joe Overfield), *The Fall Classics of the 1890s* (John Phillips, account of game on 10/5/1896).

TREVOR HOFFMAN 6'1" 200-pound righty
45-44, 2.78, 352 Saves 1993 2003

Pitches, 1993–94: 1. Fastball (mid-90s) 2. Hard Slider 3. Straight Change (occasional)
Pitches, 1995: 1. Fastball (low-90s) 2. Slider 3. Curve 4. Change

Pitches, 1996–2003: 1. Change 2. Fastball (high-80s) 3. Cut Fastball 4. Slider (occasional) 5. Curve (occasional)
Source: *The Scouting Report: 1996; The Scouting Notebook* (1995, 1996, 2002, and 2003 editions); *Sports Illustrated* (5/13/2002, Tom Verducci)

Quote from *The Scouting Notebook: 2002:* "Hoffman has a reputation of having a mid-90s fastball, but the fact is that he rarely tops 90 MPH anymore with his location usually just off the plate. He also mixes in an average slider and curve to give batters something to think about. Hoffman's out pitch is his changeup, which many observers still see as one of the best—if not *the* best—off-speed pitch in the game. He has great command of the change, will throw it on any count, and will go to the pitch two, three, even four times in a row to the same hitter."

Quote from Verducci article: "Hoffman says his velocity began to drop after he developed a sore arm in 1994. He quietly rehabilitated the arm during the players' strike that year, but he never regained his youthful heat. At about the same time, though, Hoffman began perfecting the changeup as his out pitch after tweaking his grip. The pitch is now so well disguised by the speed of his arm as it comes forward that hitters think it's another one of his 88-mph fastballs.

"Hoffman has supreme faith in the changeup. He ended a game against the Dodgers on April 13 with such a nasty one to Paul LoDuca that the Los Angeles catcher, who whiffed on the pitch, said, 'It's like it has a parachute on it.' Many times the mere threat of his changeup is enough to make him effective. The night after he fanned LoDuca, Hoffman earned another save against the Dodgers, one in which he threw 13 pitches—the first 12 of which were fastballs or cut fastballs—before he finally slipped in a changeup."

CHIEF HOGSETT 6'0" 190-pound lefty
63-87, 5.02, 33 Saves 1929 1944

Pitch Selection: 1. Sinker 2. Curve/Slider 3. Spinner 4. Change
Sources: Interview with Elon Hogsett (11/3/1991, Rob Neyer); Hogsett in *In the Shadow of the Babe* (Brent Kelley, 1995)

Note: Hogsett told Kelley that his curve was the pitch later known as the slider.

Description: "Hogsett is primarily an underhand pitcher, but of late he has been slipping over a side arm delivery. He has a good sinker ball and a mystifying curve which makes him feared and respected by every left-hand batter in the American League. It breaks up and away and is called in the parlance of the game a 'butterfly.' Batters also look very feeble at times against his number two bender. This breaks down."
Source: *Baseball Magazine* (July 1933, Clifford Bloodgood)

BOBBY HOGUE 5'10" 195-pound righty
18-16, 3.97, 17 Saves 1948 1952

Key Pitch: Slider
Quote: "The best [slider] I'd seen was Bobby Hogue's, when we were on the Braves together. But his was a natural slider and he couldn't tell anyone how he threw it."
Source: *Sport* (February 1956, Al Hirshberg)

AL HOLLAND 5'11" 207-pound lefty
34-30, 2.98, 78 Saves 1977 1987

Pitch Selection: 1. Rising Fastball 2. Sinking Fastball
Source: *The Scouting Report: 1985*

AL HOLLINGSWORTH 6'0" 174-pound lefty
70-104, 3.99, 15 Saves 1935 1946

Pitch Selection, late career: 1. Curve 2. Change 3. Slow Curve (as change) 4. Fastball
Charlie Metro: "He had pinpoint control with everything. At that time he was more of a curveball pitcher. Good curve, wasn't quick at that time, had excellent control. And he had a change-up, and he changed up on his curve. He wasn't fast at that time, being near the end of the line, but his fastball moved on you."
Source: Phone interview with Metro (6/13/2002, Rob Neyer)

KEN HOLLOWAY 6'0" 185-pound righty
64-52, 4.40, 18 Saves 1922 1930

Pitches: 1. Fastball 2. Change 3. Screwball
Source: *Baseball Magazine* (July 1928, "Comprising an Interview with Ken Holloway")

BRIAN HOLMAN 6'4" 190-pound righty
37-45, 3.71, 0 Saves 1988 1991

Pitch Selection: 1. Fastball 2. Curve 3. Forkball 4. Change
Source: *1987 Montreal Expos Media Guide*

Pitch Selection: 1. Fastball (high-80s) 2. Slider 3. Curve 4. Change
Source: *The Scouting Report: 1990*

Pitch Selection: 1. Sinking Fastball 2. Slurve
Source: *The Scouting Report: 1992*

DARREN HOLMES 6'0" 200-pound righty
35-33, 4.25, 59 Saves 1990 2003

Pitch Selection: 1. Fastball 2. Slider 3. Curve
Source: *1995 Baseball Almanac*

Leo Mazzone: "Great curveball. So he practiced the fastball to make his breaking ball better. It all starts with the fastball. Regardless of velocity, that's the pitch you've got to have, along with command of it, to be a good pitcher. It's very simple."
Source: article by Jayson Stark on ESPN.com (2/25/2003); Mazzone was Holmes' pitching coach with the Braves in 2002.

CHRIS HOLT 6'4" 205-pound righty
28-51, 4.76, 1 Save 1996 2001

Pitch Selection: 1. Fastball (high-80s) 2. Curve 3. Slider 4. Change
Source: *The Scouting Notebook: 1998*

Pitch Selection: 1. Sinking Fastball (92–93) 2. Change 3. Curve
Source: *The Scouting Notebook* (2000 and 2001 editions)

MIKE HOLTZ 5'9" 185-pound lefty
16-20, 4.68, 3 Saves 1996 2002

Pitch Selection: 1. Fastball 2. Curve 3. Change
Source: *The Scouting Notebook: 1997*

Pitch Selection: 1. Slow Curve 2. Fastball (89)
Source: *The Scouting Notebook* (2001 and 2002 editions)

KEN HOLTZMAN 6'2" 175-pound lefty
174-150, 3.49, 3 Saves 1965 1979

Pitch Selection: 1. High Fastball 2. Change 3. Curve
Sources: *The Cubs of '69* (Rick Talley, 1969); *Catfish: My Life in Baseball* (Jim "Catfish" Hunter with Armen Keteyian, 1988)

RICK HONEYCUTT 6'1" 185-pound lefty
109-143, 3.72, 38 Saves 1977 1997

Pitch Selection: 1. Slider 2. Forkball
Source: *The Scouting Report 1990*

Pitch Selection: 1. Slider 2. Curve 3. Change
Source: *The Scouting Report 1992*

Note: Honeycutt was suspected of throwing a spitball.
Source: *The Sporting News* (6/6/1981, Peter Gammons)

JAY HOOK 6'2" 182-pound righty
29-62, 5.23, 1 Save 1957 1964

Pitch Selection: 1. Curve
Sources: *1963 Major League Handbook* (Don Schiffer)

Note: A *Baseball Digest* article published at almost the same time (January, 1963) says that Hook "throws a good curve ball on paper. He knows all the principles of physics that cause a baseball to spin as it goes into the plate. However, he has not as yet solved the air currents around the National League."

BURT HOOTON 6'1" 210-pound righty
151-136, 3.38, 7 Saves 1971 1985

Pitch Selection: 1. Knuckle Curve 2. Fastball
Sources: *The Sporting News* (5/24/1975, Jerome Holtzman; 6/8/1974, Richard Dozer)

JOE HORLEN 6'0" 170-pound righty
116-117, 3.11, 4 Saves 1961 1972

Pitch Selection: 1. Fastball 2. Curve
Source: *Baseball Stars of 1968* (article by Bill Furlong)

Quote from Al Lopez: "He has plenty of good stuff—a good fast ball and slider. But his best pitch is his overhand curve."
Source: *1965 Official Baseball Almanac* (Bill Wise)

RICKY HORTON 6'2" 195-pound lefty
32-27, 3.76, 15 Saves 1984 1990

Pitch Selection: 1. Fastball 2. Change 3. Slider
Source: *The Scouting Report: 1987*

Pitch Selection: 1. Change 2. Fastball 3. Curve
Source: *The Scouting Report: 1990*

DAVE HOSKINS 6'1" 180-pound righty
9-4, 3.79, 1 Save 1953 1954

Key Pitch: Curve
Source: *Crossing the Line: Black Major Leaguers, 1947–1959* (Larry Moffi and Jonathan Kronstadt, 1994)

CHARLIE HOUGH 6'2" 190-pound righty
216-216, 3.75, 61 Saves 1970 1994

Pitch Selection: 1. Knuckleball 2. Fastball 3. Slider
Source: *The Scouting Report: 1990*

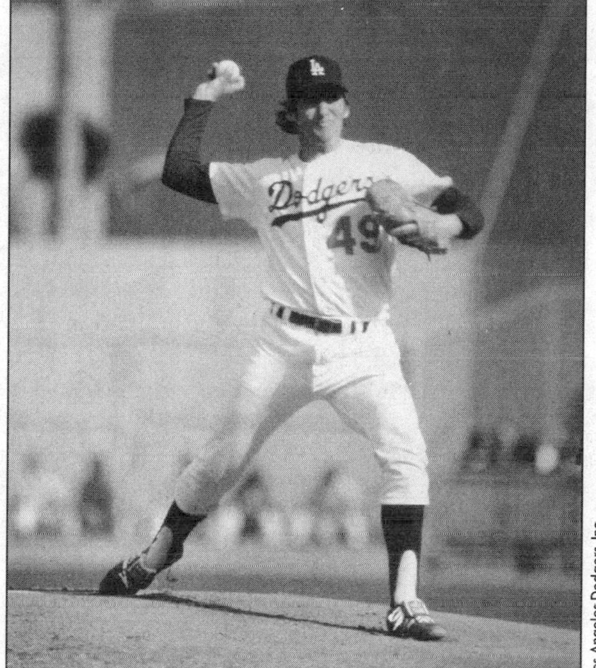

Los Angeles Dodgers, Inc.

Rough, Tough, Charlie Hough

TOM HOUSE 5'11" 190-pound lefty
29-23, 3.79, 33 Saves 1971 1978

Pitch Selection: 1. Curve 2. Screwball 3. Fastball
Quote: "I threw a fastball, curveball, and a screwball. My fastball was below average, my curveball a little above average, and my screwball average, but I threw all three with equal confidence for strikes. My screwball got right-handed hitters off my fastball. My curveball got left-handed hitters out and put me in the bullpen . . . the main reason I hung around the major leagues for seven or eight years!"
Source: e-mail message from House to Rob Neyer (1/12/2003)

Description: "On the mound he stirs memories of little Eddie Lopat, with his compact delivery and pinpoint control. Though his strikeout pitches are a wicked screwball and a 'slurve,' a cross between a curve and a slider, lately he has been taking more chances with his fastball which, says Braves catcher Johnny Oates, 'on a scale of five is a three.' "
Source: *Sports Illustrated* (7/8/1974, Ray Kennedy)

ART HOUTTEMAN 6'2" 188-pound righty
87-91, 4.14, 20 Saves 1945 1957

Pitch Selection: 1. Fastball 2. Curve 3. Slider
Source: *Sport* (August 1950, Lyall Smith)

Note: Houtteman occasionally utilized a sidearm crossfire delivery, once common but less so by the 1950s.

Pitch Selection: 1. Sharp Curve 2. Sinker
Source: *The Ballplayers* (1990, article by Jane Charnin-Aker)

Description: "Houtteman has the weapons for which pitchers sweat years. He has a 'live arm,' his sinker is deceptive, his curve sharp. But he has a tendency to get pitches 'too fat' after he has the batter at his mercy. One of the Yankees said last spring, 'Houtteman is the greatest two-strike pitcher in the majors. But then he starts messin' around, tryin' to be cute, and the first thing you know he's loused up.' "
Source: *Sport* (November 1954, Whitey Lewis)

BRUCE HOWARD 6'2" 180-pound righty
26-31, 3.18, 1 Save 1963 1968

Pitch Selection: 1. Sinking Fastball 2. Curve 3. Slider 4. Slip Pitch
Source: *A Pictorial History of the White Sox—1966 Yearbook*

STEVE HOWE 6'1" 180-pound lefty
47-41, 3.03, 91 Saves 1980 1996

Pitch Selection: 1. Four-Seam Fastball
2. Sinking Fastball 3. Slider 4. Change
Source: *Bill Mazeroski's Baseball* (1993 edition)

HARRY HOWELL 5'9" 175-pound righty
134-146, 2.74, 5 Saves 1898 1910

Key Pitch: Spitball
Sources: *Baseball Magazine* (November 1910, Arthur Cummings); Branch Rickey (Howell's catcher) quoted by John Lardner in *The Saturday Evening Post* (6/17/1950)

JAY HOWELL 6'3" 200-pound righty
58-53, 3.34, 155 Saves 1980 1994

Pitch Selection: 1. Fastball 2. Sharp Curve 3. Slider
Source: *The Scouting Report 1990*

KEN HOWELL 6'3" 220-pound righty
38-48, 3.95, 31 Saves 1984 1990

Pitch Selection: 1. Fastball (low-90s)
2. Slider (high-80s) 3. Forkball (as Change)
Source: *The Scouting Report* (1987 and 1990 editions)

BOBBY HOWRY 6'5" 220-pound righty
14-20, 3.92, 49 Saves 1998 2003

Pitch Selection: 1. Fastball (mid-90s)
2. Curve (occasional) 3. Change (occasional)
Source: *The Scouting Notebook: 2000*

LA MARR HOYT 6'3" 195-pound righty
98-68, 3.99, 10 Saves 1979 1986

Pitches: 1. Fastball (88–89) 2. Cut Fastball 3. Sinker
4. Change 5. Slider 6. Spitball
Hoyt: "My fastball is 88 or 89 miles per hour, not great but pretty good. I have a good hard sinker and I should work on it more . . . But in the past I've used my cut fastball to get out of trouble. I usually can make people pop it up and that's just as good as a grounder . . . I also need to keep working on my change-up, which I'll throw five or 10 times a game. Really, I'm only as good as my change-up . . . Aw, in the summer when it's hot, I'll throw a few 'natural spitters'—just use the sweat that's runnin' down my forehead. No big deal; it's all legal. I don't use any foreign substances—just sweat. I'm not going to live and die with the pitch; it's too hard on your arm. But if it's hot and I'm tired, I'll use it. It's just sweat. It's legal . . ."
Source: *The Sporting News* (4/22/1985, Dave Nightingale)

Pitch Selection: 1. Slider 2. Curve 3. Sinker
Source: *The Sporting News* (8/23/1980, Robert Markus)

Pitch Selection: 1. Change 2. Slow Curve 3. Fastball
Source: *The Scouting Report: 1987*

WAITE HOYT 6'0" 180-pound righty
237-182, 3.59, 52 Saves 1918 1938

Pitch Selection: 1. Fastball 2. Curve 3. Change
4. Developed a Slider late in his career
Sources: *The New York Yankees* (Frank Graham, page 66), *Babe Ruth's Own Book of Baseball* (Ruth, 1928), *Baseball Between the Wars* (Eugene Murdock, 1992)

AL HRABOSKY 5'11" 185-pound lefty
64-35, 3.10, 97 Saves 1970 1982

Pitch Selection: 1. Fastball 2. Forkball (added in 1974)
Source: *The Sporting News* (7/13/1974, Neal Russo)

CARL HUBBELL 6'0" 170-pound lefty
253-154, 2.98, 33 Saves 1928 1943

Pitch Selection: 1. Screwballs (25%) 2. Fastball
3. Curve
Source: *Baseball's Famous Pitchers* (Ira L. Smith, 1954), *Baseball Magazine* (August 1935, F.C. Lane)

Hubbell in 1933: "Hard work did it. I saw other pitchers work with the screw ball mainly as a change of pace ball. I decided to make it my big specialty and this finally achieved my goal. I was able to pitch the screw ball with three speeds. That, and experience, did the trick."
Source: *Baseball Magazine* (November 1933, Daniel M. Daniel, "The Star of the Series")

Hubbell in 1934: "Sometimes, almost every ball I throw is a screw ball. That is when the game is close and the hitters, coming up one after another, are dangerous. In other games, where I have some margin to work on, I may not throw more than a half dozen screw balls."

Source: *Baseball Magazine* (October 1934, Frank Graham, "The Wizard of the Screw Ball")

Quote from Lane article: "Hubbell seldom uses his famous screw ball except in the pinch or against certain batters. 'I suppose I'll call on it for about 25 pitches during a ball game, on average,' he says. 'If you pitched nothing but screw balls, they'd get on it . . . ' "

Umpire Emmett Ormsby: "I don't know whether you know it or not, but he hasn't one screw ball but two. The Senators had heard all about his screw ball and while they were baffled by it in the first game [of the 1933 World Series] they figured they had begun to get a line on it and that the next time they saw it they would knock the cover off it. That was the screw ball that breaks down and away from a right handed hitter. So, in the second game Carl pitched, which was the one I umpired back of the plate, they were all set for it—and Carl showed them one that came up straight as a string and then dropped as abruptly as though he had rolled it off the end of a table. I have looked at many a delivery but I never saw one like that before . . ."
Hubbell: "I suppose there are two of them, although I always have looked on them as one. It is merely that I give the ball a different twist by employing a slightly different pitching motion. For the ball that drops down and away from a right handed hitter, I use a side arm motion. For the other, I pitch over hand. This gives the ball a little more speed and a sharper break."
Source: *Baseball Magazine* (October 1934, Frank Graham)

Description: "Carl Hubbell was the greatest pitcher I ever caught. When you talk of great pitchers you always talk of a great fastball. Carl didn't have a great fastball, but he had uncanny control. He'd throw his fastball high and his screwball hard, and it would break about two feet. He also had a good curveball, but people just talk about his screwball. He was a fastball-high and screwball-low pitcher with great control. He wouldn't throw at batters; he didn't believe in it."
Source: Giants catcher Harry Danning in *Dugout to Foxhole* (Rick Van Blair, 1994)

Pepper Martin: "Look at the crooked-arm son of a gun. His left hand turns the wrong way. No wonder he's such a good pitcher. He's a freak."
Jim Murray: "The only eccentric thing about him is his left arm. He looks as if he put it on in the dark."

Source: *Super Stars of Baseball* (Bob Broeg, 1971); Hubbell's left arm was permanently disfigured because of all the screwballs he threw.

WILLIS HUDLIN 6'0" 190-pound righty
158-156, 4.41, 31 Saves 1926 1944

Key Pitch: Sinker
Note: Hudlin threw sidearm, at least some of the time.
Sources: *The Cleveland Indians* (Franklin Lewis, 1949); *How to Pitch Baseball* (Lew Fonseca, 1949)

Note: A comment in *Who's Who in the American League, 1935* (Speed Johnson) seems to confirm that Hudlin lived on the sinker. The comment says " 'Hud' remembers his game against the New York Yankees when the Indians equaled the league record for double plays in a single contest and regrets an error prevented a new mark."

Pitch Selection: 1. Fastball 2. Curve 3. Change
Note: Hudlin threw from at least three different angles.
Description: "Hudlin hasn't everything. He doesn't throw a spit ball or a knuckle ball, nor even a screw ball. His curve he calls just fair. But he has great natural speed and a troublesome, from the batter's viewpoint, delivery. Hudlin throws the ball overhand with telling effect, for a fast ball will then jump straight 'up.' But he also throws an equally fast ball with a side arm motion, and occasionally with an underhand dip of the wrist, using these three types of deliveries at will. This is an excellent combination, but Hudlin also employs a deceptive change of pace. And he uses a cross-fire ball with great effect."
Source: *Baseball Magazine* (February 1928, F.C. Lane)

Description: "Speed and a cross-fire pitch are his chief stocks in trade. Trick pitching is not to his liking. He does not employ a knuckle ball or a screw ball. He puts a hop on his fast ball, either overhand or side-arm. He has a curve, but does not use it a great deal. He thinks a fastball pitcher doesn't have to."
Source: *Who's Who in Major League Baseball* (compiled by Harold "Speed" Johnson, 1933)

CHARLES HUDSON 6'3" 185-pound righty
50-60, 4.14, 2 Saves 1983 1989

Pitch Selection: 1. Fastball 2. Slider 3. Change
Source: *The Scouting Report 1987*

SID HUDSON 6'4" 180-pound righty
104-152, 4.28, 13 Saves 1940 1954

Pitch Selection: 1. Fastball 2. Hard Curve 3. Change
Note: In 1966 Hudson patented and marketed a device intended to teach a pitcher how to throw a curve. The device consisted of "a strap of leather and a couple of pieces of elastic."
Sources: *The Sporting News* (8/15/1940, Dick Farrington; and 7/16/1966); Billy Hitchcock in *The Pastime in Turbulence: Interviews with Baseball Players of the 1940s* (Brent Kelley, 2001)

Hudson: "I had a good arm with a good curve and a good fastball."
Source: *Splendor on the Diamond* (Rich Westcott, 2000); according to the same source, Hudson threw overhand before World War II, but developed a bone spur in his shoulder while pitching for his Army team, and came back after the war as a sidearmer.

Description: "Just twenty-two years old last January 3rd, Hudson has a world of stuff, but no more so than any number of pitchers we might mention at the moment. But Hudson, despite his youth, has something more—the something that makes him a respected and feared hurler. That something is control plus confidence. He has the happy faculty of controlling his curve beautifully—feeding it to batters around the knees, but keeping it in the strike zone. That means half the battle, especially in the American League this season."
Source: *Baseball Magazine* (October 1940, Naiph J. Abodaher)

Quote from *TSN* in 1940: "Hudson is not particularly fast, nor is his curve the sharpest on the Senator staff [but] he can keep his curve low all day—and get it over the plate." Ted Lyons, an opposing pitcher, worked with him in 1940 to improve his change (or "let-up pitch"), which was his weakness when he came to the majors.
Quote from Billy Hitchcock: "Sid was a big, tall, slender right-hander, sort of a three-quarter guy, had a good sinkin' fastball."

Description: ". . . specializes in sidearm fast balls. He has a so-so curve ball but a honey of a sinker."
Source: *Baseball Digest* (January 1951, Milton Richman)

TIM HUDSON 6'1" 164-pound righty
80-33, 3.26, 0 Saves 1999 2003

Pitches: 1. Sinker (low-90s) 2. Splitter 3. Change 4. Slider 5. Curve
Sources: *The Scouting Notebook* (2000–2003 editions)

DICK HUGHES 6'3" 195-pound righty
20-9, 2.78, 8 Saves 1966 1968

Pitches: 1. Fastball 2. Slider 3. Curve 4. Screwball
Source: *Baseball Digest* (March 1967, "Official Scouting Reports on 1967 Major League Rookies")

JIM HUGHES 6'2" 185-pound righty
82-41, 3.00, 1 Save 1952 1957

Pitch Selection: 1. Fastball
Tommy Lasorda: "He was a big, tough guy. It would take him three, four pitches to get warm. After a few pitches, he was fogging it. Nothing but hard stuff. Didn't have a breaking ball."
Source: Hughes' obituary in *The New York Times* (8/18/2001)

LONG TOM HUGHES 6'1" 175-pound righty
131-175, 3.09, 17 Saves 1900 1913

Note: Leever wrote the chapter "How to Pitch a Drop" in the 1908 book *How to Pitch*.

Quote: "He is one of the most original 'goat getters' in the business. When pitching he keeps up a verbal broadside against every batter he faces."
Source: unidentified clipping from the Hall of Fame Library (March 1911)

TOMMY HUGHES 6'1" 190-pound righty
31-56, 3.92, 3 Saves 1941 1948

Pitches: 1. Fastball 2. Curve 3. Change
Description: "Tom's fast ball isn't a scorcher like Dizzy Dean's was nor does it break the way Clay Bryant's did in 1938 when the Cubs won the pennant . . . But his fast ball is always doing something. Sometimes it slides, other times it takes off and occasionally it sinks. But hardly ever does Tommy throw a 'cripple' pitch that comes down the alley straight as a string."
Source: *Baseball Magazine* (October 1942, Frank Yeutter)

JIM HUGHEY 6'0" 188-pound righty
29-83, 4.87, 2 Saves 1891 1900

Note: *Misfits!* (1991), J. Thomas Hetrick's account of the 1899 Cleveland Spiders, contains dozens of references to Hughey and accounts of games he pitched, but never actually says what pitches he threw. Our impression is that he had a decent fastball and nothing else. He was constantly referred to as "Smiling Jim" and "Coldwater Jim," and he could not field a bunt to save his soul. According to Hetrick, Hughey was "described by contemporaries as lacking in ambition and judgment."

TEX HUGHSON 6'3" 198-pound righty
96-54, 2.94, 17 Saves 1941 1949

Pitches: 1. Sinking Fastball 2. Hard Curve 3. Slider 4. Screwball 5. Knuckleball 6. Change
Sources: *Fenway* (Peter Golenbock, 1992); *Baseball Magazine* (Ed Rumill, August 1944); Red Hayworth in *The Pastime in Turbulence: Interviews with Baseball Players of the 1940s* (Brent Kelley, 2001)
Note: Hayworth says that Hughson had a "good fastball, good curve, good change, and about four or five times . . . in a ballgame he'd throw you a good knuckleball."

TOM HUME 6'1" 185-pound righty
57-71, 3.85, 92 Saves 1977 1987

Pitch Selection: 1. Fastball 2. Slider 3. Sinker
Source: *The Scouting Report 1987*

BOB HUMPHREYS 5'11" 165-pound righty
27-21, 3.36, 20 Saves 1962 1970

Pitch Selection, 1962–64: 1. Fastball 2. Curve
Pitch Selection, 1965–67: 1. Cutter/Slider 2. Fastball 3. Curve
Pitch Selection, 1968–70: 1. Knuckleball
Notes: Humphreys learned his slider (which was actually more of a cutter than a slider) from Frank Lary in 1962, and that became his best pitch after a 1964 elbow injury. He learned a knuckleball from Bob Tiefenauer while with Atlanta in 1963, but didn't throw the pitch during games at that point. Humphreys suffered a shoulder injury in 1968, and by the middle of that season he was throwing "all knuckleballs."
Source: Phone interview with Humphreys (8/1/2002, Rob Neyer)

Description: "Has odd windup and delivery. Good fast ball and control. Fair curve."
Source: *Baseball Digest* (March 1963, Page 120)

JOHNNY HUMPHRIES 6'1" 185-pound righty
52-63, 3.78, 12 Saves 1938 1946

Pitch Selection: 1. Fastball 2. Curve (ineffective)
Source: *Baseball Magazine* (April 1942, Herbert Simons)

Joe McCarthy: "That kid is great. I wish we had him. He has got a fast ball! Say, he's faster than Feller, and maybe faster than any pitcher in the league. What a future! Just a little more control and a polishing up on pitches other than his fast ball, and he will be a pip!"
Source: unidentified clipping dated May 25, 1938

Comment: "But nearly all who have seen Humphries, including Joe DiMaggio, Lou Gehrig and Joe Cronin, say that Humphries is faster than Feller."
Source: unidentified column by Bill Braucher, dated June 19, 1938

Note: When Humphries arrived in the majors in 1938, he immediately was thought to have the best fastball in the American League. He suffered arm problems in 1939, and never did learn to control his curveball.

CATFISH HUNTER 6'0" 190-pound righty
224-166, 3.26, 1 Save 1965 1979

Pitches: 1. Fastball 2. Slider 3. Change (occasional) 4. Slider (very occasional)
Source: *Catfish: My Life in Baseball* (Jim "Catfish" Hunter with Armen Keteyian, 1988); according to *Baseball: The Biographical Encyclopedia*, Hunter said after his 1968 perfect game: "I went with fastballs and sliders. I threw only three changeups and one curveball all night."

A's pitching coach Wes Stock: "You try to judge Hunter on his fastball and you're missing the point. The man is an artist. He's always ahead of the hitter because he's always got his control. Usually he doesn't show the fastball until he's got the hitter off balance. Then he pops one and it's strike three."
Ray Fosse: "He doesn't throw as hard as Vida and his ball doesn't move around as much. To right-handers, he has a super slider. He also has come up with a sort of change-up he uses, especially to left-handers."

Source: *Baseball Stars of 1974* (edited by Ray Robinson; article by Larry Bortstein)

Roger Angell: "No other pitcher in baseball settles into stride with quite this sort of nearly audible click, or, once there, throws such elegant, thoughtful, and flowing patterns—up and out, up and in, down on the hands, out and away, with each part and pitch connected, in psychology and tactics, to its predecessor and its quickly following variant."
Source: *Five Seasons* (Angell, 1977)

Hunter on his grip: "I tuck my thumb. I've only seen one other pitcher hold the ball like I do. See how my thumb's tucked under? That's the way I picked up throwing."
Source: advertisement for Puma shoes in *The Sporting News* (7/17/1976, Page 13)

BRUCE HURST 6'4" 200-pound lefty
145-113, 3.92, 0 Saves 1980 1994

Pitch Selection: 1. Fastball 2. Slow Curve 3. Forkball 4. Slider
Sources: *The Scouting Report: 1987; The Scouting Report: 1990*

JOHNNY HUTCHINGS 6'2" 250-pound righty
12-18, 3.96, 6 Saves 1940 1946

Comment: "There is no doubt that had he kept his weight down, Johnny Hutchings, who wore a tent-sized uniform last season, would have been a steady winner in the National League. Even with his tremendous waistline, John did fairly well and was quick as a cat covering his position. But a slender Hutchings would have stayed around longer, even in peace."
Source: *Baseball Magazine* (March 1947, Hub Miller)

FRED HUTCHINSON 6'2" 190-pound righty
95-71, 3.73, 7 Saves 1939 1953

Pitch Selection: 1. Fastball 2. Change 3. Curve
Source: *The Saturday Evening Post* (3/11/1939, Paul O'Neil; presumably describes Hutchinson as immature pitcher.)

Key Pitches as mature pitcher: Slider and Change
Sources: *Sport* (February 1957, Al Hirshberg); *Baseball Magazine* (August 1948, Hub Miller); *Baseball Digest* (January 1951, Milt Richman)

Gene Mauch: "You know how much stuff Hutch had? He had a nickel curve, a nickel fast ball, a purpose pitch and a million dollars worth of heart, that's what he had."
Source: *Baseball Digest* (August 1965, Clark Nealon)

Hirshberg: "Manager Fred Hutchinson of the Cardinals, who had one of the best sliders in baseball when he was an active pitcher for the Tigers, threw it off his forefinger and turned his wrist a little."

Hub Miller: "Hutchinson's early critics insisted that lack of a good fast ball would ruin his chances in the American League. A lot of scouts will ignore a young pitcher who does not have what the profession refers to as a 'high, hard one.' " Hal Wagner in the same source says that Hutchinson has "the best control and change of pace I have ever caught."

Richman: "[Hutchinson and Ed Lopat were] two birds of a feather. Both are excellent control pitchers; both keep the ball down; both set up the batters with slow breaking stuff."

Comment: ". . . the slider made [Hutchinson] a winning pitcher after he flunked his first trial with Detroit."
Source: Article by Lou Smith (6/11/1960, newspaper un-identified); article also says that Hutchinson threw two different sliders: a hard one with a sharp break and a slower one with a big break.

Billy Pierce: "He didn't have a fastball. He had a deceptively quick motion and threw a lot of change-ups. He could get a strike on you before you turned around."
Source: *We Played the Game* (Danny Peary, 1994); Pierce is describing Hutchinson in the late 1940s.

BILL HUTCHISON 5'9" 175-pound righty
181-158, 3.59, 3 Saves 1884 1897

Pitch Selection: 1. Fastball
2. Hutchison added a Curve late in his career.
Source: *Nineteenth Century Stars* (SABR, 1989, article by Harold L. Dellinger)

DICK HYDE 5'11" 170-pound righty
17-14, 3.56, 23 Saves 1955 1961

Key Pitch: Sinker

Note: Hyde threw underhanded, and taught Ted Abernathy the motion.
Quote: "Dick Hyde was the last of the legitimate submarine pitchers . . . Sometimes, in fact, it looked as though he was throwing the ball from between his legs."
Source: *The Great American Baseball Card Flipping, Trading and Bubble Gum Book*

JEFF INNIS 6'1" 170-pound righty
10-20, 3.05, 5 Saves 1987 1993

Pitch Selection: 1. Sinking Fastball 2. Slider 3. Overhand Curve 4. Riding Fastball 5. Knuckleball
Notes: Innis learned to throw the knuckleball from Joe Niekro. Innis threw sidearm on all pitches except the overhand curve.
Sources: *The Scouting Report* (1992 and 1993 editions)

HIDEKI IRABU 6'4" 250-pound righty
34-35, 5.15, 16 Saves 1997 2002

Pitch Selection: 1. Fastball (low-90s) 2. Split-Fingered Fastball
Source: *The Scouting Notebook: 1998*

Note: *The Scouting Notebook: 1999* says that Irabu threw a slow curve, and *The Scouting Notebook: 2001* mentions that he threw sliders.

JASON ISRINGHAUSEN 6'3" 230-pound righty
31-32, 3.83, 130 Saves 1995 2003

Pitches: 1. Fastball (high-80s) 2. Curve 3. Change
Source: *The Scouting Notebook: 1996*

Pitches: 1. Fastball (mid-90s) 2. Cut Fastball (added 2001) 3. Curve
Sources: *The Scouting Notebook* (2002 and 2003 editions)

Jeromy Burnitz: "It's just nasty. He was already nasty enough, but with a cutter he's just that much tougher."
Source: *New York Daily News* (6/9/2002, T.J. Quinn)

AL JACKSON 5'10" 169-pound lefty
67-99, 3.98, 10 Saves 1959 1969

Pitch Selection: 1. Slider 2. Curve 3. Fastball
Source: *View from the Dugout* (Ed Richter, 1963)
Pitch Selection: 1. Fastball 2. Low-Breaking Curve 3. Change
Sources: *1963 Major League Handbook* (Don Schiffer); *Baseball Digest* (March 1960, Page 94)

DANNY JACKSON 6'0" 205-pound lefty
112-131, 4.01, 1 Save 1983 1997

Pitch Selection: 1. Slider 2. Fastball 3. Change (developed in 1993)
Sources: *The Scouting Report* (1987 and 1994 editions); *Tom Seaver's 1989 Scouting Notebook*

Note: For most of his career, Jackson didn't bother much with change-ups, but after joining the Phillies in 1993, he started throwing more of them under the tutelage of pitching coach Johnny Podres (who was famous for both throwing and teaching the pitch).
Source: *The Scouting Report: 1994*

Keith Hernandez: "Jackson can be an effective, seasoned power pitcher—good fastball, hard slider, and a change-up that I'm sure has improved under the tutelage of Phillies pitching coach Johnny Podres, who had one of the best ever. Historically, though, Danny's problem has been that he can be a little wild around the plate, fall behind in the count, and therefore be forced to give the batter one or two good pitches to hit."
Source: *Pure Baseball: Pitch by Pitch for the Advanced Fan* (Hernandez and Mike Bryan, 1994)

GRANT JACKSON 6'0" 180-pound lefty
86-75, 3.46, 79 Saves 1965 1982

Pitch Selection as Starting Pitcher: 1. Fastball 2. Slider 3. Curve 4. Change
Pitch Selection as Reliever: 1. Fastball 2. Slider 3. Change
Source: *The Sporting News* (7/7/1973, Lou Hatter)

LARRY JACKSON 6'1" 175-pound righty
194-183, 3.40, 20 Saves 1955 1968

Pitch Selection: 1. Fastball 2. Curve 3. Slider
Source: *Baseball Stars of 1965* (article by George Vecsey)

Pitch Selection: 1. Curve
Source: *1963 Major League Handbook* (Don Schiffer)
Description: ". . . His best pitch is a fast ball (although

Jackson credits his control and an improving slider with helping him last year) and he rarely misses a turn. The fastball isn't overpowering but sinks and sails."
Source: *1965 Official Baseball Almanac* (Bill Wise)

Maury Wills: "Larry Jackson had one hell of a slider. He also had a questionable balk move that was rough on a base runner. He got away with it, though, because he was a veteran."
Source: *How to Steal a Pennant* (Wills with John Freeman, 1976)

MIKE JACKSON 6'1" 185-pound righty
60-67, 3.35, 142 Saves 1986 2002

Pitches: 1. Slider 2. Two-Seam Fastball
3. Four-Seam Fastball 4. Forkball 5. Change
Sources: *The Scouting Report: 1993; The Scouting Notebook 1999*

ROY LEE JACKSON 6'2" 190-pound righty
28-34, 3.77, 34 Saves 1977 1986

Pitch Selection: 1. Fastball (high-80s) 2. Slider
3. Curve 4. Change
Source: *The Scouting Report: 1984*

ELMER JACOBS 6'0" 165-pound righty
50-81, 3.55, 7 Saves 1914 1927

Key Pitch: Curveball ("dipsy-do")
Source: *Pacific Coast League Stars* (John E. Spalding, 1996)

Note: Jacobs' curve may have been a product of doctoring the ball, or an incredibly strong grip which he used to misshape the ball. Spalding quotes a 1931 *San Francisco Chronicle* article by Ed R. Hughes which states, "What Jacobs really did was to raise the seams a trifle by twisting the ball in the powerful grip of his two hands. That sometimes enabled him to make the ball do funny things." However, in 1926 he was suspended for ten days when umpires caught him with foreign substances on the mound.

SIG JAKUCKI 6'2" 198-pound righty
25-22, 3.79, 5 Saves 1936 1945

Pitch Selection: 1. Sinking Fastball 2. Curve
3. Knuckleball??
Source: Red Hayworth and Clint Conatser in *The Pastime in Turbulence: Interviews with Baseball Players of the 1940s* (Brent Kelley, 2001)
Note: Conatser says that Jakucki threw a knuckleball. However, Conatser's major league career does not overlap with Jakucki's. Jakucki may have thrown the knuckleball in the minor leagues, or Conatser, interviewed forty years later, may have him confused with somebody else.

BILL JAMES 6'4" 195-pound righty
65-71, 3.20, 5 Saves 1911 1919

Pitch Selection: 1. Spitball 2. Change
Source: *1915 Reach Guide* (Pages 83, 93–105)

BOB JAMES 6'4" 215-pound righty
24-26, 3.80, 73 Saves 1978 1987

Pitch Selection: 1. Fastball (low-90s) 2. Curve
Sources: *The Scouting Report* (1985 and 1987 editions)

MIKE JAMES 6'3" 200-pound righty
16-14, 3.67, 11 Saves 1995 2002

Pitches: 1. Fastball 2. Cut Fastball 3. Slider
4. Change (occasional)
Source: *The Scouting Notebook* (1998 and 2001 editions)

LARRY JANSEN 6'2" 190-pound righty
122-89, 3.58, 10 Saves 1947 1956

Pitch Selection: 1. Fastball 2. Slider
3. Overhand Curve
Sources: *Baseball Magazine* (July 1948, Ken Smith); *The Miracle of Coogan's Bluff* (Thomas Kiernan, 1975); *Stan Musial* (Musial with Bob Broeg, 1964)

Mel Ott in Smith article, describing Jansen's fastball: "His other talents were glossed over and by the time he reached the Polo Grounds people had him marked as a control pitcher only. But as a matter of fact he is quite fast. He has a good deal of speed."

Pitch Selection: 1. Curve 2. Fastball 3. Change
4. Slider (occasional) 5. Sinker (occasional)
Source: *Baseball Digest* (February 1951, Charles Dexter)

Jansen: "I pitched for the [San Francisco] Seals in 1941 and had a good year, but in 1942 I was having a rough

time, and Larry Woodall, one of our coaches, taught me the slider. The slider was not a common pitch in those days. Very few pitchers threw it. Larry Woodall had been a catcher, and I have no idea where he learned it."
Source: *Baseball's Forgotten Heroes* (Tony Salin, 1999)

Stan Musial: "He had a wonderful overhanded curve, one of the best I ever saw. He also had a good fast ball and good control."
Hank Borowy: "As far as I know, the first man to use [the slider] with really great success in the major leagues was Larry Jansen."
Source: *Sport* (February 1957, Al Hirshberg); Borowy's comment is historically questionable, as the slider was used effectively by at least a few pitchers before Jansen reached the majors, but is presented here as it may be instructive about Jansen's reliance on his slider.

Comment: "Best pitch is a sinker."
Source: *Baseball Digest* (January 1951, Milt Richman)

Note: In the August 1952 *Baseball Digest*, Tom Meany repeatedly refers to Jansen as a "curve ball pitcher."

KEVIN JARVIS 6'2" 200-pound righty
33-46, 5.83, 1 Save 1994 2003

Pitches: 1. Fastball (high-80s) 2. Slider 3. Curve 4. Change
Source: *The Scouting Notebook: 2002*

PAT JARVIS 5'10" 180-pound righty
85-73, 3.58, 3 Saves 1966 1973

Pitch Selection: 1. Fastball 2. Curve
Description: Jarvis "throws good stuff . . . owning a hard fastball and curve and mixing his speeds well."
Source: *Major League Baseball, 1969* (Jack Zanger)

LARRY JASTER 6'3" 190-pound lefty
35-33, 3.64, 3 Saves 1965 1972

Pitch Selection: 1. Fastball 2. Curve 3. Slider?
Sources: *Baseball for Brain Surgeons and Other Fans* (Tim McCarver, 1998); *Baseball Digest* (March 1963, Page 107); *Major League Baseball—1969* (Jack Zanger)

Notes: According to McCarver, Jaster was "a one-pitch pitcher." He had a curveball but, according to McCarver, a very poor one. *Baseball Digest* says that Jaster "throws a curve ball slow and deliberate. Sneaky fast ball." Jack Zanger said that Jaster also threw a slider, and three years earlier *Baseball Digest* (March 1966) said Jaster had "Fine fast ball, good slider . . ."

AL JAVERY 6'3" 183-pound righty
53-74, 3.80, 5 Saves 1940 1946

Pitch Selection: 1. Fastball 2. Change
Description: "His best stock in trade is a very fast ball made more effective by a good change of pace."
Source: *Baseball Magazine* (December 1941, Clifford Bloodgood)

JOEY JAY 6'4" 228-pound righty
99-91, 3.77, 7 Saves 1953 1966

Pitch Selection: 1. Slow Curve 2. Fastball 3. Change 4. Slider
Note: Jay has been credited with inventing two pitches, the change-up screwball and the slop slider. However, at least one earlier pitcher (Freddie Frankhouse) threw a half-speed screwball as a change, and Jay's manager, Fred Hutchinson, also threw an off-speed slider. What Jay invented was new names for these pitches.
Sources: *Pennant Race* (Jim Brosnan, 1962); *Sport* (August 1963, Roy McHugh); *Stan Musial* (Musial with Bob Broeg, 1964)

Quote: "Jay has the best slow curve I've ever seen in a young boy. He's got a good change and a slider. Besides, the hitters know he can throw a fast ball. They can't dig in. He can throw it by them."
Source: Braves pitching coach Whitlow Wyatt in *Sport* (April 1959, Dick Schaap)

MIKE JEFFCOAT 6'2" 190-pound lefty
25-26, 4.37, 7 Saves 1983 1994

Pitch Selection: 1. Sinking Fastball (87–88) 2. Curve 3. Slider 4. Change
Source: *The Scouting Report: 1985*

Pitch Selection: 1. Fastball 2. Curve 3. Split-Fingered Fastball (used as a change)
Source: *The Scouting Report: 1990*

JESSE JEFFERSON 6'3" 188-pound righty
39-81, 4.81, 1 Save 1973 1981

Pitch Selection: 1. Slider 2. Fastball 3. Curve 4. Change

Quote: "[Bobby] Mattick and pitching coach Al Widmar have made one change in Jefferson, taking away his slow curve.

"After the shutout Jefferson admitted, 'I had a good change, a good curve, and a good slider, but I didn't have any pop on my fastball. Sometimes when my fastball is good you just try to blow it by the hitters and don't concentrate.' "

Source: *The Sporting News* (8/16/1980)

FERGIE JENKINS 6'5" 205-pound righty
284-226, 3.34, 7 Saves 1965 1983

Pitches: 1. Four-Seam Fastball 2. Two-Seam Fastball 3. Slider 4. Curve 5. Forkball (as Change)

Source: *Inside Pitching* (Jenkins with Dave Fisher, 1972)

Notes: The terms "four-seam" and "two-seam" fastball were not in use at that time, but it is very clear from his description in *Inside Pitching* that Jenkins was throwing the four-seam (rising) fastball to right-handed hitters, the two-seam (sinking) fastball to lefties, and that he regarded the two as distinct pitches.

According to a chart in *Inside Pitching,* in a late-1960s game against the Cardinals, Jenkins threw 50 fastballs, 44 sliders, 20 curves . . . and zero change-ups.

Other Source: *Like Nobody Else* (Ferguson Jenkins and George Vass, 1973)

Umpire Tom Gorman: "They tell me Jenkins is now throwing what the players call a 'dirt ball,' that is, he scrubs dirt into the seams and the ball drops straight down, like a spitter. That's a new one on me. I'd never heard of a dirt ball before."

Source: *Three and Two!* (Tom Gorman as told to Jerome Holtzman, 1979)

Description: "If your elbow is even with your shoulder and your wrist above your elbow, call it three-quarters . . . Ferguson Jenkins look(s) like (a) sidearmer because (he is) so tall and reach(es) out so far, but at the point of release (he) still (has) the wrist above the elbow."

Source: *Pitching with Tom Seaver* (Seaver and Steve Jacobson, 1973).

JASON JENNINGS 6'2" 245-pound righty
32-22, 4.79, 0 Saves 2001 2003

Pitch Selection: 1. Hard Sinker 2. Change

Source: *Sports Illustrated* (9/2/2002, item by Stephen Cannella)

TOMMY JOHN 6'3" 180-pound lefty
288-231, 3.34, 4 Saves 1963 1989

Key Pitch: Sinker (or Sinking Fastball)

Notes: John threw a sinking fastball 85 to 90 percent of the time from the beginning to the end of his major league career.

He was suspected of throwing a spitball or scuffball.

Source: *The Heart of the Order* (Thomas Boswell, 1989)

Pitch Selection: 1. Sinking Fastball 2. Curves 3. Cut Fastball 4. Change (added in 1988)

John: "I threw my change-up off my pinky and ring fingers . . .

"I didn't throw my change-up until the last two years of my career, when I needed something extra in my arsenal. Until then all I ever threw was the fastball and curve. I was a two-pitch pitcher. My fastball moved and my curveball broke down and in to right-handed hitters. I'd change the break of my curve depending on how fast I threw it, and so I had a variety of curveballs. I could also cut a fastball when I needed to move it inside to a right-handed batter. These 'off' pitches served the same function for me as a change-up.

"I was blessed in that my ball naturally broke down. The sinkerball was my meal ticket. But I also learned the mechanics that added to my natural ball movement. I learned them when I was with the White Sox. Ray Berres, the pitching coach there, taught me to throw with my hand position going from straight up to straight down. It takes effort and a lot of practice to throw the ball that way, since the uncorrected tendency is to keep your hand positioned at an angle. It's called throwing high-to-low, and that's the way I pitched, driving the ball down with my hand and fingers."

Source: *TJ: My Twenty-Six Years in Baseball* (John with Dan Valenti, 1991)

CONNIE JOHNSON 6'4" 200-pound righty
40-39, 3.44, 1 Save 1953 1958

Pitch Selection: 1. Fastball 2. Slider 3. Screwball 4. Slip Pitch

Sources: *The Sporting News* (8/29/1956); *Baltimore News-Post* (circa 1957, article by John F. Steadman)

Note: *TSN* article lists Johnson as having one of the best fastballs in the league.

Key Pitch: Sweeping Sidearm Curve
Source: *Chicago White Sox Yearbook, 1954* (Arch Ward)

ERNIE JOHNSON 6'3" 190-pound righty
40-23, 3.78, 19 Saves 1950 1959

Pitches: 1. Palm Ball 2. Slider 3. Sidearm Curve 4. Fastball
Source: *Milwaukee Journal* (2/10/1963, Bob Wolf; and 6/16/1957, Wolf)

Description: "A sidearming right hander with a 'whip' delivery reminiscent of Ewell Blackwell's . . ."
Source: *Milwaukee's Miracle Braves* (Tom Meany, 1954)

HANK JOHNSON 5'11" 175-pound righty
63-56, 4.76, 11 Saves 1925 1939

Pitch Selection: 1. Fastball 2. Curve 3. Change
Note: As a child, Johnson idolized Walter Johnson, and copied his delivery, eventually becoming a carbon copy of Walter, although his fastball was not *that* good. In 1927, Miller Huggins changed Johnson's arm angle, converting him from a sidearm delivery to overhand. After he had surgery to remove bone chips from his elbow in 1934 he went back to his original delivery, and also at that time the curve became his best pitch.
Sources: Henry P. Edwards, *American League Service Bureau* (12/27/1933); *The Sporting News* (12/23/1934, Dick Farrington); *Birmingham News* (3/22/1939)

JERRY JOHNSON 6'3" 200-pound righty
48-51, 4.31, 41 Saves 1968 1977

Pitch Selection: 1. Fastball 2. Slider
Source: *The Sporting News* (7/3/1971, Pat Frizzell; 7/2/1977, Neil MacCarl)

KEN JOHNSON 6'1" 185-pound lefty
12-14, 4.58, 0 Saves 1947 1952

Key Pitch: Curve
Source: *Baseball Digest* (March 1951, Frank Yeutter)
Note: Johnson, whose nickname was "Hook," was said to throw one of the best curveballs in the majors and had a decent fastball, but, like Walter Beall, he had serious control problems.

KEN JOHNSON 6'4" 210-pound righty
91-106, 3.46, 9 Saves 1958 1970

Pitch Selection: 1. Knuckleball 2. Fastball 3. Slider
Sources: *Pennant Race* (Jim Brosnan, 1962); *Inside the Astrodome* (1965)

Description: "[Johnson is] mainly a knuckle-ball pitcher, and (can) operate overhand, sidearm and underhand."
Source: *Major League Baseball 1965* (Jack Zanger)

RANDY JOHNSON 6'10" 225-pound lefty
230-114, 3.10, 2 Saves 1988 2003

Pitches, 1990–1992: 1. Fastball (high-90s) 2. Sharp Curve 3. Change
Sources: *The Scouting Report* (1991–1993 editions)

Pitches, 1993–1997: 1. Fastball (mid-90s) 2. Hard Slider 3. Curve (occasional) 4. Change (occasional)
Sources: *1994 Baseball Almanac; The Scouting Notebook* (1996–1998 editions)

Pitches, late career: 1. Four-Seam Fastball (95–97) 2. Hard Slider 3. Two-Seam Fastball (91–93, as Change)
Johnson: "About 90 percent of the time I will throw a slider in an 0-2 or 1-2 count because it is my strikeout pitch . . ."
Source: *Randy Johnson's Power Pitching* (Randy Johnson with Jim Rosenthal, 2003); not once in Johnson's book does he mention throwing a curveball or a true change-up, and says, "I've always favored a slider over a curveball . . ." This throws the above reference to curveballs into serious doubt.

Brian Jordan on Johnson's slider: "You're thinking fastball and that rotation [on the slider] is so tight that by the time you pick it up it's too late. There's no pitch close to it in this league."
Johnson on Johnson's slider: "It's sharpness is a matter of velocity. The harder you throw it the harder it rotates, and that's what makes the ball cut down."
Source: *Sports Illustrated* (3/31/03, Page 62)

Description: "At six-foot-ten, the Big Unit has a mighty big advantage with those long legs and that big stride. He looks like a big hairy half-tarantula as he goes into the windup. Instead of throwing from sixty feet, six inches, he sometimes looks like he's delivering from about fifty feet, five inches.

"Johnson's arm is thirty-eight inches long, which means that he's actually delivering the ball three feet behind a left-handed hitter's back. The amazing part is that the ball winds up on the outside part of the plate, causing the left-handed hitter to lean so far forward that he's almost falling on his nose . . ."

Source: Umpire Durwood Merrill in *You're Out and You're Ugly, Too* (Merrill with Jim Dent, 1998)

SI JOHNSON 5'11" 185-pound righty
101-165, 4.09, 15 Saves 1928 1947

Pitch Selection, 1930–31: 1. Fastball
Pitch Selection, 1932–35: 1. Fastball 2. Nickel Curve
Pitch Selection, 1936–38: 1. Fastball 2. Improved Curve
Pitch Selection, 1940–43: 1. Slider 2. Curve 3. Fastball 4. Change
Pitch Selection, 1946–47: 1. Change 2. Pogo Pitch 3. Slider 4. Curve 5. Fastball
Sources: *Baseball Magazine* (May 1933, Clifford Bloodgood); interview with Lyall Smith in *Chicago Daily News* (1/15/1944); unidentified article in TSN Morgue, probably 1947

Commentary: The story of Si Johnson is an archetype. As a young pitcher he had an excellent fastball, which darted suddenly in and down as it crossed the plate. He made it to the majors with the fastball and nothing else, and pitched 250 innings for the Reds in 1931 and '32 while throwing nothing but fastballs and working on a curve, but nothing really he could count on. (He occasionally attempted to throw a change, but it was transparent, and usually hit hard.) He lost a lot of games that way and his fastball declined steadily, although the curve gradually came around. Returned to the minors in 1938, he won 22 games at Rochester in 1939 by learning to throw a slider and change speeds, and returned to the majors in 1940 as a cagey veteran.

The Pogo Pitch was a curve, discovered accidentally in 1946; despite the joke name, it was a key part of his repertoire as an older pitcher. Attempting to get something extra on a hard curve to Pete Reiser in 1946, he took a hop—a pogo jump—in mid-motion. The ball broke sharply, so Johnson refined and adopted the pitch, with the bunny hop off the mound. In the mid-1940s he was also accused of throwing an occasional spitball.

SYL JOHNSON 5'11" 180-pound righty
112-117, 4.06, 43 Saves 1922 1940

Pitch Selection: 1. Curve 2. Sidearm 3. Rising Fastball
Note: Johnson threw sidearm.
Sources: *Who's Who in Major League Baseball* (compiled by Harold "Speed" Johnson, 1933); *Major League Baseball* (Ethan Allen, Page 29)
Quote from *Who's Who:* "He is not a fast ball thrower, but depends principally upon a curve."
Quote from Allen: "Sylvester Johnson, a sidearm pitcher, threw a rising fast ball. This cannot be explained except that Johnson, unlike most sidearm pitchers, gripped the ball across the widest separation of seams."

WALTER JOHNSON 6'1" 200-pound righty
417-279, 2.16, 34 Saves 1907 1927

Pitch Selection: 1. Fastball 2. Curve
Note: Johnson threw sidearm. He apparently didn't master his curve until mid-way in his glory years, about 1913 or 1914.
Sources: *The Washington Senators* (Shirley Povich, 1954); *Baseball Between the Wars* (Eugene Murdock, 1992) contains numerous comments about whether and how often Walter Johnson threw something other than a fastball. Some hitters claim Johnson never threw anything else. Ed Wells claims (Murdock, Page 75) that Johnson threw a curveball only in his last two seasons.

Johnson: "I used to pitch one wiggly one to about four or five fast ones, but I could never seem to get very much on my curves, and so I have come to depend almost solely on speed."
Source: *Baseball Magazine* (November 1913, F.C. Lane)

Quote: "Walter Johnson has more stuff than I ever saw in a pitcher, and he has an easy delivery. But I think he made a mistake when he took up curve pitching. He didn't need anything more than he already had. And I don't believe he can develop good curves which will not take toll sooner or later out of his arm."
Source: Nap Rucker in *Baseball Magazine* (June 1917, Rucker in "The Biggest Mistake of My Career")

Johnson in 1919: "I have developed what I consider a pretty good curve ball. I will not attempt to say how it compares with that of other pitchers, but it has proved serviceable to me. Many days now when my fast ball is not quite as good as it used to be, I fall back on my curve. Probably I shall depend more and more on my curve as time goes on."
Source: *Baseball Magazine* (May 1919, "My Honest Opinion of My Own Pitching")

Quote: "Walter had a habit of throwing his curve ball whenever he got two strikes on a batter. He didn't *have* a curve, just a wrinkle. So I'd take two strikes and look for that little curve."
Source: Eddie Collins, quoted in *Great Baseball Pitchers* (Jim Brosnan, 1965)

Quote: "Some pitchers are fast some of the time, but Johnson is fast all the time. When he is merely fast you can hit him if you are lucky; but when he is in a hole or happens to want to dig up the red hot stuff and puts that Johnson speed into it the ball travels so fast that no one can hit it."
Source: Vean Gregg in *Baseball Magazine* (October 1913, F.C. Lane)

Comment: "Walter Johnson is ranked No. 2 by [Hughie] Jennings in the speed list. The great Washington pitcher is a side-arm thrower, long of arm, strong in control, and pitches with as little visible effort as anybody I've seen except Jack Powell, one time Yankee, Clevelander and St. Louis Brown."
Source: *Baseball Magazine* (April 1923, William B. Hanna)

Also see entry for Joe Wood.

JOHN JOHNSTONE 6'3" 210-pound righty
15-19, 4.01, 3 Saves 1993 2000

Pitch Selection: 1. Fastball (low-90s) 2. Slider 3. Split-Fingered Fastball
Source: *The Scouting Notebook: 1999*

BARRY JONES 6'4" 225-pound righty
33-33, 3.66, 23 Saves 1986 1993

Pitch Selection: 1. Fastball 2. Slider 3. Change (occasional)
Sources: *The Scouting Report* (1987 and 1993 editions)

BOBBY J. JONES 6'4" 210-pound righty
89-83, 4.36, 0 Saves 1993 2002

Pitch Selection: 1. Sinker 2. Curve 3. Change 4. Fastball 5. Cut Fastball
Source: *The Scouting Notebook: 1997*

DOUG JONES 6'3" 195-pound righty
69-79, 3.30, 303 Saves 1982 2000

Pitch Selection: 1. Slow Fastball 2. Change 3. Different Change 4. Screwball
Sources: *USA Today* (6/4/1990, Mike Terry); *The Scouting Report* (1987 and 1990 editions); *The Scouting Notebook: 1997*

Commentary: Jones threw the screwball in 1985 and '86; but didn't throw it more than once in a while the rest of his career. His stock in trade was keeping hitters off-stride with slow, slower, and even slower change-ups.

JIMMY JONES 6'2" 175-pound righty
43-39, 4.46, 0 Saves 1986 1993

Pitch Selection: 1. Fastball 2. Curve 3. Slider
Note: Learned the curve and slider from Jack Lamabe
Source: *The Scouting Report: 1987*

Pitches: 1. Fastball (88–90) 2. Curve 3. Change 4. Sinking Fastball
Note: Source claims that Jones planned to unveil a slider in 1990.
Source: *The Scouting Report: 1990*

Pitches: 1. Fastball 2. Slow Curve 3. Hard Curve 4. Change
Source: *The Scouting Report: 1992*

Pitch Selection: 1. Fastball 2. Curve 3. Change 4. Cut Fastball (added 1992)
Note: Source does not mention the fastball, but we're assuming he didn't junk it.
Source: *The Scouting Report: 1993*

PERCY JONES 5'11" 175-pound lefty
53-57, 4.33, 6 Saves 1920 1930

Pitch Selection: 1. Fastball 2. Curve
Quote: ". . . as he bears down on his fastball or releases one of his deceptive benders."
Source: *Boston Globe* (4/23/1928)

RANDY JONES 6'0" 178-pound lefty
100-123, 3.42, 2 Saves 1973 1982

Pitches: 1. Sinker (mid-70s) 2. Slider 3. Curve 4. Fastball
Padres catcher Fred Kendall: "People talk about Randy's sinker, but the pitch that makes him so effective is his slider. He busts it in on their fists when they get to leaning and looking for the sinker. The slider keeps 'em honest."
Source: *The Sporting News* (6/19/1976, Phil Collier)
Other Source: *The Sporting News* (9/6/1975, Phil Collier)

Comment: "[Jones] hardly ever exceeds 80 m.p.h. In fact, during one San Diego-Dodgers game, Jones never surpassed 80."
Source: Mark Purdy in the *New York Times* (September, 1978)

Keith Hernandez: "Perhaps more common than the hard sinker ballers are pitchers like the former Padre Randy Jones, a left-hander with a sinker that traveled in the low eighties—not hard at all, really, but that pitch broke late and sharply and killed the league. Right-handed batters lost patience, chased after it, and missed it every time. Finally some manager had the bright idea of going against the book by stacking his lineup with left-handed hitters to go against the left-hander Jones. Unheard of! But the sinker broke into their favorite hitting zone. Jones retaliated against left-handed batters with a good, sharp slider that he could break over the outside corner . . ."
Source: *Pure Baseball: Pitch by Pitch for the Advanced Fan* (Keith Hernandez and Mike Bryan, 1994)

SAD SAM JONES 6'0" 170-pound righty
229-217, 3.84, 31 Saves 1914 1935

Pitch Selection: 1. Curve 2. Slow Ball 3. Fastball
Sources: *1918: Babe Ruth and the World Champion Boston Red Sox* (Allan Wood, 2000); *The Ballplayers* (1990, article by Ed Walton); 1924 *Reach Guide* (Page 48)

Tris Speaker in 1918: "That slow ball of his simply floats up there and you swing your head off. Then he's got a fast one that's on top of you before you realize it. Plus, he's got as good a curve-ball as anyone in the league."
Source: *1918: Babe Ruth and the World Champion Boston Red Sox*

Jones: "You know, I think one reason I pitched so long is that I never wasted my arm trying to throw over to first to keep runners close to the base. There was a time there, for five years, I never *once* threw to first base to chase a runner back. Not once in five years. Ripley put that in 'Believe It or Not.' "
Source: *The Glory of Their Times* (Lawrence S. Ritter, 1966)

Quote: "Sam is the prettiest pitcher in action that I ever saw. He pitches with an absolute minimum of effort and he always knows exactly what he is doing. Sam hasn't much speed, but he doesn't need it. He has proved that there is a lot to pitching beside trying to throw the ball by the batter."
Source: Sloppy Thurston in *Baseball Magazine* (July 1933, F.C. Lane)

Note: At some point Jones added a screwball to his repertoire. In 1928 he told an interviewer, "With all due respect to Gehrig, and he is a marvelously improved ball player, I figure Ruth is the most disturbing batter in the game. But I've never had so much trouble with Ruth when I've pitched against the Yankees. I usually depend upon a screw ball and a slow curve. The screw ball, as I throw it, isn't particularly hard on my arm because I don't put so much behind it. After all, speed is of small importance compared with what you do with the ball."
Source: *Baseball Magazine* (June 1928, "Comprising an Interview with Samuel Pond Jones")

See also entry for Howard Ehmke.

SAM JONES 6'4" 192-pound righty
102-101, 3.59, 9 Saves 1951 1964

Pitch Selection: 1. Sweeping Curve 2. Fastball 3. Change
Sources: *Baseball Stars of 1959* (article by Arnold Hano); *Stan Musial* (Musial with Bob Broeg, 1964)

Pitch Selection: 1. "Wicked Curve"
Source: *Sports Illustrated* (8/31/1959 and again 9/28/1959)

Stan Musial: "Sam had the best curve ball I ever saw . . . He was quick and fast and that curve was terrific, so big it was like a change of pace. I've seen guys fall down on sweeping curves that became strikes. Righthanders thought Sam had the most wicked curve, and as a left-handed hitter, I thought that it was positively the best."

Description: "Biggest curveball in the league. If it started out behind you, it was going to be a strike . . . It wasn't the curveball so much, because you could see the spin. It was the wildness, because you weren't *sure* what the pitch was."
Source: Eddie O'Brien speaking at Northwest SABR meeting in May 2002 (recorded by Rob Neyer)

Also see Gregg Olson, comment from Frank Robinson.

TODD JONES 6'3" 200-pound righty
39-42, 4.06, 184 Saves 1993 2003

Pitch Selection: 1. Fastball 2. Curve 3. Change
Source: *The Scouting Notebook: 1997*

ORVILLE JORGENS 6'1" 180-pound righty
21-27, 4.70, 5 Saves 1935 1937

Key Pitch: Sinker
Description: "Well, Jorgens is no Mungo for 'swift,' but he has good speed when the necessity for such is demanded. He depends more, however, on a sinker ball to confuse the enemy."
Source: *Baseball Magazine* (May 1937, Clifford Bloodgood)

Comment: "Jorgens, of the Phillies, combines with his relief pitching skill the strange knack of trapping runners off first base. At this time he has caught no fewer than 21 off the bag. He has a remarkable motion for a right-hander—almost as deadly as the southpaw motion which Sherry Smith, of the Dodgers, used and with which he nipped so many off the base."
Source: *Baseball Magazine* (October 1937, Daniel M. Daniel)

ADDIE JOSS 6'3" 185-pound righty
160-97, 1.89, 5 Saves 1902 1910

Pitches: 1. Fastball 2. Hard Curve 3. Slow Ball
Quote: "Unlike so many other pitchers, he did not own a large assortment of curves. Not because he could not master and deliver them, but he believed that with a few well mastered deliveries he could acquire greater control and success with less strain on his arm. Joss did not trifle with the spitball . . . His fast ball always had that 'something on it.' His curve was a fast breaking beauty and his change of pace, viz., the slow ball, was perfect."
Source: George Moriarty in *Baseball Magazine* (August 1911, "The Greatest Pitcher I Ever Faced")

Description: "Joss not only had great speed and a fast-breaking curve, but a very effective pitching motion, bringing the ball from behind him with a complete body swing and having it on the batter almost before the latter got sight of it."
Source: *Baseball Magazine* (August 1911, "Addie Joss")

Key Pitch: Jump Ball
Note: Joss threw from a sort of corkscrew windup motion.
Sources: *The National Game* (Alfred H. Spink, 1911); *Baseball's 50 Greatest Games* (Bert Sugar, 1968)

Quote from Spink: "[Joss] gained the reputation of being the brainiest pitcher in the American League."

Description: "He was a great pitcher, that fellow. He would turn his back toward the batter as he wound up, hiding the ball all the while, and then whip around and fire it in. He threw the good fastball and the good curve. Very tough to hit."
Source: Roger Peckinpaugh in *The Man in the Dugout* (Donald Honig, 1977)

Also see Fred Fitzsimmons entry.

JEFF JUDEN 6'8" 271-pound righty
27-32, 4.81, 0 Saves 1991 1999

Pitch Selection: 1. Sinking Fastball (low-90s) 2. Cut Fastball 3. Slider
Source: *The Scouting Notebook: 1997*

Pitch Selection: 1. Fastball (low-90s) 2. Slider 3. Curve 4. Change
Source: *The Scouting Notebook: 1999*

JORGE JULIO 6'1" 190-pound righty
6-14, 3.22, 61 Saves 2001 2003

Pitches: 1. Fastball (96–98) 2. Hard Slider 3. Change (occasional)
Source: *The Scouting Notebook* (2003 edition)

JIM KAAT 6'4" 205-pound lefty
283-237, 3.45, 18 Saves 1959 1983

Pitch Selection: 1. Slider 2. Curve 3. Fastball 4. Slurve
Source: *Baseball Stars of 1967* (article by Ray Robinson)

Note: In *Me and the Spitter* (page 126), Gaylord Perry says Kaat's best pitches were a sinker and screwball.

Story: "One day, while watching Whitey Ford warm up in the bullpen for the Yankees, Kaat summoned up the nerve to ask the rival lefthander how he threw his sinking fastball. Says Kaat, 'Turns out his grip was something in between a two-seam and a four-seam grip. He showed me, I tried it out and it became my fastball grip from that point on.' "
Source: *ESPN The Magazine* (9/1/2003, Jeff Bradley)

GEORGE KAHLER 6'0" 160-pound righty
32-43, 3.17, 2 Saves 1910 1914

Key Pitch: Emery Ball
Note: Kahler was the second major league pitcher to use the emery ball. After Russ Ford discovered the scuff ball in the minor leagues and brought it to the majors, he kept it secret for several years. Kahler discovered the secret; he claimed, improbably enough, that Ford had told it to him in a dream, and this explanation appears to have been widely accepted at the time. In any case, after Kahler began throwing the pitch Ford gave up the secret, and the pitch spread rapidly around the major leagues.
Source: *The Sporting News* (10/1/1914)

SCOTT KAMIENIECKI 6'0" 200-pound righty
53-59, 4.52, 5 Saves 1991 2000

Pitch Selection: 1. Fastball 2. Curve 3. Change 4. Slider
Sources: *1994 Baseball Almanac; The Scouting Notebook 1998*

MATT KARCHNER 6'4" 220-pound righty
21-13, 4.21, 27 Saves 1995 2000

Pitch Selection: 1. Fastball (mid-90s) 2. Slider
Source: *The Scouting Notebook: 1999*

ED KARGER 5'11" 185-pound lefty
48-67, 2.79, 3 Saves 1906 1911

Pitch Selection: 1. Fastball 2. Curve
Quote: "He threw only 2 kinds of pitches—fast ball + curve."
Source: Letter from Karger's widow, Maude M. Karger, to SABR member Joe Simenic (dated 5/1/1971)

ANDY KARL 6'1½" 175-pound righty
18-23, 3.51, 26 Saves 1943 1947

Pitch Selection: 1. Knuckleball 2. Fastball 3. Knuckle Curve
Comment: "Karl has added something new to the knuckleball delivery. He never has been able to throw a good curve in the orthodox manner of snapping his wrist and letting the ball revolve over the ends of his fingers, so he has developed a 'knuckle curve,' a ball held on the tips of his fingers—like an ordinary knuckler—but one that he pushes off. The ball spins as it goes to the plate and breaks down like a drop."
Source: *The Sporting News* (8/9/1945, J.G. Taylor Spink)

SCOTT KARL 6'2" 195-pound lefty
54-56, 4.81, 0 Saves 1995 2000

Pitch Selection: 1. "Heavy" Change or Palmball 2. Curve 3. Fastball
Sources: *The Scouting Notebook* (1997 and 2000 editions)

BENNIE KARR 6'0" 175-pound righty
35-48, 4.60, 5 Saves 1920 1927

Key Pitch: Forkball (55%)
Quote: "In the old days he used to be a curve pitcher. At Boston, however, he came under the influence of Joe Bush and the famed fork ball delivery which he had invented. Karr experimented with this delivery for two years until he finally mastered it and now he considers it the corner stone of his pitching success . . . 'Now I can grip it easily and control it as well as a curve. Out of a hundred balls that I pitch, at least fifty, very often sixty, are fork balls.

" 'It is such a good delivery that I have often wondered why more pitchers don't use it. The only ones that I know of who mastered it to any degree are Joe Bush, who originated the delivery, Gaston and myself.' "

Source: *Baseball Magazine* (October 1925, "Comprising an interview with Bennie Karr")

STEVE KARSAY 6'3" 210-pound righty
31-38, 3.88, 41 Saves 1993 2002

Pitch Selection: 1. Fastball (93–94) 2. Change 3. Curve
Source: *The Scouting Notebook: 1998*

Pitch Selection: 1. Fastball (95–98) 2. Hard Curve (76–82) 3. Split-Fingered Fastball 4. Change
Note: Split-fingered fastball and change used when pitching as a starter.
Source: *The Scouting Notebook* (2000 and 2001 editions)

TONY KAUFMANN 5'11" 165-pound righty
64-62, 4.18, 12 Saves 1921 1935

Quote: ". . . dazzling the batters of [the Western Canada League] with his 'stuff.' "
Source: files of NL publicist Ford Sawyer

RAY KEATING 5'11" 185-pound righty
30-51, 3.29, 1 Save 1912 1919

Key Pitch: Emery Ball
Note: Keating's aggressive use of the emery ball led to the first major controversy about the emery ball, and thus to the first public awareness of the pitch.
Source: *The Sporting News* (10/1/1914)

JACK KEEFE 1913 1919

Pitches: 1. Fastball 2. Spitball 3. Slow Ball (occasional)
Source: *The Saturday Evening Post* (3/7/1914, Ring Lardner; 5/23/1914, Lardner)

TIM KEEFE 5'10" 185-pound righty
342-226, 2.62, 2 Saves 1880 1893

Pitch Selection: 1. Change 2. Fastball 3. Curve
Sources: *Baseball's Hall of Fame* (Robert Smith); *The Ballplayers* (1990, article by A.D. Suehsdorf); Lee Allen in *The Sporting News* (4/4/1964, Allen's "Cooperstown Corner" column); *The National Game* (Alfred H. Spink, 1911)

Allen: "Keefe had good speed and a curve and was also one of the first pitchers to employ the change-up, throwing it with the same motion as his fast one."

Description: "Tim mixed in a change of pace with the drop, and the way he could stand batsmen on their heads by pushing in the slow-drop curve on a third strike was simply paralyzing."
Source: *Baseball Magazine* (May 1911, "The Discoveries of the Curve and Drop")

Quote: "The original slow ball was merely a ball thrown slowly, the pitcher depending entirely upon a false motion to deceive the batter into believing he was pitching a fast ball. Keefe, O'Day, and most of the oldtime pitchers used that kind of a slow ball."
Source: *Touching Second* (John J. Evers and Hugh S. Fullerton, 1910)

BOB KEEGAN 6'2" 207-pound righty
40-36, 3.65, 5 Saves 1953 1958

Pitch Selection: 1. Sinking Fastball 2. Curve (occasional) 3. Slip Pitch (experimental)
Keegan: "My fast ball is my best pitch. I throw it almost exclusively. In one game last season I threw only four or five curves against the Tigers, plus a few experimental 'slip' ball pitches."
Source: *The Sporting News* (2/3/1955, Ed Prell)

MIKE KEKICH 6'1" 196-pound lefty
39-51, 4.60, 6 Saves 1965 1977

Pitch Selection: 1. Fastball 2. Curve 3. Change
Source: Mariners pitching coach Wes Stock quoted in unidentified magazine article from Kekich's Hall of Fame file

HARRY KELLEY 5'9" 170-pound righty
42-47, 4.86, 5 Saves 1925 1939

Key Pitch: Slow Curve
Comment: "Kelley's is one of the slowest curves in the majors, and has led to the supposition that he throws a knuckler."
Source: *Baseball Magazine* (September 1937, Daniel M. Daniel)

ALEX KELLNER 6'0" 200-pound lefty
101-112, 4.41, 5 Saves 1948 1959

Pitch Selection: 1. Fastball 2. Curve 3. Change
Note: Kellner threw overhand.
Source: *Baseball Stars of 1950* (article by Franklin W. Yeutter)

Quote: "Like most all kids that come up to us, Alex had to be straightened out. They usually come out of the minors throwing overhand, sidearm and underhand. You have to find their groove and make them stay in it. Kellner was doing that, so I made him come straight overhand. Only once in a while does he come sidearm, then always to a left-hand hitter. Staying in one groove improved his control. He was pretty wild before that."
Source: A's pitching coach Earle Brucker in *Baseball Magazine* (December 1949, Ed Rumill)

BILL KELSO 6'4" 215-pound righty
12-5, 3.13, 12 Saves 1964 1968

Description: "Big strong right-hander. Could be better as a movie star than as a ball player. Used to be a catcher. His marks are not good at all."
Source: *Baseball Digest* (March 1967, "Official Scouting Reports on 1967 Major League Rookies")

RUSS KEMMERER 6'2" 198-pound righty
43-59, 4.46, 8 Saves 1954 1963

Pitches: 1. Sinking Fastball 2. Slider/Cutter
3. Slip Pitch
Kemmerer: "My fastball was my best pitch. Some guys threw a real light ball, some guys threw a real heavy ball . . . I was one of those heavy-ball pitchers; catchers didn't like to catch me. My best pitch was a sinking fastball that went into a right-handed hitter, and away from the left-handed hitter. If I pitched up I was in trouble . . . I had a pretty good slider, which acted just the opposite of the fastball. I guess now they call it a cutter; we called it a slider . . . My other pitch I relied on was the slip pitch."
Source: phone interview with Kemmerer (6/6/2002, Rob Neyer)

Kemmerer: "I had a good sinking fastball that dived towards a right-handed hitter and broke down and away from a left-handed hitter. This movement of my fastball resembled the action of a spitball . . . By the way, I never did throw the spitter. For one reason or another, whenever I tried it the pitch straightened out!"
Source: *Ted Williams: 'Hey Kid, Just Get It Over the Plate!'* (Kemmerer with W.C. Madden, 2002)
Note: In his book, Kemmerer mentions throwing a fastball, curve, change, slider, and slip pitch. It appears that he moved from the curve to the slider as he aged.

BRICKYARD KENNEDY 5'11" 160-pound righty
191-154, 3.96, 5 Saves 1892 1903

Key Pitch: Curve
Source: *The Great Teams of Baseball* (MacLean Kennedy, 1929; reference is extremely weak.)

MONTE KENNEDY 6'2" 185-pound lefty
42-55, 3.84, 4 Saves 1946 1953

Key Pitch: Fastball
Stan Musial: "Monte Kennedy threw very hard for a left-hander, but he had to rely on his fast ball because he couldn't control his curve ball. Whenever he threw his curve to me, I just took it because I knew he had to come in with the fast ball. I'd wait for it and always had good luck against him."
Source: *Stan Musial: The Man's Own Story* (Musial, as told to Bob Broeg, 1964)

VERN KENNEDY 6'0" 175-pound righty
104-132, 4.67, 5 Saves 1934 1945

Pitch Selection: 1. Sinker 2. Curve 3. Fastball
Quote from Charlie Metro: "He was a very energetic type of pitcher on the mound; he worked fast. He had a little sinker ball, he had a curve ball, he had a fastball."
Source: phone interview with Metro (6/13/2002, Rob Neyer)

Pitch Selection: 1. Sinking Fastball 2. Curve
3. Knuckleball (occasional)
Sources: *Baseball Digest* (October 2002, Page 11); *Baseball Magazine* (April 1936, Clifford Bloodgood)

Comment: "Another who frequently has heard the charge of 'spitball' is Vernon Kennedy, the Cleveland Indians' pitcher. Kennedy is a nervous individual who is forever wiping the sweat from his brow with his bare hand, and opponents say he uses the moisture thus har-

vested to impart the unlawful slipperiness to the ball. Maybe he does, but he never has been caught at it."
Source: *Baseball Digest* (date unknown, article by Gordon Cobbledick)

MATT KEOUGH 6'3" 190-pound righty
58-84, 4.17, 0 Saves 1977 1986

Pitch Selection: 1. Fastball 2. Change 3. Slider
Note: Keough threw a slider prior to 1980. He was suspected of throwing an occasional spitball.
Sources: *The Sporting News* (5/10/1980, Kit Stier; 6/6/1981, Peter Gammons)

CHARLIE KERFELD 6'6" 225-pound righty
18-9, 4.20, 9 Saves 1985 1990

Key Pitch: Fastball
Source: *The National Sports Daily* (6/5/1990, Gordon Edes)

JIM KERN 6'5" 185-pound righty
53-57, 3.32, 88 Saves 1974 1986

Pitch Selection: 1. Fastball 2. Curve 3. Slider 4. Change
Source: *The Sporting News* (9/21/1974, Russ Schneider)

Pitch Selection: 1. Fastball 2. Curve 3. Change 4. Palmball
Source: *The Sporting News* (5/10/1980, Randy Galloway)

DICKIE KERR 5'7" 155-pound lefty
53-34, 3.83, 6 Saves 1919 1925

Pitch Selection: 1. Fastball 2. Curve
Source: *Eight Men Out* (Eliot Asinof, 1963); *The Great Baseball Mystery* (Victor Luhrs, 1966)

Description: "Take Dickie Kerr, now, a wee hop o' my thumb. Not much taller than a walking stick . . . the tiniest of the baseball brood. Won't weigh 90 lbs soaking wet, an astute scout once reported after a look at Kerr. Too small for a pitcher, especially for a left-handed pitcher. Two small for too much of anything, expect, perhaps, a watch charm. . . ."
Source: Damon Runyon quoted in *Eight Men Out*

JIMMY KEY 6'1" 185-pound lefty
186-117, 3.51, 10 Saves 1984 1998

Pitch Selection: 1. Curve 2. Fastball 3. Change 4. Slider
Sources: *Tom Seaver's 1989 Scouting Notebook; The Scouting Report: 1990* (article by Neil McCarl)

LEO KIELY 6'2" 180-pound lefty
26-27, 3.37, 29 Saves 1951 1960

Key Pitch: Sinking Fastball
Source: George Susce, quoted by Ed Rumill in the *Christian Science Monitor* (August 1951)

DARRYL KILE 6'5" 185-pound righty
133-119, 4.12, 0 Saves 1991 2002

Pitch Selection: 1. Curve 2. Fastball 3. Change
Sources: *1994 Baseball Almanac; The Scouting Notebook 1998*

Tim McCarver: "There are very few 12-to-6 (on a clock) downers anymore. Darryl Kile comes the closest today, throwing the tightest-wrapped, hardest-to-hit curveball in the National League. It's hard to imagine anyone throwing a curve as good as Koufax's, but Kile's overhanded curves are also of the straight-down variety, what we called 'drops' as kids. Most of the other curveballers must settle for 11:50-to-5:20 downers."
Source: *Tim McCarver's Baseball for Brain Surgeons and Other Fans* (McCarver with Danny Peary, 1998)

PAUL KILGUS 6'1" 185-pound lefty
21-34, 4.19, 4 Saves 1987 1993

Pitch Selection: 1. Curve 2. Fastball
Source: *The Scouting Report: 1990*

FRANK KILLEN 6'1" 200-pound lefty
163-124, 3.78, 4 Saves 1891 1900

Key Pitch: Fastball
Source: *Nineteenth Century Stars* (SABR, 1989, article by Robert L. Tiemann)

MATT KILROY 5'9" 175-pound lefty
141-132, 3.47, 1 Save 1886 1898

Quote: "[Kilroy was nicknamed] 'Matches' [probably] as a tribute to his blazing fastball."

Source: *The Biographic Encyclopedia of Baseball* (editors Pietrusza, Silverman, and Gershman, 2000)

Also see entry for Bert Cunningham.

BYUNG-HYUN KIM 5'9" 180-pound righty
29-27, 3.24, 86 Saves 1999 2003

Pitch Selection: 1. Fastball (88–91) 2. Slider
Note: Throws with a low sidearm or submarine delivery.
Source: *The Scouting Notebook: 2002*

ELLIS KINDER 6'0" 195-pound righty
102-71, 3.43, 102 Saves 1946 1957

Pitch Selection: 1. Change 2. Curve 3. Fastball 4. Slider 5. Spitball
Sources: *Summer of '49* (David Halberstam, 1989); *Sport* (February 1957, Al Hirshberg); *New York Post* (6/24/1956, Page 34); *The Sporting News* (3/23/1955); *Baseball Digest* (November 1949, Milt Richman)

Notes: Halberstam, describing Kinder at his peak, does not mention the slider, but Hirshberg quotes Kinder as saying that "When I was a kid, I threw a slider, only we called it an outshoot," and the *New York Post* reference says that Kinder relied heavily on his slider as a 40-year-old reliever. Kinder acknowledged throwing the spitball in the 3/23/1955 issue of *The Sporting News.* The *Baseball Digest* article says Kinder threw the best change of pace in the league at that time.

CLYDE KING 6'1" 175-pound righty
32-25, 4.14, 11 Saves 1944 1953

Pitches: 1. Curve 2. Fastball 3. Straight Change
Source: *A King's Legacy* (Clyde King with Burton Rocks, 1999)
Note: In 1951, King recorded the final out in a Dodgers victory over the Giants by throwing a "bubblegum ball" for strike three against Whitey Lockman (and yes, the bubblegum ball was exactly what it sounds like).

Umpire Tom Gorman: "Clyde King . . . was a real cutie. He'd quick-pitch, which was against the rules, and got so good at it that a lot of times he didn't get caught."
Three and Two! (Tom Gorman as told to Jerome Holtzman, 1979)

ERIC KING 6'2" 218-pound righty
52-45, 3.97, 16 Saves 1986 1992

Pitch Selection: 1. Fastball 2. Curve 3. Change
Source: *The Scouting Report: 1992*

Quote: "King is a hard thrower and throws several different pitches, including a couple of different fastballs—one that rides into a righthanded hitter and one that moves away—as well as a good hard curve."
Source: *The Scouting Report: 1990*

SILVER KING 6'0" 170-pound righty
204-154, 3.18, 5 Saves 1886 1897

Pitches: 1. Fastball 2. Curves
Silver King: "My pitching stock consisted mainly in speed. I threw some curves, but I never knew about such things as a spitball, a fadeaway, shine ball and all these tricks. You simply had to be a Colossus to stand the gaff."
Source: Interview in *The Sporting News* (1/10/1919)
Other source for fastball: *Nineteenth Century Stars* (SABR, 1989, article by Bob Tiemann)

Pitch Selection: 1. Fastball 2. Drop Ball
Source: St. Louis *Post-Dispatch* (6/30/1889), reprinted in *A Tale of Two Cities* (Jean-Pierre Caillault, 2003)

Comment: "While speed was King's best asset he is wrongly credited with having invented the crossfire style. This is not true, however, as it was used by at least four [pitchers] before he acquired fame. He was the first pitcher who used the bodyswing. He had large hands—he had been a bricklayer—which were of great aid to him while he was pitching. He inclined his body forward when he delivered the ball and was very graceful."
Source: King's obituary in the 1939 *Spalding Guide*

Description: "First he twists on his left leg, then lightly springs to the right on the other, then comes back again like a rubber ball onto his left leg, and taking an extra flip-flap fires the ball over the plate."
Source: *Kansas City Times* (10/7/1886), quoted in *One Year in the National League: An Account of the 1886 Kansas City Cowboys* (H. L. Dellinger, 1977)

BRIAN KINGMAN 6'2" 200-pound righty
23-45, 4.13, 1 Save 1979 1983

Pitches: 1. Fastball 2. Curve

Kingman: "I had probably an above-average speedball with good movement, and a good curveball, but I didn't have as good a command with the curve as I wanted."
Source: ESPN.com chat with Kingman, 9/5/2003

FRED KIPP 6'4" 200-pound lefty
6-7, 5.08, 0 Saves 1957 1960

Pitches: 1. Fastball 2. Fast Curve 3. Slow Curve 4. Change 5. Knuckleball
Source: Fresco Thompson in *The Sporting News* (11/28/1956, Roscoe McGowen)

BOB KIPPER 6'2" 200-pound lefty
27-37, 4.34, 11 Saves 1985 1992

Pitch Selection: 1. Cut Fastball 2. Slider 3. Change
Sources: *The Scouting Report* (1987 and 1990 editions)

Pitch Selection: 1. Fastball 2. Slider 3. Curve 4. Change
Source: *The Scouting Report: 1992*

CLAY KIRBY 6'3" 175-pound righty
75-104, 3.84, 0 Saves 1969 1976

Pitch Selection: 1. Fastball 2. Curve 3. Slider 4. Change
Sources: *The Sporting News* (7/3/1971, Paul Cour); *Major League Baseball: 1971* (Brenda Zanger and Dick Kaplan)

Quote: "Throws swift fastball, hard slider and concedes nothing . . ."
Source: *The Complete Handbook of Baseball* (1972 edition, edited by Zander Hollander)

BRUCE KISON 6'4" 178-pound righty
115-88, 3.66, 12 Saves 1971 1985

Pitch Selection: 1. Rising Fastball 2. Slider
Note: Kison threw sidearm.
Source: *The Suitors of Spring* (Pat Jordan, 1973)

Description: "A lanky, long-legged twenty-one-year-old who seems to have recently outgrown his uniform, Kison throws a swift, riding fast ball, delivered sidearm, that arrives from the direction of third base and sometimes ends up in a right-hand batter's ribs."
Source: Roger Angell in *The New Yorker* (reprinted in *The Summer Game,* 1972)

RON KLINE 6'3" 205-pound righty
114-144, 3.75, 108 Saves 1952 1970

Pitch Selection, early career: 1. Fastball 2. Curve
Pitch Selection, mid career: 1. Fastball 2. Slider 3. Slow Curve 4. Change
Pitch Selection, late career: 1. Slider 2. Fastball 3. Knuckleball
Notes: Late in his career Kline touched his cap, belt, and shirt before each pitch, in an attempt to distract hitters. He learned to throw Slider and Knuckleball in the Dominican Republic in winter of 1955–56. Late in his career he was accused of throwing a spitball.
Sources: *The Ballplayers* (1990, article by John L. Evers); *The Sporting News* (6/28/1969, Pat Frizzell); *Sport Magazine* (September 1957); *Sports Illustrated* (6/3/1963); *Major League Baseball—1969* (Jack Zanger); *Baseball Digest* (March 1960, Neal Russo)

Pitch Selection, late career: 1. Sinker 2. Knuckleball
Source: *Don Schiffer's Major League Baseball Handbook—1964*

STEVE KLINE 6'3" 200-pound righty
43-45, 3.26, 1 Save 1970 1977

Pitch Selection: 1. So-so Fastball 2. Roundhouse Curve 3. Sinker 4. Slider 5. Change
Source: *Major League Baseball: 1971* (Brenda Zanger and Dick Kaplan)

STEVE KLINE 6'2" 200-pound lefty
25-28, 3.46, 33 Saves 1997 2003

Pitch Selection: 1. Sinking Two-Seam Fastball 2. Hard Slider
Sources: *The Scouting Notebook* (1999 and 2000 editions)

BOB KLINGER 6'0" 180-pound righty
66-61, 3.68, 23 Saves 1938 1947

Key Pitch: Curve
Sources: unidentified clippings from the Hall of Fame Library (6/17/1938, May 1945, 4/22/1946)

Quote: "Eight Giants fanned all told, too many of them taking the Pirate's very good curve ball."

Source: unidentified clipping from the Hall of Fame Library (6/17/1938)

Quote: "Bob Klinger . . . reports from the Pacific that the war has done things to his curve ball—improved it. Bob writes that pitching on such remote islands . . . has added to his benders."
Source: unidentified clipping from the Hall of Fame Library (May 1945)

Quote: "Pittsburgh coach Johnny Gooch knew that Klinger's fast curve was not as tough as in previous years."
Source: unidentified clipping from the Hall of Fame Library (4/22/1946)

JOHNNY KLIPPSTEIN 6'1" 173-pound righty
101-118, 4.24, 66 Saves 1950 1967

Pitch Selection: 1. Curve 2. Fastball
3. Screwball (added late in '52 season)
4. Slider (but after 1952, just occasional)
Sources: *Baseball Digest* (May 1953, John C. Hoffman), *View from the Dugout* (Ed Richter, 1963); Klippstein in *We Played the Game* (Danny Peary, 1994)
Notes: Hoffman says that Klippstein's "physique belies the wickedness of his fast ball." Listed by *The Sporting News* (8/29/1956) as having one of the better fastballs in the league.

BOB KNEPPER 6'3" 195-pound lefty
146-155, 3.68, 1 Save 1976 1990

Pitch Selection: 1. Sinker 2. Cut Fastball
3. Slow Curve 4. Change
Source: *Tom Seaver's 1989 Scouting Notebook*

Description: "Lacking a blazing fastball, he is a thrower who must move the ball around and strive for what baseball people describe as 'location'; keep the hitters overswinging and overguessing. His unquestioned talent is to pitch as much with his head as his arm."
Source: *The Greatest Game Ever Played* (Jerry Eisenberg, 1987)

Vin Scully: "Sometimes when Knepper throws that big slow curve it looks like the ball might never reach the plate . . . it's very deceptive."
Source: TV broadcast of Dodgers/Astros game, 6/3/1989

CHARLIE KNEPPER 6'4" 190-pound righty
4-22, 5.78, 0 Saves 1899 1899

Pitch Selection: 1. Drop Ball or Curve 2. Fastball
Source: *Mistfits: The Cleveland Spiders in 1899* (J. Thomas Hetrick, 1991)

JACK KNOTT 6'2" 200-pound righty
82-103, 4.97, 19 Saves 1933 1946

Pitch Selection: 1. Forkball 2. Fastball 3. Curve
Sources: *The Sporting News* (10/13/1932); unidentified clippings from the Hall of Fame Library (2/1/1933 and 3/13/1936); *New York World-Telegram* (7/24/1941)

Description: "Knott, a lanky right-hander with only average natural ability, survived eleven seasons in the majors by outsmarting hitters."
Source: Phil Marchildon in *Ace: Phil Marchildon* (Marchildon with Brian Kendall, 1993)

Quote: "He . . . can throw the ball with speed and skill . . . Knott attributes his success to what he calls a 'dry spit ball.' The delivery is so called because the ball darts and hops much after the fashion of the nearly extinct spitball."
Source: *The Sporting News* (10/13/1932)

Quote: "Three years ago Knott was allowed to drift out of the Pacific Coast League although he was still a youth with a good fast ball and a fairly snappy curve."
Source: unidentified clipping from the Hall of Fame Library (2/1/1933)

Quote: "The ball broke close to the plate and 'sailed' . . . [Knott said,] 'Yes, I'm working with a "sailer." I learned a lot about it from Lyons during the month we were touring Old Mexico last fall. I hold the ball loosely with the first and second fingers spread apart. I throw it at about three-quarters speed and it breaks close to the batter . . . It looks like it's going over, until close to the plate; then it sails.' "
Source: unidentified clipping from the Hall of Fame Library (3/13/1936)

Note: In *Baseball Magazine* (September 1937), Dan Daniel placed Knott in a group of knuckleball pitchers with Fred Fitzsimmons, George Caster, Ted Lyons, and Ivy Andrews.

Quote: "Baseball men say Jack Knott throws a two-way curve. 'I grasp the ball off center so the greater proportion of it projects beyond the first finger and thumb,' explains (Knott). 'A straight overhand motion is used and terrific spin is imparted. The spin makes the ball curve downward and to the left. When that spin is spent the off-balance weight of the ball takes control and forces the change in direction.' "
Source: *New York World-Telegram* (7/24/1941)

DAROLD KNOWLES 6'0" 180-pound lefty
66-74, 3.12, 143 Saves 1965 1980

Pitch Selection: 1. Sinker 2. Slider 3. Change
Source: *The Sporting News* (4/15/1978, Ian MacDonald)

Pitch Selection: 1. Fastball 2. Knuckleball
Quote: "Throws one-finger knuckler to right-handed hitters."
Source: *Baseball Digest* (March 1963, Page 112)

BILLY KOCH 6'3" 215-pound righty
27-22, 3.82, 155 Saves 1999 2003

Pitch Selection: 1. Fastball (high-90s)
2. Slider (occasional) 3. Change (occasional)
Source: *The Scouting Notebook: 2000*

Pitch Selection: 1. Four-Seam Fastball (95–97)
2. Hard Slider 3. Hard Sinker
4. Curve (occasional)
Source: *The Scouting Notebook: 2002*

RAY KOLP 5'10" 187-pound righty
79-95, 4.08, 18 Saves 1921 1934

Key Pitch: Curve
Sources: Casey Stengel quoted in the *New York World-Telegram* (2/13/1935); George Moriarty quoted in the *New York World-Telegram* (4/28/1937)

Moriarty: "He had a fair curve ball, but it was usually wild."

Quote from Clyde Sukeforth: "Best needler of 'em all was Ray Kolp. Most jockeys work from the bench but Ray would work from the mound."
Source: unidentified clipping from the Hall of Fame Library, dated 4/22/1942

JIM KONSTANTY 6'1" 202-pound righty
66-48, 3.46, 74 Saves 1944 1956

Pitch Selection: 1. Slider 2. Screwball 3. Curve
4. Change 5. Fastball
Source: *Jim Konstanty* (Frank Yeutter, 1951); it's apparent from the other sources that Konstanty's Change refers to his Palm Ball, which was probably his best-known pitch, if not his *best*.

Andy Seminick: "Jim wins because he can control the ball and he knows what he's doing. He uses his head. When he throws a fast ball, he throws it where they can only look at it, not hit it. When they're swinging, they get a slider, screwball, palm ball or curve—some kind of breaking stuff. He really has those hitters buffaloed . . ."
Source: *Baseball Magazine* (November 1950, Ed Rumill)

Key Pitch: Slider
Comment: "The slider is the pet pitch of this head man among relief pitchers. The slider also is Konstanty's pay check and his claim to fame . . . Without it, he admits he probably would not be in the big leagues."
Source: *Baseball Digest* (November 1950, Ed Pollock)

Pitch Selection: 1. Palm Ball 2. Screwball 3. Fastball
Description: "His best pitch is a palm ball, although his screwball rates just behind. He's not too fast, but just fast enough to fool those always looking for curves. Never tries to strike out a hitter with his fast ball."
Source: *Baseball Digest* (January 1951, article by Milt Richman)

Pitch Selection: 1. Slider 2. Palm Ball 3. Change
Sources: *Baseball Digest* (September 1955); Richie Ashburn in *Legends: Conversations with Baseball Greats* (Art Rust, Jr., 1989)

Comment: "Konstanty relieved in 74 games that season, threw almost exclusively palm balls and was named the National League's Most Valuable Player."
Source: *The Philadelphia Bulletin* (4/6/1980)
Note: This was written many years after the fact, and the memory simplifies things. The other sources carry more weight.

CAL KOONCE 6'1" 185-pound righty
47-49, 3.78, 24 Saves 1962 1971

Pitch Selection: 1. Change

Quote: "Split 20 decisions . . . using changing speeds taught to him by his father."
Source: *1963 Major League Handbook* (Don Schiffer)

JERRY KOOSMAN 6'2" 205-pound lefty
222-209, 3.36, 17 Saves 1967 1985

Pitch Selection: 1. Fastball 2. Curve 3. Change 4. Slider (developed in 1974)
Note: Koosman didn't really have a good fastball from 1970 through 1973.
Sources: *The Sporting News* (8/21/76, Jack Lang; and 6/1/74, Lang)

Note: Joseph Durso in the *New York Times* says that the Mets at that time had prohibited Koosman from throwing a slider, for fear that the slider would detract from his excellent curve.

Description: "Jerry had good stuff, and he knew he had good stuff. He should have signed a contract with Louisville Sluggers. They should have paid him for all the bats he broke. This guy sawed them off.

"Jerry had a fastball, and he came off the side of the mound, and he could get that fastball in on right-handers, and I mean he ate them up. And he kind of cut it a little, too. It ran in on right-handers. Boy, you talk about eat them up! Jerry made a science out of it."
Source: Ron Swoboda in *Amazin': The Miraculous History of New York's Most Beloved Baseball Team* (Peter Golenbock, 2002)

DAVE KOSLO 5'11" 180-pound lefty
92-107, 3.68, 22 Saves 1941 1955

Stan Musial: "He had control and he could win at the Polo Grounds because he could keep the ball low and away. He wasn't overpowering, didn't have what you could call a good curve, but wouldn't walk anybody."
Source: *Stan Musial: The Man's Own Story* (Musial, as told to Bob Broeg, 1964)

Note: In 1951, Koslo added a knuckleball to his repertoire.
Source: *The Sporting News* (4/23/1952, Arch Murray)

SANDY KOUFAX 6'2" 210-pound lefty
165-87, 2.76, 9 Saves 1955 1966

Pitch Selection: 1. Fastball 2. Curve 3. Change
Sources: *Baseball Stars of 1964* (article by Ray Robinson); *Heroes of the Major Leagues* (Alexander Peters, 1967)

Quote: "Koufax still has only three pitches. Fast one, curve and change-up . . ."
Source: Dodgers pitching coach Joe Becker quoted in *1965 Official Baseball Almanac* (Bill Wise)

Walter Alston: "By now, Koufax has a good change of pace and a fork ball to go along with the others. The only doggone delivery in his repertoire that I don't care for is a soft blooper he gets the urge to throw once in a while. Luckily, I haven't seen him hurt with this pitch yet, but I'm afraid some day he will be."
Source: *Alston and the Dodgers* (Alston and Si Burick, 1966); Alston was obviously in a position to know what he was talking about, but this is the only reference we've found to the forkball or blooper, so we can assume those pitches were rarely used, and probably only very late in Koufax's career.

Roger Angell: "His fastball . . . flares upward at the last

Los Angeles Dodgers, Inc.

Sandy Koufax

instant, so that batters swinging at it often look as if they had lashed out at a bad high pitch. Koufax's best curve, by contrast, shoots down, often barely pinching a corner of the plate, inside or out, just above the knees. A typical Koufax victim—even if he is an excellent hitter—having looked bad by swinging on the first pitch and worse in letting the second go by, will often simply stand there, his bat nailed to his shoulder, for the next two or three pitches, until the umpire's right hand goes up and he is out. Or if he swings again it is with an awkward last-minute dip of the bat that is a caricature of his normal riffle. It is almost painful to watch, for Koufax, instead of merely overpowering hitters, as some fast-ball throwers do, appears to dismantle them, taking away first one and then another of their carefully developed offensive weapons and judgments, and leaving them only with the conviction that they are the victims of a total mismatch."
Source: Angell in *The New Yorker* (October 1964, reprinted in *The Summer Game*)

Umpire Jocko Conlan: "Sandy threw his curve overhand; he was the only left-hander who threw the curve ball overhand to make it drop off, straight down. There was no question that his was the greatest curve around. You couldn't hit it any distance. It was a ball you beat into the ground. That was the reason for all his victories. He struck out a lot of men, but those that got the bat on the ball hit it on the ground."
Source: *Jocko* (Jocko Conlan and Robert Creamer, 1967)

Umpire Tom Gorman: ". . . When Koufax was pitching it was either a called strike or a swinging strike. He was smart. He always tried to throw as few pitches as possible. And he had the best curveball, for a left-hander, that I ever saw, what we used to call the old drop. It broke down and in on right-handed batters. There were many times when a hitter was lucky if he was able to get a foul off him."
Source: *Three and Two!* (Tom Gorman, as told to Jerome Holtzman, 1979)

Also see entry for Bob Shaw.

JOE KRAKAUSKAS 6'1" 203-pound lefty
26-36, 4.53, 4 Saves 1937 1946

Key Pitch: Fastball
Quote: "I'm a lot more effective when I keep the ball down at the batter's knees. When I can control my pitches low, the hitters generally do not get a good piece of the ball, hence they don't tee off."
Source: *Pacific Coast Baseball News* (9/25/1948)

JACK KRALICK 6'2" 180-pound lefty
67-65, 3.56, 1 Save 1959 1967

Pitch Selection: 1. Curve 2. Fastball 3. Slider 4. Change
Source: *The New York Times* (9/7/1962)

Key Pitch: Fastball
Source: *Don Schiffer's Major League Baseball Handbook—1964*

Quote: "Birdie Tebbetts and Early Wynn took him aside in '64 and advised him to stop throwing so much junk and to go more with his blazing fast ball and excellent slider."
Source: *Major League Baseball 1965* (Jack Zanger)

JACK KRAMER 6'2" 190-pound righty
95-103, 4.24, 7 Saves 1939 1951

Pitch Selection: 1. Fastball 2. Curve
Source: *Fenway* (Peter Golenbock, 1992)

HARRY KRAUSE 5'10" 165-pound lefty
36-26, 2.50, 2 Saves 1908 1912

Key Pitch: Curve
Source: *Touching Second* (Johnny Evers and Hugh Fullerton, 1910)

LEW KRAUSSE JR. 6'0" 175-pound righty
68-91, 4.00, 21 Saves 1961 1974

Pitch Selection: 1. Slider 2. Fastball 3. Curve
Sources: *The Sporting News* (10/9/1971, Larry Whiteside); *Major League Baseball—1969* (Jack Zanger)

RAY KREMER 6'1" 190-pound righty
143-85, 3.76, 10 Saves 1924 1933

Pitch Selection, through 1929: 1. Fastball 2. Change 3. Curve 4. Screwball
Pitch Selection, in final years: 1. Curve 2. Change 3. Fastball
Sources: *Baseball Magazine* (September 1929, Ward

Mason); also, interview with Kremer in *Baseball Magazine* (1930)

Quote from 1929 article: "Kremer is essentially a fastball pitcher. Others excel him at this specialty, particularly Vance and Malone. But he has, so opposing hitters affirm, the best change of pace in the league. That in itself is enough to make him formidable. But he also has what he chooses to call a fair curve and a dependable screw ball."

Kremer in 1932: "My speed has suffered somewhat, but I can't say the same for my curve ball. I don't throw as wide a curve as I used to do when I was a kid pitcher on the sand-lots. But I think it's a better curve, a sharper breaking curve. And certainly I can control it better."
Source: *Baseball Magazine* (July 1932, "Comprising an Interview with Ray Kremer")

Commentary: Kremer, like Joe McGinnity, switched between overhand and underhand (low sidearm) deliveries. In a 1925 article, "The Pitcher With the Deceiving Delivery," John J. Ward says that in 1924 Kremer beat the Giants in a game and used only three underhand deliveries. In his next start he beat Brooklyn, throwing just three pitches *over*hand. Later articles make no mention of this, and Kremer may have switched gradually to a straight overhand style.
Source: *Baseball Magazine* (May 1925, John J. Ward)

LOU KRETLOW 6'2" 185-pound righty
27-47, 4.87, 1 Save 1946 1956

Pitch Selection: 1. Fastball 2. Curve
Sources: *The Pastime in Turbulence: Interviews with Baseball Players of the 1940s* (Brent Kelley, 2001); *The Sporting News* (8/29/1956)
Note: Both sources say that Kretlow had one of the best fastballs of his era.

BILL KRUEGER 6'5" 205-pound lefty
68-66, 4.35, 4 Saves 1983 1995

Pitch Selection: 1. Fastball 2. Slider
3. Curve (breaks straight down)
4. Change 5. Cut Fastball
Sources: *The Scouting Report* (1985 and 1993 editions)

MIKE KRUKOW 6'5" 205-pound righty
124-117, 3.90, 1 Save 1976 1989

Pitch Selection: 1. Curve 2. Fastball 3. Krukow developed a Split-Fingered Fastball under the tutelage of Roger Craig in San Francisco.
Source: *The Scouting Report: 1987*

JOHNNY KUCKS 6'3" 170-pound righty
54-56, 4.10, 7 Saves 1955 1960

Key Pitch: Sinker
Source: Ryne Duren quoted in *The Gospel According to Casey* (Ira Berkow and Jim Kaplan, 1992); Whitey Ford quoted in *Sweet Seasons* (Dom Forker, 1990)

Kucks: "I was just an average pitcher. I didn't have overpowering stuff. Control was my forte. If I didn't have it, I would make a quick exit."
Source: *Sweet Seasons*

Description: "In the spring of 1956 Kucks continued to be outstanding, throwing with a loose-jointed, easy three-quarter motion, imparting a heavy over-spin on the ball that caused hitters to break their bats and sting their hands if they didn't meet the ball just right. The fielders enjoyed playing behind Kucks because he pitched quickly. He was the antithesis of Tom Byrne, who held the ball so long before pitching. The Yankees liked to see Kucks pitch on the road because the game went so quickly, and catching a train to the next town was assured. At Yankee Stadium Harry M. Stevens, the concessionaire, hated to see Kucks pitch because short games meant fewer hot dogs and less beer sold."
Source: *Dynasty: The New York Yankees 1949–1964* (Peter Golenbock, 1975)

BOB KUZAVA 6'2" 202-pound lefty
49-44, 4.05, 13 Saves 1946 1957

Pitch Selection: 1. Fastball 2. Curve
Source: Kuzava in *Dugout to Foxhole* (Rick Van Blair, 1994)

Key Pitch: Sinking Fastball
Note: Listed as a sidearm pitcher
Source: *How to Play Winning Baseball* (Arthur Mann, 1953)

Description: "Once he was considered the fastest pitcher around but now he has switched and offers sharp breaking curves almost exclusively."
Source: *Baseball Digest* (January 1951, Milt Richman)

CLEM LABINE 6'0" 180-pound righty
77-56, 3.63, 96 Saves 1950 1962

Pitch Selection: 1. Sinker (Split-Finger) 2. Curve 3. Fastball
Sources: *When the Cheering Stops* (Heiman et al., 1990); *Bums* (Peter Golenbock, 1984); *Sports Illustrated* (6/3/1957)

Pitch Selection: 1. Fastball 2. Sinker 3. Change-up Curve
Source: *Baseball Digest* (June 1956, Charles Dexter)

Stan Musial: "Clem Labine was one of the best relief pitchers for several years because he had a wicked curve and a terrific sinker. He had powerful forearms . . . I found it difficult to pick up his curve ball and I tried to pull his fast sinker without much success."
Source: *Stan Musial: The Man's Own Story* (Musial, as told to Bob Broeg, 1964)

Umpire Jocko Conlan: "Clem Labine . . . had both a sinker and a good curveball, a downer curve. The sinker broke straight down to a right-handed batter, maybe even in a little; the curve broke down and away. He was a strong pitcher. Rosy Ryan and Freddie Fitzsimmons had curves like that, and Cliff Markle and Walter Beall . . ."
Source: *Jocko* (Conlan and Robert Creamer, 1967)

Notes: *Baseball Digest* article (January 1963, Page 46), cites Labine as throwing one of the best curves ever seen. In *The Pastime in Turbulence: Interviews with Baseball Players of the 1940s* (Brent Kelley, 2001), Wayne Terwilliger says "Clem Labine had the best curveball I ever saw."

Labine: "Sandy (Koufax) tried to keep the ball high because (Dale) Long isn't too strong on high fast balls. But I can't pitch to him there because he'll kill my fast ball. Sandy has a good fast ball; I don't."
Source: *Sports Illustrated* (6/3/1957, Bob Creamer)

MIKE LACOSS 6'5" 185-pound righty
98-103, 4.02, 12 Saves 1978 1991

Pitch Selection: 1. Fastball 2. Forkball 3. Curve 4. Sinker
Source: *The Scouting Report: 1987*

DOYLE (PORKY) LADE
5'10" 183-pound righty
25-29, 4.39, 3 Saves 1946 1950

Pitch Selection: 1. Curve 2. Fastball 3. Change 4. Slider
Source: *Baseball Magazine* (August 1947, Clifford Bloodgood)

JEFF LAHTI 6'0" 180-pound righty
17-11, 3.12, 20 Saves 1982 1986

Pitch Selection: 1. Fastball (90) 2. Slider 3. Curve (occasional)
Source: *The Scouting Report: 1983*

JOE LAKE 6'0" 185-pound righty
62-90, 2.85, 5 Saves 1908 1913

Pitch Selection: 1. Spitball 2. Fastball
Sources: *The National Game* (Alfred H. Spink, 1911); Lee Allen in *The Sporting News* (6/1/1968, Allen's "Cooperstown Corner" column)
Spink: "A fine speedy right-hander is Lake with thorough command of the ball . . . He is regarded as the best right-handed spit ball artist in the American League, barring Ed Walsh."

WAYNE LAMASTER 5'8" 170-pound lefty
19-27, 5.82, 4 Saves 1937 1938

Key Pitch: Fastball?
Description: "Wayne's pitching equipment is fairly well assorted, and he doesn't resort to any trick deliveries such as the sinker or screw ball. His best pitch is perhaps his fast ball which is deceiving in its speed."
Source: *Baseball Magazine* (July 1938, Clifford Bloodgood)

DENNIS LAMP 6'4" 200-pound righty
96-96, 3.93, 35 Saves 1977 1992

Pitch Selection: 1. Sinking Fastball 2. Slider
Source: *The Scouting Report: 1987*

LES LANCASTER 6'2" 200-pound righty
41-28, 4.05, 22 Saves 1987 1993

Pitch Selection: 1. Fastball 2. Slider 3. Change (occasional)
Source: *The Scouting Report: 1990*

Pitch Selection: 1. Fastball 2. Cut Fastball 3. Slider 4. Curve 5. Change
Source: *The Scouting Report: 1993*

BILL LANDIS 6'2" 178-pound lefty
9-8, 4.46, 4 Saves 1963 1969

Key Pitch: Sinker
Quote: "Only his sinker is outstanding. Knows how to pitch but needs more work."
Source: *Baseball Digest* (March 1967, "Official Scouting Reports on 1967 Major League Rookies")

BILL LANDRUM 6'2" 202-pound righty
18-15, 3.39, 58 Saves 1986 1993

Pitch Selection: 1. Fastball (mid-90s) 2. Change 3. Curve
Note: Learned to throw the change and curve from Pirates' pitching coach Ray Miller.
Source: *The Scouting Report: 1990*

RICK LANGFORD 6'0" 180-pound righty
73-106, 4.01, 0 Saves 1976 1986

Key Pitch: Slider
Note: Langford was suspected of throwing a spitball.
Sources: John Lowenstein in *From 33rd Street to Camden Yards* (John Eisenberg, 2001); *The Sporting News* (3/17/1979, Tom Weir; and 6/6/1981, Peter Gammons)

MARK LANGSTON 6'2" 177-pound lefty
179-158, 3.97, 0 Saves 1984 1999

Pitch Selection: 1. Fastball 2. Slider 3. Curve 4. Change
Sources: *Tom Seaver's 1989 Scouting Notebook; The Scouting Report: 1990*

MAX LANIER 5'11" 180-pound lefty
108-82, 3.01, 17 Saves 1938 1953

Pitch Selection: 1. Overhand Curve 2. Fastball 3. Change 4. Knuckleball (late career)

Lanier: "I sidearmed left-handers and pitched overhand, mostly, to right-handers. I had quite a high leg kick, and like most of the pitchers back then, I took a full windup. Mostly curveball, fastball and changeup, plus I threw a knuckleball later on in my career. That was somethin' I picked up on my own. There weren't too many pitchers in our league throwin' one, as I remember."
Source: *Redbirds Revisited* (David Craft and Tom Owens, 1990)
Other Source: *Stan Musial* (Musial with Bob Broeg, 1964)

Lanier: "I had a lot of different pitches. I mixed them up—curveball, fastball, high, low. I had a moving fastball, and I could pitch a lot of guys high because my ball took off."
Source: *Splendor on the Diamond* (Rich Westcott, 2000)

JOHNNY LANNING 6'1" 185-pound righty
58-60, 3.58, 13 Saves 1936 1947

Pitch Selection: 1. Hard Curve 2. Slow Curve
Quote: "Lanning employed a curve which was delivered with varying speed. His slow hook was just as effective as his swifter one."
Source: article by Edward T. Murphy, unidentified clipping from the Hall of Fame Library (5/26/1936)
Other Source: article by Chilly Doyle, unidentified clipping from the Hall of Fame Library (April 1946)

PAUL LAPALME 5'10" 175-pound lefty
24-45, 4.42, 14 Saves 1951 1957

Key Pitch: Knuckleball
Source: *Collier's* (10/2/1953, Tom Meany)

DAVE LAPOINT 6'3" 205-pound lefty
80-86, 4.02, 1 Save 1980 1991

Pitch Selection: 1. Change 2. Slider 3. Fastball
Sources: *The Scouting Report* (1985 and 1990 editions)

Quote from *The Scouting Report: 1985:* "LaPoint considers his off-speed pitch to be pretty much a change-up, but it has actions like a palmball or more likely a screwball."

TERRY LARKIN 6'0" 190-pound righty
89-80, 2.43, 0 Saves 1876 1880

Key Pitch: Curve

Note: Larkin was one of the first pitchers to throw a curve ball.
Quote: "Cummings, Tommy Bond, Terry Larkin and others developed the out-curve, but not before 1870."
Source: 1919 *Reach Guide* (Page 257)

DAVE LaROCHE 6'2" 200-pound lefty
65-58, 3.53, 126 Saves 1970 1983

Pitch Selection: 1. Fastball 2. Slider
3. Late in his career, LaRoche would occasionally throw a blooper pitch dubbed "La Lob."
Source: *The Sporting News* (8/2/1975, Russ Schneider)

DON LARSEN 6'4" 215-pound righty
81-91, 3.78, 23 Saves 1953 1967

Pitch Selection: 1. Fastball 2. Slider 3. Slow Curve
Source: *Diamond Greats* (Rich Westcott, 1988)
Note: Listed by *The Sporting News* (8/29/1956) as having one of the best fastballs in the league.

DAN LARSON 6'0" 175-pound righty
10-25, 4.40, 1 Save 1976 1982

Key Pitch: Curveball
Larson: "Actually, I don't like to throw more than 20-25 percent curves in a game, even though the curve is my out pitch. I like to save the curve for the crucial situations."
Source: *The Sporting News* (9/18/1976, Harry Shattuck)

FRANK LARY 5'11" 175-pound righty
128-116, 3.49, 11 Saves 1954 1965

Pitch Selection: 1. Fastball 2. Slider 3. Sinker
4. Change
Sources: Brooks Robinson in *We Played the Game* (Danny Peary, 1994); *With a Southern Exposure* (Furman Bisher, Page 49); *They Too Wore Pinstripes* (Brent Kelley, 1998); Lary in *Bombers* (Richard Lally, 2002)

Notes: Lary developed a Knuckleball during the 1956 season, and was still throwing it occasionally in 1962. Listed by *The Sporting News* (8/29/1956) as having one of the best fastballs in the league. In *They Too Wore Pinstripes,* Billy Hunter says Lary's slider "kind of exploded on you."

Lary in *Bombers*: "I threw a hard slider, didn't break real big, maybe five or seven inches, but I could change speeds on it, even easier than I did my fastball."

BILL LASKEY 6'5" 190-pound righty
42-53, 4.14, 2 Saves 1982 1988

Pitch Selection: 1. Sinking Fastball (high-80s) 2. Slider
3. Curve 4. Change
Source: *The Scouting Report* (1983 and 1984 editions)

TOMMY LASORDA 5'10" 175-pound lefty
0-4, 6.48, 1 Save 1954 1956

Pitch Selection: 1. Curve 2. Fastball
3. Knuckleball (occasional)
Source: *The Artful Dodger* (Lasorda and David Fisher, 1985)

BARRY LATMAN 6'3" 210-pound righty
59-68, 3.91, 16 Saves 1957 1967

Pitch Selection: 1. Fastball 2. Slider 3. Curve
Latman: "Once I made the majors, [White Sox pitching coach Ray] Berres taught me to throw a slider. He showed me how to put different amounts of finger pressure on the seams to make the ball move. My fastball moved upward—it had a hop to it. Now I could make it slide either way . . .

"I was a fast worker and threw 60 to 70 percent fastballs. My out pitch changed with each hitter, but more and more it became the slider Berres and [Dick] Donovan taught me. I wanted batters to swing at that because they were expecting my fastball and would either miss it or not hit it solidly."
Source: *We Played the Game* (Danny Peary, 1994)

GEORGE LAUZERIQUE 6'1" 180-pound righty
4-8, 5.00, 0 Saves 1967 1970

Description: "Good arm with above par curve, change and fielding and good control and poise. Has a slider. Majors within his possibilities."
Source: *Baseball Digest* (March 1967, "Official Scouting Reports on 1967 Major League Rookies")

GARY LAVELLE 6'2" 190-pound lefty
80-77, 2.93, 136 Saves 1974 1987

Pitch Selection: 1. Fastball 2. Slider
Source: *The Scouting Report: 1987*

JIMMY LAVENDER 5'11" 165-pound righty
63-76, 3.09, 12 Saves 1912 1917

Pitch Selection: 1. Spitball 2. Fastball 3. Curves 4. Slow Ball
Source: Lavender in *Baseball Magazine* (November 1912, F.C. Lane)

Pitch Selection: 1. Spitball 2. Emery Ball
Sources: *The Sporting News* (10/1/1914); *The Ballplayers* (1990, article by Art Ahrens)

Source: "Cubs pitcher Jimmy Lavender tried attaching sandpaper to his uniform, which worked until the umpires wanted to know why he kept scratching himself."
Source: *1918: Babe Ruth and the World Champion Boston Red Sox* (Allan Wood, 2000)

VERN LAW 6'2" 195-pound righty
162-147, 3.77, 13 Saves 1950 1967

Pitch Selection: 1. Curve 2. Slider 3. Fastball
Sources: *Sport* (April 1960, Larry Klein; and April 1962, James Joyce Donahue); *Baseball Stars of 1961* (article by Ray Robinson)

Comment: "Although brushing back hitters has become a commonplace, accepted technique for frightening and discouraging the hitters from taking a toehold at the plate, Law simply doesn't believe in it, either morally or as an efficacious instrument. He prefers to pitch his own game, throwing his well-controlled sliders, his moderately fast fast ball and his precisely aimed curve ball. He has a reputation for throwing more than his quota of home run balls . . ."
Source: *Baseball Stars of 1961*

Note: The September 1957 issue of *Sport* says that Law sometimes threw a knuckleball, and the August 10, 1955, issue of *The Sporting News* confirms that he was, indeed, throwing it then.

BROOKS LAWRENCE 6'0" 205-pound righty
69-62, 4.25, 22 Saves 1954 1960

Pitch Selection: 1. Fastball 2. Curve 3. Sinker 4. Slider
Source: *Baseball Digest* (October 1956, Charles Dexter)

Pitch Selection: 1. Slider 2. Curve 3. Fastball
Description: "His breaking stuff in general is very good. He has a good slider and a good curve, he throws a lot of sinking stuff, and he's able to keep you guessing with all of it because his fast ball is strong enough to set the other stuff up."
Source: *Sport* (May 1957, Bill Roeder)

ROXIE LAWSON 6'0" 170-pound righty
47-39, 5.37, 11 Saves 1930 1940

Pitch Selection: 1. Curve 2. Change 3. Fastball
Source: *The Sporting News* (9/5/1935)

Key Pitch: Change of Pace
Description: "Lawson is a pitcher who has a variety of stuff, the most baffling of which perhaps is an excellent change of pace. In delivering this he masks his intentions completely, the only way to make it effective."
Source: *Baseball Magazine* (September 1937, Clifford Bloodgood)

CHARLIE LEA 6'4" 194-pound righty
62-48, 3.54, 0 Saves 1980 1988

Pitch Selection: 1. Fastball 2. Curve 3. Change
Note: Lea's basic game was changing speeds on his curve.
Source: *The Scouting Report: 1985*

TERRY LEACH 6'0" 215-pound righty
38-27, 3.15, 10 Saves 1981 1993

Pitch Selection: 1. Sinker 2. Curve
Note: Leach was a submarine pitcher.
Sources: *The Scouting Report* (1990 and 1993 editions)

LUIS LEAL 6'3" 205-pound righty
51-58, 4.14, 1 Save 1980 1985

Pitch Selection: 1. Fastball 2. Slider 3. Curve 4. Change
Source: *The Scouting Report: 1983*

TIM LEARY 6'3" 205-pound righty
78-105, 4.36, 1 Save 1981 1994

Pitch Selection: 1. Forkball (1988 on) 2. Fastball 3. Curve 4. Slider
Source: *Tom Seaver's 1989 Scouting Notebook; The Scouting Report: 1990*

Quote: "Tim Leary of the Dodgers, commuting from his home in Santa Monica, Calif., had a 9-0 record and 1.24 ERA for Tijuana. He used the work to develop a split-finger pitch, which helped improve his record from 3-11 in 1987 to 17-11 in 1988."
Source: *Baseball America's 1989 Almanac* (Page 233, review of 1987–88 Mexican Winter League season)

BILL LEE 6'3" 195-pound righty
169-157, 3.54, 13 Saves 1934 1947

Pitch Selection: 1. Overhand Curve 2. Sidearm Curve 3. Change 4. Fastball
Note: Lee generally threw overhand, and his overhand curve would break almost straight down.
Sources: *Major League Baseball* (Ethan Allen, page 30); *1947 Scout Report* (Wid Matthews); Phil Cavaretta in *Wrigleyville* (Peter Golenbock, 1996)

BILL LEE 6'3" 205-pound lefty
119-90, 3.62, 19 Saves 1969 1982

Pitches: 1. Fastball 2. Curve 3. Slider 4. Change 5. Knuckleball
Source: *The Sporting News* (8/21/1971, Larry Claflin)
Notes: According to Lee, "I only threw the knuckler on the sidelines. It was a pitch I was saving for when I got older. I threw only two in a major league game, in 1979 I think, with the Expos. To Craig Swan, the pitcher for the Mets. He hit them both for stand up doubles off the wall. After that, I decided to shelve that pitch until I was 60."

Also according to Lee, his pitches were 1. Sinker (preferably low and away), 2. Overhand Curve, 3. Screwball (as Change), 4. Slider, 5. Fastball.
Source: e-mail message from Richard Lally, Lee's collaborator (10/17/2003)

Key Pitch, 1969–76: Sinker
Key Pitch, 1976–82: Slow Curve
Quote: "I have a quirk in my body: I can't throw two pitches in a row at the same speed, no matter how hard I try. I also can't throw the ball straight; it either dips or rises."
Source: Lee in *The Wrong Stuff* (Bill Lee with Dick Lally, 1984)

Commentary: Lee always considered himself a finesse/control/groundball pitcher, but after injuring his shoulder during a Red Sox–Yankees brawl in 1976, Lee lost the good velocity on his sinker and was forced to rely on his off-speed pitches even more than he had before.
Note: By the mid-1970s, Lee was also throwing a slow, lollipop curve that looked almost like, and was described by Curt Gowdy as, a blooper. That's the pitch Tony Perez hit for a home run in Game 7 of the 1975 World Series.
Source: HBO special, *The Curse of the Bambino* (first aired in September 2003)

BOB LEE 6'3" 225-pound righty
25-23, 2.70, 63 Saves 1964 1968

Pitch Selection: 1. Fastball 2. Curve
Source: *Baseball Digest* (March 1960, Page 94)

THORNTON LEE 6'3" 205-pound lefty
117-124, 3.56, 10 Saves 1933 1948

Pitch Selection: 1. Fastball 2. Curve 3. Change
Sources: *Baseball Magazine* (April 1938, Clifford Bloodgood), *The Ballplayers* (1990, article by Dennis Bingham)
Note: Bloodgood describes Lee's fastball as "a high hard one," but Bingham describes it as a sinking fastball. Bloodgood says that Muddy Ruel improved Lee's control in 1938 when he realized that Lee was over-striding when throwing his fastball.

SAM LEEVER 5'10" 175-pound righty
194-98, 2.47, 14 Saves 1898 1910

Key Pitch: Sharp Curve
Source: *The Ballplayers* (1990, article by A.D. Suehsdorf)
Note: Leever wrote the chapter, "How to Pitch the Outcurve" in the 1908 book, *How to Pitch*.

CRAIG LEFFERTS 6'1" 180-pound lefty
58-72, 3.43, 101 Saves 1983 1994

Pitch Selection: 1. Fastball 2. Slider 3. Screwball 4. Cut Fastball (developed in 1989)
Source: *The Scouting Report: 1990*

CHARLIE LEIBRANDT 6'3" 195-pound lefty
140-119, 3.71, 2 Saves 1979 1993

Pitch Selection: 1. Change 2. Slider 3. Fastball
Source: *Tom Seaver's 1989 Scouting Notebook*

DAVE LEIPER 6'1" 160-pound lefty
12-8, 3.98, 7 Saves 1984 1996

Pitch Selection: 1. Split-Fingered Fastball/Forkball 2. Sinker (high-80s)
Source: *The Scouting Notebook: 1996*

LEFTY LEIFELD 6'1" 165-pound lefty
124-97, 2.47, 7 Saves 1905 1920

Pitch Selection: 1. Fastball 2. Curve
Johnny Evers: "Leifeld seldom uses curves unless compelled to, and his high fast ball which breaks with an odd little jump, is one of the hardest for batters to hit."
Source: *Touching Second* (John J. Evers and Hugh S. Fullerton, 1910)

Christy Mathewson: ". . . Leifeld uses almost exactly the same motion to throw to first base as to pitch to the batter. These two are so nearly alike that he can change his mind after he starts and throw to the other place.

"He keeps men hugging the bag, and it is next to impossible to steal bases on him. If he gets his arm so far forward in pitching to the batter that he cannot throw to the base, he can see a man start and pitch out so the catcher has a fine chance to get the runner at second. If the signal is for a curved ball, he can make it a high curve, and the pitcher is in position to throw. Leifeld has worked this combination pitch either to first base or the plate for years, and the motion for each is so similar that even the umpires cannot detect it and never call a balk on him."
Source: *Pitching in a Pinch* (Christy Mathewson, 1912)

AL LEITER 6'2" 200-pound lefty
145-112, 3.69, 2 Saves 1987 2003

Pitches: 1. Sharp Curve 2. Fastball 3. Slow Curve 4. Slider
Source: *The Scouting Report: 1996*

Pitches: 1. Sinking Fastball 2. Cut Fastball 3. Big Curve 4. Hard Slider
Source: *The Scouting Notebook 1999*

MARK LEITER 6'3" 210-pound righty
65-73, 4.57, 26 Saves 1990 2001

Pitches: 1. Sinking Fastball 2. Hard Curve 3. Slider 4. Slow Forkball/Change 5. Circle Change
Source: *The Scouting Report: 1996*

DENNY LEMASTER 6'1" 182-pound lefty
90-105, 3.58, 8 Saves 1962 1972

Pitch Selection: 1. Fastball 2. Change 3. Slow Curve 4. Slider
Sources: *Baseball Digest* (February 1968, Joe Heiling), *Major League Baseball 1965* (Jack Zanger)

Pitch Selection: 1. Curve 2. Fastball
Source: Milwaukee Braves 1961 Guide for Press/Radio/TV

BOB LEMON 6'0" 180-pound righty
207-128, 3.23, 22 Saves 1946 1958

Pitch Selection: 1. Curve 2. Slider 3. Sinker
Lemon: "I had a pretty good curve, slider, and sinker. The slider is a breaking ball that you can control. I had one for a 3-1 count, one for a 3-2 count, and so forth. They broke differently, depending on the count."
Source: *Splendor on the Diamond* (Rich Westcott, 2000)

Pitch Selection: 1. Curve 2. Fastball
Source: *Baseball Stars of 1954* (article by Ted Merritt)

Pitch Selection: 1. Slider 2. Fastball 3. Curve
Source: *The Crooked Pitch* (Martin Quigley, 1984)

Lemon: "Technically, I have no fast ball. Everything I throw is breaking stuff. My fast ball is a natural sinker."
Source: *Sport* (May 1956, Frank Graham, Jr.)

Quote: "Bob Lemon, who may be the first man to have pitched his way into the Hall of Fame with a slider, says he learned the pitch from Mel Harder . . ."
Source: Roger Angell in *The New Yorker* (1976, reprinted in *Five Seasons*, 1977)

Quote: "[Lemon] is credited with having one of the best sliders in the majors."
Source: *Baseball Digest* (June 1956, Page 71)

Umpire Beans Reardon: "Bob Lemon has the best slider I ever saw."
Source: *Long Beach Press-Telegram* (September, 1952)

Quote: ". . . when he [Lemon] was at his peak, possessed the most effective slider in the game."
Source: *Sport* (February 1957, Al Hirshberg)

Description: "Lemon was and is blessed with one of those very rare, wonderfully 'live' arms that make a baseball perform astonishing tricks. It always has been next to impossible for him to throw a ball without something special—spin, curve, shoot, or drop—on it. You see this so seldom, even in the majors, that such a wing is worth cultivating at all cost."
Source: *Sport* (June 1950, Al Stump)

Quote from longtime pitching coach George Susce: "Pitchers like Bob Lemon [and Mel Parnell] are not very fast, but their ball does this and that, and never comes in straight. Everything they throw does something."
Source: *Christian Science Monitor* (August 1951, Ed Rumill)

Quote: "[Lemon has] the best fast ball on the Cleveland staff."
Source: *Baseball Digest* (January 1951, Milt Richman)

Note: A poll of 645 players in the book *Players' Choice* (Eugene V. McCaffrey and Roger A. McCaffrey, 1987) lists Lemon's sinker as the second-greatest ever. He received 12.7 percent of the vote, trailing only Bruce Sutter (13.4 percent).

DENNIS LEONARD 6'1" 190-pound righty
144-106, 3.70, 1 Save 1974 1986

Pitches: 1. Fastball 2. Slider 3. Change 4. Curve
Sources: *The Sporting News* (8/7/1976, Sid Bordman; 7/5/1980, Del Black)

Description: "Is the hardest thrower among the Royals' pitchers and mixes fastball well with a curve and slider."
Source: *The Complete Handbook of Baseball: 1982 Season* (edited by Zander Hollander)

DUTCH (EMIL) LEONARD 6'0" 175-pound righty
191-181, 3.25, 44 Saves 1933 1953

Pitch Selection: 1. Knuckleball 2. Slow Curve 3. Fastball 4. Screwball (added late career?)
Sources: *Chicago Tribune* (6/13/1948, shows photos of Leonard gripping each of his four pitches); *Baseball's Famous Pitchers* (Ira L. Smith, 1954); *Baseball for Everyone* (Joe DiMaggio, 1948); *Baseball Digest* (May 1953, article about Johnny Klippstein)

Jackie Robinson: "I'm glad of one thing, and that is, I don't have to hit against Dutch Leonard every day. Man, what a knuckleball that fellow has. It comes up, makes a face at you, then runs away."
Source: *The Sporting News* (11/12/1947, Page 11)

Description: "The 'butterfly ball' isn't the only thing 'Dutch' has that fools big-league batters. He has a fair fast ball, an excellent let-up pitch, and a sharp curve that could be more effective with a little more speed. No one yet has compared Leonard's curve to Tommy Bridges' nor his fast ball to Bob Feller's, although Joe DiMaggio did make a slight error when he called 'Dutch' one of the fastest pitchers in the league in his recent magazine article. 'Dutch's' fast one is not exactly fast but more of the sneaker type that catches a batter flat-footed when he is expecting a floating knuckler or a slow curve and perhaps seems faster than it really is by comparison."
Source: *Baseball Magazine* (October 1939, Al Costello)

Description: "He's big and looks fast, and he goes through an exaggerated wind-up that makes it appear as if he's going to cut loose with a Bob Grove fireball. But up dances his Sunday pitch in slow motion and the batter frequently is back on his stance by the time he readjusts his stance."
Source: *Baseball Magazine* (April 1947, Frank Yeutter)

DUTCH (HUB) LEONARD 5'10" 185-pound lefty
139-112, 2.76, 13 Saves 1913 1925

Pitch Selection: 1. Spitball 2. Fastball 3. Curve
Description: "Dutch was a left-handed spitball pitcher, the spitball was legal back in those days. I had no problem with the spitball as a rule, but Dutch Leonard was left-handed, he had a good fastball—not as fast as Walter Johnson, but he had a good fastball—and a good curve and he was mean with it. He'd knock you down."
Source: Joe Sewell in *Fields of Green* (Paul Green, 1984)

Note: Leonard was one of the "grandfathered" pitchers

who were allowed to continue to throw the spitball after it was otherwise banned in 1921.
Source: 1923 *Reach Guide* (Page 38)

DAVE LEONHARD 5'11" 165-pound righty
16-14, 3.15, 5 Saves 1967 1972

Description: "Fair change-up pitcher with hard fast one as feature. Curve can fool 'em."
Source: *Baseball Digest* (March 1967, "Official Scouting Reports on 1967 Major League Rookies")

RANDY LERCH 6'5" 190-pound lefty
60-64, 4.53, 3 Saves 1975 1986

Pitch Selection: 1. Fastball 2. Curve 3. Slider 4. Change
Note: Lerch had an above-average fastball, so-so secondary pitches, poor control of the change. He threw "halfway between straight overhand and three-quarters."
Source: *The Scouting Report: 1983*

CURTIS LESKANIC 6'0" 180-pound righty
47-29, 4.30, 51 Saves 1993 2003

Pitch Selection: 1. Fastball 2. Hard Slider 3. Cut Fastball
Source: *The Scouting Notebook 2000*

Pitch Selection: 1. Fastball (93–95) 2. Slider 3. Curve (occasional)
Source: Announcer Ryan Lefebvre in broadcast of Royals-Mariners game (7/17/2003)

AL LEVINE 6'3" 175-pound righty
21-29, 3.75, 10 Saves 1996 2003

Pitch Selection: 1. Sinking Fastball (high-80s) 2. Slider 3. Change
Source: *The Scouting Notebook: 2000*

Pitch Selection: 1. Slider 2. Sinking Fastball (mid-80s) 3. Straight Fastball (90)
Source: *The Scouting Notebook: 2002*

RICHIE LEWIS 5'10" 175-pound righty
14-15, 4.88, 2 Saves 1992 2001

Pitch Selection: 1. Overhand Curve 2. Sinking Fastball 3. Change (occasional)
Source: *The Scouting Notebook: 1997*

TED LEWIS 5'10" 158-pound righty
93-63, 3.53, 5 Saves 1896 1901

Key Pitch: Curve
Source: *Nineteenth Century Stars* (SABR, 1989, article by Rich Eldred)

JON LIEBER 6'3" 220-pound righty
86-83, 4.18, 2 Saves 1994 2002

Pitch Selection: 1. Sinking Fastball 2. Slider 3. Change
Source: *The Scouting Notebook 2000*

KERRY LIGTENBERG 6'2" 222-pound righty
16-14, 3.09, 45 Saves 1997 2003

Pitch Selection: 1. Split-Fingered Fastball 2. Slider 3. Four-Seam Fastball (low-90s)
Source: *The Scouting Notebook: 1999*

DEREK LILLIQUIST 5'10" 195-pound lefty
25-34, 4.13, 17 Saves 1989 1996

Pitch Selection: 1. Fastball 2. Curve 3. Cut Fastball (added September 1989)
Source: *The Scouting Report: 1990*

Pitch Selection: 1. Fastball 2. Slider 3. Change
Source: *The Scouting Report: 1993*

Pitch Selection: 1. Sinking Fastball 2. Slider 3. Curve
Source: *The Scouting Notebook: 1995*

JOSE LIMA 6'2" 170-pound righty
71-77, 5.13, 5 Saves 1994 2003

Pitch Selection: 1. Sinking Change 2. Sinking Fastball 3. Curve
Source: *The Scouting Notebook 2000*

Note: Lima learned to throw the slider from Royals pitching coach John Cumberland in June of 2003, and it quickly became an important pitch for him.
Source: *Kansas City Star* (6/21/2003, Joe Posnanski column)

PAUL LINDBLAD 6'1" 185-pound lefty
68-63, 3.29, 64 Saves 1965 1978

Pitch Selection: 1. Sinker 2. Change
Source: *The Sporting News* (10/4/1975, Ron Bergman)

JOHNNY LINDELL 6'4" 217-pound righty
8-18, 4.47, 1 Save 1942 1953

Pitches, 1942: 1. Fastball 2. Curve 3. Slider 4. Sinker
Key Pitch, 1953: Knuckleball (80%)
Source: *Baseball Digest* (August 1952, Emmett Watson)

Notes: Lindell arrived in the majors in 1942 as a pitcher, but in 1943 Yankees manager Joe McCarthy turned him into an outfielder. Lindell returned to the minors in 1950, and Hollywood Stars manager Fred Haney asked him to pitch. Lindell had been fooling around with a knuckleball for years, and that quickly became his best pitch. He returned to the majors in 1953 and pitched for the Pirates and Phillies with moderate success.

FRANK LINZY 6'1" 190-pound righty
62-57, 2.85, 111 Saves 1963 1974

Pitch Selection: 1. Sinker 2. Hard Slider
Source: *The Sporting News* (5/29/1971, Neal Russo)

Quote: "I like a sinkerball thrower in relief, and Linzy has the best sinker around."
Source: Unidentified National League manager in *Sport* (June 1968, John Devaney)

Description: "Burly, nearsighted right-hander with outstanding sinker."
Source: *The Complete Handbook of Baseball* (1972 edition, edited by Zander Hollander)

FELIPE LIRA 6'1" 205-pound righty
26-46, 5.32, 1 Save 1995 2001

Pitch Selection: 1. Fastball (high-80s) 2. Cut Fastball 3. Slider 4. Change
Source: *The Scouting Notebook: 1996*

HOD LISENBEE 5'11" 170-pound righty
37-58, 4.81, 1 Save 1927 1945

Pitch Selection: 1. Fastball 2. Curve 3. Change of Pace
Source: *Baseball Magazine* (January 1928, F. C. Lane)
Quote from Lane: ". . . a fine fast ball, a fair curve and a clever change of pace."

Note: Lisenbee threw mostly sidearm, but would sometimes switch to an overhand delivery, and occasionally to a straight underhand motion.

BEST SINKERS

1. Dan Quisenberry
2. Frank Linzy
3. Randy Jones
4. Kevin Brown
5. Tommy John
6. Bucky Walters
7. Kent Tekulve
8. Derek Lowe
9. Hal Schumacher
10. Mel Stottlemyre

Others: Wilcy Moore, Steve Barber, Mickey Lolich, Roger McDowell, Bill Lee, Mike Hampton, Bill Swift, Doug Corbett, Gerry Staley, Ken McBride, Bob Lemon

AD LISKA 5'11" 160-pound righty
17-18, 3.87, 3 Saves 1929 1933

Pitches: 1. Fastball 2. Curve 3. Change of Pace (occasional)
Note: Liska pitched with an underhand delivery.
Source: *Baseball Magazine* (June 1931, F.C. Lane)

Description: "Liska flings the submarine ball and it is a more under-handed delivery than that featured by any other mound artist now in the majors. In fact it is even more radical than the offering made famous by Jack Warhop and Carl Mays. Liska brings his arm up close to his side, much after the fashion of a bowler, starting the ball on its flight to the plate from his ankles."
Source: *Who's Who in Major League Baseball* (compiled by Harold "Speed" Johnson, 1933)

Quote: "I was so bad against Liska [in the Pacific Coast League] that I think even if he had walked the ball up to the plate, I couldn't have hit him. The reason he didn't stay up in the majors for a long time is because the left-handed hitters used to wear him out . . ."
Source: Dario Lodigiani in *Dugout to Foxhole* (Rick Van Blair, 1994)

Comment: "And don't think that at 40 . . . he still hasn't plenty on the ball, especially when he pitches from 'way

down under' in his true submarine form. Liska's slumps nearly all have been traceable to departure from this form, due to an odd tendency he sometimes has to throw low sidearm rather than full submarine."
Source: "Greg's Gossip" column in the Portland *Oregonian* (8/25/1947, L.H. Gregory)

MARK LITTELL 6'3" 210-pound righty
32-31, 3.32, 56 Saves 1973 1982

Pitch Selection: 1. Slider 2. Fastball
3. Littell developed a Forkball late in his career.
Source: *Redbirds Revisited* (David Craft and Tom Owens, 1990)

GRAEME LLOYD 6'7" 215-pound lefty
30-36, 4.04, 17 Saves 1993 2003

Pitch Selection: 1. Big Curve 2. Sinker 3. Slider
Source: *The Scouting Notebook: 1997*

ESTEBAN LOAIZA 6'4" 190-pound righty
90-82, 4.58, 1 Save 1995 2003

Pitch Selection, 1995–2002: 1. Fastball (low-90s)
2. Hard Slider 3. Change
Source: *The Scouting Report: 1996; The Scouting Notebook* (1998–2003 editions)

Key Pitch, 2003: Cut Fastball
Note: Loaiza started throwing the cut fastball in 2002, at the suggestion of Blue Jays pitching coach Gil Patterson, but he didn't perfect the cutter until the spring of 2003, when it quickly became his best pitch, and he claimed to have thrown 90 percent cutters in one August start.
Loaiza: "I get different movements with it going in different directions. One's going sideways, one's going down. It just depends on how I want to throw it and the count."
Source: *Chicago Tribune* (8/15/2003, Teddy Greenstein)

Description: "Loaiza's emergence as staff ace is due in part to a more diverse assortment of pitches. He has added a cut fastball and a changeup to a repertoire that already included two-seam and four-seam fastballs and a slider.

"Loaiza bores the cutter in on lefties, Mariano Rivera style, and sinks the two-seamer away. Then he turns around and uses the two pitches with the opposite effect against righties."
White Sox GM Kenny Williams: "It's not just the weapons, but how he's decided to use them. In the past he'd always reach back for the 94 or 95 when he was in trouble. Now the hitters don't know what's coming."
Source: Jerry Crasnick in ESPN.com (9/11/2003)

RON LOCKE 5'11" 168-pound lefty
1-2, 3.48, 0 Saves 1964 1964

Key Pitch: Fastball
Source: *The Sporting News* (11/2/1963)

BOB LOCKER 6'3" 200-pound righty
57-39, 2.75, 95 Saves 1965 1975

Key Pitch: Sinker or Sinking Fastball
Sources: *Champagne and Baloney* (Tom Clark, 1976); Chicago White Sox 1968 Yearbook (Page 49)

SKIP LOCKWOOD 6'1" 175-pound righty
57-97, 3.55, 68 Saves 1969 1980

Pitch Selection: 1. Fastball 2. Slow Curve 3. Slider
Sources: *The Relief Pitcher* (John Thorn, 1979); *Major League Baseball: 1971* (Brenda Zanger and Dick Kaplan)
Quote from Kaplan and Zanger: "Skip came to Milwaukee with a good fastball, a slow curve and a slider. But pitching coach Wes Stock suggested he forget his slider and slow curve and concentrate on his fast stuff for a while."

BILLY LOES 6'1" 165-pound righty
80-63, 3.89, 32 Saves 1950 1961

Pitch Selection: 1. Fastball 2. Curve 3. Change
Note: When Billy Loes signed for a large bonus in 1948, Charley Dressen said that Loes' fastball was not good enough to pitch in the major leagues. He later acknowledged (in *The Sporting News*, 8/27/1952) that he was wrong. "He's faster than the average pitcher," Dressen acknowledged. "And he looks even faster because he uses his fast ball carefully, so the hitter seldom expects it."
Bill Rigney: "Loes will have to change his style of pitching. I don't know what kind of hitters they have in the other league, but he can't pitch high in this league and

get away with it. He's going to have to keep his fast ball low."
Source: Associated Press (6/2/1960)
Other Sources: Milton Gross (February 1956, newspaper unidentified); Michael Gaven (December 1953, newspaper unidentified)
Gross: "He has more speed, better curves and greater potential than anyone the Dodgers have had in years."

BILL LOHRMAN 6'1" 185-pound righty
60-59, 3.69, 8 Saves 1934 1944

Key Pitch: Slider
Source: *Baseball Magazine* (January 1943, Harold C. Burr)

Key Pitch: Sailer
Source: Ethan Allen, by way of Lee Allen in *The Sporting News* (1/4/1969, Allen's "Cooperstown Corner" column; in the same column, Lee Allen repudiated his earlier description of Lohrman as a sinkerball pitcher)
Commentary: It's likely that in the 1930s and '40s, the words "slider" and "sailer" were sometimes (or perhaps even often) used to describe the same pitch, or two pitches that weren't easily distinguishable.

RICH LOISELLE 6'5" 245-pound righty
9-18, 4.38, 49 Saves 1996 2001

Pitch Selection: 1. Fastball (mid-90s) 2. Slider
Note: Loiselle had thrown a change-up, but abandoned that pitch in 1997.
Source: *The Scouting Notebook: 1998*

MICKEY LOLICH 6'1" 170-pound lefty
217-191, 3.44, 11 Saves 1963 1979

Pitch Selection: 1. Sinker or Slider 2. Fastball 3. Curve 4. Change
Sources: *The Summer Game* (Roger Angell, 1972); *Pitching with Tom Seaver* (Seaver with Steve Jacobson, 1973); *The New Yorker* (10/26/1968, Roger Angell); *The Sporting News* (2/3/1979 and 3/24/1979)
Tom Seaver: "[Lolich's fastball] is different than either of mine. He holds the ball with his two fingers on the slick, broad surface of the ball without contact with the seams. The ball comes up spinning oddly and then sinks as if it were a spitter."
Roger Angell: "Detroit's starter, Mickey Lolich, is a swaybacked, thick-waisted left-hander whose sinker ball becomes more difficult to hit as he grows tired in late innings."

Umpire Bill Kinnamon: "Mickey Lolich was an outstanding pitcher who was also very difficult to call because his ball would really move. Just about the time you'd make up your mind on the ball, that slider would bust in there. His ball would also ride a little bit. Nobody throws a ball hard enough to make it jump up, but a few can throw it hard enough to make it ride a little bit. Lolich could do that . . ."
Source: *The Men in Blue* (Larry Gerlach, 1980)

Lolich: ". . . I threw a fastball at 96 miles an hour. I was a power pitcher."
Source: Joey Wahler's column in MSGNetwork.com (9/26/2003)

Note: According to the aforementioned *TSN* articles, Lolich fooled around on the sidelines with a knuckleball throughout his career, perhaps throwing it occasionally in games. In 1978 he got serious about the pitch, and went to Florida in the spring of '79 to get special instruction from Hoyt Wilhelm. It's not clear how often he threw the knuckler that season (his last), but we do know that he finished with a 4.74 ERA.

TIM LOLLAR 6'3" 200-pound lefty
47-52, 4.27, 4 Saves 1980 1986

Pitch Selection: 1. Fastball (low-90s) 2. Hard Slider 3. Change (occasional)
Note: Lollar used an overhand delivery
Sources: *The Scouting Report* (1983–1985 editions)

VIC LOMBARDI 5'7" 158-pound righty
50-51, 3.62, 16 Saves 1945 1950

Key Pitch: Curve
Source: *The Sporting News* (10/30/1946, Page 20)

JIM LONBORG 6'5" 200-pound righty
157-137, 3.86, 4 Saves 1965 1979

Pitch Selection: 1. Fastball 2. Sinker 3. Curve 4. Slider
Source: *Baseball Stars of 1968* (article by Al Hirshberg)

Pitch Selection, late career: 1. Slider 2. Forkball? 3. Fastball

Source: Scout Ray Scarborough quoted in *Five Seasons* (Roger Angell, 1977)

BILL LONG 6'0" 185-pound righty
27-27, 4.37, 9 Saves 1985 1991

Key Pitch: Curve
Source: *The Scouting Report: 1990*

BRADEN LOOPER 6'3" 220-pound righty
19-17, 3.70, 46 Saves 1998 2003

Pitch Selection: 1. Two-Seam Fastball (93–98) 2. Four-Seam Fastball 3. Slider 4. Change
Source: *The Scouting Notebook: 2000*

EDDIE LOPAT 5'10" 185-pound lefty
166-112, 3.21, 3 Saves 1944 1955

Pitch Selection, 1947: 1. Curve 2. Fastball 3. Screwball 4. Slow Curve (used as Change)
Source: *Baseball Magazine* (August 1947, Ed Rumill)
Note: Rumill says the screwball is a recent addition to Lopat's repertoire, that Lopat has "a good fastball (and) a better curve," and that he learned to throw the slow curve as a change-up from watching Ted Lyons.

Pitches with Yankees: 1. Screwball 2. Fastball 3. Curve 4. Slider 5. Knuckleball (occasional, beginning in 1949 or 1952, depending on who you believe)
Sources: *The Men of Autumn* (Dom Forker, 1989); *The Sporting News* (9/24/1952, Dan Daniel); *New York Times* (July 1953, Arthur Daley); *The Sporting News* (4/13/1949, Page 40)

Comment: "Lopat, of course, made his reputation as a 'junk pitcher.' With him, it was knuckler, slider, change-up, curve and 'scroogie'—the ballplayers' term for screwball—every time out. Lopat did throw a fast ball now and then, but only as a change off his slow stuff."
Source: *Sport* (July 1956, Milton Richman, "Nobody Wins With a Fast Ball")

Quote from Daley: "I know Eddie Lopat throws [a slider], but it can't be much more than a change-of-pace pitch, buried among his assortment of junk."

Lopat on his pitching philosophy: "Never the same pitch twice, never the same place twice, never the same speed twice."
Source: *The Hurlers* (Kevin Kerrane, 1989)

Dave Philley: "Lopat? You don't *figure* him out. He had a dinky little screwball, wasn't much of one. Little slider, little breaking ball: take a little off, add a little. No pattern whatsoever you could ever figure out. And it looks so big coming up there . . . I always said this: If I take it, it gets just enough of the plate; if I swing, that joker is just enough *off* the plate. And it's always that situation. And that herky-jerky-like motion, too."
Source: *This Side of Cooperstown* (Larry Moffi, 1996)

Umpire Lee Ballanfant: "Eddie Lopat couldn't splash water, but, oh, what a screwball."
Source: *The Men in Blue* (Larry Gerlach, 1980)

Casey Stengel: "Every time he wins a game, people come down out of the stands asking for contracts."
Eddie Lopat: "Before I came over to the Yankees, Ted Lyons polished me off with the White Sox. He taught me to short-arm and long-arm my pitches. You have the same motion, but one time you extend your arm all the way while throwing, and another you just snap it through. Those two deliveries and throwing from different angles—overhead, sidearm, and three-quarters—create different pitches. So you're throwing ten, twelve, fourteen pitches if you break it down."
Source: *The Gospel According to Casey* (Ira Berkow and Jim Kaplan, 1992)
Also see entry for Fred Hutchinson.

ALBIE LOPEZ 6'2" 240-pound righty
47-58, 4.94, 4 Saves 1993 2003

Pitches: 1. Fastball (92–95) 2. Curve 3. Change 4. Cut Fastball (added 2000) 5. Slider
Source: *The Scouting Notebook* (1996, 2001, and 2002 editions)

AURELIO LOPEZ 6'0" 185-pound righty
62-36, 3.56, 93 Saves 1974 1987

Pitch Selection: 1. Fastball 2. Slider 3. Screwball
Source: *The Scouting Report: 1987*

TOM LOVETT 5'8" 162-pound righty
89-59, 3.94, 2 Saves 1885 1894

Key Pitch: Curve
Source: *The Washington Post* (5/19/1893, Page 6)

GROVER LOWDERMILK 6'4" 190-pound righty
23-39, 3.58, 0 Saves 1909 1920

Key Pitch: Fastball
Quote: "Laudermilk [*sic*] is a fearfully speedy pitcher and his only weakness is lack of control."
Source: *The National Game* (Alfred H. Spink, 1911)

DEREK LOWE 6'6" 214-pound righty
58-47, 3.57, 85 Saves 1997 2003

Pitches: 1. Hard Sinker 2. Curve 3. Change 4. Cut Fastball
Note: The Cut Fastball was added or refined in 2002, when Lowe went from relieving to starting.
Sources: *The Scouting Notebook* (2000–2003 editions); *Sports Illustrated* (7/8/2002, Tom Verducci)

TURK LOWN 6'0" 180-pound righty
55-61, 4.12, 73 Saves 1951 1962

Pitch Selection: 1. Fastball
Source: *Sports Illustrated* (9/28/1959)

Comment: "The Cubs are also looking for much better things from Turk Lown, whose only previous recommendation was a fine fast ball. Good as it was, it failed to keep him in the big leagues; but now that he's back from a stint in the minors with a new sidearm change-up, the Cubs feel he is much better equipped to stick."
Source: *Sport* (July 1956, Milton Richman, "Nobody Wins With a Fast Ball")

GARY LUCAS 6'5" 200-pound lefty
29-44, 3.01, 63 Saves 1980 1987

Pitch Selection: 1. Sinker 2. Slider 3. Fastball (mid-80s)
Source: *The Scouting Report: 1983*

RED LUCAS 5'9" 170-pound righty
157-135, 3.72, 7 Saves 1923 1938

Pitch Selection: 1. Fastball 2. Curve 3. Change
Source: *Baseball Magazine* (April 1931, F.C. Lane)

Note: Listed as a suspected spitballer
Source: *The Cincinnati Game* (Lonnie Wheeler and John Baskin, 1988)

CARL LUNDGREN 5'11" 175-pound righty
91-55, 2.42, 6 Saves 1902 1909

Key Pitch: Curves
Quote: "He had fine control, a steady nerve, and an excellent assortment of curves."
Source: *The Sporting Life* (4/21/1906)

DOLF LUQUE 5'7" 160-pound righty
194-179, 3.24, 28 Saves 1914 1935

Pitch Selection: 1. Fastball 2. Curve
Sources: *Baseball Magazine* (September 1926); *Baseball Digest* (August 1955, Tom Meany); *The Baseball Research Journal No. 19* (article by Peter Bjarkman); 1924 *Reach Guide* (Page 47)
Quote from *Baseball Magazine*: ". . . he has a good curve which he uses most judiciously. But his fast ball is his best ball."

Quote: "In later years Luque claimed that he learned *his* curve from the immortal Christy Mathewson."
Source: *Great Baseball Pitchers* (Jim Brosnan, 1965)

Luque: "Some pitchers with the count three and two will cut loose through the center of the plate. I never do."
Source: *The Hurlers* (Kevin Kerrane, 1989)

Al Lopez: "He was strictly overhand, with a curve that broke straight down—they called it a drop. He could pitch to left-handed hitters better than he could to righties by throwing them that curve."
Source: *The Man in the Dugout* (Donald Honig, 1977)

Lopez, again: "Another hurler I'll never forget was Dolf Luque. He was perfect in his pitching pattern. Nobody

Transcendental Graphics / ruckerarchive.com

was better at setting up a hitter with a couple of big sharp curves and then getting him with a fastball at the knee for a called third strike."
Source: *Legends of Baseball* (Walter M. Langford, 1987)

SPARKY LYLE 6'1" 182-pound lefty
99-76, 2.88, 238 Saves 1967 1982

Pitch Selection: 1. Slider 2. Fastball 3. Curve
Sources: *The Relief Pitcher* (John Thorn, 1979); unidentified clipping from TSN morgue (July 1979, Frederick C. Klein); *Late and Close: A History of Relief Pitching* (Paul Votano, 2002)

ED LYNCH 6'6" 230-pound righty
47-54, 4.00, 8 Saves 1980 1987

Pitch Selection: 1. Fastball 2. Curve 3. Change 4. Slurve
Source: *The Scouting Report: 1985*

JACK LYNCH 5'8" 185-pound righty
110-105, 3.69, 0 Saves 1881 1890

Pitch Selection: 1. Drop Curve 2. Inshoot (probably a Screwball)
Sources: *New York Clipper* (undated, from Hall of Fame Library); *New York Journal* (12/4/1911, Sam Crane)
Quote from *New York Clipper*: "Studying the in-and-out curves, rise and drop deliveries, he rapidly acquired a reputation as an effective and puzzling pitcher . . . He has complete control of the ball, with all the curves and varying paces in delivery, and is cool and self-possessed."
Quote from *New York Journal*: "Lynch was also the first pitcher to combine a drop curve with a speedy inshoot. He originated the combination and it was so puzzling a delivery that I have seen batters strike at balls very frequently that bounced in front of the plate . . . [Manager Ben] Douglass was, of course, greatly surprised, and asked Lynch where he had learned to pitch. 'Why, with Terry Larkin, who taught me how to curve a ball and the drop . . . For a drop curve Terry used the two middle fingers, and I do the same.' But at that time a pitcher by the rules could not swing his hand above his waist in delivering the ball. Lynch had to do so, however, to get his drop curve, and he had much trouble with umpires until the rule was changed soon after."

TED LYONS 5'11" 200-pound righty
260-230, 3.67, 23 Saves 1923 1946

Pitches, prior to 1931 arm injury: 1. Sailer 2. Knuckleball 3. Curve 4. Change
Pitches, after 1931: 1. Slow Curve 2. Knuckleball 3. Fastball 4. Slower Curve (as Change)
Source: *Baseball Magazine* (October 1927, "Comprising an interview with Ted Lyons")
Other Sources: *Baseball Players and Their Times* (Eugene C. Murdock, 1991); *Famous American Athletes of Today* (1942 edition), *Baseball Magazine* (August 1947, article about Ed Lopat)

Note: According to an article in the October 1939 issue of *Baseball Magazine,* Lyons 1) also suffered an injury in 1929, and 2) began throwing the knuckleball then, after seeing a photo of Eddie Rommel's knuckleball grip. Also, his knuckleball was "a fingernail ball and that was perfect for Ted, who has stubby fingers and can't grip the ball with the effect of pitchers who have ponderous hands."

Notes: Lyons' sailer was described as a "peculiar fast ball that . . . will swerve from a straight line as much as a foot or more, breaking somewhat like a curve. Lyons throws this ball with great speed and with an overhand motion." Also, unlike many contemporary practitioners of the knuckleball, Lyons actually threw the ball from his fingertips. According to Lyons, "In some games I'll pitch as many as 25 knucklers."
Source: October 1927 *Baseball Magazine*

Notes: Jimmy Dykes in *Baseball Digest* (Dec.–Jan. 1961) said that Lyons threw a good slider.

When he first came to the majors, Lyons relied on a "pump-handle" delivery to destroy the hitter's timing. He would pump his arms over his head sometimes one time, sometimes twice, even three or four times, so that the hitter never knew when he was going to throw the ball.

Note: When asked, in 1944, "What is your favorite pitch?" Lyons answered, "I like to throw that knuckler, but I don't do it very often. I stick mostly to my so-called fast one and my slow curve, but I have a knuckle ball in reserve and it helps mostly as a threat. They're watching for it and that helps me sneak the fast one by 'em."
Source: *Baseball Digest* (May 1946, Al Wolf)

Description: "Ted Lyons was never an overpowering pitcher. He had his knuckleball and stuff, but Ted was

probably the strongest man that I ever ran into in the big leagues. He could pick me up by my shirt and just shake my damn teeth out."
Source: Buddy Lewis in *Dugout to Foxhole* (Rick Van Blair, 1994); Lewis didn't arrive in the majors until 1935, years after the injury that cost Lyons his great fastball.

MIKE MACDOUGAL 6'4" 195-pound righty
4-7, 4.28, 27 Saves 2001 2003

Pitches: 1. Fastball (95–98) 2. Slider 3. Curve 4. Change (occasional)
Source: John Sickels at ESPN.com (4/17/2003)
Other Source: *The Scouting Notebook 2004*

Commentary: MacDougal's breaking pitches, when thrown effectively, have to rank among the most overpowering anyone has ever thrown. In 2003 he completely fooled Frank Thomas, Albert Pujols, and Barry Bonds, leaving all three standing at home plate with their bats on their shoulders on pitches that broke right over the heart of the plate. However, at this writing MacDougal rarely knows where his slider and curve will wind up.

DANNY MACFAYDEN 5'11" 170-pound righty
132-159, 3.96, 9 Saves 1926 1943

Pitch Selection: 1. Curve 2. Fastball
Source: *Who's Who in the Major Leagues* (1939 edition); *Red Sox Century* (Glenn Stout and Richard A. Johnson, 2000)

Description: "When he was young and using his fire-ball Danny MacFayden had only moderate success as a major-league hurler. Then toward the end of his career when he had lost much of his speed, he had several exceptionally good seasons. In one game that I saw in 1938 he used one of the strangest deliveries ever seen—used with success, that is. With an overhand pitch he threw the ball to the plate no faster in motion or speed of the ball than if he were engaged in an ordinary game of catch with somebody who had merely a fielder's glove. But, though not much oftener than once in five times, he let go a really fast ball with just the same easy preliminary action. The batters knew they had to be ready for that pitch. That is what made the other stuff good."
Source: Al Chapman in *Play Ball!* (Chapman and Hank Severeid, 1941)

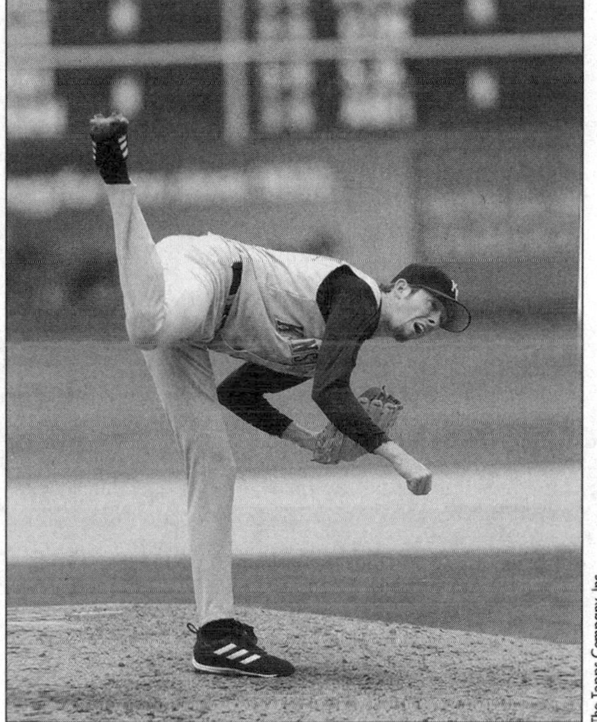

Mike MacDougal

NICK MADDOX 6'0" 175 pound righty
43-20, 2.29, 1 Save 1907 1910

Description: ". . . a well-formed youth with a face like a dried apple."
Source: William F. Kirk in the New York *American* (9/19/1908), reprinted in *The Unforgettable Season* (G.H. Fleming, 1981)

Note: Maddox pitched a shutout in his MLB debut, and one week later he pitched the first nine-inning no-hitter in Pirates history.

GREG MADDUX 6'0" 170-pound righty
289-163, 2.89, 0 Saves 1986 2003

Pitches: 1. Fastball 2. Circle Change 3. Slider 4. Cut Fastball 5. Split-Fingered Fastball 6. Sinker 7. Curve
Sources: *Tom Seaver's 1989 Scouting Notebook; The Scouting Report: 1992; 1995 Baseball Almanac; The Scouting Notebook 1999*

Commentary: Maddux has command of an exceptional number of pitches, and adds and discards pitches all the time. The Cut Fastball has been his No. 1 or No. 2 pitch since about 1995, but he was a Cy Young pitcher before he even started to throw that one.

Comment: "He was 16 when Rusty Medar, a volunteer coach in Las Vegas, watched the skinny kid throw straight over the top and told him, 'You're probably never going to throw hard enough to overpower people.' So the coach showed Maddux how to lower his arm and release the ball at what would be 10 o'clock on a clock face instead of 11—and to switch from a four-seam fastball to a two-seamer. The ball immediately began to dance, usually down and away from a left-handed hitter. It is the same fastball he throws today. It is, he says, his best pitch, even if it only averages about 85 mph, 87 on a good day. Maddux also throws a wonderfully disguised circle changeup, a cutter that bores in on the hands of lefthanded hitters and two average breaking balls: a slider and curveball."
Source: *Sports Illustrated* (8/14/1995, Tom Verducci)

Description: ". . . an 82- to 86-mph fastball (on the slow radar gun) that he throws 70 percent of the time, a decent slider, a circle-change (his strikeout pitch), a cutter (a breaking fastball to back off lefthanded hitters), and a big, slow nothing of a curve. But don't be fooled: The mixture is perfectly calculated and unrelentingly diabolical, strikingly stunningly, pitch after pitch, at the hitter's weakest points, straight for the kill—outside corner, inside corner, down and away. And always at different speeds and from that same stripped-down, monotonous delivery. Everything moving dizzily away from the center of the plate. Until the poor hitter can't even see straight. Until he's on the verge of a nervous breakdown."
Source: *The Sporting News* (10/9/1995, Michael P. Geffner)

MIKE MADDUX 6'2" 180-pound righty
39-37, 4.05, 20 Saves 1986 2000

Pitch Selection: 1. Four-Seam Fastball 2. Two-Seam Fastball 3. Slider 4. Change
Sources: *The Scouting Notebook 1999; The Scouting Report: 1996*

SAL MAGLIE 6'2" 180-pound righty
119-62, 3.15, 14 Saves 1945 1958

Pitch Selection: 1. Curve 2. Fastball 3. Slow Curve (used as Change)
Sources: *The Incredible Giants* (Tom Meany, 1955); *The Sal Maglie Story* (Milton J. Shapiro, 1957); *Sports Illustrated* (3/17/1958, "Big League Secrets")

Description: "Sal throws his hooks from three different angles—sidearm, three-quarters, and completely overhand. His fast ball is nothing to write home about and he uses it only to set up his pet curve."
Source: *Baseball Digest* (January 1951, Milt Richman)

Leo Durocher: "Sal's a great pitcher, and I'll tell you why—three curves and the guts of a burglar."
Wes Westrum: "Sal had three types of curveballs. One broke four inches, the second six inches, and the third was a big, breaking curve that moved eight inches. He wrapped the ball differently for each one and he wasn't afraid to pitch inside. He would throw a high, inside pitch to a batter, shave him close. Then when he got the

George Brace Collection

Sal Maglie

ball back from me he would play this little game. He'd say, 'This ball is slippery. Give me a new one.' As if it was the ball's fault that it came in tight."
Source: *The Giants Win the Pennant! The Giants Win the Pennant!* (Bobby Thomson with Lee Heiman and Bill Gutman, 1991)

Description: "Sal uses his fast ball high and tight to drive the batter back in the box and then curves him low and outside so he'll have to reach. The Barber's curve is probably sharper than your razor. It was inevitable that it should give rise to the allegation that he was throwing the illegal spitball."
Source: *Baseball Digest* (August 1955, "Maglie—Heir to Matty's Curve")

Umpire Tom Gorman: "There used to be a rule that whenever a pitcher would ask for a new ball we had to give it to him. Some pitchers always wanted a particular ball. Sal Maglie used to look for the high-seam ball. It gives you a better curveball. The baseballs are hand-sewn, and some of the seamstresses must be stronger than others. If they pull the stitches tighter, the seams are higher.

"Maglie would drive me crazy. I gave him a new ball once, twice, then three times. He still wasn't satisfied. So I took six balls, three in each hand, and went to the mound and said, 'Here, Sal, be my guest. Take your pick!' "
Source: *Three and Two!* (Tom Gorman as told to Jerome Holtzman, 1979)

Comment: "Dolf Luque taught Maglie the art of using the curveball. Dolf showed Sal how to work inside and outside, and not be afraid to push people back with it. That came natural to Sal. He was a nothing pitcher until he went to Mexico. And when he came back he quickly became dominant. To Sal's credit, he never hesitated to tell people that Luque was the one who turned his career around."
Source: Jack Lang in *The Giants Win the Pennant! The Giants Win the Pennant!* (Bobby Thomson with Lee Heiman and Bill Gutman, 1991)

BEST PICK-OFF MOVES

(in no particular order)

Sherry Smith
Terry Mulholland
Andy Pettitte
Orville Jorgens
Hugh McQuillan
Nick Altrock
Jim Scott
Bill Wight
Ed Walsh
Frank Miller
Art Mahaffey
Tony Mullane
Claude Passeau
Lefty Leifeld
Warren Spahn

MIKE MAGNANTE 6'1" 180-pound lefty
26-32, 4.08, 3 Saves 1991 2002

Pitch Selection: 1. Change 2. Fastball (low-80s) 3. Slider
Source: *The Scouting Notebook: 1997*

JOE MAGRANE 6'6" 225-pound lefty
57-67, 3.81, 0 Saves 1987 1996

Pitch Selection: 1. Curve 2. Fastball 3. Slider 4. Change
Source: *The Scouting Report: 1990*

ART MAHAFFEY 6'1" 185-pound righty
59-64, 4.17, 1 Save 1960 1966

Pitch Selection: 1. Fastball 2. Curve 3. Change
Source: *Baseball Digest* (March 1960, Page 91)

Quote: "Has all pitches in the book plus a lightning-quick pick-off move to first base."
Source: *1963 Major League Handbook* (Don Schiffer)

Note: In Lee Allen's "Cooperstown Corner" column in *The Sporting News* (11/16/1963), Eddie Sawyer and John Ogden also cited Mahaffey's outstanding pick-off move.

ROY MAHAFFEY 6'0" 180-pound righty
67-49, 5.01, 5 Saves 1926 1936

Key Pitch: Fast-breaking Curve

Quote: "Mahaffey had a lot of stuff, but his spot pitch, his Sunday serve, was a fast-breaking curve ball."
Note: Name pronounced "may-HAFF-ee," not "muh-HAFF-ee" like the later pitcher. Also, usually referred to as "Leroy" while active.

RICK MAHLER 6'1" 195-pound righty
96-111, 3.99, 6 Saves 1979 1991

Pitches: 1. Slow Curve 2. Fastball 3. Change 4. Slider 5. Forkball 6. Screwball
Sources: *The Scouting Report: 1987; The Scouting Report: 1990*

PAT MAHOMES 6'4" 220-pound righty
42-39, 5.47, 5 Saves 1992 2003

Pitch Selection: 1. Fastball (low-90s) 2. Slider (mid-80s) 3. Change
Source: *The Scouting Report: 1993; The Scouting Notebook: 1995*

Pitches: 1. Fastball (low-90s) 2. Curve 3. Slider (occasional) 4. Change (occasional)
Source: *The Scouting Notebook: 1996*

FRANK MAKOSKY 6'1" 185-pound righty
5-2, 4.97, 3 Saves 1937 1937

Key Pitch: Forkball
Comment: "He is the only fork-ball pitcher in the major leagues. He developed it with Newark."
Source: *Baseball Magazine* (September 1937, Daniel M. Daniel); Daniel is clearly wrong about Makosky being the only forkball pitcher, as Big Jim Weaver was also a well-known proponent, over in the National League.

PAT MALONE 6'0" 200-pound righty
134-92, 3.74, 26 Saves 1928 1937

Pitch Selection: 1. Fastball 2. Curve 3. Change of Pace (developed in 1930)
Sources: *Baseball Magazine* (April 1931, John J. Ward); *The Man in the Dugout* (Donald Honig, 1977); Riggs Stephenson in *Baseball History, An Annual of Original Research* (1989)

Malone: "I pitch quite a few curves. Some overhand and some side arm."
Source: *Baseball Magazine* (September 1932, F.C. Lane); same source says Malone "is a fast ball pitcher, one of the greatest in baseball."

Bill Dickey: "He uses a fast ball mainly, but it's a good one. He has sure saved a lot of games for us."
Source: *Baseball Magazine* (February 1937, John J. Ward)

JIM MALONEY 6'2" 190-pound righty
134-84, 3.19, 4 Saves 1960 1971

Pitch Selection: 1. Fastball 2. Curve 3. Change 4. Slip Pitch
Sources: *Baseball's Star Pitchers* (Bill Libby, 1971); Maloney in *The No-Hit Hall of Fame* (Rich Coberly, 1985)

Maloney: "I had a very good curve. Everybody remembers my throwing so hard. But my curve was a good pitch, too."
Source: *Splendor on the Diamond* (Rich Westcott, 2000); according to same source, Maloney's fastball was once clocked at 99.5 miles per hour.

Quote: " 'You can bet the percentage always has been with low-ball pitchers. The only type pitchers who can get away with the high-riding type of stuff are guys like Sandy Koufax and Jim Maloney. How many pitchers do we have like Koufax and Maloney? But if you're not the Koufax or Maloney type, you've got to start throwing the ball low or you're not going to be very successful.'

"According to Friend, there is one time when a low-ball pitcher gets in real trouble.

" 'And I'm speaking from experience,' he said. 'I've done a lot of pitching on two of the hardest infields in baseball—ours at Forbes Field and Dodger Stadium. A hard infield will not bother a Koufax or Maloney. They are strikeout pitchers with that high, hard stuff. But a pitcher like me—one who relies on the sinker ball, the hard infield can be murder.' "
Source: *The Sporting News* (3/12/1966, Til Ferdenzi)

GORDON MALTZBERGER 6'0" 170-pound righty
20-13, 2.70, 33 Saves 1943 1947

Description: "The fellow who has almost as much of a variety of stuff as Hughson is Gordon Maltzberger of the White Sox. He's the perfect relief pitcher. Fellows like Hughson and Maltzberger make it easier on the um-

pires. They pitch true with plenty on the ball, and they don't fool much with the corners."
Source: anonymous American League umpire quoted by Shirley Povich in *The Sporting News* (8/17/1944, Page 10)

AL MAMAUX 6'0" 168-pound righty
76-67, 2.90, 10 Saves 1913 1924

Key Pitch: Fastball
Source: *The Pittsburgh Pirates* (Fred Lieb, 1948)

MATT MANTEI 6'1" 198-pound righty
13-15, 3.56, 89 Saves 1995 2003

Pitches, 1995–1999: 1. Fastball (high-90s) 2. Overhand Curve
Pitches, 2000–2003: 1. Fastball (high-90s) 2. Slider
Sources: *The Scouting Notebook* (1999–2002 editions)

JOSIAS MANZANILLO 6'0" 200-pound righty
10-12, 4.56, 5 Saves 1991 2003

Pitch Selection: 1. Fastball (low-90s) 2. Slider
Source: *The Scouting Notebook: 2002*

FIRPO MARBERRY 6'1" 190-pound righty
148-88, 3.63, 101 Saves 1923 1936

Pitch Selection: 1. Rising Fastball 2. Curve 3. Change
Sources: *The Relief Pitcher* (John Thorn, 1979); *Baseball Magazine* (December 1924, F.C. Lane); *Who's Who in the American League* (1935 edition)
Marberry in *Baseball Magazine:* "I have a pretty easy motion, and specialize in speed. That's what makes a good relief hurler, a fast ball and control. A team wants someone who can go in there and get them over the plate, and at the same time fool the batters for a few innings."

Bucky Harris: "Firpo was the type of pitcher who could toss a few in the bullpen, casually saunter to the mound, and then knock the bats out of their hands with his blazing speed."
Source: Harris quoted in *Late and Close: A History of Relief Pitching* (Paul Votano, 2002)

Comment: "He originally was a fast ball caster, but has developed a new repertoire which includes effective slow stuff."
Source: 1935 *Who's Who in the American League, 1935*

PHIL MARCHILDON 5'10" 170-pound righty
68-75, 3.93, 2 Saves 1940 1950

Pitches, before World War II: 1. Fastball 2. Curve 3. Change and Slow Curve (both occasional and ineffective)
Pitches, after 1946: 1. Curve 2. Fastball 3. Forkball (unveiled on Opening Day in 1947)
Sources: Marchildon in *Ace: Phil Marchildon* (Marchildon with Brian Kendall, 1993); *Baseball Magazine* (January 1942, Frank Yeutter; and February 1948, Hub Miller); also, *Baseball Magazine* article about A's pitching coach Earle Brucker (April 1949, Frank Yeutter)

Marchildon: "Later on in the majors it was estimated that my fastball traveled about ninety-five miles per hour. The movement on it was so distinctive that it became known around the American League by the name 'Johnny Jump-Up.'

"I developed a three-quarter, slightly sidearm delivery . . .

"My curveball came around only after many hours spent experimenting with a variety of grips and deliveries until I found one that worked. When you throw as hard as I did, the fastball is always going to be your best pitch. But on a good day my curve had a wide downward break to it that made it almost as effective as my heater. Because I gripped the ball tightly, my curve was only slightly slower than my fastball, which made it even more difficult for batters to tell what was coming."

Notes: According to the *Baseball Magazine* article about Brucker, Marchildon came to the majors with just a fastball and curve. "He hated the knuckle ball when he tried it, his hand wasn't big enough for the palm ball. So the last trial was a fork ball. And Phil adopted that pitch for his 'sneaker.' " According to an article in *Sport* (July 1949, Vincent D. Lunny), Marchildon became disenchanted with his forkball in 1947, and didn't throw as many afterward.

Comment: "The secret of the Canadian's great fast ball, which is one of the most 'alive' pitches to enter the American League, is a powerful muscle that stands up like a marble at the base of his thumb and first finger. He grips the ball like a vise. His knuckle joints also are unusually large and his arms are like the Village Smithy's."
Source: *The Sporting News* (8/2/1945, Page 2)

Quote: "We had some pitchers that threw what we called a screwball in those days, but that was a hard pitch to throw, and it was hard on your arm. Phil Marchildon threw a good screwball."
Source: Carl Scheib in phone interview (5/9/2003, Rob Neyer); no other source, including Marchildon's autobiography, mentions the screwball even in passing.

JOHNNY MARCUM 5'11" 197-pound righty
65-63, 4.66, 7 Saves 1933 1939

Pitch Selection: 1. Curve 2. Change 3. Fastball 4. Screwball (against left-handed batters)
Quote: "He thought he had enough with his curve, change of pace and control . . . On the theory that practice makes perfect, he kept on pounding away—change of pace, curve and fast ball. Then it came to Johnny. 'A right-handed screwball for left-handed batters,' he said to himself . . . [Dayton manager Nick Cullop] showed Marcum how it was thrown and the big right-hander tried it . . . Thus it was that Marcum reached back and pulled the screwball out of his bag of tricks during the 1934 training trip. Marcum is a half-side-arm thrower, but in delivering the screwball he comes down overhanded."
Source: *The Sporting News* (1935)

JUAN MARICHAL 6'0" 185-pound righty
243-142, 2.89, 2 Saves 1960 1975

Pitches: 1. Slider 2. Fastball 3. Change 4. Curve 5. Screwball
Note: Marichal's motion contained an extremely high kick, and he threw anywhere from over the top to sidearm.
Source: *Sport* (9/24/1964, Al Stump)

Marichal: "I think the slider was my best pitch against righthanders. Against lefthanders my best pitch was the screwball. Candlestick Park was a lefthanded hitters' park, and I always faced lefthanded lineups, so I had to come up with that pitch. I started fooling around with it in 1960. About that time, we had a pitcher named Ruben Gomez. He threw one of the best screwballs I ever saw. I learned from him how to throw the pitch, and by 1962 I had a pretty good one."
Source: *Splendor on the Diamond* (Rich Westcott, 2000)

San Francisco Giants

Juan Marichal

Description: "Just how fast Marichal's fastball travels when he does throw it is a subject of mild controversy. 'Slower than Koufax's' is a common comment, but the truth is: as fast as he feels like throwing it. One National League hitter claims to have counted ten different speeds, and few batters have ever seen Marichal really cut loose. Cincinnati's John Edwards is one of the privileged few. After Marichal struck him out with the bases loaded last week, Giants coach Charlie Fox noted that 'Edwards obviously knew those fastballs were coming. But they were the very best in the league, and they went right by him.' "
Source: *Time* (6/10/1966); see below . . .

Marichal: "Those are kind words, but I cannot claim to have a fastball that travels at ten different speeds, as that anonymous hitter asserted. When my fastball is really working, I believe it travels at two different speeds: fast and not-quite-so-fast . . .

"In addition to two fast-ball speeds and the curve, I also use a screwball, a slider, and occasionally a floating slow pitch. Not all, but most of all, my pitches can be de-

livered in any one of three ways—overhand, three-quarter, and sidearm."
Source: *A Pitcher's Story* (Juan Marichal with Charles Einstein, 1967); note here that Marichal does *not* mention throwing a change-up.

Description: ". . . When Juan was first in the league, Charlie Dressen tried to upset him by claiming that he was pitching illegally. When a pitcher goes to a full windup, he has to have one foot on the rubber and one behind it. Marichal pitched off the end of the rubber, one foot on it and the other off to the side—off to the side but behind the line of the rubber if you extended it . . ."
Source: *Jocko* (Jocko Conlan and Robert Creamer, 1967)

Description: ". . . throws like some enormous and dangerous farm implement . . ."
Source: Roger Angell in *The New Yorker* (reprinted in *The Summer Game,* 1972)

Description: "Left-handed pitchers should be on the left side of the rubber for the same reason that a right-hander is on the right side of the rubber . . . the exception to this rule concerns pitchers who throw a screwball often. For example, Juan Marichal . . . a right-hander who uses the screwball most effectively, pitches from the left side of the rubber."
Source: *Pitching* (Bob Shaw, 1972)

Another description, same source: "Juan, like Spahn, is not completely square to home plate, but remember he too has an exaggerated high leg kick and is an overhand pitcher . . ."

Pitch Selection: 1. Fastball 2. Curve 3. Screwball
Source: *The Sporting News* (1/8/1972, Pat Frizzell)

Note: An article in the *New York Daily News* (6/9/2002, T.J. Quinn) says that Marichal's slider was actually a cut fastball.

CLIFF MARKLE 5'9" 163-pound righty
12-17, 4.10, 0 Saves 1915 1924

Key Pitch: Curve
Source: *Jocko* (Jocko Conlan and Robert Creamer, 1967); Conlan puts Markle's curveball in a class with Clem Labine's, Rosy Ryan's, Freddie Fitzsimmons', and Walter Beall's.

RUBE MARQUARD 6'3" 180-pound lefty
201-177, 3.08, 19 Saves 1908 1925

Pitches, 1908–1910: 1. Fastball 2. Curve
Pitches, post–1910: 1. Fastball 2. Curve 3. Fadeaway 4. Slow Ball
Note: Marquard was a huge disappointment in his first few seasons—he was widely derided as the "$11,000 Lemon"—so prior to spring in 1911, John McGraw asked Wilbert Robinson and Christy Mathewson to work with Marquard. And by the time the season opened, Rube had two new effective pitches.
Sources: *Rube Marquard* (Larry D. Mansch, 1998); *They Played the Game* (Harry Grayson, 1944)

Marquard: "I have always been called a speed pitcher, and I suppose speed is my main strong point. This year, however, I have developed curves to an extent where I can use them effectively and have also had good success with my slow ball. I have a good slow ball when it is working well. It twists and breaks almost the same as a spit ball would do. I have never pitched a spit ball myself and I have no desire to learn."
Source: *Baseball Magazine* (August 1912, Marquard)

John McGraw: "When right Marquard's fast ball had a peculiar jump to it that was a complete baffler to opponents. It was in the use of this ball at the right moment that he won his nineteen straight games.
Source: *My Thirty Years in Baseball* (McGraw, 1923)

Comment: "His poor record [in 1910] was due to lack of control although he possesses great speed and a wonderful array of benders . . . he is said to possess as much speed as Rusie."
Source: *The National Game* (Alfred H. Spink, 1911)

CONNIE MARRERO 5'7" 158-pound righty
39-40, 3.67, 3 Saves 1950 1954

Description: "His pleasant disposition, rich sense of humor, comical physical appearance and the plentiful assortment of slow stuff—curves, sliders and knucklers—which he throws with such gay abandon have made him something of a legend even in a country

where every man is a potential character and every situation a potentially comic one."
Source: *Sport* (September 1951, Al Silverman)
Note: According to Silverman, in Cuba Marrero's nickname was *El Curvo.*

MIKE MARSHALL 5'10" 180-pound righty
97-112, 3.14, 188 Saves 1967 1981

Pitch Selection: 1. Fastball 2. Screwball 3. Slider
Note: The Seattle Pilots forbade Marshall from throwing his screwball in 1969, and the Astros weren't wild about the pitch, either.
Sources: *Ball Four* (Jim Bouton, 1970); *The Relief Pitcher* (John Thorn, 1979); Marshall in *Talkin' Baseball: An Oral History of Baseball in the 1970s* (Phil Pepe, 1998); e-mail correspondence between Marshall and Rob Neyer (9/1/2003), in which Marshall expressly denied having thrown a palm ball (which has been attributed to him in some sources)

Description: "Marshall's 31-year-old body is unremarkable. He is short for a pitcher—only 5'10"—and he weighs 180 pounds. He has big shoulders and a weightlifter's arms, but he bulges at the middle. He has long sideburns and an impressive mustache, but his curly brown hair has thinned on top. Standing one sunny day last week in the doorway of the Lanai Coffee Shop at San Diego's Town & Country Hotel pensively chewing on a toothpick, he could have passed for a life-insurance salesman."
Source: *Sports Illustrated* (8/12/1974, Ron Fimrite)

Notes: From 1971 through 1974, Marshall recorded, in great detail, every pitch that he threw.

According to his Web site, over those four seasons Marshall threw roughly 36 percent fastballs, 39 percent screwballs, and 25 percent sliders. Of course, the percentages did change from one season to the next, with the biggest difference between 1971 and '72.

Upon analyzing his pitches after the '71 season, Marshall realized that he'd enjoyed great success with his screwball when he threw it for strikes, but had thrown it only 30 percent of the time because he had trouble controlling it. So before the '72 season he learned how to throw the screwball for strikes, and in each of the following three seasons he threw that pitch at least 38 percent of the time.

While between 30 and 40 percent of his pitches were fastballs in all four seasons, he went from throwing nearly 40 percent sliders in 1971 to throwing roughly 20 percent sliders in each of the next three seasons.
Source: www.DrMikeMarshall.com

DENNIS MARTINEZ 6'1" 160-pound righty
245-193, 3.70, 8 Saves 1976 1998

Pitches: 1. Hard Curve 2. Fastball 3. Sinking Fastball 4. Slider 5. Change
Note: Martinez threw from a variety of angles.
Sources: *The Scouting Report* (1987, 1990, and 1992 editions)

Martinez: "My stuff was decent. I had a good curveball. My fastball was decent. My curveball made my fastball better. Everyone was aware of my curveball, so my fastball went right by them. But mostly, I had a big heart."
Source: *From 33rd Street to Camden Yards: An Oral History of the Baltimore Orioles* (John Eisenberg, 2001)

PEDRO MARTINEZ 5'11" 150-pound righty
166-67, 2.58, 3 Saves 1992 2003

Pitch Selection: 1. Fastball 2. Slider 3. Change
Source: *1994 Montreal Expos Media Guide*

Pitch Selection: 1. Riding Fastball 2. Circle Change 3. Cut Fastball (breaks like a slider) 4. Hard Slider 5. Curve
Note: Martinez uses frequent changes of his arm angle to further confuse hitters.
Sources: *The Scouting Notebook* (1998 and 2000 editions); NESN broadcast of Red Sox–Orioles game (9/10/2003)

Tim McCarver: "Pedro Martinez's best two pitches are his fastball and the best change in baseball. He'll use the first pitch to make batters go backward and the other to make them go forward. He has the same arm motion for both, and batters can't protect both the front and back of the plate. Those pitches are great for getting guys out, but to get a surprise called strike he'll throw the breaking ball—his third-best pitch—when behind in the count."
Source: *Tim McCarver's Baseball for Brain Surgeons and Other Fans* (McCarver with Danny Peary, 1998)

Description: "Facing Martinez is a game of Red Sox roulette: What's coming—the mid-90s fastball or the low-80s changeup? His arm action on the changeup is no tipoff: It's the same as if he were throwing the heater. 'By the time the ball gets there, the batter has got to be ready to adjust to it,' [Martinez] says. 'Otherwise it's too late.' Even if the hitter guesses correctly, he must still deal with the late-breaking movement of the pitch. 'It tails away from lefties, in on righties with a drop at the end,' he says. 'Nothing special.' "
Source: *Sports Illustrated* (3/31/03, Page 61)

RAMON MARTINEZ 6'4" 165-pound righty
135-88, 3.67, 0 Saves 1988 2001

Pitch Selection: 1. Tailing Fastball 2. Circle Change 3. Slurve 4. Big Overhand Curve
Sources: *The Scouting Report: 1996; The Scouting Notebook 2000*

TIPPY MARTINEZ 5'10" 180-pound lefty
55-42, 3.45, 115 Saves 1974 1988

Pitch Selection: 1. Overhand Curve 2. Fastball (87-89) 3. Change (occasional)
Sources: *The Scouting Report* (1983 and 1987 editions)

MIKE MASON 6'2" 205-pound lefty
29-39, 4.53, 0 Saves 1982 1988

Pitches: 1. Fastball (low-90s) 2. Curve 3. Sinker 4. Slider
Sources: *The Scouting Report* (1985 and 1987 editions)

ROGER MASON 6'6" 226-pound righty
22-35, 4.02, 13 Saves 1984 1994

Pitch Selection: 1. Tailing Fastball 2. Split-Fingered Fastball
Source: *The Scouting Report: 1987*

Pitch Selection: 1. Fastball 2. Slider 3. Forkball (added about 1992)
Source: *The Scouting Report: 1993*

WALT MASTERSON 6'2" 189-pound righty
78-100, 4.15, 20 Saves 1939 1956

Key Pitch: Fastball
Source: *Who's Who in the Major Leagues* (1947 edition)

BOBBY MATHEWS 5'5" 140-pound righty
166-136, 3.00, 3 Saves 1876 1887

Pitch Selection: 1. Curve 2. Fastball 3. Spitball
Sources: *Nineteenth Century Stars* (SABR, article by James D. Smith, III); *The National Pastime Special Pictorial Edition* (SABR, 1986); *The National Game* (Alfred H. Spink, 1911)

Key Pitch: Spitball
Umpire Hank O'Day: "The method of delivery has not changed much during the last decade, except in the matter of the spit ball. This was scarcely ever used in years gone by, but there is no doubt it was employed by such a veteran as 'Bobby' Mathews. He would certainly spit on the palm of his hand and rub the ball in the moistness. In the course of two or three innings, the ball would be perfectly black except in the spot where it was rubbed and there it would be perfectly white. Mathews was a very effective pitcher, and there is no doubt this process of his aided him greatly in his delivery. The batsmen used to wonder how he got away with his pitching. There is no doubt at all it was the use of the spit ball that brought this about, and he was clever enough to cover this up and keep the batsmen in a quandary what it was that made him so successful."
Source: *Baseball Magazine* (June 1908, Henry O'Day, "A Big League Umpire's View")

Commentary: Mathews is sometimes credited with inventing the curve *and* the spitball. In the 1919 *Reach Guide* there is a badly edited and somewhat confusing debate about the origins of the curve ball, in which someone is apparently claiming that Mathews, in 1869, was the first pitcher to throw a curve. Someone else responds and acknowledges that Mathews did throw a curve in 1869 (when he was 18 years old), but insists that Candy Cummings was throwing it in 1868.

A quote from Spink in *The National Pastime:* "He had the same curves that Martin and Cummings had introduced a year or two before and . . . a good deal of speed and this combination made him invincible . . . Some of the players of the present day claim that the ball which Mathews was pitching then was nothing more nor less than the 'spit' ball used now by many of the best pitchers. But this is hardly possible for the 'spit' ball is fairly wearing on the pitcher and soon retires him from service."

Actually, most of the evidence suggests that 1) he was one of the first to throw the curveball effectively, and 2) he might have been the first to throw a good spitball.

GREG MATHEWS 6'2" 180-pound lefty
28-33, 4.08, 0 Saves 1986 1992

Pitch Selection: 1. Fastball (mid-80s) 2. Curve 3. Change
Source: *The Scouting Report: 1987*

T. J. MATHEWS 6'1" 225-pound righty
32-26, 3.82, 16 Saves 1995 2002

Pitch Selection: 1. Two-Seam Fastball (low-90s) 2. Four-Seam Fastball (low-90s) 3. Split-Fingered Fastball 4. Slider
Source: *The Scouting Notebook 2000*

TERRY MATHEWS 6'2" 225-pound righty
22-21, 4.25, 10 Saves 1991 1999

Pitch Selection: 1. Fastball (low-90s) 2. Curve 3. Slider 4. Split-Fingered Fastball (used as Change)
Source: *The Scouting Report: 1993*

Pitch Selection: 1. Fastball (80s) 2. Slider
Source: *The Scouting Notebook: 1998*

CHRISTY MATHEWSON 6'1" 195-pound righty
373-188, 2.13, 28 Saves 1900 1916

Pitch Selection: 1. Fadeaway 2. Fastball 3. Drop Curve
Sources: *The Unforgettable Season* (G. H. Fleming, from an excellent description by Mathewson of his pitch selection), *Baseball's Greatest Players* (Tom Meany, 1953); *Inside Baseball* (Arthur Daley, 1950)

Mathewson: "I have always thought my curve was my best pitch. At least it has been my favorite. I took to the slow ball, which I have so often called the 'fade-away,' quite naturally. I made no deliberate effort to develop this pitch. It was, I suppose, part of my natural equipment. But it is a pitch that I can control very well—and, as I have said before, I place great emphasis on control. In 1908, a year in which I yielded only 42 bases on balls in a total of 416 innings, it was my fade-away that I relied upon most."
Source: *Baseball Magazine* (December 1914, Mathewson)

Description: "Mathewson, who had a good fast ball and a pretty good curve, relied more and more on the fadeaway as he lost the hop on his high hard one but, always, the fadeaway was a psychological threat. If a hitter guessed with Matty, he was guessing with a master of control and cunning."
Source: *Super Stars of Baseball* (Bob Broeg, 1971)

Note: In the 1996 edition of *Baseball Research Journal* (Society for American Baseball Research), Dick Thompson examined the various accounts of how Mathewson learned to throw the fadeaway, and concluded that the most credible story is that Mathewson was taught to throw the pitch in 1898 by Dave Williams, his teammate on the Honesdale, Pennsylvania, team.

JON MATLACK 6'3" 205-pound lefty
125-126, 3.18, 3 Saves 1971 1983

Pitch Selection: 1. Fastball 2. Curve
Sources: *The Pitching Staff* (Steve Jacobson, 1975)

Maury Wills: "There is much to like about Jon Matlack. He has excellent control, a good breaking pitch, and what ballplayers call a long fastball that moves."
Source: *How to Steal a Pennant* (Wills with John Freeman, 1976)

Note: Matlack gave up Roberto Clemente's 3000th (and final) hit, a double to left-center field, on a full-count curveball.
Sources: Matlack in *That Was Part of Baseball Then* (Vincent Debs Jr., 2002); Tom Seaver in *Talkin' Baseball: An Oral History of Baseball in the 1970s* (Phil Pepe, 1998)

LEROY MATLOCK 5'9" 175-pound lefty
NEGRO LEAGUES 1929 1942

Pitches: 1. Curve 2. Drop Curve 3. Screwball 4. Slider 5. Fastball 6. Change
Note: Matlock was famously tough on left-handed hitters.
Sources: *Buck Leonard: The Black Lou Gehrig* (Buck Leonard and James A. Riley, 1995); Gene Benson interview in *Black Diamonds* (John B. Holway, 1989); *The Bi-*

ographical Encyclopedia of the Negro Baseball Leagues* (James A. Riley, 1994)

Note: In *The Biographical Encyclopedia*, Riley says Matlock "had a good fastball," but Buck Leonard says in his book, ". . . Matlock wasn't a fastball pitcher. He could just get me out. With other fellows, I could tell when they were going to throw me the curveball, but with Matlock, I couldn't tell when he was going to throw a curveball."

DARRELL MAY 6'2" 185-pound lefty
16-20, 4.69, 0 Saves 1995 2003

Pitches: 1. Curve 2. Fastball (high-80s) 3. Change 4. Slider
Source: *The Scouting Notebook 2003*

JACKIE MAY 5'8" 178-pound lefty
72-95, 3.88, 19 Saves 1917 1932

Description: "[May was] a fat, fun-loving southpaw who employed a side-arm delivery . . . he was blessed with a world of stuff."
Source: *The Cincinnati Reds* (Lee Allen, 1948)

RUDY MAY 6'2" 205-pound lefty
152-156, 3.46, 12 Saves 1965 1983

Key Pitch as young pitcher: Fastball
Pitches, after 30: 1. "Sharp-breaking" Curve 2. Fastball 3. Change
Sources: *The Sporting News* (6/19/1976, Phil Pepe; 5/15/1971, Dick Miller; and 9/2/1972, Miller)

Note: As a young pitcher, May had one of the best fastballs in the league, but he had a poor change-up until Andy Messersmith taught him to throw a good one in 1971.

ERSKINE MAYER 6'0" 168-pound righty
91-70, 2.96, 6 Saves 1912 1919

Pitch Selection: 1. Curve 2. Fastball
Note: Mayer threw underhand and sidearm.
Source: *Encyclopedia of Jews in Sports* (Page 46)

CARL MAYS 5'11" 195-pound righty
207-126, 2.92, 31 Saves 1915 1929

Pitch Selection: 1. Fastball 2. Curve

Notes: Mays was the only notable submarine pitcher of his era. He told Bob McGarigle the pitch that killed Ray Chapman was a high fastball.
Source: *Baseball's Great Tragedy* (Bob McGarigle, 1972); *The Pitch That Killed* (Mike Sowell, 1989)

Description: "Carl slings the pill from his toes, has a weird looking wind-up and in action looks like a cross between an octopus and a bowler. He shoots the ball in at the batter at such unexpected angles that his delivery is hard to find, generally, until along about 5 o'clock, when the hitters get accustomed to it—and when the game is about over."
Source: *Baseball Magazine* (June 1918, "Who's Who on the Diamond")

Note: In *The Cincinnati Reds* (1948), Lee Allen wrote, "A right-hander, Mays was a devotee of submarine pitching, with a fast curve ball being his best bet." Allen was certainly right about Mays throwing underhand, but nearly every other source agrees that his best pitch was the fastball.

Road West Publishing—*Baseball Magazine* Collection

Carl Mays

AL MAUL 6'0" 175-pound righty
84-81, 4.43, 1 Save 1884 1901

Comment: "Maul fooled them with his slow ball and out curve, and pitched in great form . . ."
Source: *The Washington Post* (5/16/1896, Page 4)

JOE MAYS 6'1" 192-pound righty
42-55, 4.69, 0 Saves 1999 2003

Pitch Selection: 1. Fastball (88–92) 2. Curve 3. Slider 4. Change
Source: *The Scouting Notebook: 2002*

Quote: "Facing an Angels team that had totaled 31 runs and 56 hits in unseating the Yankees, Mays clearly had his best stuff. When Gardenhire was asked what was working for Mays, he replied: 'Take less time if I tell you what wasn't working. He had everything. He had his changeup, he had his great fastball moving in and out. His curveball, he had his slider . . . That's what we envision with Joe Mays right there, going right at the hitters, making them swing the bats, going right at them, attacking.' "
Source: *Minneapolis Star-Tribune* (10/9/2002, Dan Barreiro column)

JIM McANDREW 6'2" 185-pound righty
37-53, 3.65, 4 Saves 1968 1974

Key Pitch: Sinker
Description: "Jim does not throw especially hard, nor does he have a wicked curve. His 'out' pitch is a sinker that, when he keeps it down, breaks bats and results in many ground balls."
Source: *Major League Baseball: 1971* (Brenda Zanger and Dick Kaplan)

McAndrew: "I had what you call a comfortable fastball that was live when I kept it down. When I got it up in the strike zone I got in trouble, because the pitch straightened out and I didn't throw hard enough to just throw it by a hitter."
Source: *A Magic Summer* (Stanley Cohen, 1988)

AL McBEAN 5'11" 165-pound righty
67-50, 3.13, 63 Saves 1961 1970

Pitch Selection: 1. Fastball 2. Slider 3. Curve
Source: Jack Zanger in *Major League Baseball—1969;* the 1965 edition of the same book says that McBean relied on "a buzzing fast ball and a great sinker."

KEN McBRIDE 6'1" 190-pound righty
40-50, 3.79, 3 Saves 1959 1965

Pitch Selection: 1. Sinker 2. Fastball 3. Curve
Description: "The sinker is essentially a fast ball which, upon reaching the plate, veers slightly and drops. It actually drops more than it veers, the result of spin created by the pitcher.

" . . . McBride offers no testimony that the sinker is the greatest thing since Hungarian meat balls. He sticks with the pitch, as often as 90 percent of the time . . ."
Source: *Baseball Digest* (Oct.–Nov. 1962, Melvin Durslag)

Quote: "Ken McBride's problem was that he was a sinkerball pitcher—he had probably the best sinkerball that I've ever seen outside of Mel Stottlemyre—but if his mechanics weren't just perfect he would lose his sinker, or it wouldn't be as good some days. I think that prevented him from maybe being as effective as he might have been. But he was a fine pitcher and, ooh, when he had his sinker going, there wasn't anybody that could beat him."
Source: Jack Spring in *The San Francisco Seals, 1946–1957* (Brent Kelley, 2002)

BILL McCAHAN 5'11" 200-pound righty
16-14, 3.84, 0 Saves 1946 1949

Key Pitch: Fastball
Source: *Baseball Magazine* (September 1947, Frank Yeutter)

WINDY McCALL 6'0" 180-pound lefty
11-15, 4.22, 12 Saves 1948 1957

Note: Listed by *The Sporting News* (8/29/1956) as having one of the best fastballs in the league.

KIRK McCASKILL 6'1" 190-pound righty
106-108, 4.12, 7 Saves 1985 1996

Pitch Selection: 1. Slider 2. Hard Curve 3. Sinking Fastball 4. Change

Note: McCaskill's best pitch was his fastball before arm troubles in 1987 and 1988.
Source: *The Scouting Report: 1990*

STEVE McCATTY 6'3" 195-pound righty
63-63, 3.99, 5 Saves 1977 1985

Pitch Selection: 1. Fastball 2. Curve
Source: *The Sporting News* (8/16/1980, Kit Stier)

JOE McCLAIN 6'0" 183-pound righty
8-22, 4.42, 1 Save 1961 1962

Pitch Selection: 1. "Sneaky" Fastball 2. Curve
3. Change
Source: *The Washington Post* (June 1961, Bob Addie)

DANNY McCLELLAN lefty
NEGRO LEAGUES 1903 1923

Description: "He was a smart pitcher, mixing an assortment of off-speed curves effectively to offset his lack of a substantial fastball."
Source: *The Biographical Encyclopedia of the Negro Baseball Leagues* (James A. Riley, 1994)

BOB McCLURE 5'11" 170-pound lefty
68-57, 3.81, 52 Saves 1975 1993

Pitch Selection: 1. Sharp Curve 2. Fastball 3. Change
4. Knuckleball (added in 1985)
Sources: *The Scouting Report: 1986; The Scouting Report: 1990*

Note: The Milwaukee Brewers' 1996 media guide says that Steve Sparks is the third knuckleball pitcher in Brewers' history, and lists McClure as the second (we're assuming the first was Bob Humphreys).

GEORGE McCONNELL 6'3" 190-pound righty
41-51, 2.60, 4 Saves 1909 1916

Key Pitch: Spitball
Quote: "McConnell is entirely a 'spit baller.' "
Source: *The Unforgettable Season* (G. H. Fleming, Page 154)

BILLY McCOOL 6'2" 195-pound lefty
32-42, 3.59, 58 Saves 1964 1970

Pitch Selection: 1. Fastball
2. Slider (developed in 1966)
3. Curve (occasional) 4. Change (occasional)
Sources: *The Sporting News* (7/2/1966, Earl Lawson); *The Relief Pitcher* (John Thorn, 1979); Mel Harder quoted in *The Sporting News* (3/4/1967, Lawson)

JIM McCORMICK 5'10" 215-pound righty
265-214, 2.43, 1 Save 1878 1887

Key Pitches, through 1882: 1. Fastball 2. Curve
Key Pitch, beginning 1883: "Raise Ball" (low sidearm/underhand)
Source: *The Sporting News* (4/11/1918)

Quotes and Explanation: When he came to the majors (he) was regarded as "the Apollo Belvedere in the perfection of his physical manhood, as he had an arm of steel with speed and curves that made the greatest of batsmen fall before him." After hurting his arm in 1883 he began throwing sidearm in an attempt to return more quickly, and this evolved into an underhand "raise ball," apparently thrown very hard. "No pitcher of the past or present had the 'raise ball' like Jim McCormick's," according to *The Sporting News.*

Description: "There are few tricks or embellishments to McCormick's delivery, but it is none the less effective on that account. With a firm grasp of the ball he steps quickly through the box, driving the sphere forcibly."
Source: article titled "How Men Pitch Base-Ball: The Famous Pitchers of the National League of 1886." No author or publisher is given, though the information in the article is said to have come from photographic studies done by the *New York World* newspaper.

Description: "McCormick combined speed with a good curve in his best days but among ball players he was known as a tricky pitcher, the kind who can't be figured. A batter never knew what trick McCormick might play on him. He was famous for his balk motion and many were the arguments that cropped up during his career as to whether he was pitching legitimately or not."
Source: *Baseball Magazine* (March 1931, H.H. Westlake)

MIKE McCORMICK 6'2" 195-pound lefty
134-128, 3.73, 12 Saves 1956 1971

Pitch Selection: 1. Hard Screwball (McCormick's

best pitch starting in 1967) 2. Curve
3. Slow Screwball 4. Fastball

Note: Prior to 1961 tendinitis, McCormick threw mostly fastballs.
Source: *Baseball Stars of 1968* (article by Arnold Hano)

LANCE McCULLERS 6'1" 210-pound righty
28-31, 3.25, 39 Saves 1985 1992

Pitch Selection: 1. Fastball (90–95) 2. Slider
3. Change

Source: *The Scouting Report: 1987*

LINDY McDANIEL 6'3" 195-pound righty
141-119, 3.45, 172 Saves 1955 1975

Pitch Selection: 1. Sinking Fastball 2. Hard Curve
3. Forkball

Note: McDaniel threw both sidearm and overhand.
Sources: *Redbirds Revisited* (David Craft and Tom Owens, 1990); *View from the Dugout* (Ed Richter, 1963)

Note: According to Dick Lally in *Pinstriped Summers* (1985), 1) during the 1959 season McDaniel converted from a three-quarters to an overhand delivery, and 2) the following winter he added the forkball to his repertoire.

Key Pitch: Forkball
Source: *Dog Days: The New York Yankees' Fall from Grace and Return to Glory, 1964–1976* (Philip Bashe, 1994); in *Dog Days,* McDaniel recounts a game against the Orioles on July 7, 1970, in which he threw nine straight forkballs, all for strikes (but the ninth strike became a seeing-eye single and game-winning RBI).

VON McDANIEL 6'2" 180-pound righty
7-5, 3.44, 0 Saves 1957 1958

Pitches: 1. Slider 2. Fastball 3. Change 4. Curve
Source: *Baseball Stars of 1958* (article by Jim Beach)

Commentary: McDaniel, Lindy's younger brother, ranks as one of the more spectacular flame-outs ever. In 1957, when he was eighteen, he arrived with the Cardinals, pitched a two-hit shutout in his first start, and wound up the season 7-5 with a 3.22 ERA and two shutouts. He never won another game in the majors, and by the early '60s he'd become a power-hitting infielder in the minor leagues.

MICKEY McDERMOTT 6'2" 170-pound lefty
69-69, 3.91, 14 Saves 1948 1961

Pitches: 1. Fastball (mid-90s?) 2. Curve
3. Change (occasional)

Sources: Babe Martin in *The Great Rivalry* (Ed Linn, 1991); McDermott in *Bombers* (Richard Lally, 2002)
McDermott: ". . . I loved challenging hitters. Throwing heat. I had a 100-mile-an-hour fastball and a pretty wicked curve. But in the majors, no matter how hard you throw, you need three reliable pitches. I had a pretty good change-up, but I didn't trust it. I should have worked more on it, but I was having too much fun off the field."
Source: Press release for McDermott's memoir, *A Funny Thing Happened on the Way to Cooperstown* (2003)

Description: "McDermott looks as if he hasn't a bone in his body. He's so loose that he can twist himself up like a pretzel. He does it sometimes, just to scare people. Like Ewell Blackwell, he's all arms and legs and Adam's apple. He wears a size 16 collar, and it looks too big for him."
Source: *Sport* (December 1949, Al Hirshberg)

BEN McDONALD 6'7" 212-pound righty
78-70, 3.91, 0 Saves 1989 1997

Pitch Selection: 1. Fastball 2. Curve
3. Split-Fingered Fastball (added 1993) 4. Change

Sources: *1994 Baseball Almanac; The Scouting Notebook 1997*

WEBSTER McDONALD 6'0" 190-pound righty
NEGRO LEAGUES 1920 1940

Pitch Selection: 1. Sinking Fastball 2. Rising Curveball
3. Change

Note: McDonald threw submarine style.
Source: *The Biographical Encyclopedia of the Negro Baseball Leagues* (James A. Riley, 1994)
Note: According to Riley, McDonald mixed his pitches so well that he earned the nickname "56 Varieties."

JACK McDOWELL 6'5" 180-pound righty
127-87, 3.85, 0 Saves 1987 1999

Pitches: 1. Fastball (high-80s)
2. Split-Fingered Fastball 3. Curve (occasional)

Sources: *The Scouting Report: 1992; 1994 Baseball Almanac*

Pitch Selection: 1. Split-Fingered Fastball
2. Fastball (high-80s)

Description: "Yet McDowell . . . doesn't fit the mold of the traditional power pitcher. His fastball is usually in the high 80-mph range. His best pitch is the split-fingered fastball, which he throws in the conventional overhand style as well as from the side. The latter gives the illusion of a slider except with a deeper break."

Shane Mack: "He throws a great forkball. The last guy I saw consistently do that was Mike Scott . . . McDowell's breaks like a slider away from the hitter and you've got no chance."

Greg Hibbard: "I've seen on TV that Jack's fastball almost never runs over the middle of the plate. He paints the corners constantly. So, after you take a fastball or two, you have to swing at his splitter."

Source: *The Sporting News 1994 Baseball Yearbook* (Joel Bierig and Bruce Levine)

ROGER McDOWELL 6'1" 175-pound righty
70-70, 3.30, 159 Saves 1985 1996

Pitches: 1. Sinker 2. Slider 3. Fastball 4. Change

Sources: *The Scouting Report: 1992; The Scouting Report: 1995*

SAM McDOWELL 6'5" 190-pound lefty
141-134, 3.17, 14 Saves 1961 1975

Pitches: 1. Fastball 2. Hard Curve 3. Slider
4. Change

Sources: *Star Pitchers of the Major Leagues* (Bill Libby, 1971); *Suitors of Spring* (Pat Jordan, 1973)

CHUCK McELROY 6'0" 160-pound lefty
38-30, 3.90, 17 Saves 1989 2001

Pitches: 1. Fastball 2. Curve 3. Slider (early 90s)
4. Split-Fingered Fastball or Forkball 5. Change

Sources: *The Scouting Report: 1992; The Scouting Notebook: 1997*

ANDY McGAFFIGAN 6'3" 185-pound righty
38-33, 3.38, 24 Saves 1981 1991

Pitches: 1. Fastball 2. Slider 3. Sinker 4. Curve
5. Change (added 1986)

Sources: *The Scouting Report* (1984, 1985, and 1986 editions); *1987 Montreal Expos Media Guide*

BILL McGEE 6'1" 215-pound righty
46-41, 3.74, 6 Saves 1935 1942

Pitch Selection: 1. Sidearm Sinker (added 1938)
2. Sidearm Fastball 3. Overhand Fastball
4. Overhand Curve

Description: "This year Bill has come up with a new delivery, a side-arm sinker, that is natural for him and no strain on the arm. It is a wow of a pitch for making the batters beat the ball into the dirt and thus hit into double plays. He finds it especially effective against left-hand hitters and employs it frequently in the well-known clutch. He has excellent control of this pitch and won't hesitate to throw it with the count of three and two or three and one. Bill also owns a fast side-arm ball to mix with his sinker and to further add to a batter's confusion will cross with an overhand fast ball or curve. The batter who tries to guess what Mr. McGee is going to throw is usually outwitted."

Source: *Baseball Magazine* (September 1938, Clifford Bloodgood)

Key Pitch: Hard Sinker

Mickey Owen: "I know from experience that he throws a ball that seems like a cannon ball when it comes into a catching mitt. I caught him in St. Louis. When the heavy ball he throws is hit real good by a hitter it doesn't carry like a light ball will. Look up the records and you'll see he doesn't give up many home runs."

Source: *Baseball Magazine* (July 1941, Edward T. Murphy)

WILLIE McGILL 5'6" 170-pound lefty
71-70, 4.59, 1 Save 1890 1896

Pitch Selection: 1. Curve 2. Screwball 3. Fastball

Source: *Baseball Historical Review 1981* (SABR, article by L. Robert Davids)

Description: "He is like the little girl's definition of a sugar plum, round and rosy and sweet all over, and he throws barrel hoops and corkscrews at the plate. Once in a while he varies these with a swift straight ball that is full of starch as though it had just come from the laundry."

Source: Davids quoting the Buffalo Express, date unknown

Also see Bert Cunningham entry.

DAN McGINN 6'0" 185-pound lefty
15-30, 5.11, 10 Saves 1968 1972

Key Pitch: Sinker
Source: *The Summer Game* (Roger Angell, 1972)

JUMBO McGINNIS 5'10" 197-pounder
102-79, 2.95, 0 Saves 1882 1887

Description: "An underhand speed pitcher"
Source: *Nineteenth Century Stars* (SABR, 1989, article by Robert L. Tiemann)

JOE McGINNITY 5'11" 206-pound righty
246-141, 2.66, 24 Saves 1899 1908

Pitch Selection: 1. Curve 2. Fastball
Notes: According to *Baseball's Famous Pitchers* (Ira L. Smith), McGinnity delivered his curve sidearm or underhand, but often came over the top with his fastball. According to the 1939 *Spalding Guide* (John B. Foster), McGinnity "could switch from overhand to underhand without any effort. McGinnity was not ambidextrous, as was Tony Mullane of the Cincinnatis, but when he tired of pitching overhand he would change to underhand, and it seemed to be as easy for him to strike a batter out underhand as the other way."

Description: "Joe McGinnity's 'Old Sal,' a ball that came in low and then sped up above the batter's knees, was a rising slant that came pretty near to being a patent—no one else had it, no one seemed able to steal it."
Source: *Baseball Magazine* (August 1913, "The Vagaries of Pitching")

Commentary: McGinnity was still pitching professionally in 1923, when he was 53, and in an interview with *Baseball Magazine* (March 1924) he attempted to explain his longevity: "All my life I have used a delivery which was easy on my arm. I have, therefore, avoided most of thc kinks and twists and wrenches which gradually wear out the ordinary pitcher's arm . . . In the days when I was in my pitching prime I used to pitch overhanded sometimes, but mostly underhanded. Underhanded pitching rests your arm. It's the natural way to pitch. Why there are not more pitchers who follow that style, I can not say. It's undoubtedly the natural way to pitch, and yet, I used to be the only underhanded pitcher of my time. There are few now. You may say Carl Mays is the only real underhanded pitcher in the Major Leagues.

"Pitchers have told me that the underhanded delivery was hard to control. I never found it so. Of the two, I believe I can control a ball pitched underhanded better than I can overhanded. Pitchers who find it difficult to control the ball are probably guilty of some other fault. They blame the delivery for their failure elsewhere.

"Most pitchers grip the baseball between the thumb and the first two fingers of the pitching hand held fairly close together. They can get the ball to curve easily enough and they can control its general direction; but the ball is likely to slip a little to one side or the other as they release it. It is that slip which makes the ball shoot from one side or the other and break away from the plate. It is that slip that makes it seem to them difficult to control the ball.

"Now, I have always avoided this danger by keeping the two fingers of my pitching hand somewhat apart. I grasp the ball firmly between my thumb and these two fingers. It could not slip to one side. I could thus control the ball without undue effort. It simply couldn't get away from me."

LYNN McGLOTHEN 6'2" 185-pound righty
86-93, 3.98, 2 Saves 1972 1982

Pitch Selection: 1. Fastball 2. Slow Curve 3. Big Curve
Source: *The Sporting News* (5/11/1974, Neal Russo)

JIM McGLOTHLIN 6'1" 185-pound righty
67-77, 3.61, 3 Saves 1965 1973

Pitches: 1. Curve 2. Fastball 3. Change
Notes: McGlothlin threw two fastballs: a straight fastball and a "tailing" fastball. His change-up had a screwball action. While working with Bob Lemon in 1967, he also experimented with a sidearm fastball.

According to Jack Zanger in *Major League Baseball—1969*, Lemon taught McGlothlin to throw a slider and a change.
Other Sources: *The Sporting News* (10/2/1971, Earl Lawson); *Putting It All Together* (Brooks Robinson with Fred Bauer, 1971)

TUG McGRAW 6'0" 170-pound lefty
96-92, 3.14, 180 Saves 1965 1984

Pitches: 1. Screwball 2. Fastball 3. Curve
McGraw: "And, since we're talking trade secrets, you throw the screwjie maybe a third of the time—at least I do. Mostly I'll throw fastballs. To put it in percentages, maybe 60 percent fastballs, 30 percent screwballs, and 10 percent curveballs. Nowadays I'm trying to break in the curveball more all the time so that I don't actually have to throw the screwball so much, and save the wear and tear on my arm. What the hell, it's just as effective if they look for the screwball and I throw the fastball."
Note: McGraw learned his screwball from Ralph Terry after the 1966 season, but it was years before the Mets would let him actually throw the pitch in games.
Source: *Screwball* (Tug McGraw and Joe Durso, 1974)

Pitches: 1. Screwball 2. Fastball 3. Slider 4. Curve
Sources: *The Relief Pitcher* (John Thorn, 1979); *The Team That Wouldn't Die* (Hal Bodley, 1981)

Note: Herm Starrette said that McGraw and Mike Cuellar threw the best screwballs he ever saw.

SCOTT McGREGOR 6'1" 190-pound lefty
138-108, 3.99, 5 Saves 1976 1988

Pitches: 1. Slow Curve 2. Fastball 3. Change
Sources: *The Scouting Report: 1987*; McGregor in *From 33rd Street to Camden Yards* (John Eisenberg, 2001)

Commentary: When McGregor came to the majors his fastball was in the high eighties (later it dropped into the low eighties), his curve and change both in the low seventies. Earl Weaver and George Bamberger decided they wanted McGregor's curve to be even slower than his change, and they went to work on it with a radar gun. Eventually they were able to get the curve down into the low sixties. Thus, McGregor's three pitches were thrown at dramatically different speeds, making it difficult to time him.

Description: "His secret: three pitches thrown at three distinctly different speeds yet by the same odd, across-the-body motion. He threw an 86-mph fastball, 73-mph changeup and 63-mph curve."
Source: *Rare Birds: A Look at the Baltimore Orioles from A to Z* (Chris Colston, 1998)

Rick Dempsey: "He changed his speeds, maybe only gave you 83–84, but he knew how to pitch. He was a very intelligent guy on the mound. Stuck to a game plan as good as you could do. With that slop that he threw up there, to win as many games as he did, he was very smart. Sometimes I didn't even know the difference between some of his pitches, but he had tremendous location . . ."
Source: Eisenberg

Quote: "Hitters around the league know about his change-up now, and Scotty has that great ability to know what they're expecting. He'll throw them the change-up anyway . . . only slower."
Source: Orioles pitching coach Ray Miller in *The Hurlers* (Kevin Kerrane, 1989)

HARRY McINTIRE 5'11" 180-pound righty
71-117, 3.22, 7 Saves 1905 1913

Pitch Selection: 1. Spitball 2. Fastball 3. Curve
Sources: unidentified clippings from the Hall of Fame Library (1908, 1909)
Quote from 1908 clipping: "The thumb stiffened so that I couldn't hold the ball as I usually do—or as all other pitchers do—but was compelled to keep the thumb close to the other fingers, holding the ball in a sort of a hook . . . I began to notice that by holding the ball in this new way I was able to obtain much better control of my spit ball."
Quote from 1909 article: ". . . the famous cuspidor curver . . . He broke [the spitball] in and out. Sometimes it had a six-inch drop and again it dropped to twelve inches . . . [McIntire said,] 'I did not learn the pitch from Stricklett. I knew of it before I came to Brooklyn . . . Why, it's as easy as a fast ball for me. A curve gives my arm a jerk . . . I don't pitch more than one or two curves in a game.' "

Note: McIntire threw sidearm.
Sources: unidentified clippings from the Hall of Fame Library (1910, 10/22/1932)

DOC McJAMES 6'2" 170-pound righty
80-80, 3.43, 3 Saves 1895 1901

Key Pitch: "Intricate Curve Ball"
Source: *Where They Ain't* (Burt Solomon, 1999). We have absolutely no idea what an "intricate" curve ball

might be, and frankly, neither does Solomon, but we're sure he got the description from somewhere.

DENNY McLAIN 6'1" 185-pound righty
131-91, 3.39, 2 Saves 1963 1972

Pitches: 1. Fastball 2. Change 3. Curve 4. Slider (1968 on)
Source: *Nobody's Perfect* (Denny McLain with Dave Diles, 1975)

Ted Williams: "He's a craftsman. He has a good overhand curve, good motion, good changeup and control, and he can spot his fastball. With that he should win quite a few games."
Source: *Kiss It Goodbye* (Shelby Whitfield, 1973)

BO McLAUGHLIN 6'5" 210-pound righty
10-20, 4.49, 9 Saves 1976 1982

Pitch Selection: 1. Slow Curve 2. Fastball
Note: McLaughlin threw with a deceptive, herky-jerky motion.
Source: *The Sporting News* (9/18/1976, Harry Shattuck)

JOEY McLAUGHLIN 6'2" 205-pound righty
29-28, 3.85, 36 Saves 1977 1984

Pitches: 1. Fastball (high-80s) 2. Knuckle Curve 3. Slider 4. Change
Sources: *The Scouting Report* (1983 and 1984 editions)

CAL McLISH 6'0" 179-pound righty
92-92, 4.01, 6 Saves 1944 1964

Pitch Selection: 1. Curve 2. Slider 3. Fastball 4. Change
Sources: *View from the Dugout* (Ed Richter, 1963); McLish quoted in *This Side of Cooperstown* (Larry Moffi, 1996)

Pitches: 1. Change 2. Sinking Fastball 3. Screwball 4. Curves 5. Slider
Comment: "It is the completeness of his game that makes him effective. He throws a fast ball that is not as fast as it was in 1944, but which moves downward, as Bob Lemon's once did, and becomes a sinker. He throws a workable slider, a combination of curves, an effective screwball (which often as not is his Uncle Charlie), and an excellent change of pace. (In spring training this year, at manager Gordon's request, Cal conducted a class on the change-up for the Cleveland pitching staff.)"
Source: *Sport* (September 1959, Irv Goodman)

Description: "McLish is noted for his ambidexterity. He throws right, but can sling them in from the left on occasion. Cal believes his control is better as a righthander but he's got more stuff as a southpaw. He throws orthodox style in actual play. The lean young Indian has an excellent curve ball and a fast one sufficiently speedy to give him a good mixture."
Source: *Pacific Coast Baseball News* (8/10/1949)

DON McMAHON 6'2" 215-pound righty
90-68, 2.96, 153 Saves 1957 1974

Pitch Selection: 1. Fastball 2. Slider
Sources: *The Sporting News* (6/29/1974, Pat Frizzell); Milwaukee Braves 1961 Media Guide

Pitch Selection: 1. Fastball 2. Curve
Source: *Late and Close: A History of Relief Pitching* (Paul Votano, 2002)

SADIE McMAHON 5'9" 165-pound righty
173-126, 3.51, 4 Saves 1889 1897

Pitch Selection: 1. High Fastball 2. Overhand Drop Ball
Source: *Nineteenth Century Stars* (SABR, 1989, article by Robert L. Tiemann)

GREG McMICHAEL 6'3" 195-pound righty
31-29, 3.25, 53 Saves 1993 2000

Pitch Selection: 1. Change 2. Fastball (high-80s) 3. Slider
Note: Throws with a sidearm delivery.
Sources: *The Scouting Notebook: 1995; The Scouting Notebook: 1996*

Pitch Selection: 1. Change 2. Slider 3. Fastball (very occasionally)
Quote: "McMichael pitches like he prays to a statue of Doug Jones."
Source: *The Scouting Notebook: 1997*

CRAIG McMURTRY 6'5" 192-pound righty
28-42, 4.08, 4 Saves 1983 1995

Pitches: 1. Fastball (high-80s) 2. Slider 3. Sinker 4. Curve 5. Change
Sources: *The Scouting Report* (1984 and 1985 editions)

Pitch Selection: 1. Fastball 2. Slider 3. Change
Source: *The Scouting Report: 1990*

DAVE McNALLY 5'11" 185-pound lefty
184-119, 3.24, 2 Saves 1962 1975

Pitches: 1. Curve 2. Fastball 3. Slider 4. Palm Ball (as Change)
Note: McNally switched to a different change in 1970.
Sources: *The Education of a Baseball Player* (Mickey Mantle with Bob Smith, 1967); Doug Brown for the Associated Press (September, 1968); *The Sporting News* (8/17/1968, Doug Brown; 9/14/1968, Brown; and 3/28/1970, Lowell Reidenbaugh)

Note: McNally's turning the corner in 1968 was widely attributed to his rediscovering his slider (or "short curve"), which he had thrown in the minor leagues, but had been unable to throw in his first few years in the majors. His slider was outstanding, although it was his third pitch until his last year or two.

Mickey Mantle: "McNally, who has just about the best curve ball in the league, will throw that curve any time, no matter what the situation."

McNally: "My change-up, though, is what might be called a palmball. Instead of gripping the ball mainly with my fingers, I hold it way back in the palm, with the fingers wrapped around it. So I throw hard, but the ball comes out dragging."
Source: *Sports Illustrated Baseball* (1972, by editors of *Sports Illustrated*)

Jim Palmer: "My ex-teammate, Dave McNally, a lefty, is one of the few three-quarter pitchers with an outstanding curve ball; I guess he was born with the ability. He throws a very hard one. Dave has some other things going for him, too: a fast ball that runs away really well from right-handed hitters and a very effective flat slider."
Source: Palmer in *Pitching* (edited by Joel H. Cohen, 1975)

GEORGE McQUILLAN 5'11" 175-pound righty
85-89, 2.38, 14 Saves 1907 1918

Description: "He had . . . as much 'stuff' as any twirler in fast company . . . has control, speed and a wise head."
Source: *Baseball Magazine* (August 1914)

HUGH McQUILLAN 6'0" 170-pound righty
88-94, 3.83, 16 Saves 1918 1927

Pitch Selection: 1. Fastball 2. Curve 3. Change
Sources: *The New York Giants* (Frank Graham, 1952) and the 1923 *Reach Guide* (Page 196)

Note: McQuillan apparently had one of the greatest pickoff moves of his time. In *Jocko* (Jocko Conlan and Robert Creamer, 1967), Conlan says, "Hughie McQuillan . . . had pitched with the Giants and then he joined the Newark team I was with in the International League. They told us that when Hughie was with the Giants and it was a close game, if the other team got a man on base in a late inning McGraw would yank his pitcher and put Hughie in. Hughie would pick the runner off base, and McGraw would send another pitcher in to finish up. It was a good story, but it seemed fantastic to me. Yet Walter Johnson did exactly that with McQuillan at Newark when I was there. He took Hughie right out of the dugout—he didn't even warm up—and sent him out to the mound. Hughie took his five or six practice pitches from the mound, and then got ready to pitch. There was a base runner on second. Boom. McQuillan caught the man off second, and then Johnson took him out. I saw it happen."

LARRY McWILLIAMS 6'5" 180-pound lefty
78-90, 3.99, 3 Saves 1978 1990

Pitches: 1. Forkball 2. Fastball 3. Curve 4. Knuckleball (occasional)
Note: McWilliams worked very fast, and learned his herky-jerky motion from Johnny Sain, his minor-league pitching coach.

Duke Snider: "McWilliams is a broadcaster's dream—he pitches as if he's double-parked. All those dips and doodles in his motion distract a hitter. With a pitcher like him, sometimes a hitter finds himself watching the motion, not the ball."
Source: *The Scouting Report: 1984*

Pitches: 1. Fastball 2. Curve 3. Slider 4. Forkball
Source: *The Scouting Report: 1987*

RUSTY MEACHAM 6'2" 180-pound righty
23-17, 4.43, 9 Saves 1991 2001

Pitch Selection: 1. Forkball 2. Slider 3. Fastball
Source: *Bill Mazeroski's Baseball* (1993 edition)

Pitch Selection: 1. Sinking Fastball 2. Slider
Source: *The Scouting Notebook: 1996*

BRIAN MEADOWS 6'3" 236-pound righty
39-51, 5.24, 1 Save 1998 2003

Pitches: 1. Fastball (87–90) 2. Slider 3. Curve 4. Change
Source: *The Scouting Notebook* (1999–2001 editions)

LEE MEADOWS 6'0" 190-pound righty
188-180, 3.37, 7 Saves 1915 1929

Pitch Selection: 1. Curve 2. Spitball
Quote: "Utilizing a sidearm delivery, Meadows' best pitch was a devastating curveball that he mixed with a spitball, still legal at the time."
Source: *Cardinals Collection: 100 Years of St. Louis Cardinals Photos* (Mark Stang, Page 34)

JIM MECIR 6'1" 230-pound righty
28-26, 3.86, 10 Saves 1995 2003

Pitches: 1. Screwball 2. Fastball (low-90s) 3. Slider 4. Split-Fingered Fastball (occasional)
Source: *The Scouting Notebook 2002*

DOC MEDICH 6'5" 225-pound righty
124-105, 3.78, 2 Saves 1972 1982

Pitch Selection: 1. Sinker 2. Slider 3. Change
Source: Richard Lally interview with baseball writer Billy Altman (6/6/2002)

JOUETT MEEKIN 6'1" 180-pound righty
156-137, 4.07, 2 Saves 1891 1900

Key Pitch: Fastball
Sources: *The Fall Classics of the 1890s* (mimeographed publication by John Phillips); *The National Game* (Alfred H. Spink, 1911)
Description: "Meekin, who throws almost all fastballs . . ."
Source: Phillips, quoting un-identified newspaper article of October 5, 1894
Quote from Spink: "[Doc] Farrell will tell you now that Meekin had more speed than any pitcher he ever caught, and he caught the whirlwind Rusie."

Hughie Jennings: "Meekin was about as fast as Rusie. Some players think he was faster, but I don't. And I know he didn't have the wonderful curve Rusie did, the fastest curve ever known and the widest. Meekin didn't have much of a curve, but he had a corking good cross fire. He was a side-arm pitcher. Rusie had a three-quarter delivery."
Source: *Baseball Magazine* (April 1923, William B. Hanna)

HEINIE MEINE 5'11" 180-pound righty
66-50, 3.95, 3 Saves 1922 1934

Pitch Selection: 1. Curve 2. Fastball 3. Change
Source: *Baseball Magazine* (March 1933, John J. Ward)

Note: Meine broke into baseball as a spitball pitcher. He was in the minor leagues, but owned by the Browns, when the spitball was banned. Failing to make the "exempt" list (pitchers allowed to continue throwing the spitter), Meine later said, meant "I had to learn pitching all over again."

CLIFF MELTON 6'5" 203-pound lefty
86-80, 3.42, 16 Saves 1937 1944

Pitch Selection: 1. Fastball 2. Curve
Source: *Baltimore Sun* (6/29/1936, Jesse A. Linthicum); *The Sporting News* (9/2/1937, Tom Meany)
Quote from Meany article: "Melton has a loose and easy wind-up, which adds greatly to his effectiveness. His fast ball is deceptive and, aided by his long stride, is on the batter before the latter is able to gauge it. Sometimes his fast one sinks sharply and other times it skips, like a stone skimmed over a millpond. Furthermore, Cliff has a crossfire which baffles left-handed hitters."

JOSE MENDEZ 5'8" 160-pound righty
NEGRO LEAGUES 1908 1926

Key Pitch: Fastball
Description: "He threw the ball with such ease that it

amounted almost to a change-of-pace. You couldn't gauge it and the ball came so fast that it was very deceptive. I would say that Mendez—and this is just a personal judgment—I would say that Mendez was faster than Smoky Joe Williams."
Source: Arthur W. Hardy in *Only the Ball Was White* (Robert Peterson, 1970)

Description: "This idea of varying the height of the ball is best shown by Mendez, the black Cuban pitcher. I have seen Mendez work three slow balls, getting a strike on each, and each a long distance from where the one before it sailed, while he does the same thing with fast deliveries."
Source: *Baseball Magazine* (August 1913, "The Vagaries of Pitching")

RAMIRO MENDOZA 6'2" 195-pound righty
57-39, 4.32, 16 Saves 1996 2003

Pitches: 1. Sinking Fastball (low-90s) 2. Slider 3. Change
Sources: *The Scouting Notebook* (1998 and 1999 editions)

Pitches: 1. Sinker 2. Fastball 3. Change
Sources: *The Scouting Notebook* (2001–2003 editions)
Note: Mendoza's four-seamer (Fastball) and change-up were mostly for show, as he depended mainly on his two-seam fastball (Sinker).

JOCK MENEFEE 6'0" 165 pound righty
58-69, 3.82, 0 Saves 1892 1903

Pitch Selection: 1. Fastball 2. Curve 3. Change
Menefee: "I used a fast ball, a curve and a slow pitch ball . . . We didn't monkey around with anything else."
Source: unidentified clipping from Hall of Fame Library (circa 1948, possibly *The Sporting News*)

JOSE MERCEDES 6'1" 180-pound righty
33-39, 4.75, 0 Saves 1994 2003

Pitch Selection: 1. Fastball (88–90) 2. Cut Fastball 3. Curve
Source: *The Scouting Notebook: 2001*

WIN MERCER 5'7" 140-pound righty
134-160, 3.97, 9 Saves 1894 1902

Pitch Selection: 1. Slow Ball 2. Fastball 3. Drop

Description: "A feature of the afternoon's practice, one of the few surprises of the training campaign at Hampton, was Winnie Mercer's wily concoction of 'slows,' 'straights,' and 'drops' in his four-inning turn at pitching."
Source: *The Washington Post* (4/9/1899, Page 8)

Description: "Mercer had only a fair amount of speed, he being of slender build, but Win had a head as long as a baseball bat which he used advantageously. Mercer developed a tantalizing slow ball, over which he had absolute control. He sandwiched it between his swift ones and many backs were strained in the endeavor to connect with his lazy floater."
Source: *Baseball Magazine* (May 1919, Edmund K. Goldsborough)

KENT MERCKER 6'1" 175-pound lefty
66-64, 4.27, 20 Saves 1989 2003

Pitches: 1. Cut Fastball (low-90s) 2. Sinking Fastball (low-90s) 3. Curve 4. Change 5. Slider
Sources: *The Scouting Notebook* (1997–2000 editions)

Pitches, 2002: 1. Fastball 2. Slider 3. Change
Note: Upon becoming a situational reliever in 2002, Mercker began dropping down to sidearm, especially against left-handed hitters.
Source: *Sports Illustrated* (4/19/2003)

JIM MERRITT 6'3" 175-pound lefty
81-86, 3.65, 7 Saves 1965 1975

Pitches: 1. Slow Curve 2. Slider 3. Fastball 4. Knuckleball (occasional)
Pete Rose: You don't really know what his best pitch is. You don't know what he is going to throw you—a one, two or three. You look for a slow curve and he'll blow a fastball by you. If he gets you thinking, he has got you. He messes your mind up."
Source: *Sport* (November 1970, John Devaney)

JOSE MESA 6'3" 170-pound righty
70-91, 4.32, 249 Saves 1987 2003

Pitches: 1. Two-Seam Sinking Fastball 2. Fastball (mid-90s) 3. Split-Fingered Fastball 4. Curve
Source: *The Scouting Notebook: 1996*

Commentary: Mesa threw four pitches as a starter, when he wasn't very successful. He became a highly successful reliever after ditching the splitter and the curve, and working with the first two pitches.

ANDY MESSERSMITH 6'1" 200-pound righty
130-99, 2.86, 15 Saves 1968 1979

Pitches: 1. Curve 2. Change 3. Fastball 4. Slider
Note: Messersmith had an excellent fastball, but always regarded himself as a breaking-ball pitcher. He always used the fastball to set up the off-speed pitches, which were also excellent. One source says that he threw two distinct change-ups.
Sources: *The Sporting News* (8/9/1969, John Wiebusch; 1/31/1970, Wiebusch; 8/29/1970, Ross Newhan; 5/15/1971, Dick Miller; 1/6/1973); *Major League Baseball: 1971* (Brenda Zanger and Dick Kaplan)

Pitches: 1. Change 2. Fastball (high-80s)
Keith Hernandez: "The guy who always amazed me because he did get by with just two pitches—thrived, in fact—was Andy Messersmith of the Dodgers and the Braves. He featured a regular fastball—I don't imagine it ever reached 90 mph—and the greatest change-up I've seen or heard about. That pitch just stunned me and a lot of other hitters. It was not a sinking change-up, either. It stayed pretty much on course, but the change of speeds was unbelievably effective. Andy was the rare pitcher who used his change-up to set up his fastball . . ."
Source: *Pure Baseball: Pitch by Pitch for the Advanced Fan* (Hernandez and Mike Bryan, 1994)

JACK MEYER 6'1" 175-pound righty
24-34, 3.92, 21 Saves 1955 1961

Pitches: 1. Fastball 2. Curve
Robin Roberts: "Jack Meyer had Nolan Ryan–type stuff with a sharp curveball to go with a blazing fastball. I remember Willie Mays wanted no part of him."
Source: *My Life in Baseball* (Robin Roberts with C. Paul Rogers III, 2003)

Note: Listed by *The Sporting News* (8/29/1956) as having one of the best fastballs in the league.

RUSS MEYER 6'1" 175-pound righty
94-73, 3.99, 5 Saves 1946 1959

Pitch Selection: 1. Overhand Curve 2. Fastball
Source: *1947 Scout Report—National League* (Wid Matthews, Page 45)

Description: "Russ Meyer had a good curveball, and he also threw one of the best screwballs in the league."
Source: Eddie Sawyer in *The Man in the Dugout* (Donald Honig, 1977)

DANNY MICELI 6'1" 185-pound righty
35-42, 4.59, 33 Saves 1993 2003

Pitch Selection: 1. Fastball (mid-90s) 2. Hard Curve
Source: *The Scouting Notebook 1999*

PETE MIKKELSEN 6'2" 210-pound righty
45-40, 3.38, 49 Saves 1964 1972

Pitch Selection: 1. Sinker 2. Palm Ball
3. Curve (added about 1970)
Sources: *The Sporting News* (6/2/1966, Page 8); *Major League Baseball: 1971* (Brenda Zanger and Dick Kaplan). Also, TSN (3/21/1964, Til Ferdenzi) cites Mikkelsen's "exceptional sinker ball."

BOB MILACKI 6'4" 230-pound righty
39-47, 4.38, 1 Save 1988 1996

Pitches: 1. Two-Seam Fastball 2. Four-Seam Fastball
3. Curve 4. Slider 5. Change
Source: *The Scouting Report: 1992*

SAM MILITELLO 6'3" 200-pound righty
4-4, 3.89, 0 Saves 1992 1993

Pitch Selection: 1. Fastball (mid-80s) 2. Slow Curve
3. Hard Curve
Description: "Possessing savvy that belies his age, Militello doesn't rattle, changes speeds expertly, and relies on two curveballs, one tantalizingly slow, the other with a harder, quicker break. Late hopping action makes his mid-80s fastball a deceptive pitch . . ."
Source: *Bill Mazeroski's Baseball* (1993 edition)

JOHNNY MILJUS 6'1" 178-pound righty
29-26, 3.92, 5 Saves 1915 1929

Pitch Selection: 1. Outstanding Fastball
2. Overhand Curve 3. Sidearm Curve
Sources: *Baseball Complete* (Russ Hodges, 1952); Carmen Hill in *Baseball Between the Wars* (Eugene Murdock, 1992)

BOB MILLER 6'3" 190-pound righty
42-42, 3.96, 15 Saves 1949 1958

Pitch Selection: 1. Sinker 2. Fastball
Sources: *The Whiz Kids and the 1950 Pennant* (Robin Roberts and C. Paul Rogers III, page 212); *Sport* (June 1964, Harry Paxton)
Note: Roberts says Miller had a "sizzling" fastball.

BOB MILLER 6'1" 180-pound righty
69-81, 3.37, 51 Saves 1957 1974

Pitch Selection: 1. Fastball 2. Palm Ball
Source: *The Pitching Staff* (Steve Jacobson, 1975)

Description: "Miller's motion is economical. His pitches are more sidearm than Marichal's, and his deceptive speed comes from a big twist of the torso toward left field just before he delivers the pitch."
Source: Roger Angell in *The New Yorker* (June 1962, and reprinted in *The Summer Game*)

FRANK MILLER 6'0" 188-pound righty
52-66, 3.01, 4 Saves 1913 1923

Key Pitch: Fastball
Quote: "He was known around the National League circuit as 'Bullet' Miller because of his fast ball."
Source: unidentified clipping from the Hall of Fame Library (9/25/1941)

Quote: "Rogers Hornsby . . . once said Miller had the fastest ball he had ever seen . . . [Miller said,] 'Carey complained that I had a half-balk move to first base that allowed me to pick so many men off base.' "
Source: *South Haven (MI) Daily Tribune* (1/22/1972)

Key Pitch: Knuckleball
Quote: "I don't think any of them had ever seen a knuckle ball before."
Source: Miller, recalling a 1913 exhibition game in the *Alleghan County (Michigan) Photo-Journal* (12/15/1971)

JAKE MILLER 6'2" 170-pound lefty
60-58, 4.09, 3 Saves 1924 1933

Key Pitch: Slow Curve
Quote: "Miller [had] a slow, deliberate motion that irked the batters as much as the stuff he put on his assortment of foolers . . . Most of the time he threw a slow curve that broke over the plate."
Source: *Chicago Tribune* (5/21/1933)

STU MILLER 5'11" 165-pound righty
105-103, 3.24, 154 Saves 1952 1968

Pitch Selection: 1. Change 2. Slow Curve 3. Fastball
Source: *The Relief Pitcher* (John Thorn, 1979); *Stan Musial* (Musial with Bob Broeg, 1964)

Quote: "There is nothing so enjoyable as watching him frustrate an opposing slugger with that head fake and his annoying assortment of slow pitches."
Source: *The Sporting News* (7/27/1963, Page 6)

Harmon Killebrew: "I could hit most pitchers, but Stu Miller was the toughest. He had such an uncanny way of changing speeds. And his motion was incredible. It was

Baltimore Orioles

Stu Miller

so different than anybody else's. I think I got two hits off him in the five years I faced him."
Source: *Splendor on the Diamond* (Rich Westcott, 2000)

Billy Pierce: "Our relief ace, Stu Miller, was amazing. He'd jerk his head and throw the ball and have these big guys swinging helplessly. He had the greatest change-up in the world, without any question."
Source: *We Played the Game* (edited by Danny Peary, 1994)

Milt Pappas: "He had three speeds for his pitches: slow, slower, and slowest. He had a phenomenal career for a guy that couldn't break a pane of glass with his fastball. He would frustrate the hell out of the hitters. His best fastball was probably about 45 miles per hour, and then it got worse. But he had a change-up curve, a regular change-up, a change-up off his fastball, and a change-up off that fastball. He would just totally frustrate hitters.

"Stu had a herky-jerky wind-up, too. He would wobble his head back and forth before releasing the ball. If the hitter was watching him, the poor schmuck didn't have a chance of hitting the ball."
Source: *Out at Home* (Pappas with Wayne Mausser and Larry Names, 2000)

Frank Robinson: ". . . I still don't see how Stu Miller threw the ball that soft and got it to home plate. It was unbelievable. If it wasn't the best change-up ever, it was one of the best. Because hitters knew what was coming, and they still couldn't hit it. Then he'd jam them with his seventy-five-mile-per-hour fastball."

Dick Hall: "Stu Miller had the best change-up ever. He held it just like a fastball, and right at the last second he was able to break his wrist backwards so he had that real good fastball arm motion, and the ball had a fastball spin, but it never got there. They'd sit around waiting for the change-up, but it took so long to get there that they went on and swung anyway. Then he'd pop the fastball. He was really good."
Source: *From 33rd Street to Camden Yards* (John Eisenberg, 2001)

Note: A poll of 645 players in the book *Players' Choice* (Eugene V. McCaffrey and Roger A. McCaffrey, 1987) lists Miller's changeup as the greatest ever.

TRAVIS MILLER 6'3" 215-pound lefty
7-18, 5.05, 1 Save 1996 2002

Pitches: 1. Fastball (89–90) 2. Slider 3. Change (occasional)
Source: *The Scouting Notebook: 2001*

ALAN MILLS 6'1" 190-pound righty
39-32, 4.12, 15 Saves 1990 2001

Pitches: 1. Slider 2. Fastball 3. Sinker (added 1998)
Sources: *The Scouting Report: 1993; The Scouting Notebook 1999*

LEFTY MILLS 6'1" 187-pound lefty
15-30, 6.06, 2 Saves 1934 1940

Pitch Selection: 1. Fastball 2. Curve
Description: "Mills is a steel-nerved, easy-working pitcher with a loose side-arm delivery. He has a zippy fast one, which he frequently throws from a three-quarter over-hand delivery. He also shoots the fast ball from the side-arm angle, mixing it up with a sneaky curve. His deliberate style reminds older fans somewhat of Tom Zachary's when the latter was south-pawing."
Source: *The Sporting News* (9/15/1938, Dick Farrington)

Description: "He's big, strong and has his greatest control while pitching side-armed. He has a strong tendency to become wild when pitching over-handed, but usually managed to strike out more than he walked, which is a test of any good pitcher's control."
Source: *Baseball Magazine* (April 1939, Charlie Casper)

KEVIN MILLWOOD 6'4" 205-pound righty
89-58, 3.78, 0 Saves 1997 2003

Pitches: 1. Fastball 2. Hard Slider 3. Change 4. Curve
Source: *The Scouting Notebook 2000*

Pitches: 1. Four-Seam Fastball 2. Two-Seam Fastball 3. Cut Fastball 4. Slider 5. 12-to-6 Curve
Quote: "He will ride his hard slider in on the thumbs of lefthanders. He uses his four-seamer for consistent first-pitch strikes and as an out pitch. He challenges right-handed hitters inside with either a four-seamer or a two-seamer, preferring the heavy two-seamer. He chal-

lenges lefthanded hitters down and in with a hard slider. He mainly uses his four-seamer, sinker and cutter during the early innings, breaking balls in the middle innings and fastballs again in innings 6 and 7. He mixes his pitches well. He shows a loose motion from a three-quarters arm slot; he sometimes goes to a high three-quarters arm slot from a high overhand windup. He began using the high windup during the 2002 season to work out a kink in his delivery. His beefy trunk is that of a workhorse. He forces hitters to put the ball in play and get themselves out."
Source: Scouting report by scout Lewis Shaw in *The Sporting News* (6/2/2003)

Note: In his no-hitter on April 27, 2003, 81 of Millwood's 108 pitches were fastballs.
Source: Associated Press game account (Ron Maaddi, 4/28/2003)

AL MILNAR 6'2" 195-pound lefty
57-58, 4.22, 7 Saves 1936 1946

Key Pitch: Slider
Phil Rizzuto: "When I came up in 1941, Al Milnar of Cleveland was the only pitcher who threw the slider regularly."
Source: *New York Times* (Joe Durso in September, 1968)

ERIC MILTON 6'3" 225-pound lefty
57-51, 4.76, 0 Saves 1988 2003

Pitches: 1. Fastball (low-90s) 2. Curve 3. Slider
4. Change
Source: *The Scouting Notebook* (1999–2003 editions)

STEVE MINGORI 5'10" 165-pound lefty
18-33, 3.03, 42 Saves 1970 1979

Pitch Selection, early '70s: 1. Sinking Fastball 2. Slider
Pitches, late '70s: 1. Sinking Fastball 2. Screwball
3. Knuckle Curve
Source: *The Sporting News* (8/7/1976, Sid Bordman)
Mingori in *The Sporting News:* "Whitey [Herzog] told me not to try to throw too hard, and I think he's serious. My fast ball has to sink. I can't say I've got a good fast ball—but I guess it's sneaky. I'm a corner pitcher. I try never to give the hitter the middle of the plate."

PAUL MINNER 6'5" 200-pound lefty
69-84, 3.94, 10 Saves 1946 1956

Key Pitch prior to 1949 injury: Fastball
Pitches, beginning 1950: 1. Hard Curve
2. Slow Curve 3. Palm Ball 4. Fastball
5. Screwball 6. Blooper (occasional)
Source: *The New Era Cubs* (Eddie Gold and Art Ahrens, 1985)

GREG MINTON 6'2" 180-pound righty
59-65, 3.10, 150 Saves 1975 1990

Pitches: 1. Sinker 2. Fastball 3. Change 4. Slider
Source: *The Scouting Report: 1990*

Description: "Sinkerball specialist . . ."
Source: *The Complete Handbook of Baseball: 1982 Season* (edited by Zander Hollander)

PAUL MIRABELLA 6'1" 190-pound lefty
19-29, 4.45, 13 Saves 1978 1990

Pitch Selection: 1. Fastball (83–84) 2. Curve 3. Slider
Source: *The Scouting Report: 1983*

CLARENCE MITCHELL 5'11" 190-pound lefty
125-139, 4.12, 9 Saves 1911 1932

Pitch Selection: 1. Spitball 2. Fastball
3. Curve (occasional)
4. Knuckleball (added in 1931)
Note: Mitchell was one of the "grandfathered" pitchers allowed to continue to throw the spitball after it was otherwise banned in 1921.
Sources: 1924 *Reach Guide* (Page 48); 1923 *Reach Guide* (Page 38); *The Cincinnati Reds* (Lee Allen, 1948); *Baseball Magazine* (March 1932, William E. Brandt article about knuckleball pitchers)
Quote from 1924 *Reach Guide:* "Mitchell uses it [the spitball] almost exclusively . . . He said, for example, that if he had pitched 120 balls during the game 75 or 80 of them were 'spitters.' A majority of the remainder were fast balls while a few were curves."

WILLIE MITCHELL 6'0" 176-pound lefty
84-92, 2.88, 4 Saves 1909 1919

Pitch Selection: 1. Fastball 2. Curve

Description: "Willie is a southpaw with a wonderful curve ball and plenty of speed."
Source: unidentified clipping from the Hall of Fame Library (December 1914)

Description: "He is a left-hander, with a lot of speed but wild."
Source: *The Sporting News* (8/17/1916)

VINEGAR BEND MIZELL 6'3" 205-pound lefty
90-88, 3.85, 0 Saves 1952 1962

Pitch Selection: 1. Fastball 2. Sweeping Curve
Source: *Diamond Greats* (Rich Westcott, 1988)

Note: Listed by *The Sporting News* (8/29/1956) as having one of the best fastballs in the league.

DAVE MLICKI 6'4" 185-pound righty
66-80, 4.72, 1 Save 1992 2002

Pitches: 1. Sinking Fastball (low-90s) 2. Curve 3. Knuckle Curve 4. Slider 5. Change
Source: *The Scouting Report* (1996–1998 editions)

Pitches: 1. Fastball (low-90s) 2. Curve 3. Change 4. Slider
Source: *The Scouting Notebook* (1999–2001 editions)

Pitches: 1. Slider 2. Fastball (high-80s) 3. Change 4. Curve
Source: *The Scouting Notebook: 2002*

BRIAN MOEHLER 6'3" 235-pound righty
50-56, 4.57, 0 Saves 1996 2003

Pitches: 1. Cut Fastball 2. Sinker (88–90) 3. Change 4. Slider
Sources: *The Scouting Notebook* (1998, 1999, 2002, and 2003 editions)

RANDY MOFFITT 6'3" 190-pound righty
43-52, 3.65, 96 Saves 1972 1983

Pitch Selection: 1. Fastball 2. Slider
Note: Moffitt threw overhand, sidearm, and three-quarters.
Source: *The Sporting News* (5/11/1974, Pat Frizzell)

GEORGE MOGRIDGE 6'2" 165-pound lefty
132-131, 3.23, 20 Saves 1911 1927

Pitch Selection: 1. Fastball 2. Curve
Source: *The No-Hit Hall of Fame* (Rich Coberly, 1985)

Comment: "[Mogridge] is an adept at 'getting the goat' of a batsman by compelling him to wait for unduly long periods between deliveries. He has learned that an over-anxious hitter is the easiest to dispose of."
Source: 1925 *Reach Guide* (Francis C. Richter)

MIKE MOHLER 6'2" 208-pound lefty
14-27, 4.99, 10 Saves 1993 2001

Pitches: 1. Sinker 2. Forkball 3. Change 4. Fastball (occasional)
Source: *The Scouting Notebook: 1996*

DALE MOHORCIC 6'3" 220-pound righty
16-21, 3.49, 33 Saves 1986 1990

Pitches: 1. Sinker 2. Fastball 3. Curve 4. Slider
Source: *The Scouting Report: 1987*

BILL MONBOUQUETTE 5'11" 190-pound righty
114-112, 3.68, 3 Saves 1958 1968

Pitch Selection: 1. Fastball 2. Slider 3. Curve
Source: Monbouquette quoted in *The No-Hit Hall of Fame* (Rich Coberly, 1985)

Note: In the January 1963 issue, *Baseball Digest* said that Monbouquette has the best slider in the American League.

SID MONGE 6'2" 185-pound lefty
49-40, 3.53, 56 Saves 1975 1984

Pitches: 1. Fastball 2. Slider 3. Curve 4. Screwball
Source: *The Scouting Report: 1984*

JOHN MONTEFUSCO 6'1" 180-pound righty
90-83, 3.54, 5 Saves 1974 1986

Pitch Selection, before 1977 ankle injury: 1. Fastball 2. Slider/Slurve
Pitch Selection, after ankle injury: 1. Sinker 2. Change 3. Forkball
Note: Montefusco pitched a no-hitter at the end of the 1976 season, and said afterward that 92 of his 97 pitches

had been sinking fastballs. And many years later, he told interviewer Bill Ballew, "Frank Funk taught me a sinker and that was the first day that I used it. I got a lot of ground balls, and I did not have my best stuff that day."
Source: Montefusco in *The Pastime in the Seventies* (Bill Ballew, 2002)

RICH MONTELEONE 6'2" 214-pound righty
24-17, 3.87, 0 Saves 1987 1996

Pitch Selection: 1. Fastball 2. Slider 3. Change
Source: *The Scouting Report: 1993*

JEFF MONTGOMERY 5'11" 170-pound righty
46-52, 3.27, 304 Saves 1987 1999

Pitches: 1. Fastball 2. Slider 3. Curve 4. Change
Source: *The Scouting Report: 1992*

Montgomery: "My best pitch was a strike. I don't know that I had one pitch that was better for a strike than any other. If I had to narrow it down, I got more quality outs over my career on a slider."
Source: *Kansas City Star* (12/5/2002, Bob Dutton)

Commentary: Montgomery was very odd, in that he was the only relief ace we know of who was a four-pitch pitcher throughout his career. Most relief aces work with one or two key pitches, because they have to know what's working when they hit the mound. Montgomery had no key pitch; he had a different pattern to each hitter.

CY MOORE 6'1" 178-pound righty
16-26, 4.86, 3 Saves 1929 1934

Pitch Selection: 1. Fastball 2. Curve 3. Knuckleball
Source: *The Sporting News* (3/17/1932)

DONNIE MOORE 6'0" 185-pound righty
43-40, 3.67, 89 Saves 1975 1988

Pitches: 1. Fastball 2. Hard Forkball 3. Slurve 4. Change
Source: *The Scouting Report: 1987*

EARL MOORE 6'0" 195-pound righty
162-154, 2.78, 7 Saves 1901 1914

Pitch Selection: 1. Sidearm Curve 2. Fastball

Comment: "Earl Moore was a pitcher of the Philadelphia National League team, and his reputation still remains as the most famous crossfire pitcher in major league history."
Moore: "Even pitchers seldom shift their position. They rely absolutely on curves and change of pace. Both are essential to success, but how much better they might succeed if they would only change from one side of the pitcher's plate to the other. That is what constitutes the crossfire, in addition to the ability to stand with one foot on the extreme corner of the plate and step out and deliver the ball at the same time."
Source: *How to Pitch* (J.E. Wray, 1928)

Note: Moore threw with a cross-fire delivery, and has been credited with originating it.
Source: *The Cleveland Indians* (Franklin Lewis, 1949)

LLOYD (WHITEY) MOORE
6'1" 195-pound righty
30-29, 3.75, 4 Saves 1936 1942

Pitch Selection: 1. Fastball 2. Curve (occasional)
Note: Moore switched from sidearm to an overhand delivery in 1938.
Source: *Baseball Magazine* (May 1939, Stan Witwer)

MIKE MOORE 6'4" 205-pound righty
161-176, 4.39, 2 Saves 1982 1995

Pitch Selection: 1. Sinking Fastball 2. Forkball (1989 on)
Source: *The Scouting Report: 1990*

Pitch Selection, 1992: 1. Forkball 2. Slider 3. Fastball
Source: *Bill Mazeroski's Baseball* (1993 edition)

RAY MOORE 6'0" 195-pound righty
63-59, 4.06, 46 Saves 1952 1963

Pitch Selection: 1. Fastball or Curve 3. Slider
Sources: *The Ballplayers* (1990, article by Norman Macht); *Baseball Digest* (Dec.–Jan. 1961, Page 44)

WILCY MOORE 6'0" 195-pound righty
51-44, 3.70, 49 Saves 1927 1933

Key Pitch: Sinking Fastball
Source: *Babe Ruth's Own Book of Baseball* (Ruth, 1928)
Quote: "Cy Moore owed his relief success to his strange

sinker, which he never could explain. It was a natural delivery and he really did not know how to throw it."
Source: *Baseball Magazine* (September 1937, Daniel M. Daniel)

BOB MOOSE 6'0" 200-pound righty
76-71, 3.50, 19 Saves 1967 1976

Pitch Selection: 1. Fastball 2. Slider
3. Knuckleball (as Change, developed in 1969)
Note: As a 20-year-old kid in August 1968, Moose was caught applying pine tar to the ball.
Sources: *The Sporting News* (8/10/1968, Les Biederman); *Pittsburgh Press* (8/31/1968, Biederman); *The Sporting News* (11/29/1969, Charley Feeney)

Description: "[Moose is] not overpoweringly fast (but) has an excellent slider."
Source: *Major League Baseball—1969* (Jack Zanger)

LEW MOREN 5'11" 150-pound righty
48-57, 2.95, 3 Saves 1903 1910

Key Pitch: Knuckleball
Quote: "The knuckle ball got a bad advertisement, Moren, its inventor, being knocked out in the fifth inning."
Source: *The Unforgettable Season* (G.H. Fleming, Page 43)

ROGER MORET 6'4" 170-pound lefty
47-27, 3.66, 12 Saves 1970 1978

Pitch Selection: 1. Fastball 2. Slow Curve 3. Change
Description: "When Rogelio Moret pitches, he looks like he is falling out of a tree. But the tall, floppy lefthander with a ragdoll arm has the ability to throw a ball hard . . . very hard."
Source: *The Sporting News* (11/2/1974, Peter Gammons)
Other Sources: *The Sporting News* (8/11/1973, Larry Claflin); *Boston Record* (8/28/1971, Fred Ciampa)

CY MORGAN 6'0" 175-pound righty
79-78, 2.51, 3 Saves 1903 1913

Key Pitch: Spitball
Sources: *Connie Mack* (Fred Lieb, 1945); 1911 *Reach Guide* (Page 223); *The National Game* (Alfred H. Spink, 1911)
Quote from Spink: "Morgan uses the spit ball with tremendous speed. He is also a fine fielding pitcher . . . he is now one of the steadiest as well as one of the speediest pitchers in the business."

MIKE MORGAN 6'3" 195-pound righty
141-186, 4.23, 8 Saves 1978 2002

Pitches: 1. Fastball (88–90) 2. Overhand Curve
3. Slider 4. Change
Source: *The Scouting Report* (1983, 1984, and 1987 editions)

Pitches: 1. Fastball 2. Change 3. Slider 4. Curve
Source: *Tom Seaver's Scouting Notebook* (1989 and 1990 editions); *The Scouting Report: 1990*

Pitches: 1. Two-Seam Fastball 2. Four-Seam Fastball
3. Slider
Description: "He displayed command of his two fastballs, and his slider was continually beaten into the ground, making Morgan the third most frequent groundball pitcher in the league behind teammate [Greg] Maddux and the Giants' Bill Swift. The two-seam fastball that he has used to great success the last three seasons was moving well all year . . ."
Source: *The Scouting Report: 1993*
Other Sources: *The Scouting Report* (1992 and 1994 editions)

Pitches: 1. Slow Curve 2. Sinking Fastball 3. Curve
4. Slider 5. Change
Source: *The Scouting Report: 1995*

Pitch Selection: 1. Fastball (low-90s) 2. Sinker
3. Slider
Source: *The Scouting Notebook 1998*

TOM MORGAN 6'1" 180-pound righty
67-47, 3.61, 64 Saves 1951 1963

Key Pitch: Sinking Fastball
Source: *Dynasty* (Peter Golenbock, 1975)

ED MORRIS 5'7" 165-pound lefty
171-122, 2.82, 1 Save 1884 1890

Pitch Selection: 1. Fastball 2. Curve 3. Change

Source: *Nineteenth Century Stars* (SABR, 1989, article by Robert L. Tiemann)

JACK MORRIS 6'3" 195-pound righty
254-186, 3.90, 0 Saves 1977 1994

Pitch Selection, 1977–1981: 1. Fastball (94) 2. Slider (89)
Pitch Selection, 1982: 1. Fastball (88–89) 2. Slider (83–84) 3. Change
Pitch Selection, after 1982: 1. Fastball 2. Slider 3. Forkball
Sources: Roger Craig quoted in *Baseball Digest* (July 1983, Peter Gammons); *The Scouting Report* (1987 and 1990 editions); *Inside Sports* (February 1992, Page 52)

Quote: "Fastball has been clocked at 94 mph."
Source: *The Complete Handbook of Baseball: 1982 Season* (edited by Zander Hollander)

JIM MORRIS 6'3" 215-pound lefty
0-0, 4.80, 0 Saves 1999 2000

Pitches: 1. Fastball (mid-90s) 2. Slider
Source: documentary about Morris included on *The Rookie* DVD
Note: In 1999, Morris became the oldest pitcher to make his major-league debut since Diomedes Olivo in 1960.

MATT MORRIS 6'5" 220-pound righty
72-42, 3.28, 4 Saves 1997 2003

Pitches: 1. Four-Seam Fastball (mid-90s) 2. Two-Seam Fastball 3. Overhand Curve 4. Straight Change
Source: *The Scouting Notebook: 2001*

JOHNNY MORRISON 5'11" 188-pound righty
103-80, 3.65, 19 Saves 1920 1930

Pitch Selection: 1. Curve 2. Fastball
Sources: *Babe Ruth's Own Book of Baseball* (Ruth, 1928); *The Cincinnati Reds* (Lee Allen, 1948); 1924 *Reach Guide* (Pages 47–48); 1926 *Reach Guide; Baseball Magazine* (September 1923)

Quote: "Zack Wheat, the Brooklyn Captain who ought to know pitching when he sees it, says that Morrison has the best curve ball since Mordecai Brown . . .

"Morrison does not use his curve ball exclusively by any means. He has a good fast ball. But he delights to give the batter who is expecting a fastball one of his dizzying curves. It is a most effective delivery."
Source: *Baseball Magazine* (September 1923, John J. Ward)

Note: Morrison's "jughandle" curve was one of the most famous pitches of the 1920s.

CARL MORTON 6'0" 200-pound righty
87-92, 3.73, 1 Save 1969 1976

Pitch Selection: 1. Fastball 2. Screwball (developed in 1975) 3. Straight Change (developed in 1975)
Source: *The Sporting News* (8/9/1975, Wayne Minshew)

GUY MORTON 6'1" 175-pound righty
98-88, 3.13, 6 Saves 1914 1924

Pitch Selection: 1. Curve 2. Fastball
Sources: unidentified clippings from the Hall of Fame Library (May 1915); *Baseball Magazine* (August 1915); *The Sporting Life* (9/4/1915 and 7/8/1916); press release (June 1916); *Florence (AL) Times* (10/18/1934); *Lorain (OH) Morning Journal* (7/18/2001); *Baseball Digest* (May 1946, Al Wolf)

Description: ". . . Morton has about as much speed as any pitcher in the American League, except of course, for Johnson."
Source: *Baseball Magazine* (October 1918, "Who's Who on the Diamond")

Description: "[He] still looked good because of his great speed and his curve, which is said to break faster than that of any pitcher in the league."
Source: unidentified clipping from the Hall of Fame Library (May 1915)

Story: "In slipping the three-strike knockout to Boone the other day here, Guy Morton showed something new, according to Boone and others. With two strikes and two balls on Lute, Guy took a long windup and then cut loose with an underhand delivery, throwing the ball much the same way a small boy 'skips' a rock on the surface of the water. The ball took a crazy break, up and out, and Boone missed his swing by a foot or more. 'I don't know what that ball was,' confessed catcher Steve O'Neill after the game. 'I signed for a fast one and that's

what he gave me.' Morton himself was just as much at a loss to explain the freak ball. 'I just took a notion to cut loose with an underhand ball,' confessed Guy, 'and I was certainly surprised to see the funny break I got on it.' However, there's not much danger that Guy's going to be allowed to bother much with that ball, for it's delivered with a jerky motion that it is bound to be wearing on the arm."
Source: *The Sporting Life* (9/4/1915), quoting a Cleveland writer

Description: "He has wonderful speed, some perfect curves, great control and, in baseball parlance, 'a noodle.' "
Source: press release (June 1916)

Quote: "The raw-boned Alabama youth had terrific speed, but all he knew was to stand there on the rubber and burn his fast boy through . . . He has developed into a hurler who knows all the tricks of the trade."
Source: *The Sporting Life* (7/8/1916)

Quote: "Known for a devastating curveball and a fastball that baseball people from that era compared with Walter Johnson."
Source: *Lorain (OH) Morning Journal* (7/18/2001)

Note: When asked, in 1946, who had the best curve he ever saw, Ted Lyons responded, "Walter Beall, Pete Appleton and Guy Morton. The first two had trouble getting their hooks over the plate, though."
Source: *Baseball Digest* (May 1946, Al Wolf)

DON MOSSI 6'1" 195-pound lefty
101-80, 3.43, 50 Saves 1954 1965

Pitches, up to 1960: 1. Curve 2. Fastball 3. Slider
Pitches, in 1960s: 1. Curve 2. Slider 3. Fastball 4. Change
Sources: *The Dallas Morning News* (April 1952, Bill Rives); *Baseball Digest* (October 1955, Hal Lebovitz); *The Sporting News* (4/1/1959, Hal Middlesworth)

Commentary: Mossi's fastball and curve were both outstanding, and as a reliever he didn't need anything else, although he did experiment with a slider.

Note: Listed by *The Sporting News* (8/29/1956) as having one of the best fastballs in the league.

FRANK MOUNTAIN 5'11" 185-pound righty
58-83, 3.47, 1 Save 1880 1886

Pitch Selection: 1. Fastball 2. Curve
Quote: "He has a swift delivery, coupled with a remarkable command of the ball, somewhat resembling in that respect [Jim] Whitney, the Boston phenomenal pitcher. He does not depend entirely on his speed, but has some very clever curves."
Source: *New York Clipper* (10/14/1882)

JAMIE MOYER 6'0" 170-pound lefty
185-132, 4.07, 0 Saves 1986 2003

Pitches: 1. Fastball 2. Change 3. Other Change 4. Slow, Sweeping Curve 5. Sharper Curve
Sources: *The Scouting Report: 1990*; *The Scouting Notebook* (1997 and 2000 editions)

Notes: When Moyer won 12 games in 1987 his fastball was in the high 80s. By the time he emerged with Seattle almost ten years later, it was in the low to mid eighties.

According to the *Seattle Times* (10/15/2001), Moyer in 2001 threw 50 percent fastballs, 28 percent changeups, 14 percent sliders, and eight percent curves. According to the same article, Moyer threw three fastballs: a four-seamer thrown 85–87 miles per hour, a two-seam sinker thrown 83–85, and a cutter thrown 82–84. His curve was slow with an 11-to-5 break, and his slider was actually a slurve, thrown 72–78 mph. His changeup had a slight sink to it.

Two seasons later, Moyer's velocity was down yet further, with his fastball topping out at 84 miles an hour.

Jerry Hairston: "Normally, guys are throwing in the mid-90s and the changeup is like 85 or 84. That is his fastball. His changeup I saw a couple times at 72. That's more like a double changeup. You see it and go after it to attack the ball and it's not there yet."
Source: Hairston quoted in AP story on Mariners-Orioles game, 5/26/2002

Description: "Jamie Moyer is the unusual lefthander who actually is more effective against righthanded batters. Lefthanders can take away his best pitch—the changeup—because it has a tendency to fade down and in to them, exactly where many like the ball. Moyer also has trouble throwing his cutter to lefties; he tends to leave it up in the strike zone when he tries to get it inside.

"Against righthanders, he trusts the change enough to throw it high and away. He can throw it with a stiff or loose wrist, which can vary the movement from dive-and-fade to dive-and-cut. Because he also can change speeds on the changeup, he can turn one pitch into three or four. He's not afraid to throw the changeup—or any of his pitches, for that matter—on any count, and he uses the change as his No. 1 out pitch.

"He has definite pitching patterns: Against righties, he works away on the first couple of pitches, then comes inside; he starts lefties off away, then tries to go backdoor for the second strike."

Source: Scout Lewis Shaw in *The Sporting News* (8/25/2003)

Jason Giambi: "He will throw that changeup at any time in the count, and there aren't a lot of guys who will do that. It's harder to play the game within the game with Jamie because he's not afraid to throw that pitch at any time. Even if he throws what I'm looking for, it might be at a different speed or location."

Source: *The Sporting News* (8/25/2003, Stan McNeal)

HUGH MULCAHY 6'2" 190-pound righty
45-89, 4.49, 9 Saves 1935 1947

Pitch Selection, pre-1937: 1. Fastball 2. Fast Curve 3. Hard Sinker

Pitch Selection, post-1937: 1. Fastball 2. Slower Curve 3. Change 4. Sinker

Source: *Baseball Magazine* (February 1940)

Billy Herman: "Of course, there were certain kinds of pitchers who gave me a lot of trouble, and I would remember them. I always had trouble with the right-handed, sinkerball pitchers. Thank God, there weren't a lot of them around. Guys like Bucky Walters, Hal Schumacher, and Hugh Mulcahy gave me trouble. I never really knew how to hit the sinker."

Source: *Splendor on the Diamond* (Rich Westcott, 2000)

Note: When he came to the majors, Mulcahy threw "half underhand" and threw everything hard. In 1937, Jimmie Wilson converted Mulcahy to a three-quarters delivery, and taught him to vary the speed on his pitches.

TERRY MULHOLLAND 6'3" 200-pound lefty
119-131, 4.37, 5 Saves 1986 2003

Pitch Selection, 1988–1993: 1. Sinking Fastball 2. Slider

Pitch Selection, 1994–forward: 1. Slider 2. Change 3. Split-Fingered Fastball 4. Fastball

Sources: *The Scouting Notebook 1997* and *2000; The Scouting Report: 1992*

Note: Mulholland had the best pickoff move of his generation, and was almost impossible to run against.

TONY MULLANE 5'11" 165-pound righty
287-214, 3.05, 14 Saves 1881 1894

Pitch Selection: 1. Fastball 2. Drop Ball

Source: *Nineteenth Century Stars* (SABR, 1989, article by Dennis Goldstein, L. Bob Davids, and Lefty Blasco)

Quote: " 'The answer to the effectiveness of Mullane was his violation of all pitching rules. He threw from the shoulder every time but the appeals of Cuthbert were treated with utter contempt by the umpire and yells and hoots from the hoodlums.' "

Source: *Baseball (1882) From the Newspaper Accounts* (Preston D. Orem, 1966)

Note: Pitched with both hands on July 18, 1882, June 5, 1892, and July 14, 1893.

GEORGE MULLIN 5'11" 188-pound righty
227-196, 2.82, 8 Saves 1902 1915

Pitch Selection: 1. Fastball 2. Curve

Sources: *Baseball's Famous Pitchers* (Ira L. Smith, 1954); *The National Game* (Alfred H. Spink, 1910)

Description: ". . . [H]e mostly was a fast ball pitcher with a good curve. He didn't do as much with the ball as a lot of other fellows did in those days. George used more straight stuff than most of the others."

Source: Tigers catcher Oscar Stanage in *Baseball Digest* (August 1952, Lyall Smith)

Quote from Spink: "Keen baseball men now rank Mullin with Mordecai Brown, Christy Mathewson and William Dinneen, three of the greatest pitchers that ever curved a ball over the plate."

Quote: "All curves are developments of the 'barrel hoop,' the same principle entering into each, whether it is Mordecai Brown's marvelous 'hook' curve, George Mullin's meteoric shoot, or the wonderful curves of Camnitz, Overall, Wiltse, Krause, Adams, Ferguson, and others."
Source: *Touching Second* (John J. Evers and Hugh S. Fullerton, 1910)

BOB MUNCRIEF 6'2" 190-pound righty
80-82, 3.80, 9 Saves 1937 1951

Pitch Selection: 1. Fastball 2. Sharp Curve 3. Change
Sources: *Baseball Magazine* (August 1943, Clifford Bloodgood); *The Great Rivalry* (Ed Linn, 1991)
Quote from Bloodgood article: "Muncrief is something of a pitching oddity in that he doesn't fool around with any sinkers or sliders, or butterfly or fork balls that are so much in vogue . . . he depends on nothing but good, old fashioned, orthodox stuff."

Quote: "The big difference now is the slider, which was just coming in when I was pitching. A few pitchers had it back then—Bob Muncrief, he was one of them. We called it the short curve."
Source: Ray Scarborough in *Five Seasons* (Roger Angell, 1977)

RED MUNGER 6'2" 200-pound righty
77-56, 3.83, 12 Saves 1943 1956

Pitches: 1. Fastball 2. Curves 3. Change 4. Slider
Quote: "The tobacco-chewing strikeout artist relies chiefly on his fast ball, but mixes it up with curves, a change of pace, and a slider."
Source: *Baseball Magazine* (October 1947, Ellis J. Veach)

Pitch Selection against Jackie Robinson: 1. Slider 2. Cut Fastball
Munger: "I tried to get Jackie out with good sliders and a cut fastball. I would pitch him up and in and then go away with the slider."
Source: Munger in *Jackie Robinson: A Life Remembered* (Maury Allen, 1987)

Stan Musial: "Red Munger was older than the book showed, I'm sure, and that, plus the weight he put on, accounted for the fact he went pretty quickly. Munger had good stuff and an exceptionally good pickoff motion for a right-handed pitcher, but he was a happy-go-lucky guy who lacked the killer instinct."
Source: *Stan Musial: The Man's Own Story* (Musial, as told to Bob Broeg, 1964); if Munger was lying about his age, nobody's yet found him out.

VAN MUNGO 6'2" 185-pound righty
120-115, 3.47, 16 Saves 1931 1945

Pitch Selection: 1. Fastball 2. Curve
Source: *Baseball's Famous Pitchers* (Ira L. Smith, 1954)

Comment: "Probably, he is faster than any other pitcher in the major leagues today. On an off-day last season, he went up to West Point with a party of pitchers, among them Lefty Gomez, to have his speed measured by the apparatus used at the military academy to test the speed of bullets. Gomez made a creditable showing—but Mungo, when he cut loose, almost broke the machine."
Source: *Baseball Magazine* (May 1935, Tommy Holmes); this is the earliest mention we've found of somebody trying to scientifically measure the speed of a pitch.

Comment: "There is the case of Van Lingle Mungo, the Brooklyn Ace. Tested by a mechanism which registered the speed of swiftly moving objects, Mungo's fast ball outstripped that of all competitors. He is regarded, and justly we think, as the speediest fast ball pitcher in the National League. Not only has he tremendous speed, but he has developed a smoking curve that breaks down, knee high. Burleigh Grimes is the authority for the statement that this curve is almost unhittable. Why isn't Mungo another Dazzy Vance?"
Source: F.C. Lane in *Baseball Magazine* (November 1937)

Al Lopez: "Of all the pitchers I caught, I believe the fastest was Mungo. The trouble was that Mungo's ball didn't move. It came in straight as a string. So, when he got a little tired in the late innings, the batter would catch up with him and knock him out."
Source: *Legends of Baseball* (Walter M. Langford, 1987)

Quote: "If there was one pitcher that I really didn't want to face, it was Brooklyn's Van Lingle Mungo. Oh, was he fast! He threw bullets! Bob Feller was just as fast, but Feller had better control than Van Mungo . . ."

Source: Pinky May in *Dugout to Foxhole* (Rick Van Blair, 1994)

Description: "There wasn't another pitcher in the National League who had speed that could match Mungo's. How he poured his fast balls up to hitters! Going through his wind-up he would raise his long and powerful left leg 'way up and his strong right arm would send a ball hurtling toward the plate with the speed of a rifle shot. It wasn't pleasant for hitters to swing against the smoke balls he fired and he would glare at any batsman who did make a hit off his delivery."
Source: *Baseball Magazine* (September 1940, Edward T. Murphy, "Brooklyn's Forgotten Man")

MIKE MUNOZ 6'2" 190-pound lefty
18-20, 5.19, 11 Saves 1989 2000

Pitch Selection: 1. Screwball 2. Fastball 3. Change
Sources: *1995 Baseball Almanac; The Scouting Notebook 2000*

STEVE MURA 6'2" 188-pound righty
30-39, 4.00, 5 Saves 1978 1985

Pitch Selection: 1. Fastball 2. Overhand Curve 3. Slider 4. Slow Curve
Source: *The Scouting Report: 1983*

MASANORI MURAKAMI 6'0" 180-pound lefty
5-1, 3.44, 9 Saves 1964 1965

Pitches: 1. Curve 2. Fastball
Murakami: "I throw fast ball and curve. But no change. The change-up no good. Relief pitcher come in, men on bases. Throw change. Boom! Long ball. No good!"
Source: *The Sporting News* (9/19/1964, Bob Stevens)

Quote: "He showed me a major league curve from the start. It breaks big and it breaks fast."
Source: Fresno manager Bill Werle in *The Sporting News* (10/3/1964, Jack McDonald)

JOHNNY MURPHY 6'2" 190-pound righty
93-53, 3.50, 107 Saves 1932 1947

Pitch Selection: 1. Curve 2. Fastball 3. Change
Source: *The Relief Pitcher* (John Thorn, 1979)

ROB MURPHY 6'2" 200-pound lefty
32-38, 3.64, 30 Saves 1985 1995

Pitch Selection: 1. Fastball 2. Slider
Source: *The Scouting Report: 1990*

TOM MURPHY 6'3" 185-pound righty
68-101, 3.78, 59 Saves 1968 1979

Pitch Selection: 1. Curve 2. Fastball
Ted Simmons: "Murph had a really fine curveball, that was his best pitch, and he had a fastball."
Source: phone interview with Simmons (10/8/2002, Rob Neyer)

DALE MURRAY 6'4" 205-pound righty
53-50, 3.85, 60 Saves 1974 1985

Pitch Selection: 1. Fastball 2. Sinker 3. Forkball
Source: *The Scouting Report: 1983*

Note: *The Scouting Report: 1983* says that Murray's sinker and forkball were recent additions, but does not say what other pitches Murray threw before adding them. Murray was often accused of throwing the spitball.

MIKE MUSSINA 6'2" 185-pound righty
199-110, 3.53, 0 Saves 1991 2003

Pitches: 1. Two-Seam Fastball 2. Four-Seam Fastball 3. Knuckle Curve 4. Cut Fastball 5. Overhand Curve 6. Change 7. Slider
Sources: *The Scouting Report: 1993; 1994 Baseball Almanac; The Scouting Report: 1996; The Scouting Notebook 1999*

Tim McCarver on Mussina's knuckle curve: "Mussina, who has thrown it since he was eight, holds the ball with the index and middle fingers as if he were going to throw a knuckler, only with this pitch the ring finger is never involved. He actually flips the ball out of his hand. It's amazing. He holds it with his fingertips, and in order to keep it from rolling, he uses the seam, and actually flicks or flips the ball toward the plate. It's beyond me how he gets that type of rotation on a flicker. You have to have awfully strong fingers to do that."
Source: *Tim McCarver's Baseball for Brain Surgeons and Other Fans* (McCarver with Danny Peary, 1998)
Notes: According to the *Seattle Times* (10/18/2001),

The Topps Company, Inc.

Mike Mussina

Mussina in 2001 threw 57 percent fastballs, 24 percent curves, 10 percent sliders and 9 percent changeups. According to the same source, Mussina threw three fastballs: a four-seamer thrown 89–93, a cutter thrown 84–85, and a two-seam sinker. His curves were a knuckle curve and a sharp curve with a 12-to-6 (downward) break, thrown 72 to 80 m.p.h. His change-up was a sinker and his slider was thrown 78 to 81 m.p.h. and broke late.

According to Jon Miller and Joe Morgan in an ESPN broadcast on October 1, 2003, Mussina—who already threw as many different pitches as anybody—added a splitter to his repertoire in the middle of the 2003 season.

ELMER MYERS 6'2" 185-pound righty
55-72, 4.06, 7 Saves 1915 1922

Pitch Selection: 1. Fastball 2. Curve 3. Change
Sources: unidentified clipping from the Hall of Fame Library (article by Joe Vila, May 1916); Connie Mack, quoted in the *Philadelphia Enquirer* (6/7/1916)
Quote from Vila: "He is a right-hander and he delivers the ball with so little exertion that the best hitters in the American League have been fooled by his wonderful speed. Furthermore, Myers has a curve ball and a drop which, in time, will make him take rank with such famous boxmen as Walter Johnson, Mathewson, Alexander and others."
Quote from Mack: "He has a fast ball and a curve that are puzzling. He also has a good change in pace."

MIKE MYERS 6'3" 197-pound lefty
12-20, 4.37, 14 Saves 1995 2003

Pitch Selection: 1. Sinking Fastball 2. Slider
Note: Myers began pitching from low sidearm/submarine at the suggestion of Al Kaline.
Source: *The Scouting Notebook: 2002*

RANDY MYERS 6'1" 190-pound lefty
44-63, 3.19, 347 Saves 1985 1998

Pitch Selection: 1. Fastball 2. Slider
Source: *The Scouting Report: 1990*

CHRIS NABHOLZ 6'5" 215-pound lefty
37-35, 3.94, 0 Saves 1990 1995

Pitch Selection: 1. Sinking Fastball 2. Curve
3. Change
Source: *The Scouting Report: 1992*

CHARLES NAGY 6'3" 200-pound righty
129-105, 4.51, 0 Saves 1990 2003

Pitch Selection, to 1993: 1. Slider 2. Sinking Fastball
3. Splitter 4. Change
Pitch Selection, post-1993: 1. Sinker 2. Slurve
3. Split-Fingered Fastball 4. Change
Sources: *The Scouting Report: 1993; The Scouting Notebook 1997*

Pitch Selection: 1. Slider 2. Fastball
3. Forkball (as Change)
Source: *Bill Mazeroski's Baseball* (1993 edition)

MIKE NAGY 6'3" 195-pound righty
20-13, 4.15, 0 Saves 1969 1974

Pitch Selection: 1. Sinker 2. Curve
Source: *Major League Baseball: 1971* (Brenda Zanger and Dick Kaplan)

STEVE NAGY 5'9" 174-pound lefty
3-8, 6.42, 0 Saves 1947 1950

Pitch Selection: 1. Fastball 2. Curve
Quote: ". . . has blazing speed and a good curve."
Source: *Pacific Coast Baseball News* (5/25/1949)

SAM NAHEM 6'1" 190-pound righty
10-8, 4.69, 1 Save 1938 1948

Pitch Selection vs. RH Batters: 1. Slider 2. Fastball
Pitch Selection vs. LH Batters: 1. Overhand Curve 2. Fastball
Note: Nahem threw submarine style against the right-handed hitters, overhand against lefties.
Source: Phone interview with Neyer (1/30/2004)

Nahem: "I often wish that God had given me movement on my fastball, but He didn't."
Source: *The Whiz Kids and the 1950 Pennant* (Robin Roberts and C. Paul Rogers III)

RAY NARLESKI 6'1" 175-pound righty
43-33, 3.60, 58 Saves 1954 1959

Pitch Selection: 1. High Fastball, Rode in on a Right-Hander 2. Slider 3. Sailer (another Fastball) 4. Curve 5. Change
Source: *Baseball Digest* (October 1955, Hal Lebovitz)

Narleski: "I had a rising fastball that I could throw 95–100 miles per hour. The batters would hit underneath it and pop it up. I had a knuckle-curve in the minors, but Bill Norman, one of my managers, said to forget it. I had a slider, too. Mel Harder taught me how to throw a curve later on. He also helped me with my motion."
Source: *Splendor on the Diamond* (Rich Westcott, 2000)

Note: Listed by *The Sporting News* (8/29/1956) as having one of the best fastballs in the league.

JIM NASH 6'5" 215-pound righty
68-64, 3.58, 4 Saves 1966 1972

Pitch Selection: 1. Fastball 2. Curve 3. Change 4. Slider (developed in 1970)
Sources: *The Sporting News* (6/6/1970, Wayne Minshew); *Major League Baseball—1969* (Jack Zanger)

Description: "As a rookie Nash relied on pinpoint control of his 91-mph fastball to get batters out. Later in his career he developed an off-speed curve . . ."
Source: *Sports Illustrated* (2/3/2003, Stephen Cannella)

JAIME NAVARRO 6'4" 210-pound righty
116-126, 4.72, 2 Saves 1989 2000

Pitch Selection: 1. Slider 2. Fastball 3. Change 4. Forkball
Sources: *The Scouting Report: 1993; The Scouting Notebook 1997*

JULIO NAVARRO 5'11" 190-pound righty
7-9, 3.65, 17 Saves 1962 1970

Pitch Selection: 1. Sidearm Fastball 2. Slider
Source: *Don Schiffer's Major League Baseball Handbook—1964*

DENNY NEAGLE 6'4" 200-pound lefty
124-92, 4.24, 3 Saves 1991 2003

Pitch Selection: 1. Fastball 2. Circle Change 3. Straight Change
Source: *The Scouting Notebook 1998*

Pitches: 1. Circle Change 2. Fastballs (2-seam and 4-seam) 3. Little Slider 4. Big Curve
Source: *Pitch Like a Pro* (Leo Mazzone and Jim Rosenthal, 1999)

Pitch Selection: 1. Change 2. Fastball (90) 3. Cut Fastball 4. Overhand Curve
Source: *The Scouting Notebook: 2002*

RON NECCIAI 6'5" 185-pound righty
1-6, 7.08, 0 Saves 1952 1952

Pitches: 1. High Fastball 2. Overhand Curve (Drop) 3. Sidearm Curve 4. Change
Source: *Baseball Digest* (August 1952, Tom Siler)

Note: Necciai became famous in 1952 after striking out 27 batters in a game in the Class D Appalachian League.

Branch Rickey: "I've seen a lot of baseball in my time. There have been only two young pitchers I was certain were destined for greatness, simply because they had the meanest fastball a batter can face. One of those boys was

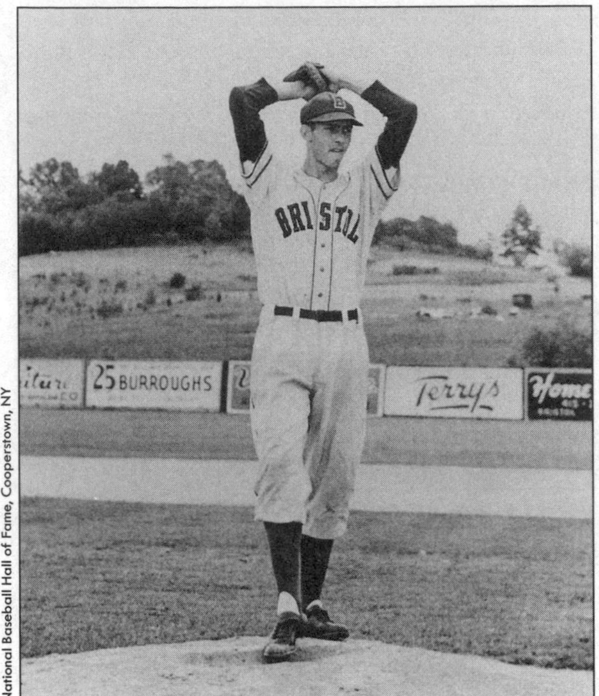

National Baseball Hall of Fame, Cooperstown, NY

Ron Necciai

Dizzy Dean. The other is Ron Necciai. And Necciai is harder to hit."
Source: *Branch Rickey's Little Blue Book* (edited by John J. Monteleone, 1995)

Necciai on his Curve: "We used to call it a 'drop.' Straight up and down. I found that I could throw it backwards easier and it was a whole lot more effective. It looked like a fastball but went straight down."
Source: *A Glimpse of Fame* (Dennis Snelling, 1993)

ART NEHF 5'9" 176-pound lefty
184-120, 3.20, 13 Saves 1915 1929

Key Pitch: 1. Curves 2. Fastball 3. Change
Sources: *Great Baseball Pitchers* (Jim Brosnan, 1965); 1923 *Reach Guide* (Pages 181 and 198)
Notes: The 1923 *Reach*, reporting on the 1922 World Series, says that "Nehf outpitched Bush and used his curve ball to utmost advantage."

Giants scout Dick Kinsella, after seeing Carl Hubbell pitch for the first time, wired John McGraw, "Reminds me of Art Nehf."

Description: "His principal stock in trade is speed and curves, and his speed is certainly most effective and his curves baffling to the batsman. Most of the time he uses a puzzling underhand or side-arm delivery, alternating occasionally with an overhand movement to still further hamper the man at the plate."
Source: *Baseball Magazine* (November 1915; no author listed)

GENE NELSON 6'0" 172-pound righty
53-64, 4.13, 28 Saves 1981 1993

Pitch Selection: 1. Low Fastball 2. Slider 3. Forkball
Source: *The Scouting Report: 1990*

JEFF NELSON 6'8" 225-pound righty
46-39, 3.32, 31 Saves 1992 2003

Pitch Selection: 1. Slider 2. Cut Fastball 3. Fastball
Note: Nelson throws sidearm.
Source: *The Scouting Notebook 1998*

LYNN NELSON 5'10" 170-pound righty
33-42, 5.25, 6 Saves 1930 1940

Key Pitch: Curve
Description: "Lynn employs about everything that's legal to baffle the batters but leans much to curves."
Source: *Baseball Magazine* (December 1938, Robert C. Milne)

Note: Nelson's nickname was "Line Drive," not because he gave them up, but rather because he hit so many of them.

ROGER NELSON 6'3" 200-pound righty
29-32, 3.06, 4 Saves 1967 1976

Quote: "Throws hard, fields well, has a nice curve—but needs another pitch. If he comes up with one, he could make the majors overnight."
Source: *Baseball Digest* (March 1967, "Official Scouting Reports on 1967 Major League Rookies")

ROBB NEN 6'4" 190-pound righty
45-42, 2.98, 314 Saves 1993 2002

Pitch Selection: 1. Fastball (97) 2. Slider 3. Split-Fingered Fastball 4. Curve

Sources: *1995 Baseball Almanac; The Scouting Notebook 1999*

DON NEWCOMBE 6'4" 220-pound righty
149-90, 3.56, 7 Saves 1949 1960

Pitch Selection: 1. High Fastball 2. Curve 3. Change
Source: *Baseball Digest* (September 1955, Charles Dexter)

Yogi Berra: "Big Don Newcombe, when he was young and strong, was rough. He was a fast-ball pitcher, but he had good control, too. He didn't have much of a curve, but he had a fair slider and a pretty good change-up. His strike-out pitch, though, was the fast ball, and he could put it exactly where he wanted it."
Source: *Yogi: The Autobiography of a Professional Baseball Player* (Berra and Ed Fitzgerald, 1961)

Branch Rickey: "The difference between a poor and good fielding pitcher is in the moving of the pivot foot. Don Newcombe brings himself into a beautiful fielding position every time. He steps and then, boom—he brings over his pivot foot even with his stepping foot, in perfect balance."
Source: *Branch Rickey's Little Blue Book* (edited by John J. Monteleone, 1995)

Notes: As an older pitcher, Newcombe may have thrown a spitball (*We Played the Game,* Danny Peary, 1994).

Baseball Digest (January 1963) says that "Newcombe's slider backed up on him a lot, which is a danger; it straightened out [and] became real fat over the plate."

In the *New York Journal-American* (1/14/1953), Newcombe was quoted as telling Vin Scully that he did *not* throw a slider, that the pitch that people often thought was a slider was actually his curve (see Branch Rickey quote below).

Listed by *The Sporting News* (8/29/1956) as having one of the best fastballs in the league.

Branch Rickey: "Don Newcombe has been publicized as the daddy of the pitch now commonly called a slider. His was a velocity pitch (hard to differentiate from his fast ball) which slid from the line of a fast ball in the direction of a curve. It was very effective. But it was Newcombe's curve ball."
Source: *The American Diamond* (Branch Rickey, 1965)

HAL NEWHOUSER 6'2" 180-pound lefty
207-150, 3.06, 26 Saves 1939 1955

Pitch Selection: 1. Fastball 2. Sweeping Curve 3. Change
Sources: *A Tiger in His Time: Hal Newhouser and the Burden of Wartime Ball* (David M. Jordan, 1990); *The Best in Baseball* (Robert H. Shoemaker, 1949)

Description: "Newhouser, tall, blond and curly-haired, is a sort of right-handed Lefty Grove. He has a good fast ball that does things as it flutters across the letters on a batter's shirt. He has a good curve, too, and during a couple of games in the spring training season, broke off a couple that were reminiscent of the curve of Tommy Bridges, which is regarded as Grade A-1."
Source: *Baseball Magazine* (September 1940, Charles P. Ward)

BOBO NEWSOM 6'3" 200-pound righty
211-222, 3.98, 21 Saves 1929 1953

Pitch Selection: 1. Fastball 2. Sharp Curve 3. Change 4. Blooper (1945 on)
Notes: Newsom began his career as a submarine pitcher, but was converted to overhand by Wilbert Robinson. He would also pitch sidearm and three-quarters. There are two sources for the Blooper, which he apparently threw occasionally from about 1945 to the end of his career, basically to entertain himself and the fans.
Sources: John Lardner in *The Second Fireside Book of Baseball; Who's Who in the Major Leagues* (1935 ed.); *20 Years Too Soon* (Quincey Trouppe); Harold Kaese article (unidentified newspaper, March 1956, TSN morgue)

Story: "Crazy Bobo had more rituals than any pitcher I've ever seen. Without fail he would spit in his glove when leaving the bench, touch the ground on either side of the foul line, pull a blade of grass from the infield, then handle the rosin bag. He hated even the smallest piece of litter on the pitching mound, and would hold up the proceedings until he had put everything just right. To throw Bobo off his game, and for the sheer enjoyment of watching him go berserk, opposing infielders sometimes dropped confetti on the mound as they headed to the dugout between innings."
Source: Phil Marchildon in *Ace: Phil Marchildon* (Marchildon with Brian Kendall, 1993)

Comment: "The lone American League windmiller is 'Bobo' Newsom."
Source: *Baseball Digest* (September 1947, Harry Sheer)

DICK NEWSOME 6'0" 185-pound righty
35-33, 4.50, 0 Saves 1941 1943

Key Pitch: Knuckleball
Source: *Baseball Magazine* (September 1944, Ed Rumill article on knuckleballers, in which Rumill lists Newsome along with Dutch Leonard, Johnny Niggeling, Jim Tobin, and Roger Wolff as pitchers who "have been tying the sluggers into knots of various shapes and sizes with the so-called 'butterfly' . . .")

CHET NICHOLS, JR. 6'1" 165-pound lefty
34-36, 3.64, 10 Saves 1951 1964

Key Pitch: Curve
Source: Bob Bolin quoted in *We Played the Game* (Danny Peary, 1994)

Notes: As a rookie in 1951, Nichols led the National League with a 2.88 ERA (granted, he just barely pitched enough innings to qualify). He got drafted into the service after the season, and was never the same after returning to the majors in 1953.

Nichols' father, Chet Sr., pitched in forty-four major league games and went 1-8 with a nifty 7.19 ERA.

KID NICHOLS 5'10" 175-pound righty
360-205, 2.95, 18 Saves 1890 1906

Pitch Selection: 1. Fastball 2. Curve
3. Change (occasional)
Sources: *Baseball's Famous Pitchers* (Ira L. Smith, 1954); *The National Game* (Alfred H. Spink, 1910)

Comment: "A fast ball with a jump was claimed by several pitchers, but worked by Charley Nichols while with Boston to better advantage than ever before."
Source: *How to Play Baseball* (revised by John B. Foster, 1938)

Quote: "There have been a few pitchers in the history of baseball who could 'get by' in the majors with nothing more than a good fast ball. I remember seeing Charlie Nichols, old Boston National hurler, go through nine innings with just four curves and all the rest fast balls. Asked on one occasion why he threw so few curves, Charlie replied, 'They say the batters like speed. Well, maybe they do if you don't give them too much. I figure that I've got that little too much.' "
Source: Cincinnati Reds scout Al Chapman in *Play Ball!* (Charles L. Chapman and Henry L. Severeid, 1941)

Comment: "I have yet to learn that Nichols has any wonderful, elusive curves and quick-breaking shoots, but he has one thing that makes an effective pitcher, and that is command of the ball and the speed to back it up."
Source: nineteenth-century outfielder Patsy Donovan quoted in *The Boston Braves* (Harold Kaese, 1948)
Description: "Charlie Nichols, who endured so long, was a poem in motion as he pitched the ball, a perfect overhand delivery with a full 'follow through' as they say in golf."
Source: *Baseball Magazine* (June 1909, J.B. Sheridan)

TOM NIEDENFUER 6'5" 225-pound righty
36-46, 3.29, 97 Saves 1981 1990

Pitch Selection: 1. Rising Fastball 2. Slider
Source: *The Scouting Report: 1987*

JOE NIEKRO 6'1" 185-pound righty
221-204, 3.59, 16 Saves 1967 1988

Pitches, 1967–1971: 1. Slider 2. Fastball 3. Curve
Pitches, 1972–1975: 1. Fastball 2. Knuckleball
3. Slider 4. Curve 5. Change
Pitches, 1976–1988: 1. Knuckleball 2. Slider
3. Fastball 4. Curve (occasional)
Sources: *The Sporting News* (8/20/1977, Harry Shattuck; and 7/28/1979, Shattuck); *The Scouting Report* (1983, 1985, and 1987 editions)

Commentary: Niekro began experimenting with the knuckleball in 1971, but didn't perfect it until 1978. Even before then, however, he considered the knuckler his best pitch and described himself as a "knuckleball pitcher." (Listing 1976 as the first season during which the knuckleball was Niekro's No. 1 pitch is pretty arbitrary; it might well have happened earlier. On the other hand, in one of his best starts in 1979—his best season—Niekro threw fifty percent sliders.) Niekro pitched into his early forties, and as he aged he threw a higher and higher percentage of knuckleballs.

Note: According to both Niekro and teammate Archie Reynolds in *Take Me Out to the Cubs Game* (John C.

Skipper, 2000), the Cubs strongly discouraged Niekro from throwing his knuckleball when he pitched for them (1967–1969).

Niekro in 1976: "The slider used to be my best pitch, but Billy Martin got me away from it in 1972. Martin decided that year to make me a spitball pitcher. He was tired of us getting beat all the time by Gaylord Perry's spitter. So he decided I would beat Perry at his own game."
Source: *The Sporting News* (4/10/1976, Harry Shattuck); same article, Shattuck refers to Niekro's knuckleball as "his bread-and-butter" pitch.

PHIL NIEKRO 6'1" 180-pound righty
318-274, 3.35, 29 Saves 1964 1987

Pitch Selection: 1. Knuckleball 2. Fastball 3. Slider
Source: *The Sporting News* (9/9/1972, Wayne Minshew)

Comment: "Added pitch almost as baffling as his knuckler last season . . . It's a floater without a name . . . Left trail of sluggers twisted like pretzel with the pitch . . . Pitch developed in winter instructional league where Niekro went to learn the slip pitch after first losing season in majors . . ."
Source: *The Complete Handbook of Baseball* (1972 edition, edited by Zander Hollander)

JOHNNY NIGGELING 6'0" 170-pound righty
64-69, 3.22, 2 Saves 1938 1946

Pitch Selection: 1. Knuckleball 2. Fastball
Comment: "Niggeling, unlike Leonard and Wolff, doesn't have to rely completely on his knuckler. He has a fast ball with which he can get by very nicely."
Source: *The Sporting News* (12/23/1943, Shirley Povich)

Dan Daniel: " 'Niggeling is the closest we have seen to Eddie Rommel,' said Harry Geisel. 'He's a better knuckleball thrower than Emil Leonard of the Senators,' chimed in Johnny Quinn. 'He's very tough to work with,' smiled Bill Grieve. 'That butterfly of Niggeling's does all sorts of tricks.' The Yankees said Niggeling made the ball hop and dip. It came out of one side, then out of the other, and you either [illegible] it and whaled the seams off it or Niggeling made you look like a drunk in a shooting gallery."

AL NIPPER 6'0" 188-pound righty
46-50, 4.52, 1 Save 1983 1990

Pitches: 1. Fastball (mid-80s) 2. Curve 3. Slider 4. Change
Note: Nipper added a knuckleball in 1986 and threw it occasionally until 1990, when he tried, with very little success, to become a "true" knuckleball pitcher.
Sources: *The Scouting Report* (1985–1987 and 1991 editions)

RON NISCHWITZ 6'3" 205-pound lefty
5-8, 4.21, 6 Saves 1961 1965

Key Pitch: Sinking Fastball
Source: *1963 Major League Handbook* (Don Schiffer)

C.J. NITKOWSKI 6'3" 205-pound lefty
16-31, 5.33, 3 Saves 1995 2003

Pitch Selection: 1. Sinking Fastball (87–89) 2. Slider
Source: *The Scouting Notebook: 1996*
Note: According to *The Scouting Notebook: 2001*, Nitkowski's fastball velocity was in the low 90s.

WILLARD NIXON 6'2" 195-pound righty
69-72, 4.39, 3 Saves 1950 1958

Pitch Selection: 1. Curve 2. Fastball 3. Change
Source: *The Boston Red Sox* (Tom Meany, 1956)

Key Pitch: Slider
Source: *Sport* (February 1957, Al Hirshberg)
Note: Meany's book was published in 1956, probably written in 1955, implying that Nixon may have developed the slider in 1956.

GARY NOLAN 6'2" 197-pound righty
110-70, 3.08, 0 Saves 1967 1977

Pitch Selection: 1. Change 2. Curve 3. Fastball
Note: Nolan's best pitch was his fastball prior to 1968 and 1969 arm problems.
Source: *The Big Red Machine* (Bob Hertzel, 1976)

Note: *Putting It All Together* (Brooks Robinson with Fred Bauer, 1971) has an excellent scouting report on Nolan, noting that his change "has screwball action," that he sometimes drops to three-quarters to throw the fastball and curve, that he uses the slider a little bit, and that he throws a pitch that drops sharply and might be a spitball.

THE ONLY NOLAN 5'8" 171-pound righty
23-52, 2.98, 0 Saves 1878 1885

Pitch Selection: 1. Underhand Fastball
2. Lateral Curve (Inward and Outward)
Quote: "Nolan, known as 'The Only,' looked to Boston like simply a swift underhand thrower like Devlin, McCormick and many others. But their speed as compared with that of Nolan's was 'like the velocity of a ball from an old smooth bore would compare with a ball from a Winchester rifle.' Nolan was 'also a clever master of the lateral curve, both inward and outward and, on the whole, fairly deserves his sobriquet of 'The Terror.' "
Source: *Baseball (1845–1881) from the Newspaper Accounts* (Preston D. Orem, 1961)

DICKIE NOLES 6'2" 160-pound righty
36-53, 4.56, 11 Saves 1979 1990

Pitch Selection: 1. Fastball (90) 2. Curve 3. Slider
Source: *The Scouting Report: 1983*

HIDEO NOMO 6'2" 210-pound righty
114-90, 3.85, 0 Saves 1995 2003

Pitch Selection: 1. Fastball 2. Forkball 3. Curve
Notes: Nomo is aided by a unique twisting delivery. The curve is basically a waste pitch.
Source: *The Scouting Report: 1996*

Quote: "Although his fastball wasn't the Nomo specialty of old, he was clocked at 89 mph, fast enough to complement a suddenly rejuvenated curveball . . . 'I'd like to take credit,' says Brewers pitching coach Bill Campbell. 'But it's not as if we found a mistake and changed it. We've done nothing. The only thing I can figure is that he's gotten used to throwing less hard. There's a big difference between 94 mph and 89, but not if you locate your pitches. He's been doing that."
Source: *Sports Illustrated* (7/12/1999, note credited to Stephen Cannella and Jeff Pearlman)

JERRY NOPS 5'8" 168-pound lefty
72-43, 3.70, 1 Save 1896 1901

Note: unidentified clipping of Temple Cup game (October 4, 1897) describes Nops as "slowballer," and also notes that he could pitch well when not drinking.
Source: *The Fall Classics of the 1890s* (mimeographed publication by John Phillips)

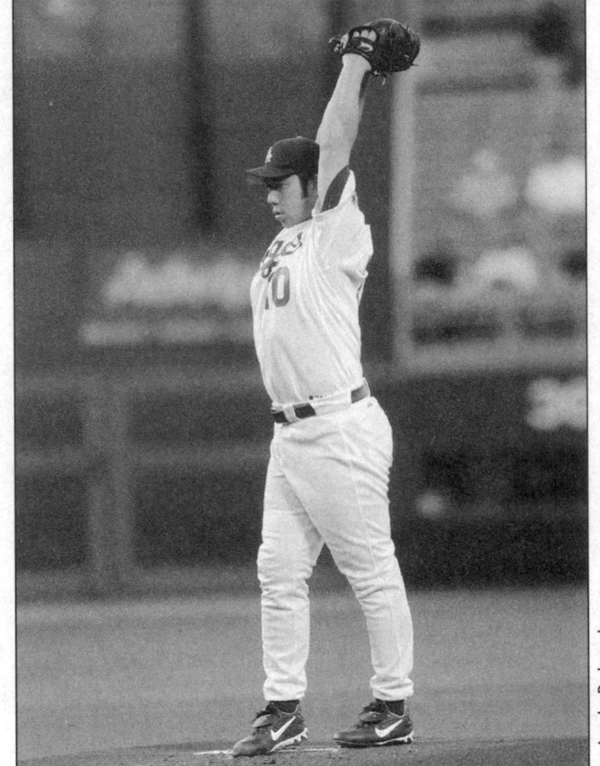
Los Angeles Dodgers, Inc.

Hideo Nomo

FRED NORMAN 5'8" 155-pound lefty
104-103, 3.64, 8 Saves 1962 1980

Key Pitch, 1962–70: Fastball
Pitches, 1971–80: 1. Screwball 2. Fastball 3. Curve
4. Slider 5. Change
Note: When Norman pitched in the Cubs' system (1964–1966), they forbade him from throwing his screwball, and so he lost confidence in the pitch. However, in 1970 his manager in Tulsa was Warren Spahn, and Spahn told Norman his screwball was good enough for the major leagues. In 1971 Norman joined the Padres, where pitching coach Roger Craig helped him refine the screwball, and that became his best pitch.
Sources: *Men of the Machine* (Ritter Collett, 1977); *The Sporting News* (7/10/1976, Jerome Holtzman column); *The Sporting News* (5/20/1978, Earl Lawson)

MIKE NORRIS 6'2" 175-pound righty
58-59, 3.89, 0 Saves 1975 1990

Pitch Selection: 1. Screwball 2. Fastball 3. Curve 4. Change
Note: Norris was suspected of throwing a spitball.
Sources: *The Sporting News* (6/6/1981, Peter Gammons); *Late Innings* (Roger Angell, Page 322)

DON NOTTEBART 6'1" 190-pound righty
36-51, 3.65, 21 Saves 1960 1969

Pitch Selection: 1. Slider 2. Sinking Fastball
Sources: *1963 Major League Handbook* (Don Schiffer); Milwaukee Braves 1961 Guide for Press/Radio/TV; *Baseball Digest* (March 1960, Page 89)

Key Pitch: Sinker
Source: *Tim McCarver's Baseball for Brain Surgeons and Other Fans* (McCarver with Danny Peary, 1998)

CHET NOURSE 6'3" 185-pound righty
0-0, 7.20, 0 Saves 1909 1909

Note: The March 1911 issue of *Baseball Magazine* reported, "Nourse recently had the third finger of his right hand amputated to prevent the spread of blood poisoning. It is said the loss of the digit will not affect his power as a pitcher and may make him more formidable."

Nourse, who had pitched briefly for the Red Sox in 1909, never pitched in the majors again.

EDWIN NUÑEZ 6'5" 235-pound righty
28-36, 4.19, 54 Saves 1982 1994

Pitch Selection: 1. Fastball 2. Splitter
Sources: *The Scouting Report: 1990; The Scouting Report: 1992*

JOE NUXHALL 6'3" 195-pound lefty
135-117, 3.90, 19 Saves 1944 1966

Pitch Selection: 1. Fastball 2. Slider
Source: *Baseball Digest* (June 1956, Arthur Daley)
Note: Listed by *The Sporting News* (8/29/1956) as having one of the best fastballs in the league.

BUCK O'BRIEN 5'10" 188-pound righty
29-25, 2.63, 0 Saves 1911 1913

Key Pitch: Spitball
Source: *The Boston Red Sox* (Fred Lieb, 1947)

DARBY O'BRIEN 5'10" 165-pound righty
59-65, 3.68, 2 Saves 1888 1891

Key Pitch: Fastball
Quote: "With his face turned toward center field, he would get a grip on the ball and with an elegant swing of his good right arm he would send the sphere with lightning like speed over the plate. Seldom did his face turn toward the plate until the delivery was completed and on this account all batsmen feared him for none knew where to expect to receive the ball."
Source: *The Sporting News* (3/19/1892)

Comment: "His delivery was, without any doubt, the most peculiar of any right hand pitcher who ever played ball."
Source: *The Sporting Life* (3/19/1892)

HANK O'DAY 6'0" 180-pound righty
73-110, 3.74, 4 Saves 1884 1890

Key Pitch: Fastball
Source: *A Tale of Four Cities* (Jean-Pierre Caillault, 2003)

Note: According to Norman Macht in *Baseball's First Stars* (SABR, 1989), O'Day was "primarily a slowball pitcher." However, Macht quotes Deacon McGuire, who broke in with O'Day, as saying that O'Day "had a world of stuff" and "threw the heaviest and hardest ball I ever caught. It was like lead and it came to me like a shell from a cannon." This seems incompatible with the "slowball" description, and we are uncertain as to why Macht described him in this way.

See Tim Keefe entry

BILLY O'DELL 5'11" 170-pound lefty
105-100, 3.29, 48 Saves 1954 1967

Pitch Selection: 1. Fastball 2. Slider 3. Curve 4. Change
O'Dell: "My fast ball and slider are still my two best pitches. But I've been working on the change, and I think my curve is coming back to me, too. It was breaking a lot better last season, right before the doctors told me to call it quits for the year."
Source: *Sport* (May 1959, John Steadman)

Pitch Selection: 1. Slider 2. Fastball 3. Sinker 4. Curve

Source: *Baseball Stars of 1959* (article by Ernie Harwell)

BLUE MOON ODOM 6'0" 178-pound righty
84-85, 3.70, 1 Save 1964 1976

Key Pitch: Sinking Fastball
Source: *Catfish: My Life in Baseball* (James A. Hunter and Armen Keteyian, 1988); *The Sporting News* (6/14/1969, Ron Bergman)

Al Kaline: "There aren't many pitchers of any age who are tougher. Most guys who throw real hard throw straight. The harder they throw, the straighter their ball gets. Odom throws hard, but his ball always moves. The harder he throws, the more it moves. I think he's the best young pitcher in baseball."
Odom: "I throw hard, but two, three pitchers in this league are faster. Jim Hunter and Chuck Dobson on this club, Sam McDowell on the Cleveland club, maybe. But I think my fastball moves more than any other pitcher's. It sinks mostly. People think I'm wild, but I'm not. It's just that my pitches move so much, it's hard for me to control them."
Source: *Sport* (September 1969, Bill Libby)

Comment: "Odom credits pitching coach Bill Posedel with helping him adjust his delivery, as he was finally able to get his curve over last year . . . Blue Moon also throws a strangely sinking fastball."
Source: *Major League Baseball 1969* (Jack Zanger)

JOHN O'DONOGHUE 6'4" 203-pound lefty
39-55, 4.07, 10 Saves 1963 1971

Key Pitch: Slow Curve
Source: *Baseball Digest* (March 1960, Page 75)

JOE OESCHGER 6'0" 190-pound righty
82-116, 3.81, 8 Saves 1914 1925

Key Pitch: Fastball
Source: *The Ol'Ball Game* (article by Norman Macht)

CHAD OGEA 6'2" 220-pound righty
37-35, 4.88, 0 Saves 1994 1999

Pitch Selection: 1. Change 2. Curve 3. Fastball (87–91)
Note: Ogea threw a slider early in his career, but scrapped it in 1996 and concentrated on his curveball.
Sources: *The Scouting Notebook* (1997–2000 editions)

BOBBY OJEDA 6'1" 185-pound lefty
115-98, 3.65, 1 Save 1980 1994

Pitch Selection: 1. Change 2. Fastball 3. Curve 4. Screwball
Source: *Tom Seaver's 1989 Scouting Notebook*

OMAR OLIVARES 6'1" 185-pound righty
77-86, 4.67, 4 Saves 1990 2001

Pitch Selection: 1. Change 2. Slow Curve 3. Fastball
Source: *The Scouting Notebook 2000*

DARREN OLIVER 6'0" 170-pound lefty
84-76, 5.02, 2 Saves 1993 2003

Pitch Selection: 1. Change 2. Hard Curve 3. Fastball
Source: *The Scouting Notebook: 1997*

DIOMEDES OLIVO 6'1" 195-pound lefty
5-6, 3.10, 7 Saves 1960 1963

Pitch Selection: 1. Fastball 2. Curve 3. Change
Source: *The Sporting News* (5/23/1962, Harry Keck)

Note: Olivo debuted in the major leagues when he was 41 years old, and enjoyed his only full season (1963) when he was 43.

VERN OLSEN 6'0" 175-pound lefty
30-26, 3.40, 2 Saves 1939 1946

Key Pitch: Sinker
Quote: "He is the only left-hander I can remember who has a good sinker while throwing overhand."
Source: Cubs coach George Uhle in *Baseball Magazine* (April 1941, Herbert Simons)

GREGG OLSON 6'4" 210-pound righty
40-39, 3.46, 217 Saves 1988 2001

Pitch Selection: 1. Curve 2. Fastball (low-90s) 3. Sinker (added in 1992) 4. Change
Sources: Baltimore Orioles 1992 Media Guide; *From 33rd Street to Camden Yards* (John Eisenberg, 2001); *The Scouting Report* (1993 and 1994 editions)

Frank Robinson: "It had been a long time since I saw a pitcher who could lock hitters like that with his curveball. The last one before Olson was 'Sad Sam' Jones back in the '50s."
Gregg Olson: "If you're looking at a clock, my normal [curve] was probably one o'clock to seven going down."
Source: Eisenberg

EMMETT O'NEILL 6'3" 185-pound righty
15-26, 4.76, 0 Saves 1943 1946

Key Pitch: Fastball
Source: Jim Turner in *Baseball Magazine* (September 1945, Ed Rumill)

STEVE ONTIVEROS 6'0" 190-pound righty
34-31, 3.67, 19 Saves 1985 2000

Pitch Selection: 1. Fastball (high-80s) 2. Slider
Source: *The Scouting Report: 1987*

Pitch Selection: 1. Sinking Fastball (mid-80s)
2. Cut Fastball 3. Overhand Curve 4. Slider
5. Forkball
Source: *The Scouting Notebook: 1995*

MIKE OQUIST 6'2" 190-pound righty
25-31, 5.46, 0 Saves 1993 1999

Pitches: 1. Slider 2. Change 3. Curve
3. Fastball (mid-80s)
Sources: *The Scouting Notebook* (1995 and 1998 editions)

JESSE OROSCO 6'2" 174-pound lefty
87-80, 3.16, 144 Saves 1979 2003

Pitch Selection: 1. Fastball 2. Hard Slider
3. Change-up Slider 4. Orosco threw a Split-Fingered Fastball in 1981 and '82.
Source: *The Scouting Report: 1987*

Pitch Selection, late career: 1. Slider 2. Fastball
3. Curve (against right-handed batters)
Source: *The Scouting Notebook: 2000*

Quote: "When his velocity dropped off, he depended more on his slider, and when his slider began to flatten, he picked up a split-finger changeup that has become his out pitch."
Source: *Sports Illustrated* (3/10/2003, Jeff Pearlman)

PHIL ORTEGA 6'2" 170-pound righty
46-62, 4.43, 2 Saves 1960 1969

Pitch Selection: 1. Fastball 2. Slider
Source: *The Sporting News* (7/2/1966, Bob Addie)

AL ORTH 6'0" 200-pound righty
203-184, 3.37, 9 Saves 1895 1909

Key Pitch: Slow Ball
Comment: "Albert Orth was one of the most famous 'slow ball' pitchers ever in major league base ball. To the spectators Orth pitched a ball that it seemed must be easy to hit, yet year after year he kept on 'fooling' the batsmen."
Source: *How to Pitch* (J. E. Wray, 1928)

George Brace Collection

Al Orth

Key Pitch: Thumb Ball (submarine spitball)
Sources: *The Year They Called Off the World Series* (Benton Stark, 1991)

Notes: According to Branch Rickey in *The Saturday Evening Post* (6/17/1950), Orth's spitter broke out, rather than down—the only pitcher Rickey ever saw with a sideways spitball. Orth's nickname was "The Curveless Wonder."

RUSS ORTIZ 6'1" 208-pound righty
88-51, 3.97, 0 Saves 1998 2003

Pitches: 1. Fastball (90–94) 2. Hard Curve 3. Slider (occasional) 4. Change (occasional, but more in 2003)
Sources: *The Scouting Notebook* (1999–2003 editions); *Athens Banner-Herald* (4/7/2003); Steve Lyons during Fox broadcast of Braves-Cubs Division Series Game (9/30/2003)

DONOVAN OSBORNE 6'2" 210-pound lefty
47-46, 3.96, 0 Saves 1992 2002

Pitch Selection: 1. Fastball (90) 2. Slider 3. Change
Sources: *The Scouting Report: 1993; The Scouting Notebook: 1999*

CLAUDE OSTEEN 5'11" 160-pound lefty
196-195, 3.30, 1 Save 1957 1975

Pitch Selection: 1. Slider 2. Sinking Fastball 3. Curve 4. Change
Source: *Glory Days with the Dodgers* (Roseboro with Bill Libby, Page 196)

Description: "[Osteen threw] a tricky (fastball) that runs in on lefthanded hitters and away from righthanders."
Source: *Major League Baseball: 1971* (Brenda Zanger and Dick Kaplan)

Description: "Claudc, or 'Gomcr' as we call him, is a good control pitcher and throws a mean sinker, curve ball, and slider."
Source: *Phil Regan* (Phil Regan as told to Jim Hefley, 1968)

FRITZ OSTERMUELLER 5'11" 175-pound lefty
114-115, 3.99, 15 Saves 1934 1948

Description, early career: "Ostermueller has a lot of stuff and he flips it with a delivery similar to that of Bob Grove."
Source: *The Sporting News* (7/19/1934, Page 1)

Pitch Selection, late career: 1. Curve 2. Change 3. Fastball
Comment: "One of Fred's best pitches is his change of pace, which he calls his 'take off,' meaning he takes sometimes a little, sometimes a lot off the speed of his fast ball."
Source: *Baseball Magazine* (December 1946, Ed Rumill)

Description: " 'Old Folks,' as his Pirate teammates called him, was one of the slowest-working pitchers in the game. As a result of an elbow injury suffered in 1943, he developed a long, drawn-out windup. The delivery took time, but as Fritz said, 'I don't care if it takes me three hours to pitch a game. I don't have anything else to do all day.' "
Source: Ostermueller's obituary in *The Sporting News* (12/17/1957)

Note: According to Stan Musial, Ostermueller "had one of the first lefthanded sliders."
Source: *Stan Musial: The Man's Own Story* (Musial, as told to Bob Broeg, 1964)

AL OSUNA 6'3" 200-pound lefty
18-10, 3.83, 14 Saves 1990 1996

Pitch Selection: 1. Screwball 2. Fastball (88) 3. Big Slider 4. Short Slider
Source: *The Scouting Report: 1992*

Pitch Selection: 1. Fastball (80s) 2. Slider 3. Change 4. Curve
Source: *The Scouting Report: 1993*

ANTONIO OSUNA 5'11" 200-pound righty
34-28, 3.58, 21 Saves 1995 2003

Pitch Selection: 1. Four-Seam Fastball 2. Change 3. Curve
Note: ". . . managers voted his fastball as the third best in the National League, behind those of Mark Wohlers and Robb Nen."
Source: *The Scouting Notebook: 1997*

JIM O'TOOLE 6'0" 190-pound lefty
98-84, 3.57, 4 Saves 1958 1967

Pitch Selection: 1. Fastball 2. Slider 3. Overhand Curve 4. Three-Quarters Curve/Change
Sources: *We Played the Game* (Danny Peary, 1994); *1963 Major League Handbook* (Don Schiffer); *Pennant Race* (Jim Brosnan, 1962)

Quote: "His fast ball is alive, say the Cincinnati catchers, and his slider really moves."
Source: *1965 Official Baseball Almanac* (Bill Wise)

MARTY O'TOOLE 5'11" 175-pound righty
27-36, 3.21, 2 Saves 1908 1914

Pitches: 1. Spitball 2. Fastball 3. Knuckleball (occasional) 4. Curve (occasional)
Sources: *Baseball Magazine* (August 1912, O'Toole; and October 1914, F.C. Lane)

O'Toole in 1912 *Baseball Magazine:* "The secret of whatever success I may have had as a pitcher is largely due to the spitball. I am a spitball pitcher, though not so much as I used to be. Originally I was a curve pitcher, though I always depended a good deal on speed and change of pace. I well remember the first time I ever pitched a spitball. Of course, I had practiced with it considerably, but the first professional game I ever used it was against Worcester in 1907 . . . About one out of every three balls I pitch is a spitball. The others are curves, slow balls, or straight fast ones. I have had pretty good success with my slow ball this year, and have always taken to curves. One of my favorite tricks is to follow a couple of spitballs which drop sharply when they cross the plate by a straight fast one, which invariably jumps as it reaches the batter."

O'Toole in 1914 *Baseball Magazine:* "The slow ball, of which there are several types, I pitch as a Knuckle Ball. I dig my fingers into the seams of the ball, and let it roll off my knuckles . . . As a matter of fact, the slow ball does act in a puzzling way, properly delivered. It should come floating up to the batter without rotating at all. But it has a tendency to rotate away from the pitcher and while this tendency is struggling to assert itself the ball will vacillate from side to side as it meets the opposing air currents."

Description: "Marty in his usual game goes along swimmingly, striking out man after man, but for every strikeout he gives a base on balls. His delivery is almost unhittable when going at full speed, but he has great difficulty in controlling the delivery, and if he slows down in an effort to locate the plate he passes at once into the batter's range and is likely to be hit hard. O'Toole is much in the position of a man who possesses an ungovernable horse. The animal is a superb steed, with all the possibilities of a valuable mount, but its strength is a loss rather than a gain until it has been thoroughly broken to the bit. The spit-ball in the hands of a man like O'Toole is a treasure, but its very strong points are also its weaknesses, and the failure of the batters to hit it is also reflected in the failure of the pitcher to control it."
Source: *Baseball Magazine* (March 1913, F.C. Lane article about Ed Walsh)

Note: In his time, O'Toole was quite famous because the Pirates paid the record sum of $22,500 to obtain him from the St. Paul club.

ORVAL OVERALL 6'2" 214-pound righty
108-72, 2.23, 12 Saves 1905 1913

Pitch Selection: 1. Drop Curve 2. Spitball 3. Fastball
Sources: *Touching Second* (John J. Evers and Hugh S. Fullerton, 1910); *Baseball Magazine* (May 1911, no author listed)
Quote from *Baseball Magazine:* "He says the ligaments that bothered him last fall have apparently grown back into their normal condition, for he has experienced not the slightest pain when throwing either his spitter or drop curve."

STUBBY OVERMIRE 5'7" 170-pound lefty
58-67, 3.96, 10 Saves 1943 1952

Pitch Selection: 1. Curve 2. Slow Curve (as Change) 3. Sailer
Sources: *Safe by a Mile* (Charlie Metro with Tom Altherr, 2002); phone interview with Charlie Metro (6/13/2002, Rob Neyer)

Metro in *Safe by a Mile:* ". . . We were playing in Detroit, and I was feeling pretty good. The bases were loaded. Stubby Overmire was pitching for the Tigers. I knew what Stubby was going to throw me. He was going to throw me that change-up of his. He had a dandy. It was kind of a little bit of a curve, like a change-up on a curve ball, and it was real slow . . ."

Metro in interview: "He had a real good curve, he would throw it about three or four speeds. Where Ed Lopat would throw his curve at seven or eight different speeds, Stubby might throw it four different speeds. He had a little bit of a cut fastball. He had stubby fingers, he wasn't a tall guy; he'd cut the fastball a little. They call that a cut fastball now, but it's what we used to call a sailer. He was a very clever pitcher and he had excellent control."

FRANK OWEN 5'11" 160-pound righty
82-67, 2.55, 2 Saves 1901 1909

Pitch Selection: 1. Speedy Curve 2. Slow Curve
Quote: "He has a puzzling delivery, mixes up his speedy and slow curves in tantalizing style, and is as good as anybody in fielding his position."
Source: unidentified clipping from the Hall of Fame Library

JOE PAGE 6'3" 200-pound lefty
57-49, 3.53, 76 Saves 1944 1954

Pitch Selection: 1. Rising Fastball 2. Spitball 3. Curve 3. Forkball
Sources: *The Relief Pitcher* (John Thorn, 1979); Roy Face quoted in *Maz and the '60 Bucs* (Jim O'Brien, 1993); Spider Jorgensen quoted in *We Played the Game* (Danny Peary, 1994)

Comment: ". . . Joe Page, who was one pitch away from being sent to the minors in 1947. Page had a fast ball and little else. When his ball was alive, he could win. When it wasn't, he was in imminent danger of being beheaded by line drives—until in desperation he adopted the spitter as his payoff pitch.

"With its selective use, Page helped win a pennant for the Yankees in 1947. As we went along undetected that season, he became less secretive about employing the illegal pitch. When he used it for an out pitch at a crucial stage, he would defiantly spit in his glove, and those of us who traveled with the Yankees at the time would wait for the moment Page thought was the big one."
Source: *Sport* (October 1956, Milton Gross, "Are They Still Throwing the Spitter?")

Face on Page's forkball: "Page would move the ball so that one of his fingers would catch on one of the seams and he'd get a little pull on the seam to break it in or break it out."

Commentary: The reference to the curve (Jorgensen) is weak, and Face saw Page pitch in 1954, years after his heyday with the Yankees. By all accounts, in his prime Page relied on an outstanding fastball and didn't bother with much else.

Note: Preacher Roe created a firestorm in July of 1955 when he confessed in a magazine interview that he had thrown the spitball as a key part of his repertoire. On July 31, 1955, Page confessed to Jimmy Cannon in the *New York Post* that he, also, had thrown the spitball.

SATCHEL PAIGE 6'4" 180-pound righty
28-31, 3.29, 32 Saves 1948 1965

Pitches, 1926–1938: 1. Fastballs 2. Curve (occasional)
Commentary: Until relatively late in his Negro Leagues career, Paige was famous for three things: his amazing control, his fastball, and his near-complete lack of any pitch aside from the fastball. He threw his curve very rarely; in his autobiography, he claimed that three curves he threw to Dizzy Dean in a 1934 exhibition were close to the first he'd ever thrown in a game. But Satchel didn't really need a curve, because he had great control of two fastballs, his "bee ball" and his "jump ball" (he also frequently referred to his "trouble ball," which may have been a general term for his fastballs). Paige's description: "I throw both overhand, only the bee ball goes off my fingers on the smooth hide of the ball and rides on the level, and my jump ball I throw with my fingers across the seam and that makes it jump four to six inches."

Pitch Selection, 1939–1949: 1. Sneaky Fastball 2. Slow Curve 3. Change
Commentary: Paige suffered a severe arm injury in the winter of 1938/1939—he once claimed that the injury came because he tried to learn to throw a curveball in Mexico City—and though he eventually recovered, his fastball was never again what it had been. He began to throw other pitches, and he also mixed his deliveries, throwing submarine, sidearm, and overhand. However, beginning in 1948 when he reached the recently-integrated American League, the evidence suggests that he 1) mostly threw overhand, 2) occasionally threw

National Baseball Hall of Fame, Cooperstown, NY

Satchel Paige

rine style.

Commentary: In 1943, Paige developed his famous "hesitation pitch." His description: "The idea came to me in a game, when the guy at bat was all tighted up waiting for my fast ball. I knew he'd swing as soon as I just barely moved. So when I stretched, I paused just a little longer with my arms above my head. Then I threw my left foot forward but I didn't come around with my arm right away. I put that foot of mine down, stopping for a second, before the ball left my hand.

"When my foot hit the ground that boy started swinging, so by the time I came around with the whip he was way off stride and couldn't get anywhere near the ball.

"I had me a strikeout."

Paige displayed the hesitation pitch in his debut with the Indians in 1948, after which American League president Will Harridge, on somewhat questionable grounds, banned the pitch.

Pitches, 1951–1965: Everything, including the kitchen sink.

Commentary: By the mid-1950s, Paige was throwing virtually every pitch from virtually every angle. He still threw both of his fastballs, his curve, and his change of pace ("nothing ball"), but he also fooled around with a screwball, a sidearm/submarine forkball ("whipsy-dipsy-do"), a slider, a knuckleball that he called his "bat-dodger," a blooper, and anything else he happened to think of on a given day.

Sources: *Maybe I'll Pitch Forever* (LeRoy "Satchel" Paige as told to David Lipman, 1961); *Pitchin' Man: Satchel Paige's Own Story* (LeRoy "Satchel" Paige as told to Hal Lebovitz, 1948); Ted Page in *Voices from the Great Black Baseball Leagues* (John Holway, 1975); Wally Berger and Cool Papa Bell in *Josh and Satch* (John B. Holway, 1991); many other sources were used for this entry.

Quote: "He had more patience than any pitcher I have ever seen in my life because he never made a pitch until in his mind he knew exactly where he wanted it to go, what he wanted to do with it, and what speed he wanted it to go. I saw him one Sunday afternoon in Buffalo, New York, take nine minutes to make four pitches to Luke Easter and pop him up for the third out."
Source: Bubba Church in *For the Love of the Game* (Cynthia J. Wilber, 1992)

LANCE PAINTER 6'1" 200-pound lefty
25-18, 5.24, 3 Saves 1993 2003

Pitch Selection: 1. Fastball 2. Slider 3. Change
Source: *The Scouting Notebook: 1995*

ERV PALICA 6'1" 180-pound righty
41-55, 4.23, 12 Saves 1947 1956

Pitches: 1. Fastball 2. Curve 3. Change of Pace 4. Knuckleball (occasional)

Source: *The Sporting News* (7/15/1953, Roscoe McGowen)

Comment: "Erv probably had the best stuff of any pitcher that I've ever seen."
Source: Clem Labine in *Bums: An Oral History of the Brooklyn Dodgers* (Peter Golenbock, 1984)

DONN PALL 6'1" 180-pound righty
24-23, 3.63, 10 Saves 1988 1998

Pitch Selection: 1. Split-Fingered Fastball
2. Fastball (high-80s)
Source: *The Scouting Report: 1990*

Pitch Selection: 1. Split-Fingered Fastball
2. Slider (added 1991) 3. Curve
Source: *The Scouting Report: 1992*

DAVID PALMER 6'1" 195-pound righty
64-59, 3.78, 2 Saves 1978 1989

Key Pitch: 1. Cut Fastball 2. Curve 3. Slider
Sources: *The Ballplayers* (1990, article by Jane Charnin-Aker); *The Scouting Report: 1987*

JIM PALMER 6'3" 190-pound righty
268-152, 2.86, 4 Saves 1965 1984

Pitch Selection: 1. Fastball 2. Slow Curve 3. Slider
Sources: *The Sporting News* (5/31/1975, Jim Henneman; and 9/20/1975, Henneman)

Comment: "Although Palmer's best pitch during the first decade of his career was a high fastball, which is ordinarily considered a strikeout pitch, he was never especially concerned with his strikeout totals. Strikeouts, he asserted, are only important in certain situations; 'otherwise, they're just something glamorous and not particularly significant.'

"That philosophy served Jim well on days when he didn't have his best fastball. Rather than switching exclusively to breaking pitches, he would slow his other pitches down so that the fastball seemed to be thrown at normal speed. This unusual tactic worked for him more often than not."
Source: *Baseball's Greatest Players: The Saga Continues* (David Shiner, 2001)

Tom Seaver: "You may also want to flick your gloved hand into the batter's line of sight with every pitch. It can disrupt the batter's timing slightly but significantly. Jim Palmer is a master of that quick glove flick."
Source: *The Art of Pitching* (Seaver with Lee Lowenfish, 1984)

Note: Palmer is famous for having never given up a grand slam in his career, but what's not widely known is that Palmer was *generally* effective with the bases loaded. He faced 254 batters with the bases loaded, and gave up only thirty-six hits (.195 batting average), six doubles and one triple (.233 slugging average), and fourteen walks (.233 on-base average).
Source: Retrosheet

JOSE PANIAGUA 6'2" 195-pound righty
18-21, 4.49, 13 Saves 1996 2003

Pitch Selection: 1. Hard Sinker (low-90s)
2. Four-Seam Fastball 3. Slider
Source: *The Scouting Notebook: 2000*

Pitch Selection: 1. Cut Fastball (low-90s) 2. Forkball
3. Slider
Source: *The Scouting Notebook: 2002*

AL PAPAI 6'3" 185-pound righty
9-14, 5.36, 4 Saves 1948 1955

Key Pitch: Knuckleball
Source: *The Diamond Appraised* (Craig Wright and Tom House, 1989)

MILT PAPPAS 6'3" 190-pound righty
209-164, 3.40, 4 Saves 1957 1973

Pitch Selection: 1. Fastball 2. Slider 3. Slip Pitch
(refined in 1971)
Sources: *The Ballplayers* (1990, article by Shepard C. Long); Brooks Robinson in *We Played the Game* (Danny Peary, 1994); SABR-L Posting of January 21, 2002, comments posted by Gary Collard on behalf of John Holway; *Out at Home* (Pappas with Wayne Mausser and Larry Names, 2000)

Pappas on his Slip Pitch: "Paul Richards taught it to me, but I hadn't used it very often as an out pitch in my pitching repertoire yet. Basically, I palmed the ball and threw it with the same motion as the fastball except I didn't snap my wrist in the delivery."
Source: *Out at Home*

Notes: According to the *1963 Major League Handbook* (Don Schiffer), Pappas "has to keep his curve ball low to be effective." Other references do not mention Pappas throwing a curve, and Schiffer is not overpoweringly reliable.

According to Randy Hundley, interviewed by John Holway, Pappas "got a lot of outs" by taking something off his slider, as a sort of an off-beat change.

Harry Brecheen: ". . . In fact I think Milt has more hard stuff than anyone in the league. He can use his fastball more than most pitchers because he has one that sinks and one that rises. The batters don't get used to it quickly."
Source: Brecheen, then the Orioles pitching coach, quoted in *1965 Official Baseball Almanac* (Bill Wise)

CHAN HO PARK 6'2" 185-pound righty
90-65, 4.09, 0 Saves 1994 2003

Pitch Selection: 1. Fastball (mid-90s) 2. Curve 3. Change
Source: *The Scouting Notebook 1999*

HARRY PARKER 6'3" 190-pound righty
15-21, 3.85, 12 Saves 1970 1976

Key Pitch: Curve
Note: Parker threw an exceptional curveball, the best on the Mets' staff in 1973 and '74.
Source: *The Pitching Staff* (Steve Jacobson, 1975)

ROY PARMELEE 6'1" 190-pound righty
59-55, 4.27, 3 Saves 1929 1939

Pitch Selection: 1. Moving Fastball 2. Curve
Description: "His powerful arm can throw a ball with a swiftness that would do credit to the greatest speed pitcher of the game. In sheer stuff, he outranks all other pitchers of the Giant staff, even the glittering Schumacher. Parmelee's fast ball is a fearful and sometimes a wonderful thing. It comes with terrific speed and sheers out along a pathway that none may safely predict. The wild and freakish hops and swerves of Parmelee's fast ball have become proverbial in the National League. Not only does the fast ball elude the batter, but it frequently eludes the catcher also.

". . . This freakish fast ball swerves inward toward a left-handed batter, away from a right-hander."
Source: *Baseball Magazine* (June 1934, F.C. Lane)

Quote: "In Roy Parmelee, the Giants have a pitcher with more stuff than any other hurler in the league. He is big and strong, with fine hands, and has a wealth of natural stuff . . . Parmelee pitches a slideball. It is a fast delivery that breaks away from the hitter. And it is a natural delivery. Like Schumacher's, it is pitched low."
Source: *The Sporting News* (4/12/1934, Daniel M. Daniel)

Key Pitch: Sinker
Quote: "The toughest pitcher I ever caught . . . was Roy Parmelee. I used to say that he was the only pitcher who could pitch one-third of the game under home plate. He hit me all over. He could throw hard. He would throw that sinker, which would hit on the front end of the plate and it would get you in the arms . . . he had a tremendous arm."
Source: Ray Hayworth in *Baseball Between the Wars* (Eugene Murdock, 1992)

Description: "He had a sailing slider-fastball kind of pitch which was effective."
Source: Paul Richards in *The Man in the Dugout* (Donald Honig, 1977)

MEL PARNELL 6'0" 180-pound lefty
123-75, 3.50, 10 Saves 1947 1956

Pitches: 1. Slider 2. Fastball 3. Curve 4. Sinker
Parnell: "Most times, my slider was my out pitch. I also used a fastball, curve, and sinker, depending on which one was working best on a particular day . . . I basically mixed the slider with the three other pitches. What I would do was use the slider to back a righthanded hitter off the plate a bit, then come back with a sinker outside. If he moved up again, I'd return to the slider. So I kept working in and out, always giving the hitters a lot of movement and changing speeds."
Source: *When the Cheering Stops* (Heiman et al., 1990)
Other source: *Diamond Greats* (Rich Westcott, 1988)

Parnell: "Coming up in the Red Sox organization, I was a fastball pitcher. However, when I got to Fenway Park I figured I had to do more than just throw the fastball. So I went to the slider and sinker and worked more on my curveball. The fastball was a pitch you didn't want to give them to hit in Fenway Park. You wanted to keep that ball moving in on 'em all the way. I concentrated so much on the right-hander that I got a little too relaxed on the left-handed hitter . . .

"Of course, I was one that threw from as high as I could get, and my reason for it was, the higher I could get—and throwing to the lower part of the strike zone—the ball's going out of the line of vision. The hitter's seeing the top of the ball and not the whole baseball. That's what I thought. That was my theory of pitching.

"And I didn't toe the rubber like a lot of other pitchers. A lot of them would turn their foot sideways and pitch from the whole foot. I didn't. I went up on my toes on the rubber, to get a little more height. That was my feeling: the higher I could deliver from, the better it was for me. Then, in throwing the curveball or the sinker, it gave it a chance to get a little more breakage. We all have different theories, but that was the one that I had when I was pitching."
Source: Parnell in *This Side of Cooperstown* (Larry Moffi, 1996)

Description: ". . . uses his fast ball most (but) lately, he has been toying with a slider."
Source: *Baseball Digest* (January 1951, Milt Richman)

Parnell: "My three best pitches are a hook, a slider and a sinker."
Source: *Sport* (July 1956, Milton Richman)

JIM PARQUE 5'11" 170-pound lefty
31-34, 5.42, 0 Saves 1998 2003

Pitch Selection: 1. Fastball (90) 2. Change 3. Curve 4. Slider
Source: *The Scouting Report: 1999*

JEFF PARRETT 6'4" 185-pound righty
56-43, 3.80, 22 Saves 1986 1996

Pitch Selection: 1. Fastball 2. Slider 3. Palm Ball
Source: *1987 Montreal Expos Media Guide*

Pitch Selection: 1. Fastball (90) 2. Slider 3. Split-Fingered Fastball (as Change)
Sources: *The Scouting Report* (1990 and 1993 editions)

STEVE PARRIS 6'0" 195-pound righty
44-49, 4.75, 0 Saves 1995 2003

Pitch Selection: 1. Curve 2. Sinking Fastball (90) 3. Slider 4. Change
Source: *The Scouting Notebook: 1996*

CAMILO PASCUAL 5'11" 170-pound righty
174-170, 3.63, 10 Saves 1954 1971

Pitch Selection: 1. Overhand Curve 2. Fastball 3. Change
Source: *Diamond Greats* (Rich Westcott, 1988)

Comment: "Still no one close to him in quality and quantity of curve balls . . ."
Source: *1963 Major League Handbook* (Don Schiffer)

Note: Pete Runnels, on moving to the National League in 1963, was asked about the speed of Sandy Koufax.

"He's fast," said Runnels, "but how can anybody hum 'em in there faster than Camilo Pascual of the Twins?"
Source: *The Sporting News* (4/27/1963, Jack McDonald)

Description: "It also helps to have a crackling fast ball, a razor-sharp curve and a baffling change-up. Pascual has all of this equipment . . ."
Ted Williams: "I've seen guys with better curves, and some with better fast balls. But I've never seen a pitcher who could throw both as well as Pascual."
Source: *1964 Official Baseball Almanac* (Don Wise)

Description: "Without a doubt the Cuban had the most feared curveball in the American League for 18 years. Camilo had a direct overhand delivery and a high leg kick that shielded the ball from the hitter until the last possible moment. To make it more deceptive he twisted his body around almost to second base before delivering the ball to the plate. Pascual had a blazing fastball that he kept high in the strike zone. His curve started out at the same level and broke straight down ending up about knee high."
Source: *Ted Williams: 'Hey Kid, Just Get It Over the Plate!'* (Russ Kemmerer with W.C. Madden, 2002)

CLAUDE PASSEAU 6'3" 198-pound righty
162-150, 3.32, 21 Saves 1935 1947

Pitch Selection: 1. Sinker 2. Slurve 3. Knuckleball (occasional)
Sources: *Stan Musial* (Musial with Bob Broeg, 1964); *The New Era Cubs* (Eddie Gold and Art Ahrens, 1985); *Baseball Magazine* (September 1944, Ed Rumill on knuckleball pitchers)

Pitch Selection: 1. Fastball 2. Curve 3. Change
Description: "Claude's main stock in trade is a great fast ball with plenty of hop on it, but also totes a fair curve

and change of pace. He is a pitcher who is good at keeping baserunners glued to the bag, although he is a right hander."
Source: *Baseball Magazine* (March 1938, Arthur O. W. Anderson)

Umpire Bill Stewart: "The best so-called spitballs of recent years were thrown by Claude Passeau and Rip Sewell, but Passeau's was much better because he had a perfect chance to cover it up. Passeau's left hand was partially withered, and he couldn't moisten the ball by rubbing it together in his hands. Because of that, he had special permission to wear his glove when he rubbed up the ball. I never caught him at it and neither did anyone else, but it would have been a simple matter for Passeau to put a little slippery elm into his glove."
Source: *The Sporting News* (7/20/1955)

Comment: "There's hardly a game Passeau pitches in which there isn't at least one protest made to the umpires that he is throwing the 'spitter,' a delivery every fan knows was made illegal back in 1920. Every such protest naturally results in an examination of the ball and also in Passeau's complete acquittal."
Source: *Baseball Magazine* (November 1940, Herbert Simons)

Stan Musial: "His ball really went down. I thought it was a spitter, just as others did, but Passeau, a mean competitor, always insisted it was a sinker. Wet or dry, it was a helluva pitch."
Source: *Stan Musial: The Man's Own Story* (Musial, as told to Bob Broeg, 1964)

Notes: Passeau's sinker was widely suspected of being a spitball.

However, in *The New Era Cubs*, written long after Passeau had any incentive to lie about it, Passeau vigorously denied that he ever threw a spitball, and said that "I wouldn't know what to do with a wet baseball." Passeau also says (same source) that he never threw a curveball.

Description: "Claude Passeau was a respected veteran right-hander whom Leo Durocher held up as an example to us young pitchers. Had a great move to first base and could pick you off just looking at you."
Source: *Rex Barney's Thank Youuuu for 50 Years in Baseball from Brooklyn to Baltimore* (Barney with Norman L. Macht, 1993)

FRANK PASTORE 6'2" 188-pound righty
48-58, 4.29, 6 Saves 1979 1986

Pitch Selection: 1. Fastball 2. Slider 3. Off-Speed Curve
Source: *The Scouting Report: 1984*

Story: "When Seaver was with the Reds, one of their young pitchers, Frank Pastore, practiced his delivery so much that the only way you could tell the difference between his and Seaver's was to look at their faces."
Source: *This Ain't Brain Surgery: How to Win the Pennant Without Losing Your Mind* (Larry Dierker, 2003)

JOE PATE 5'10" 184-pound lefty
9-3, 3.50, 12 Saves 1926 1927

Key Pitch: Knuckleball
Source: *The Sporting News* (7/13/1955, Don Donaghey)

Comment: "Pate, who was with the Athletics some years ago, had the best knuckle ball I ever saw. I've seen him put it right over the heart of the plate and make a clean miss of the catcher's glove. Even his own backstop couldn't follow the course of that ball."
Source: Hod Lisenbee in *Baseball Magazine* (August 1930, "Comprising an Interview with Horace Lisenbee")

Notes: Cy Perkins and Ira Thomas both caught Pate with the Athletics, and both confirmed to Donaghey that Pate's "meat-and-potatoes pitch was the knuckler or 'raw-raw' as the flutter was then known to the trade."

Pate made a splash in 1926 when, as a thirty-four-year-old rookie, he went 9-0 with a 2.71 ERA out of the Athletics' bullpen.

CASE PATTEN 6'0" 175-pound lefty
105-128, 3.36, 5 Saves 1901 1908

Pitches: 1. Fastball 2. Drop Ball 3. Fast Curve 4. Spitball
Comment: "The rusty-topped youth had everything on the calendar yesterday. His speed left a trail of fire behind it, and Umpire Sheridan called for the ball a couple of times to see if it was all there, because when it left Case's south paw it looked like a shriveled-up pea."
Source: *The Washington Post* (6/4/1902, Page 9)

Comment: "Winter opposed Patten on the rubber. Both used the spitball almost exclusively . . ."
Source: *The Washington Post* (4/29/1905, Page 9)

BOB PATTERSON 6'2" 185-pound lefty
39-40, 4.08, 28 Saves 1985 1998

Pitch Selection: 1. So-So Fastball 2. Curve 3. Slider
Sources: *The Scouting Report: 1992; The Scouting Notebook 1998*

DANNY PATTERSON 6'0" 190-pound righty
24-18, 4.07, 7 Saves 1996 2003

Pitch Selection: 1. "Vulcan" Splitter 2. Hard Sinker 3. Slider
Note: Patterson gripped his splitter between his middle and ring fingers.
Sources: *The Scouting Notebook* (1998 and 1999 editions)

Pitch Selection: 1. Sinking Fastball (high-80s) 2. Slider 3. Split-Fingered Fastball (as Change)
Source: *The Scouting Notebook* (2001 and 2002 editions)

Note: It's quite likely that Patterson's split-fingered fastball referenced here is the "Vulcan" pitch, but these latter sources don't describe it as such.

DARYL PATTERSON 6'4" 192-pound righty
11-9, 4.09, 11 Saves 1968 1974

Description: "Good fast ball, curve is sharp. Must develop another pitch. Has major league arm but has not been able to use it after two previous trials."
Source: *Baseball Digest* (March 1967, "Official Scouting Reports on 1967 Major League Rookies")

KEN PATTERSON 6'4" 222-pound lefty
14-8, 3.88, 5 Saves 1988 1994

Pitch Selection: 1. Fastball (low-90s) 2. Hard Curve
Source: *The Scouting Report: 1990*

ROY PATTERSON 6'0" 185-pound righty
81-73, 2.75, 2 Saves 1901 1907

Key Pitch: Spitball
Source: *On to Nicollet: The Glory and Fame of the Minneapolis Millers* (Stew Thornley, 1988)

MARTY PATTIN 5'11" 180-pound righty
114-109, 3.62, 25 Saves 1968 1980

Pitch Selection: 1. Rising Fastball 2. Overhand Curve
Source: *Ball Four* (Jim Bouton, 1970)

Pitch Selection: 1. Slider 2. Fastball 3. Change
Source: *The Sporting News* (4/27/1974, Joe McGuff)

ROGER PAVLIK 6'2" 220-pound righty
47-39, 4.58, 1 Save 1992 1998

Pitch Selection: 1. Fastball (89–90) 2. Slider 3. Curve 4. Change
Note: Change used only occasionally in 1992.
Source: *The Scouting Report: 1993; The Scouting Notebook: 1995*

Pitch Selection: 1. Fastball 2. Split-Fingered Fastball 3. Curve 4. Change
Note: Pavlik used an across-the-body delivery.
Source: *The Scouting Notebook: 1996*

Note: *The Scouting Notebook: 1997* says that Pavlik has a sinker that acts like a split-fingered fastball.

GEORGE PEARCE 5'10" 175-pound lefty
35-27, 3.10, 1 Save 1912 1917

Key Pitch: Spitball
Description: "Pierce [*sic*] is hard to hit, has good control for a southpaw spitballer, but seems to get tapped for about one long, crashing drive at fatal times."
Source: *Baseball Magazine* (July 1914, William A. Phelon)

MONTE PEARSON 6'0" 175-pound righty
100-61, 4.00, 4 Saves 1932 1941

Pitch Selection: 1. Curve 2. Fastball
Sources: *The No-Hit Hall of Fame* (Rich Coberly, 1985); Bobby Doerr in *Fenway* (Peter Golenbock, 1992); *Baseball Magazine* (August 1943, Harold C. Burr)
Note: The Burr article states that Pearson had "one of the sharpest-breaking curve balls in history" despite the fact that he had small, ladylike hands which were considered a liability to a curveball pitcher.

ALEJANDRO PEÑA 6'1" 200-pound righty
56-52, 3.11, 74 Saves 1981 1996

Pitch Selection: 1. Fastball (low-90s) 2. Curve 3. Forkball (occasional)
Source: *The Scouting Report: 1990*

Pitch Selection: 1. Fastball 2. Change 3. Slider
Source: *The Scouting Report: 1992*

ORLANDO PEÑA 5'11" 154-pound righty
56-77, 3.71, 40 Saves 1958 1975

Key Pitch: Cuban Fork Ball
Note: Pena's "Cuban Fork Ball" was widely believed to be a spitball.
Sources: *Sports Illustrated* (6/3/1963); *Me and the Spitter* (Gaylord Perry with Bob Sudyk, 1974)

Description: "The skinniest of all flamethrowers is Orlando Guevera Pena, the 155-pound leftyash who's built like a vertical pretzel . . . He has a wide assortment of pitches and can effectively use two or three types of throwing motions."
Source: *Don Schiffer's Major League Baseball Handbook—1964*

Also see entry for Pedro Ramos.

HERB PENNOCK 6'0" 160-pound lefty
241-162, 3.60, 33 Saves 1912 1934

Pitch Selection: 1. Overhand Curve 2. Sidearm Curve 3. Change 4. Fastball 5. Screwball
Sources: *Babe Ruth's Own Book of Baseball* (Ruth, 1928; Waite Hoyt in *Baseball Between the Wars* (Eugene Murdock, 1992); *Baseball Magazine* (December 1923, John J. Ward)
Note: According to Ed Wells in Murdock's book, Pennock snapped his wrist so hard when he threw the curve ball that you could hear his wrist snap if you were sitting on the bench.

Pennock: "I think curve pitching is on the whole the most effective delivery. There are some batters who like curve, but the great majority do not. Of course you cannot use curves exclusively. No pitcher's arm would stand that. You must mix them up with something else, so I have learned to depend very greatly upon a change of pace. This, mixed up with my curves, is the secret of my delivery, such as it is."
Source: *Baseball Magazine* (Ward article)

Pennock: "When I broke into the professional game, I did not have any great speed. I was not and I never have been a speed pitcher . . . There are many pitchers who can throw a faster ball than I can. But there is still a great difference between my fast ball, unimpressive as it may seem, and my screw ball. For example, I use a screw ball mainly as a change of pace. If I can get it over the plate, and I am frequently successful in doing so, it's a tough ball to hit."
Source: *Baseball Magazine* (February 1929, F.C. Lane)

Description: "Pennock throws the ball to the batter with an arm motion that is so twisting of itself that the ball begins to take the curve almost from the moment that it leaves his hand. His control is admirable. That, combined with a drop ball that is baffling to the best of batters, makes him one of the best left-hand pitchers of all time."
Source: *How to Pitch* (J.E. Wray, 1928)

Description: "The New York Yankees have an illustrious brother of the fleshless type of hurler in Herb Pennock, one of the greatest pitchers who ever curved a ball. Pennock's arm is as thin as a high school girl's from shoulder to wrist. His biceps is conspicuous by its absence. In fact, his arm appears so frail that it would impress the observer as quite unsuited to the grilling labor of the hurling mound. And yet, Pennock himself, far from considering his meagre attenuated arm as a disadvantage, is inclined to rate it as a distanced help. 'A thin wrist,' he says, 'is a good thing in curve pitching. Pitching anyway requires no great strength of arm.' "
Source: *Baseball Magazine* (July 1930, F.C. Lane)

Description: "Pennock produced sweeping curves from overhand and three-quarter deliveries, and almost always with the thumb tucked under. He was not speedy fast, and so used thumb-end and finger-tip for the fast ball grip. Batters, even umpires, were constantly perplexed by the wide arc of Pennock's curves . . .

"Pennock also possessed a flexible wrist, which he would occasionally flip gracefully in mid-air, and in different ways during delivery to let the ball go from the side or off the fingers on a diagonal. At times he would turn the wrist so that his palm faced up. From this posi-

tion, and with the wrist flip, he would deliver a downbreaking curve from the sharpest angle used by any lefthander. And with the thumb tucked under!"
Source: *How to Play Winning Baseball* (Arthur Mann, 1953)

Comment: "One famous batter . . . said that in an entire series Herbert Pennock never threw him two balls of the same kind. There was always a difference in position or speed or direction, just enough to throw him off balance and mix him up in his stride or swing."
Source: Sam Jones in *Baseball Magazine* (September 1930)

TROY PERCIVAL 6'3" 200-pound righty
27-35, 3.00, 283 Saves 1995 2003

Pitch Selection: 1. Fastball (high-90s) 2. Curve 3. Change
Sources: *The Scouting Notebook: 1997; The Scouting Notebook 2000*

CARLOS PEREZ 6'3" 210-pound lefty
40-53, 4.44, 0 Saves 1995 2000

Pitches: 1. Fastball (86–90) 2. Change 3. Slider 4. Split-Fingered Fastball
Sources: *1996 Montreal Expos Media Guide; The Scouting Notebook* (1996 and 1998 editions)

MELIDO PEREZ 6'4" 180-pound righty
78-85, 4.17, 1 Save 1987 1995

Pitch Selection: 1. Fastball 2. Forkball
Source: *The Scouting Report: 1993*

MIKE PEREZ 6'0" 187-pound righty
24-16, 3.56, 22 Saves 1990 1997

Pitch Selection: 1. Fastball 2. Curve 3. Slider (occasional)
Source: *The Scouting Notebook: 1996*

PASCUAL PEREZ 6'2" 162-pound righty
67-68, 3.44, 0 Saves 1980 1991

Pitch Selection: 1. Slider 2. Fastball 3. Change 4. Curve
Note: Perez would throw an eephus pitch a couple of times a game.
Sources: *Tom Seaver's 1989 Scouting Notebook; The Scouting Report* (1990 and 1992 editions)

YORKIS PEREZ 6'0" 213-pound lefty
14-15, 4.44, 2 Saves 1991 2002

Pitch Selection: 1. Fastball 2. Slider 3. Change
Source: *1990 Montreal Expos Media Guide*

Pitch Selection: 1. Fastball 2. Curve 3. Slider
Sources: *The Scouting Notebook: 1995* and *1996*

RON PERRANOSKI 6'0" 180-pound lefty
79-74, 2.79, 179 Saves 1961 1973

Pitch Selection: 1. Sinker 2. Curve 3. Fastball 4. Change
Sources: *The Relief Pitcher* (John Thorn, 1979); Perranoski in *Baseball Digest* (January 1962, Charlie Park), *Baseball Stars of 1964* (article by George Vecsey), *Major League Baseball: 1971* (Brenda Zanger and Dick Kaplan)

Perranoski: "Most relief pitchers who didn't last relied on fast balls. I've got a good hummer but I rely on my curve and change-up too. Breaking stuff. That's what gets them."
Source: *1964 Official Baseball Almanac* (Don Wise)

Description: ". . . Ron Perranoski threw a curveball that broke in enormous proportions, both horizontally and vertically. He also threw from a 'drag-arm' delivery. His arm came around a count after he took his stride, an instant later than the batter expected it."
Source: *The Pitching Staff* (Steve Jacobson, 1975)

POL PERRITT 6'2" 168-pound righty
92-78, 2.89, 8 Saves 1912 1921

Pitch Selection: 1. Fastball 2. Curve 3. Slow Ball
Description: "Perritt is possessed of wonderful speed and an exceptional curve ball to supplement it . . . Heretofore this human slat thought only of buzzing his fast ball past the hitter. Now he mixes up his delivery. And he has a pretty fair sort of slow ball to toss in with the speed and the hook."
Source: unidentified source from the Hall of Fame Library, September 1917

Note: Perritt threw sidearm.
Source: *The Sporting Life* (1/16/1915)

GAYLORD PERRY 6'4" 205-pound righty
314-265, 3.11, 11 Saves 1962 1983

Pitches: 1. Spitball 2. Slider 3. Fastball 4. Curve 5. Forkball (developed in 1970) 6. Change
Source: *Me and the Spitter* (Perry with Bob Sudyk, 1974)

Pitches, 1981: 1. Spitball 2. Forkball 3. Sinker 4. Slow Curve 5. Change
Source: *The Sporting News* (5/9/1981, Tim Tucker); also, early in 1981 Perry threw the "puff ball," which he invented. Tucker wrote, "As the 'puff ball' is thrown, a cloud of resin dust emerges, distracting the hitter, if not rendering him helpless." The Puff Ball was outlawed in mid-May of that season.

Note: Late in the 1965 season, Perry refined his slider with the help of Giants pitching coach Larry Jansen, and the slider became one of his better pitches.
Source: *Baseball Digest* (March 1967, Jack McDonald)

Quote: "Oh, he may throw [the spitball] once in a while. But really, he throws a real good sinker. That thing about the spitter is mostly psychological."
Source: Pirates pitching coach Don Osborn in *Sport* (November 1972, Lou Prato)

JIM PERRY 6'4" 190-pound righty
215-174, 3.45, 10 Saves 1959 1975

Pitch Selection: 1. Fastball 2. Curve 3. Slider
Source: *Baseball Digest* (September 1960)

Pitch Selection: 1. Fastball 2. Slider
Source: *The Sporting News* (9/11/1971, Bob Fowler)

ROBERT PERSON 6'0" 193-pound righty
51-42, 4.64, 9 Saves 1995 2003

Pitches: 1. Fastball (90) 2. Hard Slider 3. Straight Change
Source: *The Scouting Notebook: 1997*

Pitches: 1. Fastball (mid-90s) 2. Slider 3. Split-Fingered Fastball 4. Curve 5. Change
Source: *The Scouting Notebook: 2002*

GARY PETERS 6'2" 200-pound lefty
124-103, 3.25, 5 Saves 1959 1972

Pitch Selection: 1. Sinking Fastball 2. Slider 3. Change 4. Curve
Sources: *Baseball Stars of 1964* (article by Bill Furlong); *Baseball Stars of 1965* (article by Furlong); *When the Cheering Stops* (Heiman et al., 1990)

FRITZ PETERSON 6'0" 185-pound lefty
133-131, 3.30, 1 Save 1966 1976

Pitch Selection: 1. Fastball 2. Curve 3. Slider 4. Screwball (added 1971)
Sources: *The Ballplayers* (1990, article by George D. Wolf); *Major League Baseball: 1971* (Brenda Zanger and Dick Kaplan)

MARK PETKOVSEK 6'0" 198-pound righty
46-28, 4.74, 5 Saves 1991 2001

Pitch Selection: 1. Sinking Fastball 2. Change 3. Curve (occasional)
Source: *The Scouting Notebook 2000*

DAN PETRY 6'4" 185-pound righty
125-104, 3.95, 1 Save 1979 1991

Pitch Selection: 1. Fastball 2. Slider 3. Change 4. Curve
Sources: *The Scouting Report: 1987; Tom Seaver's 1989 Scouting Notebook; The Scouting Report: 1990*

ANDY PETTITTE 6'5" 235-pound lefty
149-78, 3.94, 0 Saves 1995 2003

Pitch Selection: 1. Fastball 2. Sinker 3. Hard Curve 4. Cut Fastball 5. Change
Sources: *The Scouting Notebook* (1997 and 2000 editions)

Note: In 2001, Pettitte threw 64 percent fastballs, 20 percent curves, 10 percent sliders and 6 percent change-ups. According to the same source, Pettitte threw two fastballs, a four-seamer thrown 87–94 miles per hour, and a cutter thrown 84–88. His curve had a big 12-to-6 break and was thrown 69–77 m.p.h. He threw a sweeping slider 80–85 m.p.h. and a change-up with a slight sink, thrown 75–79 m.p.h.
Source: *The Seattle Times* (10/17/2001)

JESSE PETTY 6'0" 195-pound lefty
67-78, 3.68, 4 Saves 1921 1930

Pitch Selection: 1. Fastball 2. Curve 3. Change 4. Knuckleball (occasional)

Sources: *Baseball Magazine* (July 1927, John J. Ward; and August 1929, Ward); *Minneapolis Star* (4/12/1935)
Note: In Ward's 1927 article, Petty credited his success as a major league pitcher to Joe Wood, who (in 1920) helped him change from a sidearm delivery to three-quarters.
Petty in Ward's 1929 article: "My fast ball has always been my best ball. I have a good curve, and I can throw a knuckle ball . . . Very few pitchers can depend upon getting the knuckle ball over the plate. I can't myself."

PRETZEL PEZZULLO 5'11" 180-pound lefty
3-5, 6.38, 1 Save 1935 1936

Description: "And then there is John Pezzullo, a young left-hander with the Phillies, who still is quite a sight. Ballplayers say that the young man . . . first throws out a shoe. Then a glove appears, a hip swings out and an arm comes around. The ball is thrown, finally, to a batter who is sometimes so bewildered by the whole business that he forgets to swing. No wonder! Players swear the ball Pezzullo tosses up, finally, jumps, glides, sinks and sometimes collapses."
Source: *Baseball Magazine* (June 1936, Hugh Bradley, "Freak Pitching Deliveries—Past and Present")

JEFF PFEFFER 6'3" 210-pound righty
158-112, 2.77, 10 Saves 1911 1924

Key Pitch: Fastball
Source: *The Brooklyn Dodgers* (Frank Graham, 1947)

JACK PFIESTER 5'11" 180-pound lefty
70-44, 2.02, 0 Saves 1903 1911

Description: "A side-wheeling left hander with a great pick-off move to first base . . ."
Source: *Deadball Stars of the National League* (SABR, 2004; article includes a photo that vividly shows Pfiester throwing with a low sidearm motion.)

Quote: "Jack Pfiester is chosen in advance by Manager Chance to occupy the slab in the crucial game as the New Yorkers have been found less effective against the sidewheel delivery."
Source: *The Unforgettable Season* (G.H. Fleming, Page 302)

DAN PFISTER 6'0" 187-pound righty
6-19, 4.87, 1 Save 1961 1964

Description: "AL batters insist that Dan Pfister has more baffling pitches than any K.C. hurler . . . has a quantity of curves."
Source: *1963 Major League Handbook* (Don Schiffer)

DEACON PHILLIPPE 6'0" 180-pound righty
189-109, 2.59, 12 Saves 1899 1911

Pitch Selection: 1. Fastball 2. Curve
Source: *Honus Wagner: A Biography* (Dennis De Valeria and Jeanne Burke-De Valeria, 1995)

TOM PHOEBUS 5'8" 185-pound righty
56-52, 3.33, 6 Saves 1966 1972

Pitch Selection: 1. Fastball 2. Curve 3. Slider
Source: *The No-Hit Hall of Fame* (Rich Coberly, 1985)
Pitch Selection: "Strong overhand curve and a good fastball."
Source: *Major League Baseball—1969* (Jack Zanger)

HIPOLITO PICHARDO 6'1" 195-pound righty
50-44, 4.44, 20 Saves 1992 2002

Pitches: 1. Sinking Fastball (low-90s) 2. Slider 3. Change
Source: *The Scouting Report: 1993*

Pitches: 1. Sinking Fastball (low-90s) 2. Split-Fingered Fastball 3. Slider 4. Change
Sources: *The Scouting Notebook* (1996, 1997, and 1999 editions)

RON PICHE 5'11" 165-pound righty
10-16, 4.19, 12 Saves 1960 1966

Pitch Selection: 1. Sinking Fastball
Source: Milwaukee Braves 1961 Guide for Press/Radio/TV

BILLY PIERCE 5'10" 160-pound lefty
211-169, 3.27, 32 Saves 1945 1964

Pitches: 1. Fastball 2. Curve 3. Slider (added in 1951) 4. Change
Sources: *Baseball Digest* (September 1956, John C. Hoffman); *The Sporting News* (6/5/1957, Edgar Mun-

zel); *The Sporting News* (8/29/1956, Page 4); Paul Richards in *The Man in the Dugout* (Donald Honig, 1977); many other sources; the Slider probably replaced the Curve as Pierce's second-best pitch at some point after 1951.

Note: According to Al Hirshberg in *Sport Magazine* (February 1957), Pierce threw his slider off the motion that he had used to throw the curve, rather than throwing it as a fastball.

Note: Listed by *The Sporting News* (8/29/1956) as having one of the best fastballs in the league.

Also see entries on Bob Shaw and Ted Gray.

TONY PIERCE 6'1" 190-pound lefty
4-6, 3.25, 8 Saves 1967 1968

Key Pitch: Curve
Source: *Baseball Digest* (July 1967, Sid Bordman)

Description: "Good control, curve, but his fast ball is not good enough to carry him through. A good-looking boy but you can't give him a fast ball if he doesn't have one."
Source: *Baseball Digest* (March 1967, "Official Scouting Reports on 1967 Major League Rookies")

DUANE PILLETTE 6'3" 195-pound righty
38-66, 4.40, 2 Saves 1949 1956

Pitches: 1. Sinker 2. Slider 3. Curve 4. Fastball
Pillette: "I was basically a three-quarters pitcher from the time I started out. I hurt my elbow in spring training in 1947, pitching for Newark. So I had to change my delivery a little bit, so it didn't hurt so much. My fastball had tailed off real good to right-handers anyhow, so I developed a great sinker. I became a sinkerball-sliderball pitcher more than a fastball-change pitcher. And I'd throw the curve maybe six or eight times a game, for a strike when I wanted one. The fastball was just to show 'em something, brush 'em back or something . . . My sinker, I'd throw with four seams, but I'd turn it over. The slider, I'd throw to the center of the plate, and it would break to the left. Same thing with the sinker, but it would break the other way. Basically, I was effective because I didn't have to throw to the corners; everything I threw would just nick the corners . . . The curveball was big, and I could throw it for strikes."
Source: interview with Duane Pillette (8/2/2003, Rob Neyer)

GEORGE PIPGRAS 6'1" 185-pound righty
102-73, 4.09, 12 Saves 1923 1935

Pitch Selection: 1. Fastball 2. Knuckleball 3. Screwball 4. Curve
Sources: Pipgras in *Baseball When the Grass Was Real* (Donald Honig, 1975); *Babe Ruth's Own Book of Baseball* (Ruth and Ford Frick, 1928)
Quote from Ruth book: "Most of the pitchers in the league today have a screw ball of some sort or another. George Pipgras, the youngster who made good with the Yankees last year, has as a good a one as any—though George's knuckle ball is even more effective than his screw ball."

Comment: "He pitches a lot of balls, more than almost any other pitcher in either league. Somehow, his curves break too much or the fast ball hops a little too far. But this wildness is not an unmixed blessing. It tends to make him difficult to hit.

"Pipgras has a knuckle ball which he uses mainly as a change of pace. He also has a pretty good curve. But his main dependency is a sizzling, fast ball. There are few pitchers who have anything on George Pipgras, when he is burning them over the platter."
Source: *Baseball Magazine* (May 1930, John J. Ward)

Note: About Pipgras's performance in Game 2 of the 1927 World Series, umpire George Moriarty wrote, "The most noteworthy feature of his work was his almost curveless pitching. He threw only six curves during the nine frames. While he is primarily what the profession calls a 'fast ball pitcher,' he has an effective curve. The average pitcher uses between twenty and forty curves in a game."
Source: *Baseball Magazine* (February 1928)

Note: According to Pipgras in *The Men in Blue* (Larry Gerlach, 1980), he learned his curveball from Herb Pennock.

TOGIE PITTINGER 6'2" 175-pound righty
115-113, 3.10, 3 Saves 1900 1907

Pitch Selection: 1. Fastball 2. Curve
Quote: "In his prime he had great speed, sharp curves and good command."
Source: *The Sporting Life* (1/23/1909)

JUAN PIZARRO 5'11" 170-pound lefty
131-105, 3.43, 28 Saves 1957 1974

Pitch Selection: 1. Fastball 2. Slow Curve 3. Spitball
Note: Prior to 1961, Pizarro also threw a screwball and knuckleball, and for a while all the stories about Pizarro mentioned that he'd been convinced to abandon the screwball.
Sources: *Baseball Stars of 1965* (article by Bill Furlong); *Nobody's Perfect* (Denny McLain with Dave Diles, 1975); *1963 Major League Handbook* (Don Schiffer)

Quote: ". . . then, last season, he developed a slow curve . . . Says Chicago manager Al Lopez, 'When Pizarro first joined the club in 1961 he was fooling around with a screwball. Here was a young pitcher with control trouble, so I told him to concentrate on finding the plate with his fastball and curve and forget about the screwball. He had enough stuff without it.' "
Source: *1964 Official Baseball Almanac* (Don Wise)

Description: "With Juan Pizarro, I think in his case his potential was that he could throw the ball at ninety-five miles per hour. Well, that's not necessarily potential, that's somebody with a good fastball . . . It was just, throw the ball hard and then turn that little screwball over at times. But I don't think that he was consistent in getting the pitches where he needed to get them in times of trouble."
Source: Braves catcher Del Crandall in *This Side of Cooperstown* (Larry Moffi, 1996)

EDDIE PLANK 5'11" 175-pound lefty
326-194, 2.35, 23 Saves 1901 1917

Pitch Selection: 1. Curve 2. Fastball
Source: Bob Shawkey in *The Man in the Dugout* (Donald Honig, 1977)

Ty Cobb: "Now, that is Plank's biggest weakness. He has a bad move toward first base, and is one of the few pitchers with a bad motion to hold runners near the bag who has been really great. This is well known in the American League."
Source: *Busting 'Em and Other Big League Stories* (Ty Cobb, ghostwritten by John Wheeler, 1914)

Quote: ". . . The cross-fire pitcher steps sideways instead of straight ahead, with the forward foot. Such foot action obliges him to pitch to the plate from an angle instead of a straight line, which latter style is pursued by the majority of moundsmen.

"Cross-firing, therefore, is done for effectiveness but cannot be gained otherwise. It is undoubtedly harder to possess control in this manner, because a pitcher is off balance on each effort before the ball leaves his hands. Many pitchers have made reputations with this odd delivery, one of the foremost of whom was Eddie Plank, the old Mack southpaw . . ."
Source: Umpire George Moriarty in *Baseball Magazine* (July 1927)

DAN PLESAC 6'5" 205-pound lefty
65-71, 3.64, 158 Saves 1986 2003

Pitch Selection: 1. Fastball 2. Hard Slider
Sources: *The Scouting Report: 1990; The Scouting Report: 1992*

ERIC PLUNK 6'5" 210-pound righty
72-58, 3.82, 35 Saves 1986 1999

Pitches, early career: 1. Fastball 2. Curve 3. Slider 4. Slow Curve/Change
Pitch Selection, late 1990s: 1. Wide-Breaking Slider 2. Fastball
Sources: *The Scouting Report: 1990; The Scouting Notebook 2000*

JOHNNY PODRES 5'11" 170-pound lefty
148-116, 3.68, 11 Saves 1953 1969

Pitch Selection: 1. Curve 2. Fastball 3. Change
Sources: *Sporting News* (7/27/1963, Page 21), *Sport* (August 1963, Bill Libby); *Splendor on the Diamond* (Rich Westcott, 2000)

Podres in 1963: "I have four pitches: slow curve, fast curve, fast ball and change-up."
Source: *Baseball Digest* (May 1963, Frank Reagan)

Pitch Selection: 1. Fastball 2. Change
Podres: "Right behind my fast ball, I rate my change-up. I don't know, maybe my change is better than my fast ball but I still feel more confident in a tight spot with my fast ball. I will say this, though. I started becoming a pitcher instead of a thrower right after Charlie Dressen taught me the change three seasons back . . . The change and the fast ball make a good combination. I re-

ally learned how to mix them up right against the Yankees in the Series."

Gil McDougald: "Well, he's not as fast as Herb Score, but he'll do."
Source: *Sport* (July 1956, Milton Richman)

Quote: "Johnny Podres was extraordinarily fast in 1953 . . . Podres is a more rounded pitcher now, but not quite so fast."
Source: *1964 Official Baseball Almanac* (Don Wise)

Quote: "In a normal nine-inning game, Podres estimates that sixty-five percent of his pitches are fast balls, twenty-five percent curves, and the remaining ten percent changes off either his fast ball or his curve."
Source: *Famous American Athletes of Today* (F.E. Whitmarsh, 14th Series, October 1956)

Tim McCarver: "Brooklyn Dodgers left-hander Johnny Podres threw the most effective circle change, and it still serves as the prototype. He gripped the ball with only his last three fingers while his thumb and index finger formed a circle halfway up on the ball. It was a change-up that he could throw on any count."
Source: *Tim McCarver's Baseball for Brain Surgeons and Other Fans* (McCarver with Danny Peary, 1998)

Commentary: Though contemporary sources did *not* stress the quality of Podres' change-up (taught to him by Charlie Dressen), by the early 1990s—when Podres was the Phillies' pitching coach—he was often described as the master of the change-up.

TOM POHOLSKY 6'3" 205-pound righty
31-52, 3.93, 1 Save 1950 1957

Pitches: 1. Sneaky Fastball 2. Curve 3. Change
Comment: "Poholsky doesn't bother with any of the trick pitches—knucklers, screwballs and all that. He sticks to the standard equipment, mixing up the fastball, curve and change-up."
Marty Marion: "He's a master of changing speeds already. I have watched him when his control was a little off and he'd get behind a hitter, two and nothing. He might come right in with the change-up, a tricky slow curve. And he'll get it where he wants it. Man, you won't see many old-timers with the nerve to do that."
Max Lanier: "Tom will fool you. He has such an easy way of throwing you get the idea he's not fast. But he is, and that ball of his is always doing things. It moves."
Source: *The Sporting News* (6/6/1951, W. Vernon Tietjen)
Note: Listed by *The Sporting News* (8/29/1956) as having one of the best fastballs in the league.

HOWIE POLLETT 6'1" 175-pound lefty
131-116, 3.51, 20 Saves 1941 1956

Pitch Selection: 1. Fastball 2. Change 3. Slow Curve
Source: *Stan Musial* (Musial with Bob Broeg, 1964)

Description: "Used to terrorize the hitters with his fine fast ball but not any longer. Now considered strictly a 'junk' pitcher."
Source: *Baseball Digest* (January 1951, Milt Richman)

Quote: "[Pollett] is one of the few 'survivors' of the windmill tradition."
Source: *Baseball Digest* (September 1947, Harry Sheer)

ELMER PONDER 6'0" 178-pound righty
17-27, 3.21, 0 Saves 1917 1921

Key Pitch: Slow Curve
Quote: "Elmer was another to whom the curve 'came natural.' He threw 'the hook' much more than [Tommy] Bridges does—at least nine curves to every ten pitches. At spring camp Ponder always started out with curves, the reason he cited, 'because they're so much easier on the arm.' Other pitchers who didn't find them that way would shake their heads as Ponder unfurled big slow 'spinners' from opening day on; but unwise though his method might have been for them, it certainly worked well for him."
Source: "Greg's Gossip" column in the Portland *Oregonian* (5/20/1947, L.H. Gregory).

SIDNEY PONSON 6'1" 249-pound righty
58-65, 4.54, 1 Save 1998 2003

Pitch Selection: 1. Fastball (92) 2. Slider 3. Curve 4. Change
Source: *The Scouting Notebook: 2000*

JIM POOLE 6'2" 190-pound lefty
22-12, 4.31, 4 Saves 1990 2000

Pitch Selection: 1. Slow Curve 2. Fastball 3. Forkball
Source: *The Scouting Report: 1996*

BOB PORTERFIELD 6'0" 190-pound righty
87-97, 3.79, 8 Saves 1948 1959

Pitch Selection: 1. Fastball 2. Change 3. Curve 4. Slider (learned in 1954)
Source: *The Boston Red Sox* (Tom Meany); *Baseball Stars of 1953* (article by Shirley Povich); *Sport* (February 1957, Page 72)

Note: Listed by *The Sporting News* (8/29/1956) as having one of the best fastballs in the league.

MARK PORTUGAL 6'0" 170-pound righty
109-95, 4.03, 5 Saves 1985 1999

Pitch Selection: 1. Curve 2. Slider 3. Fastball 4. Change
Sources: *The 1994 Baseball Almanac; The Scouting Notebook 1999*

NELS POTTER 5'11" 180-pound righty
92-97, 3.99, 22 Saves 1936 1949

Pitches 1. Screwball 2. Fastball 3. Curve 4. Change 5. Slider
Sources: *Baseball Magazine* (November 1944, Herbert Simons); *Stan Musial* (Musial with Bob Broeg, 1964); *Baseball's 50 Greatest Games* (Bert Sugar, page 172); *We Played the Game* (Danny Peary, 1994); Clint Conatser in *The Pastime in Turbulence: Interviews with Baseball Players of the 1940s* (Brent Kelley, 2001)

Key Pitch: Knuckleball
Source: *1949 Who's Who in Baseball* (Page 72)

Note: The 1944 *Baseball Magazine* article gives a near-perfect account of Potter's pitch selection at that time, stating that

1) he learned to throw the screwball in 1936,

2) he began throwing it regularly a couple of years later,

3) he picked up a slider at Louisville in 1942, and

4) he threw the screwball about one pitch in four.

Commentary: According to *The Sporting News* (5/1/1957), Potter was once ejected from a game by Cal Hubbard and suspended by the league for throwing a spitball. According to *The Saturday Evening Post* (6/17/1950), this occurred in 1944, and came about because Luke Sewell, Browns manager, was getting nowhere protesting that Hank Borowy was throwing a spitter. Frustrated, he ordered his own pitchers to retaliate. Potter did—and was suspended for ten days by the league. There's not a lot of evidence that Potter threw a spitball as a matter of course, and in 1945 umpire Bill Summers told Dan Daniel that Potter "definitely does not throw the spitter. He doesn't know how." On the other hand, in Phil Marchildon's autobiography he says Potter's "repertoire included a screwball, a slider and the occasional spitter."

The Knuckleball citation has only the single source, and is highly suspect.

DENNIS POWELL 6'3" 175-pound lefty
11-22, 4.95, 3 Saves 1985 1993

Pitch Selection: 1. Fastball 2. Slider 3. Curve
Source: *The Scouting Report: 1990*

JACK POWELL 5'11" 195-pound righty
244-256, 2.97, 16 Saves 1897 1912

Key Pitch: Fastball
Quote: "Powell's great forte is pitching with fearful speed."
Source: *The National Game* (Alfred H. Spink, 1911)

Note: According to *The Ballplayers* (1990, article by Jack Kavanaugh), Powell threw sidearm.

Also see Walter Johnson entry.

JAY POWELL 6'4" 225-pound righty
35-22, 4.23, 22 Saves 1995 2003

Pitch Selection: 1. Sinking Fastball (low-90s) 2. Cut Fastball
Source: *The Scouting Notebook: 1997*

Pitch Selection: 1. Sinking Fastball (91–96) 2. Slider
Sources: *The Scouting Notebook: 1999* and *2000*

TED POWER 6'4" 215-pound righty
68-69, 4.00, 70 Saves 1981 1993

Pitch Selection: 1. Fastball 2. Slider 3. Sinker
Sources: *The Scouting Report* (1987 and 1990 editions)

JOE PRESKO 5'9" 165-pound righty
25-37, 4.59, 5 Saves 1951 1958

Description: "Presko has a sneaky fast ball like Brecheen's and has adopted many of his tutor's [Brecheen's] man-

nerisms. When the youngster peers intently at the catcher's signal, goes into his business-like, unspectacular windup and cuts loose with the ball, he looks like Brecheen pitching from the opposite side."
Source: *New York Sun Telegram* (7/2/1951)

TOT PRESSNELL 5'10" 175-pound righty
32-30, 3.80, 12 Saves 1938 1942

Pitch Selection: 1. Knuckleball 2. Curve 3. Fastball
Source: *Milwaukee Brewers: Pennant Winners American Association 1936* (Howard Purser, 1937); Ray Hayworth in *Baseball Between the Wars* (Eugene Murdock, 1992)

JOE PRICE 6'4" 220-pound lefty
45-49, 3.65, 13 Saves 1980 1990

Pitches: 1. Fastball (86–88) 2. Curve 3. Slider 4. Change
Source: *The Scouting Report: 1984*

RAY PRIM 6'0" 178-pound lefty
22-21, 3.56, 4 Saves 1933 1946

Pitch Selection: 1. Fastball 2. Screwball
Description: "Although he's known chiefly for his screwball—which he picked up from a hurler he can't identify in his Piedmont League days—Prim prefers a fast ball for his clutch pitch. 'You make fewer bad pitches with a fast ball,' he stresses. However, the screwball, which he may throw merely three or four times in one game and then maybe ten or twelve times in three innings the next, is a lethal weapon."
Source: *Baseball Magazine* (March 1946, Herbert Simons)

MARK PRIOR 6'5" 230-pound righty
24-12, 2.74, 0 Saves 2002 2003

Pitches: 1. Fastball (93–97) 2. Hard Curve 3. Slider
Note: Prior's mid-90s fastball usually moves from right to left.
Source: Observation of WGN broadcast, 7/19/2002 (Rob Neyer)

MIKE PROLY 6'0" 185-pound righty
22-29, 3.23, 22 Saves 1976 1983

Pitch Selection: 1. Sinking Fastball 2. Slider 3. Change 4. Curve (occasional)
Source: *The Scouting Report: 1983*

HUB PRUETT 5'10" 165-pound lefty
29-48, 4.63, 13 Saves 1922 1932

Pitches: 1. Screwball 2. Fastball 3. Curve
Quote: "In late July (Lee) Fohl had given Pruett a two-week rest and indicated that the rookie would be used only for relief work for the rest of the season. However, recent relief appearances had shown that his 'screwball' or 'fadeaway' did not break and he relied mainly on his curve and fastball. With his pitching inventory thus reduced the University of Missouri grad was much less effective."
Source: *The 1922 St. Louis Browns* (Roger A. Godin, 1991)
Other Source: *Baseball Digest* (December–January 1961, Page 45)

Note: Pruett was famous for one thing: his success against Babe Ruth. Pruett's obituary in the *New York Times* (1/30/1982) reported that he struck Ruth out 15 of the 30 times he faced him.

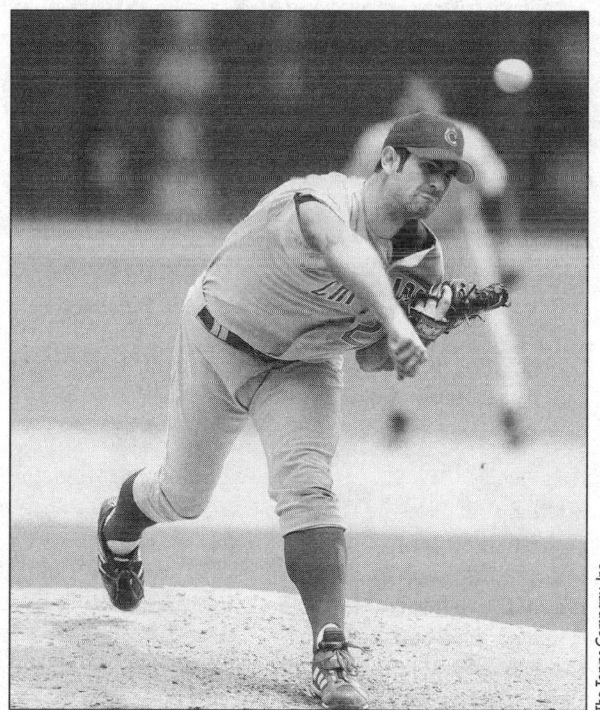

Mark Prior

CHARLIE PULEO 6'2" 190-pound righty
29-39, 4.25, 2 Saves 1981 1989

Pitch Selection: 1. Fastball (84–87) 2. Slider 3. Curve
Source: *The Scouting Report* (1983–1985 editions)

BOB PURKEY 6'2" 175-pound righty
129-115, 3.79, 9 Saves 1954 1966

Pitch Selection: 1. Slider 2. Knuckleball 3. Fastball 4. Sinker
Sources: *Baseball Stars of 1959* (article by Dick Kaplan); *Pennant Race* (Jim Brosnan, 1962); *Don Schiffer's Major League Baseball Handbook—1964*

Pitches, 1962: 1. Knuckleball 2. Fastball 3. Slider 4. Straight Change 5. Slow Curve 6. Sinker
Purkey: "The tail end of last year, I hit a bad streak where nothing was working. I came up to a game against Pittsburgh determined to get myself back in the groove or shake up the hitters. Seven years before, Mr. (Branch) Rickey took me aside for ten pitches and taught me how to throw a knuckleball. I'd been fooling around with it ever since, but I didn't have confidence in getting it over. Against Pittsburgh that day I threw 96 knuckleballs. I got beat 3-1 on two unearned runs, but from then on I've known I can get it over the plate."
Description: "The Purkey knuckleball (which he grips with the index and middle finger on top of the ball) thus joined the Purkey slider, the straight change, the off-speed curve, the sinker, and 'a fastball that moves.'

" 'I wouldn't trade my fastball,' asserts Purkey, 'for a lot of others in this league that are thrown faster but straighter. My fastball moves 'in' to a righthanded batter. It moves this much . . .'

"Here Purkey gauges a six-inch break. (Gil Hodges, commenting on Purkey, said the fastball 'moves this much . . . ' and held his hands even further apart.)"
Source: *Sport* (October 1962, Steve Perkins)

Ron Fairly: "He used to throw everything but the kitchen sink. Now he throws the sink, too."
Roberto Clemente: "Everything he throws you is the same—same motion, same angle—but you don't know where the ball is going. All you know is it's going to be a strike, so you got to be alive."
Ernie Banks: "He's got a sinker ball that drops out of sight. I think he could drill for oil with it."
Purkey: ". . . So I started to experiment with the knuckler. That was in 1955. By 1958 I was able to throw it effectively. Sometimes, if I'm accomplishing nothing with my fastball or curve or if I'm in trouble, getting myself belted on the mound, I try the knuckler. But that doesn't mean it's my best pitch. If I'm right, I can set up any batter with almost any type of pitch . . ."
Purkey: "I don't depend mainly on any one pitch. My knuckler isn't as good as Hoyt Wilhelm's, my fastball not so overpowering as Ryne Duren's, my curve not so sharp as Vernon Law's. But put them all together, and they give me a pretty fair repertoire."
Quote from author Herb Kamm on Game 3 of 1961 World Series: "Purkey was pitching as if he could go on forever, mixing sliders and flutterballs with fastballs so effectively the Yanks were slamming their bats into the dugout in disgust."
Source: *Baseball's Greatest Players Today* (edited by Jack Orr, 1963)

PAUL QUANTRILL 6'1" 175-pound righty
59-73, 3.65, 20 Saves 1992 2003

Pitch Selection: 1. Sinking Fastball 2. Slider 3. Change 4. Curve
Sources: *The Scouting Report: 1996* and *The Scouting Notebook 1999*

MEL QUEEN 6'1" 197-pound righty
20-17, 3.14, 14 Saves 1966 1972

Key Pitch: Fastball
Queen: "I just went to the mound and threw as hard as I could."
Source: *Go Pro Baseball Wise* (P.J. Dragseth, 1999)

JACK QUINN 6'0" 196-pound righty
247-218, 3.29, 57 Saves 1909 1933

Pitch Selection, 1909–1915: 1. Fastball 2. Curve 3. Spitball
Pitch Selection, 1920–1933: 1. Spitball 2. Curve 3. Change
Note: Quinn was one of the "grandfathered" pitchers allowed to continue to throw the spitball after it was otherwise banned in 1921.
Sources: *The National Game* (Alfred H. Spink, 1911); *Baseball Magazine* (July 1927, W. R. Hoefer); *The Relief*

Pitcher (John Thorn, 1979); *The Crooked Pitch* (Martin Quigley, 1984); 1923 *Reach Guide* (Page 38)

Description: "There are pitchers who are easy to catch and pitchers who are hard to catch. The easiest pitcher I ever handled is Jack Quinn. His control is well nigh perfect."
Source: Athletics catcher Cy Perkins in *Baseball Magazine* (October 1930, F.C. Lane)

DAN QUISENBERRY 6'2" 170-pound righty
56-46, 2.76, 244 Saves 1979 1990

Pitch Selection: 1. Sinker 2. Curve
3. Change (developed in 1984)
4. Knuckleball (rare)
Note: Quisenberry converted from sidearmer to submariner in 1980.
Source: *Season Ticket* (Roger Angell, Page 205)

DICK RADATZ 6'6" 230-pound righty
52-43, 3.13, 122 Saves 1962 1969

Pitch Selection: 1. Fastball 2. Slider
Quote: ". . . whipping in a sidearm concoction of blue darts and sharp hooks."
Sources: *The Relief Pitcher* (John Thorn, 1979); Radatz in *Fenway* (Peter Golenbock, 1992); *1963 Major League Handbook* (Don Schiffer)

Pitch Selection: 1. Fastball (80%) 2. Slider 3. Change
Joe Adcock: "He has three things going for him: his fast ball moves, he gets it over the plate, and he has a deceptive delivery."
Al Kaline: "He takes a very slow windup. Then all of a sudden the ball is in on top of you. That windup fools me. I never expect the ball to get to the plate as quickly as it does."
Source: *Late and Close: The History of Relief Pitching* (Paul Votano, 2002)

Description: "His blazing fastball (which he throws about 80 percent of the time), slider, and change-ups were striking out batsmen at the rate of better than one an inning . . ."
Source: *1964 Official Baseball Almanac* (Don Wise)

Radatz: "Ted Williams had said that I needed another pitch. So I tried adding a pitch in '65. It got me into control problems. I changed my arm position, and came up with a sinker. I started using it when I shouldn't have, and it was all downhill after that. It was a classic case of, if the wheel's not broke, don't fix it. I tried changing something, and it became a nightmare for me."
Source: *Splendor on the Diamond* (Rich Westcott, 2000)

Radatz: "I throw overhand to lefthanded batters and sidearm to righthanded hitters."
Source: *1965 Official Baseball Almanac* (Bill Wise)

OLD HOSS RADBOURN 5'9" 168-pound righty
309-196, 2.67, 2 Saves 1881 1891

Pitch Selection: 1. Rising Fastball 2. Dry Spitball
3. Inshoot 4. Slow Change
5. Fadeaway (Screwball) 6. Sinker
Sources: *The National Game* (Alfred H. Spink, 1911); *Heroes of Baseball* (Robert Smith, Page 137), *The Sporting News* (4/11/1918)

Commentary: Radbourn pitched like Marichal, Pedro Martinez, David Cone, or El Duque, throwing a bewildering mix of pitches from a variety of arm angles, thrown hard with outstanding control. Alfred H. Spink, who saw him pitch, wrote, "He was an athlete in figure as well as in action and beside being able to send the ball in with terrific speed, to curve it in any direction, he was always in complete control of his delivery." The best description, however, was offered by the redoubtable Ted Sullivan, who managed Radbourn, also by way of Spink. " 'Rad' was continually inventing some new delivery and trying to get control of it . . . Radbourne, as the posted followers of the game know, was the master of curves and deliveries. He had all of what they have to-day, and one or two that they have not. He had a jump to a high, fast ball, and an inshoot to a left-handed batter. He had a drop ball that he did not have to spit on, and called it a 'spit ball.' Added to that, he had a perplexing slow ball that was never duplicated on the ball field. The nearest approach to him in this delivery was by John Clarkson and Tim Keefe of Rad's time. To this slow ball he could give a lot of speed. It would come toward you and then change its route all of a sudden. It was the delivery they call today the 'fadeaway.' "

Quote: "The 'prince of hurlers,' as Rad is often called, is noted for the entire absence of effort which characterizes his delivery. The ball is thrown with an easy underhand movement, at a pace which the over-confident

batsman soon discovers to be very deceptive. Change in speed and a wide 'out curve' are the strong points of Radbourne's work."
Source: Article titled "How Men Pitch Base-Ball: The Famous Pitchers of the National League of 1886." No author or publisher is given, though the information in the article is said to have come from photographic studies done by the *New York World* newspaper.

Comment: "In the early days the pitcher delivered a straight ball, varying only in speed and, with the development of batting skill, the game promised to become a farce, due to the enormous scores. Arthur Cummings, Jim Devlin and other pitchers, had been experimenting with a twist or curve, but it remained for Radbourne to perfect and put into execution the in and out shoots, the drop and the upshoots and marvelous deceptions in speed, besides a system of watching bases, which gave the game an extraordinary zest. 'Rad' was also the first to conceive the idea of walking the heavy hitters and then fanning the light weights."
Source: *Baseball Magazine* (August 1917, E.E. Pierson); without actually doing the work to check, we'll assume that Radbourn here is being given a bit more credit than he deserves.

Description: "When Radbourne reported to Providence in 1882 he had a slow ball which, to the amazement of the batters who faced him, revolved rapidly until it reached the plate and then simply seemed to die away and fall toward the ground. A fast ball acting in this manner would not have fooled them so much but as Radbourne always threw his fast ball, his curve and this queer fast-spinning slow ball with the same motion, the National League batsmen found him a hard nut to crack."
Source: *Baseball Magazine* (May 1931, H.H. Westlake)

TED "DOUBLE DUTY" RADCLIFFE

5'10" 190-pound righty
NEGRO LEAGUES 1928 1950

Pitch Selection: 1. Emery Ball 2. Fastball 3. Curve
Source: Radcliffe interview in *Voices from the Great Black Baseball Leagues* (John Holway, 1975)

Quote: "The fact is Double Duty could cut the ball. It wasn't any secret. This is called cheating. A cut baseball is extremely tough to hit because if the pitcher throws it one way, it'll sink and if he throws it another way, it'll sail. You'd wait to hit it, and it would either drop or jump and you never knew which until it was too late. It was an illegal pitch."
Source: *Catching Dreams: My Life in the Negro Baseball Leagues* (Frazier "Slow" Robinson with Paul Bauer, 1999)

SCOTT RADINSKY 6'3" 190-pound lefty

42-25, 3.44, 52 Saves 1990 2001

Pitch Selection: 1. Fastball (low-90s) 2. Slurve
Note: Pitched with a low three-quarters delivery.
Source: *Bill Mazeroski's Baseball* (1993 edition)

Pitch Selection: 1. Fastball 2. Slider
Source: *The Scouting Notebook 1999*

BRAD RADKE 6'2" 186-pound righty

116-110, 4.32, 0 Saves 1995 2003

Pitch Selection: 1. Fastball 2. Curve 3. Slider 4. Change
Source: *The Scouting Notebook 1998*

KEN RAFFENSBERGER 6'2" 185-pound lefty

119-154, 3.60, 16 Saves 1939 1954

Key Pitch, early career: Rising Fastball
Pitches, as veteran: 1. Forkball 2. Slow Curve 3. Fastball 4. Change
Note: By 1944, Raffensberger had come up with a dependable forkball, and by the late 1940s that was probably his best pitch.
Sources: *Stan Musial* (Musial with Bob Broeg, 1964); *Baseball Magazine* (February 1945, Clifford Bloodgood)
Musial: "Raffy had nothing except slow stuff, and a fork ball, but, with changing speeds and control, he made those pitches seem so fat when they weren't. The fork ball looked as big as a grapefruit, but fell off the table, low. I stubbornly tried to slug with him and didn't have much success. The challenge to go for the long ball off soft stuff hurt me—and the Cardinals—against crafty Raffy."

Description: "Ken Raffensburger was another cutie, another Preacher Roe; couldn't blacken your eye with a pitch. The ball would come up there looking like a basketball, then all of a sudden it wasn't there."
Source: *Rex Barney's Thank Youuuu for 50 Years in Base-*

ball from Brooklyn to Baltimore (Barney with Norman L. Macht, 1993)

Description: "Raffensberger, whose six-two height is accentuated by his slimness, has what is probably the widest range of pitching delivery in the majors, from decidedly underhanded to completely overhanded, with varying degrees of side-arm and three-quarters."
Source: *Baseball Magazine* (April 1941, Herbert Simons)

PAT RAGAN 5'10" 185 pound righty
77-104, 2.99, 6 Saves 1909 1923

Description: "While the great Mathewson failed to show winning form, young Ragan furnished a delightful surprise for the spectators. Ragan was purchased from the Brooklyn club principally because he had proved effective against the Giants, and the way he manipulated his curves and shoots yesterday made it plain that Manager Stallings had 'doped' the kid's work out to a nicety, for Ragan held the Giants to two hits, both in the fifth inning, a clean liner by Robertson and a scratch bunt single by Merkle."
Source: *Boston Evening Globe* (6/1/1915)

CHUCK RAINEY 5'11" 190-pound righty
43-35, 4.50, 2 Saves 1979 1984

Pitch Selection: 1. Fastball (83–85) 2. Slider 3. Curve
Source: *The Scouting Report: 1983*

ED RAKOW 5'11" 178-pound righty
36-47, 4.33, 5 Saves 1960 1967

Pitch Selection: 1. Fastball 2. Curve
Quote: "This hard thrower has a curve which bends in half and his fast one has a deceptive hop."
Source: *1963 Major League Handbook* (Don Schiffer)

PEDRO RAMOS 6'0" 175-pound righty
117-160, 4.08, 55 Saves 1955 1970

Pitch Selection: 1. Fastball 2. Spitball 3. Curve
Quote: "Secondly, he brought the pitch he calls a Cuban palmball. He learned it throwing rocks at the Iglesia brothers, who lived down the street. Today Pedro has a good fastball, a rubber arm and that Cuban palmball that sometimes breaks a good deal more than the hitter expects.

"Some hitters and managers around the American League have suggested—even insisted—that the good curveball was a spitter. True to the pitchers' code, Ramos says, 'Who, me?' But he laughs just a little more and protests just a little less than the other pitchers. 'A spitter?' he says. 'That's illegal. I would try anything and everything to improve myself and win. It's a Cuban palmball."
Source: *Sport* (January 1965, Steve Jacobson)

Ramos on his spitball: "When they'd say I threw a spitter, I'd say it was my 'Cuban palmball.' I never threw a palmball. Now I can say that I did wet it a little bit. Jim Bunning used to put grease in his pants, Whitey Ford used to mark and scuff the ball. A lot of pitchers did things to the ball. So I decided if I could get away with that, I was going to do it. My curve wasn't that effective, so I needed another pitch to help me get by in tough situations where I didn't want to use my heater. I needed a ball that would sink so I could get double-play grounders instead of 2-run homers. I heard from other pitchers that if you just wet the tips of the fingers, the ball would move. So I started working on the side with it and started developing a pretty good 'Cuban palmball.' I did throw some and was never caught."
Source: *We Played the Game* (Danny Peary, 1994)

Pitch Selection: 1. Fastball 2. Knuckleball
Description: ". . . Ramos has a better than average fast ball, which rises, and a knuckler. Most baseball observers agree that his greatest asset, though, is his ability to change speeds . . .

"Ramos throws his knuckler in the conventional way, with his thumb alongside the ball and the fingernails of his index and middle fingers on the seams. He grips the ball as tightly as he can and throws it with a stiff wrist."
Source: *Sport* (September 1959, Bob Addie)

Umpire Bill McKinley: "Now you had to watch some of those pitchers because they'd give you the business with the ball. The worst was Pedro Ramos of the Washington Senators. We had to watch him like a clock. He would go to his mouth with his hand and then pass it down over his shirt before he pitched. His fingers never touched his shirt, but you couldn't tell that from behind the plate.

The first thing you knew, that ball was all brown and sticky."
Source: *The Men in Blue* (Larry Gerlach, 1980)

Note: In the late 1950s and early '60s, Ramos was widely regarded as one of the fastest *runners* in the American League.

WILLARD RAMSDELL 5'11" 165-pound righty
24-39, 3.83, 5 Saves 1947 1952

Pitch Selection: 1. Knuckleball 2. Slow Curve 3. Fastball
Source: *The Sporting News* (7/23/1952)

Story: "It's just like catching without signals. When Ramsdell's on the mound there's a three-way guessing game going on between the batter, me and Ramsdell himself on what the ball is going to do. On one pitch in Seattle, apparently headed over the plate, the ball suddenly broke at a right angle and hit Heinz Becker squarely on the chest. Walt Dropo of Sacramento hit a knuckler that didn't knuckle over the centerfield wall at Gilmore [Field, in Hollywood] but in the same game Will had him swinging on a third strike that fluttered clear over my head and into the backstop. I sure have to stay loose back there."
Source: Hollywood Stars catcher Al Unser in *Pacific Coast Baseball News* (6/25/1949); same article claims that Ramsdell "throws nothing but 'dipsey-doo' pitches."

TOAD RAMSEY 6'1" 190-pound lefty
113-124, 3.29, 0 Saves 1885 1890

Pitch Selection: 1. Drop Ball 2. Fastball
Quote: "Ramsay [*sic*], the greatest strike-out pitcher among all the left-handers, was strong for the strike-out theory, and worked with an immense drop ball that the enemy would miss by wholesale."
Source: *Baseball Magazine* (November 1910, George Morton)
Other Source: *Baseball Magazine* (February 1937, George Bulkley)

Quote: ". . . baseball's first knuckleball pitcher, but that the pitch was then known as a 'drop curve.' "
Source: *Nineteenth Century Stars* (SABR)

Note: *Heroes of Baseball* (Monk Sherlock, 1954) contains an article about Ramsey titled "The First Knuckle Baller," and says that Ramsey's index finger was permanently bent so that he had an unusual grip on the ball.

Note: The *Baseball Cyclopedia* (Ernest Lanigan) says that Ramsey was "a bricklayer before he took up the Pastime" and "seemed to have acquired phenomenal strength in his arm and fingers laying brick, [which] he used to good advantage when he pitched. His speed was nothing terrible, but he had a drop ball that would break a foot at least."

Commentary: It's extremely unlikely that Ramsey threw a knuckleball, in anything like the modern sense of the term. Ramsey was moderately famous at the turn of the century, and if he'd thrown the dancing variety of the knuckleball, people would have said that when Ed Summers and Eddie Cicotte arrived in the majors. What's likely is that Ramsey threw some variety of what we know as the knuckle-curve.

PAT RAPP 6'3" 195-pound righty
70-91, 4.68, 0 Saves 1992 2001

Pitch Selection: 1. Fastball (88–90) 2. Slider 3. Curve 4. Change
Source: *The Scouting Notebook 2000*

VIC RASCHI 6'1" 205-pound righty
132-66, 3.72, 3 Saves 1946 1955

Pitch Selection: 1. High Fastball 2. Slider (post-1948) 3. Slow Curve
Sources: Raschi in *The Men of Autumn* (Dom Forker, 1989); Raschi quoted in *The Sporting News* (7/20/1968, Lee Allen's column); *My Life in Baseball* (Robin Roberts with C. Paul Rogers III, 2003)

Note: According to Raschi in the Lee Allen column, ". . . I never had a curve. Never a curve at all. It was learning a slider from Johnny Schulte that made me a winning pitcher."

Raschi in 1948: "I do not pitch the slider. I have it. I could use it with telling effect. But after having acquired the pitch, I never used it in an American League game.

"I made use of the slider as a curative agency, and then put it in a pigeonhole for possible reference and use later on. I do not now contemplate using it.

"Why? Well, if you are not the complete master of

the slider, it becomes a Frankenstein monster. It turns into a gopher ball.

"I have enough confidence in my fast ball and curve and change to keep away from extra stuff."

Source: *The Sporting News* (9/15/1948, J.G. Taylor Spink column)

Quote: "Vic had the faculty, when he was in trouble, to throw his fastball a foot farther. And he got it over."

Source: Tom Ferrick in *The Men of Autumn*

Mel Parnell: "Vic Raschi was a high-ball pitcher, a Robin Roberts type. His high fastball would rise and the batter was constantly hitting underneath it, hit it up in the air."

Source: *This Side of Cooperstown* (Larry Moffi, 1996)

Description: "His best and most frequent pitch is a high fastball. He often changes the speeds on his fastball and generally comes in with a slow curve when he gets behind."

Source: *Baseball Digest* (January 1951, Milt Richman)

Robin Roberts: "Yogi Berra once told me that Vic Raschi . . . developed a big, slow curve to help him get through the start of the game when he couldn't get his rhythm for his fastball. Once he gets going, he would throw about 90 percent fastballs and pretty much ignore his curveball."

Source: *My Life in Baseball*

DENNIS RASMUSSEN 6'7" 230-pound lefty
91-77, 4.15, 0 Saves 1983 1995

Pitch Selection: 1. Fastball 2. Slow Curve 3. Change

Source: *Tom Seaver's 1989 Scouting Notebook*

ERIC RASMUSSEN 6'3" 205-pound righty
50-77, 3.85, 5 Saves 1975 1983

Pitch Selection: 1. Fastball 2. Slider

Ted Simmons: "Rasmussen came with a fastball and a pretty good slider, and there for a while he had some success with just those two pitches. He didn't have a third pitch, though. He didn't have a change-up, and after a while the hitters will figure you out if you're just throwing hard and hard, unless your fastball's 97 and your slider's 91 or something."

Source: phone interview with Simmons (10/8/2002, Rob Neyer)

Note: In 1977, Rasmussen developed a cut fastball under the tutelage of Cardinals pitching coach Claude Osteen.

Sources: *The Sporting News* (7/16/1977, Neal Russo; 2/3/1979, Phil Collier)

DOUG RAU 6'2" 175-pound lefty
81-60, 3.35, 3 Saves 1972 1981

Pitches: 1. Change 2. Fastball 3. Curve

Note: Rau experimented with a sinker in 1975, but dropped it because it interfered with his change.

Sources: *The Sporting News* (9/23/1972, Bob Hunter; 9/14/1974, Gordon Verrell; and 5/22/1976, Verrell)

SHANE RAWLEY 6'0" 170-pound lefty
111-118, 4.02, 40 Saves 1978 1989

Pitch Selection: 1. Fastball 2. Slider 3. Curve 4. Change

Sources: *The Scouting Report: 1987; Tom Seaver's 1990 Scouting Notebook*

JIM RAY 6'1" 185-pound righty
43-30, 3.61, 25 Saves 1965 1974

Pitch Selection: 1. Slider 2. Curve 3. Fastball

Source: *Baseball Digest* (March 1966, "Scouting Reports on 1966 Major League Rookies")

BUGS RAYMOND 5'10" 180-pound righty
45-57, 2.49, 2 Saves 1904 1911

Pitch Selection: 1. Hard Spitball 2. Fastball 3. Curve 4. Change

Source: *The National Game* (Alfred H. Spink, 1911)

Quote from Spink: "He is a man of wonderful physique and fearful strength. He has terrific speed and is really one of the fastest pitchers in America . . . Raymond read of the marvelous success Elmer Stricklett was having with [the spitball], and immediately determined to become famous as a spitball pitcher . . . Raymond is a clever pitcher and relies upon this cleverness to win games, as well as he does on his strength, speed and curves. Fully half the ball players in the National League to-day give Raymond no credit for possessing brains at all, and these same players are the easiest victims for the big fellow."

Description: "Raymond, when pitching, chewed slippery elm incessantly and the spittle thus produced when applied to the ball gave it an extraordinary sharp break."
Source: *Baseball Magazine* (May 1913, P.A. Meaney)

CLAUDE RAYMOND 5'10" 175-pound righty
46-53, 3.66, 83 Saves 1959 1971

Pitch Selection: 1. Fastball 2. Change 3. Curve
Source: *Inside the Astrodome* (1965)

JEFF REARDON 6'0" 190-pound righty
73-77, 3.16, 367 Saves 1979 1994

Pitch Selection: 1. Fastball 2. Slider 3. Curve
Sources: *The Scouting Report: 1983; The Scouting Report: 1990*
Note: Later in his career Reardon pretty much dumped the slider, and worked mostly with curves and fastballs.

DICK REDDING 6'4" 210-pound righty
NEGRO LEAGUES 1911 1938

Pitch Selection: 1. Fastball 2. Curve
Note: Redding did not develop the curve until late in his career.
Source: *Blackball Stars* (John Holway, 1988)

Quote: "Now Satchel didn't throw as hard as Dick Redding. You should have seen *him* turn the ball loose."
Source: Jesse Hubbard, quoted by Holway in the 1980 *Baseball Research Journal* (SABR)

Quote: "Redding was like Walter Johnson. Nothing but speed. That's the reason they called him Cannonball. He just blew the ball by you."
Source: Frank Forbes, quoted by Holway in the 1980 *Baseball Research Journal* (SABR)

JERRY REED 6'1" 190-pound righty
20-19, 3.94, 18 Saves 1981 1990

Pitch Selection: 1. Fastball (high-80s) 2. Curve 3. Slider
Source: *The Scouting Report: 1990*

RICK REED 6'0" 195-pound righty
93-76, 4.03, 1 Save 1988 2003

Pitch Selection: 1. Two-Seam Fastball 2. Cut Fastball 3. Curve 4. Change
Source: *The Scouting Notebook 1999*

RON REED 6'6" 215-pound righty
146-140, 3.46, 103 Saves 1966 1984

Pitch Selection: 1. Fastball 2. Slider 3. Curve 4. Slip Pitch
Hank Aaron: "The last kid I saw coming up with so many pitches was Juan Marichal. Most kids have one or two pitches when they come up but Reed has several. And he can control all of them. In that respect, he reminds me of Robin Roberts, although he doesn't have Roberts' fastball."

Description: "Because of his lanky build and the exaggerated windup [Lum] Harris helped him develop, Reed doesn't seem to need a Roberts' fastball. His delivery, which confuses the batter with arms, legs and elbows coming from all directions, makes him deceptively fast."
Source: *Sport* (September 1968, Lou Prato)

Pitch Selection: 1. Fastball 2. Slider
Source: *The Sporting News* (5/19/1979, Hal Bodley)

Description: "He isn't real fast. But he has fine control of his change-up and that makes his fast ball look quicker."
Source: Braves manager Lum Harris in *Baseball Digest* (August 1968, Ed Rumill); same source says that Reed's change-up was the Slip Pitch, taught to him by Paul Richards (of course), who then was the president of the Braves.

Note: Reed played in the NBA for two seasons, beginning in 1965, then quit basketball and earned a spot on the National League All-Star team as a rookie in 1968.

STEVE REED 6'2" 200-pound righty
45-34, 3.50, 18 Saves 1992 2003

Pitch Selection: 1. Sinker 2. Curve 3. Slider 4. Change
Note: Reed is basically a submarine pitcher, sometimes going up to a three-quarters delivery.
Sources: *1994 Baseball Almanac; The Scouting Report: 1996; The Scouting Notebook 1999; The Scouting Notebook 2000*

PHIL REGAN 6'3" 200-pound righty
96-81, 3.84, 92 Saves 1960 1972

Pitches, 1960–1962: 1. Hard Slider 2. Sinking Fastball 3. Overhand Curve

Pitches, 1963–1965: 1. Sinking Fastball
2. Overhand Curve 3. Slider
Pitches, 1966–1972: 1. Hard Slider 2. Sinking Fastball
3. Spitball
Source: *Phil Regan* (Regan as told to Jim Hefley, 1968)

Commentary: Regan learned his slider—he said it was "different from sliders that most pitchers throw. Mine breaks only a little, sharp and down."—from Schoolboy Rowe in the minors. When Charlie Dressen took over as manager of the Tigers in 1963, he told Regan to stop throwing his slider so often and concentrate on his overhand curve. Regan had decent success throwing the curve that season, but couldn't throw it where he wanted in 1964 and '65, resulting in a career crisis. But he was traded to the Dodgers, sent to the bullpen and allowed to throw his slider, and lasted another seven seasons as a reliever.

Pitch Selection: 1. Spitball 2. Slider
Sources: *The Cubs of '69* (Rick Talley, 1983), *Me and the Spitter* (Gaylord Perry with Bob Sudyk, 1974)

Description: ". . . Regan was one of a kind. He had an awkward diving delivery, and his out pitch was a moist one that went with a tough slider. Because Regan threw what might be called a clean spitter, allowing the perspiration to run down his arms onto the ball, umpires were never able to bust him, despite their certainties that the ball was coming in less than arid."
Source: *Durocher's Cubs: The Greatest Team That Didn't Win* (David Claerbaut, 2000)

Umpire Tom Gorman: "Regan, of course, needed the spitter. It was his out pitch."
Source: *Three and Two!* (Tom Gorman as told to Jerome Holtzman, 1979)

DOC REISLING 5'10" 180-pound righty
15-19, 2.45, 1 Save 1904 1910

Description: "He is a medium sized man with plenty of strength and all the curves."
Source: *The National Game* (Alfred H. Spink, 1911)

BRYAN REKAR 6'3" 220-pound righty
25-49, 5.62, 0 Saves 1995 2002

Pitch Selection: 1. Fastball (low-90s) 2. Slider
3. Curve 4. Change

Description: "He has a Hideo Nomo like turn in his windup that can disrupt a hitter's timing."
Source: *The Scouting Notebook: 2002*
Other Sources: *The Scouting Notebook* (1996 and 1998 editions)

MIKE REMLINGER 6'0" 195-pound lefty
50-46, 3.78, 16 Saves 1991 2003

Pitch Selection: 1. Fastball (low-90s) 2. Hard Slider
3. Change (added about 1997)
Source: *The Scouting Notebook: 1998*

STEVE RENKO 6'5" 230-pound righty
134-146, 3.99, 6 Saves 1969 1983

Pitch Selection: 1. Cut Fastball 2. Knuckle Curve
Source: *Baseball Digest* (July 1983, Mike McKenzie)

ED REULBACH 6'1" 190-pound righty
182-106, 2.28, 13 Saves 1905 1917

Pitch Selection: 1. Fastball 2. Curve
Quote: "John Evers claims that Reulbach was not inferior even to Walter Johnson in speed."
Source: *Baseball Magazine* (May 1915)

Pitch Selection: 1. Curve 2. Drop Curve
Sources: *Baseball Research Journal 1982* (article by Cappy Gagnon); *My Life in Baseball: The True Record* (Ty Cobb with Al Stump, 1961)

Description: "Ames and Reulbach have the best and sharpest curves and the best assortment of them, but both have suffered terribly from this very fact, especially in the early spring. Their shoots have such strange 'hops' that they fool the umpire, and ball after ball is called when the curves really break over the plate. Much of the reputation of Ames and Reulbach for wildness is due to the vision of the umpires. In summer, when Reulbach and Ames seem to be going invincibly, they are really using the same stuff, but the umps can see them better."
Source: *Baseball Magazine* (August 1913, "The Vagaries of Pitching")

Commentary: While there's little doubt that Reulbach showed fine curveballs, there's also little doubt that he was very fast. In an October 1913 *Baseball Magazine* article about the physiology of speed pitching, a photo of Reulbach is captioned, "Ed Reulbach, Who Boasts the

Swiftest Delivery in the National League. Note His Long Clean Cut Arm and Shoulders, an Ideal Build for Speed Pitching."

RICK REUSCHEL 6'3" 215-pound righty
214-191, 3.37, 5 Saves 1972 1991

Pitch Selection: 1. Sinker 2. Slider 3. Curve
Sources: *Tom Seaver's 1989 Scouting Notebook; The Scouting Report: 1990*

Pitch Selection: 1. Fastball 2. Cut Fastball 3. Curve 4. Sinker
Source: *USA Today* (6/14/1989, Rod Beaton)

JERRY REUSS 6'5" 200-pound lefty
220-191, 3.64, 11 Saves 1969 1990

Key Pitch until mid-'80s: Fastball
Quote: "I'll bet he didn't throw more than two or three curves all day."
Source: Dodgers catcher Steve Yeager after Reuss pitched a five-hitter to beat the Yankees in Game 5 of the 1981 World Series, quoted in *The Sporting News* (11/7/1981, Page 21). A year later in TSN (9/27/1982, Gordon Verrell), Dodgers pitching coach Ron Perranoski called Reuss's fastball "his bread-and-butter pitch" and said it "was breaking this far" (holding his hands a foot apart).

Pitches, following three elbow operations in mid-'80s:
1. Cut or Sinking Fastball 2. Slow Curve 3. Change
Sources: *The Scouting Report* (1987 and 1990 editions); *Tom Seaver's 1989 Scouting Notebook*

CARLOS REYES 6'0" 190-pound righty
20-36, 4.66, 4 Saves 1994 2003

Pitch Selection: 1. Change 2. Slider 3. Fastball
Sources: *The Scouting Notebook: 1995* and *1996*

Pitch Selection: 1. Sinker 2. Slider 3. Fastball (low-80s)
Sources: *The Scouting Notebook: 1997* and *2000*

DENNYS REYES 6'3" 245-pound righty
15-21, 4.77, 2 Saves 1997 2003

Pitch Selection: 1. Cut Fastball 2. Overhand Curve
Source: *The Scouting Notebook: 2000*

ALLIE REYNOLDS 6'0" 195-pound righty
182-107, 3.30, 49 Saves 1942 1954

Pitches: 1. Fastball 2. Slider 3. Slow Curve 4. Spitball
Sources: *The Men of Autumn* (Dom Forker, 1989); Reynolds quoted in *The No-Hit Hall of Fame* (Rich Coberly, 1985); Gus Zernial quoted in the *Kansas City Star* (3/26/1957, Page 14); *Allie Reynolds: Super Chief* (Royce Parr, 2002)

Reynolds: "Different pitchers grip the ball different ways. I used to hold the ball across the seams, using all four of them. I felt it gave my ball a rise and a good break on the curve. I was kind of a dart thrower. I didn't have a long, loose motion like Raschi's. I did pick up a slider with the Yankees. I tried to pick up a change-up like Lopat's, but I didn't have quite the motion—too short."
Source: *The Gospel According to Casey* (Ira Berkow and Jim Kaplan, 1992)

Note: Described by *The Sporting News* (12/1/1954) as one of the hardest throwers in baseball.

SHANE REYNOLDS 6'3" 210-pound righty
114-95, 4.09, 0 Saves 1992 2003

Pitch Selection: 1. Split-Fingered Fastball 2. Fastball 3. Curve
Source: *The Scouting Notebook 1999*

ARMANDO REYNOSO 6'0" 186-pound righty
68-62, 4.74, 1 Save 1991 2002

Pitch Selection: 1. Cut Fastball 2. Screwball 3. Forkball 4. Curve
Source: *The Scouting Notebook 2000*

FLINT RHEM 6'2" 180-pound righty
105-97, 4.20, 10 Saves 1924 1936

Pitch Selection: 1. Fastball 2. Overhand Curve 3. Knuckleball (occasional)
Quote: "Rhem developed an over-hand curveball to complement his blazing fastball."
Source: *Cardinals Collection: 100 Years of St. Louis Cardinals Photos* (Mark Stang, Page 16)
Other Source for Fastball: *The St. Louis Cardinals* (Fred Lieb, 1945)
Source for Knuckleball: *Baseball Magazine* (May 1928)

Jesse Haines in *Baseball Magazine:* "Flint Rhem has a knuckle ball that would make your hair stand on end. But catchers don't like to have him use it for neither they, nor he, nor anyone else knows just where it's going when he cuts loose with it."

BILLY RHINES 5'11" 168-pound righty
112-107, 3.48, 4 Saves 1890 1899

Pitch Selection: 1. Curve 2. Upcurve
Note: Rhines threw sidearm, except for the "upcurve" which was thrown underhanded, and appeared to break upwards. Our impression is that Rhines threw hard, although Zeman's article does not specifically say so.
Source: *Baseball's First Stars* (SABR, 1996, article by David Zeman)

BOB RHOADS 6'1" 215-pound righty
97-82, 2.61, 2 Saves 1902 1909

Quote: "After [the fourth inning] Rhoads was never in real danger, although he started the sixth by hitting Speaker with a fast inshoot, but the latter was caught between second and third on Thoney's grounder. From that time never a visitor reached first base."
Source: *Boston Globe* (9/19/08)

Comment: "If 'Dusty' Rhoades possessed greater speed, he would be a great pitcher."
Source: *The Sporting News* (11/5/1908)

RICK RHODEN 6'3" 195-pound righty
151-125, 3.59, 1 Save 1974 1989

Pitch Selection, early career: 1. Fastball 2. Slider
Source: *The Sporting News* (9/18/1976, Gordon Verrell)

Pitches, later career: 1. Slider 2. Fastball 3. Curve 4. Change
Source: *The Scouting Report: 1987*

ARTHUR RHODES 6'2" 190-pound lefty
69-51, 4.33, 17 Saves 1991 2003

Pitches: 1. Fastball 2. Curve 3. Change
Source: *The Scouting Notebook 2000*

Pitches: 1. Fastball (mid-90s) 2. Slider 3. Curve 4. Change
Source: *The Scouting Notebook 2003*

GORDON RHODES 6'0" 187-pound righty
43–74, 4.85, 5 Saves 1929 1936

Key Pitch: Fastball
Source: *Los Angeles Times* (7/20/1928, Page 11)

DENNIS RIBANT 5'11" 165-pound righty
24-29, 3.87, 9 Saves 1964 1969

Pitch Selection: 1. Big, Slow Curve 2. Slider
Source: *Baseball Digest* (March 1963, Page 99)

WOODY RICH 6'2" 185-pound righty
6-4, 5.06, 1 Save 1939 1944

Pitch Selection: 1. Sinker 2. Fastball
Comment: "A big, strong right-hander, Woody had the natural sinker and fastball of a great pitcher . . . But Rich's fame was short-lived. He did stay with the [Red Sox] long enough to win a few games and, at times, showed flashes of greatness. But the boy had such an uncontrollable appetite that he soon was fat and well beyond big league hurling condition. It was not long before he even had trouble winning in the higher minors."
Source: *Baseball Magazine* (March 1947, Hub Miller)

J.R. RICHARD 6'8" 222-pound righty
107-71, 3.15, 0 Saves 1971 1980

Pitch Selection: 1. Slider 2. Fastball
Source: *The Sporting News* (5/26/1979, Harry Shattuck)

Quote: "James Rodney Richard threw the hardest slider of any pitcher in history."
Source: Rick Sutcliffe during ESPN broadcast of Cardinals-Cubs game, 7/28/2002

Comment: "Former big leaguers James Rodney Richard and Larry Andersen had the best sliders of any pitchers that I ever coached."
Source: *Think Better Baseball* (Bob Cluck, 2002)

PETE RICHERT 5'11" 165-pound lefty
80-73, 3.19, 51 Saves 1962 1974

Pitch Selection: 1. Fastball 2. Slider
Source: *The Ballplayers* (1990, article by Jane Charnin-Aker)

Pitch Selection: 1. Rising Fastball 2. Sinking Fastball 3. Curve
Source: *Sport* (May 1961, "Waiting and Hoping")

Comment: "Richert hopes to (add) an extra pitch to go along with his fastball and slider. If he's lacked a definite identity, he's also lacked variety in his pitches."
Source: *Major League Baseball—1969* (Jack Zanger)

LEE RICHMOND 5'10" 155-pound lefty
75-100, 3.06, 3 Saves 1879 1886

Pitch Selection: 1. Fast Jump Ball 2. Half Stride Ball
Richmond: "I did have a fast jump ball that was hard to hit when it was working right . . . It is a singular thing that of that first no-man-reach-first-base game in 1880 I can remember almost nothing except that my jump ball and my half stride ball were working splendidly and that Bennett and the boys behind me gave me perfect support." (The half stride ball, we would assume, was a primitive change. Richmond's phrasing, thinly parsed, seems to imply that he had other pitches as well.)
Source: *The National Game* (Alfred H. Spink, 1911)

Pitch Selection: 1. Fast Jump Ball 2. Half Stride Ball 3. Curve
Source: *Perfect* (Ronald A. Mayer, 1991)
Note: Mayer uses the same quote as above but cites the Cleveland Press (no date) as the source. He also relates the familiar tale of the nineteenth-century pitcher while in college convincing the school's physics professor that a curve ball actually does curve. In this case the school was Brown, and the professor, Walter Greene.

ELMER RIDDLE 5'11" 170-pound righty
65-52, 3.40, 8 Saves 1939 1949

Pitch Selection: 1. Curve 2. Sinker 3. Change 4. Fastball
Sources: Jack Miley, King Features Syndicate (1941); *Baseball Magazine* (August 1942, Clifford Bloodgood)
Quote from Miley article: "His ace in the hole is one of the big league's best fast curves. It breaks as if it rolls off a rooftop. Even his best friends wouldn't call Elmer a Bob Feller. He can get that ball up to the plate without bouncing it, but he breaks no speed records in doing so."

STEVE RIDZIK 5'11" 170-pound righty
39-38, 3.79, 11 Saves 1950 1966

Note: Listed by *The Sporting News* (8/29/1956) as having one of the best fastballs in the league.

DAVE RIGHETTI 6'4" 195-pound lefty
82-79, 3.46, 252 Saves 1979 1995

Pitch Selection: 1. Fastball 2. Slider
Note: Righetti also threw a curve and change as a starter.
Source: *The Scouting Report: 1990*

Pitch Selection: 1. Fastball 2. Curve 3. Slider 4. Sinker 5. Change
Source: *The Scouting Report: 1992*

JOHNNY RIGNEY 6'2" 190-pound righty
63-64, 3.59, 8 Saves 1937 1947

Ted Williams: "The trouble with the average pitcher is his hardheadedness. He has too inflated an opinion of what he's got. Say it's a fastball. He thinks he can throw it by you any time, any place, anywhere. If you hit it, he gives it to you again.

"Johnny Rigney was like that. He would put it in there, and you would ride it out . . . All the great hitters could hit fastballs, no matter how fast the pitcher was."
Source: *My Turn at Bat* (Ted Williams with John Underwood, 1969)

JOSE RIJO 6'1" 200-pound righty
116-91, 3.24, 3 Saves 1984 2002

Pitch Selection: 1. Fastball 2. Slider 3. Forkball 4. Change
Sources: *The Scouting Report 1990; The Scouting Report: 1992*

RICARDO RINCON 5'9" 190-pound lefty
19-22, 3.42, 21 Saves 1997 2003

Pitch Selection: 1. Slider (83–88) 2. Sinking Fastball (low-90s)
Sources: *The Scouting Notebook: 1999* and *2002*

JIMMY RING 6'1" 170-pound righty
118-149, 4.12, 11 Saves 1917 1928

Pitch Selection: 1. Fastball 2. Curve
Sources: *The Cincinnati Reds* (Lee Allen, 1948); *The Great Baseball Mystery* (Victor Luhrs, 1966)

TODD RITCHIE 6'3" 210-pound righty
43-52, 4.67, 0 Saves 1997 2003

Pitch Selection: 1. Sinking Fastball (low-90s) 2. Hard Slider 3. Curve 4. Change

Sources: *The Scouting Notebook* (1998, 2000–2002 editions)
Note: The 2002 *Scouting Notebook* says that Ritchie's change-up was a split-fingered fastball.

KEVIN RITZ 6'4" 229-pound righty
45-56, 5.35, 2 Saves 1989 1998

Pitch Selection: 1. Fastball (high-80s) 2. Curve 3. Change 4. Slider (occasional)
Source: *The Scouting Report: 1990*

Pitch Selection: 1. Fastball (high-80s) 2. Slider 3. Change
Sources: *The Scouting Notebook* (1996–1998 editions)

MARIANO RIVERA 6'2" 168-pound righty
43-29, 2.49, 283 Saves 1995 2003

Pitch Selection: 1. Cut Fastball 2. Fastball
Sources: *New York Daily News* (6/9/2002, T.J. Quinn); *The Scouting Notebook 2000*
Note: Quinn article says Rivera learned to throw cut fastball from John Wetteland.

Quote: "You can gauge the movement on Rivera's cutter by counting the number of broken bats. When it's working properly, the pitch approaches like a fastball, then seemingly takes a lefthand turn, sawing off lefty hitters. 'I want ground balls,' he says. 'They're better than strikeouts.' And hitters better be looking for the cutter from the time they step into the box. 'I'll throw the first pitch of the at bat or the last pitch,' he says. 'It doesn't make a difference to me.' "
Source: *Sports Illustrated* (3/31/03, Page 63)

Quote: "That cutter is as heavy as any sinker. He's the only one I know of that's got it."
Source: Bret Boone during eighth inning of Fox broadcast of ALCS Game 3 (October 11, 2003)

EPPA RIXEY 6'5" 210-pound lefty
266-251, 3.15, 14 Saves 1912 1933

Pitch Selection: 1. Fastball 2. Hard Curve 3. Change
Source: *The Ballplayers* (1990, article by A.D. Suehsdorf)

Rixey in 1927: "How dumb can the hitters in this league get? I've been doing this for *fifteen* years. When they're batting with the count two balls and no strikes, or three and one, they're always looking for the fastball. And they *never* get it."
Source: *Voices of Baseball* (ed. Bob Chieger, 1983)

Comment: "Rixey . . . pitches a lot of balls. One hundred and twenty or one hundred and thirty in nine innings is a very fair showing for him."
Source: F.C. Lane in *Baseball Magazine* (February 1930)

Notes: In *Masters of the Diamond* (Rich Westcott, 1994), Ethan Allen repeatedly refers to Rixey throwing a screwball.

According to J.C. Kofoed in *Baseball Magazine*, the 6'6" Rixey was the tallest pitcher in the major leagues.

DAVE ROBERTS 6'3" 195-pound lefty
103-125, 3.78, 15 Saves 1969 1981

Pitch Selection: 1. Fastball 2. Curve 3. Change 4. Slider 5. Knuckleball
Source: *The Sporting News* (9/14/1974, Joe Heiling)

ROBIN ROBERTS 6'0" 190-pound righty
286-245, 3.41, 25 Saves 1948 1966

Pitches, 1948–1951: 1. Rising Fastball 2. Slow Curve 3. Sinker (occasional)

George Brace Collection

Robin Roberts

Pitches, 1952–1966: 1. Rising Fastball 2. Hard Curve 3. Slow Curve (as Change) 4. Sinker (occasional)

Note: On Opening Day in 1952, Roberts decided that his slow curve wasn't nearly as effective as Sal Maglie's hard curve, so he decided to adopt Maglie's hard curve. And shortly thereafter, he did.

Roberts: "I was mainly a one-pitch pitcher, although sometimes I mixed in a curveball when I was ahead in the count. I could put my fastball where I wanted it, but I was sometimes criticized for not pitching inside more and not knocking hitters down . . . Well, lots of people talked about knocking batters down, but few did it. And it just wasn't me. I just went after people with my best stuff and let the batters hit it if they could. That was my act, and it got me through 18 years in the big leagues."

Source: *My Life in Baseball* (Robin Roberts with C. Paul Rogers III, 2003)

Quote: "Robin admits to only three pitches—a fast ball, a curve and a change-of-pace, which is just a weak version of his curve. He makes maximum and intelligent use of each of them. Batters say that when they think they've seen everything Roberts throws, he sticks his curve in a different place or slips one by them that looks suspiciously like a slider."

Source: *Sport* (September 1953, "How Roberts Does It")

Roberts: "Many hitters insist I throw a slider, but I really don't. What they think is a slider is actually another kind of curve I throw. It breaks a little slower than my first curve. I'm not nearly fast enough to try to blow the ball by the hitter."

Source: *Sport* (July 1956, Milton Richman)

Phillies manager Eddie Sawyer: "He would never throw at hitters. They knew this and would go up there and take a toehold, but he would still get them out. He did it with speed, control, and stamina. He seldom threw a ball above the belt, and most of the time he was right across the knees with it. And he had the ability to draw back and throw a little bit harder when he had to.

"He had a very easy delivery. I call it symmetry of motion. It just flowed, pitch after pitch. He made it look easy."

Source: *The Man in the Dugout* (Donald Honig, 1977)

Umpire Jocko Conlan: ". . . Roberts was a great pitcher. He was an umpire's delight to work the plate with because he had uncanny control. The ball was always in or near the strike zone, and he had the players swinging at the ball all the time. They weren't waiting for bases on balls because Roberts didn't give up bases on balls, or very few of them. You'd get a fast ball game when he pitched, two hours or less, and a very well-pitched game, too . . .

". . . I didn't like Robin Roberts, but he was a great pitcher and I never saw him throw at a batter."

Source: *Jocko* (Conlan and Robert Creamer, 1967)

Quote: "[Tom] Seaver has the control to be a 30-game winner. His pitching style is similar to that of Robin Roberts, the old Phillie sensation. Seaver is not as fast as Fireball Roberts was, but his curve is better."

Source: *Baseball Digest* (June 1970, Dave Condon); in Roberts' autobiography, he discusses the first time he saw Seaver pitch on TV, in 1967, and realizing immediately that Seaver pitched just as he had.

Also see Curt Simmons entry.

CHARLIE ROBERTSON 6'0" 175-pound righty 49-80, 4.44, 1 Save 1919 1928

Pitch Selection: 1. Slow Curve 2. Rising Fastball 3. Shine Ball/Grease Ball (?)

Quote: "Besides uncanny control, Robertson had a slow curve and a fast ball, a peculiar fast ball that broke sharply upwards. The fact that it broke upwards disproves the charges that the ball was tampered with . . . On nearly every batter Robertson first served his slow curve for a first strike. Sometimes this curve was high, other times low, outside or inside, all depending upon the batsman. And then he generally came back with the fast ball . . ."

Source: *Baseball Magazine* (July 1922, H.G. Salsinger describing Robertson's perfect game); see below for Shine Ball references.

Key Pitch: Shine Ball

Sources: *Paris Texas News* (8/30/1917); *The American* (5/1/1922)

Description from *Paris Texas News:* ". . . Pitcher Robertson, a college recruit and shine ball expert . . ."

Quote from *The American:* "It is a pity that such a magnificent game as that pitched by Charley Robertson yesterday—perhaps the best game in the history of the world—may be barred because it is tainted.

"Umpire Nallin will submit a number of balls, the side of which had been smeared with a substance resembling crude oil, to Ban Johnson.

"Nallin threw out balls perfectly clean. After a few pitched a Tiger player would call for a ball, and lo, its pristine beauty had been destroyed by a great splotch of black oil, it is declared. Robertson denied tampering with the ball . . .

"Dr. Keene, the Detroit physician, is the authority for the statement that balls had been discolored by crude oil. He would not charge Robertson with it, but he did assert that oil was smeared on almost every ball pitched."

DON ROBINSON 6'4" 225-pound righty
109-106, 3.79, 57 Saves 1978 1992

Pitches: 1. Curve 2. Fastball 3. Palmball
Sources: *The Scouting Report* (1985 and 1986 editions)

Pitches: 1. Fastball (low-90s) 2. Slider 3. Forkball
Sources: *The Scouting Report: 1987; Tom Seaver's 1989 Scouting Notebook*

Pitch Selection: 1. Sinking Fastball 2. Curve 3. Slider 4. Change
Sources: *The Scouting Report* (1990 and 1991 editions)

JEFF D. ROBINSON 6'6" 235-pound righty
47-40, 4.79, 0 Saves 1987 1992

Pitch Selection: 1. Split-Fingered Fastball 2. Fastball 3. Big Curve
Sources: *The Scouting Report: 1990; The Scouting Report: 1992*

JEFF M. ROBINSON 6'4" 195-pound righty
46-57, 3.79, 39 Saves 1984 1992

Pitch Selection: 1. Fastball (91–94) 2. Slider 3. Split-Fingered Fastball
Note: Learned to throw split-fingered fastball from Roger Craig.
Source: *The Scouting Report: 1990*

RON ROBINSON 6'4" 235-pound righty
48-39, 3.63, 19 Saves 1984 1992

Pitch Selection: 1. Fastball 2. Curve 3. Change 4. Slider
Source: *The Scouting Report: 1985*

Note: By 1989, the curve was Robinson's #1 pitch.
Source: *The Scouting Report, 1990*

JOHN ROCKER 6'4" 225-pound lefty
13-22, 3.42, 88 Saves 1998 2003

Pitch Selection: 1. Fastball (high-90s) 2. Slider 3. Change (occasional) 4. Curve (occasional)
Description: "Rocker's delivery contains a high leg kick and lots of arm movement . . ."
Source: *The Scouting Notebook: 1999*
Other Sources: *The Scouting Notebook* (2000–2002 editions)

FELIX RODRIGUEZ 6'1" 198-pound righty
32-17, 3.43, 10 Saves 1995 2003

Pitch Selection: 1. Fastball (93–98) 2. Slider (high-80s) 3. Change (occasional)
Source: *The Scouting Notebook* (1998–2003 editions)
Note: Rodriguez relied almost exclusively on his outstanding fastball, having never really got the hang of the slider or change-up.

FRANCISCO RODRIGUEZ
6'0" 185-pound righty
8-3, 2.85, 2 Saves 2002 2003

Pitches: 1. Slider (83) 2. Fastball (mid-90s) 3. Change (occasional)

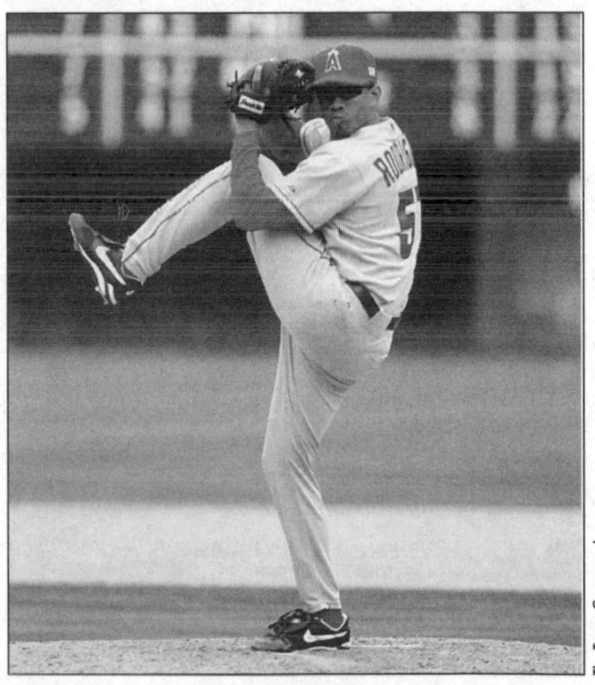

Francisco Rodriguez

Sources: *Sports Illustrated* (6/2/2003); *The Scouting Notebook 2003*

FRANK RODRIGUEZ 6'0" 210-pound righty
29-39, 5.53, 5 Saves 1995 2001

Pitches: 1. Fastball (90s) 2. Hard Curve 3. Slider 4. Change (occasional)
Source: *The Scouting Notebook: 1996*

RICH RODRIGUEZ 5'11" 200-pound lefty
31-22, 3.81, 8 Saves 1990 2003

Pitches: 1. Fastball 2. Change 3. Sinker 4. Slider
Source: *The Scouting Report: 1996*
Key Pitch: Screwball
Source: *The Scouting Notebook 1998*

ROBERTO RODRIGUEZ 6'3" 185-pound righty
4-3, 4.81, 7 Saves 1967 1970

Pitch Selection: 1. Curve 2. Fastball
Source: *Baseball Digest* (March 1967, "Official Scouting Reports on 1967 Major League Rookies")

PREACHER ROE 6'2" 170-pound lefty
127-84, 3.43, 10 Saves 1938 1954

Pitches: 1. Curve 2. Screwball 3. Spitball 4. Fastball
Note: Roe was a power pitcher before suffering a fractured skull while refereeing a basketball game in the late 1940s.
Sources: *Stan Musial* (Musial with Bob Broeg, 1964); Bill Bruton in *When the Cheering Stops* (1990); see below for others.

Pitches: 1. Fastball 2. Curve 3. Slider 4. Spitball
Source: *The Boys of Summer* (Roger Kahn, 1971)

Yogi Berra: "As for Preacher Roe, he wrote a magazine article admitting his money pitch was the spitter. But he also threw a good fast ball, curve, and slider. I was always eager to hit against him, but it was mostly in my mind. He was a lot like Eddie Lopat, with real good control, and the ball seemed to come in big and fat. But even when you were telling everybody how you couldn't wait for your next lick, you were going oh-for-four against him."
Source: *Yogi: The Autobiography of a Professional Baseball Player* (Berra and Ed Fitzgerald, 1961)

Quote from *The Boys of Summer*: "Roe underplayed his talents. 'I got three pitches,' he said. 'My change; my change off my change; and my change off my change off my change.' In essence, slow, slower, and slowest. But he could throw hard and, after watching him for a while, one saw in this sharp-nosed, bony, fidgety man an absolute manner of guile. Even his fidgeting was planned. It was essential to his spitball.

"When wetting a pitch, Roe touched his cap and his sleeve, tugged his pants, dabbed his brow and, as his fingers rested at the forehead, he spat quickly into the heel of his hand. Then he pretended to pull his belt with his pitching hand. In the process his fingertips touched wet heel. Now he was ready to throw the spitter."

Description: "Chief stock in trade is his uncanny control. He has a tricky sinker, a slow-breaking curve to go with it, and is a genuine wizard with slow stuff. Always look for breaking stuff when facing Roe."
Source: *Baseball Digest* (January 1951, Milton Richman)

Commentary: The spitball may have been more important than that, particularly toward the end of his career. Roe described how he threw the spitter in a 1955 article for *Sports Illustrated*. There is also an excellent description of Roe's pitching style in Arthur Daley's *Sports of the Times* (1959), which includes the quote from Roe that "I try to keep the hitters off balance, never giving them a decent pitch. When I put one over the middle of the plate, it's an accident and you read about it in the papers."

ED ROEBUCK 6'2" 185-pound righty
52-31, 3.35, 62 Saves 1955 1966

Key Pitch: Sinker
Source: Roebuck in *We Played the Game* (Danny Peary, 1994)

BULLET ROGAN 5'7" 180-pound righty
Negro Leagues 1917 1938

Pitch Selection: 1. Drop Curve 2. Fastball 3. Palm Ball (used as a change) 4. Spitball 5. Fork Ball 6. "Slider" 7. Side-arm Curve
Chet Brewer: "Rogan could throw a curve ball faster than most pitchers could throw a fast ball. And he was the inventor of the palm ball. He had such a terrific fast ball, then he'd palm the ball and just walk it up there.

Hitters were well off stride. I saw him one winter just make Al Simmons crawl trying to hit that ball."

Babe Herman: "He was the best colored pitcher I hit against, had one of the best curve balls I ever saw and a good, live fast ball. I always said he was much better than Satchel Paige. Satchel was real fast, but he had a lousy curve, and his fast ball was pretty straight. Rogan's fast ball was just *alive!* Did you ever see Luque play? I think Rogan must have learned his curve ball from him. Broke straight down."

Frank Duncan: "I'd say Rogan and Satchel threw the fastest balls I ever saw, but Rogan also had a great curve with a three-foot drop on it. Bullet had a little more steam on the ball than Paige, and he had a better breaking curve ball. The batters thought it was a fast ball heading for them and they'd jump back from the plate, and all of a sudden, it would break sharply for a strike. I've never seen a pitcher like him, and I've caught some of the best."

Comment: "Rogan threw an assortment of fast balls, curves, change-ups, and spitters . . . Rogan was the first of the no-windup pitchers who delivered straight from the shoulder."

Source: *Blackball Stars* (John Holway, 1988)

KENNY ROGERS 6'1" 200-pound lefty
158-114, 4.23, 28 Saves 1989 2003

Pitch Selection: 1. Sinking Fastball 2. Straight Change 3. Curve 4. Cut Fastball

Sources: *The Scouting Report: 1996; The Scouting Notebook 1999*

STEVE ROGERS 6'2" 175-pound righty
158-152, 3.17, 2 Saves 1973 1985

Pitch Selection: 1. Sinker 2. Fastball 3. Slider 4. Curve 5. Change

Sources: *The Expos Inside Out* (Dan Turner, 1983); *The Art of Pitching* (Tom Seaver with Lee Lowenfish, 1984)

Tom Seaver: "Steve Rogers has a somewhat unorthodox, stiff-legged delivery, but he demonstrates that there are many paths to pitching success if you are creative and consistent in your efforts. He achieves tremendous hip rotation, generated by the turning of his left knee at the height of his lift. Steve hides the ball very well and keeps it invisible to the batter until very late in his delivery."

Seaver, again: "Steve Rogers . . . has one of the most devastating sinkers in today's game. He has a natural sink to his fastball, but he has made his sinker even more effective by constantly experimenting with different grips and pressure points. As I do, he usually throws his sinker off his index finger."

Source: *The Art of Pitching*

Umpire Ron Luciano: "He's a sinkerball pitcher, and like all things that sink, they tend to get wet once in a while."

Source: *Voices of Baseball* (ed. Bob Chieger, 1983)

SAUL ROGOVIN 6'2" 205-pound righty
48-48, 4.06, 2 Saves 1949 1957

Pitches: 1. Curve 2. Fastball 3. Change of Pace

Source: *Sport* (May 1952, Milton Richman)

Quote: "Rogovin's curve and fast ball are good enough to make him a better-than-average pitcher, but it's his deceptive motion that makes him a standout."

Source: Sam Zoldak in 1952 *Sport*

Description: ". . . Saul Rogovin, who once led the American League in earned-run averages mainly by using his fast ball. Now, by using his head, he is getting his second major-league wind with the Phillies, and causing considerable surprise with a newly-acquired sinker and change-up."

Rogovin: "Somebody cracked that I now throw with three speeds—slow, slower and stop. But who cares, as long as I'm winning? They can have the fastball."

Source: *Sport* (July 1956, Milton Richman)

BILLY ROHR 6'3" 170-pound lefty
3-3, 5.64, 1 Save 1967 1968

Pitch Selection: 1. Sneaky Fastball 2. Curve 3. Change

Source: Leonard Koppett quoted in *A Glimpse of Fame* (Dennis Snelling, 1993)

MEL ROJAS 5'11" 175-pound righty
34-31, 3.82, 126 Saves 1990 1999

Pitch Selection: 1. Fastball 2. Forkball 3. Slider

Sources: *1995 Baseball Almanac; The Scouting Notebook: 1997; 1990 Montreal Expos Media Guide*

RON ROMANICK 6'4" 195-pound righty
31-29, 4.24, 0 Saves 1984 1986

Pitch Selection: 1. Fastball (high-80s) 2. Change 3. Curve 4. Slider
Source: *The Scouting Report: 1985*

EDDIE ROMMEL 6'2" 197-pound righty
171-119, 3.54, 29 Saves 1920 1932

Pitches, 1920–1921: 1. Fastball 2. Curve 3. Knuckleball
Pitches, 1922–1932: 1. Knuckleball 2. Fastball 3. Curve
Rommel: "Roughly speaking, I throw a knuckle ball perhaps once out of every three tries on the slab. The remaining two tries will be about evenly divided between curves and fast balls."
Source: *Baseball Magazine* (July 1923, F.C. Lane)

Note: According to another *Baseball Magazine* article (September 1926, F.C. Lane), in a 1-0 loss to Walter Johnson on Opening Day in 1926, Rommel pitched fifteen innings and didn't throw even one knuckleball.

Note: According to Ed Wells in *Baseball Between the Wars* (Eugene Murdock, 1992), Rommel had very short fingers, which gave him a kind of "natural knuckleball."

Also see article about Rommel on page 75.

ENRIQUE ROMO 5'11" 185-pound righty
44-33, 3.45, 52 Saves 1977 1982

Key Pitch: Palm Ball
Source: *The Philadelphia Bulletin* (4/6/1980, Page 13)

VICENTE ROMO 6'1" 180-pound righty
32-33, 3.36, 52 Saves 1968 1982

Description: "He possesses an elaborate windmill motion (similar to Luis Tiant's) that seems to deliver a thousand different pitches from a thousand different angles."
Source: *The Suitors of Spring* (Pat Jordan, 1973)

JIM ROOKER 6'0" 195-pound lefty
103-109, 3.46, 7 Saves 1968 1980

Pitches: 1. Fastball 2. Curve 3. Slider (added 1971) 4. Change
Note: Rooker experimented with a Knuckleball in 1980, but pitched only four games that season.
Sources: *The Sporting News* (8/23/1969, Paul O'Boynick; 2/27/1971; and 3/1/1980, Charley Feeney)

CHARLIE ROOT 5'10" 190-pound righty
201-160, 3.59, 40 Saves 1923 1941

Pitch Selection: 1. Sidearm Fastball 2. Curve
Sources: Riggs Stephenson in *Baseball History, An Annual of Original Research* (1989), *Babe Ruth's Own Book of Baseball* (Ruth, 1928); *Who's Who in the Major Leagues* (1936 edition), Phil Cavaretta in *Wrigleyville* (Peter Golenbock, 1996)

Notes: Ray Kremer in *Baseball Magazine* in 1930 cited Root as having one of the best fastballs in the league. C. William Duncan in *Baseball Magazine* (August, 1927) described Root as a "fast ball artist." Lew Fonseca in *How to Pitch Baseball* (1942) listed Root among three "present-day pitchers who successfully employ the sidearm type of delivery."

Root: "The hardest ball to hit is one whose velocity and course are both difficult to gauge. Hence, I suppose the hardest ball for a good hitter to hit is a slow curve. But right there you haven't enough to keep fooling the batter. You must mix them up. Hence, the pitcher who really puts the most 'stuff' on the ball is the one who gets it to swerve most from a straight line, to one side or another, up or down, and at the same time changes frequently from one speed to another. Change of pace has come to mean a lot to most pitchers. Personally, I've not been content to stop even there. A ball that shoots and hops isn't enough for me. A ball whose velocity varies from one pitch to another isn't enough. I also have a third element of uncertainty by varying the angle at which I release the ball. When I'm facing right-handed batters I'm inclined to use what might be termed a cross-fire ball. At such a time I'll stand at the extreme left of the pitching slab, step forward when I hurl the ball, but step to one side. When the ball leaves my hand, it may be two feet outside the slab.

". . . In order to make a fast ball jump, I grip it hard, just as I release it. I have practiced this so much that I can take a perfectly new ball and make it sail, as the batters say, just as though it had been roughened or treated to a dose of emery. I can also take a brand new ball and pitch

a sinker, that is, a ball that sinks as it crosses the plate. It is the grip of the fingers which imparts curious twists to the ball rather than any strength of pitching arm."
Source: *Baseball Magazine* (March 1929, "Comprising an Interview with Charles Root")

JOSE ROSADO 6'0" 185-pound lefty
37-45, 4.27, 1 Save 1996 2001

Pitch Selection: 1. Fastball (88–92) 2. Cut Fastball 3. Change 4. Curve
Source: *The Scouting Notebook* (1998–2001 editions)
Commentary: Rosado's chief strength was his willingness and ability to throw his fastball inside to right-handed hitters.

BUCK ROSS 6'2" 170-pound righty
56-95, 4.94, 2 Saves 1936 1945

Pitch Selection: 1. Change 2. Fastball
Source: *The Ballplayers* (1990, article by Ed Walton)

SCHOOLBOY ROWE 6'4" 210-pound righty
158-101, 3.87, 12 Saves 1933 1949

Pitch Selection, early career: 1. Fastball 2. Overhand Curve 3. Change
Note: Rowe threw straight overhand, and his curve would break almost straight down.
Sources: *Major League Baseball* (Ethan Allen, Page 30); Charlie Gehringer in *Cobb Would Have Caught It* (Richard Bak, 1991), *New York Times* (5/22/1936, account of game in which Rowe struck out Joe DiMaggio twice in a row with slow curves); *Baseball Magazine* (September 1934, Clifford Bloodgood)
Pitch Selection, late career: 1. Change 2. Screwball 3. Sneaky Fastball 4. Knuckleball (added in 1940)
Description: "The Schoolhouse no longer tries to blow it past the hitter. Once he overpowered them with speed. Now he confuses them with the taunting cunning of unexpected pitches. He irritates them with the change-up and the screwball and when they're looking for the soft stuff he will come in with a sneaky fast ball."
Source: *Baseball Digest* (September 1947, Jimmy Cannon)
Sources for Knuckleball citation: *Baseball Magazine* (April 1947, Frank Yeutter) and *The Sporting News* (10/3/1940, H.G. Salsinger)

Description: "Rowe was a pitcher with a variety of styles in 1933. This season he has been entirely overhand. He has speed. He has curves. And the best change of pace in the American League. His control is exemplary."
Source: Dan Daniel in "Daniel's Dope" column, just before 1934 World Series

Description: "Great speed, fine control, a good enough curve, and a corking letup ball . . ."
Source: Johnny Murphy in Dan Daniel's *New York World-Telegram* column (5/16/1935)

DAVE ROZEMA 6'4" 185-pound righty
60-53, 3.47, 17 Saves 1977 1986

Pitch Selection: 1. Sinker 2. Sidearm Curve 3. Split-Fingered Fastball
Source: *Inside Pitch* (Roger Craig with Vern Plagenhoef, Page 41)

DAVE RUCKER 6'1" 185-pound lefty
16-20, 3.94, 1 Save 1981 1988

Pitch Selection: 1. Fastball (90) 2. Slider 3. Forkball
Source: *The Scouting Report: 1984*

NAP RUCKER 5'11" 190-pound lefty
134-134, 2.42, 14 Saves 1907 1916

Pitch Selection: 1. Fastball 2. Overhand Drop Curve 3. Knuckleball 4. Slow Ball
Source: A booklet edited by Irving M. Howe in 1914 and titled "Pitching Course" provides an almost perfect description of Rucker's pitching.
Other Sources: *The Brooklyn Dodgers* (Frank Graham, 1945); *Atlanta Constitution* (2/28/1934 and 3/1/1934, columns by Jimmy Jones)

Description of Rucker's Knuckleball: "The knuckle ball is what its name implies. It is thrown with the hand all double, not unlike a pig's knuckle, and merely floats to the plate without a twist or turn. No speed can be put on it, the cramped position of the hand preventing that. It is safe to use only with a change of pace from a swift ball, and then when a pitcher has the batter in a hole."
Source: *The Unforgettable Season* (G.H. Fleming, 1981) quoting the *New York Evening Journal* of March 24, 1908; it should be noted that by 1914, at the very latest, Rucker was throwing a knuckleball not unlike that thrown 90 years later by Tim Wakefield and Steve Sparks, with his index and middle fingertips gripping the ball.

Rucker in Howe booklet: "The Knuckler and an ordinary slow ball are my change of pace deliveries. Combining these with an overhand drop and a fast ball, all started with the same swing enables me to cope with the sluggers of the National League with some success.

"By alternating the Knuckler, which is a slow drop curve, with my fast ball or a slow ball with an overhand curve the average batter experiences great difficulty in timing his swing, with the result that a fielder is usually given an easy chance."

John McGraw: "Rucker was easily the greatest slow-ball pitcher that I have ever seen. He relied on that tantalizing floater almost solely in critical moments. Occasionally he would serve a swifter ball, but even that was only a half-speed delivery—just enough to be a foil for his teasers.

"Of course, you know that Rucker was a southpaw. Originally he used considerable speed, but as his arm became weaker he was wise enough to appreciate that he could not last much longer unless he conserved his strength. Thereupon he shifted to his slow ball and with perfect control was a better pitcher than ever. Rucker utilized a 'sailer' that seemed to hang in the air as if he had tied a string to it. Many a batter almost broke his back swinging at that ball before it got to him. He felt sure that he could knock it out of the lot, it appeared so big and so easy.

"There have been other slow-ball pitchers of note, but Rucker had the most aggravating delivery of them all."

Source: *My Thirty Years in Baseball* (John McGraw, 1923); the slow ball—"floater"—that McGraw refers to is quite likely Rucker's knuckleball (see below).

Note: The following is part of W.R. Hoefer's "Diamond Dust," a regular feature that ran for a time in *Baseball Magazine.* This appeared in the December 1916 issue, and describes in verse Rucker's pitching repertoire at that late point in his career. The "fork-hand floater" mentioned is *not* a forkball—which hadn't yet been invented—but rather Rucker's knuckleball.

"NAP RUCKER"

He used to pitch a ball with lots of smoke; and the stock of curves he carried was no joke. In the days of yesteryear he could burn the atmosphere as he made the slugging biffers swear and choke. But the sizzling speed has left his ancient wing and he throws a floating ball that doesn't sing. Yet he fools the swatters still with his hesitation pill, smiling grimly as the clouters fail to bing. All the stuff he has is just a dinky curve with a clever head and lots of sand and nerve, but the way the batters fall for his foolish looking ball shows he's still a winning Hurling Hill Reserve. Nap lobs his fork-hand floaters o'er the plate and the batter sees 'em forty minutes late . . .

Also see Sherry Smith entry.

DICK RUDOLPH 5'9" 160-pound righty
121-109, 2.66, 8 Saves 1910 1927

Pitch Selection: 1. Fastball 2. Curve 3. Spitball 4. Slow Ball

Rudolph: "I use a fast ball a good deal, in spite of what they say. I also use curves, spit balls, and slow balls. True, I used spit balls mostly as a blind. But the batter can never tell when I am bluffing and when I am actually going to cut loose with a spit ball, so it has the same effect as though I used it more frequently.

"My slow ball is my ace in the hole. I use it on the spur of the moment when conditions seem to call for it, and often without a signal from the catcher. Half the time, when I wind up, I don't know myself that I am going to throw a slow ball. Oftentimes the catcher will signal for a fast ball. I will intend to give him a fast ball. But the batter will shift his feet or change his position or give me some indication at the last minute, that it would be a good stunt to feed him a slow ball. And so I will give him one . . ."

Source: *Baseball Magazine* (May 1918, article credited to Rudolph)

Comment: "Dick Rudolph is a wise pitcher who uses almost everything that is lawful for the pitcher. He is too wise to depend overmuch on the spit ball, but he does throw a spitter occasionally, just often enough to remind the batter that he can expect a freak break once in a while. What Rudolph does do, however, is to bluff at throwing the spitter, and this is just as bad as actually using the twister, so far as batting is concerned."

Source: *Baseball Magazine* (June 1919, F.C. Lane, "Should the Spit Ball Be Abolished?")

Pitch Selection: 1. Spitball 2. Curve
Note: Rudolph was listed among the "grandfathered" pitchers allowed to throw the spitball after it was otherwise banned in 1921.
Sources: *The Boston Braves* (Harold Kaese, 1948); 1915 *Reach Guide* (Page 83); 1923 *Reach Guide* (Page 38)

DON RUDOLPH 5'11" 195-pound lefty
18-32, 4.00, 3 Saves 1957 1964

Pitch Selection: 1. Curve 2. Fastball 3. Slider
Source: *1963 Major League Handbook* (Don Schiffer); *Baseball Digest* (May 1963, Larry Fox)
Description by Fox: "Rudolph's fast ball would have trouble chipping a Dresden china vase. His slider resembles a ripple on a very quiet lake. But he's got control, heart and a mastery of his trade even though he won't impress warming up on the sidelines."
Note: According to Fox, in 1962 Rudolph pitched one game that lasted one hour and thirty-two minutes, and five others that were completed in less than one hour and fifty minutes, making him the fastest worker in the majors.

KIRK RUETER 6'3" 190-pound lefty
119-73, 4.11, 0 Saves 1993 2003

Pitch Selection: 1. Change 2. Fastball (82–84) 3. Curve 4. Cut Fastball (added 1999)
Sources: *The Scouting Notebook 1998; The Scouting Notebook 2000*

DUTCH RUETHER 6'1" 180-pound lefty
137-95, 3.50, 8 Saves 1917 1927

Note: Apparently had a deceptive delivery.
Quote: "I don't know what he had but when he started twisting those arms around himself I'd get all caught up in the fancy knots he was making and the ball would be over the plate before I even knew he was ready to throw."
Source: Charley Grimm in *Great American Sports Humor* (Mac Davis)

BRUCE RUFFIN 6'2" 205-pound lefty
60-82, 4.19, 63 Saves 1986 1997

Pitch Selection: 1. Hard Sinker 2. Fastball 3. Slurve
Sources: *The Scouting Report: 1987* and *1992*

RED RUFFING 6'1" 205-pound righty
273-225, 3.80, 16 Saves 1924 1947

Pitch Selection: 1. Fastball 2. Sharp Curve 3. Slider
Sources: *Cooperstown* (published by *The Sporting News*, Page 225); source for Slider is *Famous American Athletes* (Ninth series, 1945), which says that Ruffing taught Spud Chandler "how to throw his slider." Also, *The Sporting News* (9/24/1952, Page 4) says Ruffing was "one of the early experts with the slider."

Ruffing: "I pitch three or four fast balls for every curve. I have a pretty good curve, pretty good control, pretty good everything except luck."
Source: *Baseball Magazine* (April 1931, F.C. Lane)

Umpire Joe Paparella: "The first game I ever worked behind the plate in the major leagues was against the guy who invented the slider and had the best slider ever seen—Red Ruffing."
Source: *The Men in Blue* (Larry Gerlach, 1980); there's very little evidence that Ruffing did invent the slider, but there's an abundance of evidence suggesting that he was

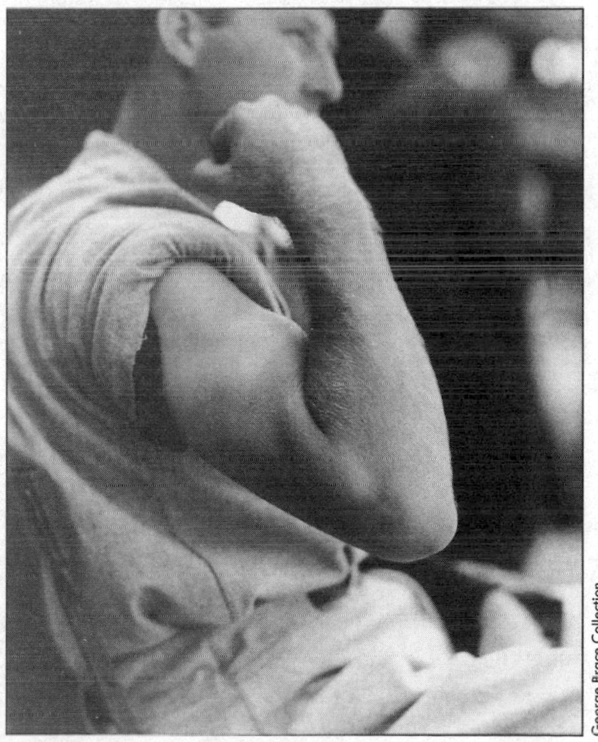
George Brace Collection

Red Ruffing

among the first to throw a good one. For example, in 1945 umpire Bill Summers told Dan Daniel, "Later, on account of Red Ruffing, the slider got to be the thing."

Commentary: According to Bob Shawkey in *The Man in the Dugout* (Donald Honig, 1977), Ruffing's early-career problems with the Red Sox were due to a pitching motion that placed undue strain on his arm, and resulted in fatigue after the fifth or sixth inning. The Yankees traded for him on Shawkey's recommendation, Shawkey taught Ruffing to use his arm less and his body more, and Ruffing wound up in the Hall of Fame.

VERN RUHLE 6'1" 185-pound righty
67-88, 3.73, 11 Saves 1974 1986

Pitch Selection: 1. Sinker 2. Slider
Source: *Late Innings* (Roger Angell, Page 319)

GLENDON RUSCH 6'1" 223-pound lefty
42-76, 5.11, 2 Saves 1997 2003

Pitch Selection: 1. Curve 2. Cut Fastball 3. Change 4. Fastball (high-80s)
Source: *The Scouting Notebook: 1999*

Pitch Selection: 1. Fastball (high-80s) 2. Curve 3. Change 4. Cut Fastball
Source: *The Scouting Notebook: 2002*

BOB RUSH 6'4" 205-pound righty
127-152, 3.65, 8 Saves 1948 1960

Pitch Selection: 1. Fastball 2. Curve 3. Change
Sources: *Baseball Magazine* (November 1949, Clifford Bloodgood); *The Sporting News* (12/1/1954 and 8/29/1956); *Baseball Stars of 1953* (article by Edgar Munzel); Hank Sauer quoted in *Take Me Out to the Cubs Game* (John C. Skipper, 2000)

Note: According to Rich Westcott in *Splendor on the Diamond* (2000), Rush's fastball was a sinker the batters described as a "heavy ball."

Quote from *Baseball Magazine* article: "Bob doesn't go in for fancy deliveries such as the sinker, slider or any trick stuff . . . he rears back and lets go a fast ball that has the admiration of every scout that sees it."

Quote: "Facing Rush, the batters rarely or never look for a curve."
Source: *Baseball Digest* (January 1951, Milt Richman)

Note: Listed by *The Sporting News* as having one of the best fastballs in the league, on December 1, 1954, and again on August 29, 1956.

AMOS RUSIE 6'1" 200-pound righty
248-167, 3.07, 5 Saves 1889 1901

Pitch Selection: 1. Fastball 2. Hard Curve 3. Slow Ball
Sources: *My Thirty Years in Baseball* (John McGraw, 1923); *Baseball's Famous Pitchers* (Ira L. Smith, 1954); *The History of Baseball* (Danzig and Reichler, Page 214); 1892 *Spalding Guide* (Page 32)

John McGraw in *My Thirty Years in Baseball:* "Rusie had tremendous speed and a wonderful curve. He could throw a fast ball almost as fast as his regular fast one. Not only that, but he had the nerve and confidence to whip his curve over the plate when in a hole. As a rule, pitchers do not dare try a curve when the count is two strikes and three balls. They've got to get the ball over, and to be sure they usually use their fast one. Rusie had no such misgivings. If in such a hole he would deliberately pitch his curve ball with every ounce of steam he could put on it. Usually he stood batters on their ears by that kind of pitching."

Also see Jouett Meekin entry.

ALLAN RUSSELL 5'11" 165-pound righty
70-76, 3.52, 42 Saves 1915 1925

Key Pitch: Spitball
Note: Russell was one of the "grandfathered" pitchers allowed to continue to throw the spitball after it was otherwise banned in 1921.
Sources: *The Washington Senators* (Shirley Povich, 1954); *The Relief Pitcher* (John Thorn, 1979); *Baseball Between the Wars* (Eugene Murdoch, 1992); 1923 *Reach Guide* (Page 38)

JACK RUSSELL 6'1" 178-pound righty
85-141, 4.46, 38 Saves 1926 1940

Pitch Selection: 1. Sinker 2. Change
Russell: "When (Dickie) Kerr was with the White Sox, he worked out with our high school team before going to spring training. He showed me how to pitch. He showed me the proper motion, taught me how to throw a change of pace."
Source: *Diamond Greats* (Rich Westcott, 1988)

Description: "Russell employs a simple wind-up and has a free delivery which is easy on the arm."
Source: *Baseball Magazine* (October 1933, Clifford Bloodgood)

JEFF RUSSELL 6'4" 200-pound righty
56-73, 3.75, 186 Saves 1983 1996

Pitch Selection: 1. Fastball 2. Hard Slider 3. Change
Source: *The Scouting Report 1990*

REB RUSSELL 5'11" 185-pound lefty
81-59, 2.33, 13 Saves 1913 1919

Pitch Selection: 1. Fastball 2. Curve 3. Slow Ball
Sources: unidentified source from the Hall of Fame Library (July 1913); *Baseball Magazine* (October 1914); letter from Russell to Lee Allen (1/15/1965)

Quote from unidentified 1913 source: "He had a lot of speed and stuff . . . He does not use the broad sweeping curve of the usual left-hander, although he has a good sharp break to his bender."
Russell in *Baseball Magazine*: "Speed is my favorite delivery . . . I have always seemed more successful with the fast ball than with anything else. Most left-handed pitchers use curves a good deal and I am no exception. I use a good many curves, though I don't like them so well and haven't had as much success with them, usually, as I do with sheer speed. I have cultivated a slow ball with fair success. I can get a pretty good break on this ball when I am right, though I hate to use it and seldom do. As for the spitball, I will leave that to Ed Walsh . . . I have never yet got to the point where I felt like using it in a regular game."
Quote from Russell in letter to Lee Allen: "I pitched my fast ball high, slow ball low on the outside corner, very few curve balls."

MARIUS RUSSO 6'1" 190-pound lefty
45-34, 3.13, 5 Saves 1939 1946

Pitches: 1. Sinking Fastball 2. Curve
Description: "Russo has what it takes with his side arm or overhand deliveries and a fast ball that sinks and has the batters knocking it into the dirt a lot. He has good curves, but uses them sparingly, maybe only one in a half-dozen pitches."
Source: *Baseball Magazine* (July 1942, Clifford Bloodgood)

BABE RUTH 6'2" 215-pound lefty
94-46, 2.28, 4 Saves 1914 1933

Pitch Selection: 1. Fastball 2. Curve
Source: Casey Stengel quoted in *Babe* (Robert Creamer, 1974)

DAMON RUTHERFORD

Pitch Selection: 1. Fastball 2. Hard Curve
Note: In Season LVI, Rutherford was killed by a pitched ball from Knickerbocker rookie Jock Casey.
Source: *The Universal Baseball Association, Inc. J. Henry Waugh, Prop.* (Robert Coover, 1968)

DICK RUTHVEN 6'3" 190-pound righty
123-127, 4.14, 1 Save 1973 1986

Pitch Selection: 1. Fastball 2. Curve
Source: *The Sporting News* (9/21/1974, Ray Kelly)

KEN RYAN 6'3" 225-pound righty
14-16, 3.91, 30 Saves 1992 1999

Pitch Selection: 1. Fastball (low-90s)
2. Overhand Curve 3. Slider
Note: Threw with a herky-jerky motion.
Source: *The Scouting Notebook: 1995*
Other Sources: *The Scouting Report* (1995 and 1996 editions); *The Scouting Notebook: 1997*

NOLAN RYAN 6'2" 170-pound righty
324-292, 3.19, 3 Saves 1966 1993

Pitch Selection: 1. Fastball 2. Curve
3. Circle Change (added in 1986)
Sources: *Throwing Heat* (Ryan with Harvey Frommer); *The Scout* (Red Murff with Mike Capps, 1996; according to Murff, he taught Ryan both the circle change and a cutter in 1986).

Umpire Durwood Merrill: "Contrary to what some people said, Nolan wasn't a one-dimensional pitcher. There were nights when the fastball was clocking in the upper nineties and the curveball was hitting eighty-nine on the

radar gun. At that speed, the curve would break so hard that it'd take your stomach away."
Source: *You're Out and You're Ugly, Too* (Merrill with Jim Dent, 1998)

Tom Seaver: "Nolan Ryan, who throws a great curve but no slider, says that one of the secrets of his success has been that he threw nothing but fastballs until he was twenty-three . . . The secret to Nolan's curveball is that he throws it with almost the same velocity as his fastball. When the ball breaks downward before the hitting zone, the hitter is almost helpless . . . Nolan does not cock or 'wrap' his wrist on his curveball. He uses a straight, relaxed wrist that has probably accounted for the durability of his arm. Many curveballers like me and Don Sutton simply cannot control the pitch with the straight wrist."
Source: *The Art of Pitching* (Seaver with Lee Lowenfish, 1984)

ROSY RYAN 6'0" 185-pound righty
52-47, 4.14, 19 Saves 1919 1933

Pitch Selection: 1. Curve 2. Fastball
Sources: *Baseball Magazine* (September 1927, Page 450); *The Relief Pitcher* (John Thorn, 1979)

Virgil Barnes in *Baseball Magazine:* "Curve pitching is very popular on this club. Perhaps I ought to say it's too common. Most pitchers, I believe, don't like to throw many curves because they are hard on the arm. McGraw, however, is a great believer in curve pitching and what he says goes. I once saw 'Rosy' Ryan get into a game, pitch 57 curve balls and only 17 fast balls. That's a pretty tough proportion."

Comment: "[Ryan] was also a pre-1920 spitballer, but John McGraw failed to designate him as such—no doubt deliberately—leaving Ryan no choice but to develop a curve, which proved the making of his career."
Source: Thorn

C.C. SABATHIA 6'7" 290-pound lefty
43-25, 4.12, 0 Saves 2001 2003

Pitch Selection: 1. Fastball (92–96) 2. Curve (83–86) 3. Change (78–82)
Source: *The Scouting Notebook: 2002*

BRET SABERHAGEN 6'1" 160-pound righty
167-117, 3.34, 1 Save 1984 2001

Pitch Selection: 1. Fastball 2. Curve 3. Slider 4. Change
Sources: *The Scouting Report: 1987; The Scouting Report: 1990*

Description: "Nasty, nasty, nasty stuff, maybe the best in the league. He cannot throw a ball straight, yet his control is so good, he almost always has a hitter down in the count."
Source: *Bill Mazeroski's Baseball* (1993 edition)

RAY SADECKI 5'11" 180-pound lefty
135-131, 3.78, 7 Saves 1960 1977

Key Pitch: Fastball
Source: *1963 Major League Handbook* (Don Schiffer)

Billy Williams: "But one of the toughest for me was Ray Sadecki. When he first came to the Cardinals, he threw

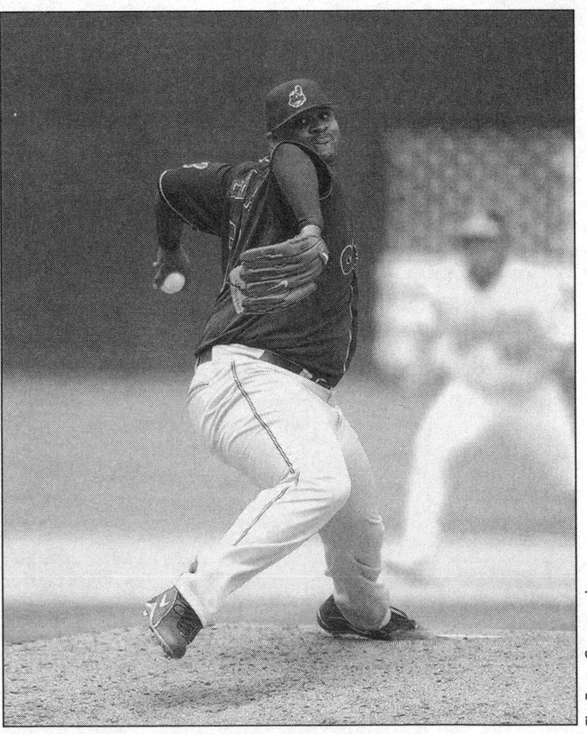

C.C. Sabathia

really well. He threw a lot of junk that always kept me off balance. I wanted guys to come at me hard."
Source: *Splendor on the Diamond* (Rich Westcott, 2000)

JOHNNY SAIN 6'2" 185-pound righty
139-116, 3.49, 51 Saves 1942 1955

Pitch Selection: 1. Overhand Curve 2. Fastball 3. Change
Sources: *1947 Scout Report* (Wid Matthews); Spider Jorgensen in *We Played the Game* (Danny Peary, 1994); Billy Southworth quoted in *Baseball Magazine* (January 1947, article by Ed Rumill)

Spider Jorgensen: "On the first day against Johnny Sain, [Rex Barney] told me, 'All you're going to get is curveballs, curveballs—if he throws a fastball, don't swing because it will be a ball.' He was exactly right."
Sain: "I was released four times in Class A because I didn't have velocity. But in the end, I made it, and I did it by throwing breaking and off-speed pitches."
Source: *A Baseball Winter* (edited by Terry Pluto and Jeffrey Neumann, 1986)

Description: "Johnny Sain is a big, tobacco-chewing, rough-looking hillbilly from Havana, Arkansas, who knows more about pitching than anybody can catalog. If you said hello to him, you might get a grunt in response on a good day. One night in Brooklyn he threw thirty-two straight curveballs from thirty-two different directions: underhand, overhand, sidearm, three-quarters, behind his back almost. The whole world knew what was coming. Didn't matter. We haven't hit one of them yet. He could drop a curve in a coffee mug."
Source: *Rex Barney's Thank Youuuu for 50 Years in Baseball from Brooklyn to Baltimore* (Barney with Norman L. Macht, 1993)

Description: "Mr. Sain, a curveball-throwing fool if there ever was one . . ."
Source: *You're Missin' a Great Game* (Whitey Herzog and Jonathan Pitts, 1999)

Description: "[Sain] used to be a fast ball pitcher but now deals strictly in curves. Also goes in for slider a lot."
Source: *Baseball Digest* (article by Milt Richman)

Description: "Sain is one of the few 'survivors' of the windmill tradition."
Source: *Baseball Digest* (September 1947, Harry Sheer)

Commentary: In 1942, when he walked 63 men in 97 innings, Sain varied his arm angle constantly, and would use a cross-fire motion for every third or fourth pitch. He stopped doing this, during the war years, because he realized it was causing him control trouble. After the war the only time he would vary his delivery would be to (occasionally) drop down sidearm when he was ahead of the hitter. The rest of the time, he used a straight overhand delivery.

SLIM SALLEE 6'3" 180-pound lefty
174-143, 2.56, 36 Saves 1908 1921

Pitch Selection: 1. Floater 2. Fastball 3. Curve 4. Change
Note: Sallee threw with a crossfire delivery.
Sources: *The St. Louis Cardinals* (Fred Lieb, 1945); *The Baseball Research Journal* 19 (article by A.D. Suehsdorf and Richard J. Thompson)

Key Pitch: Curve
Sallee: "Outside of control which came naturally to me and which I have done all I could to cultivate, I have been successful mainly as a curve pitcher. Good curves

Road West Publishing—*Baseball Magazine* Collection

Slim Sallee

combined with good control will carry a pitcher a long ways. I have never tried to use the spitball. This style of delivery needs a man who is rather heavy and speedy. It requires a good deal of strength. A successful spitball pitcher uses an overhand motion and puts much strength behind the effort. A pitcher who uses the spitball successfully must practice all the time. He is seldom good for anything else."
Source: *Baseball Magazine* (February 1913, M.V.B. Lyons)

Description: "Some pitchers depend largely on their motions to fool batters. 'Motion pitchers' they might be called. Such an elaborate wind-up is developed that it is hard for a hitter to tell when and from where the ball is coming. 'Slim' Sallee of the St. Louis Nationals hasn't any curve to mention and he lacks speed, but he wins a lot of ball games on his motion.

" 'It's a crime,' says McGraw, 'to let a fellow like that beat you. Why, he has so little on the ball that it looks like one of those Salome dancers when it comes up to the plate, and actually makes me blush.'

"But Sallee will take a long wind-up and shoot one off his shoe tops and another from his shoulder while he is facing second base. He has good control, has catalogued the weaknesses of the batters, and can work the corners. With his capital, he was winning ball games for the Cardinals in 1911 until he fell off the water wagon. He is different from [Bugs] Raymond in that respect. When he is on the vehicle, he is on it, and, when he is off, he is distinctly a pedestrian."
Source: *Pitching in a Pinch* (Christy Mathewson, ghosted by John N. Wheeler, 1912)

Virgil Barnes: "When I came to New York and had to handle a clean new ball almost every pitch, I found myself helpless. Slim Sallee was on the club then and he taught me, in a five minute conversation, more than I ever knew about pitching . . . Sallee was a wise old pitcher and what he didn't know about pitching wasn't worth knowing."
Source: *Baseball Magazine* (September 1926)

JACK SALVESON 6'0" 180-pound righty
9-9, 3.99, 4 Saves 1933 1945

Key Pitch: Fastball
Note: Salveson pitched mostly out of the bullpen while in the major leagues, but for many years he was a top starter in the Pacific Coast League, and became famous for throwing very few pitches. Lefty O'Doul once called Salveson "the great conservationist."
Salveson: "I don't monkey around with those fancy pitches. I think those screwballs, knucklers and sliders are freak pitches."
Source: Salveson's obituary in *The Sporting News*

MANNY SALVO 6'4" 210-pound righty
33-50, 3.69, 1 Save 1939 1943

Pitch Selection: 1. High Fastball 2. Change of Pace 3. Curve
Sources: *New York World-Telegram* (2/25/1939, Tom Meany; and 6/2/1939, Meany)

Salvo: "I use a pitching style all my own, I guess, but after seeing pictures of Johnny Vander Meer pitching, I see we both use the same style."
Source: *New York Herald Tribune* (1/31/1939, Arthur E. Patterson)

JOE SAMBITO 6'1" 185-pound lefty
37-38, 3.03, 84 Saves 1976 1987

Sambito: "I have to rely on a sinking fastball and changing speeds and I have to have control of my off-speed pitches to win. If I get behind the hitters, they'll wait for my hard stuff and I won't get it by them."
Source: *The Sporting News* (9/18/1976, Harry Shattuck)

Pitch Selection: 1. Fastball 2. Slider
Source: *The Scouting Report: 1987*

RAUL SANCHEZ 6'0" 150-pound righty
5-3, 4.62, 5 Saves 1952 1960

Note: Listed as a suspected spitball pitcher
Source: *The Cincinnati Game* (Lonnie Wheeler and John Baskin, 1988)

BEN SANDERS 6'0" 210-pound righty
80-70, 3.24, 2 Saves 1888 1892

Description: "One of his strong points as a pitcher was his control . . . he was an awkward fielder, particularly on bunts. Most of his fielding problems seemed due to his unorthodox delivery, which found him falling off the mound with his back to the plate after hurling the ball."

Source: *Baseball's First Stars* (SABR, 1996, article by Joe Klein)

KEN SANDERS 5'11" 168-pound righty
29-45, 2.97, 86 Saves 1964 1976

Pitches: 1. Sinker 2. Slider 3. Curve 4. Change
Sanders: "My best pitch is my sinker and even if I know the batter likes sinkers I am going to pit my strength against his. I also throw a slider, breaking pitch, and change of pace."
Source: *Late and Close: A History of Relief Pitching* (Paul Votano, 2002)

SCOTT SANDERS 6'4" 220-pound righty
34-45, 4.86, 5 Saves 1993 1999

Pitches: 1. Fastball 2. Slider 3. Change
Note: Sanders' changeup was never an effective pitch, and he scuttled it when he moved to the bullpen in 1998.
Sources: *The Scouting Notebook: 1997; The Scouting Notebook 2000*

SCOTT SANDERSON 6'5" 195-pound righty
163-143, 3.84, 5 Saves 1978 1996

Pitch Selection: 1. Fastball 2. Slow Curve 3. Forkball 4. Change
Sources: *The Scouting Report* (1990 and 1992 editions)

JACK SANFORD 6'0" 190-pound righty
137-101, 3.69, 11 Saves 1956 1967

Pitch Selection: 1. Rising Fastball 2. Slow Curve 3. Slider 4. Change
Sources: *Baseball Stars of 1963* (article by Jack Zanger), *Sport* (March 1963, Bill Libby); *Stan Musial: The Man's Own Story* (Musial with Bob Broeg, 1964)

Pitch Selection: 1. Slider
Source: *1963 Major League Handbook* (Don Schiffer)

Description: "Sanford owns a curve ball, a slider, and a change-up, but the fast ball is his big stick, coming back every time a hitter starts to get ideas."
Source: Bob Purkey in *Baseball's Greatest Players Today* (edited by Jack Orr, 1963)

Comment: "[Whitlow] Wyatt, incidentally, is credited by Sanford with 'straightening out' his curve ball. By that he means that the placid Georgian, a former Dodger pitching star, taught him how to throw it downward without getting it into the dirt, and how to throw it upward without losing it in the stands. Wyatt also gave Sanford some pointers in the art of throwing a slow and medium curve. What it boils down to is that Sanford is no longer just a 'thrower'—although he told a New York *Times* writer that he was no more than that—but a crafty pitcher who knows what to do with his pitching repertoire . . .

". . . Unlike a lot of righthanders, Sanford has no particular trouble with lefthanded sluggers. This is because he can make his fast ball move equally well to the right or to the left."
Source: *Sport* (December 1957, Hugh Brown)

JOHAN SANTANA 6'0" 195-pound lefty
23-12, 3.97, 1 Save 2000 2003

Pitches: 1. Fastball (mid-90s) 2. Slider 3. Circle Change
Sources: *The Scouting Notebook 2003;* Jon Miller during ESPN broadcast of Twins-Yankees Division Series game on September 30, 2003.

JOSE SANTIAGO 6'2" 185-pound righty
34-29, 3.74, 8 Saves 1963 1970

Key Pitch: Fastball
Quote: "Has a real good fastball. Comes overhand, three-quarters, sidearm . . . and when he comes sidearm, I flinch a little bit up here in this booth."
Source: Pee Wee Reese during NBC broadcast of Red Sox vs. Angels on August 19, 1967

KAZUHIRO SASAKI 6'4" 220-pound righty
7-16, 3.14, 129 Saves 2000 2003

Pitches: 1. Splitter 2. Fastball (low 90s) 3. Curve (occasional)
Source: *The Scouting Notebook* (2001–2004 editions)

SCOTT SAUERBECK 6'3" 200-pound lefty
19-16, 3.71, 5 Saves 1999 2003

Pitch Selection: 1. Curve 2. Sinking Fastball 3. Change (occasional)
Source: *The Scouting Notebook: 2000*

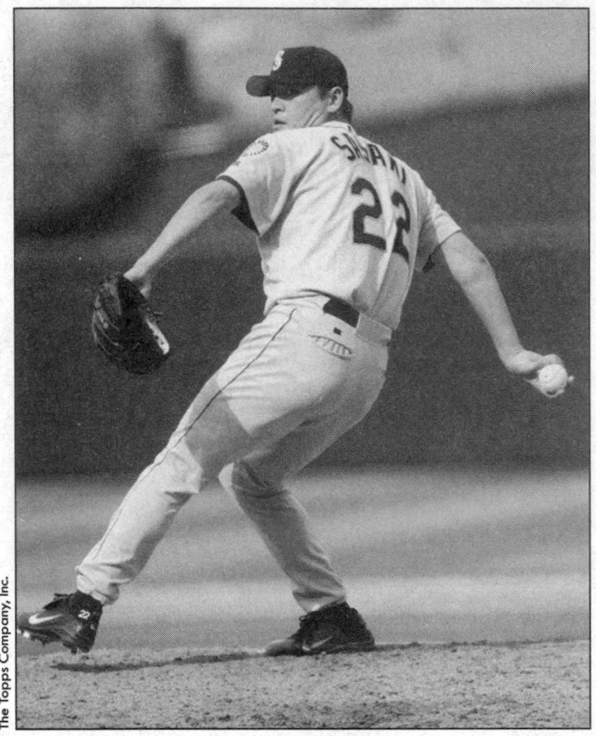

The Topps Company, Inc.

Kazuhiro Sasaki

BOB SAVAGE 6'2" 180-pound righty
16-27, 4.32, 9 Saves 1942 1949

Pitch Selection: 1. Fastball 2. Palm Ball
Source: A's pitching coach Earle Brucker in *Baseball Magazine* (September 1947, Frank Yeutter)

BOB SCANLAN 6'7" 215-pound righty
20-34, 4.63, 17 Saves 1991 2001

Pitches: 1. Fastball (low-90s) 2. Curve 3. Slider 4. Splitter 5. Change
Sources: *The Scouting Report* (1992–1995 editions)

PAT SCANTLEBURY 6'0" 178-pound lefty
NEGRO LEAGUES 1944 1950

Key Pitch: Spitball
Bob Feller: "[Scantlebury's spitter] looked like a pigeon coming out of a barn."
Source: *Invisible Men* (Donn Rogosin, 1983)

RAY SCARBOROUGH 6'0" 185-pound righty
80-85, 4.13, 14 Saves 1942 1953

Pitches: 1. Curve 2. Fastball 3. Change 4. Knuckleball (occasional) 5. Slider (developed in 1953)
Sources: *Baseball Magazine* (July 1949, Ed Rumill); *Baseball Digest* (May 1953, Hy Goldberg)

Ted Williams: "He keeps me guessing. Just as he is coming around with his arm, he sort of crooks his wrist and I think it's going to be a curve. But 50 percent of the time it's a fast ball. He's tough."
Source: *Baseball Magazine* (October 1949, Ed Rumill)

Scarborough: "The big difference now is the slider, which was just coming in when I was pitching. A few pitchers had it back then—Bob Muncrief, he was one of them. We called it the short curve. I was a curveball pitcher, but mine was a real old-fashioned curve, and that took a lot more effort to throw."
Source: Scarborough in *Five Seasons* (Roger Angell, 1977)

CHARLEY "HIPPO" SCHANZ
6'3" 215-pound righty
28-43, 4.34, 14 Saves 1944 1950

Key Pitch: Fastball
Description: "Charley is fast—very fast . . ."
Source: *Pacific Coast Baseball News* (6/10/1949)

Note: The nickname "Hippo" doesn't show up in the encyclopedias, but it does appear every time Schanz appears in the *Pacific Coast Baseball News.*

DAN SCHATZEDER 6'0" 185-pound lefty
69-68, 3.74, 10 Saves 1977 1991

Pitch Selection: 1. Curve 2. Slider 3. Fastball
Source: *The Scouting Report: 1990*

CARL SCHEIB 6'1" 192-pound righty
45-65, 4.88, 17 Saves 1943 1954

Pitches: 1. Fastball 2. Curve 3. Straight Change 4. Slider (late career)
Scheib: "In those days, we didn't mess around with forkballs and stuff like that. We were taught fastball, curveball, and change. I had a real good curveball, a big

curveball. I really don't know how hard I threw. I would guess that if we could have timed it, it would have been around 90. I used the fastball mostly. In those days, we were taught, 'Give 'em your best stuff and let 'em hit it.' For my change off the fastball, I held it deep in my hand, almost against the palm . . . Later on in years, I started trying to throw a slider."
Source: phone interview with Scheib (5/9/2003, Rob Neyer)

Quote: "He's a smart kid. You show him a thing once and he's got it. He hasn't much of a curve ball but he's about as fast as any kid I've ever seen except Bob Feller.

"The surprising part about him is that a change of pace came to him natural as could be."
Source: A's pitching coach Earle Brucker in *Baseball Magazine* (September 1947, Frank Yeutter)

BILL SCHERRER 6'4" 170-pound lefty
8-10, 4.08, 11 Saves 1982 1988

Pitch Selection: 1. Curve 2. Fastball (85) 3. Slider
Source: *The Scouting Report: 1984*

CURT SCHILLING 6'5" 205-pound righty
163-117, 3.33, 13 Saves 1988 2003

Pitch Selection: 1. Fastball (low-90s) 2. Slider 3. Split-Fingered Fastball 4. Change
Note: The splitter moved up the list in 1997, triggering Schilling's 1997 increase in strikeouts.
Sources: *The Scouting Report* (1993, 1995, and 1996 editions); *The Scouting Notebook 1998*

Tim McCarver: "Schilling has changed from being an occasional sinkerballer who would throw the slower two-seamer down in the strike zone after getting two strikes on the batter. Now he is a pitcher who almost always will stick with the high four-seam ninety-five mph fastball with two strikes. He didn't get 319 strikeouts in 1997 with sinkers."
Source: *Tim McCarver's Baseball for Brain Surgeons and Other Fans* (McCarver with Danny Peary, 1998)

CALVIN SCHIRALDI 6'5" 215-pound righty
32-39, 4.28, 21 Saves 1984 1991

Pitches: 1. Fastball (low-90s) 2. Slow Curve 3. Slider
Source: *The Scouting Report* (1987 and 1990 editions); *One Pitch Away* (Mike Sowell, 1995)

BIFF SCHLITZER 5'11" 175-pound righty
10-15, 3.60, 1 Save 1908 1914

Key Pitch: Spitball
Source: *The Sporting News* (9/24/1908)

DAVE SCHMIDT 6'1" 185-pound righty
54-55, 3.88, 50 Saves 1981 1992

Pitch Selection: 1. Slider 2. Change 3. Sinker 4. Fastball
Source: *The Scouting Report 1987*

Pitch Selection: 1. Fastball 2. Slider 3. Palmball
Source: *1990 Montreal Expos Media Guide*

HENRY SCHMIDT 5'11" 170-pound righty
22-13, 3.83, 2 Saves 1903 1903

Key Pitch: Curve Ball
Source: *The Baseball Research Journal,* Number 22 (1993, article by Joseph Cardello)
Note: Schmidt is the only major leaguer to pitch only one season and win twenty or more games.

Curt Schilling

JASON SCHMIDT 6'5" 185-pound righty
86-67, 4.02, 0 Saves 1995 2003

Pitch Selection: 1. Fastball (94) 2. Slider (86) 3. Change 4. Curve
Source: *The Scouting Notebook: 1997*

WILLARD SCHMIDT 6'1" 187-pound righty
31-29, 3.93, 2 Saves 1952 1959

Pitch Selection: 1. Fastball 2. Curve 3. Slider (added in 1954)
Source: *The Sporting News* (9/8/1954, Page 36)
Note: Listed by *The Sporting News* (8/29/1956) as having one of the better fastballs in the league.

JOHNNY SCHMITZ 6'0" 170-pound lefty
93-114, 3.55, 19 Saves 1941 1956

Pitches: 1. Big Curve 2. Slow Curve 3. Fastball (85–87) 4. Change 5. Sinker
Schmitz: "I threw a big curveball and a change-up curve . . . I threw a curveball, fastball, change-'em-up, and a sinkerball."
Source: Interview conducted by Gene DeLisio (April, 2003); in same interview, Schmitz said he learned to throw his sinker from teammate Emil Kush.

Pitch Selection: 1. Curve 2. Sinking Fastball 3. Change
Sources: *1947 Scout Report* (Wid Matthews); *Baseball Magazine* (September 1947, Ed Rumill); *Stan Musial* (Musial with Bob Broeg, 1964); Rumill quotes an unidentified hitter as saying that Schmitz "has a big curve ball. It's as tough as any you look at in our league."

Description: "Johnny Schmitz, left-hand curveballer, owned the Dodgers . . . I can close my eyes and see that curve; three inches in front of home plate it was up around your head, and the catcher wound up catching it by your feet. Damnedest curve I've ever seen."
Source: *Rex Barney's Thank Youuuu for 50 Years in Baseball from Brooklyn to Baltimore* (Barney with Norman L. Macht, 1993)

PETE SCHNEIDER 6'1" 194-pound righty
58-86, 2.64, 4 Saves 1914 1919

Pitch Selection: 1. Fastball 2. Curve 3. Change
Sources: *Baseball Magazine* (February 1919, "Leading Stars of the Winter Trades"); *Seattle Times* (4/10/1914)
Quote from *Baseball Magazine:* "Schneider was noted at Cincinnati for his great speed and his hard luck."
Quote from *Seattle Times:* "Pete is going to burn up the league this season . . . He has a swell curve, and a nice change of pace."

MIKE SCHOOLER 6'3" 220-pound righty
15-29, 3.49, 98 Saves 1988 1993

Pitch Selection: 1. Fastball (low-90s) 2. Slider 3. Curve
Sources: *The Scouting Report: 1990* and *1992*

GENE SCHOTT 6'2" 185-pound righty
28-41, 3.73, 4 Saves 1935 1939

Key Pitch: Fastball
Source: *Baseball Magazine* (May 1937, Franklin Pollock)

PETE SCHOUREK 6'5" 195-pound lefty
66-77, 4.59, 2 Saves 1991 2001

Pitch Selection: 1. Fastball 2. Change 3. Slow Curve
Source: *The Scouting Notebook: 1996*

PAUL SCHREIBER 6'2" 180-pound righty
0-0, 3.98, 1 Save 1922 1945

Key Pitch, 1945: Knuckleball
Source: *Baseball Dynasties* (Rob Neyer and Eddie Epstein, 1998)

Note: Schreiber pitched a few innings for the Dodgers in 1922 and '23, at which point his major-league career seemed to end. But in 1945, Schreiber, forty-two years old and working as the Yankees' batting-practice pitcher, pitched in two September games against the Tigers.

KEN SCHROM 6'2" 195-pound righty
51-51, 4.81, 1 Save 1980 1987

Pitch Selection: 1. Fastball (88) 2. Curve 3. Straight Change
Source: *The Scouting Report: 1984*

BARNEY SCHULTZ 6'2" 200-pound righty
20-20, 3.63, 35 Saves 1955 1965

Key Pitch: Knuckleball
Source: *The Sporting News* (9/5/1964, Page 18)

HAL SCHUMACHER 6'0" 190-pound righty
158-121, 3.36, 7 Saves 1931 1946

Pitches: 1. Sinker 2. Overhand Curve
3. Palmball (developed after 1935 arm injury)
Sources: *Major League Baseball* (Ethan Allen, Page 29); *Under Coogan's Bluff* (Fred Stein, 1978); *Who's Who in the Major Leagues* (1936 edition); *Baseball for Everyone* (Tom Meany, 1948)

Description: "Schumacher's unique delivery is a fast ball thrown with an overhand motion that breaks down like a screw ball. No one else has a fast ball quite like his, for the typical fast ball jumps or shoots to one side or the other. Schumacher's breaks down, for some unknown reason, and opposing batters are still wondering why it acts so."
Source: *Baseball Magazine* (September 1933, F.C. Lane)

Comment: "There are only two overhand sinker-ball pitchers—Hal Schumacher, of the Giants, and Spurgeon Chandler, of the Yankees. This variety of the pitch entails tremendous strain on the arm. The overhand sinker has no complete follow through. Watch Schumacher, if you can, and you will note that he pitches out of the arm socket and not with the force of his body."
Source: *Baseball Magazine* (September 1937, Daniel M. Daniel)

Harry Danning: "Hal Schumacher had a great fastball and was a low-ball pitcher. He also had a good, fast curveball; his used to break a foot. Hal threw a heavy ball that would tear a catcher's hand off."
Source: *Dugout to Foxhole* (Rick Van Blair, 1994)

Al Lopez: "He had a very fast sinker, a heavy ball that always bore into the batter."
Source: *The Greatest Team of All Time* (Nicholas Acocella and Donald Dewey, 1994)

FERDIE SCHUPP 5'10" 150-pound lefty
61-39, 3.32, 6 Saves 1913 1922

Pitch Selection: 1. Fastball 2. Curve 3. Slow Ball
Description: "Fairly tall, willowy, left-handed, with a lot of speed and a curve ball that broke away out to here, or away in here, right under the batter's fists. But not knowing, always, when he let the ball go, where it was going. And not inclined to worry over much where it went . . ."
Source: *The New York Giants* (Frank Graham, 1952 edition)
Other Source: *Baseball Magazine* (July 1917, J.J. Ward)

Description from *Baseball Magazine*: "After carefully looking for flaws in his style, noting the amount of 'stuff' he totes in his south side pitching flipper and observing the coolness he displays with runners on the bags, our personal opinion is this: Schupp's form is well-nigh perfect. His pitching repertoire is as extensive as any hurler extant . . . Schupp has about everything a hurler can use except a spitter and cross-fire ball, and with his control he is as well equipped a gunner as you'll see from Brooklyn to Shanghai. If he had any more control he couldn't very well be left handed and human, and if that south side fin of his packed any more 'stuff' it would break out with a rash.

"Schupp has nice speed, and gets it with apparently little effort. He has a good slow ball and delivers it with the same motion as his fast one. He has a stylish looking curve with a sharp break that behaves like a loving child and he makes a runner stick to first base like a porous plaster; he does this by employing a peculiar, half-kick motion, as he delivers the ball, that looks as though he intended to throw to first."

DON SCHWALL 6'6" 200-pound righty
49-48, 3.72, 4 Saves 1961 1967

Pitch Selection: 1. Sinker 2. Fastball 3. Slider
Comment: "Still, it was Don's sinkerball—his natural fastball thrown off a three-quarter motion (his overhand fastball sails)—that made him so successful. 'I've thrown my sinkerball as much as 90 percent of the time in some games,' Schwall said last summer."
Source: *Inside Baseball* (1962, "Produced by the Editors of Sport Magazine")

HERB SCORE 6'2" 185-pound lefty
55-46, 3.36, 3 Saves 1955 1962

Pitches, 1955–1959: 1. Fastball 2. Overhand Curve
3. Slider
Pitches, 1960: 1. Fastball 2. Overhand Curve

Quote: "I told Score to abandon two pitches, the sidearm and the slider. The sidearm delivery was unnatural for him, and the slider could hurt his arm and was not needed. I said 'Herb, your fastball and your curve,

coming straight overhand, are all you need, at least until you get re-established. Then we will have another talk."
Source: White Sox manager Al Lopez in *New York World-Telegram* (5/9/1960, column by Dan Daniel)

JACK SCOTT 6'2" 199-pound righty
103-109, 3.85, 19 Saves 1916 1929

Key Pitch: Curve
Sources: *Baseball's Greatest Drama* (Joseph J. Krueger, 1946 edition); 1923 *Reach Guide*

Note: Scott pitched a four-hit shutout in the third game of the 1922 World Series, his most famous feat. The 1923 *Reach Guide* says Scott "used only a curve" (page 209), and also, in a separate article, says that "Scott's brilliant curve-ball pitching had the Yankees completely buffaloed" (page 194). Krueger reports that Scott "curved the Yankees into submission."

Another source, Noel Hynd's *The Giants of the Polo Grounds*, says that Scott, in Game 3, threw "nothing but high heat." Hynd was writing many years after the fact, and I regard the other sources as far more likely to have it right.

JIM SCOTT 6'1" 235-pound righty
107-113, 2.30, 8 Saves 1909 1917

Pitch Selection: 1. Spitball 2. Fadeaway
Source: *The Ballplayers* (1990, article by Richard C. Lindberg)

Quote: "On the way to Arizona, Jim Scott regaled the pitchers on both teams with horror stories of pitching in the thin desert mountain air. In the high Arizona desert, curve balls did not curve, at least for a few days, by which time the pitcher could grow accustomed to the atmospheric conditions and finally figure out how to make a curve ball break."
Source: *The Tour to End All Tours: The Story of Major League Baseball's 1913–1914 World Tour* (James E. Elfters, 2003). There is no specific reference for this quote. However, the notes do include a newspaper article, "Rarified Air Hampers Pitchers at Douglas," by G.W. Axelson and published in the *Chicago Record-Herald*.

Quote: "Who had the best pickoff motion? That's easy, Sherry Smith. The best by a righthander was that of Death Valley Jim Scott. Today's best, left or right, is Warren Spahn."
Source: John Ogden in *The Sporting News* (11/16/1963, Lee Allen's "Cooperstown Corner" column)

MIKE SCOTT 6'2" 210-pound righty
124-108, 3.54, 3 Saves 1979 1991

Pitches, 1979–1984: 1. Fastball (mid-90s) 2. Slider 3. Change 4. Curve
Pitches, 1985–1991: 1. Split-Fingered Fastball 2. Fastball (low-90s) 3. Slider
Note: Scott pretty much abandoned his slider during the 1984 season, and, with his career at a crossroads, prior to the '85 season he learned the split-finger pitch from Roger Craig. Immediately, he became one of the better pitchers in the league.
Sources: *The Scouting Report* (1983, 1985, 1986, and 1990 editions)

Note: During the successful part of Scott's career, and particularly in 1986, everybody who faced Scott was convinced that his best pitch was, rather than a Splitter, an illegal pitch that he achieved by scuffing the ball. The Mets were especially adamant about this, but Scott was never caught in the act.

TIM SCOTT 6'2" 205-pound righty
24-13, 4.13, 5 Saves 1991 1997

Pitch Selection: 1. Fastball (high-80s) 2. Slider 3. Change 4. Forkball
Source: *The Scouting Report: 1993*

Pitch Selection: 1. Fastball (low-90s) 2. Split-Fingered Fastball
Source: *The Scouting Notebook: 1996*

SCOTT SCUDDER 6'2" 180-pound righty
21-34, 4.80, 1 Save 1989 1993

Pitch Selection: 1. Sinking Fastball 2. Hard Slider 3. Curve
Quote: "Scudder throws a lot of different pitches, but has mastered few and makes too many mistakes."
Source: *Bill Mazeroski's Baseball* (1993 edition)

ROD SCURRY 6'2" 180-pound lefty
19-32, 3.24, 39 Saves 1980 1988

Pitches: 1. Curve 2. Fastball 3. Change (occasional)
Sources: *The Scouting Report* (1983–1985 editions)

Note: All sources report that Scurry's curve was among the best in baseball.

RUDY SEANEZ 5'11" 205-pound righty
17-17, 4.54, 11 Saves 1989 2003

Pitch Selection: 1. Fastball (low-90s) 2. Hard Slider 3. Curve
Source: *The Scouting Notebook: 1996*

RAY SEARAGE 6'1" 180-pound lefty
11-13, 3.50, 11 Saves 1981 1990

Quote: "He has a good fastball and an assortment of breaking pitches."
Source: *The Scouting Report: 1990*

TOM SEATON 6'0" 175-pound righty
93-65, 3.14, 11 Saves 1912 1917

Key Pitch: Knuckleball
Source: Dan Daniel in the *New York World-Telegram* (6/6/1940)
Daniel: "Tracing the origins of specialties like the spitter, screwball and knuckler is a hazardous job, because there are so many false claimants—and they holler the loudest. But it seems likely that the first knuckleball hurler was Tom Seaton, with the Phillies." (This clearly isn't true, though Seaton might have been the first National League knuckleballer.)

TOM SEATS 5'11" 190-pound lefty
12-9, 4.47, 1 Save 1940 1945

Pitch Selection: 1. Fastball 2. Curve
Note: Seats threw overhand until 1947, when he switched to three-quarters (though by that point he was in the minors for good).
Source: *Pacific Coast League Baseball News* (8/15/1947 and 9/10/1948)

TOM SEAVER 6'1" 195-pound righty
311-205, 2.86, 1 Save 1967 1986

Pitch Selection: 1. Rising (Four-Seam) Fastball 2. Sinking (Two-Seam) Fastball 3. Slider 4. Curve 5. Change
Sources: *Pitching with Tom Seaver* (Seaver with Steve Jacobson, 1973), *Sport World* (August 1976, S.M. Horsting)

Note: According to Frederick C. Klein in a July 1979 clipping from an unidentified newspaper in the *TSN* morgue, Seaver added the curve only in 1979, when his fastball and slider began to fade a little. However, the 1973 book with Steve Jacobson has a photo showing how he gripped his curve. He probably didn't use the curve a lot until the late 1970s.

Seaver: "I've got four [pitches]—fast ball, curve ball, slider and change-up—but I've got a couple of different kinds of fast balls and three different curve balls and a slider and two change-ups. So it's seven or eight pitches that I have, though there are only four different signals for them. I might show four different kinds of curve ball."
Source: *Inside Corner: Talks with Tom Seaver* (edited by Joel H. Cohen, 1974)

Seaver: "In the early years of my career, I did not have a straight change-up but used at least three different speeds of fastball . . . The change-up will require a lot of discipline and dedication to perfect, but if you work at it, you will experience the great joy of discovery. I remember the moment when I worked out my basic change-up grip. I was throwing in the outfield one day between starts with my teammate Jon Matlack of the Mets, and 'Eureka!,' after countless attempts, I found the grip that worked for me."
Source: *The Art of Pitching* (Seaver with Lee Lowenfish, 1984)

DIEGO SEGUI 6'0" 190-pound righty
92-111, 3.81, 71 Saves 1962 1977

Pitch Selection: 1. Forkball 2. Fastball 3. Overhand Curve (added 1970)
Sources: *Catfish: My Life in Baseball* (Jim "Catfish" Hunter with Armen Keteyian, 1988); *Major League Baseball: 1971* (Brenda Zanger and Dick Kaplan)

SOCKS SEIBOLD 5'8" 162-pound righty
48-86, 4.43, 5 Saves 1916 1933

Seibold: "The curve used to be my best ball. But now I find a screw ball mighty useful, and a knuckle ball helps out, too. The only trouble with the knuckle ball is con-

trol, but I discovered you can't throw at the plate. You throw at the catcher. If it gets over the batter has something to worry about."
Source: *Baseball Magazine* (June 1932, F.C. Lane)

AARON SELE 6'5" 205-pound righty
122-88, 4.48, 0 Saves 1993 2003

Pitch Selection: 1. Overhand Curve 2. Fastball (high-80s) 3. Cut Fastball 4. Other Curve
Sources: *The Scouting Notebook 1998; The Scouting Notebook 2000*

Note: According to the *Seattle Times* on October 17, 2001, that season Sele threw 63 percent fastballs, 23 percent curves, 9 percent sliders and five percent change-ups. According to the same source, Sele threw three types of fastballs: four-seamer thrown 88–92 m.p.h., two-seamer thrown 83–87, and a cutter. His curve had a big 12-to-6 break and was thrown 65–75. His change-up had a slight sink and was thrown 78–83, and his slider was actually a "hard slurve" thrown 78–84.

DICK SELMA 5'11" 160-pound righty
42-54, 3.62, 31 Saves 1965 1974

Pitch Selection: 1. Fastball 2. Curve 3. Slider
Sources: *The Sporting News* (11/2/1963, Barney Kremenko); *Major League Baseball—1969* (Jack Zanger); *Baseball Digest* (March 1966, "Scouting Reports on 1966 Major League Rookies")

CARROLL SEMBERA 6'0" 155-pound righty
3-11, 4.70, 6 Saves 1965 1970

Key Pitch: Sinking Fastball
Description: "Has possibilities in middle relief in majors. Fast ball moves well and sinks, but he's not fast enough to be a starter."
Source: *Baseball Digest* (March 1967, "Official Scouting Reports on 1967 Major League Rookies"; and in 99 games in the majors, Sembera started exactly once.)

SCOTT SERVICE 6'6" 240-pound righty
19-21, 4.89, 16 Saves 1988 2003

Pitch Selection: 1. Fastball (low-90s) 2. Hard Slider 3. Split-Fingered Fastball
Source: *The Scouting Notebook: 1999*

FRANK SEWARD 6'3" 200-pound righty
3-3, 5.15, 0 Saves 1943 1944

Pitches: 1. Fastball 2. Curve/Slider
Source: Seward in *The San Francisco Seals, 1946–1957* (Brent Kelley, 2002)

RIP SEWELL 6'1" 180-pound righty
143-97, 3.48, 15 Saves 1932 1949

Pitches: 1. Slider 2. Fastball 3. Curve 4. Blooper 5. Knuckleball (occasional)
Note: After a 1941 hunting accident, Sewell was forced to pitch straight overhand, and developed the blooper pitch. According to longtime umpire Bill Stewart in *The Sporting News* (7/20/1955), Sewell also threw one of the best spitballs he ever saw.
Sources: Sewell in *Baseball When the Grass Was Real* (Donald Honig, 1975); *The Blooper Man* (Elson Smith, Page 45); *Baseball Magazine* (September 1943, Clifford Bloodgood; and September 1944, Ed Rumill)
Quote from Bloodgood article: "Rip monkeyed around with a new pitch last season, further developed it this spring and unveiled it in competition shortly after the present campaign began. It is a tantalizing slow ball that describes an arc on the way to the plate. It may rise twenty feet in the air and descends over the pan on a slant. The catcher will grab it only a foot or so off the ground. Rip has no name for this delivery of his, but his teammates have dubbed it 'Skyscraper,' 'Dodo' and 'Dewdrop.' . . . He has good control of his floater and can put it over the plate for strikes five times out of seven. He may throw it fifteen times during the course of a ball game, and the fans get a big kick out of it." (This describes Sewell's blooper in 1943; in later years he probably threw it higher and more often.)

Comment: "And now, as if things weren't bad enough, Sewell is experimenting with a new pitch—an underhand knuckler. When he has it perfected his crazy repertory will read as follows:

"1—Fast ball, 2—curve ball, 3—slider, 4—blooper, 5—half-blooper, 6—change of pace, 7—knuckler, 8—underhand knuckler."
Source: Arthur E. Patterson, Director of National League Service Bureau, quoted in *The Sporting News* (4/19/1945, Page 12)

Umpire Lee Ballanfant: "Now that damned blooper pitch Rip Sewell used to throw was the hardest thing to judge. You're supposed to call the ball as it comes over the plate, but what do you do if it comes straight down? He just pushed it up there; wasn't hard enough to break a pane of glass. It was the damnedest thing you ever saw; I missed a lot of calls. He'd throw it fifteen, twenty times a game, especially if he didn't want to give a guy a good pitch. It sure looked big coming up there, and sometimes they'd pop it up because their timing was off. But if the batter was looking for it, it wasn't even a good batting-practice pitch."
Source: *The Men in Blue* (Larry Gerlach, 1980)

Description: "What made Sewell's pitch so effective, so utterly baffling, is that he threw it in the same motion as his fastball. He merely put three fingers on the ball instead of four and it would come off his finger tips with a tremendous back spin."
Note: According to Sewell, the blooper was called the "Eephus Pitch," so named by teammate Maurice Van Robays. Sewell introduced the pitch in an exhibition game against the Tigers in Muncie, Indiana. He had experimented with it in the bullpen and was encouraged by his catcher, Al Lopez, to throw it in a game.
Source: *Baseball Digest* (July 1975, Joe Falls)

Description of Sewell in 1939: "Sewell should go far for he has had long experience and possesses a wide variety of stuff, very deceptive, including a sinker and a slider pitch. That slider pitch is his ace in the hole and it looks to the batter as if he were merely throwing an ordinary fast ball, but it has a sharp break with a bit of a spin on it just as it reaches the batter. He finds it especially effective against left handers. Mixing that with his sinker ball which breaks the opposite way, and his fast ball and curve Sewell can handcuff the best."
Source: *Baseball Magazine* (July 1939, Clifford Bloodgood)

CY SEYMOUR 6'0" 200-pound lefty
60-53, 3.76, 3 Saves 1896 1902

Pitch Selection: 1. Fastball 2. Curve 3. Screwball
Quote: "The New York press said that he had the best curve in the league."
Source: *Baseball Research Journal* 29 (SABR, 2000, article by Bill Kirwin)

Comment: "There have been innumerable pitchers possessing incredible speed who would certainly have carved their names indelibly on baseball's archives, if only they had been blessed with that indispensable asset—control. Such a pitcher was Cy Seymour, who had lightning speed, but was unable to control it, which was partly due, it was said, to the fact that his hands were small. Cy finally realized that he would never make a consistent moundsman, and turned his attention to the outfield, where he developed into a star."
Source: *Baseball Magazine* (May 1919, Edmund K. Goldsborough, "Famous Speed Kings of the Past")

Note: *Baseball: The Biographic Encyclopedia* (ed. Pietrusza, et al., 2000) says that Seymour "received his nickname (short for 'Cyclone') as a tribute to his fastball." However, the term "Cyclone Pitch" was a nickname used in the 1890s for a hard curve, a "cyclone" curve; thus, I am uncertain as to the validity of this observation.

BOBBY SHANTZ 5'6" 139-pound lefty
119-99, 3.38, 48 Saves 1949 1964

Pitch Selection: 1. Curve
2. Knuckleball (added in 1951)
3. Fastball 4. Change
Source: *The Story of Bobby Shantz* (Shantz, as told to Ralph Bernstein, 1953); *Baseball Digest* (August 1952, Carl Lundquist)

Shantz on his knuckleball: "I like to throw it, too, when I get two strikes on a batter. I've got a pretty good fast ball, but I don't like to throw that one then because the darned thing usually goes down the middle too good where the batter can tee off on it.

"But the knuckler is a good waste pitch and if it comes close to the plate, the batter usually goes for it, and even if he hits it, he has a hard time getting a very good piece of it."
Source: 1952 *Baseball Digest*

Note: An article in *Baseball Digest* (January 1963) says that Shantz never threw a slider, although many hitters believed that he did because he sometimes threw his curve hard. *The Sporting News* (9/24/1952, Page 3) said Shantz "has a curve, a fair fast ball, a great change of pace, and a pitch the Cubans call Mariposa Blanco, the White Butterfly" (with the latter pitch presumably being his knuckleball).

JOE SHAUTE 6'0" 190-pound lefty
99-109, 4.15, 18 Saves 1922 1934

Key Pitch, 1922–1930: Fastball
Key Pitch, after 1930 arm injury: Curve
Source: *Who's Who in Major League Baseball* (compiled by Harold "Speed" Johnson, 1933)

BOB SHAW 6'2" 195-pound righty
108-98, 3.52, 32 Saves 1957 1967

Pitch Selection: 1. Fastball 2. Slider 3. Curve 4. Change
Sources: *View From the Dugout* (Ed Richter, 1963); *The Sporting News* (4/3/1965, Jack McDonald)

Note: Shaw gripped his change-up with three fingers, somewhat like the circle change that became so popular after he retired.
Shaw: "I had a slightly open stance as did Wynn; we both had three-quarter-arm deliveries. Koufax and Pierce both dropped their back shoulders more than I did because they threw overhand . . ."
Source: *Pitching* (Bob Shaw, 1972)

Note: According to Gaylord Perry in *Me and the Spitter,* Shaw frequently threw a spitball.

DON SHAW 6'0" 180-pound lefty
13-14, 4.01, 6 Saves 1967 1972

Key Pitch: Sinker
Source: *Baseball Digest* (March 1967, "Official Scouting Reports on 1967 Major League Rookies")

DUPEE SHAW 5'8" 165-pound lefty
83-121, 3.10, 0 Saves 1883 1888

Key Pitch: Curve
Source: *The Baseball Cyclopedia* (Ernest Lanigan, Page 78)

JEFF SHAW 6'2" 185-pound righty
34-54, 3.54, 203 Saves 1990 2001

Pitch Selection: 1. Split-Fingered Fastball 2. Sinking Fastball 3. Slider (occasional)
Sources: *The Scouting Notebook 1998; The Scouting Notebook 2000*

BOB SHAWKEY 5'11" 168-pound righty
196-150, 3.09, 29 Saves 1913 1927

Pitch Selection: 1. Curves 2. Fastball 3. Change
Sources: *Babe Ruth's Own Book of Baseball* (Ruth, 1928); Waite Hoyt in *Baseball Between the Wars* (Eugene Murdock, 1992)
Hoyt: "Shawkey threw two curves and his fastball and a change of pace."

Description: "Shawkey broke into the League as a speed ball pitcher with a world of stuff, but changing conditions brought about a complete readjustment of his hurling methods and he is now generally considered a curve ball pitcher."
Source: *Baseball Magazine* (July 1926, "Comprising an Interview with Bob Shawkey")

Description: "Shawkey has the hardest arm motion of any major league pitcher. He puts all his body from his waist up into his pitching motion and twists himself on his pivot foot long before he lets the ball get away. The result is a very wide curve that is hard to bat, especially when Shawkey has a good day and his speed is at its highest development. His delivery is not advised for a young pitcher to copy, although his finger positions are all right."
Source: *How to Pitch* (J.E. Wray, 1928)

FRANK SHEA 6'0" 195-pound righty
56-46, 3.80, 5 Saves 1947 1955

Description: "His curve isn't as good as Newhouser's and his fast ball is not as fast as Feller's, but every pitch he throws is 'live' and does something."
Source: *Baseball Digest* (September 1947, Shirley Povich)

JIM SHELLENBACK 6'2" 200-pound lefty
16-30, 3.81, 2 Saves 1966 1977

Description: "Very good fast ball. Change of speed pitcher. Has slider and good curve. Knows how to pitch. Good chance to hit the top."
Source: *Baseball Digest* (March 1967, "Official Scouting Reports on 1967 Major League Rookies")

Note: Shellenback's uncle, Frank Shellenback, was a legendary spitballer who pitched for the White Sox in 1918 and '19, then won 295 games in the Pacific Coast League.

BILL SHERDEL 5'10" 160-pound lefty
165-146, 3.72, 26 Saves 1918 1932

Pitch Selection: 1. Slow Ball 2. Fastball 3. Sidearm Curve 4. Slow Curve
Sources: *Baseball Magazine* (July 1927; and September 1928); *The St. Louis Star* (5/31/1929, Harry T. Brundidge); Thomas S. Rice in the *Brooklyn Eagle* (date unidentified, TSN morgue); two other unidentified articles, TSN morgue

Commentary: Sherdel, a very small man, was not an effective pitcher in the minor leagues, and the baseball world was puzzled by the fact that Branch Rickey wanted him for the Cardinals. Rickey saw that Sherdel was throwing everything the same speed, and that while he was a very poor fastball pitcher, he could be made into an extremely effective change-of-pace pitcher. He threw more fastballs than slow balls, easily, but his slow ball was the pitch for which he was famous, and was by far his most effective pitch. His fastball was decent, and had a hop to it.

Quote from *Baseball Magazine,* 1928: "There's really no mystery about this slow ball of mine. It's not registered in the Patent Office and any pitcher is at liberty to copy it, if he so desires. I throw the ball with exactly the same motion as I would throw a fast ball, but with this important difference. Just as I let go of the ball my fingers 'give' a bit. I fail to impart to the ball that spinning motion which makes it 'shoot' if it's a fast ball. So it comes up to the batter looking as big as a house but not coming as fast as it seems. And just before it gets to the plate it's apt to duck."

LARRY SHERRY 6'2" 180-pound righty
53-44, 3.67, 82 Saves 1958 1968

Pitch Selection: 1. Fastball 2. Slider 3. Curve
Sources: *Sports Illustrated* (10/19/1959); Walter Alston quoted in *Sport* (July 1960, Dick Young)

BOB SHIRLEY 5'11" 180-pound lefty
67-94, 3.82, 18 Saves 1977 1987

Pitch Selection: 1. Fastball 2. Slider
3. Shirley developed a Forkball in 1980.
Source: *The Sporting News* (6/14/1980, Phil Collier)

URBAN SHOCKER 5'10" 170-pound righty
187-117, 3.17, 25 Saves 1916 1928

Pitch Selection: 1. Fastball 2. Curve 3. Spitball
Note: Shocker was on the list of pitchers allowed to continue throwing the spitball after 1920, and so there are numerous sources which list him primarily as a spitball pitcher. However, the most authoritative source that we found, the 1924 *Reach Guide* (p. 48), says that Shocker "frequently will go through a game throwing just five or six spitballs. Of course, he will do a lot of bluffing, but usually it is a fast one or a curve." The same source also tells of a game in which Shocker pitched well when the home plate umpire was Ed Walsh, the master spitballer. Asked to evaluate Shocker's spitball, Walsh replied that Shocker was a great pitcher, but not a great spitball pitcher, and added that he had thrown only four spitballs in the game.

Pitch Selection: 1. Spitball 2. Slow Ball
3. Slow Spitball
Comment: "Urban Shocker, who died a year ago, was one of the great spitball artists because he successfully mixed a slow ball with his wet delivery. Shocker also slowed up his spitter, and in that manner used it as a change of pace."
Source: Umpire George Moriarty in *Baseball Magazine* (December 1929)

Ty Cobb: "Shocker had a peculiar head motion that used to dazzle base-runners. He'd stand out there and shake his head toward first base—as a boxer feints. This entranced many a runner, who kept watching Shocker's head. His purpose was to hold a man near the base—but not to pick him off. When the steal attempt came, Shocker's catcher had a much better chance to nail the runner at second."
Source: *My Life in Baseball: The True Record* (Cobb with Al Stump, 1961)

ERNIE SHORE 6'4" 220-pound righty
66-43, 2.47, 5 Saves 1912 1920

Key Pitch: Sinking Fastball
Shore: "My particular stock in trade is a fast ball which I have trained so that it has a peculiar break. The average fast ball will shoot to one side or the other as it crosses the plate, and in some cases where thrown with suffi-

cient speed, will actually rise. My fast ball, on the other hand, drops sharply. It will not break as much as a curve, but the drop will be much more sudden."
Source: *Baseball Magazine* (September 1917, "A Pitcher's Day Dreams")

Description: "Ernest Shore had peculiar fingers which, in his opinion, were the basis of his freaky fast ball. This fast ball had a break unlike the usual type of a pitcher's repertoire and was a thorn in the side of the batter when Shore was in his prime."
Source: *Baseball Magazine* (October 1925, Page 496)

BILL SHORES 6'0" 185-pound righty
26-15, 4.17, 7 Saves 1928 1936

Pitch Selection: 1. Curve 2. Fastball
Source: *The Sporting News* (4/12/1934, Daniel M. Daniel)

Key Pitch, 1937–1939: Knuckleball
Source: *The Sporting News* (1/27/1938, Ed. R. Hughes; and 6/8/1939, Jim McGee); by this point, Shores was in the minor leagues for good, but it seems likely that he'd thrown the knuckleball at least occasionally while in the majors.

CHRIS SHORT 6'4" 205-pound lefty
135-132, 3.43, 18 Saves 1959 1973

Pitch Selection: 1. Fastball 2. Curve 3. Change
Sources: *Baseball Digest* (March 1960, Page 92); *Major League Baseball 1965* (Jack Zanger)
Quote from *Baseball Digest:* "No one pitch is outstanding but has a little of it all. Good fast ball and curve. Needs some help on changes."
Quote from Zanger: "[Short] possesses a humming fast ball, along with a dandy curve and change-up." (This essentially confirms the pitch selection, but discusses Short as a successful pitcher.)

Note: Don Schiffer's *1963 Major League Handbook* gives a substantially different description, saying that Short had developed a new curve and improved his slider in late 1962, and also that "Working from a three-quarters motion exclusively and adding a slider to his repertoire has made a better man of Chris Short."
Gene Mauch: "Short can get more than one pitch over for strikes. He uses a fast ball, change-up and quick and slow curves."
Source: *1965 Official Baseball Almanac* (Bill Wise)

CLYDE SHOUN 6'1" 188-pound lefty
73-59, 3.91, 29 Saves 1935 1949

Pitch Selection: 1. Fastball 2. Curve
Sources: *The Sporting News* (7/18/1935; 8/1/1935); Tommy Holmes quoted in an unidentified source from the Hall of Fame Library (1/4/1936); *New York World-Telegram* (6/3/1937); media release, 1938; *New York Times* (6/18/1940)
Quote from TSN (8/1/1935): "He burns in a smoking fast ball and down in the cotton belt they compare him to Lefty Grove . . . He has better control than the average young left-hander."
Quote from *New York World-Telegram:* "Shoun, to all outward appearances, is a young southpaw with a fair fast ball and a fair curve."
Quote from 1938 media release: "Clyde . . . showed a good fast ball and a pretty fair curve."

ERIC SHOW 6'1" 185-pound righty
101-89, 3.66, 7 Saves 1981 1991

Pitch Selection: 1. Sinking Fastball 2. Slider 3. Change 4. Curve
Sources: *The Scouting Report: 1987; Tom Seaver's 1989 Scouting Notebook; The Scouting Report: 1990*

PAUL SHUEY 6'3" 215-pound righty
45-27, 3.57, 22 Saves 1994 2003

Pitch Selection: 1. Fastball (92–97) 2. Split-Fingered Fastball (low-90s) 3. Curve
Sources: *The Scouting Notebook* (1998–2003 editions)

SONNY SIEBERT 6'3" 190-pound righty
140-114, 3.21, 16 Saves 1964 1975

Pitch Selection: 1. Curve 2. Live Fastball
Sources: *The Ballplayers* (1990, article by Morris Eckhouse); *Baseball Digest* (March 1963, Page 119)

BILL SIMAS 6'3" 235-pound righty
18-19, 3.83, 23 Saves 1995 2000

Pitch Selection: 1. Fastball (90s) 2. Slider 3. Change
Source: *The Scouting Notebook: 1997*

CURT SIMMONS 5'11" 175-pound lefty
193-183, 3.54, 5 Saves 1947 1967

Pitch Selection: 1. Fastball 2. Slow Curve 3. Change
Note: Simmons threw with a herky-jerky delivery.
Sources: Eddie Sawyer in *The Man in the Dugout* (Donald Honig, 1977); *Stan Musial* (Musial with Bob Broeg, 1964); I Had a Hammer (Hank Aaron with Lonnie Wheeler, 1991)

Note: The above is probably a more accurate description of Curt Simmons post-comeback, in the early 1960s. As a young player, Simmons threw *extremely* hard with excellent movement, and relied heavily on his fastball.
Source: Richie Ashburn in *Legends: Conversations with Baseball Greats* (Art Rust Jr., 1989)

Quote: "[Robin] Roberts had less dazzling stuff than Simmons, but he was nearly three years older and more mature."
Source: *Sport* (June 1964, Harry Paxton)

Whitey Lockman: "The toughest guy for me to hit was Curt Simmons . . . a cross-firing guy and he could throw hard. Some guys throw heavy balls, some guys throw lighter balls; his ball was a heavy ball and even when I hit it, I felt like I hit a rock."
Source: *The Pastime in Turbulence: Interviews with Baseball Players of the 1940s* (Brent Kelley, 2001)

Robin Roberts: "He certainly did not disappoint, throwing harder and with more movement on the ball than anyone I had ever seen. He also had a peculiar delivery that hid the ball from the batter."
Source: *My Life in Baseball* (Robin Roberts with C. Paul Rogers III, 2003)

Description: "For eight innings [of Game 3 of the 1964 World Series], Curt Simmons and Jim Bouton pitched marvelously—Simmons, the veteran, with a selection of soft, in-and-out sliders, curves, and other junk, and Bouton with a rearing fast ball delivered with such energy that his cap flew off on every second or third pitch."
Source: Roger Angell in *The New Yorker* (October 1964, and reprinted in *The Summer Game*)

Description: "His herky-jerky motion prevented batters from picking up the ball readily. Moreover, the left-handed Simmons's crossfire delivery, which came from the direction of first base, intimidated left-handed hitters. His pitching repertoire consisted of two fastballs—one that took off and another that dipped—an excellent change-up, and a hard-breaking curve."
Source: *Baseball's Pivotal Era 1945–1951* (William Marshall, 1999)

WAYNE SIMPSON 6'3" 220-pound righty
36-31, 4.37, 0 Saves 1970 1977

Description: "Simpson throws an unusual fastball. When he throws it from the batter's waist down, it breaks down. When he throws it above the waist, it rises." (In modern terminology, this probably means simply that Simpson threw both a two-seam and a four-seam fastball.)
Source: *Major League Baseball: 1971* (Brenda Zanger and Dick Kaplan)

BILL SINGER 6'4" 184-pound righty
118-127, 3.39, 2 Saves 1964 1977

Pitch Selection: 1. Fastball 2. Spitball 3. Slider
4. Sidearm Curve
Sources: *The Sporting News* (6/30/1973, Dick Miller); *Glory Days With the Dodgers* (John Roseboro with Bill Libby, Page 197); *The No-Hit Hall of Fame* (Rich Coberly, 1985)

ELMER SINGLETON 6'2" 174-pound righty
11-17, 4.83, 4 Saves 1945 1959

Key Pitch, early career: Sinking Fastball
Pitches, late career: 1. Slider 2. Sinking Fastball
3. Knuckleball 4. Screwball (occasional)
Source: *The Sporting News* (7/26/1955, Page 23)

MIKE SIROTKA 6'1" 200-pound lefty
45-42, 4.31, 0 Saves 1995 2000

Pitch Selection: 1. Fastball (90) 2. Slider 3. Change
Sources: *The Scouting Notebook: 1999; The Scouting Notebook: 2000*

Pitch Selection: 1. Fastball 2. Curve 3. Change
4. Slider (occasional)
Sources: *The Scouting Notebook: 2001; The Scouting Notebook: 2002*

DOUG SISK 6'2" 210-pound righty
22-20, 3.27, 33 Saves 1982 1991

Pitch Selection: 1. Sinker 2. Slider 3. Fastball
Source: *The Scouting Report: 1987*

JIM SLATON 6'0" 185-pound righty
151-158, 4.03, 14 Saves 1971 1986

Pitches, early career: 1. Fastball 2. Curve 3. Change
Pitches, mid career: 1. Fastball 2. Slider 3. Curve 4. Change
Pitches, late career: 1. Fastball 2. Slurve 3. Change
Slaton: "I didn't throw a slider my first couple of years, was just fastball, curve, change. Cal McLish taught me the slider. Later on my slider turned into a slower slider, and they started calling it a slurve. I kinda used that as my one breaking pitch and didn't use my curve later in my career. Top pitch varied from outing to outing; fastball was probably my best pitch, although other people said my slider was. We didn't have the circle-change back then, so for a changeup I just took something off my two-seam fastball."
Source: Interview with Slaton (7/20/2002, Tacoma Rainers broadcaster Mike Curto)

LOU SLEATER 5'10" 185-pound lefty
12-18, 4.70, 5 Saves 1950 1958

Key Pitch: Knuckleball
Source: *The Sporting News* (5/22/1957)

HEATHCLIFF SLOCUMB 6'3" 210-pound righty
28-37, 4.08, 98 Saves 1991 2000

Pitch Selection: 1. Hard Sinker 2. Hard Slider 3. Forkball
Source: *The Scouting Notebook: 1997*

JOHN SMILEY 6'4" 180-pound lefty
126-103, 3.80, 4 Saves 1986 1997

Pitch Selection: 1. Fastball 2. Slider 3. Change 4. Overhand Curve
Note: After Smiley's 1993 arm trouble the change replaced the slider as Smiley's No. 2 pitch.
Sources: *The Scouting Report: 1992; The Scouting Notebook: 1996*

Description: "He came up with an outstanding change-up two years ago. He throws 88 to 90 mph and has a good curve, but that change really made him."
Source: *Bill Mazeroski's Baseball* (1993 edition)

AL SMITH 5'11" 180-pound lefty
99-101, 3.72, 17 Saves 1934 1945

Pitch Selection: 1. Curve 2. Screwball 3. Change 4. Fastball
Description: "Smith hasn't got much of a fast ball. At least he hasn't got fast ball enough to get him by without the help it gets from a curve, a screw ball, a change of pace, amazing control—and a head into which is packed the wisdom that can come only from long experience and painstaking study."
Source: *Baseball Digest* (August 1943, Gordon Cobbledick). According to Bob Feller in *Strikeout Story,* Smith developed the screwball after having arm trouble in 1939.

BOB SMITH 5'10" 175-pound righty
106-139, 3.94, 40 Saves 1925 1937

Pitch Selection: 1. Fastball 2. Change
Source: *Baseball Players and Their Times* (Eugene Murdock, 1991)
Note: Referred to by Ethan Allen in *Masters of the Diamond* (Rich Westcott, 1994) as a "slowball pitcher."

BRYN SMITH 6'2" 200-pound righty
108-94, 3.53, 6 Saves 1981 1993

Pitches: 1. Palmball 2. Fastball 3. Slider 4. Curve
Sources: *The Scouting Report* (1984–1987 editions)
Note: Smith's palmball described as behaving "like a change-up/curve."

Pitches: 1. Sinker 2. Palmball 3. Slider 4. Curve 5. Fastball
Source: *The Scouting Report: 1990; Tom Seaver's 1989 Scouting Notebook*

CHARLIE SMITH 6'1" 185-pound righty
66-87, 2.81, 3 Saves 1902 1914

Quote: "Smith is a right-hander and a cool proposition under fire."

Source: unidentified article from the Hall of Fame Library, 1909

DAVE SMITH 6'1" 195-pound righty
53-53, 2.67, 216 Saves 1980 1992

Pitch Selection: 1. Fastball 2. Sinker 3. Curve 4. Forkball
Sources: *The Scouting Report 1987; The Scouting Report 1990*

EDDIE SMITH 5'10" 174-pound lefty
73-113, 3.82, 12 Saves 1936 1947

Pitch Selection: 1. Fastball 2. Curve
Smith: "I could throw pretty hard . . . I could throw my fastball through a brick wall . . . Rube Walberg [taught] me how to throw a curveball."
Source: Smith interviewed in *Masters of the Diamond* (Rich Westcott, 1994)

ELMER SMITH 5'11" 178-pound lefty
76-58, 3.35, 0 Saves 1886 1898

Key Pitch: Fastball
Source: *Nineteenth Century Stars* (SABR, 1989, article by Robert L. Tiemann)

FRANK SMITH 5'10" 194-pound righty
138-112, 2.59, 6 Saves 1904 1915

Key Pitch: Spitball
Quote: "Smith and Walsh are two of the game's greatest spit ball pitchers and both are as noted for stamina as for skill."
Source: *The Sporting News* (9/24/1908, Page 1)

Pitch Selection: 1. Drop Ball 2. Curve
Source: *The No-Hit Hall of Fame* (Rich Coberly, 1985)

Ty Cobb: "A good many pitchers have a knee move. Frank Smith, formerly of the White Sox, always looked toward third base when he was going to throw to first with a runner on. Any time he looked at the catcher, it was a safe bet he would not throw over again, and a runner could get his start."
Source: *Busting 'Em and Other Big League Stories* (Ty Cobb, ghostwritten by John Wheeler, 1914)

GEORGE SMITH 6'2" 163-pound righty
41-81, 3.89, 4 Saves 1916 1923

Quote: "He drove the hitters back and dusted them off when they crowded the plate again."
Source: article by Frank Graham (unidentified source, 8/14/1936)

HAL SMITH 6'3" 195-pound righty
12-11, 3.77, 1 Save 1932 1935

Pitch Selection: 1. Sinker 2. Curve 3. Change of Pace
Description: "Hal counts up his victories by depending largely upon a sinker ball, but he uses a curve a lot to make the sinker more effective. His curve calms down the left hand hitters, while his side-arm delivery is hard for right-hand batsmen to follow. He has a fair change of pace, but it doesn't render the best of service for he can't depend on where the ball will go. Otherwise his control is good."
Source: *Baseball Magazine* (April 1934, Clifford Bloodgood)

HILTON SMITH 6'2" 180-pound righty
NEGRO LEAGUES 1932 1948

Pitch Selection: 1. Curve 2. Fastball 3. Slider 4. Sinker 5. Change
Note: Hilton threw all of his pitches both sidearm and overhand.
Sources: Hilton Smith in *Voices from the Great Black Baseball Leagues* (John Holway, 1975); *The Biographical Encyclopedia of the Negro Baseball Leagues* (James A. Riley, 1994); *Catching Dreams* (Frazier "Slow" Robinson with Paul Bauer, 1999)
Slow Robinson in *Catching Dreams:* "We had Hilton Smith who threw an excellent curveball and a very good fastball to go with it . . . Hilton Smith had the best curveball that I ever saw and a good pick off move too."
Hilton Smith in *Voices from the Great Black Baseball Leagues:* "I guess I had a curve ball as good as anybody's in baseball at that time. My fast ball ran, it just jumped . . . We had to have two curve balls, a big one and a small one. Now they call it a slider, but those guys were throwing it years and years back."

LEE SMITH 6'5" 220-pound righty
71-92, 3.03, 478 Saves 1980 1997

Pitch Selection: 1. Rising Fastball 2. Slider
3. Cut Fastball 4. Forkball (used as a change)
Sources: *The Scouting Report: 1987; The Scouting Report: 1995*

PETE SMITH 6'2" 185-pound righty
47-71, 4.55, 1 Save 1987 1998

Pitch Selection: 1. Fastball 2. Hard Slider 3. Curve
4. Circle Change (added 1989)
5. Splitter (added early 1990s)
Note: By the late 1990s, the Splitter had replaced the fastball as Smith's best pitch.
Sources: *The Scouting Report: 1990; The Scouting Notebook 1998*

Keith Hernandez: "When Pete gets that slightly off-speed sinker away for strikes against left-handers and throws enough fastballs hard and in, he can be very effective . . ."
Source: *Pure Baseball: Pitch by Pitch for the Advanced Fan* (Keith Hernandez and Mike Bryan, 1994)

PHENOMENAL SMITH 5'6" 161-pound lefty
54-77, 3.89, 1 Save 1884 1891

Key Pitch: Rough Pitch
Quote: "A washout in two previous years, Smith picked up a 'rough' pitch in 1886 that brought him success and controversy. Similar to an emery ball, the pitch was subjected to lawsuits and injunctions."
Source: *Who's Who in Baseball History* (Lloyd Johnson and Brenda Ward, 1994)

RIVERBOAT SMITH 6'0" 185-pound lefty
4-4, 4.75, 0 Saves 1958 1959

Pitches: 1. Fastball 2. Curve (early career) and
Slider (late) 3. Change
Smith: "I wish they'd've had a gun. I'd say I was middle 90s. I could throw. I was probably as fast at the time as Herb Score. I could throw as hard as he could."
Source: Smith in *The San Francisco Seals, 1946–1957* (Brent Kelley, 2002)

ROY SMITH 6'3" 217-pound righty
30-31, 4.60, 1 Save 1984 1991

Pitch Selection: 1. Fastball (88–90) 2. Slow Curve
Note: Learned slow curve in Florida Instructional League after the 1983 season.
Source: *The Scouting Report: 1985*

SHERRY SMITH 6'1" 170-pound lefty
114-118, 3.32, 21 Saves 1911 1927

Pitches: 1. Curve 2. Fastball 3. Change
4. Knuckleball
Sources: *Atlanta Constitution* (3/1/1934); George Moriarty in 1928 article copyrighted by North American Newspaper Alliance; *Baseball Magazine* (August 1926, John J. Ward)
Quote from *Atlanta Constitution:* "Sherry Smith . . . had everything as a pitcher, including a great curve, fast ball and change of pace . . . Smith had a marvelous assortment of stuff, practically everything that Nap Rucker had, including a knuckle ball. He probably never had Rucker's speed, but he was no mean hand at burning the ball in there."
Quote from *Baseball Magazine:* ". . . he puts over the ball with an easy, almost careless flip of his pitching arm. He has practically no windup and he never seems to exert himself in the least. In fact, so smooth and even is his delivery that some people have accused Sherry of not taking a proper interest in the game. This is pure error . . ."
Note: All three cited articles and others (see below) say that Smith had the best pickoff move of his generation, and was virtually impossible to steal bases against.

Quote: "Sherry Smith, a left-hander who pitched for the Dodgers back around 1920, had one of the greatest moves to first. You know they say of some pitchers that they can look over at first base and if the runner happens to be tapping his foot on the bag, the pitcher will get him between taps. They used to say about Sherry Smith that if the base runner was only thinking about taking a lead Sherry would throw over and get him between thoughts."
Source: Jocko Conlan in *Jocko* (Conlan and Robert Creamer, 1967)

Description: "Sherry Smith . . . who passed out of the big leagues some years ago, had no wind-up at all. He

merely hunched his shoulders, threw back his left hand, brought it forward with a bend of his big body and released the ball. He said, 'Wind-up is a waste of time.' "
Source: *Baseball Magazine* (June 1935, F.C. Lane)

ZANE SMITH 6'2" 185-pound lefty
100-115, 3.74, 3 Saves 1984 1996

Pitches: 1. Sinking Fastball 2. Slider 3. Curve 4. Change
Sources: *The Scouting Report* (1990 and 1992 editions)

MIKE SMITHSON 6'8" 215-pound righty
76-86, 4.58, 2 Saves 1982 1989

Pitch Selection: 1. Sinking Fastball 2. Slider 3. Change
Sources: *The Scouting Report: 1987; The Scouting Report: 1990*

JOHN SMOLTZ 6'3" 210-pound righty
163-120, 3.29, 110 Saves 1988 2003

Pitch Selection, 1988: 1. Fastball 2. Curve
Pitch Selection, 1989: 1. Fastball 2. Curve 3. Change
Pitches, 1990: 1. Fastball 2. Curve 3. Change 4. Slider
Pitches, 1991: 1. Fastball 2. Slider 3. Curve 4. Change
Pitches, 1992–1994: 1. Fastball 2. Slider 3. Circle Change 4. Curve 5. Straight Change
Pitches, 1995: 1. Two-Seam Fastball 2. Four-Seam Fastball 3. Hard Slider 4. Curve 5. Circle Change 6. Split-Fingered Fastball
Pitches, 1996–1997: Hard to say. Everything working. Splitter developed into an outstanding pitch, and he threw it more than he had before. He dumped the splitter in 1998 because of the pressure it put on his elbow.
Pitches, 1998: 1. Fastball 2. Change 3. Slider 4. Curve 5. Other Fastball
Pitches, 1999: Same stuff but added a three-quarters delivery and began experimenting with a Knuckleball (and he threw a few in games).
Pitches as reliever, 2001–2003: 1. Slider 2. Fastball (98) 3. Split-Fingered Fastball (90) 4. Change
Sources: *The Scouting Report* (1990, 1992, 1993, 1995, and 1996 editions); *The Scouting Notebook* (1995–2000 editions); ESPN.com article by Tony Gwynn (8/2/2002)
Gwynn: "Smoltz has four pitches—fastball, slider, splitter and change-up. His slider is his best pitch, but he also still throws the fastball at 98 mph and the splitty at 90. Then he even has the ability to make pitches up when he's on the mound. It's almost unfair trying to hit against him."

Craig Biggio: "He uses that splitter like a sinker. It's firm, and as hard as he throws it, you don't have much time to react."
Smoltz on his Splitter: "It's thrown hard and has such late-breaking movement that it gives guys less chance to recognize it. I want the splitter to start where my fastball ends up and disappear."
Source: *Sports Illustrated* (3/31/03, Page 65)

LARY SORENSEN 6'2" 200-pound righty
93-103, 4.15, 6 Saves 1977 1988

Pitch Selection: 1. Sinker 2. Slider
Sources: *The Sporting News* (8/2/1980, Tom Flaherty)

VIC SORRELL 5'10" 180-pound righty
92-101, 4.43, 10 Saves 1928 1937

Pitch Selection: 1. Fastball 2. Curve 3. Change
Description: "Sorrell is a fast ball pitcher who uses a moderate number of curves and a change of pace."
Source: *Baseball Magazine* (June 1933, "Comprising an Interview with Victor Sorrell)
Other Source: *Who's Who in Major League Baseball* (compiled by Harold "Speed" Johnson, 1933)

Sorrell: "My curve is just fair. Some of the players tell me it's pretty good, but I fear they're giving me the best of the argument. One thing I have done, however, is to develop a moderately effective change of pace."
Source: *Baseball Magazine* (July 1930, John J. Ward)

ELIAS SOSA 6'2" 186-pound righty
59-51, 3.32, 83 Saves 1972 1983

Pitches: 1. Fastball (88–90, 65%) 2. Slider (25%) 3. Curve 4. Forkball or Palmball
Source: *The Scouting Report: 1983*

ALLEN SOTHORON 5'11" 182-pound righty
91-100, 3.31, 9 Saves 1914 1926

Key Pitch: Spitball
Note: Sothoron was one of the "grandfathered" pitchers allowed to continue to throw the spitball after it was otherwise banned in 1921.
Sources: *The Crooked Pitch* (Martin Quigley, 1984); *Baseball Magazine* (June 1951, Ellis J. Veech); 1923 *Reach Guide* (Page 38)

Quote: "Sothoron came next, with a trick ball that acted very much like the emery ball of Russel Ford. In time his secret was discovered but before we had done so he had made a great record. He worked it by raising a corrugation on the side of the ball without the aid of any foreign substance. By the use of a strong forefinger and thumb Sothoron would work up the seam of the ball until it stood out."
Source: *Memoirs of Twenty Years in Baseball* (Ty Cobb, Page 69)

MARIO SOTO 6'0" 174-pound righty
100-92, 3.47, 4 Saves 1977 1988

Pitch Selection: 1. Fastball 2. Change
Source: *The Scouting Report: 1987*

WARREN SPAHN 6'0" 172-pound lefty
363-245, 3.09, 29 Saves 1942 1965

Pitches, early career: 1. Fastball 2. Curve 3. Change 4. Sinker
Pitches, later career: 1. "Screwball" (added in 1955) 2. Curve 3. Slider (refined in 1958) 4. Fastball 5. Palm Ball 6. Knuckleball (unveiled in 1963)
Note: Prior to knee problems in 1953 and '54, Spahn's best pitch was his fastball.
Sources: *Super Stars of Baseball* (Bob Broeg, 1971); *Warren Spahn: Immortal Southpaw* (Al Silverman, Page 22); *The Warren Spahn Story* (Bob Cutter, Page 19); *Baseball Digest* (January 1951, Milt Richman)

Spahn: "When I came up, I was a fastball pitcher with a curve and a change-up. In the beginning, the fastball was always the barometer for every game I pitched. The hitter tells you the story. When you're throwing well, you're literally throwing the ball by the hitter. When they can't pull your fastball, you're throwing pretty well. But when they start hitting line drives, you know the ball's not moving. That was when I started playing around with the screwball.

"I particularly wanted the screwball to combat righthanded hitters. I found that it complemented the fastball and vice versa. On given days, I could throw the fastball as well as I ever did, but I didn't have to rely on it. I had weapons for both lefthanders and righthanders."
Source: *Splendor on the Diamond* (Rich Westcott, 2000)

Commentary: While everybody *knew* that Spahn threw a great screwball in the latter part of his career, Spahn himself often denied throwing a screwball at all. And in fact, it seems likely that he was actually throwing the pitch that's now known as the Circle Change. As Roger Angell relates in *Season Ticket* (1988), " 'Look, it's easy,' Spahnie said. 'You just do this.' His left thumb and forefinger were making a circle, with the three other fingers pointing up, exactly as if he were flashing the 'O.K.' sign to someone nearby. The ball was tucked comfortably up against the circle, without being held by it, and the other fingers stayed up and apart, keeping only a loose grip on the pill. Thrown that way, he said, the ball departed naturally off the inside, or little-finger side, of the middle finger, and would then sink and break to the left as it crossed the plate. 'There's nothing to it,' he said optimistically. 'Just let her go, and remember to keep your hand up so it stays inside your elbow. Throw it like that, and you turn it over naturally—a nice, easy movement, and the arm follows through on the same track.' "

Sounds exactly like the Circle Change, though Angell calls the pitch a "sinker-screwball."

Description: "A good curve, fast ball, change of pace, and control of all three. Every ball he throws does something. He simply has good stuff, plus that confidence I just mentioned. That's always a winning combination in any league."
Source: Billy Southworth in *Baseball Magazine* (November 1947, Ed Rumill)

Description: "At one time, wonderful Spahn was a blow 'em down pitcher whose rising fast ball alone was a considerable weapon. His curve ball was just pretty good and he had a pretty good change."
Johnny Sain: "Spahn became great because of these things and because he's one of the smartest men ever to play the game. He came up with a screwball to help

when his fast ball began to fade and then he added the slider . . ."
Source: *Super Stars of Baseball*

Comment: "Now using a slider more than ever . . ."
Source: *1963 Major League Handbook* (Don Schiffer)

Description: "Spahn perfected his motion in boyhood, through endless games of catch with his father. His windup began with a big arm pump, swinging both hands back dramatically to head height. In mid-delivery he hid the ball behind a straight front leg, but that leg flexed rapidly and led into a graceful drop and drive launch. Spahn's follow-through was perfectly balanced, and he ended his motion in perfect fielding position."
Source: *The Hurlers* (Kevin Kerrane, 1989)

Description: "Warren swung his hands back high during his preliminary motion, which was quite picturesque . . . he had a high leg kick, slightly toward home plate, and was an overhand pitcher."
Source: *Pitching* (Bob Shaw, 1972)

Note: Spahn listed as "one of the few 'survivors' of the windmill tradition."
Source: *Baseball Digest* (September 1947, Harry Sheer)

Comment: "No story about Spahn would be complete without a description of his ability to hold runners on base, his 'move,' as they call it in the trade. It is one of the best in the business, if not the best. It certainly is the best in the National League and only Bill Wight in the American League can challenge it.

"When Spahn pitches, he kicks his right leg high in the air, hiding the ball from the batter. He has a knack of kicking up the leg, too, as he strides toward first but the movement is entirely legal. As a matter of fact, Spahn has had only one balk called against him since he came into the National League in 1946."
Source: *Milwaukee's Miracle Braves* (Tom Meany, 1954)

Maury Wills: "The toughest pitcher of all for me to run against was Warren Spahn, a left-hander. But would have been just as tough going right-handed. Spahn's moves were so deceptive that I often found myself guessing . . ."
Source: *How to Steal a Pennant* (Wills with John Freeman, 1976)

Note: Listed by *The Sporting News* (8/29/1956) as having one of the best fastballs in the league.

AL SPALDING 6'1" 170-pound righty
48-12, 1.78, 1 Save 1876 1878

Pitch Selection: 1. Fastball 2. Change
Source: *Baseball and Mr. Spalding* (Arthur Bartlett, 1951)

Notes: According to *The National Game,* Spalding pitched *underhand,* releasing the ball from below his waist. In reporting on a game played June 3, 1870, the *New York Times* said that "Spalding has a troublesome delivery, made all the more so by a peculiar attitude or pose assumed just before his final swing."
Sources: *The National Game* (Alfred H. Spink, 1911); *Baseball: 1845–1881* (Preston D. Orem)

STEVE SPARKS 6'0" 180-pound righty
56-69, 4.77, 3 Saves 1995 2003

Pitch Selection: 1. Knuckleball 2. Slider
3. Fastball (low-80s)
Source: *The Scouting Notebook: 2002*

TULLY SPARKS 6'2" 175-pound righty
123-136, 2.79, 8 Saves 1897 1910

Key Pitch: Slow Ball
Source: *Touching Second* (Johnny Evers and Hugh Fullerton, 1910)

Sparks: "It is not essential that the slow ball should be a curve. Some seem to cling to that opinion, but I have frequently demonstrated to my own satisfaction that as much is to be gained by pitching a straight slow ball as one with a curve. The main thing is to catch a batter napping. Be sure that the same motion is used in pitching a slow ball as a fast one, and the batter is quite certain to be fooled when they are judiciously used."
Source: *How to Pitch* (edited by John B. Foster, 1908)

JOE SPARMA 6'1" 190-pound righty
52-52, 3.94, 0 Saves 1964 1970

Pitches: 1. Rising Fastball 2. Fast Curve (Slider)
3. Sinking Fastball 4. Overhand Curve 5. Change
Source: Johnny Sain in *The Sporting News* (4/15/1967, Warren Spoelstra)

Comment: "Sparma got away strong with the new hard curve he learned under pitching John Sain. When Joe

slipped over the breaking pitch, he became more formidable. By most estimates, Sparma's fastball velocity is not exceeded in the American League."
Source: Warren Spoelstra in *The Sporting News* (6/17/1967)

Note: In 1969, Sparma began to suffer from something like Steve Blass Disease, and in 1970 his affliction led to a rules change. According to *The Biographical History of Baseball*, "Montreal manager Gene Mauch assigned one of his infielders to a spot behind the catcher during a 1970 game while the base on balls was being doled out. The National League subsequently intervened to rule more specifically that only 'a catcher could be standing in foul territory with the delivery of a pitch.'"

DAN SPILLNER 6'1" 190-pound righty
75-89, 4.21, 50 Saves 1974 1985

Pitch Selection: 1. Fastball 2. Slider 3. Slow Curve
Source: *The Scouting Report: 1983*

PAUL SPLITTORFF 6'3" 205-pound lefty
166-143, 3.81, 1 Save 1970 1984

Pitch Selection: 1. Fastball 2. Slider 3. Curve 4. Change
Source: *The Sporting News* (7/1/1978, Del Black)

KARL SPOONER 6'0" 185-pound lefty
10-6, 3.09, 2 Saves 1954 1955

Pitch Selection: 1. Fastball 2. Curve
Clem Labine: "That man had a fastball that was unbelievable, not for sheer speed, but for how much the ball moved."
Source: *Bums* (Peter Goldenbock, 1984)

Key Pitch: Extraordinary Fastball
Source: *New York Times* (July 1955, article by Arthur Daley)

JERRY SPRADLIN 6'7" 246-pound righty
17-19, 4.75, 11 Saves 1993 2000

Key Pitch: Fastball (90s)
Source: *The Scouting Notebook: 2000*

JACK SPRING 6'1" 175-pound lefty
12-5, 4.26, 8 Saves 1955 1965

Pitches: 1. Sneaky Fastball 2. Curve 3. Change 4. Slider (late career)
Spring: "I was a pretty generic pitcher. I was sneaky fast, but I think my best asset was my control . . . I threw a changeup and late in my career I started throwing a slider, but I didn't throw it a lot, and, of course, a curveball. The four generic pitches, but if I was gonna get you out it was gonna be a fastball to a spot."
Source: *The San Francisco Seals, 1946–1957* (Brent Kelley, 2002)

DENNIS SPRINGER 5'10" 185-pound righty
24-48, 5.18, 1 Save 1995 2002

Pitch Selection: 1. Knuckleball 2. Fastball (78) 3. Slider
Source: *The Scouting Notebook: 2000*

RUSS SPRINGER 6'4" 211-pound righty
20-33, 5.18, 8 Saves 1992 2003

Pitch Selection: 1. Sinking Fastball (91) 2. Slurve 3. Slider
Source: *The Scouting Notebook: 1995*

RANDY ST. CLAIRE 6'2" 190-pound righty
12-6, 4.14, 9 Saves 1984 1994

Pitches: 1. Two-Seam Fastball 2. Slider 3. Three-Finger Change
St. Claire: "I threw the three basic pitches, and I probably threw my two-seam fastball eighty-five to ninety percent of the time. The fastball ranged from 87 up to 91 or occasionally 92 when I was younger, but I mostly worked in the upper 80s. My change-up? It was a three-finger change, two fingers on one side of the horseshoe and the third on the other side."
Source: phone interview with St. Claire (9/4/2003, Rob Neyer)

BILL STAFFORD 6'1" 188-pound righty
43-40, 3.52, 9 Saves 1960 1967

Key Pitch: Curve
Source: *Don Schiffer's Major League Baseball Handbook—1964*

GERRY STALEY 6'0" 195-pound righty
134-111, 3.70, 61 Saves 1947 1961

Pitches: 1. Sinker 2. Curve 3. Screwball 4. Fastball 5. Knuckleball
Source: *The Sporting News* (2/17/1960, Jerome Holtzman)

Pitches: 1. Sinker 2. Knuckleball 3. Slider 4. Curve
Description: "To throw those low strikes, Staley's best pitch is his sinker, which he developed after joining the White Sox. This is a fastball released off the middle finger with a little extra spin. His sidearm delivery helps the sinker to break low and forces the hitters to beat it into the ground."
Staley: "So many guys hit my first pitch I always wondered if they knew I had anything else but a sinker. I also throw a slider, a curve and the knuckler."
Al Lopez: "There's no question about it—the sinker is his best pitch. He should throw it frequently and quickly."
Source: *Sport* (September 1960, Hal Lebovitz)

Pitch Selection as reliever: 1. Sinker 2. Knuckleball
Source: *Stan Musial: The Man's Own Story* (Musial with Bob Broeg, 1964)

Description: "Staley throws an assortment of knuckle balls and curves."
Source: *Sports Illustrated* (9/28/1959)

Key Pitch: Sinking Fastball
Note: Listed as a sidearm pitcher.
Source: *How to Play Winning Baseball* (Arthur Mann, 1953)

HARRY STALEY 5'10" 175-pound righty
137-120, 3.80, 2 Saves 1888 1895

Note: Staley was known for his pickoff move.
Source: *Who's Who in Baseball* (Lloyd Johnson and Brenda Ward, 1994)

TRACY STALLARD 6'5" 204-pound righty
30-57, 4.17, 4 Saves 1960 1966

Pitch Selection: 1. Curve 2. Fastball
Source: *Baseball Digest* (January 1963, Page 50)

LEE STANGE 5'10" 170-pound righty
62-61, 3.56, 21 Saves 1961 1970

Pitches: 1. Slider 2. Fastball 3. Curve
Comment: "Until 1962 he essentially was a two-pitch pitcher, fastball and curve. Then one day when he was with the Twins, he was warming up on the sidelines with Hal Naragon. Naragon taught him to throw a slider."
Source: *Lost Summer: The '67 Red Sox and the Impossible Dream* (Bill Reynolds, 1992)

DON STANHOUSE 6'2" 185-pound righty
38-54, 3.84, 64 Saves 1972 1982

Pitch Selection: 1. Fastball 2. Slider
Source: *Kansas City Times* (10/9/1979)
Note: Stanhouse was the slowest-working pitcher of his time.

BOB STANLEY 6'4" 210-pound righty
115-97, 3.64, 132 Saves 1977 1989

Pitch Selection: 1. Sinking Fastball 2. Slider 3. Palmball
Note: Stanley supposedly threw spitballs early in his career.
Sources: *The Scouting Report: 1987; Tom Seaver's 1989 Scouting Notebook; The Sporting News* (6/6/1981, Peter Gammons)

MIKE STANTON 6'2" 205-pound righty
13-22, 4.61, 31 Saves 1975 1985

Pitches: 1. Fastball (low-90s) 2. Hard Slider 3. Hard Sinker
Note: Threw with a herky-jerky motion.
Sources: *The Scouting Report* (1983–1985 editions)

MIKE STANTON 6'1" 190-pound lefty
55-44, 3.81, 76 Saves 1989 2003

Pitches: 1. Fastball 2. Curve 3. Slider
Sources: *The Scouting Report: 1992; The Scouting Notebook 1999*

RAY STARR 6'1" 178-pound righty
37-35, 3.53, 4 Saves 1932 1945

Pitch Selection: 1. Knuckleball 2. Big Curve 3. Small Curve 4. Change

Note: Starr threw from a variety of arm angles to keep hitters off balance.
Source: *Baseball Magazine* (August 1943, Frank Y. Grayson)

Note: Starr pitched briefly in the major leagues in 1932 and '33, then went back to the minors for seven seasons before returning to the majors in 1941. The pitches above describe his repertoire in the '40s; in the early '30s, Starr did throw a knuckleball but his best pitch was his fastball.
Source: *The Sporting News* (3/3/1932)

DAVE STENHOUSE 6'0" 195-pound righty
16-28, 4.14, 1 Save 1962 1964

Pitches: 1. Knuckle-curve 2. Sinker 3. Slider 4. Curve (occasional) 5. Change (occasional)
Stenhouse on his knuckle-curve: "The way I came about the pitch, I was in high school and playing catch with a friend of mine. I had a pretty good arm and he said, 'Why don't you throw a knuckleball?' Now you're supposed to throw a knuckleball different than all the other pitches. But not me, I put my knuckles on the ball and threw it like you'd throw a fastball. And so when I threw the knuckleball, it had a semi-knuckleball, semi-fastball spin on it. And the pitch came in and broke straight down. I said to myself, 'Geez, that's a pretty good pitch.' So starting in high school, I developed this knuckle-curve. I threw my fastball 88 or 89, and I'd guess the knuckle-curve came in around 82–83, almost the same speed as my slider. Everybody thought I was throwing a spitball when I came up to the majors. They'd ask to check the baseball all the time, and it wasn't until I'd been around the league a few times that everybody realized that was just how my pitch moved. We used to call it the K-D, the knuckle drop. I had five pitches. I used three of 'em a lot. I had a sinker, I had a good slider, I had the knuckle-curve. I had a curveball, a lousy curve, but I'd only throw four or five a game. And I threw a change-up, but usually I'd just take a little off my knuckle-curve when I wanted to change speeds."
Source: phone interview with Stenhouse (6/7/2002, Rob Neyer)

Quote: "Knucklers and curves are standard pitching equipment, but something new is the knuckler-curve of Dave Stenhouse."
Source: *1963 Major League Handbook* (Don Schiffer)

Description: "Breaking Ball Pitcher. Fast ball is just fair but has some life."
Source: *Baseball Digest* (March 1960, Page 84)

DAVE STEWART 6'2" 200-pound righty
168-129, 3.95, 19 Saves 1978 1995

Pitch Selection: 1. Rising Fastball 2. Slider 3. Forkball (1986 on)
Source: *The Scouting Report: 1990*

WALTER (LEFTY) STEWART
5'10" 160-pound lefty
101-98, 4.19, 8 Saves 1921 1935

Key Pitch: Curve
Quote: "Stewart depends upon a nimble brain, unflagging zest and an assortment of deceptive curve balls." It is clear from the article that Stewart did not throw hard, but worked ahead of the hitters and had good movement on his fastball.
Source: *Baseball Magazine* (February 1931, Clifford Bloodgood)

SAMMY STEWART 6'3" 200-pound righty
59-48, 3.59, 45 Saves 1978 1987

Pitch Selection: 1. Fastball (93) 2. Curve 3. Slider 4. Straight Change
Source: *The Scouting Report: 1985*

DAVE STIEB 6'0" 185-pound righty
176-137, 3.44, 3 Saves 1979 1998

Pitches: 1. Slider 2. Sinking Fastball 3. High Fastball 4. Curve 5. Change
Blue Jays manager Bobby Cox: "He isn't a Nolan Ryan, who overpowers you. But he throws two outstanding fastballs, one that sinks and one he throws by batters up. He has that awesome slider, a curveball and a change-up, throws them all for strikes and isn't afraid to throw any of them at any time."
Source: *The Sporting News* (6/13/1983, Peter Gammons)

Pitches: 1. Slider 2. Fastball 3. Overhand Curve 4. Change
Sources: *The Scouting Report: 1987; Tomorrow I'll Be Perfect* (Stieb with Kevin Boland, 1986)

DICK STIGMAN 6'3" 200-pound lefty
46-54, 4.03, 16 Saves 1960 1966

Pitch Selection: 1. Curve
Source: *1963 Major League Handbook* (Don Schiffer)

Key Pitch: Fastball
Note: Described as "fireballing left-hander."
Source: *Don Schiffer's Major League Baseball Handbook—1964*

JACK STIVETTS 6'2" 185-pound righty
201-127, 3.74, 9 Saves 1889 1899

Pitch Selection: 1. Fastball
Sources: *Nineteenth Century Stars* (SABR, 1989, article by Robert L. Tiemann); *A Tale of Four Cities* (Jean-Pierre Caillault, 2003)

CHUCK STOBBS 6'1" 185-pound lefty
107-130, 4.29, 19 Saves 1947 1961

Early Years with Boston: 1. Fastball 2. Change 3. Curve
Mid-Career: 1. Change 2. Slider
Source: *When the Cheering Stops* (Lee Heiman et al., 1990)

TIM STODDARD 6'7" 230-pound righty
41-35, 3.95, 76 Saves 1975 1989

Pitch Selection: 1. Fastball 2. Slider
Source: *The Scouting Report 1987*

GEORGE STONE 6'3" 205-pound lefty
60-57, 3.89, 5 Saves 1967 1975

Pitches: 1. Change 2. Sneaky Fastball 3. Curve
Description: ". . . ¾ arm slot with sneaky fastball, good curveball and a great change-up. He was above average with command (think of George as a blue-collar Tom Glavine)."
Source: e-mail message from Tom House to Rob Neyer (1/13/2003)

STEVE STONE 5'10" 175-pound righty
107-93, 3.97, 1 Save 1971 1981

Pitch Selection: 1. Curve 2. High Fastball
Source: *Weaver on Strategy* (Weaver with Terry Pluto, 1984)

Notes: When Stone won the Cy Young Award in 1980, he attributed his success, in part, to somehow gaining five miles per hour on his fastball, giving him a high-80s fastball for the first time since the late 1960s, when he was pitching in the minors.

Stone also threw his curveball significantly more often in 1980 than he had before; according to Peter Gammons in *The Sporting News* (7/19/1980), Stone threw 73 curves in one game and 74 in another.

BILL STONEMAN 5'10" 170-pound righty
54-85, 4.08, 5 Saves 1967 1974

Pitches: 1. Four-Seam Fastball 2. Curve 3. Slider 4. Two-Seam Fastball 5. Change (occasional)
Stoneman: "When I first broke into the major leagues, I was a two-pitch pitcher, four-seam fastball and curveball. I was a power pitcher without terrific control. I became a starter in 1969 and threw my first no-hitter with just those two pitches, the four-seam fastball and the curveball. I threw my second no-hitter in '72 with four pitches: the four-seam fastball and the curveball still, but I'd added a slider and a two-seam fastball. I rarely threw a change-up. I did throw a straight change, but I usually changed off my curveball. I had better control of my curveball than most people. So to guys who were susceptible to the change-up, what I usually did was take something off my curveball."
Source: phone interview with Stoneman (11/21/2002, Rob Neyer)

Pitch Selection: 1. Curve 2. Fastball
Notes: By 1972, the slider had replaced the curve as Stoneman's primary breaking pitch. He also began throwing a change in the early 1970s.
Sources: *The No-Hit Hall of Fame* (Rich Coberly, 1985); *Like Nobody Else* (Ferguson Jenkins and George Vass, 1973); and *Major League Baseball: 1971* (Brenda Zanger and Dick Kaplan)

Quote: "Possesses live fast ball and crackling overhand curve."
Source: *The Complete Handbook of Baseball* (1972 edition, edited by Zander Hollander)

LIL STONER 5'9" 180-pound righty
50-58, 4.76, 14 Saves 1922 1931

Pitch Selection: 1. Fastball 2. Curve
Sources: unidentified article from the Hall of Fame Library (1/6/1929); 1931 press release
Quote from 1929 article: "He has a good curve, a fair amount of speed and is reputed to be a quick thinker."
Quote from 1931 press release: "Lil is known as a fastball and curve-ball pitcher. Possessing speed beyond the ordinary, he struck out 105 men."

MEL STOTTLEMYRE 6'1" 178-pound righty
164-139, 2.97, 1 Save 1964 1974

Pitches: 1. Sinker 2. Fastball 3. Slider 4. Curve
Source: *The Sporting News* (10/24/1964, Til Ferdenzi)

Quote: ". . . the best slider I ever caught is thrown by Mel Stottlemyre."
Source: *Catching* (Elston Howard)

TODD STOTTLEMYRE 6'3" 195-pound righty
138-121, 4.28, 1 Save 1988 2002

Pitches: 1. Fastball 2. Curve 3. Slider 4. Change
Note: Stottlemyre changes speeds on all of his pitches.
Sources: *The Scouting Report: 1992*, *The Scouting Notebook: 1995* and *The Scouting Notebook: 1997*

MONTY STRATTON 6'5" 180-pound righty
36-23, 3.71, 2 Saves 1934 1938

Pitch Selection: 1. Fastballs 2. Curve 3. Change
Description: "He possesses a fast ball that breaks in or sinks according to the way he lets it leave his hand, a good curve and an effective change of pace. He pitches side-arm to right-handed batters, overhand to the lefties. He has confidence that his change of pace ball will confuse the hitters and throw them off in their timing, especially when he keeps it low."
Source: *Baseball Magazine* (September 1938, Clifford Bloodgood)

Notes: In a photo that appeared in *The Sporting News* (6/17/1937), Stratton is shown gripping a ball in what would now be called a "two-seam fastball" grip.

Also in 1937, columnist John P. Carmichael said Stratton's "best pitch, then and now, is his low sidearm sinker."

Quote: "He was the nearest thing to Grover Cleveland Alexander I ever saw . . . the same control, the same 'dip' on every pitch, the same smooth, confident motion . . ."
Source: Charlie Grimm quoted in undated clipping from the late 1940s, story by John P. Carmichael; Stratton certainly was a fine pitcher, but his career was ended by a hunting accident that resulted in the amputation of his right leg. And Grimm was probably romanticizing Stratton's talent, just a bit.

ELMER STRICKLETT 5'6" 140-pound righty
35-51, 2.84, 6 Saves 1904 1907

Key Pitch: Spitball
Commentary: Stricklett owns a place in history like that of Fred Martin or Bobby Castillo. Although his career was modest, he was the first pitcher to regularly throw a spitball with any degree of success in the major leagues. Both Jack Chesbro and Ed Walsh saw Stricklett and developed outstanding spitballs of their own, which cast a large shadow in major league baseball between 1904 and 1920.
Sources: *Baseball Magazine* (March 1913, F.C. Lane article about Walsh, "The Spit-Ball King"; and May 1913, P.A. Meaney article, "Who Invented the Spit Ball?")

BRENT STROM 6'3" 190-pound lefty
22-39, 3.95, 0 Saves 1972 1977

Pitches: 1. Curve 2. Fastball 3. Change
Source: e-mail message from Strom (11/5/2003)

TOM STURDIVANT 6'0" 170-pound righty
59-51, 3.74, 17 Saves 1955 1964

Pitch Selection: 1. Knuckleball 2. Fastball
Note: Sturdivant developed the knuckleball in 1959, and it became his primary pitch.
Sources: *Pennant Race* (Jim Brosnan, 1962); *Sweet Seasons* (Dom Forker, 1989)
Note: However, Bob Addie wrote, in the *Washington Post* in June 1961, that Sturdivant's knuckleball was at its best in 1956 and '57, when he won 16 games each year. Sturdivant learned a curve in spring training, 1961, near the end of his career.

WILLIE SUDHOFF 5'7" 165-pound righty
103-135, 3.56, 3 Saves 1897 1906

Pitch Selection: 1. Curve 2. Fastball
Source: *Misfits! The Cleveland Spiders in 1899* (J. Thomas Hetrick, 1991)

Note: According to *The Sporting News* (5/17/1917) Sudhoff lived by "curves, speed, and remarkable mental ability."

GEORGE SUGGS 5'7" 168-pound righty
101-91, 3.11, 17 Saves 1908 1915

Key Pitch: Fastball
Source: unidentified article (November, 1913) from the Hall of Fame Library

FLEURY SULLIVAN
16-35, 4.20, 0 Saves 1884 1884

Description: "Sullivan was a speedy pitcher . . ."
Source: *The National Game* (Alfred H. Spink, 1911)

FRANK SULLIVAN 6'6" 215-pound righty
97-100, 3.60, 18 Saves 1953 1963

Pitch Selection: 1. Fastball 2. Curve
3. Hesitation Pitch
Sources: *Baseball Digest* (December 1955, Max Morgan); Harold Kaese article in unidentified newspaper (TSN morgue, March 1956)
Note: Listed by *The Sporting News* (8/29/1956) as having one of the best fastballs in the league.

JOE SULLIVAN 5'11" 175-pound lefty
30-37, 4.01, 4 Saves 1935 1941

Description: "As a matter of fact Sullivan doesn't have anything in the way of equipment that would cause a stampede in the dugout to watch his stuff. What gets him by is a good assortment of everything which he knows how to use to the best advantage. He is always putting something in there at the plate that looks highly tempting, but is just enough different to throw batters off their stride. He pitches well to spots."
Source: *Baseball Magazine* (September 1935, Clifford Bloodgood)

SCOTT SULLIVAN 6'4" 210-pound righty
37-24, 3.91, 9 Saves 1995 2003

Pitch Selection: 1. Fastball (low-90s)
2. Cut Fastball (added 2000) 3. Slider
Source: *The Scouting Notebook: 2001*

ED SUMMERS 6'2" 180-pound righty
68-45, 2.42, 3 Saves 1908 1912

Key Pitch: Finger-Nail Ball
Source: *Baseball Magazine* (July 1908, James C. Mills)

Commentary: Though Summers relied on a pitch very much like the pitch we know today as the knuckleball, in 1908 the pitch was brand-new, and a distinction was made between the pitch thrown with the fingertips and the pitch thrown off the knuckles. Another source refers to Summers' new pitch as a Dry Spitter, but that nomenclature didn't stick, while Finger-Nail Ball continued to poke its head around the corner for decades.

JEFF SUPPAN 6'2" 210-pound righty
62-75, 4.90, 0 Saves 1995 2003

Pitches: 1. Fastball (four-seam & two-seam)
2. 12-to-6 Curve 3. Fosh Change 4. Slider
Note: Learned to throw the fosh change from Al Nipper in 1995.
Sources: *The Scouting Notebook* (1997, 1999, 2000, and 2003 editions); Jerry Remy during broadcast of Red Sox–Phillies game, 9/1/2003.

MAX SURKONT 6'1" 195-pound righty
61-76, 4.38, 8 Saves 1949 1957

Key Pitch: Fastball
Stan Musial: "He could throw as hard as anybody I ever saw."
Source: *Stan Musial* (Musial with Bob Broeg, 1964)
Note: In 1956, *Sport* published, in the May issue, the results of a poll in which players on all sixteen major-league teams were asked which pitchers threw a spitball. Fifteen pitchers were mentioned, and Surkont tied with Lou Burdette for first place.

RICK SUTCLIFFE 6'7" 215-pound righty
171-139, 4.08, 6 Saves 1976 1994

Pitches, 1979–1981: 1. Fastball 2. Curve 3. Change

Pitches, 1982–1991: 1. Fastball 2. Slider 3. Curve 4. Change

Sources: *The Scouting Report* (1990 and 1992 editions); ESPN.com chat session (9/10/2003)

Quote from ESPN.com chat: "After I won the Rookie of the Year in '79, Tommy Lasorda took me out of the rotation in 1980 and put me in the bullpen . . . But I was too inconsistent with my curve ball. I continued to struggle until 1982, when I [learned?] to throw a slider. My curve ball was too big and a lot of times the umps would miss it. The slider was a tighter breaking ball that I got to work for me and once I did that, no one ever mentioned the bullpen to me again."

BRUCE SUTTER 6'2" 190-pound righty
68-71, 2.83, 300 Saves 1976 1988

Pitches: 1. Split-Fingered Fastball 2. Fastball 3. Slider (occasional)

Note: Sutter learned his split-fingered fastball in 1973, from Cubs minor-league instructor Fred Martin.

Sources: *Sports Illustrated* (9/17/1979, Ron Firmrite); *The Scouting Report: 1983*

Barry Foote in *Sports Illustrated:* "Bruce's pitch looks like a fastball when it leaves his hand, because of the arm speed, but it gets to the plate like a change, and then it drops down like a spitter or forkball."

Tim McCarver: "Think of the split-finger fastball. The reason it's so effective is that it gives the illusion of a strike. Bruce Sutter, who popularized the pitch in 1977, almost never threw it for a strike."

Source: *Oh, Baby, I Love It!* (McCarver with Ray Robinson, 1987)

Comment: "In the last few years, I have noticed that many short-relief specialists like Bruce Sutter have taken to pitching from the stretch even with no runners on base."

Source: *The Art of Pitching* (Tom Seaver with Lee Lowenfish, 1984)

Note: A poll of 645 players in the book *Players' Choice* (Eugene V. McCaffrey and Roger A. McCaffrey, 1987) lists Sutter's "sinker"—referring to his splitter—as the greatest ever. He received 13.4 percent of the vote.

DON SUTTON 6'1" 185-pound righty
324-256, 3.26, 5 Saves 1966 1988

Pitch Selection: 1. Curve 2. Fastball

Note: Sutton was frequently accused of doctoring the baseball.

Sources: *The Sporting News* (7/2/1966, Bob Hunter), *The Heart of the Order* (Thomas Boswell, Page 266), *You're Missin' a Great Game* (Whitey Herzog and Jonathan Pitts, 1998)

Comment: "Sutton . . . has refined his curve to a point where it's a half-knuckler. He crimps his index finger atop the ball which makes the ball appear to dive for the ground like a crashing airplane. He can throw this malicious mischief for a strike."

Source: *Baseball Digest* (July 1967, Jim Murray); it's apparent that Sutton threw a pitch very much like, if not identical to, Mike Mussina's Knuckle Curve.

Pitches: 1. Curve 2. Fastball 3. Slider 4. Screwball 5. Change

Walter Alston: "I don't think too many pitchers have mastered as many pitches as he has."

Source: *Winningest Pitchers: Baseball's 300-Game Winners* (Rich Westcott, 2002)

Umpire Tom Gorman: "The hassle over illegal pitches is eternal, endless. Last summer Doug Harvey . . . tried to clean up Sutton's act. Sutton is a very good pitcher, been with the Dodgers for years, a big winner. But he has this habit of defacing and cutting the ball. Been doing it for years. Harvey never caught him in the act, but in one game he penalized him ten or fifteen times."

Source: *Three and Two!* (Tom Gorman as told to Jerome Holtzman, 1979)

Keith Hernandez: "When you see the pitcher swipe at his leg with his glove as he stares in at the plate, he's asking for another sign . . . It's too bad Don Sutton is not still pitching or you could go out and watch him call the entire game this way. He's one of the few pitchers I ever saw do this, and I don't know of any active pitchers who consistently call the game from the mound. Some will do it off and on. With Sutton, the catcher—Steve Yeager or Joe Ferguson—would drop the sign—'1' for fastball, '2' for curve, '3' for slider, '4' for change-up, traditionally. Sutton had complete control of all four pitches, and he didn't care what Yeager or Ferguson called for. If he

wanted something else, he signaled back with his glove swiped across his chest or down his thigh. Swipes on the chest meant add that number to the sign called: If the catcher flashed '1' and Don swiped twice on his chest, he was throwing '3,' the slider. Swipes down his thigh meant subtract that number of swipes from the sign the catcher just flashed . . . If you notice a pitcher swiping in this manner with any regularity, that's what he's up to. He's giving the signs."
Source: *Pure Baseball: Pitch by Pitch for the Advanced Fan* (Keith Hernandez and Mike Bryan, 1994)

MAC SUZUKI 6'3" 205-pound righty
16-31, 5.72, 0 Saves 1996 2002

Pitch Selection: 1. Fastball 2. Slider
3. Split-finger Fastball
4. Curve (occasional; added 2001)
Quote: "Suzuki's two-seam fastball usually breaks away from a right-handed hitter but not always . . . And it's usually low enough to induce a ground ball . . . Suzuki has added a curveball to his fastball, slider and split-finger but doesn't throw it all that often. 'I just try to let them know I have four pitches,' he said."
Source: *Kansas City Star* (5/26/2002, Dick Kaegel)

CRAIG SWAN 6'3" 215-pound righty
59-72, 3.74, 2 Saves 1973 1984

Pitch Selection: 1. Fastball 2. Slider 3. Curve
Source: *The Pitching Staff* (Steve Jacobson, 1975)

CHARLIE SWEENEY 5'10" 181-pound righty
64-52, 2.87, 1 Save 1883 1887

Pitch Selection: 1. Fastball 2. Curve
Sources: *Heroes of Baseball* (Robert Smith, 1952), *Baseball Research Journal 1985* (article by Frederick Ivor-Campbell)

Comment: "So far as it is known, Charlie Sweeney is the father of the 'fadeaway.' At any rate, it was that style of delivery that he used when he immortalized himself, when pitching for Providence, in 1884, by fanning 19 batters in that nine-frame contest. However, that very feat nearly ended Charlie's career as a boxman, because it affected his arm. He never tried it again."
Source: *A Century of Baseball* (A.H. Tarvin, 1938)

Note: John Phillips in *When Lajoie Came to Town*, entry for April 3, reports the death of Sweeney and quotes an un-named paper describing him as "one of the first successful curveballers."

LES SWEETLAND 5'11" 155-pound lefty
33-58, 6.10, 4 Saves 1927 1931

Key Pitch: Sinker
Source: Lee Allen in *The Sporting News* (12/30/1967, "Cooperstown Corner" column)

STEVE SWETONIC 5'11" 185-pound righty
37-36, 3.80, 11 Saves 1929 1933

Pitches: 1. Fastball 2. Curve 3. Change
Description: "Swetonic hasn't a fast ball like Dazzy Vance and that youthful marvel, Lonnie Warneke. He hasn't a vicious hook like Lefty Clark. In fact, to watch him pitch he hasn't any outstanding talents. But he has what is more important, a wide assortment of stuff and the shrewdness to make that assortment effective. The catchers say that Swetonic is good at everything, fast ball, curve, change of pace, control, knowledge of what to pitch to the batters and that rarer gift of pitching the right kind of ball at the right time. This is an enviable repertoire."
Source: *Baseball Magazine* (February 1933, John J. Ward); Swetonic studied engineering at the University of Pittsburgh, and Ward notes that Swetonic was especially interested in knowing not only how to make a baseball curve, but *why* it curves.

BILL SWIFT 6'0" 170-pound righty
95-82, 3.58, 20 Saves 1932 1943

Pitch Selection: 1. Fastball 2. Change of Pace
Source: *Who's Who in Major League Baseball* (compiled by Harold "Speed" Johnson, 1933)

Notes: Swift arrived in the majors as an overhand pitcher, but by 1932 was throwing exclusively sidearm against right-handed hitters. He considered the fastball his best pitch, but developed a sinker and used it frequently against the right-handers.
Source: *Baseball Magazine* (November 1932, Clifford Bloodgood)

BILL SWIFT 6'1" 192-pound righty
94-78, 3.95, 27 Saves 1985 1998

Pitch Selection: 1. Sinking Fastball 2. Slider 3. Curve 4. Forkball (used as Change)
Sources: *The Scouting Report: 1993; The Scouting Notebook: 1995*

GREG SWINDELL 6'2" 225-pound lefty
123-122, 3.86, 7 Saves 1986 2002

Pitch Selection: 1. Fastball 2. Slider 3. Curve 4. Change
Source: *Men at Work* (George Will, 1990)

FRANK TANANA 6'2" 180-pound lefty
240-236, 3.66, 1 Save 1973 1993

Pitch Selection, first half of career: 1. Fastball 2. Hard Curve
Pitch Selection, second half: 1. Slow Curve 2. Fastball 3. Change
Source: *Tom Seaver's 1989 Scouting Notebook*

JESSE TANNEHILL 5'8" 150-pound lefty
195-117, 2.79, 8 Saves 1894 1911

Key Pitch: Slow Curve
Source: *The Chicago Daily Tribune* (8/18/1904, reprinted in Rich Coberly's *The No-Hit Hall of Fame*)

KEVIN TAPANI 6'0" 180-pound righty
143-125, 4.35, 0 Saves 1989 2001

Pitches: 1. Fastball 2. Slider 3. Change 4. Forkball or Splitter
Sources: *The Scouting Report: 1992; The Scouting Notebook 1999*

Description: "Tapani is a legitimate three-pitch guy. He has a fastball in the upper-80s, a solid slider, and a forkball good enough to stand as his No. 2 pitch when his slider isn't sliding . . . A quick worker with an effortless, compact delivery . . ."
Source: *Bill Mazeroski's Baseball* (1993 edition)

KEN TATUM 6'2" 205-pound righty
16-12, 2.93, 52 Saves 1969 1974

Pitch Selection: 1. Fastball 2. Slider
Source: *The Sporting News* (1/12/1974)

JULIAN TAVAREZ 6'2" 165-pound righty
63-48, 4.52, 13 Saves 1993 2003

Pitch Selection: 1. Fastball (89–93) 2. Sinker 3. Slider
Source: *The Scouting Notebook: 1996*

Pitch Selection: 1. Sinking Fastball (low-90s) 2. Slider 3. Split-Fingered Fastball
Source: *The Scouting Notebook: 1998*

BILLY TAYLOR 6'8" 235-pound righty
16-28, 4.21, 100 Saves 1994 2001

Pitch Selection: 1. Fastball (90) 2. Split-Fingered Fastball 3. Slider 4. Change
Source: *The Scouting Notebook: 1995*

Pitch Selection: 1. Sinking Fastball (high-80s) 2. Slider 3. Change
Sources: *The Scouting Notebook* (1997 and 1999 editions)

JACK TAYLOR 6'1" 190-pound righty
119-110, 4.23, 10 Saves 1891 1899

Pitch Selection: 1. Fastball 2. Curve
Source: unpublished manuscript by Peter Mancuso
Quotes from Mancuso's manuscript: "He relied heavily on his fastball . . . He was in his position throwing the ball with lightning velocity [from Lebanon, PA *Daily News*, 5/8/1891] . . . The big Brooklyn's banged Jack's benders like he was an amateur [from Cincinnati *Enquirer*, 5/1/1899] . . . He had speed and a curve that had a break as abrupt as a rich man's no to a book agent [from Cincinnati *Enquirer*, 8/3/1899] . . . He has all the speed he ever had and he put in a nice assortment of benders [from Cincinnati *Enquirer*, 9/1/1899] . . . Taylor's size and strength, no doubt, aided the delivery of his devastating fastball. In time he became a very sophisticated pitcher capable of a variety of pitches and speeds."

JACK TAYLOR 5'10" 170-pound righty
152-140, 2.66, 5 Saves 1898 1907

Key Pitch: Fastball
Note: Taylor threw sidearm.
Sources: *Baseball Research Journal 1976* (article by Art Ahrens), *Misfits* (J. Thomas Hetrick, 1991)

Description: "Corner working is his forte. He mixes up pitches. Fast and slow come along with almost the same motion."
Source: Contemporary writer, quoted in *Deadball Stars of the National League* (SABR, 2004)

LUTHER (DUMMY) TAYLOR
6'1" 160-pound righty
116-106, 2.74, 3 Saves 1900 1908

Key Pitch: Fastball
Source: *The Cleveland Blues. 1902 (When Lajoie Came to Town)* (John Phillips, 1988)

RON TAYLOR 6'1" 195-pound righty
45-43, 3.93, 72 Saves 1962 1972

Pitch Selection: 1. Sinker/Sinking Fastball 2. Slider 3. Curve 4. Fastball 5. Forkball
Sources: *The Sporting News* (12/29/1962; 7/13/1963; 9/14/1963; 12/7/1963; 7/4/1964; 10/24/1964; 12/5/1964; 3/25/1967; 11/6/1971)
Quote from 12/7/1963 TSN: "Relying on a sinker as his No. 1 pitch, but owning a pretty good fast ball and good breaking pitches as well, Taylor had worked in 25 games."
Quote from Johnny Keane in *TSN* 12/7/1963: "Now, with the forkball he's working on, the fast curve, sinker, and slider, Ron will have four pitches going for him instead of two."

Comment: "After all, Ron even went to the Florida Instructional League following his excellent rookie season. He went to work on a curve to supplement both his bread-and-butter pitch, the sinker, and his slider."
Quote from coach Joe Schulz: "In trying to better his curve, Ron changed his delivery. Just a little, but even a variance of a couple of inches can make such a big difference in a pitcher's control, I mean putting the ball where he wants to. That's what Ron is working on in winter ball."
Source: *The Sporting News* (12/5/1964)

Quote: "Almost sidearm delivery but comes up with overhand pitches to left-handers."
Source: *Baseball Digest* (March 1963, Page 108)

KENT TEKULVE 6'4" 180-pound righty
94-90, 2.85, 184 Saves 1974 1989

Pitch Selection: 1. Sinker 2. Slider 3. Tekulve developed a Change in 1986.
Source: *The Scouting Report: 1987*

Pitches: 1. Sinker 2. Slider 3. Slow Curve (as Change)
Source: *The Sporting News* (5/10/1980, Lowell Reidenbaugh)

Note: Tekulve threw between sidearm and submarine.

ANTHONY TELFORD 6'0" 195-pound righty
22-25, 4.17, 8 Saves 1990 2002

Pitches: 1. Fastball 2. Slider 3. Curve 4. Cut Fastball (added 1997) 5. Change (occasional)
Sources: *The Scouting Notebook* (1998–2001 editions)

WALT TERRELL 6'2" 205-pound righty
111-124, 4.22, 0 Saves 1982 1992

Pitch Selection: 1. Sinking Fastball 2. Slider 3. Palmball
Sources: *The Scouting Report: 1987; Tom Seaver's 1989 Scouting Notebook; The Scouting Report: 1990*

ADONIS TERRY 5'11" 168-pound righty
199-202, 3.72, 7 Saves 1884 1897

Key Pitch: Curves
Note: McMahon (below) says that Terry "was known for his wide assortment of puzzling curves, including what *Sporting Life* called 'the sharpest and speediest outcurve ever seen.' "
Source: *Baseball's First Stars* (SABR, 1996, article by William E. McMahon)

RALPH TERRY 6'3" 195-pound righty
107-99, 3.62, 11 Saves 1956 1967

Pitch Selection: 1. Fastball 2. Curve 3. Slider 4. Change
Sources: *Season of Glory* (Ralph Houk with Bob Creamer, 1988), *Baseball Digest* (January 1963, Page 8)

Pitch Selection: 1. Curve 2. Slider 3. Fastball 4. Change
Source: *The Sporting News* (6/23/1962, Til Ferdenzi)

Allie Reynolds: "At one time Terry had seven pitches. He blew a 6-1 lead in Kansas City by throwing some sliders. I told him, 'Forget your slider, work on your curve and bring up your change and fastball.' "
Source: *The Gospel According to Casey* (Ira Berkow and Jim Kaplan, 1992)

Description: "Had reputation of constantly attempting new pitches, but now sticks to basic fast ball, curve and slider."
Source: *1963 Major League Handbook* (Don Schiffer)

SCOTT TERRY 5'11" 195-pound righty
24-28, 3.73, 8 Saves 1986 1991

Pitch Selection: 1. Fastball 2. Slider 3. Change
Source: *The Scouting Report: 1990*

JEFF TESREAU 6'2" 218-pound righty
115-72, 2.43, 9 Saves 1912 1918

Pitch Selection: 1. Spitball (70%) 2. Fastball 3. Slow Ball
Source: Tesreau's obituary in *The Sporting News* (11/2/1946); *Baseball Magazine* (November 1913, John J. Ward); *The Sporting News* (10/10/1912)
Tesreau in *Baseball Magazine*: "I suppose seven out of ten of the balls I pitch are spit-balls . . .

"I have a fair slow ball and pretty good speed, but I have never been able to develop much of a curve. I don't know why; it seems hard for me to learn it. And since I don't appear to need it I probably never will be much of a curve pitcher now."

Description: "Tesreau's massive strength enables him to do work of the most laborious kind with little fatigue. Again, he has a peculiar body swing in his delivery which takes much of the muscular tension off his arm. Fans who have seen him pitch will remember that the burly boxman seems to all but lie down on his face in the forward heave he gives his shoulders as he releases the ball. This body swing, once patented by Coombs, and used by various pitchers, is a beautiful scheme to nurse the arm."
Source: Ward in *Baseball Magazine*

Note: Many pitchers in Tesreau's time threw a spitball or even relied on the pitch, but Tesreau's was famous for its speed.

BOB TEWKSBURY 6'4" 200-pound righty
110-102, 3.92, 1 Save 1986 1998

Pitch Selection: 1. Sinking Fastball (low-80s) 2. Curve 3. Slider
Sources: *The Scouting Report: 1993; The Scouting Notebook: 1995*

Description: "His arm diminished by surgery earlier in his career. Tewksbury, 32, has become a righthanded John Tudor. He takes control of the count with his curveball, then gets out with his fastball. Tewksbury uses two curves, one at 80–81-mph that has a sharp bite, the other a 74–75-mph teaser. His fastball rarely cracks 85 mph, but doesn't get hit because he locates it so well. Often, Tewksbury will get ahead 0-2 with breaking stuff, then busts a fastball on a hitter's fists. See ya later."
Source: *Bill Mazeroski's Baseball* (1993 edition)

BOBBY THIGPEN 6'3" 195-pound righty
31-36, 3.43, 201 Saves 1986 1994

Pitch Selection: 1. Fastball 2. Slider 3. Curve 4. Change
Sources: *The Scouting Report* (1990 and 1992 editions)

MYLES THOMAS 5'9" 170-pound righty
23-22, 4.64, 2 Saves 1926 1930

Key Pitch: Forkball
Source: Jim Turner in *Yesterday's Heroes* (Marty Appel, 1988)

TOMMY THOMAS 5'10" 175-pound righty
117-128, 4.11, 12 Saves 1926 1937

Pitches: 1. Fastball 2. Nickel Curve
Note: In his prime, Thomas was regarded as having one of the best fastballs in baseball.
Sources: Luke Appling in *Sport* (June 1983, David Whitford), *Who's Who in the Major Leagues* (1936 edition)

Description: "He is a typical fast ball pitcher. From preference, he uses few curves, though he doubtless will employ this unpopular twister more frequently than in his Baltimore days. But shooting the ball across the corners of the plate with enough stuff on it to fool the batters is Thomas' favorite stunt. Speed and still more speed is his pitching slogan."

Source: *Baseball Magazine* (September 1927, "Comprising an Interview with Al Thomas")

JUNIOR THOMPSON 6'1" 185-pound righty
47-35, 3.26, 7 Saves 1939 1947

Pitch Selection: 1–2. Curveball and Fastball
Thompson: "Sometimes I was considered a fastball pitcher, sometimes a curveball pitcher. I threw a lot of breaking stuff, cross-fired some, a little unorthodox at times."
Source: *The Pastime in Turbulence: Interviews with Baseball Players of the 1940s* (Brent Kelley, 2001)

JUSTIN THOMPSON 6'4" 215-pound lefty
36-43, 3.98, 0 Saves 1996 1999

Pitch Selection: 1. Sinking Fastball (90) 2. Cut Fastball 3. Curve 4. Straight Change
Source: *The Scouting Notebook: 1997*

Pitch Selection: 1. Two-Seam Fastball 2. Four-Seam Fastball 3. Change 4. Curve
Source: *The Scouting Notebook: 1998*

MARK THURMOND 6'0" 180-pound lefty
40-46, 3.69, 21 Saves 1983 1990

Pitches: 1. Fastball 2. Curve 3. Slider 4. Change
Source: *The Scouting Report: 1985*

Pitch Selection: 1. Cut Fastball 2. Slider 3. Change
Source: *The Scouting Report: 1990*

SLOPPY THURSTON 5'11" 165-pound righty
89-86, 4.24, 13 Saves 1923 1933

Pitches: 1. Fadeaway (25%) 2. Fastball 3. Curve
Sources: *Baseball Magazine* (October 1924, John J. Ward; July 1933, F.C. Lane)
Thurston, in Ward article: "My favorite ball is a kind of fade-away that breaks away from a left-handed batter. It's a slow ball and I use a lot of them. Perhaps out of a hundred pitched balls, I'll use as many as twenty-five slow balls . . . I have only a fair fast ball, but a fast ball, even without much hop on it, will get by if you have perfect control."
Johnny Evers, in Ward article: "The two most important things a pitcher can have are guts and a slow ball. Thurston has both and a lot besides. He has not only a slow ball, but he has a slower ball and he knows how to mix them up."
Max Carey, in Ward article: "I like speed as well as anyone, but I've always had a weakness for a pitcher who was foxy enough to use his head and who won games in spite of a lack of stuff on the ball."
F. C. Lane: "His fast ball is not conspicuous and he impresses the observer from the stands as a pitcher who ought to be easy to hit."

LUIS TIANT, SR. 5'11" 175-pound lefty
NEGRO LEAGUES 1930 1947

Pitch Selection: 1. Screwball 2. Change 3. Fastball 4. Curve 5. Slider
Note: Tiant was famous for his screwball and his pickoff move, and legend holds that he once struck out a batter while throwing to first base.
Sources: *The Biographical Encyclopedia of the Negro Baseball Leagues* (James A. Riley, 1994; interview with Ted Page in *Voices from the Great Black Baseball Leagues* (John Holway, 1975)

Frazier "Slow" Robinson: "I hit most left-handers good but old man Tiant. Anybody that threw overhanded like this was easy for me to hit. I'd see it all the way. But if you come kind of sidearm, it's kind of hard to pick up the ball. That's why I always had a little trouble out of old man Tiant . . . His boy was just like him with that herky-jerky delivery and junk he'd throw."
Source: *Catching Dreams: My Life in the Negro Baseball Leagues* (Frazier "Slow" Robinson with Paul Bauer, 1999)

Note: In the September, 1968 issue of *Sport*, Arnold Hano describes Sr. as "one of the finest spitball pitchers in the history of the Negro American league."

LUIS TIANT, JR. 6'0" 180-pound righty
229-172, 3.30, 15 Saves 1964 1982

Pitch Selection: 1. Fastball 2. Curve 3. Slider 4. Change
Note: Tiant would pitch from a variety of angles, and sometimes featured a barely legal hesitation pitch.
Source: *El Tiante* (Tiant and Joe Fitzgerald, 1976)

Pitches, 1975: 1. Fastball 2. Slider 3. Curve 4. Slow Curve (as Change) 5. Palm Ball 6. Knuckleball

Quote: "The Oakland scouting report on him warned he had six pitches—fastball, slider, curve, change-up curve, palm ball, and knuckler—all of which he could serve up from the sidearm, three-quarter, or overhand sectors, and points in between, but on this particular afternoon [Game 1 of the 1975 American League Championship Series] his fastball was so lively that he eschewed the upper ranges of virtuosity."
Source: Roger Angell in *Five Seasons: A Baseball Companion* (1977, Page 292; a few pages later, Angell provides a virtuoso's catalogue of Tiant's various gyrations on the mound.)

Description: "Equipped with a slider, a good curve and his best pitch—a fastball that really explodes—the husky Cuban seems a sure bet for big league success."
Source: *1965 Official Baseball Almanac* (Bill Wise)

Tony Kubek: "I batted against him when he was with Cleveland, when he first came up. There were very few that could throw harder, and his ball moved."
Source: NBC broadcast of Red Sox–Athletics game on July 22, 1972

JAY TIBBS 6'3" 185-pound righty
39-54, 4.20, 0 Saves 1984 1990

Pitch Selection: 1. Fastball (mid-80s) 2. Slider
3. Curve (abandoned in 1989) 4. Change
5. Slider
Source: *The Scouting Report* (1985, 1987, and 1990 editions); *1987 Montreal Expos Media Guide*

DICK TIDROW 6'4" 210-pound righty
100-94, 3.68, 55 Saves 1972 1984

Pitch Selection: 1. Screwball 2. Slider
Source: *The Sporting News* (8/2/1980, Joe Goddard)

BOB TIEFENAUER 6'2" 185-pound righty
9-25, 3.84, 23 Saves 1952 1968

Pitch Selection: 1. Knuckleball (75%) 2. Sinker
Sources: *The Sporting News* (8/24/1963, Page 18); a 1951 note in TSN also listed Tiefenauer's pitches as 1. Knuckleball, 2. Sinker.

THAD TILLOTSON 6'2" 195-pound righty
4-9, 4.06, 2 Saves 1967 1968

Note: Named by Brooks Robinson as throwing "constant" spitballs.
Source: *The Sporting News* (12/23/1967)

MIKE TIMLIN 6'4" 205-pound righty
51-55, 3.56, 116 Saves 1991 2003

Pitch Selection: 1. Two-Seam Sinking Fastball
2. Slider (1993)
Sources: *The Scouting Report* (1992 and 1995 editions); *The Scouting Notebook 1999*

BUD TINNING 5'11" 198-pound righty
22-15, 3.19, 4 Saves 1932 1935

Key Pitch: Curve
Source: *Baseball Magazine* (March 1934, Clifford Bloodgood)

JIM TOBIN 6'0" 185-pound righty
105-112, 3.44, 5 Saves 1937 1945

Pitches: 1. Knuckleball 2. Fastball 3. Slider (occasional) 4. Curve (*very* occasional)
Notes: In Tobin's 1944 no-hitter against the Dodgers, approximately 80 of his 98 pitches were knuckleballs. Also, beginning in 1943 (and quite possibly in other seasons) Tobin threw his knuckler sidearm to right-handed hitters and overhand to left-handed hitters.
Source: *Baseball Digest* (July 1944, Harold Kaese); *Baseball Magazine* (July 1944, Hub Miller)

Tobin: "I grasp the ball with the thumb on bottom and first two fingers on top, same as for a fast ball or curve, so as not to tip off the delivery. At the ball of the windup, I shift the ball back against the palm and move the top two fingers so the fingertips dig into the seam. Gripping the ball hard with the inside of my thumb and ring finger, I release it without breaking the wrist. That sends it floating up without any spin, and it catches on an air pocket for a sudden swerve about five feet from the plate."
Source: *The Sporting News* (7/2/1942, Page 8)

Description: ". . . Tobin's butterfly looms more prominent than ever when you realize that he is laboring with-

out a fast ball and with only a ripple of a curve. The knuckler is his one payoff pitch; his only weapon against the hitter. Jim would be the first to admit that without his fluttering delivery, he would be hidden in the minors, or perhaps out of baseball entirely."
Source: Miller in *Baseball Magazine*

Note: Tobin developed his knuckleball in 1939. Just prior to that season, Clifford Bloodgood wrote, "Jim has a fair amount of stuff . . ." and didn't mention a knuckleball at all.
Source: *Baseball Magazine* (February 1939, Bloodgood)
Other Sources: *The Braves, The Pick and the Shovel* (Al Hirshberg, 1948); *The No-Hit Hall of Fame* (Rich Coberly, 1985)

BRETT TOMKO 6'4" 215-pound righty
62-51, 4.62, 1 Save 1997 2003

Pitch Selection: 1. Hard Sinker (low-90s)
2. Cut Fastball (90) 3. Change
Source: *The Scouting Notebook: 1998*

Pitches: 1. Sinking Fastball (low-90s)
2. Cut Fastball (90s) 3. Straight Change
4. Curve (occasional)
Source: *The Scouting Notebook: 1999*

Pitch Selection: 1. Sinker (88–91) 2. Fastball
3. Slider
Quote: "His mechanics are good; his arm speed is average. His best pitch is a sinker, which he throws 88 to 91 mph with late life. His fastball has little movement, and he overuses his slider."
Source: Scout Lewis Shaw in *The Sporting News* (4/21/2003)

DAVE TOMLIN 6'2" 180-pound lefty
25-12, 3.82, 12 Saves 1972 1986

Pitch Selection: 1. Sinking Fastball 2. Sweeping Slurve
3. Change
Quote: "Funky delivery with above average fastball with sink, a sweeping slurve and a so-so change-up."
Source: e-mail message from Tom House to Rob Neyer (1/13/2003)

Sparky Anderson: "Tomlin will be a short relief man. He's got a good breaking ball and his fast ball runs good."
Source: *The Sporting News* (4/15/1978, Earl Lawson)

RANDY TOMLIN 5'10" 182-pound lefty
30-31, 3.43, 0 Saves 1990 1994

Pitch Selection: 1. Vulcan Change
2. Fastball (84)
Quote on the Vulcan change: "He jams the ball between his middle and ring fingers, reminiscent of the Vulcan sign in 'Star Trek.' "
Source: *The Scouting Report: 1992*

Pitch Selection: 1. Vulcan Change 2. Fastball
3. Slider 4. Curve
Source: *The Scouting Report: 1993*

FRED TONEY 6'6" 245-pound righty
137-102, 2.69, 12 Saves 1911 1923

Pitch Selection: 1. Spitball 2. Fastball 3. Curve
4. Overhand Sinker
Source: *Baseball's 10 Greatest Games* (John Thorn, 1981)

Story: "They tell a story about Fred Toney, who once pitched for John McGraw. Fred, like the Babe, was not shrinking violet at the dinner table. He ate long and often.

"Toney was scheduled to open a series at St. Louis one day, so he got himself ready for the battle of the heat by putting away an enormous breakfast, starting with the usual fruit, toast and bacon and eggs, and ending with a steak. On the way to Sportsman's Park with George Burns, Fred complained of feeling a little weak, so George suggested a hot dog. Toney felt obliged to follow this suggestion. In fact, he had several hot dogs, washed down by several bottles of pop, and topped off by several boxes of ice cream.

"But Toney was not convinced he had the strength to endure the St. Louis heat through nine innings, so reinforced himself in the clubhouse with more hot dogs and more pop. Then, just before going out to warm up, he cooled himself off with a long drink of ice water.

"Did Toney win that day? An answer in the affirmative would make interesting reading. But he neither won or lost. As a matter of fact, he threw just one ball and collapsed in a heap on the mound."
Source: *Baseball Magazine* (March 1947, Hub Miller)

MIKE TORREZ 6'5" 220-pound righty
185-160, 3.96, 0 Saves 1967 1984

Pitch Selection: 1. Slider 2. Fastball
3. Slow Curve (developed in 1975) 4. Change
Sources: *Weaver on Strategy* (Earl Weaver with Terry Pluto, 1984); TV broadcast of American League East playoff game in 1978

Note: In the 1977 World Series, Torrez was clocked at 94 on his fastball, 89 on his slider.
Source: *Los Angeles Times* (September, 1978, Mark Purdy)

Note: Bucky Dent's homer in 1978 came off a fastball that tailed over the plate.
Source: Torrez in *Talkin' Baseball: An Oral History of Baseball in the 1970s* (Phil Pepe, 1998)

HAPPY TOWNSEND 6'0" 190-pound righty
34-82, 3.59, 0 Saves 1901 1906

Key Pitch: Fastball
Quote: "Taylor has a good sinking fast ball, a good slider and excellent control . . . He needs an off-speed pitch."
Source: unidentified Wilmington, Delaware newspaper (12/23/1963)
Other Source: *The Sporting News* (1/4/1964)

STEVE TRACHSEL 6'3" 185-pound righty
106-118, 4.26, 0 Saves 1993 2003

Pitch Selection: 1. Two-Seam Fastball
2. Four-Seam Fastball 3. Split-Fingered Fastball (used as Change) 4. Curve
Source: *The Scouting Notebook 1999*

BILL TRAVERS 6'4" 187-pound lefty
65-71, 4.10, 1 Save 1974 1983

Pitch Selection: 1. Forkball 2. Fastball
Travers on his forkball: "Sometimes it flutters like a knuckleball. Sometimes—and this is what I like—it drops off sharply, like a spitter. And even when it doesn't move, it's a good change."
Source: *The Sporting News* (7/24/1976, Lou Chapman)
Other Source: *The Sporting News* (6/26/1976, Chapman)

TED TRENT 6'3" 185-pound righty
NEGRO LEAGUES 1927 1939

Pitch Selection: 1. Drop Curve 2. Curve 3. Fastball
Sources: *Catching Dreams: My Life in the Negro Baseball Leagues* (Frazier "Slow" Robinson with Paul Bauer, 1999); George Giles in *Black Diamonds* (John Holway, 1989)
Slow Robinson: "They say an old timer named Trent had the best (curve) of all . . . He was a tall right-hander who came right over the top. They said he had *several* different curveballs . . ."

MIKE TROMBLEY 6'2" 200-pound righty
37-47, 4.48, 44 Saves 1992 2002

Pitch Selection: 1. Split-Fingered Fastball 2. Curve
3. Fastball
Source: *The Scouting Notebook 2000*

DIZZY TROUT 6'2" 195-pound righty
170-161, 3.23, 35 Saves 1939 1957

Pitch Selection: 1. Fastball 2. Forkball 3. Sinker
4. Curve 5. Knuckleball 6. Screwball 7. Change
Sources: *New York Herald-Tribune* (3/13/1937); *The Sporting News* (December 1938; 8/31/1944; 9/20/1945; 8/30/1950; 3/18/1932); AL Service Bureau press release (Henry P. Edwards, 1/28/1940); *Baseball Magazine* (July 1940); *New York World-Telegram* (1/2/1945); *Saturday Evening Post* (3/31/1945); scout Wish Egan in *Detroit News* (12/14/1948); *Baltimore Evening Sun* (9/2/1957)

Trout: "I'm not so much on that fancy stuff, but I can breeze that fast one in there so it looks like an aspirin tablet. And when that fork ball of mine comes up to those left-handers, you'll see them trotting back to the dugout disgusted."
Source: *New York Herald Tribune* (3/13/1937)

Description: "He has a sizzling fast ball and developed a neat change of pace . . . His curve ball was not so good, but he doesn't need one, with his speed."
Source: *The Sporting News* (December 1938)

Description: "He liked to experiment with this or that delivery. One never knew whether he intended to throw over hand, side arm or under hand. He really does not need to experiment as he has a great fast ball."

Source: AL Service Bureau press release (Henry P. Edwards, 1/28/1940)

Description: "He let his fast ball and sinker do most of his talking. He has a nice 'hop' on his high hard one and the sinker is good for inducing players to hit into the dirt."
Source: *Baseball Magazine* (July 1940)

Description: "It never seemed to matter what sign he got. He was going to come at you the only way he knew how—as fast as he could, as hard as he could, with every ounce of energy in his body . . . He'd go into the big rocking motion, back and forth, and here'd be that high hard one roaring across the plate."
Source: *The Sporting News* (3/18/1972)

Key Pitch: Fastball
Charlie Gehringer: "Paul [Dean] could throw harder than Dizzy [Dean], but he didn't have the curve or know-how. He was just a Dizzy Trout–type pitcher—just go out there and throw as hard as he could for as long as he could."
Source: *Cobb Would Have Caught It* (Richard Bak, 1991)

Quote: "Diz used to throw a fork ball. Now they call it a split-fingered fastball, but it's the same pitch. He could control it. He had big hands, so he could spread those fingers across the ball."
Source: Barney McCosky in *Cobb Would Have Caught It*

STEVE TROUT 6'4" 195-pound lefty
88-92, 4.18, 4 Saves 1978 1989

Key Pitch: Sinker
Source: *The Scouting Report: 1987*

BOB TROWBRIDGE 6'1" 190-pound righty
13-13, 3.95, 5 Saves 1956 1960

Pitch Selection: 1. Fastball 2. Curve 3. Slider (experimental)
Source: *The Sporting News* (6/15/1955, Eddie Jones)

VIRGIL TRUCKS 5'11" 198-pound righty
177-135, 3.39, 30 Saves 1941 1958

Pitch Selection: 1. Fastball 2. Curve 3. Slider 4. Change 5. Knuckleball 6. Slip Pitch (early 1950s)
Sources: *The DiMaggio Albums* (Richard Whittingham, Page 474, article by Frank Graham contains excellent description of Trucks' stuff); *Baseball Stars of 1954* (article by Virgil Trucks); *The Sporting News* (3/23/1955, Page 2); Trucks in *Masters of the Diamond* (Rich Westcott, 1994); *Baseball Magazine* (July 1946, Hub Miller)
Trucks in *Masters of the Diamond:* "I was clocked at one hundred five miles per hour . . . I developed the slip pitch. Paul Richards taught it to me. I threw that sixty miles an hour."

Trucks in 1956: "It took me 12 years to become a 20-game winner in the majors and I still wouldn't have done it if I hadn't perfected a slider."
Source: *Sport* (July 1956, Milton Richman)

Notes: In 1938, Trucks set a professional record (at the modern pitching distance) with 418 strikeouts while pitching in the Alabama-Florida League.

Listed by *The Sporting News* as still having one of the best fastballs in the league, December 1, 1954 and again on August 29, 1956.

JOHN TSITOURIS 6'0" 175-pound righty
34-38, 4.13, 3 Saves 1957 1968

Key Pitch: Fastball
Source: *Sport* (July 1960, Milton Richman)

JOHN TUDOR 6'0" 185-pound lefty
117-72, 3.12, 1 Save 1979 1990

Pitch Selection: 1. Fastball 2. Slider 3. Curve 4. Change
Source: *The Sporting News* (8/2/1980, Joe Giulotti)

Pitch Selection: 1. Change 2. Fastball
Source: *The Scouting Report: 1987*

Whitey Herzog: ". . . in five years with the Cardinals, John Tudor never threw his curveball to a righthanded batter . . . Breaking stuff wasn't his main attraction anyway. John lived off changeups."
Source: *You're Missin' a Great Game* (Herzog and Jonathan Pitts, 1998)

GEORGE TURBEVILLE 6'1" 275-pound lefty
2-12, 6.14, 0 Saves 1935 1937

Pitch Selection: 1. Fastball 2. Knuckleball

Source: *The Sporting News* (8/29/1935, James C. Isaminger)

BOB TURLEY 6'2" 215-pound righty
101-85, 3.64, 12 Saves 1951 1963

Pitch Selection: 1. Fastball 2. Slider 3. Sinker 4. Change 5. Hard Curve
Sources: *New York Times* (July 1955, article by Arthur Daley); *The Sporting News* (8/29/1956, Page 4); *Baseball Digest* (August 1958, Page 10); *Sweet Seasons* (Dom Forker, 1989); *Baseball Stars of 1959* (article by Dick Kaplan); *Dynasty* (Peter Golenbock, 1975); *The Sporting News* (9/7/1974)

Comment: "The story of Turley's early career in the majors has been a spectacular but disappointing one. For five or six innings, he would rack up one strikeout victim after another, but there were always too many walks and a perceptible weakening as the game grew older. Turley is putting in a lot of work and hours on his other pitches now. When he gets them down pat, he should become, like Score, a big winner."
Source: *Sport* (July 1956, Milton Richman, "Nobody Wins With a Fast Ball")

Note: Turley ranks with Herb Score and Ryne Duren as the hardest-throwing pitchers in baseball in the mid-1950s. *The Sporting News* stated flatly on December 1, 1954, that Turley was then the hardest-throwing pitcher in baseball. He was timed at 94.2 MPH in 1958 (at that time the third-fastest pitch ever recorded) and at 90.75 in 1960.

JIM TURNER 6'0" 185-pound righty
69-60, 3.22, 20 Saves 1937 1945

Key Pitch: Fastball
Source: *The Braves: The Pick and the Shovel* (Al Hirshberg, 1948)
Note: Hirshberg describes Turner as "a hard-working fast ball pitcher," but in *The Ballplayers,* Norman Macht writes that Turner relied "on control and a low curveball." Make of these what you will.

Comment: "Neither Turner nor [teammate Lou] Fette was a strike-out pitcher. Both relied on good control. They kept the ball low, so that enemy batters hit the ball on the ground, which was kept damp and slow by the canny McKechnie."
Source: *The Boston Braves* (Harold Kaese, 1948)

WAYNE TWITCHELL 6'6" 215-pound righty
48-65, 3.98, 2 Saves 1970 1979

Pitch Selection: 1. Fastball 2. Curve 3. Slider 4. Circle Change (late in career, occasional)
Source: Phone interview with Twitchell (6/10/2002, Rob Neyer)

LEFTY TYLER 6'0" 175-pound lefty
127-116, 2.95, 7 Saves 1910 1921

Key Pitch: Slow Ball
Sources: *New York Tribune* (5/22/1921); unidentified source from the Hall of Fame Library (5/22/1921)

Note: The *Biographic Encyclopedia of Baseball* (Pietrusza, Silverman and Gershman, 2000) says Tyler used a "crossfire delivery."

GEORGE UHLE 6'0" 190-pound righty
200-166, 3.99, 25 Saves 1919 1936

Pitch Selection: 1. Fastball 2. Overhand Curve 3. Slider (developed late in career)
Sources: Uhle in *Cobb Would Have Caught It* (Richard Bak, 1991), Waite Hoyt and Ed Wells in *Baseball Between the Wars* (Eugene Murdock, 1992)

Umpire George Moriarty: "Uhle, when right, is a masterful pitcher. No predecessor or contemporary ever knew more about the science and technique of box work than this veteran. It is an unusual treat to watch him slip out of danger in a pinch."
Source: *Baseball Magazine* (July 1930)

Notes: Uhle, by his own description, did *not* throw a screwball. He did not call any of his own pitches a screwball. However, other people sometimes referred to one of his pitches as a screwball. *Babe Ruth's Own Book of Baseball* (page 86) and Gene Murdock's *Baseball Between the Wars* (pages 48 and 83) both say that Uhle threw a screwball, and so we may assume that he threw something that *looked* like a screwball. But Uhle was very specific in stating that he did not throw a screwball.

Also, Waite Hoyt credits Uhle with inventing the

slider. In *Baseball Digest* (January 1963), Sal Maglie reported that he was working with Uhle in 1939, and asked Uhle to teach him the slider. But Uhle refused, saying that Maglie had too good a curve to mess with.

FRANK ULRICH 6'2" 195-pound righty
19-27, 3.48, 2 Saves 1925 1927

Pitch Selection: 1. Fastball 2. Knuckleball
Quote: "Ulrich had speed with his knuckler. He blazed through the National League in the last two months of 1927."
Source: *Baseball Magazine* (March 1932, William E. Brandt)

TOM UNDERWOOD 5'11" 170-pound lefty
86-87, 3.89, 18 Saves 1974 1984

Pitch Selection: 1. Curve 2. Fastball
Source: *The Sporting News* (9/27/1975, Ray Kelly)

CECIL UPSHAW 6'6" 205-pound righty
34-36, 3.13, 86 Saves 1966 1975

Pitches: 1. Sinking Fastball 2. Running/Rising Curve 3. Slip Pitch 4. Screwball 5. Slider 6. Change 7. Fastball
Note: Upshaw usually threw sidearm.
Sources: *The Sporting News* (7/13/1968; 4/12/1969; 6/28/1969; 9/5/1970; 10/31/1970; 2/13/1971; 3/27/1971; 5/12/1973); *Atlanta Braves Scorebook 1982; Sports Collectors' Digest* (3/4/1994); *Baseball Digest* (March 1967, "Official Scouting Reports on 1967 Major League Rookies")
Quote from *TSN* 4/12/1969: "The added pitch late last year was a screwball. Upshaw had been fooling around with it for some time, but could get no downward break. It was 'flat.' Then one day he decided to exaggerate his follow-through and really put rotation on the ball. Voila! A screwjie!"

". . . He also throws a 'running' curve, a sinker and slider."
Note: The same *TSN* article (4/12/1969) discusses how, during spring training in 1969, Upshaw began throwing his slip pitch overhand instead of sidearm.
Quote from *TSN* 10/31/1970: "The fall session gave Upshaw a chance to try all his tested pitches—sinking fast ball, screwball, curve, change-up—under game conditions . . . 'I wanted to work on an overhand slider, too, but I didn't get the chance.' "
Quote from *Atlanta Braves Scorebook:* "It's a funny story about how I started throwing sidearmed. I just couldn't become a strikeout pitcher. I was getting two strikes on everybody and then couldn't get that third strike. I started dropping my arm down on two-strike pitches and the strikeouts came. It worked."
Quote from *Sports Collectors' Digest:* "My real dead-out pitch was my sinkerball . . . My strikeout pitch was my rising curve, and I threw it about three different ways. I could make it go straight up. I could make it go up and away or up and in."

Note: In the minors, Upshaw frequently threw a Knuckleball. In 1966, a scouting report in *Baseball Digest* said, "Throws knuckler but fast ball is not fast and curve needs help."

UGUETH URBINA 6'0" 205-pound righty
35-37, 3.32, 206 Saves 1995 2003

Pitch Selection: 1. Fastball (high-90s) 2. Slider 3. Change (occasional)
Source: *The Scouting Notebook: 1998*

Pitch Selection: 1. Fastball 2. Slider 3. Split-Fingered Fastball (occasional) 4. Change (occasional)
Source: *The Scouting Notebook: 2002*

Commentary: Watching Urbina pitch in the 2003 World Series, it's almost all fastballs (92–93) and change-ups (78–82), with a slider occasionally mixed in.

ISMAEL VALDES 6'3" 183-pound righty
88-94, 3.93, 1 Save 1994 2003

Pitches: 1. Overhand Curve 2. Two-Seam Fastball 3. Four-Seam Fastball 4. Three-Quarters Curve 5. Change
Sources: *The Scouting Notebook: 1997; The Scouting Notebook 2000*

FERNANDO VALENZUELA 5'11" 180-pound lefty
173-153, 3.54, 2 Saves 1980 1997

Pitches: 1. Hard Screwball 2. Slow Screwball 3. Fastball 4. Curve 5. Slider

Source: *The Scouting Report: 1987*

Quote: "He learned the screwball from teammate Bobby Castillo . . ."
Source: *The Sporting News* (7/11/1983, Ken Gurnick)

RUSS VAN ATTA 6'0" 184-pound lefty
33-41, 5.59, 6 Saves 1933 1939

Pitch Selection: 1. Fastball 2. Curve
Van Atta: "In the Association my best ball was my fast ball, but now I think that my curve is just as good. I owe the development of that to Herb Pennock, who taught me many invaluable tricks including the proper hold and the right pressure of the middle finger on the ball."
Source: *Baseball Magazine* (May 1934, Clifford Bloodgood)

TODD VAN POPPEL 6'5" 240-pound righty
36-46, 5.50, 4 Saves 1991 2003

Pitches, early career (as starter): 1. Fastball (high-80s) 2. Overhand Curve 3. Circle Change
Pitches, late career (as reliever): 1. Fastball (low-90s) 2. Slider 3. Change
Source: *The Scouting Notebook* (1995–1997, 2003 editions)

DAZZY VANCE 6'2" 200-pound righty
197-140, 3.24, 11 Saves 1915 1935

Pitch Selection: 1. High Fastball 2. Overhand Curve
Sources: *Baseball's Famous Pitchers* (Ira L. Smith, 1954); 1924 *Reach Guide* (pages 47 and 48); Vance interviewed in *Baseball Magazine* (April 1926)

Notes: In the 1926 Interview, Vance says that he is one of the few pitchers in the league who throws straight overhand, and that most fastball pitchers throw at least somewhat sidearm. "I pitch side arm myself, when I feel like it," Vance says, "but when I'm really in the hole and have got to hump up my back and get out of it, I pitch overhand.

"Most pitchers try to save their arm. They won't put much stuff on the ball except in the pinch. I generally put a lot of stuff on every thing I throw. That's my theory of getting results with the least effort in the long run. But I always plan to have something up my sleeve. I don't cut loose with everything I've got more than four or five times a game. When the bases are full and you've got two and three on the batter, you're pretty apt to let fly and get your shoulder blades, your ears and your tonsils behind that pitch. But I don't like to cut loose with everything. It's like speeding in an automobile. Something may give."

Ray Kremer in *Baseball Magazine* (July 1932) said, "I used to consider Dazzy Vance the fastest pitcher in our league. I guess he still is, though Dazzy, like myself, is growing old. But Dazzy had a remarkable curve with his speed, the best curve, I would say, that I ever looked at." Ward Mason in *Baseball Magazine* in September 1929 described Dazzy's delivery as a "sweeping forward lunge and blinding speed."

In the *Baseball Digest* in September 1947, Charlie Grimm is quoted as saying that Vance had "the best windmill (motion) I ever saw."

Comment: "The best curve ball I ever saw was pitched by Dazzy Vance. When that big fellow brings his arm over, straight down and lets go of one of his hooks, it will drop not inches but feet."
Source: Hod Lisenbee in *Baseball Magazine* (August 1930, "Comprising an Interview with Horace Lisenbee")

Description: "Vance threw both that high hard one and the curve with exactly the same motion and on his best days the batter rarely knew what was coming until it had gone by."
Source: *Baseball Magazine* (October 1938, John Drebinger)

Comment: "Vance throws about four [knuckleballs] a game, and is very choosy just when to throw them, although he is credited with chucking a very mean one."
Note: *Baseball Magazine* (March 1932, William E. Brandt)

Riggs Stephenson: "Dazzy Vance pitched off a high mound and he was already a big man, so the ball came down at you instead of straight toward you. And his fastball would rise, too. He also had a sharp overhand curve, the kind we used to call a drop. Then, to make things even harder on the hitter, he'd cut his shirt around the right arm so you couldn't pick up the ball with those shreds of a sleeve flapping around."
Source: *The Greatest Team of All Time* (Nicholas Acocella and Donald Dewey, 1994)

ED VANDE BERG 6'2" 175-pound lefty
25-28, 3.92, 22 Saves 1982 1988

Pitch Selection: 1. Slider 2. Fastball 3. Curve
Sources: *The Scouting Report: 1983; The Scouting Report: 1987*

JOHNNY VANDER MEER 6'1" 190-pound lefty
119-121, 3.44, 2 Saves 1937 1951

Pitch Selection: 1. Fastball 2. Curve 3. Change
Sources: *1947 Scout Report* (Wid Matthews); Vander Meer in *Diamond Greats* (Rich Westcott, 1988); Bucky Walters in *Baseball When the Grass Was Real* (Donald Honig, 1975)

Note: According to Clifford Bloodgood in *Baseball Magazine* (August 1938), prior to the '38 season Reds manager Bill McKechnie changed Vander Meer's style "from half sidearm to overhand."

ELAM VANGILDER 6'1" 192-pound righty
99-102, 4.28, 19 Saves 1919 1929

Pitches: 1. Fastball 2. Curve 3. Change
Quote: "Van Gilder's fast ball is his main defence. He has, however, a pretty good curve and a fairly effective change of pace."
Source: *Baseball Magazine* (February 1928, F.C. Lane)

HIPPO VAUGHN 6'4" 215-pound lefty
178-137, 2.49, 5 Saves 1908 1921

Pitch Selection: 1. Fastball 2. Curve 3. Slow Ball
Sources: Vaughn in *Baseball Magazine* (November

Transcendental Graphics / ruckerarchive.com

Big Jim Vaughn

1917); *New York Press* (1910); unidentified source from the Hall of Fame Library (1911); *Baseball's 10 Greatest Games* (John Thorn, 1981)
Quote from *New York Press:* "Ball players say the Highland southpaw has more speed than any other left-hander in the American League."
Vaughn in 1917 *Baseball Magazine:* "In my case I can control a curve better than I can a fast one . . ."

Vaughn: "Personally I like the side arm delivery although I use the overhand type most of the time when I want to be sure of my control. There are not many side-arm pitchers. In fact, I do not consider even Johnson a true side-arm pitcher. He uses a half side-arm motion, but his arms are so long he is in a class by himself. Alexander, however, is a true side-arm pitcher."
Source: *Baseball Magazine* (August 1919, F.C. Lane)

Pete Alexander: "Big Jim Vaughn used to pitch the particular kind of ball a batter liked best just to show him that he couldn't hit it. Nothing pleased him better than to strike a man out pitching to his strength."
Source: *Batting* (F.C. Lane, 1925; reprinted by SABR in 2001)

JAVIER VAZQUEZ 6'2" 205-pound righty
64-68, 4.16, 0 Saves 1998 2003

Pitch Selection: 1. Change
2. Sinking Fastball (low-90s) 3. Curve
Source: *The Scouting Notebook: 1999*

Pitch Selection: 1. Sinking Two-Seam Fastball
2. Rising Four-Seam Fastball 3. Curve 4. Change
Source: *The Scouting Notebook: 2000*

Pitch Selection: 1. Fastball (low-90s) 2. Change
3. Cut Fastball (added 2000) 4. Curve
Source: *The Scouting Notebook: 2001*

Pitch Selection: 1. Fastball 2. Slider 3. Curve
4. Change 5. Cut Fastball
Source: *The Scouting Notebook: 2002*

BOB VEALE 6'6" 212-pound lefty
120-95, 3.07, 21 Saves 1962 1974

Pitch Selection: 1. Fastball 2. Curve 3. Slider
Sources: *When the Cheering Stops* (Heiman et al., 1990); *Major League Baseball—1969* (Jack Zanger)
Quote from Zanger: ". . . one of the National League's hardest throwers . . . he also throws what he calls his 'angry ball' when he is upset with himself on the mound."

Description: "He has four pitches—great fast ball, real good curve, a fine change-up and his biggest pitch now is control . . ."
Source: Larry Shepard in *1965 Official Baseball Almanac* (Bill Wise)

Pitches: 1. Fastball 2. Sinking Fastball 3. Slider
4. Change 5. Curve
Veale: "I was a power pitcher and I was all over the place. You might get it inside two feet or outside. Wildness can be beneficial to a pitcher. My best pitches were my fastball and low fastball, but most of the outs came on sliders. I came up with a pretty good change-up and a pretty curveball later on."
Source: *Twin Killing: The Bill Mazeroski Story* (John T. Bird, 1995)

MIKE VENAFRO 5'10" 180-pound lefty
14-10, 4.11, 5 Saves 1999 2003

Pitch Selection: 1. Fastball (90) 2. Curve 3. Change
Source: *The Scouting Notebook: 2000*

JOE VERBANIC 6'0" 155-pound righty
12-11, 3.26, 6 Saves 1966 1970

Description: "Good fast ball. Has control and a slider. Pitches sinking fast ball with an overhand delivery. Ready for majors."
Source: *Baseball Digest* (March 1967, "Official Scouting Reports on 1967 Major League Rookies")

DAVE VERES 6'1" 195-pound righty
36-35, 3.44, 95 Saves 1994 2003

Pitch Selection: 1. Fastball 2. Slider
3. Split-Fingered Fastball 4. Change
Source: *1996 Montreal Expos Media Guide*

Pitch Selection: 1. Split-Fingered Fastball
2. Fastball (low-90s) 3. Hard Slider
Source: *The Scouting Notebook 1999*

LEE VIAU 5'4" 160-pound righty
83-78, 3.33, 2 Saves 1888 1892

Pitch Selection: 1. Fastball 2. Curve
Sources: *The Sporting News* (January 1948); unidentified manuscript titled "A Green Mountain Boy of Summer: Leon Viau of Corinth VT."
Quote from *TSN:* "Using a sidearm delivery and throwing with apparent little effort, Viau, nevertheless, worked rapidly and was esteemed as the fastest pitcher in the long line of Cincinnati's old-time hurlers."
Quote from manuscript: "Reported to be very fast, he pitched with an effortless side-arm delivery . . . A 'deceptive curve' complemented the blazing fastball."

RON VILLONE 6'3" 243-pound lefty
39-43, 4.95, 5 Saves 1995 2003

Pitch Selection: 1. Fastball (low-90s) 2. Change
Source: *The Scouting Notebook: 1996*

Pitch Selection: 1. Fastball (mid-90s)
2. Split-Fingered Fastball
Source: *The Scouting Notebook: 1997*

Pitch Selection: 1. Fastball (90s) 2. Change 3. Slider
Source: *The Scouting Notebook: 1998*

Pitch Selection: 1. Fastball (low-90s) 2. Curve
3. Change
Source: *The Scouting Notebook: 2000*

FRANK VIOLA 6'4" 200-pound lefty
176-150, 3.73, 0 Saves 1982 1996

Pitch Selection: 1. Fastball 2. Change 3. Curve
Sources: *The Scouting Report: 1987; The Scouting Report: 1990*

BILL VOISELLE 6'4" 200-pound righty
74-84, 3.83, 3 Saves 1942 1950

Pitch Selection: 1. Overhand Fastball 2. Change
3. Hard Curve 4. Slow Curve
Voiselle: "I could always throw pretty hard. I threw straight overhand . . . I just showed a curve once in a while to let them know I had one."
Source: *Masters of the Diamond* (Rich Westcott, 1994)

BRUCE VON HOFF 6'0" 187-pound righty
0-3, 5.06, 0 Saves 1965 1967

Description: "Fast ball and curve might get him by. Sidearm delivery. Can be an outstanding relief man when he learns to stay downstairs."
Source: *Baseball Digest* (March 1967, "Official Scouting Reports on 1967 Major League Rookies")

ED VOSBERG 6'1" 210-pound lefty
10-15, 4.32, 13 Saves 1986 2002

Pitch Selection: 1. Curve 2. Fastball
Source: *The Scouting Notebook: 1997*

PETE VUCKOVICH 6'4" 215-pound righty
93-69, 3.66, 10 Saves 1975 1986

Pitch Selection: 1. Fastball 2. Slider 3. Curve
4. Change
Note: Vuckovich threw from a variety of angles.
Sources: *Why Time Begins on Opening Day* (Tom Boswell, Page 297); *Nine Innings* (Dan Okrent, 1985)

Description: In the middle of Vuckovich's motion, he brought his hands behind his left foot, which he kicked toward the third-base dugout.
Source: Observation of Brewers-Tigers game of 10/3/1981 (aired on ESPN Classic, 9/17/2003)

RUBE WADDELL 6'1" 196-pound lefty
193-143, 2.16, 5 Saves 1897 1910

Pitch Selection: 1. Fastball 2. Hard Curve
Sources: *The Fireballers* (Jack Newcombe, 1964); *The National Game* (Alfred H. Spink, 1911)

Connie Mack: ". . . curve was even better than his speed . . . [He] had the fastest and deepest curve I've ever seen."
Source: *Kings of the Diamond* (Lee Allen and Tom Meany, 1965)

BILLY WAGNER 5'11" 195-pound lefty
26-29, 2.53, 225 Saves 1995 2003

Pitches, 1995–1998: 1. Fastball (95–98)
2. Curve (occasional)
Pitches, 1999–2003: 1. Fastball (96–100)
2. Slider (occasional) 3. Curve (rarely)

Billy Wagner

Note: In 1999, it was widely reported that during Randy Johnson's two-month stint with the Astros, he taught his slider to Wagner. However, later sources suggest that Wagner never quite got the hang of the pitch, and continued to work with the curve.
Sources: *The Scouting Notebook* (1997–2003 editions)

Matt Williams: "He doesn't need another pitch. His fastball is already so good and dominating. Plus, he hides the ball so well that it all works to his advantage. You don't have a lot of time to know what he's throwing. Everything he throws is from the side of his body. He doesn't need a slider. If he keeps developing it, it's not going to be fun facing him. It'll be challenging, but it won't be fun."
Source: *The Sporting News* (6/7/1999, Michael Knisley)

CHARLIE WAGNER 5'11" 170-pound righty
32-23, 3.91, 0 Saves 1938 1946

Pitch Selection: 1. Curve 2. Fastball 3. Change
Source: *Baseball Magazine* (May 1947, Harold Winerip)

PAUL WAGNER 6'1" 210-pound righty
29-45, 4.83, 3 Saves 1992 1999

Pitches: 1. Fastball (low-90s) 2. Slider (88) 3. Curve
Source: *The Scouting Notebook* (1995–1997 editions)
Note: According to 1997 edition, Wagner "experimented with a straight change, palmball, and forkball without much success."

RICK WAITS 6'3" 194-pound lefty
79-92, 4.25, 8 Saves 1973 1985

Pitches: 1. Fastball 2. Curve 3. Slider 4. Change
Note: Waits also threw a screwball in the early 1980s.
Sources: *The Sporting News* (7/29/1978, Russ Schneider; 9/15/1979, Bob Sudyk; and 5/17/1980, Bob Sudyk); *The Scouting Report* (1983–1985 editions)

TIM WAKEFIELD 6'2" 195-pound righty
116-101, 4.24, 22 Saves 1992 2003

Pitches: 1. Fast Knuckleball 2. Slow Knuckleball
3. Slow Curve (used as a change)
4. "Straight Ball" or "Non-Fastball" 5. Slider
Sources: *The Scouting Report: 1996; The Scouting Notebook 1999*

RUBE WALBERG 6'1" 190-pound lefty
155-141, 4.16, 32 Saves 1923 1937

Pitch Selection: 1. Fastball 2. Hard Curve
Source: *Babe Ruth's Own Book of Baseball* (Ruth, 1928)
Note: Walberg had unusually large hands, which enabled him to grip the ball in unusual ways.

Quote: " 'Walberg ought to be the greatest pitcher on the diamond,' said one of his own team mates whose name we won't divulge. 'He has nearly as much sheer speed as Lefty Grove and a much better curve ball. In fact, he has the greatest assortment of stuff of any left hander in baseball.' "
Walberg: "I pitch overhand both for speed and direction. When I drop down to a side arm delivery, which I sometimes do unconsciously, I'm not so good."
Source: *Baseball Magazine* (September 1928, F.C. Lane)

Comment: ". . . Connie Mack had three great pitchers—Grove, Earnshaw and Walberg. Walberg was the most brilliant and the least effective of the trio. Mickey

Cochrane, who caught them all and is certainly a good judge of pitchers, repeatedly contended that Walberg had as much stuff as Grove, with a greater natural assortment and a more deceptive delivery. Walberg did win a lot of ball games, but he was not the dependable performer that he should have been."
Source: F.C. Lane in *Baseball Magazine* (November 1937); it's apparent that Cochrane was probably Lane's source for the 1928 quote above.

Umpire Bill Summers: "Rube Walberg, once of the Athletics, got away with many a spitter, but in those days it was up to the opposition to make the squawk. Now the umpire is charged with policing the pitching."
Source: *New York World Telegram* (4/7/1945, "Daniel's Dope" column)

BOB WALK 6'3" 185-pound righty
105-81, 4.03, 5 Saves 1980 1993

Pitch Selection: 1. Hard Curve 2. Sinking Fastball 3. Slider 4. Change
Sources: *The Scouting Report* (1990 and 1992 editions)

BILL WALKER 6'0" 175-pound lefty
97-77, 3.59, 8 Saves 1927 1936

Pitch Selection: 1. Fastball 2. Hard Curve 3. Slow Curve 4. Change
Sources: *The Sporting News* (11/17/1932, Harry T. Brundidge); transcript of Walker interview on KMOX radio, 1/7/1933 (TSN morgue); *The Sporting News* (2/2/1933)
Quote from KMOX interview: "I generally use the three standard deliveries, a fast ball, a curve, and a change of pace. I never went in for freak deliveries, such as the screw ball or the knuckle ball . . . generally speaking, I rely mostly on my fast ball."
Note: Walker also credited Carl Mays with teaching him how to pitch—perhaps the only nice thing ever said about Carl Mays.

Notes: Walker had serious heart trouble as a child, suffering what was diagnosed as a heart attack at age 7, another at age 15. He never played baseball until his late teens, but could throw hard as soon as he took up the game. He had no heart trouble as an adult.

Cited by Ray Kremer in *Baseball Magazine* (1930) as having one of the best fastballs in the league.

DIXIE WALKER 6'0" 192-pound righty
25-31, 3.52, 0 Saves 1909 1912

Quote: "He is a big fellow and possessor of great speed."
Source: *The National Game* (Alfred H. Spink, 1911)

JERRY WALKER 6'1" 195-pound righty
37-44, 4.36, 13 Saves 1957 1964

Note: In *Baseball Digest* (Dec.–Jan. 1961), Paul Richards complained about Walker throwing sliders, which caused him to lose control of his Curve, which Richards felt strongly was a better pitch.

LUKE WALKER 6'2" 190-pound lefty
45-47, 3.65, 9 Saves 1965 1974

Pitch Selection: 1. Fastball 2. Curve 3. Slider
Description: "Very good fast ball and curve. Throws slider."
Source: *Baseball Digest* (March 1967, "Official Scouting Reports on 1967 Major League Rookies")

DONNE WALL 6'1" 205-pound righty
31-28, 4.20, 2 Saves 1995 2002

Pitches: 1. Fastball (90) 2. Change 3. Slider 4. Splitter 5. Overhand Curve
Source: *The Scouting Notebook* (1999–2001)

Larry Dierker: "Donne didn't throw hard and didn't have a good breaking ball. He had to hit corners with his fastball and use his excellent change-up to be effective."
Source: *This Ain't Brain Surgery: How to Win the Pennant Without Losing Your Mind* (Dierker, 2003)

ED WALSH 6'1" 193-pound righty
195-126, 1.82, 34 Saves 1904 1917

Pitches: 1. Spitball 2. Fastball
3. Slow Ball (occasional)
4. Curve (*very* occasional)
Source: *Baseball's Famous Pitchers* (Ira L. Smith); *The National Game* (Alfred H. Spink, 1911 edition); see below for other sources.

Walsh: "Few outside of the players on the team know how much I use the [spitball] in actual games. Well, sometimes nine out of ten balls I throw are of that style of delivery."

Source: *Baseball Magazine* (February 1912, "The Spit Ball")

Walsh: "I have pitched two curves in seven years. Somehow or other I haven't missed them."
Source: *Baseball Magazine* (March 1913, F.C. Lane)

Walter Johnson: "Walsh, in my opinion, has solved the great secret of throwing the spit-ball. This secret, as I have observed it, is to throw a ball not over waist high. When it is thrown thus and thrown right, it breaks below a man's knee. Of course, it is not a strike at all in such a case, but in nine cases out of ten, when the batter sees a swift, erratic, spit-ball coming toward him with all the earmarks of a perfect strike, he will hit at it with his whole strength and be properly angry when the ball ducks his swing and dives below his knees. Walsh, it will be noticed, throws all his spit-balls low when he is in first-class pitching trim. It is then that he is so dreaded by all opposing batsmen on the diamond. That fast, breaking ball of his, which comes in with such terrific speed, and unerringly dives just as if it knew what it was about and tried to dodge the hitter's bat, is about the most tantalizing delivery in baseball. For it is the supreme recommendation of a spit-ball that while a batter's eye can always follow a straight ball and can, if trained acutely, follow a curve as well, it cannot follow a spit-ball at all when it is breaking good."
Source: *Baseball Magazine* (November 1913, F.C. Lane)

Quote from *The National Game:* "Walsh's great effectiveness as a pitcher consists mainly of his ability to pitch what is called the spit ball. He uses a trifle of slippery elm bark in his mouth and moistens a spot an inch square between the seams of the ball. His thumb he clinches tightly lengthwise on the opposite seam, and swinging his arm straight overhead with terrific force, he drives the ball straight at the plate. At times it will dart two feet down and out, depending upon the way his arm is swung . . . Sometimes Walsh is known as 'the spitball trust.' He uses the spitball more than any other man, and he is its best booster."

Sam Crawford on Walsh's overhand spitball: "I think that ball disintegrated on the way to the plate and the catcher put it back together again. I swear, when it went past the plate it was just the spit went by."
Source: *The Hurlers* (Kevin Kerrane, 1989)

Ty Cobb: " 'Ed' Walsh has one of the best [moves] in the American League, a move that has nipped many a runner and is so near a balk that players have frequently urged umpires to call it on him. Walsh will raise his shoulder slightly, an action that in most men is a sure sign they are going to deliver the ball to the batter, and then he swings and drives it to first base. It has caught many a runner flat footed. And the peculiar thing about it is that this move would not get a poor base runner who does not have sense enough to look for the little things. Walsh grabs off the best base runners in his league right along, in spite of the fact that his efficiency in this specialty is universally known."
Source: *Busting 'Em and Other Big League Stories* (Ty Cobb, ghostwritten by John Wheeler, 1914)

Clyde Milan: "Ed Walsh was, in my mind, the most successful pitcher I ever saw at catching the runner off first base, and this was owing largely to his bluff motion which was at least a half balk."
Source: *Baseball Magazine* (May 1914, F.C. Lane)

Comment: "New York scribes abused the Yankee batsmen for not 'waiting out' Ed Walsh's pitching. Two of them were criticized for swinging with the count three balls and one strike. Just why any hitter should wait on 'Big Ed' is not made clear. Mr. Walsh has been known to get three balls on a batter and then strike him out with three spitballs. The policy of the wise batsmen has always been to hit whatever Walsh serves up that is possible to hit. It's foolish to 'wait out' a pitcher whose control is as nearly perfect as Ed's. It would be equally foolish in the case of Mordecai Brown or Christy Mathewson."
Source: *Baseball Magazine* (January 1912, page 100)

Walsh on his spitball: "Some of these young pitchers give the spit ball a black eye by slobbering it all over. That isn't necessary. When I throw the spit ball I moisten a place on one side, no larger than a half dollar. But the time that ball gets to the fielders if it does, it is so nearly dried, that it wouldn't bother anyone."
Source: *Baseball Magazine* (June 1919, F.C. Lane, "Should the Spit Ball Be Abolished?")

BUCKY WALTERS 6'1" 180-pound righty
198-160, 3.30, 4 Saves 1934 1950

Pitches: 1. Sinker 2. Slider 3. Fastball 4. Curve 5. Knuckleball (occasional)

Sources: *Stan Musial: The Man's Own Story* (Musial with Bob Broeg, 1964); *Diamond Greats* (Rich Westcott, 1988); *Memories of a Ballplayer* (Bill Werber with C. Paul Rogers III, 2001); *Baseball Magazine* (September 1944, Ed Rumill article on knuckleball pitchers)
Quote from Werber: His sinker "bore in on right-handed hitters."

Description: "Walters is a sinker ball pitcher. It comes natural with him. His fast ball dips low and inside and is tricky. His curve is better than average. He has better control than his base on balls record indicates. He sometimes experiments around with his pitches, especially if he's out in front . . ."
Source: *Baseball Magazine* (October 1939, George Kirksey)

Note: Walters was taught to throw the slider by Chief Bender in 1935. At the time, neither Bender nor Walters had a name for the pitch, which later became known as the slider.
Source: unidentified newspaper clipping from April 1953 in *TSN* morgue

Quote: "In the National League the best sinker is that which Bucky Walters, of the Reds, serves up to annoy opposing batsmen."
Source: *Baseball Magazine* (July 1941, Edward T. Murphy)

DICK WARD 6'1" 198-pound righty
0-0, 3.00, 0 Saves 1934 1935

Key Pitch: Forkball
Source: *Baseball Digest* (Herbert Simons, "The 'V for Victory' Pitch")
Note: Ward pitched just briefly in the major leagues, but in 1933 he won 25 games in the Pacific Coast League.

DUANE WARD 6'4" 185-pound righty
32-37, 3.28, 121 Saves 1986 1995

Pitch Selection: 1. Fastball 2. Hard Slider
Source: *The Scouting Report: 1992*

MONTE WARD 5'9" 165-pound righty
164-102, 2.10, 3 Saves 1878 1884

Pitch Selection: 1. Hard Curve 2. Slow Curve 3. Change 4. Fastball
Note: Ward used a "spinning" delivery.
Source: *A Clever Base-Ballist: The Life and Times of John Montgomery Ward* (Bryan DiSalvatore, 1999)

JACK WARHOP 5'9" 168-pound righty
69-93, 3.12, 7 Saves 1908 1915

Pitch Selection: 1. Fastball 2. Curve 3. Change
Quote: "His underhand shoot has a peculiar whirl . . . His fast ball and curve, though fair, are not extraordinary, but the way he mixes them with his slow ball—combined with his extraordinary control—would make him a valuable asset to any club."
Source: *Baseball Magazine* (August 1915)

Description: "He is the speedy right-hander of the Highlanders . . ."
Source: *The National Game* (Alfred H. Spink, 1911)

LON WARNEKE 6'2" 185-pound righty
192-121, 3.18, 13 Saves 1930 1945

Pitch Selection, 1930–1935: 1. Fastball 2. Curve 3. Change 4. Screwball
Pitch Selection, 1936–1945: 1. Curve 2. Change 3. Fastball 4. Screwball 5. Knuckleball
Sources: *Baseball Magazine* (July 1949, Ed Rumill); Billy Herman in *Baseball Digest* (50th Anniversary, Page 39); countless articles in Hall of Fame clipping file. Phil Cavaretta gives a detailed (but not precisely accurate) description of Warneke's pitches in Peter Golenbock's *Wrigleyville* (1996). The source for the knuckleball note is that Warneke told Barney Kremenko of the *New York Journal American* (April, 1955), "I was a fast ball pitcher and I didn't have too good of a breaking curve." Warneke said that he worked hard to develop a knuckleball because he needed a breaking pitch, but never could master the knuckler.

Pitch Selection: 1. Fastball 2. Change
Description: "Warneke is a side-arm pitcher with a tendency to keep his fast ball low. It is a difficult target for the worried batter. Warneke makes it doubly difficult because, young as he is, he has mastered a most effective change of pace. He is one of those rare pitchers who, as his teammates unanimously affirm, 'Has everything.' "
Source: *Baseball Magazine* (November 1942, F.C. Lane)

Pitch Selection: 1. Curve 2. Fastball
Source: *Baseball Magazine* (July 1949, Ed Rumill)

JOHN WASDIN 6'2" 196-pound righty
31-30, 5.22, 3 Saves 1995 2003

Pitch Selection: 1. Fastball (mid-80s) 2. Curve
3. Slider
Source: *The Scouting Notebook: 1997*

Pitch Selection: 1. Fastball (90) 2. Slider 3. Change
Source: *The Scouting Notebook: 1999*

JARROD WASHBURN 6'1" 195-pound lefty
56-41, 3.96, 0 Saves 1998 2003

Pitch Selection: 1. Four-Seam Fastball 2. Slider
3. Change
Washburn: "I throw a four-seam fastball; I throw that probably 90 percent of the game. Once in a while it cuts, once in a while it sinks. I don't know which way it's going to go. It's just the luck of the draw.

I hope it moves one way or the other, and not go straight."
Sources: ESPN broadcast of Angels-Mariners game, 7/21/2002
Other Source: *The Scouting Notebook: 2002*

RAY WASHBURN 6'1" 205-pound righty
72-64, 3.53, 5 Saves 1961 1970

Pitch Selection: 1. Fastball 2. Slider
3. Curve (used beginning 1967 or '68)
Sources: *1963 Major League Handbook* (Don Schiffer); *The Sporting News* (7/2/1966, Neal Russo)

Notes: Schiffer wrote in 1963 that Washburn "must polish his curve and slider to match his priceless fast ball."

Russo wrote in 1966, when Washburn was near his prime, that he was "mixing an excellent slider with a fastball." In *Major League Baseball—1969*, Jack Zanger wrote that Washburn is "no longer a flamethrower (and) now depends on a hard slider and a slow curve."

Pitch Selection: 1. Hard Curve 2. Sinker
Source: Washburn in *Redbirds Revisited* (David Craft and Tom Owens, 1990)

GARY WASLEWSKI 6'4" 190-pound righty
11-26, 3.44, 5 Saves 1967 1972

Description: "Curve quite inconsistent in break and control. Fast ball average. Doubt whether he's a big league prospect."
Source: *Baseball Digest* (March 1967, "Official Scouting Reports on 1967 Major League Rookies")

ALLEN WATSON 6'1" 224-pound lefty
51-55, 5.03, 1 Save 1993 2000

Pitch Selection: 1. Fastball 2. Curve 3. Change
Source: *The Scouting Notebook 1998*

MULE WATSON 6'1½" 185-pound righty
50-53, 4.03, 4 Saves 1918 1924

Pitches: 1. Fastball 2. Slow Ball 3. Curve 4. Drop
5. Change of Pace
Source: Cardinals scout Bob Connery in *Baseball Magazine* (May 1917, W.R. Hoefer)

EDDIE WATT 5'10" 183-pound righty
38-36, 2.91, 80 Saves 1966 1975

Pitch Selection: 1. "Short Curve" (Slider)
2. Sinking Fastball 3. Curve 4. "Reverse Change"
5. Straight Change
Notes: Cal Ripken Sr. taught Watt to throw a slider at Aberdeen in 1964, and also taught him to vary his delivery to throw the hitter off stride. He sometimes threw three-quarters; sometimes overhand. These things made him a major-league pitcher.

Watt threw a unique "changeup," which was that when he was in trouble, he would throw *harder.* Everybody knows that you can't do that, you'll just get yourself in deeper trouble, but it worked for him.
Sources: Oscar Kahen in *The Sporting News* (May 1965); Ed Rumill in *The Christian Science Monitor* (8/19/1966)
Quote from Kahen: "Watt is not a 'blazeball' pitcher by any means. But he's cunning on the mound. He moves the ball around, seldom giving the batter two pitches alike."

GARY WAYNE 6'3" 200-pound lefty
14-14, 3.93, 4 Saves 1989 1994

Pitch Selection: 1. Fastball (mid-80s)
2. Split-Fingered Fastball (used as change)
Note: Threw with a herky-jerky delivery.
Source: *The Scouting Report: 1990*

Pitch Selection: 1. Fastball (high-80s)
2. Overhand Curve 3. Change

Note: Abandoned herky-jerky motion in 1992.
Source: *The Scouting Report: 1993*

DAVID WEATHERS 6'3" 205-pound righty
45-55, 4.49, 14 Saves 1991 2003

Pitches: 1. Sinking Fastball (low-90s)
2. Slider (low-80s) 3. Fastball 4. Change
Sources: *The Scouting Notebook* (1995, 1996, 2000, 2002, and 2003 editions)

JEFF WEAVER 6'5" 200-pound righty
51-63, 4.59, 2 Saves 1999 2003

Pitch Selection: 1. Fastball (low-90s) 2. Slider
3. Change
Sources: *The Scouting Notebook* (2000, 2002, and 2003 editions)

Note: After giving up a walk-off home run to Alex Gonzalez in Game 4 of the 2003 World Series, Weaver told reporters, "It was a sinker that ran back over and I was trying to go down and away. It just didn't go my way there. It's 3-2, I've got to go with my best pitch and that's my sinker."
Source: Anthony McCarron column in the New York *Daily News* (10/23/2003)

The Topps Company, Inc.

Jeff Weaver

JIM WEAVER 6'6" 230-pound righty
57-36, 3.88, 3 Saves 1928 1939

Pitches: 1. Forkball 2. Fastball 3. Curve (occasional)
Note: Weaver said he threw his forkball roughly a third of the time.
Source: *Baseball Magazine* (June 1936, F.C. Lane)

MONTE WEAVER 6'0" 170-pound righty
71-50, 4.36, 4 Saves 1931 1939

Pitch Selection: 1. Overhand Curve 2. Fastball
Sources: *Baseball Magazine* (February 1933, John J. Ward); *Who's Who in the Major Leagues* (1939 ed.); *Baseball Digest* (May 1992)
Ward in *Baseball Magazine:* "Curve and speed are all that I have. Change of pace would, no doubt, be valuable to me, but unfortunately, I have never been able to perfect a change of pace that was better than merely fair."
Quote from *Who's Who:* "One of the greatest curve-ball artists in the majors."

Quote: "Weaver pitches either sidearm or overhand and can throw his fast ball and curve both ways. 'It is a queer thing,' [he] says, 'but I threw curves long before I acquired a good fast ball.' "
Source: *Who's Who in Major League Baseball* (compiled by Harold "Speed" Johnson, 1933)

BRANDON WEBB 6'2" 228-pound righty
10-9, 2.84, 0 Saves 2003 2003

Pitches: 1. Sinker (84–90) 2. Curve 3. Change
Source: Joe Morgan during ESPN broadcast of Diamondbacks-Giants game, 8/31/2003.
Commentary: During the same game, Webb had an amazing streak ended: ninety-five straight outs, over the course of nearly a month, that were not recorded by an outfielder. Also, watching the broadcast it was apparent that Webb is particularly skilled at varying the speed on all three of his pitches, especially the sinker.

Description: "Webb is the rare pitcher who baffles hitters without changing speeds. More than 80% of his

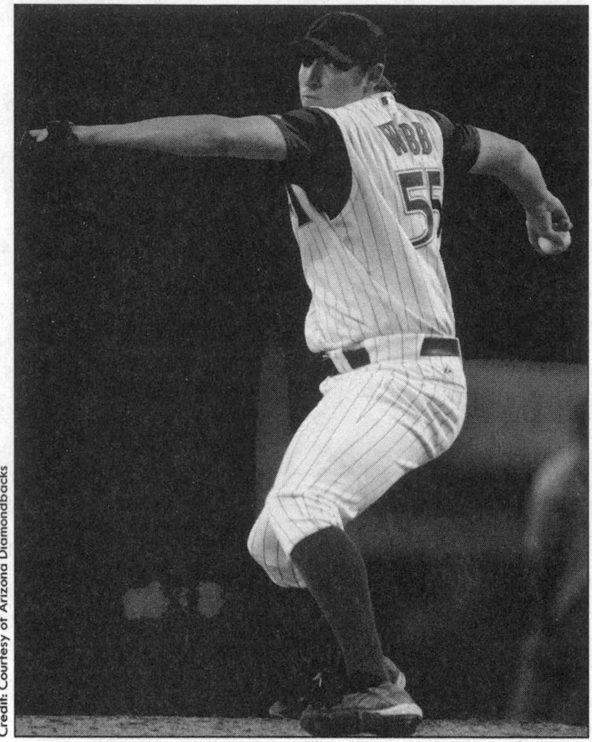

Credit: Courtesy of Arizona Diamondbacks

Brandon Webb

pitches are two-seam sinking fastballs that have so much movement that he hasn't had to throw many off-speed pitches. Webb doesn't throw particularly hard—he tops out in the low 90s—but his stuff is nasty. 'Big league hitters aren't dumb,' says first baseman Mark Grace. 'They know what's coming. They still can't touch him.' "
Source: *Sports Illustrated* (7/14/2003, Albert Chen)

MIKE WEGENER 6'4" 215-pound righty
8-20, 4.73, 0 Saves 1969 1970

Description: "Three-quarters delivery, live fast ball, fair curve. Worth watching."
Source: *Baseball Digest* (March 1967, "Official Scouting Reports on 1967 Major League Rookies")

BILL WEGMAN 6'5" 200-pound righty
81-90, 4.16, 2 Saves 1985 1995

Pitch Selection: 1. Fastball 2. Slider 3. Change
Sources: *The Scouting Report: 1987* and *1993*
Note: After arm trouble in 1989 Wegman's best pitch was probably his slider.

HERM WEHMEIER 6'2" 185-pound righty
92-108, 4.80, 9 Saves 1945 1958

Pitch Selection: 1. Fastball 2. Change 3. Curve
Source: *Baseball Magazine* (December 1950, Ed Rumill)
Notes: Listed by *The Sporting News* as having one of the best fastballs in the league, August 29, 1956 (which also confirms the change and curve.) Milt Richman in *Baseball Digest* (January 1951) says that Wehmeier (early in his career) "throws fast balls almost exclusively."

BOB WEILAND 6'4" 215-pound lefty
62-94, 4.24, 7 Saves 1928 1940

Key Pitch: Fastball
Source: *The Ballplayers* (1990, article by Jack Kavanaugh)

CARL WEILMAN 6'5" 187-pound lefty
85-95, 2.67, 10 Saves 1912 1920

Pitch Selection: 1. Fastball 2. Curve
Quote: "He had an ambition to pitch and put in a lot of time, practicing curves and benders . . . He has great speed and wonderful control, and his remarkable height makes his cross-fire delivery a very puzzling one."
Source: unidentified clipping from the Hall of Fame Library (February 1913)

JAKE WEIMER 5'11" 175-pound lefty
97-69, 2.23, 2 Saves 1903 1909

Pitch Selection: 1. Fastball 2. Curve
Sources: *The Sporting Life* (9/29/1906); unidentified clipping from the Hall of Fame Library
Quote from *The Sporting Life:* "[Weimer has] curveful cunning."
Quote from unidentified clipping: "He has no peer among the side-wheelers . . . [He has] more speed than a bullet and control that is marvelous."

BOB WELCH 6'3" 190-pound righty
211-146, 3.47, 8 Saves 1978 1994

Pitch Selection: 1. Fastball 2. Cut Fastball 3. Curve 4. Change 5. Welch developed a Forkball in 1988
Source: *The Scouting Report: 1990*

MICKEY WELCH 5'8" 160-pound righty
308-214, 2.71, 5 Saves 1880 1892

Pitch Selection: 1. Curves 2. Change 3. Fastball
Welch: "I was a little fellow, and I had to use my head. I studied the hitters and I knew how to pitch to all of them, and I worked hard to perfect my control. I had a pretty good fast ball, but I depended chiefly on change of pace and an assortment of curve balls."
Source: Welch quoted in *Baseball's First Stars* (SABR, 1996, article by Irv Bergman)

Description: "Facing the batsman, Welch advances the left foot, holding the ball at his breast. With a characteristic hop he shifts his weight from his right foot to the left, delivering the sphere in the act."
Source: Article titled "How Men Pitch Base-Ball: The Famous Pitchers of the National League of 1886." No author or publisher is given, though the information in the article is said to have come from photographic studies done by the *New York World* newspaper.

Description: "Welch, of the New Yorks, is always smiling. He plants his right foot forward and scrapes a pile of dirt, then expectorates, and a moment later wipes the perspiration from his brow, when suddenly he doubles himself up and throws with all his might. Batters say that he is the best pitcher in the league."
Source: Brooklyn *Daily Eagle* (11/25/1888), reprinted in *A Tale of Four Cities* (Jean-Pierre Caillault, 2003)

BOB WELLS 6'0" 180-pound righty
40-28, 5.03, 15 Saves 1994 2002

Pitch Selection: 1. Fastball 2. Slider 3. Change
Sources: *The Scouting Notebook: 1997; The Scouting Notebook 2000*

DAVID WELLS 6'3" 187-pound lefty
200-128, 4.06, 13 Saves 1987 2003

Pitches, early career: 1. Fastball (low-90s)
2. Overhand Curve 3. Slider
4. Change (used as starter; added about 1990)
Pitches, later career: 1. Sweeping Curve
2. Sinking Fastball (high-80s) 3. Change 4. Slider
Sources: *The Scouting Report* (1990, 1991, 1995, and 1996 editions); *The Scouting Notebook* (1995–2003 editions)

The Scouting Notebook: 2001: "There used to be two versions of Wells, both of which were equally effective. One featured a fastball in the 93–94 MPH range; the other used his pinpoint control to compensate for a fastball that peaked in the high-80s. It appears we've seen the last of the former version."

ED WELLS 6'1" 183-pound lefty
68-69, 4.65, 13 Saves 1923 1934

Pitches: 1. Fastball 2. Slow Curve/Change
3. Nickel Curve/Slider
Sources: Wells in *Cobb Would Have Caught It* (Richard Bak, 1991) and *Baseball Between the Wars* (Eugene Murdock, 1992)

Pitches: 1. Fastball 2. Slow Ball 3. Curve
Description: "Wells has an excellent fast ball, a fair curve, a better slow ball and still better control."
Source: *Baseball Magazine* (May 1927, F.C. Lane)

Comment: ". . . the sober minded Wells saw before he became a professional ballplayer that an effective slow ball was a disturbing element to most hitters. So he spent ten grim years developing this baffling ball. Today it is his most deceptive delivery. He throws it with exactly the same motion as a fast ball and a batter can never tell when it is coming. Therein lies its effectiveness. Many pitchers would have yielded to despondency and given up the idea of mastering a change of pace."
Source: *Baseball Magazine* (June 1931, Clifford Bloodgood)

CHRIS WELSH 6'2" 185-pound lefty
22-31, 4.45, 0 Saves 1981 1986

Pitch Selection: 1. Overhand Curve
2. Fastball (two-seam: 83–84; four-seam: 86)
3. Change
Welsh: "Sometimes I would cut the four-seamer in to righties. I threw a change-up with a weird split-finger/screwball grip with the pressure on my index finger. It was pretty effective vs. righties. I also threw a sharp breaking curve (over the top). I think this was the pitch that got me to the big leagues. I could throw it for strikes in most any count and it was a strikeout pitch in the minors but not so in the majors."
Source: e-mail correspondence between Welsh and Rob Neyer (4/29/2002)

TURK WENDELL 6'2" 180-pound righty
36-33, 3.85, 33 Saves 1993 2003

Pitch Selection: 1. Hard Slider 2. Softer Slider 3. Fastball 4. Change
Sources: *The Scouting Notebook: 1997; The Scouting Notebook 2000*

BUTCH WENSLOFF 5'11" 185-pound righty
16-13, 2.60, 1 Save 1943 1948

Pitch Selection: 1. Fastball 2. Curve 3. Knuckleball
Description: "Wensloff has more stuff than any other new pitcher in the major leagues. He is fast, has control, boasts a fine curve and mixes in a tough knuckler."
Source: *The Sporting News* (7/15/1943, Dan Daniel)

BILL WERLE 6'2" 182-pound lefty
29-39, 4.69, 15 Saves 1949 1954

Pitch Selection: 1. Curve 2. Fastball 3. Forkball
Werle: "I've added a fork ball to my curve and fast one which helps keep batters guessing . . . Most of my stuff is down around the hitter's knees—very few homers are hit off me—and with the swatters hitting most of the balls into the dirt, our great infield eats 'em up."
Source: *Pacific Coast Baseball News* (8/10/1948); Werle actually gave up a fair number of homers after he reached the majors the next season.

Key Pitch: Sinking Fastball
Note: Listed as a sidearm pitcher
Source: *How to Play Winning Baseball* (Arthur Mann, 1953); also Jack Brewer in *The San Francisco Seals, 1946–1957* (Brent Kelley, 2002) confirms that Werle's best pitch was the sinker.

Description: "One of the few pitchers around who occasionally throws underhanded. He . . . likes to experiment with many kinds of curves."
Source: *Baseball Digest* (January 1951, Milt Richman)

DAVID WEST 6'6" 247-pound lefty
31-38, 4.66, 3 Saves 1988 1998

Pitch Selection: 1. Fastball (high-80s) 2. Curve 3. Change
Source: *The Scouting Report: 1990*

JOHN WETTELAND 6'2" 195-pound righty
48-45, 2.93, 330 Saves 1989 2000

Pitches, 1992–93: 1. Fastball 2. Curve 3. Slider 4. Cut Fastball
Pitches, 1994–95: 1. Fastball 2. Slider 3. Curve
Pitches, 1996–99: 1. Fastball 2. Curve 3. Slider 4. Sinker 5. Change 6. Splitter
Sources: *The Scouting Report* (1993 and 1996 editions); *The 1995 Baseball Almanac; The Scouting Report* (1997 and 2000 editions)

Pitch Selection: 1. Fastball 2. Curve 3. Change
Source: *1993 Montreal Expos Media Guide*

GUS WEYHING 5'10" 145-pound righty
265-234, 3.89, 3 Saves 1887 1901

Pitch Selection: 1. Curve 2. Drop Curve
Source: *Misfits!* (J. Thomas Hetrick, 1991, relying on the *Washington Post* of 7/21/1899)

DOC WHITE 6'1" 150-pound lefty
187-156, 2.39, 5 Saves 1901 1913

Key Pitch: Drop Ball
Quote: "Doc White gave me trouble for a long time. He had a drop ball that fooled me continually. It broke very sharply and was apt to fool anybody who stood well up in the box . . . I discovered that this drop ball would travel two feet over the plate after it dropped."
Source: *Memories of Twenty Years in Baseball* (Ty Cobb, Page 112)

Key Pitch: Slow Ball
Source: *Touching Second* (Johnny Evers and Hugh Fullerton, 1910); *Baseball Magazine* (April 1913, "White Sox Notes")

GABE WHITE 6'2" 204-pound lefty
33-23, 4.26, 16 Saves 1994 2003

Pitch Selection: 1. Fastball 2. Sinker 3. Change
Source: *The Scouting Notebook: 1999*

Pitch Selection: 1. Fastball (90) 2. Change
Source: *The Scouting Notebook: 2002*

RICK WHITE 6'4" 230-pound righty
28-40, 4.17, 12 Saves 1994 2003

Pitches: 1. Fastball (low-90s) 2. Slider 3. Split-Fingered Fastball 4. Curve 5. Change

Sources: *The Scouting Notebook* (1995, 2000, 2002, and 2003 editions)

WILL WHITE 5'9" 175-pound righty
229-166, 2.28, 0 Saves 1877 1886

Key Pitch: Curve
Sources: letter from White's niece Ruth McKee to Lee Allen (9/6/1962); *Biographical Dictionary of American Sports: Baseball*
Quote from Ruth McKee's letter: "Uncle Will was the one to throw the first curved ball and [another relative has] some proof or story about it."
Quote from *Biographical Dictionary:* "By age 17, the right-hander had mastered the curve ball and could curve a ball around a post in the ground."

JOHN WHITEHEAD 6'2" 195-pound righty
49-54, 4.60, 4 Saves 1935 1942

Key Pitch: Fastball
Description: "His best ball, so he says, is his fast ball. This, he admits, isn't amazingly fast, but he mixes it up and employs good control."
Source: *Baseball Magazine* (March 1936, John J. Ward)

EARL WHITEHILL 5'9" 174-pound lefty
218-185, 4.36, 11 Saves 1923 1939

Pitches: 1. Curve 2. Fastball
Sources: *Baseball Magazine* (May 1925, "Comprising an interview with Earl Whitehill"); *Who's Who in the Major Leagues* (1937); Eddie Wells in *Cobb Would Have Caught It* (Richard Bak, 1991)
Whitehill in *Baseball Magazine:* "I was acquainted with [Johnny] Morrison before he came up to Pittsburgh. He had a very good curve in those days, but no doubt he has developed it since. I was particularly interested in his delivery for a curve is my own best bet in the pinch. In fact, I depend upon my curve much more than I do upon a fast ball."
Quote from *Who's Who* (1937): "He is considered the proprietor of the slickest left-handed curveball in the junior circuit."
Wells in *Cobb Would Have Caught It:* "[Whitehill] had a crackerjack of a curveball."

Key Pitch: Forkball
Source: *Who's Who in the American League* (1935 edition)

Transcendental Graphics / ruckerarchive.com

Jim Whitney

Quote: "Everybody insists the best of all windmills belonged to Earl Whitehill, the former Tiger."
Source: *Baseball Digest* (September 1947, Harry Sheer)

MATT WHITESIDE 6'0" 200-pound righty
18-15, 5.10, 9 Saves 1992 2001

Pitches: 1. Sinking Fastball (low-90s) 2. Slider 3. Change
Source: *The Scouting Report* (1993 and 1995 editions)

JIM WHITNEY 6'2" 172-pound righty
191-204, 2.97, 2 Saves 1881 1890

Key Pitch: Fastball
Source: *Nineteenth Century Stars* (SABR, 1989 article by Harold Dellinger)

ED WHITSON 6'3" 195-pound righty
126-123, 3.79, 8 Saves 1977 1991

Pitches, 1977–1982: 1. Fastball (88–90) 2. Slider 3. Curve 4. Palmball (occasional)
Pitches, 1983–1987: 1. Slider 2. Fastball (88–90) 3. Palmball (refined in 1983)
Pitches, 1988–1991: 1. Slider 2. Curve 3. Change 4. Fastball (several speeds)
Note: Whitson began to rely on his palmball in 1983, when he cut his finger on a soda can and didn't want to miss a start. However, he lost the feel for that pitch in the mid-'80s and apparently went to a more conventional change-up in the late '80s.
Sources: *The Scouting Notebook* (1983–1987 editions); *Tom Seaver's 1989 Scouting Notebook; The Scouting Report* (1990 and 1991 editions)

DAVE WICKERSHAM 6'3" 188-pound righty
68-57, 3.66, 18 Saves 1960 1969

Pitch Selection: 1. Screwball 2. Slider
3. Sinking Fastball
4. Fastball that rode in on a right-handed hitter
5. Slow Curve
Notes: Wickersham was taught to throw the Screwball by Willis Hudlin in 1961. Wickersham's fastballs were so-so, and he did not throw the hard curve that almost all starting pitchers of the 1960s leaned heavily upon. He kept an extensive book on opposing hitters, and used all four of his best pitches about the same amount. The slow curve was used mostly as a change.
Sources: *Kansas City Star* (June 1962, article by Joe McGuff); *The Sporting News* (4/6/1963, Joe McGuff); *The Sporting News* (6/6/1964, cover story by Joe Falls)

Wickersham: "At first, all I had were a sinker and a slider but Lopat showed me how to throw a screwball, exactly what I needed to win up here."
Comment: "The Tigers intended to use sidewheeling Dave solely in relief . . ."
Source: *1965 Official Baseball Almanac* (Bill Wise)

BOB WICKMAN 6'1" 207-pound righty
59-45, 3.68, 156 Saves 1992 2002

Pitch Selection: 1. Sinking Fastball 2. Slider 3. Cut Fastball (to lefties) 4. Change
Sources: *The Scouting Report: 1995; The Scouting Notebook 2000*

Description: "He throws a slider and is learning a change-up, but relies mostly on a fastball that has exceptional movement. Wickman snaps the pitch off his deformed index finger, the tip of which was cut off in a childhood accident."
Source: *Bill Mazeroski's Baseball* (1993 edition)

STUMP WIEDMAN 5'8" 165-pound righty
101-156, 3.60, 2 Saves 1880 1888

Key Pitch: Fastball
Quote: "He was a man of medium stature, but he had great speed and strength as a pitcher. He had in fact all of the skill possessed by the cleverest pitcher of to-day and wonderful command of the ball."
Source: *The National Game* (Alfred H. Spink, 1911)

Key Pitch: Drop Curve
Quote: "Weidman's delivery is characteristic, and marked by many little peculiarities. Facing second base, he pivots around on the left foot, executes a sort of pigeon-toed double-shuffle as he moves through the box, and lets the ball go with a round arm swing. With a man on base 'Weedy' watches the runner like a cat, facing the bag which is occupied and rarely allowing a steal. Like many other 'twirlers' he is partial to the 'drop curve.' "
Source: Article titled "How Men Pitch Base-Ball: The Famous Pitchers of the National League of 1886." No author or publisher is given, though the information in the article is said to have come from photographic studies done by the *New York World* newspaper.

BOB WIESLER 6'3" 188-pound lefty
7-19, 5.74, 0 Saves 1951 1958

Note: Listed by *The Sporting News* as having one of the best fastballs in the league, August 29, 1956, with the comment that he nonetheless experimented with a lot of off-speed stuff.

HENRY WIGGEN 6'3" 195-pound lefty
247-151, 3.26, 16 Saves 1951 1971

Pitches, early career: 1. Fastball 2. Screwball 3. Curve 4. Half-Speed Fastball (as Change)
Pitch Selection, late career: 1. Sharp Curve 2. Fastball

Sources: *The Southpaw* (Mark Harris, 1953); *It Looked Like For Ever* (Harris, 1979)

Note: On July 1, 1956, Wiggen struck out the side on nine pitches.
Source: *It Looked Like For Ever*

BILL WIGHT 6'1" 180-pound lefty
77-99, 3.95, 8 Saves 1946 1958

Key Pitch: Curve
Source: *Baseball Magazine* (July 1950, Hub Miller)

Description: "Wight didn't throw hard at all. He had one of the best pickoff moves to first."
Source: Bob Cain in *We Played the Game* (Danny Peary, 1994)

Note: Wight had the best pickoff move of his time, or one of the best, along with Parnell and Spahn.

MILT WILCOX 6'2" 185-pound righty
119-113, 4.07, 6 Saves 1970 1986

Pitch Selection: 1. Fastball 2. Slurve
3. Split-Fingered Fastball (added in 1981)
4. Knuckle Curve
Note: Wilcox threw a slider until 1981.
Source: *Inside Pitch* (Roger Craig)

HOYT WILHELM 6'0" 190-pound righty
143-122, 2.52, 227 Saves 1952 1972

Pitch Selection: 1. Knuckleball 2. Fastball 3. Curve
4. Slider
Source: *The Relief Pitcher* (John Thorn, 1979)

Description: "The ball sailed up, made a sudden small swerve, like a moth in a hallway, and flumped feebly into the catcher's glove . . . Wilhelm does not have to think too hard about his work, since he has no more idea than the batter which way the spinless ball will jump, and he delivers the pitch with approximately the same effort as a man tossing a pair of socks into a laundry hamper."
Source: Roger Angell in *The New Yorker* (4/13/1968)

Umpire Bill Kinnamon: "Hoyt Wilhelm was as tough as any pitcher who ever lived. He was so difficult to call because there wasn't any way his ball couldn't go. You never saw everything he had because the ball never did the same thing twice. When he released the ball, only the Good Lord knew where it was going. He never tried to finesse you—throw it low or throw it high, inside or outside. He just threw it right at the center of the plate, and the ball did whatever it did. You had to wait until after the catcher caught the ball before making the call. I've seen him throw balls that were head-high and then all of a sudden drop down for a strike. He was by far the best knuckleballer that ever lived."
Source: *The Men in Blue* (Larry Gerlach, 1980)

KAISER WILHELM 6'0" 162-pound righty
56-105, 3.44, 5 Saves 1903 1921

Pitch Selection: 1. Spitball
Source: *Baseball in Chicago* (SABR, 1986, article by Arthur R. Ahrens)

MARC WILKINS 5'11" 212-pound righty
19-14, 4.28, 3 Saves 1996 2001

Pitch Selection: 1. Fastball (low-90s) 2. Curve
3. Change
Source: *The Scouting Notebook: 1997*
Pitch Selection: 1. Sinking Fastball (low-90s) 2. Curve
3. Slider
Source: *The Scouting Notebook: 1998*

TED WILKS 5'9" 178-pound righty
59-30, 3.26, 46 Saves 1944 1953

Key Pitch: Fastball
Stan Musial: "He just poured it over the plate, making sure he had plenty on the ball. I still don't know of better pitching philosophy for a short-order man coming in from the bullpen with the ball game on the bases."
Source: *Stan Musial: The Man's Own Story* (Musial, as told to Bob Broeg, 1964)

Description: "Ted gives the batters something a little different. They never know what to expect. He may pitch overhand, sidearm, or come up with a submarine delivery. He thinks his sinker ball is best to serve left-handed batters in a pinch, and he prefers to sidearm to starboard swingers."
Source: *Baseball Magazine* (October 1949, Clifford Bloodgood)

ED WILLETT 6'0" 183-pound righty
102-99, 3.08, 5 Saves 1906 1915

Pitch Selection: 1. Sidearm Curve 2. Fastball 3. Underhand floater
Source: *Baseball Magazine* (May 1924, George Moriarty)
Note: Moriarty argues that the slow underhand pitch was extremely effective, and that Willett could have had a much better career had he been more willing to use it, but that Willett just insisted, despite the advice of teammates, on throwing the sidearm curve and fastball.

Comment: "No less an authority than the master batsman, Wee Willie Keeler, once opined that Willett could have ranked with the top-notchers if he had adhered exclusively to his under-handed stuff in the tight spots."
Source: George Moriarty in *Baseball Magazine* (September 1930, Moriarty's "Calling Them" column)

CARLTON WILLEY 6'0" 175-pound righty
38-58, 3.76, 1 Save 1958 1965

Key Pitch: Fastball
Quote: "Willey has a terrific fast ball. He's a lot smaller than [Joey] Jay, but he's faster. He doesn't use a slider. He can win without it. The main thing for Carl is to work on improving what he's got. He's really learned how to pitch."
Source: Braves pitching coach Whitlow Wyatt in *Sport* (April 1959, Dick Schaap)

AL WILLIAMS 6'4" 190-pound righty
35-38, 4.24, 2 Saves 1980 1984

Pitch Selection: 1. Curve 2. Fastball (high-80s) 3. Change
Sources: *The Scouting Report: 1983* and *1984*

BRIAN WILLIAMS 6'3" 230-pound righty
26-38, 5.37, 6 Saves 1991 2000

Pitch Selection: 1. Fastball 2. Curve 3. Slider 4. Change 5. Circle Change
Source: *The Scouting Report: 1993*

Pitch Selection: 1. Fastball (91–93) 2. Slider 3. Curve 4. Straight Change
Source: *The Scouting Notebook: 2000*

DAVE WILLIAMS 167-pound lefty
0-0, 5.30, 0 Saves 1902 1902

Note: According to Dick Thompson in the 1996 *Baseball Research Journal*, Williams, who pitched only 17 innings in the major leagues, taught Christy Mathewson to throw the fadeaway.

FRANK WILLIAMS 6'1" 205-pound righty
24-14, 3.00, 8 Saves 1984 1989

Pitch Selection: 1. Fastball 2. Curve
Note: Throws with a sidearm delivery.
Source: *The Scouting Report: 1985*

LEFTY WILLIAMS 5'9" 160-pound lefty
82-48, 3.13, 5 Saves 1913 1920

Pitch Selection: 1. Fastball 2. Slow Ball 3. Curve
Source: *The Great Baseball Mystery* (Victor Luhrs, 1966)

MIKE WILLIAMS 6'2" 190-pound righty
32-54, 4.45, 144 Saves 1992 2003

Pitches, 1999–2002: 1. Slider 2. Fastball (88–91) 3. Change 4. Sinker
Quote: "After struggling as a starter earlier in his career with Philadelphia, Williams has thrived as a reliever, relying on his sharp-breaking slider, which he throws with a curveball grip. He's mastered the slider to the point where he adeptly changes speeds and breaks with it . . . He became more effective last season because he started throwing more fastballs to righthanded hitters, while using more changeups against lefthanders."
Source: *The Scouting Notebook: 2003*
Other Sources: *The Scouting Notebook* (2000 and 2002 editions)

MITCH WILLIAMS 6'3" 180-pound lefty
45-58, 3.63, 192 Saves 1986 1997

Pitches: 1. Fastball 2. Hard Slider
Note: Williams did not throw exceptionally hard, but hid the ball extremely well. Batters could not pick the

ball up coming out of his hand, and often thought that he was throwing much harder than he actually was.
Source: *The Scouting Report: 1992*

SMOKEY JOE WILLIAMS 6'4" 190-pound righty
NEGRO LEAGUES 1905 1932

Pitch Selection: 1. Fastball 2. Slider (Nickel Curve) 3. Change
Quote from semipro catcher Robert Berman, who supposedly saw Williams and Johnson in their primes: "Joe Williams had the physique of Walter Johnson. Tall, beautifully built, long arms. Very, very fast. Weight about 205; Walter only weighed about 197–198 . . . I think Johnson was faster than Williams. But what made Williams appear fast was the fact he had other pitches too. Johnson didn't start throwing a curve until the middle '20s. Everybody knew what he was throwing. Joe had a combination of pitches—a curve, a change-up, and a fast ball . . . It gripes me when the papers claim that Satchel Paige was the fastest black pitcher that ever lived. Smokey Joe Williams, to my mind, was the fastest."
Quote from catcher Sam Streeter: "They talk about Satchel and them throwing hard, but I think Joe threw harder. It used to take two catchers to hold him. By the time the fifth inning was over, that catcher's hand would be all swollen. He'd have to have another catcher back there the rest of the game . . . He pitched just like Don Larsen, right from the shoulder. He didn't twist or anything.
Source: *Blackball Stars* (John Holway, 1988)

STAN WILLIAMS 6'5" 230-pound righty
109-94, 3.48, 43 Saves 1958 1972

Pitch Selection with Dodgers: 1. Fastball 2. Slider 3. Spitball
Sources: *Pennant Race* (Jim Brosnan, 1962); *Glory Days with the Dodgers* (John Roseboro with Bill Libby, Page 196); *We Played the Game* (Danny Peary, 1994)
Pitches, during late-career comeback: 1. Fastball 2. Curve 3. Slider 4. Screwball
Source: *Major League Baseball—1969* (Jack Zanger)

WOODY WILLIAMS 6'0" 180-pound righty
92-76, 4.04, 0 Saves 1993 2003

Pitch Selection: 1. Four-Seam Fastball 2. Cut Fastball 3. Curve 4. Slider 5. Change
Source: *The Scouting Notebook 2000*

MARK WILLIAMSON 6'0" 177-pound righty
46-35, 3.86, 21 Saves 1987 1994

Pitch Selection: 1. Fastball (88–89) 2. Slider 3. Palmball
Source: *The Scouting Report: 1990*

SCOTT WILLIAMSON 6'0" 185-pound righty
25-23, 3.13, 54 Saves 1999 2003

Pitches: 1. Fastball (mid-90s) 2. Slider (high-80s) 3. Split-Fingered Fastball 4. Change (occasional)
Note: Williamson learned his splitter from Bruce Sutter's son, his roommate at Tulane.
Sources: Ross Porter during broadcast of Dodgers-Reds game (8/1/2002); FOX broadcast of 2003 ALCS Game 3; *The Scouting Notebook: 2000*

CARL WILLIS 6'4" 213-pound righty
22-16, 4.25, 13 Saves 1984 1995

Pitch Selection: 1. Split-Fingered Fastball 2. Fastball 3. Change
Quote: "Wills relies on a split-fingered fastball that some opposing hitters have accused of being a spitter."
Source: *The Scouting Report: 1993*

DONTRELLE WILLIS 6'4" 195-pound righty
14-6, 3.30, 0 Saves 2003 2003

Pitches: 1. Fastball (low-90s) 2. Change (low-80s) 3. Slider (low-80s)
Description: "At the apex of Dontrelle Willis' delivery, his right foot is nose high, his right knee just below his chin. His chest and head are twisted so that he is facing right field, his eyes aimed upward. His intention is to throw the ball in almost the complete opposite direction, where he is not looking. The hitter cannot see the ball at this instant; the ball is only a part of the hitter's imagination. It is hidden, behind Willis' shoulder, behind his head, inside of his glove, and the hitter won't see the

Florida Marlins, Denis Bancroft

Florida Marlins, Denis Bancroft

Dontrelle Willis

ball until Willis' delivery begins to unravel—the feet, the legs, the hands and the glove, all exploding at the hitter. Then the hitter finally sees the ball. By then, it's almost too late to do anything about it."
Source: Buster Olney at ESPN.com, 6/17/2003

RON WILLIS 6'2" 185-pound righty
11-12, 3.32, 19 Saves 1966 1970

Description: "Sidearm delivery. Shows sinker at times."
Source: *Baseball Digest* (March 1967, "Official Scouting Reports on 1967 Major League Rookies")

VIC WILLIS 6'2" 185-pound righty
248-208, 2.63, 11 Saves 1898 1910

Pitch Selection: 1. Slow Curve 2. Slow Ball
Sources: *The Boston Braves* (Harold Kaese, 1948); *Baseball Research Journal* 18 (article by Stephen Cunerd); *Touching Second* (Johnny Evers and Hugh Fullerton, 1910)

BILL WILSON 6'2" 195-pound righty
9-15, 4.22, 17 Saves 1969 1973

Key Pitch: Slider
Description: "Control is best asset so could make it as relief pitcher. Comes in with good slider."
Source: *Baseball Digest* (March 1967, "Official Scouting Reports on 1967 Major League Rookies")

DON WILSON 6'2" 195-pound righty
104-92, 3.15, 2 Saves 1966 1974

Pitch Selection: 1. Fastball 2. Hard Slider 3. Curve 4. Change
Sources: *The Sporting News* (six articles by John Wilson: 11/18/1967, 7/27/1968, 10/12/1968, 1/31/1970, 1/2/1971, and 6/12/1971); *Christian Science Monitor* (January 1974, article by Larry Bortstein); *The No-Hit Hall of Fame* (Rich Coberly, 1985)

Commentary: Wilson had many spectacular games in his career—two no-hitters, an 18-strikeout effort, other great games. In most of his best games, Wilson threw nothing or almost nothing but fastballs. His fastball was fast, about 93, and it had fantastic movement—sometimes diving, sometimes sailing, sometimes breaking sharply out on a right-handed hitter. When his fastball was moving, he just aimed for the middle of the plate and threw fastballs. Although he experimented with a curve and a changeup from 1967 until his death, neither of these pitches ever amounted to much. He did have to rely on off-speed pitches in 1970, when he had arm trouble, and did surprisingly well.

EARL WILSON 6'3" 216-pound righty
121-109, 3.69, 0 Saves 1959 1970

Pitch Selection: 1. High Fastball 2. Marginal Curve
Sources: *The Ballplayers* (1990, article by Morris Eckhouse), *Baseball Digest* (March 1960, Page 8)
Note: Mentioned by *Sports Illustrated* (6/3/1963) as possibly throwing a spitball.

Late-career Quote: "Earl pitches more with his head these days than his arm . . . He sticks mostly to his slider and curve, using the fastball as his off-speed pitch."
Source: *Major League Baseball—1969* (Jack Zanger)

JACK WILSON 5'11" 210-pound righty
68-72, 4.59, 20 Saves 1934 1942

Pitch Selection: 1. Fastball 2. Curve
3. Knuckleball (added in 1940)
Sources: Henry P. Edwards, American League Service Bureau (12/26/1937); *The Sporting News* (2/20/1941, Carl T. Felker)
Source for Knuckleball citation: *The Sporting News* (2/27/1941, Jack Malancy)
Note: Edwards described Wilson's fast ball as "sensational," and says that Wilson "blazed his fast one by 137 batsmen." *TSN* source also says that Wilson had an outstanding fastball. He did not throw a curve when he first reached the majors, but was taught to throw one by Herb Pennock at Syracuse in 1935.

JIM WILSON 6'1" 200-pound righty
86-89, 4.01, 2 Saves 1945 1958

Pitches: 1. Slider 2. Slow Curve 3. Slip Pitch
4. Other Curve Ball
Sources: Dave Philley and Bill Wight in *From 33rd Street to Camden Yards: An Oral History of the Baltimore Orioles* (John Eisenberg, 2001); *The Milwaukee Braves* (Bob Buege, 1988)

Pitch Selection: 1. Fastball 2. Sharp Curve 3. Change
Quote: "Many believe Jim's live fast ball is responsible for his winning efforts. According to Paul Richards, Seattle skipper, Wilson does have a good fast ball but his success is due to the ability to mix his fast ball with a sharp curve and change-of-pace pitch thus getting the batter off-stride and guessing. A hitter can't get set for Wilson because the pitcher has so much variety plus good control . . . an unbeatable combination."
Source: *Pacific Coast Baseball News* (7/25/1950)

Note: In 1956 (May issue), *Sport* published the results of a poll in which players on all sixteen major-league teams were asked which pitchers threw a spitball. Fifteen pitchers were mentioned, and Wilson drew the most "support" among the American Leaguers.

STEVE WILSON 6'4" 224-pound lefty
13-18, 4.40, 6 Saves 1988 1993

Pitches: 1. Fastball 2. Change 3. Curve
Source: *The Scouting Report* (1990 and 1993 editions)

TREVOR WILSON 6'0" 192-pound lefty
41-46, 3.87, 0 Saves 1988 1998

Pitch Selection: 1. Fastball 2. Hard Slider
Source: *The Scouting Report: 1990*

Pitch Selection: 1. Fastball 2. Curve 3. Slider
4. Change
Source: *The Scouting Report: 1992*

HOOKS WILTSE 6'0" 185-pound lefty
139-90, 2.47, 34 Saves 1904 1915

Key Pitch: Curve
Sources: *New York Times* (2/26/1955, Arthur Daley); unidentified (typewritten) article in Wiltse's file in TSN morgue (1938); *Baseball in the Big Leagues* (Johnny Evers, Page 104)

Comment: There are some side-arm left-hand pitchers, but few of them ever have found that they could last in the major leagues. One of the most notable of that type was Wiltse of the Giants . . . he used a side-arm delivery with much success."
Source: *How to Pitch* (J. E. Wray, 1928)

Description: "Some pitchers have a peculiar hook delivery, a species of curve which owes its chief baffling influence to the fact that it comes from an unexpected angle while the eye is deceived by a complicated windup motion. Wiltse of the Giants is generally known as Hooks on account of his delivery . . . Needless to say, the pitchers who are proficient at this art are left-handers."
Source: *Baseball Magazine* (November 1913, F.C. Lane)

Quote: "McGraw will risk Wiltse against left-handers who bunt or slug, and will send him against right-handers who play a hurry-up game. He will not try Wiltse on any team, left or right-handed, that does the waiting act and dawdles at the plate, for Wiltse is slender and none too muscular. He must win quickly or not at all."
Source: W.A. Phelon in *Baseball Magazine* (November 1910)

GEORGE WINTER 5'8" 132-pound righty
83-102, 2.87, 4 Saves 1901 1908

Pitches: 1. Fastball 2. Drop Ball 3. Outcurve
4. Fadeaway
Description: "He had great speed from start to finish, a sharp drop and B and O curves in plenty." An O curve was possibly an "Outcurve," a common term at the time. I have taken the term "B curve" to mean a back curve, a fadeaway, but this could be incorrect.
Source: *The Sporting News* (4/4/1943, Don Basenfelder)
Note: The thirteen-page, typewritten original of the Basenfelder article can be found in the TSN morgue, and is an invaluable source of information about this otherwise forgotten pitcher, who was a college roommate and lifelong friend of Eddie Plank. There is also a fascinating story, completely unknown, about behind-the-scenes wrangling over the money from the first World Series, and a humorous anecdote about the 131-pound Winter pitching his first major-league game in oversized borrowed shoes and a uniform borrowed from Cy Young, who weighed about 220 at the time.

Winter also claims that when the American League first introduced the cork center baseball, it would get lopsided after it was hit a couple of times, and would curve like a son of a gun, and often would break erratically even when the pitcher threw a fastball.

NIP WINTERS 6'5" 225-pound lefty
NEGRO LEAGUES 1920 1933

Pitch Selection: 1. Curve 2. Fastball
Source: *The Biographical Encyclopedia of the Negro Baseball Leagues* (James A. Riley, 1994)

RICK WISE 6'1" 180-pound righty
188-181, 3.69, 0 Saves 1964 1982

Pitch Selection: 1. Fastball 2. Curve 3. Slider
4. Change
Sources: Wise in *Splendor on the Diamond* (Rich Westcott, 2000); *The Sporting News* (6/26/1976, Larry Whiteside)

BOBBY WITT 6'2" 190-pound righty
142-157, 4.83, 0 Saves 1986 2001

Pitch Selection: 1. Fastball 2. Slider 3. Curve
4. Split-Fingered Fastball (added about 1994)
5. Change
Note: A sinker added in 1996 was his best pitch in that season, when he won 16 games. About 1998 he began using his splitter as a change, calling it a "split-change."
Sources: *The Scouting Report: 1987; The Scouting Report: 1990; The Scouting Report: 1995; The Scouting Notebook 1997; The Scouting Notebook 2000*

GEORGE WITT 6'3" 185-pound righty
11-16, 4.32, 0 Saves 1957 1962

Pitches: 1. Fastball 2. Curve 3. Change
Chuck Dressen: "He could win in the majors right now. He's got one of the smoothest deliveries I've seen in a long time."
Source: *The Sporting News* (8/14/1957, Frank Finch)

Notes: According to a Pirates press release, in 1957 Witt threw 58⅓ consecutive innings without allowing an earned run, while pitching for the Hollywood Stars in the PCL.

As a rookie with the Pirates in 1958, Witt went 9-2 with a 1.61 ERA in 106 innings. The rest of his career, he was 2-14 with a 6.66 ERA in 123 innings.

MIKE WITT 6'7" 185-pound righty
117-116, 3.83, 6 Saves 1981 1993

Pitch Selection: 1. Hard Curve 2. Fastball 3. Change
Note: Witt threw over the top.

Sources: *The Scouting Report: 1987; The Scouting Report: 1990*

MARK WOHLERS 6'4" 207-pound righty
39-29, 3.97, 119 Saves 1991 2002

Pitch Selection: 1. Fastball 2. Slider
3. Split-Fingered Fastball
Source: *The Scouting Notebook 1998*

RANDY WOLF 6'0" 194-pound lefty
54-48, 4.10, 0 Saves 1999 2003

Pitch Selection: 1. Fastball (high-80s) 2. Change
3. Curve
Source: *The Scouting Notebook: 2000*

ROGER WOLFF 6'0" 208-pound righty
52-69, 3.41, 13 Saves 1941 1947

Pitch Selection: 1. Knuckleball 2. Fastball
3. Slider (added in 1945)
Sources: *The Crooked Pitch* (Martin Quigley, 1984); *The Washington Post* (4/16/1946, Shirley Povich column)
Source for Slider: *The Sporting News* (3/19/1947, Page 8); in 1945, the slider might have been one of Wolff's two best pitches, along with the knuckleball.

MELLIE WOLFGANG 5'9" 160-pound righty
15-14, 2.18, 0 Saves 1914 1918

Key Pitch: Spitball
Source: *The 1917 White Sox* (Warren N. Wilbert and William C. Hageman, 2003)

JOE WOOD 5'11" 180-pound righty
116-57, 2.03, 11 Saves 1908 1920

Pitch Selection: 1. Fastball 2. Curve
3. Slow Ball (occasional)
Sources: 1914 booklet edited by Irving M. Howe, titled "Pitching Course"; *Baseball Magazine* (November 1912, John J. Ward; and January 1916, F. C. Lane)
Wood in *Pitching Course:* "I sometimes use a curve ball, but the occasions are rare, indeed, and it is effective only for the reason that I have established a reputation as a pitcher of a fast ball . . . Perhaps I throw a curve ball once in ten times."
Ward in 1912 *Baseball Magazine:* "Wood has tremendous speed. He pitches with an over-arm motion; Johnson generally with a side-arm motion. Wood is faultlessly clever, brilliantly fast, a marvel of pitching grace."
Walter Johnson in 1916 *Baseball Magazine:* "When I used to see Wood pitch, although I admired his speed and control, it made my own shoulders ache to watch his delivery. That pitching with the arm alone, that wrenching of the muscles in the shoulder, would wear out my arm, I am sure, much quicker than the easy, swinging motion I always aim to use."

Comment: "Joe Wood . . . has always been troubled by his slow ball. Wood has a slow ball which is very effective at times, but, like Johnson, experiences difficulty in controlling it."
Source: *Baseball Magazine* article about Jean Dubuc (January 1913, F.C. Lane)

KERRY WOOD 6'5" 225-pound righty
59-41, 3.62, 0 Saves 1998 2003

Pitch Selection: 1. Fastball (high-90s) 2. Curve
3. Slider 4. Change
Source: *The Scouting Notebook: 1999*

Pitch Selection: 1. Fastball 2. Curve 3. Cut Fastball
4. Slider 5. Fosh Change
Source: *The Scouting Notebook: 2002*

SPADES WOOD 5'10" 150-pound lefty
6-9, 5.61, 0 Saves 1930 1931

Key Pitch: Curve
Ray Kremer: "Wood, of our own club, has a great curve, a remarkable curve, but he can't always get it over the plate."
Source: *Baseball Magazine* (1930)

WILBUR WOOD 6'0" 180-pound lefty
164-156, 3.24, 57 Saves 1961 1978

Pitch Selection: 1. Knuckleball 2. Fastball 3. Curve
Source: *Baseball Stars of 1973* (article by William Barry Furlong)

Description: "Everything about Wilbur Wood is disarming. On the mound, he displays a comfortable expanse of tum and the stiffish-looking knees of a confirmed indoorsman, and thus resembles a left-handed accountant or pastry chef on a Sunday outing. Even the knuckler—

which he throws, sensibly, on nearly every pitch—looks almost modest, for it does not leap and quiver like Hoyt Wilhelm's old hooked trout."
Source: Roger Angell in *The New Yorker* (1973, reprinted in *Five Seasons,* 1977)

STEVE WOODARD 6'4" 210-pound righty
32-36, 4.94, 0 Saves 1997 2003

Pitch Selection: 1. Fastball 2. Curve 3. Change
Source: *The Scouting Notebook: 1999*

Pitch Selection: 1. Two-Seam Fastball (high-80s) 2. Four-Seam Fastball (high-80s) 3. Change 4. Curve
Source: *The Scouting Notebook: 2001*

HAL WOODESHICK 6'3" 200-pound lefty
44-62, 3.56, 61 Saves 1956 1967

Pitch Selection: 1. Sinking Fastball 2. Curve 3. Slider
Source: *The Sporting News* (7/27/1963, Page 3)

Comment: "Strictly a fastballer at one time, he started to throw a curve in earnest in 1962, and is now an artist at low snapping hooks."
Source: *Don Schiffer's Major League Baseball Handbook—1964*

TIM WORRELL 6'4" 210-pound righty
39-49, 3.90, 45 Saves 1993 2003

Pitch Selection: 1. Fastball 2. Slider
Source: *The Scouting Notebook: 1997*

TODD WORRELL 6'5" 215-pound righty
50-52, 3.09, 256 Saves 1985 1997

Pitch Selection: 1. Fastball 2. Slider 3. Change
Source: *The Scouting Report: 1990*

AL WORTHINGTON 6'2" 195-pound righty
75-82, 3.39, 110 Saves 1953 1969

Pitch Selection: 1. Slider 2. Fastball
Sources: *New York Times* (July 1953, Arthur Daley); *Sport* (September 1957, Page 72)

Pitches, 1964: 1. Knuckleball 2. Sidearm Curve (to right-handed hitters) 3. Overhand Curve (to left-handed hitters) 4. Sliding Fastball
Source: *The Sporting News* (8/29/1964, Max Nichols)

Description: "Worthington is a rarity among pitchers: his fastball is a natural slider. It drops and curves into left-handed batters and away from right-handers. That natural gift, though, has been both a curse and a blessing for many years."
Source: *Sport* (December 1965, John Devaney)

CLYDE WRIGHT 6'1" 180-pound lefty
100-111, 3.50, 3 Saves 1966 1975

Pitch Selection: 1. Fast Curve 2. Slow Curve 3. Fastball 4. Wright developed a Screwball prior to the 1970 season, and used that as a change.
Sources: *The Sporting News* (7/2/1966, Ross Newhan); *The No-Hit Hall of Fame* (Rich Coberly, 1985); *Major League Baseball: 1971* (Brenda Zanger and Dick Kaplan)

JAMEY WRIGHT 6'5" 203-pound righty
51-69, 5.15, 0 Saves 1996 2003

Pitch Selection: 1. Sinker (low-90s) 2. Slider 3. Curve 4. Straight Change
Sources: *The Scouting Notebook* (1998, 2000–2003 editions)

Description: "Wright's pitches have so much movement that he's tough to hit even when he's behind in the count. However, he often finds himself in that situation, which is one downside of his pitches' tremendous life. With a 90-MPH sinker, a tight slider, hard curveball and changeup, Wright gets tons of groundballs and is tough to take deep . . ."
Source: Mat Olkin in *The Scouting Notebook 2002*

JARET WRIGHT 6'2" 230-pound righty
37-37, 5.68, 2 Saves 1997 2003

Pitch Selection: 1. Fastball (mid-90s) 2. Slider 3. Slow Curve 4. Change 5. Splitter (developed in 2003)
Sources: *The Scouting Notebook 1998; The Scouting Notebook 2000;* discussion with Portland Beavers broadcaster Rich Burk (7/7/2003, Rob Neyer)

RASTY WRIGHT 5'11" 160-pound righty
24-19, 4.05, 5 Saves 1917 1923

Key Pitch: Knuckleball
Source: *The 1922 St. Louis Browns* (Roger A. Godin, 1991)

JOHN WYATT 5'11" 200-pound righty
42-44, 3.47, 103 Saves 1961 1969

Key Pitch: Fastball
Quote: "Wyatt's big pitch is his fast ball and when he's right he's willing to challenge anyone in the league with it. At the same time he is also working on a curve and slider and they have been of help to him.

" 'The side-arm curve has helped me a lot,' Wyatt said. 'Lopat got me to throw it and gave me confidence in it. When the right-handed hitters start digging in on me that side-arm curve makes 'em stop and think.

" 'I don't like to throw my regular curve ball much on 3 and 2 because I still hang it too much and if I'm going to get beat I want to get beat with my best pitch. I have confidence in my fast ball. When I've had my good fast ball I've only had one home run hit against it all year.' "
Source: *The Kansas City Star* (8/9/1962, Joe McCuff)

Pitch Selection: 1. "Forkball" 2. Fastball
Notes: Wyatt's "forkball" was almost certainly a spitball or a Vaseline ball.
Sources: *Major League Baseball: 1966* (Jack Zanger); *Major League Baseball: 1967* (Jack Zanger); *Major League Baseball: 1968* (Jack Zanger)

WHIT WYATT 6'1" 185-pound righty
106-95, 3.79, 13 Saves 1929 1945

Pitch Selection: 1. Rising Fastball 2. Slow Curve 3. Slider
Notes: Wyatt learned the slider in 1934, but did not know what to call it at the time. In 1958, while coaching for the Braves, Wyatt helped Warren Spahn refine his slider. (See also Dick Donovan.)
Sources: *Stan Musial* (Musial with Bob Broeg, 1964); *Dodger Classics* (Bob Tiemann, 1983); January 1964 article by Sandy Grady, unidentified newspaper, *TSN* morgue, *Baseball Digest* (July 1950, Page 60); *Super Stars of Baseball* (Bob Broeg, 1971)
Wyatt in *Baseball Digest* article: "My slow curve was the pitch that had brought me back to the major leagues [in 1939 with the Dodgers]."

Umpire Lee Ballanfant: "Whitlow Wyatt was the best competitor. He went out there with blood in his eye and a frown on his face, and he never cracked a smile during that ball game—he was there to *beat* you."
Source: *The Men in Blue* (Larry Gerlach, 1980)

JOHN WYCKOFF 6'1" 175-pound righty
23-34, 3.55, 3 Saves 1913 1918

Key Pitch: Curve
Source: 1915 *Reach Guide* (Page 93)

EARLY WYNN 6'0" 190-pound righty
300-244, 3.54, 15 Saves 1939 1963

Pitches, pre-1949: 1. Fastball 2. Change 3. Knuckleball (occasional) 4. Curve (occasional) 5. Blooper (occasional)
Pitches, post-1948: 1. Fastball 2. Curve 3. Change 4. Slider 5. Knuckleball
Sources: See below.

Description: "He pitches more like Red Ruffing than anybody else. Chunky like Ruffing and sneaky-fast like Ruffing. He still doesn't have much of a curve, but he has come up with something else just about as valuable, a clever letup ball."
Source: *Baseball Digest* (March 1944, Shirley Povich)

Description: "He could throw a fast ball from the time he reported to the Washington club. In later years he came up with not only a curve, but also a change of pace and even a blooper ball that Buck Newsom taught him."
Source: *Baseball Digest* (April 1948, Shirley Povich)

Quote: ". . . I'll tell you something, he didn't become a real good pitcher until we traded him to Cleveland. When he pitched for me in the early forties, he had a good fastball, but that was it. When he went to Cleveland, Mel Harder got hold of him and taught him how to throw the good curveball and change-up, and that's when Early became a great pitcher."
Source: Ossie Bluege in *The Man in the Dugout* (Donald Honig, 1977)

Quote: "We got Early Wynn from Washington in 1949 and he was strictly a fastball and knuckleball pitcher. Those are the pitches he relied on. When he joined Cleveland, Early and I talked quite a bit. I told him he had to throw the curveball and a change-up and forget about the knuckleball. So he ended up being quite a pitcher because he improved so quickly."
Source: Mel Harder in *Voices from the Pastime* (Nick Wilson, 2000)

Wynn: "I didn't have [a curveball] till I got to Cleveland [in 1949] and Mel Harder showed me how to throw one . . .

"Whenever I tried to throw a curve, I'd come up with a nothing ball, a bad slider. So I was just throwing fast balls and change-ups. I had the knuckler, but I just threw it on the sidelines. That's another pitch I didn't really use until I got to Cleveland."
Source: *Sport* (March 1956, Roger Kahn); it's unlikely that this was literally true. Wynn probably did have a curveball before he went to the Indians, but it probably wasn't worth much.

Description: "Here's a guy who has gone 'cute' in the past two seasons. He always changes speeds, works the corners carefully and keeps the batters guessing. His curve ball is of the ten cent variety."
Source: *Baseball Digest* (January 1951, Milt Richman)

Quote: "I caught Early in '52 and I know that he threw a curve, fast ball, knuckler, slider, sinker, and a change of speed."
Source: *20 Years Too Soon* (Quincy Trouppe, Page 243)

Description: "Wynn throws all the pitches—knucklers, sliders, curves and fast balls—and he keeps the ball high. This is exactly what young pitchers are told not to do."
Source: *Sports Illustrated* (9/28/1959)

Quote: "Wynn got by for a long time on a fast ball, a change-up and a two-penny curve. Later he developed a slider and a knuckler. He never tried a sinker."
Source: *Baseball Digest* (September 1962)

Note: Another *Baseball Digest* article (January 1963) says that Wynn was the only pitcher who was able to change speeds on his slider without getting hurt by it.

Wynn in 1972, on how to effectively employ a high slider: "Start with a bad [slider], that breaks wide. Bad pitch, but till it breaks it looks okay. He goes for it and misses and you have your strike. Try with something else, the curve, or for me the knuckler, and you can get a second strike. Now throw a spinner—not a slider but a ball that spins looks like it's gonna slide—just where you threw that first pitch. He thinks it will break wide again. He doesn't swing, and you've got called strike three. Of course, you've got to put something on the ball."
Source: *A Season in the Sun* (Roger Kahn, 1977); by the way, this quote suggests that perhaps Wynn's knuckleball was more important in his post-1948 repertoire than we've got it.

Wynn in 1953: "I believed 'em when they said [the knuckleball] would ruin my arm, and I never even tried a knuckler until after I was traded from Washington to Cleveland in 1949. I remembered how well Leonard, Wolff, Haefner and Niggeling got by with the Senators and I decided to try it once in a while. I find it a good pitch, when I have a hitter two strikes and no balls. And on days when it's breaking good, I'll use it any time—to start a hitter off or even when the count is three-and-two."
Source: *Collier's* (10/2/1953, Tom Meany); this quote directly contradicts other sources that Wynn regularly threw a knuckleball before 1949.

Description: ". . . throws from a three-quarter-arm delivery."
Source: *Pitching* (Bob Shaw, 1972)
Also see Bob Shaw entry.

BILLY WYNNE 6'3" 205-pound righty
8-11, 4.33, 0 Saves 1967 1971

Description: "Fair curve, good fast ball and fair change. Has control problem. Needs to get ball over plate to warrant consideration."
Source: *Baseball Digest* (March 1967, "Official Scouting Reports on 1967 Major League Rookies")

HANK WYSE 5'11" 185-pound righty
79-70, 3.52, 8 Saves 1942 1951

Pitches: 1. Sinker 2. Screwball 3. Fastball 4. Curve 5. Change
Source: *Baseball Magazine* (September 1945, Herbert Simons)

ESTEBAN YAN 6'4" 255-pound righty
28-32, 5.41, 43 Saves 1996 2003

Pitch Selection: 1. Fastball 2. Curve 3. Change
Source: *1996 Montreal Expos Media Guide*

Pitch Selection: 1. Fastball (mid-90s) 2. Slider 3. Change
Source: *The Scouting Notebook: 1999*

Pitch Selection: 1. Fastball (up to 98) 2. Slider 3. Split-Fingered Fastball
Source: *The Scouting Notebook: 2002*

EMIL YDE 5'11" 165-pound lefty
49-25, 4.02, 4 Saves 1924 1929

Key Pitch: Fastball
Source: *Baseball Magazine* (February 1925, F.C. Lane)

MOSE YELLOWHORSE 5'10" 180-pound righty
8-4, 3.93, 1 Save 1921 1922

Pitch Selection: 1. Fastball 2. Curve
Note: Kid Elberfeld supposedly said that YellowHorse's fastball ranked with Walter Johnson's (which of course is something that was said, almost always inaccurately, about many, many pitchers of Johnson's era).
Source: *60 Feet Six Inches and Other Distances from Home: the (Baseball) Life of Mose YellowHorse* (Todd Fuller, 2002)

MASATO YOSHII 6'2" 215-pound righty
32-47, 4.62, 0 Saves 1998 2002

Pitch Selection: 1. Two-Seam Fastball 2. Forkball 3. Curve 4. Change
Source: *The Scouting Notebook 2000*

FLOYD YOUMANS 6'2" 180-pound righty
30-34, 3.74, 0 Saves 1985 1989

Pitch Selection: 1. Fastball (90+) 2. Hard Slider 3. Change 4. Curve (abandoned 1986)
Source: *The Scouting Report: 1987*

CURT YOUNG 6'1" 175-pound lefty
69-53, 4.31, 0 Saves 1983 1993

Pitch Selection: 1. Overhand Curve 2. Fastball 3. Change (added 1986)
Source: *The Scouting Report: 1987*

CY YOUNG 6'2" 210-pound righty
511-316, 2.63, 19 Saves 1890 1911

Pitch Selection: 1. Jump Ball (Fastball) 2. Curves 3. Change 4. Spitball (occasional)
Sources: *Cy Young: A Baseball Life* (Reed Browning, 2000); Young in *The No-Hit Hall of Fame* (Rich Coberly, 1985), *Pitching in a Pinch* (Christy Mathewson, 1912); *My 66 Years in the Big Leagues* (Connie Mack, 1950)

Cy Young: "I had excellent control, throwing with four different deliveries and wheeling on the batter to hide the ball. I saw some fast ones—Amos Rusie, Walter Johnson, Lefty Grove and Feller, among others—but I was among them, too. My favorite pitch was a whistler right under the chin, and, as Ty Cobb said, I had a couple of good curve balls, an overhanded pitch that broke sharply down and a sweeping, sidearmed curve."
Source: Young in *Super Stars of Baseball* (Bob Broeg, 1971)

Description: "What can we infer from contemporary accounts about Young's stylish windup in his prime? First off, he did not raise his left leg high; his stride was closer to a big step than a kick, and today we would probably call it a slide step. Second, when his left leg was raised, he briefly pivoted away from the plate on his right leg, turning some of his back toward the batter. This movement allowed him briefly to hide his ball and glove. Third, after releasing the ball he did not fling his right arm far across his body, preferring to get his raised right foot back down to the ground and so to plant himself to be able to deal with any batted ball. Finally—and this had been true from the beginning of his professional career—his basic delivery was released overhand, not from the shoulders or side arm. Many years later, and certainly by 1908, he sometimes pitched balls sidearm in order to alter his release point and give an unexpected axis of revolution to a pitch. And throughout his career—we should probably recall that the teenaged Young began to learn his craft when under-handed deliveries were the only lawful ones—he occasionally startled a batter with a submarine pitch . . . By Cap Anson's testimony, when Young made a pitch, it seemed as if 'the ball was shooting down from the hands of a giant.' "
Source: Browning

Cy Young: "It always depended on the batter. If a right-handed crowded my plate [Young always called the plate 'his'], I side-armed him with a curve, and then, when he stepped back, I'd throw an overhand fast ball low and outside. I was fortunate in having good speed from overhand, three-quarter or side-arm. I had a variety of curves—threw a so-called screwball or indrop, too—and I used whatever delivery seemed best. And I never

had but one sore arm. That was in 1911, my last, and the sore arm forced me to quit."
Source: *How to Play Winning Baseball* (Arthur Mann, 1953)

Notes: According to Mathewson, Young was strictly a fastball pitcher in the National League, but when he lost his fastball and left the NL, he developed a wonderful curve. The citation for the spitball is from Connie Mack: "He had a fast ball, a curve, and a spitter that almost hypnotized the batter." Honus Wagner, according to the same source, said that "Walter Johnson was fast, but no faster than Rusie. And Rusie was no faster than Johnson. But Young was faster than both of 'em!"

MATT YOUNG 6'3" 205-pound lefty
55-95, 4.40, 25 Saves 1983 1993

Pitch Selection: 1. Fastball 2. Slider 3. Curve
Sources: *The Scouting Report: 1987; The Scouting Report: 1990*

TOM ZACHARY 6'1" 187-pound lefty
186-191, 3.73, 22 Saves 1918 1936

Key Pitch: Knuckleball
Source: *Baseball's 50 Greatest Games* (Bert Sugar, Page 17)

Quote: "This grizzled southpaw has been firing assorted benders since 'way back in 1919."
Source: *Who's Who in the Major Leagues* (1936 edition)

Commentary: Our attempts to find better information about Zachary's pitches were fruitless, though he did enjoy a long and productive career. We found many magazine and newspaper articles about Zachary, none of which mention which pitches he favored, though he did mention his curve and fastball in no particular order. This leads one to believe that while he *might* have relied on the knuckleball, it's more likely that his repertoire was conventional.

PAT ZACHRY 6'5" 180-pound righty
69-67, 3.52, 3 Saves 1976 1985

Pitch Selection: 1. Slider 2. Change 3. Fastball
Source: *The Scouting Report: 1983*

GEOFF ZAHN 6'1" 180-pound lefty
111-109, 3.74, 1 Save 1973 1985

Key Pitch: Sinking Fastball
Source: *The Sporting News* (8/30/1980, Patrick Reusse)

Zahn: "I thank Gene Mauch for reviving my career. I'm no longer a power pitcher, but since I've learned to use more changeups, I'm more effective and consistent."
Source: *The Complete Handbook of Baseball: 1982 Season* (edited by Zander Hollander)

JEFF ZIMMERMAN 6'1" 200-pound righty
17-12, 3.27, 32 Saves 1999 2001

Pitch Selection: 1. Fastball (93–94) 2. Slider
Note: Fastball has a natural screwball action.
Source: *The Scouting Notebook: 2000*

BARRY ZITO 6'4" 215-pound lefty
61-29, 3.12, 0 Saves 2000 2003

Pitch Selection: 1. Overhand Curve 2. Change 3. Fastball (high-80s)
Source: *The Scouting Notebook: 2002*

Zito: "It [the curve] has been my go-to pitch. It's weird . . . growing up it was, but now it is hittable by big league hitters when they know it is coming. My change-up is actually my go-to pitch right now. But it's nice to know that guys are aware I have that curveball in my backpocket."
Source: ESPN.com chat session (8/1/2002)

Jason Giambi: "A lot of times it's [Zito's curveball] high in the strike zone and you give up on it. You may think at first it's a high fastball and then it drops in on you."
Zito: "Pulling down with the middle finger is the key, because all a curveball is is rotation. If I can throw a curve that starts at his eyes and drops in for a strike, the hitter processes that as a strike. Then I can throw a high fastball, and he thinks that's a strike too."
Source: *Sports Illustrated* (3/31/03, Page 60)

Scott Williamson: "He definitely has one of the best curves in the game. And he uses his fastball real well. It's not very powerful, but he makes it powerful because his curve and changeup are so good."
Source: *The Boston Globe* (10/3/2003, Tim Casey)

BILL ZUBER 6'2" 195-pound righty
43-42, 4.28, 6 Saves 1936 1947

Pitch Selection: 1. Fastball 2. Curve
3. Sidearm Sinker 4. Slider (added in 1946)
5. Change

Notes: Zuber learned his change-up from Dutch Leonard in 1941 or '42, and his slider from Spud Chandler; Zuber's sinker was often described in the press as the "Zuber Zinker."

Source: *Now Pitching: Bill Zuber from Amana* (Cliff Trumpold, 1992)

Note: According to Russ Hodges in *Baseball Complete* (1952), Spud Chandler said that Zuber could throw harder than Bob Feller.

GEORGE ZUVERINK 6'4" 195-pound righty
32-36, 3.54, 40 Saves 1951 1959

Key Pitch: Sinker

Source: Bill Wight in *From 33rd Street to Camden Yards: An Oral History of the Baltimore Orioles* (John Eisenberg, 2001)

MAJOR-LEAGUE KNUCKLEBALLERS: THE SEVENTY WE KNOW

ROB NEYER

What constitutes a "knuckleballer"? Well, that's obviously open to interpretation. But at this particular moment, I consider a knuckleballer any pitcher 1) who would not have been in the majors without his knuckleball, *or* 2) whose knuckleball was considered his best pitch, at least for a time.

Did we find all of them? Hell no. I'm sure we've found most of them, and I'm confident that we've found nearly all of them who pitched more than a few innings in the majors. But I discovered a couple of dozen just while researching this book, and I'm sure there are a few more out there.

Also, I should mention that literally hundreds of major leaguers have made the knuckleball a part of their regular repertoire. It's unheard of now, but in the 1940s and early '50s, probably something like half the pitchers in the majors threw a knuckler at least occasionally. These aren't those guys. These are the guys who were *known* for throwing the knuckleball, and probably needed it . . .

JOHN ANDERSON *Said to throw his knuckleball sidearm, got brief trials with four different teams and failed all of them.*

GENE BEARDEN *In 1948, the rookie with the Purple Heart and the aluminum plate in his head won 20 games—including the playoff for the American League pennant—and paced A.L. with 2.43 ERA. Never had anything like that kind of season again, though.*

CLARENCE BEERS *Pitched two-thirds of an inning for the Cardinals in 1948.*

DAN BOONE (1990) *Yes, he's related to that Daniel Boone. Threw knuckleball as complementary pitch in early '80s, was out of baseball for a long spell, then got "discovered" while relying on his knuckler in the Senior League and returned to majors in 1990.*

JIM BOUTON (1969–1978) *His story is well-known, though it's easy to forget that years after the events related in* Ball Four, *Bouton made a brief comeback with the Braves, when he was thirty-nine.*

JOE BOWMAN (late career) *Pitched for nearly a dozen seasons in the majors, but didn't go to his knuckleball until the last season or two.*

HAL BROWN *Career record looked pretty good until 1964, when he went 3-15 for the Colt .45s in his last season.*

WALLY BURNETTE *Made splash with Athletics as rookie in 1956, posting 2.89 ERA after coming up in the middle of July.*

TOM CANDIOTTI *Tim Wakefield notwithstanding, Candiotti's the best knuckleballer we've seen since Charlie Hough; tutored by Phil Niekro in Cleveland.*

LEW CARPENTER *Didn't give up a run in four games, but sent down anyway and never made it back. One of* ***six***

knuckleballers (at least) who pitched for the Senators in 1943.

GEORGE CASTER *After going 4-19 as starter in 1940, shifted to bullpen in '42 and enjoyed three outstanding seasons, including league-best twelve saves in 1944 with pennant-winning Browns.*

EDDIE CICOTTE *Might have invented the knuckleball, and it was his best pitch before he discovered the shine ball.*

GLENN COX *Incredibly consistent in the International League from 1954 through '59, but had big problems in the American.*

JIM DAVIS *Must be one of the few post-1950 pitchers to throw a knuckleball* and *a screwball.*

VERN FEAR *Four games and eight innings for the Cubs in 1952.*

JARED FERNANDEZ *Still trying to establish himself, but at thirty-two he's still a young man by the standards of his profession.*

EDDIE FISHER *Overshadowed by fellow reliever and sometime teammate Hoyt Wilhelm, but Fisher was a fine pitcher for many years.*

FREDDIE FITZSIMMONS *He's here because he was famous for his "knuckleball," but it was a spinning pitch that might more properly be called a "knuckle curve."*

BEN FLOWERS *In 1953, set MLB record (since broken) by relieving in eight straight games, then followed up with a shutout in his first start.*

WES FLOWERS *In one of baseball's great coincidences—right up there with Hank Aaron being the first major leaguer, alphabetically, and Jeff Bagwell and Frank Thomas being born on the same day—Ben and Wes Flowers, the only two "Flowers" to pitch in the major leagues since the early 1870s, both relied on the knuckleball.*

LARRY FRENCH (1942) *French learned his knuckleball from Fitzsimmons . . . so was it really a knuckleball?*

MARION FRICANO *Arrived in 1953 as thirty-year-old rookie and did well; didn't* always *throw soft, and in '54 he beaned Cass Michaels, essentially ending Michaels' career.*

SAM GIBSON *Started with a couple of solid seasons in 1927 and '28, fell apart quickly afterward.*

MICKEY HAEFNER *Like three of his Washington teammates, relied on his knuckleball, but Haefner had plenty of other pitches, too.*

JESSE HAINES *If he hadn't got blisters throwing his knuckleball—which was probably more like Hooton's knuckle curve—Alexander never would have struck out Lazzeri.*

GRANNY HAMNER *Odd career path took him from shortstop to pitcher to shortstop to minor-league manager to minor-league pitcher/manager to (briefly) major-league pitcher.*

LUM HARRIS *Had a pretty good fastball and perhaps doesn't belong on this list, but notable for throwing both a knuckleball* and *his own version of the knuckle curve. Later managed the Braves to a division title in 1969.*

EARL HARRIST *First pitcher to face Larry Doby in the American League, and struck him out.*

KIRBY HIGBE (late career) *Made his name with great fastball while pitching for Dodgers, wound up throwing mostly knucklers for Giants.*

CHARLIE HOUGH *Rough, tough Charlie Hough pitched in the majors until he was forty-six, and looked sixty-six.*

BOB HUMPHREYS (1968-1970) *Hurt his arm early in '68 and somehow managed to hang around for a few seasons by throwing mostly knuckleballs.*

KEN JOHNSON *Essentially the only pure knuckleballer who started a lot of games between the late 1940s and the middle '60s.*

ANDY KARL *Also developed a "knuckle curve" which might (or might not) have resembled the "knuckleball" previously thrown by Haines and Fitzsimmons.*

PAUL LaPALME *Tossed a shutout against the Braves in his first MLB start, and pitched only one more in his career.*

DUTCH (EMIL) LEONARD *Easily the best-known knuckleballer between Fitzsimmons and Wilhelm.*

JOHNNY LINDELL (1953) *Began career as conventional pitcher, became everyday outfielder for some excellent Yankees teams, then returned to Pacific Coast League and refined his knuckleball well enough to earn return trip to majors.*

TED LYONS (later career) *When Lyons came back from the Marines in 1945, he said, "Just as long as I have that knuckler and three fast outfielders, I'll get by." And he did, completing all twenty of his '45 starts and posting a 2.10 ERA.*

PHIL McCULLOUGH *Pitched in one game for the Senators in 1942, and was one of something like a dozen knuckleballers who pitched for that club during the war.*

LEW MOREN *Along with Cicotte and Summers, among the first to throw the knuckler.*

DICK MULLIGAN *Reached the majors at the end of the '41 season, then spent four seasons in the service; came back in '46 and pitched reasonably well, but pro career quickly petered out.*

DICK NEWSOME *After winning twenty-three games with San Diego in 1940, went 19-10 as Red Sox rookie in '41. But he struggled in '42 and '43, was placed on the voluntarily retired list and never pitched again.*

JOE NIEKRO (second half of career) *Was dissuaded from throwing his knuckleball while still a young man; otherwise, might have won nearly as many games as his big brother.*

PHIL NIEKRO *If anybody knows why Knucksie didn't get elected to the Hall of Fame until his fifth year of eligibility, please let me know.*

JOHNNY NIGGELING *One of Washington's knuckleballing quartet in '44 and '45–and the only one to throw his knuckler off just one fingertip–was still pitching effectively at forty-three (in '46), but got drummed out of the majors anyway. Eventually became a barber, and hung himself in a hotel room.*

AL PAPAI *He got roughed up in the majors, but pitched in the minors into his early forties and four times won twenty or more games.*

JOE PATE *As thirty-four-year-old rookie in 1926, went 9-0 with 2.71 ERA. As thirty-five-year-old sophomore in 1927, went 0-3 with 5.20 ERA and was never glimpsed again.*

TOT PRESSNELL *His career was going nicely until 1942, when it ended for no apparent reason.*

BOB PURKEY *He threw a lot of different pitches, but it was his mastery of the knuckleball that allowed him to win twenty-three games in 1962.*

WILLARD RAMSDELL *"Willie the Knuck" first developed his knuckleball because he had problems throwing his curveball in the thin air of the West Texas–New Mexico League.*

EDDIE ROMMEL *The greatest real knuckleballer until Hoyt Wilhelm came along.*

NAP RUCKER (late career) *Rucker threw hard early in his career, but he also threw a knuckleball, which came in real handy when his fastball went away.*

OWEN SCHEETZ *Yes, another of Washington's war-time flutterballers; got into six games and saved one of them.*

PAUL SCHREIBER (1945) *Working as batting-practice pitcher for Yankees, pitched in two games for Yankees at the age of forty-two.*

BARNEY SCHULTZ *Journeyman's career distinguished by 1964, when he saved fifteen games and posted 1.64 ERA to help Cardinals win flag.*

TOM SEATON *Won twenty-seven games in 1913, then jumped to the Federal League and won 25 more in 1914 before his career nosedived.*

BOBBY SHANTZ *Like Purkey, Shantz certainly would have been in the major leagues without his knuckler, but he wouldn't have been nearly as good.*

LOU SLEATER *In relatively brief career, pitched for six different teams and didn't throw strikes for any of them.*

STEVE SPARKS *Will even his mom remember that Sparks led the major leagues with eight complete games in 2001?*

DENNIS SPRINGER *Once snubbed me for an interview, but I was flustered and called him "Steve," so I probably deserved it.*

RAY STARR *Dick Starr—no relation—also threw the knuckler (beginning in 1950), but didn't rely on the pitch as Ray did.*

TOM STURDIVANT *Suffered torn rotator cuff in 1958 and was never anything like the same, but did refine his knuckleball in '59 and was able to hang around for another five years.*

JOE SULLIVAN *Just when his career might have taken off—during World War II—Sullivan quit baseball for a job in a Puget Sound shipyard; once pitched twelve straight innings of scoreless relief.*

ED SUMMERS *"Kickapoo" was in the neighborhood when the knuckleball was invented, and might even have been involved.*

JIM TOBIN *Among his many accomplishments, tossed a couple of no-hitters and once hit three home runs in one game.*

TIM WAKEFIELD *Bears passing resemblance to John Cusack, who 1) was born five weeks before Wakefield, and 2) once played Eddie Cicotte's teammate in a movie.*

HOYT WILHELM *How many games might he have won as a starter? We'll never know, but in fifty-two career starts, Wilhelm went 19-19 with a 2.55 ERA. So we might roughly guess, "A lot."*

JIM WINFORD *In his only real shot, went 11-10 for Cardinals in 1936; in '37, described in* The Sporting News *as "a master of the knuckle ball."*

ROGER WOLFF *Generally referred to as "pudgy," which was fair enough; went 4-15 for Senators in 1944, then 20-10 in '45 as Nats nearly won pennant.*

WILBUR WOOD *Last man to start both ends of a doubleheader.*

RASTY WRIGHT *Pitched brilliantly, albeit in limited duty, in 1922 for Browns team that very nearly won their first pennant.*

BONUS LIST: A FEW MINOR LEAGUERS

This is an incredibly incomplete list of knuckleballers who never did reach the majors, or who did but aren't known to have thrown the knuckleball in the majors. It's not much, but it's a starting point (which is something).

BILL BRENNER *Started career as power-hitting minor-league catcher, spent a few years in the service during World War II, and eventually became a pitcher, winning sixty-four games over a three-season span (1952–1954) in the Western International League.*

ART EVANS *Actually had cup of coffee with the Cubs in 1932, but we don't know if he was throwing the knuckleball then.*

RICK HUISMANN *Reliever posted solid numbers in minors with conventional repertoire but struggled in major-league trials, attempted conversion to knuckleballing but that didn't work, either.*

BILL ISRAEL *Spent most of his short professional career in the Alabama State League, perhaps because of World War II.*

BILL KOSZAREK *Learned to throw knuckler from photo in* The Sporting News *of Roger Wolff's three-finger grip.*

JIMMY LYONS *In 1936, he went 1-11 in the Pacific Coast League and 11-3 in the Texas League (though not necessarily in that order).*

JOE MALMAN *In 1940, went 21-6 with the Topeka Owls in the Western Association.*

DAVE MCKINNEY *From 1936 through '38, did reasonably well with Jacksonville in the Sally League, but career fizzled afterward.*

PAUL MORSE *Nineteenth-round draft pick wasn't going anywhere after a few seasons, decided to become a knuckleball pitcher. Worked with Charlie Hough for a summer and wound up spending some time in Triple-A, but never learned to throw strikes with the pitch.*

TONY PONCE *Spent six seasons in the high minors, but enjoyed his best seasons with Phoenix in the Arizona-Texas League in the late '40s and early '50s.*

GARLAND SHIFFLETT *Missed the better part of three seasons in the middle of his professional career because of a salary dispute and a fear of flying, then added a knuckleball in 1963 and earned a brief trip to the majors (though we don't know how often he threw his knuckler while pitching for the Twins in '64).*

HAL TURPIN *Beginning in 1939, won eighty-nine games in four-year stretch for Seattle Rainiers.*

CHARLIE ZINK *Our Great Young Hope, Zink took up the knuckleball last year at twenty-three, and quickly got the knack.*

SUBMARINERS

BILL JAMES

A Chronological List of Submarine/Underhand/Low-Sidearm Pitchers 1901–2002

CY YOUNG (1890–1911) *Once in a blue moon would throw underhanded.*

JOE MCGINNITY (1899–1908) *Alternated between overhand and underhand deliveries.*

RUBE FOSTER (1902–1926) *Threw underhand just occasionally.*

THREE FINGER BROWN (1903–1916) *Would fire off an occasional underhand pitch.*

ED WILLETT (1906–1913) *Made limited use of an effective underhand floater, and everybody thought he should have thrown that way all the time.*

CHIEF BENDER (1903–1925) *Just once in a while would throw underhand.*

JACK WARHOP (1908–1915) *Is that a great name for a submarine pitcher or what? Sometimes his hand scraped the ground as he delivered.*

DIZZY DISMUKES (1910–1930) *Full-time submariner, threw hard.*

ERSKINE MAYER (1912–1919) *Threw underhand and sidearm.*

GUY MORTON (1914–1924) *Fooled around with underhand throws.*

CARL MAYS (1915–1929) *The only (white) true submariner between Warhop and Auker.*

ART NEHF (1915–1929) *Mixed in some underhand throws, mostly early in his career.*

SLIM HARRISS (1920–1928) *Threw scary low sidearm fastball, similar to Mays but not as low.*

SHERIFF BLAKE (1920–1937) *Occasionally threw underhand after 1928 injury.*

WEBSTER MCDONALD (1920–1940) *Negro League workman nicknamed "56 Varieties."*

REMY KREMER (1924–1933) *Mixed underhand throws with overhand; sometimes pitched whole games underhanded.*

SATCHEL PAIGE (1926–1966) *Threw a few pitches underhanded.*

HOD LISENBEE (1927–1945) *Just occasionally threw one underhand.*

CLINT BROWN (1928–1942) *Developed a submarine screwball in early 1930s.*

AD LISKA (1929–1933) *Largely a full-time submarine pitcher, but did occasionally come overhand for a hopping fastball.*

CHIEF HOGSETT (1929–1944) *One probably-not-reliable source says he threw underhand; more likely threw sidearm, perhaps low sidearm.*

Lawrence Journal World, Kansas Collection, Kenneth Spencer Research Library, University of Kansas Libraries

Dan Quisenberry

BOBO NEWSOM (1929–1953) *Stories say that he* began *his career as submarine pitcher, converted out of it in 1930 or thereabouts. Of course, stories about Bobo say all kinds of things.*

PAT CARAWAY (1930–1932) *Unclear how often he threw underhand—maybe all the time—but we do know he's one of the few submariners who regularly threw a knuckleball.*

TEX CARLETON (1932–1940) *A sidearm pitcher who would occasionally sag.*

ELDEN AUKER (1933–1942) *Switched to underhand delivery after a college football injury.*

SAM NAHEM (1938–1948) *Threw from his knees.*

KEN RAFFENSBERGER (1939–1954) *Liked to experiment with arm angles.*

DIZZY TROUT (1939–1957) *Could throw 100, but occasionally threw underhanded. They didn't call him "Dizzy" for nothing.*

MURRY DICKSON (1939–1959) *Would occasionally throw underhand, among many other tricks.*

RUSS CHRISTOPHER (1942–1948) *Earle Brucker made him a submariner, full time.*

TED WILKS (1944–1953) *Late in career would occasionally throw underhand to keep hitters off stride.*

BILL WERLE (1949–1954) *Occasionally flipped it to the plate underhanded.*

DICK HYDE (1955–1961) *Was true submariner, but Jekyll always threw overhand.*

TED ABERNATHY (1955–1972) *Full-time submariner after a 1957 injury.*

KEN JOHNSON (1958–1970) *Occasionally threw underhand, according to one occasionally reliable source.*

The Topps Company, Inc.

Chad Bradford

ANDY HASSLER (1971–1985) *Dabbled in nether pitching at the very end of his career.*

KENT TEKULVE (1974–1989) *Successful career triggered 1980s revival of underhand style.*

DAN QUISENBERRY (1979–1990) *Humorist, poet, and submariner. We miss ya, buddy.*

BOB LONG (1981–1985) *Pitched well for M's in his only real chance, but didn't get another.*

TERRY LEACH (1981–1993) *A true submariner.*

MARK EICHHORN (1982–1996) *Switched to low sidearm after 1983 shoulder injury.*

STEVE REED (1992–2003) *Low sidearm/marginal underhand.*

BRAD CLONTZ (1995–2000) *No relation to Wayne Fonts.*

MIKE MYERS (1995–2002) *Al Kaline persuaded him to use the underhand style.*

CHAD BRADFORD (1998–2003) *Michael Lewis' favorite pitcher.*

BYUNG-HYUN KIM (1999–2003) *Has devastating inverse slider.*

MIKE VENAFRO (1999–2003) *Broadcasters loved to exclaim about his "Frisbee slider."*

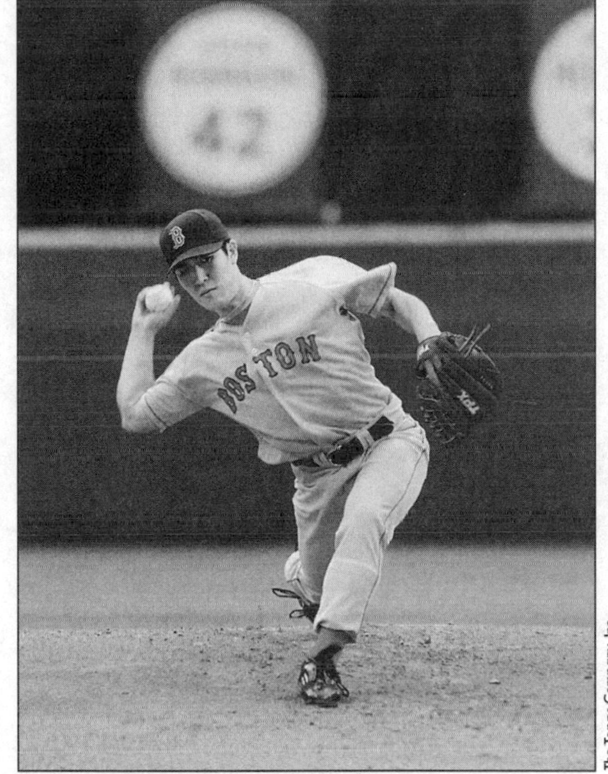

The Topps Company, Inc.

Byung-Hyun Kim

KELLY WUNSCH (2000–2003) *Has absolutely the worst delivery I have ever seen, except possibly Floyd Youmans.*

EDDIE OROPESA (2001–2002) *The Diamondbacks love submariners.*

BRETT PRINZ (2001–2002) *Ditto.*

PART III
PITCHING

ABUSE AND DURABILITY

BILL JAMES

I. Background

For more than twenty years, momentum has been building within the sabermetric community for the belief that having a pitcher throw an excessive number of pitches in a game is dangerous and counter-productive. This belief traces back essentially to the work of my longtime friend Craig Wright, who was employed in the early 1980s by the Texas Rangers. As Craig wrote in his 1989 book *The Diamond Appraised*, "I grew up as a Tigers fan. What happened to (Mark) Fidrych made a strong impression on me. It made me realize that in trying to protect the modern pitcher we can no longer rely on innings pitched as our sole measure of a pitcher's workload. We also have to consider how often he's pushed past his endurance level within his starts."

Seven years before *The Diamond Appraised*, on pages 59–60 of the 1982 *Baseball Abstract*, I had discussed the issue of whether Billy Martin, then manager of the Oakland Athletics, was riding his starting pitchers too hard, and was going to ruin their arms:

> The most conspicuous pattern among Martin's teams has to do with the handling of his pitchers . . . Martin concentrates an enormous number of innings in a very few pitchers. Is he over-doing it? Is he abusing these few arms in the interest of winning a couple of extra games?

The subsequent discussion answered this question in the affirmative: Martin *was* abusing the arms of his top starters, and would pay a heavy price for it in 1982, a prediction which proved accurate. Whether my thinking even at that time was influenced by Craig's, or whether we were merely thinking separately along the same lines, I no longer remember, but certainly by 1984 both Craig and I were advocating the belief that some major-league pitchers were being subjected to workloads that they could not long sustain.

At that time we had few counts of the number of pitches thrown by a pitcher in a game or in a season. Even in the absence of such data, it was apparent to Craig, and to me, that there was a huge difference between having a pitcher pitch 200 innings in 35 starts—less than six innings per start—and having a pitcher pitch 200 innings in 25 starts (eight innings per start). What was significant, we believed, was not the *innings* the pitcher worked, but the innings that he worked when he might have been tired. I should stop speaking for Craig, it being a matter of time until I misstate his beliefs, but in any case Craig developed the concept of BFS (Batters Faced per Start) as a measure of the "strain" on a pitcher, and introduced this concept to the public in *The Diamond Appraised*. Craig also related BFS to pitches per game, arguing that "For ages twenty to twenty-two, (pitchers) should average no more than 105 pitches per start for a season (105 pitches is the rough equivalent of 30.0 BFS.) A single-game ceiling should be set at 130 pitches." (Quote is from page 211 of *The Diamond Appraised.*)

By 1990 pitch counts for every game and season were entering the public record, and the discussion quickly began to revolve around those pitch counts. However, while Craig had produced lists of pitchers whose arms were "abused" in their formative years, and others who were not abused but went on to long careers, he never did establish a specific format by which a third party could determine reliably whether a specific pitcher should be regarded as abused. I'm not second-guessing him; he had his reasons for not taking that step, and that's fine but . . . it remained undone. And, because that remained undone, we were never in position to take the critical next step of documenting that a specific usage pattern carried a specified and quantifiable risk.

I believe that it was in the 1999 edition of the *Baseball Prospectus* that Rany Jazayerli and Keith Woolner first introduced the concept of "Pitcher Abuse Points" . . . actually, I have never seen the 1999 edition of the *Baseball Prospectus* and don't know whether there was a 1998 edition; I was in hiding at the time, and am just figuring this out from the later editions, which I read from cover to cover and attempted to memorize. Anyway, Rany's and Keith's method was a simple and logical implementation of Craig's thesis, or at least it seems so to me. In the first version of his system that I have been able to memorize, Rany charged one "Pitcher Abuse Point" for each pitch thrown by a pitcher in a start over the level of 100, a second Pitcher abuse Point for each pitch after 110, a third for each pitch after 120, etc. . . . a pitcher throwing 115 pitches in a game would be charged with 20 Pitcher Abuse Points (PAP), while a pitcher throwing 140 pitches in a game would have 100 PAP, a pitcher throwing 162 pitches in a game would be charged with 224 PAP, and a pitcher throwing 400 pitches in a game would be Leon Cadore.

Jazayerli and Woolner then totaled up the season Pitcher Abuse Points for each pitcher, modified this by a scale intended to factor in the pitcher's age, divided by the pitcher's games started, and produced a "Workload" for each pitcher. By this method, they were able to produce an objective list of the "most abused" pitchers of each season.

Meanwhile, the concept of pitch limits had become so generally accepted, within the popular culture, that any manager who let his starting pitcher work more than seven innings was risking the wrath of the post-game callers. In every city there are injured pitchers, and in every city there is a quasi-permanent coalition of fans in quest of the manager's hide. For those fans, pitch counts had become a club with which to beat the manager. For every starting pitcher who had an injury, there was a game to which it could be traced—that time in July, when the pitcher threw 132 pitches on a hot day with the game already decided, or that time last April, when the pitcher threw 132 pitches on a cold day because the bullpen wasn't ready.

But while this was happening, my thinking on this issue was drifting away from the mainstream of the sabermetric community. Writing about Bert Blyleven in the New Historical Abstract, I offered the following reflection:

> In the early 1970s there were a number of pitchers, particularly American League pitchers, who pitched huge numbers of innings, not only more innings than anyone has pitched since then, but also more than anyone had thrown for fifty years before then . . . Looking back at it from this vantage point, there is surprisingly little evidence that pitching 320 to 350 innings did much to shorten any of these pitchers' careers, except maybe Mickey Lolich. Bert Blyleven, a young pitcher at that time, lasted another 20 years after the fact. Gaylord Perry, Steve Carlton, Nolan Ryan, and Fergie Jenkins, who all pitched huge numbers of innings, all were effective pitchers until they were near (and in some cases past) 40. Catfish Hunter lasted long enough to win 224 games, Jim Palmer (323 innings in 1975) lasted. Wilbur Wood lasted long enough to win 164 major league games although he was fat, spent half of his career as a reliever, had a shattered kneecap on a line drive, and pitched 377 innings in a season. Mickey Lolich won 217 major league games, including 76 after he pitched 376 innings in 1971, although he was even fatter than Wilbur Wood. That generation produced more 300-game winners than the rest of baseball history since 1920, plus several other pitchers who won 260 or more. If pitching 325 innings was destructive to any of these pitchers, the fact is surprisingly subtle in history.

Responding to this, another friend (David Srinivasan of *The Sporting News*) argued that pushing pitchers that hard *was* dangerous, was destructive of their arms, and referenced the Jazayerli/Woolner articles, which, he said, produced lists of pitchers which he had relied upon, with good success, to be strong candidates for arm trouble. In 1998, for example, the Jazayerli/Woolner method had identified Tony Saunders and Kerry Wood as over-used pitchers. Wood was injured in 1999, while

Saunders' career disappeared faster than the backroom bartender in a raid on a whorehouse. In 1999 they had pegged as abused Jason Schmidt and Jamey Wright, both of whom did have arm trouble in 2000, and in 2000 Jazayerli and Woolner had tagged as abused Rick Heiling (who had a poor season) and Garrett Stephenson, who missed the 2001 season entirely.

Well, yes, I replied, but in *any* group of young pitchers there are a substantial number whose careers are going to flame out suddenly, usually due to arm injuries. The question isn't whether they identified as abused some pitchers who later had injuries, but whether those pitchers tagged as abused had a *greater* risk of injury than comparable pitchers.

By the summer of 2002, then, all of the pieces necessary to do this study were finally in place:

1) Rany and Keith had produced an objective list of abused pitchers,

2) Enough time had passed to enable us to look back at those lists and evaluate what had happened to those pitchers,

3) I had published the Win Shares system, which enabled us to identify pitchers of approximately the same age and the same value pattern up to the time of the alleged abuse, and

4) I had become skeptical as to whether the high pitch counts did in fact have the deleterious effects which had long been alleged.

II. Method

What I essentially did was to take all of Woolner and Jazayerli's lists of abused pitchers, and to identify for each "abused" pitcher the most comparable pitcher, in terms of his age and value pattern up to that point in his career, who was not listed as abused, and who had not already been claimed by another partner in the study. I then looked at the following seasons, to see whether or to what extent the "abused" pitchers suffered greater declines in value than the "non-abused" pitchers matched with them.

First, you need to wash your mind of the "similarity scores" method that I developed a long time ago, which is used by various people to identify similar pitchers or similar position players. That's not what I'm doing here. If a pitcher has gone 14-12 with 139 strikeouts and a 3.78 ERA, I don't look for another pitcher who has gone about 14-12 with 139 strikeouts and a 3.78 ERA. That method, were it applied here, would have a strong tendency to identify as most-similar to the abused pitchers . . . another set of abused pitchers.

What I was doing here was looking for similar *value patterns,* without respect to performance specifics. For example, since Al Leiter had earned 11 Win Shares in 1999, 17 in the year 2000, had earned 106 in his career through the year 2000, and was born in the second half of 1965, I tried to match him, ideally, with another pitcher who also earned 11 Win Shares in 1999, 17 in 2000, 106 in his career, and was also born in the second half of 1965. Of course, there was no other such pitcher, but the best match turned out to be with Kenny Rogers, who had earned 12 Win Shares in 1999, 15 in 2000, 128 in his career through 2000, and who was born in November 1964. The specific algorithm by which similarity was determined was:

1000 points,

Minus 5 points for each 1 difference in Win Shares in the focus year of the study,

Minus 2 points for each 1 difference in Win Shares in the previous season,

Minus one-half of one point for each difference in career Win Shares at the conclusion of the focus season,

Minus 10 points for each year of difference in age between the two pitchers.

"Age" was entered in six-month chunks, so that a pitcher born in the second half of 1965 would have a five-point penalty compared to a pitcher born in the first half of 1965 or the first half of 1966, a ten-point penalty when compared to a pitcher born in the second half of 1964 or 1966.

Leiter and Rogers . . . you have to admit, that's a good match. These are their season and career records up through the 2000 campaign:

	2000 Season			**Career**		
	IP	**W-L**	**ERA**	**Won-Lost**	**Pct**	**ERA**
Leiter	208	16-8	3.20	106-79	.573	3.73
Rogers	227	13-13	4.55	127-91	.583	4.11

But that wasn't how they were picked as being similar. Leiter earned 17 Win Shares in 2000; Rogers, 15—a 10 point penalty. Leiter had earned 11 Win Shares the previous season, Rogers 12—a 2 point penalty. Leiter had earned 106 Win Shares in his career, Rogers 128, an 11 point penalty. Rogers was one year older than Leiter, a 10 point penalty. The penalties totaling up to 33, the similarity between them was scored at 967, which made Leiter more similar to Rogers than to any other major league pitcher, by our method.

Thus, when Leiter—identified by Jazayerli/Woolner as a high-stress pitcher in 2000—went on to earn 14 Win Shares in 2000, while Rogers earned only 2, this was entered into the ledger as 14 Win Shares in the followup season for the "abused" pitcher, and 2 for the matched pitcher.

III. Results

Surprising as it may be, and surprising as it certainly was to me, the pitchers identified by Keith and Rany as "abused" performed consistently and dramatically *better* in subsequent seasons than did the most-comparable pitchers. Not worse, not even "as well," which would have been sufficient to question the method, but *better*—consistently, and by wide margins.

If you are willing to accept this statement as true, you have no particular reason to read the rest of this section . . . jump now to "IV. Meaning?" If, at any time, you get tired of the dry details of the study, and want to ask "so what?" then just jump ahead to that point.

I was eventually to do eight studies related to this issue, the first seven using similar or overlapping methods.

Study 1

I started with the 2000 list, which was published on page 515 of the 2001 *Baseball Prospectus* under the title "Table 9: 25 Highest Pitchers by Workload Stress Rate."

Of the 25 pitchers on their list, one (Ruben Quevedo) could not be used in my study, because he had no career value . . . his career value up to the point at which he was identified as being all stressed out 'n stuff was zero. As such, he is regarded as a perfect match for every other pitcher in his age group who had never done anything, either—indeed, in theory, as a perfect match for every other human being on the planet in his age group, except those relative few who could actually pitch. Since the purpose of the study is to examine whether the Jazayerli/Woolner method predicts future *declines* in value, Quevedo is simply of no use to us.

The 24 matches in the original study, with the "abused" pitcher listed on top, were:

		1999	2000	Career	Age
1.	Livan Hernandez	9	14	38	25.0
	Kris Benson	12	14	26	25.5
		1999	2000	Career	Age
2.	Randy Johnson	26	26	200	36.5
	Kevin Brown	19	20	200	35.0
		1999	2000	Career	Age
3.	Jason Schmidt	13	1	35	27.0
	Jose Rosado	13	1	44	25.5
		1999	2000	Career	Age
4.	Rick Helling	12	15	53	29.5
	Mike Sirotka	13	14	40	29.0
		1999	2000	Career	Age
5.	Ron Villone	8	5	25	30.0
	Tim Crabtree	7	5	29	30.5
		1999	2000	Career	Age
6.	Al Leiter	11	17	106	34.5
	Kenny Rogers	12	15	128	35.5
		1999	2000	Career	Age
7.	Roger Clemens	10	16	333	37.5
	Chuck Finley	14	16	201	37.5
		1999	2000	Career	Age
8.	Sterling Hitchcock	10	1	45	29.0
	Scott Karl	9	1	47	28.5
		1999	2000	Career	Age
9.	Randy Wolf	4	13	17	23.5
	Javier Vazquez	8	14	22	23.5
		1999	2000	Career	Age
10.	Pedro Martinez	27	29	155	28.5
	Mike Hampton	26	19	93	27.5
		1999	2000	Career	Age
11.	Scott Elarton	10	11	26	24.0
	Jim Parque	7	11	22	24.0

		1999	2000	Career	Age
12.	Kevin Appier	9	11	160	32.5
	Andy Benes	8	8	132	32.5

		1999	2000	Career	Age
13.	Doug Davis	0	5	5	24.5
	Valerio de los Santos	0	3	5	24.5

		1999	2000	Career	Age
14.	Wade Miller	0	4	4	23.5
	Matt Anderson	1	4	10	23.5

		1999	2000	Career	Age
15.	Jeff Suppan	12	12	31	25.0
	Eric Milton	12	11	29	24.5

		1999	2000	Career	Age
16.	Mike Mussina	17	18	161	31.5
	Curt Schilling	15	16	139	33.5

		1999	2000	Career	Age
17.	Woody Williams	10	12	59	33.5
	Dave Veres	11	14	61	33.5

		1999	2000	Career	Age
18.	Kevin Tapani	6	6	117	36.0
	Todd Stottlemyre	6	6	115	35.0

		1999	2000	Career	Age
19.	Pedro Astacio	19	11	89	30.5
	Aaron Sele	13	12	77	30.0

		1999	2000	Career	Age
20.	Sidney Ponson	10	11	26	23.5
	Jeff Weaver	7	12	19	23.5

		1999	2000	Career	Age
21.	Kelvim Escobar	7	8	28	24.0
	Carl Pavano	3	8	17	24.0

		1999	2000	Career	Age
22.	Blake Stein	4	7	11	26.5
	Octavio Dotel	3	7	10	26.5

		1999	2000	Career	Age
23.	Garrett Stephenson	5	11	26	28.0
	Bryan Rekar	3	11	21	28.0

		1999	2000	Career	Age
24.	Albie Lopez	4	13	32	28.5
	Gabe White	3	15	29	28.5

This study was based on comparable pitchers through the 2000 season. In the 2001 season, the 24 pitchers identified by Jazayerli and Woolner as having been worked hard earned 235 Win Shares, a decline in value of 15% from their 2000 performance. The 24 most-comparable pitchers, in terms of their age and previous value pattern, earned 144 Win Shares, a decline in value of 44%. The "abused" pitchers outperformed their "non-abused" partners by 63% (235 to 144):

Stressed Pitchers		Best Matches	
Livan Hernandez	5	Kris Benson	0
Randy Johnson	26	Kevin Brown	11
Jason Schmidt	9	Jose Rosado	0
Rick Helling	7	Mike Sirotka	0
Ron Villone	3	Tim Crabtree	0
Al Leiter	14	Kenny Rogers	2
Roger Clemens	19	Chuck Finley	3
Sterling Hitchcock	2	Scott Karl	0
Randy Wolf	11	Javier Vazquez	21
Kevin Appier	15	Andy Benes	0
Pedro Martinez	12	Mike Hampton	11
Scott Elarton	0	Jim Parque	0
Doug Davis	8	Valerio de los Santos	0
Wade Miller	17	Matt Anderson	8
Jeff Suppan	12	Eric Milton	15
Mike Mussina	20	Curt Schilling	24
Woody Williams	11	Dave Veres	7
Kevin Tapani	7	Todd Stottlemyre	0
Pedro Astacio	7	Aaron Sele	14
Sidney Ponson	4	Jeff Weaver	13
Kelvim Escobar	11	Carl Pavano	0
Blake Stein	7	Octavio Dotel	12
Garrett Stephenson	0	Bryan Rekar	1
Albie Lopez	8	Gabe White	2
Totals	235		144

Sixteen of the 24 "abused" pitchers outperformed their best value comp in the followup season.

Garrett Stephenson and Bryan Rekar . . . I had a "that can't be right" reaction to that one, as I'm sure many of you did. Stephenson went 16-9 in 2000; Rekar, 7-10. However, Rekar had a better ERA (4.41 vs. 4.49) despite playing in a league with a higher ERA . . . thus, they are credited with the same Win Shares for the season, and, since they are the same age, they wind up as man and match.

Study 2

Now, there are all kinds of problems with that study. I know that, you know that . . . that's kind of the nature of the research bidness, things don't work out the way you might hope. To start with, there are two easily identifiable problems:

1) It doesn't look right to have starting pitchers matched with relievers,

2) Some of the "abused" pitchers are one-of-a-kind superstars who have no good matches. Kevin Brown is a good pitcher; he's not Randy Johnson. Chuck Finley is a good pitcher; he's not Roger Clemens. Mike Hampton is a good pitcher; he's not Pedro Martinez.

With regard to the relievers . . . if I wanted to be obstreperous, I could well argue that there is no reason, within our guidelines, why relievers should not be matched against starting pitchers. They're all pitchers; they all do the same thing once they get to the mound, and they all have value. If relieving is less "stressful" on the arm than starting, isn't that what we're supposed to be measuring? There's really no reason why a starting pitcher *shouldn't* be matched against a reliever in a study of the effects of high stress versus low stress.

Not wishing to be obstreperous, I got rid of the relievers in the second study, and in all subsequent "comp" studies (three through seven), except study number four.

The second problem is what is known as "quality leakage" . . . it happens in all matched-set studies. Even though you may *intend* to match players, sealing out all non-germane differences between the groups, differences in quality have a strong tendency to leak into the study, simply because very good players are unusual, and are hard to match.

Although it seems extremely unlikely that quality leakage could explain the very large difference between these two groups of players, it is nonetheless clear that it fouls the study, and should be eliminated. To offset the effects of quality leakage, in the second study I attempted to identify matched players who were not *equal* to the abused pitchers, but slightly *better*—very similar, but slightly better, rather than simply very similar. I did this by looking to identify players who had:

1) One more Win Share in the focus season.
2) One more Win Share in the previous season, and
3) 10% more Win Shares in their careers.

That is, for Al Leiter, rather than looking for a pitcher with 11 Win Shares in 1999, 17 Win Shares in 2000 and 106 in his career, I looked for a pitcher with 12 Win Shares in 1999, 18 in 2000, and 117 in his career.

Of course, for Randy Johnson, Roger Clemens, and Pedro Martinez, this makes no difference. Whether you look for a pitcher as good as Randy Johnson, slightly better than Randy Johnson or slightly worse than Randy Johnson makes no difference, because there aren't any more of him and there aren't any better than him, so you're going to wind up with a weak match for him no matter what you do. Most often it makes no difference . . . most of the time you wind up with the same pitcher, anyway. It's just that, once in awhile, it flips the data so that a pitcher is matched against a slightly stronger candidate, which offsets the cases where a pitcher must be matched against a slightly weaker candidate.

In the second study, twelve pitchers wound up with new partners. Some of this is just shuffling the deck . . . Livan Hernandez is matched up against Tim Hudson, rather than Kris Benson. However, this causes Jeff Suppan to be matched up with Kris Benson, rather than Eric Milton, which causes Scott Elarton to be matched up with Eric Milton, rather than Jim Parque, and that causes Kelvim Escobar to be matched against Jim Parque, rather than Carl Pavano . . . four changes, but really, all we have done is to replace Carl Pavano with Tim Hudson.

The other eight changes are:

Jason Schmidt is matched against Jose Lima, rather than Jose Rosado.
Blake Stein is matched against Jarrod Washburn, rather than Octavio Dotel.
Doug Davis is matched with Tomokazu Ohka, rather than Valerio de los Santos.
Albie Lopez is matched against Brian Anderson, rather than Gabe White.
Woody Williams is matched with Dave Burba, rather than Dave Veres.
Wade Miller is matched against A. J. Burnett, rather than Matt Anderson, and

Ron Villone is matched against Bobby Jones (of the Mets), rather than Tim Crabtree.

These changes reduce slightly the degree to which the "abused" pitchers outperform their best matches in 2001. In 1999, the abused pitchers recorded 243 Win Shares; their best matches 246. In 2000—the base year of this study—the abused pitchers recorded 277 Win Shares, the best matches 269.

In 2001, the abused pitchers recorded 235 Win Shares; the best matches 173. The abused pitchers declined in value by 15% (the same figure as before . . . it is the same list of pitchers), while the control group declined by 36%. The abused pitchers also outperformed their non-abused counterparts by 36% (235/173).

Study 3

At this point, I thought perhaps that there was simply something odd about the "matches" that I had selected, which could perhaps be cured by searching for a new and non-overlapping group of comparable pitchers. On that theory, I then repeated the search for comparable pitchers for those on the 2000 list, but eliminated from the study anyone who had been included in the second study. As in the second study, I also eliminated relief pitchers, and I again looked for pitchers slightly *better* than those on the abused list, to offset the effects of quality leakage.

I call this the "second best matches" study. In this study:

Livan Hernandez was matched with Jeff D'Amico.
Randy Johnson was matched with Tom Glavine.
Jason Schmidt was matched back with Jose Rosado.
Rick Helling was matched with Bartolo Colon.
Ron Villone was matched with Tanyon Sturtze.
Al Leiter was matched with Denny Neagle.
Roger Clemens was matched with David Wells.
Sterling Hitchcock was matched with Darren Oliver.
Randy Wolf was matched with Ryan Dempster.
Kevin Appier was matched with Pat Hentgen.
Pedro Martinez was matched with Brad Radke.
Scott Elarton was now matched with Carl Pavano.
Doug Davis was matched with Jesus Sanchez.
Wade Miller was matched with Mark Mulder.
Jeff Suppan was matched with Mac Suzuki.
Mike Mussina was matched with Darryl Kile.
Woody Williams was matched with Rick Reed.
Kevin Tapani was matched with John Burkett.
Pedro Astacio was matched with Jon Lieber.
Sidney (keep your) Ponson was matched with Freddy Garcia.
Kelvim Escobar was matched with Jamey Wright.
Blake Stein was matched with Scott Schoeneweis.
Garrett Stephenson was matched with Darren Dreifort.
Albie Lopez was matched with Esteban Loaiza.

In this study, bringing in pitchers like Mark Mulder, Freddy Garcia, Bartolo Colon and Tom Glavine, the "matched" pitchers did essentially as well, in the followup season, as the "abused" pitchers. The data for the "abused" pitchers, of course, remains the same—277 Win Shares in the focus year, 235 in the followup season, a 15% decline. The matched pitchers declined from 253 Win Shares to 215, also a 15% decline. This was the one study of the seven in which the matched pitchers performed as well as the supposedly abused pitchers.

Study 4

At this point, I thought that we were ready to conclude that those pitchers who were subjected to heavy workloads in the 2000 season did not, in fact, decline to any unexpected extent in 2001. However, at this point we had studied only 24 "overworked" pitchers, from a single list of pitchers. We had 50-some "comps" to those 24 pitchers, but only 24 in the study group. Clearly, this is not enough to sustain any general conclusion—and, to be honest, at this point in the research I still expected to find that the 2000 season was simply an aberration, and that all I had done was to measure the aberration from three different angles.

I then switched my attention to what Rany and Keith had introduced as "the Danger Dozen—the 12 Most-Abused Pitchers of 1999," which list, of course, I had memorized from page 14 of the 2000 *Baseball Prospectus.* This list contains some now-familiar names: Livan Hernandez, Russ Ortiz, Freddy Garcia, Pedro Martinez, Jose Rosado, Randy Wolf, Randy Johnson, Bartolo Colon, Pedro Astacio, Jason Schmidt, Jamey Wright, and Shawn Estes. The following chart summarizes these twelve pitchers, and the most-comparable pitchers to them (in terms of value) from the 1999 season:

Abused Pitchers					Best 1999 Matches				
Player	'98	'99	Car	Age	Player	'98	'99	Car	Age
Livan Hernandez	6	9	24	24	Steve Woodard	9	9	19	24
Russ Ortiz	3	12	15	24.5	Kris Benson	0	12	12	24.5
Freddy Garcia	0	16	16	22.5	Scott Williamson	8	17	17	23
Pedro Martinez	21	27	126	27.5	Mike Hampton	15	26	74	26.5
Jose Rosado	10	13	43	24.5	Ugueth Urbina	17	14	49	25
Randy Wolf	0	4	4	22.5	Jeremy Powell	0	4	4	23
Randy Johnson	19	26	174	35.5	Kevin Brown	26	19	180	34
Bartolo Colon	16	16	34	26	Omar Daal	12	16	38	27
Pedro Astacio	6	19	78	29.5	Mariano Rivera	14	17	66	29.5
Jason Schmidt	11	13	34	26	Dustin Hermanson	13	12	35	26.5
Jamey Wright	8	7	23	24.5	Kelvim Escobar	7	7	20	23
Shawn Estes	3	6	29	26	C. J. Nitkowski	4	6	10	26
	103	168	600			117	159	524	

The obscure title "Car" means "Career through 1999" . . . you probably figured that out, but I worry that maybe there's a dumb guy reading the book. In any case, this chart compares the performance of these very comparable pitchers in the two following seasons, the 2000 and 2001 seasons:

Player	2000	2001	Player	2000	2001
Hernandez, Livan	14	5	Woodard, Steve	2	4
Ortiz, Russ	7	15	Benson, Kris	14	
Garcia, Freddy	8	18	Williamson, Scott	11	0
Martinez, Pedro	29	12	Hampton, Mike	19	11
Rosado, Jose	1		Urbina, Ugueth	2	11
Wolf, Randy	13	11	Powell, Jeremy	1	
Johnson, Randy	26	26	Brown, Kevin	20	11
Colon, Bartolo	15	14	Daal, Omar	5	11
Astacio, Pedro	11	7	Rivera, Mariano	16	19
Schmidt, Jason	1	9	Hermanson, Dustin	9	8
Wright, Jamey	9	7	Escobar, Kelvim	8	11
Estes, Shawn	10	7	Nitkowski, C.J.	3	2
	144	131		110	88

One of the 1999 abused pitchers, Jose Rosado, did drop off the face of the earth, and another one, Jason Schmidt, had serious arm trouble in 2000, as was noted by my friend Srinivasan at the onset of this article.

However, as a group, the "abused" pitchers once more performed substantially better in 2000 and 2001 than did the best-matched pitchers who were not listed as abused. In 1999 the "abused" pitchers were credited with 168 Win Shares; the control group, with 159. In 2000, the abused pitchers declined to 144—a 14% decline—while the "unabused" pitchers declined to 110, a drop of 31%.

In the second followup season, the "abused" pitchers declined to 131 Win Shares, an additional decline of slightly less than 10%. The "non-abused" pitchers declined from 110 to 88, an additional decline of 20%. In sum, this study is consistent with the evaluation of the 2000 list.

Study 5

In Study 4, we used the same method as in Study 1, and encountered the same problems: quality leakage, and starting pitchers compared to relievers. To get rid of these, we made the same adjustment as we made from Study-1 to Study-2—that is, we got rid of the relievers, and used the same method outlined before to look for comparable pitchers who were slightly *better* than those on the "abused" list.

This produced wholesale changes in the list of comparable pitchers:

For Russ Ortiz, Jeff Suppan rather than Kris Benson.

For Freddy Garcia, Tim Hudson rather than Scott Williamson.

For Jose Rosado, Ismael Valdes rather than Ugueth Urbina.

For Randy Wolf, Kyle Farnsworth rather than Jeremy Powell.

For Randy Johnson, David Cone rather than Kevin Brown.

For Bartolo Colon, Jose Lima rather than Omar Daal.

For Pedro Astacio, Wilson Alvarez rather than Mariano Rivera.

For Jamey Wright, Chris Carpenter rather than Kelvim Escobar.

For Shawn Estes, Brett Tomko rather than C. J. Nitkowski.

However, the new list of comparable pitchers performed far worse, in 2000, than the original list (in Study-4). While the original pitchers declined to 110 Win Shares in 2000, 88 in 2001, the new control group declined to 71 Win Shares in 2000, recovering somewhat to 97 in 2001. As in the previous studies, the "abused" pitchers performed far better, in the followup seasons, than their counterparts who had not been abused.

Study 6

Study 6 deals with a list of pitchers given on page 13 of the 2000 *Baseball Prospectus,* which is introduced as a list of "the winners of the Most-Abused Pitcher Award for each year from 1988–98." For this study, I'm going to deal with the pitchers one at a time, because this was the study that convinced me that I was not dealing with a fluke outcome, but with a real phenomenon.

1. Bobby Witt, 1988

Bobby Witt in 1988 was 8–10 with a 3.92 ERA in 174 innings, giving him a career record at that time of 27–29, 4.74 ERA. We credit him with 6 Win Shares in 1987, 10 in 1988, 19 to that point in his career, and he was born in May 1964.

The most-comparable pitcher to Witt at that point was Scott Bankhead, who in 1988 was 7–9 with a 3.07 ERA in 135 innings, giving him a career record of 24–26, 4.35 ERA. We credit him with 6 Win Shares in 1987—the same as Witt—and 10 Win Shares in 1988, again the same as Witt. He had 22 Win Shares to that point in his career, and he was born in July 1963. We score this similarity as 993.5, making him the best comp to Witt, and also the best match for any of the eleven pitchers in Study 6.

The Jazayerli/Woolner article discusses Witt for three paragraphs, and makes the point that "in 1991, he blew out his arm and has never been the same." This is quite true, but it is also true that Witt pitched in the majors until 2001, and won 142 games in his career. Bankhead, the most comparable pitcher to him at the point at which Witt was tagged as abused, ended his career in 1996 with 57 wins.

2. Roger Clemens, 1989

Roger Clemens in 1988 was 18-12, 2.93 ERA; in 1989 he was 17-11, 3.13 ERA. His career record to that point was 95-45 with a 3.06 ERA.

The most comparable pitcher to Clemens at that point in his career was Mark Gubicza. I know that, after all Clemens has done in the last decade, it is difficult to think of Mark Gubicza as ever having been in the same class with him, but Gubicza was an excellent comp for Clemens at that time. Gubicza in 1988 was 20-8, 2.70 ERA; in 1989 he was 15-11, 3.04 ERA. He pitched six more innings than Clemens in 1988 (270-264), and two more in 1989 (255-253).

Gubicza's career record at that point was "only" 84-67—a good record, but 16 and a half games behind Clemens. While Clemens *had* outperformed Gubicza in previous seasons, however, Gubicza's value was higher than Clemens' in both 1989 (19-18) and 1988 (24-22). Clemens led in career Win Shares, 113 to 95, and both pitchers were born in August 1962. They are an excellent match (982) at the point at which Clemens was listed as the most-abused pitcher of the year.

Obviously, Clemens has outperformed Gubicza by a very wide margin since that point in time.

3. Ramon Martinez, 1990

(The book actually says Pedro, but I'm pretty sure they meant Ramon.) Ramon went 20-6 in 1990, his first full season in the majors, and has become one of the poster children of the movement to end arm abuse.

However, the most-comparable pitcher to Martinez at that time—and frankly, we do have a quality leakage problem here—was Mike Harkey of the Cubs. Harkey, a year and a half older than Martinez, also had his first full season in the majors, and also pitched well, going 12-6 with a 3.26 ERA in 174 innings. Harkey's ERA in Wrigley Field is actually more impressive than Martinez' in Dodger Stadium (2.92), and we credit Martinez with 17 Win Shares (three less than his actual wins), Harkey with 15 (three more than his actual wins). We score the similarity between them at 962.

While Martinez did struggle in the rest of his career, while he did fail to achieve what he seemed to be capable of, his post-1990 career is far better than that of the most-comparable pitcher to him at the point at which he was listed as abused.

4. Jose DeJesus, 1991

Jose DeJesus in 1991 went 10-9 with a 3.42 ERA; his career record to that point in his career was 17–18, 3.77 ERA, and he was born in January 1965.

The best comp to DeJesus at that point in his career was Trevor Wilson, who in 1991 was 13-11, 3.56 ERA, giving him a career record of 23-23, 3.81 ERA; he was born in June 1966. Each pitcher was credited with 11 Win Shares in 1991, giving Wilson a career total of 17; DeJesus, a total of 18. The similarity between the two of them was scored at 985.5.

DeJesus, who I think clearly was pushed beyond his breaking point, earned only 2 Win Shares in the rest of his career. However, Wilson, who had some very unusual medical problems, didn't do a whole lot better, earning only 14 Win Shares in the rest of his career.

5. Randy Johnson, 1992

Randy Johnson *now* is hard to match, a unique pitcher. At that point in his career, 1992, he was not hard to match in terms of quality. In 1992 he went 12–14, 3.77 ERA; his career record at that time was 49-48, 3.95 ERA. He was regarded as a hard thrower with no control, and time was running out on him to develop, as he turned 29 in September of that season.

The most-comparable pitcher to him, in terms of value pattern through 1992, was Terry Mulholland. A few months older than Johnson, he had gone 13-11 in 1992, 3.81 ERA, giving him a career mark of 45–49, 3.87 ERA. In terms of value, age, performance in 1991, performance in 1992, and career performance up to that point, he is an excellent match for Randy Johnson at the point at which Johnson was first identified as the most-abused pitcher of the season.

While Mulholland has had a long and creditable career, obviously he has not recently been compared to Randy Johnson.

6. Cal Eldred, 1993

After making three starts in 1991, Cal Eldred came to the majors in mid-season, 1992, and was sensational, going 11-2 with a 1.79 ERA. In 1993 he led the American League in starts (36) and innings pitched (258), finishing 16-16 with a 4.01 ERA.

The most-comparable pitcher to him at that time was Ben McDonald, who had gone 13-14 with Baltimore with a 3.39 ERA, making 34 starts. McDonald was the number one draft pick in the country in 1989, when Eldred was also picked in the first round, and was born on the same day as Eldred—November 24, 1967. The similarity between them was scored at 988.

Eldred, another of the poster children of the arm abuse movement, had earned 37 Win Shares in the rest of his career (through 2001). McDonald, an extremely comparable pitcher at that point in time, earned 41.

7. Randy Johnson, 1994

By 1994, when the "most-abused" tag returned to him for its second visit, Randy Johnson had begun to separate himself from the herd, going 19-8 in 1993, 13-8 in 1994, with respectable ERAs (3.24 and 3.19).

However, while he was *good* in those years, he was not *so* good that he was terribly hard to match. Chuck Finley, a year older than Johnson, had gone 16-14 in 1993, 10-10 in 1994 with a 3.15 ERA in '93, but 4.32 in '94. Finley's career record at that point (99-86, 3.50 ERA) was a little better than Johnson's (81-62, 3.70 ERA).

While Finley has continued to be a quality pitcher up to the present time, obviously he has not become the superstar that Randy has, since the second point at which Johnson was identified as the most abused pitcher in the major leagues.

8–9. Alex Fernandez, 1995 and 1996

A rotation anchor for the White Sox since 1990, Alex Fernandez was 18-9 in 1993, then 11-7 in 1994, 12-8 in 1995, giving him a career record at that point of 63-53, 3.88 ERA.

In 1995 the most comparable pitcher to Fernandez was Tom Gordon of Kansas City, then exclusively a starting pitcher. Gordon was 11-7 in 1994 (the same as Fernandez) and 12-12 in 1995, giving him a career record of 79-71, 4.02 ERA. He was 21 months older than Fernandez, a 20-point penalty which lowers the similarity between them to 967.5.

While Fernandez has had significant arm trouble since 1995, so has Gordon. Gordon has earned 52 Win Shares from 1995 through 2001; Fernandez, 49.

In 1996, after being tagged as heavily abused in 1995, Fernandez pitched 258 innings for the White Sox, going 16-10 with 200 strikeouts. At that point, the most-comparable pitcher to him in the major leagues, in terms of value pattern, was Chuck Nagy of Cleveland, who went 17-5 with a 3.41 ERA. Nagy then owned a career record of 74-54, 3.86 ERA; Fernandez, of 79-63, 3.78 ERA.

Nagy was two-and-a-half years older than Fernandez, a 25-point penalty, but was the best available comp. Both pitchers have had serious arm trouble since that time, Nagy earning 34 additional Win Shares; Fernandez, 30.

10. Pedro Martinez, 1997

The tenth pitcher listed by Rany and Keith as the most-abused man of the year was Pedro Martinez, who is of course very difficult to match. Pedro went 17-8 that season with a 1.90 ERA (his first great season), giving him a career record at that time of 65-39, 3.00 ERA.

The best match to Pedro at that time was Andy Pettitte, who was 18-7 that year, 2.88 ERA, giving him a career mark of 51-24, 3.58 ERA. He was (and is, as far as I know) eight months younger than Pedro.

This match, which scores at 942.5, is the weakest pairing of the 11 in Study 6. Since 1997 both pitchers have continued to pitch well, Pedro earning an additional 89 Win Shares, and Pettitte an additional 50.

11. Livan Hernandez, 1998

After pitching three innings in 1996, Livan Hernandez was called up in mid-season, 1997, and . . . well, you all know that story. He did not pitch particularly well in 1998, finished 10-12 with a 4.72 ERA for a bad team, but he did pitch a whole bunch, 234 innings, including 265 hits allowed, giving him a career record of 19-15, 4.23 ERA.

Hernandez' value pattern to that point was 1-8-6, total of 15. The most comparable value pattern at that point in time belongs to Glendon Rusch, whose value pattern was 0-5-5, total of 10, and who was about three months older than Hernandez.

Rusch had an ugly record at that point—6-15 in 1998, 5.88 ERA, giving him a career mark of 12-24, 5.68. But remember this: while Livan had pitched for one bad team and one World Championship team, Rusch had pitched for two bad teams. Also, while Hernandez was pitching in a league with a 4.23 ERA and in a park with a park factor of .90 (for that one season), Rusch was pitching in a league with a 4.65 ERA and in a park with a park factor of 1.07. In context, Rusch's ERA is not significantly worse than Hernandez'. In any case, we asked the system to pick the one most similar pitcher to Hernandez, and this is the answer it gives us.

In the three seasons since then, Hernandez has earned 28 Win Shares. Rusch has earned 17.

Summary

Of these 11 pitchers who have been cited as the most-abused of each season, 1988 to 1998, there is not a single case in which the most-abused pitcher has performed *significantly* worse, in subsequent seasons, than the most-comparable major-league pitcher in terms of his career value pattern up to that point. Seven of the "abused" pitchers have done better than their partners, four have done worse, but all four of the "wins" for the "non-abused" pitchers are by very small margins.

In sum, the "abused" pitchers in this study have earned 975 career Win Shares subsequent to their designation as abused. The most-comparable pitchers have earned 458:

Most-Abused Pitcher		Best Value Match	
Bobby Witt	83	Scott Bankhead	34
Roger Clemens	239	Mark Gubicza	46
Ramon Martinez	87	Mike Harkey	16
Jose DeJesus	2	Trevor Wilson	15
Randy Johnson	184	Terry Mulholland	64
Cal Eldred	37	Ben McDonald	41
Randy Johnson	147	Chuck Finley	89
Alex Fernandez	49	Flash Gordon	52
Alex Fernandez	30	Charles Nagy	34
Pedro Martinez	89	Andy Pettitte	50
Livan Hernandez	28	Glendon Rusch	17
	975		458

The "abused" pitchers have outperformed their non-abused counterparts, in subsequent seasons, by 113%.

If, for some reason, we declare Randy Johnson to be a freak of nature and a pitcher who can't be matched, and we take his two entries out of the study, the abused pitchers have still outperformed their counterparts by 111%.

If we also take Pedro Martinez out of the study, it goes back up to 118%.

If we take Roger Clemens out of the study (as well as Johnson and Martinez), the abused pitchers have still outperformed their non-abused counterparts by 51% (316 to 209).

The abused pitchers have outperformed their unabused counterparts in the first subsequent season by 78% (167-94), in the second subsequent season by 58% (125-79), in the third subsequent season by 55% (135-87), in the fourth subsequent season by 26% (88-70), in the fifth subsequent season by 134% (96-41), and in the sixth subsequent season by 29% (71-55). After the sixth subsequent season, the "abused" pitchers have outperformed their unabused matches by 816% (293-32).

Study 7

At this point it seems fairly clear that the pitchers listed by Rany and Keith as abused do not, in fact, have any unusual tendency to collapse quivering on the floor after having been worked so hard. However, there is one more list that can be studied, and so, for the sake of thoroughness, we will study it.

That list is of the twelve highest Workloads of the 1998 season, which is discussed on pages 12 and 13 of the 2000 *Baseball Prospectus.* The list is Livan Hernandez, Kelvim Escobar, Pedro Martinez, Kerry Wood, Rafael Medina, Randy Johnson, Bartolo Colon, Curt Schilling, Orlando Hernandez, Jason Schmidt, Andy Pettitte and Tony Saunders.

Almost all of these pitchers had some injuries or periods of ineffectiveness in 1999, and the article discusses each of these failures. To match these players, I put in the "look for someone slightly BETTER" element to counteract quality leakage, which causes Livan Hernandez, who previously was matched against Glendon Rusch, to come out matched against Jamey Wright.

We have another Ruben Quevedo here. Rafael Medina, like Quevedo in 1999, had no value, consequently cannot be used in our study. The other matches are:

Kelvim Escobar to Jaret Wright
Pedro Martinez to Mike Mussina
Kerry Wood to Chris Carpenter
Randy Johnson to David Cone
Bartolo Colon to Jose Lima
Curt Schilling to Tom Glavine
Orlando Hernandez to Juan Acevedo
Jason Schmidt to Dustin Hermanson
Andy Pettitte to Brad Radke
Tony Saunders to Kevin Millwood

This study produced the same result as before, but with an interesting wrinkle. In this case the "abused" pitchers performed neither better nor worse than the best matches in the first subsequent season, 1999; each group earned 137 Win Shares. However, the "abused" pitchers then moved far ahead in the second subsequent season (142-98) and the third (131-102). Since 1998, the 11 abused pitchers have been credited with 410 Win Shares. The 11 pitchers who match them best have been credited with 337.

Study 8

This study is different from the other seven, being not an attempt to find comparable pitchers to those listed as abused, but an examination of an underlying question.

The underlying question is this: what is a normal rate of decline for a pitcher? The seven studies here, of four different lists of pitchers, show a decline in performance in the following seasons, for all the "abused" pitchers on the four lists, of 10.3%, from 761 Win Shares to 683. The seven lists of "comparable" pitchers declined by 32%, from 1,382 Win Shares to 944. This raises an obvious question: what is a normal rate of decline? Which of these figures is out of line?

Of course, the "normal" rate of decline is no doubt different for every group of pitchers . . . it is no doubt different for a 37-year-old pitcher who earns 20 Win Shares than it is for a 27-year-old pitcher who earns 10 Win Shares. Since the pitchers listed as abused are of all different ages and levels of value, we would not be able to establish clearly what sort of expectation we should have for them without doing an immense amount of work.

Taking all levels of performance from 1 Win Share to 30 and all ages from 19 to 42, we could generate 720 "cells" of information, some of which would be void, and many more of which would be based on limited information. I don't want to get into that, for obvious reasons, but what if we chose a limited number of cells where there would be reasonably good data, and estimated the decline rate for each of those locations?

I chose four ages and four levels of performance, resulting in 16 estimates of the normal rates of decline. I chose the ages 24, 27, 30, and 33, and the performance levels of 8, 12, 16, and 20 Win Shares. I then asked, for example, what is the normal rate of decline for a 33-year-old pitcher who earns 16 Win Shares?

I eliminated two groups of pitchers:

a) those born before 1900, who may have aberrant data in any number of ways, and

b) those who were at the target age in 2001, for whom there is as yet no "next season" to study.

There have been only five pitchers born since 1900 who earned exactly 20 Win Shares at the age of 24 (not counting Javier Vazquez, who did this in 2001. The other five are Tom Bradley, Joe Coleman Jr., Rick Reuschel, Kevin Appier, and Johnny Rigney.) Anyway, obviously I can't get much out of five players, so I expanded that group to include 24-year-old pitchers who earned 19 or 21 Win Shares, the only time it was necessary to do that (and I still got a funny-looking result in that cell.)

Anyway, these are the estimates of the decline rates for each of these 16 cells:

	Age 24	Age 27	Age 30	Age 33
20 Win Shares	19%	41%	43%	14%
16 Win Shares	35%	40%	24%	23%
12 Win Shares	23%	22%	5%	32%
8 Win Shares	6%	18%	24%	30%

The overall rate of decline for all players in these 16 cells is 23%.

IV. Meaning?

Ok, why are we getting these results?

Let me begin by explaining what I do and do not question about this area of research.

First, I do not question that there is a risk of working a young pitcher too hard and destroying his arm, robbing him of his future, and I do not question that this has in fact happened to countless young pitchers in the history of baseball—Steve Busby, Gary Nolan, Wally Bunker, Mark Fidrych, Larry Dierker, Dave Rozema, Britt Burns, John Fulgham, Jose Rosado, Jose Guzman, Edwin Correa, etc.

Second, I do not question that the pitch counts are a potentially useful tool in steering clear of this disastrous result.

Third, I do not question that Rany and Keith's studies were done in good faith and with the best of intentions, and I think that actually they were done with both intelligence and good sense. Had I been doing the same studies, I would have done them essentially the same way that Rany and Keith did them, and I believe that I would have reached essentially the same conclusions.

But those conclusions are not valid. Something has gone wrong. Somewhere, between 1982 and the present, this research has gone off-track, and has begun to run in an unproductive direction.

As to *where* exactly this happened, I honestly don't know. I'm just guessing. Nobody knows; we have to have some hypothesis to start with.

One reason that the "abused" pitchers show up as substantially *better* than the non-abused pitchers, I believe, is that the pitch-count system has a tendency to identify power pitchers as abused pitchers, which is counter-productive, since power pitchers have greater durability and consistency than non-strikeout type pitchers.

However, if you remove that factor—if, somehow, you could "correct" for it—the best you could possibly do is get back to zero. At zero, we have nothing—the "abused" pitchers are no more likely to get hurt than non-abused pitchers—and frankly, I don't think you could get back to zero. So that's not going to lead anywhere.

One problem with my studies, which I haven't discussed yet, is that they are inclined to identify as "comparable" to the abused pitcher another pitcher who is also on one of the abused lists at some other point in time. For example, on the 2000 "non-abused" list we have Jose Rosado, who was on the abused list in 1999, and for Pedro Martinez in 1997 we have paired him with Andy Pettitte, who would then make the abused list in 1998.

This sort of thing happens a lot in these studies, and certainly, it is a matter of concern. There are many cases where players are "partnered" with pitchers who probably were also abused at some other point in their careers, although they don't happen to have appeared on any of the lists . . . Kevin Appier in one study is paired with Andy Benes, who certainly would turn up on some "abused" lists somewhere, sometime. I'm not suggesting that my studies are perfect, by any means; if you want to study the issue some other way, be my guest. But

a) there are so many pitchers who are listed as "abused" somewhere that to do a "comparables" study which steers clear of all of them is probably like trying to go bowling without running into anybody wearing a funny shirt, and

b) it's not going to make any difference anyway.

If you went through all of these studies and took out every "comparable" pitcher who was "also" abused, you would have much smaller and therefore less convincing studies, but otherwise exactly the same conclusion.

Also, if you think about it logically, you'll realize that the inclusion of some pitchers in Group "B" who *should* be in Group "A" would not likely cause Group A to perform better than Group B. If the average of Group A is 100 and the average of Group B is 50, and you accidentally include some pitchers from Group B in Group A, that *reduces* the measured difference between Group A and Group B. It doesn't increase it.

The problem isn't in the comparables; the problem

is that what Rany and Keith are saying simply is not true: the pitchers that they list as abused simply do not have any unnatural tendency to decline in subsequent seasons, and you are never going to be able to prove that they do. The pitchers that Jazayerli and Woolner identify as "abused" declined in value by 10% in the following season. That can't possibly be an unnatural decline. *This system simply does not identify at-risk pitchers, period.* That's what I believe. It may not identify pitchers who have unusually *good* durability, or it may, but it does not identify pitchers who have a high risk of losing value.

In the 2001 edition, Jazayerli and Woolner revised their system to change somewhat how they identified an abused pitcher. Again, in my opinion, that can't possibly make any real difference. The changes are not large enough to explain the findings.

Another issue of marginal concern here is the "age" factor in the Woolner/Jazayerli method. If you look back to Craig Wright's earliest writings on this issue, it is clear that Craig was concerned mostly with the effect of hard usage on *young* pitchers. Craig wrote, and I've already quoted it, that a 20- to 22-year-old pitcher should never throw more than 130 pitches in a game.

Well, hell, I have no problem with that. You have a 21-year-old pitcher throwing 140 pitches, I'd tend to think that the manager was crazy.

The problem is that we have raced way past that, where now we are second-guessing managers for giving 120, 125 pitches to a mature pitcher. Woolner and Jazayerli attempted, in their method, to build in an "age" adjustment by multiplying the raw pitch-count score by a factor increasing gradually back in time from age 32.

I believe that this "age adjustment" may be inadequate, and that this may be one of the reasons that their system misrepresents the effects of throwing a lot of pitches. Craig's original work, I believe, suggests that pitch counts of 130 to 150 may be perfectly OK for mature pitchers with no history of an impingement syndrome, but that they should be assiduously avoided for immature pitchers, and for certain other "vulnerable" pitchers. That still sounds very reasonable to me.

But again, I don't really think that fixing this "age" adjustment is going to make this method work. I think that the problems are more fundamental than that. I think, in essence, that we have driven a long way here down a blind alley, and that we're not going to fix it by backing up a few feet and trying again.

The problem is not with our *method;* the problem is with our *thinking.* The method is fine; it's our thinking about the whole issue of pitch counts that is messed up. Throwing 120, 130 pitches a game, for a healthy, mature pitcher, simply isn't dangerous. It's probably good for them.

This research is built on *assumptions.* There is, to the best of my knowledge, no sabermetric research anywhere that backs up those assumptions.

Here's the note that struck me, in reading the 2000 article in the *Baseball Prospectus* (page 12):

> Why is 100 used as the threshold? It's certainly not because every pitcher should come out after 100 pitches, or that outings longer than that are foolish and reckless. But repeated outings that go beyond 100 pitches can, over time, cause the kind of chronic overuse injury which may render the pitcher incapacitated or ineffective.

Chronic overuse injury. *Chronic Overuse Injury.* Are there actually a lot of mature major league pitchers who are incapacitated by a chronic overuse injury?

I don't think that there are. There are *some,* certainly, and there is nothing wrong with keeping an eye out for those.

Here's what I think . . . in fact, I'm going to break it off and make that a separate section, because I've thought about this for several days, and I'm pretty convinced that I should say this.

V. Where We Went Wrong

> *It's hard for people to buy into the fact that throwing will strengthen your arm. A lot of them think that rest will strengthen it. It won't. It might make it feel better but it won't strengthen it.*
>
> —*Tommy John*

I think that there is a natural balancing of risks, in almost any physical activity, and that this balancing of risks, with respect to the use of pitchers, has gotten out of whack.

About fourteen months ago, I realized that I had gotten terribly out of shape, and that my good health was at risk if I didn't make an effort to do better. This didn't happen suddenly, either the getting out of the shape or

Lawrence Journal World, Kansas Collection, Kenneth Spencer Research Library, University of Kansas Libraries

Tommy John

the realization that it had happened, but let's not get into that.

Thinking about how to work myself back into better shape, two things were obvious:

1) That I was going to have to spend some quality time with a treadmill, and

2) That I had to be careful not to overdo it right away.

Fifty-two-year-old man weighing close to 300 pounds, you don't want to hop on that bugger and see how fast you can run in the first week. If I had tried to run, at any point in the first three months, I would have been inviting a heart attack. I had to be careful to stay well within the limits established by my previous conditioning routine—none—while at the same time pushing myself to work harder, to do more, and to build up my body's tolerance for exercise.

Suppose that you can deadlift 40 pounds, and you want to build that up to where you can clean and jerk a couple of hundred. What do you do?

Well, you don't go out and push yourself to body's limit right away, or you're going to have a pulled muscle in your shoulder, or a displaced vertebrae, or some other injury to your spine or muscular system which sounds cold and clinical but hurts like bloody hell for a long time. You have to stay within the limits of your body, but you also have to push yourself hard enough that you build up those limits, and change them gradually over time.

Well, it's the same thing here. *Most* injuries to pitchers are not the result of chronic overuse; some are, particularly to young pitchers, but most are not. They're catastrophic events, just like a heart attack or a torn muscle. They happen suddenly, and they happen when a pitcher goes outside the envelope of his previous conditioning.

Backing away from the pitcher's limits *too far* doesn't make a pitcher *less* vulnerable; it makes him *more* vulnerable. And pushing the envelope, while it *may* lead to a catastrophic event, is more likely to enhance the pitcher's durability than to destroy it.

What I believe has happened is that this "balancing of risks" has just gone completely haywire. Two things have happened to cause it to go haywire:

1) We have introduced new information—pitch counts—into a previously organized way of thinking about the issue, and

2) We have focused undue attention on the risk of chronic overuse, which in reality is merely one of many potential problems for a pitcher.

There is a natural balancing of risks, between avoiding a catastrophic event, and developing a tolerance for more work. In order to develop a real understanding of this issue, we are going to have to take account of both ends of the injury spectrum.

A RESPONSE IN DEFENSE OF PAP

RANY JAZAYERLI AND KEITH WOOLNER

It was a mixed blessing when we heard from Bill James that he had written a critique of our PAP system for his new book. It's possible neither one of us would be writing about baseball today if it weren't for Bill's influence, so certainly his words carry weight with us. That he invited us to write a rebuttal in his (and Rob's) own book is testament to his graciousness. Which we will now exploit by pointing out all the holes in his argument.

First off, we must quibble with Bill's methodology. In particular, his first three studies relied on the exact same list of abused pitchers that was printed in the 1999 and 2000 editions of *Baseball Prospectus.* Those lists were generated using a formula that we already know was imperfect. When PAP was introduced, we freely admitted that it was done without any empiric evidence to back it up, but we presented it as a framework to spur further research on the topic.

That research was done by Keith in BP 2001, which resulted in a complete overhaul in the way PAP scores were calculated. Bill is correct when he concludes that the lists generated from the first iteration of PAP don't work. That's why we created a second iteration.

More pertinent to the issue of whether PAP works is that the conundrum that Bill exposes—that looking forward, abused pitchers pitch better as a group than any control group that you compare them with—is something we discovered while working on the updated version of PAP. In fact, we wrote about it on page 491 of BP 2001:

> Evaluating the effectiveness of PAP is not as simple as identifying the pitchers with the highest PAP scores and then looking to see if they got injured or lost their effectiveness more than the average pitcher. If you look at the pitchers with the highest PAP scores, you're staring at Randy Johnson, Roger Clemens, Pedro Martinez, and others—the best pitchers in baseball, players who have tallied the highest PAP scores because they've earned them . . . Pedro Martinez was worked a lot harder than Omar Olivares in 1999; that Olivares was the one who fell apart in 2000 doesn't really tell us anything other than the fact that Omar Olivares is no Pedro Martinez.

Put plainly, pitchers who are entrusted with the highest workloads are different from other pitchers, and no amount of massaging the names of the pitchers in the control group is going to make them comparable.

Bill writes of Randy Johnson, "at that point in his career, 1992, he was not hard to match in terms of quality." Perhaps, but Johnson was (and is) almost impossible to match as a physical specimen. Terry Mulholland may have been equally valuable at the time, but even then, no one would have claimed that Mulholland was equally durable.

Bill compares Roger Clemens to Mark Gubicza. We remember Mark Gubicza. We were fans of Mark Gubicza. Mark Gubicza was no Roger Clemens.

This is a theme that insinuates itself into every level of this study. Almost every pitcher that earned a place on the most-abused list did so because his team thought he had the stamina and the stuff to handle the workload. Almost every pitcher selected for the control group was on that list because his team thought he didn't. Even after controlling for value, the two groups simply aren't comparable.

This bias is so pervasive that we found it nearly impossible to remove it completely. As Bill himself wrote many years ago, on a completely different topic, "All of you who work with statistics know that once in a while the numbers themselves will seem to conspire to obfuscate the truth, and this is one of those times."

At this juncture, we had two options. We could throw up our hands, proclaim the issue unsolvable, and walk away. Or we could get creative.

We got creative. Since we couldn't find any pitcher to compare to Randy Johnson, we decided to compare the Big Unit to himself. We compared Johnson's performance in games following a 130-pitch start with his performance after throwing 120, or 106, or 58 pitches. We did this for every pitcher from 1988 through 1998, actually—the exact process was complicated, but the details can be found in BP 2001.

And when you look at the issue this way, you find that pitch counts above 100 *are* associated with a short-term decline. The trend of this decline, in fact, is what was responsible for changing the formula used to calculate PAP.

Of course, even a proven short-term decline does not necessarily lead to a long-term injury risk. So with our new formula in hand, we studied the issue of whether there was a correlation between high PAP scores and injury risk.

The method we used was significantly different than Bill's, and we feel was a more relevant one. In our minds, Bill is assessing "comparability" along the wrong dimension. He defines comparable pitchers by Win Share value, not the amount of work they performed. If injury is related to throwing too many pitches while tired, comparable pitchers are ones who performed similar amounts of work, but with a lower proportion of "tired work." To truly find comparable pitchers, you need to compare pitchers with similar career total pitches thrown, but with lower career PAP scores.

Keith performed this very comparison in BP 2001. He identified pitchers who actually had arm injuries, and compared them to all major-league pitchers of similar age and workload. "Stress," defined as the average amount of PAP per pitch thrown over his career, was demonstrated to be correlated with a higher chance of injury.

Having defended our system, we don't mean to imply that Bill's work is completely without merit. Bill is almost certainly right when he states that almost all of the risk inherent in throwing too many pitches occurs in a pitcher's formative years. The connection between overuse and catastrophic injury seems to drop off quickly past age 25 or so. The abused pitchers who *did* suffer catastrophic injuries—Jose Rosado, Jose DeJesus, Scott Elarton, Ramon Martinez—were all in their early 20s when they had the abuse heaped upon them.

Second, it's clear that pitch counts are only one factor in determining a pitcher's injury risk. A pitcher's mechanics, his workout regimen, his body habitus—all are factors which play a part in determining how many pitches is too much. Which is why we're continuing to push the envelope in assessing pitchers' injury risk. Our colleague at BP, Will Carroll, has started what he calls "The Velocity Project" in an attempt to determine whether a subtle decline in a pitcher's velocity is a harbinger of fatigue and loss of effectiveness.

So there is clearly a danger in relying on pitch counts as the sole arbiter of a pitcher's risk. For instance, we are *not* particularly concerned about Mark Prior's arm—even though he had the third-highest Stress score in baseball last season—because his pitching mechanics are as close to drop-dead perfect as anyone has ever seen.

In the end, we feel that the notion that lowering pitch counts can reduce injury risk will be vindicated in the clearest way possible: on the playing field. Perhaps the most under-reported development in baseball over the last five years has been the dramatic decline in high pitch counts. As recently as 2000, a pitcher threw 122 or more pitches in a game 323 times. In 2003, that number was reached just 149 times—a decrease of fifty-four percent.

For the first time in baseball history, teams are being proactive in protecting their young pitchers before fatigue and injury set in. As a rookie, C.C. Sabathia was the youngest left-hander to win 17 games in over 80 years. In any other era, his team would have seized upon his success by pushing him to the very limits of his endurance. But in three seasons, the Indians have yet to let Sabathia throw more than 125 pitches in any start. Sabathia has yet to visit the DL, and his ERA has improved each season. The Oakland A's Big Three—Mark Mulder, Barry Zito, and Tim Hudson—have combined for just three starts of more than 127 pitches in their career. None of them has suffered a significant arm injury.

A revolution in the management of starting pitchers is underway, and the early signs suggest that the revolution may well lead to fewer injuries. If it succeeds, if baseball teams find a way to prevent even a fraction of the injuries which befell so many top pitching prospects, we may see a new era of baseball, less tilted towards the hitting pyrotechnics of the past decade—and, along with it, a better product on the field.

E = M CY SQUARED

BILL JAMES

Is it possible to write a "Cy Young Formula" which will predict reliably who will win the Cy Young Award? Those of you who have read my littershure over the years know that I am always fooling around with questions like this . . . looking for formulas to predict MVP voting, or Hall of Fame voting, or most any kind of voting that doesn't involve Florida (I'm not crazy). It has been a while since I have taken on the Cy Young Award, and we have a book about pitching here, so . . .

Our goal is to produce a simple, cogent formula which reliably predicts Cy Young voting, in such a form that we can "track" the Cy Young contest over the course of the season. What we want, in other words, is to be able to look at the statistics of the leading pitchers on June 21 or July 21 or August 21, do a few simple calculations, and make a reasonable conclusion about who is "ahead" in the Cy Young race, how far ahead they are, and what the other pitchers have to do to catch up.

I think I have come up with such a formula. It is:

Wins times 6
minus Losses times 2
plus Strikeouts divided by 12
plus Saves times 2.5
plus Shutouts
plus Runs Saved
plus 12 points for pitching for a first-place team.

Runs Saved are figured as "runs not allowed by the pitcher, compared to a pitcher with a 5.00 ERA."

In the American League in 2002, in the murkiest Cy Young race in years, the top two candidates were Barry Zito and Pedro Martinez. Zito went 23-5; that's 128 points (138 minus 10), while Martinez went 20-4, which is 112 points (120 minus 8). Usually, 23 and 5 beats 20 and 4 in Cy Young voting.

Zito had 182 strikeouts, which are worth 15.17 points, while Pedro had 239, which are worth 19.92 points; that makes it 143.17 to 131.92, Zito still ahead. Neither pitcher had any saves, and, surprisingly enough, neither pitcher had any shutouts. Zito had a 2.75 ERA in 229 innings; that's 5 minus 2.75 (2.25), divided by 9 (.2500), times 229; that's another 57.25 points, giving him 200.42 "Cy Young points." Pedro had a 2.26 ERA in 199 innings, that's .3044 times 199, which is 60.58, which gives him 192.50.

Zito would be ahead anyway, 200.42 to 192.50, but he also gets a 12-point bonus for "leading his team to the pennant" (yeah, right). This is the point counts for the top pitchers in the league, and the voting:

Formula Points		**Voting**	
1. Zito	212.42	1. Barry Zito	114
2. Martinez	192.50	2. Pedro Martinez	96
3. Lowe	180.47	3. Derek Lowe	41
4. Halladay	169.97	4. Jarrod Washburn	1
5. Mulder	161.44		
6. Wells	153.03		
7. Hudson	152.08		
8. Washburn	149.93		

Barry Zito is predicted to win the Award, which of course he did. The voting pretty well matches the formula; according to the 1986 Resolution of the International Council of Sports Analysts, I am allowed to point this out for purposes of illustration, so long as I don't try to convince you that the system ALWAYS works that well.

It doesn't, of course, but the system picks the actual winner of the Cy Young Award more than 80 percent of the time, and often picks the top finishers in something near their voting order. Since the Cy Young Award sprang from the forebrow of Ford Frick in 1956, there have been 83 Cy Young Awards given . . . one per year for eleven years, two per year since, leaving us permanently stuck on an odd number. For sixty-seven of those races, our formula picks the correct winner. One year (American League, 1969) the voting ended in a tie; our formula picks the top two finishers 1-2 in the league (and well ahead of anybody else), so we give ourselves half-credit for that one, and claim to be 81 percent accurate in picking the Award.

This claim is conservative, for the modern vote. The system missed ten or eleven awards from 1969 through 1984. We had a lot of trouble with relief pitchers in that era, when

a) quite a few relievers were winning Cy Young Awards, and

b) the role of a relief ace was in a dynamic transition, and the voters didn't quite know what they were supposed to think (now they do).

Setting those years aside, we've been much more than 80 percent accurate, missing on only five other awards. This chart compares the formula's "top three" picks with the top three in the voting for all awards since 1990:

1990 American

Formula	Voting
1. Bob Welch	1. Bob Welch
2. Roger Clemens	2. Roger Clemens
3. Dave Stewart	3. Dave Stewart

1990 National

Formula	Voting
1. Doug Drabek	1. Doug Drabek
2. Ramon Martinez	2. Ramon Martinez
3. Frank Viola	3. Frank Viola

1991 American

Formula	Voting
1. Roger Clemens	1. Roger Clemens
2. Scott Erickson	2. Scott Erickson
3. Mark Langston	3. Jim Abbott

1991 National

Formula	Voting
1. Tom Glavine	1. Tom Glavine
2. Lee Smith	2. Lee Smith
3. John Smiley	3. John Smiley

1992 American

Formula	Voting
1. Dennis Eckersley	1. Dennis Eckersley
2. Roger Clemens	2. Jack McDowell
3. Mike Mussina	3. Roger Clemens

1992 National

Formula	Voting
1. Greg Maddux	1. Greg Maddux
2. Tom Glavine	2. Tom Glavine
3. Doug Jones	3. Bob Tewksbury

1993 American

Formula	Voting
1. Jack McDowell	1. Jack McDowell
2. Randy Johnson	2. Randy Johnson
3. Jeff Montgomery	3. Kevin Appier

1993 National

Formula	Voting
1. Greg Maddux	1. Greg Maddux
2. John Wetteland	2. Bill Swift
3. Tom Glavine	3. Tom Glavine

1994 American

Formula	Voting
1. Jimmie Key	1. David Cone
2. David Cone	2. Jimmy Key
3. Randy Johnson	3. Mike Mussina

1994 National

Formula	Voting
1. Greg Maddux	1. Greg Maddux
2. Ken Hill	2. Ken Hill
3. Bret Saberhagen	3. Bret Saberhagen

1995 American

Formula	Voting
1. Randy Johnson	1. Randy Johnson
2. Jose Mesa	2. Jose Mesa
3. Mike Mussina	3. Tim Wakefield

Lawrence Journal World, Kansas Collection, Kenneth Spencer Research Library, University of Kansas Libraries

Bret Saberhagen

1995 National

Formula	Voting
1. Greg Maddux	1. Greg Maddux
2. Pete Schourek	2. Pete Schourek
3. Hideo Nomo	3. Tom Glavine

1996 American

Formula	Voting
1. Pat Hentgen	1. Pat Hentgen
2. Andy Pettitte	2. Andy Pettitte
3. Charles Nagy	3. Mariano Rivera

1996 National

Formula	Voting
1. John Smoltz	1. John Smoltz
2. Trevor Hoffman	2. Kevin Brown
3. Kevin Brown	3. Andy Benes

1997 American

Formula	Voting
1. Roger Clemens	1. Roger Clemens
2. Randy Johnson	2. Randy Johnson
3. Mariano Rivera	3. Brad Radke

1997 National

Formula	Voting
1. Greg Maddux	1. Pedro Martinez
2. Darryl Kile	2. Greg Maddux
3. Pedro Martinez	3. Denny Neagle

1998 American

Formula	Voting
1. Roger Clemens	1. Roger Clemens
2. Pedro Martinez	2. Pedro Martinez
3. Tom Gordon	3. David Wells

1998 National

Formula	Voting
1. Kevin Brown	1. Tom Glavine
2. Greg Maddux	2. Trevor Hoffman
3. Tom Glavine	3. Kevin Brown

1999 American

Formula	Voting
1. Pedro Martinez	1. Pedro Martinez
2. Mariano Rivera	2. Mike Mussina
3. Bartolo Colon	3. Mariano Rivera

1999 National

Formula	Voting
1. Mike Hampton	1. Randy Johnson
2. Randy Johnson	2. Mike Hampton
3. Kevin Millwood	3. Kevin Millwood

2000 American

Formula	Voting
1. Pedro Martinez	1. Pedro Martinez
2. Tim Hudson	2. Tim Hudson
3. Derek Lowe	3. David Wells

2000 National

Formula	Voting
1. Randy Johnson	1. Randy Johnson
2. Greg Maddux	2. Tom Glavine
3. Tom Glavine	3. Greg Maddux

2001 American

Formula	Voting
1. Roger Clemens	1. Roger Clemens
2. Mariano Rivera	2. Mark Mulder
3. Freddy Garcia	3. Freddy Garcia

2001 National

Formula	Voting
1. Randy Johnson	1. Randy Johnson
2. Curt Schilling	2. Curt Schilling
3. Matt Morris	3. Matt Morris

2002 American

Formula	Voting
1. Barry Zito	1. Barry Zito
2. Pedro Martinez	2. Pedro Martinez
3. Derek Lowe	3. Derek Lowe

2002 National

Formula	Voting
1. Randy Johnson	1. Randy Johnson
2. Curt Schilling	2. Curt Schilling
3. Eric Gagne	3. John Smoltz

The formula still has trouble with relief pitchers, actually. Whatever it is that causes a relief pitcher to ring bells with the voters, the formula doesn't reliably quantify it.

Another fun thing you can do with this formula is use it to make more accurate guesses as to who would have won the Cy Young Award in earlier years, had there been such an award. Of course, a thousand people have already picked retroactive Cy Young Awards, and, since there is no compelling evidence that the voting would have worked out the way the formula says it would, there is no obvious reason to retrace those steps.

Since the Cy Young Award began in 1956, the top ten "Cy Young seasons" are as follows:

Year	Name	W	L	SO	ERA	Points
1968	Denny McLain	31	6	280	1.96	329
1965	Sandy Koufax	26	8	382	2.04	307
1966	Sandy Koufax	27	9	317	1.73	305
1963	Sandy Koufax	25	5	306	1.88	296
1968	Bob Gibson	22	9	268	1.12	293
1972	Steve Carlton	27	10	310	1.97	292
1978	Ron Guidry	25	3	248	1.74	285
1971	Vida Blue	24	8	301	1.82	283
1985	Dwight Gooden	24	4	268	1.53	273
1972	Gaylord Perry	24	16	234	1.92	256

As we have gone forward in time, the numbers have gotten lower; Randy Johnson's 2002 season (255 points) is the highest-scoring in almost twenty years, but fails to make the list in direct competition with the 1960s and 1970s numbers. Going back in time, of course, the numbers get even larger. The top ten Cy Young seasons of all time are, of course, all from the 1870s and 1880s:

Pitcher	Year	W	L	IP	ERA	SO	Points
Hoss Radbourn	1884	59	12	679	1.38	441	665
John Clarkson	1885	53	16	623	1.85	308	552
Guy Hecker	1884	52	20	671	1.80	385	549
George Bradley	1876	45	19	573	1.23	103	497
Pud Galvin	1884	46	22	636	1.99	369	488
Silver King	1888	45	21	586	1.64	258	486
Charlie Buffinton	1884	48	16	587	2.15	417	485
Hoss Radbourn	1883	48	25	632	2.05	315	478
Jim McCormick	1880	45	28	658	1.85	260	473
Al Spalding	1876	47	12	529	1.75	39	472

While the top-scoring seasons of the twentieth century were all from the dead ball era:

Pitcher	Year	W	L	IP	ERA	SO	Points
Ed Walsh	1908	40	15	464	1.42	269	443
Jack Chesbro	1904	41	12	455	1.82	239	409
Christy Mathewson	1908	37	11	391	1.43	259	400
Joe McGinnity	1904	35	8	408	1.61	144	393
Walter Johnson	1913	36	7	346	1.14	243	387
Grover Alexander	1915	31	10	376	1.22	241	376
Grover Alexander	1916	33	12	389	1.55	167	361
Jack Coombs	1910	31	9	353	1.30	224	359
Walter Johnson	1912	33	12	369	1.39	303	359
Joe Wood	1912	34	5	344	1.91	258	358

The highest-scoring season since 1920 was McLain's, followed by Lefty Grove in 1931.

Also, since this is a simple, straightforward system with no squares or square roots or anything, there is no barrier to using the same system to score careers. The Cy Young pitcher of all time, appropriately enough, is Cy Young. Young is followed by Walter Johnson, Christy Mathewson, Pete Alexander . . . it pretty much traces the career wins list, up to a point, although Dennis Eckersley, with only 197 wins, vaults to twenty-first on the list due to his saves total, and rates ahead of guys like Early Wynn, Ferguson Jenkins, Robin Roberts, Jim Kaat, and Tommy John, who won more than 280 games.

Of course, this formula likely will not work quite as well in future seasons as it has in the past. This is just the nature of retrofit calculations; it is much easier to predict the past than it is to predict the future. But I just thought it would be fun to be able to say clearly, "This is where the Cy Young race stands, as of today." Right or wrong, I developed this formula to enable us to do that.

(The 2003 season now being over, it is apparent that our formula is going to miss the American League Cy Young Award, although we expect it will hit on the National League. But that's just standard procedure. If you introduced a formula predicting that Democrats and Republicans would quarrel, they would immediately make peace for three days just to show you up.)

LUCKY BASTARDS

BILL JAMES

Who was the luckiest pitcher of all time?

In 1989, Storm Davis, backed by the best team in baseball, posted a won-lost record of 19-7 despite pitching only 169 innings, frankly not very well. His ERA was half a run worse than the league norm, in Oakland, with a bad strikeout-to-walk ratio.

Nonetheless the Kansas City Royals, at that time perhaps the only people in the Western Hemisphere unable to figure this out, signed Davis, a free agent after that season, to a multi-year contract. Asked the next spring about Davis' rotten ERA, pitching coach Billy Connors said, "We're not interested in ERA; we're interested in wins. Davis is a veteran pitcher who knows how to win." At least, that's what I remember him saying . . . this was more than ten years ago, but the quote is accurate to the best of my recollection, and after all, it wasn't Connors who made the decision to sign him; he was just defending the idiocy of his front office. Anyway, that way of thinking about pitcher records is by now so thoroughly discredited, within the community of people who read books like this one, that it's probably no longer necessary to make the supporting arguments.

In the *New Historical Abstract*, I picked a "Tough-Luck Season" for each decade . . . the Tough-Luck Season of the 1970s was by Dave Roberts in 1971, when Roberts went 14–17 with a 2.10 ERA. These picks, however, were just intuitive; I just looked through the records of the decade, and found pitchers whose won-lost records didn't match their ERAs.

Later, it occurred to me that there is no reason we couldn't address the same question ("Who was the unluckiest pitcher of the decade?") in a reasoned, systematic way. Since we know what each pitcher's won-lost record is, and since we know how to estimate what his won-lost record should have been given the number of runs he allowed and the run context, it is simply a matter of slogging through the math to actually figure out who the luckiest pitcher of all time was, who the unluckiest was, etc.

Most of the method for doing this was so straightforward that I'm not even going to explain it, other than to say that we used the Pythagorean system to project winning percentages and made park adjustments. There is one wrinkle I have to deal with. I looked at the won-lost records of all pitchers in history pitching 150 or more innings in a season (thus eliminating from consideration Roy Face, 1959, Cal Eldred, 1992, and almost all other relievers and mid-season callups), and I looked at the discrepancy between the pitcher's ACTUAL and his EXPECTED winning percentage.

If you just look at the winning-percentage discrepancy, the two luckiest pitchers of all time were Ed Wells, 1930, and Byron Houck, 1913.

Pitcher	ERA	League ERA	W-L	WPct	Deserved WPct
Wells, 1930	5.20	4.65	12-3	.800	.398
Houck, 1913	4.15	2.93	14-6	.700	.334

Wells, who deserved to go about 6–9, was carried by Murderers Row to a 12-3 record, while Houck, who walked 122 men in 176 innings and had the second-worst ERA in the league, was carried by the $100,000 Infield to 14-6.

The problem is that we're using a 150-inning cutoff. Wells pitched 151 innings; Houck, not a lot more. Using this method, the list of the luckiest pitchers ever is dominated by pitchers pitching just over 150 innings. If we cut off eligibility at 140 innings, it would be dominated by pitchers pitching just over 140 innings; the same is true at 200 innings, or whatever. Who we would select as the luckiest pitcher of all time (or the unluckiest) would be largely determined by where we set the arbitrary cutoff. A top ten list of lucky pitchers, by such a method, includes nine pitchers pitching between 150 and 180 innings.

We could look at the discrepancy in terms of WINS, rather than WINNING PERCENTAGE. Wells, with 15 decisions and a .398 deserved winning percentage, had an expectation of 5.97 wins. He exceeded this by 6.03 wins.

By this method, the luckiest pitcher of all time was Monte Ward in 1879; Ward exceeded his expectation by 11.99 Wins. This method, however, has the opposite problem: the list is entirely dominated by nineteenth-century pitchers pitching 500 or more innings. We want a list which is dominated neither by the pitchers pitching the most innings, nor by the pitchers who barely qualify for the list. We want a list to which all pitchers have reasonable access.

George Brace Collection

Ed Wells

I achieved this in the following way. There are 8,620 pitchers in history who pitched 150 (or more) innings in a season, through 2002. I simply ranked them 1 through 8,620

a) by the discrepancy between their actual and expected winning percentages, and

b) by the discrepancy between their actual and expected win totals.

I then did an average rank of the two lists—one discriminating in favor of short seasons, the other discriminating in favor of long seasons.

The luckiest pitcher of all time was, it turns out: Wild Bill Donovan in 1907. Yeah, I know; it's a crappy answer, because nobody has any real interest in Bill Donovan. I was hoping the answer would turn out to be Storm Davis, or Bob Welch in 1990, or Steve Stone in 1980, or some season that modern fans could relate to at least a little bit, but you take what you can get. These are the twelve luckiest pitcher-seasons of all time:

Rank	Pitcher, Season	W-L	ERA	League ERA	Deserved W-L
1.	Wild Bill Donovan, 1907	25-4	2.19	2.69	16-13
2.	Fred Klobedanz, 1897	26-7	4.60	4.31	16–17
3.	Catfish Hunter, 1973	21-5	3.34	3.82	13-13
4.	Whitey Ford, 1961	25-4	3.21	4.02	17-12
5.	Lefty Gomez, 1932	24-7	4.21	4.48	15–16
6.	Byron Hauck, 1913	14-6	4.15	2.93	7-13
7.	Joe Bush, 1913	15-6	3.82	2.93	8–13
8.	Jack Morris, 1992	21-6	4.04	3.95	13–14
9.	Jack Coombs, 1911	28-12	3.53	3.34	18–22
10.	Hooks Dauss, 1919	21-9	3.55	3.22	13–17
11.	Paul Abbott, 2001	17-4	4.25	4.48	10–11
12.	Fred Goldsmith, 1880	21-3	1.75	2.37	14-10

Storm Davis is in 13th place. All of these pitchers, without exception, pitched for exceptional teams with very strong offenses, and in every case it is also apparent that the pitcher's individual won-lost record is out of context with his team. Whitey Ford in 1961 was backed by Maris and Mantle's 115-homer outburst, but he also had an ERA a half a run higher than his teammate Bill Stafford. Stafford finished 14-9, while Ford was 25-4. The fact that all of the twentieth-century pitchers on

George Brace Collection

Bill Donovan

this list were in the American League is just a fluke. Other recent pitchers who rank in the top 75 include Bob Welch, 1990 (27-6), John Burkett, 1993 (22-7), Kevin Tapani, 1998 (19-9), Dwight Gooden, 1990 (19-7), Roger Clemens, 2001 (20-3), and C. C. Sabathia, 2001 (17-5).

An accounting note: of the 8,620 pitcher/seasons in the study, 1,367 (or 16 percent) had exactly the won-lost record they deserved. Twenty-seven percent of the seasons were either +1 or –1 game (and split evenly, of course), while 25 percent were +2 or –2—thus, 68 percent of the seasons were within two games of the expected won-lost record. A fuller chart:

Even	+/–1	+/–2	+/–3	+/–4	+/–5	+/–6	+/–7	+/–8	+/–9
16%	27%	25%	14%	9%	5%	2%	1%	½%	Trace

The un-luckiest pitcher/season of all time was by Buster Brown in 1910—a season which is, if possible, of even less general interest than Donovan's in 1907:

Rank	Pitcher, Season	W-L	ERA	League ERA	Deserved W-L
1.	Buster Brown, 1910	9-23	2.67	3.02	19-13
2.	Frank Allen, 1913	4-18	2.83	3.20	12-10
3.	Jack Nabors, 1916	1-20	3.47	2.82	9-12
4.	Walt Dickson, 1912	3-19	3.86	3.40	11-11
5.	Ned Garvin, 1904	5-16	1.72	2.73	13-8
6.	Paul Derringer, 1933	7-27	3.30	3.33	17-17
7.	Jim Abbott, 1992	7-15	2.77	3.95	15-7
8.	Dutch Henry, 1930	2-17	4.88	4.65	9-10
9.	Cliff Curtis, 1910	6-24	3.55	3.02	15-15
10.	Eddie Smith, 1937	4-17	3.94	4.62	12-9

Warren Brown wrote a poem about Eddie Smith . . . Under a spreading luckless spell/The White Sox Ed Smith works/He's beaten by the best there is/He's beaten by the jerks. Actually, he was pitching for the A's in 1937, but his luck with the White Sox wasn't a lot better a few years later, when he went 7-20 with a 3.98 ERA.

Smith, Brown, and Garvin were not lucky in these years, nor were they lucky in general. Ned Garvin was probably the unluckiest pitcher in major-league history, taking in the whole of his career:

Rank	Pitcher, Seasons	W-L	ERA	League ERA	Deserved W-L
1.	Ned Garvin, 1896–1904	57-97	2.72	3.48	86-68
2.	Buster Brown, 1905–1913	51-103	3.21	2.94	76-78
3.	Eddie Smith, 1936–1947	73-113	3.82	4.11	98-88
4.	Milt Gaston, 1924–1934	97-164	4.55	4.31	126-135
5.	Egyptian Healy, 1885–1892	78-136	3.84	3.54	101-113
6.	Ned Garver, 1948–1961	129-157	3.73	4.01	158-128
7.	Jack Russell, 1926–1940	85-141	4.46	4.31	109-117
8.	Skip Lockwood, 1969–1980	57-97	3.55	3.60	76-78
9.	Ken Raffensberger, 1939–1954	119-154	3.60	3.89	146-127
10.	George Smith, 1916–1923	41-81	3.89	3.40	59-63

I considered "eligible" for the list the 1000 pitchers who had pitched the most major-league innings through 2002, and used the same procedure of ranking them by the winning-percentage disparity and the wins disparity, then averaging the two lists. Other unlucky pitchers of note: Bob Barr, Dizzy Trout, Jose DeLeon, Rick Honeycutt, Bob Friend, Roger Craig, and Mike Morgan. The unluckiest Hall of Fame pitcher was Walter Johnson, whose career won-lost log is about thirty games worse than he deserves.

Road West Publishing—*Baseball Magazine* Collection

Paul Derringer and Bucky Walters

The luckiest pitchers of all time . . . "The secret of success as a pitcher," said Waite Hoyt, "lies in getting a job with the Yankees." Vic Raschi was a good pitcher, but it is probably not a coincidence that his career record (132-66) breaks down as 120-50 while with the Yankees, but 12–16 with other teams:

Rank	Pitcher, Seasons	W-L	ERA	League ERA	Deserved W-L
1.	Vic Raschi, 1946–1955	132-66	3.72	4.10	104-94
2.	Lew Burdette, 1950–1967	203-144	3.66	3.84	170-177
3.	Tommy Bond, 1876–1884	193-115	2.25	2.55	163-145
4.	Larry Corcoran, 1880–1887	177-89	2.36	2.85	150-116
5.	Chief Bender, 1903–1925	212-127	2.45	2.72	185-154
6.	Dave Foutz, 1884–1894	147-66	2.84	3.49	123-90
7.	Dwight Gooden, 1984–2000	194-112	3.51	3.96	166-140
8.	Ross Grimsley, 1971–1982	124-99	3.81	3.70	101-122
9.	Don Gullett, 1970–1978	109-50	3.11	3.67	89-70
10.	Jack Coombs, 1906–1920	158-110	2.78	2.79	133-135

The luckiest Hall of Fame pitcher, other than Bender (who's in the table), was Herb Pennock, whose 240-162 career record

a) is about 30 games better than it ought to be, and

b) isn't a Hall of Fame record anyway.

UNIQUE RECORDS

BILL JAMES

Randy Johnson in 2002 did something that no major-league pitcher has ever done before.

Well, now, that is a piss-poor lead sentence, because Randy Johnson in 2002 no doubt did a hundred things no major-league pitcher had ever done before—won his fourth straight Cy Young Award, struck out 300 batters for the fifth straight year, averaged better than a strike-out per inning for the twelfth straight year, had at least 70 more strikeouts than innings pitched for the fifth straight year . . . some of these things must be unique, although I don't know which ones. Let me back up and run at this from a different direction.

It is my habit, when doing anything, to break the task down into portions, and to represent the portions as they pass by comparing them to the won-lost records of pitchers. If I am mowing the lawn (to use just one of many possible examples), I estimate (or know from experience) that it will require eight passes along each of the four borders of the lawn, a total of 32 passes with the lawn mower, to render this particular patch of shaggy weeds into a rectangle of green neatness. As I pass the markers toward verdant nirvana, I mark them off by comparing them to the won-lost records of known pitchers . . . 11 and 21, that's Bucky Walters in 1936; 12 and 20, that's Orlando Peña in 1963; 13 and 19, that's Paul Splittorff in 1974; 14 and 18, that's Larry Jackson in 1963 or Grant Jackson in '69, etc.

Sometimes I do this with tasks that pass by at a rate of one per second or even two per second—exercises, for example; if you touch your toes 33 times in 40 seconds, it gives you about a second to come up with somebody who went 23 and 10 before it's time to start working on 24 and 9. And I try not to use any Yankees.

Now, I wish to emphasize, lest there should occur any misunderstanding about this, that I am NOT fantasizing about being a major-league pitcher as I do this; I am merely using won-lost records to mark the passage of the task. It has absolutely, totally, completely, 100 percent NOTHING to do with fantasizing about being a major-league pitcher, at least most of the time. But anyway, I need to come up with these records, and occasionally I hit blank spots on the grid, and can't come up with a pitcher who went 16 and 17. If anybody posted the needed record in the early 1960s, I'm covered, but if somebody did it before 1940 or since 1980, where it wouldn't be closely associated in my mind with a specific baseball card, I might not be able to come up with it.

So then I decided to make an organized effort to fill in the gaps, which gets us back to Randy Johnson. Randy Johnson last year filled in a gap: he was the first pitcher in major-league history to finish a season 24-5. It's a unique record: there is one, and only one, pitcher in major-league history to finish a season at 24 and 5. Pitchers had gone 23-5, 25-5, 26-5, 24-4, 23-6, 25-4 . . . but never 24 and 5.

Randy became the first pitcher since 1999 to break out a new won-lost record. In 1999 Pedro Martinez went 23 and 4, and Mike Hampton went 22 and 4—both new won-lost records in major-league history. My source in compiling these charts was Lee Sinins' Sabermetric Encyclopedia; different sources have different information for nineteenth-century pitchers, even a few pitchers early in the twentieth century. Anyway, the most wins ever by a pitcher, according to Sinins, is 59, by Old Hoss Radbourn in 1884 (of course, some sources list him at 60). The most losses ever were 48, by John Coleman in 1883 (12-48).

If you construct a matrix which has all of the possible won-lost records up to 59 wins and up to 48 losses, there are 2,940 cells in the matrix—60 by 49, since you have to leave slots for zeros. Thus, there are 2,940 "possible" won-lost records for a pitcher in a season, if you assume that any win total up to 59 is possible, and any loss total up to 48 is possible.

Of course, there are no pitchers in baseball history who have gone 59-48, since that would be 107 decisions, so that isn't really a "possible" won-lost record; none the less, there is a cell there waiting for it if it happens to occur, if Mickey Lolich comes out of retirement or something. But of those 2,940 records, how many are actual won-lost records which have been compiled by actual major-league pitchers?

839, it turns out; all of the pitchers in major-league history have created 839 distinct won-lost records, through 2002. The other 2,101 cells in the matrix are still empty. Of the 839 "open" records, 250 are "unique" records, held by only one pitcher in one season, like Randy Johnson in 2002.

Well, not all that much like Randy Johnson in 2002. Actually, the great majority of them were more like Old Hoss Radbourn in 1884, and even more like Old Hoss Radbourn in 1882 or 1886. Of the 250 unique records in baseball history, the great majority were nineteenth-century pitchers who posted records which, by 1905 or 1910, had become impossible to duplicate, like 30-22, 32-15, or 46-19. Of the 250 unique records, 177 were posted before 1900, and 208 were posted no later than 1910. This is the breakdown, by decades, of unique records:

1876–1879	17
1880–1889	112
1890–1899	48
1900–1909	28
1910–1919	8
1920–1929	3
1930–1939	8
1940–1949	2
1950–1959	5
1960–1969	4
1970–1979	4
1980–1989	4
1990–1999	6
2000–2002	1

The unique records which have been posted since 1910 are:

First	Last	Year	W-L
George	Bell	1910	10-27
Buster	Brown	1910	9-23
Cliff	Curtis	1910	6-24
Ed	Walsh	1911	27-18
Joe	Wood	1912	34-5
Walter	Johnson	1913	36-7
Jack	Nabors	1916	1-20
Eddie	Cicotte	1919	29-7
Eddie	Rommel	1921	16-23
Charles	Ruffing	1928	10-25
Tom	Zachary	1928	12-0
Lefty	Grove	1930	28-5
Lefty	Grove	1931	31-4
Paul	Derringer	1933	7-27
Dizzy	Dean	1934	30-7
Lefty	Gomez	1934	26-5
Si	Johnson	1934	7-22
Ben	Cantwell	1935	4-25
Johnny	Allen	1937	15-1
Freddie	Fitzsimmons	1940	16-2
Howie	Krist	1941	10-0
Preacher	Roe	1951	22-3
Robin	Roberts	1952	28-7
Don	Larsen	1954	3-21
Don	Newcombe	1956	27-7
Elroy	Face	1959	18-1
Sandy	Koufax	1963	25-5
Roger	Craig	1963	5-22
Jack	Fisher	1965	8-24
Phil	Regan	1966	14-1
Rogelio	Moret	1973	13-2
Ron	Guidry	1978	25-3
Bob	Stanley	1978	15-2
Phil	Niekro	1979	21-20
Terry	Felton	1982	0-13
Orel	Hershiser	1985	19-3
Jose	DeLeon	1985	2-19
Dennis	Lamp	1985	11-0
Bob	Welch	1990	27-6
Greg	Maddux	1995	19-2
Jim	Abbott	1995	2-18

(continues)

First	Last	Year	W-L
Randy	Johnson	1995	18-2
Pedro	Martinez	1999	23-4
Mike	Hampton	1999	22-4
Randy	Johnson	2002	24-5

Randy thus becomes the first pitcher since Lefty Grove to be the proud owner of two unique records—18-2, the record he posted in 1995, and 24-5.

Actually, that may not be true; there may have been somebody else in there who HELD two unique records, but lost one of them or both of them. New unique records are posted, but records also cease to be unique. Roger Clemens has personally wiped two uniquers—both New York Mets—off the books. Dwight Gooden in 1985 became the first major-league pitcher to post a record of 24-4. Roger in 1986 jumped onto his slot. David Cone in 1988 became the only pitcher ever to go 20-3. Clemens in 2001 squatted next to him, as well.

As you can see, the only way to post a unique record now is to post a winning percentage so high or so low that there is a very small population of pitchers around you. Then, if you happen to hit the right number of decisions, you may find a niche. Almost all of the unique records in baseball history have one of the following three qualities:

1) A winning percentage of .800 or above,
2) A winning percentage of .200 or below, or
3) 35 or more decisions.

Of the 250 unique records, 197 were by pitchers posting 35 or more decisions, and the great majority of those, of course, were by pitchers pitching before 1910. 31 of the unique records were by pitchers with winning percentages of .800 or above, and 22 were by pitchers with winning percentages of .200 or below.

That would appear to account for all of the pitchers, except that some of these pitchers had 35 decisions AND very high or very low winning percentages. The double-dippers are:

First	Pitcher	Year	W-L	Dec	WPct
John	Coleman	1883	12-48	60	.200
Hoss	Radbourn	1884	59-12	71	.831
Mickey	Welch	1885	44-11	55	.800
John	Ewing	1889	6-30	36	.167
Joe	McGinnity	1905	35-8	43	.814
Joe	Wood	1912	34-5	39	.872
Walter	Johnson	1913	36-7	43	.837
Eddie	Cicotte	1919	29-7	36	.806
Lefty	Grove	1931	31-4	35	.886
Dizzy	Dean	1934	30-7	37	.811
Robin	Roberts	1952	28-7	35	.800

If you ask, "What is the most unique won-lost record in major-league history?" . . . well, I'm not sure that you can get any more unique than unique, but if you can, these would appear to be the best candidates, the "double-unique" records which involve both an unusual number of decisions and an unusual winning percentage. The "most unique" won-lost record in major league history is probably Radbourn's 59-12 record in 1884.

Stories about Old Hoss Radbourn in 1884 almost always focus on how *much* he pitched, the day-after-day starting grind that left him unable to lift his arm to brush his hair in the morning, but still able to pitch in the afternoon. These stories, it seems to me, miss what is really remarkable about his season: not that he *pitched* so much, but that he *won* so much. Radbourn had 71 decisions in 1884, which is not a terribly unusual number for that era. Guy Hecker had 72 decisions that same year (52-20), Pud Galvin had 75 decisions in 1883 (46-29) and 68 more in '84 (46-22), Jim McCormick had 73 decisions in 1880 (45-28), Will White had 74 in 1879 (43-31), and Radbourn himself had had 73 decisions the previous year (48-25). In that era, 71 decisions is just not a particularly unusual number. He did pitch a lot of innings, but even there, he doesn't hold the record (Will White in 1879), and he pitched only a few innings more than most of these other pitchers. What is remarkable about Radbourn's season in 1884 is not that he pitched every day, but that he pitched *and won* almost every day.

Anyway, as an accounting issue, I left open eleven records—the eleven which met none of the three standards which otherwise define the group. One of those was Don Newcombe in 1956, 27 and 7. Newk missed 35 decisions by one, and missed an .800 winning percentage by one win; he is one game different from Robin Roberts four years earlier, but Roberts hits two of the standards, Newk none.

The other ten were: big losers. The other ten were all pitchers who won 6 to 9 games, but lost 22 to 27 games—totaling up less than 35 decisions, but more than a .200 winning percentage. And all of those were in 1910 or before, except Paul Derringer, 1933, Si Johnson, 1934, and Jack Fisher, 1965, who were charted above.

Randy Johnson's 24-5 mark is part of a kind of interesting series:

Randy Johnson, 2002	Only pitcher to go 24-5
Sandy Koufax, 1963	Only pitcher to go 25-5
Lefty Gomez, 1933	Only pitcher to go 26-5
Lefty Grove, 1930	Only pitcher to go 28-5

If we can find a skinny left-hander with a 99 MPH fastball to go 27-5 in about 2032, we'll fill in the straight flush. Three pitchers have gone 23-5, including Barry Zito last year, but 22 and 5 is still an open slot; nobody has done that.

In fact, that's one of the most "common" or "accessible" records in baseball history which no one happens to have hit. If a pitcher wants to make this list in 2004, what is the easiest way to do it? I don't know, and I don't know how to figure it, but these are the obvious candidates, the easiest of the virgin records:

0 and 11
13 and 0
0 and 14
13 and 1
1 and 14
1 and 17
17 and 2
18 and 3
3 and 20
21 and 4
23 and 3
22 and 5
6 and 22
24 and 6

0-and-11 is probably the easiest record to reach, actually. Pitchers have gone 0-and-10, 11-and-0, 0-and-12, 12-and-0, even 0-and-13—but 0 and 11 has been overlooked (my money's on Albie Lopez).

18-and-3 is another kind of odd oversight; no one has ever gone 18-and-3 in a season, although, improbably enough, there was a pitcher who wound up with a *career* mark of 18-3. Luis Aloma, a Cuban who pitched for the White Sox from 1950 through 1953, went 7-2, 6-0, 3-1, 2-0—a total of 18-3. He is probably known to table-gamers for his memorable 1951 season, when he not only went 6-0 with a 1.83 ERA, but also hit .350 with a double and a walk, producing, one would suppose, some nice table-game replications.

Anyway, 18-and-3 . . . that's the kind of record somebody could hit in the modern game, probably will within a few years. As recently as 1984, while the record 16-3 had been fairly common, the record 17-3 was uniquely held by Chief Bender in 1914, and 18-3, 19-3 and 20-3 were all open cells. But since then this path has clogged up considerably; Hershiser found 19 and 3, Smoltz joined Bender at 17-3, Cone and then Clemens went 20-3. Eighteen and three is still waiting (my money's on Pedro).

The other side of that coin is, what is the most unusual record which is *not* unique?

Probably 29-34; Matt Kilroy in 1886 went 29-34, and probably wasn't at all disappointed, excited, or even interested when Amos Rusie posted the exact same record four years later. But it hasn't been done since, except perhaps by a few lawn mowers cutting seven-sided lawns. Another good candidate is 39-24—two nineteenth-century studs did that—and another is 35-19.

The most common won-lost record for a major league pitcher in a season is, of course, 0 and 0. This isn't easy to figure, and I don't have any real confidence that I'm right, but my belief is that, through 2002, there have been 31,375 pitcher/seasons in major-league history. Of those 31,375, 4,377 (or 13 percent) finished the season 0-0.

What is the most common "real" won-lost record, involving a win or a loss? That's obvious; it's 0 and 1. These are the accumulated totals for the ten most common records, as best I know:

0-0	4,377 times
0-1	1,433 times
1-0	1,015 times
1-1	928 times
0-2	867 times
1-2	668 times
2-1	467 times
2-2	438 times
1-3	402 times
2-3	383 times

The ten most common won-lost records involving double-digit wins or double-digit losses are:

9-10	100 times
8-10	93 times
10-10	91 times
12-11	90 times
11-10	89 times
10-9	88 times
10-6	85 times
7-10	85 times
11-12	84 times
7-11	84 times

The most common record for a 20-game winner is 20-12 or 20-9, each of which has been done 34 times in baseball history.

None of this, of course, means anything; it's pure trash sabermetrics. I wanted to know this stuff, so I looked it up. That's all.

PITCHER CODES

BILL JAMES

Do you want to dream a little bit?

To a Kansas City Royals fan, the question "Do you want to dream a little bit?" is a subtle joke, or perhaps a tribute to our longtime announcer Fred White. Sometimes the Royals would get dreadfully behind in a game, 8-1 let's say, but as soon as they would get a runner on base, Fred would say, "Well, if you want to dream a little bit, get another couple of baserunners here and George Brett comes up; we could be right back in the game." When the Royals turned into a bad team in the 1990s we would hear that phrase two or three times every week, and it became a kind of symbol of the disarray of the organization.

But, getting well ahead of ourselves . . .

In theory, it is possible to draw up a "code" which would describe the *abilities* of any major-league pitcher at any moment. Not the *performance;* statistics describe performance. I'm talking about describing skills, not outcomes. The way it works is this:

First, we code the pitcher "L" or "R": left or right.

Second, we enter the recorded speed of the pitcher's normal fastball. If a guy throws 94–96, we enter that as "95"; if he throws 88–90, we enter that as "89" (working with historical pitchers for whom good speed estimates are not available, we code their fastballs "A," "B," etc., based on the best evidence we've got).

Third, we enter a code identifying the pitcher's best pitch, his No. 1 pitch. The code list is as follows:

B—Blooper (Or Eephus, or Lob)
C—Straight Change
D—Drop Curve
E—Empty
F—Four-Seam Fastball (Rising Fastball)
H—Hard Curve
J—Screw Ball
K—Knuckle Ball
L—Splitter (or Hard Forkball)
M—Slow Curve
N—Sinker
O—Overhand Curve
P—Palm Ball (or Slip Pitch)
Q—Spitball (or Scratched/Defaced Baseball)
R—Knuckle Curve
S—Slider (Tight-breaking slider)
T—Two-Seam Fastball
U—Cut Fastball (Breaks in like screwball)
V—Cut Fastball (Breaks out like slider)
W—Wide Breaking Slider/Slurve
X—Unknown
Y—Circle Change
Z—Slow Forkball or Fosh

If a guy simply does not have a third pitch or a fourth pitch—we'll be coding more pitches as we go along—we code that as "E" for empty. If we don't *know* whether or not the guy has a third or fourth pitch, we list that as "X" for unknown. Some guys have funny names for pitches . . . there's a guy now throwing a pitch he calls the "shuuto." I haven't seen it, but from the descriptions of it, it's just some version of a screwball. For our purposes here, we code the pitch by what it does, not by what the guy calls it.

That's the third element of the thirteen-element code, the identifier for the first pitch. The fourth element is a value judgment about the pitch. If it is a "plus" pitch at the major-league level, we would code that as "1." If it's a decent pitch but not an out pitch, that's a "2." If it's a poor pitch for a major league pitcher, that's a "3," and if it's a pitch you can't really throw in the majors, that's a "4."

The fifth element of the code is the pitch code (from the chart above) for his No. 2 pitch. The sixth element is a 1-4 evaluation of the second pitch. The seventh element is the guy's third pitch; the eighth is a 1-4 evaluation of his third pitch.

The ninth element of the code is the fourth pitch, if the guy has one, and the tenth element is the 1-4 evaluation of the fourth pitch. If a guy doesn't have a third pitch or a fourth pitch, we just enter that as "X 4" . . . otherwise the codes for the third and fourth pitch are the same as the codes for the first pitch. A two-pitch pitcher with a good fastball, a so-so change, and no third or fourth pitch would be coded F 1 C 2 X 4 X 4. If he is a right-hander who hits 93–95 on the gun, he's coded R 94 F 1 C 2 X 4 X 4: right-hander, 94-m.p.h. fastball, best pitch is a fastball which is a plus pitch, also has a pretty good change-up, has no third pitch (or fourth pitch, obviously).

We've got three elements left. The eleventh code element is the arm angle:

A Straight Over the Top
B Almost Straight Over the Top
C Three Quarters
D High Sidearm
E Straight Sidearm
F Low Sidearm
G Submarine
H Intentionally Varies His Arm Angle

The twelfth code element is a 1-3 evaluation of the pitcher's Command and Control (actually 1-4, but "4" means "clearly not at a major league level"). "Command," to me, means that the pitcher can reliably make the pitch break the way it is supposed to break; the curve doesn't hang, the fastball doesn't straighten out, the slider doesn't stray where it doesn't belong. "Control" means that the pitcher can put the pitch where he wants it. Command and control are clearly distinct things, but they're related.

The thirteenth code element is a 1-3 evaluation (4, again, meaning "not major league") of the pitcher's understanding of how to approach a hitter. If the pitcher knows how to mix up his pitches, work on the hitter's timing, make the hitter move his hands, make the hitter move his eyes, that's a "1." If he really doesn't have any understanding of that stuff, that's a "3" or even a "4."

Let's code somebody. Robin Roberts, 1952. He's a right-hander, so his code starts out "R." We don't have a radar reading on his fastball, but we know that it was very, very good, so that's code "A."

His best pitch was a Rising Fastball (Code F), and obviously that was a very, very good pitch, which we code as "1." Here's what we have so far:

Robin Roberts, 1952 R A F-1

Again, that tells us he's a right-handed pitcher with a Grade A fastball, his best pitch an outstanding rising fastball.

His second pitch, which he actually developed early in the 1952 season, was a hard curve. A hard curve is "H." It wasn't a "plus" pitch; it was an okay major-league pitch, so that makes it H-2. This is Roberts' code now:

Robin Roberts, 1952 R A F-1 H-2

His third pitch (which was his second pitch before 1952) was a slow curve, which he used as a change of pace. A slow curve is "M," and this, again, was an okay pitch, nothing sensational, so we'll enter it as "M-2." This makes Roberts' code:

Robin Roberts, 1952 R A F-1 H-2 M-2

He could also throw a sinker, but it wasn't really a quality pitch, and he rarely threw it. A sinker is "N," and the question is whether this was N-3 or N-4, but we'll make it N-3:

Robin Roberts, 1952 R A F-1 H-2 M-2 N-3

Roberts, I *think*, was almost straight over the top; anyway I am going to assume that he was, and if I'm wrong somebody can correct me. Almost straight over the top is "B":

Robin Roberts, 1952 R A F-1 H-2 M-2 N-3 B

Roberts' command and control was outstanding, so that's a "1," and his knowledge of how to approach a hitter was outstanding, so that's also a "1." This, then, is the complete code for Robin Roberts, 1952:

Robin Roberts, 1952 R A F-1 H-2 M-2 N-3 B 1 1

Summing up, we know that 1) Roberts was a right-handed pitcher with an excellent fastball, 2) his best pitch was a rising fastball, 3) he threw a pretty good hard curve and a decent enough slow curve, 4) he fooled around with a sinker, but it wasn't a pitch he could rely on, 5) he threw from almost over the top, 6) his command and control were both outstanding, and 7) his knowledge of how to approach a hitter was outstanding.

Which is to say, if you understand the coding system, then you can "read" a fairly complete description of the pitcher's skills in one line.

Let's do another one . . . Orel Hershiser, 1988. No, no . . . that's too good; we don't want to do another Cy Young winner . . . Let's do a .500 pitcher: Steve Trachsel, 2002. This is the code for Trachsel:

Steve Trachsel, 2002 R C T-2 M-2 Y-2 L-2 B 2 1

What does that mean? R means that he was right-handed at that time; C means that he had a "C" fastball, nothing special. T-2 means that his best pitch was a two-seam fastball, and that it was an average major-league pitch, and not what the scouts call a "plus" pitch. (A "plus pitch" can loosely be described as a pitch nobody can hit if you get it where you want it.) He also threw a slow curve (M), a circle change (Y), and a splitter (L), all of which were OK pitches, major league pitches, nothing special (M-2 Y-2 L-2).

He came almost over the top (B, which, these days, is the most common arm slot). His command and control were okay, nothing exceptional (2), but he was a veteran pitcher who knows how to pitch (1).

All of that information can be stored in—and read out of—one line. Isn't that cool?

If you want to dream a little bit, there really isn't any reason why "codes" like this could not be created for every major-league pitcher in every season in history. If you combine the type of research that Rob and I have done with an intelligent reading of the player's record, you can fill in most of the blanks. There will be some X's ("I don't know") and some E's (empty), but you can figure out most of it. If a guy has a great fastball, but walks 105 people and finishes 11–16, you can figure out what his command and control is and what his understanding of how to pitch is. If a pitcher's strikeout rate drops, you can figure his fastball has gone back on him, and you'll be right 99 percent of the time. The rest of it is just legwork.

If we had those codes, they would be immensely valuable for a million different research purposes. Suppose, for example, that you have a young pitcher whose code might be:

Young pitcher, 2002 R A T-1 F-1 O-2 Y-3 C 2 2

Young pitcher has a Grade A fast ball, throws an excellent two-seam fastball and an excellent four-seamer, other pitches are so-so, command and control isn't a problem or a positive, knowledge of how to pitch is pretty good for a young pitcher. What is the chance that this young pitcher will develop into a star? What is the chance that he will develop into a star in one year, in two years, in three years?

More importantly, what will it take for him to step forward as a star? How important is the third pitch? How important is command and control? How important is an understanding of how to work the hitter?

That's actually the code for Josh Beckett, 2002, and, as it turned out, his chance to become a star was pretty good. But if you had these codes, you could study an unimaginable array of questions. What is the injury rate for a pitcher who throws a screwball as his No. 1 pitch? What's the difference in the success rate for a pitcher with a "B" fastball (a 90–93 m.p.h. fastball, leaving aside the question of movement) as opposed to a "C" fastball (86–89). What percentage of pitchers with "B" fastballs become successful major-league starting pitchers? Is there a connection between the arm slot and the injury rate?

What is the difference between the ERA and won-lost record of a pitcher with a given code on a bad team, and a pitcher with the same code on a good team?

Are pitchers who throw big curve balls as their number-two pitch more successful than those who throw sliders?

Such codes, if we had them, would make it practical to create a simulation—a game—which started not with outcome frequencies, but with skill sets.

You might think, at a glance, that we have attempted to summarize all of the things that distinguish pitchers into one line. This is far from true. There are many, many things that separate one pitcher from another that we have made no allowance for in this code. We have made no mention of

Size
Strength
Holding Baserunners
Endurance

Durability
Concentration
Control of Emotions
Ability to Hide the Ball
Consistency of Motion (Arm Slot)
Wasted Motion (Noise in the Delivery)
Competitiveness
Toughness
Pitching Philosophy
Injury History

There's a lot of things that distinguish one pitcher from another that we haven't made any place for in this code. I'm just trying to focus on the most basic facts about a pitcher, and make a succinct summary of them. If the code goes on any longer than this, it's going to become a novel.

I actually thought about, and Neyer and I talked briefly about, the possibility of creating "codes" for all of the pitchers in this book. Not every year, of course, but career codes. Once we thought about it, it became apparent that we couldn't do it. Apart from the massive work load it would have added to putting the book together, it would have necessarily involved a certain amount of guesswork. Thus, we would have been presenting to the reader speculative information, cheek by jowl with the hard facts that we have so carefully documented. This would have created confusion in the reader's mind about what we were attempting to do, and would have led some people to think that the entire exercise was just a lot of guesswork. We couldn't do that to the research.

Still, if you want to dream a little bit, wouldn't it be fun to have an "encyclopedia" of pitchers which had the codes for every pitcher every year? You could compare Josh Beckett at age 23 to . . . let's see, who would be comparable to Josh Beckett at the same age? Don Sutton would be very comparable. You could ask and answer the hypothetical question: What would happen to Jarrod Washburn if he came up with a really good screwball?

To tell you the truth, I've already figured the codes for every major-league pitcher in 2002, and I know the answers to a couple of the questions I have posed here. One season done; 126 to go. We're down 126 to 1, but if you want to dream a little bit . . .

Florida Marlins, Denis Bancroft

Josh Beckett